LBS-4

The Practice of Modern Internal Auditing

The Practice
of Modern
Internal Auditing

Second Edition, Revised and Enlarged

Lawrence B. Sawyer

The Institute of Internal Auditors, Inc.
Altamonte Springs, Florida

International Standard Book Number: 0-89413-092-7
Library of Congress Catalog Card Number: 81-810325

The Institute of Internal Auditors, Inc.
Altamonte Springs, Florida 32701

First Edition published 1973
Second Edition, Revised and Enlarged, published 1981

Printed in the United States of America
80260 JUL81
81245 DEC81

To Esther

my wife, my love, my best friend — always.

Contents

Preface   page ix
Acknowledgements   page xiii

Part 1
Introduction to Internal Auditing
1.   Development of Internal Auditing   3
2.   The Profession of Internal Auditing   17
3.   Control   53

Part 2
Techniques of Internal Auditing
4.   Performing the Preliminary Survey   87
5.   Audit Programs   143
6.   Field Work   169
7.   Deficiency Findings   213
8.   Working Papers   243

Part 3
Scientific Methods

9. Sampling   279
10. Quantification   325
11. Computer Auditing   343
12. Computer-Assisted Auditing   415

Part 4
Reporting

13. Reports   431
14. Audit Report Reviews and Replies   493
15. Reports to Executive Management and the Board   513

Part 5
Administration

16. Establishing the Internal Auditing Organization   539
17. Selecting and Developing the Staff   567
18. Preparing Long-Range Schedules   607
19. Controlling Audit Projects   631
20. Quality Control   659

Part 6
Other Matters Relating to Internal Auditing

21. Principles of Management   677
22. Employee and Management Fraud   713
23. Dealing with People   747
24. Relationships with External Auditors   773
25. Relationships with Boards of Directors   787

Appendix A   811
Appendix B   828
Appendix C   834
Appendix D   835
Appendix E   843
Appendix F   846
Appendix G   857
Index   867

Preface

Internal auditing is an emerging profession. It is expanding and growing with each passing day. The literature on the subject seeks to keep pace with the new concepts and techniques developed for internal auditors and with the new responsibilities thrust upon them.

That is why it is necessary to revise, expand, update, and add to the original *Practice of Modern Internal Auditing*. To date, internal auditors have had to learn their job by practicing it. The courses of study in universities are accounting-oriented instead of operations-oriented. So practitioners of modern internal auditing — management-oriented internal auditing — acquired their education on the job instead of in the classroom.

That is still the path most candidates for professional internal auditing positions must take. This book provides the reader with some of the theory and a good deal of the practical application of modern, management-oriented internal auditing. It describes the way modern internal auditors practice their craft — the empirical approach to appraising the diverse activities of an entity. In effect, the reader will be looking over the shoulders of practitioners and following them as they plan an audit, perform preliminary surveys, prepare audit programs, carry out field work, develop and sell audit findings, compose their working papers, write their audit reports, review them with auditees, evaluate replies, follow up on corrective action, and submit summary reports to executives.

But internal auditors are responsible for more than the performance of audit assignments. They are now called upon to be conversant with disciplines and fields far beyond what was accepted practice at the start of the '70s.

Several recent developments that have had a profound effect on the responsibilities of internal auditors include the establishment of a program of certification, the adoption by The Institute of Internal Auditors, Inc., of the *Standards for the Professional Practice of Internal Auditing,* and the passage of the U.S. Foreign Corrupt Practices Act of 1977. These events increased internal audit's stature, sped the growth of internal auditing in public and private enterprises, and enhanced its professional status.

Along with growth, however, comes expanded authority and increased responsibility; and so the discipline broadens to cover new fields with a greater accountability. This new edition, therefore, seeks to reflect this expansion.

The revised text has grown from 13 to 25 chapters. It is divided into six parts, as follows:

Part One introduces internal auditing. The first chapter provides a history of internal auditing and shows how it differs from such other disciplines as public accounting and industrial engineering. The second chapter describes the professional characteristics of internal auditing and the means of obtaining the Certified Internal Auditor designation. The third chapter is devoted to the all-important subject of control, the internal auditor's stock in trade. An understanding of the anatomy of control is essential at the very outset as the subject is threaded through most chapters in the book. All three chapters are new.

Part Two is devoted to the techniques of internal auditing — to the tools internal auditors use to develop information and to evaluate both control and performance. The chapters on preliminary surveys, audit programs, field work, and working papers appeared in the first edition; but they are expanded and updated here. The chapter on deficiency findings is new. We believe the subject is sufficiently important to be afforded separate treatment.

Part Three deals with scientific methods. Chapters on sampling and computers appeared in the first edition. The chapter on sampling has been updated. The one on computers is completely new and takes a different approach. It is structured around the standards developed by the Comptroller General of the United States that set forth internal audit responsibilities for auditing computer systems and applications. The remaining two chapters on quantification and computer-assisted audits are new; these acknowledge the technological advances made since the first edition was written.

Part Four deals with reports — preparing audit reports, reviewing such reports with auditees and accepting responsibility for follow-up of replies, and summary reporting for senior management and the board. These chapters appeared in the first edition. They have been updated here and include new illustrations and examples.

The chapters in Part Five relate to the administration of the internal auditing department. The first four are revisions of similar chapters which appeared in the first edition. The fifth, dealing with quality control, is new. It is the result of new requirements incorporated in the *Standards for the Professional Practice of Internal Auditing*. The *Standards* state that directors of internal auditing should establish means of assessing the ability of their departments to perform professionally.

Part Six comprises five new chapters. These seek to keep pace with the state of the art. The chapter on management briefly describes the functions of management and shows how internal auditors can assist managers in the tasks of managing. The chapter on fraud describes how fraud occurs; it explores the internal auditor's responsibilities regarding fraud and points to the signs of fraud and the hazards fraud presents. The chapter on dealing with people examines internal auditing's effect on individuals and points to ways of softening the harsh effects. The chapter on relationships with external auditors emphasizes the need for a closer relation between external and internal auditors and the need to coordinate their efforts. The chapter on relationships with boards of directors describes the awakening of board members to more stringent responsibilities, the growth of audit committees, and the ways in which internal auditors can provide needed assistance and comfort to such committees.

The breadth of the material has uses for a variety of readers:

Entry level internal auditors will find it helpful as a means of acquainting themselves with management-oriented internal auditing.

Instructors can use it for a college-level or a graduate course on the concepts and the practice of modern internal auditing.

Experienced internal auditors will find it useful as a refresher course and as a mirror reflecting how internal auditing is practiced in forward-looking organizations.

Internal auditors developing new internal auditing departments or seeking to upgrade existing ones will find in one book examples of charters, statements of responsibilities, job descriptions, suggestions for audit manuals and forms, and a host of other materials to help them.

External auditors will find a means of developing constructive relationships with internal auditors and the internal auditing organizations.

Executives and board members will find helpful information in determining what they can or should expect of their internal auditors.

Other control groups, such as safety engineers, quality control engineers, and industrial engineers will gain insights into internal auditing and into the means of sharpening their own information-gathering and evaluation techniques.

As a study guide, the book is designed to ease the tasks of generating class discussion, assigning homework, and giving examinations by providing problems, multiple choice questions, and case studies after each chapter. Special assignments can be based on the suggested readings listed at the end of the text material in each chapter.

Practitioners will find the questions and case studies useful since they focus on the more salient features of the chapter which they follow. Many of the questions were adapted from Certified Internal Auditing Examinations. Researching the answers to the questions will be an especially valuable exercise for those readers interested in sitting for the Examination.

Internal auditing is not an exact science. It is practiced in different ways by different internal auditors. Hence the views expressed in this book will not necessarily reflect the philosophies of all internal auditors and all internal auditing organizations. Some of those philosophies may be narrow to mirror the restricted charters some managements have imposed on their internal auditors. Some may follow a rigorous, aloof approach that sees no place for participative auditing. Others may not require of their auditors the professional conduct of audits nor the documentation of audit results.

For these reasons, we solicited the ideas and the assistance of a broad spectrum of practitioners, seeking to reconcile the varying viewpoints. The names and organizations mentioned in the acknowledgments which follow this preface indicate the scope of our search for diverse views and attitudes. We have earnestly sought advice and counsel in preparing this book. But the decisions made as to what to include or exclude, what to emphasize and what not to emphasize, which avenues to explore or to neglect, and which style to use in presenting the ideas, had to be ours. So we accept the full responsibility for the course this book has taken.

Lawrence B. Sawyer
Camarillo, Calif.
1981

Acknowledgments

The first edition of *The Practice of Modern Internal Auditing* had about five years to garner critical comment when we decided to revise it. That edition was a case of first impression. We used information then available to supplement personal experience. Both the information and the experience have mushroomed since then. Besides, suggestions to improve the book were not lacking from practitioners and academicians alike.

When we began gathering material for the new edition, we asked for advice, guidance, and material from academics who used the text in courses, or were familiar with it, and from practicing internal auditors. The ready responses and helpful contributions gave us a wealth of ideas and illustrative material to sharpen and expand the original book.

All the material received could not be used because of space limitations. But the material offered and the guidance given made the writing of this book much easier.

I offer my sincere thanks to the following practitioners who stand in the forefront of our profession and who responded to my plea for help: D. K. Booth of Kodak, W. A. Bradshaw of the Office of the Auditor General of Canada, J. D. Bradt of Imperial Oil Ltd., C. L. Brown of J. C. Penney, R. N. Carolus of Northwest Bancorporation, W. J. Duane of Manufacturers Hanover Trust Co., W. B. Haase of Arthur Young and Company, W. J. Harmeyer of the California Institute of Technology, P. E. Heeschen of Lockheed, Odd Hunsbedt of As Denofa Og Lilleborg, J. E. Kohl of Gulf Oil, A. C. Levingston of Florida Department of Transportation, George Maroulis of Canadian National Railway, J. P. Marusak of ITT Grinnell Corp., R. J. Mitchell of Caterpillar of Australia Ltd., E. E. Mullineaux of Standard Oil Co. (Indiana), R. A. Reese of Shell Oil Corp., R. L. Richmond of B. F. Goodrich Company, D. L. Scantlebury of the U.S. General Accounting Office, Aaron Schneider of Pet Incorporated, B. L. Smeltzer of McDonnell Douglas Corp., J. P. Soderberg of Singapore Petroleum, W. E. Swanson of Owens-Illinois, D. L. Sweeney of the American Institute of Certified Public Accountants, W. E. Thompson of Alabama Bancorporation, W. W. Warrick of the Aluminum Corporation of America, D. D. Weiss of International Multifoods, J. P. Wesberry of the Organization of American States, and R. A. Wolvert of Portland General Electric.

Members of academe who advised me or supplied material for the revision include Morris Friedman of Spring Garden College, G. R. Hodges of the New School for Social Research, F. E. Mints of Cal State Los Angeles, F. L. Neumann of the University of Illinois of Urbana-Champaign, G. A. Pfeiffer of Loyola College in Maryland, B. J. Schwieger of St. Cloud State University, H. F. Stettler of the University of Kansas, and G. C. Yost of the University of West Florida.

I am especially grateful to those members of the profession who offered their time and considerable talents in reviewing all or parts of the manuscript and who gave me invaluable ideas for improving the form and substance of the book. Paul E. Heeschen and Rodney A. White reviewed every chapter. Dr. Frederic E. Mints reviewed most of them. The dedication and wise counsel of these good friends kept me from making more than my share of blunders. Leon R. Radde reviewed the chapters on control, preliminary surveys, and audit findings. William E. Wilkerson and Frank K. Gentile of the Department of Health, Education, and Welfare gave their excellent talents to the chapter on sampling. C. O. "Bill" Smith of the U.S. General Accounting Office, a master in the field, provided invaluable material for, and a thorough editing of, the extensive chapter on computers and the companion chapter on computer-assisted audits; and L. F. Haynes, F. W. Lyons, and C. R. Basa of The Institute of Internal Auditors helpfully supplemented C. O. Smith's reviews. Dr. H. J. Podell of the U.S. General Accounting Office and Dr. S. L. Newman of The Institute of Internal Auditors reviewed the chapter on quantification, filling in with their mastery of the subject those places where my knowledge was lacking.

A special word of thanks goes to Ceel Pasternak, who edited the final draft. I shall be ever grateful for her untiring efforts, her keen grasp of the subject, and her consummate technical ability. I am grateful, also, to Don Cadwallader for his meticulous attention to editorial detail, and to William J. Stafford and Lee Hansen, who masterfully piloted the production of the book through the storms and cross-currents which inevitably beset a publication of such magnitude.

All these people gave me the benefit of their technical capability, their up-to-date knowledge of the profession of internal auditing, and their friendship. But the entire venture would have foundered if I did not have the support, the sense of what is fitting and reasonable, and the dedication of my Esther. She typed manuscripts, reviewed copy, asked the hard questions, and bucked me up when there seemed to be no end to the task.

LBS

Part 1

Introduction to
Internal Auditing

1
Development
of Internal Auditing

The roots of internal auditing — Mesopotamia, the Egyptians, Persians, and Hebrews; Greece and Rome; Italian commerce. England and the industrial revolution. Crossing the seas. World War I. The bankers and the railroads. The securities acts. A shadow of the external auditor. The Institute of Internal Auditors, Inc. The struggle for identity. The term *internal auditor*. The expanding statements of responsibility. Internal auditing defined. Comprehensive internal auditing of operations. Internal auditing versus external auditing and industrial or efficiency engineering. The varied objectives. Management-oriented internal auditing. The lessons each discipline can learn from the others. Examples of internal auditing approaches.

History

Ancient Times

Internal auditing has its roots in antiquity. Only recently has the tree begun to blossom. The story of modern internal auditing bespeaks a painfully slow growth since its ancient beginnings. The buds did not begin to show until 1941 when The Institute of Internal Auditors, Inc., was formed; then a distinctive discipline began to flower.

Evidence of verification of transactions — now only one of internal auditing's activities — goes back over 5,500 years. The records of a Mesopotamian civilization about 3600 B.C. show tiny marks at the side of numbers relating to financial transactions. The dots, checks, and tick marks portray a system of verification. One scribe prepared summaries of transactions; another verified them. It was probably here that the control systems of verification and division of duties originated.

3

Early Egyptian, Persian, and Hebrew records show similar systems. The Egyptians, for example, required the actual witnessing of corn brought to the granaries and demanded that receipts of corn be certified.

The Greeks were strong believers in control over finances. Their records show that transactions required authorization and verification. Their systems of control included peculiarly direct methods. They preferred slaves over freemen as record keepers since slaves could be tortured to reveal the truth. With brutal logic, the Greeks regarded torture as a more trustworthy means of extracting information than questioning a freeman under oath.

Ancient Rome employed the "hearing of accounts." One official would compare his records with those of another. This oral verification was designed to keep officials in charge of monies from committing fraudulent acts. Indeed the task of hearing accounts gave rise to the term *audit*, from the Latin *auditus* ("a hearing"). *Quaestors* ("one who inquires") would examine the accounts of provincial governors, seeking to detect fraud and the misuse of funds.

The Middle Ages

When Rome fell, so did monetary systems and controls. Not until the end of the Dark Ages did rulers demand proof that they were obtaining the revenues owed them. Barons and justices made the first audits; appointed officials made them later.

An expanding Italian commerce during the 13th century demanded more sophisticated record keeping. Thus was born the double-entry system of bookkeeping — an answer to an essential need. This system helped merchants control transactions with customers and suppliers and check on the work of employees. Auditing was taken seriously. An auditor representing Queen Isabella accompanied Columbus to the New World.[1]

The Industrial Revolution

Auditing, as we now know it, began during the industrial revolution in England. Companies hired accountants to check the records. Audit verification became less a matter of personal accountability and stewardship. It became more a matter of scrutinizing written records and comparing entries in the books of account with documentary evidence. The concern was with the records rather than with the people who prepared them.

Recent Times

Auditing crossed the seas to the United States during the 19th century along with British investments. Wealthy Englishmen invested substantial amounts in United States corporations, especially breweries. They wanted an independent check on their investments. The English auditors brought with them methods and procedures which the Colonials adapted to their own needs. The British requirements arose under the statutory dictates of the British Companies Act calling for accountability to investors. The United States had no such dictates; hence, auditing served the needs of the entrepreneur. These needs gave rise to the balance-sheet audit, stressing a more analytical approach to accounts.

Auditing in the United States

After World War I, the United States' economy escalated. Many corporations, although not required to do so, published audited financial statements. But, by and large, auditing was for the benefit of the bankers who feared the overly optimistic balance sheets and needed an independent verification on which they could rely.[2] The railroads were among the first to adopt a farflung internal auditing program. Railroad executives needed assurances that their station masters across the country were handling receipts properly.

Congressional Action

Auditing received a great push forward when the United States Congress enacted the Securities Act in 1933, the Securities and Exchange Act in 1934, the Public Holding Company Act in 1935, and the Investment Company Act in 1940. The purpose of this legislation was to regulate publicly traded securities and to use accounting and auditing as a means toward that end. Corporations could not rely entirely on the external accountants because they needed in-depth analyses that those accountants were not always in a position to give. Therefore, they hired internal auditors to help in the verification of accounting records and to determine compliance with accounting controls.

The Internal Auditor's Struggle for Identity

The outside auditors usually controlled the internal auditors. The latter were shadows of the former, shadows with little prestige or identity.

Modern internal auditing began to evolve in 1941 when The Institute of Internal Auditors, Inc., was formed. Only then did the shackles that bound it to the books of account start to break down. Only then did it assume an upright posture, no longer genuflecting to the professional outside accountant.

The terms *internal auditor* and *internal auditing* had a pettifogging, nit-picking connotation to some of the founders of The Institute. They sought for a term or phrase that would better describe the expanding role of the internal auditor, but none emerged. And so John B. Thurston, one of The Institute's founders, said in 1941:

> You will all recognize the unhappy inadequacy of the phrase "internal auditor." Years ago it was probably satisfactorily descriptive of our earlier predecessors in the profession. But today, auditing, in the precise meaning of the word, is only one of the functions of the internal auditor. Your organizing committee gave much thought to the possibility of using some other phrase or term, and finally reached the conclusion that we must bow to historical precedent.[3]

The founders hoped that the actions rather than the description of the profession would help it achieve its separate identity. But 1941 did not give birth to an Athena springing fully formed from the brow of Zeus. Rather it sparked the glint in the eyes of the founders who dreamed of a profession concerned more with assisting management in all its activities, not merely verifying accounting transactions. The glint presaged a lusty infant — management-oriented auditing — and the infant has made steady progress.

That progress is depicted in the various changes the Statement of Responsibilities of the Internal Auditor underwent from 1947 to 1976 (discussed in Chapter 2).

Definition

Many terms have been used instead of *internal auditing*. It has been called management auditing, operational auditing, program auditing, results auditing, operations appraisals, and the like. But the title internal auditing bespeaks the function; it is the umbrella term that covers all forms of appraisals of activities undertaken by auditors working for and within an organization.

The definition that we believe best describes the broad-ranging appraisals contemplated by modern internal auditors is this:

An independent appraisal of the diverse operations and controls within an organization to determine whether acceptable policies and procedures are followed, established standards are met, resources are used efficiently and economically, and the organization's objectives are being achieved.

This definition embraces both opportunities and responsibilities. It elevates the internal auditor's sights, and it demands a management-oriented approach to audit appraisals.

The definition calls for these things:

Professional objectivity and a status within the organization which promotes consideration of the auditors' findings and action on their recommendations.

A broad scope of operations and the authority to have unrestricted access to all relevant papers, properties, and people.

Going beyond mere compliance with rules to find out whether the rules are adequate and appropriate and are carrying out the organization's current objectives.

Reviewing compliance with laws and regulations, both internal and external, and finding out if financial operations are properly conducted and financial and operating reports are accurate, timely, and meaningful.

Reviewing the management of people, money, and materials to throw the spotlight on inefficient and uneconomical practices so that corrections can be made, while at the same time reporting and commending good performance.

Evaluating planned missions and programs to find out if projects and activities are achieving what was intended.

Making sure the internal auditor's outlook is on the same level as that of managers in all echelons of the organization.

This definition depicts more than the popular stereotype which the term *internal auditor* and its history conjure. It bespeaks an extension of management, not merely the eyes and ears of management, but its outlook and dreams as well. Management-oriented internal auditors are expected to go beyond fault finding, beyond merely seeing if rules are being followed and records are accurate. They are expected to find out also whether the rules are valid and whether the records are necessary. They are, of course, concerned with whether things are done right (economy and efficiency). But above all they must be concerned with whether the right things are being done (effectiveness).

Auditing Operations

Many auditing departments have waded into the sea of nonfinancial operations in their organizations. Many are performing top-flight, management-oriented audits in areas unconnected with the financial branch of the entity. But in their enthusiasm with the beneficial effects of these audits, they must not permit the pendulum to swing too far. They must not neglect the bread-and-butter audits of financial records and transactions.

Financial activities, in fact, remain a significant part of the operations of the entity. They represent the entity's nervous system, and controls over that system are essential. Internal auditors, no matter how management-oriented they have become, must include in their long-range schedule the reviews of the adequacy and the effectiveness of accounting controls. They must also make whatever verifications and tests are necessary to inform management that the controls are proper and are working well or that action is needed to improve controls or performance or both.

Similarly, internal auditors must not be carried away by their status in the organization. Even though they may report directly to the chief executive officer and even though they have the ear of the chairman of the board of directors, they are still staff. They are not line. They have no operating responsibilities and no operating authority. They have no right to give orders. They cannot demand that operating people carry out audit recommendations; only that they consider them and take whatever action is needed to correct the conditions that the recommendations were calculated to improve.

Internal Auditing and Related Disciplines

Internal auditors sometimes have difficulty explaining their function. When the uninitiated hear the term *internal auditor*, the comment usually is, "Oh, you check on the company's books." When internal auditors try to explain their expanded scope of operations, the comment may be, "I see. You're an efficiency expert."

The modern internal auditor is neither of these. Internal auditing is a distinctive discipline. The purpose and the scope of modern internal auditing is different; its desired outcomes are different.

The Internal Auditor and the External Auditor

The External Auditor's Mission

Internal auditors are often recruited from the public accounting profession. A great many internal auditors have prior public accounting experience. This prior experience is valuable. It provides important training in developing audit programs, in evaluating systems, in analyzing transactions, and in identifying defects. But if these transplanted auditors were to try to apply public accounting techniques without change to their internal auditing projects, their results might be ineffectual; they might miss the point of the entire audit. The activities of the two disciplines — internal and external auditing — may overlap in some areas, such as reviewing the adequacy of accounting controls; but the overall differences are greater than the similarities because the objectives are different.

The primary responsibility of the independent public accountants is to examine a company's financial statements. Their objective is to determine whether these statements present fairly the financial position of the company and the results of its operations for the year. Also, they must satisfy themselves that the statements are prepared in conformity with generally accepted principles applied consistently with those applied in the previous year. [4]

Recent legislation, such as the U.S. Foreign Corrupt Practices Act, draws a sharp bead on corporate financial controls. Some influential external auditors believe that the internal auditor's forays into nonfinancial operations are a waste of time; they should be focusing on accounting internal controls, not performing operational audits. This view, we believe, casts a blind eye on the expanded scope of the internal auditor.

The Differences

Internal reviews of accounting controls are important, and internal auditors must be involved in them; but that is not their entire mission. The losses resulting from poor production, engineering, marketing, or inventory management of resources are incalculably greater than those suffered from financial peculations. Management controls over financial activities have been greatly strengthened through the years. The same cannot always be said of controls elsewhere in the enterprise. Embezzlement can hurt a corporation; poor management of its resources can bankrupt it. Therein lies one of the basic differences between external auditing and management-oriented internal auditing: the first is narrowly focused, the second is comprehensive.

True, the external auditor performs management services and submits management letters which recommend improvements in systems and controls. By and large, however, these are financially oriented. The occasional sally into nonfinancial operations may not reflect the depth and understanding of the resident internal auditor who is intimately familiar with the organization's systems, people, and objectives.

Also, the external auditor may not be vitally concerned with fraud or waste that does not have a significant effect on the financial statements — is not "material." The internal auditor, however, is desperately concerned with all manner of waste and fraud, no matter how small. That concern does not stem from the need to check every minor deviation. Rather it is rooted in the understanding that the tiny cloud can mushroom into a tempest that may rock the pillars of the enterprise. The minor impropriety may not be so material as to affect the financial statements of a multimillion or multibillion dollar corporation. But to the experienced internal auditor it may be more than a random human error; it may be an indicator of poor morale, poor systems, poor policies, or a poor understanding of management philosophy.

The internal auditor and external auditor must coordinate their efforts. Their techniques in financial audits may be similar, but their aims and intended outcomes vary. They represent two distinct professions which must respect each other and make use of each other's talents. They must develop a relationship that is strong and enduring (discussed in Chapter 23). Here is an example comparing the different approaches by internal and external auditors in an audit of cash. The external auditor will normally take these steps:

Follow the transactions from the place of their origin to the final balance in the books of account.

Review the cash balance for reasonableness.

Determine that deposits are promptly banked.

Review cash disbursement cutoffs.

Count cash on hand; follow undeposited collections to the bank.

Confirm bank balances.

Verify the mathematical accuracy of bank reconciliations.

Obtain a cutoff bank statement directly from the bank, tracing bank reconciliation items to the statement.

Compare checks written before the year's end and clear with the cutoff bank statement the list of outstanding checks supporting the bank reconciliation.

Compare with cash disbursement records those checks not clearing with the cutoff statement.

Account for checks outstanding last year that did not clear with that year's bank cutoff statement.[5]

If cash defalcation is suspected, additional steps may be taken; but generally the normal external audit techniques are those just listed. The internal auditors may do the same if they audit cash themselves, or they may assist the external auditor in these steps. But their interest goes beyond these essential but pedestrian steps. Here are two examples:

1. One company paid large *ad valorem* taxes. Operating capital was costly, so how can they pay taxes as required by law and still conserve cash? The internal auditor puzzled out the problem.

   Some states permitted installment payments. The auditor recommended an appropriate procedure for paying taxes piecemeal instead of in advance in one lump sum.

   Some payments were paid early to earn a discount, but the value of money had risen. Short term investments yielded more favorable results. The auditor pointed out the obvious, discounts were forfeited, and property taxes were paid on the precise day due.

   As a result, working funds were freed to earn $50,000 a year.[6]

2. One internal auditor recognized that cash, besides being protected, must be regarded as a nonearning asset. He understood that idle bank balances must be kept to a minimum. He saw that this could be done by good cash forecasting and progressive bank relations. He also saw that management did not have such a sophisticated view. Therefore he obtained a computer run which analyzed two years of cash receipts and disbursements. He wanted to know when cash was available for even a few days.

   Here's what he found: General bank accounts contained several million dollars more than was needed for day-to-day operations. Several local banks were used for noninterest-bearing "good will" accounts to help employees cash paychecks. Few employees needed the service. The company was not taking advantage of investment techniques which permit investment of funds over weekends. Investments were primarily in United States securities, but high-grade commercial paper offered higher yields.

   The internal auditor presented his findings and recommendations to higher management. The managers, evidently impressed, accepted the auditor's counsel. Through some changes in procedures, they were able to increase income from short-term investments by about $400,000 a year.[7]

To summarize the principal distinctions between the internal and the external auditors, here is a tabulation of the differing positions and concerns of the modern internal auditor on the one hand, and the external auditor — engaged solely in balance sheet audits — on the other:

Internal Auditor	External Auditor
An organization's employee.	An independent contractor.
Serves management and the board of directors.	Serves third parties who need reliable financial information.

Reviews all operations and controls in an organization for efficiency, economy, and effectiveness.	Reviews balance sheet and income statement accounts. Reviews operations and internal controls to determine scope of examination and reliability of financial data.
Is directly concerned with the prevention of fraud in any form or extent in any activity audited.	Is incidentally concerned with the prevention and detection of fraud in general, but is directly concerned when financial statements may be materially affected.
Is independent of the activities audited, but is ready to respond to the needs and desires of all elements of management.	Is independent of management and the board of directors both in fact and in mental attitude.
Reviews activities continually.	Reviews records supporting financial statements periodically — usually once a year.[8]

The Management-Oriented Approach

The two cases of cash audits by internal auditors, discussed previously, go beyond pedestrian checking. But even these are just a beginning. The opportunities for still greater service will broaden with the internal auditor's increased acceptance by executive management and the boards of directors. It would have been unheard of in the 1940s and the 1950s for the internal auditors to affect management decisions or even receive a hearing in the top echelons of the enterprise. From 1942 to 1955, Montgomery Ward's buildup of cash balances and short term investments rose from 16 million to 325 million dollars. In the meantime, Sears Roebuck made maximum use of its idle funds to build sales outlets and strengthen its market position. The internal auditors who would have pointed out Sears' use of its cash to their Montgomery Ward executives might have been given a dismissal notice. Today, with broadened acceptance and with the ear of the audit committee of the board of directors, the internal auditor's recommendations to make use of such idle cash might be given a sympathetic and respectful hearing.

The examples of modern internal audits of cash underscore the management-oriented approach to internal auditing and contrast with the financially oriented approach. Each approach is significant. Each is necessary. Each provides an essential service. But they are quite different. They represent two separate disciplines that can work together productively and in harmony — neither subservient to the other — when they understand each other's functions and coordinate them carefully.

The Internal Auditor and the Industrial Engineer

The Differences

Internal auditors and industrial engineers — the latter were once called efficiency experts — represent two different crafts. Internal auditors are not efficiency experts or industrial engineers, although on occasion they make use of their techniques.

An efficiency expert or engineer is defined as one who analyzes methods, procedures, and jobs in order to devise means for securing maximum efficiency of equipment and personnel. The industrial engineer is a step higher on the professional ladder. Maynard defines industrial engineering as that branch of engineering knowledge and practice which analyzes, measures, and improves the methods of performing duties assigned to individuals; designs and installs better systems of integrating duties assigned to a group; and specifies, predicts, and evaluates the results obtained.[9]

Internal auditors perform some of these activities. They analyze, measure, and recommend methods to improve the performance of tasks. But they do not design and install systems. They may suggest the inclusion of needed controls when systems are being designed. They may evaluate those systems to see whether they are functioning as intended when they are completed. But they should not design them; that is not their function and it would destroy their objectivity. It is a fact of life that we hesitate to criticize our own offspring.

The Similarities

The internal auditor has much to learn from efficiency experts and industrial engineers. The early pioneers of motion study had a common goal: to study a task and then make the operation simpler or physically easier, to eliminate unneeded operations, to lessen fatigue, and to reduce the time and cost of accomplishing the task. The studies of Frank and Lillian Gilbreth, David Porter, and Henry L. Gantt are worth the internal auditor's attention. All are calculated to enhance profits — a vital concern of internal auditors. Profits increase when manufacturing methods are improved, labor or material is saved, waste is prevented, defective work is reduced, product quality is enhanced, working conditions are improved, hazards are reduced, unnecessary records are eliminated, equipment is made more efficient, and methods to increase productivity are installed.[10]

These are important aspects of the internal auditor's work. Yes, it is useful to improve some function or to assemble some product more economically and more efficiently. But is this particular function or product really needed? That is the additional question the internal auditor must ask, therefore going beyond economy and efficiency to look for effectiveness. There are other questions: Why is it done here? Why is it done now? Does it really contribute to company objectives? Does it continue to function because it is truly needed, or because executive management forgot it is there?

Here are just two examples of improvement in nonfinancial activities, which are similar to those which concern industrial engineers, but which were recommended by internal auditors:

1. A state auditor observed delays in a series of street-widening projects. In one such project, utility poles and utilities were not being removed promptly. The work had not been scheduled correctly. First of all, the poles presented an unsightly and hazardous condition in an otherwise widened street. Secondly, the general contractor for that one project was paid $600 a month for one year — $7,200 — to remain on the job because the utility poles were not removed. The cost for all projects affected by these delays was enormous. The fault lay in city management leadership's failing to schedule and coordinate work. As a result of the internal audit recommendations, specifications would in future contain a street-by-street schedule of site improvements, coordinating the work of the utility companies and the contractors.[11]

2. An internal auditor's observation of rejected materials brought to light the scrapping of expensive assemblies in the last phase of work. He found that inexperienced people were assigned to this critical assembly phase. He recommended that only experienced people be used in that stage of work because a large amount of labor had already been invested. To put the last phase of the expensive assembly in the hands of inexperienced people was ludicrous. Estimated savings totaled $80,000 in the first year.[12]

Internal Audit Concerns

Internal auditors can learn from the methods of the external auditor and the industrial engineer, then incorporate them into their own internal audit programs. However, internal audit functions are more comprehensive, and internal auditors' objectives are different. In addition to finance and production, they are concerned with planning, organizing, marketing, research and development, purchasing, industrial relations, engineering, and a host of other activities; in short, with anything that concerns executive management.

That is why to refer to the modern internal auditor as an accountant or as an efficiency expert is to miss the point entirely.

Conclusion

Internal auditing is a distinctive discipline. Its roots are the same as those of the independent accountant, but it is a completely separate trunk. The work of these two disciplines can be and should be coordinated, but their objectives are different.

The work of the internal auditor and the so-called efficiency (or industrial engineering) expert is different. Each can learn from the other; each can help the other. But the scope of their activities and their responsibilities is not the same. The efficiency expert is concerned with evaluating and developing processes and systems. Internal auditors are concerned with appraising them after they are installed. Their interests are more managerial than mechanical.

All these disciplines work together for the benefit of the enterprise, but internal auditors can become ineffective if their identities are merged with those of the other two disciplines.

References

1. Gordon McIntyre, "Auditing for Management Control," *The Internal Auditor*, May/June 1975, p.37.
2. A. H. Adelberg, "Auditing on the March: Ancient Times to the Twentieth Century," *The Internal Auditor*, November/December 1975, p. 40.
3. D. E. Dooley, "Nothing New Under the Sun?" *The Internal Auditor*, Summer 1965, p. 10.
4. John W. Winter, "Coordination Between Internal and External Auditors," *The Internal Auditor*, December 1976, p. 18.
5. H. F. Stettler, *Auditing Principles* (Englewood Cliffs, N.J.: Prentice-Hall, Inc., 1977), pp. 213, 214.
6. "The Round Table," *The Internal Auditor*, January/February 1975, p. 74.
7. "How to Save $14,500,000 Through Internal Auditing," H. J. Mintern, ed. (Orlando, Fla.: The Institute of Internal Auditors, 1975), p. 33.
8. Stettler, p. 100.
9. H. B. Maynard, *Industrial Engineering Handbook* (New York: McGraw-Hill, 1971), pp. 1-5.
10. L. K. Maguire, "What Promise Does Industrial Engineering Hold for Internal Auditing?" *The Internal Auditor*, February 1978, pp. 43, 44.
11. The Comptroller General of the United States, "Examples of Findings From Governmental Audits," *Audit Standards Supplement, Series No. 4* (1973), pp. 21, 22.
12. "The Round Table," *The Internal Auditor*, March/April 1971, p. 80.

Supplementary Reading

Adelberg, A. H. "Auditing on the March: Ancient Times to the Twentieth Century." *The Internal Auditor*. November/December 1975, p. 40-47.

Cadmus, Bradford. *Operational Auditing Handbook*. New York: The Institute of Internal Auditors, 1964, Ch. I.

Brink, V. Z. with J. A. Cashin and Herbert Witt. *Modern Internal Auditing — An Operational Approach*. New York: The Ronald Press Company, 1973, pp. 1-11.

Lindberg and Cohn. *Operations Auditing*. New York: AMACOM, 1972, pp. 3-10.

Sawyer, L. B. "Observations on the 1971 Revision of the Statement of Responsibilities of the Internal Auditor." *The Internal Auditor*, September/October 1971, pp. 8-11.

For further study

Discussion problems

1. Modern internal auditing has been referred to as simply a state of mind. Comment.

2. To what circumstances would you attribute the expanding role of modern internal auditing?

3. Do you believe the terms *internal auditor* and *internal auditing* best describe their modern functions? If not, what terms would you recommend? Is the label of a function that significant?

4. What is the significant change incorporated into the 1971 Statement of Responsibilities of the Internal Auditor? Do you think that the excerpt quoted in the text can be further improved? How?

5. The internal auditor has been called "the eyes and ears of management." What impression does that phrase convey to you?

6. Which of these audit objectives are directed toward compliance? toward efficiency? toward effectiveness?

a. To find out whether payments to creditors are managed so as to best conserve the company's cash.
b. To find out whether expenditures are distributed to the right account.
c. To find out whether accounts payable files permit prompt retrieval of records and information.

7. Contrast the objectives of:

a. The classic, financially oriented internal auditor.
b. The modern internal auditor.
c. The public accountant.
d. The efficiency expert (engineer).

Multiple choice problems

1. Determining whether 16-pound stationery stock can replace 20-pound stock relates to:
a. Effectiveness.
b. Economy.
c. Efficiency.
d. Compliance.
e. Propriety.

2. Since internal auditors are experts in controls, they should have the authority:
a. To develop accounting systems.
b. Direct accounting personnel to make corrections and adjustments.
c. Order changes in accounting systems.
d. All of the above.
e. None of the above.

3. The internal auditor's concern about fraud within the enterprise:
a. Is the same as that of the external auditor.
b. Involves matters of financial materiality only.
c. Relates to what the fraud, big or little, implies.
d. Is determined by its effect on the financial statement.
e. None of the above.

4. Internal auditing is a term which includes:
a. Management auditing.
b. Operational auditing.
c. Comprehensive auditing.
d. All of the above.
e. None of the above.

5. Modern internal auditing determines whether:
a. Procedures are complied with.
b. The procedures themselves are appropriate.
c. Things are done right.
d. The rights things are done.
e. All of the above.

Case Study

1-1 To Study Production Scheduling

The Gordon Manufacturing Company produces farm equipment. Its sales were about $50,000,000 last year. Ingrid Austin has been an internal auditor at Gordon for three years. She has an MBA degree and has completed successfully a number of internal auditing projects at Gordon. Most of her work, however, as well as that of her three fellow internal auditors, has been in financial and administrative activities. The internal auditors have done little work in other operating areas, but they are anxious to move into more challenging assignments.

The company has a good reputation in the industry, turning out good products on schedule at reasonable prices. Recently, however, the Production Department has been having difficulty in meeting its schedules. Top management, upset by customer complaints, called for outside help. The company's public accountants made a survey of the production activities and submitted a report of their findings and recommendations. Management was not convinced of the results; it did not feel that the suggested actions would solve the problems and so the report was ignored.

Ingrid was therefore assigned to make an internal audit of Gordon's scheduling activities in the hope that she could identify the difficulties. As her first step she gained an audience with the department manager, David Prodder. Here are some excerpts from their conversation:

David: What's your background, Ingrid?

Ingrid: I've an MBA from State College, and after two years with a national accounting firm, I came to Gordon three years ago.

David: What kinds of audits have you made at Gordon?

Ingrid: I've done audits of data processing, accounts payable, cash management, travel expenses, shipping, sales promotion, and blueprints.

David: It doesn't seem to me that you've had any experience in factory work. We've just been through an audit with the outside accountants. They made all sorts of analyses, asked a ton of irrelevant questions, told my people what to do, and drove my managers crazy. I wouldn't want to live through that again. And they had assured me that they had successfully completed a similar project at the Woven Textile Company. Now here you are — another accountant. What assurance do I have that your audit would be any different from the one the external auditors carried out?

Required: (1) What could Ingrid do to make sure her own audit reports earn a better reception? (2) What arguments can she present to David about her approach and how it differs from the public accountant's approach? (3) What audit steps could she discuss with David so as to ease his mind about her ability?

2
The Profession
of Internal Auditing

Profession defined. Internal auditing as a profession. The Institute of Internal Auditors, Inc. The expanded Statement of Responsibilities. Reviewing all operations. Complying with a code of ethics. Independence and objectivity. Reviews of proposed controls. The two codes of ethics for Institute members and for Certified Internal Auditors. Obligation to the public. Provision for disciplining. The Common Body of Knowledge. The levels of knowledge required. The certification program. Benefits. Requirements. Study guides. Examples of questions. Review material. The need for a structured college curriculum. Emerging curricula. Pass/fail rates. Courses in internal auditing. Suggested approaches. The new *Standards*. Purpose of the *Standards*. Service to the organization. Practical independence. Requirements for professional proficiency. The meaning of due professional care. The full-scope audit. Quality performance. Quality control.

Professionalism

What is a Profession?

As generally understood, a profession is a pursuit that requires prolonged study and training before one is ready to follow it as a means of livelihood. The term also often implies that one has undergone tests of one's fitness and has won a degree, or has given proof of one's qualifications and has been licensed to practice. It often also implies devotion to an end other than that of earning a livelihood.

Certain professions are bound together in a common discipline. The requirements of these professions — their codes of conduct, such as the Hippocratic Oath of doctors and the Canon of Ethics for attorneys — create a spirit of fraternity, scholarship, and public service. In their case, the rule of *caveat emptor* ("buyer beware") does not apply.

The client or customer is not as skilled in the discipline as the practitioner, whose level of skill is usually beyond the ability of the layman to assess. Those who seek such professional skill and service must therefore rely on the reputation of the practitioner or on a professional code to which the practitioner subscribes.

Internal Auditing as a Profession

Where does modern internal auditing stand in terms of representing a profession? In the minds of the public it is not regarded as a full-blown profession such as law, medicine, dentistry, public accounting, or teaching. But in its short span it has established criteria of excellence and codes of conduct for its practitioners. It has made significant progress toward a spirit of fraternity and scholarship. It has sought public acceptance and has demonstrated a concern for public service. What forms has this progress taken? Because the discipline is so new and often not understood, it is necessary to examine the separate documents of the profession and their interpretations.

The Professional Organization of Internal Auditing

The Separation from Independent Accounting

The need for a professional organization stemmed from the emergence of internal auditing as a distinctive discipline. In the early part of the 20th century, internal auditors were usually employed in the accounting department where they checked routine financial activities. They sought to determine whether other employees were complying with financial and accounting procedures, whether assets were maintained under appropriate security, and whether there were any indications of fraud or other wrongdoing.

In some organizations the status of internal auditors was enhanced when they reached out to serve management in more imaginative and innovative ways. These internal auditors advanced their own interests by developing contacts with others in their discipline and by sharing their problems and accomplishments. The forum for such contacts was limited, however, to associations in the public utility industry, namely, the Edison Electric Institute and the American Gas Association. Each of these associations had an accounting section with a number of subcommittees, but internal auditing was not recognized as a separate activity in either the Institute or the Association. So two people who had expanded the role of internal auditing in their own utility companies — John B. Thurston of the North American Company and John G. Ivers of Detroit Edison — established an internal audit subcommittee of the general accounting committees of both professional organizations.[1]

The Birth of The Institute of Internal Auditors

Thurston was not satisfied. He foresaw the usefulness of a national body devoted to the needs of internal auditors alone. He enlisted the cooperation of leading internal auditing practitioners, and in 1941 they formed The Institute of Internal Auditors, Inc. The Institute was incorporated pursuant to the Membership Corporation Law of the State of New York. The purposes of The Institute, set forth in its articles of incorporation, are these:

> To cultivate, promote and disseminate knowledge and information concerning internal auditing and subjects related thereto; to establish and maintain high standards of integrity, honor and character among internal auditors; to furnish information regarding internal auditing and the practice and methods thereof to its members, and to other persons interested therein, and to the general public; to cause the publication of articles, relating to internal auditing and practices and methods thereof; to establish and maintain a library and reading rooms, meeting rooms and social rooms for the use of its members; to promote social intercourse among its members; and to do any and all things which shall be lawful and appropriate in furtherance of any of the purposes hereinbefore expressed.[2]

The first annual meeting of The Institute was held on December 9, 1941. To promote the spirit of fraternity and scholarship, The Institute adopted the motto "Progress Through Sharing" and showed the lamp of learning on its official seal.

The Growth of The Institute

The Institute grew mightily after 1941. In 38 years — a mere moment in the lives of most other professional organizations — it surged from one chapter in New York to over 156 chapters and 7 audit clubs around the world; from 24 charter members to over 23,000 members in 1981. The Institute was originally headquartered in New York, but in 1970, its educational arm was established in Winter Park, Florida. With membership needs and services expanding, the New York staff relocated there also. Since then the headquarters office moved to Altamonte Springs, Florida, where The Institute owns its own facility. In the meantime, the staff and the services to members expanded. Directors were employed to deal with education, professional practice, communications and public relations, chapter and membership services, certification, governmental and public affairs, finance and planning, and personnel and facilities.

Publications

The Institute is the spokesman for its practitioners and the source of information on internal auditing theory and practice. It publishes a professional journal *The Internal Auditor* and it engages in research studies and publishes the results in research bulletins. The subjects explored range as wide as the field of internal auditing — from "Behavioral Patterns in Internal Auditing Relationships"[3] to *Foozles and Frauds;*[4] from "Internal Audit of Inventory Control and Management"[5] to *Systems Auditability and Control Study — Data Processing Audit Practices Report.*[6]

Through its educational programs, The Institute offers seminars and training sessions on subjects of interest to internal auditors, ranging from the elements of internal auditing to advanced data processing audit techniques.

Statement of Responsibilities

Transitions

The first Statement of Responsibilities of Internal Auditors was published in 1947 (see Exhibit 2-1 for current statement). It heralded the break with other related disciplines. The definition of internal auditing, which opens the Statement, was a daring step forward for the times. It gave the first hint that internal auditing was not necessarily an adjunct of financial record keeping:

> It [internal auditing] deals primarily with accounting and financial matters but it may also properly deal with matters of an operating nature.

How gingerly the drafters of the 1947 Statement dipped their toes into the sea of operations! Even that hesitant step was a mighty leap for those starry-eyed internal auditors who saw more to internal auditing than a primary allegiance to the chief accountant. Strengthened by this small victory, the Statement was revised in 1957 with another step forward:

> Internal auditing is an independent appraisal activity within an organization for the review of accounting, financial, and other operations. . . .

The step was a small one. Acounting and financial matters still came first. They were still identified as the principal operations for internal audit review, but the 1957 Statement, like its predecessor, implicitly acknowledged that the evolution of the profession calls for revisions to express the expanded concepts of modern internal auditing.

The Broadened Role

The 1971 revision of the Statement finally cut the umbilical cord to the books of account. W. James Harmeyer, member of a research subcommittee which drafted the document, proposed that the first sentence of the new Statement be simplified, changing "accounting, financial, and other operations" to simply "operations." The first section of the Statement, under the heading of "Nature," then read:

> Internal auditing is an independent appraisal activity within an organization for the review of operations as a service to management. It is a managerial control which functions by measuring and evaluating the effectiveness of other controls.

The word *operations* is intended to encompass the entire spectrum of activities that an organization carries on. The change symbolized the internal auditor's equal concern with every significant aspect of the organization's operations.

Removing the words *financial* and *accounting* does not exclude those activities from the internal auditor's purview; these functions are covered by the generic term *operations*. The change did proclaim, however, the internal auditor's equal interest in whatever activities affect the entire enterprise.[7]

Exhibit 2-1.

STATEMENT OF RESPONSIBILITIES
OF INTERNAL AUDITORS

NATURE
Internal auditing is an independent appraisal activity within an organization for the review of operations as a service to management. It is a managerial control which functions by measuring and evaluating the effectiveness of other controls.

OBJECTIVE AND SCOPE
The objective of internal auditing is to assist all members of management in the effective discharge of their responsibilities by furnishing them with analyses, appraisals, recommendations and pertinent comments concerning the activities reviewed. Internal auditors are concerned with any phase of business activity in which they may be of service to management. This involves going beyond the accounting and financial records to obtain a full understanding of the operations under review. The attainment of this overall objective involves such activities as:

- Reviewing and appraising the soundness, adequacy, and application of accounting, financial, and other operating controls, and promoting effective control at reasonable cost.

- Ascertaining the extent of compliance with established policies, plans, and procedures.

- Ascertaining the extent to which company assets are accounted for and safeguarded from losses of all kinds.

- Ascertaining the reliability of management data developed within the organization.

- Appraising the quality of performance in carrying out assigned responsibilities.

- Recommending operating improvements.

RESPONSIBILITY AND AUTHORITY
The responsibilities of internal auditing in the organization should be clearly established by management policy. The related authority should provide the internal auditor full access to all of the organization's records, properties, and personnel relevant to the subject under review. The internal auditor should be free to review and appraise policies, plans, procedures, and records.

The internal auditor's responsibilities should be:

- To inform and advise management, and to discharge this responsibility in a manner that is consistent with the Code of Ethics of The Institute of Internal Auditors.

- To coordinate internal audit activities with others so as to best achieve the audit objectives and the objectives of the organization.

In performing their functions, internal auditors have no direct responsibilities for nor authority over any of the activities reviewed. Therefore, the internal audit re-

---

Exhibit 2-1. (Cont.)

view and appraisal does not in any way relieve other persons in the organization of the responsibilities assigned to them.

INDEPENDENCE

Independence is essential to the effectiveness of internal auditing. This independence is obtained primarily through organizational status and objectivity:

- The organizational status of the internal auditing function and the support accorded to it by management are major determinants of its range and value. The head of the internal auditing function, therefore, should be responsible to an officer whose authority is sufficient to assure both a broad range of audit coverage and the adequate consideration of and effective action on the audit findings and recommendations.

- Objectivity is essential to the audit function. Therefore, internal auditors should not develop and install procedures, prepare records, or engage in any other activity which they would normally review and appraise and which could reasonably be construed to compromise the independence of the internal auditor. The internal auditor's objectivity need not be adversely affected, however, by determining and recommending standards of control to be applied in the development of the systems and procedures being reviewed.

The Statement of Responsibilities of Internal Auditors was originally issued by The Institute of Internal Auditors in 1947. The continuing development of the profession has resulted in three revisions: 1957, 1971, and 1976. The current statement embodies the concepts previously established and includes such changes as are deemed advisable in light of the present status of the profession.

Objective and Scope

Four substantive changes were made in the Objective and Scope section of the 1971 Statement to indicate the management-oriented thinking of the practitioners of modern internal auditing:

First, the Statement places emphasis on the internal auditors' needs to transcend accounting records to obtain a full understanding of the operations under review. Internal auditors are concerned not only with the map, but also with the terrain it represents. They must go beyond representations to reality, beyond the historical data to the actual operations which are reflected in or affect the accounting records.

Second, the internal auditors are cautioned that in promoting effective control they must consider the cost. They must balance the price tag for control on the one hand with the risks to be guarded against on the other. And they must be concerned with controls in relation to the objectives they seek to accomplish — not merely with control for control's sake.

Third, the phrase "accounting and other data" was changed to "management data" — another indication of the modern internal auditor's vista since data generated in nonfinancial activities can have a profound effect on management decisions.

Fourth, a new responsibility is listed: "Recommending operating improvement." This addition emphasizes the constructive as well as the protective aspect of the internal auditor's work. This constructive role can be more income-producing or cost-reducing than the protective and the detective aspects of internal auditing.

Responsibility and Authority

The Responsibility and Authority section makes it clear that the internal auditors' responsibility for their assignments, and their authority to carry them out, must be set forth in management policy statements. The internal auditors must have free and unrestricted access to all records, properties, and personnel relevant to their review. Then, two additional matters were included in this section.

First, it was stated categorically that the internal auditors will carry out their responsibilities in a manner consistent with the Code of Ethics of The Institute. This moved internal auditing another step forward toward complete professionalism. True professionals have a responsibility not only to their clients, but also to their own professional standards of conduct. They are obligated to make sure that they will not knowingly be a part of any illegal activity.

Second, it specified that internal auditors are responsible for coordinating their activities with others. Many respondents to the first draft of the 1971 Statement felt the need to show the desirability of coordinating the work of the internal auditor with the public accountant. The drafters of the 1971 Statement believed that the internal auditor should be coordinated with other disciplines both inside and outside the organization; therefore, the clause was written in general terms to permit the broadest interpretation.

Independence

The final provision of the 1957 Statement read:

> Since complete objectivity is essential to the audit function, internal auditors should not develop and install procedures, prepare records, or engage in any other activity which they normally would be expected to review and appraise.

This provision was revised in the 1971 Statement to emphasize the internal auditors' concern with control. As consultants on control, they may be called upon to advise on standards of control for new procedures or operations. For example, in their work with electronic data processing applications, they are often asked to review and evaluate a system before it is put into effect. For that reason the 1971 Statement included the following sentence: "His objectivity need not be adversely affected, however, by his determination and recommendation of the standards of control to be applied to the development of systems and procedures under his review."[8]

The 1976 Statement

In 1976, the Statement was rewritten to take into account the welcome influx of women into the profession (see Exhibit 2-1). No substantive changes were made, but all references to the masculine gender were eliminated.

Code of Ethics

The Institute's Code

The Institute's first Code of Ethics was adopted on December 13, 1968, and affects all members of The Institute of Internal Auditors, Inc.[9] (see Exhibit 2-2). It outlines criteria of professional behavior and expects members of The Institute to maintain standards of competence, morality, and dignity.

The Code recognizes that ethics are an important consideration in the practice of modern internal auditing and charges members to exercise honesty, objectivity, diligence, and loyalty to employers; to avoid conflicts of interest and not to accept fees or gifts without the knowledge of senior management; to treat information gained as confidential; to factually support their opinions; to reveal all material facts known to them; and to seek self-improvement.

The Statement of Responsibilities has no policing provisions and contains no legal requirements for internal auditors. Nevertheless, many charters developed by organizations for their internal auditors incorporate, or are based on, it. That Statement incorporates the Code of Ethics by reference. Organizations, therefore, whose charters by implication refer to the Code of Ethics, could reasonably expect their internal auditors to meet the criteria enunciated in the Code. This is particularly true when the internal auditors are members of The Institute.

Section 240 of the *Standards for the Professional Practice of Internal Auditing* (see Appendix A) provides that "internal auditors should comply with professional standards of conduct." It refers specifically to The Code of Ethics of The Institute of Internal Auditors. It would seem reasonable that, in an issue subject to adjudication in the courts, the Code could come into play. Whenever courts have had to rule on professional conduct, their only source for criteria of acceptable conduct has been the general standards set by the profession itself.

It follows, then, that anyone in fact practicing internal auditing — whether a member of The Institute or not, whether self-termed an internal auditor or known by some other designation — who wrongs someone through the practice of his or her profession, might be held accountable when conduct is not consistent with the Code.

Some might argue that internal auditing responsibilities differ widely among organizations, thus making a common code impossible. The com-

Exhibit 2-2.

THE INSTITUTE OF INTERNAL AUDITORS, INC.
CODE OF ETHICS

INTRODUCTION: Recognizing that ethics are an important consideration in the practice of internal auditing and that the moral principles followed by members of *The Institute of Internal Auditors, Inc.*, should be formalized, the Board of Directors at its regular meeting in New Orleans on December 13, 1968, received and adopted the following resolution:

WHEREAS the members of *The Institute of Internal Auditors, Inc.*, represent the profession of internal auditing; and

WHEREAS managements rely on the profession of internal auditing to assist in the fulfillment of their management stewardship; and

WHEREAS said members must maintain high standards of conduct, honor and character in order to carry on proper and meaningful internal auditing practice:

THEREFORE BE IT RESOLVED that a Code of Ethics be now set forth, outlining the standards of professional behavior for the guidance of each member of *The Institute of Internal Auditors, Inc.*

In accordance with this resolution, the Board of Directors further approved of the principles set forth.

INTERPRETATION OF PRINCIPLES: The provisions of this Code of Ethics cover basic principles in the various disciplines of internal auditing practice. Members shall realize that individual judgment is required in the application of these principles. They have a responsibility to conduct themselves so that their good faith and integrity should not be open to question. While having due regard for the limit of their technical skills, they will promote the highest possible internal auditing standards to the end of advancing the interest of their company or organization.

ARTICLES:

I. Members shall have an obligation to exercise honesty, objectivity, and diligence in the performance of their duties and responsibilities.

II. Members, in holding the trust of their employers, shall exhibit loyalty in all matters pertaining to the affairs of the employer or to whomever they may be rendering a service. However, members shall not knowingly be a part to any illegal or improper activity.

III. Members shall refrain from entering into any activity which may be in conflict with the interest of their employers or which would prejudice their ability to carry out objectively their duties and responsibilities.

IV. Members shall not accept a fee or a gift from an employee, a client, a customer, or a business associate of their employer without the knowledge and consent of their senior management.

V. Members shall be prudent in the use of information acquired in the course of their duties. They shall not use confidential information for any personal

---

Exhibit 2-2. (Cont.)

gain nor in a manner which would be detrimental to the welfare of their employer.

VI. Members, in expressing an opinion, shall use all reasonable care to obtain sufficient factual evidence to warrant such expression. In their reporting, members shall reveal such material facts known to them, which, if not revealed, could either distort the report of the results of operations under review or conceal unlawful practice.

VII. Members shall continually strive for improvement in the proficiency and effectiveness of their service.

VIII. Members shall abide by the bylaws and uphold the objectives of *The Institute of Internal Auditors, Inc.* In the practice of their profession, they shall be ever mindful of their obligation to maintain the high standard of competence, morality, and dignity which *The Institute of Internal Auditors, Inc.*, and its members have established.

---

mittee drafting the Code decided, however, that while responsibilities might vary — some narrow, some broad — internal auditors all have common purposes. Thus, the Code, as written, could be an acceptable guide for personal discipline and conduct.[10]

The Certified Internal Auditor's Code

Awarding the designation of Certified Internal Auditor (CIA) is conditioned, in part, on the candidate's certification that he or she has "read and will abide by the CIA Code of Ethics" (see Exhibit 2-3).

The articles of the two codes are virtually the same. The CIA Code does not contain The Institute's Article VIII, which concerns upholding Institute objectives and maintaining Institute standards. One reason for eliminating Article VIII is this: Requiring membership in The Institute as a condition to certification would contravene United States laws. An applicant in the United States does not have to be an Institute member to take and pass the CIA Examination and be awarded the designation Certified Internal Auditor.

While the articles of the two codes are much the same, there are some significant differences between other parts of The Institute and CIA Codes.

First, the CIA Code, as befits a professional pronouncement, points to the CIA's obligation to the general public to maintain high standards of conduct, one of the attributes of a lofty profession.

Second, the CIA Code has teeth: "A Certified Internal Auditor who is judged by the Board of Directors of The Institute to be in violation of the

Exhibit 2-3.

 Certified
Internal
Auditor

CODE OF ETHICS

The Certified Internal Auditor has an obligation to the profession, management, and stockholders and to the general public to maintain high standards of professional conduct. In recognition of this obligation, The Institute of Internal Auditors, Inc., adopted this Code of Ethics for Certified Internal Auditors.

Adherence to this Code, which is based on the Code of Ethics for members of The Institute, is a prerequisite to maintaining the designation Certified Internal Auditor. A Certified Internal Auditor who is judged by the Board of Directors of The Institute to be in violation of the provisions of the Code shall forfeit the Certified Internal Auditor designation.

Preamble

The provisions of this Code of Ethics cover basic principles in the various disciplines of internal auditing practice. Certified Internal Auditors shall realize that their individual judgment is required in the application of these principles. They have a responsibility to conduct themselves in a manner so that their good faith and integrity should not be open to question. Furthermore, they shall use the "Certified Internal Auditor" designation with discretion and in a dignified manner, fully aware of what the designation denotes and in a manner consistent with all statutory requirements. While having due regard for the limit of their technical skills, they will promote the highest possible internal auditing standards to the end of advancing the interest of their company or organization.

Articles

I. Certified Internal Auditors shall have an obligation to exercise honesty, objectivity and diligence in the performance of their duties and responsibilities.

II. Certified Internal Auditors, in holding the trust of their employer, shall exhibit loyalty in all matters pertaining to the affairs of the employer or to whomever they may be rendering a service. However, a Certified Internal Auditor shall not knowingly be a party to any illegal or improper activity.

III. Certified Internal Auditors shall refrain from entering into any activity which may be in conflict with the interest of their employer or which would prejudice their ability to carry out objectively their duties and responsibilities.

IV. Certified Internal Auditors shall not accept a fee or a gift from an employee, a client, a customer or a business associate of their employer without the knowledge and consent of senior management.

V. Certified Internal Auditors shall be prudent in their use of information acquired in the course of their duties. They shall not use confidential information for

---

Exhibit 2-3. (Cont.)

any personal gain or in a manner which would be detrimental to the welfare of their employer.

VI. Certified Internal Auditors, in expressing an opinion, shall use all reasonable care to obtain sufficient factual evidence to warrant such expression. In reporting, Certified Internal Auditors shall reveal such material facts known to them which, if not revealed, could either distort the report of the results of operations under review or conceal unlawful practice.

VII. Certified Internal Auditors shall continually strive for improvements in the proficiency and effectiveness of their service.

---

provisions of the Code shall forfeit the Certified Internal Auditor designation."

Third, Certified Internal Auditors "shall use the 'Certified Internal Auditor' designation with discretion and in a dignified manner." This is a significant provision. The internal auditor who qualifies for the designation is "board certified." That board is The Institute of Internal Auditors, Inc. The certification is not awarded by a state agency, and many states have statutes prohibiting the use of any designations which could be confused with the state-awarded CPA, PA, or, in British countries, the CA. Thus, CIAs must be careful in their letterheads or business cards not to contravene state laws by creating the proscribed impressions. A reasonably safe procedure for such items as documents, cards, and letterheads circulated outside the umbrella of The Institute, would be to use the entire designation, Certified Internal Auditor. This use has other benefits. The initials, to most people, are not associated with auditing. The full name describes the designation; there is no confusion with any government agency.

The discipline of internal auditing still has a mountain to climb. Doctors, lawyers, and certified public accountants may not practice their profession unless they take an oath binding them to established professional ethics. Today, uncertified internal auditors are not so bound. Internal auditors who are not certified can ply their craft without concern for disciplinary action if they violate any of the precepts laid down by the present codes. When the dishonest or incompetent internal auditor will be faced with official censure for his or her misdeeds or ineptitude, the profession as a whole will have moved up to the top rungs of professionalism.

The Common Body of Knowledge

The Approach

An essential building block in the structure of a profession is a common body of knowledge. It forms the conceptual foundation of the discipline. It serves as the standard for education and for training, recruiting, and testing the competence of those who aspire to enter the profession.

The Institute's certification program demands high standards of education for applicants. In 1971, a subcommittee of The Institute's Education Committee was formed under the leadership of Robert E. Gobeil, then of Domtar Limited in Canada, to develop a common body of knowledge for internal auditors. Besides reviewing the auditing literature, the subcommittee analyzed the common bodies of knowledge and the educational guidelines of a number of professional organizations in the field of management.[11]

The Results

The subcommittee's survey disclosed the following broad areas that would apply to a common body of knowledge for internal auditors: accounting and finance, auditing, behavioral science, communication, computer systems and equipment, economics, legal aspects of business, quantitative methods, and systems and procedures.

Within each of these areas were certain subheads. For example, accounting and finance was subdivided into elementary accounting, financial accounting, cost accounting, and accounting for management planning and control. Questionnaires sent to practitioners evoked a consensus of the levels of knowledge needed for subjects appropriate to a common body of knowledge for internal auditors.

The questionnaires, when prepared, expanded the nine subjects into seventeen. It soon became apparent that it would be a rare individual who could apply with equal facility all the subjects in the common body. Indeed, there would be no need to acquire and maintain a high level of knowledge in all these subjects because many of them do not arise in the day-to-day work of internal auditors. Yet all of them do arise every once in a while, and internal auditors should not be ignorant of any of them. So the levels of knowledge were finally set at three in number and were defined as follows:[12]

Level One. A general appreciation of the broad nature and the fundamentals involved. The ability to recognize the existence, or the likelihood of existence, of special features and problems in various business transactions and to determine what further study or research must be undertaken under various conditions.

Level Two. A sound appreciation of the broad aspects of practices and procedures and an awareness of the problems relating to more detailed aspects. The ability to apply such broad knowledge to situations likely to be encountered, to recognize the more detailed aspects which must be considered, and to carry out research and studies necessary to come to a reasonable solution.

Level Three. A sound understanding of principles, practices, and procedures. The ability to apply such knowledge to situations likely to be encountered and to deal with all aspects of the subject without extensive recourse to technical research and assistance.

A consensus is almost always a compromise, so the questionnaire results, when tabulated, came within ranges that ran from 2.31 down to less than one. Some elements within a subject were at the first level, some at the second level, and others at the third. It seemed obvious to the compilers that the responses from practitioners were founded on what they were actually practicing rather than what they should be practicing. But the responses, nevertheless, were indicative.

Within the range of Level Three (2 to 3) were auditing first, then accounting and finance.

Within the range of Level Two (1 to 1.99) were behavioral science, communication, computers and systems, law and taxes, business management, finance and control, production, quantitative methods, and systems and procedures.

Within the range of Level One (.01 to .99) were economics, external relations, marketing, personnel administration, secretarial and legal, and research and development.

Three international committees of The Institute — Education, Professional Development, and Research — in joint session adopted the draft of the Common Body of Knowledge on June 17, 1972. The members unanimously agreed to "accept and support the Common Body of Knowledge study as an initial step in developing educational requirements for internal auditors." They also agreed that the study should serve as the basis for The Institute's certification program.

When the certification program was inaugurated, the Board of Regents rearranged the subjects into four groupings which represented the four parts of the Certified Internal Auditor Examination.

Certification Program

Initiating the Program

Once the Common Body of Knowledge was adopted, the way was clear for a certification program. Many practitioners opposed the program since they could see no benefit to themselves from such an undertaking. Still, the majority recognized that current benefits were much less important than the benefits down the road. They realized that any claims for professionalism were idle wishes without a testing and certification of the professionals. So, despite much opposition, the Board of Directors of The Institute adopted the program in 1972 and the first examination was held on August 16 and 17, 1974.

In the meantime, about 7,900 internal auditors, out of about 8,500 who applied, received the Certified Internal Auditor designation under the so-called Grandfather clause. The successful candidates demonstrated that they had practiced internal auditing in a decision-making capacity and agreed to abide by the CIA Code of Ethics. In October 1973, they were awarded certificates designating them as Certified Internal Auditors.[13] In

March 1975, the CIA designation was awarded to 122 out of 654 candidates who sat for the first Certified Internal Auditor examination in 1974.

The Benefits of the Program

William S. Smith, a former international president of The Institute and the certification program's driving force, gave these reasons for taking the examination: participation in a recognized profession, higher level of professional training, recognition by one's peers, better acceptance in the job market, and personal satisfaction.[14]

Other tangible benefits have resulted from the program. First, the Comptroller General of the United States has drafted "form" legislation for states wishing to inaugurate internal auditing programs which provides that the general auditor in the state should be a CPA or a CIA. Second, the United States Civil Service Commission has decreed that any applicant for an auditing position in the federal government who has an **earned** CIA designation would be excused from taking a written examination.

Requirements to Sit for the CIA Examination

A "Certified Internal Auditor Program and Study Guide," published by The Institute, describes the examination and the subjects on which candidates will be examined. The requirements are summarized as follows:

All candidates in the United States shall hold a baccalaureate degree from an accredited college-level institution. Qualifications of candidates outside the United States will be judged on their merits by the Board of Regents of the CIA program in terms of equivalency to the United States baccalaureate degree.

All candidates shall have a minimum of two years work experience in internal auditing before they will be awarded their certificates.

Each registration must be accompanied by a statement from a Certified Internal Auditor or supervisor attesting to internal auditing experience.

Each applicant must subscribe to the CIA Code of Ethics and submit a character reference from a Certified Internal Auditor or from a supervisor.

Qualified candidates must successfully pass all parts of an examination which at this time is in four parts. Candidates must sit for at least two parts of the examination in their initial sitting. They may reapply to repeat those parts they fail. Those who fail to pass all parts of the examination within five successive examinations will lose credit for any parts successfully completed.

The Examination

The examination is given primarily in the United States and Canada, but it is also given in any other place in the world where sufficient applications are received to warrant holding the examination. It has been given in May of each year since 1974; beginning in 1982, however, it is expected that the examination will be given twice each year.

The examination, based on the Common Body of Knowledge for Internal Auditors, is divided into the following four parts as of this writing:

I Principles of Internal Auditing

II Internal Audit Techniques

III Principles of Management

IV Disciplines Related to Internal Auditing

Questions in Part I deal with such matters as the nature of internal auditing; administering the internal audit department and the individual audit assignments; principles of internal control, including computer controls; and the internal auditor's environment, including behavioral science, communication, and external relations. Here are two typical questions:

Multiple Choice (Estimated time for multiple choice questions averages about 1½ minutes a question.) (Question 10, 1976)

The charter for an internal auditing department should indicate responsibility for:

a. Reconciling bank accounts.

b. Developing standards of control in a new EDP system.

c. Developing job descriptions in any department under review where there are no job descriptions.

d. Correcting any deficient condition.

e. None of the above.

Narrative (Estimated time: 5 minutes) (Question 15, 1975)

An internal auditor is pressed for time. He has discussed his findings with the auditee. As a result of the discussion, he suspects that there may be certain failures in complying with the company's policies and procedures. He cannot take the time to verify the situation.

Required: What course of action would you recommend which would be in keeping with the Code of Ethics for Certified Internal Auditors and which would not adversely affect good auditor-auditee relationships?

Questions in Part II cover the tools and techniques of internal auditing, such as applications of internal control, computers, preliminary surveys, flowcharts, audit programs, field work, working papers, and audit reports. Covered also is the auditing of various functions of an organization, such as accounting, marketing, production, personnel administration, purchasing, and research and development. Here are two typical questions:

Multiple Choice (Question 5, 1975)

The reentry of all data rejected by the computer may be monitored by:

a. Instructions issued over the signature of an executive officer.

b. A sound training program.
c. Placing the responsibility for reentry on the user department.
d. A tape inventory of errors.
e. All of the above.

Narrative (Estimated time: 25 minutes) (Question 33, 1978)
A senior auditor completed a preliminary survey of certain marketing activities for a company. The following situations were disclosed: One, billings from the advertising agency for insertions in magazines and newspapers are approved for payment without adequate review by advertising department personnel. Two, purchases of advertising materials and artwork are made by one employee of the advertising department. Three, company-owned materials, such as artwork, furniture, company products, and other items used for photographic sets, are retained by the advertising agency.

Required: For each of the three situations, prepare four audit steps to be included in the audit program.

Questions in Part III deal with the auditor's environment; the nature of management; and the management processes of planning, organizing, directing, and controlling. Here are two typical questions:

Multiple Choice (Question 14, 1978)
Which of the following would normally be considered a line position?
a. Credit manager in a retail store.
b. Computer programmer in a brokerage firm.
c. Secretary in an accounting department.
d. Internal auditor in a public utility.
e. Salesperson in a manufacturing company.

Narrative (Estimated time: 15 minutes) (Question 19, 1978)
When people work together for some time, they tend to form informal groups.

Required: State whether informal groups should be discouraged by management. Explain your answer. Give a condition or situation which is conducive to informal group formation. List three common characteristics of informal groups.

Questions in Part IV deal with managerial or financial accounting, economics, law, corporate taxation, finance, quantitative methods, and information systems. Two typical questions are as follows:

Multiple Choice (Question 12, 1976)
Which of the following is not an essential step in using a linear programming model?
a. Quantify the maximization coefficient inflows.
b. Determine the objective function.

   c. Establish the basic relationships between the variables and the constants.

   d. Identify the feasible alternatives.

   e. Solve the equations to find the optimum alternative.

Narrative (Estimated time: 11 minutes) (Question 18, 1974)

In a standard cost system of a manufacturer, at what point in the operating cycle would you recognize, for the purpose of recording, each of the two variances for raw materials? Give reasons for your answer.

As this book goes to press, the Board of Regents is considering changing the structure of the examination to increase the emphasis on computers and quantification, and reduce the emphasis on management principles, law, and taxation.

Preparing for the Examination

A serious difficulty facing candidates for the Certified Internal Auditor Examination is the absence of structured university curricula covering the common body of knowledge for internal auditors. To fill the gap temporarily, The Institute prepared a suggested readings list of the subject areas of the CIA Examination (see Exhibit 2-4).

Chapters of The Institute, several universities, and a few entrepreneurs are providing review courses for the CIA Examination. For candidates having a solid educational background in the subjects covered by the examination, the review courses can be a valuable refresher. At this writing, the sources of information needed to pass the CIA Examination are still fractionated. So at least for the present, the candidate most likely to pass the examination is an experienced internal auditor with a master's degree in business administration who recently took a CIA review course. This combined experience and study provide knowledge of most of the subjects in the exam.

Internal auditing is a skilled profession, and the attaining of certification calls for more than study of digested review material. Many people who took the CIA Exam were not prepared to do so; the pass/fail rate tends to support that assertion. Here are some statistics on the CIA Examinations given as of this writing, showing the number of candidates who took all four parts of the examination and the number and percentage who passed:

Year	Number of Candidates	Number Passing	Percentage Passing
1974	490	122	24.9
1975	257	63	24.5
1976	420	136	32.4
1977	361	67	18.6
1978	607	136	22.4
1979	633	150	23.7
1980	902	157	17.4

Despite its difficulty, the interest in the CIA Examination has grown steadily. From 1974 through 1980, the number of candidates who took the examination increased each year. The number who passed all four parts of the examination, some with more than one try, is as follows:

Year	Total Candidates	Passing All Four Parts Over the Years
1974	654	122
1975	719	159
1976	1099	299
1977	1227	200
1978	2091	332
1979	2250	431
1980	2653	514
Totals	10693	2057
Special Certification (Grandfathers)		7880
Total Certified Internal Auditors		9937

The grand total of 10,693 candidates includes those who repeated parts of the examination which they had failed. The dramatic increase of total candidates in 1978 can be attributed, in part, to a desire to make application before a new requirement went into effect. Starting in 1979, all candidates must have a baccalaureate degree if they sit for the examination in the United States, and an equivalent to such a degree if they sit for it elsewhere.

As the years go by and the scope of the profession deepens and broadens while the literature becomes more extensive and varied, the examination is bound to become more taxing. But that only serves to make the earned certification a more respected reward for the time and effort invested. Still, a full-fledged course in internal auditing is a necessity.

Courses in Modern Internal Auditing

Internal auditing has long been discussed in accounting literature, but by and large it was financially oriented. So were the courses the prospective CIA candidates took.

With the advent of the new profession of internal auditing, a need evolved for literature and for college courses devoted to appraisals of all the operations of an organization. The literature began to appear (see Exhibit 2-4).

The courses, for the most part, however, have been one-semester evening courses. These are helpful, but they are not complete solutions. They do not go into sufficient depth and breadth to qualify the student to sit for the entire CIA Examination. At best they are useful for Parts I and II.

In 1968, The Institute of Internal Auditors, Inc., established an educational program to provide useful seminars on internal auditing. These seminars are directed primarily toward improving the skills of working internal auditors. They are concerned with those subjects covered in Parts I and II of the examination, with computers, and with audit sampling.

The fields of management and the disciplines related to internal auditing are taught, if at all, in courses here and there, but the relationship to internal auditing is not stressed.

Few schools have courses of study that focus on the subject with a view to integrating the disparate pieces and producing appraisers of all operations of the enterprise. For a long time the closest thing to such a course was a master's degree in business administration with a major in accounting. But that did not touch on the heart of modern internal auditing which is tested in Parts I and II.

A substantial number of accounting students are not planning on becoming external auditors. They would rather be employed in business or government. Too often they do not learn of this new profession of internal auditing until after they have left school. When they become aware of the rich store of varied experiences and opportunities awaiting them, they learn how internal auditing can be a rewarding career for life or serve as a springboard into management positions. When they do learn of this new profession, they must take more courses to prepare themselves properly. That and on-the-job training are all the preparation now specifically available to acquire a discipline whose principles and techniques are diverse and warrant study at the university level. [15]

Many thoughtful educators who truly understand the needs of their students conceive of a branching trail for the accounting student — one which will allow a choice and provide better preparation for those whose interests lie in fields other than public accounting. These educators foresee a curriculum providing first for a sound foundation in accounting for all Business Administration candidates majoring in accounting. After receiving this foundation, the candidates will have the option of traveling either of two different paths: one leading toward public accounting, with all the related auditing courses pointing in that direction; the second leading toward private or governmental accounting, management, and internal auditing, with auditing courses covering appraisals of all operations in the organization. [16]

Accounting is important to both internal auditors and managers. But it is not their *sine qua non*. Other management-related courses are equally important. For those who enter public accounting and then decide to pursue a career in internal auditing, there should be an established series of classes to come back to. If such courses were available, those who plan to sit for the Certified Internal Auditor Examination would be better prepared for it.

There are stirrings in the universities for such courses, prompted by demands from companies for well-qualified internal auditors. Probably the first was proposed by Australia's Royal Melbourne Institute of Technology in its school of business. Plans are for a two-year course of study leading to a graduate diploma in internal auditing at the postgraduate level. Prerequisites are a degree from a college of advanced education or equivalent qualification with at least four units of accountancy. The aims of the course are to provide a program to meet perceived needs of internal auditors and to examine the objectives, theory, and practice of internal auditing.

The entire course calls for 350 hours of study, a little over eight United States semester equivalents. The first year's course includes:

Subjects	Hours	U.S. Semester Equivalents
Internal Auditing I	84	2
Quantitative Methods	56	1⅓
An elective	42	1
Total, first year	·182	4⅓

The second year's course includes:

Internal Auditing II	84	2
Integrated studies	84	2
Total, second year	168	4
Grand total	350	8⅓

The courses span a broad range. Among the many subjects covered are these: principles and techniques of internal auditing; internal control; communication; administering both the internal auditing department and the internal audit assignment; audits of varied functions in industry, commerce, and government through case studies; linear programming; critical path method (CPM) and program evaluation and review technique (PERT); regression analysis; macroeconomic planning devices; management; forecasting; assessment of profit opportunities and risks; social conscience; and leadership. Also included is a thorough indoctrination in business systems with heavy emphasis on computers. As of this writing, the course is still in the planning stage with implementation, we are told, awaiting the necessary funding.

Universities in the United States are also hearing the call for courses which will lead to a degree in internal auditing or at least provide the education needed to sit for the CIA Examination with a reasonable prospect of success.

The Catholic University of America in Washington, D.C., has instituted a specialized graduate program leading to a master's in internal auditing. The reason for the program was explained in the proposal by the Department of Economics and Business Management of the University: "There is a definite need for a graduate program which would offer a well integrated and academically acceptable master's program and at the same time provide the training for the achievement of the certification in internal auditing (CIA)."

The program calls for 36 credit hours made up of six required courses, five elective courses, and an internship equal to one course. Applicants able to prove their practical experience in internal auditing are released from the requirement of the internship. That reduces the total credit hours from 36 to 33. The required courses include auditing, internal auditing, computer control audit, and advanced internal auditing. Also included are computer theory and behavior, management of organizations, and Graduate Statistics I. The electives are selected from the fields of economics, accounting, business law, and management.

In 1978, the College of Business Administration of the University of South Carolina took a hard look at courses in accountancy and decided that the curriculum was too narrow and did not apply to a broad group of accountants who are not necessarily interested in a career in public accounting. This group includes accountants in industry and government, management accountants, systems and procedures specialists, internal auditors, and management advisory specialists. The university has designed its curriculum to fill a "need for increased professionalism in accounting education."

South Carolina's "Professional Accounting Program" is a ten-semester (160-163 hours) course with the objective of educating people for entry into the practice of professional accounting as distinguished from a purely CPA orientation. Of these credit hours, 130-133 are taken at the baccalaureate degree level and 30 at the graduate level. The principal subject areas include: financial accounting, managerial accounting, management information and accounting systems, tax planning and accounting, and auditing (internal and public).

A specialization program provides for 15 additional hours of graduate-level, individually arranged courses directed toward a number of goals. One of these goals is internal auditing. This specialization program therefore gives consideration to the needs of candidates for the professional designations of CIA, CMA (Certificate in Management Accounting), and CPA.

In 1979, the Graduate School of Management and Urban Professions of the New School for Social Research, began to offer a course leading to a Master of Professional Studies in Management Auditing. The course is held in New York City and Washington, D. C. In addition to a baccalaureate degree prerequisite, the course requires 48 credits for completion — 18 credits of required courses, 6 credits for a Master's Project, and 24 credits of electives. The curriculum encompasses a variety of courses (3 credits each) aimed at providing students with expertise in:

The tools and techniques needed for effective management audits including quantitative methods, information systems and computer applications, managerial accounting; audit programs, computer audits, internal control questionnaires; audit reports, planning and control systems;

The principles of management, the manager's concerns, the tools for making decisions and administering the matters for which they are responsible, and the factors affecting accomplishment of an organization's objectives;

Organizational behavior; diagnosis, organizational intervention and change, and planning and systems control;

Administration of the management audit; planning the management audit; selection, training, and evaluation of staff; measurement and evaluation of audit accomplishments; the auditor's environment; organizational and procedural controls; auditing ethics;

Communications, reporting the results of management audits, reporting formats and techniques, communication skills, interviewing and fact-finding, utilizing management results in management decision making.

Curricula like these, carried out as planned, will fill the vacuum long existing between courses provided in universities and the needs of the professional accountant and the professional internal auditor. It will be another step toward converting internal auditing from a craft to a respected profession.

The certification program and the growth of courses in internal auditing do point to a dilemma. Internal auditing may be regarded as a profession, but all its practitioners are not necessarily professional people. Strictly speaking, a professional is one who has been certified as having certain qualifications; yet many people who practice internal auditing are free to do so without being certified. This is a dilemma the years will have to solve. In time, internal auditors will be regarded as professionals only if they have obtained a degree in internal auditing and have passed an examination on the subject. This then, will put them on the same footing as the doctor, the lawyer, and the certified public accountant.

Standards for the Professional Practice of Internal Auditing

Adoption of the Standards

In June 1978, at The Institute of Internal Auditor's International Conference in San Francisco, The Institute's Board of Directors formally adopted a set of standards for internal auditors (see Appendix A). This was a remarkable step, carried off successfully by the International Standards and Responsibilities Committee, chaired by Roger N. Carolus of Northwest Bancorporation. These Standards apply to all internal auditors.

Differences in Application

Internal auditors around the world have been practicing their craft in different ways. Most have been functioning under the direction of the people to whom they report, running the gamut from chief accountants to audit committees of boards of directors. Some practitioners have access to all records, properties, and personnel within the enterprise. Others are confined to the accounting department.

Certainly, no set of standards can dictate mangement's disposition of its internal auditors' efforts, and the Standards carefully avoid imposing criteria on managers or board members. Standards for internal auditors can bind only internal auditors, and the *Standards* made it plain in its Introduction that implementation "will be governed by the environment in which the internal auditing department carries out its assigned responsibilities." But the Introduction states quite specifically that " . . . compliance with the concepts enunciated by these *Standards* is essential before the responsibilities of internal auditors can be met."

The Management Problem

Through the published *Standards*, management and the board of directors were, in effect, given this notice: Certainly, you hold the purse strings and call the plays, but you have no right to tell the world that you have a team of internal auditors who meet professional standards if you keep them shackled to the books of account, if you have them reporting to a level of management that renders them impotent, or if you have a host of activities that you keep your internal auditors from appraising.

This is no idle notice. Government regulatory agency officials, like Harold M. Williams, former chairman, United States Securities and Exchange Commission, saw the qualified internal audit department as a powerful force for good in the organization.[17] External auditors will rely on the work of internal auditors — and thereby reduce their work and their fees — only if that work meets professional standards. And courts, which judge the level of due care exercised by a profession, usually have little to rely on other than the profession's own statement of standards and code of ethics, as long as they are in accord with criteria considered applicable to any profession.

The Purposes and Thrust of the *Standards*

The committee developing the *Standards* saw these purposes for their development — to establish a basis for consistent measurement of internal auditing operations; to unify internal auditing throughout the world; to encourage improved internal auditing; to assist in communicating to others the role, scope, performance, and objectives of internal auditing; and to provide a vehicle by which internal auditing can be fully recognized as a profession.[18]

The *Standards* are divided into the following five sections:

○ Independence
○ Professional Proficiency
○ Scope of Work
○ Performance of Audit Work
○ Management of the Internal Audit Department

Here are some of the more significant concepts raised by the *Standards*. (The numerical references identify the sections.)

100. *Independence*

The *Standards* recognize the shift from "a service to management" to "a service to the organization." *Organization* in this sense comprises both management and the board of directors, and the *Standards* see the internal auditor as owing a duty to both.

The *Standards* point out the need for practical independence. Certainly, the internal auditor's paycheck is still signed by a member of management; but a concerted effort must be made to see that internal auditors in an organization are perceived to be independent of the activities they audit. To that end the *Standards* point out that independence is enhanced when the board of directors concurs in the appointment or removal of the director of internal auditing.

The *Standards* also recommend direct communication with the board of directors including the submission of reports showing the audit work intended and accomplished, as well as the significant findings of the audit.

200. Professional Proficiency

This section places requirements on both the internal auditing department and the internal auditor.

The *Standards* expect of the department reasonable assurance of the proficiency of prospective auditors, calling for knowledge and skills within the department sufficient to carry out audit responsibilities. The *Standards* require adequate supervision of the audit work.

Of the individual internal auditor the *Standards* expect compliance, skill in dealing with people and communicating audit results, the maintenance of technical competence through continuing education, and the exercise of professional care.

The *Standards* define *due professional care* in the same way as the courts would: "The care and skill expected of a reasonably prudent and competent internal auditor in the same or similar circumstances." This does not mean infallibility or extraordinary performance. It does not mean that the internal auditor can be held to be an insurer against all forms of wrongdoing within the enterprise. Such a responsibility for internal auditors would be as ludicrous as requiring a doctor to assure patients that they would never get sick or requiring a lawyer to assure clients that they would never be sued.

Due professional care requires alertness to the risk areas — to those potential conditions which promote or invite improprieties. To that extent, due professional care by internal auditors is not a static thing. As the profession grows more sophisticated, as the literature expands to point out indicators or new ways of developing indicators of things amiss, the professional internal auditor will be expected to make use of them. If a new, specific drug for cancer were developed and hailed in the medical journals and approved by the Food and Drug Administration, and a doctor failed to prescribe it to a patient suffering from cancer where such a prescription was clearly indicated, the doctor could be held guilty of negligence.

Similarly, if internal auditors fail to make use of techniques their professional literature discusses and their peers are using to reveal wrongdoing, they could be considered negligent. The right to be called a professional carries burdens. One cannot claim the name without playing the game.

But the drafters of the *Standards* were careful to point out that if internal auditors suspect irregularities, they should inform "the appropriate authorities **within** the organization." (Emphasis added.) The *Standards* place no responsibility upon internal auditors to inform other authorities outside the organization.

300. Scope of Work

Not all internal auditors have the charter or the skill to make a full-scope audit. The *Standards* recognize this, and the drafters were well aware that internal auditors must function within the fences their superiors construct for them or else seek other forms or places of employment.

But the *Standards* also state, at least implicitly, that the audit scope should ideally encompass four elements:

1. Integrity of information systems — accuracy, timeliness, and usefulness of accounting and operating records and reports.

2. Compliance with policies, plans, procedures, laws, and regulations — whether operating rules and regulations are still useful and appropriate.

3. Economical and efficient use of resources and safeguarding of assets — whether what is being done is done in the best and least expensive way, and whether the resources of the organization are under adequate surveillance and control.

4. Adequacy of operating objectives and goals and the effectiveness of results — whether operating aims coincide with overall organizational aims, whether satisfactory objectives and goals are being met, whether assigned missions are being accomplished, and whether the control systems throughout the organization are functioning effectively and are designed to see that goals are being met.

The fourth element is the most difficult to accomplish because many auditors may not yet have the needed skills. Many organizations do not give their internal auditors that much authority, but professional internal auditing could not possibly turn its eyes away when an operation that is being done efficiently and economically is the wrong operation to begin with.

400. Performance of Audit Work

The *Standards* expect certain qualities of performance from professional internal auditors. They should plan their work before they start it, and they should document those plans and their accomplishment. They should support their opinions and reports with sufficient, competent, and relevant information. The information should have enough depth to be compelling, have enough reliability to be believable, and have enough applicability to the issue at hand to be useful.

The audit work accomplished should be reported to those entitled to know of it. And professional internal auditors are obligated to report findings and opinions clearly enough to be understood and compellingly enough to make the need for action abundantly evident.

Professional internal auditors should follow up their work to see that appropriate action is taken on reported audit findings. It is important to differentiate between "appropriate action . . . on reported audit findings" on the one hand and "acceptance of internal audit recommendations" on the other. Managers are responsible for correcting defects in their organizations or operations in whatever manner they consider best; that is a management prerogative. Internal auditors are responsible for seeing that the defects have been corrected in whatever manner management considers appropriate.

500. Management of the Internal Auditing Department

Internal auditing departments have been managed as long as there have been internal auditing operations and managers. This section makes certain things about the auditing department specific and raises one new issue.

Made specific are establishing a charter for the department, planning for the audits to be carried out, providing policies and procedures to guide the staff, and staffing the department and training the people.

The new issue raised in Section 500 is the quality assurance program. Professional internal auditors are expected to provide for a review of their performance. They should be able to answer convincingly the question: "Who audits the internal auditors?" This is really not very different from the peer reviews made in academe. Peers are asked to review the work of academicians and express opinions on whether academic standards are being met. Similar reviews are required for CPAs. The *Standards* propose three elements for a quality assurance program:

1. Current supervision of the audit work.

2. Internal reviews performed by one or more of the staff members who would examine the working papers and reports issued by other members of the staff.

3. External reviews by persons independent of the internal auditing department. Such reviews could be performed by internal auditors of other enterprises, by public accountants, or by qualified consultants. Many large internal auditing organizations have already undergone such reviews.

(Quality assurance is also discussed in Chapter 20.)

Meeting the *Standards*

The question is often raised about the difficulties faced by an internal auditing department made up of only one or two internal auditors. Obviously they would find it much more difficult to meet the *Standards* than

Exhibit 2-4.

Suggested References for the Certified Internal Auditor Examination

The following is a list of suggested references which has been published to assist candidates who are preparing for the Certified Internal Auditor Examination. Although the authors of the references listed provide information relevant to areas covered in the examination, examination questions are not limited to information from these books. Candidates who are familiar with other books with similar coverage should use them.

Candidates should be knowledgeable of current research reports and other professional publications of The Institute of Internal Auditors, Inc., and the Foundation for Auditability Research and Education as they relate to specific examination parts. Candidates should keep informed of current developments by reading periodicals such as *The Internal Auditor, The Financial Executive, Management Accounting, Journal of Accountancy, Management Review, The Wall Street Journal*, and similar publications. Candidates should also be familiar with new legislation and pronouncements of regulatory bodies which affect the internal auditing profession.

	Part			
	I	II	III	IV
Arens, Alvin A., and Loebbecke, James K. *Auditing: An Integrated Approach.* 2nd ed. Englewood Cliffs, New Jersey: Prentice-Hall, Inc., 1980.	✓	✓		
Arkin, Herbert. *Handbook of Sampling for Auditing and Accounting.* 2nd ed. New York: McGraw-Hill Book Co., 1974.		✓		✓
Awad, Elias M. *Business Data Processing.* 5th ed. Englewood Cliffs, New Jersey: Prentice-Hall, Inc., 1980.				✓
Bierman, H.; Bonini, C.; and Hausman, W. *Quantitative Analysis for Business Decisions.* 5th ed. Homewood, Illinois: Richard D. Irwin, Inc., 1977.		✓		✓
Brink, Victor Z.; Cashin, James A.; and Witt, Herbert. *Modern Internal Auditing — An Operational Approach.* 3rd ed. New York: Ronald Press Co., 1973.	✓	✓		
Burch, John G., Jr., and Sardinas, Joseph L., Jr. *Computer Control and Audit: A Total Systems Approach.* 2nd ed. New York: John Wiley & Sons, Inc., 1978.		✓		✓
Burch, John G., Jr.; Strater, Felix R.; and Grudnitski, Gary. *Information Systems: Theory and Practice.* 2nd ed. New York: John Wiley & Sons, Inc., 1979.				✓

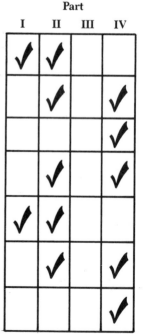

Exhibit 2-4. (Cont.)

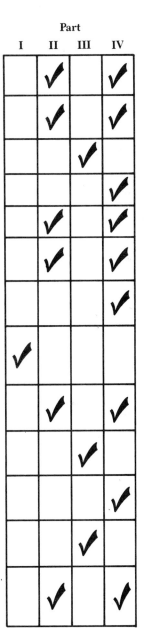

	Part I	II	III	IV
Canadian Institute of Chartered Accountants. *Computer Audit Guidelines.* Toronto, Ontario: Canadian Institute of Chartered Accountants, 1975.		✓		✓
Canadian Institute of Chartered Accountants. *Computer Control Guidelines.* Toronto, Ontario: Canadian Institute of Chartered Accountants, 1970.		✓		✓
Dale, Ernest. *Management Theory and Practice.* 4th ed. New York: McGraw-Hill Book Co., 1978.			✓	
Davis, Gordon B. *Computer Data Processing.* 2nd ed. New York: McGraw-Hill Book Co., 1973.				✓
Ernst & Whinney. *Audit Sampling.* Cleveland, Ohio: Ernst & Whinney, 1979.		✓		✓
Gallagher, Charles A., and Watson, Hugh J. *Quantitative Methods for Business Decisions.* New York: McGraw-Hill Book Co., 1980.		✓		✓
Horngren, C. T. *Cost Accounting: A Managerial Emphasis.* 4th ed. Englewood Cliffs, New Jersey: Prentice-Hall, Inc., 1977.				✓
Institute of Internal Audiotors. *Standards for the Professional Practice of Internal Auditing.* Altamonte Springs, Florida: The Institute of Internal Auditors, Inc., 1978.	✓			
Institute of Internal Auditors. *Systems Auditability & Control.* 3 vols. Altamonte Springs, Florida: The Institute of Internal Auditors, Inc., 1977.		✓		✓
Ivancevich, John M.; Donnelly, James H., Jr.; and Gibson, James L. *Managing for Performance.* Dallas, Texas: Business Publications, Inc., 1980.			✓	
Kieso, Donald E., and Weygandt, Jerry J. *Intermediate Accounting.* 3rd ed. New York: John Wiley & Sons, Inc., 1980.				✓
Koontz, Harold; O'Donnell, Cyril; and Weihrich, Heinz. *Management.* 7th ed. New York: McGraw-Hill Book Co., 1979.			✓	
Leslie, Donald A.; Teitlebaum, Albert D.; and Anderson, Rodney J. *Dollar-Unit Sampling: A Practical Guide for Auditors.* Toronto, Ontario: Copp Clark Pitman, 1979.		✓		✓

Exhibit 2-4. (Cont.)

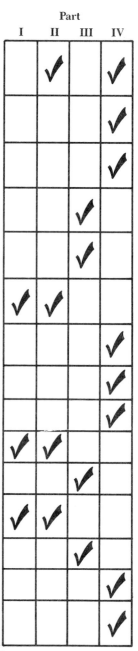

	Part			
	I	II	III	IV
Mair, William C.; Wood, Donald R.; and Davis, Keagle W. *Computer Control & Audit.* 2nd ed. Altamonte Springs, Florida: The Institute of Internal Auditors, Inc., 1978.		✓		✓
McConnell, Campbell R. *Economics: Principles, Problems, and Policies.* 7th ed. New York: McGraw-Hill Book Co., 1978.				✓
Meigs, Walter B.; Mosich, A. N.; and Johnson, Charles E. *Intermediate Accounting.* 4th ed. New York: McGraw-Hill Book Co., 1978.				✓
Rue, Leslie W., and Byars, Lloyd L. *Management: Theory and Application.* Homewood, Illinois: Richard D. Irwin, Inc., 1977.			✓	
Sawyer, Lawrence B. *The Manager and the Modern Internal Auditor: A Problem-Solving Partnership.* New York: AMACOM, 1979.			✓	
Sawyer, Lawrence B. *The Practice of Modern Internal Auditing,* 2nd ed., rev. and enl. Altamonte Springs, Florida: The Institute of Internal Auditors, Inc., 1981.	✓	✓		
Senn, James A. *Information Systems in Management.* Belmont, California: Wadsworth Publishing Co., Inc., 1978.				✓
Shillinglaw, Gordon. *Managerial Cost Accounting.* 4th ed. Homewood, Illinois: Richard D. Irwin, Inc., 1977.				✓
Spencer, Milton H. *Contemporary Economics.* 4th ed. New York: Worth Publishers, Inc., 1980.				✓
Stettler, Howard F. *Auditing Principles.* 4th ed. Englewood Cliffs, New Jersey: Prentice-Hall, Inc., 1977.	✓	✓		
Stoner, James A. F. *Management.* Englewood Cliffs, New Jersey: Prentice-Hall, Inc., 1978.			✓	
Taylor, Donald H., and Glezen, G. William. *Auditing: Integrated Concepts and Procedures.* New York: John Wiley & Sons, Inc., 1979.	✓	✓		
Terry, George R. *Principles of Management.* 7th ed. Homewood, Illinois: Richard D. Irwin, Inc., 1977.			✓	
VanHorne, James C. *Fundamentals of Financial Management.* 4th ed. New York: Prentice-Hall, Inc., 1980.				✓
Weston, Fred J., and Brigham, Eugene F. *Essentials of Managerial Finance.* 5th ed. New York: Holt, Rinehart & Winston, Inc., 1979.				✓

SOURCE: The Institute of Internal Auditors, Inc., January, 1981.

would large internal auditing departments. Their scope of audit might be restricted by their charters. Indeed, they might not have a charter. Direct supervision of the audit work could be much more difficult — or even impossible: Who supervises the work of a one-auditor internal auditing department?

It is a knotty problem, but if internal auditing is to be raised to the level of a learned profession, the standards must be high. Those internal auditors who are handicapped by lack of training or shackled by the restrictive rules of their enterprises will simply have to strive harder to meet the *Standards* if they aspire to professionalism. Calling oneself an internal auditor does not in and of itself make one a professional. A paramedic practices a form of medicine; a paralegal clerk practices a form of law, as does a real estate agent and a notary public. But these people are not professional doctors or lawyers; they are not equipped to render professional judgments and opinions. The same is true of people who claim to be internal auditors, but do not meet the *Standards* and the qualifications set for their profession.

Conclusion

Internal auditing has achieved professional status. It measures up to certain standards set for professions: A statement of responsibilities, two codes of ethics, a common body of knowledge, a certification program, and courses of study. Curricula have been developed at some universities leading to a degree in internal auditing. What was once a narrow discipline, descended from public accounting, is now a profession in its own right with standards to measure its practitioners and, for certified internal auditors, with a means of policing its membership.

References

1. V. Z. Brink, *Foundations for Unlimited Horizons — The Institute of Internal Auditors, 1941-1976* (Altamonte Springs, Fla.: The Institute of Internal Auditors, Inc., 1977), pp. 3, 4.
2. *Ibid.*, p. 6.
3. F. E. Mints, "Behavioral Patterns in Internal Auditing Relationships," Research Committee Report 17 (New York: The Institute of Internal Auditors, Inc., 1972).
4. H. F. Russell, *Foozles and Frauds* (Altamonte Springs, Fla.: The Institute of Internal Auditors, Inc., 1977).
5. R. L. Grinaker, "Internal Audit of Inventory Control and Management," Research Committee Report 16 (New York: The Institute of Internal Auditors, Inc., 1970).
6. "Systems Auditability & Control — Data Processing Audit Practices Report," Prepared for The Institute of Internal Auditors, Inc., by Brian Buder, T. S. Eason, M. E. See, and S. H. Russell of the Stanford Research Institute under a grant from The International Business Machine Corporation.
7. L. B. Sawyer, "Observations on the 1971 Revision of the Statement of Responsibilities of the Internal Auditor," *The Internal Auditor*, September/October 1971, p. 9.
8. *Ibid.*, pp. 10, 11.
9. W. B. Pitts, "Introduction to the Code of Ethics," *The Internal Auditor*, May/June 1969, pp. 42-45.

10. *Ibid.*, p. 43.
11. R. E. Gobeil, "The Common Body of Knowledge for Internal Auditors," *The Internal Auditor*, November/December 1972, p. 21.
12. *Ibid.*, pp. 20-28.
13. D. E. Wilson, "Highlights of the First Certified Internal Auditor Examination," *The Internal Auditor*, March/April 1975, p. 15.
14. W. S. Smith, "Certification, A Giant Step," *The Internal Auditor*, November/December 1972, p. 18.
15. L. B. Sawyer, "Modern Internal Auditing — The New Profession," *The Accounting Review*, January 1975, pp. 176-178.
16. L. B. Sawyer, "Tomorrow's Internal Auditor," *The Internal Auditor*, June 1978, pp. 14-16.
17. H. M. Williams, "The Emerging Responsibility of the Internal Auditor," *The Internal Auditor*, October 1978, p. 45.
18. R. H. Carolus and M. J. Barrett, "The Development of the Standards for the Professional Practice of Internal Auditing," *The Internal Auditor*, December 1977, p. 13.

Supplementary Reading

"Certified Internal Auditor Examination - Personal Review Course." Orlando, Fla.: The Institute of Internal Auditors, Inc., 1976.

Brink, V. Z., *Foundations for Unlimited Horizons - The Institute of Internal Auditors, 1941-1976.* Altamonte Springs, Fla.: The Institute of Internal Auditors, Inc., 1977.

Booker, J. A., with J. F. Bussman and J. D. Marquardt. "The CIA Examination: A Topical Profile and Index," *The Internal Auditor*, June 1977, pp. 8-14.

Gleim, Irvin N. *CIA Examination Review Manual.* Gainesville, Fla.: Accounting Publications, Inc., 1981.

Joseph, Joseph J., Jr. *Comprehensive Review Manual.* New York: Person-Wolinsky Professional Development, Inc., 1981.

For further study

Discussion Problems

1. To which person or persons in an organization should the director of internal auditing be responsible?

2. What actions are required of internal auditors who suspect fraud? What responsibility do internal auditors owe to the public in the event they encounter fraud in high places in their organization?

3. What are some reasons for a formal charter for internal auditors within a company?

4. What would be your response to the statement that internal auditing organizations should include only CPAs or people with accounting experience?

5. If internal auditors in a corporation have unrestricted access to all of its operations, how could they successfully respond to the assertion that they should be held responsible for the prevention and detection of all fraud within the corporation?

6. Discuss three factors that internal audit supervisors should consider when overseeing staff auditors on internal audit assignments.

7. What do you consider to be the major objective of internal auditing?

8. What are the responsibilities of an

internal auditor with respect to deficiency findings that have been reported to management? How do these responsibilities square with the auditor's role as staff and not line?

9. What assurances should directors of internal auditing have so that their independence cannot be successfully questioned?

10. Contrast efficiency, economy, and effectiveness. Give examples.

Multiple Choice Problems

1. The 1971 Statement of Responsibilities of Internal Auditors states that internal auditing:
a. " . . . may also deal with matters of an operating nature."
b. Provides for "the review of accounting, financial and other operations . . . "
c. Provides for " . . . the review of operations as a service to management."
d. Provides for " . . . the review of operations as a service to the organization."
e. Provides for " . . . independent reviews of the organization's activities."

2. The 1976 Statement of Responsibilities was rewritten to:
a. Make certain substantive changes.
b. Change "service to management" to "service to the organization."
c. Conform with the *Standards for the Professional Practice of Internal Auditing.*
d. Remove all references to gender.
e. None of the above.

3. The CIA Code of Ethics varies from the Code affecting all members of The Institute in that the CIA Code:
a. Does not require upholding Institute standards.
b. States that it applies to both men and women.

c. Is applicable to Institute members only.
d. Requires annual reaffirmation.
e. None of the above.

4. The U. S. Civil Service Commission has decreed that applicants for auditing positions in the federal government are excused from taking a written examination if:
a. They are Certified Internal Auditors.
b. They have an earned CIA designation.
c. They are members of The Institute of Internal Auditors, Inc.
d. They passed the CIA Examination.
e. All of the above.

5. The purposes of the *Standards for the Professional Practice of Internal Auditing* are to:
a. Unify internal auditing throughout the world.
b. Promote the recognition of internal auditing as a profession.
c. Encourage improved internal auditing.
d. Permit consistent measurement of internal auditing operations.
e. All of the above.

Case Studies

2-1 Staff vs. Line Work

Your company's management is considering a proposal which would require the internal auditors to participate in collecting the bids and controlling the competitive bidding practices in the purchasing department.

Required: Discuss your response to the above proposal to involve the internal auditors in a line function in relation to: (1) A short-term assignment. (2) A long-term assignment. (3) Its possible impact on the effectiveness of your normal audit program in the purchasing area.

2-2 Conflict of Interest

Ian Austin is a certified internal auditor working for the ABC Life Insurance Company. Ian is energetic, ambitious, helpful, and competent. His energies do not seem completely tapped by undeniably excellent work as a staff auditor. It has come to the attention of his superiors that Ian has engaged in the following practices:

a. Designed an accounting system for a general agent of ABC Life.
b. Entered into a partnership engaged in land development.
c. Assisted members of a fraternal organization, of which Ian is a member, in planning life insurance coverage.

Required: Is Ian guilty of any violations of the Statement of Responsibilities or the Code of Ethics? Explain.

2-3 Obligation to the Public

You are a CIA and the director of internal auditing in a publicly held manufacturing corporation, Conprod, which deals in consumer products. The company has developed a new line of baby carriages. Large sums have been spent on the research, development, and marketing of the product. The end result of the research is an attractive and exceptionally comfortable carriage. A great deal of the comfort is attributable to Product X material with which the carriages are padded. The padding makes for comfort and for protection of the infant from any sharp corners or hard edges.

Your auditors have made a review of the new processes developed for the product. During their review of documents, they found several memoranda signed by Sander Deems, the company's manager of the safety department, to Dion Manfred, director of manufacturing. Sander is directly responsible to Dion in the organizational hierarchy. In the memoranda, Sander pointed out that Product X is inflammable and dangerous. Dion has ignored the warnings.

Your auditors have done some additional research on the subject and have confirmed Sander's fears. Accordingly, they discussed the matter with Dion. He firmly rejected any change in the material used to pad the carriages. Hundreds of pounds of Product X had already been purchased, the production lines were already operating, costs were poking through the budgeted amounts, and schedules were tight. You talked the matter over with Dion, but he remained adamant. He said that the carriages were to be produced as designed. Customers were already clamoring for them; he had a commitment to Charles E. Osgood, president and chief executive officer of Conprod, to get the carriages out on time and at reasonable cost; and no internal auditors were going to keep him from meeting his commitment. You told Dion that you felt obligated to discuss the matter with Mr. Osgood. Dion said, "Be my guest."

Accordingly, you set up a meeting with Mr. Osgood and presented the facts to him. Osgood was not only negative to your presentation, he was furious. "This is a technical matter and your people are not safety or production technicians. Your people have no business poking their noses in matters which are beyond their competence. Besides, I know of no danger from Product X. It's been used for years. Get your people off the audit and let Dion produce his carriages as he sees fit."

You were stunned by Mr. Osgood's reaction. But you were convinced of the danger and felt you could not in good conscience turn your eyes away. So you said, "Mr. Osgood, I deeply wish I could let the matter drop. But I'm convinced we have a problem that needs resolving, and I must tell you that I'll have to bring it before the audit committee of the board of directors." Mr. Osgood looked at you furiously, but he said nothing, turning to the pages on his desk. He was well aware of your charter that gave you access, free and unfettered, to the audit committee.

You then gained an audience with the audit committee and presented your case to them. You had asked Sander to accompany you, but Sander declined. Off-the-record, however, Sander assured you that the danger was real, and he even supplied you with independent studies supporting his thesis that Product X was inflammable and extremely toxic when it burned.

The members of the audit committee, none of whom were members of Conprod's management, listened attentively and politely to your presentation. When you were through, they conferred briefly and told you that they would bring the matter up before the whole board and give you their decision. Two days later you were called before the audit committee. They informed you that it was the opinion of the board that the production line would not be stopped. They said that they were aware of no serious accidents involving Product X and that it would be unfair to the company and its stockholders to scrap what seemed like a lucrative program. They therefore had no intention of intervening.

Required: What are your responsibilities as a certified internal auditor under such circumstances?

3
Control

The internal auditor's Open Sesame. Installing controls. Objectivity. Technical activities. Pressures for improved control. Concerns of board members. The change from restricting to assisting controls. Self-measurement. Removing temptation. The evolving definition of control. Definition for internal auditors. Different types of controls. Controls to prevent and detect improprieties. Examples. Objectives, standards, comparisons, corrections. Various means of control. The Foreign Corrupt Practices Act of 1977 — a misnomer. The Act and accounting literature. ASR No. 242. The Canadian version. Controls and objectives. Cycle audits of internal accounting controls. The cycles. Control procedures and techniques. Management-oriented reviews. Operating controls and the functions of management. Examples of nonfinancial controls. Excessive controls. Management overrides of controls. Company directive on control.

The Significance of Control
Importance for the Internal Auditor

For the internal auditor, control is both an opportunity and a responsibility.

Broad-based internal auditing pushes internal auditors into unfamiliar terrain. They could not possibly become instant experts in advertising, agriculture, customs duties, engineering, international trade, pensions, quality assurance, safety, transportation, welfare, and the hosts of other disciplines, both public and private, where they must make objective appraisals.

But competent internal auditors have an open sesame which gives them an opportunity to make useful contributions to all these disciplines. With it they can open doors to which only the technical experts normally gain entrance. With it they can help solve many of the problems that lie behind those doors.

This Open Sesame, this key, is control. Control is a force. It sees that things get done. Controls are the physical means through which the force is exerted. Control and controls are used to make sure that technical objectives will be met. Internal auditors may not be advertising specialists, but they can be perfectly at home in determining and evaluating the controls needed to see that advertising people carry out their functions efficiently, economically, and effectively. They may not be production specialists, but they can determine the kind of information the production specialist needs to see whether products are being manufactured within budget, at acceptable quality, and on time.

Besides, internal auditors are given a much better reception by managers of nonfinancial activities when they have allayed some of their fears — when they assure managers that they will not second-guess their technical decisions and accomplishments. Rather they will be concerned primarily with the answers to two questions: Are operations satisfactorily controlled? Are the means used to help managers control both adequate and effective?

And when the auditees see before them an emissary of high-level management — someone privy to what executive management is interested in and concerned about, someone who understands top management's broad policies and procedures, someone who has had experience in examining controls over many other operations of the enterprise, someone who is willing to share the knowledge of and experience with internal control, someone who may be able to point out pitfalls and thereby save the auditees bruised shins or a bloody nose — then the auditees begin to see an associate and not a policeman, a constructive business consultant and not a threat, a management-oriented auditor and not a picker of nits.[1]

Control is an internal auditing responsibility as well. Internal auditors are expected to be monitors of the organization's control systems. Where control systems are adequate and are working as intended, internal auditors should be able to assure executive management on that score. Where controls are lacking or are not functioning properly, they are expected to alert management to the need for corrective action.

Managers are responsible for installing control systems. Indeed, internal auditors are cautioned that they should never design or install systems that they will someday evaluate. Clearly, appraising one's own brainchild cannot be regarded as an objective exercise. The tendency is to praise what one has created, to be partial to it, not to regard it with objectivity.

So some independent, unbiased observer must supply the objectivity and the capability to evaluate control systems throughout the organization. This is what senior management needs, this is what it expects, and this is one of the major reasons it establishes the internal auditing function.

Concerns About Financial Controls

Pressures weigh heavily on both internal and external auditors to monitor the effectiveness of internal financial controls. Here are some of the reasons:

In most large business organizations, corporate audit committees are responsible for the functioning of financial controls within the enterprise. They cannot shrug off unpleasant happenings in their companies. They are charged with knowing about them whether they actually know or not. Ignorance is no excuse. So their interest in controls designed to prevent unpleasantness is immediate and continuing.

The so-called "sensitive payments" — those illegal or questionable payments to promote sales — have embarrassed many board members and executives. Therefore, they are vitally concerned with the means employed to prevent such payments or to promptly disclose those made.

The U.S. Foreign Corrupt Practices Act laid down stringent requirements about internal accounting controls. One board of directors passed the following resolution about internal control:

Resolved: That management of the company is hereby directed to:
(1) Retain the company's independent public accountants to conduct a review of the company's system of internal accounting controls, and subject to any recommendations that may result from such a review,
(2) To effect such changes in the company's system of internal accounting controls that may be deemed necessary or advisable in order to provide reasonable assurance that the internal control meets the requirements set forth in the U.S. Foreign Corrupt Practices Act of 1977.[2]

The public sector must likewise be concerned with internal controls. Fiscal crises at both the national and local level have raised outcries for greater accountability on the part of government officials. Internal auditors are called upon to provide the test for such accountability, and that test includes the evaluation of internal controls. The cost of ineffective controls can be staggering. Many factors probably played a part in the New York City financial crisis; but clearly the lack of adequate financial controls aggravated the problem and brought on charges that public officials had engaged in "accounting and budget gimmickry."[3] And as late as February 13, 1979, the Wall Street Journal reported that New York City had been criticized by external auditors for the weaknesses in the city's internal controls.

The Benefits of Controls

Controls need not be exclusively restrictive. They do not have to be a straitjacket that confines a victim. They can be an aid to managers. The approach to controls has changed in modern times. In Henri Fayol's day controls were seen as solely preventive. The man regarded as the father of classical management theory said:

In an enterprise, control consists in checking to see if everything is going according to the program adopted, the orders given and the accepted principles. Its object is to indicate shortcomings and mistakes so they can be corrected and not repeated. It applies to everything, things, persons, actions.[4]

But modern management philosophy regards control as an aid rather than a constriction. It looks at control as a means of integrating personal and enterprise objectives to help people meet their goals. It advocates inviting the person controlled to help devise the controls. It regards controls as the means of measuring oneself — determining whether standards have been met, whether one has accomplished the job intended.

Control devices thereby become the means of auto-control. They are used for self measurement. And they can activate individuals to improve their performance — not just get by with what they are doing.

Controls from a restrictive view can also be beneficial. They can help to remove temptation. For example, it is well accepted that three conditions must exist before a person will embezzle an employer's funds: Unusual need (actual or perceived), opportunity, and rationalization. Management can do little about how an employee perceives his or her needs. But by adequate control the opportunity to embezzle can be removed or diminished. The need must become desperate indeed before the employee will seek to embezzle by trying to break a thoroughly controlled system. But where funds are left wide open to peculation, the employee can readily rationalize that he or she has been invited to partake of the feast.

So good controls not only protect the enterprise, they protect the employee as well. Management is morally obligated to see that temptation is not placed in the way of their people. Most employees will respect a well-controlled operation. Control weaknesses breed contempt; they make it easy for employees to rationalize that since management does not care, why shouldn't they take what is there for the taking?

As an example, complete concentration of all parts of an operation in one individual is dangerous — it is bad for the organization and just as bad for the individual. The clerk who receives cash, records the receipts, carries the funds to the bank, and reconciles the bank statements may be honest as the day is long. But let some inadvertent error occur or let someone else take funds dishonestly, and where will the blame fall? On the honest, overburdened clerk and none other. So management owes that clerk the segregation of some of the clerical duties, even if management itself must assume a portion of those duties.

Control Defined

Early Definitions

Control, also spelled "controul," first appeared in the English lexicon around 1600 and was defined as "the copie of a roll [of account], a paralell [sic] of the same qualitie and content with the originall." It derived from the

Latin *contrarotulus* from *contra*, "against," and *rotula*, "a roll."[5] Samuel Johnson sums up this original meaning as "a register or account kept by another officer, that each may be examined by the other."[6]

The importance of control to auditors (or "internal check" as it was first called) was recognized by L. R. Dicksee as early as 1905. He pointed out that a suitable system of internal check should eliminate the need for a detailed audit. He viewed control as a composite of three elements: division of work, the use of accounting records, and the rotation of personnel.[7]

In 1930, George E. Bennett defined internal control (internal check) this way:

> A system of internal check may be defined as the coordination of a system of accounts and related office procedures in such a manner that the work of one employee independently performing his own prescribed duties continually checks the work of another as to certain elements involving the possibility of fraud.[8]

So we're back to *contrarotulus* and controul. But in 1949, a special report entitled "Internal Control — Elements of a Coordinated System and its Importance to Management and the Independent Accountant," by the AICPA Committee on Auditing Procedure, defined internal control as follows:

> Internal control comprises the plan of organization and all of the coordinate methods and measures adopted within a business to safeguard its assets, check the accuracy and reliability of its accounting data, promote operational efficiency, and encourage adherence to prescribed managerial policies. This definition [continued the Committee] possibly is broader than the meaning sometimes attributed to the term. It recognizes that a system of internal control extends beyond those matters which relate directly to the functions of the accounting and financial department.

Definitions for Public Accountants

Independent auditors in the United States, however, saw the definition as too broad for their purposes. After all, they were primarily concerned with internal control as it relates to the reliability of financial statements or to the aims of authorization, accounting, and asset safeguarding. So internal control was subdivided into *administrative' control* and *accounting control*. These are defined in section 320.27-.28 (1973) of the AICPA's Professional Standards, taken from the Statement of Auditing Standards (SAS) No. 1:

> *Administrative control* includes, but is not limited to, the plan of organization and the procedures and records that are concerned with the decision processes leading to management's authorization of transactions. Such authorization is a management function directly associated with the responsibility for achieving the objectives of the organization and is the starting point for establishing accounting control of transactions.

> *Accounting control* comprises the plan of organization and the procedures and records that are concerned with the safeguarding of assets and the reliability of financial records and consequently are designed to give reasonable assurance that:

> a. Transactions are executed in accordance with management's general or specific authorization.

b. Transactions are recorded as necessary (1) to permit preparation of financial statements in conformity with generally accepted accounting principles or any other criteria applicable to such statements and (2) to maintain accountability for assets.
c. Access to assets is permitted only in accordance with management's authorization.
d. The recorded accountability for assets is compared with the existing assets at reasonable intervals and appropriate action is taken with respect to any differences.

It will be observed that the definition of administrative control links such control to management objectives. The definition of accounting control does not.

The Canadian Institute of Chartered Accountants remedies this lack by proposing its own definition in Section 5200.05-06 of its Auditing Recommendation of December 1977:

Internal control comprises the plan of organization and all the coordinate systems established by the management of an enterprise to assist in achieving management's objective of ensuring, as far as practical, the orderly and efficient conduct of its business, including the safeguarding of assets, the reliability of accounting records and the timely preparation of reliable financial information.

Internal control within an enterprise consists of many systems, each of which is designed to help management to achieve its particular objectives. Each system comprises numerous internal controls, of which some are interdependent and others function independently. Each system, in order to be effective, must be well-designed and properly operated.

The Canadian definition is helpful in acknowledging that controls do not exist in a vacuum. They have usefulness and meaning only if they are designed to achieve an objective. Therefore, to speak of controls without discussing the aims they are designed to meet is to tell only half the story and to dilute their importance. That independent accountants now recognize this relationship is brought out in the current "cycle" theory of evaluating internal controls, discussed later in this chapter.

Definitions for Internal Auditors

The definitions just given tend to blur the distinction between *control* as a verb and *control* as a noun. In the world of business and government, these words have developed specific meanings, and it is well to maintain the distinction between them: The verb represents the action of seeing that what should be done will be done; that established management objectives will be met. The noun represents the means used to help the "controller" control.

Internal auditors, who should be management-oriented and objective-oriented, need a definition of their own — a definition that ties the management function of control and controlling to the means used to exercise that function in any activity of the organization. Thus, the internal auditor may regard control and controls as follows:

Control is the employment of all the means devised in an enterprise to promote, direct, restrain, govern, and check upon its various activities for the purpose of seeing that enterprise objectives are met. These means of control include, but are not limited to, form of organization, policies, systems, procedures, instructions, standards, committees, charts of account, forecasts, budgets, schedules, reports, records, checklists, methods, devices, and internal auditing.[9]

But definitions of control are less significant than the purpose of control. What internal auditors must keep in mind is that controls are adequate and useful only if they are designed to attain an objective. And internal auditors must know the objective before they can properly evaluate the means of control.

Prevention and Detection Controls

Controls may be categorized in two ways: Those which are designed to prevent undesirable outcomes and those which detect them when they occur. These categories are particularly applicable to computers.

Prevention controls are more cost effective than detection controls. When built into a system, prevention controls forestall errors and thereby avoid the cost of correcting them. Here are some examples of preventive controls: trustworthy, competent people; segregation of duties to prevent intentional wrongdoing; proper authorization to prevent improper use of enterprise resources; adequate documentation and records as well as proper record-keeping procedures to deter improper transactions; and physical control over assets to deter the improper conversion or use of assets.

Detection controls are more expensive than protection controls, but they too are essential. First, they measure the effectiveness of the prevention controls. Second, some errors cannot be effectively controlled through a system of prevention; they must be detected when they occur. Detection controls include records of performance and independent checks on performance. They also include such control devices as bank reconciliations; confirmation of bank balances; cash counts; reconciliations of accounts receivable details to accounts receivable control accounts; physical counts of inventories and analyses of variances; confirmation with suppliers of accounts payable; and systems of review.

Prevention controls may not always be noticeable; they are usually built into the system. Detection controls, however, are generally obvious. For example, executive management will review monthly financial or operating reports, comparing them with budgets or forecasts. When variances are found, the executive will want to know why they occurred and what is being done to recover from adverse conditions. The requests for information on that score can be highly visible. Some examples of built-in protection controls and visible detection controls follow in Exhibit 3-1.

Elements of Control

Common Control Devices

Control is an action taken to see that something will be accomplished. Controls are the means used to see that the action is effective. Both control

Exhibit 3-1. PROTECTION AND DETECTION CONTROLS

Activity	Protection Controls	Detection Controls
Cash	A record of cash received established at the earliest possible moment. Practical safeguards to see that the record is properly made.	Surprise cash counts. Frequent cash balancing and pickups. Reconciliation of bank statements. Reconciliations of cash register tapes and deposit slips. Reviews of endorsements on checks.
Accounts Receivable	Receivable ledgers controlled by general ledger accounts, and periodic proof that the amounts in the subsidiary ledgers agree with the control account.	Adequate procedures requiring reports to management on the status of collectibility of receivables.
Inventory	Inventories kept in storerooms under lock and key and under the control of responsible people. Stores issued on basis of approved requisitions only.	Provision for physical inventories. Periodic reports to management of inventories on hand. Reconciliations of detail property records to related general ledger accounts.

and the means of control should be directed toward some aim or objective to be attained.

For example, comfort in the home is a desired aim. To achieve that aim the homeowner seeks to control the environment by supplying cold or heat when necessary. If the homeowner feels excessive cold or excessive heat, he can turn on his furnace or his air conditioner to bring the temperature to a comfortable level.

He can do these things manually, or he can use a control device to help him control the temperature. One such device is a thermostat. His objective, of course, is comfort in the home. Deciding on an **objective** is the first step in any control process. Then he can set the thermostat at a desired temperature. The setting is the **standard** — the second element of control.

As the thermostat rises above or falls below the standard, the thermostat observes the difference between the actual temperature and the desired temperature. This is the third element of control — **comparing** what is with what should be. Since the comparison shows an unsatisfactory condition, the thermostat commands the heating or cooling elements to turn on. This returns the room temperature to the desired levels. This is the fourth element of control — **corrective action.**

Analysis of the Elements

All control devices work the same way: Some objective to be met; a standard of what is desirable; information to provide a comparison between standards and actual conditions; action to meet the standards so that the objectives can be achieved. If any of these elements are lacking, the control system is inadequate or ineffective or both. Let us analyze these elements further:

Objectives to be achieved. Objectives for the entire organization are set by senior management, the board of directors, or the legislature. Operating objectives are usually set at the operating level. These objectives should be compatible with the organization's overall objectives. And, of extreme importance, all relevant objectives should be communicated to those people whose work is being controlled. Otherwise, they may fight the controls as being unneeded, restrictive, or irrelevant.

Standards to be met. Standards should be designed so that they will help managers make appropriate decisions. Whatever is superfluous to this requirement should be eliminated. It may not be easy to establish performance standards in all situations. Without them, however, managers cannot control rationally and consistently. They will not know what is acceptable or desirable; hence, they may overcontrol or undercontrol. Performance standards that get the best results have these attributes:

1. They are attainable — neither impossible dreams nor conservative underguesses.

2. They are understood — people must know what the standards are and the reasons for them.

3. They are accepted and used — those who use the standards or are measured by them must be committed to them and willing to extend themselves to meet them.

Standards and results compared. Comparisons call for information. Indeed, some writers show information as a separate element of control, but information and comparisons are so closely tied together that it would seem illogical to separate them. At any rate, such information should be responsive and relevant to the standards established. The information system should supply facts that are accurate, timely, and usable. The data supplied should be summarized so that managers will not be flooded with excessive detail. The system of comparisons should highlight all variances. And the system should call for an investigation of significant variances. The investigation should be directed toward seeking the causes for the differences and then underscoring any adverse trends. Only if causes are isolated can cures be prescribed. Only the identification of unfavorable trends will emphasize the need for prompt corrective action to return conditions to the desired track.

Discrepancies to be corrected. Finding variances and investigating their causes without doing something about it is an exercise in futility. It is like bemoaning the dripping of a faucet, but not replacing the worn washer. The identification of serious differences should trigger a call to action, and that action should be effective. Correcting the symptom of a defect is good, but eliminating the cause is better. Defects can recur. They are prevented from recurring by removing their cause.

A System That Failed

All these elements must be present for a system to be adequate and to work effectively. Here is an example of a control system which was adequate in its conception, but which failed because some of the elements were not implemented:

> A manufacturing company had a production plant and a scrap sales yard. Two miles separated them. The production plant generated metal scrap. At the plant, carts were filled with the scrap which included such expensive metals as stainless steel, molybdenum, copper, titanium, and beryllium. Periodically, the carts were hooked to a tractor and hauled from the production plant to the scrap sales yard for sale to scrap dealers.
>
> Because of the value of the scrap, a control system was installed to safeguard it en route. The objective was to provide reasonable assurance that the transported scrap would safely reach its destination without any of it being dropped off on the way. The standard established was the time it should reasonably take to haul the scrap, directly and without stops, from the production plant to the scrap sales yard. The information on whether the standard was met was to be included on tags accompanying the scrap. As the tractor passed the guard at the gate of the production plant, he was to enter on the tags the exact time the driver

left the plant. A guard at the scrap sales yard was to enter the exact time the tractor reached that point. The two entries were then to be compared. Any significant variances between the standard and the actual elapsed time were to be investigated. On paper, the control system contained all the elements of an adequate control system.

The audit disclosed, however, that the guards were not entering the times of departure and arrival on the tags. Without that information, the control system was valueless. The guards were asked if they had been instructed to enter the time on the tags, and if so, why they weren't doing so.

Both said that the instructions made no sense to them and that they were not about to spend time on nonsense. Obviously, they had been ordered to gather the information without being told about the objective of the control system. The auditors pointed out that if the tractor driver stopped to hand over scrap illegally to a confederate, the difference between the standard time and the actual time elapsed would point up the improper stop. The guards' eyes widened and they agreed enthusiastically to gather the data. The information needed now made sense to them.

Because the objectives had not been explained to the guards, the information was not gathered, the comparisons could not be made, any variances could not be investigated, and any needed corrective action could not be taken. A control system, adequate in concept, was completely ineffective.

Means of Achieving Control

Some of the means by which managers can control functions within an enterprise are these:[10]

○ Organization
○ Policies
○ Procedures
○ Personnel
○ Accounting
○ Budgeting
○ Reporting
○ Internal review

Here are some criteria for each of these means of control — criteria which internal auditors can use in evaluating the adequacy and the effectiveness of control systems.

Organization

Organization, as a means of control, is an intentional structure of roles assigned to people within the enterprise so as to achieve the objectives of the enterprise efficiently and economically.

Responsibilities should be divided so that no one person will control all phases of any transaction.

Each manager should have the authority to take the action necessary to discharge his or her responsibility.

Individual responsibility should always be clearly defined so that it can neither be sidestepped nor exceeded.

An official who assigns responsibility and delegates authority to subordinates should have an effective system of follow-up to make sure that tasks assigned are properly carried out.

The individuals to whom authority is delegated should be required to exercise that authority without close supervision. But they should check with their superiors in case of exception.

People should be required to account to their superiors for the manner in which they have discharged their responsibilities.

The organization should be flexible enough to permit changes in its structure when operating plans, policies, and objectives change.

The organizational structures should be as simple as possible.

Organization charts and manuals should be prepared to help in planning, controlling changes in, and providing better understanding of the form of organization, chain of authority, and assignments of responsibilities.

Policies

A policy is any rule which requires, guides, or restricts action. Policies should follow certain principles:

Policies should be clearly stated in writing and systematically organized in handbooks, manuals, or other publications.

They should be systematically communicated to all officials and employees of the organization.

They must conform with applicable laws and regulations, and they should be consistent with objectives and general policies prescribed at higher levels.

They should be designed to promote the conduct of authorized activities in an effective, efficient, and economical manner and to provide a satisfactory degree of assurance that the resources of the enterprise are suitably safeguarded.

They should be periodically reviewed, and they should be revised when circumstances change.

Procedures

Procedures are methods employed to carry out activities in conformity with prescribed policies. The same principles applicable to policies are also applicable to procedures. In addition:

To reduce the possibility of fraud and error, procedures should be so coordinated that one employee's work is automatically checked by another who is independently performing their own prescribed duties. In determining the extent to which automatic internal checks should be built into the system of control, such factors as degree of risk of loss or error, cost of preventive procedures, availability of personnel, and feasibility should be considered.

For nonmechanical operations, prescribed procedures should not be so detailed as to stifle the use of judgment.

To promote maximum efficiency and economy, prescribed procedures should be as simple and as inexpensive as possible.

Procedures should not be overlapping, conflicting, or duplicative.

Procedures should be periodically reviewed and improved as necessary.

Personnel

People hired or assigned should have the qualifications to do the jobs assigned to them. The best form of control over the performance of individuals is supervision. Hence, high standards of supervision should be established. The following practices help improve control:

Employees should be given training and refresher courses to provide the opportunity for improving competence and to keep them informed of new policies and procedures.

Employees should be given information on the duties and responsibilities of other segments of the organization so that they may better understand how and where their jobs fit into the organization as a whole.

The performance of all employees should be periodically reviewed to see whether all essential requirements of their jobs are being met. Superior performance should be given appropriate recognition. Shortcomings should be discussed with employees so that they are given an opportunity to improve their performance or upgrade their skills.

Accounting

Accounting is the indispensable means of financial control over activities and resources. It furnishes a framework which can be fitted to assignments of responsibility. It is the financial scorekeeper of the enterprise. The problem lies in what scores to keep. Here are some basic principles for accounting systems:

Accounting should fit the needs of managers for rational decision making rather than the dictates of some textbook or canned check list.

It should be based on lines of responsibility.

Financial reports of operating results should parallel the organizational units responsible for carrying out operations.

Budgeting

A budget is a statement of expected results expressed in numerical terms. As a control, it sets a standard of what should be achieved.

Those who are responsible for meeting a budget should participate in its preparation.

They should be provided with adequate information that compares budgets with actual events and shows reasons for any significant variances.

All subsidiary budgets should tie into the overall budget for the enterprise.

Budgets should set measurable objectives; they are meaningless unless managers know what they are budgeting for.

They should help sharpen the organizational structure because objective budgeting standards are difficult to set in a confused combination of subsystems. Budgeting is therefore a form of discipline.

Reporting

In most organizations, management functions and makes decisions on the basis of the reports it receives. Reports should therefore be timely, accurate, meaningful, and economical. Here are some principles for establishing a satisfactory internal reporting system:

The reports should be made in accordance with assigned responsibilities.

Individuals or units should be required to report only on those matters for which they are responsible.

The cost of accumulating data and preparing reports should be weighted against the benefits to be obtained from them.

Reports should be as simple as possible, and consistent with the nature of the subject matter. They should include only information which serves the needs of the readers. Common classifications and terminology should be used as much as possible to avoid confusion.

When appropriate, performance reports should show comparisons with predetermined standards of cost, quality, and quantity.

When performance cannot be reported in quantitative terms, the reports should be designed to emphasize exceptions or other matters requiring management attention.

Reports should be timely to be of maximum value. Timely reports based partly on estimates may be more useful than delayed reports that are more precise.

Report recipients should be polled periodically to see if they still need the reports they are receiving.

Internal Review

The uninspected inevitably deteriorates. All operations should be periodically reviewed by people who are independent of those operations. Internal auditing is one such form of review. Here are some principles for a system of internal review:

Top management should devise an internal review system and organization that will best suit its needs.

All types of review activity within an organization, such as inspections and internal audits, should be coordinated. The work done by each review group should be clearly defined to avoid duplication and jurisdictional disputes.

Organizational needs for internal review vary. The scope of work cannot, therefore, be standardized, but should be set by each company's management.

The duties, responsibilities, and the stature of the review agency should be clearly defined so that the review authority is recognized.

Review authority should be independent of the operations reviewed. Thus, the manager of Quality Control should not report to the Director of Manufacturing.

The internal review operation should not replace line authority and responsibility. Operating managers must remain responsible for doing and supervising their own jobs.

Internal review is a staff function. Internal reviewers should not control or direct action — their responsibility is advisory: to provide information as a basis for decision making and action.

Review work should be planned, and the plans should be approved by top management.

All internal review work should meet professional standards of competence, reliability, and objectivity.

Internal reviewers should place primary emphasis on promoting improvement of operations, rather than on fault finding.

Findings should be reviewed with the people whose work is being appraised except where the possibility of fraud requires different treatment.

Suitable follow-up procedures should be devised to see whether findings and recommendations have been considered, corrective action has been taken, and results are satisfactory.

The U.S. Foreign Corrupt Practices Act of 1977

The Great Change

Internal controls were once an exclusive management prerogative. Corporate executives decided what controls they needed or did not need to carry on their businesses. If controls were deemed to be onerous or costly or undesirable, management would not install them or would eliminate them. If this brought on risks, management on its own initiative would decide whether to install the control or take the risk.

The U.S. Foreign Corrupt Practices Act of 1977, 91 Stat. 1494, signed into law December 19, 1977, has curtailed management's initatives in that country. Now the ways a publicly held United States enterprise is controlled, and how it keeps it records, are subject to legal constraints. Offenders may be fined or jailed under Section 32(a) of the U.S. Securities and Exchange Act.

Requirements of the Act

The Act's most far-reaching implications to domestic firms are not the provisions prohibiting the corruption of foreign officials. Rather they are the requirements for record keeping imposed on United States companies. To that extent, the title of the Act is a misnomer. The Act in general says this: Internal accounting controls shall be examined, and if material weaknesses are found, controls must be strengthened or additional ones installed. Bribes or questionable conduct shall cease, and funds for such bribes and conduct must not be made available.

Internal auditors find themselves concerned with both these requirements, but this chapter shall address the matter of internal accounting controls. That part of the Act reads as follows:

Sec. 102. Section 13(b) of the Securities Exchange Act of 1934 (15 U.C.S. 78q(b) is amended by inserting "(1)" after "(b)" and by adding to the end thereof the following:
(2) Every issuer which has a class of securities registered pursuant to section 12 of this title and every issuer which is required to file reports pursuant to section 15(d) of this title shall —
(a) make and keep books, records, and accounts, which, in reasonable detail, accurately and fairly reflect the transactions and dispositions of the assets of the issuer; and
(b) devise and maintain a system of internal accounting controls sufficient to provide reasonable assurances that —
(i) transactions are executed in accordance with management's general or specific authorization;
(ii) transactions are recorded as necessary (I) to permit preparation of financial statements in conformity with generally accepted accounting principles or any other criteria applicable to such statements and (II) to maintain accountability for assets;
(iii) access to assets is permitted only in accordance with management's general or specific authorization; and
(iv) the recorded accountability for assets is compared with the existing assets at reasonable intervals and appropriate action is taken with respect to any difference.

It is pertinent to note that the Act recognizes the importance of professional auditing literature. Section 102(2)(b) of the Act is taken without change from the AICPA's Statement on Auditing Standards No. 1 (SAS No. 1), section 320.8. The Act has not broadened those responsibilities. SAS No. 1 was issued to guide external auditors in the study of internal accounting control for one purpose — to serve as a basis for setting the scope of the examination of financial statements. External auditors test only those controls on which they intend to rely; they are not responsible for those controls on which they do not intend to rely. But the Act gives management, and therefore internal auditors, a wider concern — devising and maintaining a system of internal accounting controls that provide reasonable assurance that transactions are authorized and accounted for and that assets are safeguarded.

ASR No. 242

Following the enactment of this law, the U.S. Securities and Exchange Commission issued Accounting Series Release No. 242 (ASR No. 242) on February 16, 1978 — Securities Exchange Act Release No. 14478, entitled "Notification of Enactment of Foreign Corrupt Practices Act of 1977." The release said in part that:

> . . . because the Act became effective on signing, it is important that issuers subject to the new requirements review their accounting procedures, systems of internal accounting controls, and business practices in order that they may take any actions necessary to comply with the requirements contained in the Act.

The Canadian Law

The accounting provisions of the Foreign Corrupt Practices Act are not unique to the United States. For example, the Canada Business Corporations Act lays down requirements similar to those now in effect in the United States. Section 20(2) of the Canadian Act states that "a corporation shall prepare and maintain adequate accounting records," and Section 22(2) states that: "A corporation and its agents shall take reasonable precautions to (a) prevent loss or destruction of, (b) prevent falsification of entries in, and (c) facilitate detection and correction of inaccuracies in the records and registers required by this Act to be prepared and maintained."

The Internal Auditor's Role

Internal auditors in the United States and Canada can become powerful tools for management by evaluating control systems and by pointing out weaknesses in internal control that need strengthening. But internal auditors, it should be remembered, are tools of management; they are not themselves managers. This raises a significant caveat in terms of compliance with the United States and Canadian acts regarding internal accounting controls.

Evidence of compliance with these acts resides in appropriate documentation. When systems of control are well documented, an organization can more readily demonstrate compliance with relevant statutes. Good documentation is an internal audit stock in trade. Management is prone, therefore, to instruct its internal auditors, "Document our internal accounting controls systems so that we can prove to the government that we are complying with the law."

That is a trap, and the internal auditor should try to avoid it. Compliance with a statute is by definition a legal and not an audit matter. The internal auditor is not equipped to tell regulatory agencies, "We are complying with the law." That is a function of management with the advice and counsel of its legal people. Internal auditors can evaluate the documentation just as they can evaluate any other activity in the company, but they are not responsible for rendering legal opinions on compliance with the law.

These acts apply to the United States and Canada. But internal auditors in other countries, even though not under legislative mandate, will still have a responsibility for evaluating internal accounting controls and for pointing out weaknesses to management.

In evaluating both internal accounting controls and other internal controls of the enterprise, the internal auditor must heed the admonition previously given: Controls must be designed to achieve a management objective.

The Cycle Approach to Internal Accounting Controls

In 1979, the AICPA issued a "Report of the Special Advisory Committee on Internal Accounting Control." Although the Committee was formed before the adoption of the Foreign Corrupt Practices Act of 1977, it believes that its report should be useful to management and to boards of directors when considering whether their companies are complying with the provisions of the Act.

The committee, as do many accounting firms, advocated the "cycle" approach to the evaluation of control procedures and techniques. The approach is eminently reasonable. It gives consideration to objectives and makes use of standards. It is linked to the cycles of business transactions, following such transactions throughout the organization's systems of control. For example, the "expenditure cycle" for goods purchased starts with authorization to use certain suppliers, then covers the supplier selection process, the receipt of goods, and the payments to suppliers, and winds up with the recording of payments.

The control objectives — authorization, accounting, and asset safeguarding — are those stated in the U. S. Foreign Corrupt Practices Act and in accounting literature.

The criteria are those that are appropriate for transactions which fall within each transaction cycle. The approach suggested three steps: Classify transactions according to the cycles into which they can be conveniently grouped, identify the criteria (standards) of internal control appropriate for the transactions according to the objectives to be met, and measure the existing control procedures and techniques against the criteria.

Cycles can vary from company to company. The committee suggests, however, that the transactions of most companies can be grouped into these five cycles:

Cycles	Examples of Transactions
Revenues	Customer acceptance, credit, shipping, sales, sales deductions, cash receipts, receivables, warranties, allowance for doubtful accounts.

Expenditures	Purchasing, payroll, cash disbursements, accounts payable, accrued expenses.
Production or Conversion	Production, inventory planning, property and deferred cost accounting, and cost accounting.
Financing	Capital stock and debt, investments, treasury stock, stock options, dividends.
External Financial Reporting	Preparation of financial statements and related disclosures of other financial information including, for example, controls over financial statement valuation and estimation decisions, selection of accounting principles, unusual or nonrecurring activities and decisions, and those which are not transactional in nature such as contingencies.

For each of these types of transactions there are criteria of acceptable internal controls set forth in the committee's report. These criteria are grouped according to the control objectives to be met — authorization, accounting, and asset safeguarding. For each criterion there are control procedures and techniques which are designed to see that the control objectives are met. Exhibit 3-2 shows examples for two of the five cycles, Revenues and Expenditures.[11]

The Rule of Reason

Internal auditors must keep in mind that good auditing is not done by rote. No two organizations are the same. Indeed, no organization is the same today as it was yesterday. Managers are replaced, supervisors are reassigned, new employees are hired, and procedures are revised. Good controls are dependent on good people, well motivated and well trained; and people, their motivation and their training, can change.

Further, ostensibly good controls can be circumscribed either by employee collusion or management override; on the other hand, good controls may be too good. They may be more costly than that which they seek to control. They may be unnecessarily redundant, or they may be so ironclad that they restrict people's imagination, initiative, and innovativeness.

The internal auditor must review internal accounting controls through the eyes of top management, giving consideration to the people, the times, the environment, the risks, and the circumstances.

Internal Operating Controls

Controls, Criteria, and Objectives

Internal auditors should be as expert in dealing with operating controls as

Exhibit 3-2. REVENUE CYCLE

Criteria	Selected Control Procedures and Techniques
Authorization Objectives	
The prices and other terms of sale of goods and services should be properly authorized.	Approved sales catalogs or similar documents containing current price information and policies on matters such as discounts, sales taxes, freight service, warranties, and returned goods.
	Use of appropriate control forms.
	Procedures for approval of individually priced sales.
Accounting Objectives	
Cash receipts should be accounted for properly and on a timely basis.	Provision for comparing initial record of cash receipts with bank deposits and accounting entries and for investigating any unusual delays in depositing receipts.
Asset Safeguarding Objectives	
Access to cash receipts and cash receipt records, accounts receivable records, and billing and shipping records should be suitably controlled to prevent, or detect within a timely period, the interception of unrecorded cash receipts or the abstraction of recorded cash receipts.	Independent control of cash upon receipt (through, for example, lock box arrangements, cash registers, prenumbered cash receipt forms)
	Restrictive endorsement of checks upon receipt.
	Segregation of duties between access to cash receipts and keeping records of sales, customer credits, cash receipts, and accounts receivable.

EXPENDITURE CYCLE

Authorization Objectives	
Disbursements should be made for properly authorized expenditures only.	Formal designation of authority to sign checks, including establishment of requirement for dual signatures.
	Examination of supporting documentation by the individual authorized to sign checks, possibly on a test basis in accordance with established criteria, supporting cash disbursement.
	Independent mailing of signed checks.
	Use of imprest bank accounts and comparison of the deposits to such accounts.

Exhibit 3-2. (Cont.)

Criteria	Selected Control Procedures and Techniques

Investigation of unusual amounts charged to "purchase discounts lost."

Accounting Objectives

Disbursements should be recorded in the appropriate amount and in the appropriate period and should be properly classified in the accounts.

Policies and procedures covering accounting routines and related approval procedures for major disbursement functions.

Accounting for all checks issued.

A suitable chart of accounts and standard journal entries.

Asset Safeguarding Objectives

Access to cash and cash disbursement records should be suitably controlled to prevent or detect, within a timely period, duplicate or improper amounts.

Segregation of duties between the accounts payable and cash disbursement functions; segregation of duties within the cash disbursement function between the issuance of checks or disbursement of cash and the maintenance of the cash disbursement records.

Safekeeping procedures for blank checks and facsimile signature plates.

Safekeeping procedures over the signing of checks (dual signatures, control over signing equipment and signature plates).

Reconciliation of the number of checks issued on a facsimile signature machine to the number of checks prepared.

Mutilation and retention of spoiled checks.

Independent bank reconciliations including comparison, possibly on a test basis, of paid checks with cash disbursement records; and examination, possibly on a test basis, of paid checks for alterations, unauthorized signatures, and unusual endorsements.

Surprise counts of cash funds on hand.

they are with accounting or financial controls. Indeed, inadequate or ineffective controls in a production or marketing department can result in greater dollar losses than those in the accounting department. Millions can be wasted in ineffective programs. Errors in payments or abstractions of receipts in the accounting or financial sections rarely result in such losses.

Operating controls are more difficult to assess. Financial controls have been written about and accepted for many years, but operating controls are not as clear or obvious. Often no criteria or standards have been set for what constitutes appropriate control procedures and techniques. This, then, is where internal auditors can demonstrate their professional ability by recommending and reaching agreement with the auditee on appropriate criteria and controls. To this end, the *Standards for the Professional Practice of Internal Auditing* provide the following guidelines:

280.05 Due professional care includes evaluating established operating standards and determining whether those standards are acceptable and are being met. When such standards are vague, authoritative interpretations should be sought. If internal auditors are required to interpret or select operating standards, they should seek agreement with auditees as to the standards needed to measure operating performance.

As with financial controls, those controls over nonfinancial activities must be keyed to objectives and criteria. Where financial controls are established in consonance with generally acceptable accounting procedures, nonfinancial controls should be established in consonance with accepted management principles and techniques. Hence, in any nonfinancial activities, the auditor who thinks like a manager will determine what control techniques and procedures the manager should have to help him or her plan, organize, direct, and control the activity; for these are the four functions of management.

Management Functions and Control

Within each of the four management functions there should be criteria of acceptable performance which, if met, would give reasonable assurance that the objective would be achieved. Exhibit 3-3 gives some examples of the criteria and suggested control procedures in a research and development (R & D) activity. Through such techniques the control system within an organization can be analyzed and evaluated. The means of control may often be similar for unrelated activities.

In terms of planning, control of R & D activities, for example, calls for formal procedures to create development plans; similarly, control of purchasing activities would call for formal procedures for selecting potential suppliers.

In terms of organizing, R & D personnel should have their responsibilities clearly assigned; in purchasing, procedures should provide explicitly for clear levels of purchase order approvals based on the values of the orders.

Exhibit 3-3. RESEARCH AND DEVELOPMENT

Criteria	Selected Control Procedures and Techniques

Planning Function

R & D work should be planned in adequate detail and the plans should be reduced to writing.	The objectives and goals of R & D are set forth in writing.
	A formal procedure is used to create the development plan and consider inputs from all parts of the organization affected by R & D activities.
	Measurable goals are included in the plans for R & D.
	Each project is uniquely identified and budgeted in the plan, and project milestones are clearly set.
	The R & D budget is properly balanced as to new products, product maintenance, and cost reduction programs.

Organizing Function

The R & D department should be organized so as to be able to carry out its objectives to create new products or improve existing products.	Responsibility for R & D is clearly set forth in written job descriptions covering all personnel assigned to the activity.
	The technological requirements for development work have been identified and the personnel involved in R & D have the necessary knowledge and skills in these technologies.
	Personnel records include complete data for each person assigned to R & D work.
	Where in-house technological capability is lacking, provision is made to use competent outside consultants.
	Special test facilities and equipment essential to R & D work have been identified and are available.

Directing Function

Personnel should be motivated to do imaginative, innovative work.	Personnel are promptly informed of the issuance of procedures and directives which affect their activities.

Continued

Exhibit 3-3. (Cont.)

Criteria	Selected Control Procedures and Techniques
	Personnel are encouraged to participate in professional organizations.
	Personnel are encouraged to publish articles in professional journals.
	The atmosphere within the R & D unit is conducive to open and frank exchanges of opinion.
	"Rap" sessions are held to permit and encourage the airing of views.

Controlling Function

Criteria	Selected Control Procedures and Techniques
The manager of R & D should be provided with adequate information to administer the department effectively.	The manager is supplied with timely, accurate, useful reports on R & D costs.
	Comparisons are made between budgets and costs, and significant variances are investigated.
	Provision is made for giving information on field operation performance to the R & D manager.
	An adequate system of coordination is in force for R & D projects throughout the entire enterprise.
	Records are maintained of the department's accomplishments.
	A formal process exists for authorizing changes in scope of work or expenditures defined by plans.

In terms of directing, R & D personnel should be promptly informed of procedures and directives affecting their activities. Purchasing personnel, similarly, should be informed in ample time of long-lead-time products on the drawing boards which they will be called upon to purchase in whole or in part.

In terms of controlling, the R & D manager should be supplied with timely, accurate, useful reports on R & D costs. Buyers should be supplied with timely, accurate, useful reports on products received, accepted, or rejected.

In the same manner, the "cycle" approach to financial activities can be equally useful in the analysis of nonfinancial controls. Transaction cycles can be identified in advertising, engineering, quality control, and production activities as well as in accounting activities, and they too can be related to the functions of management.

Overcontrolling

One fear that followed the impact of the U.S. Foreign Corrupt Practices Act of 1977 is that of excessive, redundant, useless, and/or inordinately expensive controls. When a difficulty arises, the tendency is sometimes to throw money at it in hopes that it will thereby subside. But too much control can be as bad as too little. A structure of expensive, restrictive controls can stifle performance and initiative. Protection is bought at the price of repression.

A mine superintendent who received a 200-page "cost sheet" had this wry comment: "You people slaved two weeks on this bundle of figures and all I ever look at are the first four [summary] pages. They tell me whether I'll keep my job. The rest is damn wasted motion."[12]

Perhaps he was justified. Reports in many instances can be accused of being overplus. Control reports, those means of control which are supposed to help managers control their own activities, are often guilty of being:

Too voluminous — they should be condensed to the bare essentials.

Too complex — they should be useful to the reader and should emphasize what is significant, not merely provide "interesting information."

Too misleading — they should reach definite conclusions.

Too generalized — they should focus on one direction and not be guilty of "report sprawl."

Too stereotyped — they should be elastic, and if uncommon matters are reported, these should be defined.

Management Overrides

Internal auditors have long claimed to be experts on control, and with good reason. They usually demonstrate their expertise with each audit of an operational activity which focuses on the controls rather than on technical performance. Their claims are now more readily accepted by management. The penalties for poor controls are escalating and there are few other people in the organization that management can turn to for expert, objective advice on control systems. But with the increased responsibilty comes increased accountability.

Internal auditors will be expected to be more aware of control weaknesses and control breakdowns. When losses occur because of poor control, the internal auditors will be taken to task because management relied on them and took them at their word when they claimed to be the experts on control.

But what of problems resulting from management overrides of internal control systems — overrides of which the internal auditors are not aware? What of contempt for controls, merely reflecting at the operating level what is felt at the executive level? These conditions can make the job of the internal auditor well nigh impossible to carry out.

Some enlightened organizations have seen the risk and met it with top-level policy statements. Exhibit 3-4 is an example of one such statement. It acknowledges the requirements of the U.S. Foreign Corrupt Practices Act of 1977. It defines internal control for all to see. It reemphasizes the company's compliance with ethical standards, adherence to acceptable control procedures, oversights by the audit committee of the board of directors, and reviews of controls by the internal audit staff and the independent auditors.

Significantly, it prohibits "management override of any control designed to prevent or detect transactions that are illegal, improper, unethical, or against the social conventions of the United States." And it provides that "All other management overrides of internal control systems must be authorized in writing by the responsible executive and filed with the General Auditor and Corporate Controller."

Exhibit 3-4. CORPORATE POLICY ON INTERNAL CONTROL

Need for a Policy

In view of the importance of internal control in the orderly and efficient conduct of the Company's business and, in view of the emphasis on internal control by law and by the Securities and Exchange Commission, a statement has been issued to focus the Company's traditional requirements for adequate internal control.

Statement of Policy

It is the policy of the Company that the management of the Corporation and all divisions and subsidiaries maintain systems of internal control which are designed to ensure, as far as it is practical, that the objectives of the Company are achieved and to comply with applicable law. Within the perspective of internal control, in the broad sense, management is expected to maintain adequate internal accounting control over all aspects of the Company's operations.

Definitions

Internal control is the composite total of all organizational and operating plans, systems, policies, procedures and practices, as well as the attitudes and behavior of executive management and other employees, occurring within the Company, established by executive management with the approval of the Audit Committee of the Board of Directors, to achieve the basic objective of ensuring the disciplined and efficient conduct of the Company's business in general, and specifically:

    a) to assure the Company's assets are accounted for and safeguarded from losses of all kinds,

    b) to assure the accuracy and reliability of accounting and financial information generated within the Company and to assure the fiscal integrity of resulting financial reports released to the public and other media,

    c) to promote operating efficiency of all Company conponents, and

    d) to inform and encourage adherence by all Company employees to prescribed managerial policies.

Exhibit 3-4. (Cont.)

There is a distinction between the exercise of internal control and the determination of business policies. Even though internal control includes all the controls established by management to achieve its objectives, it does not encompass all management activities. For example, determining a sales policy is a business decision; monitoring and recording the results achieved by such a decision is a function of internal control.

An accounting system is an important element of internal control but is not in itself an internal control system. An internal control system includes comparisons, determination of discrepancies and decisions as to corrective action, as well as controls over the accounting system.

Application of Policy

As guidance to management in the evaluation of internal accounting control, the Company considers the following components to be essential to an adequate system of internal accounting control:

1. Compliance with ethical standards in all of the Company's affairs as set forth in Corporate Directive Policy No. 2.

2. Trustworthy personnel with the ability, training and experience required to perform satisfactorily the responsibilities assigned to them.

3. Enforcement of Corporate Directive Policies on Conflict of Interest (No. 5) and Antitrust (No. 3).

4. A plan of organization including delegation and coordination of assigned responsibilities with proper regard to the segregation of incompatible functions.

5. An adequate accounting structure at each operating entity including budgetary and cost accounting techniques, a chart and text of accounts, procedural manuals and, where applicable, charts depicting the flow of transactions.

6. Proper procedures for authorization of transactions.

7. Recording of transactions in reasonable detail and with promptness and accuracy.

8. Thorough review in the preparation of financial statements and other financial information for internal use and external reporting.

9. Adequate physical facilities and safeguards to prevent improper movement of property and to protect the accounting records of the Company.

10. Regular monitoring by corporate and operating unit management.

11. Review of the Company's systems and controls by an extensive program of audits by the Company's internal auditing staff and independent auditors.

12. Close coordination of the internal audit and independent audit effort by a member of Corporate management under the oversight of the Audit Committee of the Board of Directors.

13. Continuous evaluation of the costs of controls in relation to the expected benefits of those controls. Management is authorized to forego specific

Exhibit 3-4. (Cont.)

controls where the magnitude of risk incurred by the absence of individual controls, or combinations of controls, does not justify the cost of maintaining such controls. Magnitude of risk shall be a subjective judgment gauged to the total operations and assets of the Company.

14. Prohibition against management override of any control designed to prevent or detect transactions that are illegal, improper, unethical, or against the social conventions of the United States.

15. All other management overrides of internal control systems must be authorized in writing by the responsible executive and filed with the General Auditor and Corporate Controller.

Responsibility and Authority

The Management Committee, acting with the approval of and under the surveillance of the Audit Committee of the Board of Directors, has the prime authority and responsibility for the Company's internal control systems. The Corporate Controller, as the chief accounting officer for the Company, has the authority and responsibility for the internal accounting controls and systems of the Company and its wholly-owned and majority-owned subsidiaries. Each manager and executive of the Company and its divisions and subsidiaries is responsible for maintaining internal controls which establish accountability and safeguard against misuse of Company assets under his or her charge. Such internal controls are to at least reflect the standards set forth by the Management Comittee and, in the case of internal accounting controls, by the Corporate Controller.

Specifically with regard to internal accounting controls, each Division Controller or Vice President-Analysis and Control is directly responsible to the Corporate Controller for the accounting and accounting systems and controls of the division. Further, each plant and subsidiary within the division shall designate a chief accounting executive acceptable and responsible directly to the Division Controller or Vice President-Analysis and Control for the accounting and internal accounting controls of such plant or subsidiary. Such lines of responsibility and authority are to be communicated in writing to those involved with a copy to the Corporate Controller.

Conclusion

Internal auditors have long been experts on financial and accounting activities. They have reached the audit of nonfinancial activities via a bridge called control. Designing controls is a management prerogative. Appraising their adequacy and effectiveness is the internal auditor's responsibility. The Foreign Corrupt Practices Act of 1977 has heightened management's interest in controls. Management now faces serious risks if controls do not meet reasonable standards. Internal auditors must therefore improve their expertise in studying, evaluating, and expressing opinions on internal controls throughout the enterprise.

References

1. L. B. Sawyer, "Internal Control — The Internal Auditor's 'Open Sesame'," *The Internal Auditor*, January/February 1970, p. 36.
2. R. H. Benson, "Changing Demands on Internal and External Auditors," *The Internal Auditor*, February 1979, p. 55.

3. J. P. Callahan, "Audit of Financial Controls," *The Internal Auditor*, June 1976, pp. 70-72.
4. Henri Fayol, *General and Industrial Management* (New York: Pitman Publishing Corp., 1949, trans. from the French, originally published in 1916).
5. Oxford English Dictionary.
6. Samuel Johnson, *Dictionary of the English Language*, 1755.
7. R. H. Montgomery, "Dicksee's Auditing," quoted in C. P. A. Handbook, American Institute of Certified Public Accountants, 1956.
8. G. E. Bennett, *Fraud — Its Control Through Accounts* (New York: Appleton Century Co., 1930).
9. L. B. Sawyer, "The Anatomy of Control," *The Internal Auditor*, Spring 1964, pp. 15, 16.
10. U.S. General Accounting Office, "Comprehensive Audit Manual," Chapter 9.
11. *Report of the Special Advisory Committee on Internal Accounting Control*, 1979, issued by the American Institute of Certified Public Accountants.
12. J. F. Arnold, "The Dynamics of Internal Control," *The Internal Auditor*, May/June 1970, p. 29.

Supplementary Reading

AICPA. "Tentative Report of the Special Advisory Committee on Internal Accounting Control."

Arthur Anderson & Co. "A Guide for Studying and Evaluating Internal Accounting Controls," January 1978.

Davies, D. H. "Controls vs. Control." *The Internal Auditor*, August 1976, pp. 17-25.

The Foreign Corrupt Practices Act of 1977, P.L. 95-213, December 19, 1977, 91 Stat. 1494.

Morfin, J. G. "The Function of Control and Internal Control." *The Internal Auditor*, January/February 1973, pp. 42-55.

Peat, Marwick, Mitchell & Co. "Evaluating Internal Accounting Controls." 1978.

Securities and Exchange Commission Release No. 242, February 16, 1978. "Notification of Enactment of Foreign Corrupt Practices Act of 1977."

Touche Ross & Co. "The New Management Imperative — Compliance With the Accounting Requirements of the Foreign Corrupt Practices Act," 1978.

For further study

Discussion Problems

1. What principles of internal control are violated in a company where the bookkeeper deposits receipts, the buyer doubles as accounts payable clerk, and the inventory clerk authorizes inventory write offs?

2. Why are the objectives of internal control satisfied if a buyer is permitted to negotiate prices but are not satisfied if he approves invoices for payment?

3. What principles of internal control are violated when programmers are given unrestricted access to EDP operating equipment?

4. An internal auditor was assigned to the audit of a receiving operation. He found that no performance standards had been set. So he eliminated the test from his audit program, since field work implies measurement and an

auditor cannot measure without standards. Comment.

5. An example of internal accounting control is:

a. Long-range planning
b. Internal auditing
c. A system of authorization and approval
d. A statement of function and responsibility
e. All of the above

6. What three circumstances have made it increasingly significant for the internal auditor to evaluate internal controls?

7. The director of internal auditing of a large corporation was asked by the audit committee of a company to provide written advice to their board of directors as to whether the company maintains its records and internal accounting controls to the extent and manner required by the U.S. Foreign Corrupt Practices Act of 1977. What would be an appropriate response?

8. Describe the change in the way internal control is regarded since Henri Fayol defined control.

9. A manager says to you: "Give me timely, accurate information on performance and that's all I need to exercise proper control. Information is synonymous with internal control." Comment.

10. The chairman of the audit committee of the board of directors of your company says to you, "The U.S. Foreign Corrupt Practices Act of 1977 is causing me much concern. Its provisions are not precise. It does not provide standards of what good internal accounting control should be, yet we shall be held to compliance with the provisions of the Act. What do you recommend we do to avoid being penalized for noncompliance?" How would you respond?

11. You are the director of internal auditing in a broad-based organization. Operating personnel in manufacturing, procurement, and receiving have accused your internal auditors of tying their hands with unnecessary controls which, in their view, are so much red tape.
Considering the standards of good internal auditing practice, discuss the accusation that the internal auditor bears responsibility for the controls which the operating personnel resent.

12. In a large manufacturing organization supplying goods and services, several departments may be involved in the processing of customer complaints and the issuance of any resulting credit memos. Those departments are: receiving, sales, production, customer service, and accounts receivable.

Explain briefly the control function each of these departments performs when processing complaints and issuing credit memos.

13. Both internal and external auditors have a responsibility to study and evaluate internal control.

Required: (a) Define internal control. (b) State the type of control that is concerned with the safeguarding of assets and the processing of authorized transactions. (c) Explain the relationship between internal control and the responsibilities of the internal auditor as outlined in the Statement of Responsibilities of Internal Auditors. (d) List two objectives of the internal auditor in evaluating internal control. (e) List two objectives of the external auditor in evaluating internal control.

14. There are seven or more steps in a sales (revenue) cycle. Internal auditors expect to find one or more controls to assure performance of each step. One step is the acceptance of a customer's

order. This step should be controlled by proper authorization.

Required: List three additional steps in the sales (revenue) cycle; and, for each step, list one control the internal auditor would expect to find for that step.

15. Provide the reasons for the following criteria of internal control:

Organization criteria: The individual to whom authority is delegated should be required to exercise that authority, but should check with a superior in case of exception.

Policies criteria: Policies should be clearly stated in writing and systematically organized in handbooks, manuals, or other publications.

Multiple Choice Problems

1. An appropriate internal control for the payroll function would be segregation of duties for distributing payroll checks and:
a. Keeping records of absenteeism.
b. Batch processing time cards.
c. Preparing payroll tax returns.
d. Reconciling hours worked to hours paid.
e. Hiring personnel.

2. Which of the following is least likely to be detected by an internal control system?
a. Duplicate payments to suppliers.
b. Deviations from written procedures.
c. Fraudulent actions by an individual employee.
d. Fraudulent actions by a group of employees.
e. Unauthorized disbursements.

3. Which of the following internal controls would most likely prevent payment of vendors' duplicate invoices?
a. Cancelling invoices by means of a

"Paid" stamp or perforation prior to approval.
b. Prenumbering unused voucher forms and periodically checking for missing numbers.
c. Sending cancelled checks to the bank reconciliation unit.
d. Determining that vouchers are properly authorized and approved and include original receiving documentation prior to check preparation.
e. Requiring two authorized signatures for voucher checks.

4. Which of the following is the most important internal control procedure for acquisitions of property, plant, and equipment?
a. Establishing a written company policy to distinguish between capital and revenue expenditures.
b. Using a budget to plan, authorize, and control acquisitions.
c. Analyzing monthly variances between authorized expenditures and actual costs.
d. Establishing a property ledger.
e. Requiring approval of capital expenditures by the chief financial officer.

5. Administrative control in an internal auditing department includes:
a. Preparation of audit programs.
b. Proper supervision of assistants.
c. Maintenance of audit time records.
d. Explanation of significant audit budget variances.
e. All of the above.

6. Organization charts of the activity being audited are useful to the internal auditor because they:
a. Depict informal lines of communication.
b. Provide good internal control.
c. Ensure a proper allocation of responsibilities.
d. Provide a basis for reviewing controls.

e. Provide a listing of auditee personnel.

7. After preparing a flowchart of a local government's procurement system, an auditor should next:
a. Select a random sample of transactions to audit.
b. Identify the control points.
c. Prepare a report listing any weaknesses in the system.
d. Determine the possibility of fraud occurring.
e. Evaluate whether the system provides adequate control.

8. Internal control is enhanced when employees are placed on the payroll upon the approval of:
a. The requesting department.
b. The personnel department.
c. The payroll department.
d. Both a and b.
e. None of the above.

9. The auditor, in recommending controls, should always consider the cost of the control in relation to the risk. Which of the following controls best reflects this philosophy with respect to a large dollar investment in heavy machine tools?
a. A monthly physical inventory.
b. Security guards on duty 24 hours a day.
c. A controlled identification number on each tool.
d. All dispositions approved by the vice president of sales.
e. None of the above.

10. Good internal control over the receipt of material requires:
a. Detailed quantity checks by the using department.
b. Package counts at the receiving dock.
c. Sample inspections for quality.
d. All of the above.
e. None of the above.

11. Good internal control is provided when wage and salary advances for vacation are approved by:
a. The section supervisor.
b. The department manager.
c. The payroll department.
d. All of the above.
e. None of the above.

12. The practice that would most likely improve inventory control would be:
a. To investigate thoroughly all significant inventory adjustments.
b. To write off inventory adjustments to general profit and loss.
c. To charge operating departments for estimated inventory adjustments.
d. All of the above.
e. None of the above.

Case Studies
3-1 Internal Auditing and Internal Control
Internal auditing is an important part of an organization's system of internal control.
Required: (1) List three major objectives of internal control. (2) For each of the objectives listed in (1), above, briefly describe two of the internal auditor's examination responsibilities.

3-2 Agency Agreements Under the FCPA
You are making an audit of the marketing branch. You find that your company has embarked on a program to penetrate the foreign market with its products. To do so it has hired an agent living and doing business in the foreign country where sales are to be made. You are concerned with whether the marketing people took all reasonable steps to demonstrate that the agency agreement did not violate the anti-corruption provisions of the FCPA (U.S. Foreign Corrupt Practices Act).
Required: Describe at least three actions that the marketing people should have taken to demonstrate compliance with the relevant provisions of the Act.

Part 2

Techniques of
Internal Auditing

4

Performing the Preliminary Survey

Familiarization. Foundation for the internal audit. Answering the key questions. The skills to acquire. Responsibility for identifying risks. Employee integrity is no constant. Violations of administrative controls. Assessing management. Indications of poor management. A catalogue of risks. Risks in the purchasing and payroll departments. Controls designed to reduce risks. Differentiating among objectives, goals, and standards. Evaluating them. Searching for the key controls. Guarding against purchasing and payroll risks. Quantitative risk assessments. Planning the audit. Reminder lists. Questionnaires. The first meeting with operating management. Setting the tone of the audit. Interview techniques. Survey information and the elements of management. Potential problems. Information sources. The people in the operating organization. Personal observations. "Walk-throughs." Security inspection. Flowcharting. Different forms of flowcharts. Summarizing and reporting survey results.

The Purpose of the Preliminary Survey

Simply stated, the purpose of the preliminary survey is familiarization; but familiarization for internal auditors is different from familiarization for the casual observer. Auditors must not only view the scene and read the words, they must hear the music too. They must do more than perceive the flow of work, they must perceive the true objectives, they must identify the risks, they must pinpoint the key controls, they must understand the management style, they must look into the background of employees. Only then will the auditors be able to determine significant control points, develop a thoughtful audit program tailored to the needs of that particular audit, deploy audit efforts economically, and form a firm foundation for the examination that follows.

Inadequate familiarization can result in a lack of understanding of what the audit assignment really is; in an inept audit program; in spending too much time on one activity and too little on another; in overemphasizing the insignificant; in not comprehending the information being gathered; in not understanding the needs and problems of the people to be dealt with, therefore not being able to deal with them; in short, it can bring about frustration.

A poor preliminary survey, or no survey at all, can result in a poor audit or a wasted one. A good survey may not guarantee a brilliant analysis, but it will provide reasonable assurance of a workmanlike audit examination. Indeed, it may sometimes be sufficient to substitute for many parts of the detailed examination. It may even support a decision to make no further audit at all.

Yet the preliminary survey is very often given short shrift by the auditor. More's the pity, because it is one of the most useful and vital tools available to cut through the mystifying mass of detail that blocks a clear view of the audit objectives — to start the audit job quickly and in the right direction.

Many operations in large companies and government agencies are extremely complex. Often, the people engaged in an activity can spend years working on it without truly understanding all its facets — much less the interface between their activities and others. Clearly, the internal auditor who seeks not only to understand the activity, but also to evaluate it and suggest improvements, has a baffling path to follow. The path gets rockier and thornier as government and business activities become more complex; as the computer injects itself into more and more activities; as managers learn to use more sophisticated management techniques, such as operations research and statistical inference; as the external environment, such as legal restrictions, political atmosphere, ecology, public relations, employee relations, market conditions, changing technology, safety requirements, and stockholder concerns, impinges on the internal operation of the activity; as management styles change; and as middle management turns and twists to adjust to new executive postures.

It is a baffling path, indeed a forbidding one. The human mind, with its limitations on absorbing and remembering, is boggled by the mass of information, nuances, relationships, causes, and effects that must be gathered, sorted out, absorbed, and put to practical use. But no mass of data has yet been accumulated that cannot be given some semblance of order and in some way be arrayed, summarized, and evaluated — if done in a logical, organized, and methodical manner. That is what the preliminary survey is all about. Collect information, array it, summarize it, evaluate it, and put it to use in developing an audit program; and throughout, learn to understand the people doing the work and the managers who seek to lead them.

Put in simpler terms, the preliminary survey should answer these questions about an activity:

What is the job?	Where is it done?
Who does it?	When is it done?
Why is it done?	How is it monitored?
How is it done?	How much does it cost?

A good deal of work goes into a preliminary survey. So that it fulfills its purpose, it should be approached professionally. The questions to be asked should be jotted down in advance to make sure they are not forgotten. The information gathered should be documented in the audit working papers. The end result will be worth the effort because the competent preliminary survey will permit more realistic decisions on audit objectives, staffing, scheduling, audit budgets, locations to be covered or not to be covered, the detailed tests to be made, and whether a detailed audit examination is worthwhile.

To carry out preliminary surveys accurately, completely, and economically, internal auditors should have or acquire the following skills:

They must be able to identify the risks that lie beneath the surface of an activity or are implicit in its operations.

They must understand objective-oriented management. Without clear-cut objectives and goals, activities may drift and flounder. If internal auditors do not understand an activity's objectives, their audits may also drift and flounder.

They must understand the theory and means of control — the anatomy of control and the various control techniques.

They must be able to equip themselves for the preliminary survey so as to be able to ask intelligent questions.

They must be able to set a cooperative, participative tone for the audit during the preliminary meeting.

They must have a clear understanding of the information needed, the sources of that information, and the means of obtaining it.

They should be adept at the techniques of flowcharting so as to draw clear pictures of complex operations that do not lend themselves to narrative descriptions.

They must know how to assess the way an activity is managed and how to evaluate the backgrounds of the people who perform it.

They must be adept at making physical inspections of operations.

They should be able to present post-survey reports orally or in writing so as to identify weaknesses and promote prompt corrective action.

Risks

The Internal Auditor's Responsibilities

The *Standards for the Professional Practice of Internal Auditing* call for professional care — the kind of care and skill expected of a reasonably prudent and competent internal auditor. They do not require internal auditors to be omniscient or to be insurers against all and any noncompliance or wrongdoing which might be occurring in their companies or agencies. They require reasonable care and compliance — not infallibility or extraordinary performance.

Professional care does include considering the possibility of material irregularities or noncompliance. Whenever internal auditors undertake audit assignments, they must be aware of the risks, the potential traps, and the stones under which lie the scorpions poised to strike. Infinite awareness and insight no; but professional competence yes. The layman may see no harm in the same employee ordering and receiving supplies, but the professional internal auditor must immediately perceive the inherent risks.

Just as the competent physician will detect the telltale signs of an illness with a single glance at a patient, just as an able attorney will detect the dangers in the language of a homemade will at a quick scanning, so professional internal auditors will be able to clearly identify the hazards that lurk in some activities.

Deliberate wrongdoing is not the only or the most significant hazard. Records or transactions are mishandled less through dishonesty or malice than by people making mistakes, not following the rules, not understanding instructions, or not being properly monitored.[1] When the improprieties are deliberate, the losses are generally attributable more to employees misusing systems than to outsiders gaining unlawful entry. Those who steal from inventory usually work in inventory control. Those who work in payroll do not usually steal from inventory or from accounts receivable. Most improprieties involving property are perpetuated by the people working in the activities where the thefts or embezzlements occur.

Internal auditors, concerned with potential risks, look for the safeguards that will help prevent losses from such risks. They must not be swayed by the tenure of the employees, by their past history of sterling behavior, or by the high repute in which they are held by others. Individual personal integrity is not a constant. It varies with time and circumstances and changes as conflicts arise. The desire to be honest may yield to the need to pay for an urgently required operation for child. The highly motivated employees — pillars of probity who feel that they were passed over for promotion — may decide to get those increases in a manner of their own choosing.

So internal auditors place their reliance on adequate systems, effective monitoring, and competent management. They are responsible for identifying inadequate controls, for appraising managerial effectiveness, for assessing the quality of people, and for pinpointing the common risks.

Inadequate Controls

Inadequate controls present hazards. People do things wrong — either carelessly or intentionally — if their work is not monitored or if systems are ineptly designed. Everybody needs a reviewer — either a human reviewer or a system which shouts "Tilt!" when something is done improperly.

Internal auditors keep in the cubby holes of their minds the kinds of management controls that will help prevent the errors and the improprieties. Improprieties can be catalogued under the four generally accepted elements of management: planning, organizing, directing, and controlling (see Chapter 21). Internal auditors analyze systems and activities with management-control principles in mind. When they see the principles violated, they focus their field work on the errors likely to result. Violations of principles of good adminstration are red flags which alert internal auditors to the possibility of errors or intentional wrongdoing. Here are some of the violations:

Planning

Not giving planning primacy over all other functions.

Failing to communicate planning premises to subordinates.

Not setting or updating goals or standards.

Not prescribing a system of review and approval.

Developing plans that are incompatible with company objectives.

Not providing for the receipt or submission of new and relevant information.

Not providing for the measurement of the performance needed to carry out plans.

Not providing for the periodic reappraisal of plans.

Organizing

Failing to establish unity of objectives within organizational units of the enterprise.

Failing to maintain a reasonable span of control.

Failing to provide equality of authority and responsibility.

Failing to establish clear lines of responsibility which extend from the top of the organization to the lowest level of supervision.

Failure to ensure unity of command: one person, one boss.

Failure to provide for a mix of ages so that retirements will not adversely affect the functioning of the organization.

Failure to ensure adequate balance in the organization.

Failure to provide flexibility within the organization.

Failure to delegate authority so as to permit decisions to be made at the lowest practicable level of management.

Directing

Not training or instructing subordinates.

Not making sure that people read and understand instructions.

Not maintaining current information on the work and location of employees.

Not providing for coordination of plans, objectives, policies and procedures of the unit with those of the company and interfacing units.

Not periodically reviewing the needs of serviced units.

Not providing information on breakdowns in cooperation.

Controlling

Not providing schedules and budgets for each job.

Not establishing a central control (charts, logs, registers, sales or work orders, and the like).

Not highlighting oldest, off-schedule, or overbudget jobs.

Not setting priorities for incoming work.

Not fixing responsibility for work performed.

Not providing for approvals commensurate with the importance of the work.

Not providing for feedback on the quality and acceptability of the work performed.

Not comparing results with expectations and investigating variances.

Not reporting variances to those responsible for correcting them.

Not following up on work in process.

Ineffective Management

Assessing the adequacy of management is a dangerous pursuit. Pointing the finger at a manager may bring repercussions which could make the jobs of internal auditors difficult or impossible to accomplish. They may develop a reputation as headhunters or spies. Besides, such appraisals tend to become subjective and therefore may be regarded as failing to display the impartiality expected of internal auditors.

Yet internal auditors cannot turn a blind eye to management effectiveness. It remains the most significant means of control in any activity. Competent management, watchful management, respected management can counterbalance a host of system inadequacies. But incompetent management, management which disassociates itself from operations, management which does not have the respect of its employees, can render the best of systems ineffective.

Internal auditors must be able to detect the signs of poor management. Not to point their fingers at the managers themselves, but to use the signs to point the auditors' noses in the right directions — to document, objectively, the tangible results of poor management. The subjective evaluation of people should never be reported, but the objective evidence of the results of poor management is something else. The thing must speak for itself. The deficient conditions, objectively reported, will carry a clear message to higher managment.

Managerial difficulties can be listed under two headings: One concerns the indications of inadequate operating management, the other deals with the problems operating managers face because of constraints placed upon them by higher authority. Here are some of the indicators:

Inadequate Operating Management

Giving perfunctory approvals — authorizing an action without really understanding what is involved.

Not knowing what their people are doing.

Not comparing accomplishment with goals and analyzing variances.

Not providing adequate instruction to employees.

Not providing adequate indoctrination for new employees.

Not keeping control records accurate, current, and complete.

Not keeping written procedures up-to-date.

Not following up on assigned tasks.

Not obtaining reports from subordinates on task accomplishment.

Lack of adequate knowledge of related functions in interfacing organizations.

Lack of adequate feedback to highlight inadequate output.

Lack of provision for evaluating significant jobs at key milestones.

Lack of a system of self-evaluation.

Not monitoring the ongoing process.

Not subordinating departmental objectives to company objectives.

Lack of adequate statistics on the volume of work and the accomplishment of objectives.

Not developing backup personnel.

Not providing employees with the tools and resources to do their jobs.

Not accepting the responsibilities assigned.

Not seeking out information on the probable amount of work to be received in the future.

Constraints on Good Management

Requiring managers to spend their time correcting problems rather than planning for the prevention of problems.

Withholding the resources needed to do an acceptable job.

Assigning responsibility without delegating the necessary authority.

Emphasizing schedule over everything — quality, cost, safety, ecology, and the needs of people.

Not including operating management and supervision in the setting of goals and objectives.

Generating the fear syndrome throughout the enterprise.

Stifling creativity.

Not providing managers with the information needed to measure their own productivity.

Not informing managers about future plans, objectives, and goals of the enterprise.

Not putting the right manager into the right job.

The Common and Unique Risks

A complete compendium of common risks to be found in all activities of all companies and agencies probably does not exist. A knowledge of these risks can be gained from auditing and accounting literature and from the ability to translate accounting and financial risks into risks applying to other operations in the organization. For example, failure to separate duties will create a risk which will be equally applicable in the accounting department and the medical department. The person who receives cash should not be the same one who records the receipts. Similarly, the person who orders medical supplies should not also receive them, record them, inventory them, and make record adjustments.

It would be impractical to try to catalogue all such risks in a book such as this. But those which present the greatest hazards to the organization should be identified, listed formally, and referenced to the audit projects in which they are to be reviewed. Here is a listing of some common risk areas or activities which a manufacturing company has identified for periodic audits:

Payments to or for Employees

Undelivered payroll checks

Wage and salary adjustments

Blank check stock

Expense advances

Expense reports

Entertainment expense

Credit cards

Airline tickets

Approval of overtime

Facsimile signature plates

Rotation and vacation schedules of key employees (applies in other areas as well)

Payments to employees in sensitive areas

Payments to Suppliers

Processing payments for supplies received

Blank check stock

Invoices approved by executives without evidence of receipt

Facsimile signature plates

Mailing accounts payable checks

Undelivered checks

Credit and no-charge sales

Freight drafts

Authorization of new suppliers

Time and material contracts

Cash

Bank reconciliations

Cashier funds

Travelers checks

Petty cash funds

Wire transfers of funds

Cash received by the mail room

Import and export of currency

Metered postage

Plant Security

Inspection of vehicles driven in and out of the plant

Rotation of guards

Locksmith activities

Purchasing
Selection of suppliers

Product changes

Changes to purchase orders

Receipts of gifts and gratuities

Scrap and Salvage Generation and Disposition
Segregation of scrap at source

Procedures for evaluating bids from scrap dealers

Other Risk Areas
Preparation of specifications for supplies

Supplies particularly susceptible to pilferage

Supplies or services delivered directly to using departments

Conflict of interest programs

Dealing with agents

Safeguarding company's proprietary data

Physical control over fixed assets

Professional services

Computer room security

Remote computer terminal security

It will be observed that in some cases exposures to risk can be assessed during an audit directed exclusively to the enumerated risk. That is, the risk or risks may be the subject of the complete audit. In other cases, the exposures should be reviewed during an audit of a broader subject which includes those risks and other matters as well.

Each organization has its unique problems. In a manufacturing organization, for example, product changes are accompanied by significant risks. When purchased parts incorporated into a product are changed, there is a real risk that the purchase orders for the superseded parts will not be canceled; unneeded parts will be received and paid for. In an insurance company, changes to policy provisions present a risk that claims processors or insurance agents will not be promptly instructed as to their roles with respect to the changes.

At the same time, most companies have common operations. Purchasing and payroll department activities, for example, will present very much the same kinds of risks — with some variations — no matter how diverse the organization's products or services:

Purchasing

Receipt of substandard supplies.

Purchases from suppliers related to buyers or other company people.

Purchases made from foreign suppliers in violation of import quotas.

Purchases in excess of need.

Goods purchased too far in advance, straining working capital, raising warehouse costs, and running the risk of obsolescence.

Low-cost suppliers not asked to bid.

Supplies or services ordered by people not authorized to do so.

Significant purchases under agreements not reviewed by legal counsel.

Goods received in excess of that ordered.

Rush orders left on receiving dock because paper work is not forwarded promptly to the receiving department.

Payroll

Employees hired for sensitive positions without checking backgrounds.

Nonexistent employees added to payroll.

Separated employees not removed from payroll.

Laws and government regulations not followed, resulting in fines, penalties, or contingent liabilities.

Payments in amounts not authorized.

Unauthorized overtime.

Unauthorized deductions.

Labor used to do things not authorized — building an addition to an executive's home, for example.

Labor charged to improper accounts or contracts.

Personnel records not safeguarded.

The purpose of being aware of the risks is to make sure controls have been established to guard against them. Controls do not exist for their own sake; they are established to see that an objective is met. And one significant objective for controls is to eliminate or reduce losses resulting from known risks.

When internal auditors perceive risks, they should search out the controls designed to protect against them. If controls are inadequate or ineffective, they should be discussed then and there with the auditee-manager. If agreement on corrective action is reached and if adequate corrective action is taken, further audit effort would be pointless. If, however, the manager remains unconvinced and needs proof that the risks are real and the controls are weak, the auditor should program a purposive test — rather than a test by random sample — to support the existence and significance of the weaknesses.

The preliminary survey, with its overview of the entire operation instead of nibbling at corners, provides a firm foundation for the preparation of a thoughtful audit program that concentrates on those matters which are of vital interest to management: Have the key risks been identified? Are the key risks being monitored? Are inadequate controls being brought to light and corrected? Which activities presenting unmonitored hazards should be audited in depth?

Identifying Objectives, Goals, and Standards

During their preliminary surveys, internal auditors should seek to determine the objectives of the activity under audit. Unless those objectives are clearly understood, the audit may miss its mark. Taking a clear, sharp picture of the activity's objectives — its mission within the entity — is the hallmark of professional internal auditors. They are not swayed or influenced by the functions described in statements of function and responsibility. These may be obsolete or they may be self-serving declarations designed to elevate status. They may not get to the marrow of the activity.

Internal auditors must differentiate among objectives, goals, and standards. **Objectives** represent the entity's missions and broad purposes. **Goals** are measurable units to be achieved in meeting the objectives. **Standards** are the gauges of excellence in terms of cost, schedule, and quality. For example, service is an objective of a department of water and power. Installing 1,000 new water meters in the coming year might be a goal. Keeping the cost of the average installation under $25, the time of installation under an hour, and improper installations under one percent could be standards.

Objectives are more difficult to isolate than goals or standards. For example, a statement of function may declare that the accounts payable department shall process invoices for payment. Quite true, but it doesn't really hit the mark. All it calls for is seeing that invoices are supported by evidence of terms (contracts or purchase orders) and evidence of receipt (receiving memos or signed approvals). But actually the objective of accounts payable is to approve for payment what is due, when due, while achieving maximum conservation of company funds. Perceiving that objective will lead internal auditors into more productive examinations than those which merely call for comparing pieces of paper.

Goals, specific and measurable goals, are what operating managers are expected to achieve or intend to achieve. Well-constructed goals will include the standards by which the accomplishment of the goals will be measured. For example, an organization intends to produce 15,000 units by April 15, with a rejection rate not over 2%, at a cost not to exceed $5 a unit. These are clearly defined goals and standards. Accomplishment can be readily measured. The standards are plain to see and understand. Both managers and internal auditors can determine after April 15 whether the mission has been accomplished as intended.

During the preliminary survey, internal auditors should evaluate objectives and goals. Are they set forth formally? Are they understood by those charged with meeting them? Do they incorporate standards of excellence so that all involved understand precisely what is expected of them? If the internal auditors cannot measure accomplishment, how can the manager or the manager's people? Oh yes, the manager can obtain a general impression of whether things are going badly or well; but this can be affected by bias, unreasonable demands, or how the manager happens to be feeling that day.

Internal auditors should know the goals of those programs and activities they intend to review before they proceed to their programming and field work. If goals and standards cannot be satisfactorily established, detailed review may become a chancy exercise.

In audits of economy and efficiency, goals are generally implied. All organizations are expected to keep costs down and schedules in line without sacrificing effective performance. But even here goals and standards can provide reasonably precise gauges of performance. How many cases should a welfare case worker handle in a month? How many invoices should an accounts payable clerk process in a week? How many letters or pages should a typist produce in a day? What percentage of errors should a draftsman be allowed per blueprint? In seeking out standards, auditors may often obtain realistic ones from other organizations doing similar work.

For program results, goals usually represent what the authorizing body — the legislature, the board of directors, the chief executive officer, or other people in authority — intends to accomplish. Information on these goals is critical. An internal audit that does not report the extent that objectives and goals have been met, does not measure up to a management-oriented audit.

Defining goals and standards is not a simple task. Objectives may be imprecisely stated. Quantitative indicators or standards for measuring performance may not have been established. Data for measuring performance may not be available. When these conditions exist, internal auditors owe it to executive management to seek out the reasons why they exist so that objectives, goals, and standards can be improved. Here are some of the causes of imprecisely stated aims:

Enabling legislation or management policies and procedures did not identify program objectives clearly.

Goals and standards may not have been properly understood by those responsible for meeting them.

Premises, such as sociological, economical, or human factors, were not thoroughly examined in setting goals and standards.

The original objectives and goals may have changed without changing those that had been formally stated.

It must be remembered, however, that internal auditors are staff, not line. They have neither the authority nor the responsibility to set objectives, goals, and standards for operating people. Yet without a clear understanding and agreement on these, an audit might be fruitless. Thus, as stated in *The Standards for the Professional Practice of Internal Auditing*:

280.05 Due professional care includes evaluating established operating standards and determining whether those standards are acceptable and are being met. When such standards are vague, authoritative interpretations should be sought. If internal auditors are required to interpret or select operating standards, they should seek agreement with auditees as to the standards needed to measure operating performance.

This does not mean dictating goals and standards. Rather it means identifying them and gaining their acceptance. Thus, if the auditee agrees to them, they become the goals and the standards of the auditee and not of the auditor.

When goals and standards have not been set and no agreement can be reached on them, that in itself is a deficiency — the absence of goals and standards by which management can be measured or, more important, can measure itself. It is basic to good business practice and to accepted principles of management that managers have a responsibility to set goals and standards for themselves and their people. When this has not been done, the internal auditor can point to a failure to carry out a primary management function.

Thus, throughout their surveys, internal auditors will be sorting out in their minds precisely what objectives, goals, and standards the auditee organization should be or is working toward. Auditors should seek to find out:

Whether formal statements of objectives have been prepared for the auditee organization.

Whether these objectives are in consonance with company directives — the entity's grand design.

Whether those who will be bound by objectives, goals, and standards participated in setting them.

Whether these are known to all who will participate in their achievement.

Whether these realistically consider the activity's available resources.

Whether these may run the activity aground on the shoals of external constraints and controls.

Whether established goals and standards will motivate people to reach beyond what they think is within their grasp.

Whether the goals and standards are measurable.

Whether periodic, formal reports are being prepared to show how well the objectives are being achieved and the goals and standards are being met.

Whether objectives, goals, and standards are periodically reevaluated and redefined.

The controls applicable to a system are directly related to the objectives, goals, and standards of the system. For example, if the primary objective of an activity is to process something promptly, the controls devised should be centered on ensuring timeliness and meeting established schedules. If, on the other hand, the objective of precision and timeliness is secondary, the controls should be concerned with accuracy and adherence to established standards of quality.

Controls Related to Objectives

Once objectives, goals, and standards have been identified and agreed upon during the preliminary survey, the next step is to determine what controls are or should be in effect to see that the desired results will be achieved.

Internal auditors are faced with a host of potential controls when they perform a preliminary survey. These take the form of company or agency policies, procedures, manuals, special instructions, reports, logs, registers, forms, division of duties, approval systems, supervision, and others. To attempt to read and comprehend all of them can stultify the brain and blur the eyes. The effect spent on seeking to absorb the literature on a myriad of controls is often a waste. When read without relevance to a particular problem they appear unconnected to reality.

But when a control is sought out because the internal auditor sees a need for it, then it will appear to have some meaning. So the most productive way of identifying and evaluating controls is to look first for the problem areas and then for the controls that should have identified or prevented those problems, or the controls that should reduce a perceived risk.

One way of identifying problem areas is through conversations with people in the activity being audited or with people in downstream activities who bear the brunt of difficulties flowing from their upstream neighbor. A skimming of production and performance reports also provides indicators of actual or potential problems.

Once these problems have been brought to light, internal auditors can study the procedures or methods in effect and determine why they did not prevent the improper actions. Perhaps people were not following valid procedures or systems. In that case, supervision or training — two significant means of control — were either inadequate or ineffective. Or perhaps the procedures and systems were inadequate for the job. In either event, the defects should be brought to management's attention.

Another way of linking the problem to the control is to make use of what the internal auditors identified at the outset of the survey: the risks. Wherever a risk is known to exist, a control should be in effect to help prevent the adverse effects. Determining the adequacy of the control is a matter of professional competence. Based on experience, training, and sound business judgment, the professional internal auditor should be able to judge whether an existing control is sufficient to diminish or guard against the risk. Determining the actual existence of controls — whether purported controls are actually in effect and are working — is a function of the "walk-through." Determining the effectiveness of the controls — whether they are actually doing the job for which they were designed — is a function of the tests of transactions carried out during the field work.

Exhibit 4-1 illustrates some of the previously designated risks in the purchasing and payroll activities and the controls that can guard against risk:

Exhibit 4-1.   CONTROLS TO REDUCE RISK

Risks	Controls
Purchasing	
Receipt of substandard supplies.	Suppliers' quality control systems are to be reviewed by quality assurance engineers. Inspection of all receipts by receiving inspectors.
Purchases made from suppliers related to buyers or other company people.	An approved-vendor file. Supervisory approval of bidders lists. Conflict of interest program.
Purchases of supplies in violation of import quotas.	Legal approval of foreign purchases. Written procedures and instructions on foreign purchases. Supervisory approval or review of all foreign purchases.
Purchases in excess of need.	Provision that only materials on bills of material will be ordered, and quantities of materials ordered should not result in on-hand inventory exceeding stated levels. Using departments, not buyers, should determine quantities to be ordered except where quantity discounts become a factor.

Continued

Exhibit 4-1. (Cont.)

Risks	Controls
Goods purchased far in advance, straining working capital and warehouse facilities.	Analysis of lead time experienced vs. lead time desired. Requirement for using department to show need dates on requisitions.

Payroll

Risks	Controls
Employees hired for sensitive positions without checking backgrounds.	Statements of criteria for each job and formal job descriptions. Verification of applications for positions by obtaining credit reports, checking references, or contacting former employees.
Nonexistent employees added to payroll.	Payroll additions only by written authorization of employment department. Payroll checks delivered to employees. Periodic floor checks of employees on payroll.
Separated employees still on payroll.	Reconciliation of payroll and timekeeping records. Undelivered checks returned to cashier. Witnessing of check distributions.
Laws and government regulations not followed.	Documented and up-to-date payroll tax tables. Schedules of voluntary deductions supported by signed authorizations. Requirement that legal department inform payroll department of all relevant new or revised laws and regulations.
Payments in amounts not authorized.	Reconciliation of hours between timecards and attendance logs. Reasonableness tests or computerized limit checks for such conditions as excessive hours worked, higher than expected payroll rates, and deductions that exceed gross pay or a given percentage of gross pay.

Risk Assessment

Internal auditors cannot make unreasonable demands for onerous controls which would cost more than the risks to be guarded against. A control costing $100,000 a year should not be recommended to prevent a hazard which could not exceed $10,000 a year. This sounds simple, but comparing potential risks and costs can be perplexing.

One interesting technique, published in IBM's TR-21.700, "Security Risk Assessment in Electronic Data Processing Systems," has been developed by Robert H. Courtney, Jr., of IBM's System Communication Division, Kingston, N.Y. 12401.

The technique involves a computation whereby dollar values are assigned to potential risks, and estimates are made of the frequency with which those risks might breed difficulties. Internal auditors and management should try to reach agreement on the assigned values and estimated frequencies. These may be subjective, but a consensus can produce an acceptable degree of reliability. It is argued that the method is better than no estimates at all.

The potential impact of an event is given a value (v) of from 1 to 7:

	Amount	v
$	10 =	1
	100 =	2
	1,000 =	3
	10,000 =	4
	100,000 =	5
	1,000,000 =	6
	10,000,000 =	7

The estimated frequency of occurrence is given a rating (p) of from 1 to 8:

Frequency		p
Once in 300 years	=	1
Once in 30 years	=	2
Once in 3 years	=	3
Once in 100 days	=	4
Once in 10 days	=	5
One per day	=	6
10 times a day	=	7
100 times a day	=	8

The following formula yields the estimated loss in dollars per year (E) for the assigned value and frequency if an undesirable event occurs:

$$E = \frac{10^{(p + v - 3)}}{3}$$

For example, if it is assumed that some disastrous event could cost a company $1,000,000 and that it might happen once in 30 years, then $v = 6$ and $p = 2$. The solution, therefore, would be as follows:

$$E = \frac{10^{(2 + 6 - 3)}}{3}$$
$$= \frac{10^5}{3}$$
$$= \frac{100,000}{3}$$
$$= \$33,333$$

Thus, the control designed to guard against the risk should cost less than $33,333 a year.

If internal auditors or managers, or both together, can assign values to a potential dollar effect of an unwanted occurrence, and if they can estimate how often that occurrence would reasonably take place, they could arrive at the potential annual cost of the risk. This could then be compared with the cost of a control designed to reduce the risk. The decision to control or not to control, and how much to control, could then be supported mathematically.

The U.S. Foreign Corrupt Practices Act requires applicable organizations to maintain systems of "internal accounting controls sufficient to provide reasonable assurances that . . . ." What is "reasonable" calls for a management decision. But those decisions will have to be documented. Management will have to be able to demonstrate that a neglected control was omitted deliberately for valid reasons. One reason would be that the cost of the control exceeded the cost of the risk, and demonstrating that decision mathematically would be a powerful argument for the soundness of the management decision.

Preparing for the Preliminary Survey

The Mechanics of Planning

Get what's important and get it fast. That is the essence of a good preliminary survey. Focus on the highlights; the detail comes later. To help gather this information, internal auditors use or develop techniques that will get the job moving.

Planning an audit can be either disheartening or productive, depending on how well the internal auditor proceeds through the preliminary phases of the audit project. While each internal audit is likely to be different from the others, there are many initial steps that are common to all. These steps should be set forth in a reminder list that will ease the launching of the job.

The reminder list is in no way designed to inhibit initiative or creativity. It will merely make the planning easier. Without such a list auditors have a tendency to say "Where do I start?" or "What do I do next?" and waste time. With it they can rapidly perform the necessary mechanical chores needed to get the project going in an organized fashion and gradually ease into the preliminary survey with a minimum of false starts. It will help them organize their working papers more methodically and make the subsequent audit steps easier to perform. Exhibit 4-2 is an example of such a reminder list.

Before following the instructions in the list, internal auditors can take an initial step to make tangible inroads into the planning phase of the audit — preparing a table of contents for the first part of their working papers. This will discipline them to provide for certain matters to be covered as the job progresses and to establish working paper references. The table of contents, and the documents and records to which they refer, will be applicable with little variation in most internal audit projects. Here is an example table of contents with explanatory comments in parentheses:

Table of Contents

Subject	Working paper reference

Referenced report draft — A-1
(Copy of the draft from which the final audit report was prepared, with marginal references to the applicable supporting
working papers.)

Report outline — A-2
(The skeletal structure of the proposed report, to be reviewed
by the supervisor before the report is drafted.)

Review notes — A-3
(Notes on reviews of report drafts with the audited management personnel.)

Assignment sheet — A-4
(The formal audit assignment.)

Notes from permanent file — A-5
(Notes inserted in the permanent file, since the last audit, to
indicate areas to be covered, problems encountered, people to
talk to, etc.)

Audit instructions — A-6
(Notes on discussions with the supervisor or audit manager on
the conduct of the audit.)

Prior audit report and replies — A-7
(Removed from the permanent file for ready reference during
the audit examination.)

Time record — A-8
(Record of time budgeted and used.)

Project reminder list — A-9
(List of steps to take in performing the audit project. See Exhibit 4-2.)

Notes on preliminary contacts — A-10
(Record of discussions with or telephone calls to management
personnel telling them of the proposed audit project.)

Organization charts — A-11
(Copies of the major organization charts covering the audit
area.)

Policy statements, directives, procedures — A-12

Table of Contents (Cont.)

Subject	Working paper reference
Tentative audit program (Primarily, a brief record of the intended purpose, scope, and theory of the proposed audit and a preliminary assessment of its thrust and course.)	A-13
Audit program (The formal audit program, prepared after the preliminary survey.)	A-14
Summary of prior audit findings and suggestions (A list of all such matters brought out by the prior audit. The purpose is to determine whether corrective action has been effective or whether deficient conditions have recurred.)	A-15
Glossary of terms and abbreviations (Each activity in a company has its own jargon. The auditors will pick up their terms or abbreviations and sprinkle them throughout their working papers. A glossary is needed for the uninitiated reviewer of the papers.)	A-16
Questionnaires and responses (Formal or informal lists of questions asked of or mailed to the auditees, and the answers.)	B-1
Volume statistics (Data showing the volume of transactions or other values relevant to the audit.)	B-2
Flowcharts (New or updated charts — charts from prior audits can be used, either intact or with some updating.)	B-3
Records of Audit Findings (Reports of each individual deficiency finding and records of corrective action taken.)	B-4
Miscellaneous (Any other information not relevent to individual audit segments or tests.)	B-5

Audit Project Reminder List

Because of the host of matters requiring attention to get many audit projects under way, it is desirable to have them conveniently listed so that they are not overlooked.

The needs of different companies will be satisfied only by lists tailored to their individual activities and methods, and so no general list will be applicable to every company or operating entity. Nevertheless, a guide to the preparation of such a list is set forth as Exhibit 4-2.

The sample list is divided into three parts. The first part covers the planning phase and is relevant to the matters just listed in the pro forma table of contents for working papers. The second part covers certain matters, common to most projects, which would arise during the field work. The third part relates to the preparation of the audit report and the closing of the project (see Chapter 13).

Cost Reductions

There can be little doubt that cost reductions are close and dear to the heart of executive management. If a report of the correction of a serious deficiency ranks in the management mind at seven on a scale of ten, then a solid cost reduction will rank at the very top or mighty close to it.

Some of the auditor's cost reductions will emerge from a combination of an existing condition, good luck, and a sparkle of insight. These events, however, like comets, flash but rarely across the auditor's sky. Yet this does not mean that cost reductions must always await a fortuitous union of occurrences. They can be hunted systematically, if the hunter knows where and how to look.

In many instances, cost reductions come about simply because a methodical auditor looked hard at a piece of equipment, a form, an EDP-prepared report, a manually prepared report, or a register, and then asked:

How can these activities be simplified?

How can this process be improved?

How can this form be combined with another?

How can this flow of work be rerouted?

How can this step be abolished entirely?

How can this amount of copying be done away with?

The results of consistent, organized, methodical attacks on waste and duplication far exceed the rare flashes of genius. Thus, educating the staff to direct its efforts and attention to those records and activities where excessive cost may exist can have long-range benefits — for the company, and for the auditor in the eyes of management.

One such effort is through a cost reduction reminder list to be used in each appropriate audit. An example of such a list is shown as Exhibit 4-3.

Records of Impressions

Still another list is included in the auditor's catalogue of reminders. It helps provide a special service to management because it is information which will not ordinarily appear in the auditor's formal report. It is a record of the auditor's observations and impressions gained during the audit. An example of such a form is shown as Exhibit 4-4.

Exhibit 4-2. AUDIT PROJECT REMINDER LIST

	Completed	
Planning	**(Date)**	**(NA)**

Permanent file reviewed for:

- Audit Analysis sheet (Exhibit 18-3) of prior examination _____
- Prior audit report and related replies _____
- Notes and comments _____

Prepared a summary of the prior deficiencies and suggestions _____

Obtained Project Assignment Order (Exhibit 19-1) _____

Reviewed related reports from other audit organizations within the company _____

Reviewed the *Bibliography of Internal Auditing* for articles or research publications touching on the subject to be reviewed _____

Interviewed manager of organization(s) to be audited _____

Analyzed applicable organization charts, procedural instructions, and directives _____

Conducted preliminary survey _____

Prepared the audit program, making provision, where applicable, for

- Examination of assigned ledger accounts _____
- Review of applicable management reports _____
- Determination whether EDP reports received by the organization are needed _____
- Determination whether input provided to Data Processing by the organization is accurate, authentic, and timely _____
- Consideration of factors affecting income and other taxes _____
- Allocation of project work-days to audit program segments _____
- Use of statistical sampling _____
- Plans for issuance of interim reports _____
- Review of compliance with record retention provisions and security regulations _____
- Use of flowcharts to evaluate control system _____

Reviewed audit program and this check list with the supervisor _____

_____   _____
         Date   Supervisor

Continued

Exhibit 4-2. (Cont.)

	Completed
Field Work	(Date) (NA)

Posted project time record each day and reported time each week to the supervising auditor _____

Forecasted calendar date of field work completion at mid-point of the field work _____

Discussed with client management personnel their availability for review of findings and of draft reports so as to anticipate vacations and other absences _____

Final

Completed record of audit findings and report outline, and reviewed them with the supervising auditor _____

Prepared audit report draft and cross-referenced it to the working papers _____

Transferred appropriate records to the permanent file _____

Prepared Audit Analysis sheet (Exhibit 18-3) _____

Described matters for consideration in other audit projects in writing and placed notes of such matters in the appropriate permanent files _____

Scheduled reviews of the draft report with client personnel _____

Confirmed status of completed and open deficiency findings either by test or by review with client personnel _____

Performed final verification of the draft report, as modified by reviews with client or otherwise, before submitting it for final typing _____

Prepared staff rating forms for assistants and reviewed them with the supervising auditor _____

Examined prior audit working papers and suggested to supervising auditor which should be retained and which destroyed _____

Completed current audit working papers and submitted them to the supervising auditor before filing them _____

Placed record of open findings in a follow-up file so that they would be monitored until considered closed _____

Returned all documents taken from office files to those files _____

_____   _____
Date   Auditor-in-Charge

Exhibit 4-3. REMINDER LIST FOR COST REDUCTION
(Indicate Matters Reviewed)

Records	Eliminate	Combine	Simplify	Improve	Reroute	Elim. Copying	W/P Ref.
Forms							
Tabulated reports							
Manually prepared reports							
Logs and registers							
Equipment usage							

Exhibit 4-4. RECORD OF IMPRESSIONS

_____   _____

Audit Project   Title

_____

Organization Audited

This record will serve to document your impressions of certain aspects of the organization you have reviewed. Complete it after each audit. Use it for each organization substantially involved in a functional review of many organizations. We plan to summarize the data so as to determine whether there are any general trends or problems throughout the company which should be brought to management's attention. Thus, unless there is an impression which directly relates to a specific deficiency finding, do not discuss the record with client personnel. If you feel you do not have sufficient information to answer a question, so state beneath each question.

Yes or No

Employee Morale
Do employees seem to have a good attitude toward their fellow employees, their jobs, their supervisors, and the company?   _____

Do they accept their assignments readily?   _____

Do they appear to support departmental and company goals?   _____

Working Habits
Do people appear to be working at a reasonable tempo?   _____

Do they appear to be conducting an excessive amount of personal business at work?   _____

Are working hours, lunch hours, and coffee breaks observed?   _____

Is supervision sympathetic toward employee complaints? Is supervision willing to take appropriate corrective action?   _____

Does the manager seem to keep the employees informed?   _____

Continued

Exhibit 4-4. (Cont.)

Organization and Staffing
Does the organization seem to be well organized to accomplish objectives? _____

Are tasks segregated properly? _____

Does work appear to flow in an orderly and economical manner? _____

Do employees appear to be working within their job classifications? _____

Do new employees appear to be receiving sufficient orientation and training? _____

Supervision
Do supervisors appear to know their jobs, and do they have the respect of their employees? _____

Do supervisors seem to be exercising control and providing direction to employees? _____

Interface with Other Organizations
Does the organization seem to communicate effectively with interfacing organizations? _____

Are there any obvious conflicts? _____

Does there seem to be evidence of genuine cooperation? _____

Working Areas
Do working areas seem to be properly laid out and maintained? _____

Do location, noise levels, lighting, temperature, and housekeeping seem adequate and lend themselves to an effective operation? _____

Does machinery and equipment seem to be properly maintained? _____

Do employees seem to have adequate equipment? _____

In the following space explain any adverse ratings. If specific deficiency findings appear relevant to any of the adverse ratings, reference them.

_____   _____   _____
Supervisor   Auditor-in-Charge   Date

The information recorded on the form does not constitute the usual, objective compilation of well-documented facts. It is valuable nevertheless because management is not only concerned about the hard facts of the audit, but also about its people. The auditor is in an especially advantageous position to provide such information.

Very often, poor performance cannot be traced solely to inoperative controls or inadequate instructions. It can sometimes be the result of slovenly habits, poor morale, inappropriate organizational structure or work flow, indifferent supervision, clashes with interfacing organizations, badly maintained facilities and equipment, and general environment. Such inadequacies can have a profound effect on production. Where conditions like these exist, the auditor has a duty to bring them to management's attention.

Obviously, this concept involves some delicate and sensitive balances. The impressions should not be recorded lightly. They should be based on more than one fleeting observation. They should not be broadcast to line personnel because the practice could easily evoke the cry of "company spy."

On the other hand, when the defects are the direct cause of reportable deficiencies — and can be readily demonstrated — they should be promptly discussed with line management, along with the objectively established deficiency. In general these reports should not be presented individually to higher management. Rather, they should be summarized periodically to determine whether they represent undesirable trends throughout the organization — symptoms of a general malaise deserving special attention to improve employee relations and working conditions.

These reports should be handled with discretion; but properly used, they can perform a special service to management.

Developing Questionnaires

The internal auditors' review of material in their own offices should provide enough insight about an activity selected for audit to enable them to ask reasonably intelligent questions. Nobody expects internal auditors to be experts in the activity's affairs at the outset; but they are expected to have a general familiarity with where it stands in the company or agency hierarchy and what it is supposed to be doing.

The result of the in-office review will be a list generally developed from the following records: the permanent file (see Chapter 19), the prior audit report, and management's charter for the activity to be reviewed.

From this material auditors can devise questions to suit their audit objectives and to pose to the auditee-manager at their first meeting. But let haste not interfere with the orderly listing of questions; for without a methodical guide the conversation will ramble, the manager's time will be wasted, and the first impression the manager receives will be one of disorganization. A useful form for this purpose — which is, in effect, an agenda for the meeting — is the "split page," with questions on the left-hand side and space for jotted responses on the right. The pages can then be placed in the working papers without recopying them. Some of the questions that can be asked, depending on the audit purpose, are as follows:

How many sections within your activity?

How many people?

What activities do you carry out?

Which activities do you consider the most important? the most trouble-some?

How do you exercise control over your organization?

What control reports do you receive from your own people?

What standards have you set for your people?

How do you train your people?

How do you evaluate their performance?

How do the supervisors help to improve employee performance?

What is the employee turnover rate?

How do you set priorities for your work?

What is the extent and nature of your backlog?

To whom do you report?

What reports do you prepare for your own management? How often?

What organizations do you interface with?

What kind of feedback do you get from them?

What major changes have occurred since the last audit?

What is the status of the deficiency findings last reported?

What areas do you think need the most attention?

This informal questionnaire may be expanded or contracted, according to the circumstances. The nature of the questions will vary, depending on whether the proposed audit is organizational (completely within a single organizational unit) or functional (following a function from beginning to end and crossing organizational lines). In the organizational audit, people-oriented questions will predominate. In the functional audit, the questions will deal more with work flow, interface with other organizations, and feedback.

Formal questionnaires, transmitted in advance of the auditor's arrival, may sometimes be useful. They can provide ample preparation for the auditor's arrival. They can involve the auditee's supervisory personnel in the audit — a sort of collegial approach. They can give management personnel an opportunity to take a good hard look at themselves since, if it is properly prepared, the questionnaire can be a good self-evaluation form. It can provide substantial economies, since the leg work will have been mainly done by those most competent to do it rapidly, and the auditors need but analyze the answers and the supporting data and then ask amplifying questions of the auditee personnel.

Such questionnaires may be sent out under the cover of a memorandum signed by the executive, located at the company headquarters, to whom the off-site manager reports. This will obtain the involvement of executive management and will add a touch of authority to the request. The memorandum should be drafted by the auditor for the signature of the executive. The memorandum will introduce the auditor or audit team, give the time of arrival, ask for cooperation, and let it be known that the questions should not only be answered fully and openly but should be supported by copies of relevant reports and other pertinent documents, to await the arrival of the auditor.

A copy of a sample transmittal memorandum is shown in Exhibit 4-5. A copy of a sample questionnaire for an off-base manufacturing plant — whose accounting records are, in the main, handled by the headquarters office — is shown in Exhibit 4-6.

Exhibit 4-5.

To: Manager, Plant X
From: Vice President, Off-Site Plants
Subject: Audit of Plant X Activities

The Internal Auditing Department is planning to perform its periodic audit of activities at Plant X in the very near future. The audit will be performed by two auditors: John A. Smith is the auditor-in-charge, and William B. Jones will assist him.

The auditors will arrive at Plant X on or about November 9. Mr. Smith will call you a few days before his arrival to tell you the exact date.

To save the time of both the auditors and your staff, they have developed a set of questionnaires which should elicit a good deal of the information they will need. If the answers to the questions could be prepared in advance of their visit, it would simplify the audit and reduce the length of the auditors' stay at Plant X.

The questions are divided into the areas of Administration, Manufacturing Services, Production, and Quality Control — conforming to the Plant X organization — and so can be assigned to several people for response, thereby reducing the burden on any one individual. The auditors have asked that you attach any relevant reports and records to the answered questions to illustrate the documentation being used.

Hold the answered questions pending the auditors' visit. After they have had an opportunity to review the replies and the supporting documentation, please assign someone to provide them with a "walk-through" of the Plant X facility, to answer any further questions they may have, and to assist them through the remainder of their audit.

I shall appreciate your according full cooperation to the auditors and providing them with any assistance they may need.

                                Vice President, Off-Site Plants

cc: J. A. Smith

Exhibit 4-6. CONTROL QUESTIONNAIRE

Administration

What means are used for recording employees' attendance?

What means are used for recording employees' time charges?

What means of monitoring are used to ensure the accuracy of the attendance records and time charges?

How are attendance and labor hours balanced?

What is the basis for redistributing labor charges from pool work orders to ultimate work orders?

What methods are used to control payments to suppliers?

What methods are used to safeguard assets and facilities?

How are the entrance and exit of personnel controlled?

How are the entrance and exit of materials controlled?

How are valuable documents controlled?

How is the need for repetitive reports determined?

How are telephone and telegram expenses controlled?

How are files kept up-to-date?

How are insurable valuables determined?

Production Services

What methods are used to schedule and control the manufacture of assemblies?

How are behind-schedule conditions determined and reported?

What assurance is provided that current, accurate planning documents (shop orders, tool orders, etc.) are used?

What provision is made that the latest blueprints will be used?

What are the methods used to forecast needs for component parts and other materials and supplies?

What provision is made for scheduling and taking cycle inventories?

What methods are used to evaluate employee productivity?

What provisions have been made to procure materials and services at the most favorable prices?

What provisions have been made to account for and safeguard severable fixed assets?

What provisions have been made for issuing, safeguarding, and accounting for standard tools and supplies?

What provisions have been made to identify tools?

How are tools inventoried?

What provision has been made for preventive and corrective maintenance?

Exhibit 4-6. (Cont.)

Production

What means are used to control vehicles and gasoline and to provide for appropriate maintenance?

What provisions have been made for the detection, accumulation, and disposition of scrapped and surplus materials?

What means are used to ensure the prompt shipment of completed assemblies?

What methods are used to expedite the receipt of parts and the reporting of parts shortages?

What means are used to maintain parts and stock bins?

What provision has been made to detect the excess usage of material?

What are the methods employed to control high-value stock levels?

Quality Control

What methods are used in the inspection of assemblies to assure compliance with quality standards and engineering drawings and specifications?

What records of rejection are maintained?

What are the procedures for reviewing and evaluating discrepant parts and materials?

What provision has been made for the inspection of production tooling?

How are production and inspection stamps controlled?

What provision has been made for the certification of gauges and equipment?

Some companies use such questionnaires in advance of undertaking large operational reviews. Although the questionnaires are sometimes considered to constitute an onerous task by the recipient, the auditor's position is that the auditee-manager should have the requested information readily at hand in order to be able to manage effectively. Exhibit 4-7 gives an example of such a questionnaire for a purchasing department and a marketing department.

Each question calls for a narrative response. Yes or no answers are usually of little value because the full burden is then placed on the internal auditors to support and evaluate the propriety of the responses. Narrative statements can be more readily documented and evaluated.

The Preliminary Meeting

Advance Notice

The preliminary meeting should be arranged in advance. Whenever possible, surprise visits should be avoided. On occasion, surprise audits may be necessary — cash audits, security audits, or other matters of extreme sensitivity. In the absence of such circumstances, advance notice is a courtesy which will be appreciated and will do no serious harm.

Exhibit 4-7. QUESTIONNAIRE

Purchasing Operations

What proportion of the company's purchases are "off the shelf" items, and what proportion are made to the company's design?

What procedures have been developed for conducting surveys of supplier operations and claims?

What procedures have been developed to cover negotiations with suppliers?

Which purchase negotiations, if any, have been delegated to other company organizations?

What means are used to follow up on supplier deliveries? What authority does the buyer have to expend additional funds to expedite delayed deliveries?

What kind of regular reports does the Purchasing Department issue on its follow-up activities?

How does the Purchasing Department judge the quality of supplier performance? What standards of performance have been set?

What steps are taken to develop alternatives to sole source suppliers?

What controls have been installed to make sure that the company receives credit for short shipments, rejected parts and materials, etc.?

What procedures have been developed on purchase order documentation?

What approvals are required before a purchase order may be issued?

Are there any reciprocal agreements with certain suppliers? If so, which suppliers, and what are the agreements?

What procedures govern supplier overshipments?

What procedures apply when invoice and purchase order prices differ?

What procedures apply when suppliers ship in advance of requested dates?

How are price and source files kept up to date?

How does the Purchase Department participate in "make or buy" decisions?

What are the procedures for controlling, recording, and recalling company-owned tools supplied to suppliers, or made by suppliers and held at their plants?

What termination procedures have been developed for canceled orders?

What reports are prepared on the amounts of orders issued to various suppliers?

How is the Purchasing Department Manual kept up to date?

What has been the ratio of Purchasing Department employees to total company employees during the past three years?

What has been the volume of purchases per Purchasing Department employee during the past three years?

What Purchasing Department training programs are in effect?

What is the policy towards encouraging purchasing personnel to attend technical seminars and conferences?

Continued

Exhibit 4-7. (Cont.)

To what extent has the Purchasing Department cooperated with suppliers to have them undertake cost reduction and value engineering programs of their own?

What are the three most important problems facing the company — from the Purchasing manager's viewpoint?

What type of assistance is received from corporate headquarters?

What additional type of assistance would the department like to receive?

Marketing Operations

List the major products sold and their approximate share of the market.

Give your ideas about each product's future.

Who are the company's major customers, and what kinds of products are sold to each?

To what extent does the company use dealers, agents, and distributors?

Who are the strongest competitors in the company's major product lines?

What was the sales and profit trend over the past three years, by important territorial, product, and customer groups?

Does marketing management systematically and regularly compare sales forecasts with performance, and does it attempt to determine the reason for the differences?

What kind of regular and current reports are prepared for marketing management which compare actual sales and profits with forecasted sales and profits for each marketed item?

What market analysis functions are now in use?

Which of the company's product lines have required the most intensive marketing effort? Why?

To what extent has intensive marketing effort on weak product lines paid off in improved profitability?

How is your advertising program coordinated with other selling efforts?

On what basis is the overall advertising budget allocated so as to control spending for highest total profitability and allow monthly comparisons between actual expenditures and budgeted expenditures?

How is the company's catalog kept up to date?

What training programs does the Marketing Department have in effect?

How are prices set on company products?

How are prices set on spare parts?

What latitude do salesmen have in setting prices?

How is the performance of salesmen measured?

How frequently are the regular marketing publications issued, and to whom are they distributed?

What analyses are made of sales returns to determine causes?

Continued

Exhibit 4-7. (Cont.)

What is the approximate number and value of items that are shipped but not billed?

What is Marketing's procedure to review sales stock for excess and obsolete parts?

What are the amounts of inventory write-offs for excess and obsolete inventory for the past three years?

Do salesmen set delivery schedules? If so, on what basis?

To whom has the Marketing Manual been distributed?

What procedures are followed to see that the Marketing Manual is kept up to date?

What written procedures have been developed for internal departmental operations?

What approvals are required to initiate changes in sales policies and procedures?

What are the two or three most important problems facing the company — from the Marketing manager's viewpoint?

What types of marketing assistance does the department receive from corporate headquarters?

What additional assistance would it like to have?

The objection is sometimes raised that advance notice will precipitate the correction of defective conditions before the internal auditors arrive on the scene. The rejoinder to that objection is: That's fine. If this is the affect the auditors have, it is a beneficial effect. Both the internal auditors and the operating people are working for the same overall organization. Whatever improves conditions is welcome. The seriously defective transactions probably could not escape a competent substantive test. Correction of inadequate control systems or of minor deviations are desirable no matter when accomplished.

The preliminary meeting will most likely set the tone for the audit. That tone should be one of cooperation. Internal auditors should be open and candid about their audit objectives. They should pose their questions with the tone of a seeker of information, not an inquisitor. No disputes, discords, or challenges should mar this first meeting. By and large, auditee-managers wish only to be treated fairly, viewed objectively, have findings placed in proper perspective, and make sure that all deficiencies encountered will be reviewed with them. Auditors should adopt this as their purpose as well.

Of course, internal auditors should not let themselves be led down the garden path of false assurances. The airy comment from management that "We were fully aware of this condition and are working on it" should be challenged with: "When did that work begin? Can we see evidence of the plans or instructions to correct the difficulty? What is the time frame for correction?"

When the responses to those questions produce valid evidence of corrective action, the internal auditor should give management appropriate credit for the awareness. If it is significant enough, the matter should be included in the internal audit report. Where the assurances are merely attempts to hoodwink the auditor, the matter should be reported as the internal auditor's finding.

Interviewing

Interface with people at all levels is what helps make the job of internal auditing stimulating. Conferences with managers can raise their perception of internal auditors or lower it, depending on the way the auditors conduct their interviews. So the professional internal auditor must be adept at:

Knowing what information to offer or obtain.

Projecting a personality that puts people at ease.

Presenting a professional, assured manner.

Developing a sensitivity to the way people are reacting.

Knowing when the information has been gained or transmitted and not protracting the interview.

In an interesting article on audit interviews, Harmeyer and Wood list some do's and don't's for internal auditors that should be kept in mind if audit interviews are to be successful.[2] Their techniques are summarized as follows:

Do	**Don't**
Preparing	
Homework.	Ever go in "cold."
Write basic questions.	
Organize and consolidate questions.	
Learn something about the people and the activities in advance.	
Scheduling	
Give plenty of lead time.	Get discouraged if there is no immediate contact.
Set a specific time, place, and duration.	Force a meeting on the auditee.
Have a one-to-one meeting if possible.	Schedule the meeting late in the day, just before or after lunch, or just before a weekend or vacation.

<u>Do</u>   <u>Don't</u>

Opening

<u>Do</u>	<u>Don't</u>
Arrive on time.	Fail to apologize for delays.
Put auditee at ease.	Begin too abruptly.
Control small talk.	Waste time on preliminaries when
State purpose clearly.	the ice is broken.
Assure confidentiality.	

Conducting

<u>Do</u>	<u>Don't</u>
Ask to repeat if something is not understood.	Debate.
Ask for concrete examples.	Amplify on the criticism offered.
Allow periods of silence for think-ing.	React negatively to new ideas.
Distinguish between opinions and facts.	Jump to conclusions.
Define what is "important."	Ask loaded questions.
Stimulate interviewee to ask ques-tions.	Ask yes or no questions.
Beware of answers that:	Use sarcasm or subtle humor.
Are too pat.	Contradict in front of others.
Too agreeably fit your ideas.	Waste time in disagreeing on any
Contain unfamiliar or complex terms.	one point no matter how impor-tant.
You don't understand.	
Give the appearance that you're in-terested in what is being said.	

Closing

<u>Do</u>	<u>Don't</u>
Terminate quickly if there is a clash of personalities.	Let the session drag out.
Stick to the schedule.	Discourage the interviewee if he or she wants to extend the inter-view.
Make the last few minutes count.	
Thank interviewee for his or her time.	Close the interview on a negative note.

Recording

Record the information immedi-ately while it is still fresh in your mind.

Obtaining Information

What Information to Obtain

    Preliminary surveys will move along swiftly, smoothly, and systemati-cally if internal auditors have a clear idea of what they want. In management-oriented audits, that information can readily be classified under the basic functions of management: for example, planning, organizing, directing, and controlling.

Planning

Identify the objectives of the activity or organization — long range and short range.

Obtain copies of policies, directives, and procedures.

Obtain copies of budgets.

Determine what special projects or studies are underway.

Determine whether plans for the future have been developed.

Ask if people have advanced any ideas for improvement that remain undeveloped.

Determine how goals are set and who developed or helped develop them.

Organizing

Obtain copies of organization charts.

Obtain copies of position descriptions.

Inquire about the relations with interfacing organizations.

Review the physical layout, the equipment records, and the location of assets.

Determine what organizational changes were made recently or since the last audit.

Obtain information on the authority and responsibility permitted to be exercised.

Obtain information on the location, nature, and size of field offices.

Directing

Obtain copies of operating instructions to employees.

Ask employees if instructions are clear and understandable.

Determine whether the spans of management supervisory control permit adequate direction of the work.

In government agencies, identify important problems which would interest the legislature or the public.

Identify any restrictions on the organization's ability to carry out its assigned duties.

Controlling

Obtain copies of written standards and performance guides.

Review systems and work flow. Be alert to signs of waste and extravagance, backlogs, excess equipment or material, idle personnel, extensive repair and rework, excessive scrap, and poor working conditions (see Flowcharting in this chapter).

Review historical financial data, seeking to identify trends.

Review financial operating reports: one, budgets compared with revenues and expenditures; two, progress in relation to time and cost objectives; three, increasing or decreasing productivity — units produced compared with number of employees; four, comparisons between benefits and costs; and five, volume of receipts and expenditures, indicating trends. (Note: If managers do not have this information, ask what other means they use to control the work in their departments.)

Identify the specific activities or procedures to be illustrated by means of a flowchart: for example, awarding contracts, examining loan applications, approving or disapproving loans, selling assets, entering into leases, advertising, fixing prices, hiring employees, borrowing money, selecting suppliers. These actions or procedures should be representative of the activities under review. Representation is more important than volume.

But merely cataloguing information mechanically is not enough. Experienced internal auditors seek not only to list and array data but also to understand its implications. The one is clerical; the other is professional. So while obtaining information during the preliminary survey, they are alert to obvious and potential difficulties. These will become the focus of the audit program. They are looking for:

Duplication of effort and records.

Unbudgeted purchases.

Not accepting responsibility for duties assigned.

Not receiving authority to do the job.

Not exercising control over activities.

Cumbersome or extravagant organizational patterns.

People without the background, education, or training to do the work.

Ineffective use of people or resources.

Records or reports seldom consulted or serving no useful purpose.

Unnecessary reporting or excessive copies of reports.

Excessive backlogs or no backlogs at all where some would be expected.

The possibility of using data processing instead of manual methods.

Standards, goals, and budgets to work toward.

Unclear instructions.

Customer complaints.

Poor inventory ratios.

Prolonged poor quality from suppliers.

Delays between the time of receipt of unsatisfactory materials and the issuance of debit memos.

Increases in the volume of returns and allowances.

Critical field service reports.

Excessive rework costs.

When a significant number of these items or deficiencies seems to be indicated, they are recorded for inclusion in the audit program and developed during the field work. Seeking to develop them during the survey defeats its purpose and slows it down; but if management appears amenable to suggestions and is willing to take corrective action, there is no point in withholding the information.

Sources of Information

The sources of information to be tapped during the preliminary survey will vary depending on the nature of the information and the forms of organization. Sources for government auditors will differ to some extent from sources for auditors in the private sector. Here are some sources, selected at random:

Discussions with operating supervisors and employees engaged in the activities under review.

Discussions with managers in downstream and upstream organizations.

Legislative histories and hearings of congressional committees.

Reorganization plans.

Correspondence files.

Reports submitted to and by the auditee manager.

Budget data.

Statements of short-range and long-range objectives and reports to show the accomplishment of those objectives.

Policy statements and procedure manuals.

Reports by government control agencies — state and federal.

Records of self-appraisals or reports of audits by other agencies.

People

People are the muscle of every organization. Good controls, in and of themselves, are powerless to see that an activity is successfully carried out if competent people are not there to do the work. Internal auditors seek objectivity in expressing their opinions, but they must consider the people engaged in an activity while surveying the activity itself and determining the extent of their audit.

For this reason, the preliminary survey may include a review of personnel records and practices in appropriate cases. This review may not permit auditors to make definitive determinations, but it may raise danger signals and influence the audit program. Here are some of the things that auditors might try to find out:

Has there been a rapid turnover of personnel?

Is the organization peopled with new and inexperienced people?

Is the educational background appropriate for the kind of work performed?

Is the training program for new employees adequate?

Is there a mix of ages so that some time in the near future the staff will not be decimated by retirements?

Does each key position, including the manager's, have a backup in the event of disability or retirement?

Is there a system of rotation so that a person knows more than one job?

Is there a formal system of in-job training for higher-level positions?

Are people kept informed of what is going on in the company?

Is the requirement to take vacations enforced so that improper practices are not kept hidden?

Is there an unusual level of overtime?

The answers obtained through these questions may have a significant effect on the size of the samples the auditors will examine during the field work. When the answers indicate a satisfactory condition, the auditors may reduce the high levels of sample reliability which they might otherwise demand from test results; in other words, they may be justified in examining smaller samples. Where the survey indicates unsatisfactory personnel practices, auditors may have to make tests more rigorous, expand their samples, and be on the lookout for ineffective, inefficient job performance.

Physical Inspections

Abstractions are difficult to comprehend and impossible to picture. Someone else's descriptions cannot substitute for personal observation. Descriptions have gaps and flaws. They cannot portray everything and, besides, they are second hand. Observations, personal observations, create pictures that are impressed on the mind. So internal auditors have to go out and see for themselves the facilities, the physical layouts, the processes, and the flow of materials and documents.

Personal observation tells what is going on and how it is going on. Also, it proves to internal auditors whether what was purported to exist actually does. Physical observations should be in two phases.

In the first phase, internal auditors should tour facilities to obtain a better understanding of location and layout. This will be a bird's eye view — a frame of reference for policies, procedures, and organization charts. At this point, people will be met, introductions will be made, and questions can be asked. Some of the questions may be:

Is the work coming to you on schedule, and is it of acceptable quality?

Are there any informal reports or records of difficulties with the work received?

What corrective action was taken on problems encountered?

Has the action proved effective? If not, why not?

Are there any safety problems? Have there been any reviews by Occupational Safety and Health Administration inspectors?

Are there any security problems?

Are cabinets containing classified information equipped with a full-length bar and combination lock (if that is the procedure)?

Is the lock kept secured at all times, whether the cabinet is open or closed?

Are "Open" and "Closed" signs properly used to indicate the locked or unlocked condition of the cabinet?

Are people who have access to classified information properly cleared by the security department?

Do people using classified documents guard their contents from people not authorized to see them?

In relatively simple operations, this tour may be enough of an inspection. In complex operations, internal auditors may find it necessary to go on to the next phase.

The second phase may be used in conjunction with preparing flowcharts. This type of inspection is often referred to as a "walk-through." Auditors will review a few representative work activities from beginning to end. By tracing how acts, steps, processes, and work flow through the system, internal auditors can gain practical working information on:

How the program or activity is actually carried out.

The need or usefulness of the various steps of a process.

The results of the work in terms of company or agency objectives, legal requirements, and plain common sense.

The existence or the absence of needed management controls.

A walk-through helps internal auditors determine whether procedures are actually followed, policies and procedures are being applied, and control points are really functioning. It will not tell how well transactions are being processed; that must await the substantive tests. But it is far more effective than a general review of manuals and operating instructions. Besides, it provides a faster and more efficient identification of weaknesses and potential problem areas.

Internal auditors should not walk through every type of document processed by the auditee organization. They should test only those they believe to be significant in terms of the organization's objectives. The results of this walk-through may readily be documented in flowcharts.

Flowcharting

A flowchart is a portrait of a process. Flowcharting is a combination of science and art, but chiefly it is an art. Like most arts, it takes time to develop a facility for it. Some people take to flowcharting readily and do well with it; to others it is a dreary chore. With practice it can become a useful instrument for all auditors. It provides a visual grasp of the system and a means for analyzing complex operations that cannot be achieved by detailed narratives.

Formal flowcharting should be standardized in an auditing department. All the auditors should use the same templates and follow the same basic instructions. It is usually helpful to coordinate flowcharting techniques with the external auditor — the independent accountant — so that each can use the work of the other.

Exhibit 4-8 shows certain standardized flowchart symbols, and a legend describing each. These symbols will be used in this book for formal flowcharts.

Not all flowcharts, however, need be detailed, formal, and extensive. The auditors may find their needs satisfied by a simple layout that will give them an easily read overview of the system. Exhibit 4-9 provides the key steps involved in the process that starts with the procurement and ends with the storage of purchased materials. This may be adequate in some circumstances.

On the other hand, the system under review may be so complex or so fraught with risk that a detailed and formal flowchart is needed to ensure exact knowledge of every step of the way. Exhibit 4-10 depicts a formal flowchart of a direct delivery system. This system is part of the receiving operation, but because materials bypass the normal receiving routines, with their usual safeguards, and are delivered by suppliers directly to the using departments, the system presents certain risks. Therefore, it is beneficial to auditors to know every part of the delivery routine and to identify the control points and the risk areas.

Exhibit 4-8. STANDARD FLOWCHART SYMBOLS

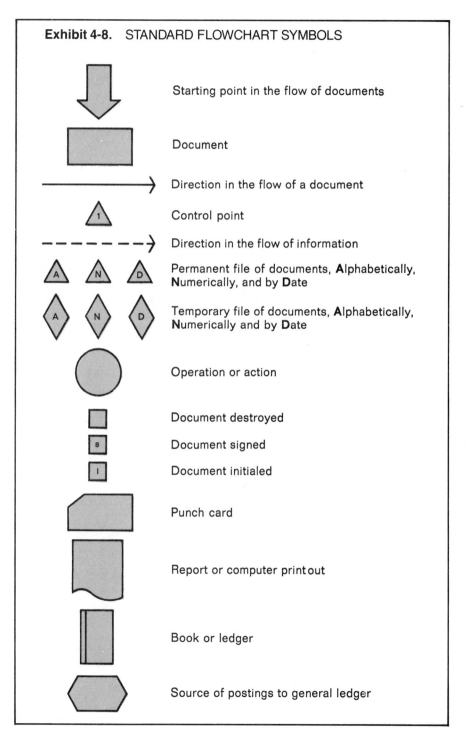

Starting point in the flow of documents

Document

Direction in the flow of a document

Control point

Direction in the flow of information

Permanent file of documents, **A**lphabetically, **N**umerically, and by **D**ate

Temporary file of documents, **A**lphabetically, **N**umerically and by **D**ate

Operation or action

Document destroyed

Document signed

Document initialed

Punch card

Report or computer print out

Book or ledger

Source of postings to general ledger

Exhibit 4-9. INFORMAL FLOWCHART
Procurement of Materials

PURCH. DEPT.	RECEIVING DEPT. OFFICE	RECEIVING DEPT. DOCK	HOLD AREA	A/C PAYABLE	INSPECTION	STORES
Purchase Orders and changes are prepared and sent to: 1. Supplier 2. Accounts Payable 3. Receiving Dep't. 4. Buyer 5. Purchasing Files	The master P.O. is held in temporary files awaiting receipt of materials and shipping notice. Upon receipt of shipping notice, the receiving information is added to the ditto master of the P.O. to create the Receiving Memo.	Materials and shipping notice are received. The shipping notice is sent to Receiving office. The materials are sent to the hold area.	Materials are held until the Receiving Memo is prepared. Thereupon the materials are sent to Inspection.	Evidence of receipt is matched with copy of P.O. No invoice is required. If match is satisfactory, payment to supplier is approved.	Material is inspected. Unsatisfactory material is sent to hold area. Satisfactory material is sent to stores.	Materials are stored awaiting requisitions from using departments.

Besides picturing the processing of documentation, the flowchart brings into sharper focus the key controls on which auditors should concentrate their tests. Based on an analysis of the chart, they can pinpoint the controls. An analysis of Exhibit 4-10 shows them the importance of the following matters:

The control over procurement and direct delivery stamps should be operating and effective. If any individuals in the company could avail themselves of those stamps, they could easily subvert the system to their own use.

The system of checking the approval signatures through review in a control agency will help prevent the unauthorized use of the direct delivery system.

Packing slips signed by the same employee who is authorized to issue or approve requests to purchase defeat the assurances gained by a division of authority.

Payments to suppliers should not be made without evidence of actual receipt. Otherwise, collusion between a supplier and an employee is made easy.

An accurate commitment record is a strong control over the determination of cash needs and the overextending of the capacity of a supplier, as determined by the credit department.

Check signing should be separated from the authority to consummate the commitment for which the check is issued.

Delays in processing documents can have an adverse effect on earned discounts; and the surest way to accelerate the processing flow is to show the managers responsible just how their organizations are preventing prompt payment.

Similarly, reports on violations of rules relating to direct deliveries will have a beneficial effect on compliance.

Some organizations use a combination of narrative and symbols to prepare their flowcharts. The benefits of this method include a written description that parallels the symbols, thereby making the chart more readily understood. The shortcomings include the need for a great many pages to tell the story; hence, a broad picture may not be gained at a glance. A one-page adaptation from such a flowchart is shown in Exhibit 4-11. It depicts part of an ordering and receiving operation.[3]

Summarizing Survey Results

A properly conducted survey usually produces a considerable amount of useful information. It can identify important issues and problem areas and

Exhibit 4-10. FORMAL FLOWCHART

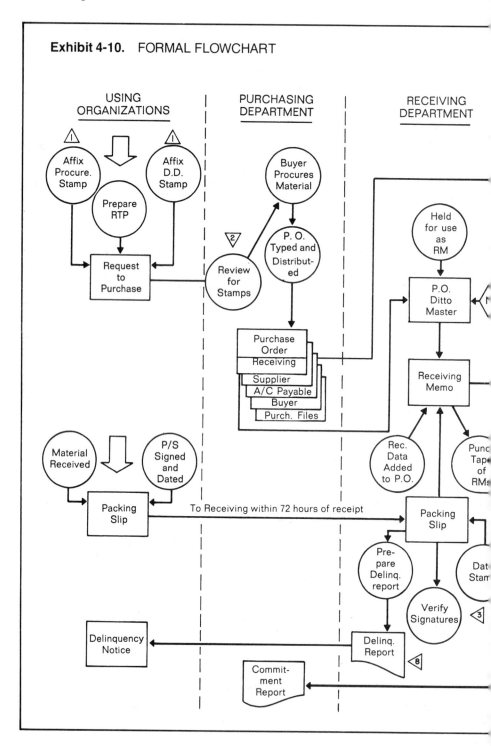

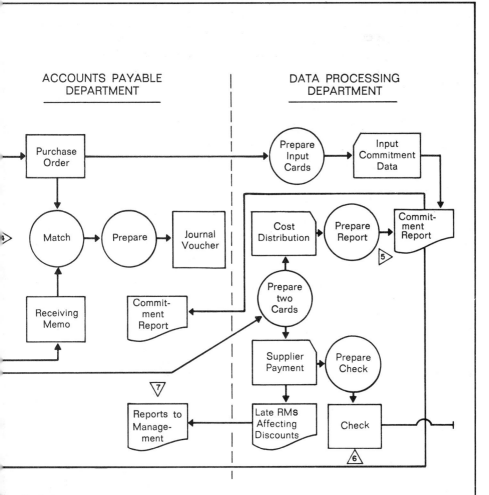

ACCOUNTS PAYABLE
DEPARTMENT

DATA PROCESSING
DEPARTMENT

Key Controls:

△1 Stamps controlled by registers in Purch. Department. Only authorized Departments and personnel may validate RTPs or use D.D. system.

△2 Unvalidated requests are returned to requesters.

△3 Improperly approved P/S's challenged.

△4 Payments not made without proof of receipt. Invoices not required.

△5 Record of commitments helps establish cash needs.

△6 Check signed in Finance Department (not on chart) where it is mailed to supplier.

△7 Reports to cognizant managers on unearned discounts monitors timeliness of processing P.O.'s, P/S's, RMs and payments to suppliers.

△8 Reports warn that D.D. privileges may be withdrawn.

Abbreviations:

D.D — Direct Delivery
P.O. — Purchase Order
P/S — Packing Slip
RM — Receiving Memo
RTP — Request to Purchase

Exhibit 4-11. Narrative	Op. No.	

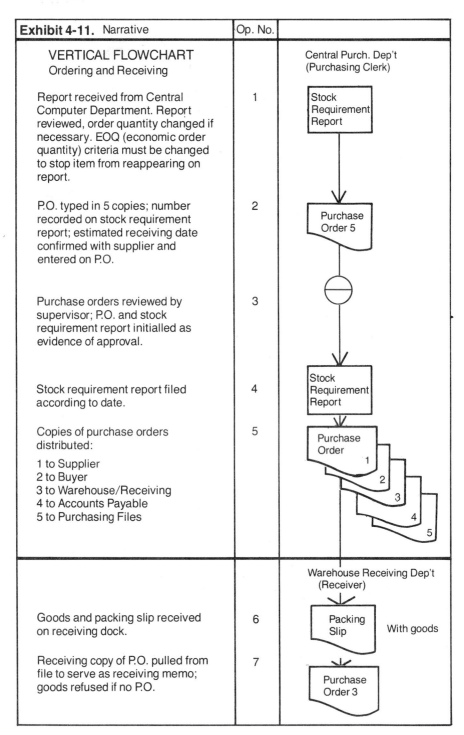

VERTICAL FLOWCHART
Ordering and Receiving

Central Purch. Dep't
(Purchasing Clerk)

Report received from Central Computer Department. Report reviewed, order quantity changed if necessary. EOQ (economic order quantity) criteria must be changed to stop item from reappearing on report. — **1** — Stock Requirement Report

P.O. typed in 5 copies; number recorded on stock requirement report; estimated receiving date confirmed with supplier and entered on P.O. — **2** — Purchase Order 5

Purchase orders reviewed by supervisor; P.O. and stock requirement report initialled as evidence of approval. — **3**

Stock requirement report filed according to date. — **4** — Stock Requirement Report

Copies of purchase orders distributed: — **5** — Purchase Order

1 to Supplier
2 to Buyer
3 to Warehouse/Receiving
4 to Accounts Payable
5 to Purchasing Files

Warehouse Receiving Dep't
(Receiver)

Goods and packing slip received on receiving dock. — **6** — Packing Slip — With goods

Receiving copy of P.O. pulled from file to serve as receiving memo; goods refused if no P.O. — **7** — Purchase Order 3 help decide what further investigation is needed. Indeed, if the survey provides assurances of good systems, good controls, good surveillance, and good management, it may form the basis for a "no audit" decision.

Audit resources are usually scarce. Most internal auditing organizations have more audit projects on tap than they have auditors to carry them out. So why waste precious audit hours on doggedly pursuing the testing of transactions where there is a good likelihood that the control system itself will bring all materially deficient transactions to light?

Most internal auditors consider it advisable to issue an audit report even if they contemplate no audit beyond the survey. With the information gleaned during the survey, a respectable report can most likely be prepared. It would be wise, however, to carefully delineate the scope of the audit, concentrating on the adequacy — not the effectiveness — of the system of controls, and pointing to the basis for the decision to proceed no further with the audit.

Even when an audit program will be prepared and field work will be carried out, it may be useful and helpful to summarize the survey results and report them informally to management. Sometimes enough information will be obtained during a survey to recommend improvements even before substantive tests are made. In such cases, the internal auditor's preliminary observations should be discussed with the auditee-manager before the audit program is prepared. If the manager is satisfied with the auditor's analysis and is willing to take corrective action, those survey results may be considered final, subject to the normal follow-up for any corrective action.

During the review of the results of the survey with management, it is conducive to good auditor-auditee relations to report positive as well as negative findings. This carries forward what all internal auditors seek to convey: a healthy, objective, unbiased, cooperative attitude toward the appraisal of operations.

When survey results dictate further auditing, auditors should include in their summaries: suggested audit steps and the reason for them; activities which the auditor decides not to audit, and the reasons; preliminary estimates of time and resource requirements; and target dates for the field work and reporting phase of the audit.

Conclusion

The preliminary survey offers many benefits. It familiarizes the internal auditor with the entire operation under review. It provides information on the audit tests to be made, the resources to deploy, the extent of the audit examination, and how much or how little to test. In appropriate cases it will buttress a "no audit" decision.

It helps pinpoint the objectives, goals, and standards of the activity being audited, the actual or potential risks to the organization, and the controls needed to diminish or guard against them. It provides insights to management style and the kind of control managers exercise over their organizations. It helps set the tone of the audit and promotes a cooperative attitude on the part of both auditor and auditee. Through flowcharting it provides a graphic layout of the entire operation and any hazards implicit in its systems and processes.

Of equal importance, when carried out properly, it can be the means of displaying the auditor's professionalism at work.

References

1. R. H. Courtney, Jr., *Security Risk Assessment in Electronic Data Processing Systems*, TR 21.700 (Kingston, N.Y.: IBM System.Communications Division, 1978), p. 14.
2. W. J. Harmeyer and R. A. Wood, "Audit Interview Techniques: A Behavioral Approach," *The Internal Auditor*, January/February 1975, pp. 13-22.
3. The Institute of Internal Auditors, Inc., FARE, *Proceedings of the Conferences on the Foreign Corrupt Practices Act of 1977*, pp. 255, 256.

Supplementary Reading

Anderson, R. J. "Analytical Auditing — Does It Work?" *The Internal Auditor*, July/August 1972, pp. 36-54.

Courtney, R. H., Jr. *Security Risk Assessment in Electronic Data Processing Systems*, TR 21.700. Kingston, N.Y.: IBM System Communications Division, 1978.

Crouse, D. W. "Risk Analysis in an EDP Environment." *The Internal Auditor*, December 1979, pp. 69-77.

Finke, D. B. "The Audit Interview: Key to Successful Evaluation." *The Internal Auditor*, July/August 1968, pp. 37-45.

Harmeyer, W. J. and R. A. Wood. "Audit Interview Techniques: A Behavioral Approach. *The Internal Auditor*, January/February 1975, pp. 13-22.

U.S. General Accounting Office. "The Audit Survey." Audit Standards Supplement Number 11.

Weil, J. J. "System Flowcharting Techniques for the Internal Auditor." *The Internal Auditor*, April 1977, pp. 52-58.

For further study

Discussion Problems

1. What are the dangers of making an audit without an adequate preliminary survey?

2. List five questions the preliminary survey can answer for internal auditors.

3. What is the essence of a good preliminary survey?

4. Give three benefits of the split-page questionnaire.

5. What steps could the internal auditor take to save time when assigned to audit an off-site location?

6. Describe a walk-through and point out its benefits.

7. Using Courtney's risk assessment method, estimate the annual cost of risks under the following circumstances:

Amount	Frequency
$ 10,000	Once in 3 years
1,000,000	Once in 30 years

8. What hazards are likely to result from the following violations of good management control?

a. Accounts payable not kept current with changes in purchase order terms.

b. Marketing personnel are authorized to deal directly with suppliers.

c. Quality control department is organizationally responsible to the director of production.

d. Receiving department people are not telling purchasing department people that they are holding goods on the receiving dock pending receipt of copies of purchase orders.

e. Waiting until the end of a long-term project before checking on its status.

9. If a manager is doing an inept job of managing, that matter should be included in the formal audit report. Comment.

10. What are the hazards when accounts payable personnel pay invoices on executive approvals?

Multiple Choice Problems

1. In reviewing flowcharts for a sales-receivable operation, the internal auditor's **primary** concern is to determine whether there is:

a. A continuity of shipping or sales order numbers.

b. An appropriate retention of billing and shipping documents.

c. A system to ensure the invoicing of all goods shipped.

d. An adequate control of access to the shipping area.

e. All of the above.

2. A properly prepared flowchart should:

a. Follow a transaction after it leaves the system.

b. Avoid the interrelationship of sequential functions.

c. Emphasize the individual responsible for the steps in the transactions.

d. Follow a transaction from initiation to disposition.

e. All of the above.

3. Which of the following questions is phrased in a manner most likely to provide useful information?

a. Do you find the computer printouts delivered to you to be meaningful?

b. What use do you make of the computer-generated reports?

c. Have the computer reports been delivered to you on time?

d. Have you found the information provided by the computer to be accurate?

e. Are you satisfied with the format of the computer printouts?

4. A well-conducted preliminary survey tends to produce:

a. An economical audit program.

b. An effective audit report.

c. The effective deployment of audit resources.

d. All of the above.

e. Both a and c above.

5. In carrying out a preliminary survey, an internal auditor should:

a. Test key controls.

b. Become familiar with the areas and activities to be audited.

c. Report on the attainment of goals by the activity.

d. Select a statistical sample of transactions.

e. All of the above.

6. A decision that items produced will not exceed a tolerance of $\pm.0001$ inches relates to:

a. An objective.

b. A goal.

c. A standard.

d. An aim.

e. A hope.

7. Written questionnaires to off-site locations should be transmitted over the signature of an operating manager or executive in authority because:
a. He or she should be aware of what is going on.
b. There is a greater likelihood that the questionnaire will be answered.
c. It simplifies the audit.
d. He or she should approve the questions being asked.
e. All of the above.

8. One of the matters that a review of personnel records in an organizational audit is **not** designed to disclose is whether:
a. There is a rapid turnover in personnel.
b. The educational background is appropriate for the work being performed.
c. There is a system of rotation so that a person knows more than one job.
d. The manager has a better education than his or her subordinates.
e. There is a proper mix of ages.

9. As they review objectives and goals, internal auditors will want to know whether:
a. Objectives realistically consider the activity's available resources.
b. Work is scheduled in a reasonable fashion.
c. A system of feedback has been devised.
d. There is an adequate backup chart in the organization.
e. Personnel have adequate educational backgrounds.

10. Flowcharts are particularly appropriate where:
a. Supervisors in the activity do not want to talk to the auditors.
b. The auditor is equipped with standard flowcharting stencils.
c. The system is complex.

d. The system lends itself to flowcharting.
e. Processes are well documented.

Case Studies
4-1 Shipping

When a shipment is made, the Shipping Department prepares a shipping order form in three copies. The first copy is sent out with the goods to the customer as a packing slip, the second copy is forwarded to the Billing Department, and the third copy is sent to Accounting. The Billing Department, before filing the order, uses the information to prepare a two-part sales invoice. The first copy of the sales invoice is sent to the customer, and the second copy is forwarded to Accounting. Periodically, Accounting matches its copy of the shipping order with its copy of the sales invoice and files them alphabetically by customer name. Before doing so, however, Accounting uses the copy of the sales invoice to post the sales entry in the subsidiary accounts receivable ledger.

Required: (1) For use in appraising internal control, prepare a flowchart covering the flow of documents just described. (2) List those deficiencies and/or omissions revealed by the flowchart which would lead you to question the internal control.

4-2 Registration Procedures

You were recently appointed internal auditor for a private college. Your first assignment is to appraise the adequacy and effectiveness of the student registration procedures. You have completed your preliminary survey. Based on your interviews and walkthrough of the student registration operation, you prepared an informal flowchart.

Required: Examine the following informal flowchart and list **five** internal control weaknesses (such as omissions of certain steps or measures) in the student registration procedures.

INFORMAL FLOWCHART ADMISSION-PROCESSING OF REGISTRATIONS

Mail Room

Opens all mail, prepares remittance advices and remittance listings.

Sends copies of advices and listings to:

a. Cashier (with cash and checks).

b. Accounts receivable clerk.

c. General Accounting.

Destroys other copies of advices and listings.

Registration Clerk

Receives three copies of completed registration forms from students.

Checks for counselor's or similar approval.

Records appropriate fee from official class catalog.

If completed properly, forms are approved and students are sent with registration form to cashier.

If not completed properly, forms are returned to student for follow-up and reapplication.

Cashier

Collects funds or forwards two copies of registration forms to billing clerk.

Records cash receipts in daily receipts record.

Prepares and makes daily deposits.

Forwards duplicate receipted deposit slips and daily receipts records to General Accounting.

Destroys copies of daily receipt records.

Billing Clerk

Receives two copies of registration form, prepares bill, and makes entries in registration (sales) journal.

Forwards copies of billings and registration forms to accounts receivable clerk and forwards copies of bill to General Accounting.

Accounts Receivable Clerk

Posts accounts receivable subsidiary ledger detailed accounts from remittance listings.

Matches billings and registration forms and posts accounts receivable subsidiary ledger detailed accounts.

General Accounting

Journalizes and posts cash receipts and applicable registrations to general ledger.

Enters registration (sales) journal data in general ledger.

4-3 Objectives

In performing the preliminary survey of an activity, the internal auditor should identify the key objectives of that activity. For example, the key objectives of the accounts payable function would be to process for payment what is due, when due, to distribute expenditures to appropriate accounts, and to facilitate the conservation of the organization's funds.

Required: Identify two *key* objectives for each of the following activities:

(1) Purchasing
(2) Petty cash
(3) Production control
(4) Safe deposit services
(5) Quality control
(6) Inventory stores
(7) Approving travel expense vouchers

4-4 Post-Survey Meeting

Before you began your audit of a complex operation, you held a preliminary meeting with the responsible manager (auditee). The purpose was to set a cooperative tone for the audit and pave the way for a productive preliminary survey.

You have now completed the preliminary survey and believe it is appropriate to hold another meeting with the auditee before drafting your audit program and beginning your field work.

Required: (1) State briefly **two** benefits you would expect to derive from holding such a meeting with the auditee. (2) Identify **three** specific subjects which would be useful to discuss at that meeting.

4-5 The Initial Meeting

"Howard," said Bob, his supervisor, "your next job is the audit of the Materials and Processes Department."

"What in the world is that?" asked Howard.

"It's made up of engineers who analyze materials and processes and decide which ones will be used in our company," explained Bob.

"How do they make their analyses?"

"They make them in laboratories, by reading brochures, by studying materials and processes, by talking to suppliers, and by visiting suppliers' plants."

"Do they tell Purchasing what it can or cannot buy?"

"Yes, indeed. They record their findings in a manual which sets forth what types of plastics or alloys or metals or parts will be acceptable for our products. They also list the suppliers capable of supplying them."

"Do some of the suppliers get to be sole sources?"

"Right. In some cases Purchasing is permitted to buy from only one designated supplier."

"Wow! That's a lot of power. What else do they do?"

"They provide services to other engineers or manufacturing people in the company who need answers to technical problems involving materials and processes."

"Anything else?"

"Yes. They prepare technical reports on acceptable materials and processes, including ways in which materials should be tested by receiving inspectors."

"Sounds like a pretty important group of engineers."

"It sure is," agreed Bob. "And they have a lot of clout. It's about time we gave them the benefit of an audit of their operations."

"You mean we've never audited them before?" asked Howard. "There are no prior reports or working papers?"

"That's quite right," said Bob. "You are Mr. Stanley about to meet Dr. Livingstone in darkest engineering. And you're just the guy who can do it. I've set up a meeting for you with Roger Semple, the head of the department. You'll meet next Wednesday at 8:30. That should give you time to prepare for it. I'll be out of town on a vendor audit that seems to be going sour. All you have to do is convince Roger that you are perfectly capable of performing an audit of his operation. By the way, I think I ought to tell you that Roger asked me how a coven of accountants could make an intelligent appraisal of his activities. I told him you'd be able to explain all that."

"Thanks a lot," said Howard. But he immediately started reading up on the Materials and Processes Department and putting together some notes for his meeting with Roger Semple.

Required: Prepare an outline of the presentation Howard will make to Roger: the modern internal auditing approach; concepts of administrative control; the function of the preliminary survey; the responsibilities of the internal auditor; and how the internal auditor perceives the objectives of the Materials and Processes Department.

5

Audit Programs

The road map. The audit program — a guide and a means of self control. The benefits of the well-constructed audit program. When to prepare the program. Field trials of pro forma programs. Programming responsibilities. Audit scope and the objectives of internal control. Contrasting economy, efficiency, and effectiveness. The audit thrust. The different theories of the audit — pedestrian and imaginative. Background information. Combining objectives, risks, and controls. Examples of programs for audits of purchasing, marketing, traffic, and safety deposit boxes. Standards for audit programs. Shunning ambiguities in audit programs. The meaning of terms used in audit programs. Time estimates. Program changes. Audit programs for small audit staffs.

Introduction

The Map

An audit program is like a road map. It shows the route the internal auditor intends to take. Like a good map, it should fit the needs of the traveler. An experienced traveler who has driven the road before needs little more than reminders of the highway routes, junctions, and turning points. An inexperienced traveler who is completely unfamiliar with the territory needs a detailed map which includes street names, alternate routes, and specific instructions.

Internal auditors without audit programs, like travelers without maps, may go in the wrong directions, miss the fastest highways, or get sidetracked on unpaved roads. They may finally reach their destination (most people do) but at excessive cost to themselves and their audit objectives, and nobody else could ever retrace their routes.

A good program is a guide, a lifeline, and a means of self control for internal auditors. Apart from keeping them on track, it will help them stay on budget and on schedule; and it will alert them to the need to evaluate their travel plans when some aspects of the audit may require expansion. They then will have the basis for deciding whether to reduce other aspects to compensate or to request increases in budget and extensions of time.

In audits of operations, which usually vary from time to time or from location to location, the audit program can rarely be of the pro forma type — one that is prepared for general use and is applied without change over and over again. In complex or changing operations, the program must be tailored to the particular circumstances.

On the other hand, some functions continue year after year, in much the same manner. Also, some operations are carried out with much the same objectives and controls in many different locations. In such circumstances the pro forma program — the so-called "canned" program — can save time, assure uniformity, and provide for minimum coverage at each location.

The Benefits

Well-constructed audit programs have much to commend them:

For each phase of the audit work they set forth a systematic plan which can be communicated both to audit supervisors and to audit staff people.

They provide a basis for assigning work to audit assistants.

They permit audit supervisors and managers to compare what was performed with what was planned.

They materially assist in training inexperienced staff members in the work steps of an audit.

They may be used to provide a summary record of work done.

Programs for past audits help familiarize subsequent auditors with the kind of audit work that was carried out.

They benefit supervisors by reducing the amount of direct supervision needed.

They present appraisers of the internal audit function with a starting point from which to evaluate the audit effort.

These potential benefits should not lead internal auditors into a slavish adherence to specific audit steps — a checklist form of audit. Audit programs should never stifle initiative, imagination, and resourcefulness. An ounce of common sense is better than a pound of specific instructions.

When to Prepare the Program

The well-tailored audit program should not be delayed. It should be prepared immediately after the preliminary survey. At that point the audit which is to follow must be structured and given form. It is just as unreasonable to delay preparing the program until later in the audit as it is for a navigator to first look at charts well into the voyage.

Immediately after the survey, when the objectives of the operation are fresh in mind and the prior audit program has been reviewed, the new audit program should be carefully developed. This form of planning requires unhurried thought, for nothing of significance should be omitted. Later, in the often feverish careening through the actual examination, the air of deliberation will have dissipated. Programs prepared later may turn out to be marred by gaps and inadequacies and may fail to give priority to significant subjects.

The pro forma program used on repeated audits of similar operations often evolves over a period of years, gradually accommodating itself to the problems encountered in the field. At other times, the program may be developed in advance to obtain particular information at many localities or to fit new or changed circumstances.

New pro forma programs which are to be followed at many locations should be prepared sufficiently in advance to permit them to be purged of errors, unreasonable demands, and unnecessary steps. What is conceived in the ivory tower often fails in the arena. Consequently, to prevent confusion on many fronts, new pro forma programs should be given field trials or pilot runs. The trials permit defects to surface early and to be corrected before the programs are sent out for actual use.

Audit Responsibilities

The *Standards for the Professional Practice of Internal Auditing,* Section 410, holds internal auditors responsible for planning audit assignments, stating:

.01   Planning should be documented and should include:

    .1   Establishing audit objectives and scope of work.

    .2   Obtaining background information about the activities to be audited.

    .3   Determining the resources necessary to perform the audit.

    .4   Communicating with all who need to know about the audit.

    .5   Performing, as appropriate, an on-site survey to become familiar with the activities and controls to be audited, to identify areas for audit emphasis, and to invite auditee comments and suggestions.

.6   Writing the audit program.

.7   Determining how, when, and to whom audit results will be communicated.

.8   Obtaining approval of the audit work plan.

(Items .2, .4, and .5 are discussed in Chapter 4.)

Audit Scope

The audit program should indicate the scope of the audit work. Professional internal auditors are held responsible by their *Standards* to examine and evaluate the adequacy and effectiveness of an organization's system of internal control and the quality of performance in carrying out assigned responsibilities (see Section 200 of the *Standards*).

The *Standards* recognize that management and the board of directors provide general direction with respect to audit scope (Section 210.01). Some internal auditors are authorized to audit all facets of an organization's activities. Others may be restricted to accounting and financial matters. Between the two poles lie several regions, each a sort of stepping stone from relatively straightforward verifications to a management-oriented assessment of mission accomplishment.

The *Standards* (Section 300.05) refer to these regions as the primary objectives of internal control ensuring:

.1   The reliability and integrity of information.

.2   Compliance with policies, plans, procedures, laws, and regulations.

.3   The safeguarding of assets.

.4   The economical and efficient use of resources.

.5   The accomplishment of established objectives and goals for operations or programs.

A comprehensive, unrestricted internal audit may cover all these objectives. Certainly, internal auditors should prepare their audit programs with these responsibilities in mind; but they must not overlook the audit authority vested in them by their superiors.

In an audit of an expenditure cycle — the business cycle that runs from the ordering to the receipt of and payment for goods and services — all five primary objectives of internal control may be examined. For example:

The distribution to the appropriate accounts of expenditures for goods and services.

The compliance by buyers with rules regarding selection of suppliers and approval of purchases and with relevant government regulations.

The safeguarding of goods on the receiving docks and in warehouses.

The purchase of economical order quantities and the effective operation of a value engineering program.

The assistance in meeting production goals by obtaining goods and services on time, and in meeting financial and warehousing objectives by not bringing goods in too early.

Improved audit ability is needed as internal auditors progress from accounting and compliance audits to the comprehensive audits of the economy, efficiency, and effectiveness of operations.

Defining Economy, Efficiency, and Effectiveness

The terms *economy, efficiency,* and *effectiveness* have become buzz-words — they are not always recognized as discrete terms with separate meanings. Their meanings sometimes overlap; they are all related. Because of their continual use in terms of operations, it would be well to clarify their meanings, and to show their differences and similarities.

Economy is often used interchangeably with *thriftiness*; but it can imply more than *saving*. Its chief implication is "prudent management" or "use to the best advantage without waste" — meanings which also apply to *efficiency*. It is more widely applicable than *thrifty* which refers only to persons or their expenditures. For example, it can be stated that sea power is the most mobile and therefore the most economical form of military force. In that sentence the term *economical* could probably be replaced by *efficient* without doing violence to the intent of the statement. Webster defines *economical* as "the prudent use of things to their best advantage." At the same time, Webster defines an *efficient operation* as "being one which is measured by a comparison of actual results with the energy expended to achieve those results." Not too wide a chasm separates the two terms.

Efficiency implies acting in su(` a manner as to minimize loss or waste of energy in effecting, producing, or functioning. When referring to people, the term *efficient* suggests exercising skill, taking pains, and keeping vigilance and often becomes synonymous with *capable* and *competent*. In some cases the term *efficient* can be applied to a person who is competent and capable of producing desired results.

Effective emphasizes the actual production of an effect or the power to produce a given effect. Something may be effective without being efficient or economical. Yet a program to make a system more efficient or economical may also turn out to be more effective.

The overlap is there, but with careful writing, one may be able to distinguish among the three terms. A system of processing records may be effective in producing accurate and properly approved documents. But the route the records take from desk to desk may be inefficient because it is circuitous and involves unnecessary backtracking. Besides, the operation may be uneconomical if six copies of the documents are produced when only five are needed.

Since audit programs usually address these concepts, internal auditors should keep the definitions in mind as they develop their programs.

The Audit Objective

Deliberation and early program development are needed to evolve what lawyers call "the theory of the case," which is the particular thrust, method, slant, and concept which lawyers will use in trying a law suit. In the same way, internal auditors need to develop the theory, thrust, and major objective of the audit. The theory or major objective is the central theme of the audit — all the audit steps are merely variations.

As an example of the "thrust of the audit," consider two approaches, one pedestrian, another imaginative, to the examination of a payroll. Neither example is exhaustive. They merely provide indications of different audit theories and objectives. The pedestrian theory of the audit includes the following steps:

Review internal checks designed to prevent improper additions of names to the payroll and the prompt deletion of the names of those separated from the rolls; assure the accuracy of the hours worked; control the mechanics of calculating gross and net pay; and protect against the misuse of check stock and signature plates.

Review the legislation concerning various deductions.

Analyze the distribution of labor costs to operating or overhead areas.

Examine wage rates and related matters defined in the union agreements.

In addition to those audit steps necessary to cover certain basic features of the payroll system, an imaginative theory of the audit includes these four steps:

1. An examination of the payroll department's assignment of duties, organization, staffing, and work flow. (Payroll work is subject to peak loads followed by sharp dips in activity. Management tends to staff for the peaks. The valleys will see overstaffing, lowered efficiency, and loss of morale. Lowered efficiency will affect the peaks, calling for still further staffing. The cycle could be vicious. The internal auditor may ask what efforts have been made to smooth the highs and the lows.)

2. An analysis of overtime payments — when and why they occurred. (Why, for example, should an employee work 35 hours in one week and 45 hours in the next? Does this happen often? Does this happen in a number of departments? Which ones? Are there indications of poor planning and workloading?)

3. An evaluation of labor turnover — whether it is high, low, or average for the industry, the region, or the nation. (What reasons are advanced or determined for high turnover?)

4. A check of night premium payments. (Why, for instance, are only 20 percent of the maintenance people on night premium when 70 percent of routine maintenance can be dealt with more effectively after the operating departments are shut down?)

The decision to give serious consideration to the theory of the audit and the key objectives at the outset has a tendency to raise the internal auditor's sights and stimulate him or her to think like a manager.

Preparing the Audit Program

Background Information

The background information gained through the preliminary survey will help dictate the programmed audit coverage. Certainly any broad operation, with its many interrelationships and processes, could keep an audit team occupied for a long time if it decides to examine every activity being carried out. But economical programs focus on what is essential to meet the operation's objectives and not on what is merely interesting.

Identifying Objectives, Risks, and Controls

Internal auditors should prepare audit progams that will focus on what is hazardous to the health of the organization. Not every door need be opened — only those likely to conceal problems and difficulties. The professional internal auditor should be able to identify the objectives of an operation, the risks that lie in the path leading to the objectives, and the key controls in effect, or needed, to help achieve the objectives. At this point it is important that the internal auditor be able to distinguish between audit objectives and the objectives of the operations being audited. The first is what the auditor intends to accomplish. The second is what management expects its people to accomplish, and these vary with each operation and with similar operations in different locations. That is why the tailor-made programs will be more relevant to an operation than some generalized program. The latter does not necessarily take into account the variations resulting from changing circumstances, varied conditions, and different people. But a careful analysis spells out the objectives, identifies the actual or potential risks, and determines the controls appropriate to the circumstances. Such an analysis can produce a thoughtful, relevant, and economical audit program. Such an audit program makes good sense to a company or agency executive, because it is management-oriented and because it deals with the larger issues — those which concern management.

Some examples will explain this approach more clearly than a written description. Let us examine how this analytical approach to the elements of objectives, risks, and controls applies to the functions of purchasing and marketing.

Exhibit 5-1. EXCERPTS FROM AN AUDIT PROGRAM FOR A PURCHASING DEPARTMENT

Audit segment: Costs and goods and services   Objective of operation: To obtain goods and services at the right price.

Audit budget: 5 days

*The letters in parentheses indicate the degree of risk, running from high risk (A) to low risk (G).

Risks	Controls	Tests - (Recommendations)	W/P Ref.	Comments
Make or Buy Committee does not have a written charter or set of procedures. (F)*	Committees should include people from Manufacturing, Quality Control, Engineering, and Procurement. They should meet regularly to arrive at make-or-buy decisions on new products and programs. Decisions should be based on plant capacity, continual cost information, and appropriate trade-offs.	Examine records of Committee to determine whether principal procurements have been considered and adequate support has been provided for the decisions.		
Absence of quantitative and qualitative yardsticks on purchasing activities. No information or standards by which management can judge procurement activity. Uncontrolled buying. Higher prices and possible deterioration of buyer discipline. (E)	Monthly commitment reports by each buyer on such matters as: Total dollars committed. Commitments based on competitive bids. Reasons for no competition. Dollars spent on noncompetitive buys. Savings achieved through competitive bids, negotiation, new supply sources, innovative procedures, and substitute materials.	Determine by sample the volume of non-competitive bids. Ask for reasons. Inquire of buyers the procedures they follow in obtaining reduced prices. (Recommend new system of reporting to provide management with such information.		
Lack of provision for rotation of buyer assignments, permitting buyers to have long-term dealings	Provision for periodic rotation of assignments. Requirement that all buyers take vacations. Formal ro-	Examine rotation and vacation schedules. Investigate any instances where vacations were not		

Exhibit 5-1. (Cont.) EXCERPTS FROM AN AUDIT PROGRAM FOR A PURCHASING DEPARTMENT

Risks	Controls	Tests - (Recommendations)	W/P Ref.	Comments
with particular suppliers and favoring them. (C)	tation and vacation schedules.	taken or assignments were not rotated.		
Purchasing made aware of new equipment requirements on receipt of completed engineering drawings. Thus, Purchasing does not have time to obtain competitive bids on long-lead-time items. (D)	A committee, including Purchasing people, to establish schedules for equipment items to deal with long-lead-time procurements. Purchasing should be party to establishing schedules on such items.	For a sample of long-lead-time items, determine whether schedules were set, were realistic, and provided ample time for soliciting competitive bids.		
Absence of a value analysis program whereby goods are investigated to relate value to function, not cost. (G)	System by which items procured must pass tests as to appropriate form, is cost proportionate to usefulness, is there a need for all the features the item has, availability of standard parts, etc.	Determine who is responsible for value analysis. Review reports on savings. From sample determine whether items were subjected to value analysis.		
Excessive number of confirming orders, meaning that using departments instead of Purchasing are selecting suppliers and ordering goods, thereby evading procurement controls and leading to favoritism and higher prices. (A)	Provision for reports on such orders, determining reasons, and taking appropriate disciplinary action. Management directive giving Purchasing sole authority to commit company funds for services and supplies obtained from suppliers.	Determine ratio of confirming orders to total orders. Determine what is done to reduce their number. From a sample, inquire of buyers and using departments the reasons for the confirming orders.		
No provision for records showing prior purchases for same products, thereby witholding valuable information from buyers in assessing bids and quotations. (B)	System for recording on cards or on electronic equipment the procurement activity on each individual item on which there are repeated purchases.	For purchase orders sampled, trace prior purchases for same items. Investigate significant variances. (Recommend maintenance of price history records.)		

Purchasing

The generally accepted management objectives of a purchasing operation are to obtain the right goods or services at the right price, at the right time, in the right quantity, at the right quality, in the right place.

These objectives can form the framework of the audit program. Each can head a separate segment of the program. For example, obtaining goods and services at the right price can represent a separate part of the audit program and the audit work. Then the auditor can list any actual risks disclosed during the preliminary survey and the potential risks inherent in any purchasing operation relating to establishing the right prices for goods and services.

Exhibit 5-1 shows part of an audit devoted to prices. It does not list every conceivable risk and control; such a comprehensive audit program could be unnecessarily expensive. Instead it spells out those risks which are applicable to a particular purchasing organization at the time of audit as determined by the preliminary survey. For example, assume that the preliminary survey showed and documented close adherence to excellent bidding procedures. Accordingly, to expend an inordinate amount of audit effort on bidding practices would be wasteful. Instead, the program identifies existing and potential problems and concentrates on them.

In any audit of operations, internal auditors must go beyond the five kinds of operating objectives we enumerated for the purchasing function. Another significant objective exists in any activity or department: that it be well managed. Accordingly, one segment of a program for procurement would be related to the administration of the activity. The administrative risks revealed during the preliminary survey might be as follows:

Organization charts for Purchasing have not been prepared. (May result in confusion as to which buyer is responsible for purchasing particular products or services.)

Lack of a directive on Purchasing's authority and responsibility. (Other organizations may assume the authority to deal directly with suppliers.)

Lack of a Purchasing manual. (Buyers may perform in accordance with their personal desires rather than in a consistent, approved fashion.)

Absence of a procedure by which people are authorized to sign requisitions for supplies and services. (Orders may be issued by people for their own use or for the wrong materials or quantities.)

Risks vary in degrees of intensity and in different contexts. Obviously, auditors should be sure to review risks offering the greatest dangers before they deal with those which are less hazardous. Internal auditors may find it burdensome to prepare a program which lists risks in the order of decreasing intensity. But once the risks, controls, and program steps have been put into the program, auditors should be able to review what they listed and indicate the severity of the risk.

Accordingly, they may rate the intensity by placing some form of indicator after the listed risk. For example, A might indicate the greatest risk, B the next, and so forth. In that way auditors will be alerted to review major risks before they work on minor ones. Thus, they would not put themselves in the unfortunate position of having failed to examine a serious risk before their audit budget was exhausted.

Marketing

Some of the more important objectives of a marketing organization might be these: determining the market potential for the company's products and services (market research); imparting information, developing consumer attitudes, and inducing action beneficial to the company (advertising); and inducing distributors to give extra attention to the sales of company products and persuading customers to buy those products (sales promotion).

Thus market research, advertising, and sales promotion might each be a separate segment of the audit of a marketing function. Some of the risks, related controls, and suggested tests associated with an advertising activity will be found in Exhibit 5-2.

Both programs illustrated provide a column for reference to the working papers ("W/P Ref."), which are the records of tests and reviews. This reference is extremely important for ready access to the evidence of work done. Audit supervisors, external auditors, and other reviewers will generally use the audit program as a starting point for appraising the adequacy of the audit work accomplished.

The program also provides a column for the auditors' comments. These can be brief statements indicating the results of the audit work, and can be very useful in providing an overview of audit results. The comments should be brief, such as, "Controls adequate," "No exceptions," "Excellent system," "Substantially correct"; or they should make reference to a record of an audit finding such as "RAF-7" (see Chapter 7).

Comprehensive Audits

Under some circumstances internal auditors may wish to make comprehensive audits of an operation. Perhaps the first audit of an operation may warrant an audit of all activities whether or not they present serious risks or hazards. Or the auditors may wish to document an entire system to determine whether it conforms to the internal accounting control requirements of the U.S. Foreign Corrupt Practices Act of 1977.

The tailor-made program may still be the best course, but in such cases, since the risks are not the primary basis for the extent and approach of the audit, the focus will be on controls. The audit will be directed toward determining the controls that exist or should exist to see that the operation's

Exhibit 5-2. EXCERPTS FROM AN AUDIT PROGRAM FOR A MARKETING DEPARTMENT

Audit Segment: Advertising
Objective of operation: To impart information; develop consumer attitudes, and induce action beneficial to the company.
Audit budget: 10 days
*The letters in parentheses indicate the degree of risk, running from high risk (A) to low risk (G).

Risks	Controls	Tests - (Recommendations)	W/P Ref.	Comments
Company is advertising in various media but has a single expense account. Hence budgets become useless as a control device. (F)*	Establish separate budgets and accounts for such matters as magazine and newspaper space, television and radio, television talent and production, with written descriptions on what should be charged to each account.	Compare budgets and costs. Investigate significant differences. Determine that overruns have been properly approved. (Recommend separate accounts.)		
Complete comparisons between budgets and actual advertising costs are made at the end of a fiscal year. Thus, advertising trends are not identified in time to take corrective action. (G)	Prompt recording of both commitments and expenditures; monthly reports comparing budgets and actuals.	Review reports for accuracy, timeliness and meaningfulness. Determine what action was taken on adverse trends. (Recommend monthly comparisons.)		
Absence of written agreement with advertising agency. Leads to uncertainty and disputes. No right to review agency records. (A)	Written agreement containing provisions as to charges and expenses billable, records to be maintained, and right of audit of systems and records.	Review agency charges for reasonableness and applicability to advertising work. (Recommend written agreement.)		

Exhibit 5-2. (Cont.) EXCERPTS FROM AN AUDIT PROGRAM FOR A MARKETING DEPARTMENT

Risks	Controls	Tests - (Recommendations)	W/P Ref.	Comments
Absence of a detailed estimate of charges for each advertising project. Hence, agency may make expenditures exceeding budget. Lack of information on adverse cost trends. (D)	Provision for costs of individual jobs or projects to be itemized on the estimates and subjected to frequent comparisons with actual costs incurred.	Without estimates, tests may be meaningless. Examine whatever means management uses to determine propriety of charges. (Recommend provision for written estimates and comparison of charges with the estimates.)		
The same agency employee is responsible for placing advertising orders and also verifying related charges. Hence, excessive authority given to one individual; potential for manipulation. (E)	Separation of duties. It is as important in an advertising agency as it is in the auditor's company.	Review system. See what supervision the employee receives. Test transactions from ordering to receipt. (Recommend separation of duties.)		
Artwork and company property left with agency for photographic sets. Hence, possible loss of valuable materials. (C)	Provision for inventory records of all property with sufficient value to warrant control. Insurance coverage for valuable property.	Test system of control exercised by the Advertising group. Trace records of items shipped to agency. Compare records and physical items. Question retention by agency of property for unreasonable lengths of time.		
For nonmedia purchases, the Advertising group deals directly with suppliers and contracts with them for supplies. (B)	Purchasing Department must have the responsibility and the authority to make all commitments for supplies. For repetitive purchases of items needed expeditiously, the Purchasing Department should negotiate blanket orders for the Advertising Group.	Examine a sample of transactions. Determine whether appropriate bidding, ordering, and receiving practices were used. (Recommend that Advertising deal with Purchasing for all supplies.)		

Exhibit 5-3. EXCERPTS FROM AN AUDIT PROGRAM FOR A TRAFFIC DEPARTMENT

Audit Segment: Routine Inbound and Outbound Shipments

Objective of operation: To select carriers and routes which will provide the most economical and timely shipments of supplies and finished goods.

Audit Budget: 8 days

Optimum Means of Control	Risks	Audit Tests	W/P Ref.	Comments
Inbound Shipments		Select at random documents covering a representative number of routings and determine whether:		
Provision for close coordination with the Purchasing Department and for review by Traffic personnel of requests to purchase.	Inefficient and uneconomical routings.	Routing was approved by traffic.		
Requirement for special approvals for premium transportation.	Excessive use of more costly transportation.	Premium traffic was properly authorized.		
Provision to consolidate shipments to obtain carload rates.	Unnecessarily expensive shipments.	Items received in large quantities, and subject to carload rates, were received in carload lots and not LCL (less than carload).		
Standard time spans for the ordering of goods to allow adequate time for nonpremium routings.	Excessive premium routings to meet production schedules.	Sufficient time was allowed by ordering and purchasing departments between shipping and required dates.		
Preparation by Traffic for Purchasing of information on routings and rates for major suppliers.	Purchase orders providing uneconomical routing instructions.	Suppliers made allowances for transportation costs when purchase orders provided for carload shipments and part of shipment was LCL.		

Exhibit 5-3. (Cont.) EXCERPTS FROM AN AUDIT PROGRAM FOR A TRAFFIC DEPARTMENT

Optimum Means of Control	Risks	Audit Tests	W/P Ref.	Comments
Outbound Shipments		Determine whether:		
Provision for Traffic to specify means of shipment.	Best means of shipment might not be used.	Routing was specified by Traffic.		
Maintenance of current routing and rate guides.	Errors in routing.	Routing and rate guides were up to date.		
Provision to charge customer for more expensive routing when such routing is requested.	Customer may not be billed for requested routing.	Customer was billed for more expensive routing requested.		
Provision for adequate support for premium shipments.	Unauthorized premium shipments.	Premium rates were supported by ■ Reason for routing ■ Authorization for premium shipment ■ Appropriate accounting distribution.		
Provision to review and report on the use of premium shipments.	Failure to detect any unfavorable trends. Excessive premium shipments.	Results anticipated by premium transportation were actually gained.		

objectives will be met. Exhibit 5-3 provides an excerpt from one of the segments of such a program for a traffic department.

Pro Forma Programs

Pro forma programs are useful, even essential, when audits will be carried out by inexperienced auditors whose work must be closely monitored. They are also useful if the same kind of audit will be performed at a number of different locations, when comparable information is needed for each location, and where similar reports or consolidated reports will be issued.

An example of such a program, for the audit of safety deposit boxes in a bank, is shown as Exhibit 5-4. The program focuses on detailed verifications, and also provides the auditors with background information, indicating the objectives of the operation and the prescribed system of control. It is a useful audit program, helpful to the auditors and capable of producing all the information needed for a comprehensive evaluation of the activity under review.

Criteria for Audit Programs

Audit programs should conform to certain criteria if they are to meet the objectives of the internal audit department. The following standards are illustrative:[1]

The objectives of the operation under review should be carefully stated and agreed to by the auditee.

Programs should be tailor-made to the audit assignment unless compelling reasons dictate otherwise.

Each programmed work step should show the reason behind it; i.e., the objective of the operation and the controls to be tested.

Work steps should include positive instructions. They should not be stated in the form of questions. (General questions, particularly those calling for yes or no answers, do not lead to effective auditing. They usually result in superficial answers rather than in-depth analyses and evaluations. Moreover, the way that the questions are framed may call for answers with an undesirable slant or bias. This rule does not reject the use of yes or no questions as mind-joggers for the auditor to be certain that significant audit objectives are not overlooked. As a practical matter, experienced auditors will jot down such questions to make sure they remember to look at all important aspects of an operation. But the work steps leading to an objective, unbiased audit opinion, should be positive.)

Whenever practicable, the audit program should indicate the relative priority of the work steps. Thus, the more important parts of the program will be completed within the allotted time or other restrictions.

Audit programs should be flexible and permit the use of initiative and sound

Exhibit 5-4. EXCERPTS FROM AUDIT PROGRAM FOR
SAFE DEPOSIT DEPARTMENT

General Information

Boxes are rented to customers for the safekeeping of personal property. Each safe deposit box has two separate locks. The box can be opened only when the key to each of these locks is used at the same time. When a box is rented, two keys to one of these locks are given to the customer. There are no duplicates available. The keys to the other lock, which are called "Guard Keys," are kept by the bank. No customer can gain admittance to a box without proper identification.

Purpose of Audit

To determine whether all boxes that are supposed to be rented are actually rented and that proper rental fees are being received.

To determine whether there is strict adherence to operating procedures.

To determine whether rental collections are credited to the proper income account.

Lease Agreements

Review exceptions noted in the last audit.

Prepare a list of all safe numbers in the vault. If a prepared list is included with the working papers, make a visual check to verify the numbers.

Review lease agreements for rented boxes. Place audit mark opposite the number on the list for each agreement held.

If the agreement is new since the previous audit, check for proper completion and correctness of form used. Initial and yeardate on the agreement to the left of the safe number. (An alteration of safe number on the rental agreement should be initialed by the renter.)

Check all court orders of guardianship and trusteeship covering new lease agreements.

If a box is subject to restricted access because of a deceased depositor, two or more should be present or, if there is an attachment, list the number on a work sheet.

- Check to see that the agreement card is jacketed.
- Check to see that there is a plug in the lock of the customer's box.
- Test-check access slips, for boxes requiring two or more to be present, by comparing signatures with the agreement card.

Review customer access procedure with the safe deposit attendant.

- Ask attendant to outline procedure followed in admitting customer to box.
- Review current access slips for proper processing and filing.

At offices where a separate audit is made of the safe deposit department, indicate on the office rating sheet the number of boxes available and number of boxes rented. For example: "Of the 5,268 total number of boxes, 4,183 were rented on the date of our audit."

Additional segments of audit program include:
Keys ▪ Annual Rental Cards ▪ Contents of Drilled Boxes ▪ Storage ▪ Night Depository ▪ Articles Found on Bank Premises ▪ Vacant Boxes.

judgment in deviating from prescribed procedures or extending the work done, but audit supervisors should be informed promptly of major deviations.

Programs should not be cluttered with material from sources readily available to the staff. Incorporate by reference if feasible.

Unnecessary information should be avoided. Include only what is needed to perform the audit work. Excessive detail wastes the time of those who prepare the programs and those who read them.

Audit programs should bear evidence of supervisory approval before they are carried out. Significant changes should also be approved in advance.

Ambiguities

Precise instructions are most likely to produce precise audit information. Words like *adequate, sufficient,* and *thorough* mean different things to different people. To tell an auditor to "determine whether adequate competition was obtained" is to say nothing and to invite different responses from different auditors.

For example, assume that an audit program is to be carried out by audit teams in different locations. Assume further that their audit programs tell them to "determine whether the installation has an adequate payroll system."

Some staffs might appraise every single part of the system. They may be doing more work than intended. Other staffs might decide that the program wants them to determine only that employees were properly paid — no more. Still other staffs, in their tests of payments to employees, may see errors in vacations paid or travel expenses reimbursed. They might decide to concentrate on these known hazards and do very little auditing of the payroll system. Besides, staff people might be confused and spend unnecessary time discussing the ambiguous program steps when they could be devoting their time to productive audits.

Instead of the broad ambiguous instructions about "an adequate payroll system," the program could call for these specific steps:

Determine whether payments to employees are in accordance with approved time cards.

Determine whether employees are paid the correct amounts due.

Determine whether total salaries and wages paid are in agreement with the direct and indirect labor charged to appropriate contracts and accounts.

Most auditors would be likely to get answers to such program steps without further instructions, and they still would have plenty of latitude to decide how they would meet these program objectives.[2]

Ambiguities are reduced if internal auditing departments adopt uniform meanings for the various terms used in audit programs. Here are some definitions which can help eliminate confusion and build a sound bridge between the programmer and the staff auditor.[3]

Analyze. To break into significant component parts to determine the nature of something.

Check. To compare or recalculate, as necessary, to establish accuracy or reasonableness.

Confirm. To prove to be true or accurate, usually by written inquiry or by inspection.

Evaluate. To reach a conclusion as to worth, effectiveness, or usefulness.

Examine. To look at or into closely and carefully for the purpose of arriving at accurate, proper, and appropriate opinions.

Inspect. To examine physically.

Investigate. To ascertain facts about suspected or alleged conditions.

Review. To study critically.

Scan. To look over rapidly for the purpose of testing general conformity to pattern, noting apparent irregularities, unusual items, or other circumstances appearing to require further study.

Substantiate. To prove conclusively.

Test. To examine representative items or samples for the purpose of arriving at a conclusion regarding the group from which the sample is selected.

Verify. To establish accuracy.

The term *audit* is too general to use in referring to a work step.

Relation to the Final Audit Report

Audit steps which produce information that will not be reported are usually wasteful. The audit program stage is not too soon to think about the final audit report. Some organizations even develop a standard report outline — a sort of digest — to indicate the subjects to be covered in the final report. This provides a useful discipline and sense of direction while carrying out the review and eliminates unnecessary audit work. Even if no such digest is prepared, auditors should keep in mind the general structure of the report and the programmed scope of audit. Economy and efficiency are qualities desirable in internal auditing also.

Some internal auditors find it efficient and helpful to write segments of their audit reports as the audit progresses. In large audit projects, progress reports provide early information to auditees and make the final audit report easier to write. And if the audit report is kept in mind as the program is written, the format of the program itself will make the outline of the formal report easier to prepare.

Program Mechanics

The audit program should include estimates of the time required to carry out each of the segments of the audit. These are preliminary estimates, of course, but they help the auditor in charge and the audit supervisor to control and review the progress of the work. The estimates also help determine how many staff people should be assigned to the audit in order to complete the work in a reasonable time.

Adjustments to the estimates may have to be made as the audit progresses if circumstances encountered differ markedly from circumstances anticipated.

Audit supervisors or managers should approve all audit programs. They should also approve all significant changes. Audit programs tend to be evolutionary. It is rare indeed for the programmer to be able to anticipate every circumstance or condition that will be encountered in the audit. A small rock seen in the preliminary survey may turn out to be but the tip of a huge boulder when the auditors start digging.

In actual practice, the audit evolves from the initial programmed step. So audit programs should be updated periodically as the work progresses. If actual conditions are not those that were foreseen, it may be necessary to revise plans or even to discontinue the audit. Any significant changes should be reduced to writing, the reasons should be shown, and the changes should be approved at the same level of authority which approved the original program. Experience has shown that important information is overlooked when changes in audit scope or direction are not recorded.

The audit program should document the progress of the audit work. A simple method is to make reference in the audit program to the working papers where tests are carried out — each programmed audit step should bear a working paper reference. This will show what work was done and what still remains to be done. Also, it helps the auditor make sure no steps were omitted inadvertently. If a step is deliberately omitted, the reason is shown.

Small Audit Staffs

Audit staffs composed of one or two auditors may object to the time required to prepare audit programs. These objections have no merit.

An audit report is usually written by one person. The good report writer will prepare a careful outline before writing the report. The outline is the program for the written report. Similarly, even a one-person audit department should prepare audit programs for the audit projects. It is just as easy for that individual to forget or omit significant audit steps as it is for junior members in large audit departments.

Besides, even small companies will want the external auditors to make use of the work of their internal auditors so as to reduce external audit costs. But external auditors will have little respect for internal auditors whose audit work is not programmed and whose audit scope and objectives are not defined (see Chapter 24).

Obviously, an audit program prepared by the internal auditor who will carry it out in its entirety need not be as detailed as one written for a junior auditor; but it should set forth the objectives of the operation being audited and it should show the audit steps to be taken. These can be listed in the form of audit objectives. ("Determine the adequacy and effectiveness of the controls designed to see that the names of people leaving the company are promptly removed from the payroll.") But however the auditor decides to show the work steps, they should be listed and they should be carried out.

Guidelines for Preparing Audit Programs

The task of preparing audit programs has its own methodology. When properly followed, it should result in an acceptable, usable audit program. Each professional, experienced internal auditor will have his or her programming methods. For the new internal auditor, here are some guidelines:

1. Review audit program for prior audit, if any, to determine what was covered, how it was covered, in what depth, and with what results. Also, determine what was eliminated from the scope of the prior audit.

2. Carry forward any routine checklists and questionnaires.

3. Perform a preliminary survey to determine objectives of the operation, existing systems of control, and apparent risks.

4. Review internal audit literature which touches on the operation to be reviewed and which may provide programming ideas:
   - Research Studies of The Institute of Internal Auditors, Inc.
   - Bibliography of *The Internal Auditor* for articles on the operation being audited.
   - *Modern Internal Auditing — An Operational Approach,* by Brink, Cashin, and Witt, for suggested audit steps.

5. Obtain agreement with the auditee on the objectives of the various segments of the proposed audit.

6. For each segment of the audit, prepare a program worksheet showing, as needed, title of the audit project; title of the audit segment; objective of the operation; and audit budget based on prior audit, an educated guess, or the available time allotted for the entire audit.

7. List the risks that must be covered using symbols that will identify the seriousness of each risk, such as letter A to indicate the greatest risk, etc.

8. For each risk to be examined, show the controls already in force **or that are needed** to meet the operation's objectives and protect against the indicated risk.

9. For each of the listed controls, show the work steps required to test the effectiveness of those in existence, or indicate the recommendations that will have to be made to install needed controls now missing.

10. Provide columns for working paper references and comments on the audit findings.

Conclusion

An audit program is as useful to an auditor as an outline is to a report writer. It provides the structure and the approach to the audit. Its benefits extend beyond the auditor to the people who will have occasion to review the results of the audit. With the growing interdependence of external and internal auditors, the audit program is an important step toward reliance on the work of the internal auditor.

Audit programs should take into account the requirements of the U.S. Foreign Corrupt Practices Act: They can identify existing risks and the controls in effect or needed to guard against the risks; and the resulting working papers can be useful documentation either to show compliance with the Act or to highlight control weaknesses needing correction.

In most audits of operations, an economical and effective audit program focuses on the risks that can be harmful and avoids a complete analysis of an operation which contains activities not potentially hazardous to the health of the organization. The useful audit program combines the concepts of objectives, risks, and controls. The management-oriented audit program should begin with an identification of the operation's objectives. The audit objectives will then list the steps needed to determine whether the organization's objectives are being met.

All auditors should prepare audit programs, even those in one-person audit departments. These need not be as formal as those prepared in large internal audit organizations, but they still are needed as an audit guide and as a form of self control.

References

1. United States General Accounting Office, "Comprehensive Audit Manual," July 1976, pp. 18-8, 9.
2. D. L. Scantlebury and R. B. Raaum, *Operational Auditing* (Arlington, Va: The Association of Government Accountants, 1978), p. 45.
3. GAO, p. 8-11.

Supplementary Reading

Cadmus, Bradford. *Operational Auditing Handbook.* New York: The Institute of Internal Auditors, Inc., 1964.

Brink, V. Z., J. A. Cashin, and Herbert Witt. *Modern Internal Auditing.* New York: The Ronald Press Company, 1973.

Glenn, E. S. "Toward Better Internal Auditing." *The Internal Auditor*, April 1977, pp. 16-26.

Holstrum, G. L., and W. A. Collins. "Operational Audits of Production Control" Research Report 20. Altamonte Springs, Fla.: The Institute of Internal Auditors, Inc., 1978.

Scantlebury, D. L., and R. B. Raaum. *Operational Auditing.* Arlington, Va: The Association of Government Accountants, 1978, pp. 37-45.

U.S. General Accounting Office. *Comprehensive Audit Manual.* July 1976.

Warfield, J. S. "Audit Program for Organizational Control and Effectiveness." *The Internal Auditor*, October 1979, pp. 42-48.

For further study

Discussion Problems

1. What characterizes an audit at the managerial level and one at the compliance level?

2. Why is it necessary to identify the key objectives in developing the audit program?

3. What should the internal auditor include in an individual, tailor-made program?

4. When should an audit program be prepared? Why?

5. What would you consider to be the chief objectives of the following activities?
   a. Production
   b. Accounts Receivable
   c. Payroll
   d. Receiving
   e. Scrap
   f. Pricing
   g. Insurance
   h. Customer Service

6. What types of activities are good candidates for a pro forma program?

7. Some of the objectives of the accounts payable function may be regarded as making sure that (a) goods and services to be paid for have been received, (b) amounts billed are contractually authorized, (c) amounts due are mathematically correct, and (d) amounts approved for payment are distributed to the appropriate accounts. For each of these four objectives, list two key steps you would include in your audit program to determine whether the controls designed to achieve those objectives are operating effectively.

8. List five specific internal control measures you would expect to find in a well-controlled billing operation.

9. A preliminary survey of a maintenance service operation for office machines and equipment produced the following information: (a) The manager of the maintenance service operation said that in his opinion the objective of the operation was to respond to calls for service in a minimum time; (b) More experienced repairmen were used to respond to second calls when the original repairs were not effective; (c) A comprehensive perpetual inventory system was maintained for all repair parts and supplies. For each of the three situations described, list two questions relating to the operation which the internal auditor would attempt to answer when performing the audit.

10. Contrast audit objectives and audit steps. Give an example of each in terms of a purchasing function.

Multiple Choice Problems

1. The internal audit program for an organization or function should be:
a. Taken from a book of standard internal audit programs.
b. Prepared before the preliminary survey.
c. So devised that it can be used without change on all subsequent audits.
d. Followed without deviation by the internal auditor.
e. None of the above.

2. The internal audit program used for a previous audit of an organization or function should be:
a. Discarded.
b. Updated at the end of the next audit.
c. Followed exactly during the next audit.
d. Reviewed before the preliminary survey.
e. None of the above.

3. Programs prepared during the audit tests:
a. Best capture the flavor of the audit.
b. Never need rewriting.
c. Can be marred by gaps.
d. Are the easiest to prepare.
e. Both a. and d. above.

4. All audit programs should be developed to determine whether:
a. Management's objectives are being met.
b. The general ledger and subsidiary ledger are in balance.
c. There is a proper mix of ages in the audited department.
d. There is a proper rotation of personnel.
e. None of the above.

5. As they prepare their audit programs, auditors should keep in mind:
a. The budgeted audit days of the prior job.
b. Their vacation schedule.
c. Their current budget.
d. The final audit report.
e. The weaknesses previously reported.

6. To purge pro forma programs of error, they should be:
a. Typewritten.
b. Given a trial run.
c. Reviewed by the audit department manager.
d. Thoroughly proofread.
e. Reviewed by the auditee.

7. After the program has been prepared, it should be approved by:
a. The supervisor of the prior audit.
b. The manager of the audited department.
c. The auditor's current supervisor.
d. The auditor in charge.
e. The external auditor.

8. Which of the following is an objective of an operation?
a. To assure the quality of materials produced.
b. To compare materials with specifications.
c. To determine whether materials meet standards.
d. To determine whether specifications are current.
e. None of the above.

9. Which of the following is an audit objective?
a. To distribute EDP printouts to those with a need to know.
b. To inquire of report recipients whether they use the EDP printouts.
c. To verify the timeliness of one month's EDP printouts.
d. To trace the process of EDP printout preparation.
e. To determine whether EDP printouts are useful to the recipients.

10. Which of the following is an audit step?

a. Determine whether agreements with advertising agencies contain appropriate provisions.

b. Trace agency billings for media service to underlying invoices from the media.

c. Ensure the preparation of written agreements with advertising agencies.

d. Control costs by comparisons with budgets.

e. Appraise the merits of the organization of the sales effort.

Case Studies

5-1 Weaknesses in a Marketing Activity

A senior auditor completed a preliminary survey of certain marketing activities of a company. The following conditions were disclosed:

1. Billings from the advertising agency for insertions in magazines and newspapers are approved for payment without adequate review by advertising department personnel.

2. Purchases of advertising materials and artwork are made by one employee of the advertising department.

3. Company-owned materials such as artwork, furniture, company products, and other items used for photographic sets are retained by the advertising agency.

Required: For each of the three conditions, prepare four audit steps to be included in the audit program.

5-2 Weaknesses in an Inventory Management Function

You are auditing the inventory management function of a large mainte-

nance operation for city-owned vehicles. During your preliminary survey you obtained the following information:

1. Vehicle maintenance records indicate that the number of inoperative trucks waiting for spare parts is increasing, even though the total number of trucks is decreasing.

2. Stockroom employees have been unable to find some parts, even though the perpetual inventory system shows them as being on hand.

3. The investment of spare-parts inventory has remained the same since the last audit three years ago.

4. Many of the spare parts can be used for passenger cars.

5. The perpetual inventory is maintained on inventory record cards by a clerk in the parts warehouse office.

Required: Prepare two audit steps to be included in the audit program for each of the five conditions.

5-3 Can the Internal Auditor Avoid the Problem?

Earl Naismith, performing an audit of the receiving organization, called his supervisor, Rod Gray.

"Rod," he said, "I've run into something that bothers me."

"What is it?" asked Rod.

"It's the 'not downs,' " said Earl.

"What in the world are they?" asked Rod.

"As you know, when a purchase order is written, a duplicate master copy of the purchase order goes to receiving and is used as the receiving memo."

"Right."

"If the RM doesn't reach receiving, they have no basis for accepting the items covered by the PO."

"So?"

"There's been an awful lot of delay

between the time the buyers telephone their orders to the suppliers and the time they get around to writing up their POs," explained Earl.

"So I guess the items come in and then find no POs to greet them," said Rod.

"Exactly. And if the POs are not sent down from purchasing, the condition is called a 'not down.' "

"What's your problem?" asked Rod.

"Well, it means that badly needed items just sit on the receiving dock. I think I ought to run down the reasons for the 'not downs,' " said Earl.

"Hey," said Rod, "that would mean you'd have to go into purchasing. And that's not on your program, or your budget, or your audit schedule."

"I know that," Earl agreed, "and that's why I'm calling you. This is a real problem, and I think I ought to run it down."

"Not on your life," said Rod. "That's another job altogether. It's a purchasing problem."

"But I'd feel like a fool," protested Earl, "to just hide the thing under the rug."

"Look, Earl, your job is to audit receiving, not purchasing. If we go dashing off in all directions, we'll never get our annual program completed. We've got to handle these things in accordance with our long-range audit plan or we'll be completely disorganized. I'm not asking you to sweep the 'not downs' under the rug. You'll prepare a memo on them and put it in the permanent file for purchasing. It will be covered in that audit at that time."

"That's ridiculous," said Earl. "The problem is here and now. The using departments are not getting their materials on time. I've got the beast by the tail and I don't see any reason to let go."

Required: State how you think the matter should be handled.

6

Field Work

The purpose of field work. Measurement and evaluation. Units of measurement and standards. Measuring diverse operations. Developing standards where they did not exist. Evaluating results of measurements. Evaluating standards. Auditing for quality, cost, and schedule. When to survey and when to test. Steps in testing. Implicit and explicit standards. Defining the population in terms of the audit objectives. Audit samples. The six forms of field work: observing, questioning, analyzing, verifying, investigating, and evaluating. The audit modes: functional audits, organizational audits, management studies, and program audits. Using consultants. Contract audits. Types of contracts: lump-sum, cost-type, and unit-cost. Indicators which highlight relationships and trends. Legal evidence: best evidence, secondary evidence, direct evidence, circumstantial evidence, conclusive evidence, corroborative evidence, opinion evidence, and hearsay evidence. Audit evidence: physical, testimonial, documentary, and analytical. Standards of audit evidence: sufficiency, compliance, and relevance. The effect of The U.S. Foreign Corrupt Practices Act of 1977 on field work.

The Nature of Field Work

Carrying Out the Program

Field work is the term used for the detailed part of the audit. It is chiefly concerned with gathering and evaluating data. Its purpose is to carry out the programmed audit steps and achieve the audit objectives. It encompasses all the efforts of the internal auditor to accumulate, classify, and appraise information so as to support an opinion and to make any needed recommendations for improvement. It includes collecting, arraying, and analyzing data and records anywhere inside or outside the enterprise. It consumes by far the greatest part of the auditor's time.

Field work, when reduced to its barest essentials, is simply measurement and evaluation. The concept of measurement has a special significance for internal auditors. When they have fully grasped this concept, they can successfully examine virtually any operation in the organization. But they must understand that they cannot audit an operation in a vacuum. They cannot observe a process and make an offhand decision that it is good or bad. They must look at the operation in terms of units of measurement and standards. The units of measurement are the discrete elements that apply to the operation — the dollars, days, pounds, degrees, people, documents, machines, or other quantifiable things — by which it can be objectively gauged. The standards are those qualities of acceptability to which the measured things will be compared in order to judge their success or failure.

Each audit subject, each operation, must be approached with the thought that it can be dealt with by determining its size, extent, or other quality in terms of units of measurement; and by comparing the results with acceptable standards for that operation.

Then internal auditors can measure objectively and effectively. But where they cannot measure, they had better tread lightly because they will be able to produce only a subjective observation — not an objective conclusion.

Audit Measurement

An example of a routine examination will illustrate the concept of audit measurement. Suppose the auditors wish to evaluate the promptness with which purchased materials clear receiving inspection. The unit of measurement is an hour or a day. The standard may be what management considers acceptable as stated in job instructions. It may be the needs of the production department as set out in production schedules. Or it may be some other logical criterion that is keyed to a company objective. The auditors will apply the unit of measurement to each transaction — to each delivered shipment in the audit sample. They will then compare the results with the standard. Finally, they will determine whether the sum total of their findings portrays a good or bad condition by evaluating the results of their measurement.

Now let us take a less common audit situation. Assume that internal auditors wish to determine whether the records show that test pilots are reporting defects in the aircraft they are testing when they should. Pilots fill in check sheets as they fly the plane and read the instruments before them. Some entries relate to pressure readings. The pressure instruments are calibrated in terms of pounds per square inch. The pilot is asked to read a particular instrument at a given altitude and power setting and to enter the reading on the check sheet. If the reading is outside acceptable limits, the pilot must prepare a "squawk" sheet which will trigger an investigation of the reason for the unacceptable reading.

To make their determination, the auditors will read the pilot's check sheet. The units of measurement are there — the pounds per square inch shown on the instruments and on the pilot's check sheet. Yet if the auditors were to examine the pilot's readings without reference to a standard, they would be wasting their time. They could draw no acceptable conclusions. A reading of 80 or 100 or 120 might all seem equally appropriate.

But if the auditors consulted engineering specifications and found, for example, that fuel pressure at 20,000 feet and a power setting of 85% should be between 90 and 100 pounds, they have a standard. Then, if the pilot's entry on the check sheet is 100, the auditors can be quite satisfied that no action was needed; but if the entry were 130 pounds, then the auditors would expect to see a squawk sheet. If one had not been prepared, they would record a deficient condition, and they could do so confidently.

To make a meaningful examination, auditors look for a unit of measurement and then for a standard. The standards can be found in job instructions, company directives, budgets, product specifications, trade practices, minimum standards of internal control, generally accepted accounting principles, contracts, statutes, sound business practices, or even in the multiplication tables. Then, by comparing their findings of fact with the standards, they can arrive at an objective conclusion.

Developing Standards

As internal auditors wade deeper and deeper into the stream of operations, and as they begin evaluating management functions for which standards have not been established, they find themselves faced with the need to develop their own. This may not be a simple task, but if done with care it may lead to audit results often thought beyond the auditor's reach.

The standards should match the objectives of the operation reviewed. If the subject is technical, the standards should be validated by one who is technically qualified, and then accepted by auditee management. An example of this approach involved an audit of a company's system of safety control. Since no standards existed, the auditors constructed them. Then, to obtain adequate assurance that the standards were reasonable and relevant, they asked a representative of the National Safety Council to review them. The validated standards were discussed with auditee management and accepted. The auditors were then able to use those standards with confidence in making their measurements.

Relevant excerpts follow from the resulting audit report, demonstrating the auditors' methods.

To evaluate the adequacy of the organizational structure as a means for dealing with potential disasters and with matters of safety, we constructed a set of criteria to use as a yardstick in measuring the adequacy of the control system. Our criteria covered matters of industrial safety and were as follows:

Committee structure, composition, and operation.

Have appropriate committees been constituted to provide policy guidance and direction over disaster and safety control?

Are the line organizations which are responsible for industrial safety operations adequately represented on the committees?

Are committee activities carried out in a businesslike manner, including the advance scheduling of meetings, the provision for detailed agendas, the recording, assigning, and resolution of action items, and the preparation and distribution of minutes?

Is there assurance that safety problems at the hourly employee level will receive proper attention and will be followed to a satisfactory conclusion?

Is there a means of obtaining interface among the various committees for handling related problems?

Plans, programs, practices, and implementation instructions.

Have emergency and/or disaster plans been developed and have appropriate instructions been issued to implement the plans?

Have industrial safety programs been established for the promotion of safety through accident prevention?

Have adequate provisions been made for the implementation of the requirements of the Occupational Safety and Health Act which became effective April 28, 1971?

Monitoring, inspecting, and reporting activities.

Have specific hazards been identified and has provision been made to monitor them?

Are physical inspections of plants and facilities being made, and are reports on the inspections being distributed?

Is the workmen's compensation insurance company with which our company deals represented at general safety meetings, and is the insurance company being provided with minutes of all safety meetings and reports of the inspections?

Is corrective action being taken on deficiencies reported as a result of inspections?

To obtain assurance that our criteria have provided us with adequate yardsticks, we submitted them to the occupational safety director of the local chapter of the National Safety Council. He informed us that in his judgment our criteria were both reasonable and complete and that an organizational structure together with appropriate plans and programs, which measure up to those criteria, would represent an adequate system of control.

Evaluation

Measurement is only one of the two phases of field work. Having made their measurements, the internal auditors must then evaluate the results to arrive at professional judgments.

Evaluation suggests an intent to arrive at a mathematically correct judgment; to express that judgment in terms of what is known. It seldom suggests the determination of a thing's monetary worth, but rather finding its mathematical equivalent in more familiar terms, such as the timeliness with which invoices are being processed, or their mathematical accuracy, or the accuracy with which receipts of goods are inspected.

The mathematical connotation permits measurement and evaluation — the key to field work — to walk side by side down the audit trail with perfect compatibility.

Throughout all their field work, as they apply standards, internal auditors should not fail to evaluate the standards themselves. The fact that such standards have been established and approved as criteria for satisfactory operating performance does not necessarily raise them above all reproach. Standards developed yesterday may not be applicable today. Changing circumstances may require new or revised statutes, contracts, regulations, procedures, or instructions. In other words standards, too, should be measured, and the measuring stick is their adequacy in meeting the organization's objectives and goals, and the applicability of the standards in the real world of today.

Aspects of an Operation

The internal auditor's measurements will normally be directed to three principal aspects of an organization; quality, cost, and schedule. As a simple example, assume that the auditor is examining controls over the purchasing operation. Included among the measurements will be:

Quality. Determine whether purchase orders have been properly approved and contain all required terms. Determine whether changes in specifications have been submitted to the supplier.

Cost. Determine whether bidders' lists have been approved by buying supervisors. Determine whether competitive bids are used whenever possible.

Schedule. Determine whether dates when goods are needed are shown on the purchase orders and whether the dates agree with those requested by the using organization. Determine whether buyers follow up regularly with suppliers to obtain purchased products on time.

The Forms of Field Work

The form of field work depends on the subject under examination and the circumstances of the particular situation. Under some circumstances, detailed verification of transactions is essential. In other circumstances, surveys with minimal verification will suffice.

If auditors foresee high risks and serious consequences from the improper functioning of an activity, they should seek thorough and detailed support for their opinions. The survey form of examination in such a situation may not be enough. A substantial verification of transactions would be needed to provide them with requisite assurance. For example:

In an audit of compliance with conflict of interest programs, auditors must understand that even one conflict might present management with serious problems. Determining that adequate controls have been provided is not enough. The auditors would most likely want to examine a large sample to provide reasonable assurance that the system of control is effective and that it will detect instances of potential conflict. If suspicions are aroused, they may have to look under every stone.

Sales of scrap traditionally present problems and can represent significant amounts of money. Auditors would wish to examine in detail representative samples of transactions before they would express an opinion that the system is working as intended.

On the other hand, the subject may not be fraught with high risk; or self-checking devices may have been installed to highlight defects and alert management to control breakdowns. Then the auditors may be willing to place reliance on the system and concentrate on the effectiveness of the checking devices. For example:

A stock room has a system of self-checks. Supervisors are required to make periodic tests of stores and related records. They are responsible for reporting their tests and results in writing to the department manager. He or she provides evidence of having reviewed those tests and the follow-through of action items. Here the auditors may reduce their tests. They may evalute the adequacy of the check lists, the frequency of the tests, and the correction of observed defects. These reviews, together with minimal tests of transactions to provide assurance that the system is indeed functioning as prescribed, should give the auditor adequate support for an opinion on the operations.

A document security department is subject to quarterly reviews by government inspectors who provide written reports of all defects. Also, department personnel use a comprehensive check list to make examinations of every document control station in the company once a year. Personnel charged with the conduct of the document control stations are provided with indoctrination and periodic reindoctrination courses. In such circumstances, the auditor's review may be restricted to providing assurance that the control system is functioning and that all prescribed self-checks are being made.

Between the two extremes of surveys on the one hand and the detailed tests on the other are a multitude of variations. Auditors must dip into their store of audit techniques for the appropriate instrument to make their measurements and obtain their assurances.

Testing

The Purpose of Testing

Auditors achieve audit objectives by a process known as testing. *Testing* implies placing activities or transactions on trial, putting them to the proof, and revealing their inherent qualities or characteristics.

Testing to the internal auditor implies the measurement of selected transactions or processes and the comparison of the results of those measurements with established standards. The purpose is to provide the auditor with the basis for forming an audit opinion.

The audit test usually implies evaluating transactions, records, activities, functions, and assertions by examining all or part of them. In today's complex world, the examination of an entire entity in detail is usually impracticable or uneconomical. But testing — when viewed as putting something to proof — does not necessarily exclude a complete examination. It is anything which supplies the auditor with sufficient proof to support an audit opinion.

Circumstances will vary the steps to be taken in this audit function, but usually the steps include:

○ Determining standards.
○ Defining the population.
○ Selecting a sample of transactions or processes.
○ Examining the selected transactions or processes.

Determining the Standards

Standards are explicit or implicit. They are explicit when they are set forth clearly in directives, job instructions, specifications, or laws. Instructions may state categorically, for example, that time spans shall not exceed five days, or that competitive bids must be obtained on all procurements over $1,000, or that production lots must be rejected when error rates exceed 5%, or that the advertising budget may not exceed 1% of projected sales. Auditors in such cases have well-calibrated measuring sticks for their comparisons: units of measurement and established standards.

Standards are implicit when management may have established, or may be working toward, objectives and goals, but has not set forth with particularity how they will be achieved. In those cases, auditors, after reviewing the objectives and goals and determining the controls established or needed, will have to consult with management on what it considers to be satisfactory performance. To make tests without coming to agreement on units of measurement and on standards of acceptability may result in wasted work and fruitless argument — there can be no meaningful measurement, and without measurement, field work becomes conjecture and not fact.

Defining the Test Population

The population to be tested must be considered in terms of the audit objectives. If the objective is to form an opinion on the transactions which took place since the last audit, the totality of such transactions since then represents the population. If the objective is to form an opinion on the adequacy, effectiveness, and efficiency of existing systems of control, the population may be more restricted. Under the latter circumstances, management is not interested in past history. It is concerned with the here and now. Is the system working the way it should? If not, how can we improve it?

In either event, auditors should seek to obtain reasonable ideas of the number of transactions involved: purchase orders, receiving memos, invoices, billings, shipping tickets, shop orders, rejections, sales slips, contracts, travel vouchers, blueprints, change orders, manifests, and so forth.

They should seek to determine the character and location of the population to see if any documents can be missing and to help them decide on the appropriate selection plan. How are the documents filed? Are they in random order? Are file receipts supposed to be substituted for all items removed from the files? Is there good control over the files? Are the transactions stratified according to value or other quality? Are the documents serially numbered?

Selecting the Sample

The sample selection should follow the plan which best fits the audit objectives, judgmental or statistical. The most reliable selections are made from lists which are separate from the records of transactions themselves. In that way the auditors have better assurance that items which may have been removed from the filed will not be overlooked (see Chapter 9).

Examining Transactions

Auditors examine transactions and processes to get the facts and to reach conclusions. The term *examination* includes both measurement and evaluation. Auditors have many techniques at their disposal to help them achieve this audit objective. Just what those techniques should be called is a moot point among auditors. They are grouped here under six headings which can carry the auditors from the beginning to the end of their field work.

These headings are defined relevant to audit examination rather than to their common usage. Of the six forms of field work, the first five may be considered as part of the measurement process. The last, evaluation, gives meaning to the information that the auditor has gathered.
- Observing
- Questioning
- Analyzing
- Verifying
- Investigating
- Evaluating

Observing

To the auditor, observing means seeing, noticing, and not passing over. It implies a careful, knowledgeable look at people and things. It means a visual examination with a purpose, a mental comparison with standards, an evaluative sighting.

It differs from analysis because analysis implies setting down and arraying data. Observation, on the other hand, means seeing and making mental notes and judgments. Since all auditing, including observing, is largely measurement, proper observation is probably one of the most difficult of audit techniques; for auditors are measuring what they see with what they have in their minds. The broader their experience, the more standards they retain, the more alert they are to deviations from the norm, the better observers they can become.

While observing is important, it is generally preliminary to other techniques. It usually requires confirmation through analysis or investigation. It takes place during the preliminary survey when auditors familiarize themselves with the physical plant and with systems and processes, but it can also take place during questioning and interviewing, when auditors note the reactions and behavior of those with whom they deal. It can take place, as well, when they are obtaining impressions of work tempo, facilities, staffing, and plant conditions.

Observations can be useful in noting clerical filing practices or work flow for unnecessary effort or tortuous routing. Auditors can observe the condition of rejected material as a start to backtracking for causes. They can tour a plant and observe idle equipment or idle facilities. They can observe security precautions on the perimeter of a plant or inside a bank or store. They can observe dangerous conditions and safety violations. They can observe cluttered stock rooms and evidence of backlogs. They can observe poorly stored or dangerously stacked materials. They can observe storerooms left unlocked. They can observe lack of adequate maintenance. They can observe trucks leaving the plant without being halted by guards. The list is without end.

Knowledgeable observations can provide keen insights, but auditors must be careful how they use them in citing deficient conditions. If such visual examinations are reported without confirmation, they should be clearly labeled as observations and impressions. They will seldom withstand a frontal attack by the auditee. If the auditee agrees with the observations and takes corrective action, they need not be followed up with detailed analysis.

Here is an example of how auditors followed through with a thoughtful, imaginative analysis of an observation made during an audit examination:

> Internal auditors were reviewing an operation involving returnable containers. They observed that strong but heavy returnable containers could be stacked two high in the rail cars used to return them. The cardboard containers used could be stacked only one high. The authors consulted the rail rates and learned that weight was no problem: The cost of shipping 140,000 pounds of commodity per car was no more than shipping 100,000 pounds. Management accepted the audit recommendations to eliminate nonstackable cardboard containers. By carrying out the recommendation about $500,000 was saved each year.[1]

Questioning
Questioning is probably the most pervasive technique of the auditor who

is reviewing operations. Questioning is carried on throughout the audit and may be oral or written.

Oral questions are usually the most common, yet they are probably the most difficult to pose. Obtaining information can be raised to the level of an art. To get the facts and to do so without upsetting the auditees is sometimes not an easy task. If the auditees detect an inquisitorial tone or perceive a cross-examining attitude, they may raise their defenses and be reluctant to part with the truth. The information they then give may be wrong or incomplete; or answers may not be forthcoming at all. So if auditors can understand how the average auditee sees them — as a potential threat to job security — and can modify their manner to allay fears, their chances for obtaining adequate information will improve.

At the same time, the auditors' concern for the auditee's feelings should not deter them from insisting on getting the facts. To that end they should not put words in the auditee's mouth. A question such as this will usually produce an affirmative response, true or not: "Do you always keep the doors to the storeroom locked?" A question like "How do you protect stores?" might bring a more satisfactory answer. When audit decisions depend on answers to oral questions, a good rule to follow is to confirm the information by putting the same question to at least two people. Good reporters never believe what the first person tells them. Here is an example of the result of some persistent questioning:

> An auditor found that identical raw materials cost $400 more per carload when purchased from one supplier than from another. The auditor questioned the purchasing agent and was told that the difference lay in the method of equalizing freight, prepaying it, and adding it to the invoice. The purchasing agent explained that freight equalization was based on the nearest producing point from a given manufacturer for a given item.
> But the auditor was not satisfied and questioned the manufacturer who said that freight equalization should be based on the nearest producing point of a given item regardless of the manufacturer. During the past five years the manufacturer had been equalizing freight on the basis of its own nearest producing facility. This resulted in an overcharge for freight of $75,000. As a result of the auditor's persistent questioning — not believing what the first person told him — that amount was recovered.[2]

Questions may sometimes be the most satisfactory way of determining how well or how poorly an activity is being conducted. The test of whether a service is acceptable rests on the opinions of those served. This is especially true of technical operations, where only the technicians are qualified to evaluate the manner in which a service or product meets their expectations or standards.

For example, regarding the usefulness of reports, auditors can prepare a questionnaire along the following lines:

Do you receive the report on time for it to be of value to you?

Does the report seem readily understandable?

Does it give you the information you need?

What use do you make of the report?

What was the last time you used it to help you in your work?

Have you ever found the report inaccurate or misleading?

If so, what did you do about it?

What would you do if you no longer received the report?

Questions such as these can be submitted in writing, used as a poll over the telephone, or asked face to face. Some of the questions ask for a yes-or-no answer — something we previously cautioned against — but here the people questioned have no vested interest in the preparation of the reports. Yes-or-no questions would not be objectionable in this case.

Analyzing

Analyzing implies a detailed examination. It stresses dividing a complex entity for the purpose of determining its true nature. It contemplates laying bare the inner working of some function, activity, or mass of transactions and determining the relationships between the individual parts.

Analyzing suggests the intent to discover or uncover qualities, causes, effects, motives, and possibilities, often as a springboard to further searching or as a basis for judgment. By analyzing an account, auditors who examine financial records separate, array, and spread out the individual elements that constitute the account. In this way, they can see which elements are significant, which recur, which are minimal, and which need further attention.

Internal auditors who examine operations do much the same. The principles are no different, only the subject matter. Auditors can see significant relationships and make precise measurements by parading before their audit microscopes the individual elements which make up the activity they examine. In contrast, when the entities are examined as a whole, the mind cannot perceive the intricate interrelationships between the diverse and varied elements that make up a complex function or a large population.

In audits of operations, the subject matter can span a broad spectrum and so can the types of analyses the modern internal auditor may use in making evaluations.

Auditors can list a sample of purchase orders on a spread sheet and analyze each one in terms of bids, sole source procurements, approvals, past history of particular purchases, freight routing, cost analysis, schedules, accurate purchase order preparation, make-or-buy decisions, and other matters.

Similarly, auditors can analyze a directive, a statute, a contract, or a statement of policy. Here, too, they can spread out the document, read each word, underline what is significant, measure it in terms of good business practice or real-world conditions, or measure existing practices in terms of the requirements set forth in the document. A simple reading is not enough. Auditors must identify and highlight significant elements and determine what they mean.

Also auditors may analyze the work of committees having related functions in carrying out broad programs. A company's safety program is an example. In any large company a number of committees can have responsibilities for different aspects of company and employee safety. Auditors might analyze the program by arraying the functions of committees in a matrix which shows for each committee where the committee gets its authority, what its precise functions are, who the chairman and vice chairman are, to whom it reports, how often it meets, who prepares the minutes and what happens to them, how action items are assigned and monitored, and how the various committees interface. In this way, auditors can observe administrative failings, decide whether there is overlap among committees, and see whether some essential function has somehow been overlooked.

Any composite can be analyzed by division, by breaking it into elements, by observing trends, making comparisons, and isolating aberrant transactions or conditions. Auditors do it by arraying data on work sheets, verifying the validity of the data, and evaluating the results. This is the essence of the auditor's art. Auditors step into modern internal auditing when they apply these techniques to operating matters which are a far cry from account analysis. This precise analysis, this ability to isolate, identify, quantify, and measure, makes the audit results useful, sound, and unassailable.

Here is an example of analyzing by developing standards or benchmarks, gathering data, comparing what is with what should be, and investigating variances:

> One auditor was examining the revenues of a hotel which was operated for the auditor's company by independent agents under a management agreement. Obviously, the lower the revenues reported, the less the return to the company. The question was how to develop a reliable indicator to test the accuracy of the revenues reported. The auditor concluded that the reports of hotel rooms cleaned would be difficult to manipulate; probably nobody would see any reason to manipulate them. The auditor's analysis of four month's revenues and of the related cleaning records for that period showed that the revenue was much less than what the rooms should have generated. The analysis showed that the management operator had diverted $258,000 from the hotel's funds.[3]

Verifying

Verifying suggests attesting to the truth, accuracy, genuineness, or validity of something. It is the auditor's oldest tool. It is most often used in establishing the correspondence of the actual facts or details to those given in an account or in a statement. It implies the deliberate effort to establish the accuracy or validity of some affirmation by putting it to the test, such as a comparison with ascertainable facts, with an original, or with some standard.

Verification also includes corroboration and comparison when statements of one person are confirmed by discussions with others or one document is compared with a substantiating document or documents. It also includes confirmation, which implies the removal of all doubts through independent validations by objective parties.

Auditors verify an accounting entry by comparing it with supporting detail. They verify an amount due by confirming it with a creditor. They verify an approval by consulting directives that establish levels of approval and by comparing the approval signatures with those on signature cards. They verify the propriety of a purchase by assuring themselves that the requirement for the purchased item was established by someone other than the buyer; that the number of items procured did not exceed those called for in a bill of materials; that the items were procured on time, but not in advance of need, by referring to production schedules; that the items were actually received, by referring to a receiving memo, by visiting the stores department, or by examining the end product.

Verifying has not only certain unique qualities of its own, but it also has some of the attributes of the other audit techniques the auditor uses. Here is an example:

> A company's policy was not to verify the propriety of charges of certain bonus-sharing construction contracts, but the auditors decided to verify charges incurred in one contract which showed an underrun of $1,700,000. The company and the contractor were to share the underrun equally. The verification of charges showed that not all reductions were due to the efforts of the contractor. In fact, the underrun was due largely to reductions in the scope of work and an unused contingency reserve. These were hardly bonuses for the contractor to share in as a reward for sterling effort. On top of that, the contractor had charged to the project $200,000 that related to a completely different project.
>
> The results of the audit verifications were discussed with the contractor. Recoveries exceeded $500,000. The auditors are now verifying charges on all such contracts.[4]

Investigating

Investigating is a term that generally applies to an inquiry which has for its aim the uncovering of hidden facts and the establishing of the truth. It implies a systematic tracking down of something that the auditor hopes to discover or needs to know. It includes, but is not limited to, probing, which applies to investigations that search deeply and extensively with the intent to detect wrongdoing.

Auditors may investigate, but investigating is different from auditing. Audits imply objectivity. Investigations seek to establish evidence of improprieties. Investigations therefore have more pointed direction than analyses and verifications, which imply the review of data having relatively unknown qualities until examined. This book will regard investigations as dealing with conditions that are suspect.

Probes are specifically related to wrongdoing, and here auditors must be careful not to go beyond their depth. Probes often involve legal and criminal considerations. After obtaining some inkling of serious impropriety, auditors should refer the matter to those who are experienced in interrogations. Auditors who do not heed such warnings may find themselves violating an individual's rights and laying their company open to prosecution for libel, slander, defamation of character, malicious prosecution, or false imprisonment. In such matters, therefore, it is wise to consult with their company's security people or legal counsel (see Chapter 22).

Here is an example of investigating:

> An audit of a time and material contract disclosed that a significant amount of sewer pipe was transferred to salvage after the job was completed. The only bid for the scrapped pipe was from the plumbing contractor. The auditors decided to investigate the entire transaction. They found that the material estimate was prepared by the owner's facilities manager. The estimate included excess materials over and above what would be reasonably needed. That excess was exactly what was transferred to salvage. The plumber admitted that he planned to use the materials in the construction of a bunkhouse in which some company executives had an interest. The amount of salvaged pipe was the amount needed for the bunkhouse. As a result, instead of buying the salvage at prevailing scrap prices, the plumber agreed to pay the owner's cost. The difference amounted to $19,000.[5]

Evaluating

Evaluating, as well as its kindred term *appraising*, implies estimating worth. In auditing, it means arriving at a judgment. It conveys the thought of weighing what has been analyzed and determining its adequacy, its efficiency, and its effectiveness. It is the step between analysis and verification on the one hand and an audit opinion on the other. It represents the conclusions the auditors draw from the facts they have accumulated.

Evaluation implies professional judgment, and it is the thread that runs through the entire fabric of the audit. In the early stages of the audit examination, auditors must evaluate the risk of eliminating an activity from their review by comparing the amount of the risk with the cost of examining it. In their programs they must evaluate the need for a detailed test in place of a survey or a walk-through. In their sampling procedures, they must evaluate the precision and confidence level required to achieve the degree of sample reliability they believe they need. As they compare a transaction with a standard and find a variance, they must evaluate the significance of the difference and determine whether corrective action is necessary. As they summarize the results of the audit examination, they must evaluate what those results imply.

Fact-finding without evaluating becomes a clerical function. Proper evaluations lift the audit from what may be a detailed check to a management appraisal. As has been said, the auditors first observe the facts through the bottom part of their bifocals — the verification half — and then evaluate them through the top part — the management half.

No auditor can become a full professional without evaluating everything audited in terms of objectives and standards. Arrayed data, no matter how artfully arranged, is merely rough ore until it has been transformed into something useful through evaluation.

Evaluation, obviously, calls for judgment. The mature, experienced auditor, the veteran of many audit examinations, the participant of many a report draft view, the wise observer of the company's course and objectives, evaluates audit findings almost intuitively, and usually is correct. But even such auditors can benefit from a structured, organized approach to the evaluation of what the findings mean. For example, in evaluating deviations from the norm — the failure to meet standards — they might ask themselves these questions:

How significant are these deviations?

Who or what has been hurt or could be hurt?

How bad was or could be the damage?

Have the deviations prevented the organization or function from achieving its objectives and goals?

If corrective action is not taken, is the deviation likely to recur?

Why did the deviation take place?

What is the cause? What event or combination of events threw the process off its track?

Has the cause been truly ascertained and precisely described? Will the event or combination of events cause the observed result every time? Does the cause satisfactorily explain every aspect of the deviation?

Clearly, auditors are bound to think of how to alleviate ailments as they diagnose them. In order to consider their proposals in an organized manner, they might ask themselves these questions:

What course of action will most practically and economically cure the defect?

What objectives should we keep in mind in recommending corrective action? What should management be trying to achieve in setting forth an improved course of action?

What choices are open? How do they measure up when compared with the objectives?

What tentative alternate has been selected and what injurious side effects might be expected?

Which is the best choice with the least unsatisfactory side effects?

What mechanism should be suggested to control the corrective action after it is taken? How can one make sure that the corrective action is taken; that it will be carried to a conclusion; that future deviations will be referred back to someone authorized to remove impediments from the proper fulfillment of the suggested course of action?

The auditor owes management a duty not only to suggest corrective action to cure defects, but also to point the way to ensuring continued efficacy of that action.

Here is a situation in which auditors discovered some relatively minor defects, but their evaluation of the activity which included those defects disclosed a significant problem that needed management attention:

> Auditors were reviewing state employment insurance charges and found several that were improper. Some of the people for whom unemployment insurance had been charged had never worked for the company. Employees who worked but half a week received a full week's insurance. One employee had actually been working while receiving unemployment insurance.
>
> But the evaluation of the total unemployment insurance picture — an evaluation stemming from the findings of loose practices — is what brought the greatest benefits. Many of the employees released as the result of an austerity program were available for rehire. Not only were they qualified and experienced, but their recall reduced unemployment insurance charges. Besides, employment agency fees were eliminated and the costs of training were minimized. Employees who refused to return to work were reported to the Department of Labor and their unemployment insurance benefits were terminated.[6]

Audit Modes

The Approaches

The techniques of observing, questioning, analyzing, verifying, investigating, and evaluating are applied under varied circumstances. They are used whenever auditors perform an examination. By and large, however, they are applied within broad frameworks, or audit modes, which indicate the direction or scope of the audit. The end results are the same — an audit opinion and recommendations; but the approach to the audit will differ according to the auditor's particular plan of attack.

Most audit projects will be carried out under one of four audit modes. In addition, internal auditors often engage in audits of costs on subcontracted projects, including construction contracts. The modes are identified as follows:

- Functional audits
- Organizational audits
- Management studies
- Program audits
- Consultants
- Contract audits

Functional Audits

As discussed here, a functional audit is one which follows a process from beginning to end, crossing organizational lines. Functional audits tend to concentrate more on operations and processes than on administration and people. They seek to determine how well all the organizations concerned with a function will interface and cooperate to see that is carried out effectively and efficiently. Some functional audits that can be of value in an organization are:

Scrap accumulation, segregation, and sale.

The incorporation of changes into products.

The ordering, receiving, and paying for materials and supplies.

Safety controls and practices.

Programs to detect conflicts of interest.

Direct deliveries of supplies or services to using departments.

Functional audits present special difficulties because of their breadth and scope. Auditors are required to define the parameters of the job, keeping it within reasonable bounds, yet covering all significant aspects of the function. They must deal with a number of organizations, each perhaps with objectives which might be in conflict with the objectives of downstream or upstream organizations.

Yet functional audits can provide special benefits to management: varying viewpoints can be identified, bottlenecks can be exposed, differing objectives can be reconciled, and duplications can be highlighted.

An example of the benefits of the functional audit is given in the following case history:

A manufacturing company had developed procedures and assigned responsibilities for the accumulation, segregation, and sale of scrap metals. In general, the responsibilities were as follows:

The machine shops where the scrap metal was generated were responsible for segregating the scrap according to types of metals.

The Reclamation Department was charged with supplying carts bearing signs to show the categories of scrap to be deposited in the carts. Reclamation was to ticket the carts when they were ready to be transported to the salvage sales yards or to truck bodies which had been supplied by scrap dealers under contract with the company.

The Transportation Department was responsible for transporting the carts either to the company's Salvage Sales yard (for mixed metals) or to the truck bodies (for large volumes of metal turnings or chips).

The Salvage Sales yard was held responsible for obtaining the best prices for scrap and for rejecting those carts which contained improperly segregated scrap and returning the carts with the mixed scrap to the scrap-generating departments.

The Procurement Department was to issue reports on sales of different types of scrap, showing the prices received for each.

The auditors followed the process from the point of scrap generation to the point of sale. They examined scrap placed in the carts, rode in trucks, talked to people, and compared the amounts received for scrap with prices listed in a technical publication dealing with metals. As they carried on their examination, they became aware of a considerable amount of parochialism, with excessive concern for individual departmental goals and with indifference to or lack of understanding for the needs of other organizations or of the company's overall goals. For example:

At scrap generating points, production supervisors gave little thought to the need for scrap segregation. They were not aware of the value of properly segregated scrap as compared with the value of contaminated scrap. They were resentful of having to segregate scrap when Reclamation refused to accept carts with contaminated scrap or when Salvage Sales returned carts containing improperly mixed metals.

Reclamation supplied carts, but was not always careful to supply the identifying signs that would facilitate segregation.

Salvage Sales was concerned solely with the highest dollar return for scrap and rejected any carts which carried contaminated scrap.

The Procurement Department prepared reports of scrap sales, but submitted the reports to its own management only.

As a result of conflicting goals, lack of good communication, and the failure to understand the goals of others and the objectives of the company as a whole, the auditors found the following conditions:

The cost of segregation in some instances exceeded the value of the segregated metals.

Rejected carts were shuttled back and forth because Salvage Sales was concerned only with cash returns and not with the cost of resegregating scrap.

Since Procurement sent reports of sales receipts to its own management only, others were not aware of the amounts of return that could be received for properly segregated scrap as against contaminated scrap.

At the conclusion of the audit, the auditors held meetings with the managers responsible for the processing and sale of scrap metals. As a result the following corrective action was taken:

Company procedures were revised to emphasize company objectives and to establish reasonable rules for scrap segregation, accumulation, and sale.

Carts were properly identified.

Generating departments were supplied with reports of scrap sales and were given the authority to segregate or not segregate metals, based on the volume of scrap generated and the potential return.

The shuttling back and forth of the carts was discontinued; but to keep generating departments informed of their derelictions, Salvage Sales would send them memos informing them of the losses in revenue that were suffered because of improperly segregated scrap.

The auditors managed to resolve conflicts, reconcile differences, and generate a better net return for scrap. They made a follow-up review about six months after the new procedures went into effect. They were amazed at the turnabout in attitude, cooperation, and results. People were willingly following policies that made sense to them. The system was functioning smoothly, effectively, and economically.

The functional audit can achieve similar results for other systems and processes in the company, so long as the auditor keeps his eye on overall company objectives and manages to bridge the gaps between the various organizations concerned with the function.

Organizational Audits

Organizational audits are concerned not only with the activities performed within an organization but also with the administrative controls used to make sure they will be carried out. The auditor is interested, therefore, with how well the organization's manager is meeting the objectives of the organization with the resources at hand. An incisive organizational approach can often provide insights into operations transcending those insights obtained solely by testing transactions.

Especially in large organizations with a multiplicity of operations and functions, the auditor is better advised to determine how well management is managing than how well transactions flow or trickle through the organization's pipeline. The audit measuring stick, the standards applied in appraising an organization's operations, is constructed from the elements that make up acceptable principles of administrative control.

It is a rare organization indeed that is so managed that it operates in accordance with all or even most of the theoretical precepts of good administrative control. Yet internal auditors, in performing organizational audits, should have those precepts in mind. Often an unsatisfactory condition can be the direct result of the violation of an accepted principle of good administration.

If auditors keep these principles in mind, they will begin to function at the management level. They should have a working knowledge of administrative, or management, control within a business. As auditors carry out organizational audits, they will be putting the principles of management control to work. They should be able to "flesh out" the skeletal structure drawn in Chapter 4. A clear picture of the completed structure, engraved on the mind's eye, can have a profound effect on how auditors view the administration of the organization and on the questions they ask when they perform their audits. The nature of those questions will contribute mightily to increasing the auditor's stature in the eyes of operating management.

Internal auditors should be conversant with the principle of planning — with setting objectives, developing policies and procedures, maintaining continuity, and reappraising plans and goals in the light of changed conditions.

They should be conversant with the principle of organizing — with the assignment of responsibility, the delegation of authority, and the development of staff.

They should be conversant with the principle of directing — with leadership, motivation, and communication.

They should be conversant with the principle of controlling — with setting standards; maintaining standards; training people to comply with standards; prescribing an approval and review system; ensuring compliance with standards; devising systems of records, reports, and master control; and monitoring the entire ongoing process (see Chapter 21).

Management Studies

Functional and organizational audits form the framework of the long-range audit program. The individual audits that are generally repeated at appropriate intervals represent the bread and butter of the auditor's fare. Another aspect of auditing may well be the caviar and champagne. It is the audit directed toward solving problems for management.

Many companies call upon outside consultants to perform studies, make evaluations, and offer recommendations for improvement in problem areas of the business. Some of these companies have benefited from the experience and knowledge that consultants bring to bear on the problems they are asked to solve. Others have not. The disappointments are the result of a number of factors. Some of them are as follows:

Employees may regard the consultants as strangers who have no feel for the company's life style or personality. Both employees and managers may be resentful and secretive, preventing the consultants from obtaining a complete understanding of the problems they are engaged to solve.

The consultants have a long and expensive training period to go through. No matter how experienced they may be, they still have to learn the company's geography, its organizational structure, its ingrained methods and procedures, and the personalities, strengths, weaknesses, and predilections of its management.

The outside consultant's recommendations, usually first communicated in an exit interview or in an elaborate report, may get a defensive reaction. Company personnel may spend more time in defending entrenched operations than in implementing what may very well be worthwhile suggestions.

Outside consultants generally charge sizable fees which in most cases would exceed the cost of using existing talent already in the company.

A top-notch internal audit staff, experienced in audits of operations, familiar with the company's objectives, policies, organization, and people, is a natural source of talent for this kind of consulting work. Internal auditors are already well versed in the techniques needed for problem solving: fact gathering, analysis, and objective evaluation. They developed these techniques in their regular audits. These are the same that are needed for solving management problems.

Further, they will have developed an understanding of management principles and philosophy essential to the dissection and evaluation of matters concerning management. If they have developed a proper image within the company, they have the reputation for objectivity, fairness, and personal concern for the company's interests. They will not feel impelled to generate a host of recommendations — warranted or not — merely to justify a fee.

Internal auditors then, who feel competent to take on special studies within the company, should accept the opportunity when it is presented to them. Indeed, they should be close enough to the councils of management to know when the opportunity arises and to offer their services in appropriate circumstances and under appropriate conditions.

Of course, the problem should be one that internal auditors have a chance of solving. Matters that are completely technical, or which depend entirely on executive judgment, should probably be avoided. They may not yield to the tools auditors possess or which are available to them.

On the other hand, the fact that the problem is difficult or extensive should be an inducement and not a deterrent. If some aspects of the engagement are technical, they may be dealt with through the assistance of technicians assigned to help the auditor over the technical hurdles.

These engagements should be requested and endorsed by executive management. Their scope and breadth will usually require backing at that level. It must be made clear to all employees and operating managers that this is a management project operating under a special management charter. In fact, it will function best as a task force, nominally headed by a vice president or another executive manager, with the audit manager conducting the actual work.

The auditors should, from the outset and throughout the engagement, employ all the techniques of salesmanship that they possess — keeping management informed and selling recommendations at the grassroots level before presenting them to management.

As soon as possible after they have taken the measure of the situation, they should make a formal presentation to management on how they view the problem and how they propose to attack it. This presentation can be enhanced by flip charts or view graphs. It should be carefully thought through and it should be carried out in a professional fashion. The presentation of the parameters of the problem, and the theory of the case as the auditor sees it, can have several benefits. It may force management to consider the aspect of the problem in a light it had not considered before because the problem had not been laid out visibly and in a logical manner. It can save the auditor from pursuing matters or running down avenues that are of no special interest to management. It can develop better rapport with management and draw executive management more solidly into a problem-solving partnership.

The study itself must be in depth. It cannot be a broad-stroke pass at the problem. It will require extensive reviews and thorough research. It must be able to produce authoritative answers to any relevant questions management poses. It must be able to provide a stout defense for any recommendations that it makes. It must be based on a thorough understanding of the following matters, among others:

What is the problem? (Not necessarily what management thought it was, but what it really is.)

What are the relevant facts? (The statistics, the processes, the systems, the procedures, the policies, the organizations, the people, the past, the present, the probable future, what has been written on the subject, and what is being done at other companies.)

What are the causes? (The number and variety of causes, the root causes and the surface causes, when they began to affect the problem.)

What are the possible solutions? (The alternatives, the costs, the answers to associated local problems within affected operating organizations, the solution or solutions to the generic problem with company-wide implications, the possible side effects of proposed solutions.)

A management study of broad scope will have a general cleansing effect. As the audit teams probe and query and analyze, they may find systems and performance defects. The audit team should promptly reduce each of these matters to writing, discuss it with the people concerned, and issue a memorandum that identifies the particular problem, provides adequate detail, sets forth the views of those interviewed, and proposes solutions. A format for such a memorandum is shown in Exhibit 6-1. Each memorandum would identify an individual problem, indicate the people with whom the problem was discussed, set out their views, and offer solutions.

Each week, or every two weeks, appropriate management personnel should be provided with a summary showing the status of the management study memorandums. Separate summaries should be prepared for each major organization. The form for such a summary — using the Procurement organization as an example — might be as follows:

			Status		
MSM No.	**Date**	**Summary of Condition**	**Initiated**	**Completed**	**Under Consideration**

Record of Management Study Memorandums
Procurement

Exhibit 6-1. MANAGEMENT STUDY MEMORANDUM

No: _____

Date: _____

Organizations Concerned:	(Show all the organizations involved in or affected by the condition or its solution.)
Summary of Condition:	(Provide a capsule comment that identifies the condition.)
Details of Condition:	(Describe the condition in sufficient detail to explain its significance, its causes, and its actual or probable effect.)
Proposed Solution:	(Supply the various alternatives that are available to cure the condition.)
Discussed with:	(List the names and identities of all management and supervisory personnel with whom the matter was discussed.)
Results of Discussions:	(Summarize the comments of each person with whom the matter was discussed, indicating whether he or she agreed with the statement of condition and/or the solution.)
Distributed to:	(Distribute the memo to all management personnel with whom the condition was discussed, and their superiors, as well as to the executives responsible for the task force.)

The Record of Management Study Memorandums keeps the study in the forefront of management's attention. Those matters requiring action remain flagged until corrected; the study is not permitted to fade into the background.

Every month, the audit manager may give a progress report to executive management on the status of the study. That report may:

Summarize the number of management study memorandums issued and their status.

Show the number of people — both auditors and technicians — who are involved in the study and the number of teams to which they are assigned.

Identify the more significant problems that either have been solved or remain unsolved.

Discuss in general terms the progress of the work.

Provide an estimate of the time required to complete the study.

When the task is completed, the results should be incorporated in a final report. The report should be a professional piece of work, giving the matter the aura of importance that it deserves. It might have a hard cover, comb or spiral bindings, with a double-spaced summary and single-spaced detail. It should be inviting to read. The detail may very well be a listing of the management study memorandums, as shown in the Records of Management Study Memorandums, minus the final three columns (initiated, completed, under consideration), supported by copies of the memorandums themselves. The report should discuss the matters that have been corrected and those remaining uncorrected.

Program Audits

On their own volition or at the request of executive management, internal auditors may undertake special reviews of ongoing programs. *Program* is a broad term that encompasses any funded effort which is collateral to the normal ongoing activities of an organization — an expansion program, a new employee benefit program, a new contract, a governmental health or training program, a new EDP application, or the like.

The audit goal is to provide management with information on the costs and results of the program and to make the evaluations as informative, useful, and objective as possible. In such reviews it is helpful for all concerned to have a common understanding of the terms used. Here are some:[7]

Evaluation. Ascertaining the value of something by comparing accomplishment with a standard or goal.

Program evaluation. In its broadest sense it implies both what is being accomplished in relation to cost and, beyond that, whether the objectives of the program are proper and suitable. Auditors would want a special authorization to question the latter.

Cost benefit study. This considers the relationship between costs (inputs) and benefits (outputs). Auditors may have to explore alternative ways of achieving a program objective. The auditors' aim is to identify the best choice in terms of dollars — the greatest benefits for a given cost or the required level of benefits at the lowest cost.

Cost effectiveness study. These studies are used when the benefits cannot be measured in terms of dollars — the benefits of a new apprenticeship program or the teaching of handicapped students.

Essentially, internal auditors would want to determine three things in a program audit: What was accomplished? Was the program successful? Is there an adequate system to ensure future success? In the private sector, accomplishment is generally measured in terms of revenues and profits. In the public sector, internal auditors would be concerned with three indicators: outputs, benefits, and impacts.[8]

Outputs

Outputs include such matters as services rendered, goods produced, and assistance given. Examples are students taught, cases processed, investigations made, reports completed, and examinations conducted. It sometimes takes considerable imagination to develop and apply standards and criteria for measurement.

Benefits

Benefits represent the effect of the outputs. For example, the number of students taught is an output. But the increased knowledge, skills, motivation, and aspiration levels of students are benefits. Benefits are more difficult to measure than outputs; but, obviously, they are more relevant to the evaluation of a program.

Impacts

Impacts are the effects of the program on a community, society, or even the world. These are extremely difficult to measure. They represent the lasting effect of a program, and are a challenge for an administrator to devise standards of measurement or a means of appraisal.

Clearly, in program reviews, objectives, goals, and standards must be identified quite specifically; otherwise auditors will have nothing to measure against, and what results from the audit would be opinions subject to dispute rather than well-supported conclusions. These objectives, goals, and standards are not easy to identify when:

Management or the legislature has not clearly defined the objectives.

Objectives overlap or are interdependent.

The people responsible for achieving the objectives, goals, or standards do not really understand them.

The apparent intent of management or the legislature has not been followed.

The real program objectives have changed even though the stated ones remain constant.

When such difficulties arise, auditors must understand that they cannot make an objective evaluation until the problems have been resolved. When no reasonable understanding of objectives, goals, and standards can be reached, it may be best to report that an evaluation would be fruitless. The yardsticks must be made clear and concrete and be agreed on.

The responsibility for continually evaluating their programs lies with operating and program management. Essentially, the auditor is concerned with determining how well the managers are carrying out that function. All programs are different, but certain common threads run through them. Internal auditors, in their program evaluations, seek answers to the following questions:

Are program objectives sufficiently clear to permit program managers to tell whether they are accomplishing the desired results? Are component program objectives in gear with overall program objectives?

How valid were the data used to justify the program to top management or to the legislature?

To what extent is the program accomplishing intended results? How closely is it meeting its schedules?

How well is the program succeeding within the costs budgeted or appropriated?

What variances are there between expenditures made and expenditures authorized?

What kind of information system (reports and the like) is in effect to keep top management informed about the program?

What form of internal monitoring system is in effect to keep program managers informed of program accomplishments and problems?

What conflicts, if any, exist between the program being evaluated and similar or parallel programs?

How closely related are program costs to program benefits?

To what extent were alternative programs considered to achieve the same benefits?

What might happen if the program were to be discontinued?

How accurate are the results being reported to top management or the legislature?

Consultants

Some programs and activities are quite technical or have technical aspects. A thorough audit evaluation will require the services of technical consultants. Auditors must remember that consultants assist; they do not take over the evaluation or shoulder the auditor's responsibilities. Hence, there are some rules internal auditors should follow in dealing with consultants:

The consultant and the auditors must have complete agreement on program scope and objectives before they prepare the audit or work program.

Staff should be assigned to work with consultants to monitor their activities and discuss problems with them.

Auditors must understand the nature of the consultant's work — the reasoning underlying their analytical choices, the risks inherent in their data and analyses, and whether the work done by the consultant conforms with what was intended.

The final audit report is the internal auditor's. It expresses the auditor's opinion, even though it is buttressed by the results of the consultant's studies. Consultants' opinions should be quoted only when the subject matter is clearly beyond the competence of the internal auditor and relates to completely technical matters.

Technical assistance may be solicited for the duration of the assignment or on an as-needed basis. The internal auditor must be in charge. The technical consultant is needed to clarify esoteric matters, point toward the areas that need probing, and protect the auditors from being given inaccurate information or self-serving declarations by line personnel; but technicians may not have the ability to gather evidence, array facts, and examine data so as to impel logical conclusions.

Contract Audits

Construction contracts often involve large amounts of money; such contracts are not part of the regular business of the organization for which the construction work is done. Hence, management may not be as familiar with construction costs and operations as they would for in-house production. Internal auditors can therefore be particularly helpful in auditing such contracts. For example:

> A major contract between the auditor's company and a prime contractor for a construction project provided for sharing escalation costs. But a subcontractor had billed the project and had been paid for total escalation costs for the past five years in violation of contract terms. When the internal auditor brought the matter to management's attention, the result was a recovery of $1.2 million.[9]

Construction contracts which auditors deal with generally fall into three types: lump-sum, cost-type, and unit-price.

Under lump-sum contracts, contractors agree to perform work for a fixed amount. If the work is done according to the agreement, there is little for the auditor to review. Rarely are large lump-sum contracts that simple. They often contain escalation clauses, progress payments, and adjustments for field labor costs. If actual field labor exceeds that agreed upon, any additional cost is borne by the company letting the contract. Also, lump-sum contracts may provide for reimbursement of premium time to obtain a sufficient labor supply.

Most vexing can be the changes. Large construction contracts are seldom completed without a host of changes. These as well as other collateral matters call for close audit surveillance.

Cost-type contracts may be the most economical way of dealing with a construction project, because of the many unknowns that attend such projects. Cost-type contracts do not require built-in hedges for the unknowns. They may be written to reimburse the contractor for costs plus a fixed fee or costs plus a fee based on percentage of costs. Some cost-type contracts provide for maximum costs and a splitting of any savings. Cost-type contracts are not self-policed with an incentive for efficiency or economy, so the costs the contractor is required to record need close surveillance.

Unit-price contracts are useful when a project requires large amounts of work of a uniform nature. Examples are cleaning land by the acre, removing earth by the cubic yard, and driving pilings by the foot. A price is agreed to for each unit. The problem is one of keeping proper records on the amount of work accomplished.

All these forms of contracts, cost-type in particular, benefit from audit surveillance. Internal auditors should not wait until the project is underway to protect their company's interests. Early participation is vital to evaluate bidding procedures, cost estimates, contractors' accounting systems, budgeting, financial forecasting, tax treatment, cost control, financial reporting, and systems of internal control.

Of crucial importance is provision in the construction contract for the right of system review and cost audits. Without these rights, the company is at the mercy of the contractor — especially under cost-type contracts. It is true that the company will usually have a project engineer and even an accountant on the job. But these people may not be conversant with the fine points of contract auditing; and continued attendance on the job, while working closely with the contractor, can diminish objectivity.

Construction projects are seldom alike, so a checklist approach to contract audits generally results in sterile reviews. As in other audits, the experienced internal auditors are aware of the hazards that exist in a particular project or can exist in any project. The auditors focus their audit effort on protecting their companies from potential risks rather than on checking numbers and documents.

Here are some of the risks and risk areas in contract agreements that should concern internal auditors:

In lump-sum contracts —
Inadequate competition.

Inadequate insurance coverage.

Certification of completion when work is not completed.

Charges for equipment that is not received.

Escalation provisions.

Changes in specifications or prices.

Authorization for extras and revisions.

Extras and revisions that are already part of the original contract.

Overhead items included as additional charges.

In cost-type contracts —
Overhead costs billed directly.

Inadequate internal controls by contractor over charges for people, materials, and services.

Unreasonable charges for contractor-owned equipment.

Excessive manning of project.

No effort to obtain best prices for materials and equipment.

Billings in excess of the amounts the contractor pays for labor or material.

Failure to credit project for discounts, insurance rate refunds, returned or salvaged material.

Duplication of effort or costs between headquarters and field offices.

Inadequate jobsite supervision by contractor.

Inadequate communication and follow-up from headquarters office.

Unreliable cost accounting and reporting procedures by contractor.

Billing supervision as direct labor in violation of contract terms.

Idle equipment.

Poor work practices.

Poor quality.

Extravagant use of materials and supplies.

Excessively high standards for materials and equipment.

Poor physical protection of materials and equipment.

Lack of control over absences of contractor's employees.

Cost-type work of contractor going on simultaneously with fixed-type work.

Excessive costs incurred because of contractor's negligence.

Uncontrolled overtime.

In unit-price contracts —
Excessive progress payments.

Improper reporting of units completed.

Prices bearing no relation to cost.

Changes to the original contract.

Escalation adjustments.

Inaccurate field records.

Extension of unit prices.

Auditing literature has documented a wide variety of recoveries made as a result of contract audits. Here are a few:

> Because of high inflation, a company agreed to compensate a contractor for 90% of increased costs of direct material over the bid price. When the internal auditors examined the detail supporting the increased costs, they found that the contractor had included overhead items, such as supplies and small tools. This was contrary to the agreement and resulted in a recovery of $60,663.[10]

Internal auditors observed a great deal of idle labor at a project to build a dam under a cost-type contract. They talked to the workers and found that tools and materials were lacking. Further investigation revealed the reason. Supply trucks came to the jobsite along a narrow road. Crews at the top of the road would receive the materials and tools, taking whatever they wanted. By the time the truck arrived at the more remote sites, most of the tools and materials were gone; hence the idle workers. The auditors recommended setting up a receiving and warehousing operation at a central location to deliver materials to specific crews. The labor losses had been running about $20,000. The losses were eliminated by using the central facility.[11]

Under a unit-cost contract for excavation and foundation work, a contractor was being paid for each ton of fill. But the contract called for payment by the cubic yard. By examining records of soil density tests, the internal auditors found that the method of payment — contrary to contract terms — benefitted the contractor unfairly. As a result, $25,000 was recovered and an additional $25,000 was avoided.[12]

Indicators

Certain analyses of operating data can provide revealing insights into business functions. Such analyses highlight relationships and trends, and permit valuable comparisons. They may form the basis for action or indicate the need for audit investigation and further analysis.

Standard financial anaylsis (the various balance sheet and income statement ratios, for example) has long been used to show trends and potential trouble spots. But there are other analyses that are available and useful to internal auditors and that involve the operating areas of the company.

Management usually works with a great many records and reports. Internal auditors can use the data in these reports as indicators to identify existing or potential problems. Some examples follow.

Fixed Assets

In examining the controls over fixed assets, internal auditors would want to know whether property has been aged by class and whether the cost of maintenance is shown for each class. Do the reports show where the maintenance people spend the bulk of their time? Have analyses been made of the relative economics of purchase versus lease? Do the reports show machine hours between breakdowns? Do they show maintenance hours and cost of major repairs related to replacement cost? Such analyses may disclose either excessively liberal replacement policies or excessive preventive maintenance.

Personnel Statistics

Reports can be analyzed to show various relationships between numbers of employees and other company trends; for example, ratios between hourly to salary personnel, direct to indirect personnel, sales to nonsales personnel, truck drivers to shipping personnel, supervisory to nonsupervisory personnel, total personnel to sales, and total personnel to profit.

Reports of different branches can be studied to disclose variances in procedures or the efficiency of personnel deployment. The results of the analyses may not be an end in themselves, but rather indicators for more studies in depth.

Inventory Turnover

Turnover is generally reported as a lump figure, often embracing a number of accounts or stores. But even within a single account or store, unfortunate conditions can be hidden. For example, unless inventories are periodically aged by class of item, many individual slow-moving or obsolete items can be overlooked. An overall turnover rate of four times a year, say, may conceal the fact that 30% of the items turn over only two times a year or less.

An analysis of turnover rates, including an examination of the records of specific items, may disclose how many items in inventory are over a year old. It may point to buying errors that are hidden in inventory and are protected by a satisfactory overall turnover ratio.

Employment Costs and Employee Turnover

The cost and time involved for the average hire, by class of employee, is often a matter of interest. Also of interest in the turnover rate by department or branch, and a comparison of the company's turnover rate with that in other companies in the same business.

Rolling Stock

Of importance are computations of the relationship between mileage traveled and the average life of tires, batteries, and plugs; analyses of the comparative cost of using personal versus company cars; and comparisons of manpower or dock and warehouse space with loading and unloading times, standby time, and delivery time between points.

Stationery and Supply Stores

It is often interesting to compare usage and stock balances. Also, it is useful to compare usage with the number of using personnel, particularly where items are attractive for use at home and where physical control over the stock leaves something to be desired.

Material Records

The auditor can analyze reports prepared to show the number of storeroom requisitions processed for the purpose of distributing material costs. In some cases the average unit prices may be too low to warrant the extensive paper flow. Why spend $50,000 to distribute $500,000 worth of material a year when approximations based on samples can accomplish the same results at far less cost?

Telephones

The auditor could analyze and determine the ratios of the number of telephone instruments to the number of people, the number of outside calls made, the number of toll calls, the average length of calls, and the number of restricted phones in each department. Periodic reports of the results of these analyses to operating management can have a salutary effect in reducing the number and length of calls.

The auditors must use caution in making any such analyses. These may produce data which impel false or superficial conclusions. The auditors should seek to measure their findings against norms — norms that may already have been developed in the company or in the industry. Statistics in a vacuum are meaningless. Used, however, to show deviations from norms, variances between similar operations, or adverse trends, they may be significant, and they can then point the way to further investigation to establish causes and effects.

Legal Evidence

Relation to Audit Evidence

Legal evidence and audit evidence have much in common. They both have the same objective — to give proof, to bring to the mind an honest belief about the truth or falsity of any proposition at issue. Belief is produced by the consideration of something presented to the mind. The matter thus presented, in whatever shape it may come, is evidence.

The focus in audit evidence differs somewhat from that in legal evidence. Legal evidence relies heavily on oral testimony. Audit evidence relies more on documentary evidence. Legal evidence permits certain presumptions; for example, it is conclusively presumed *at law* (that means no evidence, no matter how strong, can be brought in to the contrary) that facts recited in a written instrument, between parties and successors of interest, are true. Auditors, however, are not bound by any presumptions; they should question anything until they themselves are satisfied with its truth or falsity.

Internal auditors should understand the common forms of legal evidence. This knowledge will be useful in fraud cases, in any situations where they gather facts for legal counsel, and even in their routine audit work. What follows is a brief commentary on some of the forms of legal evidence.

Best Evidence

Best evidence, often referred to as primary evidence, is that which is the most natural and satisfactory proof of the fact under investigation. It has a strong relation to reliability. It is confined generally to documentary evidence, and it applies mostly to the proof of the content of a writing. If the original writing is available, the best evidence rule prevents a party from proving the content of a writing by oral testimony. The rule is designed to foreclose possible erroneous interpretations of a writing by requiring the production of the original writing when it is available. Oral evidence, for example, may not be used to dispute a written instrument such as a contract or a deed; however, oral evidence can be used to explain the meaning of the instrument where such instrument is reasonably capable of more than one interpretation.

Secondary Evidence

Secondary evidence is inferior to primary evidence and cannot be given the same reliance. Secondary evidence may include a copy of a writing or oral evidence of its contents. A copy of a writing is admissible, generally, if the original writing is lost or has been destroyed without fraudulent intent on the part of the proponent of the copy; if the writing is not reasonably procurable by the proponent of the copy by use of legal process or other available means; or the writing is controlled by a public entity. It must be shown that the copy is a proper representation of the original writing.

Oral testimony or written summaries are generally considered inferior to copies of writings. These are not barred by the best evidence rule if the writing consists of numerous accounts or other writings; the accounts cannot be examined in court without a great loss of time; or the accounts or other writings are produced for inspection by an adverse party if the court, in its discretion, requires such production.

Direct Evidence

Direct evidence proves a fact without having to use presumptions or inference to find the existence of a fact. The testimony of a witness to a fact is direct evidence — no inference is required. For example, a witness who states that he or she observed a receiving inspector sign for the receipt of goods, when in fact the goods received were less than that signed for, is giving direct evidence.

Circumstantial Evidence

Circumstantial evidence proves an intermediate fact, or group of facts, from which one can infer the existence of some other fact that is significant to the issue under consideration. It does not directly prove the existence of a fact, but merely gives rise to a logical inference that it exists. Short receipts that have cleared through the receiving department, and an inspector's stamp on the receiving memo, are circumstantial evidence that the receiving inspector was negligent. Internal auditors must always be wary of circumstantial evidence. For example, in the case of the receiving inspector it is possible that the inspector was not on duty the day the goods were received and that someone else used the inspector's stamp.

Conclusive Evidence

This is evidence which is incontrovertible, irrespective of its nature. It is so strong that it overbears all other evidence. It is evidence from which only one reasonable conclusion can be drawn. It cannot be contradicted and needs no corroboration. As Thoreau said, "Some circumstantial evidence is very strong, as when you find a trout in the milk." It can be conclusively presumed that the trout did not come from a cow.

Corroborative Evidence

Corroborative evidence is additional evidence of a different character concerning the same point. It is evidence supplementary to that already given and tends to strengthen or confirm it. For example, oral evidence not inconsistent with a written instrument, and offered merely to confirm it or show the truth of the matter contained in the instrument, is corroborative evidence and is considered acceptable. Oral evidence, given by an inspection supervisor, that the receiving inspector was on duty the day of the short receipts, and that nobody else had access to the inspector's stamp, corroborates the evidence of the receiving stamp.

Opinion Evidence

The opinion rule holds that witnesses must ordinarily testify to fact only — to what they actually saw or heard. Auditors should filter out opinions and gather and evaluate facts only — those items that tend to prove truth or falsity. Opinions offered by others may be useful to point the right direction for fact gathering; but opinions may be biased, self-serving, or uninformed.

There is an exception to the opinion rule, however, which relates to the testimony of experts. Under that exception an expert is permitted to offer his or her own opinion on the facts because it is the only way the jury will understand them — the only way the jury will get to the truth. Some safeguards have been set up with respect to opinion testimony, however. These safeguards require two elements to be present. First, the subject on which the opinion is expressed must be distinctly related to some science, profession, business, or occupation that is beyond the understanding of the average layman. Second, the expert witness must have such skill, knowledge, or experience in that field or calling that his or her opinion will probably help the jurors or the court in their search for the truth.

Auditors should keep the opinion rule in mind when they encounter matters outside their ken. They should understand that the opinions of others are valid when they come within the scope of the expert opinion rule — that those opinions are not valid unless they include essential elements: first, a subject beyond what the auditor is expected to understand, and second, an acknowledged expert in the field. As a practical matter, the auditor should include a third element: freedom from potential bias. In business situations the expert is often a company employee. The auditor should, if possible, select one who is outside the department or division involved in the audit. An engineer whose opinion is solicited on a matter involving Project A should be selected from Project B or C. Of course, in some companies the only expert may be working on the project under review. In that case, the auditor must take into account the possibility that the expert's testimony may not be completely free from bias.

Hearsay Evidence

The hearsay rule renders objectionable any statements made by someone other than a witness to prove the truth of the matter stated. Put another way, it refers to any oral or written evidence brought **into** court, which is offered as proof of things said **out of** court. It is second-hand evidence.

The reason that hearsay is generally inadmissible is that one of the best ways of getting at the truth or falsity of an assertion is to put witnesses under oath and cross examine them about what they personally saw or heard. Cross examination has a way of bringing to light the untrustworthiness and the many possible deficiencies, suppressions, and sources of error that lie under the bare, untested assertions of a witness.

Internal auditors must put themselves in the position of the court as they ask questions and examine records. If Smith says to the auditor "I personally saw Jones sign the receiving memo," it is direct evidence and it is not hearsay. Smith is in the presence of the auditor who can "cross-examine" him by asking questions designed to elicit information which will tend to prove the truth or falsity of Smith's statement. The auditor could ask, "Do you know Jones when you see her? Were you able to see Jones signing the receiving memo? How do you know this is the same receiving memo? When did she sign it?" and so forth.

If Smith were to tell the auditor "Thompson told me he saw Jones signing the receiving memo," that is hearsay. Thompson is not there to answer the auditor's questions. The auditor is unable to query Thompson as to the truth or falsity of the statement. All the auditor can be sure of is whether Smith heard Thompson's words exactly: "Is that word-for-word what Thompson said? Where were you at the time? What brought up the conversation? How can you remember so precisely?" As to the truth or falsity of Thompson's statement, however, that is hearsay.

What about a written statement — a sales slip, a purchase order, a discrepancy report, or any of the myriad business documents that are prepared, signed, and processed by people? They too are hearsay. They also represent statements by people not in court (or not in the presence of the internal auditor) about some transaction. But business documents come under one of the various exceptions to the hearsay rule. The exception holds that business records made during the ordinary course of business are admissible in court as evidence. That is because records made during regular business routines are usually trustworthy. Such business entries as sales slips, purchase orders, and discrepancy reports are therefore considered admissible evidence. But there should be testimony from the custodian of the records or from some other qualified witness to identify the record and describe its mode of preparation. The testimony should show that the record was prepared in the regular course of business at or near the time of the event recorded.

The trend in the courts today is to follow the methods of ordinary business by assuming the validity of records kept as daily commercial routine until they are actually discredited. In other words, the validity of the business record is rebuttable — the document is not unassailable merely because it is a so-called business record. With proper proof it can be found to be invalid or incorrect. Thus, when auditors find that the document or record represents critical evidence, they would wish to discuss it with the person responsible for preparing it and satisfy themselves of its truth or falsity by "cross-examination."

Photographs also represent hearsay evidence, but they will be considered admissible if properly authenticated. Photographs may be authenticated by the testimony of one or more witnesses, who are familiar with the subject portrayed, that the photograph is a good representation of the person, place, object, or condition. Auditors who observe the act of photographing, or take the photographs themselves, are competent witnesses. If they have a photographer take the picture, they should have the photographer record on the reverse of the photograph his or her signature, the date, the time, a brief description of the subject matter — in fact, anything that would help authenticate the photograph at a later date after memory has grown dim.

Audit Evidence

Nature

Audit evidence is the information internal auditors obtain through observing conditions, interviewing people, and examining records. Audit evidence should provide a factual basis for audit opinions, conclusions, and recommendations. Audit evidence has been categorized as: physical, testimonial, documentary, and analytical.[13]

Physical Evidence

Physical evidence is obtained by observing people, property, and events. The evidence can take the form of photographs, charts, maps, graphs, or other pictorial representations. Graphic evidence is persuasive. A picture of an unsafe condition is far more compelling than a written description. All observations should, if possible, be supported by documented examples. When the observation is the sole evidence, it is preferable to have two or more auditors make important physical observations. If possible, representatives of the auditee should accompany the auditors on such inspections.

Testimonial Evidence

Testimonial evidence takes the form of letters or statements in response to inquiries or interviews. These, standing alone, are not conclusive; they should be supported by documentation if possible. Auditee statements can be important leads not always obtainable by independent audit testing.

Documentary Evidence

This is the most common form of audit evidence. It may be external or internal. External documentary evidence includes letters or memorandums received by the auditee, suppliers' invoices, and packing sheets. Internal documentary evidence originates within the auditee organization. It includes accounting records, copies of outgoing correspondence, receiving reports, and the like.

The source of documentary evidence will affect its reliability. An external document obtained directly from its source (a confirmation, for example) is more reliable than a document obtained from the auditee. The possibility always exists that internal documents can be altered. Other matters affecting reliability include the circulation of documents through outside parties (canceled checks), satisfactory internal review procedures, and corroboration by other evidence.

Internal procedures have an important effect. For example, the reliability of a time card is significantly improved if employees are forbidden from punching a fellow employee's card, supervisors review the cards, the payroll section checks time cards against job tickets, and surprise floor checks are made.

Analytical Evidence

This type of evidence stems from analysis and verification. The sources of such evidence are computations; comparisons with prescribed standards, past operations, similar operations, and laws or regulations; reasoning; and breaking down information into its components.

Standards of Evidence

All audit evidence should stand the tests of sufficiency, competence, and relevance.

Sufficiency. Evidence is sufficient if it is so factual, adequate, and convincing that it would lead a prudent person to the same conclusions as the auditor. This, of course, would be a matter of judgment, but the judgment should be objective. Hence, when samples are used, the samples should be the result of objective, acceptable sampling methods. The samples selected should be such so as to provide reasonable assurance that they are representative of the population from which they were selected.

Competence. Competent evidence is reliable evidence. It should be the best obtainable. An original document is more competent than a copy. A corroborated oral statement is more competent than one standing alone. Direct evidence is superior to hearsay evidence. The best evidence rule should apply to audit evidence as well.

Relevance. Relevance refers to the relationship of the information to its use. The facts and opinions used to prove or disprove an issue must have a logical sensible relationship to that issue. An original purchase order, properly approved and issued, has no relevance to the issue of whether the goods procured have been received. A receiving memorandum certifying to the receipt of a certain number of items has no relevance to the issue of whether those items met stipulated specifications.

Whenever evidence does not meet the standards of sufficiency, competence, and relevance, the auditor's work remains unfinished. Corroboration or additional evidence may be required. When the internal auditor expresses an opinion, it must be based on incontrovertible evidence.

The U.S. Foreign Corrupt Practices Act of 1977

The U.S. Foreign Corrupt Practices Act is having a profound effect on internal audit field work in that country. However, internal auditors have no cause to shoulder all the responsibilities for compliance with the Act (see Chapter 3). They do have a responsibility to "assist members of the organization in the effective discharge of their responsibilities. To this end, internal auditing furnishes them with analyses, appraisals, counsel, and information concerning the activities reviewed."[14] Internal auditors are reliable judges of whether systems of control are effective — are doing the job that systems are supposed to be doing. The field work, the audit documentation, and the audit reports are valuable sources of information on which management decisions can be made concerning the efficacy of the systems mandated by the Act.

So internal audit field work, in appropriate cases, should be directed to testing systems of control and to reporting objectively whether they are effective or ineffective.

The audit program directed towards controls (see Chapter 5) is useful to determine whether controls are adequate. In matters of legal compliance, however, internal auditors must tread carefully. Declaring a control to be ineffective may bring about possibilities of liability under the Act. Determining whether a system of control provides the reasonable assurances called for by the Act requires decisions by managers and lawyers. When internal auditors detect weaknesses requiring management action, they should consider consulting with the attorneys and the managers to make sure the company is not unnecessarily laid open to external criticism.

This is not to say that internal auditors are to hide weaknesses. That is contrary to their training and their professional responsibilities. They should be cautious. They should refrain from undertaking a responsibility or taking over an authority — in terms of the Act — which is not legally theirs and which they are not competent to exercise.

Conclusion

Field work primarily carries out the basic instructions in the audit program. Essentially it is directed toward measurement and evaluation, and measurement cannot be objective unless standards of measurement have been established and units of measurement have been identified. Without standards, audit results are subjective opinions instead of objective conclusions. Internal auditors cannot accept standards blindly. They must evaluate them as well, and the evaluation of a standard is based on how well it relates to an operation's goals and objectives. Internal auditors perform field work by observing, questioning, analyzing, verifying, investigating, and evaluating. These are arbitrary terms, but in general they span the spectrum of all field work. Field work is carried out in several modes, depending on the audit objective. Internal auditors may review a single organizational unit or a function that threads many organizations. They may carry out studies for management or they may review how well programs are being managed. Audits of construction contracts are a separate mode and often yield considerable financial benefits. Internal auditors should have a working knowledge of both legal and audit evidence. And, as they perform their field work, they should consider the impact of governmental regulations, including in the United States The Foreign Corrupt Practices Act of 1977.

References

1. "The Round Table," *The Internal Auditor*, August 1979, p. 70.
2. "The Round Table," August 1979, p. 71.
3. "The Round Table," December 1979, p. 66.
4. "The Round Table," June 1979, p. 78.
5. "The Round Table," June 1978, p. 72.
6. "The Round Table," December 1979, p. 65.
7. United States General Accounting Office, "Comprehensive Audit Manual," October 31, 1972, p. 12-3.
8. L. M. Knighton, "Auditing for Effectiveness," *The Internal Auditor*, January/February 1975, pp. 81, 82.
9. "The Round Table," February 1977, p. 66.
10. "The Round Table," February 1979, p. 69.
11. "The Round Table," October 1978, p. 99.
12. "The Round Table," February 1979, p. 70.
13. GAO Manual, p. 8-1.
14. "Introduction," *Standards for the Professional Practice of Internal Auditing*, Altamonte Springs, Fla.: The Institute of Internal Auditors, Inc., 1980.

Supplementary Reading

Brink, V. Z., J. A. Cashin, and Herbert Witt. *Modern Internal Auditing, An Operational Approach*. New York: The Ronald Press Company, 1973. Part II.

Scantlebury, D. L., and R. B. Raaum. "Operational Auditing." *AGA Monograph Series, Number One*. Arlington, Virginia: The Association of Government Accountants, 1978. Ch. VII.

U.S. General Accounting Office. "Comprehensive Audit Manual." Chapters 8, 10, 12.

For further study

Discussion Problems

1. What two factors does the term *measurement*, as used in the text, imply?

2. What units of measurement and standards might an internal auditor employ in an audit of automobile maintenance?

3. Describe tests of quality, cost, and schedule in an audit of plant maintenance.

4. Describe circumstances under which internal auditors should use a survey method of field work and a detailed test of transactions.

5. The four steps in making tests of transactions, as set forth in the text, are determining standards, defining the population, selecting a sample, and examining the sample transactions. How would they apply in an audit of a receiving operation?

6. The six forms of field work are observing, questioning, analyzing, verifying, investigating, and evaluating. How would you use these concepts in an audit of stores containing miscellaneous small parts?

7. Four audit modes are functional audits, organizational audits, management studies, and program audits. Give an example of each.

8. When an auditor is asked to perform a broad management study, what should be the content of the first presentation to management?

9. What are indicators? What would be an indicator of the amount of receipts a hotel should report?

10. What is evidence and why is it important to internal auditors?

11. Why is hearsay evidence suspect?

12. What two elements must be present to invoke the "expert testimony rule"?

13. In making appraisals, how should internal auditors view the results of their tests?

14. Before setting out to obtain corrective action for deficient conditions, what questions should internal auditors ask themselves about the significance of their findings?

15. What impact has the U.S. Foreign Corrupt Practices Act of 1977 had on audit field work?

Multiple Choice Problems

1. In auditing an operating unit, the internal auditor would seek answers to the following questions:
   1. Why are the results what they are?
   2. How could performance be improved?
   3. What results are being achieved?

   What is the chronological order in which the above questions should be answered?
   a. 3 - 1 - 2
   b. 1 - 3 - 2
   c. 3 - 2 - 1
   d. 1 - 2 - 3
   e. 2 - 3 - 1

2. In testing the internal controls over accounts receivable, the internal auditor should determine whether:
   a. Noncash credits are properly authorized.
   b. The general ledger and subsidiary ledger are reconciled regularly.
   c. The write-offs of bad debts are properly approved.

d. Accounts are aged at regular intervals and the results are reported to management.
e. All of the above.

3. To audit operations for efficiency, an internal auditor should have available:
a. A procedures manual.
b. Performance standards.
c. Volume statistics.
d. Flowcharts.
e. An organization chart.

4. An internal auditor's statement, "I personally counted the cash," is an example of which kind of evidence?
a. Circumstantial.
b. Direct.
c. Primary.
d. Secondary.
e. Corroborative.

5. Field work may be defined as:
a. Measuring and evaluating the adequacy and effectiveness of internal controls.
b. Developing deficiency findings.
c. Gathering data for the internal audit report.
d. Obtaining corrective action as soon as possible.
e. All of the above.

6. The first step an internal auditor should take in performing a management study to help the director of marketing determine the optimum allocation of advertising budget to company products is to:
a. Analyze prior years' advertising costs.
b. Hold discussions with media personnel.
c. Establish and discuss with the director the key objectives of the study.
d. Determine the amount of projected sales for the purpose of establishing the proposed sales budget.
e. Both a and b above.

7. When the auditor seeks to determine whether purchase orders were properly approved, were issued in compliance with competitive bidding procedures, and were prepared in time to prevent production halts, the audit tests of the procurement process are concerned with:
a. Quality.
b. Cost.
c. Schedule.
d. All of the above.
e. None of the above.

8. Verification does *not* include:
a. Corroboration.
b. Confirmation.
c. Comparison.
d. Connotation.
e. All of the above.

9. Which of the following statements is hearsay?
a. "I did it."
b. "I saw him do it."
c. "He told me he did it."
d. "I know who did it."
e. "I don't know who did it."

10. Documentary evidence includes:
a. Flowcharts.
b. Audit conclusions.
c. Receiving memorandums.
d. Work sheets showing the results of tests.
e. Records of interviews.

11. A test designed to achieve a sample reliability that would withstand criticism is directed toward:
a. Sufficiency.
b. Relevance.
c. Competence
d. Documentation.
e. None of the above.

12. In terms of the U.S. Foreign Corrupt Practices Act of 1977, internal auditors are responsible for:

a. Determining whether systems of control comply with the requirements of the Act.
b. Seeing that controls are sufficient to provide reasonable assurance that the objectives of the controls are being met.
c. Assisting managers by providing them with counsel on internal control.
d. Developing control systems.
e. Documenting the adequacy of the control systems.

Case Studies

6-1 Physical Inventories

Following the observation of a physical inventory, the internal auditor compared the physical inventory counts with the perpetual inventory records and noted that there were apparent shortages. These shortages were materially greater than those found at the end of the previous year.

Required: (1) Identify four possible causes, other than theft, for the differences between the physical counts and the perpetual inventory records. (2) Briefly describe three potentially adverse effects on the organization which could be caused by the differences. (3) Assuming that the cause of the differences was theft, give three recommendations to prevent theft.

6-2 Accounts Receivable

The internal auditor for a pharmaceutical manufacturer was reviewing the accounts receivable activities. The auditor ascertained that controls provided reasonable assurance that:

1. Sales are billed accurately and promptly.
2. Accounts receivable are recorded properly.
3. Accounts receivable are aged and followed up to ensure prompt collections.

Required: For each of the three activities stated above, list three internal audit work steps to determine whether these activities are being carried out satisfactorily; that is, whether the controls are working as intended.

6-3 Subcontracts

You have been conducting an internal audit of the various operations of a subsidiary of your organization. During your audit, your survey and tests disclosed that under cost reimbursement subcontracts between the subsidiary and its suppliers, substantial and unanticipated cost overruns were encountered.

Required: List five recommendations to avoid recurrence of such conditions other than recommending that employees be admonished to be more careful or that supervisors pay closer attention to the work of employees.

6-4 Controlled Tests

Controlled tests of a manual system call for the deliberate introduction of false or inaccurate documents into the system to determine whether the system or the people operating it will detect the spurious documents. There is considerable difference of opinion among practitioners as to the propriety of such a program.

Required: (1) Give three reasons for the use of controlled tests with fictitious documents in a non-EDP system. (2) Give three reasons against the use of such tests.

6-5 Raw Material Inventory

During the audit at a manufacturing plant, the following facts relative to a particular raw material inventory are disclosed:

1. The quantity on hand is equal to six months production requirements.

2. A recent large purchase of this raw material was made, causing the six-month supply to be on hand. Prior inventories were generally at the two-month level.

3. The factory warehouse has sufficient space to store only two months' raw material needs; therefore, outside warehouse space was leased to store the remaining four months' supply.

4. The purchasing agent agreed that various suppliers had been satisfactorily delivering this raw material on a 30-day schedule but said he took advantage of one supplier's offer to reduce prices if six months' supply was purchased at that time.

Required: Describe the approach you would take in your audit to determine whether the purchasing agent followed good business practice with this quantity purchase.

6-6 Rework

When a supplier's parts or components fail on the production line, they are examined by a review committee made up of production, inspection, and procurement people. If the failure is considered to be the supplier's fault, and if the item cannot be returned to the supplier (generally because of schedule constraints), the committee asks the accounting department to issue a rework order to accumulate the costs of reworking the item in-house. Procurement notifies the supplier. Accounting accumulates the costs and submits them to Procurement where the responsible buyer negotiates a settlement with the supplier.

Required: List five matters to be taken into account to determine whether all rejections that are the supplier's fault are properly considered, whether costs are properly accumulated, and whether settlements are reasonable.

6-7 Lifting Equipment

Your company uses all manner of lifting equipment in its shops. The equipment includes overhead cranes, hoists, and various slings and cables. An EDP printout lists all the 15,000 items of equipment in use in the shops, according to their location. Maintenance regulations call for periodic tests and evidence of those tests for each item of equipment — from braided wire slings to huge overhead cranes. Unsafe equipment, obviously, can present extreme hazards.

Required: List five questions you might ask yourself as you set out to do your field work.

7

Deficiency Findings

Deficiencies defined. The different forms of deficiencies. "Finding" — a misnomer. Contrasting defects and improvements. Management's response to recommendations and to suggestions. The characteristics of a properly developed deficiency finding. Seeing findings through management's eyes. Factors used in assessing deficiencies. Major, minor, and insignificant deficiencies. Chief elements of a deficiency finding. Goals and standards, conditions, procedures and practices, cause, effect, conclusions, and recommendations. Discussions with operating people. Records of audit findings. Abstracts of findings. The importance of supervisory reviews of audit findings. Reporting deficiencies to management. Follow-up. The internal auditor's responsibility and authority for corrective action. Selling audit findings. Dealing with the recalcitrant operating manager.

The Nature of Deficiency Findings

Forms of Defects

Deficiency findings describe conditions or actions that are not what they should be. They include systems that do not achieve desired objectives. They also include actions that were taken improperly, actions that should have been taken but weren't, and actions that should not have been taken but were. In short, they are deviations from expected norms or established standards.

Findings which most readily capture the attention describe transactions which caused large, tangible losses. But deficiencies also include weaknesses in systems or controls where losses cannot be explicitly shown but where the possibility of loss exists. The latter, because they are usually continuing, can represent a greater risk to the enterprise — even though specific dollar losses cannot be demonstrated.

Deficiency findings are probably the most tangible and graphic evidences of the internal auditor's work. Yet the word *finding* is a misnomer. It is not necessarily what the auditor literally found. The condition existed when the auditor appeared on the scene and may even have been known to the auditee. Rather, it represents a logical assessment of information which the auditor has pulled together. The auditor's determinations can then show that certain systems or actions have an adverse effect on operations. Here are some examples, taken from internal auditing literature:

Unsatisfactory systems. An audit of dormant accounts in a bank disclosed that the system in effect was too costly. The auditors recommended that the bank absorb all accounts under $50 into income, discontinue paying interest on those accounts, and levy a service charge for handling each dormant account. After the recommendations were adopted, annual earnings increased by $32,000 as a result of the revised system.[1]

Actions taken improperly. Auditors reviewed a health plan in their company. They found that 17 employees, listed as active and covered by health premiums, had actually left the company. Unnecessary premium payments for the terminated emloyees totaled $39,000.[2]

Action not taken at all. An internal auditor reviewed a supply inventory containing test meters and probes worth $30,000. These items could have been depreciated for tax purposes, but weren't. Also, an investment tax credit could have been taken, but wasn't.[3]

Prohibited action taken. An internal auditor, checking time and material payments, found that the contractor had been submitting duplicate invoices from suppliers. The overcharges totaled $148,000. As a result of the audit, the entire amount was recovered. A review of documents on subsequent construction projects disclosed similar overcharges totaling $250,000.[4]

Suggestions for Improvement

A deficiency finding describes something that was or is wrong or is likely to go wrong. Auditors also encounter transactions or conditions which may not be intrinsically wrong, but which can stand improvement. For example, paying for products that were never received is just plain wrong. If there is enough money involved, it is a reportable deficiency. Using a receiving memo form which is awkward to use in recording receipts of products could not reasonably be considered a deficiency — especially when the internal auditor cannot point to any errors in the counting of receipts.

Reasonable operating managers will agree that payments for goods not received are deficiencies. But it would be unfair to apply the same label to a suggested improvement in the receiving memo when no errors can be demonstrated. Such improvements come under a separate classification. In some companies these are labeled suggestions for improvement — as contrasted to recommendations to correct defects — and do not carry the fault-finding connotation of a deficiency.

The question for auditors in separating deficiencies from suggestions for improvement is whether a condition is contrary to some acceptable standard of conduct or whether it is acceptable but could be improved in some way because new knowledge about the subject has come to light. The dividing line between the two is not always easy to draw. Operating managers will seek to persuade the internal auditor that a particular finding merely represents an opportunity to improve an otherwise satisfactory condition. The internal auditor may see it as a deficiency, but this is a matter of professional judgment. That judgment cannot be relinquished to operating managers. The internal auditor will have to make a fair decision based on a full appraisal of the facts — and then hold to that decision.

There are other implications as well. On the one hand, what is deficient must be corrected. The operating manager can be given no option on whether he or she must take corrective action. On the other hand, a suggestion to improve a condition which does not violate some established rule or standard is something else. In such cases, managers should have the right to decide whether to implement or not to implement the suggestion.

An excessive number of errors in processing documents manually represents a deficient condition. It cannot be tolerated and must be corrected. The proposal to automate the system is a suggestion for improvement which the operating manager should have the authority to accept or reject. It could well be that there are other ways to cure the commission of an excessive number of errors: better supervision, better cross-checks, or better employee training. Perhaps the expense of automation need not be incurred. If a manager is to be given the responsibility to run an operation, he or she should have the authority to decide how to run it, and so suggestions for improvement should be so regarded and drafted that they do not fall into the same category as deficiencies.

Characteristics

Not every deficiency discovered and developed by an internal auditor is a reportable audit finding. Some matters are insignificant and not worthy of the attention of management. Others may not be solidly buttressed by objective, sound evidence. Still others may be half-baked, without sufficient audit work to assure a thorough understanding of the conditions reported. Even those that are reportable may not be sufficiently well presented so as to compel belief and action. Hence all reportable deficiency findings should have these characteristics:

They should be significant enough to deserve being reported to management.

They should be documented by facts, not opinions, and by evidence that is sufficient, competent, and relevant.

They should be objectively developed without bias or preconceived ideas.

They should be convincing enough so that the conclusions reached are reasonable, logical, and based on the facts presented; they should compel action to correct the defective condition.

Obviously, these characteristics will be interpreted subjectively. What is a significant deviation to one individual may be insignificant to someone else. Words like *objective, convincing, reasonable,* and *logical* have different connotations to different people. The test, then, must be how the defect would be regarded by a reasonable, prudent person under the same or similar circumstances. A key question internal auditors must ask themselves as they appraise a deficient condition is, "If this were my company or agency, if I were its president or director and were appraising this condition, what would I do about it?"

If, as president, or director, they would feel that there is substantial compliance with procedures and instructions, that the procedures and instructions themselves are reasonably calculated to carry out organizational goals and objectives, and that operations are functioning in a reasonable manner despite minor imperfections, then the reported condition should not be regarded as deficient. If, however, they feel corrective action is needed, then internal auditors must press forward and bring the defects to the attention of whatever level of management is responsible for taking corrective action or seeing that it is taken.

The careful, intelligent appraisal of audit findings is the sign of the professional internal auditor. This is what constitutes so-called management auditing — seeing the finding through the eyes of a manager. Eager, inexperienced auditors, in hot pursuit of deficiency findings, gauging their own worth by the quantity of defects unearthed — never mind the quality — are the bane, not the aid of management. Such internal auditors must be taught to raise their sights.

Approach

Developing a significant, reportable deficiency finding is an acquired skill. It takes discrimination based on experience. What may seem like a serious shortcoming to a layman may be seen as a trifling deviation to the professional internal auditor.

Finding minor deviations in any ongoing process is relatively easy. Perfection is a rare commodity. Its price is often far too high. The effort needed to achieve the last 5 degrees of purity can exceed the cost of achieving the first 95. Internal auditors must be realistic. They must be fair in their judgments and conclusions. They must bring good business sense to the development of their findings. Therefore, as they approach the formulation and the communication of deficiency findings, they should consider these factors:

Hindsight and Monday-morning quarterbacking can be unfair and unrealistic. Internal auditors should consider the circumstances existing at the time the defect occurred. Management decisions are based on the facts available at the time. Internal auditors should not criticize those decisions merely because they disagree with them or because they have information not available to the decision maker. Internal auditors should not substitute audit judgment for management judgment.

The auditor, not the auditee, must assume the burden of proof. If a deficiency has not been thoroughly proved to the satisfaction of an objective, reasonable person, it is not reportable.

Internal auditors should certainly be interested in improvements in performance, but performance that is less than 100% does not necessarily deserve criticism.

Internal auditors, flushed with the success of unearthing an apparent defect, should step back from their product and play the devil's advocate. They should seek objectively to analyze their discovery for possible flaws and fallacious reasoning. Internal auditors, like any other proponents of an idea, are tempted to rationalize interpretations that will support their findings. The investment of a great deal of time and effort gives rise to protecting the investment and defending the finding against perfectly logical questions, but those findings may not stand the test of time or of shrewd scrutiny.

Internal auditors cannot take the position that a condition is defective because they have in their wisdom so labeled it. The development of a finding must conclusively demonstrate to others the propriety and reasonableness of the stated deficiency.

Degrees of Significance

No two deficiency findings are exactly the same. They will represent various degrees of actual or potential loss or risk. Giving the same audit emphasis to several random clerical errors and to an overpayment of $100,000 is clearly illogical. Internal auditors should consider the degree of damage a deficient condition can cause before communicating it to management.

An insignificant deviation — the sort of clerical misstep which all organizations experience — does not warrant formal action. Indeed, including it in a formal audit report would be counterproductive. First, it would tarnish the truly significant findings in the report, implying that the internal auditor could not discern the difference between a flyspeck and a spreading blot. Second, it would perpetuate an undesirable stereotype: the internal auditor as a nitpicker.

The insignificant errors should not be hidden or overlooked. The acceptable course of action is to discuss the error with the individual responsible for it, see that corrective action is taken, record the matter briefly in the working papers, and keep these slight deviations out of the internal audit report.

Does this mean that random, clerical errors should never be reported? Not at all. If these errors are symptomatic of a larger problem, then the course of action should be different. If the errors are a direct result of poor employee training, ineffective supervision, or unclear written instructions, then those things constitute the deficiency. The errors are merely evidence that the deficiency exists. They bolster the auditor's contention that the larger defect should be corrected.

But even in nonrandom errors, in more serious, reportable defects, there is a difference between what shakes the pillars of the enterprise and what causes less shocking tremors. An employee who commingles personal funds and company petty cash has violated both company rules and good business practice. Certainly the matter should be reported and corrected or else it may continue or become widespread. But how does that compare with a defective system of internal control in accounts payable which permitted payments totaling $500,000 in one year for goods and services that were never received?

These two types of defects should be differentiated. They should be treated in audit reports so as to show that one is a minor defect and the other is a major one. They need not be so labeled explicitly, but they should not command the same amount of space in the reports.

Obviously, deficiency findings could be put in an infinite number of categories, depending on the degree of their severity, but that would bring about more disputes than resolutions. A usable formula is to divide reportable deficiency findings into major and minor classifications.

A major finding is considered to be one which would prevent an organization or a unit in an organization from meeting a major objective. A major objective for an accounts payable department is to pay only what is rightfully due. The defective system of control that resulted in duplicate payments of $500,000 is a defect which prevented the department from meeting a major objective. Ergo, it is a major deficiency. No one could successfully dispute that.

A minor deficiency is regarded as one which requires reporting because it is more than a matter of random human errors, it will continue to have adverse effects if not corrected, and it is of sufficient significance to bring to the attention of management. Yet it does not thwart the meeting of a **major** objective of the enterprise or of one of its units. The petty-cash deficiency is an example of such a finding.

The line between major and minor findings can become exceedingly fine. Audit judgment is applied to differentiate between them. If the benchmarks just described are reasonably applied, the internal auditors can successfully defend their classification of findings.

These classifications are useful in deciding what weight and emphasis to give a finding. They are also useful in periodic reports to management which list or report the volume of defects encountered in internal audits. Fair reporting would require a segregation between reportable deficiencies, which caused or could cause major damage to the enterprise, and those which were of less severity.

Elements of a Deficiency Finding

General

The propriety of any action is best measured by comparing it with some standard of what is acceptable. The development of a deficiency finding is no different. If the developed finding meets all acceptable standards it will be logical, reasonable, compelling, and a means of motivating corrective action. If something is missing, the finding may be disputed or it may result in grudging action or no action at all.

All reportable deficiency findings should contain certain elements. Internal auditors and their supervisors should be intimately aware of those elements and they should not be satisfied until they are there, explicitly or implicitly. These elements are summarized as follows:

- *Standards.* What the operation is supposed to accomplish.
- *Condition.* What the operation was actually accomplishing.
- *Procedures or Practices.* What people were supposed to do or what they were actually doing.
- *Cause.* Why the deviation from standards occurred.
- *Effect.* What happened or could happen because conditions did not meet standards.
- *Conclusion.* The need for corrective action.
- *Recommendation.* What is needed to correct the condition.

Any deficiency finding which properly includes these elements will represent a strong argument for corrective action. It will leave no rock unturned. It will have no gaps or holes that will permit successful dispute. Both internal auditors and their supervisors will be satisfied that they had done all that was necessary to develop the finding.

Internal auditors are not omniscient — no more so than any other professional. They cannot be expected to be completely knowledgeable about all the systems, interrelationships, and technologies of an enterprise or of a unit within an enterprise. Most operating people have spent years learning how to deal with these matters. They are often not even aware of all the elements and nuances of their operations, otherwise the defects identified by the internal auditors might have been dealt with before the internal auditors arrived on the scene.

Knowledge about a reportable deficiency finding is something else again — here the internal auditors are disputing the status quo. They are singling out some system or transaction which did not meet standards. So with respect to deficiency findings, internal auditors should know as much or more about their findings than anyone else. Their knowledge should encompass all the elements of a finding. Auditors should be prepared to answer any questions about them, their facts should be unassailable, the standards should be accepted, and the auditor's logic should be convincing.

Here is a more thorough discussion of the elements just identified, along with a segment of an audit finding to illustrate each element. All the segments were adapted from a single deficiency finding.

Standards

A first and significant step in developing an audit finding is to include, in the concept of the standards, goals and objectives that represent what management wishes accomplished and the quality of the accomplishment. Not to understand the goals or objectives of an operation is like appraising a sculpture while blindfolded. Touching it gives only a partial appreciation; it does not put the part touched in context. Not to determine acceptable standards or criteria is to measure with an elastic ruler. The measurement will depend on who measures and how far the ruler is stretched.

In any audit of an activity, the goals of efficiency, economy, and effectiveness are implied. All resources should be used with a minimum of waste to accomplish some desired or desirable end. These become goals in themselves. To see how efficient, how economical, and how effective an operation is, auditors must have standards of measurement. They will have to identify valid standards or criteria of performance. They must know what should be, before they can criticize what is.

Standards may already exist. For example, management may have decreed that the rejection rate for certain products should not exceed 2%. Before accepting the standard, however, the internal auditor should appraise its validity. This can be done by searching out its basis and comparing it with industry norms, with those employed in other organizations, and with reasonableness in meeting enterprise goals.

On the other hand, management may not have established standards. In that case, the internal auditor will have to determine what is reasonable to meet enterprise goals, but such standards should not be applied until agreement is reached with the auditee. For example:

> Water meters in a community are installed to measure water usage. They therefore should be accurate so as to charge customers for the right amount of water used in order to obtain the revenue needed to maintain the water distribution system. Water meters in use should not vary from a master meter by more than a stated percentage. In the instant case the percentage was set forth in legal requirements.[5]

Condition

The term *condition* is used to connote what is. It describes what the internal auditor found through observation, questions, analysis, verification, and investigation. The condition is the heart of the finding. It is a photograph of what the auditor saw. The information gathered should be sufficient, competent, and relevant. It must be able to withstand any attack. It must be representative of the total population or system under review or, if an isolated instance, it should be a significant defect. The auditee should agree with the facts presented.

Auditees may and do disagree with audit conclusions and interpretations, but never should there be disagreement with the facts on which the opinions are based. A finding cannot be considered properly developed if the auditee can assert that the internal auditors did not get their facts right. All else becomes irrelevant. Thus, conditions must be properly assessed and they should be discussed early on with those in a position to know the facts. Any disputes about the facts should be resolved before the finding is reported. The evidence must be irrefutable. Whatever steps are needed to make the evidence conclusive must be taken, using methods that are objective and productive of representative results. Internal auditors must develop the reputation that "If the internal auditor says it then it must be true." For example:

> Internal auditors used stratified random sampling to select meters for testing. The meters selected were replaced and were then subjected to laboratory tests. The tests showed that 17% of the meters tested did not work at all and that an additional 23% ran slower than the standards specified by legal requirements.

Procedures and Practices

Procedures and practices refer to established ways of doing things to meet goals and standards. Procedures are management's instructions, usually in writing. Practices are the way things are being done — right or wrong. Both terms are usually related to the conditions in the finding. Procedures may contribute to an unsatisfactory condition, or practices may violate an adequate procedure. In developing findings, auditors should seek to determine what the procedures are, or should be, and what practices are being followed. Internal auditors should determine whether:

Established procedures or existing practices are designed to attain desired goals.

Established procedures are being followed. (Often the root of the problem is the failure to follow adequate procedures.)

Procedures and practices are complete. Do they include all the steps needed to get a job done economically and efficiently?

The existence or absence of procedures and practices may be the reason corrective action is needed. Yet it takes considerable skill to report procedures and practices without making dull reading. Only the highlights should be reported, leaving out unessential detail. For example:

Water meter inspectors pick up their assignments at the central office. They then go into the field, read meters, prepare reports, and go home after they have read the required number of meters. Supervisors compile performance figures for management, spending most of their time in the office. They rarely go out into the field. There is no procedure to check on the proper functioning of meters, to report on meters that are suspiciously slow, or to make comparisons among meters. Inspectors spend only half a day on the job, going home after they read the assigned number of meters.

Cause

The underlying cause explains why standards were deviated from, why goals were not met, and why objectives were not attained. The identification of the cause is essential to the cure. Unless it is known, the recommendations for corrective action may address only the symptom and not the disease. Every deficiency finding can be traceable to a departure from what is expected. Only when causes are known and the departures identified can the problem be resolved. Determining causes is an exercise in problem solving. The rules are the same:

Identify the problem — look for the deviation.

Specify the problem with particularity. What is the deviation? Where is the deviation? When did it occur? How big is it?

Test for possible causes — those that completely explain the deviation, that would make it happen every time, that answer all parts of the deviation.

Set out the objectives of corrective action.

Compare alternative actions with the objectives and tentatively select the best.

Think of the adverse circumstances that the selected action triggers. Consider the "what ifs?" What effect would it have to send supervisors out to see that inspectors stay on the job until the proper quitting time?

Recommend controls that will see that the best action is actually carried out. For example:

Using multiple regression analysis, the auditors established a definite correlation between the condition of meters and their age. After the meters had been in operation for a certain number of years they had a tendency to slow down and then gradually fail. By talking to managers of other utility companies the auditors learned that the practice followed in the activities audited were not calculated to focus on aging meters, to make the best use of inspectors, to make them alert to meters which were failing, or to exercise needed supervision.

Effect

Effect answers the "so what" question: assuming that all the facts are as represented, so what? Who or what gets hurt, and how badly? Internal auditors must be able to demonstrate the results of the conditions which do not meet standards and which prevent operations from meeting their goals.

Those adverse results should be significant — not merely some deviation from a procedure.

Effect is the element needed to convince auditees and higher management that the undesirable condition, if permitted to continue, will cause serious harm and would cost more than the action needed to correct the problem.

In economy and efficiency findings, the effect is usually measured in dollars. In effectiveness findings the effect is usually the inability to accomplish some desired or mandated end result. Effect is the convincer. It is indispensable in any audit finding. If it is not adequately presented to management, the chances are slim that corrective action will be taken. For example:

> The internal auditors were able to determine and demonstrate by their sample that revenues totaling $2 million a year were being lost. They were also able to document that the water rates were unnecessarily high by at least $1.5 million annually.

Conclusions

Conclusions must be buttressed by the facts. Conclusions are professional judgments, not a reciting of details. Conclusions should present potential courses of action and point out that the cost of correcting the defects will be exceeded by the benefits. Conclusions use the quantified effects as a springboard to show the need for action. For example:

> The findings led the auditors to conclude that the procedures should be improved so as to monitor meters over a certain age, to replace those that do not meet standards, and to provide necessary instruction and surveillance for inspectors so as to improve their performance.

Recommendations

Recommendations describe the course of action management should consider to rectify conditions that have gone awry and to strengthen weaknesses in systems and controls. Recommendations should be positive in nature, should be specific as possible, and should identify who is to act on them.

Audit recommendations carry the seeds of danger. If they are so couched as to tell management that the course recommended by the auditors is the only course to take, the action may return to haunt the auditors. Identifying an unsatisfactory condition is an audit responsibility. Correcting that condition is a management responsibility. Auditors should not usurp that management prerogative lest they take on a responsibility that is not theirs. They can be properly criticized if the recommended action fails.

It is far more preferable for internal auditors to propose a method or alternative methods for correcting a condition. They should make it clear that selecting a course of corrective action is management's job. The audit recommendations should be **considered,** not blindly taken. The internal auditor's recommendation is a potential course that should be considered with other courses, for management and not the internal auditor will have to live with the corrective action.

The most satisfactory means of resolving an audit deficiency is to discuss it with management before the written audit report is published. At that time, agreement should be obtained on the facts and on some reasonable course of action to cure the defect. Thereafter the formal report could contain a statement something along these lines: "We discussed our findings with management and, as a result, action was taken which we believe is calculated to correct the condition described (or, action was taken which corrected the condition described)." This approach takes nothing away from the auditor, and it builds a problem-solving partnership between auditor and auditee.

We are firmly convinced that this form of reporting is preferable to a series of audit recommendations which seem to emphasize auditee derelictions and display the auditor as some superior, omniscient creature issuing commandments engraved in granite. An example:

> The internal auditors discussed their findings and conclusions with management personnel. As a result, management took action to replace 25,000 aging or inoperative meters at a cost of $1 million. Management was satisfied that this action would yield $2 million a year of additional revenues and reduce water rates by about $1.5 million annually.
>
> Also, management took steps to dispatch a team to several utility companies to study the methods employed in inspecting meters, supervising meter inspection, and monitoring meters to detect those which were beginning to slow down.

Discussing Findings

During their development of deficiency findings, and especially when they contemplate their recommendations, internal auditors must be aware of their own fallibility. Conditions may not be interpreted correctly. Procedures may not be read as intended. What looks like an improper action may have a valid reason behind it. Hence, internal auditors should constantly be checking their understanding of what they have found by talking with those most likely to know the facts. Discussions with knowledgeable people can save auditors considerable pain and mortification. Things are not always what they seem. The auditee's intepretations should be welcome and should be carefully recorded.

Especially welcome should be the opinions of experienced employees or managers on the results of recommended action. Within any organization, no single activity is an isolated island. It is somehow connected with many other activities. Changing a process in the receiving department may have an unwanted effect in the accounts payable or the purchasing departments. The experienced internal auditor will seek out knowledgeable people in the organization who have a wide-ranging grasp of the operations in question and say: "Here's the problem. It needs correcting or improvement. What would happen if we recommended this course of action?" Many experienced internal auditors can recount tales of how such questions saved them embarrassment.

Summaries of Findings

Internal auditors who want to make sure that they have taken the most significant elements of a deficiency finding into account can make use of a device that acts as a safeguard. The device can take different forms, but whatever its form, it can keep the auditors on track and give their supervisors a means of knowing that all needed steps were taken to produce a well-developed deficiency finding.

One of the devices is shown in Exhibit 7-1, the Record of Audit Finding (RAF). It embodies most of the elements we have just discussed and provides space for:

Identifying the organization responsible.

Providing an identifying number for the particular finding and a reference to the supporting working papers.

A capsule comment of the finding — a brief statement of condition.

The standards applied in assessing the condition.

An indication of whether the finding was a repetition of something found in the prior audit.

A citation to the directive, procedure, or job instruction involved in the finding.

A summary of the extent of the audit tests and the number of discrepancies found.

The causes — why the deviation occurred.

The effect, actual or potential, of the condition.

A statement of the corrective action proposed or taken.

A record of the discussions with auditee personnel, and space to note their comments — usually whether they agree with the auditor's facts, conclusions, and recommendations — and what is the nature of the action, if any, they propose to take.

The form provides flexibility — a number of RAFs can be sorted and re-sorted to facilitate reporting. It provides a ready reference for discussion since it contains on one sheet most of the information needed to describe the problem. It functions as a guide to remind auditors to do all that is necessary to obtain the information needed for a thoroughly developed finding.

Some organizations have expanded the use of the Record of Audit Finding beyond a working paper document. They use it to communicate the finding promptly to the auditee and obtain written comments. In this way, disagreements can be more readily resolved and promises of corrective action can be made a matter of record. The auditee's response and the record

Exhibit 7-1.   INTERNAL AUDIT DEPARTMENT
RECORD OF AUDIT FINDING

Organization_____   RAF No._____
                                          W/P Ref._____

Condition_____
_____
_____

Standards_____
_____

Same finding last examination: Yes _____   No _____

Procedures or practices_____
_____
_____

Method of sample selection_____

Pop. size _____ Sample size _____ No. of discrepancies _____ % of sample _____

Causes_____
_____
_____

Effect_____
_____
_____

Recommendation_____
_____
_____

Corrective action_____
_____
_____

Discussions:

	Name	Title	Department	Date	Auditor
(1)					
Comments					
(2)					
Comments					
(3)					
Comments					
(4)					
Comments					

_____   _____
        Auditor   Date

Exhibit 7-2.　　INTERNAL AUDIT DEPARTMENT
RECORD OF AUDIT FINDING
COMMENTS AND ACTION

Management Comments:

(Use reverse side for additional comments)

Name: _____ Title: _____ Date: _____

Corrective action:

Effective date of corrective action _____

Name: _____ Title: _____ Date: _____

Auditor's appraisal:
Proposed action satisfactory _____ Unsatisfactory _____

Auditor: _____ Date: _____

Follow-up of corrective action:

Auditor: _____ Date: _____

Results of corrective action (evaluated during subsequent audit)

Auditor: _____ Date: _____

of action taken or promised is contained in an attachment to the RAF (Exhibit 7-2).

Many organizations issue a memorandum for each audit finding to report condition, criteria, cause, effect, and management's response.

An example called an Abstract of Finding (Exhibit 7-3) was adapted from one used by a government agency to report audit findings.[6] These memorandums are given wide distribution throughout the agency. The proponents of such abstracts say that they offer these benefits:

Senior managers are given a quick means of learning about current problems and the action taken to resolve them.

Managers in field offices are kept informed of problems likely to affect them as well; thus, internal auditing is able to reach more areas with the same expenditure of resources.

The abstracts are analyzed periodically to disclose trends. When brought to the attention of senior management, overall action can be taken to reverse adverse trends. A relatively minor problem in one office may be serious when it crops up in many.

The discipline of preparing abstracts before writing the audit report helps internal auditors pinpoint any shortcomings in their development of deficiency findings. Care in preparing abstracts eases the subsequent preparation of the final audit report.

A central review of abstracts helps to maintain a quality assurance program designed to improve internal auditing.

Supervisory Reviews

Audit supervision remains the key control over the professional development of deficiency findings. Each reportable deficiency finding should be subjected to close supervisory review. Nothing reduces the credibility of an internal auditing department as much as an ineptly developed finding that collapses under attack. A deficiency finding is a criticism, and the natural defensive mechanism of those criticized prompts an attack on the critic. Findings must therefore be beyond reproach. Audit supervisors can see that the desired end is accomplished by approaching any deficiency finding with these questions:[7]

Are any elements of the finding missing? Why? What can be done to seek out the missing elements? Are these defects a result of poor presentation or of incomplete audit work?

Are the elements mixed up so that clarity is clouded? Are opinions substituted for statements of condition? Are causes confused with effect? Are recommendations simply a recital of facts?

Are recommendations to improve a condition where procedures are not fol-

Exhibit 7-3. ABSTRACT OF FINDING

Office: Northeast District
Subject: Travel Expenses
Report Title: Fiscal Accounting

Condition: Travel advances exceeded prescribed maximum amounts allowed. We found that 133 of 175 accounts exceeded the allowable maximum advance of $2,500. These excessive balances ranged from $2,640 to $4,750. The excess totaled about $300,000.

Criteria: Company policy provides advance travel funds to employees authorized to travel. Advances are not to exceed expenses anticipated for a period of 45 days. Normal per diem rates are $50. Thus, the maximum for 45 days is $2,250. An additional amount up to $250 may be included to cover estimated mileage when travelers use their personally owned automobiles.

Cause: Company procedures do not require specific justification for large travel advances. The Fiscal Accounting Office relies primarily on employees' supervisors to make sure advances do not exceed needs. Inconsistencies can occur because requests are approved by different supervisors, and none of them follow the same rules.

Effect: Employees can and do accumulate large, unneeded advances. These accumulations can adversely affect the company's cash position. In addition, collections become difficult when employees holding large advances leave the company. Fiscal Accounting is now in the process of trying to collect over $15,000 from employees no longer with the company.

Management's response: The accounting department will compare travel claims with outstanding advances to identify employees with advances in excess of needs. Those employees will be required to justify the amounts advanced to them or reduce the advances to the amounts of their actual expenses. Supervisors will be given specific instruction about the amounts of advances they are authorized to approve.

_____
Audit Manager

lowed merely a lame statement that the procedures **should** be followed? Do the recommendations go to the heart of the problem? Would it be more useful to recommend clearer instructions, closer supervision, more constant monitoring, or other means of control which will promptly identify deviations from procedures?

Are the audit criteria clear, convincing, and objective? Are the criteria or standards cited reasonable? Are they designed to meet a management objective? Do they make good sense?

Is information on causes complete or is it superficial? Does it go to the heart of the problem? Will the cause trigger the same undesirable effect each time?

Is the effect exaggerated, or is it understated? Is it sufficiently quantified? Are intangibles adequately recognized and sufficiently explained?

Is the recommendation definite or does it merely say, "Improve controls?" Is it too rigid, insisting on the internal auditor's course of action? Does it address the past but ignore the future? Is it punitive rather than constructive? Is it out of harmony with the cause? Does it include a means of monitoring conditions so that the adverse effects will not recur?

Reporting Deficiencies

Abstracts or Records of Audit Findings (RAF) have been put to uses beyond recording the finding or communicating it currently to the auditee. Some audit organizations have made them the primary basis for the internal audit report. All the abstracts or RAFs are accumulated in a logical order, grouped by subject, location, or audited unit. These are then submitted to management by means of a one-page executive summary. The summary describes briefly the scope of the audit, offers an overall audit opinion, and provides comments regarding the auditor's assessment of the operation audited. It also lists, briefly, the reportable findings. The documented findings are represented by the abstracts or RAFs.

This form of reporting concentrates on deficiencies. It does have the advantage of permitting prompt reporting after the field work has been completed, but what is gained in speedy reporting may be lost in unfavorable auditor-auditee relations. The auditor may assume the aspect of a carping critic — not an objective observer who can see and report the good as well as the bad.

Follow-up

Responsibility

Section 440 of the *Standards for the Professional Practice of Internal Auditing* is as follows:

440. Following Up

Internal auditors should follow up to ascertain that appropriate action is taken on reported audit findings.

.01 Internal auditing should determine that corrective action was taken and is achieving the desired results, or that management or the board has assumed the risk of not taking corrective action on reported findings.

Views are not unanimous about this responsibility. Some writers and practitioners believe that internal auditors merely identify deficient conditions; it is up to management to take the corrective action, determine its adequacy, and monitor it. This view is not consistent, however, with the broader responsibility of internal auditors as stated in the Introduction to the *Standards*:

> Internal auditing is an independent appraisal function established within an organization to examine and evaluate its activities as a service to the organization.

Implicit in that statement is the responsibility to identify and report on both actual and potential risks to the enterprise. Internal auditors who are aware of defects and risks of defects are required to report them to appropriate levels of management. The failure to do so would be a clear shirking of that responsibility.

A deficiency finding, accepted as valid by management, obviously has described a risk to the enterprise. And the condition remains a risk until it has been fully corrected. Failing to monitor that risk until it is corrected — or until senior management has stated it will assume the risk — must be regarded as the abandonment of an audit responsibility.

The Statement of Responsibilities of Internal Auditors holds that internal auditing is a managerial control which functions by measuring and evaluating the effectiveness of other controls. Internal auditing is responsible for appraising operating management's quality of performance in carrying out its responsibilities. It is thus an extension of top management. It is management's antenna tuned to all the various controls and operations in the enterprise. To be effective, the antenna must maintain its vigil as long as the controls or the operations need surveillance. This is underscored by the sentence in the Statement which says, "Internal auditors are concerned with any phase of business activity in which they may be of service to management."

So broad a mandate asserts that the antenna must be tuned to the measures needed or taken to correct weaknesses in controls or performance. The antenna cannot be turned away until these are judged satisfactory. It would be inconsistent for the auditor to be charged with detecting a systems defect in the initial examination and then be excused or prevented from detecting defects in the means used to correct the defect, or from highlighting the failure to achieve correction.

Another argument advanced against internal auditors' following up on corrective action is that they are staff, not line. That is true, and internal auditors should not take on line functions. But following up on corrective action is not a line function. It is a staff function designed to assess action by the line function. It is carrying out its own responsibility for appraising the quality of performance in carrying out assigned responsibilities.

There is little value in applying rigid rules to judging the propriety of corrective action. Certainly it should be **responsive** to the reported defect, it should be **complete** in correcting all aspects of the defect, it should be **continuing,** and it should be **monitored** so as to ensure effectiveness and prevent recurrence. Here is an example of corrective action that did not meet these four criteria:

> A company used various forms of explosives in its operations. Handling explosives, as one might expect, requires care and experience. That lesson was learned in a shocking way when a careless, untrained worker blew off his own arm and blinded a co-worker.
>
> After that accident it became company policy to require all explosives handlers to complete a course on the subject, to be certified in explosives handling, and to be given a card attesting to the certification. The handlers were to be re-certified each year after being tested for their knowledge and ability in dealing with explosives.
>
> The internal auditors examined the certification procedures and the status of certification for a number of the handlers. They found that no system existed to inform the handlers or their supervisors that their annual examinations were due. Also, they questioned 30 out of the 100 explosives handlers and found that two had not been certified at all and that the certification of three others had expired. All five were engaged in daily explosives handling.
>
> The internal auditors promptly reported their findings. In response, the production manager had the five employees tested and certified. He then reported that information to the internal auditors, stating that he had thereby corrected the deficient condition.

The corrective action was inadequate on all counts and was rejected by the internal auditors for the following reasons:

It was not **responsive.** It did not deal with the controls over certification.

It was not **complete.** Only the handlers in the auditors' tests were considered.

It was not **continuing.** No system had been installed to make sure that handlers and their supervisors were notified about pending expirations of their certificates.

It was not **monitored.** There was no provision — other than periodic internal audits — to see that people handling explosives were trained and certified.

The auditors explained the defects in the corrective action to appropriate personnel. As a result, the following additional corrective action was taken:

A card record containing the names and the certification expiration dates for each handler was set up in the personnel department, which was responsible for the training and certification.

All 100 handlers were checked for valid, up-to-date certification cards.

One month before the expiration of a handler's certification, the manager of each handler was to be notified that recertification was required. They were also to be notified of any handlers whose certifications had expired.

The chief safety engineer instructed his engineers, who toured the plant to detect safety violations, to verify that anyone seen handling explosives had a current card evidencing certification.

Authority

Responsibility cannot be carried out without commensurate authority. The audit responsibility to appraise the adequacy and effectiveness of corrective action is meaningless if the auditor is not authorized to do so. Busy operating managers in such circumstances are likely to respond to auditors' objections with "I'm running my shop. I took what action I thought appropriate. It satisfies me. What authority do you have to tell me differently?"

These are the kinds of comments the internal auditors are likely to hear unless senior management clearly delegates authority to them to be the judges of whether proposed corrective action is calculated to correct reported deficiencies. This authority must be spelled out clearly in the internal audit charter (see Chapter 16). All managers should be made abundantly aware that corrective action must be real and effective or else the auditors have the authority to reject it.

Of course, internal auditors may not dictate the precise form of corrective action. If an operating manager proposes or takes action that does not square with what the auditors recommend, they should give it a chance to succeed or fail — unless it is clearly unacceptable or does not meet the four criteria just discussed.

If internal auditors are given the right to follow up on their findings, they should exercise that right properly. Mere promises of corrective action should be regarded as insufficient. Many an operating manager wants the auditor rather than the problem to go away. Thus, audit projects should not be closed until the defective condition has been completely cured.

Not all defects can be promptly corrected, however. Some require research, procedural work, or reorganization — all of which may take some time. However long the action takes to complete, operating managers must get accustomed to the idea that internal auditors do not relax their vigilance until the job is done. Promises for improved controls should be fulfilled with the actual installation of those controls. Promises for a reduced incidence of error may have to be checked out by additional tests of transactions.

Operating managers must learn that internal auditors will not permit themselves to be led down the garden trail with empty promises; assurances of corrective action will be thoroughly verified. In some audit departments, interim audits are made of major deficiencies to make sure the corrective action has remained effective. Because of their restricted scope, these audits are usually assigned to assistant auditors as training grounds to test their ability to handle an audit assignment on their own. Such audits should be formally assigned and should result in formal — albeit brief — audit reports.

Selling Audit Findings

People tend to gag on what is thrust down their throats. "You must!" is sure to raise hackles. The very same course of action that people would espouse if they thought of it themselves may be rejected, or at least resented, if recommended by another. The fact that a defect is valid and that the audit recommendation to correct it is logical and reasonable does not guarantee its acceptance by the auditee. The built-in resentment of an auditee being appraised and criticized may explode in the face of the auditor's statement: "Here's what I think you should do." Auditees convinced against their will are of the same opinion still. Such is the nature of human beings. Resentment can cause auditees to work harder to scuttle a good recommendation than to carry it out.

So it is clearly to the internal auditor's benefit to sell rather than tell, and the selling process should start early on. At the preliminary meeting, auditors should assure the auditees that they will be told promptly of every defect they encounter. The finding and the support for it would be thoroughly discussed. Any questions as to the facts would be resolved before the matter is reported. The auditee would be given every opportunity to initiate corrective action. In the final audit report, prominent space would be given to any action completed or started. The audit finding would be reported as "our finding" rather than the auditor's finding, if at all possible. No finding would be given any more weight or stress than it deserves. Minor findings would not be puffed up into major ones. Insignificant findings would not be formally reported at all, so long as they are corrected.

With that attitude on the part of the auditor, most auditees will go along with the proffered problem-solving partnership. The possibility of selling findings is further improved if they are fully and clearly communicated so that the auditee and auditor have a common view of the facts and their interpretation. This may require oral presentations, including charts and exhibits. The sale can benefit also from interim reports or memorandums similar to those previously discussed.

The desirability of selling a finding to the auditee should never deter the auditors from their primary purpose — to see that the defect is corrected. Some auditees, despite the best efforts of the auditors, may be recalcitrant and unconvinced. In such circumstances, the auditors may have to see the auditee's superiors. Very often, the higher up the management ladder the auditors have to climb, the more their findings will be regarded objectively.

At the higher level of management, auditors should carefully prepare their case. Senior management may not have the intimate knowledge of conditions that the operating managers have. Hence, the presentation should be clear, understandable, and convincing. Flip chart presentations have been found useful in explaining the problems and demonstrating the need for corrective action. It is especially important to make sure the presentations properly explain the goals and standards for the operation in question, the conditions, the procedures and practices, the cause and effect, and the conclusions and recommendations.

Conclusion

Deficiency findings describe conditions that are wrong and that must be corrected. Suggestions for improvement are helpful hints which managers may or may not adopt. Deficiency findings are implied criticism. They must therefore be carefully developed lest they themselves be subject to criticism. They should be accurate, significant, logical, and so presented as to promote action. The human element is especially important in dealing with deficiencies. Nobody likes criticism, yet few people will object to seeing a weakness strengthened. The secret in getting deficiency findings accepted is to avoid the implication of the pointed finger. If auditees see a condition as "our finding" and "our corrective action," they are more likely to accept the finding and take the needed action.

Internal auditors have an inherent responsibility for following up on corrective action. It is integral to identifying risks. Hence, as long as a risk remains and is known, internal auditors may not relax their vigilance. The internal auditor's responsibility cannot be dodged if an operating manager refuses to listen to reason. Internal auditors must take whatever steps are needed to get significant defects corrected, even if it means taking the matter to the highest councils of the enterprise. Internal auditors are excused from following up until a finding is corrected only if senior management or the board states that it is willing to accept the risk.

References

1. "The Round Table," *The Internal Auditor*, August 1979, p. 71.
2. "The Round Table," December 1979, p. 67.
3. "The Round Table," December 1979, p. 66.
4. "The Round Table," June 1979, p. 79.
5. "The Round Table," August 1978, p. 72.
6. F. J. Kenney, "Abstracts of Findings Offer Communication Techniques for Internal Audit Reporting," *The Internal Auditor*, December 1979, p. 78.
7. E. W. Stepnick, "The Nature and Development of Audit Findings," *The Internal Auditor*, December 1976, p. 35.

Supplementary Reading

Bradt, J. D. "Effectively Presenting the Audit." *The Internal Auditor*, July/August 1969, pp. 43-49.

Hallinan, A. J. "There Is No Escape From Follow-up Except . . . ." *The Internal Auditor*, January/February 1974, pp. 31-38.

Kenney, F. J. "Abstracts of Findings Offer Communication Techniques for Improved Audit Reporting." *The Internal Auditor*, December 1979, pp. 78-80.

Sawyer, L. B. "What's a Deficiency Finding?" *The Internal Auditor*, July/August 1971, pp. 68-70.

Scantlebury, D. L. and R. B. Raaum. *Operational Auditing.* AGA Monograph Series, Number One. Arlington, Virginia: The Association of Government Accountants, 1978, pp. 5-17.

Stepnick, E. W. "The Nature and Development of Audit Findings." *The Internal Auditor*, December 1976, pp. 30-35.

For further study

Discussion Problems

1. Give an illustration for each of the following types of deficiencies. Do not give any of the illustrations shown in this chapter.

a. An unsatisfactory system,

b. An action taken improperly,

c. A required action not taken at all,

d. An action that was taken although prohibited.

2. Contrast recommendations and suggestions as used in this chapter.

3. Are the following matters recommendations to correct deficiencies or suggestions to improve otherwise acceptable conditions?

a. Use a copy of the purchase order as a receiving memorandum.

b. Have the legal department inform the purchasing department of all new laws affecting the procurement of supplies and services.

c. Install a system to see that safety laws are being followed.

d. Improve supervision to reduce the number of errors found.

e. Install a conflict-of-interest program whereby employees annually assert in writing that they are not involved in any interests which conflict with their duties.

f. Install a log to record transactions which were being lost.

g. Issue instructions forbidding hourly employees from punching time clocks for fellow employees.

In connection with items b, c, e, and g, the audits disclosed no improper transactions. Would your answer be different if they did?

4. Why must action be taken on a deficiency but not necessarily on a suggestion for improvement?

5. Contrast insignificant, minor, and major deficiency findings.

6. Internal auditors should be concerned with improving conditions but they should not demand perfection. Why?

7. How should insignificant deficiencies be reported?

8. If one random human error is insignificant and one each of many random human errors is also insignificant, how

should the latter be treated in reports to management?

9. Identify each of the following findings as major, minor, or insignificant:

a. The personnel department was not obtaining required approvals from the medical department for extensions of prolonged leaves of absence due to medical reasons.

b. The information counter of the group insurance department was not staffed during relief periods.

c. The purchasing department entered into cost reimbursement contracts without verifying — or having internal auditing verify — that the suppliers' records were adequate to record costs accurately.

d. Processing time for group insurance claims is considered adequate if it is less than 7 days. Tests disclosed only 46% were processed in that time. About 15% took over 30 days to process.

e. Because of inadequate controls, the names of 2 out of 24 employees who had been discharged with recommendations not to rehire were not added to the screening file of the investigations unit.

f. The records did not always give explanations for the amounts paid to employees in settlement of grievances resulting from layoffs.

g. Personal funds totaling $160 were commingled with the authorized fund of $250 in the petty cash box.

h. When materials are sent out to suppliers for processing, the procurement action is not always properly documented.

i. Purchase orders for the procurement of contract labor were not being routed to the chief accountant's office for approval of terms and accounting procedures.

10. State whether the following statements describe conditions, standards, causes, effects, or recommendations.

a. Supervisors were not reviewing employees' work to detect errors.

b. Because the supervisors were not reviewing employees' work, discounts totaling $18,000 were not earned.

c. Of the 400 vouchers the internal auditor reviewed, 250 were paid after the discount periods had expired.

d. All invoices are to be paid within the discount period.

e. We believe that invoices should be filed in chronological order to facilitate the taking of discounts.

11. What benefits accrue from reporting deficiency findings currently to management?

12 Explain why internal auditors, rather than executive management, operating management, or the systems and procedures people, should follow up on corrective action.

13. Describe the attributes of corrective action.

14. What authority should internal auditors be accorded in terms of corrective action?

15. For the following reported statements of deficient conditions, describe (1) the evidence of corrective action you would consider satisfactory and (2) the steps you would take to see that corrective action has in fact been taken.
The buying organization within your company is staffed by about 100 buyers. They are assigned to five different groups and report to five different managers, each of whom is responsible for the procurement of different types

of products. You have made a test of 100 purchase orders involving purchases large enough to require written bids. You have found that:

a. Bids were being mailed by the buyers rather than by an independent person.
b. The bid forms were being delivered directly to the buyers by the mailroom, after completion by the bidders, instead of to an independent person.
c. The bids were not stamped with the dates of receipt.
d. Requests to purchase — prepared by the organizations needing the purchased materials — were held by the buyers pending receipt of the bids and not by an independent person.
e. Bids were being opened and posted to the bid record as received and were not being held until closing date.

Multiple Choice Problems

1. After internal auditors report deficiency findings that have not yet been corrected, they should:
a. Correct the defect themselves.
b. Dismiss the matter from further consideration.
c. Evaluate the corrective action after it has been taken.
d. Prescribe the action to be taken.
e. Inform top management that it should monitor the corrective action.

2. Discussing audit findings with an auditee in advance of drafting a report is most advantageous when:
a. There is agreement on the facts.
b. Fraud is suspected.
c. Corrective action is needed.
d. The findings are significant to operations.
e. Management previously took corrective action.

3. During the preliminary meeting with the auditee, internal auditors should:
a. Discuss the audit approach.
b. Seek to set a cooperative tone for the audit.
c. Discuss the audit objectives.
d. Discuss the treatment of findings.
e. All of the above.

4. Oral reports of significant audit findings:
a. Require a lower level of factual support than is required for written reports.
b. Should be used only when timeliness is a factor.
c. Do not need the careful organization used for written findings.
d. Eliminate any need for visual aids.
e. None of the above.

5. In seeking to demonstrate the support for an audit finding, and where audit objectives are not compromised, internal auditors may:
a. Show their charter to the auditee.
b. Show their working papers to the auditee.
c. Enlist the aid of an expert.
d. Present copies of relevent tab runs.
e. Bring into the meeting the person who was responsible for the defect.

6. Deficiency findings are reportable only if they are:
a. Documented by evidence which is sufficient, competent, and irrelevant.
b. Supported by sound audit opinions.
c. Buttressed by leads gained during the preliminary survey.
d. Capable of being given a dollar value.
e. None of the above.

7. A major deficiency finding is one which:
a. Involves losses of more than $500.

b. Involves more than five transactions.

c. Is repetitive.

d. Prevents the meeting of a significant operating objective.

e. Would shock the conscience of a reasonable person.

8. Once the facts relating to a deficiency have been gathered,

a. The finding should be reported in writing to management.

b. The reasoning behind it should be analyzed.

c. It should be included in the audit report.

d. It should be reported orally to management.

e. All of the above.

9. The following statement describes the condition (facts) in a finding:

a. We tested 100 invoices and found that 14 had been improperly paid.

b. As a result, $4,380 had been overpaid.

c. Accounts payable employees had not received current copies of purchase order changes.

d. Buyers are required to prepare change orders immediately and send copies to accounts payable the same day.

e. Buyers' supervisors had not been monitoring the prompt issuance of change orders.

10. Internal auditors should follow up on action taken to correct reported deficiency findings,

a. Because internal auditors are line personnel.

b. Because internal auditors are staff personnel.

c. Because a deficient condition represents a perceived risk.

d. When executive management specifically tells them to.

e. When operating managers will not otherwise take the required action.

Case Studies

7-1 Aircraft Maintenance

The following statement of a deficiency appeared in a final audit report: Company aircraft were not being maintained adequately. Our tests of maintenance records showed that none of the five aircraft were being maintained within proper time spans. Records showed that all aircraft were given routine maintenance at intervals of from seven to eight months. The cause was failure to schedule maintenance periods properly. The effect may be failure of the equipment. We recommend that records be established for the prompt and periodic maintenance of aircraft.

Required: What element of a completely developed deficiency finding is missing from this statement?

7-2 Charges for Parts-Repair Work

The following deficiency finding is included in an interim audit report prepared during the course of the audit:

Subject: Controls over the billing of charges for parts-repair work.

Current procedures provide for using prenumbered sales order forms and recording sales orders for repairs in manually maintained logs. These procedures also provide for creating manually serialized shipping documents. These shipping documents are recorded in the sales order log, which closes the sales order and may give rise to a billing for the repair work. (Some work is done on a "no-charge" basis.)

Our examination of the sales order log disclosed a significant number of sales order numbers unmatched by shipping document numbers for the past two years. As a result, it is uncertain whether the repair work performed for those orders had been authorized. Specifically, we found that the sales order logs showed "no entry" for 71 (about 18%) sales order serial numbers spread randomly over a range of about 400 serial numbers covering a recent twelve-month period. This indicated that billing personnel had not received sales orders for, or information about, the disposition of those serial numbers. Further investigation disclosed that 50 of the serial numbers showing "no entry" related to sales orders which had been voided or related to billings which had been closed at no charge. In addition, 16 other serial numbers related to sales orders which, in fact, were issued and were still open. However, we were unable to account for the remaining 15 serial numbers.

The interim report contains errors made by the internal auditor. The errors involve numbers, computations, and logic.

Required: Identify three errors made by the internal auditor and state how you would correct each one.

7-3 Bank Reconciliations

Internal auditors should recognize and take into account certain attributes when reporting an audit finding requiring corrective action. These attributes are:

a. Criteria — what should be done
b. Facts — what was wrong
c. Cause — what created the deficiency
d. Effect — the potential or actual adverse results and their materiality
e. Recommendation — the action needed or taken to correct the deficiency
f. Action — the action taken before the issuance of the report

The ten sentences which follow were selected from an auditor's working papers. Some of these are relevant to the formulation of an audit finding. The sentences are numbered for ready identification:

1. After the reconciliations were made, four bank errors that had gone undetected for as long as five months were disclosed.

2. Accounting Procedure 101.1 calls for the general accounting department to make monthly reconciliations of all bank accounts.

3. The bank statements and canceled checks are delivered to general accounting on the 5th of each month.

4. We found that the last reconciliation of the payroll account had been made six months before the date of our audit.

5. The differences between the bank balance and the ledger balances totaled $19,876.

6. A discovery sample of 437 canceled payroll checks gave us a 94.5% assurance that we would have found an improper item, assuming the existence of 25 improper items.

7. We discussed the matter with the manager of the General Accounting Department, and as a result, he issued instructions to have the bank and ledger accounts promptly reconciled.

8. Before we completed our audit, the accounts were reconciled.

9. The manager of the General Accounting Department had given a low priority to bank reconciliations.

10. A senior accounting clerk was assigned the responsibility for keeping reconciliations current.

Required: You are asked to construct an audit finding that includes all those sentences essential for an understanding of the finding but that excludes matters which, while interesting, are not directly relevant. List the sentence numbers 1 to 10. After each number, show the letter of the attribute represented by the sentence. If a sentence is irrelevant to the finding, show the letter g after the number.

7-4 Purchase Order Approvals

You have made an audit of buying activities in a large purchasing organization employing buyers, buying supervisors, buying managers, and a director of purchasing. One of your audit objectives was to test the approval procedures, which call for written approvals of the buying actions at varying levels, depending on the dollar values of the purchases. You have examined 50 purchase orders and have found that in 15 instances involving several buyers the purchase orders were typed and issued to the suppliers without the written approvals at the prescribed levels.

In her required written response to the audit report discussing the condition you found, the director of purchasing stated that she would issue instructions to her people to be more careful in the future about complying with approval procedures.

Required: (1) Describe two major shortcomings of the director's response and (2) give two additional steps the director of purchasing could prescribe that would help prevent a recurrence of the condition.

7-5 Getting Management to Take Action

Marv Johnson called his supervisor Bob Wolcott and told him he had a problem.

"What's up?" asked Bob.

"I've run into a problem on this payroll job I'm on," said Marv.

"You mean that retroactive adjustment?"

"Right," answered Marv. "As you know, when the company and the union agreed on the new contract, one of the clauses called for a retroactive increase for all hourly represented employees back to the effective date of the contract."

"I remember," replied Bob. "I understand that it was all handled by EDP. What's the difficulty?"

"Well, during the retroactive period, a number of changes occurred. Lots of salaried people were cut back to hourly. There are also problems with shift differentials and other matters, all of which are beyond the capacity of the computer program set up to take care of the retroactive pay. As a result, all the computer can do is spit out a tab run of exceptions."

"So?"

"The exceptions have to be worked over manually," said Marv.

"Are there many?" asked Bob.

"There are 849 of the blasted things!" roared Marv.

"No need to get emotional about it," said Bob. "Do they amount to anything in terms of dollars?"

"The individual ones come out to an average of about $3.50 owing to employees and about $3.25 owing from employees. That's a rough estimate based on a small sample. But some of the adjustments go as high as $15 either way."

"Why don't they work them off?" asked Bob.

"Payroll's short handed and the department manager, Tod Hicks, said he'll be hanged if he's going to spend precious hours on that chore. He'll pay employees who complain and forget about the rest."

"What does Jay Raynor, the chief

accountant, have to say about that? He's Tod's boss."

"Jay said that he made a management decision to go along with Tod's way of solving the problem," said Marv.

"Where does he think he gets off?" snarled Bob. "He's got no authority to do that."

"Now who's getting emotional?" asked Marv. "At any rate, Jay thinks he's got the authority."

"If the union got wind of this, they'd nail us to the wall," protested Bob. "And John Thompson, the vice president-controller, would want to know where in the world the internal auditors were."

"I'm with you," agreed Marv. "I've got a tiger by the tail and can't let go."

"I'll set up a meeting with Jay and Tod and we'll hash this thing out with them. I see this as a major deficiency because it's a people problem that involves the union. It will have to be reported," said Bob.

"Jay thinks it's no deficiency at all; and even if it were, it would only be a minor one."

"We'll see about that," said Bob.

Required: Set forth the steps the internal auditors should take to convince Jay and Tod to take corrective action. Do you consider this a major or a minor finding? Why?

8

Working Papers

Working papers — the documentation for the audit. The many purposes of working papers. Neat, uniform, understandable, relevant, and economical working papers. Reasonable completeness. Simple wording. Logical arrangement. Minimum information for audit segments and for individual worksheets. Information on the covers of working paper files. The importance of summarizing information gathered. The different forms of summaries: statistics, meetings, audit programs, deficiency findings. Indexing standards: simplicity and flexibility. Pro forma working papers — the benefits and the dangers. Suggestions for pro forma papers. Reviewing working papers. Protecting and safeguarding the audit working papers. A sample set of working papers. Writing as the audit proceeds. Retaining and destroying working papers.

Introduction

What They Are

Working papers document the audit. They contain the records of preliminary planning and surveys, the audit program, the results of field work, and other documents relating to the audit. Working papers are prepared from the time auditors first launch their assignments until they write the final reports.

Skillfully prepared working papers are the trademark of the professionals — the experienced internal auditors who have learned from past audits how fleeting memory can be. Such seasoned auditors are rarely distracted by the pressures of field work, budgets, or intriguing investigations.

They carefully and currently record their findings and conclusions. Just as the scientist meticulously documents experiments, so do experienced auditors document their work and the supporting detail for their conclusions and opinions. Careful documentation is as much a part of the techniques of the internal auditor as it is of a research chemist.

What They Do

Internal auditors prepare working papers for a number of different purposes:

To serve as the repository of information obtained through questioning people, reviewing instructions and directives, analyzing systems and processes, and examining transactions.

To identify and document deficiency findings, accumulating the evidence needed to determine the existence and extent of the deficient conditions.

To help perform the audit in an orderly fashion, documenting what has been done, indicating what is still to be done, and giving reasons for what will be left undone.

To give support for discussions with operating personnel. Operations can be quite complex. Interrelationships of systems and organizations can be difficult to retain in memory. Rules and exceptions to rules can be legion. Well-documented explanations and charts in the working papers, indexed for ready access, can put the internal auditor on an equal footing with the people who live with the operations and understand them intimately.

To provide support for the audit report. Well-structured working papers make it easier to transfer material written during the audit to the pages of the interim and final audit reports. The auditor can develop a discipline that moves the field work documentation and the audit report on the same assembly line so as to reduce rephrasing and restructuring to a minimum and thereby cut the report-writing effort. The experienced auditor has one eye on the report throughout the entire audit project, keeping the field work relevant and pointed in the right direction.

To serve as a line of defense when audit conclusions and recommendations are challenged. Criticism, expressed or implied, is rarely taken kindly. It can lead to challenges from the one criticized. Such challenges must be rebutted with facts and proof. The working papers, properly developed and referenced, readily accessible with a minimum of fumbling, lend stalwart support to the auditor and a warm feeling of security.

To give a basis for supervisory review of the audit's progress and accomplishment. Supervision of the audit project should be current and continual. The working papers, as evidence of work done and to be done, are a much better index of accomplishment than unsupported oral assertations which may easily become general, distorted, or superficial. The supervisor's review of working papers can be specific and can materially benefit the audit. This review of work progress is seriously diminished in value if it is based solely upon conversation with the auditor. Further, the supervisory review itself should be documented. It is a means of control over the audit and an integral part of it.

To create background and reference data for subsequent reviews. Audit projects are usually repeated or followed up. Professional working papers make the repeat audit much easier and more economical. There is no need to plow the same ground and dig the same holes. The subsequent review can build on the earlier one and not have to start from ground zero.

To provide a means by which external auditors can evaluate the internal audit work and use it in their own assessment of the company's system of control. The best evidence available to external auditors is the internal auditor's working papers. The papers must therefore portray professionalism. Inadequate working papers will breed skepticism about the value of the underlying work. Acceptable working papers lend credibility to the internal audit work and can afford the external auditors a basis for reducing their own work.

To help facilitate peer reviews. More and more internal auditing organizations are becoming involved in quality control programs — self-evaluations. Either external auditors or consultants or other internal organizations are called upon to evaluate the internal auditing activity. Again, the internal audit working papers are a major factor in drawing conclusions about the internal audit work.

To serve as part of the documentation required by the U.S. Foreign Corrupt Practices Act. The Act requires an issuer to "devise and maintain a system of internal accounting controls sufficient to provide reasonable assurances" that certain objectives relating to management authorization, recording of transactions, access to assets, and accountability for assets are being met. Evidence of compliance must be documented. Part of that documentation can well be the working papers of internal auditors, but such working papers must be capable of standing the sharpest scrutiny.

The arguments for professional working papers are so numerous and compelling that internal auditors must prepare papers that are accurate, clear, organized, and professional, taking the following matters into account:

○ Documentation, including working paper arrangement
○ Summaries, including records of deficiency findings
○ Indexing and cross-referencing
○ Pro forma working papers

○ Supervisory review of working papers

○ Control over working papers

○ Sample working papers

○ Writing as the audit progresses

○ Retention of working papers

Documentation

Working papers should follow a reasonably consistent form and arrangement. Once auditors become accustomed to a workable format, they can give less thought to how the working papers are laid out and more to what they have to say.

Working papers should be economical — economical to prepare and review. It is easy to dump every scrap of information and every form and procedure into the papers, but they then become a confused mixture of miscellany which is difficult to assimilate and use. Working papers should be a **usable** record of work done — spare but complete. The professional auditor includes only what is essential and makes each worksheet serve a purpose that fits into the audit objectives.

Keep Papers Neat

Working papers should be easy on the eye. Preparing neat working papers is a form of discipline which professional auditors have developed painstakingly because they consider it important — and in the long run, economical. They regard neat working papers as a mirror of neat thinking.

With this attitude, auditors will consider carefully what they want to say in their papers before they say it. In that way they write just once, and what they write is neatly laid out and not crowded. Paper is cheaper than the time of both the auditors and their reviewers. Many auditors write on every other line of their papers as they develop their narrative comments so that interlineations needed later can be entered without crowding. It is far better to use more paper in the beginning — leaving parts of sheets unused — than to discard a partially completed sheet and have to start over again when not enough space was allowed.

To avoid confusion and error, all names and titles should be printed clearly and neatly. Only one side of a worksheet should be used. Material on the reverse side can easily be overlooked. Not everyone is blessed with clear handwriting. Budget pressures tend to speed up the writing and make it still less legible, so many auditors have learned to print as they prepare their working papers. With practice, they can print with reasonable speed and improved legibility. Working papers have been known to end up in courts of law. Sloppy papers lose their worth as evidence.

Keep Papers Uniform

All working papers should be prepared on paper of uniform size and appearance. When it becomes necessary to include pieces of paper that are smaller than the standard size, the small sheet should be fastened to a standard sheet. Larger pieces of paper should be folded in a manner that simplifies their later review.

Three-ringed binders are used successfully for audit working papers. They keep the papers from getting lost, and papers can be sorted, re-sorted, added to, or removed without difficulty. Dividers can be inserted to separate significant segments of the audit documents.

Keep Papers Understandable

Working papers should be clear and understandable. They should need no supplementary information. Anyone picking up the papers should be able to tell, without asking many questions, what the auditors set out to do, what they did, what they found, what they concluded, and what they decided not to do. Conciseness is important, of course; but clarity should not be sacrificed just to save time and paper.

Information obtained orally is rarely recorded verbatim. Auditors who paraphrase auditee comments should also record their understanding or interpretation of what the auditee meant. Then, to make sure there is no misunderstanding, the auditee should be asked to confirm the auditor's interpretations.

Keep Papers Relevant

Working papers should be restricted to matters which are relevant and material. They should be directly related to the audit objectives. The specific audit objectives should always be kept in mind. Matters which may be interesting but not relevant to these objectives should not appear in the working papers. Well-organized audit programs and effective instruction by supervisors can help insure the inclusion of relevant documents only. Where an audit approach was contemplated but abandoned, the reason for abandonment should be explained, and the related working papers should be retained.

The practice of having all working papers contain clear statements of purpose tends to assure relevance. If the purpose of the particular audit job cannot be spelled out, the information gained is likely to be irrelevant. If a mass of immaterial or irrelevant information is assembled, important information might well be overlooked or obscured.

Forms and directives should be included only when they are relevant to the audit or to the audit finding. Written directives may often contain much information that is not germane to the audit; only a few lines may be directly related to the audit purposes. On the first reading, therefore, the relevant portions should be underlined — in red or some other contrasting color — so that they stand out on subsequent review. Where the precise wording of a procedure is not needed to support a finding, it may be referred to in the working papers without taking the time or effort to reproduce it.

Keep Papers Economical

Auditors should avoid unnecessary listing and scheduling. To this end they will use copies of client's records or computer printouts as much as possible. They can show by distinctive tick marks what audit steps were carried out, recording their audit comments in the margins.

To keep their papers economical, auditors should try to cover as many tests as are feasible on the worksheet. The same sample can thus be used for a number of analyses. In many situations, several different tests can be combined on one set of worksheets, using the same sample documents. This saves field work time, saves worksheets, and also saves time in both supervisory reviews and in subsequent references to the working papers.

Internal auditors should not try to answer every conceivable question that can be raised. This is particularly true where tests indicate satisfactory conditions. Of course, if auditors find and intend to report weaknesses, they should be prepared to meet any challenge to their findings.

Internal auditors should make full use of the working papers developed in the prior audit. Flowcharts, system descriptions, and other data may still be valid. Those papers which remain useful should be transferred to the current working papers. They should be updated with current information, renumbered, rereferenced, initialed, and dated by the current auditors. The updated working papers are now the current auditors' working papers and they bear full responsibility for them. If there is anything moved forward from the prior working papers that does not reflect current conditions, and if there is anything with which the current auditors do not agree, they are charged with the responsibility for making any necessary changes.

Keep Papers Reasonably Complete

Working papers should leave nothing hanging. No questions asked should go unanswered. Nothing is so frustrating to a reviewer as finding a course of inquiry dropped without explanation. If a space has been left for a cross reference, it should be filled in. If a question is raised, it should be answered, or the reason for not answering it should be shown.

Auditors should keep a "to do" list with their papers on which they note matters still to be covered, new thoughts worth pursuing, and any other items not specifically set out in the program but warranting audit action. Then, each item on the "to do" list should be answered or otherwise commented on.

Every time supervisors review working papers, they should record their review notes or questions preferably on the left-hand side of a fresh worksheet. The auditors should answer each note and then record their answering comments on the other side of the sheet. The "to do" list and the notes become a part of the auditor's working papers.

Prior deficiency findings, at least from the prior audit, should be followed up. Management is generally quite interested in whether deficiencies previously reported have again come to light. The working papers should contain summaries of prior deficiencies as well as notes on their current status.

Keep the Writing Simple

Working papers should be simple and readily understandable to an uninitiated reviewer. Jargon should be avoided. If it is used, it should be explained in a separate part of the working papers — in a Glossary of Terms — along with all the other technical and arcane terms used in the activity and in the working papers.

Simplicity and clarity in the working papers do not demand perfect syntax. The strict narrative form is not essential. Brief telegraphic sentences can get the ideas across and save a lot of time.

The final test of a set of good working papers is whether another internal auditor, who had nothing to do with the assignment, could step into the job in midstream, pick up the papers, understand what was done, and proceed with the examination without wasted effort.

Use a Logical Working Paper Arrangement

Working papers ahould be arranged in a manner that makes them parallel with the audit program, with audited subjects arranged in the same order in the working paper file. Each distinct subject should be covered by a separate segment of the papers. The parallel relationship between the program and the working papers will afford ready reference during and after the audit.

For each segment of the audit the auditor should provide some general information in narrative form at the beginning of that part of the papers. Such information should include the objective of the operation being audited and background information — organization, volume statistics, and the control system.

For each audit segment, the auditors should spell out in the working papers the detailed purposes of the audit as they relate to that segment. These purposes should include, and where necessary expand on, the relevant matters set out in the audit program.

Also, auditors should explain in the working papers the scope of their audit — what they covered and what they did not cover. In this part of their papers, the auditors will discuss the sample selection methods they used and the size of their sample.

After they have made their tests and analyzed the results, auditors should record their findings. The findings should be restricted to the facts — the good as well as the bad. There should be no intrusion of an audit opinion at this time. This is not the point at which to draw conclusions. Rather, it is the time to set down the bald facts from which the conclusions will be drawn. Drawing conclusions before the facts are gathered and summarized can lead to bias. Auditors should try to segregate control from performance findings since control defects will generally require different kinds of correction than performance defects.

After the statement of the findings, auditors should then draw their conclusions based on what they found and make them a matter of record in their papers. Supported by their findings on control and performance — in terms of comparisons with standards — the auditors should state whether the conditions which they found are satisfactory or unsatisfactory; that is, whether the operation's goals were or were not being met. These conclusions, in the aggregate, will support the auditor's opinion on the entire organization or function reviewed.

Finally, auditors should document in their working papers recommendations to correct the conditions they found and the corrective action taken by the auditee.

Behind the narrative comments will be the records of the audit: the flowcharts of the control system, the schedules of audit tests, and the summaries of the findings. Each worksheet should generally contain the following information:

A descriptive heading. The heading should identify the company, organization, or function audited and indicate the nature of the data continued in the paper.

A reference to the audit project. This reference is to identify the number of the audit assignment.

Tick marks and other symbols. Tick marks and other symbols should be uniform throughout the audit. They should be small and neatly placed, useful but unobtrusive, and they should be explained in footnotes.

The date of preparation and the auditor's initials. The date should indicate when the worksheet was completed. The auditor's initials should appear on each worksheet. A separate sheet in the working papers should list the names of all the auditors on the assignment and their initials.

The reference number of the working papers. Working papers should be referenced as they are prepared and should be kept in logical groupings. There is nothing so discouraging — both to the auditor and the reviewer — as a mass of working papers unnumbered and uncontrolled.

Working papers may be prepared in pencil or pen. Pencil is preferred for schedules containing figures which may be changed. Narrative comments are neater when written in ink. Some internal auditors give their working papers a special look of professionalism by writing the worksheet and column headings in ink — these rarely change — and the remainder of the schedules in pencil.

Sources of the information appearing on a worksheet should be clearly identified. An independent reviewer should be able to retrace the auditor's steps without needing to ask for supplemental information.

To the extent practicable, worksheets should be cross-referenced to other related working papers and to the audit program. Effective cross-referencing often reduces the need to duplicate data. Where the data is especially important, column totals, cross-footed totals, and computations should be independently verified.

The cover of each file of working papers should show such identification as project number and code number, name of organization or function, subject matter, audit period or other applicable date, security classification if applicable, and volume number if more than one volume.

Each working paper file should contain a table of contents. The first file should also contain a summary table of contents, identifying the other files.

Summarization

Although we have touched on summarization briefly, it is worth special mention because of its importance in working paper presentation.

Auditors in their dash down the audit trail are reluctant to disrupt the tempo of their audit to summarize. If they fail to summarize often and currently, they are making a sad mistake. What they think they have grasped fully may be dispelled by the passage of time. The mind can be a rebellious servant, often retaining what it wishes rather than what is.

The process of summarizing provides an objective overview. It hauls back the mind to hard facts. It helps put findings in perspective. It distills the valuable findings from the dross. It focuses on what is significant and relevant and helps put in its proper place what is trivial and irrelevant. Auditors who periodically summarize their findings, both the good and the bad, retain firm control over their audit projects.

Summaries are beneficial, also, in tying together groups of working papers which relate to a particular point. They provide an orderly and logical flow to the various related papers and facilitate supervisory or other reviews of particular work segments.

Through indexing and cross-referencing, the summaries become the focal point in the working papers for any particular work segment. They thereby provide a mechanical control over the underlying working papers.

They also afford newer staff auditors opportunities to become acquainted with the exactness and preciseness required to analyze information. Summaries teach these auditors the need for clarity, conciseness, readability, and organization essential to the preparation of draft reports. Summaries often present the rationale and original thinking leading to the positions taken in audit reports, so the experience in preparing usable summaries provides valuable training in developing skills in analysis and writing.

Because of the diverse nature and scope of internal audits, auditors should be flexible in the design and preparation of summaries. Each should be tailor-made to the needs of the audit segment. A summary should be recognized as a working tool. It is a means to an end — not the end itself. It should be designed to assist auditors in the orderly progression of audit assignments. Although each auditor will have to decide on which summaries to use, here are some forms of summaries that can be helpful:

Summaries of Audit Segments

Each segment of an audit should be summarized in narrative form to show the audit subject, the audit purpose and scope, the findings, the conclusions and recommendations of the auditor, and any corrective action taken by the auditee. These types of summaries were discussed in connection with using logical working paper arrangements.

Statistical Summaries

Auditors often use statistical summaries which bring together the results of audit tests. The data scattered through the test schedules are built into a cohesive unit which is easy to read and deal with.

These summaries should be treated as a pyramid, with the final, compacted data gradually expanding out into the test schedules. The secret of good statistical summaries is the care with which they are structured. From the top summary to the individual test items, reviewers can move surely and accurately without having to use a pencil to compute or summarize data. The auditors have done it for them.

Summaries of Meetings

Discussions with the auditees — their observations, agreements, disagreements, and suggestions — should be summarized promptly to recall things exactly as they were said, not as they filtered through diminished recollection. The dates and the hours of the discussions may be valuable in case of later dispute.

Summaries in the Audit Program

As auditors complete a segment of their audit, they should make appropriate comments about their findings in the audit programs, comments which encapsulate their conclusions about the activity audited. The comments should be brief and explicit. As they read through the audit program, auditors will be aware of the course the audit is taking. It will tell them where they have been and where they must still go. It can tune them in to the quality of the operation's controls and performance. It can help them control the audit, and can be a cumulative thumbnail sketch of how they feel about the operation they are reviewing. Some brief examples are as follows:

Program Steps	W/P Ref.	Comments
Examine a representative number of drawings to see whether they are:		
Being properly checked	C-8	Unsatisfactory at Project A. See RAF-1*. Satisfactory at Projects B and C.

(*"RAF" refers to the Record of Audit Findings.)

| Meeting specifications | C-8 | Unsatisfactory at Project A. See RAF-2.* Satisfactory at Projects B and C. |
| Meeting schedule | C-8 | Unsatisfactory at Projects A and C. See RAFs 3 and 4. Satisfactory at Project B. |

(*"RAF" refers to the Record of Audit Findings.)

Summaries of Deficiencies

Perhaps the most important summary is of the deficiency findings. These matters need the most support. They result in the most discussion. The summary should place at the auditor's fingertips the relevant and significant facts about a finding. An illustration of a completed Record of Audit Findings is shown in Exhibit 8-1.

Indexing and Cross-Referencing

Good cross-referencing serves many purposes. First, it simplifies the supervisory review of the working papers. Although the internal auditor may have all relevant facts about an issue clearly in mind, the relationships between facts may not be that clear to someone else. The references should lead reviewers easily to the related facts in other parts of the working papers.

Second, it eases the path of the next auditor who uses the working papers for a follow-up review.

Third, it simplifies reference to the papers by the auditors when they later review their papers. In a heated review with the auditee, good cross-referencing helps prevent fumbling and bumbling — those terrible "stage waits" after the auditee has asked a pertinent and pointed question and the auditor frantically flips work sheets back and forth while the whole room sits in impatient silence.

And fourth, it improves the final product: the internal audit report. As the auditor prepares the draft of the report, the well-referenced papers reveal their supporting information readily and helpfully. The ill-referenced papers hide their secrets.

The system of indexing should be simple and flexible. Different kinds of reviews will call for different indexing patterns, but certain principles should apply. The system to be used in a particular examination should be considered and devised as soon as the audit program has been developed so the working papers can be referenced as the audit proceeds. The auditor thus avoids dealing with a mass of unreferenced papers where it is almost impossible to find anything.

One simple index system form is to use a capital letter to designate broad segments of the audit and Arabic numerals for the worksheets within the

---

Exhibit 8-1. RECORD OF AUDIT FINDING

RAF No. 4
W/P REF. No. C5, C8, C9

Organization: Eng. Branch — Project C Eng. Dep't:

Nature of Finding: No provision had been made to monitor drawings sent to the Checking Dep't. As a result, a large percentage of the drawings included in our test had been held by the Checking Department beyond the prescribed 20-day period.

Same finding disclosed in last audit: Yes_____ No___X___

Directives or procedures involved: Eng. Proc. D-79 permits only 20 working days from drawing completion to release.

Tests made:

    Population size_140___   Sample size_20____

    Method of selection of sample _Every 7th, with random start_

    Discrepancies: No._8___   %_14___

Causes: Project management had not considered the need for schedule control over drawings sent to check.

Corrective action: Controls were established to monitor drawings sent to check. See C-15 and C-16.

Discussion with auditee personnel:

Name	Title	Department	Date	Auditor
(1) R. Roe	Administrator	Proj. C Eng.	2/3/8X	LBS
(2) P. Snow	Proj. Engineer	Proj. C Eng.	2/3/8X	LBS
(3)				
(4)				

Comments by auditee personnel:

(1) Roe corroborated the accuracy of our findings and the cause of the delay.

(2) Snow agreed with the need for corrective action. He said he'd install the same kinds of controls as those used in Project B.

(3)

(4)

____LBS____	___2/4/8X___
Auditor	**Date**

---

segments. Some auditors make use of Roman numerals. This may be satisfactory for external broad divisions of a large audit project, but when the numbers go beyond I, II, and III, the auditors accustomed to Arabic numerals must translate the Roman numerals to the Arabic numerals in their minds. Indexing and cross-referencing are tedious enough without the added problem of translation.

Thus, capital letters and Arabic numerals are usually sufficient. They stand the test of good indexing systems: simplicity and infinite expansion. The capital letters can be repeated if the alphabet of A, B, C, etc., is exhausted in the first series of segments. For the next series, the auditor can use AA, BB, CC, and so on. The Arabic numerals can also be expanded to infinity. A1 can become A1.1 or A1.1.1 or A1.1.1.1.

We find this simple system much more preferable to some forms of indexing which can get to look like algebraic formulas. For example:

$$\frac{IX - A - 1 - a}{(a) - (1)}$$

The auditor should constantly strive for simplicity. A complete audit segment can run as simply as C1, C2, C3, C4, right through the entire segment. Breakdowns within the segment are seldom necessary. If the auditor needs to add worksheets, the system permits for ready expansion. For example, if a worksheet is to be added between C2 and C3, the C2 becomes C2.1 and the added sheet can be indexed C2.2.

The auditor in charge should expect assistants to keep their working papers currently referenced. But if they are to do the referencing within the scope of the project, they should be assigned a symbol at the same time they are assigned a task. The number of segments should be planned in the audit program. The letters of the alphabet can be assigned to the segments in the program. When assistants are given the appropriate symbol, D or D.1 for example, they can then be held responsible for indexing their papers and cross-referencing them within their segment, or a section within the segment.

Cross-referencing within working papers should be complete and accurate. Professional auditors sprinkle their references copiously throughout their working papers. The references are usually in red, or some other contrasting color so that they will stand out clearly. The references readily provide direct access to the working papers. This can be extremely important when the report is reviewed in draft form with the auditee. The auditee's request for amplification or supporting documentation can be promptly answered if the marginal references can send the auditor directly to the worksheet containing the desired information. Also, when the auditors are making their painstaking verification of the final report, the marginal references can save much valuable time and help prevent overlooking relevant material.

Pro Forma Working Papers

Budget and schedule often combine to make internal auditors cut corners. The most tempting corner to cut is the preparation of working papers which will meet professional standards.

Recognizing the dilemma, some audit organizations have developed working papers which contain preprinted information reminding the auditor of the key points to be covered in the audit. One internal audit organization developed some pro forma working papers which can be helpful.[1] In the following example, an index sheet identifies the segments of the audit and provides the initial reference symbol for each segment.

Item	Description	Ref.
Reports	Transmittal letter, audit report, replies	A
Plans	Audit objectives, steps to meet objectives, executive contact letter and pre-audit meeting	B
Flowcharts	Flowcharts and sampling plan	C
References	Procedures and practices	D
Prior audit	Reports and replies	E
Final meeting	Records and flip charts	F
Time	Estimated and actual	G
Administration	Audit control sheet, draft report, etc.	H

Forms were also developed for the audit program. Each sheet of the program is in two parts — the first provides space for the audit objective, the second provides space for the steps needed to achieve the objective. By using the form, auditors are required to state unequivocally what they are setting out to achieve. The audit steps then have to tie in to the objectives.

The audit worksheets provide for three sets of narrative comments. These are headed: Purpose of the Work, Work Done, and What the Auditor Concluded. Here again the auditors are compelled to show why they took certain steps, what the steps were, and what was concluded.

Separate pro forma sheets are used for interviews. The head of each sheet provides for information on the persons interviewed: their names, titles, and functions. Spaces are also provided for the location of the interview, the date, the start/stop time, and a heading for the Record of Interview, and for Key Points to Bring Up. The record of the final audit meeting provides space to show the location, date, and start/stop times for the meeting; the people attending; and the record of discussion.

Each auditing organization using pro forma working papers has to develop forms most suitable to its needs. The forms should be helpful and not restrictive. They should guide the auditors and make sure they cover all significant points — not just follow routines because the pro forma worksheet demands them. If these rules are obeyed, a system of pro forma working papers can be useful and can save valuable time.

Working Paper Reviews

As in many other activities, the best control is surveillance by knowledgeable supervisors. All working papers, therefore, should be reviewed. The review should be evidenced on each worksheet by the name of the supervisor and the date reviewed. The questions which the supervisors raised should be included with each group of working papers, and the papers should not be accepted until the questions have been answered to the supervisor's satisfaction.

The review process is essential because there must be assurance that the work on which audit opinions are based is clear, demonstrable, and objectively evidenced.

As supervisors review working papers, they should be concerned with whether the audit program was followed and any specific instructions to the auditors were complied with; the papers were accurate and reliable (they evidence adequate work performed, and they sufficiently support the audit findings); the conclusions reached were reasonable and valid; reviews with auditees were carried out and adequately recorded, and disputes were resolved; the auditing department's rules on working papers were followed.

Supervisors should review working papers as soon as possible after the papers are completed. In that way, disruption to the work is reduced and problems are resolved before reports are written and auditors are reassigned.

One auditing organization uses a special form to evidence the final review of audit working papers. Here are some of the standards that are shown on the form:[2]

Reports

Reported findings sufficiently cross-referenced to adequate supporting documentation.

Evidence that the full scope of the audit was carried out.

Plans

An adequate audit program developed.

The pre-audit planning documented.

Omissions of steps called for in the audit program explained.

Estimated and actual audit time adequately documented.

General

Flowcharts prepared.

Documentation on sampling plans sufficiently informative.

Reference material (policies, procedures, etc.) retained serves a constructive purpose.

Prior audit reports and replies included.

Prior deficiency findings investigated.

Post-audit meeting documented.

Administrative data completed.

Field Work

Each working paper section summarized as to work done and findings developed.

Summaries cross-referenced to appropriate supporting material.

Purpose, scope, and nature of work properly identified.

Auditor's conclusions shown.

Control Over Working Papers

The working papers are the auditors' property and should be kept under their control. The auditors should know exactly where the papers are during the conduct of the audit. Where there is danger of loss, they should be kept in a locked file or in a locked desk overnight. If they are taken to a hotel room they should be kept in padlocked brief cases or in locked suitcases. They should not be available to people who have no authority to use them. To do so invites people to misuse them, to remove information from them, to change information in them, or to read information not for their eyes.

This does not mean that auditors may not show their working papers to auditees under appropriate circumstances. It can sometimes be quite useful for the auditors to spread the results of their review before the auditee — where there are no indications of fraud, of course, or any damaging comments — so that the auditors are helped to evaluate significance, perspective, accuracy, and relevance. If company policy permits, internal auditors may let external auditors or government auditors see their papers — even copy them — to avoid duplicate work. But internal auditors must always know who has access to their papers.

Audit management must take a direct interest in the control auditors exercise over their working papers. There have been instances where a set of working papers — in the middle of the audit — have been lost. What a waste of money and time this can entail! Audit management should also be concerned with the ability of a substitute auditor to pick up the work done by an auditor who suddenly becomes unavailable. The rule should be: "Keep your working papers so guarded, so organized, so indexed and cross-referenced that the audit job can be picked up by the next auditor with a minimum of program interruptions."

Sample Working Papers

Exhibits 8-2 thru 8-11 are a sample segment of working papers. The exhibits demonstrate the preparation of papers in an audit of an engineering function. This segment deals with the release of engineering drawings after they have been prepared by the draftsmen.

Under "General Information" will be found the objectives of the activity, background information, and a discussion of the control system. The objectives of the activity will dictate the approach the auditors take in their review. The background information contains only enough to provide an understanding of the tests. The explanation of the control system is supported by a simple flowchart.

The "Scope" statement shows the source of information or records used in tests and the sample selection technique. The "Purpose" statement can be related to the objectives of the activity, because obviously the auditors are mainly interested in whether the activity's objectives are being carried out.

The "Findings" answer each item in the Purpose. They provide factual information only, since it is important in subsequent reviews to distinguish between provable facts and matters of audit judgment. The "Opinion" covers all the findings and provides the auditor's assessment of the findings. The "Recommendations" cover all significant defects found in the audit and indicate the action taken by the auditee to improve conditions requiring correction.

The supporting schedules describe the tests and highlight the deficient items. The schedules are then summarized in workable form. The corrective action is documented at the end of the working papers.

The format and arrangement shown in Exhibits 8-2 through 8-11 may not be applicable in all companies or in all circumstances. Yet such working papers have proved effective in many situations and are easy to prepare after only a little practice.

By following a standard working paper arrangement, the auditors will be able to complete one segment of the audit before going on to another — they will know just what each segment requires. They will leave no trailing ends. They will wrap up each segment completely. Even when they must leave the audit segment for a while to wait for data not currently available, the practice of completing sections of papers to the extent possible makes the return to them much easier.

Writing as the Audit Progresses

The internal auditors who are constantly pressed for time may doubt their ability to turn out working papers such as those illustrated in the exhibits, but good field work organization will do it. The secret is to write down comments while performing the field work.

The initial comments about objectives, background, controls, purpose, and scope can be prepared as soon as the auditors have made an initial review of the operation. They do not have to wait until the end of their audit of the segment. By that time, the chore becomes far too heavy and many of the facts become blurred in their minds. The findings can be summarized right after the tests have been made. The results are then immediately usable in discussions with the auditee.

Time pressures are an excuse, not a reason. If internal auditors wish to be

Exhibit 8-2. SAMPLE WORKING PAPERS: RELEASE OF
ENGINEERING DRAWINGS

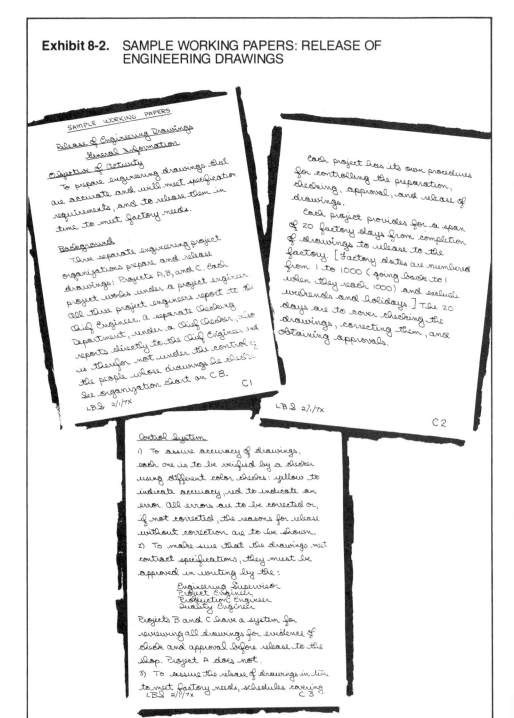

Exhibit 8-2. (Cont.)

drafting provide for completion of the drawings within 20 days of factory need dates. Project B has a follow-up system. Projects A and C do not.

4) All projects use registers to record completed drawings. All projects show release dates. Only Project B shows receipt dates. (See flow chart on C9)

Purpose

To determine whether control system is adequate to meet objectives of:

1. Accuracy
2. Meeting specification requirements
3. Meeting schedules

To determine whether performance is effective in that:

- All drawings are checked and corrected
- All drawings bear evidence of

LBS 2/1/7X   C4

---

approval

All drawings are released within 20 days of completion.

Scope

We took a judgment sample for our preliminary review of drawings released during the last half of 197X. We made a selection at random, using the interval selection technique, from the registers of released drawings maintained at each project. We decided to take a sample of 20 drawings as a preliminary test and expand our test if necessary. Since our findings were conclusive at each project, we decided not to expand the tests.

Control   Findings

1) Accuracy
2) Meeting Specs   Project A had no
    LBS 2/4/7X   provision for reviewing
                   C5

---

drawings before release or for evidence of checks and of approvals. Projects B and C did. C9.

Projects A and C had no follow-up system for drawings in process of checking. Project B did. C9.

3) Schedule

Performance

1) Accuracy
2) Meeting Specs

At Project A: 4 drawings by-passed the checks; 3 drawings had a total of 7 dimension errors. 13 drawings did not have the signatures of the Production Engineer.

At Projects B & C we found no errors. C10.

3) Schedule

At Project A -- 5 out of 20 drawings were 21 to 50 days late.

At Project C -- 8 out of 50 drawings were 10 to 30 days late.

At Project B -- all   C6

LBS 2/4/7X

---

drawings in sample were released on time C10.

Opinion

Project A — Controls over accuracy, meeting specs and schedule inadequate

Project B — Controls satisfactory

Project C — Controls over schedule inadequate

Recommendations

Install at Projects A and C the same system of control in effect at Project B.

The Project Engineers at A and C agreed with our recommendation. They issued instructions to their administrative assistants to that effect. See C15 and C16.

Subsequent reviews showed that the new controls were in actual operation.

LBS 2/4/7X

            C7

Exhibit 8-3. ORGANIZATION CHART:
TEST OF ENGINEERING DRAWINGS

Test of Engineering Drawings
For Timeliness and Release and Adequacy of
Check and Approval

ORGANIZATION CHART

PRESIDENT

CHIEF ENGINEER

PROJECT A
PROJECT ENGINEER
SECRETARY — 1
ADMINISTRATOR — 1
ENGINEERS — 5
DRAFTSMEN — 3

PROJECT B
PROJECT ENGINEER
SECRETARY — 1
ADMINISTRATOR — 1
ENGINEERS — 4
DRAFTSMEN — 2

PROJECT C
PROJECT ENGINEER
SECRETARY — 1
ADMINISTRATOR — 1
ENGINEERS — 5
DRAFTSMEN — 3

CHECKING DEPT
CHIEF CHECKER
SECRETARY — 1
CHECKERS — 4

C 8

LBS 2/1/7X

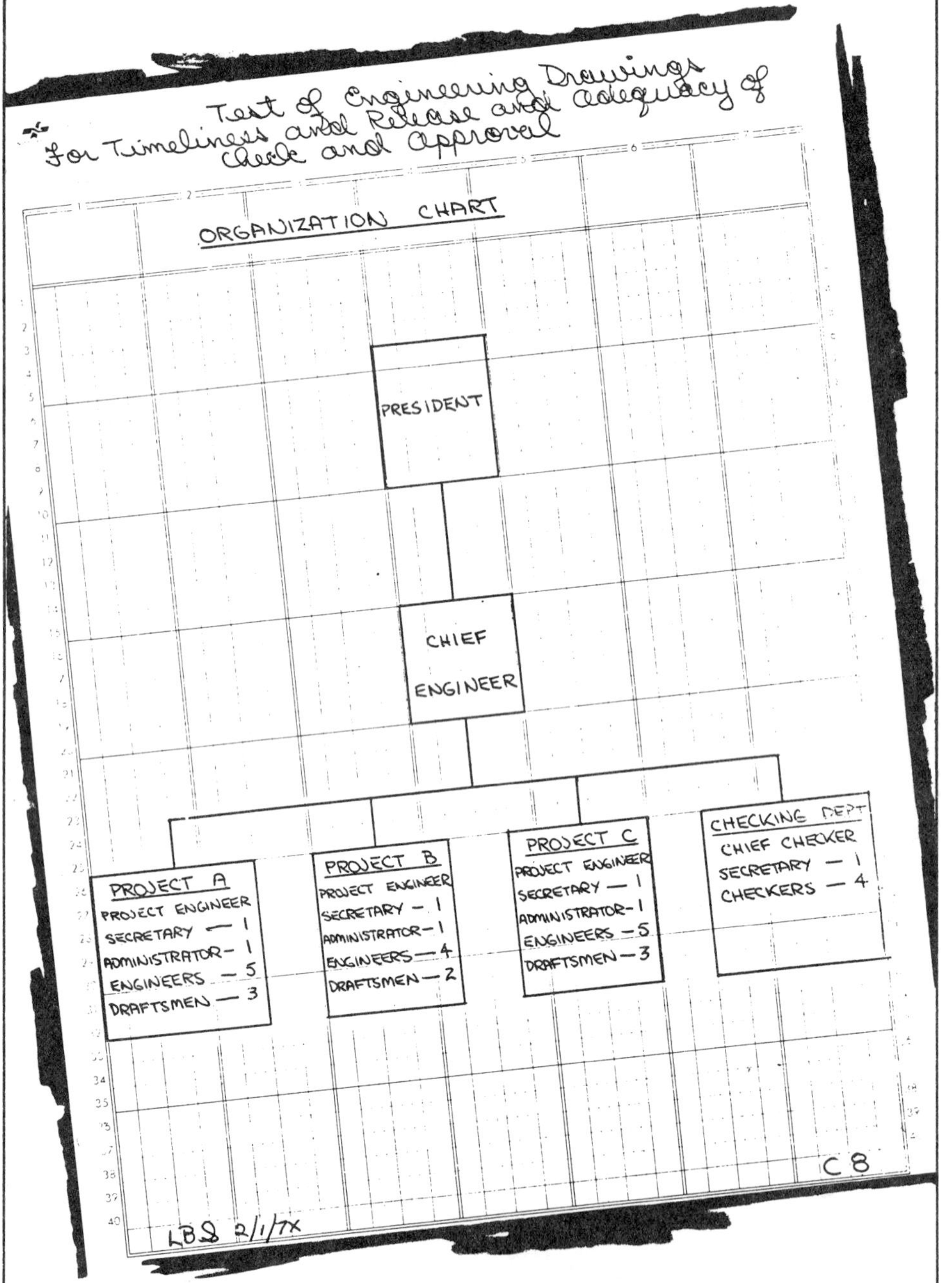

Exhibit 8-4. FLOWCHART:
RELEASE OF ENGINEERING DRAWINGS

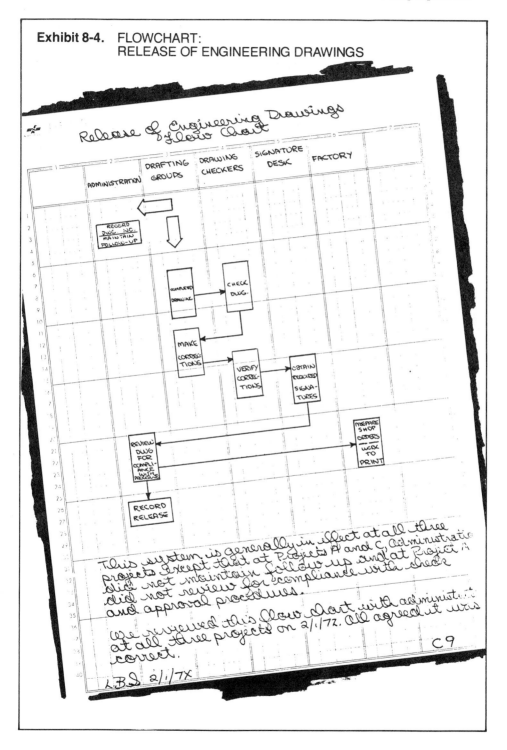

Exhibit 8-5. SUMMARY OF TESTS
OF ENGINEERING DRAWINGS

Test of Engineering Drawings
for Timeliness of Release and Adequacy of
Check and Approval

SUMMARY OF TESTS

			PROJECTS			TOTAL
		A	B	C		
				140		420
POPULATION: DWGS. ISSUED LAST 6 MOS, 197X		150	130			
SAMPLE: JUDGMENT SAMPLE, SELECTED AT RANDOM BY INTERVAL SAMPLING FROM DRAWING RELEASE REGISTERS SELECTED EVERY NTH STARTING WITH:		#3 20	#6 20	#1 20		60
	DELAYS	—	—	2		2
				2		3
10 TO 20 DAYS LATE "		1	—	2		4
21 TO 30 " " "		1	—	3		4
31 TO 40 " " "		3	—	1		4
41 TO 50 " " "		5	—	8		13

DRAWINGS BY-PASSING CHECK

4

UNCORRECTED ERRORS
NO. DWGS.   NO. ERRORS
3   7

UNOBTAINED SIGNATURES
NO. DWGS.   NO. SIG'S.
3   3

REASONS FOR DEFICIENCIES

DELAYS } PROJECTS A & C HAD NO SYSTEM OF FOLLOW-UP CONTROL
         PROJECT B HAD AN EFFECTIVE SYSTEM

BY-PASSING CHECKERS
UNCORRECTED ERRORS }
NO SIGNATURES } PROJECT A DID NOT PROVIDE FOR A REVIEW OF
                DRAWINGS BEFORE RELEASE TO FACTORY
                PROJECTS B AND C HAD AN EFFECTIVE SYSTEM

REFER TO C11

C10

LBQ 2/3/7X

Exhibit 8-6. LIST OF DISCREPANT ITEMS:
TEST OF ENGINEERING DRAWINGS

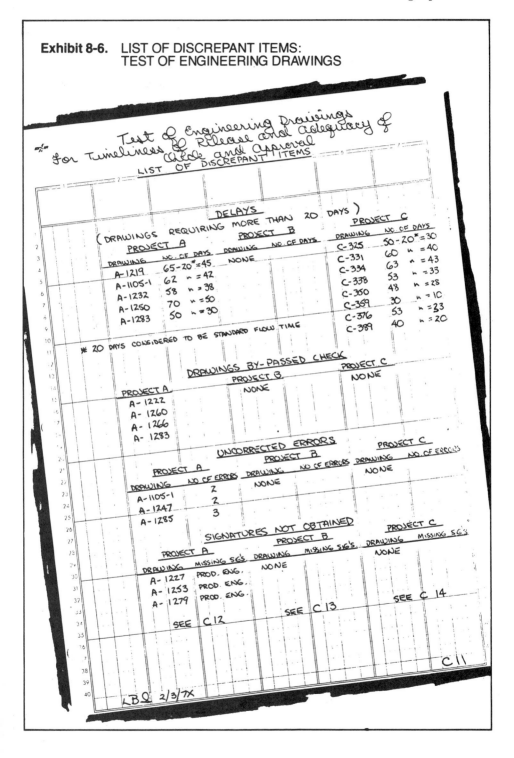

Exhibit 8-7. PROJECT A:
TEST OF ENGINEERING DRAWINGS

Test of Engineering Drawings
for Timeliness of Release and adequacy of
Check and approval
PROJECT A

DRAWING NUMBER	FACTORY DWG. PREP'D	DATE WAS REL'D	NO. OF DAYS BETWEEN PREP. & REL.	NO. OF DEFECTS PER CHECKER	COR-RECTED	REQUIRED APPROVALS SHOWN	COMMENTS
A-1206	605	615	10	3	3	YES	DWG. DELAYED IN CHECK
A-1219	550	615	65	7	7	YES	DWG BYPASSED CHECK IN ERROR
A-1222	600	616	16	0	0	YES	DWG. DELAYED IN CHECK. 2 ERRORS UNCORRECTED (NO REASON SHOWN)
A-1105-1	555	617	62	4	2	YES	PROD. ENG. DID NOT SIGN
A-1227	607	617	10	4	4	NO	DWG DELAYED IN CHECK
A-1232	560	618	58	5	5	YES	
A-1240	604	618	14	3	3	YES	2 ERRORS UNCORRECTED (NO REASON SHOWN)
A-1247	605	618	13	6	4	YES	DWG. DELAYED IN CHECK
A-1250	549	619	70	9	9	YES	PROD. ENG. DID NOT SIGN
A-1253	612	621	9	2	2	NO	DWG BYPASSED CHECK IN ERROR
A-1260	614	622	8	0	0	YES	DWG. BYPASSED CHECK IN ERROR
A-1266	612	622	10	0	0	YES	
A-1270	610	622	12	3	3	YES	
A-1274	611	622	11	4	4	YES	PROD. ENG. DID NOT SIGN
A-1279	612	624	12	3	3	NO	DWG BYPASSED CHECK (NO REASON SHOWN) PROD ENG. DID NOT SIGN, 3 ERRORS UNCORRECTED (NO REASON)
A-1283	575	625	50	6	6	YES	
A-1285	615	625	10	4	1	YES	
A-1290	617	627	10	3	3	YES	
A-1292	618	627	9	3	3	YES	
A-1296	619	628	9	2	2	YES	

ALL DIFFERENCES REVIEWED WITH ADMINISTRATOR JOHN DOE 2/3/72. WE AGREED WITH OUR FINDINGS.

LBJ 2/6/7X

C 12

Exhibit 8-8. PROJECT B:
TEST OF ENGINEERING DRAWINGS

Test of Engineering Drawings
for Timeliness of Release and Adequacy of
Check and Approval
PROJECT B

DRAWING NUMBER	FACTORY DWG. WAS PREP'D	DATE REL'D	NO. OF DAYS BETWEEN PREP & REL.	NO. OF DEFECTS PER CHECKER	COR-RECTED	REQUIRED APPROVALS SHOWN	COMMENTS
B-614	606	616	10	4	4	YES	
B-615	614	617	3	5	5	YES	
B-619	610	620	10	5	5	YES	
B-622	609	620	11	6	6	YES	
B-626	609	620	11	3	3	YES	
B-629	612	623	11	2	2	YES	
B-632	620	627	7	7	7	YES	
B-639	621	627	6	2	2	YES	
B-642	620	627	7	2	2	YES	
B-645	619	630	11	5	5	YES	
B-647	619	630	11	5	5	YES	
B-649	626	632	6	5	5	YES	
B-661	626	632	6	3	3	YES	
B-662	622	632	10	2	2	YES	
B-671	624	634	10	7	7	YES	
B-680	627	634	7	6	6	YES	
B-692	628	635	7	8	8	YES	
B-693	628	636	8	3	3	YES	
B-695	626	636	10	4	4	YES	
B-698	625	636	11	2	2	YES	

LBS 2/2/7X

C 13

Exhibit 8-9. PROJECT C:
TEST OF ENGINEERING DRAWINGS

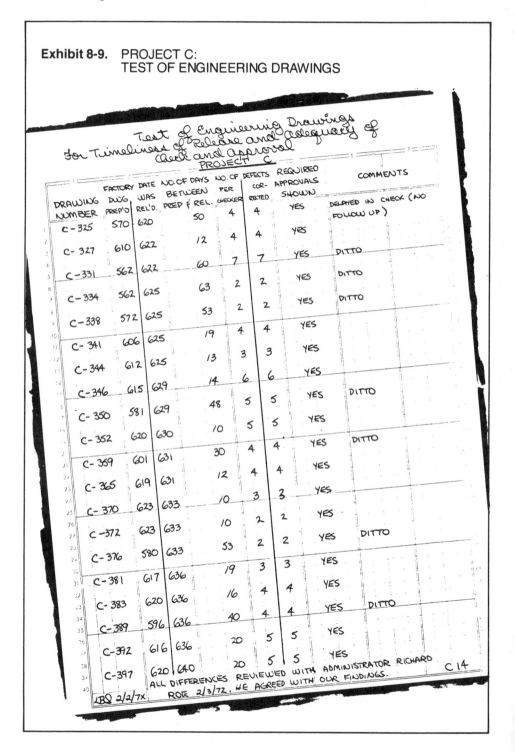

Test of Engineering Drawings
for Timeliness of Release and adequacy of
Check and approval
PROJECT C

DRAWING NUMBER	FACTORY DWG PREP'D	DATE WAS REL'D	NO. OF DAYS BETWEEN PREP & REL.	NO. OF DEFECTS PER CHECKER	CORRECTED	REQUIRED APPROVALS SHOWN	COMMENTS
C-325	570	620	50	4	4	YES	DELAYED IN CHECK (NO FOLLOW UP)
C-327	610	622	12	4	4	YES	
C-331	562	622	60	7	7	YES	DITTO
C-334	562	625	63	2	2	YES	DITTO
C-338	572	625	53	2	2	YES	DITTO
C-341	606	625	19	4	4	YES	
C-344	612	625	13	3	3	YES	
C-346	615	629	14	6	6	YES	
C-350	581	629	48	5	5	YES	DITTO
C-352	620	630	10	5	5	YES	
C-359	601	631	30	4	4	YES	DITTO
C-365	619	631	12	4	4	YES	
C-370	623	633	10	3	3	YES	
C-372	623	633	10	2	2	YES	
C-376	580	633	53	2	2	YES	DITTO
C-381	617	636	19	3	3	YES	
C-383	620	636	16	4	4	YES	
C-389	596	636	40	4	4	YES	DITTO
C-392	616	636	20	5	5	YES	
C-397	620	640	20	5	5	YES	

ALL DIFFERENCES REVIEWED WITH ADMINISTRATOR RICHARD
ROE 2/3/72. HE AGREED WITH OUR FINDINGS.

LBQ 2/2/7x

C 14

Exhibit 8-10.

To: Administrator, Project A
From: Project Engineer, Project A
Subject: Control over Drawings — Check, Approvals, Follow-up

An audit of our operations has disclosed that:
  Some drawings had bypassed the checkers,
  Some drawings did not bear all required approvals, and
  Some drawings had been delayed in check without proper follow-up.

The following procedures will be put into effect immediately, pending the issuance of suitable job instructions covering these matters:
  All drawings being released to production shall clear over the administrator's desk. He shall initial and date the release document to show that he has reviewed the document for evidence of: (1) check and (2) appropriate approvals. All documents not checked or approved shall be returned to the responsible individual by a brief memo, with copy to this office.

  The administrator shall establish and maintain a record of all drawings sent to check, showing the dates of release to and from check. Each week, the administrator shall prepare a report listing all drawings in check for more than 20 days. One copy of the report shall be sent to this office and one copy to the Chief Checker.

> /s/ P. Snow
> Project Engineer
> Project A

Exhibit 8-11.

To: Administrator, Project C
From: Project Engineer, Project C
Subject: Control over Drawings in Check

An audit of our administrative procedures has shown that drawings were delayed in the checking process without adequate follow-up.

Please install the following procedures immediately, pending the issuance of a job instruction:
  The administrator shall establish and maintain a record of all drawings sent to check, showing the dates of release to and from check. Each week, the administrator shall prepare a report listing all drawings in check for over 20 days. One copy of the report shall be sent to this office and one copy to the Chief Checker.

> /s/ T. Blow
> Project Engineer
> Project C

regarded as professionals, the evidence of their work must be professional. Internal auditors must have their work accepted by external auditors. It must pass peer reviews, and it should be acceptable as documentation within the requirements of the U.S. Foreign Corrupt Practices Act. Working paper techniques similar to those illustrated are therefore indispensable.

Retention of Working Papers

Working papers should be disposed of when they are of no further use. Once the subsequent audit of an operation has been completed, auditors should make a determination, approved by their supervisors, as to whether those papers should be retained or destroyed. When the prior working papers contain systems documentation or other material of continuing use, those sections of the papers should be carried forward to the current papers.

Some one-time audits, such as those relating to major contracts, may be held for a considerable period of time. Contractual or legal provisions may demand retention. A retention procedure and schedule for the internal auditing department should therefore be prepared and approved by legal counsel. Documentation evidencing compliance with the U.S. Foreign Corrupt Practices Act may have to be kept in separate files.

Conclusion

Nothing evidences the professional competence of an internal auditor as do working papers. The most significant findings, the most brilliant analyses, and the soundest conclusions will be lost unless they are carefully and clearly documented. Internal auditors must spend time during their apprenticeship in developing disciplines of professional working paper preparation. With practice, adequate working papers can become the accepted pattern rather than a dreary chore. The effort in turning out professional working papers is repaid by less fumbling, less wasted time trying to find elusive information, and less writing time needed for the audit report supporting the documented information.

As greater reliance is placed on the work of internal auditors by external auditors, the importance of adequate working papers escalates. Similarly, peer reviews will demand adequate evidence and documentation of the audit work. The demands of the U.S. Foreign Corrupt Practices Act also require documented evaluations of internal control systems. These pressures make it completely unacceptable for internal auditors to say they did not take the time to document their work adequately. The spoken word endures like yesterday's wind. Only what is clearly written can be lasting and useful.

References

1. C. W. Cater, Jr., "Standards for Working Papers," *The Internal Auditor*, April 1978, pp. 68-75.
2. Cater, p. 75.

Supplementary Reading

Aitchison, Tom. "Working Papers — Stepping Stones or Stumbling Blocks?" *The Internal Auditor*, March/April 1974, pp. 16-20.

Cater, C. W., Jr. "Standards for Working Papers." *The Internal Auditor*, April 1978, pp. 68-75.

Patillo, J. W. "Audit Working Papers." *Handbook for Auditors*, J. A. Cashin, ed. New York: McGraw-Hill Book Company, 1971, pp. 14-1 — 14-27.

For further study

Discussion Problems

1. Why is a consistent working paper format useful?

2. Why should working papers be neat?

3. What are some of the ways that the cost of preparing working papers can be kept at an economical level?

4. How can internal auditors economically summarize their audit findings as they proceed with the audit?

5. What are the standards for a good indexing system?

6. What are the minimum requirements for a reasonably complete set of working papers?

7. When should working papers be destroyed?

8. What should each worksheet contain besides the audit information?

9. How can the audit program be used to summarize audit work performed?

10. An auditor uses capital letters and Arabic numbers to index her working papers. She decides to insert two worksheets between worksheets C-5 and C-6, and one worksheet between D-8 and D-9. How should the inserted sheets be indexed?

Multiple Choice Problems

1. Control over working papers involves:

a. Cooperating with the auditee by granting unlimited access to the working papers.

b. Permitting review by external auditors only.

c. Placing the working papers overnight in the desk at which the auditor is working.

d. Discarding working papers in an office wastebasket.

e. Limiting access to appropriate personnel.

2. In the review of working papers, the supervisory auditor will look for:

a. Records of discussions of all deficiency findings.

b. Preparation of the working papers in a professional manner.

c. Adequate documentation of findings.

d. All of the above.

e. Both a and b above.

3. The **primary** purpose of audit working papers is to provide:

a. Evidence of the analysis of internal control.

b. Support for the auditor's report.

c. A basis for evaluating audit personnel.

d. A guide for subsequent examinations.

e. None of the above.

4. Which of the following excerpts from working papers would adequately

support a conclusion in an audit report?

a. "We are of the opinion that control over stores is adequate."
b. "A physical inventory disclosed a 9% shortage."
c. "The storekeeper appears to be doing a commendable job."
d. "We are of the opinion that requisitioning procedures are inadequate."
e. All of the above.

5. Good cross-referencing of working papers:

a. Requires the use of letters and Arabic numerals.
b. Calls for notation in red pencil.
c. Permits the elimination of an index for the working papers.
d. Facilitates independent review.
e. All of the above.

6. In discussing the audit findings, the internal auditor may show the audit working papers to the auditee when:

a. Performing an audit of negotiable securities.
b. Audit objectives are not compromised.
c. The auditee asks to see them.
d. The auditee would not otherwise take corrective action.
e. None of the above.

7. The internal auditor prepares summaries of data in working papers to:

a. Assist reviewers by assembling significant information.
b. Accumulate individual items into increasingly comprehensive digests.
c. Provide material for permanent retention.
d. All of the above.
e. a and b above.

8. Cross-referencing for working papers should be:

a. Done after completing the field work.
b. Used to confirm data previously recorded.
c. Consistently applied.
d. Referred to in the audit report.
e. a and c above.

9. Working papers should:

a. Document audit work performed.
b. Omit names of individuals.
c. Support conclusions and recommendations.
d. All of the above.
e. a and c above.

10. Working papers should be so maintained and referenced that they:

a. Represent a good historical document.
b. Can be readily filed and retrieved.
c. Can be readily completed by another auditor if the current auditor becomes unavailable.
d. Are a credit to the auditor in charge.
e. Do not get misplaced or lost.

Case Studies

8-1 Rules for Working Papers

You are an audit supervisor who has just received from an auditor a set of working papers. The auditor has obeyed some of the rules for preparing working papers but has violated others. You plan to compliment the auditor on what was done correctly and explain the reasons for your critical comment on what was done incorrectly. Accordingly, you have made the following notes on the review of the working papers, covering what you considered satisfactory and what you found unsatisfactory.

1. The auditor used only one side of each worksheet.

2. Each worksheet contained, in addition to the test information, a descriptive heading, a legend of tick marks and symbols, and the auditor's initials.

3. The working papers contained the auditor's handwritten transcriptions of pertinent procedures and job instructions.

4. The working papers were made up of 8½" x 14" worksheets. When smaller pieces of paper were used, they were fastened to those worksheets.

5. When appropriate information could be obtained, it was included in the working papers. Where information was unavailable, the auditor so indicated with a large question mark in red pencil.

6. Copies of all policy statements which had any relationship to the activity being audited were included in the working papers.

Required: For each of the above items (1) state the accepted practice for working paper techniques and (2) indicate whether the practice was observed or violated.

8-2 Improving the Working Papers

As audit supervisor, you are reviewing a set of working papers covering a completed audit assignment. The working papers consist solely of columnar schedules containing no narrative comments. All the tests set forth in the audit program were carefully carried out. All test items are listed and identified, and the tests performed are clearly indicated by appropriate tick marks properly identified in a legend on the worksheets. Items listed in the schedules to which the auditor took exception are underlined in red. The schedules contained proper headings, cross-references, dates, and initials.

Required: Give three suggestions you would make to improve these working papers.

8-3 Let's Make Sense Out of These Working Papers

Marv Johnson, auditor in charge in the audit of receiving operations, warmly greeted Phil Goldsmith, the assistant just assigned to his job.

"Man, do I need you," he said. "Art Lash got yanked off this job to do some emergency audits of patent royalties, and he left me in midstream."

"Art's pretty good at those royalty audits," replied Phil. "What was he working on for you?"

"Direct deliveries," answered Marv.

"Oh, those deliveries that bypass the receiving department," said Phil.

"That's right," said Marv. "I'm glad you know all about them."

"Hold on," Phil cautioned. "I don't know beans about them, except that they exist. Maybe Art's working papers will fill me in."

"You've just put your finger on it," said Marv.

"I did?"

"You bet. Art left me with a mess of scrap notes that will have to be put into shape."

"Didn't he write up the procedures?" queried Phil.

"No," said Marv. "And I could kick myself for not being on top of things. He really did a good job of sampling, and testing, and getting corrective action. But he didn't complete his papers. And that's what I'd like you to do. Here are his notes."

Marv handed Phil a 7-column worksheet that was partly completed, and a pile of different-sized pieces of paper containing Art's scrawls.

Phil looked at the accumulation briefly, and then said, "The worksheet seems okay, as far as it goes, but I can't even read what Art's got on his scrap notes."

"Okay," offered Marv. "I've gotten used to his scrawls. Let me read the stuff to you and you can make notes. Then you can complete the 7-column worksheet and put together a proper set of papers showing general information, purpose, scope, findings, opinion, recommendations, a summary of Art's tests and a record of audit findings."

"Fair enough," agreed Phil, and opened a pad of comment paper, with pencil at the ready.

"Art's job was to take a random sample of 40 receiving memos (RMs) and check the timeliness with which documents for direct deliveries were processed," said Marv.

"Any particular reason?" asked Phil.

"Yes. Accounts payable is crying about the delays in getting evidence of receipt of direct deliveries. As a result, they're not earning discounts, the suppliers are screaming, and some of them won't even deal with us any more."

"Sounds serious," said Phil. "Let's start at the beginning. Can anybody ask for a direct delivery?"

"No sir! The user department must be authorized to do so. Those authorized are provided with a 'direct delivery' (DD) stamp which they use to imprint the authorization on their requests to purchase (RTPs) that they prepare. The girls in procurement services will reject any DD request that is unauthorized."

"Can anything be delivered direct?"

"Almost always the item ordered is something that's off the shelf, that's needed immediately, and that's delivered the same day that the buyer orders it. All the items in our test were that way."

"What happens in procurement?" asked Phil.

"The buyer gets the RTP from procurement services, calls the supplier, and tells him what's needed and where to deliver it. Then procurement is required by purchasing directive 123 to get the purchase order (PO) issued and have it in the hands of receiving people no later than three days after the order is placed."

"Why so fast?"

"If the PO is not down there, the receiving people can't write an RM and get it to accounts payable in time to earn the discount," Marv answered.

"How long do the receiving people have to write an RM?" asked Phil.

"Two days after they get a packing sheet (P/S) from the user — the one who asked for the direct delivery. The P/S, of course, accompanies the item on the truck from the supplier."

"Of course. But how long does the user have to get the P/S to receiving?" asked Phil.

"Within two days after he gets the direct delivery and signs the P/S — giving the copy back to the truck driver — he has to send the approved P/S to receiving."

"I'd be willing to bet that the users take their own sweet time about it."

"They used to," said Marv, "but we've got a new receiving department manager. And he told the users flat out that anyone who doesn't follow the rules gets his DD privileges taken away. So just about everybody has fallen into line."

"How did Art make his tests?" queried Phil.

"He took a random sample of 40 RMs issued for DDs in the last month."

"And then?"

"He showed on his worksheet the dates the users received the P/Ss, the dates receiving got the P/Ss from the users, the dates the POs came to receiving from procurement, and the dates that receiving prepared the RMs."

"Is that what Art's schedule shows?" asked Phil.

"Yes," said Marv. "And that's all it shows. He never finished the damn thing. Look at it."

Marv then showed Phil the worksheet (Figure 1). "You can see that he put in the manufacturing dates of the various actions. You know about manufacturing dates, don't you Phil?"

"Oh, yes. Those are the consecutive numbers from 1-1000 given to all working days. They exclude Saturdays, Sundays, and holidays. They're much easier to work with than calendar days."

"Right. He got to that. But he never showed the spans between the dates. They still have to be entered on the right-hand side of the worksheet."

"What are the numbers in parentheses in the worksheet headings?" asked Phil.

"Oh, they show the allowable number of days. In column 2, the (2) means that the user has 2 days to get the P/S to receiving. In column 3 the (3) shows that the buyer has 3 days from the date of his order — same day, almost invariably, as the day the user receives the P/S — to get the PO to receiving. In column 4, the (2) shows that receiving has 2 days after the receipt of the P/S from the user, to prepared the RM."

"How about getting the RM to accounts payable?" asked Phil.

"We found that without fail receiving personnel hand-carry all those RMs to accounts payable at the end of every day."

"So when does accounts payable start hurting?" asked Phil.

"The discount terms on these items are always 1%, 10 days. Accounts payable must have 5 days to process payment after receipt of the RM. That leaves 3 days for the PO to get to re-ceiving and 2 days thereafter for receiving to issue its RM. So if procurement takes more than the allotted time and/or if receiving does, then we can't earn the discount."

"How about the user?"

"He is required to get the P/S to receiving in two days. But if he stretched it to three days, he'd still be okay — because the processing of the PO and the P/S start at the same time."

"How big was the population?" asked Phil.

"About 550 DDs for the month," said Marv. "I told Art to start with a sample of 40."

"Was that enough?" asked Phil.

"He thought so," said Marv, "because he promptly isolated the problem, just by scanning his figures on the worksheet."

"Did he carry through?" asked Phil.

"I've got to hand it to him. He sure did. He got Noel Benson, receiving department manager, to report all late POs to John Carr of procurement. He got John to monitor his buyers and raise hell if they don't get those POs out in three days. He talked to Noel last Tuesday and to John last Wednesday, if you want the dates for your record of audit findings. I'd say that the matter's corrected. But let's make sense out of the working papers, Okay?"

"Can do," replied Phil. "I'll complete the worksheet, summarize the statistics, write up the story in our usual style, prepare a simple flowchart, write up a record of audit findings, and let you have the whole segment before the day is out. What letter shall I use for the working paper references?"

"I've assigned G to that segment," said Marv. "Carry on, old boy, it's a pleasure to have you on board."

Required: Complete the working papers in line with the assignment that Phil has undertaken.

FIG. 1
CASE STUDY 8-3
WORK SHEET

Receiving Department Direct Deliveries

	Receiving Memo Number	Manufacturing Dates				Days Late & Organization Responsible					
						User		Purchaser		Receiving	
		P/S Rec'd by User (2)	Rec	P.O. Rec'd by Rec (3)	Rec. Memo Prepared (2)	Total Days	Days Late	Total Days	Days Late	Total Days	Days Late
1	2005	235	237	238	240						
2	2017	235	237	240	242						
3	2131	236	238	249	251						
4	2222	236	239	242	244						
5	3314	233	235	241	243						
6	3315	237	239	246	249						
7	3417	237	239	247	249						
8	3421	237	239	240	242						
9	3493	237	239	245	247						
10	4061	239	240	242	244						
11	4062	239	239	245	247						
12	4069	239	239	247	249						
13	4113	240	241	248	250						
14	4115	240	242	242	244						
15	4428	240	242	249	251						
16	4430	240	242	251	253						
17	4491	240	242	251	253						
18	4501	241	243	260	262						
19	4512	241	243	244	246						
20	4524	241	243	244	246						
21	4536	241	242	243	246						
22	4542	241	242	247	249						
23	4549	241	243	245	247						
24	4760	242	244	249	251						
25	4792	242	244	248	249						
26	4807	243	246	249	251						
27	4811	243	245	249	251						
28	4814	243	245	245	247						
29	4819	243	245	248	250						
30	4350	243	245	249	251						
31	4904	246	248	248	250						
32	5103	247	249	255	257						
33	5107	247	249	256	258						
34	5112	247	248	255	257						
35	5205	248	250	260	262						
36	5237	248	250	259	261						
37	5362	249	251	258	260						
38	5381	249	251	259	261						
39	5454	250	252	260	262						
40	5550	250	252	261	263						

Part 3

Scientific Methods

9

Sampling

The essence of sampling. A means to an end. Its importance to managers and internal auditors. Selecting samples. Directed versus random samples. Basic principles. Audit populations and objectives. Random numbers. EDP printouts. Stratification. Clusters and multistages. Confidence level and precision. Population variability — error rates. The normal curve. Attributes. A simple formula. Variables. Standard deviations. Tables for variables sampling. Formula for variables sampling. Dollar unit sampling. Caveats. Stop-or-go sampling. Discovery sampling. Judgment sampling. Evaluations of sample results. Proportions of items within a population — known and unknown populations. Ten commandments for audit sampling.

Introduction

Scientific sampling isn't all that hard. There's really no great trick to understanding it. In fact, the biggest barrier to becoming familiar with it is probably its name — statistical sampling. That name conjures up visions of formidable formulas and abstruse mathematical concepts. For our purposes let us call the subject sampling — just sampling; something auditors do all their professional lives.

Sampling, in essence, is the process of learning about a great deal by looking at a little. In auditing, it is used mostly to help form an opinion or recommend action on a totality (the population) by examining a part of it (a sample of the population). Sampling is just another tool that auditors use to shape their opinions. It is not an end in itself — it is only a means toward an end. The sample and the sample results are merely raw data; data that must be weighed and sifted. It must be analyzed for materiality, for reasons, for causes, and for effects. The sample is but the first step on the road to an informed audit opinion. Sometimes that opinion cannot be formed without a little help from mathematics, but the mathematics need not be difficult.

Veteran auditors with thousands of samplings behind them may well ask, "I've done all right so far, so why do I have to learn this scientific mumbo jumbo?" That question, in today's environment, is readily answered: The samples used must be defended. Most likely in the past nobody knew enough to dispute samples — samples which may not have been representative of the population sampled, whose results could not be objectively measured, or indeed, which might have been excessive. There is little doubt that a shrewd challenge to many of the veteran's samples could have left him or her floundering and defenseless.

Modern managers are becoming mathematically literate. Included in that competence today is a good grounding in probability theory on which all scientific sampling is based. Auditors who attack a manager's operations with samples that cannot be defended may find themselves having to back down.

Moreover, executive management may look to the auditor when faced with problems related to or generated by sampling. Their own assistants may present proposals for courses of action based on samples or sampling theory. On the surface, the proposals may hold promise; but the executive, a pragmatist, is sure to ask, "How good are they, really?" So they will naturally turn for assistance to the auditors, their objective advisors; for shouldn't the auditors be experts on sampling?

Auditors from governmental agencies or from prime contractors, auditing the company's transactions, may assert claims or allege discrepancies on the strength of samples. Whom do managers turn to for protection? Their own auditors, of course.

If internal auditors have a firm grasp of some of the basic principles of scientific sampling, they can provide the assistance management feels it has a right to expect of them. To begin with, the beast is easier to grasp if one understands that audit sampling stands on three legs: deciding how many sample units to select, selecting the sample units, and evaluating the sample results.

Volumes have been written on the subject. For the purposes of this book, a survey of the key sampling techniques and plans will suffice, together with a discussion of the evaluation of population proportions and approximation, a helpful audit technique.

For a more detailed discussion, see the supplementary reading list at the end of this chapter.

Where long-range, complex scientific sampling plans are undertaken — as, for example, substituting sampling for the complete examination of inventories — it is wise to coordinate the sampling program with such people as the company's public accountant, the cognizant EDP manager, the financial operations manager, and/or a qualified statistician.

Sample Selection

When auditors select samples, they may take at least two paths. The first leads to the directed sample; the second leads to the random sample.

The directed or purposive sample is used when auditors suspect serious error or manipulation and want either to obtain evidence to support their suspicions or to find as many of the suspected items as they can. This has nothing to do with scientific sampling. It is pure detective work. And the better the sleuth the auditor is, the better his or her sample will be. But auditors may not draw conclusions about a population from a directed sample. Such conclusions are completely unwarranted because the sample did not represent the population.

The random sample seeks to represent, as closely as possible, the population from which it was drawn. When auditors take a random sample they are trying to take a picture in miniature of the great mass of records or data that make up the population from which the sample is selected. The larger the sample the more closely it depicts the population. In audit argot, the sample is termed *representative*.

Taking the Sample

There are certain rules for taking a representative sample. Here are two fundamental rules of selection that are quite reasonable and make good sense:

1. Know your population, because audit opinions may be based only on what has been sampled.
2. Let every item in the population have an equal (or known) chance of being selected.

The mass of data, records, or documents from which the auditor selects a sample is variously referred to as population, universe, and field. They all mean the same thing. They also imply something that is central to good sampling: Know what you are testing. Identify specifically the population to be audited and clearly define the audit objective. The initial questions must be, "What is the population I want to test?" and "What are the objectives of my audit?" These are most significant questions, having as much to do with good audit practice as with statistical sampling. If this principle is violated, the tests are open to serious question on technical grounds; and opinions are without objective support.

Consider, for example, the auditor who wishes to estimate the annual fuel consumption of the company's automotive fleet. The fleet is made up of:

> 50 12-wheel trucks
> 100 pickup trucks
> 100 forklift trucks
> 200 passenger cars
> 300 motor scooters
> 750 pieces of automotive equipment

Let us assume in this example that the fleet has been well maintained and that there are no "gas eaters" within each group. Since the motor scooters were the most numerous, the auditor decided to select a sample of 50 motor scooters, examine fuel consumption for those 50, and project the findings to all 750 pieces of equipment. Stated this way, the results are clearly ludicrous. Yet auditors fall into similar traps in their sampling every day. For example:

They might select a sample of invoices from all those paid in July and use that test to form an opinion of all invoices paid during the year.

They might select a sample of travel vouchers for local travel only and project their findings to a population which includes foreign travel as well.

They might select a sample of purchase orders from a population which excludes all orders under $5,000 and express opinions on all purchase orders issued by the purchasing department — from $1 on up.

They might sample inventory records in one tool crib and express an opinion on the records of tool cribs in all the many locations within the company.

Each of these opinions and projections — unless properly qualified — is without support and just plain wrong. In the case of the motor vehicles, the auditor either should have sampled from all the various types of equipment or should have restricted the audit opinion to scooters alone.

Hence, auditors must always remember to define the population before starting to take their sample. They must always consider the nature of the population in terms of their audit objectives. For example, the population of the 750 vehicles can have a different meaning, depending on the audit objective. If the audit objective were to determine whether all vehicles are being maintained regularly — and let us assume that every item of equipment, be it scooter or truck, must be periodically maintained — the population assumes a different character than if the audit objective were to estimate fuel consumption. When the population is improperly defined, in the light of the audit objective, the result is bad sampling and bad auditing. When the population is properly defined — and this may take some hard thinking and a lot of questioning — the whole audit thrust and approach improve.

The principles on which scientific sampling are based operate only if the sample is selected at random. There are several ways in which random selection can be accomplished. Each method has its advantages and its drawbacks. The two basic methods are referred to as random number sampling and interval (systematic) sampling. Two other methods are called stratified random samples and cluster samples.

Random Number Sampling

Random number sampling is generally considered the most likely to result in a random sample. It makes use of tables of digits that have been scientifically "randomized." The tables provide substantially complete assurance that every item in the population has an equal chance of being selected. Many such tables have been compiled. One is the Table of 150,000 Random Decimal Digits, developed by the Interstate Commerce Commission. Appendix B contains the first six pages from that table.

The line numbers of the random digits are indicated at the left margin. Column numbers are shown in parentheses across the top of the page. The digits have been arranged in groups of five by five, only because the eye would become confused if no spaces were allowed. The spaces are for eye appeal only. They do not mean that the tables are made up of five-digit numbers. The tables are easy to use if some simple rules are followed:

Enter the tables by opening them at random and, with eyes averted, place a pencil point on the page. Start the number selection with the digit closest to the pencil point.

Use as many digits in a line as there are digits in the reference numbers of the documents being selected. For example, if receiving memos being tested have a maximum of seven digits in their numbers, use seven adjoining numbers from the tables.

Once a starting point has been selected, proceed through the tables in a predetermined order — down the columns or across the columns — without deviation, because deviation implies personal bias.

If an applicable number does not appear, continue on to the next.

For example, assume a population of rejection memos numbered from 50 to 500. The auditor wishes to select a sample of five from that population. The pencil point rests on the number 6 in column 5, line 6, of Appendix B-1. It was decided beforehand that the number on which the pencil fell would be the first digit of the number selected and that the auditor would proceed down the columns. Number 653 is inapplicable, being outside the range of 50 to 500. Thus the first applicable number is 231 (2 from column 5, line 7, and 31 from column 6, line 7). The columns considered, the five numbers selected and the numbers rejected are as follows:

Columns Considered		Inapplicable Numbers	Applicable Numbers
27756	53498	653	
98872	31016		231
18876	20922	620	
17453	18103		318
53060	59533		059
70997	79936	779	
49626	69445	669	
88974	33488		433
48237	52267	752	
77233	13916		313

The reader will observe that:

Inapplicable numbers — those outside the range of 50 to 500 — are skipped. Three digits are consistently used, so 059 becomes 59.

The numbers selected can then be arranged in numerical order for ease in locating the documents bearing those numbers, assuming the documents themselves are filed in numerical sequence.

Random number sampling can sometimes be difficult to use. Documents may be unnumbered or may resist ready identification, or the identification numbers assigned may be quite long; thus it would be an almost impossible task to match random digits with the identification numbers.

The selection job is simplified, however, if the population of items are listed in an EDP printout. Then, the random number tables could be used to select a page and a line. For example, assume a printout of 250 pages with 52 lines to a page. The auditor might want to use the first three digits of a column of random digits to identify a page and the last two digits to identify a line.

Let's see how this would work. Assume we jab the point of a pencil at the digits in column 3, line 66, of the random number tables in Appendix B-2. The first three digits, 298, are inapplicable (they're over 250). We skip them and start with the next, 020. As we go down the table we skip the inapplicable numbers and list the applicable ones for the pages. When we have our quota of pages, we start back at column 3, line 66, to pick up the last two digits for the lines. The first digits, 20, are within the range of 52 lines to a page. So we match those with the first three digits for the printout page. Hence our first item selection would be line 20 on page 20. We continue matching page number to line number in sequence. The first five selections would therefore be as follows:

Page	Line
20	20
66	50
74	24
240	49
54	35

Interval Sampling

Where random number sampling is completely inapplicable, another selection method may be used. It is called interval sampling — sometimes referred to as systematic sampling.

Interval sampling simply means selecting items at intervals. It is a relatively simple method, but in using it, the auditor must remember basic selection principles: Because the audit opinion may be based only on the population sampled, no items should be missing from the population. Because every item must have an equal chance of being selected, the first item in the selection process must be picked at random. Because no pattern in the population should affect the selection, the auditor may have to make two or more passes through the population, each with a random start.

Let us look at a simplified example of interval selection. We will assume that the items in the population are unnumbered. The population does contain some items not applicable to the audit purpose. We shall indicate the applicable items by an *x* and the inapplicable items by an *o*. We wish to select eight items from a mixed population of 60. Since we know from a scanning of the population that there are some inapplicable numbers, we will select every fifth item to make sure we select enough items for our examination, because some items may have to be rejected. If we select too many, we will eliminate the excess.

From a table of random numbers we have determined the random start to be four. From that fourth item we then select every fifth item, proceeding horizontally (selected items are underscored) as follows:

x	x	x	<u>x</u>	x	o	o	x	<u>x</u>	x
o	x	x	<u>o</u>*	x	x	o	o	<u>x</u>	x
x	x	x	<u>x</u>	o	x	x	x	<u>o</u>*	o
x	x	x	<u>x</u>	o	x	x	o	<u>x</u>	x
x	x	x	<u>o</u>*	x	x	x	o	<u>x</u>	o
x	o	o	<u>x</u>	x	x	o	o	<u>x</u>	x

*Inapplicable item found at selection point.

It will be observed that when the interval ends with an inapplicable item (*o*) the count for the next interval begins again by using the item immediately after the inapplicable item as the point of new departure. If not, we would violate a fundamental principle: Every item must have an equal chance of being selected.

Recall that we needed only eight items for our sample. The one excess item may be excluded, but at random. A simple method of deciding which item to exclude is through the use of the random number tables. The selected items may be given numbers as follows:

$$1 \quad 2 \quad 3 \quad 4 \quad 5 \quad 6 \quad 7 \quad 8 \quad 9$$

From the random number table, select a digit at random using the pencil-point method. If the selected digit were to be 2, for example, the second item in the sample could be excluded.

Interval sampling is the simplest selection technique to use; and if it is used with care, it can provide adequate assurance that the sample has been selected at random.

Stratified Sampling

In every population, we should look for wide variations in size, amount, or characteristics of the items making up the population. When we see such wide variations, we should consider stratification. Stratified sampling arranges the population so as to provide greater sampling efficiency. Properly used, stratified sampling will result in a smaller variance within a given sample size than simple random sampling.

In stratified sampling we separate the population into two or more strata — in effect separate populations — and then take samples from each. Auditors have always used the principles of stratification. Usually, they set aside the largest or most expensive or most significant items in a population for complete examination and then select a sample from the remainder.

It may sometimes be desirable to allocate the population to many strata so as to reduce the number of items needed to obtain a representative sample of the population. As we shall see later, it is variability in the population, not its size, that causes sharp increases in the number of samples needed to give a good picture of the population.

Obviously, if the population were composed of identical items, a sample of only one of them would be representative of the whole. For example, if we wished to estimate fuel consumption for a fleet of 1,000 cars, and each automotive unit in the fleet was exactly the same as the others, all we would need to do is study the consumption of one unit and multiply by 1,000. We would have fairly good assurance that the projection would be a pretty reliable indicator of the true condition. If, however, the fleet were made up of tiny scooters, huge trailer trucks, and many different types of units in between, we would have to select samples from each type — in other words, we would have to stratify the population.

In real life situations the quality of the population usually varies widely. The more the quality or character of the individual items differs in the characteristic under study, the greater the number of items we must select to obtain a fair representation of the population. We are seeking to obtain a good picture of the population through our sample. The picture tends to become distorted by unusual items or wide swings of variability. Sometimes — in fact, usually — the only way to get that picture is through stratification.

Stratification, then, helps the auditor in two important ways: It controls distortion and it permits smaller sample sizes.

Just how to stratify, how many strata to develop, and what items to group together, call for audit judgment. It can be done mathematically, and the methods are described in the *Sampling Manual for Auditors* and in the *Supplement to the Sampling Manual*. In most cases, however, sound audit judgment will suffice. Any reasonable stratification is better than none.

Once the population has been stratified, the sample items can be selected through random number sampling or interval sampling, depending on the circumstances.

Cluster Sampling

Cluster sampling acknowledges the shortness of life. Sometimes documents or records to be sampled are so scattered or dispersed that it is too time-consuming and costly to use simple random number sampling. In such cases auditors can use the technique of cluster sampling even though it is less efficient than simple random sampling or interval sampling in typical audit situations.

Cluster sampling is what the name implies. Clusters of items are selected at random, then the clusters are either examined in their entirety or are themselves sampled. The latter method is referred to as multistage sampling. So long as each selection is at random — first the clusters and then, if necessary, the items within the clusters — no rules are violated, since each item has been afforded an equal chance of being selected.

Clusters may be natural; that is, all the documents in a file cabinet drawer or in a bundle of records. Or the clusters may be artifical; that is, the auditor may decide that each half-inch group of cards represent a cluster at, say, 10-inch intervals.

Cluster sampling can be used to select:

A sample of tool cribs and then a sample of the tools in each crib.

A sample of stock rooms and a sample of the inventory records in each of the rooms.

A sample of file drawers and all or some of the documents filed in those drawers.

A sample of months, weeks, or days, and a sample of the documents processed during those periods.

Mechanized Sampling

The various selection techniques just discussed can also be employed by means of electronic data processing equipment. With so many records today on punched cards, tape, or other machine media, the selection of samples by electronic means is becoming increasingly popular. Programs can be purchased or developed to select samples mechanically. Both the *Sampling Manual* and the *Supplement* discuss such techniques. Chapter 12 of this book provides examples of the use of the computer for sampling.

Sample Sizes

Sample sizes can be determined practically or statistically. The decision depends on the audit objective. In many audit situations a large audit sample or a statistically determined sample size is unnecessary. Often, after a preliminary survey, auditors may be so impressed with the quality of a control system that they will be content with a review of a few hand-picked items to assure themselves that the system is actually in operation.

In such circumstances, how many items are examined? If the system is being used to process three separate types of transactions, for example, one sample of each of the three types is walked through the system, touching each of the control points. It can then be declared that the system does indeed have the purported control points and that they are in fact operating. Since the system satisfied us that aberrant items would be detected and corrected automatically, further sampling may be wasteful.

Suppose, however, that we want to feel reasonably sure in our own minds that the system is working with substantial effectiveness. What is the smallest sample we can take to give us that assurance? That is hard to say without knowing the system and the quality of the population; but we should not place undue reliance on a sample of under 30 items. Only at 30 may the sample begin to adopt the characteristics of the population. In many situations, a statistical sample of 30 or 40 items will give sufficient assurance that the system is working with reasonable effectiveness. Auditors should be aware, however, that they are counting on the system to detect errors rather than on their small sample.

But what if auditors wish to be able to measure objectively the reliability of their sample results? Now they are making a quantum jump. Now they must be willing to step into scientific sampling. With an open mind and a few basic concepts, they will soon find that they can grasp this important subject.

Scientific Statistical Theory Simplified

Auditors must understand that when they deal with sampling, they are seeking a reliable estimate, not an exact answer. For instance, let us say we examine 100 items out of a population of 1,000 — a sample of one-tenth of the population. Let us assume that we have found five errors. May we then multiply the number of errors by 10 and say with certainty that the population contains 50 errors? No! We may say, if the selection was at random, that we have a certain mathematical degree of confidence that our estimate, our projection, comes within a certain range or tolerance — that is, plus or minus some determinable percentage.

This brings us to two concepts that are pivotal to an understanding of scientific sampling: confidence level, and precision.

Confidence level is the degree to which we are justified in believing that the estimate based on a sample drawn at random will fall within a specified range. A confidence level is usually expressed as a percentage. For instance, a confidence level of 95% means that there are 95 chances out of 100 that the sample results will not vary from the true characteristics of the whole population by more than a certain specified amount; there are 5 chances out of 100 that they will.

The confidence level for a sample can never be 100%. For that degree of confidence the auditor will have to examine the entire population.

Precision is the range within which the estimate of the population characteristics will fall at the stipulated confidence level. Precision, being a range or tolerance, is usually expressed as a plus-or-minus percentage, such as ±2% or as an amount, such as ±$5,000.

Thus, the estimate obtained from a sample may permit us to say that we are 95% confident that the value of a population is X dollars ±Y dollars.

Confidence level and precision are integral parts of the same mechanism. Each has an effect on the other. The meaning of sample results cannot be understood without understanding that relationship. A simple example will go much further in showing this relationship than any definitions.

Assume that a baseball pitcher is given 100 balls and is asked to throw them over the center of home plate. Home plate is 17 inches wide and looks like this:

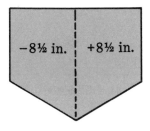

Let us assume that the pitcher can regularly get 95 of the 100 balls over the plate. It could then be said that he or she has a 95% chance (confidence level) of getting a ball over the center line ±8½ inches (precision).

But then let us say that we widen the plate to 20 inches, like this:

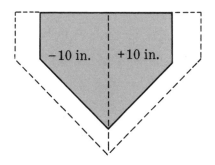

Now, with a broader range, the confidence level improves. Most likely the pitcher could get 98 or 99 balls over the center of the plate ±10 inches.

Pursuing the analogy further, let us reduce the size of the plate to 10 inches.

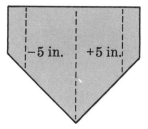

Now perhaps the pitcher can get only 80 balls over the center of the plate ±5 inches. The analogy is rough, but it points out the relationship between confidence level and precision. A change in one must change the other.

Another concept that must be understood in determining sample size is variability.

More than anything else, variability determines how large the sample must be to provide the acceptable level of confidence and range of precision. Many auditors have long believed that the size of the sample must have a direct relationship to the size of the population. In earlier days the percentage usually employed was 10%. Under that theory, a population of 100 would call for a sample of 10, and a population of a million would call for a sample of 100,000. In truth 10% of 100 is too small and 10% of a million is far too large.

Another simple example will bring the picture into sharper focus. Assume three lengths of cloth, each with a different design. The owner wishes to take a swatch from each so as to match them at the store and purchase more cloth of the same designs. This is how the lengths of cloth look:

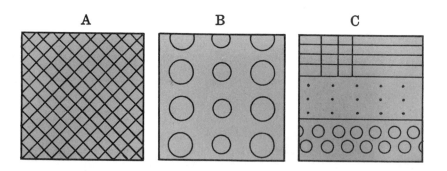

It becomes immediately apparent that although all three lengths are the same size, different sample sizes will have to be taken from each to obtain a good representation of the total design — in effect, the population. From A a very small sample will be representative. From B a much larger sample would be necessary to represent the total design. From C, unless a sample is taken from each of the four design patterns — in effect, stratification — a very large sample would be needed.

So sample size depends on three factors: confidence level, precision, and population variability.

The first two are under our control. But deciding how much reliability is needed from the sample calls for sound judgment based on the audit objectives and the nature of the associated system of internal control.

Although we may sometimes reduce variability by stratifying the population, variability is outside our control once the population to be sampled has been defined. It is part of the nature and character of the population we must deal with. That is why it is so important to "know your population."

Once the confidence level and precision have been decided, and once the variability of the population has been measured, we are in a good position to determine how large a sample we will need to give us sample results which are sufficiently reliable for our purpose. In other words, we will be able to predict how close to the true population values (determined precisely only by examining the entire population) are the values of our sample.

This ability to predict is based on principles that have been developed mathematically. The principle states, roughly, that the measurements of the values of many similar objects — when arrayed according to value or size — tend to take the shape of a bell, also known as the normal curve. And if one were to select from any population, at random, an infinite number of samples of the same size (of about 30 or more units), the frequency distribution of the means (averages) of all those samples would inevitably take the shape of a bell-shaped curve — no matter how the values of the population were distributed. Further, the mean of all the sample means would be the same as the population mean. This latter concept is important because it permits a prediction of population values based on sample values.

To pictorialize — so as to show how natural that shape is — assume a huge funnel, closed at the bottom and filled with gravel, suspended over a flat surface.

As the gravel is released from the funnel, it will invariably assume a shape somewhat as follows:

Viewed in silhouette, the pile of sand seems to have a bell-shaped curve. This shape seems natural to the viewer. Any other shape under the same circumstances might seem unnatural.

That is how the measurements of a great number of objects could be pictured. Assume the measurement of the shoe sizes of 2,000 men selected at random, plotted on a graph. The results could be as follows:

Number of
measurements

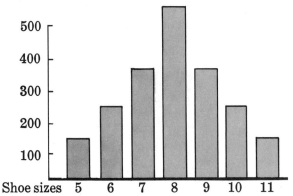

Again we see the frequency of the measurements tending to take the form of a bell-shaped curve. The shape of the curve will depict the variability of the population. A high, narrow curve will illustrate little variability; a flat, wide curve will illustrate great variability.

Variability within a population can be measured. Just as coal can be weighed by the ton, speed can be measured by miles per hour, length can be measured by yards, and time can be measured by hours — so can variability be measured by what is known as the *standard deviation*. This formidable term means simply "the measure of the variability of a particular population or of a sample from that population."

Let us break it down into its components. The standard deviation, technically, is the square root of the average of the squared deviations from the mean. It is portrayed in the following formula for a determination from a statistical sample:

$$s = \sqrt{\frac{\Sigma\,(x - \bar{x})^2}{n - 1}}$$

s = standard deviation
Σ = the sum of
x = each observation — the characteristic or value of each sample item
$\bar{x}$ = the average (arithmetical mean) of the sample item values
n = the size of the sample

To determine the standard deviation:

○ Obtain the mean (average) of the sample items
○ Subtract the mean from each item
○ Square the results and sum them
○ Divide that sum by the number of sample items — minus 1*
○ Extract the square root

The result is the standard deviation of the sample — the measure of variability of the sample — and hence an estimate of the variability of the population.

Let us determine the standard deviation, through this method, of two groups of numbers. Each has the same mean, but different variability. The resulting standard deviations will show how this measure portrays variability whereas the mean or average does not:

A					B			
Sample values	Mean†	Difference	Difference squared		Sample values	Mean†	Difference	Difference squared
17 − 20	=	−3	9		11 − 20	=	−9	81
20 − 20	=	0	0		20 − 20	=	0	0
23 − 20	=	+3	9		29 − 20	=	+9	81

$3\overline{)60}$ = 20† *$2\overline{)18}$ = 9 $3\overline{)60}$ = 20† *$2\overline{)162}$ = 81

$\sqrt{9} = 3$ $\sqrt{81} = 9$

*Note: Sample size of 3 minus 1 = 2

Although both groups of numbers have a common mean, the standard deviation of the one with the greater variability is three times that with the smaller variability.

The relationship between the bell curve, or normal distribution, and the standard deviation is an interesting one. It has been determined that in any normal distribution, the mean of the distribution, plus or minus one standard deviation, includes about 68% of the area under the normal curve; the mean plus or minus two standard deviations includes about 95.5% of the area; and the mean plus or minus three standard deviations includes about 99.7% of the area. The relationship between standard deviations and the curve can be shown as follows:

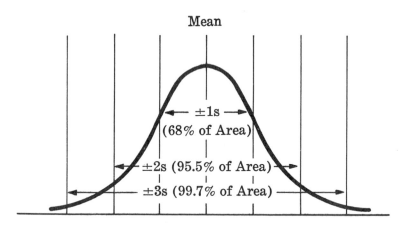

Unlike fixed units of measurement, such as an inch or a minute, the standard deviation will be different for each sample or each population because the standard deviation is the measure of variability of individual samples or populations. But regardless of the nature of the population, if we select at random a large number of samples of the same size, the distribution of the means of all those samples approximates a normal curve, and the average of the sample averages equals the average of the population.

Now let us see how this helps us in a sampling problem. Based on the principles of the normal curve, we could say that any item selected at random would fall — 68% of the time — within the range measured by the sample mean, plus or minus one standard deviation. Let us put it another way: Assuming a sample of invoices — "normally distributed" — with an arithmetic mean of $100 and a standard deviation of $10, we could say that 68% of the sampling units will fall within the value of $100 plus or minus one standard devation of $10 — from $90 to $110 at a confidence level of 68%.

If we wished to increase our confidence level to 95.5%, we must now be satisfied with a wider range — plus or minus two standard deviations. Thus:

$80 to $120 at a confidence level of 95.5%.

If we wished to increase our confidence level still further to 99.7%, we would have to be satisfied with a still wider range — plus or minus three standard deviations. Thus:

$70 to $130 at a confidence level of 99.7%.

Or if we wished a confidence level of 95% — plus or minus 1.96 standard deviations — our range would be as follows:

$80.40 to $119.60 at a confidence level of 95%.

On the normal curve, the results just enumerated could be pictured as follows:

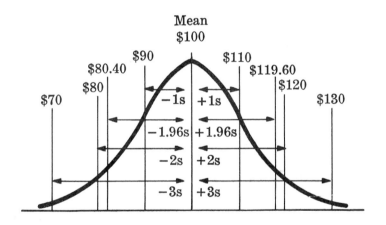

Recapitulating, then, the sample size is largely dependent on the confidence level desired, the precision wanted, and the variability found in the population.

One other factor affects sample size: the audit objective — what auditors seek to determine by tests. The objective may call for any one of several plans.

Here is a brief overview of four statistical sampling plans. The first two constitute estimation sampling and are usually referred to as sampling for attributes and sampling for variables. **Sampling for attributes** provides answers to the question "How many?" (that is, how many of this or that attribute or characteristic). **Sampling for variables** provides answers to the question "How much?" (that is, how much in terms of dollars or other variable values). The third plan is referred to as **stop-or-go sampling** and is an economical way of obtaining certain information about a population. The fourth is called **discovery** or **exploratory sampling** and is used to obtain evidence of a single item of impropriety, assuming there was more than one such impropriety in the population. The fifth sampling plan, which does not provide for statistical measurement but which is regularly used in auditing, is **judgment sampling.**

Sampling for Attributes

Sampling for attributes calls for yes-or-no, right-or-wrong answers. It is usually applied to testing systems of internal control. It is concerned with estimating the number of errors or other characteristics in a population.

It can provide an estimate of the number of engineering drawings received late by production people, but it will not give an estimate of how late — that is the function of variables sampling.

It can provide an estimate of the number of purchase orders issued to sole sources, but it will not give an estimate of their value — that too is the function of variables sampling.

Determining sample sizes is relatively easy when tables are used, and the method of using the tables is set forth in the *Sampling Manual for Auditors.* Briefly stated, the auditor first determines: the population size, the desired confidence level, the desired precision, and the expected error rate.

The principle of the expected error rate was touched on in the discussion of variability — the more variable the items in a population the larger the sample size needed. Obviously, there is no great variability in a situation where the characteristic is either "yes" or "no." If all the characteristics were "yes" it would take a test of only one to then predict that all the other items in the population were also "yes." But the more "no's" — up to 50% of the items — that are sprinkled throughout the population, the larger the sample needed to obtain a good representation of that population.

Estimating the error rate calls for judgment, but methods are available to give reasonably sound basis for an estimate:

Examine a pilot sample of about 50 items.

Review prior working papers for past experience.

Discuss the estimated number of errors being encountered with knowledgeable people.

Estimate the percentage of error it would take to automatically alert management that something is wrong.

Once the necessary decisions are made, we can proceed to the tables without difficulty, finding the one that shows the population size, confidence level, precision, and expected error rate in which we are interested.

But the available tables may not always fit the auditor's specifications. To do so would take an enormous number of tables, and auditors should never change their specifications merely to fit the tables at hand. That would be like the tail wagging the dog. A simple formula can solve the dilemma. It adjusts to any confidence level, precision, and error rate. It also adjusts to any population by applying a simple supplemental formula. It uses the standard deviation factors — here called Z factors (often referred to as t factors).

The formula has two parts, and both are simple. Neither requires the extraction of square roots. The first formula is used to obtain the sample for an infinite population. The second adjusts the formula for the population being considered.

The first formula:

$$n_{(e)} = \frac{Z^2(p)(1-p)}{A^2}$$

where:

$n_{(e)}$ = First estimate of sample size.
Z = Standard deviation factor (Appendix C)
p = Occurrence rate
A = Desired precision

The second formula uses the first estimate of sample size and adjusts it to fit the population:

$$n_{(f)} = \frac{n_{(e)}}{1+(n_{(e)}/N)}$$

$n_{(f)}$ = Final sample size
$n_{(e)}$ = First estimate of sample size
N = Population

Using these formulas, here is the computation for the sample size where the population (N) is 1,000, the desired precision (A) is ±2%, the desired confidence level (Z) is 95% and the estimated error rate (p) is not to exceed 5%:

1. $n_{(e)}$ $= \dfrac{1.96^2 \times .05 \times (1-.05)}{.02^2}$

$= \dfrac{3.8416 \times .05 \times .95}{.0004}$

$= \dfrac{.182476}{.0004}$

$= 456$

2. $n_{(f)} = \dfrac{n_{(e)}}{1+(n_{(e)}/N)}$

$= \dfrac{456}{1+(456/1000)}$

$= \dfrac{456}{1.456}$

$= 313$

The second formula, representing a "finite population correction factor," can generally be omitted if the first sample estimate is less than 5% of the universe size.[1] The second formula, in such cases, has little effect on the sample size, merely making it slightly smaller.

If we examine the sample of 313 items and find that there is indeed an error rate of 5%, then we can declare that we are 95% sure that our population of 1000 contains 950 error-free items, plus or minus 2% of 1000, or plus or minus 20 items. In other words, the number of satisfactory items in the population can be estimated to be anywhere from 930 to 970 — at a 95% confidence level.

If it turned out that the error rate in our sample is actually somewhat higher — say 6% or 7% — we would recompute the formula, using the new error rate, and determine how many more items we would have to examine to obtain an estimate with the required confidence level and precision. If the actual error rate is much higher — say 10% or more — the sampling could well be finished, since 10% of 313 items would be sufficient to indicate a real problem that needs correcting.

Sampling for Variables — Tables

This form of sampling is sometimes called dollar estimation, since it usually deals with dollar values. It can also be used for any other kinds of variable values, like time periods and weights.

Variables sampling can be used to obtain estimates — based on a sample — of the value of inventories, the value of disallowances of travel vouchers, the value of aged accounts receivable, and the like. Computing sample sizes and sample results is simplified by the use of tables. Such tables can be found in the sampling manuals referred to previously.

Here we shall make use of an alternative set of tables which allows a certain degree of flexibility often desirable in computing sample sizes.

To establish suitable sample sizes, we must determine, as we did for attributes sampling, the population size, the desired confidence level, and the desired precision. Instead of an expected error rate, however, we must determine the standard deviation.

As we pointed out in attributes sampling, the expected error rate is a measure of variability that is needed to work out the formulas for sample sizes. In variables sampling the standard deviation does the same thing.

Accordingly, for the first step in establishing the sample size needed to provide the desired degree of reliability, we must estimate the standard deviation of the population. We do that by determining the standard deviation of the sample. Just as we may take a pilot sample in attributes sampling to estimate the error rate, so we must take a pilot sample in variables sampling to determine the standard deviation.

The sample for that purpose should not be fewer than 100 units. Fewer than that number may not be representative of the population and therefore may not give a correct reading. The sample must be drawn at random, and even though it is termed a pilot sample, all the items selected can be used as a part of the additional sample items that may be required to achieve desired sample reliability.

In dealing with so many numbers, it is best to use a simplified computation in determining the standard deviation. This computation does not require subtracting the mean from the value of each sample item. The results are the same as those obtained from the formula described earlier in this chapter.

The simpler formula (easier to compute even though it looks more complicated) is as follows:

$$s = \sqrt{\frac{\Sigma(x^2) - (\Sigma x)^2/n}{n - 1}}$$

The meanings of the symbols are as follows:

s = standard deviation of the sample
Σ = sum of
x = value of each sample item
n = sample size

Using the figures in example B shown previously in determining the standard deviation:

$x =$ Sample values	$\Sigma(x^2) =$ Sum of squared sample values	$(\Sigma x) =$ Sum of sample values
11	121	11
20	400	20
29	841	29
	Total 1362	Total 60

and substituting these values in the formula, we have:

$$s = \sqrt{\frac{1362 - 60^2/3}{3 - 1}}$$
$$= \sqrt{\frac{1362 - 1200}{2}}$$
$$= \sqrt{81}$$
$$= 9$$

The standard deviation from this formula, just as it was when we used the other formula, is 9.

Once the standard deviation has been determined, the tables can be entered to determine the precision obtained through the sample. Here is what the tables have to offer.

Appendix D provides a list of precision factors for sample sizes from 30 to

300 and then at graduated intervals up to 10,000. The factors are shown at confidence levels of 80%, 90%, 95%, and 99%. A column of square roots is also provided to assist in the extraction of the square root when computing standard deviations.

The table is computed for infinite — very large — populations. Thus, if the population is not very large, it is necessary to adjust the precision by a factor which takes into account the relationship between the sample size and the population size. If the population is small, and the sample represents a large percentage of the population, then the precision obtained from Appendix D would have to be adjusted to a considerable degree. Appendix E provides the adjustment factors.

The easiest way to explain the use of the two appendices is through an example. Let us assume the following premises:

Population size	5,000
Population value	$500,000
Standard deviation determined from a sample of 100 items selected at random	$80
Desired confidence level	90%
Desired precision	±4%
Computation of precision per unit of population:	
±4% of $500,000	±$20,000
±$20,000 ÷ 5,000	±$4

We therefore need a precision of plus or minus $4 per unit before we will be satisfied with the reliability of our sample.

Appendix D-2 shows a precision factor of ±.1660 for a sample size of 100 and a confidence level of 90%.

The ratio of sample (100) to population (5,000) is .02. The finite universe correction factor in Appendix E-1 shown for .02 is .99. The precision obtained from the sample of 100 is thus the result of the following computation:

$$\$80 \times \pm.1660 \times .99 = \pm\$13.15$$

Since the sampling precision does not meet our standards, we will have to sample further. Instead of seeking to compute precise sample sizes, we may increase our initial sample of 100 in increments of 50 or 100, recomputing the precision at each increment, until we have obtained a precision range which will satisfy us. Tables to determine exact sample sizes are available in the *Sampling Manual for Auditors*.

Let us restate the problem we have just discussed, but this time let us give it some audit meaning. With the principles understood, it should be simple to follow the steps required to work out an actual audit problem.

We are asked to estimate the value of an inventory having a book value of $500,000 and composed of 5,000 line items. The average line item — kind of item, which may be composed of a number of units — therefore has a book value of $100.

We have examined 200 line items, comparing the number of units shown on the books with the actual number of units for each line item in our sample. The results are as follows:

Book value	$20,000
Value determined by physical inventory	$18,000

Through simple arithmetic, we estimate the actual value of the entire inventory. Since we examined 200 items and found their total value to be $18,000, their average value would be $90 ($18,000 ÷ 200). Since there are 5,000 items in the inventory, the estimated actual inventory would be $450,000. This compares with the book value of $500,000.

Can we be satisfied with this estimate, based on simple arithmetic? The answer is **no**. We do not yet know how reliable that estimate is.

But we can measure that reliability through statistical means. First we will determine the standard deviation of the sample of 200 items. Let us assume that it is $40. We determine the precision factor for a sample of 200 at a 90% confidence level by consulting Appendix D-5. The factor is ±.1168. We then determine the finite universe correction factor. First we divide the sample size by the population size. The result is .04. By consulting Appendix E-1 we find that the related factor is .97985. The computation is therefore:

$$\$40 \times \pm.1168 \times .97985 = \pm\$4.58$$

The amount of ±$4.58 is the precision for a single item. For the population of 5,000 items the precision is ±$22,900 (5000 × ±$4.58).

The inventory can thus be valued at $450,000 plus or minus $22,900; that is between $427,100 and $472,900. We observe, however, that the precision of ±$22,900 is over ±5% of the estimated inventory value, while our objective had been ±4%. We therefore examine another 100 items.

Let us assume that we have found the standard deviation and the differences to be substantially the same. What is our precision now?

The factor from Appendix D-7 for a sample of 300 at a 90% confidence level is ±.0954. The sampling fraction is 300/5,000 or .06, providing a correction factor of .96958. Hence:

$$\$40 \times \pm.0954 \times .96958 = \pm\$3.70$$

For the entire population (5,000 × ±$3.70) the precision would be ±$18,500, and the estimate of the corrected inventory value would be $450,000, plus or minus $18,500 or between $431,500 and $468,500.

The precision at a 90% confidence level is just about ±4%. Having substantially met our goals, we may stop sampling, satisfied with the reliability of our estimate.

Sampling for Variables — Formula

As in attributes sampling, fairly simple formulas can be used to determine sample sizes and precision (sampling error). Using the same example shown for the tables:

Population size	5,000
Population value	$500,000
Standard deviation of 200 items selected at random	$40
Desired confidence level	90%
Desired precision per unit of population	±$4

Here is the first formula:

$$n_{(e)} = \left(\frac{Zs}{A}\right)^2$$

Where:

$n_{(e)}$ = First estimate of sample size
Z = Standard deviation factor (Appendix C)
s = Standard deviation of the sample
A = Precision (sampling error)

The second is the same adjustment formula shown previously and uses the first estimate of sample size and adjusts it to fit the population:

$$n_{(f)} = \frac{n_{(e)}}{1 + (n_{(e)}/N)}$$

Using these formulas, here is the computation leading to the sample size:

1. $n_{(e)} = \left(\dfrac{1.645 \times 40}{4}\right)^2$

$= \left(\dfrac{65.8}{4}\right)^2$

$= 16.45^2$

$= 271$

2. $n_{(f)} = \dfrac{271}{1 + (271/5,000)}$

$= \dfrac{271}{1.0542}$

$= 257$

Also, as in attributes sampling, the second formula is not needed if the first sample is less than 5% of the population.

As a result of the computations, the internal auditor will select at random another 57 items to bring the total to 257. Let us assume that the examination of the sample of 257 items shows the standard deviation remains at $40. Let us also assume that the values of the sample items are as follows:

Book value	$27,000
Value determined by physical verification	23,130

The average value of the inventory items is $90 ($23,130 ÷ 257). The estimated actual inventory would be $450,000 ($90 × 5,000). The next question is: How reliable is that projection? What is the precision (sampling error) at a 90% confidence level? What is the range within which the estimated actual inventory value can be projected at the desired confidence level?

A formula can provide that answer:

$$ A = Z \frac{s}{\sqrt{n}} \left(\sqrt{1 - \frac{n}{N}} \right) $$

where:

A = Precision
Z = Standard deviation factor (Appendix C)
s = Standard deviation of the sample
n = Sample size
N = Population size

Substituting the values determined by the audit and by the desired confidence level, the value of the sampling error is reached as follows:

$$ A = 1.645 \left(\frac{40}{\sqrt{257}} \right) \left(\sqrt{1 - \frac{257}{5000}} \right) $$

$$ = 1.645 \left(\frac{40}{16.03} \right) \left(\sqrt{1 - .0514} \right) $$

$$ = 1.645 \times 2.4953 \times .97396 $$

$$ = \$4.00 $$

The precision of ±$4 for each unit computes to ±$20,000 for 5,000 units. The projected value of the entire inventory is therefore $450,000 ±$20,000. In other words, at a confidence level of 90%, the actual value of the inventory would lie within a range of $430,000 to $470,000.

Dollar Unit Sampling

A relatively new form of dollar estimation has been gaining acceptance in recent years. It goes by many different names, all meaning the same thing: DUS (dollar unit sampling), CAV (combined attributes variables sampling), and CMA (cumulative monetary amounts).

The concept of DUS gained its impetus from certain inadequacies inherent in attributes sampling. That sampling plan tells the auditor, who has taken a random sample, how many items in a population are likely to be in error. But it does not give the value of those erroneous items.

DUS combines attributes sampling and dollar estimation in one sampling plan. By using attributes selection techniques, it also provides information on "how much." It avoids the difficulty of determining standard deviations of the sample by removing the variability of the sampling unit.

In audit unit sampling, a document is the unit: a voucher, a purchase order, a receiving memo, an inventory item, an individual on the payroll, and the like. Each of these items is likely to have a different value; hence, they are variable. Any selection of such "audit units" may include large amounts and small amounts. It is quite possible for significant items to be overlooked in the sample selection process unless considerable stratification is employed. DUS gets around this problem by defining units which do not vary. Each one has the same value because each one is one dollar.

So DUS does not look at an accounts payable population as totaling $5,000,000, for example, and comprising 100,000 vouchers — the vouchers averaging $50 each and ranging from, say, $1 to $20,000. Instead it looks at that population as comprising 5,000,000 dollar bills, stretched out — dollar bill after dollar bill — for almost 500 miles.

To draw a random sample of 500 dollar bills from this population, each dollar bill must have an equal chance of selection. And so the auditor might select every 10,000th dollar after a random start. Naturally, when a selected dollar bill is drawn from the population it will not relinquish its companion dollar bills within the document where it resides. If it is a part of a $1,000 voucher, the entire voucher comes along.

The system thereby provides for automatic stratification. If every 10,000th bill is selected, then no voucher over $10,000 can be left behind. The size of vouchers certain to be selected is determined by the size of the selection intervals the auditors choose in their audit judgment. And, of course, a $20,000 account would have four times the chance of selection than a $5,000 account.

If we draw a random sample of 500 of these dollar bills and find no errors at all, then the regular attributes tables or formulas will tell us how certain we are (at, say, a 95% confidence level) that no more than a given frequency of error (say 3%) exists among these 5,000,000 dollar bills. If it turned out that after our examination we could project a 5% error rate for the population, then we could say that this represented an aggregate error of $250,000. Computer programs provide the reliability intervals for the estimate.

Credit for the technique goes to Haskins & Sells and the late Dr. Stephan of Princeton University. Certain modifications were developed by Dr. Herbert Arkin of New York University.[2]

The technique has some intriguing advantages: smaller sample sizes, an infinite degree of stratification, error frequencies convertible to dollar estimation, and the certainty of finding the large but infrequent error.

But it has disadvantages too. It generally requires the use of a computer to select the appropriate dollars. It does not focus on understatements in accounts, since the smaller the account the less chance of selecting it.

Statisticians are not in complete agreement as to how to use DUS or CAT or CMA. In an article published in the November 1974 issue of *CA Magazine*, J. L. Goodfellow, CA; J. K. Loebbecke, CPA; and J. Neter, PhD, said that they had evaluated dollar unit sampling and they acknowledged its advantages. They pointed out that a combination of attributes and variables "may well be the keystone for an effective treatment of the problem of few errors in the population." But they go on to say that based on their own studies they feel "that dollar unit sampling is not necessarily most efficient and that research is required to determine its comparative merits." They continue by saying, "It is likely that such research will indicate that auditors will need a variety of statistical tools, including combinations of attributes and variables, and cannot rely on any one approach to meet all their needs."

Our own conversations with internal auditors making extensive use of sampling methods disclosed a similar reaction. Some felt that DUS and CAV were still untried and unproved. They see it as still being "in the hands of the statisticians," awaiting resolution of some basic problems. They saw the most serious of these problems as the ease with which a "good" universe could be rejected. One use they support, however, is in populations which appear relatively error free — as a simple means of determining objectively that a "clean" population is indeed clean.

Internal auditors should keep continually alert to the potential benefits of DUS, CAV, and CMA. When the statisticians achieve agreement on accepted methodology, we will have a powerful tool to use in statistical sampling.

Stop-or-Go Sampling

Stop-or-go sampling was devised by the Air Force to permit audit decisions, with statistical reliability, that are based on relatively small samples. It applies to attributes sampling. It also applies, by and large, to fairly "clean" populations — those in which auditors want to do as little sampling as possible. Based on their knowledge of the system, the auditors may conclude that the population is relatively error-free; but they want to prove it statistically without extensive testing.

So if they can examine a small sample and find few or no errors, they will have a measurable assurance that they can discontinue their tests and accept the reasonable accuracy of the population.

Appendix F is an excerpt from the tables used in stop-or-go sampling. The first column shows the size of the sample examined. The second column shows the number of errors brought to light by the auditor's analysis of the sample. The other columns are headed by various possible maximum error rates. The columns under each of the error rates show different levels of probability (the number of times out of 100) that the true error rates in the population will be less than the indicated maximum error rates in the headings. A simple example can show how stop-or-go sampling works. Let us say that we are interested in whether receiving memorandums bear evidence that the materials received have been inspected. We shall assume that all items must be inspected. The absence of an inspector's stamp indicates no inspection.

Employees appear to be well trained. Supervisors watch the operations carefully. The manager periodically checks completed receiving memos to see that the rules are being followed. Clearly, under such a system, extensive testing would be wasteful. We take a sample of 50 items out of a population of 20,000. We stipulate that we would be satisfied if we have adequate assurance that the population has an error rate no higher than 5%.

Let us say that we examine the 50 items and find no errors. The condition is therefore as shown in the first line of the table: a 92.31% assurance (probability) that the population contains no more than a 5% error rate. If we are satisfied with that assurance, we could discontinue our tests.

But let us say that we found one error in our sample of 50. Now the condition is as in the second line: 72.06% assurance that the population contains no more than a 5% error rate. If this does not satisfy us, we might take a sample of 20 more receiving memos — a total of 70. Assume that we find no more errors. The condition is then as in the second line for a sample size of 70: 87.03% assurance. If we consider that to be adequate — taking into account the excellent system of internal control — we may discontinue our test. Otherwise we will take additional samples.

If the errors keep showing up, however, the auditor should not continue with stop-or-go sampling for sample sizes in excess of the sizes needed for attributes sampling. At that point, the auditor will want to obtain an estimate of the error rate in the population within a plus-or-minus range of precision at an appropriate confidence level.

Discovery Sampling

Discovery sampling is used when the auditor is examining populations where the existence of fraud or gross error is suspected. Such populations might include fictitious employees on the payroll, duplicate payments, unauthorized shipments of goods, or nonexistent collateral for loans.

We would not try to express an opinion on the population as a whole. We are trying, through sampling, to find at least one item with a particular characteristic, assuming a stipulated number of those items in the population. The stipulation is significant. The population would require examination item by item until the one such item was found. There would be no other choice if the item of interest were a single unique unit. But if we are willing to specify some limited, assumed number of items, we may use discovery sampling to obtain a measurable assurance that we will find at least one of that number if the actual quantity in the population is equal to or greater than the assumed quantity.

Tables have been developed for that purpose. Appendix G contains several key pages from the Air Force's table on discovery (exploratory) sampling.

Here is how the tables are used: We are examining the company records on conflict of interest. Every employee is required to complete a record designed to disclose any such conflicts. There are 10,000 employees on the rolls and we want to be 95% certain that we would locate at least one instance of impropriety — no record, wrong record, or an uninvestigated record of potential conflict.

By consulting Appendix G-4, for a population size of 10,000, we see that if we were to stipulate 50 errors in the population, we would have to examine a sample of 600 items to be 95.5% sure that our sample would include one of the erroneous items.

If our sample contained none of the errors, we would be 95.5% sure that the population included fewer than 50 erroneous items.

How many erroneous items to stipulate is a matter of judgment, taking into account the seriousness of the errors under consideration. The only alternative to discovery sampling is the examination of each item until an example has been found or the entire population has been examined. The auditor will have to evaluate the impact of the undiscovered errors in the population.

Judgment Sampling

Judgment sampling usually receives poor notices wherever statisticians deign to speak of it. But auditors have used it from time immemorial and still find that it performs signal service when statistical sampling is neither needed nor warranted.

Judgment sampling remains a significant part of the auditor's sample selection and evaluation procedures. But auditors should know when and how to use it.

Judgment sampling may be used to select examples of deficiencies to support the auditors' contention that the system is weak. They may make a purposive search for defective or improperly processed items to confirm their suspicions or support their position that the system is not capable of identifying improprieties. This is a valid use of judgment sampling. But it should not be used to estimate the number or value of such items in the total population. The auditors had not given every item in the population an equal chance of selection. The test was subjective, not objective.

Judgment sampling can be used where it is known that the population has no variability. For example, in an EDP system each item may be treated exactly the same by the computer. The transactions would be either all wrong or all right. The examination of a single judgment sample will provide the auditor with adequate assurance of the propriety or impropriety of all the items the computer processed.

Judgment sampling can provide auditors with some clues as to whether to proceed with a statistical sample. If they encounter a well-designed, well-controlled system, good management, well-trained employees, and a feedback mechanism that highlights errors, it would be extravagant to spend a great deal of time performing extensive transaction tests. A small sample — too small for stop-or-go sampling, but nevertheless selected at random to obtain some reasonable representation of the population — might suffice. If they find no errors, they may be able to say that they see no basis for examining the population further or for suspecting any material error. They may not say that they have adequate assurance that the population is truly error-free or even reasonably error-free. They have no statistical basis for such a statement. But what they can say about the functioning of the system may be sufficient for their audit purposes.

Judgment sampling has its place, so long as the auditor is aware of its limitations. Where the audit objectives are fully met by a judgment sample, there would be no valid reason to insist on the discipline of added statistical support.

Evaluating Sample Results

Internal auditors cannot content themselves with the mathematical results of their audit samples. True, these will provide them with a measurable assurance that the sample is a facsimile, in miniature, of the audited population. The results will provide them with an objective estimate of the number of errors in the population or of the true value of the population. However, this is not necessarily what management needs.

When variances occur, management wants to know why they occurred. If the book value of an inventory is $500,000, and the auditor can demonstrate that the physical inventory represented by the books is only $450,000, management wants to know — or should want to know — where the $50,000 went.

Scientific sampling helps provide the auditors with assurance that they have found out what has happened; it cannot tell them why it happened. Thus, when samples point to differences, auditors must first determine whether the differences are material, how they happened, and what can be done to prevent their recurrence.

The audit objective of modern internal auditors transcends mere scorekeeping — the number of erroneous items they find in a sample. Their objective is to determine what the score means, whether it indicates a system failure, whether it points to poor supervision, whether it is highlighting adverse trends, or whether it hints of manipulation.

So unless the sample results provide assurance of satisfactory conditions, the sample is merely a prologue to the real audit task.

A shrewd appraisal of the audit results and surrounding circumstances may give those results an entirely different character. Also, the appraisal may point to the direction the audit report should take. Here are some examples:

An examination of 200 items discloses only one error. But that error represents a significant item of a material amount. The sample results may not portray a trend, but the individual matter is of sufficient materiality to require reporting to management without reference to the sample. In other words, management may be told that the control system is functioning adequately, although this one matter needs correcting.

An examination of 100 items discloses 10 errors. The errors resulted from a control breakdown. The sample, taken from a population of 20,000, does not provide good statistical reliability. The auditor, however, feels that the job has been performed and proposes to test no further. The report to management should emphasize the control aspect, buttressed by the fact that 10% of the items were in error. There should be no implication that the error rate may reliably be projected to the entire population.

An examination of 150 items discloses only 3 errors. But each of the errors is traced to one clerk who has not been adequately trained. The auditors may then make a purposive test, in addition to their random sample, examining a substantial number of the transactions processed by that clerk to determine the seriousness of the deficiency. The results of the purposive test should not be combined with those of the random sample for the purpose of projecting results to the entire population.

An auditor selects and examines an attributes sample of 796 items out of a population of 10,000 items and finds a 10% error rate. The projection of that rate to the total population carries a 95% confidence level with a precision of $\pm 2\%$. This is extremely high reliability. The errors can be attributed to poor supervision. The auditor feels that the population should be purged of error. Management is not mathematically sophisticated and has no conception of the measurement of sample reliability. The auditor may recommend an operating review of the entire population, stating that in his or her opinion the population contains approximately 1,000 erroneous items. But the auditor would be well advised not to discuss confidence levels and precision, since this may do little more than complicate an issue that is better left simple.

Population Proportions

Auditors may have occasion to estimate the proportion of a population that possesses some property of interest. They are not concerned with error rates or sample variability; they merely wish to project the item or items of interest, found in a sample, to the entire population with some measurable degree of reliability.

For example, let us assume that certain purchases are made only after the receipt of competitive bids. Others are not. Still others are made from selected suppliers at the direction of the company's customers. It may be significant to estimate for management — with adequate reliability — what the proportions are.

There are a variety of formulas which will provide the measure of reliability for such estimates. The use of the binomial probability distribution, or the hypergeometric probability distribution for finite universes, would define the confidence limits with maximum accuracy. But confidence limits based on these distributions would involve computations so complex that they would not ordinarily be feasible without the use of a computer. Fortunately, the formula for the standard deviation of the binomial distribution can readily be used by the auditor to determine the confidence limits with a reasonably acceptable degree of accuracy. We shall discuss here two formulas based on the standard deviation of the binomial distribution. The first applies when the size of the population is known. The second applies when it is not.[3]

Known Populations

Let us assume a population of 40,000 purchase orders. Let us further assume that the auditor selected a sample of 4,000 purchase orders — every tenth order with a random start — and distributed them to the three categories just enumerated. The results of the sample are as follows:

A. Competitive bids	2,000	50%
B. No competitive bids	1,600	40%
C. Customer direction	400	10%
	4,000	100%

By simple projection, or "blow up" (multiplying each sample group by 10) the auditor estimates that the population contains 20,000 of A, 16,000 of B, and 4,000 of C. But how reliable is the estimate? In other words, what is the precision range for the estimate at a stipulated confidence level?

The auditor can obtain that statement of reliability through the following formula:

$$A = ZN \sqrt{\frac{N-n}{N \times n}} \times \sqrt{p(1-p)}$$

A = Precision
Z = Normal deviate for the desire level of confidence (Appendix C)
N = Population size
n = Sample size
p = Proportion of items of interest to sample

The computation of the range of precision, assuming a stipulated confidence level of 95.5%, is as follows:

Number in Population	40,000
Number in Sample	4,000
Z (Appendix C) at 95.5 Confidence Level	2.000
Proportion of items with a particular characteristic	
A. 2,000/4,000	.50
B. 1,600/4,000	.40
C. 400/4,000	.10

First solve:

$$ZN \sqrt{\frac{N-n}{N \times n}}$$

$$2 \times 40,000 \sqrt{\frac{40,000 - 4,000}{40,000 \times 4,000}}$$

$$80,000 \sqrt{\frac{36,000}{160,000,000}}$$

$$80,000 \sqrt{.000225}$$

$$80,000 \times .015 = 1,200$$

Then solve, for each class:

$$\sqrt{p(1-p)} \times 1,200$$

Class	p	$1-p$	$p(1-p)$	$\sqrt{p(1-p)}$ $\times$	$1,200 = A$ Precision ($\pm$) at 95% Confidence Level
A	.50	.50	.25	.5000	±600
B	.40	.60	.24	.4900	588
C	.10	.90	.09	.3000	360

Estimated Proportions And Reliability Statements

	Sample		Estimated	Precision ($\pm$) at 95% Confidence Level	
Classification	P.O.s	% of total	P.O.s in population	P.O.s	%
A. Competitive bids	2,000	50%	20,000	±600	$\pm3.0\%$
B. No competitive bids	1,600	40	16,000	588	3.7
C. Customer direction	400	10	4,000	360	9.0

It will be observed that the formula provides the best reliability when the item of interest represents a relatively high proportion of the sample.

Unknown Populations

Let us assume a large but unknown population of purchased tools. Auditors wish to estimate with reasonable reliability how many cost $100 and over.

Assume a sample of 400 tools with the division as follows:

Under $100	320
$100 and over	80
	400

Without an idea of population size, the auditors will be unable to estimate how many tools cost $100 or more. But they can estimate the proportion of items of interest. In this case they can estimate that 20% of the population contains tools costing $100 or more. They will then seek to determine the reliability of that estimate to help decide whether they have taken a large enough sample for their purposes.

The formula used to determine the precision of the estimated proportion is as follows:

$$A = \pm Z \sqrt{\frac{p(1-p)}{n}}$$

A = Precision
p = Proportion
n = Sample size
Z = Normal deviate for the desired level of confidence (Appendix C)

The computation of the reliability statement for the estimate of tools at a 95% confidence level is as follows:

$$A = \pm 1.96 \sqrt{\frac{.20(1-.20)}{400}}$$

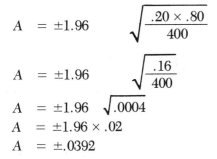

$$A = \pm1.96 \sqrt{\frac{.20 \times .80}{400}}$$

$$A = \pm1.96 \sqrt{\frac{.16}{400}}$$

$$A = \pm1.96 \sqrt{.0004}$$

$$A = \pm1.96 \times .02$$

$$A = \pm.0392$$

Thus, the precision is .20 ±.0392, or approximately from 16% to 24%. In other words, at a 95% confidence level, between 16% and 24% of the tools cost $100 or more.

If the auditors wish a more precise result, they might increase their sample size. Assuming that the sample size is doubled to 800 and the sample results remain the same, the precision would be computed as follows:

$$A = \pm1.96 \sqrt{\frac{.20\,(1-.20)}{800}}$$

$$A = \pm1.96 \sqrt{\frac{.16}{800}}$$

$$A = \pm1.96 \sqrt{.0002}$$

$$A = \pm1.96 \times .01414$$

$$A = \pm.0277$$

Now the precision, at a 95% confidence level, is ±2.77%, and the range is approximately from 17% to 23%. If this is sufficient reliability in the auditors' judgment, they may stop sampling.

Summary

In dealing with audit sampling, the auditor should keep these ten commandments in mind:

1. Know the principles of scientific sampling — but use them only when they best fit the audit objectives.
2. Know the population, and base audit opinions only on the population sampled.
3. Let every item in the population have an equal chance of being selected.
4. Do not let personal bias affect the sample.
5. Do not permit patterns in the population to affect the randomness of the sample.
6. The purposive or directed (judgment) sample has its place; but do not draw conclusions about the entire population from it.
7. Base estimates of maximum error rates on what is reasonable in the real world — try to determine at what point alarms would automatically go off.
8. Stratify wherever it would appear to reduce variability in the sample.

9. Do not set needlessly high reliability goals (confidence level and precision). Controls, supervision, feedback, self-correcting devices, and management awareness and surveillance should all be considered in seeking to reduce the extent of the audit tests.
10. Do not stop with the statistical results — know why the variances occurred.

In deciding which selection technique or sampling plan to use, the auditor should consider these applications:

Recommended Selection Technique	Character of the Population
Random Numbers	Where each of the items in the population is or can readily be numbered or is included in lists or registers which are or can be numbered.
Interval	Where items are not or cannot readily be numbered or where random number sampling would be excessively expensive. Steps must be taken to avoid any bias that may be introduced by patterns in the population or by items missing from the population.
Stratification	Where the population is composed of items which vary considerably in value or in other characteristics of interest. Where sample size can be reduced by separating the population into groups of items with reasonably similar values or characteristics.
Cluster or Multistage	Where the population is so dispersed that random number or interval sampling would be burdensome. It must be remembered that there usually may be a loss of sample reliability when cluster or multistage sampling is used, as compared with simple random number or interval sampling, and that a larger sample size may usually be required to offset that loss.
Mechanized	Where the population is, or readily can be, recorded on punched cards, magnetic tape, or other machine media.

Recommended Sampling Plan	Purpose of the Audit
Attributes	To estimate the attributes or characteristics of a population — obtaining "yes or no" answers — with a measurable degree of reliability.
Variables	To estimate the value of a population — dollars, weights, time spans, or other variable values — with a measurable degree of reliability.
Stop-or-Go	To estimate error rates or similar attributes from the smallest possible sample — discontinuing the sampling when a definitive answer is obtained.
Discovery	To identify through sampling at least one suspected item — assuming some given number of such items in the population — and discontinuing sampling when the one item is identified.
Judgment	To use samples for the purpose of obtaining information that need not be attributed to the entire population with measured reliability.

Conclusion

As managers become more mathematically literate, so must internal auditors. Whatever statistical sampling methods are useful in business and government, these should be familiar to internal auditors. Statistical sampling is an important audit technique. Internal auditors should know its uses to help them make better audits and to provide needed services to managers. They should also use dependable judgment in deciding when sampling is or is not applicable to an audit problem. Statistical sampling should not be used just because it is there, but because in a given situation it will lead to a more informed audit opinion.

Most important, the internal auditor cannot forsake audit judgment for statistics. Statistical sampling is the road towards a goal; it is not the goal itself. The auditors must interpret the numbers, decide what they mean in terms of their audit objectives, and base their audit opinions on both the facts and their interpretations of them.

References

1. W. G. Cochran, *Sampling Techniques* (New York: John Wiley & Sons, Inc., 1963), pp. 23, 24.

2. R. A. Anderson, "Audit Uses of Statistical Sampling," *The Internal Auditor*, May/June 1973, p. 37.
3. Herbert Arkin, *Handbook of Sampling for Auditing and Accounting* (New York: Mc-Graw-Hill Book Company, Inc., 1974), pp. 83, 502.

Supplementary Reading

Arkin, Herbert. *Handbook of Sampling for Auditing and Accounting.* New York: McGraw-Hill Book Company, Inc., 1974.

Auditor General, Comptroller of the Air Force, Headquarters, USAF. *Table of Probabilities for Use in Exploratory Sampling.* Attachment #5 to AGI 50-5, dated 5 August 1959.

Interstate Commerce Commission, Bureau of Transport Economics and Statistics. *Table of 105,000 Random Decimal Digits.* (Statement No. 4914, File No. 261-A-1), Washington, D.C. 20423.

The Institute of Internal Auditors, Inc. *Sampling Manual for Auditors.* Developed by Lockheed Aircraft Corporation. Altamonte Springs, Fla: The Institute of Internal Auditors, Inc., 1967.

——————. *Supplement to the Sampling Manual for Auditors.* Altamonte Springs, Fla: The Institute of Internal Auditors, Inc., 1970.

For further study

Discussion Problems

1. What is sampling?

2. Give some examples of a biased sample and indicate the attendant dangers.

3. When should the auditor avoid judgment sampling?

4. What is precision?

5. What is confidence level?

6. What happens to the confidence level when the stipulated range of precision is widened?

7. Why is it necessary to define precisely the population to be sampled?

8. What is stratification?

9. Give an example of stratifying a population of purchase orders.

10. What is the difference between random and haphazard selection?

11. In attributes sampling, why must error rates be estimated?

12. What are some of the ways of estimating the expected error rate?

13. What is the difference between acceptable and expected error rates?

14. What effect does the higher error rate have on the sample sizes needed to provide reliable sample results in attributes sampling?

15. Is the same true of discovery sampling?

16. What is a point estimate?

17. How does the point estimate compare with the range estimate or interval estimate?

18. What is the purpose of stop-or-go sampling?

19. What is the difference between stop-or-go sampling and attributes sampling?

20. To what extent should the auditors expand their stop-or-go sample as they continue to find additional errors?

21. Under what circumstances would judgment sampling be justified?

22. What is sampling for variables?

23. What is the standard deviation?

24. How much of a "normal" population will fall within one standard deviation? two standard deviations? three standard deviations?

25. What is the reliability statement?

26. What is multistage sampling?

Exercises

1. Random Number Sampling — The population to be sampled is included in a tab run comprising 225 pages, with 51 transactions on each page. Select a sample of 10 transactions, using random number sampling. Use column 2 of the table of random numbers in your test. (Use the pencil-point method to get started.) The first three digits in the column will be used to select the page number. The last two digits in the column will be used to select the comparable line numbers. Pairing the numbers in the same order that they are found, which pages and line numbers will you select? Start with Column 2, Line 1 of Appendix B-1 in the text.

2. Interval Sampling — What intervals would be used in the following circumstances?

a. Sample size of 45; population of 1006

b. Sample size of 92; population of 34,293

The auditor suspects a pattern in the population under audit. He therefore wishes to make three passes through the population as he selects his interval sample. What would the interval be to make the three passes under the following circumstances?

a. Sample size of 212; population of 12,783

b. Sample size of 94: population of 9,861.

For the sample of 212 and the population of 12,783, the auditor refers to the random number tables for numbers to provide him with random starts to his interval selection. Using the random starts 7, 163, and 200, give the numbers of the next five items after each start.

3. Stratified Sampling

a. The auditor is examining five different inventory accounts. Since each of the accounts is subject to the same systems of control, he decides to stratify his sample by allocating his sample of 100 items proportionately to the five accounts. Show the allocation of the sample to the accounts:

Account	Number of items
1	245
2	1500
3	999
4	2001
5	255
	5000

b. The auditor is examining three different groups of inventory accounts, each of which presents a different problem, as follows:

1. Large volume of items, but excellent internal control. The prior audit showed very few variances between records and the physical stock (5,000 items).

2. Items are desirable for use in the home. The prior audit disclosed a numer of variances between the records and the stock (5,000 items).

3. Large, expensive items, difficult to move and subject to periodic tests by stores personnel (200).

Assuming an initial sample of 220 items, how would you allocate the sample for a stop-or-go test? Give reasons.

4. Cluster Sampling — The auditor wishes to make a test of documents filed in 300 file drawers. He wishes to take a sample of 200 documents, but using interval or random number sampling would be too burdensome. Describe one possibility through the use of cluster sampling.

5. Attributes Sampling — Compute the sample size needed to provide a 95.5% confidence in the reliability of an estimate at ±2% precision, where the population is made up of 10,000 items of interest, and the error rate is estimated at not over 5%.

6. Stop-or-Go Sampling — Assuming the following number of items examined and errors found (shown cumulatively),

Items examined	Errors found
50	1
70	3
100	5

show the probabilities that the error rate in a universe of over 2,000 is less than 10%.

7. Discovery Sampling — Assuming a universe of 10,000, what are the probabilities of finding at least one error in the total, under the circumstances shown?

If the sample size is	and the total number of errors in the universe is:
100	40
550	10
900	25
1500	10
2000	15

8. Variable Sampling
Determine the standard deviations for the following two sets of numbers:

1	3
3	4
5	5
7	6
9	7

Determine the precision in percent under the following sets of circumstances:

	Population Size	Values
a.	5,000	$100,000
b.	10,000	$900,000
c.	20,000	$2,000,000
d.	40,000	$10,000,000

	Sample size	Desired Conf. level	Stand. dev.
a.	100	80%	$50
b.	500	90%	$80
c.	1000	95%	$100
d.	500	99%	$150

Multiple Choice Problems

1. Use random number sampling when each item in the population:
a. Is, or can readily be, numbered.
b. Is in a specified cluster.
c. Can be selected at intervals.
d. Is a random item.
e. Can be stratified.

2. When interval sampling is used,
a. The first item should be within a range of 1 to 10.
b. The first item must be selected at random.
c. Patterns in the population help protect against bias.
d. It is superior to random number sampling.
e. None of the above.

3. Auditors should know the principles of scientific sampling and use them:
a. On all their audit engagements.
b. To impress management.
c. As an exercise in algebra.
d. Only when they best fit the audit objective.
e. On most audit engagments.

4. Auditors must know their population and:

a. Base audit opinions only on the population sampled.
b. Test by using interval sampling.
c. Stratify it at all times.
d. Take samples of no fewer than 20 items.
e. Use judgment sampling.

5. To avoid bias in sample selection,
a. Every item examined should exceed a given value.
b. Every item must have an equal chance of selection.
c. Use cluster sampling.
d. Always start at the first page of the random number tables.
e. Examine the most complex transactions first.

6. Patterns in the population may:
a. Require stratification.
b. Compel the use of judgment sampling.
c. Affect the randomness of the sample.
d. Reduce the size of the standard deviation.
e. Do all these things.

7. The purposive (directed) sample has its place; but:
a. Do not use it in conjunction with random number tables.
b. Do not use it in multistage sampling.
c. Use it only to draw conclusions about the population.
d. Do not draw conclusions about the entire population from it.
e. Use it solely in cases involving suspected defalcations.

8. Estimates of maximum error rates should not be based on:
a. Pilot samples.
b. What is reasonable in the real world — when alarms are likely to go off.
c. Prior audit findings.
d. Tables of sample sizes.
e. Any of these.

9. Stratify whenever:
a. It would appear to reduce variability.
b. The sample size does not appear in available tables.
c. The audit supervisor suggests it.
d. The population exceeds 5,000 items.
e. It would appear to increase variability.

10. Do not stop with the statistical results, but
a. Take at least two separate samples.
b. Write them up in narrative form.
c. Find out why variances or deviations occur.
d. Use judgment sampling as well.
e. Summarize audit results.

11. Use attributes sampling:
a. When the population contains attributes.
b. Where it is desirable to obtain yes-or-no answers.
c. When the population has variability.
d. In a multistage situation.
e. When the population has no variability.

12. Use variables sampling to determine:
a. The number of fraudulent items in a population.
b. The point estimate of a population value based on a sample.
c. The estimated volume of liquid in a population made up of containers of different sizes.
d. The value of multistage clusters.
e. Both b. and c. above.

13. To estimate error rates or similar attributes from the smallest possible sample, use:
a. Cluster sampling.
b. Mechanized sampling.
c. Stop-or-go sampling.
d. Discovery sampling.
e. Dollar unit sampling.

14. There is a vast difference between
a. Judgment sampling and audit judgment.
b. Variables sampling and estimation sampling.
c. Discovery sampling and exploratory sampling.
d. Precision and confidence interval.
e. None of the above.

15. To identify through sampling at least one suspected item and then stop, use:
a. Stop-or-go sampling.
b. Discovery sampling.
c. Mechanized sampling.
d. Multistage sampling.
e. Judgment sampling.

16. In appraising the results of a statistical sample, the finite population correction factor:
a. Can be greater than one.
b. Has less effect as the sample becomes a larger proportion of the population.
c. Is needed when sampling is performed with replacement.
d. Is applied to the sampling error.
e. Must be used in all cases.

17. The auditor can change the standard error of the mean for a statistical sample by:
a. Stratifying the population.
b. Increasing the size of the sample.
c. Decreasing the size of the sample.
d. All of the above.
e. None of the above.

18. One measure of the variability among values in a given population is the:
a. Arithmetic mean.
b. Median.
c. Range.
d. Mode.
e. Interval.

19. In using statistical sampling for testing audit populations, rejecting a satisfactory population as unsatisfactory is an alpha error, whereas accepting an unsatisfactory population as satisfactory is a beta error. Which of the following actions is likely to result in a beta error?
a. Increasing the severity of the rejection criteria.
b. Decreasing the severity of the rejection criteria.
c. Decreasing the size of the sample.
d. b. and c. above.
e. None of the above.

20. Stop-or-go sampling has as its principal objective the detection of:
a. A fictitious employee on a payroll.
b. A duplicate payment of an invoice.
c. An unauthorized shipment of goods.
d. None of the above.
e. All of the above.

Case Study

9-1 How Can You Verify and Report on Time Charges?

Paul Eberhardt, director of internal auditing, called in his two supervisors, Bob and Rod. After they were seated he asked them:

"How good are you two at statistical sampling?"

"We've both taken The Institute's seminars, and we've both studied The Institute's sampling manuals," said Rod.

"We're fair audit samplers, but we don't pretend to be statisticians," replied Bob.

"Well, I've got a sampling problem — which means that you've got a problem," Paul explained.

"Share the wealth, I always say," said Rod.

"What's the problem?" asked Bob.

"Jan Tobias, our vice president-comptroller, called me into his office and asked my advice after he got some static from the government auditors about labor recording," said Paul.

"What kind of labor recording?" asked Rod.

"Floorchecking. The accuracy of time charges that direct employees show on their daily time cards. As you know, each direct employee gets a new time card each day, and he is required to record on it the jobs he is working on — both the start time and the stop time for each job. He identifies each job by work order number, his department number, his burden center number, and the production lot number."

"Brief me again on the principal rules," requested Rod. "I've sort of forgotten."

"The employee is not supposed to anticipate the time charges, arbitrarily allocate time charges to different jobs, delay putting his time down, or put a charge down without having an available work authorizing document — e.g., a shop order or a tool order or a maintenance order or the like," said Paul.

"What's this got to do with us?" asked Bob. "We turned that miserable chore over to the payroll people five years ago."

"Right," agreed Paul, "but the government auditors don't think the way the payroll auditors are making the verifications or recording the results is statistically sound. This involves both auditing and statistics. Jan thinks we're experts in both — or should be. And I don't want to disillusion him. I think this is a good chance to build our reputation."

"Always happy to oblige," said Rod. "How do the payroll auditors make their tests and how do they report them?"

"Well, they've tried to be as objective and unbiased as possible," said Paul.

"I would hope so. But that's not what I asked. How do they make their selection?" asked Rod.

"From a listing of all departments — there are about 250 direct departments — the payroll auditors select about 10 departments each month, using the random number tables. From each of the departments selected, they'll use interval sampling on the department's personnel list to select about 10% of the population — more or less depending on the size of the population."

"Sounds objective," said Bob.

"Then armed with the lists of people, the two labor auditors start visiting the departments. Each works independently," explained Paul.

"What do they do when they get to the departments?" asked Rod.

"The payroll auditor will introduce himself to the department manager and then set out to find each of the employees on his list."

"I can already see why the government auditors are unhappy," said Rod. "As soon as the employees know there is an auditor in the crowd, everything changes."

"Maybe so," said Paul, "but let's make up our minds after I'm through. When the payroll auditor finds an employee on his list, he asks to look at the employee's time card and see what he has recorded on it. Then he asks the employee what he's working on, looks at the work-authorizing document, and decides whether the employee put the right information on the card."

"What if the recording is wrong?" asked Bob.

"The payroll auditor discusses the error with the employee, the employee's supervisor, and the department manager, to make sure there is no disagreement as to facts."

"Then what?"

Dep't.	Number of contacts	Substantive errors	Percent	Procedural errors	Percent
B	19	5	26%	0	0%
F	26	11	42	0	0
G	8	1	13	0	0
J	23	5	22	1	4
L	26	4	15	7	27
M	28	1	4	1	4
P	27	0	0	4	15
Q	15	1	7	0	0
S	13	1	8	0	0
Z	11	0	0	3	27
	196	29	15%	16	8%

Fig. 1

"He accumulates all the data on errors and then he and his buddy turn out a monthly report," said Paul.

"What's considered an error?" asked Bob.

"There are two type of errors," said Paul, "substantive and procedural."

"Which is which?" asked Rod.

"Substantive errors are those which adversely affect our cost accumulation. Like charging the wrong contract, charging a direct work order instead of overhead — or vice versa — showing the wrong burden center, or showing the wrong production lot. Those errors will have serious adverse effects on our ability to charge accurately to contracts or to provide a sound basis for cost control or forecasts."

"What about the procedural errors?" inquired Rod.

"Those are significant in that they may indicate sloppy handling of time charges. They need to be corrected to get good discipline in our labor accumulation; but they're not as serious as the substantive errors."

"What are some examples?" asked Bob.

"Anticipating time to be worked — that is, posting time on the cards before it's worked. Missing or incomplete entries at the time of contact by the payroll auditor. Arbitrary distribution of time. Invalid authorization documents. Time cards held by the supervisor instead of the employee."

"How are the results reported to management?" asked Bob.

Very simple," said Paul. "Each month the payroll auditors list the departments tested, the number of contacts made, and the number of errors found — distributed between substantive and procedural errors (see Fig. 1).

"I'm only showing 10 departments as an illustration. Between the two payroll auditors, about 30 a month are contacted. And each month's averages are compared with those of six preceding months to see if error rates are going up or down," said Paul.

"Who gets the reports?" asked Rod.

"The vice president-comptroller, the heads of the departments audited, and the government auditors. They are available to us also, of course," said Paul.

"What does Jan do with them?" asked Rod.

"He sees if the overall average exceeds what he considers an acceptable percentage. He is aware, of course, that in matters such as these there can never be perfection. But if it exceeds his bogey of 5%, he starts asking questions. On the example I've just shown you, he'd certainly ask questions, and payroll auditing would have to tell him what was being done to bring the percentages down. The auditors asked for replies from the offending departments — in this case, all except department M."

"What's Jan upset about now?" asked Bob.

"The government auditors gave him some serious doubts about the soundness of the present methods of sampling, testing, and reporting. And that's why I called this meeting. What do you think about the situation?"

"Well," Rod replied, "I can see an awful lot of questions on all aspects of the matter. And I'll tell you this: There are many more questions than answers on audits of labor recording."

Bob agreed. "I've been involved in it myself and I have some unanswered questions."

"Fine," said Paul, "let's lay out the questions first."

Here, then, is a list of the questions that both Bob and Rod raised:

What is the population?
a. Is it all the departments in the company?
b. Is it all the direct people in the company?
c. Is it all the time charges for a day? for a week? for a year?

What is the sampling unit?
a. Is it the department in the sample selected?
b. Is it the people in that department?
c. Is it the people selected in the sample?
d. Is it the time cards?
e. Is it time charges?
f. Is it time frames for possible contacts — like 15-minute time spans during the working day?
g. Is it audit contacts?

What is management's objective?
a. Is it to keep errors under 5% company-wide?
b. Is it to get errors down to an acceptable level for every department in the company?
c. Is it to present the best possible report to the government?
d. Is it to ensure the integrity of the accounting records?
e. Is it to enforce the discipline of accurate time charging?

What are the payroll auditors' objectives:
a. Is it to improve time charges?
b. Is it to find errors?
c. Is it to report trends?
d. Is it to enforce discipline?
e. Is it to inform line management of conditions?
f. Is it to keep top management informed of conditions and trends?

What is a reasonable sample selection procedure?
a To sample with complete statistical objectivity, taking a sample each month from the entire company — that is, sampling "with replacement"?
b. To try to cover each direct department in the company — that is sampling without replacement?

What is a reasonable contact method?
a. To go into a department deliberately, with fair warning — knowing full well that when the auditor is seen, people may disappear? change their time card entries? retrieve their time cards from their supervisors who may have been adjusting them to help suit their budget realization?
b. To swoop down in force upon a department and make as many contacts as possible within a short period of time, and then leave?

How should results be interpreted?

a. Project the sample results to the entire company?

b. Report on each individual department and consider each department as a separate problem?

c. If projections are to made, would it be proper to contact fewer than 30 people in a department— knowing that samples smaller than that do not provide adequate reliability? If so, how would one deal with the 30 or 40 departments in the company whose direct employee population runs from only 3 to 15 people?

d. Seek to provide statistically sound overall figures for the company?

e. Seek to highlight all departments which exceed acceptable limits?

Should the auditor approach this audit on the theory that he will be able to provide statistically supportable estimates? If so, what can he do to stabilize a shifting, unstable population, where people may run when they see him or change their time charges before he gets to them?

After Bob and Rod had both exhausted their arsenals of questions, Paul said, "I didn't realize that the problem was quite that complex."

"Any time you're dealing with an unstable population, you've got a problem in reliable estimation," said Rod.

"Maybe our payroll auditors are trying to accomplish something that just can't be accomplished with statistical reliability," suggested Bob.

"Well," said Paul, "Jan wants an answer. He's not concerned with how tough the problem is. He just wants a solution. So why don't you two quasi-statisticians collaborate on a report for my signature to Jan, setting forth how we see the problem and suggesting some reasonable solutions."

Required: Prepare a report to Jan Tobias, setting forth how you conceive the problem, what the company's objectives should be, how the payroll auditors should construct their audit program, and how they should report audit results.

10

Quantification

Operations research — a practical tool. Models classified. Uses of models. A business model. Audits of models. Regression analysis. A study of trends and relationships. Scatter diagrams. Least squares. Simple and multiple regression analysis. Computer programs. Regression analysis of hospital services. Mathematics and common sense. Linear programming. The optimum allocation of resources. Uses of linear programming. Steps in linear programming. An application. A practical use in business. Auditing model applications. Standards to use. Data validity. Operational validity. Verifying computer models. Using consultants.

Operations Research and Models

Purpose

Internal auditors can expect to become more and more involved in the quantitative techniques to which managers turn for assistance in making business decisions. Where management goes, the internal auditor should be prepared to follow; but if management doesn't know the path, the internal auditor should be able to point the way.

The field of quantitative techniques includes what is often referred to as *operations research* (OR). OR makes use of mathematical and statistical models, designed to simulate the real thing, to help in decision making.

A model is a depiction of the interrelationships among recognized factors. In business, mathematical models seek to depict the whole business or any part of it. For example, the balance sheet and the income statement may be considered models. The balance sheet is a "static" model representing the listing of the assets and liabilities of the business at a specified point in time. The income statement is a "dynamic" model of the stream of income and expenses flowing through the business. Other models may include the entire accounting system, the production control system, the quality control system, organization charts, and plant layout.

The model concept — to represent, but not actually be, the real thing — is not new. After all, a map describes the terrain; it is not the terrain itself. What we are beginning to see is a myriad of variations, including statistical and mathematical models.

OR usually calls for an identification and definition of the central problem; an overall systems approach looking towards the results achieved through a model instead of concentrating on its integral parts; teams representing various disciplines: mathematicians, statisticians, engineers, and knowledgeable internal auditors; and the use of mathematical and statistical models as the means of analysis.

A Planning Tool

Operations research was born during World War II. Teams of mathematicians, statisticians, physicists, chemists, and military men pooled their talents to solve problems that would not yield to experience and intuition. These problems required a disciplined, structured approach. They included the search for optimum convoy sizes, repair schedules for airplane engines, and the deployment of ships to avoid or reduce losses from enemy attack.

The advent of digital computer techniques, to handle the vast number of calculations sometimes required, permitted OR to become a practical tool for management. The manager could use it as a disciplined means for discovering feasible alternatives, evaluating them, and making the best choice from among them. OR is essentially a planning and analysis tool, not a means of control.

An obsolete piece of machinery can be used superbly — through proper scheduling, maintenance, repair, and crutching by other machines — yet the overall costs might far exceed the cost of replacing the obsolete machine. OR models, therefore, can be used to tell which plan is the most appropriate under a series of different circumstances.

OR Models

OR models can be classified by their intended use, their subject matter, how they deal with time, how close they are to reality, or the techniques used in their construction. Models are used to do many things. They are identified in terms of their intended use as:

- Descriptive
- Predictive
- Planning

Descriptive. Classify variables and show their relationship.

Predictive. Predict on the basis of these relationships how the variables will behave when one or more of them are changed.

Planning. Decide the best way of combining or changing these relationships to achieve some desired result.

As pointed out, financial statements can be considered to be models. Here is an example of how such models can be used in management decision making:

A corporation wants to know its financial status so as to be able to borrow money for investments. To demonstrate to prospective lenders the financial condition of the corporation at a given time, management directs its controller to develop a balance sheet and earnings statement, using the following descriptive model (formula):

Assets = Liabilities + Net Worth

The prospective lender asks an independent auditor to test the descriptive model for accuracy and reasonableness. Having the auditor's statement based on the test, the lender uses a predictive model to compute the probability that the borrower will be able to repay the loan. The predictive model includes the various ratios used in evaluating financial condition.

Meanwhile, with the information provided by the descriptive model, the borrower/investor develops a planning model to identify the alternative effects on the balance sheet and earnings statement of investments in securities or facilities.

Internal auditors may use models in their own work. In the U.S. General Accounting Office (GAO), models have been used to compute airline costs if air fares were deregulated; forecast postal service volume, revenue, and costs; measure the benefits of auto safety standards; and determine the cost-effectiveness of military physician procurement.[1]

The GAO has also audited the models used by other government agencies to analyze:

Energy. Alternatives to achieve energy independence and to determine the technical aspects of synthetic fuel development.

Economics. National economic policies to localize economic issues.

Transportation. Interstate highway systems to develop integrated transportation plans for metropolitan areas.

Environment. The interactions of many factors affecting the total environment and the water quality in individual rivers.

Audits of model applications provide a useful service to managers who would like to use modeling techniques to improve their decision making but would like assurance that the models and their results can be relied on. Two OR, or modeling, techniques with which some internal auditing organizations are becoming involved are:

○ Regression analysis
○ Linear programming

Regression Analysis

Nature

Regression analysis is used to show relationships between two or more variable quantities. It measures the extent that a change in one of the quantities is accompanied by a change in another or others. Simple regression analysis uses only two variables. For example, the increases in the ages of children tend to be accompanied by increases in their heights.

One of the variables is called the independent variable. In the example of the children, the age is the independent variable. Another of the variables is called the dependent variable. It is associated with the independent variable — the heights of the children tend to depend on their ages.

This relationship can be plotted on a graph called a scatter diagram. The items plotted disclose the trend or historical information. Here a simple linear regression for the heights of children is plotted. The line fitted to the scattered dots represents the relation between the heights of the children at various ages (the dependent, or Y variable) and their ages (the independent, or X variable) as shown by regression analysis.

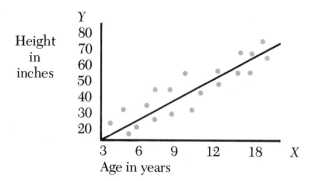

Children's heights tend to level off after 18 years so projections about heights past 18 cannot be made with this model. The "relevant range" for the model becomes 3 to 18 years. This caveat must be taken into account for all models, so the operating range must be strictly defined.

Least Squares

Merely looking at the points on a scatter diagram is not a very accurate way of defining the relationship between two variables. It does not tell which is the best fit for the line or the curve threading its way through the scattered points.

A more accurate method is to show the relationship between the two variables by the "least squares method." This method is a mathematical tool used to study the relationship between variables. If that relationship is truly linear — or close to linear — the result of using least squares is a better prediction. In the formula for determining the best fit, the dependent variable — the one we want to predict — is designated as the Y variable (the children's heights, for example). The independent variable is designated the X variable (their ages). The least squares method is based on the idea that the value which best represents (or fits) a given set of quantities is one which minimizes the sum of the squared differences between itself and these quantities.

For example, according to the least squares principle, the arithmetic mean of a set of repeated experimental measurements subject to random error is the value which best represents the set. EDP programs are available for this method.

Variables

When only two variables are involved in the analysis — one independent and one dependent — the technique is known as simple regression analysis. Where two or more independent variables are involved, the technique is called multiple regression analysis. An example of the latter is found in predicting factory overhead (the dependent variable) from such independent variables as direct labor, direct materials, and other direct charges.

In simple regression analysis, the mathematical relationship of the dependent variable Y to the independent variable X can be shown as:

$$Y = a + bX$$

where a is a fixed amount and b is the coefficient of the change in X. This carries out the basic assumption of regression analysis: Any change in the independent variable (X) produces a change of b in the value of the dependent variable (Y).

When the number of the independent variables is greater than one, the relationship between the dependent and the independent variables becomes much more complex. The relationship is shown as:

$$Y = a + b_1 X_1 + b_2 X_2 + \ldots + b_n X_n$$

In simple terms, the value of Y depends on a (a fixed amount) and b (the coefficient of change) for each of the independent variables.

Correlation

As we learned from the principles of sampling, projections are not necessarily 100% accurate. The projections will lie within some range of reliability. The corresponding question is how closely are the variables related. This relationship can be quantified with a number called the correlation coefficient, r. The number r ranges from $+1.00$ (perfect positive correlation — heights of children and foot sizes) through 0.00 (perfect random correlation — sets of two children selected at random from a school yard) to -1.00 (perfect negative correlation — ascending ages of children and amounts of baby fat).

The mathematical basis for the least squares method and regression analysis is explained in standard statistics textbooks.

The reader should be aware that the numbers must stand the test of reason. A high degree of mathematical correlation could be plotted between the import rate of bananas and the birth rate of monkeys. But reason tells us that one is not really related to the other.

Uses of Regression Analysis

Regression analysis can be employed to predict the expected. It is being used increasingly in business to disclose trends and identify aberrations.

Internal auditors can use it to help managers make predictions or to test management's predictions. Some uses of regression analysis are to analyze supply and demand, predict customer receivables, forecast burden rates, analyze markets, study price behavior, and study advance reservations.

Internal auditors can use regression analysis in their audit or investigative work. They can tell where trends may be leading and whether those trends point to aberrant conditions. The indicators so plotted might point to matters that ordinary operating reports do not identify, or the trends may point to potential danger spots.

Computer programs are available to determine the relationship between variables.[2] For example, the computer could be fed two variables: the accounts payable balances for the last twelve months and, for each of these months, the cost of direct material charged to work in progress. The computer would then determine the coefficients for individual values of the dependent variable and predict what the dependent variable would be for given independent variables. If it were known that actual material costs charged were, say, $100,000 for a particular month, the computer would predict the expected accounts payable for that month. The accounts payable prediction shown for $100,000 of material might be, for example, from $125,800 to $144,500. Among other things, this might be useful to management in forecasting cash flow or estimating cash available for investment.

Predicting Hospital Costs

An actual case involving audits of hospital costs underscores the value of regression analysis to management decision making:[3]

Government auditors were asked to study the cost of constructing and operating health facilities. The main question was whether the expense of recent innovations would reduce health costs. In some cases, the costly initial expense of innovative procedures could be less costly over the long run because of greater efficiency. But this might be true only in large hospitals. So the question involved the relationship between the volume of the hospital activity (the independent variable) and the initial investment plus lifetime operation and maintenance (dependent variables) for hospitals of different sizes.

The audit team selected a number of departments and activities for their study, including these:

Department or Activity	Methods Compared
Dietary	Conventional
	Convenience foods
Material handling	Manual
	Semiautomated
	Automated
Pharmacy	Conventional medication distribution
	Unit dose distribution

The team gathered information from 67 hospitals and obtained information from 39 manufacturers of health care systems and equipment and from six trade associations. That data included initial investment costs, annual operation and maintenance costs, and volume of activity. The data was fed into a time-sharing computer system using regression analysis formulas.

The application to the pharmacy department illustrates the use of regression analysis. In a conventional system, the pharmacy simply purchases medication and distributes it to nursing stations. But there are other elements of a total medication distribution system: filling physicians' medication orders, administering the proper dosage to patients, and recording results of patient therapy.

The unit dose system calls on the pharmacy people to do more. They maintain medication records, interpret physicians' orders, provide unit dose packages of medication at the time they are to be administered, and in certain instances, administer medication to patients. A unit dose package contains the exact dose, such as one tablet or one capsule, ordered by the patient's physician to be administered at a specified time.

In each analysis, the number of prescriptions filled annually was the independent variable and the lifetime costs (20 years) for that category was the dependent variable. For each of the alternative approaches, a separate regression analysis was performed for certain cost categories. Here are the cost categories:

Annual personnel costs

Annual medication costs

Annual supply costs

Equipment and maintenance costs

Space and maintenance costs

The regression analyses showed that the unit dose distribution system resulted in lower life-cycle costs than conventional distribution for annual prescriptions over 250,000. The major factor was the reduction in nursing time for administering unit dose medication.

Limitations

Regression analysis doesn't answer "why?" It does not prove cause and effect. The statistical determination of a relationship does not explain the reason — it merely establishes a fact. So, as in everything else, when the auditors obtain the facts they must then apply judgment.

In any mathematical technique, the procedure cannot be carried out mechanically; the assumption must be valid and the results must make sense. For example, enamored with the numbers they generate, people sometimes follow them by rote and stub their toes in the process. More important is the possibility of making the wrong assumption that relationships between variables will persist in the same way over periods of time. That is not always a valid assumption.

Linear Programming

Nature

Linear programming is employed to make the best use of scarce resources. Materials, work hours, space, products, facilities, machines, and money are invariably limited. These limitations are referred to as constraints or restraints. The trick in business is to make the most out of what one has. The question is: Which mixture of resources will provide the greatest return for the lowest allocation of available resources? But the variety of available mixes may at times boggle the mind, and intuition will almost certainly produce invalid answers.

Linear programming, however, provides the best mix of available resources to meet an objective: for example, to maximize profit or minimize cost. It derives its name from the linear algebraic equations used to describe the mix. The equations describe the relationship between variables — a relationship in which the change in one variable is accompanied by a proportional change in another or others. An example is the relationship between transportation costs and the distance traveled.

Properly used, linear programming can be employed to determine the best way to locate retail stores, achieve optimum product or material mixes, select machine and worker combinations, select the best media mix for advertising, schedule flight crews, select transportation routes, determine the least expensive routes for salespeople, blend chemical products, and use storage facilities.

Linear Programming Illustrated

Mathematicians use a number of steps to solve problems of resource allocations, but the problems must have certain characteristics. These characteristics and a simple example of each are as follows:

A stated objective. (To reduce transportation costs between scattered factories and warehouses.)

Limited resources that can be put to alternative uses. (A number of factories, each with maximum capacity, must deliver goods to a number of warehouses, each with minimum requirements.)

Problems that are subject to quantitative measurement. (The factory outputs are known in quantitative terms. The warehouse needs are similarly known. The transportation costs between each factory and each warehouse can be determined.)

The relationships must be linear. (In our transportation problem, the elements are proportional to each other: The longer the distance between a factory and a warehouse the greater the cost. A percentage increase in distance results in a percentage increase in transportation costs.)

The mathematical formulas are beyond the scope of this book; texts on OR provide them. In fact, any linear programming problem involving many variables needs a computer for solution. A simple application of linear programming to a transportation problem will illustrate the procedure:

A company is engaged in producing items in four different plants throughout the country — Plants 1, 2, 3, and 4. The company also has four warehouses for the items — Warehouses A, B, C, and D. The plant capacities and the warehouse requirements each month are as follows:

	Plant		Warehouse	
Identification	Capacity		Identification	Capacity
1	30		A	70
2	50		B	50
3	80		C	40
4	60		D	60
	220			220

The plants and warehouses are scattered all over the country. Transportation costs differ. For example, it costs $5 to ship an item from Plant 1 to Warehouse B. But it costs $8 to ship from Plant 3 to Warehouse B. To juggle all the varying costs in one's head would be nigh impossible, but a matrix helps lay out all the variable choices of this relatively simple problem. In the following matrix, the dollar amounts represent transportation costs from any plant to any warehouse; the units represent the items.

		Warehouses			Plant
Plants	A	B	C	D	Capacities
1	$5	$2	$2	$4	30 units
2	3	6	3	2	50 units
3	7	8	5	3	80 units
4	4	2	3	6	60 units
Warehouse Requirements	70	50	40	60	220 units

By using appropriate mathematical formulas, the best combinations for the matrix are determined — combinations which would lead to the lowest total transportation costs. The matrix shows the number of units transported and the destinations.

		Warehouses			Plant
Plants	A	B	C	D	Capacities
1		$2 10	$2 20		30
2	$3 50				50
3			$5 20	$3 60	80
4	$4 20	$2 40			60
Totals	70	50	40	60	220

The total costs are then determined as follows:

Plant to Warehouse		Units Number	Transp. Cost	Total Transp. Cost
1	- B	10	$2	$ 20
1	- C	20	2	40
2	- A	50	3	150
3	- C	20	5	100
3	- D	60	3	180
4	- A	20	4	80
4	- B	40	2	80
	Totals	220		$650

Because the calculations for this problem are simple, they can be carried out in a matrix. For complicated business problems, a computer would be needed to sort out all the combinations and to point to the best one. If internal auditors are asked to solve a complex problem, they would be well advised to call upon qualified mathematicians for guidance.

H. J. Heinz Company was one of the first firms in the United States to use linear programs to solve distribution problems. It was shipping products from six plants to 70 warehouses — all scattered about the country. One of the problems Heinz faced was that in the eastern half of the country demand was greater than capacity. The reverse was true in the western half. When it substituted linear programming for guesses and intuition, Heinz reduced its freight bills by thousands of dollars. [4]

Other OR Methods

Probability Theory

This theory refers to the probability that some event will occur or refers to the frequency with which an event will occur in an infinite number of trials. The expected ratio of the probable occurrences, on the one hand, to the total trials, on the other, may be based on data obtained from experience.

The probability ratio is a percentage between zero at one end (impossibility) and unity at the other (certainty). For example, the probability that the sun will rise in the east is certainty (unity or 1). The probability that it will set in the east is impossibility (or 0). The probability that the sun rising in the east will be obscured by clouds is somewhere in between.

The probability theory may be used to refine estimates of revenues and costs. It is also the basis for the sampling plans and techniques used in audit tests.

PERT/CPM

PERT stands for program evaluation and review techniques; CPM stands for critical path method. These methods are forms of network analysis. Both systems break down a project into a set of tasks and arrange them in a logical network. In actual practice, there is little to distinguish between the two methods. Network analysis provides information needed to help management plan a complex project, schedule jobs or events in a workable sequence, redeploy manpower to provide as nearly as possible a level work force, reschedule tasks to compensate for delays and bottlenecks, and determine cost-time tradeoffs (what it will cost to save or make up time).

PERT/CPM is used to schedule the field work on complex audit jobs requiring the efforts of many auditors. It can provide the audit manager with a means of directing and coordinating the many segments of the field work.

Monte Carlo Simulation

Monte Carlo simulation has been termed the unsophisticated mathematician's friend. It permits best selection from among a number of alternatives. It can be adapted to many situations as long as alternatives are specified. It is used to study such business problems as:

How many telephone trunk lines should be provided?

How many repairmen should be hired to keep production machinery operating at a maximum profit level?

How many repair parts of each kind should be kept in inventory?

What is the potential profit or loss from a revised production system?

What is the behavior of inventory stock levels under different demand patterns?

Inventory Theory

Inventory theory provides a language to describe a system which is subject to a pattern of demand and is capable of building up supplies. The demands may vary; the supply may be subject to delays and uncertainties; the inventory may be depleted by deterioration and obsolescence. Management cost will include cost of shortages, cost of replenishment, and cost of holding the inventory.

Studies of inventories have made it possible to predict demands on inventory within statistical limits and to estimate the net costs of adopting various inventory policies, even when there are many kinds of inventory, seasonal fluctuations, and unpredictable demands. Inventory theory is not restricted to inventories alone. It may be applied to staffing, workloading, parking facilities, and cash flows.

Queuing Theory

The queuing theory provides the language for distributing a system of service units. It describes how customers arrive for service, how service meets requirements in terms of average service time and variations in service time, how long customers may have to wait, and how long the service may be idle. It has been used quite successfully in devising methods of speeding up lines of customers waiting to be served by tellers at banks.

Sensitivity Analysis

Sensitivity analysis is used to test the behavior of a model to changing conditions. For example, it can be used in relation to linear programming. In formulating and solving linear programming problems, one makes certain assumptions, at least initially. It is assumed that all values of the coefficients are derived from the analysis of data and that they represent average values or best estimate values. Accordingly, it is important to analyze the sensitivity of the solution to variations in these coefficients or in the estimates of the coefficients. Stated another way, one seeks to determine the variation ranges of the coefficients over which the solution will remain optimal. Sensitivity studies of this sort are known as parametric linear programming.

Game Theory

The game theory is used to establish a basis for decision. It takes into account the consequences of the action by one party upon the actions of an opponent who is choosing from among alternatives. Game theory goes beyond the classical theory of probability, which is limited to pure chance. In game theory, strategic aspects are stressed; that is, aspects controlled by the participants. It is therefore well adapted to the study of competition where there are present several common factors such as conflicting interests, incomplete information, the interplay of rational decisions, and chance. The technique has little application to business problems.

Dynamic Programming

Dynamic programming is what is termed a "maximization theory." It is used where a whole series of states (conditions) or actions take place and where a decision in each state is dependent on the decision made in a preceding state. It permits one to determine mathematically the period-by-period consequences of decisions.

It can be used to calculate the desirability of incurring temporary losses for the sake of long term gains. For example, through dynamic programming one could calculate the benefits of expending large sums on research and development and incurring losses during immediate periods in the hope of making much greater profits in later periods.

Exponential Smoothing

The exponential smoothing technique is used to correlate later values with earlier ones in the same series. It is used to base predictions on past observations, giving the greatest weight to the latest observations. It can be applied to determining the production of optimum lot sizes to meet forecasted sales.

Auditing OR Models

Standards

Standards for acceptable models are available and there are matters the internal auditor can take into account to make a knowledgeable assessment of an OR model.[5]

Some standards the internal auditor can apply in assessing model building are these:

The documentation for the model should clearly set forth the model's assumptions, uncertainties, limitation, and capabilities.

The documentation should also disclose whether the model is understood and can be operated and maintained; and whether the model can be evaluated by an independent person or group.

The model should be developed to answer the needs of the user. The developer and user should coordinate development effort; the user should participate in the planning process; and the model should be what the user needs — no more, no less.

Model development should be adequately monitored.

Provision should be made to update the model for future use, so as not to produce outdated information.

The data needed for input into the model should be available.

The costs of building the model should be justified in terms of usefulness. How closely does the model mirror reality; that is, has the model's validity been established? Has the model's credibility been established; that is, does the documentation include, as an absolute minimum, the intended purpose of the model, the key assumptions made, a discussion of the reasonableness of the assumptions, and the basic structure of the model?

Validity

In testing the model against standards, here are some questions the internal auditor should ask in terms of validating the model:

Data Validity

Does the data identify and measure the desired problem elements?

Are the data sources clearly defined and are the responsibilities for data collection established?

Are the procedures for the collection and updating of data workable?

Is the data obtainable within reasonable time spans and at reasonable cost?

Do the data collection procedures lead to impartiality in the accurate recording of the data?

Is the resulting data representative?

Are there audit procedures for the data collection activity?

Is the data current?

Operational Validity

To what extent do the assumptions made for the model differ from actual conditions?

Would the cost of gathering the data and the need for timeliness and accuracy prevent the accumulation of needed information?

Do the logic and numerical elements of the program as transformed into the computer program result in an invalid computational process?

Are the accuracy ranges of the model's answers so wide as to make results unusable?

Are trial results inconsistent with user expectations? If so, are changes planned?

Are expected cost savings attributed to the model sufficient to justify the model? Have the costs been accurately computed? Have all elements of cost been considered?

What determination has been made of the model's responses to changes in parameter values? Is the user aware of model outputs for different possible ranges of data?

What has been done to see that the final operational environment for the model is the same as that which was assumed in the original or modified development plans?

Computer Model Verification

Are the mathematical and logical relationships internally consistent?

Are the results accurate?

Are the flow of data and the intermediate results logical and correct?

Have all important variables and relationships been included?

Does the computer program as written accurately describe the model as designed?

Is the program properly debugged on the computer?

Does the program run as expected?

The computer model verification cannot be overlooked if the internal auditor is to express an opinion on the OR model. As stated in GAO's "Guidelines for Model Evaluation":

Experience has shown that in the absence of computer model verification — at least main program flow, critical parameters, and program modules — the odds are that no one will really know what is going on. If the evaluators do not have sufficient evidence that the model has been properly verified, then they may decide to so report and to suspend their evaluation effort until the developer has satisfied the deficiency.

Employing Experts

It becomes clear from reviewing these standards and audit questions that auditing a model is not a simple process. The evaluators must have some experience with operations research and computers. Where these talents are not available within the internal auditing department, expert assistance may have to be procured from outside the department. But the internal auditor must heed this caveat: The final report on the evaluation is the internal auditor's. Management is looking to the internal auditor's opinion — not the consultant's.

It is not enough to simply hand the consultant a job to do. The internal auditors must monitor the job. They must do whatever is necessary to satisfy themselves that they and the consultants fully understand and agree on the objectives and scope of the work. The internal audit involvement should take the following forms:

Understand the nature of the work, the assumptions the consultants made, the reasoning behind their analytical choices, and the risks inherent in their data and analyses.

Make sure that the consultants' work benefits the internal auditor.

Be sure that the work the consultants do is what was intended.

If information developed by consultants is used in an internal audit report, the internal auditors should, to the extent practicable, have the consultants furnish them with sufficient supporting documentation so that they can independently satisfy themselves as to the accuracy and validity of the consultants' work.

Conclusion

Operations research and problem simulation through mathematical models can be useful. They can help managers make more rational decisions. They can help internal auditors detect trends and predict outcomes. But their complexities can leave general managers in the hands of technicians with parochial views. The models, the concepts, the assumptions, and the computer applications need validation from the viewpoint of management, based on the needs of managers. Here is where the internal auditor can provide an additional service to the manager. Any computerized model on which management relies for a far-reaching decision should be fair game for the knowledgeable internal auditor. Internal auditors should apply proven standards and audit techniques in the evaluations. Above all, numbers and formulas must always be viewed through the microscope of business judgment.

References

1. U. S. General Accounting Office, *Models and Their Role in GAO* (Washington, D. C.: U. S. General Accounting Office, October 1978), PAD-78-84.
2. C. H. Springer, et al., *Statistical Inference*, Volumes One and Two of the *Mathematics for Management* (Homewood, Ill: Richard D. Irwin, Inc., 1966), pp. 39-57.
3. U. S. General Accounting Office, Division of General Management Studies, Case Study (CS 5) *Using Regression Analysis to Estimate Costs: A Case Study* (Washington, D.C.: U. S. General Accounting Office, August 1974).
4. "The Answer, Linear Programming," *Business Week*, March 12, 1955, pp. 43-44.
5. U. S. General Accounting Office, *Guidelines for Model Evaluation*, (Washington, D.C.: U. S. General Accounting Office, January 1979), PAD-79-17.

Supplementary Reading

Albrecht, W. S. and J. C. McKeown. "Toward an Extended Use of Statistical Analytical Reviews in the Audit." *Proceedings of the University of Illinois Audit Symposium (November 1976).* Urbana: University of Illinois, August 1977.

Gallagher, C. A. and H. J. Watson. *Quantitative Methods for Business Decisions.* New York: McGraw-Hill Book Company, 1980.

Kinney, W. "The Discriminatory Power of Macro Techniques in Analytical Reviews — Some Empirical Tests." *Journal of Accounting Research 17 (Supplement 1979.)* pp. 148-155.

Lev, B. "On the Use of Index Models in Analytical Reviews by Auditors," Report No. 7838. Chicago: Center for Mathematical Studies in Business and Economics, University of Chicago, 1979.

Stringer, K. W. "A Statistical Technique for Analytical Review." *Supplement to the Journal of Accounting Research, 1975.* Chicago: University of Chicago, 1976.

U. S. General Accounting Office. *Guidelines for Model Evaluation.* Washington, D.C.: U. S. Government Accounting Office, January 1979. PAD-79-17.

For further study

Multiple Choice Problems

1. Regression analysis is:
a. A form of statistical sampling.
b. A form of estimating proportions.
c. A way of expressing relationships among observed data.
d. A way of determining relationships between two or more dependent variables.
e. None of the above.

2. Simple regression analysis is useful when:
a. There is a dependent variable we want to predict.
b. A dependent variable tends to fluctuate in response to or concurrently with an independent variable.
c. Information is available to predict the independent variable with reasonable accuracy.
d. It is desired to predict the height of people when their ages are known.
e. All of the above.

3. In predicting overhead rates, which of the following items would be the dependent variable?

a. Prior overhead rates.
b. Direct labor.
c. Direct material.
d. Indirect labor.
e. None of the above.

4. The ages and heights of children would tend to be:
a. Positively correlated.
b. Randomly correlated.
c. Negatively correlated.
d. None of the above.
e. All of the above.

5. Regression analysis answers the question:
a. What will happen?
b. What may happen?
c. Why will it happen?
d. None of the above.
e. All of the above.

6. Which of the following ways can models be classified?
a. How they mirror reality.
b. How they will be employed.
c. How they will be developed.
d. All of the above.
e. None of the above.

7. The following is a descriptive model:
a. Revenues = Income − (expenses + taxes).
b. A map.
c. An organization chart.
d. None of the above.
e. All of the above.

8. Documentation for models should show:
a. What premises were used in developing the model.
b. The degree of uncertainty associated with the assumptions.
c. The restrictions on the scope of the model.
d. All of the above.
e. None of the above.

9. When an expert, acknowledged in the field, is used to evaluate quantitative models and methods employed:

a. The internal auditor can safely relinquish his or her audit responsibilities.
b. The internal auditor can base the audit opinion on the expert's conclusions.
c. The internal auditor should base the audit opinion on the validated findings of the expert.
d. The audit report must include the expert's opinion.
e. None of the above.

10. The use of PERT or CPM might apply in planning for:
a. The construction of a new office building.
b. The installation of a new computer system.
c. The development of a new product.
d. All of the above.
e. None of the above.

11. The underlying theory of regression analysis is that:
a. No two variables are alike.
b. Dependent variables act in an unpredictable manner.
c. Independent variables never act alone.
d. The behavior of dependent variables is related to some other factor.
e. All of the above.

12. The quantitative technique that would be most helpful to an internal auditor in evaluating projected general and administrative expense is:
a. Game theory.
b. Regression analysis.
c. Probability theory.
d. Linear programming.
e. Queuing theory.

13. The most appropriate technique for developing a multiprocess production schedule is:
a. Monte Carlo method.
b. Regression analysis.
c. Queuing theory.
d. Linear programming.

e. Exponential smoothing.

14. Which of the following steps is **not** essential in using a linear programming model?
a. Quantify the maximization coefficient inflow.
b. Determine the objective function.
c. Establish the basic relationship between the variables and constraints.
d. Identify the feasible alternatives.
e. Determine the quantities involved.

15. In salary problems susceptible to linear programming, which of the following conditions or determinations should apply?
a. The purpose of the model.
b. Restraints on the decision maker's resources.
c. The problem is subject to mathematical assessment.
d. All of the above.
e. None of the above.

Case Studies

10-1 Auditing a Model

Assume that as a government auditor you have been asked to evaluate an energy growth model. The model relies on historical data and uses econo-metric techniques to estimate the parameters in the various equations. The model has one or more energy-use and price variables among the dependent variables. It includes income, capital costs, imports, and government expenditures among the primary independent variables. The model includes an assumption about the responsiveness of energy use to price change.

Required: What questions should you ask yourself in evaluating the model?

10-2 Using Consultants

You have been asked by your vice president-controller to evaluate a regression analysis model. You are expected to issue a written report on your findings, including an audit opinion. The model employs multiple regression analysis, involves a large number of equations, and is being designed for computer application. You have been authorized to employ a well-known operations research consultant.

Required: What conditions would you set for the consultant at your initial meeting?

11

Computer Auditing

The need for involvement. Internal audit "Standards." Responsibilities imposed by "Additional GAO Standards":

A. System design and development — auditor participation.

    A.1 Management policies — carried out by systems and applications.

    A.2 Audit trails — tracing transactions.

    A.3 Controls — protecting against loss or error.

    A.4 Efficiency and economy — assured by systems and applications.

    A.5 Legal requirements — compliance.

    A.6 Documentation — understanding systems and applications.

B. General controls — assuring proper design and effective operation.

    B.1 Organizational controls — meeting company or agency objectives.

    B.2 Resources and security — helping achieve effective operation.

    B.3 Operating system controls — assuring reliable processing.

    B.4 Hardware controls — detecting malfunctions.

C. Application controls — achieving timeliness, accuracy, and completeness.

    C.1 Conformance with standards and approved design — meeting established criteria.

    C.2 Tests for control weaknesses — preventing computer misuse.

Forms and causes of system changes. Intentional misuse of the computer. Computer program documentation.

Introduction

The Internal Auditor's Responsibility

The expanding field of electronic data processing (EDP) is rapidly encroaching on all of the internal auditor's territory. It is a changing, unending progression; it cannot be ignored. The old ways are going or gone. The new ways are here and now, and they are getting ever more difficult to deal with in the accustomed manner.

Some internal auditors have plunged eagerly into the exploration of this new field. Some have timidly refrained, still standing in their accustomed places, fearful of mysteries that are not really all that mysterious. Every internal auditor is in one way or another affected. As the computer and its generations grow and expand, the internal auditor must become involved to be able to function effectively in today's environment.

Computer-related expenses in many companies are the largest single item of overhead. Because of decreases in equipment cost, increased awareness of computer capabilities, and the constantly burgeoning scope of computer applications made available to potential users, computer use is extensive. Comprehensive business systems are becoming the rule. Management is relying more and more on the computer to store and furnish information for decision-making. The spreading tentacles of this automated octopus probe into every nook in large organizations and are finding footholds in small ones.

Just as management relies on the internal auditor to assure it of the efficiency and effectiveness of its other operations, so it looks to the auditor to assure it of satisfactory EDP operations and to alert it to shortcomings and pitfalls. This reliance will be sought with greater anxiety because of the mystery that surrounds EDP and the dependence management places upon it.

Executives and operating managers, hemmed in with the day-to-day problems requiring constant attention, rarely have the time to become knowledgeable and fluent in this medium with its puzzling and arcane language. Yet they are prisoners of EDP and must deal with it. Their need for the strong right arm of the modern internal auditor is increased a hundredfold as computers take over the information systems within the company.

Because of the breadth and scope of their approach, their knowledge of intracompany operations, and their independence, internal auditors are in a unique position to provide such assistance to management. Indeed, they can be held responsible for the evaluation of computer-based systems. Enunciation of this responsibility can be found in two documents. The first is the *Standards for the Professional Practice of Internal Auditing.*

310 *Reliability and Integrity of Information*

Internal auditors should review the reliability and integrity of financial and operating information and the means used to identify, measure, classify, and report such information.

.01 Information systems provide data for decision making, control, and compliance with external requirements. Therefore, internal auditors should examine information systems and, as appropriate, ascertain whether:

.1 Financial and operating records and reports contain accurate, reliable, timely, complete, and useful information.

.2 Controls over record keeping and reporting are adequate and effective.

The second document, published in 1979, became effective January 1, 1980. It is entitled "Additional GAO Standards" and is a supplement to the U. S. General Accounting Office's *Standards for Audit of Governmental Organizations, Programs, Activities & Functions* (the so-called "Yellow Book"). These supplemental standards set forth with particularity the responsibility of internal auditors for reviewing computer-based systems. They deal with the internal auditor's role as it relates to:

A. **System design and development**

B. **General controls in computer-based systems**

C. **Application controls in computer-based systems**

The GAO points out that compliance with the standards may not always be feasible. After all, internal auditors may audit only what management authorizes, but internal auditors have a duty to alert management to the potential dangers when computer-based systems are placed off limits to them. Such warnings should not be offhand comments; they should be formal communications. They should point out that in the absence of effective audits of computer systems and processes there may be no:

Built-in controls to assure proper and efficient operations.

Ability to track events through the system, and thus impeding — if not completely frustrating — audit review of the system in operation.

Compliance with generally accepted accounting principles, thereby resulting in qualifications of the independent accountant's opinion on the financial statements.

Compliance with the internal accounting controls provisions of the U.S. Foreign Corrupt Practices Act of 1977.

The GAO standards are binding on government auditors. They are not binding on internal auditors in the private sector, but they are persuasive. They set forth with specificity where the internal auditor's responsibility lies for auditing EDP systems and applications. In the absence of other standards, they will most likely be looked to as a benchmark for internal audit involvement in data-based systems.

Innumerable instances graphically underscore the need for such internal audit involvement and the reasons why internal auditors should shoulder their responsibilities for reviewing EDP systems. Here are but a few:

A computer manufacturer stored packing materials in a basement under the computer room. When the materials caught fire, heat entered the room through conduits for electrical cables. The water used to extinguish the fire increased the loss. Because the computer room had not been adequately protected, millions of dollars of computer hardware and other assets were destroyed.[1]

A large wholesaler had to raise prices as a result of inflation. But the "new" price list fed into the computer was actually a list that was six months old — it did not include the increased prices. As a result, incorrect billings were issued during a period of two months at a loss of $80,000. Collection efforts cost another $20,000.[2]

Depreciation calculations in an aerospace company resulted in assets with negative book values. The programming staff had been instructed on the various acceptable depreciation methods, but the finance people had never informed the programmers that depreciation stops when the net book value reaches zero.[3]

In a financial institution, the interest calculations on savings accounts were programmed as if each month had 31 days. A minor error? Not so. During the five months before the error was discovered, over $100,000 in excess interest was paid.[4]

It has been said that experienced auditors may expect to find programming errors in 30% of the applications they test. Rates as high as 60% have been observed. Most of the errors are not material, but some of them cost millions.

Concept of This Chapter

In recent years a flood of literature on audits of computer-based systems has inundated internal auditors. Any attempt to copy or summarize the reams of instructions would be an exercise in redundancy. It is worthwhile, however, to discuss the responsibilities of internal auditors for EDP audits, with brief descriptions of the related systems, and some of the approaches to auditing the systems.

The GAO's three EDP audit standards identify the internal auditor's responsibilities. The pamphlet in which they appear expands on the generalities and spells out specific standards. This chapter will be devoted to discussing each of the specific standards and offering some suggestions for conforming to them.*

The different standards sometimes call for similar controls or audit steps. In such cases, a control or audit step is repeated. In a few instances rather than repeat the same extended discussion in two places, the single discussion is made reference to.

---

*Author's note: Because this chapter parallels the GAO standards, the section on System Design and Development is given first place. We recognize that many auditors will deal with new applications rather than new systems. In most cases the systems will already be in place, and so auditors will be more concerned with general controls and application controls. Nevertheless, to provide comprehensive coverage in a logical pattern, the chapter begins with a discussion of the auditor's responsibility for the installation of new hardware.

A. System Design and Development*
The auditor shall actively participate in reviewing the design and development of new data processing systems or applications, and significant modifications thereto, as a normal part of the audit function.

Controls not built into a computer-based system can rarely be tacked on economically later. The expense of completely revising the system to add controls is usually prohibitive. Internal auditors should therefore work closely with the development of new computer systems and modifications of existing ones. Computer-based systems have grown, have become complex, and have developed close interrelationships and interdependences. In early days, the automated systems for personnel, payroll, and labor cost accounting were processed separately. In most large organizations they are now all part of a single complex of interwoven subsystems. The outputs for one system can be the input for another. No human hands or eyes need intervene. A control weakness in one subsystem can affect others. A modification in one subsystem can cast its shadow over all its fellows. Mistakes can cascade throughout the entire complex. Unanticipated effects can be catastrophic. The internal auditor's review is vitally needed in the development of both new systems and modifications.

A.1 Management Policies
Systems and applications should faithfully carry out the policies management has prescribed.

EDP Audit Environments
To effectively evaluate controls in an EDP system it is first necessary to gain an insight into the differing EDP audit environments. There are substantive differences in the complexity of the controls needed in a batch processing system versus a resource-sharing system.**

Simple **batch processing** is the historical and still prevalent mode of operation, wherein a number of jobs or transactions are grouped and processed as a unit. The batches are usually manually organized, and for the most part each individual job is processed to completion in the order in which it was received by the computer.

Batch-processing systems may provide local access or remote access to the computer. In local-access systems, all elements are physically located within the central computer facility; in remote-access systems, some units are geographi-

---

*These headnotes, which appear throughout this chapter, are taken directly from the "Additional GAO Standards."

**Source: *Security Controls for Computer Systems,* Report of the Defense Science Board Task Force on Computer Security, edited by Willis H. Ware; R-609-1. Reissued October 1979 by The Rand Corporation, Santa Monica, California 90406.

cally distant from the central computer facility and are connected to it by communication lines. Local-access systems are the simplest systems to control since all activities are located in one place — the central computer facility.

With the advent of resource-sharing computer systems, a new and complex dimension has been added to the problem of safeguarding computer-resident information. **Resource-sharing** systems are those that distribute the resources of a computer system (e.g., memory space, arithmetic units, peripheral equipment, channels) among a number of simultaneous users. The term includes systems commonly called *time-sharing, multiprogrammed, remote-batch, on-line, multi-access,* and where two or more processors share all of the primary memory, *multiprocessing.*

The principal distinction among the systems is whether a user must be present (at a terminal, for example) to interact with the job (time-sharing, on-line, multi-access), or whether the jobs execute autonomously (multiprogrammed, remote-batch).

Resource-sharing allows many people to use the same complex of computer equipment concurrently. The users are generally, although not necessarily, geographically separated from the central processing equipment and interact with the machine via remote terminals or consoles. Each user's program is executed in some order and for some period of time, not necessarily to completion. The central processing equipment devotes its resources to servicing users in turn, resuming with each where it left off in the previous cycle. Owing to the speed of modern computers, the individual users are rarely aware that they are receiving only a fraction of the system's attention or that a particular job is being fragmented into pieces for processing.

Multiprogramming is a technique by which resource-sharing is accomplished. Several jobs are simultaneously resident in the system, each being handled by the various system components so as to maximize efficient use of the entire configuration. The operating system (the system software which schedules work through the computer system, assigns resources to each job, accounts for resources used, etc.) switches control from one job to another in such a way to take advantage of the machine's most powerful — and most expensive — resources.

In practice, multiprogramming prevents jobs demanding large amounts of time in input or output functions (I/O bound jobs) from tying up the central processor. This is accomplished usually by allowing each job to execute until an input or output operation is required, at which point another job begins to execute concurrently with the I/O request.

On the other hand, a time-sharing system regularly interrupts each job in turn, allowing each to execute for some interval of time determined by the computer system itself rather than by the structure of the job.

These systems represent some of the latest advances in computer technology. Basically, they are intended to provide the most efficient use of expensive computing resources for the widest range of users. A single system that is able to handle several users or several sets of data simultaneously contributes to more economical operation. In addition to the direct advantages of vastly improved resource utilization and greatly increased economy of operation, these systems can drastically reduce service turn-around time, enable users with little or no formal knowledge of programming to interact directly with the machine, and extend computing capabilities to many smaller installations that would be unable to support a dedicated machine.

Internal Control

In the early days of computer applications, the EDP soufflé had a tendency to fall as soon as it was taken out of the oven. The absence of a single ingredient was the reason — involvement by executive and user managers. They avoided the feasibility studies, the setting of policies and objectives, and the development of standards. They regarded the computer as a mysterious and unmanageable beast, and they left its handling to its trainers, the EDP specialists.

But management and EDP specialists have differing objectives. Management is profit oriented. It seeks to obtain the best economic return for its investments. Many EDP specialists, on the other hand, are more concerned with solving problems. They seek technically challenging or sophisticated applications. A prime objective is to advance the state of their art. These specialists seem to obtain their greatest satisfaction by reporting to their peers an application no one has tried before. Professional achievement is paramount; economic return is an also-ran.

In one company, the EDP specialists worked zealously on a massive data-based system. They were far behind schedule. They had toiled on the system for three years and said they had another three to five years to go. A frantic management, seeing the dollars melting away, called in consultants who analyzed what was done and what was still needed. They then concluded that the entire project should be scrapped. Many parts of the project were not technically feasible. Many others had no economic value. The debacle might have been prevented by management involvement at the outset — by managers and their internal auditors asking the hard questions.[5] (Exhibit 11-1 highlights the conflicting views of management, data processing specialists, and internal auditors.)

In the middle sixties horrible examples of cost overruns in systems development plagued executive management. Often the end results were inaccurate record keeping, business interruption, erroneous management decisions, fraud, and legal sanctions because of violations of mandatory statutes or regulations.

Management can become involved through a steering committee. A member of top management should chair the committee. Of utmost importance, the users should be represented. Steering committees must meet regularly. Their functions should include approving EDP policies, approving long- and short-term plans for computer systems, considering user priorities, evaluating needs for new computer systems, and monitoring the progress of systems design, development, implementation, and operation.

Management policies should be developed during the all-important feasibility studies. These studies should be able to show the benefits to be obtained from a proposed application. They should also show the impact of the new application on the operations in the user department. They should state specifically the actual budget reductions to be experienced.

Management policies should provide for and protect the user. They should prescribe the formal system for requesting EDP assistance. They

Exhibit 11-1.

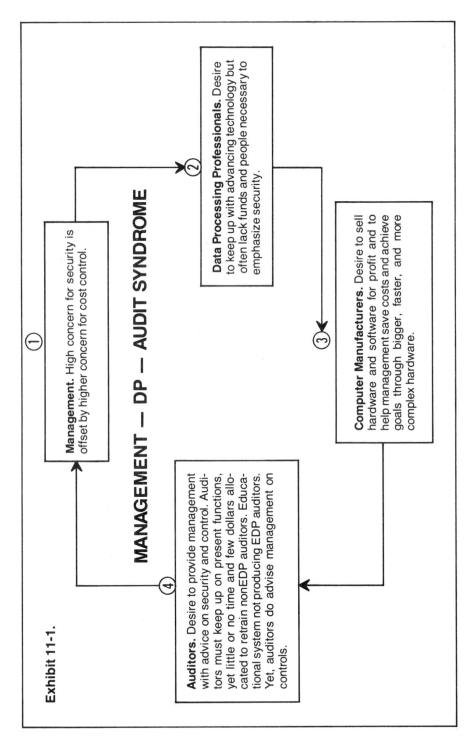

MANAGEMENT — DP — AUDIT SYNDROME

Management. High concern for security is offset by higher concern for cost control.

Data Processing Professionals. Desire to keep up with advancing technology but often lack funds and people necessary to emphasize security.

Computer Manufacturers. Desire to sell hardware and software for profit and to help management save costs and achieve goals through bigger, faster, and more complex hardware.

Auditors. Desire to provide management with advice on security and control. Auditors must keep up on present functions, yet little or no time and few dollars allocated to retrain nonEDP auditors. Educational system not producing EDP auditors. Yet, auditors do advise management on controls.

should provide for a master plan encompassing all approved development projects. They should define user needs and prepare sound cost-benefit analyses for new applications. They should call for active user participation in system definition of design and user approval of design.

Management policies set standards. Standards should be spelled out in formal statements, not informal chats. Standards should therefore be clearly stated and well documented. Vague, informal standards do not allow the prediction of results, they afford no basis for comparison, and they cannot be communicated consistently to others.

Management may not be able to appraise the technical adequacy of standards, but through its steering committee it should make sure that these have been developed.[6]

Internal Audit

The internal audit role in the feasibility and system study is not an enviable one. Internal auditors are dealing with specialists in a very specialized undertaking. They must be knowledgeable, tactful, and helpful; yet they must maintain their independence and be watchful of the company's broader goals. Not always will they be able to carry out their own function as they wish, but they will do it much better if they have a definite plan of action in mind. Here are some of the things they should try to be assured of when they participate in and review the feasibility and system study:

The study should be made by a team composed of representatives of all departments whose interests should be considered.

At least one member of the team should be an expert in the capabilities of EDP equipment.

The study should start with a thorough analysis of the preexisting manual or automated system. Sometimes the only thing wrong with the prior system is that it needed to have its problems identified and corrected.

Consideration should be given to the audit deficiencies cited against the preexisting system.

Specifications for the new system should not be so restricted as to slant them toward only one equipment manufacturer.

Workload projections should be realistic. They should not show current volume only; they should consider contemplated growth.

Consideration should be given to the risk of fraud or the loss of control.

The users should agree to the proposed system.

The budget estimates should be reasonable and supportable.

Input and output requirements should be clearly defined. The system flow should offer logical processing procedures and should be clearly presented.

Reasonable conversion plans should be formulated.

If any of these standards are not met and if the internal auditors find the EDP specialists reluctant to take corrective action, they have no alternative but to report their findings to top management.

The following case study illustrates the reasons for internal audit involvement during the feasibility study and the need to ask the hard questions:

> A large manufacturing company installed a central computer system to provide management with information on the status of operations at each of seven copying-printing centers. The system was also designed to provide the finance department with information needed to identify direct costs chargeable to customers.
>
> The department manager complained that he could not use the existing output reports because they were inaccurate, incomplete, and untimely. The internal auditor learned that controls were lacking to make sure all rejected documents were corrected and entered into the system again.
>
> The auditor tested the system and found that what he had been told during his preliminary survey was all too true. About $43,000 in chargeable costs had not been reported to finance. Besides, even if the identified defects in the entire system were corrected, the information given management on the status of operations would still be four days old. Management needed that information in two days.
>
> At the auditor's suggestion, the computer specialists eliminated the useless computer files and reports, saving $2,600 a month. He also suggested initiating a simple manual system which provided management with timely information at no additional cost.[7]

A.2 Audit Trails
Systems and applications should provide the controls needed for management, auditor, and operational review.

Internal Control

Transactions should be traceable from their initiation through all intermediate steps to final reporting. This ability permits verification of transactions and corrections of errors. In the days of manual systems, the trail was visible and continuous. Today, EDP systems have rendered those trails invisible. There is no one-to-one relation between the entry and the exit of a transaction. Auditors auditing around the computer are put at a disadvantage. They depend on the integrity of the trail through the computer. With that dependence they assume what went into the computer came out unsullied, but a smart programmer can disguise the trail within the computer.

Other problems compound the difficulty. Suppose a person is in the process of initiating a transaction and the system fails during that process. That person may not know whether the transaction was ever completed. The absence of a transaction trail may prevent correction or corroboration of results.

It has been said that trails and controls do not exist solely for the convenience of the auditor.[8] Nor are they necessarily a management tool. By and large their function is to trace and correct exceptions, so *transaction trail* is a more fitting term than audit trail. The trail helps clerical people correct errors and control the quality of transactions.

At the same time, the clerical review of the hosts of transactions clearing through the EDP system is burdensome and expensive. Computerized edits are more desirable. No system is perfect, however, and so some form of assurance of continuity from input to output is needed, even obligatory. This assurance is required to support tax transactions. Indeed, IRS recognized the desirability of machine-readable transaction trails in Revenue Ruling 71-20, holding that "machine-sensible data media may be considered records within the meaning of the revenue code."

Internal Audit

Internal auditors must contribute to the incorporation of transaction trails. They should not dictate the particular trail; that would affect their independence. But they must be able to satisfy themselves and management that needed transaction trails and controls are in force. Of course, they cannot hold themselves out as "authorizing" the system. Rather they should evaluate the proposed system, and if needed controls are lacking, they should report their absence to management.

The internal auditor also should keep in mind the needs of secondary users. For example, those in the accounting department may need certain transaction trails and controls so that they can rely upon the accuracy of the information they may need for financial reports.

In terms of transaction verification, internal auditors are most comfortable when they can walk a visible trail — from an account balance to the record of an event, from the record of an event to the account balance, and from any point within the process. Nonaccounting activities are no different.

In on-line systems, however, hard copy source documents often are lacking; transaction trails are not visible and palpable. The auditor must therefore look to the system to provide assurance that normal transactions are properly processed and that abnormal transactions are detected, rejected, and brought up for review.

Since the system is to be relied upon, changes in the system become critical to the auditor: changes in the ways data are processed within the system, changes in the environment in which the system operates, and changes in those sensors which observe the input material. For this reason, Scanlan suggests an event concept of auditing on-line systems.[9]

The event concept refers to the review of the entire EDP complex at a particular point or period of time — the audit determination of the aggregate effectiveness of all controls as the system responds to events that enter and flow through it. If the system is reliable, the transactions flowing through it must be acceptable. Clearly, a reliance on the system is conditioned on the continuity of the system. So discontinuities and changes must be given careful audit review.

For the internal auditors to be able to rely on a system as a basis for accepting the validity of transactions, they must be capable of analyzing the system and its coordinate controls. This calls for expertness in evaluating data processing systems. If the auditors are not themselves expert, they must be able to recruit such expertise.

A.3 Controls
Systems and applications should include the controls necessary to protect against loss or serious error.

Internal Control
Almost all organizations today are in thrall to the computer. Most of their records are kept on magnetic devices. The millions of records processed each day flow invisibly and without human intervention through the mysterious black boxes. Exposure to accident, error, and loss of data exists in every segment of an application: when data is transcribed from one medium to another, when data is transmitted from one location to another, while data is being processed, when data is rejected and reentered, and when data is stored.

Controls in a computer environment are the means used to reduce these exposures and to help achieve management's objectives. These means differ from those in a manual environment because:

The controls must be built into the machine.

Sources of data are sometimes independent of the users of the data.

Transaction trails from input to output are seldom visible to the human eye.

The need to be especially explicit in the absence of human judgment exists.

Documentation must be accurate and precise.

Responsibility for the user's information shifts to the EDP facilities.

To compound the difficulties, a number of factors conspire to keep an adequate control system from being developed:

Fact gathering and evaluation may be inept.

Senior management may abdicate its responsibility for the control system on the grounds that the subject is too technical.

Errors may creep into systems design.

Communication is often poor among systems people, users, and management, so users fail to specify what controls are needed to handle transactions, process data, and receive information output.

Unscrupulous programmers can incorporate minute instructions into the computer to divert assets to their own use.

A strong, unified direction may be lacking.

Yet controls must be incorporated into every system and application to reduce the everpresent exposures to poor records, to improper accounting, to interruptions of business, to bad decision making, to fraud and embezzlement, to violations of statutory or regulatory requirements, to increased costs, to loss of assets, and to loss of competitive position in the market place.

Management must therefore be aware of the controls needed to keep the computer from being used for improper purposes, to reduce the incidence of error, and to obtain the best results from computer operations. Management cannot shirk its responsibility for seeing that the controls are in fact established and working. These controls can be divided into three groups:

○ Controls over organization
○ Controls over administration
○ Controls over procedures

Controls Over Organization

Controls through division of authority are even more important in EDP systems than in other business functions. The volume is greater, the processes are faster, and great amounts are involved in terms of equipment and recorded assets.

Within the EDP organization, data files should be controlled by a librarian who should issue files only to individuals authorized to obtain them. Librarians should keep a record of file name and date and the name of the person who received the files. The library should not be accessible to anyone other than the librarian to help prevent the misfiling of records and unauthorized changes.

Using departments must participate in the study and implementation stages of computer systems. They should be required to approve the final system and its built-in controls since they will suffer the most if the system does not meet their needs.

Management must also take an active part in installing controls. Among the most important controls are the written performance standards to be set for systems design, programming, and computer operations. Management may not be able to appraise the technical adequacy of the standards, but it should make sure they have been developed and are in use. Here are some of the standards the steering committee would want to see established:

System documentation standards. These standards cover user documentation, the nature of the documentation required, how revisions should be explained, flowcharting techniques, decision tables, coding, and the particular terms used in the industry. Changes should be made under closely controlled conditions, otherwise programmers can introduce means of using computers for their own purposes.

Programming documentation standards. These standards include instructions on documenting changes to the original computer program and any subsequent changes. The standards could include logic diagrams, decision tables, coding, and a glossary of terms. Appended to this chapter are 12 categories of documentation that could be used to support computer programs (see Exhibit 11-2). All 12 categories may be used in those companies which want to include all documentation in one package with little or no need to refer to other sources. Minimum documentation, for the reasons cited in the exhibit, requires these four categories: system flowchart, logic flowchart, source program, and computer run sheet.

Operating documentation standards. These operating standards encompass changes in documentation, methods of documenting messages and halts, reconstruction and restart procedures, and procedures governing the end of the job.

Library of file documentation standards. The library accounts for documentation changes; labeling; tape, disk, and card historical records; file numbering and dating; and file storage.

Keypunching or other conversion standards. These standards cover documenting revisions; identifying codes for machine-readable records; and rules for algebraic signs, blank spaces, and other matters requiring standardized techniques.

Documentation standards for control groups. These standards include contents and format of reports and other output; methods of revising documentation; the correction, reentry, and control of previous errors; and period and cutoff arrangements.[10]

Controls Over Administration

Controls over administration comprise the means used to ensure consistency and continuity of programming and program testing.

One cannot look at a computer and determine whether the program that it is executing has been properly and completely prepared. The alternative is a well-documented trail showing how the program was prepared and describing any changes in it.

The initial control, therefore, would be a manual of programming standards which lays down specific rules on the initial preparation as well as on changes in all computer programs. The manual should be followed faithfully to give reasonable assurance that programs will be documented in an acceptable manner no matter who prepares them.

The test of good documentation is whether a typical programmer can tell what the program is supposed to do and will do, without the need for supplementary explanations. That requirement is no different from what would be expected of auditors when they document their audit examination in their working papers. Of course, the documentation tells only what the program **should** do — not what it actually does. A programmer smart enough to make self-serving modifications will hardly document those actions, thus the necessity for independent tests of the documented controls.

Program test procedures should likewise be governed by written instructions and should involve common-sense precautions. For example:

The final testing should make use of actual live data chosen to be sure the prowram will be faced with a variety of conditions, including those not specifically provided for in the program.

The test should go beyond a single cycle so as to expose the master file — a file usually required to be kept current — to updating procedures.

The test should include improper data or data which deliberately seeks to violate programmed controls, to see whether the controls are indeed functioning as intended.

The testing hierarchy begins with the testing of program routines, then continues through the testing of each program module individually; next, all modules are tested as a system; and, finally, a volume test on the entire system is performed. All problems disclosed by the tests should be thoroughly investigated and resolved.

Controls Over Procedures

Controls over procedures stand guard over the actual processing and dissemination of data. They may be subdivided into input controls, processing controls, and output controls.

Input controls. Input controls help strengthen the weak link in the chain of EDP events. All manner of checks and balances can be built into a program to assure proper processing, storage, and retrieval of data, but all of this is to no avail if the computer is presented with erroneous or incomplete data at the outset. Input controls can be devised to help. There should be assurance that whatever is received by the machine is complete. If controls are established close to the point of preparation of transactions, losses will be minimized.

A system of batch controls can provide assurance that no data is lost as it travels from place to place before it reaches the computer. One way of achieving batch control is to process all transactions for a specified period of time, total their values on an adding machine tape, and record and reconcile those totals on logs at different transfer points.

Real-time systems do not readily lend themselves to batch controls. At remote terminal systems, items entered sporadically and by different people into the terminals are not easily batched. Whether batched or not, however, each entry can be displayed on the screen for visual verification. The displayed entry can be checked against corroborative data extracted from the data base for visual tests. Also, each entry can be subjected to an edit program to make sure that each field has the proper numeric, alphabetic, or alphanumeric format. Finally, each entry can be checked for reasonableness or logic. For example, items showing more than 24 hours to a day may be rejected, or certain types of items may be originated by a particular department only.

When items have been rejected, there should be some method of ensuring the reentry of such material after it has been corrected.

Processing Controls. Processing controls apply to the machine room. Their object is to prevent or discourage the improper manipulation of data and to ensure the continued, satisfactory operation of both hardware and software.

Access to the computer should be limited to those authorized to operate the equipment. Object programs should be accessible only to the equipment operators. This separation renders it difficult to make unauthorized modifications to the program. Similarly, programmers should not have uncontrolled access to the computer locations, files, and records. Their knowledge of EDP programs makes data manipulation particularly easy.

Nor should operators have unlimited access to the machine. They should be allowed access only to that program information needed to set up the equipment and respond to programmed halts. The data processing supervisor should respond to any unprogrammed "abends" (halts) for programs that have already been tested and approved for use.

Any operator intervention should be made a matter of record. Indeed, most modern systems have a console log which will list all operator intervention within the system. Because of the everpresent possibility of wrongful manipulation, these further precautions should be considered: requiring the presence of at least two trained operators during the equipment operation and rotating assignments among operators.

Provision should be made for periodic preventive maintenance. The equipment should be maintained in accordance with schedules established by the manufacturer. Environmental controls should be provided to ensure proper temperature, humidity, and electrical power. Equipment can deteriorate when conditions exceed environmental ranges set by the manufacturer.

Information concerning computer equipment should be maintained in daily computer logs and periodic equipment utilization reports. No matter what controls are built into the hardware, machine malfunction can occur and result in errors in the processing. Thus, manual and programmed edit procedures should be provided and used to compensate for missing hardware controls or to supplement those in use.

Output controls. Output controls govern the accuracy and reasonableness of the information processed. The totals of records processed should agree with the total record input. Prenumbered forms can help control output since these can be accounted for. As an example, the number of payroll check forms can be checked against input records.

Output controls also include the proper handling of exceptions. When valid data is rejected, the fault may lie with machine malfunction or with operator error. Console typewriter sheets — a form of output — should be maintained to show the reason for rejecting valid data and the steps taken to correct errors.

Changes in Control

Internal control is not static, however. It cannot be regarded solely in terms of devices and procedures. The effectiveness of internal control can vary. The same system can be effective or ineffective depending on the presence or absence of personnel, on the degree of their motivation, on the excellence of their supervision, and on other human factors. The result is a large number of different states of nature of the internal controls during a given period, all of which management must take into account.

Internal Audit

Because controls are so essential, the design of computer systems cannot safely be left entirely to the computer specialists. Too much is at stake.

As we have already observed, many computer specialists are more concerned with solving unique and esoteric computer problems than with meeting pragmatic needs or incorporating mundane controls. Internal auditors, therefore, must look out for the needs of management and of users. They must keep company objectives in mind. And they must see that exposures are guarded against through controls built into the system before, rather than after, it becomes operational.

The internal auditor must point out to management and to computer specialists these unnerving statistics. As a rule of thumb, adding a control to a program will cost four times as much after the system is specified, eight times as much after the system is programmed, twelve times as much after the system is tested, and sixteen times as much after the system is implemented.[11]

The computer specialist is primarily concerned with new equipment, programs, and efficient performance. The internal auditor can add to these interests a rich background of company objectives and goals, and a knowledge of company needs that must be satisfied, thus providing a stabilizing influence that takes into account the entire organization, not just data processing.

Written control procedures should be completed before the system is put into operation. The caveat that bars the internal auditor from participating in the development of new systems should not be applied to EDP. The dangers are too great. The corrections are too expensive. Two examples will illustrate the point.[12]

In a large railroad company internal auditors decided that it would be a good idea to have the computer reject inaccurate data. This was after the EDP system involving freight car records had been in effect some time. The auditors developed an audit test deck. Essential data was deliberately omitted. Incorrect data was deliberately added. For example, the test deck showed cars interchanged with another railroad when their own railroad had no interchange at all with the other one. The deck showed interchanges with nonexistent railroads, with nonexistent car numbers, and in one instance a car interchanged on May 53rd. Any self-respecting computer program with appropriate edit routines would have screamed TILT when the test deck was introduced. But this program happily processed and printed out all invalid (among valid) transactions, including 22 extra days of per diem for the car interchanged on May 53rd.

The same auditors examined the computer application for the payroll. Employee pay was being machine-calculated by matching the clock numbers that were listed on the current time sheets with a purportedly "active" employee file. The auditors discovered to their horror that many of the employees in the "active" file had left the company as long as three years before. So if the clock number of the terminated employee appeared (or was placed) on the time report, there was nothing to prevent the preparation of a pay check.

The obvious solutions in those two cases were to reprogram the computer in the freight application to recognize and reject erroneous or incomplete data, and to purge the "active" file of data on terminated employees and establish a fool-proof procedure for adding and deleting data from the master file.

These eminently reasonable suggestions were taken to the data processing people. They immediately talked of the "work-years" required to reprogram — of the thousands upon thousands of dollars it would take to put into the programs the controls that should have been there from the start — the controls a knowledgeable internal auditor would have insisted upon.

As a result of this traumatic experience, the auditors learned these sad lessons:

Effective controls should be designed into a system, not tacked on afterwards.

System designers and computer programmers do not always include all the necessary controls in a new computer application. Controls designed into computer applications require time to conceive and implement. Sometimes they may be omitted for the sake of expedience — to meet a promised due date for system completion. The results can be costly and exasperating.

Auditors must participate in the evaluation of system acquisition and system design. The expense of correcting a faulty system is much too high.

The Institute of Internal Auditors, Inc., has recognized this need. In 1971 the Institute's "Statement of Responsibilities" pointed out that the internal auditor's "objectivity need not be adversely affected . . . by his determination and recommendation of the standards of control to be applied in the development of systems and procedures under his review."

The development of an EDP system demands a long, complex, and expensive study. Internal auditors must get involved at the very beginning to see that needed controls are incorporated at the most economical point in the system's development. Their successful involvement, however, will be dependent on certain conditions, and they should be abundantly aware of them.

They should be able to count on management support. (Of what use are cogent, well-buttressed suggestions that are ignored or overruled?)

They and the people who design and implement the system must be able to cooperate. (If complete and sincere cooperation is lacking, the auditors will have a lonely, frustrating road to travel. Good working relations are needed at the highest levels of the auditing and the EDP organizations.)

The systems people must be, or must be taught to be, control-oriented. Programmers who write the programs to be executed by the computer should also understand the importance of adequate controls within their programs. (This means salesmanship on the part of the internal auditors. They must be able to demonstrate the heavy penalties for inadequate controls.)

Internal auditors must know what they are talking about. They must know the EDP argot. They must be familiar with the EDP hardware. They must have a working knowledge of programming. In short, they must be able to converse on an equal level with the systems and programming people.

The internal auditor must evaluate the needs of the company — not just those of the requesting department. (Somebody must be able to ensure appropriate balance. Somebody must make sure that the demands of Department A will not be filled at the expense of Department B. Department A cannot be expected to be completely objective. It has its own needs to satisfy. The internal auditor, tuned to the overall company goals, must see to it that local demands do not create control vacuums and adversely affect interdepartmental functions.)

Patently, the auditors' task in the feasibility and system study is not an enviable one. They are dealing with specialists in a specialized and often esoteric undertaking. They must be knowledgeable, tactful, and helpful. Yet they must maintain their independence and be watchful of the company's broader goals. After all, they are probably the sole unbiased emissaries of management on the team. Not always will they be able to carry out their own function as they wish, but they will do it much better if they are aware of the risks. For example:

Maintenance men may inject improper instructions into test programs used to test for malfunctions.

Programmers who write the software can install "trapdoors" or "Trojan horses" — branches in a program that cause it to perform unauthorized processing activities, usually for some illegal purposes.

Operators have opportunities each day to tamper with the computer data and files.

Wiretaps and bugs can intercept messages or pick up the electromagnetic signals from wires and terminals.

People tapping the system may intercept passwords and masquerade as legitimate users.

People may insert so-called "piggyback" data into legitimate transmissions by hooking another computer onto a tapped line — a computer that intercepts legitimate messages and modifies them.

Legitimate users may borrow passwords to browse through other people's files.

Professional data processors often complain that integrity controls cost too much. But the techniques used to improve integrity usually improve productivity. One computerized perpetual inventory system contained inaccuracies in 70% of its on-hand balances. By expanding cycle counts, the rate was reduced to 30%. This in turn permitted a reduction of 15% in the level of inventory carried to protect against out-of-stock conditions. The reduced carrying costs saved about four times the cost of the added controls.[13]

A.4 Efficiency and Economy
Systems and operations should function efficiently and economically.

Internal Control

The more money spent on an activity the greater the payback if efficiency and economy are proportionately increased. The huge sums invested in EDP make it a fruitful source of savings that result from careful management. For that reason, top management should see that feasibility studies are carried out objectively and in depth, that a clear statement of objectives and needs is developed for each system and application, that cost-benefit analyses look without bias at costs to be incurred and the benefits to be obtained, that the EDP organization deploys its resources efficiently, and that good administrative procedures are developed and followed.

Feasibility studies for computer operations must take this concept into account. The operation will be efficient and economical if the systems and applications help management guide the organization toward established objectives and goals without wasting time, energy, and money. Hence, the feasibility study should look beyond the computer room. It should look to the needs of users and the effect on peripheral organizations. Reports that are not summarized are useless to operating managers. Designers of systems and applications must recognize that data and information are not the same. Data are the flower petals. Information is the distilled nectar. Management needs information, not data.

Systems are rarely efficient and economical when top management has not presented a sound statement of goals, when it does not supply the needed resources, when it does not develop a master plan for an EDP system, and when it does not support and become involved in the design effort. Similarly, efficiency and economy suffer when the design group does not adequately review the entire relevant organizational structure, analyze information requirements, adequately evaluate hardware and software requirements, and provide a maintainable system. Finally, to achieve economy and efficiency, users must involve themselves in the design and suggest appropriate changes to see that their needs are met. All three groups must remember that the computer machinery has for its chief objective the ability to provide service at a cost that compares favorably with alternate methods.

EDP activities need adequate cost accounting systems. These should define the specific work projects required to meet management goals. They should establish detailed methods and cost centers to track and control the progress of projects or tasks. They should accumulate data so as to measure cost, decide on how to establish billing rates, and assign costs to users. The cost system should meet three separate needs:

1. Those of the EDP managers, to measure their own cost effectiveness and efficiency, to plan future workloads, to justify the resources assigned, and to transfer costs to user units.

2. Those of senior managers, to keep abreast of costs of the EDP system and to know whether EDP results are helping meet organization goals.

3. Those of users to give them information on the cost of EDP services, to help them decide whether they can afford them, to determine how these services relate to their own activities, and to show them how they are in a position to control those costs.

Efficiency can be improved by charging user departments for EDP time used, but they should be charged only for what they can be held responsible. For example, they should not be charged for reruns that are the fault of the EDP department. Proper charges tend to force users to be more efficient; users will learn to do manually what will help reduce running time if manual operation is more economical. But economy is not enough. The EDP department should also be responsible for user satisfaction. In sum, the object is to provide computer facilities only for those applications that are cost justified and to hold the EDP department responsible for efficient and effective processing.

The enormous sums invested in computer hardware, software, and personnel demand well-controlled deployment of these resources. Just as inept production control can escalate manufacturing costs, so can poor scheduling erode the hoped-for benefits from the computer system or increase the costs of running it.

The scheduling function should be separate from other data processing activities and should not be under the domination of one particular user. The scheduling supervisor should be in a position to balance equipment capability with the user's demands on the equipment, and at the same time, be aware of broad company needs to make sure essential jobs, like payroll or production control, are not shunted aside for rush jobs having less company-wide emphasis.

The records, log, and other documentation should support and justify scheduling decisions. They should establish conformance to scheduling procedures and demonstrate whether scheduling objectives have been met.

Scheduling procedures should account for all uses of equipment and data. And they should indicate the running time for each job. The procedures should require logs to report processing, completed jobs, machine down time, uncompleted jobs and the reasons for them, summary performance statistics, EDP payroll and overtime, operator rotation and vacation schedules, and comparisons between budgeted and actual costs. (Vendor-supplied software is available to provide such records automatically.)

Internal Audit

A chief function of internal auditors is to assure management that systems and applications will operate or are operating as intended, alerting management to any failures. Senior managers do not have the time for close and constant surveillance of the EDP function. The internal auditor must therefore be management's surrogate.

Internal auditors should seek to determine whether resources of personnel, property, and space are being used efficiently and economically. They would want to know if operations produce the desired results. They would review the adequacy of the statement of mission needs and system objectives, the feasibility study and evaluation of alternative designs, the cost benefit analysis and whether these attribute specific benefits and costs to system alternatives.

Here are some questions internal auditors can ask:

Is the basis for equipment selection well supported? Has consideration been given to lowest cost, program and system reliability, and service?

Has a study been made of new equipment, new operating systems, new programming languages, multiprogramming uses, time sharing, data banks, telecommunications, and progress in the standardization of source language?

Has appropriate consideration been given to lease or purchase, including provision for (or calculation of) depreciation? cost of capital? cash flow? timing? (Lease implies steady disbursement over the years — purchase implies large initial cash outlay.) obsolescence? preparing the site? providing power facilities, air conditioning, humidity control, soundproofing, raised floors to house cables and wiring, reinforced floors and foundations, uniform and independent sources of power, and security? storage facilities for tapes, punched cards, and programs? standby equipment in the event of equipment failure? adequate protection, such as off-site storage of vital information so that it can be reproduced if necessary?

Does the study establish objectives for cost savings? efficiency? improved information? And are these objectives sufficiently detailed so that they may serve to measure system performance?

Have time-phased plans been established for site preparation? equipment delivery? development operating procedures? programming and testing? orientation of operating personnel? disaster recovery?

Have provisions been made for the multiple use of common source data? Will source data be converted to machine language at the earliest practical point? Has provision been made for management by exception?

An internal audit of the efficiency and economy of an EDP system can be made through a work sampling study. Minutes during the day can be selected by statistical sampling techniques. At those precise minutes the internal auditor can observe whether parts of the computer — Central Processing Unit (CPU), printer, card reader — are working or are idle. Less than 50% working time may indicate underuse. Potential cost reductions are available through equipment downgrade or by consolidation with another system that is also used less than 50% of the time. On the other hand, 80% may indicate that a saturation point is near and that equipment may need to be upgraded.[14]

Internal auditors have proved themselves competent and capable of improving efficiency and economy in EDP systems. Here are some samples:

An internal auditor reviewed an inventory of magnetic tapes. The inventory consisted of 4,200 tapes, but only a third were listed in the inventory records. One fourth of some 3,600 open tapes were either obsolete or duplicates. As a result of the audit, inventory records were improved and the EDP department was able to avoid ordering $10,000 worth of new tapes by using the obsolete and duplicate ones.[15]

In one organization the payroll was computerized, but the payroll account was being reconciled manually. At the internal auditor's suggestion, the company's bank helped reconcile the payroll as part of its monthly service at a cost of only $30 a month. This resulted in savings of 10 work-hours each month.[16]

In another company 17 payroll offices throughout the United States processed payrolls for 176,000 employees. An EDP audit showed that the same EDP program that created productivity reports for a payroll office also created the transaction file used to update the corporate data base. Each summary file was being processed twice by the same program but at separate locations for different purposes. The internal auditor recommended single processing for both purposes and saved 400 computer hours and $25,000 a year.[17]

A U.S. Air Force audit team reviewed a proposed EDP system. They found that the original economic analysis was inaccurate and unsubstantiated; projected manpower reduction was not realistic; user needs, system capabilities, and resources were not documented or supported; and technical and equipment specifications were not substantiated. Users said that there was little need for the proposed on-line data base. The auditors recommended revised requirements at a cost of $4.7 million. The organization was able to avoid $31.5 million in costs for a system that would not have served the users' needs.[18]

With respect to scheduling, internal auditors need to satisfy themselves that the rules regarding scheduling have been reduced to writing and that they are well understood and uniformly applied by all schedulers. Auditors would also want to know how well actual schedules agree with forecasted needs. They will be particularly interested in the basis for accepting non-scheduled work and how often established schedules are disrupted by special jobs.

A.5 Legal Requirements
Systems and applications should comply with relevant legal requirements.

Internal Control
Legal requirements can make significant impacts on EDP systems and applications. In addition to the needs of management and users, statutory and regulatory requirements must be taken into account.

In the public sector, privacy statutes have been enacted at state and federal levels. These restrict the collection and use of certain types of information. Under the Privacy Act of 1974, Public Law 93-579, 5 USC 5529, signed into law August 21, 1974, federal agencies falling within the purview of the statute are required to establish appropriate administrative, technical, and physical safeguards to ensure the privacy of personal information.[19]

The statute is primarily applicable to the federal government, but it may also apply to government contractors. Its principles could be applied in state and local governments and in private sector recordkeeping.[20] Sweden and Germany have similar laws; Norway, Denmark, and France have such laws pending.[21]

To comply with privacy statutes, each Government agency is required to, one, establish appropriate safeguards to assure the security and confidentiality of records, and two, protect against anticipated threats or hazards to their security or integrity which could result in substantial harm, embarrassment, inconvenience, or unfairness to any individual about whom information is obtained.

One of the major threats to security comes from individuals already having authorized access to the computer. Once authorized, they are permitted to browse unchallenged through personal or sensitive files. A secondary threat is from those unauthorized to have access to the computer, but who have the technical ability and the resources needed to circumvent security measures.

The risk to sensitive information varies with the types of data involved, the effectiveness of the controls exercised, and the configuration of the computer network. The potential risk increases as more personal data are centralized, the number of users proliferate, and more common data are shared.

Absolute security is a will-o'-the-wisp. But if high-level management sets security as a key objective and sees that systems are monitored, the chances of reasonable success improve. The major problem is the trade-off between the economies achievable through EDP, on the one hand, and the cost of obtaining the level of protection for personal information that is appropriate to the threats faced, on the other. By addressing the problem rationally and using appropriate oversight, as provided in the Privacy Act of 1974, a balance can be drawn.[22] On the other side of the coin are the requirements of the Freedom of Information Act. Computer systems should have the capability of providing prompt responses to legitimate requests under the statute.

In the private sector, some of the government statutes and regulations that have their impact on computer systems include the Security and Exchange Commission's requirement for quarterly reviews, national health insurance, affirmative action programs, new rules for pension reporting, and consumer protection laws. The related reports are often different from those required for managers.

The requirements of the U.S. Foreign Corrupt Practices Act also have an effect on EDP systems. The Act will require the design of systems and controls to make sure that organizations keep reasonably detailed records which accurately and fairly reflect financial activities.

Internal Audit

The primary function of the internal auditor here is communication. For example: as a working internal auditor, the author became aware of a state law, recently enacted, laying down strict rules for the purchase and use of commercial hypodermic syringes. These are often used to place drops of bonding liquid in inaccessible places on assemblies and subassemblies. Inquiries of buyers who procured the syringes and of operating people who stored, issued, and used them disclosed a vast ignorance on the subject, yet the penalties were severe. The corporation was subject to stiff fines for violation. The internal auditors asked the company attorneys what the law required. They then passed that information on to the procedure writers and the people responsible for compliance with the statute. Violations were thus prevented and fines were avoided.

The internal audit function with respect to other statutory and regulatory requirements is much the same. Auditors will have to make sure that all such requirements are known; they will have to consult legal counsel to become aware of the requirements and the steps that must be taken under them; then they will have to make sure that they are considered in the feasibility study and the system design. After the installation or application is approved and working, they will have to determine whether the statutes and regulations are in fact being complied with.

Internal auditors will be concerned not only with actual compliance but also with how such compliance can be proved if questions are asked.

The answer lies, in part, in documentation. Such documentation should demonstrate that the applicable statutes and regulations were considered. It should substantiate the incorporation of appropriate routines and controls, and should contain copies or references to the required reports. The answer also lies in tests which make certain that statutes and regulations governing the application are in fact incorporated into the software and that the software is functioning only as intended.

Probably the most extensive job of documentation will be to evidence compliance with the U.S. Foreign Corrupt Practices Act. There, the system of control, like a complete human nervous system, extends through the entire body corporate. The penalties for failing to show compliance are serious. Here the internal auditors would be well advised to work jointly with external auditors and present a common front and a unified approach to statutory compliance.

Turning once more to privacy acts, fear of violation may stampede management into excessively expensive controls. For example, cryptography can be employed to secure communication links. Cryptography in a computer network calls for the use of an encryption device at the point of data transmission and a decryption device at the point of data reception. Such devices have to be incorporated at all remote terminals, or terminal controllers, as well as at the computer facility.

The National Bureau of Standards published a standard for data encryption on January 15, 1977 (*Federal Information Processing Standard Publication 46*). This standard specifies a step-by-step procedure, an algorithm, to be implemented in electronic devices to protect computer data.

Encryption is expensive, so a definite need should be established before employing this technique. Internal auditors would want to examine a threat analysis to see if the threats to privacy warranted the cost of the devices. They would also want to know if other security safeguards, such as identification, access controls, and access auditing can be implemented before sophisticated encryption devices are procured to protect personal data. Internal auditors must always balance the cost of control with the cost of loss before taking exception to a system or making recommendations to improve it.

A.6 Documentation
Systems and applications should be so documented as to permit an understanding of the systems and applications by those who maintain and audit them.

Internal Control

Documentation should define the processes to be performed by programs in the system. It should identify the data files to be processed. It should describe the reports to be prepared for users. It should set forth the operating instructions for computer operators. It should tell users about the preparation and control of data. In short, documentation should let a reviewer, auditor, or manager know what reliance can be placed on a system.

Good documentation is a sign of a well-run data processing facility. Unfortunately, many programmers and computer specialists find the chore of documenting their work mundane and not to their liking. They would rather finish the system or application they are working on and go to the next.

Documentation is essential. It is frequently needed by management to determine the functional adequacy of a program; by programmers who have reason to make changes in a computer program; and by auditors, both internal and external, to review computer controls. In the absence of adequate documentation, it is not uncommon to find that complex and expensive computer programs had to be substantially rewritten to introduce minor changes; only one or two people — usually the original programmers no longer on the scene — were aware in detail of what the program was supposed to do; management was not informed of the specifics it needed to review the adequacy of computer programs; and extensive unauthorized changes were made in the software for illegal purposes.

Both the manual and the computerized systems should be documented. Documentation for the manual system should describe the functions and activities for which the system was responsible, the specific clerical functions carried out, the input-output documents, and the forms and records in use. It should contain a flowchart of the system before it was computerized, and it should describe all records and fields. The documentation should also describe the present security system and any backup systems. (Backup systems are those available at alternative sites to continue the processing if the primary system fails.)

A comprehensive documentation program for computerized systems includes these forms of documentation:[23]

System documentation. System objectives, flowcharts linking the manual and computer processing steps, system specifications for design and development, input forms and procedures, record formats, descriptions of transaction trails, and balancing and control procedures.

Program documentation. Descriptions and flowcharts needed to facilitate maintenance after initial installation, control cards, job control language, program listings, program test data, a testing log, input/output distribution instructions, data retention instructions, console operator instructions, and copies of change request forms.

Operations documentation. Instructions needed to run a computer application accurately and efficiently, to balance inputs and outputs, to distribute reports, and to facilitate restart and recovery.

Library documentation. Procedures for backup and retention, restrictions on access to sensitive data, and inventory recordkeeping.

User documentation. Narrative description of the system's documentation and a general flow diagram; instructions on completing input forms and transactions; control procedures on balancing, reconciling, and maintaining overall control transactions, master files, and processing results. (User documentation is, in effect, a contract between users and the EDP people. It covers what the user is to do, what decision rules to apply, what the EDP people have set out to do for the user, and how the two parties to the contract will interact.)

Control documentation. A narrative of specific points in application systems telling where the user, the internal auditor, and the data processing people can expect to find controls and the methods by which their adequacy and effectiveness can be verified.

In sum, adequate documentation has characteristics of prevention, detection, and correction. By preparing the documentation, the preparer can prevent errors through the self-checking opportunities arising from putting prescribed procedures on paper. By communicating procedures to others, detection is permitted because a medium is provided for subsequent inspection. The availability of adequate application documentation permits correction and reconstruction of practically any application process.

Internal Audit

EDP people are often lax in preparing adequate documentation, which is an additional reason for internal auditors to become involved early enough in system and application development to counteract that tendency. Management has or should have a vital interest in adequate documentation, but rarely can they afford the time for a detailed review. The responsibility, therefore, will fall on the internal auditor, an unbiased surrogate, to perform those reviews for management and to inform top managers of their findings.

Internal auditors should review existing procedures for documentation preparation. In their compliance testing they should be concerned with program documentation, system documentation, operations documentation, and user procedure documentation. Internal auditors should be particularly concerned with documentation of change control procedures, where manipulation often takes place.

In terms of the proposed systems, the internal auditor should review planning documentation to see whether it contains information on:

The objectives and goals of the system.

System flowcharts.

Descriptions of both clerical and mechanical functions.

The general (macro) logic of the programs for the new application.

A description of input data.

Copies of source documents.

A description of the output of the new system.

A catalogue of controls to be included.

Exception reporting and the action to be taken on exceptions.

A list of the files to be maintained — documents, cards, magnetic tapes.

Retention schedules.

Minimum documentation standards for computer programs.

Adequate documentation certainly simplifies an internal auditor's job, but what if the documentation is inadequate? Auditors will, of course, report this defect to management. But they may still have to move ahead to determine whether the undocumented system is adequate, efficient, and effective. They may find that people working with the system have prepared their own informal notes and descriptions for their own use. The auditors may ask for those notes that EDP people and users have in their possession. They can then fill in gaps in the system that were not otherwise documented.

If even these notes and descriptions are lacking, the internal auditor might have to make assumptions of what the system should be and test for compliance. Obviously, internal auditors do not draw conclusions or express opinions on the basis of assumptions; these should be based on their compliance tests.[24]

The internal audit of documentation can prevent future difficulties. Here is an example:

Internal auditors found that the only documentation of certain control programs were the programs themselves, and these were quite complicated. They therefore recommended that a statement be prepared describing the control procedures. The recommendations resulted in two benefits. First, the programs were documented for future use. Second, the documentation provided a training tool for computer programmers. In addition, a copy of the test file, developed by the EDP audit staff, was turned over to the user to conduct independent tests of the system.[25]

B. General Controls
The auditor shall review general controls in data processing systems to determine that (A) controls have been designed according to management direction and legal requirements and (B) such controls are operating effectively to provide reliability of, and security over, the data being processed.

General controls apply to all the processing within a computer installation. They are not affected or altered by different programs or applications. They apply to the computer organization within the company, to all its people, and to its facilities.

General controls include the authority and responsibility given to the computer division or department and to the separation of duties among its people. These controls are concerned with the physical properties of the installation, with its personnel, and with its security. They are also concerned with the protection of its software and, finally, with the installation's hardware, with malfunctions of the hardware, and with detected hardware errors.

B.1 Organizational Controls
Organizational controls should provide reasonable assurance that the EDP activity will meet company or agency objectives.

Internal Control
Organizational controls include adequate responsibility and authority for the EDP activity. Such responsibility should be sufficient to permit the EDP activity to meet organizational objectives efficiently and effectively.

The EDP activity should report to a high enough level of authority to escape the domination of the organizational units it serves. In that way it will not be compelled to carry out programs which, in its judgment, have low priority.

Within the EDP activity, efficiency is enhanced by appropriate functional groupings. The major groupings are generally as follows:

Operations and production. Converting written source documents to machine-readable form (such as key punching); operating consoles, peripheral devices, and auxiliary equipment; maintaining a library for data files and programs; and establishing a control group which starts production, keeps records, balances input and output, and sees that schedules are met.

Project development. Developing systems and designing new methods and requirements; devising procedures, forms, and instruction manuals; and applying mathematical logic and modeling techniques (including operation research) to appropriate activities within the organization.

Technical services. Selecting software and providing maintenance; analyzing equipment and comparing capabilities of new equipment; developing and maintaining EDP standards for projects, hardware, software, and operations; maintaining quality control over operations; preparing detailed coding instructions for processing applications.[26]

A significant form of control over computer operations is the separation of duties within the EDP activity. In small EDP organizations, separation of all incompatible functions may not be feasible. But managers and internal auditors must be aware of the dangers in combining incompatible functions and put them under greater surveillance. For example:

The EDP activity should be independent of the users who authorize transactions to be processed. Similarly, EDP should never initiate general or subsidiary ledger entries.

Systems and programming should be independent of computer operators.

Both systems and programming should be independent of the file library and the input/output control functions.

Programmers should not be permitted to operate the computer. When tests or assemblies require them to operate the computer, the production programs and data files should be made secure against accidental or intentional manipulation. Programmers should work with **copies** of records — an important element of internal control. They should not be in a position to change original records and files.

Computer operators should not have access to the file library or program documentation. Neither should they control input/output functions.

The EDP librarian should be independent of computer operations. At the same time, the librarian should not transport files or programs to off-site storage locations or into the computer room.

As few people as possible should know the location of off-site storage facilities.

Data processing people should not have custody of, or access to, the organization's assets.

Responsibility for sensitive applications should be rotated, and all computer people should be required to take vacations.

People in the systems function — not computer operators — should be responsible for the detection and correction of errors.

Knowledge of applications, programming, and documentation should be restricted to certain qualified people. Those people should then be given access to data files or the computer only to the extent for which they are specifically authorized.[27]

Internal Audit

The internal audit review of organizational controls normally starts with a familiarization of the system. Internal auditors can gain this familiarity by reviewing management policies, organization charts, job descriptions, manpower and overtime reports, computer operator procedures, library and storage facilities, input/output control, and data conversion.

All job positions, particularly those for librarians, computer operators, control groups, and keypunch operators should be adequately described so that there is no question as to who is responsible for what.

Internal auditors will have to observe operations to determine whether purported separations of duties are in effect. Often, organizational controls are not documented. Internal auditors, therefore, would want to know whether departments are physically segregated, machine-readable media contain external labels, the library is not open to just anyone who wants access, supervisors maintain reasonable surveillance, and only people authorized to do so are in the computer room using files needed for operations.

Internal auditors should review records of job rotation and vacation schedules. They should make sure that everyone in the EDP activity actually takes a vacation each year.

The review of the control group is designed to determine whether the group is accountable for data from the time it is received through data conversion, processing, error corrections, and reentry, to the time it is formally distributed as output to users.

B.2 Resources and Security
The EDP activity should be provided with adequate resources and with physical security.

Internal Control

Resources

The success of all activities depends on the availability of qualified people — the key resource of any undertaking. EDP personnel should be qualified, trained, and supervised. Further, management must recognize that the entire field of computers is rapidly changing and becoming more complex. Computer people, perhaps more than most others, must have a continuing program of training and education to keep up with this expanding technology.

Educating the computer people alone is not enough. Users must also understand the system, the applications, and the kind of input acceptable for conversion to machine-readable data. As programs are prepared, users should be instructed on system requirements and should be involved in developing specifications for the system. Only in that way can the computer specialists become aware of user needs. Then the users should be instructed about the new applications so that they understand them and are prepared to work with them.

The EDP people should prepare a relevant user manual describing the new system or application and telling users what the applications will do for them. The manual should set the standards for users to meet for input documents. The instructions must emphasize the need for consistently good quality, and user personnel should be tested on their understanding of these instructions.

The allocation of physical resources should be the determination of top management, with the advice of the EDP director. They should make final decisions on the physical plant, major equipment, and facilities. In postimplementation reviews, management should seek to monitor the values accruing from the resources funded and allocated. (The function of the steering committee, management's top monitoring body, was discussed under A.1 - Management Policies.)

Physical Security

Security implies the prevention of both unintentional harm to (discussed here) and intentional misuse of (discussed under B.2 - Resources and Security and C.2 - Tests for Control Weaknesses) the computer system.

Executives realize that a blow to their computer center can be like a bullet to the brain. Everything stops. A computer disaster can, as one writer put it, induce "total corporate amnesia."[28] This is not extravagant hyperbole. One dissatisfied computer center employee managed to destroy practically every file and program in his company. It was not known whether enough information could be reconstructed to keep the company alive.[29]

But despite horror stories like this, some data processing people have not truly grappled with the security problem. A poll was taken of EDP people in the United Kingdom. When asked about their computer protection, they all confidently expressed the opinion that they had formal standards of security. A poll of their users, however, indicated a less optimistic picture. The interviewers then went back to the EDP people and asked for details about the standards. None were supplied. By the time the interviewers were through asking questions, the EDP people went away with worried expressions, saying they intended to review their security procedures.[30]

Every organization depending on computers must have a detailed security plan. The plan should make provision for the safety of the computer room and the protection of records. With the infinite variety of misfortunes that can befall a computer installation, total protection is probably an impossible dream. But here are some rules that, if followed, should go a long way toward providing reasonable safeguards for the physical security of the computer room and for computer data:

Computer Room. EDP managers should issue clear job instructions assigning responsibility with security in mind.

The computer areas should not be located near open courts, stairwells, receiving docks, or manufacturing areas containing manufacturing processes capable of exploding.

The computer room air conditioning system should be separate from the regular system.

Each individual computer system should be insulated by a fireproof partition.

Generators and transformers should be located outside the computer room.

Machine cables and wiring should not pass through an area containing combustible material.

Portable fire extinguishers should be installed and their locations should be clearly marked. Internal auditors should know which extinguishers are best.

Smoking in the computer area should be prohibited.

Fire and smoke detectors should be installed.

The area should be monitored regularly by night watchmen.

Fire department and civil defense telephone numbers should be prominently posted.

Terminals outside the computer room should be placed in a lockable room, the key should be kept by the person held responsible for it, a duplicate key should be controlled, and all visitors should be logged in and out.

Telephone access should be restricted by locking the telephone dial.

Records. Duplicates of vital data files should be stored at off-site, protected locations, or should be separately stored and adequately protected within the EDP facility.*

A separate data file storage area should be under library control. The procedure should provide for logging data files in and out; keeping a current list identifying people who are authorized to receive data files; keeping records to show the precise locations of all data files at all times, inventorying the files periodically; following up to retrieve issued data files not returned to the storage area within prescribed time limits; and identifying data files that are no longer needed, in accordance with established file expiration dates.

All data files should be clearly labeled, showing the name of the file, the file number, and the jobs for which the files will be used. If files are magnetic (tape or disk), they should be kept in closed containers when they are not in use.

---

*Off-site tape units connected through telecommunications lines to the computer installation may make the maintenance of such duplicates easier. But even with duplicate copies of computer programs and information files, it may be very difficult for a computer installation to recover from a disaster. Therefore, computer room protection is of prime importance.

Files should have both internal and external labels. Internal labels can be used by the program. External labels should be affixed to the outside casing of the files. Accidental erasures should be protected against by protect rings. These provide positive protection because when they are put on a drive, they depress a switch that allows the drive to write on the reel. Therefore, "No ring, no write." Protect rings should be off the tape at all times unless the tape is supposed to be written on. Everything possible should be done to prevent unauthorized writing on tapes.

Special care should be exercised over data files for vital computer programs. The programs are usually kept on magnetic tape or disk. It is a good idea to keep duplicate programs in card form unless backup program tapes are stored off-site.

Data files should be brought to the computer room for processing only. They should then be returned immediately to the storage area.

The more computer records are relied upon the greater the need to protect them from failing. This calls for contingency plans — for means of recovering from disaster. The most likely occurrences are loss of power, loss of water supply, fire, flood, and explosion. These can be minimized by alternate power routing, private generators, private water storage, fire resistant materials, and fire suppression systems. If all else fails there must be backup facilities, and these should be tested periodically. Backup facilities usually involve somebody else's computer, and so any type of configuration change may make the backup facilities no longer compatible.

The initial security step is a recovery plan — a documented procedure understood by all who may become involved in a disaster to the computer system. Here is what the documentation should include:

A list of all off-premise master files.

Precise specifications for all hardware.

The location of and the arrangements for off-premise backup.

Names and home phone numbers of all people who should be informed of or who could help in an emergency.

A list of supplies and forms, contracts, and specifications, held off-site.

A list of copies of source codes, application run manuals, and operator manuals held off-site.

Descriptions of space, support services, and telephone lines.

Arrangements for alternate hardware-software configurations compatible with existing programs.

Copies of programs and data files in off-site locations.

The recovery plan should be layered so as to cover various forms of disruption from minor hardware failures or operator errors to destruction of the entire facility. But no paper procedure can be blindly relied upon. It must be tested.

In one company, the financial vice president tells people at the close of a day's business that they are to arrive early the next day for a drill. When they enter the computer room they see different colored cards placed on equipment. Each card tells how much damage has been done to that equipment. Personnel are then required to write memos describing the steps they would take to recover from the damage. The memos are consolidated and examined. The findings may reveal reasons to modify recovery procedures or to retrain the people.[31]

Minicomputers

An increasingly significant resource in many companies is the minicomputer. These are generally classified as having from 4,000 to 128,000 characters of main storage. In fact, present-day minicomputers have more computing capability than did the first "large" computers built in the early 1950's.

Minis can work alone or they can be composites of larger systems. They can perform limited editing and balancing so that many errors can be efficiently corrected before data is entered in the central computer. They can be interconnected with other minis and with the large computer, creating what is termed *distributive* systems. They permit local users to perform their own processing on the premises. Specific data can then be transmitted to a central facility for consolidation.

Probably the most serious exposure for minis is the lack of technical expertise. Considerable training is required for users because the mini is usually under their total control and away from the central computer room with its EDP specialists.

Control over the acquisition and system design of large computer systems applies to the same extent to minicomputers. The small unit cost of minis can be misleading. For example, a company may need several minicomputers but only one large system. As the minis become increasingly popular for their data processing capabilities, more of them will be located throughout centers of operation. Therefore, the comparatively low unit price turns into a substantial cost when the total quantity of minis in the organization is considered.

The programming costs can also be significant and could substantially increase the total cost of using the minicomputer. Normally, the advertised prices of minicomputers do not include programming costs; thus, alternatives are available which deserve careful consideration. These alternatives include having the manufacturer do the programming, doing it in-house, or contracting a third party do it.

The small size of the minis and their dispersion among many users with varying degrees of control consciousness create special problems. Computer files (programs and data) used by minis should be strictly controlled and should be given the same protection afforded comparable files for large computers. For example, backup is as essential for minis as for the larger systems.

The type of computer controls that should be exercised over minis is dependent on the way the equipment will be used. If the mini is assigned for the exclusive use of one department, it would be proper for the department to decide on the computer's use. Separation of duties within that department is important. For example, if the mini accumulates daily stock issues, the same person should not approve issues, authorize adjustments to totals accumulated by the computer, and also operate the equipment. System, program, and operating standards should also be prepared for minicomputer operations.

If minicomputer programs are prepared by company programmers, a manual of programming standards should be prepared and enforced. The programs should be as carefully documented as the programs used on large computers.

If the minicomputer is used for business applications, the procedural controls (input, processing, and output) should be followed as well. The degree of application would depend on the specific type of input, processing, output, and the kind of work to which the minicomputer is assigned.

Internal Audit
Educating the Internal Auditor
Internal auditors who wish to lay claim to being a valuable resource in computer systems and applications must be educated in the task of auditing EDP operations. They must develop an awareness of the best EDP audit tools and techniques and of the constantly changing computer technology. All internal auditors should have some awareness of data processing. One firm used the following course outline in a five-day training session for internal auditors.[32]

Elements of data processing from an internal auditor's point of view.

Overview of computer hardware: terminals, storage devices, and processers.

Overview of programming: flowcharting, decision tables, and COBOL.

Overview of documentation: types, styles, and standards.

Internal controls: objectives, methods, and audits of controls.

General controls: controls over data processing activities and data communication.

Case study of an actual audit situation.

A more advanced course is used for internal auditors with some data processing experience. A prerequisite is a knowledge of on-line systems and a course in basic control systems. Here is the course outline:[33]

Review of accepted control objectives, use of checklists.

On-line systems control, including security for terminals and controls over access.

Data communication control, including addresses, message sequencing and accounting, control totals, and error detection and correction.

Continuous operation controls relating to data, terminals, communications, and processing equipment.

Storage media/device control, including tapes and disks, internal and external labeling, and access journals.

Transaction trails.

Special audit software, including tools, techniques, and software available to meet the organization's requirements.

Computer room security.

Demonstration of new software packages.

Case study.

The more advanced courses stress on-line rather than batch control systems because of the increasing use of on-line systems and the greater risks they present.

Security

Security is of paramount importance to the internal auditor. Executive managers are not in a position to review the adequacy of security systems. The internal auditor is. Top managers can sleep a little easier if they know that internal auditors are casting a watchful eye on such systems.

Internal auditors should be aware that the most misused systems, according to the National Bureau of Standards, include payroll, accounts payable and receivable, certificates (licenses, stocks, etc.), social payments (welfare and other benefits), and operating systems (vendor-supplied systems that run the computer).[34]

The internal auditor should also be aware of the most commonly used detection and prevention safeguards. Here are some, based on a study by the Stanford Research Institute for the National Bureau of Standards.[35]

Detection Safeguards

1. User Command Log — to enable the recording of user commands and thereby monitor user activity.
2. Sensitive File Access Log — to record all accesses of files designated sensitive by security administrators so as to detect unauthorized file access.
3. Operator Console Log — to record commands at operator console so as to monitor operator's activity.
4. Media Usage Log — to record the use of removable, sensitive media by controlled external labels and times of mount and dismount according to job and user.

5. Computer Resource Usage Log — to record use of computer resources (terminals, etc.) so as to detect unauthorized disclosures (or theft) of data, programs, or service.

Prevention Safeguards

1. Application system design verification — to audit internal controls before and after installation, so as to prevent all defined misuses.
2. Application system test — to review the system before it becomes operational, so as to prevent application system failures.
3. Employee termination policy — to restrict access of terminated employees to sensitive materials and uses, thereby forestalling destruction of resources.
4. Password protection system — including initiation, disbursement, storage, and exchange of passwords, using such devices as safes and encryption, so as to prevent unauthorized modification, destruction, or disclosure of data or programs.
5. Data center access control — to list all those authorized to have access to the EDP facility and record all those entering and leaving it, so as to prevent improper modifications, destruction, or removal of equipment of supplies.
6. Fire detection and extinguishment — for all computer and user areas, obviously to prevent destruction of data, programs, equipment, and supplies.
7. Input-output data control — to monitor data moving throughout the user area and to provide for traceability and accountability so as to prevent improper modification or disclosure of data or programs.
8. Input-output data storage — to provide lockable storage for sensitive data, programs, and reports so as to prevent improper modifications, destruction, or disclosure of data and programs.

Internal audits of system security can bring significant benefits. Here is one example:

A security audit of real-time processing of receivables disclosed failings in the system. The internal auditors found unauthorized issuance of credit cards, deletion of customer balances, and changes to customers' files that were not warranted. As a result of the audit findings, the systems department made needed program changes and periodically tested the system to insure its effectiveness. [36]

Testing contingency plans cannot even be attempted if the computer center has not done an adequate job of disaster planning; there is just nothing to test. If planning has not been adequate, the internal auditor should recommend the preparation of adequate plans to top management.

The EDP installation should be prepared for any natural or man-made disaster. The internal auditor should recommend a series of plans constituting the overall disaster or contingency plan:

Emergency plan. Detecting and limiting fires or intrusion.

Backup plan. Accomplishing critical jobs in timely fashion when disaster strikes the computer room.

Recovery plan. Recovering mission capability.

Vital records plan. Identifying and protecting data vital to employees, customers, stockholders, and the national interest.

The key to a good disaster program is periodic testing. Internal auditors should therefore look for evidence that tests have been made. They should also examine the procedures and provisions designed to protect against fire, flood, and explosions. They should examine the adequacy of vaults and storage facilities, the means of preventing unauthorized access, the physical segregation of the computer room from other activities, the installation of fire extinguishing equipment, the control over the library, the control over night shift operations, insurance, and the backup for master and transaction files.

A comprehensive disaster test would simulate disaster in data processing. These tests might include retrieving and executing backup application programs stored off-site; reconstructing designated master files, using data stored off-site; testing standby electrical power sources; and executing application programs and data files at alternative computer processing facilities to see whether these are available and compatible.

When they embark on an audit of contingency plans, internal auditors must remember that the cost of control and protection should not exceed the value of what is being protected. Before recommending extensive control procedures, internal auditors should weigh the costs of developing plans and procedures, maintaining disaster storage files, and procuring protective devices, on the one hand, against the potential risks and consequences, on the other.

Each organization is different. What risks may be acceptable in a given environment is a matter for top management to decide, based on a full understanding of the circumstances.

Minicomputers

Audits of minicomputers differ little from audits of larger computers. Internal auditors can provide special assistance to management by making sure that minicomputer hardware and programming alternates have been considered. They should also verify the existence of computer security including adequate backup.

Internal auditors can usually audit more safely around the minicomputer because of less volume and more printed transaction trails. Indeed, general software packages for minis are not regularly available and auditors may find it more difficult to use computer-assisted techniques to test minis. They may have to resort to tailored programs.

B.3 Operating System Controls
Operating system controls should provide reasonable assurance of reliable computer processing.

Internal Control
Operating systems are computer software control programs supplied by the computer manufacturer which work in concert with hardware to process

application programs. They have multiprogramming ability, processing two or more application programs by interleaving the execution of individual instructions. They check file labels to see that the right files are being used. In short, they are integral to the general controls over computer systems.

Bugs or deficiencies are usually abundant in the initial releases of software packages. Preventive controls, built-in checks by the computer to reject unacceptable data, are essential when using new software; and manufacturers have been supplying such controls. (A number of these are listed under C.1 - Conformance With Standards and Approved Design.)

Two types of file labels provide a check on computer processing: File header labels permit system software to tell whether the correct file is being processed, and trailer labels are used so that the software can tell whether a file has been completely processed — no information lost or added.

In addition to these checks, organized, documented maintenance is essential. Magnetic tapes should be recertified, and disk packs should be inspected. Sad experience has demonstrated that the cost of correcting is far less than the cost of replacing.

Even with these controls in place, there is always the danger of the unpredictable human element. Superiors have the authority to override routine controls. The ostensible reason is to deal with unforeseen circumstances, but these people may have their own reasons — and these may be self-serving. Objective approval of all overrides must be obtained. Who should have the authority and the responsibility to approve overrides? In many organizations the controller and/or the internal auditors are designated to give written approval if they agree with the reasons. No approval, no override.

Even so, those systems programmers and analysts determined to have access to applications and files can gain it. They know more about the systems and the built-in controls than anyone else because they designed them. They can therefore bypass the controls almost at will, if they are unsupervised. Strong supervision is the only deterrent, sad to say, that has the capability and is constantly available to prevent bypassing operating system controls.

Internal Audit

Reviewing operating system controls calls for a fairly sophisticated knowledge of computer systems. Unfortunately that knowledge is not widespread among auditors. As a result, as disclosed by the SAC study,[37] relatively few organizations are blessed with that audit capability. Yet controls are absolutely essential if only correct information is to be accepted by computers and be processed reliably. As complicated as systems are today, they hardly even hint of the complexities of tomorrow, so internal auditors will have to keep up with this transonic technology.

The very least internal auditors can do is to learn what operating system controls are appropriate and then ask EDP people whether these have been installed. Obviously, a glib "of course" should not satisfy experienced internal auditors. They should ask for documentation and other corroboration.

Some of the matters internal auditors should seek to determine in evaluating controls ensuring reliable processing are these:[38]

Is each transaction that is entered into the computer recorded on a specially designed form?

Do written manuals describe the procedures for preparing source documents?

Is information on source documents preprinted or precoded whenever possible?

Are people properly trained in the preparation of source documents?

Does a control group receive all data for processing and see that all detected errors are corrected?

Do key identification codes use self-checking digit techniques to identify coding errors?

Is the computer itself used, whenever possible, to edit source data for accuracy?

Is access to the data or programs restricted?

Here is an example of the results of unauthorized access:

A manager in a brokerage firm programmed the computer to siphon $250,000 from a company account to two customer accounts — his own and his wife's. The computer was also programmed to show that the money went to buy stock for those two accounts. The manager accomplished the theft by going to the office Sunday mornings to punch the new computer cards and feed them into the machine. The manager ran the whole show and could bypass all systems. After the fraud was detected, and when only a fraction of the money was recovered, the system was revamped and quarterly internal audits were put into effect. [39]

B.4 Hardware Controls
Hardware controls should provide reasonable assurance that hardware malfunctions will be detected and corrected.

Internal Control
Computer hardware is usually reliable when installed, but that is no assurance it will remain reliable. The computer hardware system is extremely sensitive. Hardware failures can bring about the loss or destruction of data. Catastrophes are not the only dangers, however. Subtle malfunctions not apparent to the eye can cause logical processes to be incorrect.

The sources of hardware ailments are legion. Here are some of them:

Fire, flood, wind, and civil disorder can bring about complete breakdowns of equipment.

Components, especially plastic, can be damaged at temperatures as low as 120 degrees F.

Water from burst pipes, leaks, or firefighting efforts can cause short circuits or deposit residues that are difficult or impossible to remove.

Electrical devices, like pencil sharpeners and floor polishers, operating near tapes, disks, and computer processors — and not fitted with suppressors — may emit "noise" that interferes with accurate data processing.

Static electricity — resulting from poor grounding, floor covering not equipped with static takeoff qualities, poor humidity control, or antistatic floor cleaning products — can interfere with accurate processing.

Using steel wool for buffing can release tiny steel particles into the electronic circuitry. (In one case an employee left a cheese sandwich on the central processing unit. The heat caused the cheese to melt and run. Cleaning people tried to remove the mess with steel wool. The steel fibers from the wool entered the CPU and required its complete replacement.)[40]

Inadequate air conditioning and humidity controls can lead to corrosion of hardware.

Using hard water in humidifiers can permit metallic dust to be sprayed into the equipment. Dust can affect the accuracy of tapes.

Increases or decreases in specified electrical voltage can cause "spikes" that can adversely affect equipment.

Controls are available that reduce the chances of equipment breakdown or hardware-engendered inaccurate processing. Here are some:

Written procedures for console operators in the event of unanticipated equipment failure.

A written schedule of preventive maintenance procedures.

Preventive maintenance programs providing for periodic maintenance according to manufacturer's recommendations.

Temperature and humidity charts maintained by a continuous recorder and checked during the day.

Provision for cleaning magnetic tape drive read/write heads, capstans, and vacuum columns at least once during each 8-hour operating period.

Malfunctions described in console logs, checked by supervisors, and analyzed for recurrence.

When hardware failures occur they should be reported. A regular reporting system is an integral part of an adequate preventive maintenance program. Here are some suggested steps:

Equipment malfunctions should be logged.

The malfunctions should be reported to vendor service people.

Reported malfunctions should be followed up to see if they have been investigated and corrected.

Intermittent malfunctions should be investigated until resolved.

The program status at the appropriate restart point should be shown by the files for each hardware failure. Accordingly, a history log should contain before and after images of updated disks. Software packages are available which not only record malfunctions but also prescribe diagnostic routines.

Internal Audit

Internal auditors should make sure that hardware controls are in force and are actually working. Here are some audit steps they can take:

Interview operating people and users about the reliability of equipment. Between the two, the auditor should be able to obtain reliable information.

Determine what action is taken by computer operators (or by software) in the event of hardware malfunction.

Check downtime reports, machine-error logs, and maintenance reports to confirm the oral statements. Logs kept by maintenance engineers are a good source for determining which components failed, how often, why, and what was done to correct the difficulties.

See if temperature and humidity-control devices are installed and conform to manufacturer's environmental specifications.

Review logs generated by temperature and humidity equipment as well as operating statistics to ascertain the extent of equipment downtime and the extent of reruns because of equipment failure.

Review daily computer logs and periodic equipment utilization reports to see if manufacturer's preventive maintenance schedules are being followed.

Compare actual downtime with what would be considered normal.

Determine whether equipment is released for preventive maintenance at the most appropriate times.

Determine whether fire detection devices are in place and have been checked as required.

The fact that provisions have been made for hardware maintenance is no guarantee that it will be done. Internal auditors cannot rely on what should be, but on what is. In this example an auditor was reviewing requests for computer repairs and maintenance and found the following deficiencies:

Twenty-two percent of the time it took more than ten days before service requests were taken care of.

Although requests for maintenance were required to be in writing, they were sometimes oral.

Machine failure records designed to call attention to chronic machine trouble were not always used.

The service request procedure was not made routine and took an excessive amount of clerical time.

Preventive maintenance objectives were orally agreed to, and even these were not being met.

No objectives had been set for maintenance of tape drive units even though service requests for these units represented 43 to 50 percent of the total requirements for maintenance.

Discrepancies between nonchargeable rerun, maintenance time shown on the computer operations machine logs, and the machine maintenance logs sent to the supplier for credits on computer equipment billing had been running generally in favor of the supplier.

The internal auditor suggested several improvements in the system, was responsible for the establishment of preventive maintenance objectives for all hardware, and saw to it that controls were established to eliminate incorrect credits to the suppliers.[41]

C. Application Controls
The auditor shall review application controls of installed data processing applications to assess their reliability in processing data in a timely, accurate, and complete manner.

Applications are what the computer is designed to do. They include such things as the processing of payrolls, receivables, inventory, and deposits. Some applications are oriented toward accounting, some toward nonaccounting operations. The entire objective of the EDP function is the application activity. Thus, application controls, as distinguished from general controls, can vary from application to application.

General controls affect all aspects of the computer facility, including specific applications. And so, internal auditors should consider both forms of control when reviewing an application. A weakness in general controls might be so serious that no amount of application controls could assure reliable data processing. On the other hand, a weakness in an application control could be offset by a strong general control.

C.1 Conformance With Standards and Approved Design
Application controls should provide reasonable assurance that installed applications conform to adequate standards and approved design.

Internal Control

Application controls concern compliance with and documentation of design standards, efficient processing of data and the careful documentation of procedures, the installation and testing of internal controls, and the accuracy with which transactions are entered and converted to machine-readable form.

Design Standards

Electronic data processing usually centralizes what once was handled directly by user departments. Face-to-face communication is disappearing. Yet EDP systems need high degrees of uniformity. So rules have to be specific, they have to be in writing, and they must be understood. The standards usually set rules for input, output, and processing. Input controls generally include the following matters:

Updating transactions. These processes involve large amounts of data and are usually repetitive. Such devices as reasonableness checks and application program logic help control the input.

Inquiry. These transactions do not change a file. But they may result in updating or file maintenance as a consequence of an inquiry. Inquiry logs usually control such access to the computer.

Error correction. These transactions cause the most difficulty and are the hardest to control. Obviously a problem already exists if error correction must take place. Moreover, error corrections often result in additional errors. Correction calls for analysis of the error reports, determination of the action needed, need for new input, updating of files, entry of data into the proper files, and readjustment of balances to take the corrections into account.

Output controls include these:

Reports. These should be timely, accurate and meaningful. Confidentiality should be assured. Formats should be useful to the reader. Large amounts of data should be summarized. Recipients should be polled periodically to see whether they still need the reports.

Working documents. These take the form of checks, saving bonds, purchase orders, and the like. Security is obviously an important matter to consider, along with assurance that input is balanced with output.

Reference documents. These are used to show what was in the computer if computer services are interrupted. This kind of output can be recorded on microfilm.

Error reports. While usually small in volume, these are complex and difficult to deal with. They should be sent to the right people for corrective action and they should be controlled to make sure the action is taken and the corrected reports are returned. Follow-up is essential. Control over these reports can never be relaxed.

Design standards also set processing controls, which to a great extent implement input and output requirements, except for error correction and error reports.

Exposures. Design standards should set certain objectives. A significant objective is to reduce the risks flowing from exposures (the difficulties that can occur and that should be guarded against). Exposures that design specifications should anticipate are:

Loss of inputs. Transactions transmitted from one location to another are particularly subject to loss.

Duplication of inputs. This may occur when an input item is erroneously thought to be lost.

Inaccurate recording of inputs. Wrong numbers or wrong spellings are common examples.

Missing information. This, obviously, makes input incomplete.

Unrecorded transactions. These include not only accidental failures but also the result of theft and embezzlement.

Authorizations. Authorizations covering a composite mass of transactions may be necessary because of the sheer volume of transactions; but the absence of management focus on individual items can let some improper transactions slip through.

Transactions. Transactions initiated by the computer include such matters as automatic reorder of stock and payments to suppliers. If all is normal, the program acts as a control. But situations not anticipated in the design can create serious difficulties.

Output missent. Output information sent to the wrong people. Output sent to its destination too late to be of value.

Output that is incorrect.

Large volumes of detected errors. Complete analysis is physically impossible and/or backlogs are frustrating.

Output that cannot be supported.

Improper processing. Processing the wrong file. Processing transactions against the wrong record.

Incomplete processing. Despite the balancing of inputs against outputs.

Incorrect processing. Programming errors or clerical errors.

Processing performed too late. The processing may be correct, but the recognition of the items may not be timely.

Loss. Files lost during processing. The loss of knowledgeable people, coupled with the absence of adequate documentation.

Efficient Processing

Efficient processing is the result of well-designed applications. The designers should therefore consider the control alternatives available to them. Which controls will reasonably guard against exposures without becoming excessively burdensome or uneconomical? Designers should also see to it that the controls and processes are thoroughly documented. In this way, procedures are more likely to be followed consistently and without conflict.

Efficient processing includes such devices as dollar control totals, document counts, and line item counts. At appropriate points in the processing cycle, balances should be established. The control group should balance all input and output data to prevent the inefficiencies caused by lost data. They should monitor file control totals to make sure files are available when needed. And they should report input errors to make sure future input is efficient.

It is more efficient and more logical for users, rather than EDP people, to review error conditions because they are in the best position to know. For example, in a sales department, the person working with customer acccunts continuously can scan a file rapidly and spot unusual conditions. No computer specialist could do the same.

Means of Control

The objective of all application controls is to prevent, detect, or correct causes of exposure. Some of these objectives are to make sure that all authorized transactions are processed once only, all transaction data is complete and accurate, all transaction data is correct and appropriate, the results of computer processing are put to their intended uses, and the application will continue to function efficiently and effectively.

Application controls are varied and extensive. Here are some of the more common ones:

Hash totals. These are meaningless but highly useful because they add up numerical amounts of nonmonetary information to prevent loss during application processing.

Editing and reviewing, including a variety of checks like:

Format checks to see that data is entered in the proper mode and within designated fields.

Limit checks to see that input does not exceed a given range of acceptability.

Reasonableness checks, performed by comparing input with other information available within existing computer records.

Validity checks to see that charges are appropriate; for example, preventing a charge to a closed work order.

Field checks, for completeness of information, like an address for a new customer.

Numerical checks to see that alphabetic data are not included in fields reserved for numeric data.

Historical comparisons to see that current information is comparable with previous information.

Sequence checking to verify the alphanumeric sequence of the key field in an item to be processed.

Overflow, to prevent exceeding the capacity of a memory or file area to accept data.

Format checks to see whether input data are acceptable for the particular format defined in the application program.

Check digits, which are functions of other digits within a word or number and which are used to test for an accurate transcription.

Keystroke verification, performed by entering data into keyboards more than once. Differences between the entries cause a mechanical signal.

Authorizations and approvals. The first is advance permission. The second occurs after the fact and assumes that some edit or review took place.

Reconciliation and balancing. The first is to analyze differences. The second tests for equality.

File labels to identify transactions, files, and outputs.

Control tests by computer designers. Internal controls cannot be relied upon until they have been documented and tested. The documentation is needed to make sure that all those connected with an application understand the controls that have been installed. The tests bring out the errors, omissions, and unforseen difficulties that plague every new application. Here are some sophisticated steps that have been suggested for computer designers to test systems of computer controls, making use of the computer for that purpose. [42]

Describe quantitatively each kind of irregularity that can occur.

Identify the controls which might either detect or correct irregularities.

Chart the flow of potential irregularities through the complete application process.

Convert the diagram into a flowchart of computer logic.

Translate the computer logic flowchart into computer language code.

Gather or create any detailed transactions needed to run the computer programs, such as raw materials, price standards, or quantities shipped against representative sales orders.

Test the program for accuracy and reasonableness.

Run the program several times, setting internal control compliance levels at different feasible levels during each run.

Evaluate, quantitatively, the output generated by the computer program, such as the mean dollar value (of the net error which might result in year-end raw materials account balances) and the standard deviation (of the expected dollar error.)

All these tests can be performed by EDP personnel seeking to "debug" an application, or by internal auditors to test it:

Parallel simulation. A means of testing computer application processing by using the same input data and files as the application system and trying to produce the same results. Parallel simulation can be performed with live data without jeopardizing the file. It requires a good knowledge of the function performed and it does take time to develop a simulation program.

System test. A means of placing heavy stress on the system to make it fail. All programs, clerical procedures, test files, and people are combined to test the new application. If user personnel introduce every conceivable situation, they should be able to maximize the number of "bugs" that will surface.

Integrated test facility. Establishing a dummy entity against which data is processed — a department, an employee, a work order, or the like. After the entity is established both actual and devised transactions are processed against it. No special knowledge is needed, but the test data must be removed from the company's accounting records.

Snapshot. A form of transaction trail for specially coded inputs. The input can then be traced through the entire transaction trail.

Data Conversion

Data conversion refers to the translation of ordinary business transactions — invoices, shop orders, requisitions, and the like — into a form that the computer can deal with. The punch card was the most common means of conversion, but it is being replaced with more productive devices such as key-to-key cassettes, key-to-"floppy" cassettes and disks, key-to-conventional tapes and disks, optical character recognition (OCR), and magnetic ink character recognition (MICR).

Key-input-device operators transcribe source documents to a machine-readable medium. Being human, the operators are capable of making mistakes. They can invert digits, hit the wrong keys, and misalign data. The control procedures are designed to see that data is entered correctly and processed as designed. No data should be added erroneously or manipulated.

The initiating department — not the computer department — should control the submitted data. No one individual should be responsible for controlling all the steps. For example, no single person should establish new master files and also change and update all master records. Source documents should be retained only long enough for identification of related output records and documents. Source documents and coding sheets should be controlled once they are turned over to the transcribing department (which translates recorded information from one medium into another). The functions of coding (recording values or characters that have meanings not readily apparent), keypunching, and verifying the same document should be performed by different individuals.

The conversion program should also provide for edit checks to reject inaccurate, incomplete, or unreasonable data. A number of these editing checks are described in this chapter under the heading "Means of Control."

Internal Audit
Design Standards

To audit against loose standards is like measuring with an inaccurate ruler. When internal auditors are sufficiently involved in systems as they are developed, they can have better assurance that their subsequent audits will be directed toward evaluations of reasonable controls.

During the design phase, internal auditors can develop an in-depth knowledge of an application system. They can compare and analyze the controls associated with both the manual and the computerized systems for input, output, and processing.

They cannot dictate the controls; establishing controls is a management function. But pointing to the absence of needed controls is an auditing function. Where a significant risk is not guarded against, internal auditors must take a firm stand and report their findings to management. The final decision to install or not to install a given control rests with the users and the EDP people. If they reject the recommended control, then the internal auditor will have to reserve further action for the post implementation period. During the post audit, when transactions are actually processed, the auditor might be able to demonstrate graphically the results of failing to install a given, needed control.

While the application is being developed, the internal auditor will have to review design documentation to determine whether the application system will meet accepted standards of control. Here are some of the steps internal auditors should take:

Determine the adequacy of cost-benefit analyses. Will the proposed computer application give the organization a better and/or less expensive system than the pre-existing one?

Determine whether long-term plans were developed which took into account subsequent applications.

Determine whether users and the accounting department participated in the design development and whether their needs were taken into account.

Assess the effectiveness of segregation of duties for the application.

Assess the effectiveness of standard systems design and programming procedures.

Assess the effectiveness of the approval procedures at each major phase of the application.

Efficient Processing

In reviewing computer processing for efficiency and effectiveness, internal auditors will seek to determine whether the standards set in the design phase for input, processing, and output are working as intended. Internal auditors may witness the conversion from the normal procedures to the computerized system. They may specify test cases to the EDP specialists. They may then review test results and determine whether controls are working effectively.

Specifically, internal auditors would wish to determine whether controls are operating to:

Prevent errors of input or source data.

Prevent errors resulting from conversion of data to machine-readable form.

Assure accurate transmission of data to the computer center.

See that only valid files are used.

Make sure that the accuracy of data is maintained during processing.

Assure accuracy of program computations.

Make sure that significant errors identified at various stages in the system are properly shown in output.

Make sure all output reports are delivered promptly to the proper user department.

Testing Controls

In reviewing design standards and processing, the internal auditors will have gained an understanding of the systems and programming functions. They will then be able to identify those controls needed to provide reasonable assurance that the reliability of computer applications is not materially and adversely affected.

Compliance with controls may be tested by examining selected documentation to make sure appropriate controls have been installed. The effectiveness of the controls can be tested by interviewing users, management, and computer personnel as well as any computer auditors, to verify compliance which was not documented.

The most effective control is knowledgeable supervision along with a system of authorization. The internal auditor, therefore, should give special attention to the means employed to provide reasonable assurance that all data processed by the computer is authorized and that the people involved in the processing are properly guided and supervised. To that end, the internal auditor would:

Assess the effectiveness of the separation of the EDP department from other departments in the organization.

Evaluate the segregation of duties within the EDP department.

Verify the methods used to see that only authorized data is processed.

Make sure that input documentation bears evidence of authorization.

See that the control group reviews such evidence.

Assess the means used to see that the right file record is used with the related input/output documents.

Determine whether there are means of tracing specific items of data backwards and forwards through the processing cycle.

Data Conversion

Most internal auditors are aware of the term *garbage-in-garbage-out* (GIGO). The point at which information on documents is converted to a machine-readable form is crucial to the proper functioning of an EDP system. Internal auditors must therefore pay close attention to the controls over data conversion. Some of the steps internal auditors can take to that end are as follows:

For error correction and detection, make sure that control is established close to the potential error source.

Review the means used to reconcile input and output.

Determine that the control system provides for follow-up to see that all corrections are reentered into the system.

See whether the timing of input, output, and processing are coordinated.

Check the adequacy of logging data through the processing cycle and of maintaining balancing controls at key points so as to permit error correction and file reconstruction.

C.2 Tests for Control Weaknesses
Internal auditors should periodically test installed applications for weaknesses in controls and for system changes, and they should be alert to the possibility of computer misuse.

Knowledgeable, continuing testing of computer applications is one of the best ways of ensuring well-functioning systems. There is no guarantee that a sterling installation will retain its pristine purity. Circumstances change. People change. Modifications are made. Risks that were unanticipated suddenly surface. So internal auditors should be aware of the many difficulties that may affect the reliability of data produced.

Two types of reviews are available to the internal auditor. The first verifies the results of the computer application. The second is concerned with analyzing the actual processing operations of the computer.

When internal auditors test for results, they are inferring from accurate results that the processing controls are functioning properly. They do not delve into the controls themselves. They rely on the output they can see and verify. If, for example, the amounts of payroll checks and deductions are satisfactory, they may infer that whatever it took to achieve that result is also satisfactory.

Conversely, when the computer processes are reviewed, each key control is verified separately. For example, edit checks are reviewed to see if no unreasonable amounts can be input, proper sequences will be maintained, check digits will be working as intended, format checks will take place, and keystrokes will be verified.

As in everything else, each method is two-edged. The internal auditor should be aware of the hazards attending each form of verification. For example, a current review may show results to be completely accurate. But what assurance is there that results will prove just as accurate during a later review if the controls themselves have not been tested? Testing the processing controls gives greater assurance that the entire process is reliable and will give trustworthy results. On the other hand, control weaknesses are rarely quantifiable. It is difficult to convince EDP people or management that the nonfunctioning of a format check will result in a given dollar error in the payroll.

Each method has its benefits, and a combination of the two may provide internal auditors with the greatest assurance of satisfactory computer applications. Here are some **techniques for testing results:**

Confirmations. The confirmation technique involves matching the same transactions in the files of two different organizations. Entire files or samples of entire files may be confirmed. Confirmations include cash deposits, consigned inventories, and accounts receivable. The test relates to the present, however, not to the future. For example, confirming a receivable balance provides no indication as to what percent of those receivables will actually reach the bank.

Comparisons. The comparison technique calls for comparing records in one file with that of another file of items in the same organization. Examples are payrolls compared with personnel records, and inventory records compared with the physical properties.

Limit tests. Limit tests search for conditions that would not exist if the controls were working as they should. Examples would be payments for eight days of work in the week, or credit at a level higher than a customer is entitled to.

The **techniques for testing processing** include these:

Auditing around the computer. This technique partakes of some of the concepts of testing for results, but it is more closely related to testing the processing because it is concerned with each major step in the computer process. At each such step an internal auditor should be able to find transaction listings and trial balances for each file — before and after updating. The internal auditor would then extract samples of these transactions and verify manually every control or processing step significant to the overall process.

Test data. Test decks are sets of input data. These offer the computer a wide variety of transactions to process. The deck should contain all possible combinations of transactions and situations the computer application is likely to encounter. Obviously, the number of combinations in a complex application can be staggering. But most applications are tested this way before they are made operational. The internal auditor can therefore use such tests as a start, refining them or adding to them. The concept of test decks has been expanded to include the following methods: integrated test facilities, snapshot, sampling, and parallel simulation. (All or most of these testing methods are briefly defined in C.1-Conformance with Standards and Approved Design. They are discussed at much greater length and depth in existing literature, some of which is listed in the suggested readings appended to this chapter.)

The steps in testing a computerized application are **summarized** as follows:

Define the audit objectives. In general, these are to determine whether significant exposures have been considered and guarded against. Specifically, they are to test for the protection against more significant exposures.

Obtain a basic understanding of the application by reviewing documentation, interviewing people, and documenting the results.

Focus on specific controls, significant to the application, whose absence or weakness could have seriously unfavorable consequences.

Identify and evaluate the critical controls and processes. Determine whether the documented system is calculated to provide reliable results. Identify those controls which need verification to substantiate this reliance. Determine which investigations should be made of any apparent weaknesses.

Develop an audit program to identify the tests to be made.

Perform tests of critical controls and processes and of any exposures identified during the familiarization process.

Evaluate the test results, report any findings and conclusions, and follow up on any needed corrective action.

Another matter, not directly involving the computer process, also needs review. Clearly, an application that did not fill the user's needs is less than worthless. Enormous sums may go into an application which does not meet its prime purpose, indeed its only purpose: to help a user. Management would be vitally concerned with whether its tremendous infusion of dollars into a computer application is filling a need. If not, why change from a manual system or a prior automated system? A significant part of an application test would be to see how these needs are being met. Here are some questions an internal auditor could ask users:

For what purpose do you use the computer's end product?

How important is the end product to your work?

How easy is the product to understand?

To what extent do you have to correct, analyze, or rework the product?

On a scale of one to ten, how do you rate the product as being accurate and reliable? available when needed? up-to-date?

How can the product be improved to be more useful?

What kind of manual records do you have to maintain to supplement the computer-generated information?

To what extent does the product duplicate any other information you receive?

What information, if any, could you readily obtain from other sources?

If you have any problems with the product, what sort of help do you receive from the computer people?

Could you effectively perform your duties without the product?

Internal Control
Changes

Changes in computer systems usually stem from the maintenance of application programs. These changes may run the gamut from the alteration of a single instruction to major redesign. And changes, whether in manual or computerized systems, are fraught with peril. Whatever alters a comfortable routine can be confusing, resented, or a source for error.

Program changes can be far reaching. They may affect input, output, processing and application controls. They may involve logic, data, and procedures. They may also present serious security risks.

Changes, therefore, should be as well controlled as initial system or application development to ensure program integrity. Program change control should be a formal affair. It should be prescribed in policies, systems of authorizations, segregation of responsibilities, forms, and audit trails.

Changes usually come in two forms — mandatory changes and improvements. Mandatory changes are made to correct discrepancies or bugs, or to meet requirements such as revisions to payroll taxes. Mandatory changes leave no choice. The changes must be made. Improvements, however, are usually proposed to provide better service, to operate more efficiently, or to take advantage of new developments in hardware or software. They may be highly desirable; but management has the option to change or not to change, based on a cost/benefit analysis.

Controls applicable to each change must seek to prevent degradation of quality in the computer application. Control over changes is made almost impossible if maintenance changes are incorporated as soon as they are requested. Control over quality is more readily assured if changes are accumulated in batches and then installed and tested at intervals. Of extreme importance is a program change log which shines a searchlight on all changes and tends to reveal the surreptitious ones. Every time a program is modified, it should be documented, and the user should approve the program change before it is put into operation.

Intentional Computer Misuse

Intentional computer misuse can be defined as a willful act directed at or committed with a computer system or its associated internal data or program activities in which there is unauthorized modification, destruction, or disclosure of intellectual property (data or programs); or unauthorized modification, destruction, or theft of physical property (cash, securities, equipment, and supplies); or unauthorized use or denial of a computer service or process.

No known audit program or system of computer controls can absolutely prevent intentional computer misuse or assure management that all such misuse will be detected. Nor can any internal auditor or audit team act as an insurer that can prevent or detect all computer misuse.

Over the years, under contract with the U.S. Defense Department, the Rand Corporation and a number of other organizations have been seeking to test computer security systems. "Tiger teams" were employed to penetrate systems being considered for defense use. No major system withstood a dedicated attack by a tiger team. [43]

A 15-year old schoolboy completely cracked a security system of a major London computer time-sharing service. He gained access to the most secret files stored in the computer by other users. He could change them at will, yet he used no special gadgets and started with no special knowledge of the computer's inner workings. He relied only on ingenuity and a teletype terminal in his school. [44]

Internal auditors are bound to be alert to the risks inherent in computer systems and should be aware of the forms of control calculated to reduce the possibility of misuse.

The most useful safeguards against computer abuse are organizational. Safeguards structured around the organization emphasize to all that computer security is the responsibility of many organizational elements. Here are some standards developed in a project performed at Stanford Research Institute for the National Bureau of Standards: [45]

General management must provide a policy of security and coordinate the security activities of all people responsible for security.

The internal auditing department should include auditors who are well versed in computer activities and who will:

Monitor systems development.

Review the adequacy of test procedures.

Make operational audits of the computer installation and compliance with standards.

Evaluate the system during post-installation reviews to see whether the users' requirements were met.

Use the computer in through-the-computer audits to verify the accuracy and completeness of data, particularly auditing data stored internally in the computer system.

General management should see that internal controls and other security mechanisms are included in the system design.

General management should see that adequate insurance is taken out on the EDP facility.

General management should see that contract administrators are trained in EDP technology and terminology and are aware of the problems associated with computer programs, equipment, supplies, and services.

General management should assess the risks to particular programs. Security specialists should consider the safeguards in the context of the specific environment. In establishing a formal risk assessment, it might be well to consider two documents which are excellent foundations for a useful risk assessment program. These documents have been published by the National Bureau of Standards and are as follows:

Guidelines for Automatic Data Processing Physical Risk Assessment (FIPS PUB 31)

Automatic Data Processing Risk Assessment (NBSIR 77-1228)

Internal Audit

Changes

Internal auditors may find it physically impossible to review all changes in large computer installations. That is the responsibility of data processing supervision. They can test a representative sample of changes to see whether prescribed procedures are actually being followed. Here are some audit questions that internal auditors would want answered:[46]

Were changes adequately defined in a formal request document?

Were requests properly authorized by users and programming supervision?

Were modifications effectively made with respect to methodology and logic?

Were modifications adequately tested?

Were changes adequately documented?

Were changed programs approved by programming supervision, change control, users, and others who may be involved?

Were the changes implemented on time, were appropriate library revisions made, and did each change comply with its change request?

Were adequate transaction trails provided for user change requests, data-processing-initiated changes, source program changes, and production program implementation?

Another audit technique that can be used is for internal auditors to make periodic comparisons of two source codes (instructions to the computer in human-readable form) of programs that were produced at different times. This technique makes it relatively easy to spot discrepancies between the two codes. Then the reasons for the differences or changes can be investigated. The investigation should show whether change procedures were followed. The technique is most successfully used during regularly scheduled copying of programs. The copy of a current program can be compared with that of a prior generation program and any variances can then be investigated.[47]

Internal audits of changes are fertile ground for significant audit findings. Here is an example:

A credit card company assessed a service charge on both purchases and cash advances. The company decided to change the method of charging for its services. To implement the change, the computer program had to be modified. First, purchases needed to be separated from cash advances. Then the new method of charging had to be installed. The program did the first part well: purchases were separated from cash advances. But it slipped on the second part. It failed to assess a service charge on cash advances. An internal audit disclosed the error and resulted in preventing losses of about $30,000 a year.[48]

Intentional Computer Misuse

In testing the adequacy of a computer security system, here are some steps internal auditors can take:

Assess the effectiveness of the separation of the EDP department from the source and user departments.

Assess the degree of control exercised over the various functions within the EDP department:

Are programming and operating functions separated?

Is knowledge about the programs withheld from the operators?

Are the computer operations effectively supervised?

Are logs used at all entrances available to visitors?

Is there a planned program of rotation for operators and are sensitive applications jointly operated?

Are authorized passwords, keys, or encoded badges issued to enable the operation of time-sharing, remote job entry, and other on-line terminals?

What means are employed to protect passwords from misuse? Are they secured at three levels: identifying the user, the system, and some secret word? Are they changed frequently?

Are computer operators prohibited from making program modifications, including "patches" from the console?

What security is provided over facsimile check-signing operations and the safekeeping of signature plates?

Are machine utilization logs and console printouts reviewed?

Are data processing use meters regularly read, logged, and reviewed for unauthorized use of equipment?

Is access to the computer room and library restricted?

Do librarians control the issuance and storage of computer files?

Are key employees bonded?

Are job applicants' employment references checked?

Are job applicants checked for records with city, county, state, and federal law enforcement agencies?

Are exit interviews conducted to recover identification cards, keys, records, and manuals?

Must entrance to facilities at nonscheduled hours be approved in advance?

Are packages, briefcases, tool cases, and the like inspected when people enter and leave the facility?

Congress added another dimension to the search for preventing the misuse of computer systems when it passed the U.S. Foreign Corrupt Practices Act of 1977. The congressional intent to prevent commercial bribery, illegal payments, and questionable transactions brought about the legislated requirement for adequate internal accounting controls to reveal such payments if and when they do take place. But those controls, for all listed companies, must exist whether a company engages in foreign dealings or not. Furthermore, any weaknesses in control are suspect; the Act says nothing about materiality.

Thus, companies may be forced to prove — and in time report on — the adequacy of their internal accounting controls. In a company of any reasonable size, the computer is thoroughly involved in internal accounting controls in today's environment.

Internal auditors will be faced with new responsibilities to evaluate the adequacy of computer control systems and provide management with a basis on which to report that those systems meet the requirements of the Act.

This will call for documentation to an extent not heretofore considered necessary for computer systems. Internal auditors will have to be able to demonstrate that they have a method or a plan of gaining and identifying an understanding of controls within their companies' systems and documenting those controls. Internal auditors will have to work closely with external auditors, security people, and company counsel to be able to assure management that their existing computer systems will provide adequate internal accounting controls and that those controls are designed to meet the objectives of authorization, accounting, and asset safeguarding objectives set forth in the Act.

Exhibit 11-2. COMPUTER PROGRAM DOCUMENTATION

Opinions vary on what constitutes adequate and complete documentation of operational computer programs. It is generally agreed, however, that at least four categories of documentation are required if long and complex programs are to be significantly changed or subjected to other scrutiny.

The four categories are system flowcharts, detailed program flowcharts, source programs, and computer runsheets. Still other categories of documentation may be found when the auditor embarks on an audit of documentation supporting computer programs. The documentation may be placed in 12 different categories. They are explained here to show the relationship of various forms of documentation to the four first mentioned. The auditor is cautioned, however, that each EDP installation may not place the documentation in the precise categories described here. Some of the 12 categories may have been combined, others may have been eliminated or omitted, and still others may have been added.

1. Cover Sheet. The purpose of the cover sheet is to identify the computer program by giving such information as program name, program number, purpose (a brief nontechnical description of the problem solved by the program), source language used (such as COBOL or FORTRAN), EDP configuration that the program was designed for, programmer's name, and date of the program. Even though helpful, the cover sheet is not an absolute necessity because the information it contains is usually shown elsewhere in the documentation or is easily obtained.

2. Forms Layout. The purpose of this section is to show the content of input and output documents and reports. If it is not included in the documentation, it is usually available from other sources, such as current reports and currently used input documents.

3. Definitions. The purpose of this section is to define all symbolic names used anywhere in the program documentation. Symbolic names are abbreviated terms that are used in place of longer names, terms, or titles. For example, one of the input documents in the forms layout section may show a form space and identify its contents as "TAXDED." Reference to the definitions section might show that "TAXDED" means "Tax Deduction." This section may also contain any tables or other information the programmer feels should be defined. A table might show, for example, the number of dependents in one column and the applicable tax deduction in an adjacent column.

Exhibit 11-2. (Cont.)

Like the forms layout section, the definitions may be available from other sources if they are not defined in a separate section of documentation. As an example, definitions may be recorded on system flowcharts and detailed program flowcharts (explained later) or defined in the comments contained in the source program. Of course, the symbolic names used may have an obvious or easily determinable meaning. In that case, the definitions may not be essential.

4. System Flowchart. The purpose of the system flowchart is to show the flow of work, documents, and reports in a specific data processing job. It is designed to demonstrate how the data processing job is organized from beginning to end. It is general in nature because it does not specify the detailed and specific computer steps that are necessary for a particular processing run. (This detail is a function of the detailed program flowchart described later.)

Special data processing symbols are used in a system flowchart, along with symbolic names, previously described, and English language statements to describe flow of work, documents, and reports. By referring to the system flowchart, programmers and others can find out how the overall data processing job is organized, the source of type of input records, the point at which input records are introduced into the computer for processing, the sequence of the overall processing, all resulting output — such as printed reports — and the ultimate destination of the output.

This type of information is not usually available from another source unless it can be recalled by the people who worked on the program or unless it can be reconstructed from other detailed data processing records or current practices. Reconstruction can take a great deal of time if the data processing job is a lengthy one. Besides, it is not a good practice to rely on an individual's memory, because some important details may be forgotten or the individual may leave the company.

5. Detailed Program Flowchart. Like the system flowchart, the detailed program flowchart uses special data processing symbols, symbolic names, and English language statements. Unlike the system flowchart, however, the detailed program flowchart shows a step-by-step sequence in implementing a data processing job so that it can be made operational.

It is from the detailed program flowchart that the programmer prepares the actual computer program (called a source program) to be compiled and executed by the computer. Unless the source program is simple and only a few source program steps are required, a current detailed program flowchart is a valuable tool to the programmer in making necessary changes at a later date.

Because of its extremely detailed nature, it is important that the detailed program flowchart be kept current. Otherwise, important and minute details may be forgotten and the programmer may find it difficult or impossible to make changes in the related source program when the need arises. This is particularly true if the changes are to be made by a programmer other than the one who initially prepared the detailed program flowchart and source program. For some complex source programs, the programmer may prepare several program flowcharts, each becoming progressively more detailed until one of them possesses the detail that is necessary for writing the source program. When making program changes, the detailed program flowchart is almost always used in conjunction with the source program (described on item 7).

Exhibit 11-2. (Cont.)

6. Program Description. This section describes how the logic of the source program was developed, using the higher-level language (such as COBOL or FORTRAN) and the computer. It is a detailed flowchart in prose form. Sometimes, because COBOL is near to English, this section is not prepared for source programs written in COBOL. If it is not prepared, the same information is almost always available from the detailed program flowchart or the source program, except without the detailed and sometimes lengthy prose statements which explain why specific procedures were followed.

7. Source Program. This section contains the actual program as it is written in such higher-level languages as COBOL or FORTRAN. By comparing the detailed program flowchart with the actual source program, the programmer or others can trace each step of the computer through to a final conclusion. In reviewing and making changes in the programs, the programmer must generally refer to the source program to determine precisely how the higher-level language statements were used before the current review and change became necessary.

The detailed program flowchart is useful in determining the purpose of specific source program statements. Some EDP installations may also follow the practice of requiring programmers to include English language comments in the source program to briefly explain the purpose of each program step. Such comments are useful and, together with the detailed program flowchart, can provide a clear audit trail that shows the step-by-step procedure that was followed in developing the source program.

Sometimes, English language comments in the source program are sufficient to permit an accurate review of or change in the computer program. This, of course, depends upon the extent and clarity of the English language comments, the length and complexity of the source program, and the extent of the required review or program changes.

If a current copy of the source program is not formally kept as documentation, it can usually be obtained from punched cards that were used to introduce the source program into the computer or from other storage devices, such as magnetic tape, that may be used to hold the information.

8. List of Test Data. This section identifies the test data used by the programmer in testing the source program after it was written. The results are shown in the Test Report (described in item 10).

9. Sample Output. This section contains sample output resulting from the source program. Examples of output include reports and punched cards. If this information is not included in the documentation it is usually easily obtained by referring to recent output that resulted from EDP processing runs.

10. Test Report. This section explains the results that were obtained when the source program was tested to determine whether it was operational. If test data and test reports are not included in the documentation, the programmer can prepare other test data to determine the current effectiveness of the source program.

11. Deck Setup. This section gives the order of the source program card deck. It is similar to the source program (see item 7), but it is not in as much detail. The source program is an exact duplication of the computer program in the higher-level language. The deck setup shows the order of the related card deck, but it is usually subdivided by major category and does not outline each program step.

Exhibit 11-2. (Cont.)

This section may include such other information as requirements for peripheral equipment (magnetic tape drives, card readers, and card punchers), the time limit for the computer program when it is being executed by the computer, and special control cards needed for a successful run of the job. This information is also available from the programmer.

12. Computer Run Sheet. This section contains information needed by the console operator for running the computer program, such as the magnetic tapes or disks to be mounted, the names and usage of all input files, any central processing unit (CPU) console messages that may appear during the run, and any operator action to be taken as a result of these messages. This information is also usually available from retained copies of the CPU console messages from programmers responsible for maintaining the source program.

Conclusion

Internal auditors are responsible for determining whether systems have been designed to give reasonable assurance of the reliability and integrity of their organizations' information. A new dimension of this responsibility was added with the advent of computers. Standards now exist to provide guidance to, and at the same time define the responsibilities of, internal auditors whose organizations rely on computers for information. While the standards have been set primarily for government auditors, it is unlikely that other internal auditors can escape their impact. The standards simply put in writing those things for which many internal auditors are now being held accountable. Three aspects of computer technology are embraced by these standards: design and development of new data processing systems and their modification, general controls, and application controls.

Now that standards for computer audits have been made formal, many internal auditors will be called upon to have a working knowledge of computer controls and the means of auditing computer systems and applications. With an overview of these controls and audits and the literature available for study to expand their knowledge, internal auditors will be able to provide added assistance and safeguards for those who are responsible for the management of their organizations.

References

1. Wm. E. Mair, D. R. Wood, and K. W. Davis, *Computer Control and Audit* (Altamonte Springs, Fla.: The Institute of Internal Auditors, Inc., 1976), p. xii.
2. *Ibid.*, p. xiv.
3. *Ibid.*
4. *Ibid.*
5. Harvey Golub, "EDP and the Top Manager: A Crisis in Confidence," *The McKinsey Quarterly*, Summer 1970.

6. The Canadian Institute of Chartered Accountants, "Computer Control Guidelines," 1970, p. 88.
7. "The Round Table," *The Internal Auditor*, January/February 1976, p. 91.
8. *Computer Control and Audit*, p. 88.
9. M. J. Scanlan, "A Proposal For Alternative Procedures For Audit Of Real Time Data Systems," *The Internal Auditor*, November/December 1975, pp. 77-86.
10. The Canadian Institute of Chartered Accountants, "Computer Control Guidelines," 1970, p. 88.
11. L. George Hannye, "Auditors and DP'ers Benefit from Association in the Systems Development Process," *The Internal Auditor*, December 1977, p. 68.
12. C. A. Pauley, "Audit Responsibilities in the Design of Computerized Systems, *The Internal Auditor*, July/August 1969, p. 24.
13. *Computer Control and Audit,* p. xvi.
14. B. A. Roderick, "How to Audit the Efficiency and Economy of Computer Systems," *The Internal Auditor*, December 1977, p. 43.
15. "The Round Table," *The Internal Auditor*, February 1978, p. 82.
16. "The Round Table," *The Internal Auditor*, January/February 1976, p. 90.
17. "The Round Table," *The Internal Auditor*, October 1978, p. 98.
18. Report to the Congress by The Comptroller General of the United States, "Computer Auditing in the Executive Departments: Not Enough is Being Done," B-115369, September 28, 1977, p. 13.
19. National Bureau of Standards Special Publication 500-19, "Audit and Evaluation of Computer Security," October 1977, p. 5-4.
20. C. W. Parsons, "The Privacy Problem," *The Internal Auditor*, June 1976, p. 60.
21. NBS Special Publication 500-19, p. 5-4.
22. Report to the Congress by The Comptroller General of the United States, "Challenges of Protecting Personal Information in an Expanding Federal Computer Network Environment," B-146864, April 28, 1978, pp. 2, 17, 28.
23. Stanford Research Institute, *Systems Auditability and Control — Audit Practices* (Altamonte Springs, Fla.: The Institute of Internal Auditors, Inc., 1977), p. 85.
24. *Computer Control and Audit*, p. 88.
25. "The Round Table," *The Internal Auditor*, October 1978, p. 97.
26. *Computer Control and Audit*, p. 21.
27. *Computer Control and Audit*, p. 318.
28. Harold Weiss, "The Danger of Total Corporate Amnesia," *The Financial Executive*, June 1969, p. 63.
29. Allen Brandt, "Danger Ahead! Safeguard Your Computer," *Harvard Business Review*, November/December 1968, p. 97.
30. E. J. Howe, "Computer Security — Public and User Attitudes," *The Internal Auditor*, April 1978, p. 84.
31. *Computer Control and Audit*, p. 348.
32. *Systems Auditability and Control — Audit Practices*, p. 50.
33. *Ibid.*, p. 51.
34. National Bureau of Standards Special Publication 500-25, "An Analysis of Computer Security Safeguards for Detecting and Preventing Intentional Computer Misuse," January 1978, p. 11.
35. National Bureau of Standards Special Publication 500-25, p. 13.
36. "The Round Table," *The Internal Auditor*, September/October 1972, p. 75.
37. *Systems Auditability and Control — Audit Practices*, p. 83.
38. The Canadian Institute of Chartered Accountants, "Computer Audit Guidelines," 1975, p. 218.
39. *The Wall Street Journal*, April 5, 1968.
40. *Computer Control and Audit*, p. 322.

41. H. J. Mintern, ed., *How to Save $14,500,000 Through Internal Auditing* (Orlando, Fla.: The Institute of Internal Auditors, Inc., 1975) p. 78, 79.
42. D. C. Burns and J. K. Loebbecke, "Internal Control Evaluation. How the Computer Can Help," *The Journal of Accountancy*, August 1975, pp. 64-69.
43. Tom Alexander, "Waiting for the Great Computer Rip-off," *Fortune*, July 1974, p. 146.
44. "New Scientist," December 19, 1974, p. 881. Reprinted in *Management Auditing of Computer Operations — A Tutorial* (Long Beach, Calif.: IEEE Computer Society, 1976), p. 1-137.
45. Brian Ruder and J. D. Madden, "An Analysis of Computer Security Safeguards for Detecting and Preventing Computer Misuse," National Bureau of Standards Special Publication 500-25, January 1978, pp. 9-11.
46. Stuart Tyrnauer, "Auditing Computer Program Maintenance," *The Internal Auditor*, August 1977, p. 72.
47. *Systems Auditability and Control — Audit Practices*, p. 205.
48. "The Round Table" *The Internal Auditor*, August 1976, pp. 68, 69.

Supplementary Reading

Davis, G. B. *Auditing and EDP*. New York: American Institute of Certified Public Accountants, 1968.

Krauss, L. I. *Security Audit and Field Evaluation for Computer Facilities and Information Systems*. AMACOM, 1972.

Mair, W. C., D. R. Wood, and K. W. Davis, *Computer Control & Audit*. Altamonte Springs, Fla.: The Institute of Internal Auditors, Inc., 1976.

Management Auditing of Computer Operations: A Tutorial. Long Beach Calif.: IEEE Computer Society, 1976.

National Bureau of Standards Special Publication 500-19. *Audit and Evaluation of Computer Security*. October 1977.

Ruder, Brian, and J. D. Madden. *Computer Science & Technology: An Analysis of Computer Security Safeguards for Detecting and Preventing Intentional Computer Misuse*. National Bureau of Standards Publication 500-25, January 1978.

Stanford Research Institute. *Systems Auditability and Control Study — Data Processing Audit Practices Report*. Altamonte Springs, Fla.: The Institute of Internal Auditors, Inc., 1977.

The Canadian Institute of Chartered Accountants. *Computer Audit Guidelines*. 1975.

The Canadian Institute of Chartered Accountants. *Computer Control Guidelines*. 1970.

For further study

Discussion Problems

1. In what areas might an internal auditor be of specific assistance to management in dealing with computers?

2. What are some of the dangers that face internal auditors if they delay their involvement with the computer?

3. What are some of the conditions that will permit successful involvement by an internal auditor in computer operations?

4. What are some of the requirements for computer safety and protection?

5. What do organizational controls cover?

6. Distinguish between administrative and procedural controls.

7. What specific controls used in batch-processing systems are generally inapplicable to on-line systems?

8. How can a company guard against unauthorized use of terminals in a fast-response system?

9. Identify four different ways of auditing a fast-response system.

10. What are four aspects of computer operations that the internal auditor might be able to review without extensive knowledge of computers?

11. What problems might arise if EDP specialists make all the decisions in determining what systems and applications should be installed in the computer complex?

12. What is a steering committee, who should be members of it, and who should chair it?

13. Identify five functions of a steering committee.

14. What is another name for audit trails? Define the different audit trails.

15. Who usually makes the most use of audit trails? For what purpose?

16. What is the starting point in determining what controls should be incorporated in a computer system?

17. In many cases the objectives of management and the computer specialist vary. Explain.

18. Describe the dangers of inadequate documentation of the computer system.

19. Why are contingency plans necessary in a program of computer security?

20. Describe five kinds of checks which help ensure accurate computer input.

21. What is the difference between auditing for results and auditing for controls?

22. What kind of background in data processing do you think an internal auditor should have?

23. What requirements have the U.S. Foreign Corrupt Practices Act of 1977 placed on systems and application development?

24. What are the objectives of application controls?

25. Should internal auditors be held responsible for establishing computer controls? Give reasons for your answer.

Multiple Choice Problems

1. The auditor's objective in auditing computer operations include determining that:
a. The computer provides an adequate information base for management's needs.
b. The computer provides a more efficient form of data processing than manual means.
c. Computer programs include appropriate edit routines.
d. Management has received adequate information before approving the application.
e. All of the above.

2. Output controls relate to:
a. The operation of the machine room.
b. The accuracy and reasonableness of the information processed.
c. The weak links in the chain of events throughout the EDP system.
d. The edit checks in the computer system.
e. None of the above.

3. One method that is designed to deter an EDP equipment operator from manipulating computer records is:
a. To keep the operator out of the machine room.
b. To prevent operators from having access to object programs.

c. To assign only one operator to equipment operation.

d. To see that all operator intervention is made a matter of record.

e. None of the above.

4. The method that may be used to reconstruct files after minor processing errors or record destruction includes:

a. Relying on the judgment of well-trained operators.

b. Reference to computer registers and logs.

c. Discussions with systems analysts.

d. Reference to backup computer facilities.

e. None of the above.

5. The purpose of edit controls is:

a. To identify invalid data.

b. To assure printouts without typographical errors.

c. To detect errors in computer programs.

d. All of the above.

e. None of the above.

6. The controls designed to establish a well-documented trail showing how a computer program was prepared are a part of:

a. Input controls.

b. Processing controls.

c. Administrative controls.

d. Output controls.

e. None of the above.

7. An internal auditor should determine that header labels are used on magnetic tape files to:

a. Enable variable-length records to be processed.

b. Assure the processing of the correct files.

c. Make sure that end-of-file procedures will be followed.

d. Indicate the absence of file protection rings.

e. All of the above.

8. The technique of computer program comparison can be used by internal auditors to:

a. Verify that the computer program performs the required functions.

b. Test the efficiency of the computer program coding.

c. Disclose unauthorized changes in the computer program coding.

d. Determine that data produced by the computer program are reliable.

e. All of the above.

9. Data control activities in a computer department would appropriately include:

a. Reviewing error listings and maintaining error logs and reports.

b. Investigating deviations from standard procedures in data handling.

c. Supervising distribution of output.

d. Reviewing and balancing input and output.

e. All of the above.

10. You wish to evaluate procedural controls in your audit of the EDP department. Which of the following is not procedural in nature?

a. Batch controls.

b. Parity checks.

c. Self-checking numbers.

d. Limit checks.

e. Validity checks.

11. In a well-managed EDP installation, the internal auditor should expect to find:

a. A password protection system.

b. Duplicate files for all computer systems.

c. Computer operators with an extensive knowledge of computer programming.

d. Only computer programmers and operators permitted to have access to the computer room.

e. All of the above.

12. In an on-line computer application:

a. The system provides for a response to the user.
b. Records may be updated immediately as transactions occur.
c. Report terminals are usually an integral part of the system.
d. Response time may be virtually instantaneous.
e. All of the above.

Case Studies

11-1 On-Line Testing

As an internal auditor, you have been assigned to evaluate the controls and operation of a computer payroll system. The audit technique which you will be using is on-line testing of the computer systems and/or programs by submitting independently created test transactions with regular data in a normal production run.

Required: (1) List four advantages of this technique, and (2) list two disadvantages of this technique.

11-2 Feasibility Study

What are three major steps or considerations that should enter into a feasibility study for a new computer system?

11-3 Line Responsibility.

You are the director of internal auditing at a university. Recently, you met with the manager of administrative data processing and expressed the desire to establish a more effective interface between the two departments.

Subsequently, the manager of data processing requested your views and help on a new computerized accounts payable system being developed. The manager recommended that internal auditing assume line responsibility for auditing suppliers' invoices prior to payment. The manager also requested that internal auditing make suggestions during development of the sys-

tem, assist in its installation, and approve the completed system after making a final review.

Required: State how you would respond to the administrative data processing manager, giving the reason why you would accept or reject each of the following: (1) The recommendation that your department be responsible for the preaudit of suppliers' invoices, (2) the request that you make suggestions during development of the system, and (3) the request that you assist in the installation of the system and approve the system after making a final review.

11-4 Programmers in the Computer Room

Ed Proctor, EDP auditor, approached Manfred Davis, manager of data processing, and said, "I noted that your programmers sometimes operate computer equipment."

"So what?" asked Davis.

"That's contrary to good control procedures," said Proctor, "and it lays you open to the possibility of manipulation by the programmers."

"Do you have any evidence that there has been any manipulation?" asked Davis.

"No," answered Proctor, "and I don't need any. When the operating procedures are unsound — and I consider them unsound if the programmers have unrestricted access to operating equipment — then I'm going to say so."

"But this particular equipment is new," protested Davis. "The programs are extremely complex, and it would throw a monkey wrench into my operations if I couldn't let the programmers use the equipment at times to test their programs."

Required: What suggestions do you have to resolve this problem?

11-5 Uncontrolled Data Files

Ed Proctor was reluctant to approach the explosive Manfred Davis on the subject of control over data files. Proctor had found a large number of tape reels stored at various locations in the computer areas, many in open cabinets. There was really nothing to prevent anybody who so desired from taking any files he or she wanted. With a sigh, Parker realized he had a job to do, and so he approached Davis and explained his concern over tape security.

Predictably, Davis exploded. "I don't have to be told about my files. I know exactly where they are. We haven't lost any files and I don't need any better controls. I know what you're driving at: a librarian and a vault and all that stuff. I don't have the budget for it. I don't need it. I don't want it. Go sell your ideas elsewhere."

Required: Explain the significance of the problem. Describe Proctor's responsibility. What controls should he suggest?

11-6 Program for a Computer Audit

Alma Addison, a new assistant auditor at Able Company, approached the desk in the data processing division where Ed Proctor, senior EDP auditor, was sitting.

"Hi," said Alma. "I'm here."

Ed looked up, startled, saying, "I didn't expect you until tomorrow."

"Come on now," said Alma, "you're making me feel rejected."

"Oh, no," said Ed. "I'm glad to have you aboard; it's just that I haven't worked out my program yet, and you'll be twiddling your thumbs until I do."

"Maybe I can help," said Alma.

"You're kind of new at Able Company," said Ed.

"Right," agreed Alma. "But data processing is what I really like. I took a number of courses during my masters program. And I even taught COBOL and FORTRAN before coming to Able Company. I really mean it; I'd like to help. How far have you gotten?"

"I've made the preliminary survey," said Ed. "I've just finished writing up the controls. I was about to start preparing the program to test the controls."

"What kind of a computer application do we have here?" asked Alma.

"It's an on-line location system. The purpose is to keep track of inventories. As goods are ordered, stored, disbursed, or returned to stock, the system keeps track of them every step of the way. The system has the capability of on-line data input and inquiry with a network of remote on-line terminals located in various departments in the company."

"Is this the first time the system went on-line?" asked Alma.

"Oh, no," said Ed, "we're not that far behind the times. It used to be on the NCR 315-RMC. It's being converted to the third generation IBM 360-65 system. It's a major programming effort, though, and all programs will have to be rewritten from the NCR programming language to the Standard-COBOL language."

"Sounds like an interesting assignment," said Alma.

"You mean it?" asked Ed.

"Absolutely," replied Alma.

"Okay, I'll tell you what I'm going to do. I can easily occupy myself for a day on other things. I'll give you my write-up of the controls. What I want you to do is to give me your suggestions on how each of the controls should be tested to make sure they really exist and are functioning as intended. You game?"

"Let me at it," answered Alma.

"Nothing fancy, now," said Ed. "Just give me a statement of what you propose to do to test each of the controls I've listed."

"Where's the list?" asked Alma.

Ed then gave Alma the following description of the results of his preliminary survey:

The following system of controls has been established for the inventory system conversion:

1. A detailed planning specification package to serve as a guide to the actual programming.
2. A system of controls and reports for the data processing activities so as to maintain close surveillance over the planning and the programming phases of the conversion.
3. A comprehensive master test deck to examine all significant phases of the new system.
4. A parallel run of a single day's activity to determine whether the new system is able to accurately process the data used in regular production.
5. A comprehensive test of on-line stations to ensure the complete operation of all input and inquiry apparatus at every remote terminal location.
6. A comparison between the data base record totals of the NCR 315-RMC and those of the IBM 360-65 master files at the time of the conversion to make sure that the IBM 360-65 master files are complete when the new system starts operating.
7. An extensive review and training program provided by representa-

tives of the user organizations to appraise and supplement the new IBM 360-65 system developed in data processing and to instruct those people who will use the inventory system on the new applications.

8. A review of the operation of the system by members of data processing and user organizations immediately after conversion to make sure that it is functioning effectively.
9. A complete system documentation package to provide a detailed description of every significant phase of the new IBM 360-65 system.

As Alma lifted her head from an instant review of the control system notes, Ed said, "The control system covers some things that have been done and some that still have to be done. At this point we're at step three. We'll be able to look at the first three steps. But the audit program should cover all nine steps. We're making a concurrent review. We'll·be getting off this job to do other things, and then we'll be getting back to it as more and more steps in the conversion are completed."

"I understand," said Alma.

"So now, based on your studies, your reading, and just plain common sense — because that's mainly what internal auditing is all about — give me, in your own words, an idea how you'd go about checking out the controls."

"Will do," said Alma as she got to work.

Required: Prepare a series of audit program steps to accomplish the audit objectives. A full-blown program is not necessary. Just the specific audit steps.

12

Computer-Assisted Auditing

Reasons for computer-assisted auditing. When to use it. The need to verify internal controls. Parallel simulation. Steps in a parallel simulation audit program. Simulation techniques to solve audit problems. Example of a computer simulation. Advantages of simulation. Generalized audit software. What it can accomplish. Steps in using generalized audit software. Utility programs. Special audit programs for computers. Computer programs written by the internal auditor. File dumps. Determining which techniques to use. Examples of computer-assisted audits.

The Need to Use the Computer

Computers, increasingly responsible for storing the bulk of an organization's data, often contain the only information on its transactions. For the internal auditor to try to examine the transactions and deal with them manually is to try to grasp a ray of light. Besides, large organizations process incredible amounts of transactions in a year. The only practical way of auditing such transactions is to use the strength of the computer itself. When volume is great, when audit objectives can be parsed out in advance, and when transactions are repetitive, computers can be asked to take much of the toil and tedium out of the audit verification process. When computations are complex and numerous, the computer may be the only way to deal with them.

Internal auditors now have attained the capability of wrestling successfully with the computer and bending it to their needs. But before computers may be used in auditing, the internal auditors must satisfy themselves about the internal controls over the computer operations themselves. Obviously a well-controlled computer operation is essential if internal auditors are to turn over part of their work to the computer. A computer-assisted audit is not reliable if the computer is not adequately controlled to produce reliable information. Internal auditors must guard against the misuse of the computer by employees. They must recognize that any program flaw or system inadequacy may multiply errors enormously. The computer is not like a thinking human being who can recover from an error. It goes on happily repeating the same one until corrected. Reliance on the computer to assist the auditor presupposes assurance of adequate, effective internal control over computer operations.

Once its reliability has been established, internal auditors can take two routes to use the computer in audits:

First, the computer can be used to simulate problems. Test data can be used to check sets of transactions like payrolls, for example, through such means as parallel simulation. Also, audit or management problems can be solved through simulation techniques.

Second, computers can perform many audit functions which auditors have always had to do by hand: extract data, select samples, and make verifications and comparisons. Extensive software is available in the form of commercial audit programs for that purpose.

Let us explore both of these methods.

Simulation

Parallel Simulation

Parallel simulation calls for a separate computer application; it simply duplicates the process. It performs the same function as that performed by the application program used for regular processing.

Under the simulation program the same input data is used, the same files are used, and the same results are sought.

Thus, the two programs run in parallel. The results of the simulation program are compared with those of the live program. The technique is similar to auditing around the computer, but it does not require manual audit trails or manual processing. Besides, the auditor is better served by parallel simulation programs than by manual processing. Computer programs perform consistently. Human beings do not.

In performing parallel simulation, internal auditors can introduce transactions involving large amounts, transactions subject to error or manipulation, and a sample of the other variables. The speed of the computer permits the simulation of many transactions; it does not restrict the number of items to be tested to a number which will fit into the audit budget.

The steps in a simulation program include these:[1]

Defining the audit objective; for example, calculating the withholding tax in a payroll, verifying the automatic calculation of interest in a savings and loan institution, or reviewing overdrawn checking accounts in a bank.

Understanding the computer application being audited by obtaining descriptions of records and transactions, learning what the different codes mean, identifying the decision criteria used in the live application, and finding out the number of decimal places for calculations.

Specifying the logic to be followed. (This need not be difficult if the flowcharting under a system like STRATA is used.)

Coding the instructions; that is, telling the computer what to do in language it understands. (Specification sheets used in STRATA take the pain out of this audit step.)

Obtaining files representative of the population being reviewed, as the files (sets of related data records) should contain all the types of transactions the auditor would want to include in the audit.

Debugging the simulation program. This can be done by taking a small sample from the live file for verification.

Processing the application. By using general purpose software, the auditor can control the processing completely. Ordinarily, software programs do not require the help of computer people.

Evaluating the results.

To recapitulate: Internal auditors can extract relevant data or samples of data from a live file, then run those data through a simulation program which parallels the live program. They compare results, then investigate any differences. They can assume that the transactions with no differences are acceptable.

People expert in computer-assisted auditing find that parallel simulation provides the best balance of reliability and economy of all alternative techniques — when properly used.

Computer Simulation

Computer simulation means that internal auditors use the computer to help simulate actual conditions and seek answers to difficult audit problems. If a computer model is valid and if it truly represents the system, it can be a useful device in analyzing and evaluating systems or operations.

The computer's incredible speed and mathematical logic permit it to predict the results of many alternative actions involving a great number of calculations. When internal auditors see an audit problem that requires a great many comparisons and computations to search out an optimum choice, and they are willing to stipulate a reliability level (confidence level and precision) to estimate probable results, the computer can be a formidable ally.

Here is an example of the kind of studies internal auditors can carry out to solve audit problems:[2]

The U.S. Government Printing Office (GPO) stocked 600 different types of paper valued at about $8 million. Paper was ordered from contractors. The contracts set forth specifications of quality and quantity. Quantity variances, for example, could not exceed 30%. Paper not meeting specifications must be replaced within 14 days. Orders must be shipped within 35 calendar days. These time limits were important in determining inventory levels: The GPO's policy is to have no out-of-stock conditions because of the need to provide printing and binding services promptly to the Congress and to government departments and agencies.

Yet inventory decisions were made almost entirely on nonautomated procedures. Computers kept the records, but they did not provide information on the most economic ordering quantities. The computers told what inventory was on hand and on order; GPO officials used personal judgment in ordering paper.

To establish minimum inventory levels, the GPO gave each line item of paper a "month factor" representing the number of months of supply to be maintained in inventory — quantities on hand and on order. Factors varied from two to six, depending on the type of paper. The total factor averaged out to four months. An official determined the month factor and estimated order quantities. His guide was his experience and the average monthly use for the last six months.

The minimums to be maintained in inventory represented the reorder points. These minimums were the month factors multiplied by the average monthly use — quantities ordered were to equal one month's average use. So the average level for four month's supply was selected as the minimum quantity. However, actual inventory quantities could be and were much higher.

The auditors considered the existing inventory and ordering methods to be inefficient. They therefore sought alternative methods which would provide adequate insurance against stock-outs. Fortunately, the GPO maintained excellent historical records, and the auditors were able to obtain reliable information over a three-year period of the number of days it took to receive ordered paper and of the amount of stock on hand at any given time.

The preliminary analysis strongly suggested that minimum inventories could be reduced substantially while still insuring adequate supplies on hand. The auditors wanted some hard evidence to support their thesis, and they wanted to be able to recommend reasonable alternative procedures. They believed that a computerized model of the inventory could answer these important questions for them: What inventory procedure could be changed to reduce inventory levels? What effect could these changes have on future inventory operations? What procedures should be changed, and how could the effects of the changes be determined?

The audit analysis indicated that the month factor, then ranging from two to six, could be changed. Since it was the key to determining minimum inventory (reorder points) a small change there could mark a big change in inventory levels.

A model was designed to show the effect of ordering paper, based on different minimum order points, until a stock-out condition was reached. Historical experience was used as the test.

As a result of the information obtained from the model, the auditors recommended that the GPO use it as a basis for ordering in the future. The computer results showed that the GPO could safely use an average month factor of 2.25 instead of four. This would permit a reduction in inventory levels of about $2 million.

The model for this simulation was used on a time-sharing computer system. The language used was A Programming Language/360 (APL/360). But it could have been programmed in other mathematically oriented languages like FORTRAN, Simscript, or ALGOL.

The simulation described provided several advantages over other audit procedures. First, inventory operations spanning years could be simulated with the computer in seconds and minutes. Second, the computer could maintain complex interrelationships within statistically acceptable confidence limits. Third, the computer could present the possible effect of alternative actions without incurring the risk or cost of actually taking those actions.

Computer-Assisted Audit Techniques

Generalized Computer Audit Programs

The generalized computer audit program is the audit software. Software is able to process computer data files under the internal auditor's control and to answer the internal auditor's requirements for comparisons, calculations, reports, and summaries. The data can be on cards, magnetic tape, or disks, and can be accessed sequentially or directly.

Internal auditors can specify the types of files they want processed. They can state the processing logic to be applied, and they can dictate the reports they want to receive. The software can:[3]

Foot, cross-foot, and balance data in files.

Select specified data from files.

Perform operations on data.

Stratify data.

Specify the format of reports.

Prepare confirmation statements.

Check for duplications, missing information, or ranges of values.

Compare two different generations of a file and print out differences for investigation.

Generalized software packages have a number of advantages. They are relatively easy for internal auditors to operate, thereby making them independent of the computer people whose work they are auditing. Changes in applications have little or no effect on the software program. Complex statistical and mathematical routines are available, and they have been thoroughly tested. One such package can be used on various applications.

The packages do have some disadvantages, however. While many are available for batch processing applications, currently very few deal with on-line processing. Also, they often have limits to their logical and mathematical capabilities.

Internal auditors usually follow these six steps when they use generalized audit software packages:[4]

1. Review the system to obtain an understanding of the application to be audited, set audit objectives, and lay out an audit program specifying which data elements will be tested and the standards to be used.

2. Complete the input specification forms provided by the software supplier describing the files, records, and data elements to be processed.

3. Complete a processing specification form provided by the software supplier describing the audit processing steps the software should perform. The processing specification tells the computer what actions it must take in processing the computer files.

4. Complete the instructions on what output and reports are desired: tabulations and listings, tabulating cards, magnetic tapes, or disks.

5. Witness the computer processing, making sure the correct files are being used and review the computer program to make sure appropriate edit routines are in effect to validate input.

6. Review and evaluate test results, investigating all exceptions and documenting the results in the audit working papers.

Utility Programs

Utility programs use standard routines to merge, sort, insert, and extract data. They are available from manufacturers or software suppliers and perform one-time tasks that do not warrant special programs. Most computer installation libraries have a set of utility programs which are used to test applications. The internal auditor has the responsibility of seeing that the programs are reliable. This can be done by reviewing program documentation.

Special Audit Programs

When generalized or utility programs are not available, the internal auditor or EDP personnel may write special programs. These programs may take the following forms:

Modifications of existing programs to provide audit information simultaneously with regular processing information.

A new program not only for audit but also for management use. For example, the program may analyze fuel consumption on various types of motor vehicles — information not otherwise readily available.

A program designed to fit a specific audit requirement.

Again, the internal auditor is responsible for testing the program before using it. The audit opinion is the auditor's and the auditor's only. The basis for the opinion must be reliable. To obtain that assurance the auditor should review program documentation, test the program, and make sure there are no unnecessary interruptions or program substitutions.

Programs Written by the Internal Auditor

Few indeed are the internal auditors who can prepare their own detailed computer audit programs. If people in the internal audit department do not have the ability, others in the organization may be available for that purpose. The internal auditor, however, must participate in documenting the program. The documentation should contain a description of audit objectives, requirements, system design, programming, testing, debugging, and implementation.

File Dumps

To dump a file is to reproduce whatever may be recorded on cards, magnetic tape or disks with some other medium such as a printer. The dump provides the auditor with the ability to examine the contents of a computer-generated file.

This is an expensive method and alternative means should be considered before using file-dumping techniques. The method is useful, however, to compare two successive files so as to identify and investigate significant changes or variances. The principal advantage of file dumping is the ability to examine visually what is on cards, magnetic tapes, or disks — records which are not humanly readable — and to analyze it.

Considerations

Before reaching a decision on which computer-assisted audit technique to use, internal auditors should consider these matters:

The cost and effectiveness of the computer application as compared with manual approaches.

The availability of computer programs or of people to write them.

What training the internal auditor will have to undergo.

Which of the special audit program techniques just described is most appropriate.

The computer hardware to be used and its availability.

Example of a Computer-Assisted Audit

Computer-assisted audits have proven useful and effective in highlighting problems within the computer and determining the results of erroneous information produced. Here is a detailed description of one such audit in which the internal auditors used a software package.[5]

Information about a large fleet of vehicles had been put on the computer. The system consisted of a master file and several programs to update the master file and to produce financial and management reports.

For example, the management report listed the type of vehicle, the vehicle number, any special equipment, department assigned, purchase date, acquisition cost, depreciation expense, and operating costs.

Users were complaining about the accuracy of the reports. Also, the equipment asset control account could not be reconciled to the subsidiary ledger which the computer produced.

Accordingly, the internal auditors were called in. After surveying the system, they obtained a computer software package for their analysis. They received a copy of the file layout from the data processing department and selected the fields that contained data relevant to the audit objective. The data processing department's most current master file of the system was copied onto another tape which the auditors could access through the software package. The internal auditors were then able to extract selected data and make any needed calculations.

The computer was instructed to print a report showing information about the vehicles which included:

Vehicles with fuel use of more than 20 or less than 5 miles per gallon.

Vehicles with no year-to-date depreciation.

Vehicles with no purchase date and/or acquisition cost.

Vehicles over five years old. (Policy required the sale of all vehicles over that age.)

Vehicles with mileage over 40,000 or less than 5,000 miles.

The auditors analyzed the report and found a large number of problems:

None of the vehicles had accurate depreciation information.

Over 10 % of the fleet had miraculously achieved several hundred miles per gallon.

Some vehicles, even more miraculously, had "generated" gasoline.

Purchase dates and acquisition costs were missing for a number of vehicles.

Many vehicles on hand were more than five years old.

Many vehicles had been driven more than 40,000 or less than 5,000 miles.

The internal auditors had no difficulty concluding that the computerized files contained many inaccuracies. They then searched for the causes and found that:

There were no controls to reject unreasonable data. The controls originally installed for that purpose had been removed because so much data was rejected that processing had to be halted.

The various computer programs were designed to accept only a few types of design changes. No procedures had been developed to correct much of the erroneous data which entered the file.

Errors in some programs caused attempted file maintenance field changes to make unwanted and erroneous changes in other fields.

The internal auditors presented their finding to the data processing people. They turned out to be overly sensitive to criticism, and insisted that the problems were common to all new systems and that, as time went by, corrections would be made. Higher management took a different view, however, and insisted on immediate corrective action.

Computer-assisted audits are being made more and more frequently with considerable success. Once internal auditors become adept at using the tools available in the form of software packages or specially developed audit programs, they can ask the computer to audit any operations having a multitude of transactions. The following are some examples, briefly stated, of computer-assisted audits that have already been made.

Accounts Payable and Purchasing

The computer was used to detect duplicate payments. When suppliers submit invoices in duplicate, some of the copies can be processed in error along with the originals.

Billing

The computer was used in a service organization to verify rental billings and services rendered; the internal auditors found that the cost of servicing several items of equipment had never been billed. The computer was also used to compare contract rates with rates billed; in several instances the rates billed did not agree with those in the contracts.

Inventories

Using a generalized computer program developed by one of the large accounting firms, but modifying it to their particular purposes, internal auditors had the computer:

Extend unit prices and quantities on hand for more than 100,000 line items of inventory.

Select inventory samples.

Evaluate sample results.

Obtain a variety of statistical data.

Using the same generalized computer program, unmodified, the internal auditors analyzed 21,000 items of shop stores by having the computer:

Compute the amount of excess material included in inventory.

Compute timeliness in filling requisitions from stores.

Determine the number and percentage of overdue, unfilled requisitions.

Select a sample to determine the effect of unfilled requisitions.

Determine the volume of premature purchases of stores items.

Determine what items of material had been in storage more than 30, 60, 90, 120, and 360 days, and show their related values.

Machines — Lease or Buy?

The computer was used to analyze the costs of leasing versus purchasing certain business machines. Without the computer, the analysis for a single machine presented a formidable problem. With it, costs were accumulated, amortization schedules were produced from a few numbers applied to formulae, and extrapolations were shown for successive years.

Payroll

By using the computer to compare labor charges for certain operations over a two-month period, internal auditors were able to suggest increasing production run quantities on 78 different parts to reduce the number of expensive machine set-ups.

The computer was used to detect production overstatements by employees working on a piecework basis. The computer compared on an operation-by-operation basis production quantities with all parts reported by the employees as having been produced.

Services

By devising a computer program, internal auditors selected from 27 million entries a sample of 1,395 records. They then reviewed the records to determine whether certain services had actually been rendered and had been paid for at correct rates.

Transportation

Selecting and arraying information from freight bills — shipment dates, weights, locations, rates, total cost, destinations, and modes of shipment — provided information that resulted in rescheduling and consolidating shipments to obtain better rates, and determining the most efficient mode of transportation.

Vehicles

Through a computer program, records of six classes of vehicles were examined. The computer determined the cumulative maintenance costs for each vehicle class, compared cost per mile for each class to determine efficient use, and compared cost of in-house versus contractor-supplied maintenance care.

Training

Audit software can be very helpful to internal auditors facing mountains of transactions and hordes of computations. The computer does the spade work for the auditor. But, like a steam shovel, it needs a practiced hand on the controls. Internal auditors do not need to have programming knowledge to use such software. They will need to have a general knowledge of data processing, and some knowledge of scientific computer language and programming is helpful. Of course, a thorough knowledge of business is essential.

To use audit software successfully, internal auditors will have to understand such basic data processing documentation as application system flowcharts, logic flowcharts, and record layouts. The SAC study presented in the following table shows the kind of training internal auditors would need to deal with generalized audit software:[6]

Knowledge Area	Level*
Data processing principles and concepts	XX
Computer application system structure	X
Computer application system controls and procedures	X
Data management	X
Computer service center controls	X
Application system development controls	—
Computer application programming	—

*XX = Advanced   X = Basic   — = Not required

Computers for Auditors

Some internal auditing organizations have computers in their own offices. One internal auditing department has an office computer with 256K memory and 512 megabytes of disk storage hooked to the company's five main computers. This office computer has a distributed network system which will support up to nine distant terminals and nine printers. The director of internal auditing is planning on four of his out-of-town offices having on-line terminals and printers linked to his in-house computer.

This in-house computer has a multiprogramming environment which allows sixteen programs to operate concurrently. The company's data files are contained in some 60,000 tapes, and the system has about 60 on-line disk units. The internal audtors can readily extract any of the information from these data files and manipulate it with their computer through a system which provides the use of COBOL, BASIC, and an easier version of Assembler computer languages.

The auditors also use a number of extraction packages to analyze the data retrieved. Additional utility packages allow the auditors to compare program source and object codes to determine what changes have been made in sensitive programs since their last audit. The company — a Canadian railroad — has one on-line application which is basically an information system on car movements. With this technology the company cut freight car turnaround time from 17 days to about 8 days. The interest savings alone on the new equipment have more than repaid the cost of the system in three years.

The company's mechanized payroll system, which covers over 70,000 employees at some 3,000 pay points, is being revised. The new system will be on-line interactive; and the internal auditors plan on an interface with it. When they can handle such on-line systems, the auditors will be in a position to monitor transactions as they occur.[7]

Conclusion

Progress won't be halted. The audit assistance available from computers cannot be denied. Indeed, with so much data on tapes, disks, and cards, not readable by internal auditors, there may be no rational alternative to computer-assisted audits. Centralized audit software programs can test, examine, and balance automated records. The instructions that go with them require minimal training of internal auditors, but all internal auditors will have to receive some training in computer technology if they are to do their jobs efficiently and effectively.

Some forms of generalized audit software are helpful in performing parallel simulation and the selection of transactions for tests. The various forms of software are now widely used and will be in even greater use in the future. And while not in widespread use at present, on-line versions will achieve greater popularity as more on-line systems are developed and auditors acquire their own computers to extract and analyze data.

References

1. W. C. Mair, D. R. Wood, and K. W. Davis, *Computer Control and Audit* (Altamonte Springs, Fla: The Institute of Internal Auditors, Inc., 1976), p. 153.
2. U. S. General Accounting Office, Division of Financial and General Management Studies, "Solving Audit Problems with Computer Simulation: A Case Study," November 1972.
3. Stanford Research Institute, *Systems Auditability and Control — Audit Practices* (Altamonte Springs, Fla: The Institute of Internal Auditors, Inc., 1977), p. 143.
4. Ibid., p. 144.
5. Western Intergovernmental Audit Forum, December 1977, *The Computer as an Audit Tool*, p. V-15.
6. *Systems Auditability and Control — Audit Practices*, p. 146.
7. George Maroulis, "The Future of Internal Auditing From a Practitioner's Point of View." Speech delivered at the Institute of Internal Auditors' International Conference, July 1, 1980, in Toronto, Ontario, pp. 22-24.

Supplementary Reading

Adams, D. L. and J. F. Mullarkey. "A Survey of Audit Software." *The Journal of Accountancy*, September 1972, pp. 39-66.

Mair, W. C., D. R. Wood and K. W. Davis. *Computer Control and Audit*. Altamonte Springs, Fla: The Institute of Internal Auditors, Inc., 1976, pp. 149-160.

Perry, W. E., "The State of the Art in EDP Auditing." *The EDP Audit Control and Security Newsletter*, Vol. 4, No. 1, July 1976, p. 5.

Stanford Research Institute. *Systems Auditability and Control — Audit Practices*. Altamonte Springs, Fla: The Institute of Internal Auditors, Inc., 1977, pp. 143-147.

U. S. Department of Commerce, National Bureau of Standards. "Features of Seven Audit Software Packages — Principles and Capabilities," NBS Special Publication 500-13.

Western Intergovernmental Audit Forum, December 1977. *The Computer as an Audit Tool*, Chapters V and VI.

For further study

Discussion Problems

1. Under what circumstances should internal auditors consider using the computer as an audit tool?

2. Why should an internal auditor review computer systems and applications before using the computer as an audit tool?

3. Describe parallel simulation.

4. Contrast computer simulation and parallel simulation as used in this chapter.

5. Name two benefits of the GPO simulation discussed in this chapter.

6. Contrast generalized and utility audit programs.

7. What signficant lesson can be learned about system design from the case study describing the audit of a large fleet of vehicles?

Multiple Choice Problems

1. Internal auditors can satisfy themselves about the reliability of a computer system before engaging in computer-assisted audits, through:
a. Discussions with systems analysts.
b. Examination of the object language program.
c. Interviews with the external auditors and reviews of their working papers.
d. A review of computer documentation and a test of the application program.
e. None of the above.

2. A file dump permits an internal auditor to:
a. See what was buried in the computer.
b. Compare successive programs.
c. Examine scrapped tapes and disks.

d. Read source programs.
e. None of the above.

3. Internal auditors can use audit software:
a. If they understand basic data processing documentation.
b. By reading an instruction manual.
c. By carefully filling out forms provided by the software supplier.
d. All of the above.
e. None of the above.

4. Computer-assisted audits would be most applicable to:
a. A review of insurance policies to determine whether appropriate conditions were included.
b. A review of purchase orders to see if proper bidding procedures were employed.
c. A review to determine whether proper amounts of tax were withheld in a payroll.
d. A review of management incentive bonuses.
e. Both a. and c.

5. Which of the following steps can a generalized computer **not** perform:
a. Add data.
b. Select a statistical sample.
c. Prepare a summary of findings and conclusions.
d. Array data according to different ranges of dollar amounts.
e. Identify transactions not falling within predetermined ranges.

Case Study

12-1 Using Audit Software

Victor Price, the vice president and controller of Republic Products, called Audrey Martin, Republic's audit manager.

"Audrey, have your auditors done any work in our data processsing department?"

"Yes sir. We've done an operational review there."

"What do you mean?"

"We've looked at their organization, their scheduling methods, how the users like the reports they've been getting, and the billings from the hardware supplier for the leased equipment."

"Fine. Then you should be able to carry out this assignment."

"What assignment?"

"The computer handles our inventory of finished products. It's all on tape. We get reports on what we have on hand, what's in process, what we're due to ship, what we've shipped, and the like. We've got our problems, though."

"What kind of problems?"

"The subsidiary ledger produced by the computer does not agree with the general ledger account. Our production people don't believe the work-in-process figures. And our accounting people don't believe the financial reports. Other than that, everything is fine."

"Why can't the data processing people correct their files?"

"They've tried. They worked on it for months. I'm getting desperate. I called our external auditors, but they tell me they can't get a team out here for another five months. They did say something about a software audit package that would do the job. As soon as I heard the word audit I thought of you. Get it from them and audit our inven-

tory records."

"Well, now — "

But Price had already hung up. And Audrey had learned not to argue with him.

Audrey called the partner responsible for the external audits of Republic's accounts and made arrangements to get the software package Price had mentioned. When it arrived — tapes, instructions, and forms — she handed the package to Sam Ingalls, the senior internal auditor who had carried out the operational audit of the computer room. He was 45 years old, an experienced internal auditor, hardworking, and intelligent. Sam had attended a seminar on computer technology; but that was the extent of his computer knowledge.

Sam took the package, read the instructions, and made a date with Dred Pruitt, manager of the data processing department. Sam had not been the least bit concerned about Dred's disparaging remarks about his ability as an EDP auditor when he had made the operational audit. He had treaded on comfortable ground in that audit of the computer room. All the operations he had dealt with were little different from any other operational audit. He saw no reason why using the software package should be any more difficult. He could read instructions with the best of them. He could fill out forms. And he wasn't afraid of Dred Pruitt or any gorilla that looked and sounded like Dred. He approached his meeting with Dred confidently.

Required: (1) What do you think will be the outcome of the meeting between Ingalls and Pruitt? (2) What should Audrey have done before letting Sam meet with Dred? (3) What should Sam do before using the software package to audit the inventory system?

Part 4

Reporting

13

Reports

Getting management's attention. The ingredients of communication: perception and expectation. The essential elements of reporting: scrupulous accuracy, clear writing, conciseness and completeness, timeliness while meeting high standards, and a nonabrasive tone. The different forms of reports. The contents of formal reports: summaries, introductions, purpose and scope, opinions, and findings. The elements of a finding: authority, objectives of the activity, and conditions — both favorable and unfavorable. The components of an unfavorable finding: summary, criteria, facts, effect, cause, and recommendations. Dressing up reports with graphics. Progress reports. Oral reports and audiovisual presentations. Preparing for the oral report. Good writing calls for good thinking. Outlines for reports. Drafting the report. Language in reports. Appearance and length. Signatures and distribution. Reports which provide adjective or numerical ratings. Editing. The written performance inventory. Proofreading. Errors to watch for. Preparing a style manual. Sample reports.

What They Are And What They Do

Reports are the auditor's opportunity to get management's undivided attention. That is how auditors should regard reporting — as an opportunity — not dreary drudgery, but rather a perfect occasion to show management how auditors can help.

Much too often auditors carelessly throw away this golden chance to open management's eyes, to show management what they have accomplished and what they can accomplish, to explain what management needs to know and what it needs to do. They throw away this opportunity by using pallid prose,

431

by making mountains out of rubbish heaps, by being content with uninviting report formats, by making allegations that won't withstand assault, by drawing unsupported conclusions, and by filing complaints without solutions.

The auditors should regard their reports in the same light that salespeople regard an opportunity to present their products to the president of a company: an opening for a well-rehearsed, well-tested, well-conceived sales presentation. In this light, the audit report has two functions: first, to communicate; second, to persuade and, when necessary, sound a call to action. As Dudley E. Brown said, "We have, on the whole, an admirable story to tell — buttressed by facts and figures, and supported by analysis and reason — and it surely is one that deserves to be told often and in the right places."[1]

The audit findings and opinions are important to management. The dispassionate, objective conclusions may ease management's mind about well-functioning activities, and the recommendations may alert management to matters needing improvement.

But management must want to read or hear the reports. For communication to be effective, the channels must be clear — the medium must be incisive and easily understood. The story must be worthy of the material; much skillful and constructive audit effort flounders in the murky waters of poor reporting. Auditors who sharpen their auditing techniques but leave their reporting dull will be unable to penetrate the circles where the story should be told.

When management gives them an audience they must never forget that they are selling. So they must be consciously persuasive by the techniques of motivation and by the style they use. They must highlight what is management-oriented. They must downplay what is immaterial. They must adroitly translate the technical into the readily understandable. They must point skillfully to the need for taking action and the penalties for avoiding action.

Then management will begin to appreciate the significance of the audit product, seeing the valuable insights it can obtain and learning to accept the accuracy, the objectivity, and the plain good sense of what the auditor has to say. Then, and not until then, will the audit report become required reading for management. This will help auditors achieve one of their own objectives: to be privy to the councils of management and to have access to management's ear.

There is a small likelihood that auditors are born with the word-mastery of a Shakespeare or the crisp, lean style of a Hemingway. If they were, they would probably be in the business of writing instead of auditing. But what writing talent they have can be forged into an effective tool — with the right effort, with the right desire, with the right standards, and with the right techniques.

Communication

Reports seek to communicate. If they do not achieve communication they are without value altogether. Yet rare is the individual who understands the ingredients of communication. Most auditors take the position that if they've put it in writing they have achieved communication. More often they have thwarted communication. They've spawned words, but they have not constructed a bridge between the mind of the writer and the mind of the reader.

The difficulty begins when the report writers have thought more about the writing than about the reading. They have failed to comprehend that communication is not in the writer, the utterer; it is in the recipient. Until the recipient perceives, there is no communication — only words on paper. Perception is the key. So all report writers must ask themselves, as they put words to paper, "Is this within the scope of my reader's comprehension and perception? Have I so written my report that I have set up and met expectations?"

What is beyond the reader's perception cannot be understood. What the mind does not expect, it will not receive. A mind slanted in one direction will reject what comes from another direction.

The first rule in report writing is to know the readers. What can they perceive? What do they expect? What are they led to expect? What do they need? Once these questions are answered, the auditor can hope to achieve communication.

Top management can best perceive general concepts. It can perceive what affects the enterprise as a whole. It expects to be told of matters of significance. It expects either to have its concerns allayed or to take action to see that some risk is avoided or some significant defect is being corrected.

Operating management can perceive the details of its operations. It can comprehend discussions couched in its own familiar language. It can fully understand the details of defective conditions. But it has the right to expect not to be surprised. It has the right to see in the audit report the matters that have been discussed as the audit progressed.

So internal auditors must know that communication is in the recipient; that it is composed of perception and expectations; and that the best field work and the most brilliant analyses will remain moldering in the working papers until they are communicated.

In seeking to communicate, internal auditors must remember their principal objectives: to provide useful and timely information, both oral and written, on significant matters and to promote improvements in control and performance of enterprise operations.

Criteria for Reports

Internal audit reports can be measured; the standards or criteria of measurement have been agreed upon, by and large, by those practitioners who have written about reports. It is generally accepted that reports should have accuracy, conciseness, clarity, timeliness,[2] and tone.

Accuracy

The report must be completely and scrupulously factual. Every categorical statement, every figure, every reference must be based on hard evidence. The internal auditing organization, through unremitting effort, must develop a reputation for reliability — utter reliability must become the trademark of the internal audit report. It should be written and documented so as to compel belief and reliance. It should have character. It should speak with authority. Whatever is said, particularly in operating areas outside the auditor's normally accepted scope, must be supported or supportable. The reader must be able to rely upon the report because of its well-documented facts and inescapable logic.

Statements of fact must carry the assurance that the auditors personally observed or validated the fact. If they say there was an excessive backlog of work, it means that they personally know this to be a fact. It means they know what backlogs are considered normal and the extent of the backlog they observed. It is true that there may be conditions which auditors have not personally observed but which management should be made aware of. A statement to that effect in a report should show the source: "The department manager told us that the backlog was excessive." The reported statement is completely factual — the auditor personally heard the statement from the department manager, but the auditors themselves are not certifying to the existence or to the extent of the conditions.

Accuracy also implies perspective and objective observations, refraining from puffing up that which is not material or relevant. Executive management generally gives serious attention to audit reports. Conditions reported to be deficient may become the subject of executive wrath. It is a form of inaccuracy, therefore, to hold up as deficient one of a dozen related activities without showing how the one activity fits into the mosaic of overall functions or organization. If an operating manager is fiercely, and by and large successfully, fighting the battle of quality, schedule, and cost in his or her organization, producing an acceptable product, delivering it on time, making it within budget constraints, and training people well and knowing what they are doing — wouldn't it be a form of inaccuracy to highlight in an audit report to executive management that written job instructions could stand updating?

Accuracy implies that what is reported is material — a matter worthy of a busy manager's attention. Matters should not be included in a report as filler or merely to show the volume of audit findings. It must be demonstrated that if a reported condition is permitted to continue, it will do significant harm. A prudent person reading the finding should be impelled to say, "Yes, here is a condition that needs attention and requires correction. It cannot be overlooked."

Accuracy implies precision. Imprecise words leave a reader confused. Specificity conveys ideas more accurately than broad generalities. How much more precise it is to say: "Of the 100 items we examined, 30 were received 3 to 5 days late and 20 were 6 to 15 days late" than "Not all items were received on time."

The second statement in a report is weak and confusing. It raises vague warnings but says nothing. It is a model of imprecision and is therefore inaccurate. It conveys different thoughts to different people. It does not say what the auditor may have meant. How much is "not all"? Is utter perfection the standard? If only one item out of a thousand were a few hours late, then certainly "not all were received on time." Similarly, if five hundred out of the thousand were between two and five days late, that condition could also be described as "not all were received on time." The first is *de minimis* while the second would shock a prudent person.

Some words are too imprecise to appear without specific quantification in a self-respecting audit report: *several, a few, many, almost all, hardly ever, sometimes, a good deal.* These words may be acceptable in a lead sentence that summarizes a condition, but they should be immediately followed by the specific numbers — the population, the sample size, and the specific number of items that are unacceptable.

Clarity

Clarity implies many things. Chiefly it means putting into the mind of the reader or listener what was in the mind of the auditor. There are a host of impediments to this hoped-for clear transfer of thought. Auditors should be aware of them and they must consciously try to remove them.

Lack of clarity in the mind of the auditor is the prime impediment to clear writing. One cannot write clearly what one does not understand clearly. If we do not have a firm grasp of our subject, we are not ready to write. Until auditors know precisely what they are talking about, they should do more field work or research before taking pencil in hand.

Dull and tedious writing is another impediment to clarity. Dreary, stilted prose makes the mind turn to other things. Consider: "Reconciliation of the accounts was effected by the accounting personnel." How much clearer it comes through when we say: "The accounting people reconciled the accounts."

Poorly structured reports are impediments to clarity. An orderly procession of ideas enhances clarity. Some auditors start their reports in the middle and then go off in all directions. They may well be hiding excellent findings and recommendations in a morass of tangled sentences and paragraphs. The ideas that management desperately needs may never be communicated. For the want of an outline, the audit is lost.

Technical and jargonish terms are impediments. Skillfull translations clear the way. This means more than just substituting "rejections by inspectors" for "I-tags." It also means conveying ideas in terms that mean something to the reader. It is one thing to say that receiving memos are not being matched with invoices. It is quite another to say that there was no assurance that the company was receiving the goods it was paying for. The first statement is factual — but it paints no pictures. The second is no more factual — but it will sound sirens and galvanize management into action.

Reporting findings without setting the stage is an impediment. Giving the proper background information is sometimes essential to the understanding of a process or a condition, or to appreciate its significance. If auditors are recommending a new procedure, they should first tell what the existing one is like, what's wrong with it, and the probable effect of its continued use. Then management will be more receptive to the cogency of the auditor's proposal, and yet be in a position to make its own considered decision.

Long discussions of technical matters like the interrelationships of many different amounts are impediments to understanding. Well-designed schedules, tabulations, charts, and graphs can bring clarity. One picture can make clear what a thousand words can only obscure.

Clarity is a condition precedent to persuasiveness. Auditors must be able to convince managers of the validity of their positions, so findings must be presented convincingly. The conclusions and recommendations must flow clearly and logically from the facts presented. The reports must convince an objective reader that the findings are significant, that the conclusions are reasonable and that the recommendations are workable and acceptable.

Auditors can never take the position that "it is so because we say it is so." The burden of proof is on the auditor, not the auditee. That burden must be carried forward clearly and convincingly.

The poor organization of reported material is an impediment to clarity. Reports should flow easily from beginning to end. They should not contain closely related material in different sections. Many reports deal with complex subjects. Some report sections bear a relation to others. To the extent possible, each audit report should be so organized that all the auditor has to say on a given subject appears in only one place in the report. Summaries and digests, of course, are understandable exceptions.

Conciseness

Conciseness means cutting out what is superfluous. That does not necessarily mean making all reports short, because the subject matter may demand extended discussion. Brevity that does not inform is not a virtue. Conciseness does mean eliminating what is irrelevant and immaterial.

Conciseness means eliminating the ideas, the findings, the words, the sentences, and the paragraphs that do not help get across the central theme of the report.

At the same time, conciseness should not become such a fetish that writing is reduced to an abrupt, telegraphic style. There must still be a continuity of thought, an ease of reading, and a comfortable, integrated flow of ideas.

Auditors sometimes fall into the trap of long sentences that leave the reader puzzled and weary. If auditors really put their minds to it, they can cut the long sentences into comfortable bite sizes. They can overcome abruptness through words or thoughts of transition.

Also, conciseness does not mean using only short sentences. An uninterrupted series of short sentences creates its own sameness and dullness. A few well-constructed long sentences, sprinkled among the short ones, give a much-needed variety and tend to avoid tedium.

But one person's conciseness may be another's lack of information. What is concise enough for the operating manager who needs sufficient detail to know how to correct a condition may be overwordy to the executive who just wants to get the general idea. The report should then supply both sufficient detail for the operating manager and a summary for the executive.

Timeliness

The final, formal report is not designed to be a historical document. It is a call to action. It answers management's needs for current information. Its effect is lost, therefore, if it is not timely. Yet it must be carefully thought out. It must be impregnable. It must be incapable of being misunderstood. And this cannot be done with a stroke of the pen.

These sometimes conflicting needs — thoughtfulness and promptness — must both be met. And the informal progress report, issued while the audit is still going on, may be one answer.

Progress reports convey in writing the need for prompt action. What is written, in most big companies, produces action where the spoken word may not. As the Chinese proverb has it, "The mouth is wind. The pen leaves tracks."

Progress reports can be brief, addressing themselves to only one or two ideas. They can be labeled progress reports and contain written caveats against accepting them as the final word, thereby permitting expedited action by operating management while reserving the right of the auditors to polish and to revise.

The transmittal for the progress report can start by saying: "This progress report is designed to provide current information on conditions needing management attention. Our final report will include the matter discussed here, along with other information obtained during the remainder of our field work."

The progress report can have other salutary results. It can serve to set auditors straight on their facts or to sharpen their perspective, since the response evoked by the progress report can confirm or deny the auditor's findings to date. Operating management's studies, action, and/or replies may have a significant effect on what the auditor will finally report.

Where the auditing organization employs many young and still unseasoned auditors to perform audits away from headquarters, there may be an understandable concern about permitting them to draft and release progress reports without supervisory review. Yet prompt notice to operating management about deficient conditions — in writing — may be important. In those cases it may be advisable to develop a form similar to the Record of Audit Findings (see Chapter 7) which compels the auditor to cover all significant aspects of a deficient condition: a concise statement of condition, size of sample, extent of deficiency, causes and effects, applicable written procedures, and discussions with operating personnel.

A draft of such a progress report, specifically labeled as informal, may be of value in providing current, prompt audit information without compromising the final report.

Tone

Finally, the audit report must have a proper tone. It should be courteous. It should consider the report's effect upon subordinate operating people. It should not, therefore, identify individuals or highlight the mistakes of individuals. It should avoid pettiness and not concern itself with trivia. It should so speak that it sounds like the voice of management.

The tone should be constructive. Criticism of things past may be necessary, but the emphasis should be placed on needed improvements.

The report should be dignified without being stodgy. It should avoid slang on the one hand and high-blown language on the other; these do not stand the test of time.

The executive, pressed from all quarters by operating reports and arguments — often self-serving declarations that put the best face on questionable matters — should be able to see in the audit report a calm, objective, thoughtful, dispassionate exposition on which to rely.

Report Formats

The format of the report depends much on the kind of report being issued: formal versus informal, final versus progress, written versus oral, overall opinion versus deficiency findings only, or financial versus operational.

The format of the report will also depend on the readers: what the readers expect and how much time they can devote to reading the reports.

The format of the report will further depend on the nature and the seasoning of the auditing activity. An auditing organization just starting on reviews of nonfinancial operating areas, will feel impelled to give abundant support for its opinions and conclusions to overcome a reluctance on the part of the reader to accept audit opinions on matters that are far afield from accounting activities.

Hence, different auditing organizations will employ different report formats and divide their reports into different subsections. Whichever format is found most appropriate, it should be used with reasonable consistency.

Consistency combats confusion. Readers should know what to expect. They learn where they can readily find whatever interests them most and can turn to that part of the report without difficulty.

With each auditing organization pursuing its own ideals and objectives, it would be fruitless to define an optimum format for the formal, final written report. But the auditor should be acquainted with the different elements of an audit report that are in current use. Some or all of these elements will be found in most reports.

Formal Reports

The Summary

Summaries come in many shapes and sizes. A summary may be a simple transmittal memorandum that sends the report to the president or other executives of the company. Properly drafted, such a summary may be ideal for harried, harrassed executives, who want to read no more than they absolutely have to while reserving the right to dip into whatever detail they wish.

Some summaries are useful devices. But they may present pitfalls to unwary report writers who must be careful, as they compress the report into a brief summation, that they do not twist or distort meaning, materiality, or perspective.

An example of a brief transmittal is as follows:

Here is our report on receiving department activities. In general, the department had provided an adequate system of controls for its receiving functions. Activities were being carried out effectively and efficiently, with the following exception:

No comparisons were being made between chemicals received and billed. Our own comparisons showed that tank cars were not being completely emptied. As a result we found variances of over 8%. After we discussed the matter with operating management, systems were improved and negotiations with the supplier resulted in recoveries of about $40,000.

The Foreword or Introduction

The foreword or introduction section is the first to meet the reader's eye, It should be stated crisply and clearly so as to invite the reader to read further. It is usually a stage-setter and can be used:

To identify the audit as a regular examination or as the response to a special management request.

To identify the organizations or functions reviewed.

To refer to any relevant prior examinations.

To comment on findings or recommendations discussed in prior reports and on their current status.

To provide any explanatory information needed to acquaint the reader with the subject under examination. (A report on shipping or receiving needs no more introduction than the title of the report itself. A report on special test equipment, however, may deserve some explanatory comment.)

To set forth briefly the value or volume of transactions processed, so as to give the reader an idea of the significance of the function.

An example of a foreword section is as follows:

We have completed our regular audit of the engineering property control department. Our 19XX audit reported four deficiency findings. None of the deficient conditions then reported has recurred. The department is responsible for tools and equipment, valued at $7 million, which are used in the engineering branch.

The Statement of Purpose

The purpose describes the audit objectives. It should be in sufficient detail to help readers understand what to expect from the rest of the report.

When the purpose is spelled out with some preciseness, and when the discussions of findings that follow address themselves to each statement in the purpose, then it serves as a road map, making it easier for readers to find their way through the report.

An example of a detailed statement of purpose is as follows:

Our audit was directed toward determining whether an adequate and effective system of control had been provided over the activities of the credit department. We were concerned specifically with the following activities of the department:
Performing credit investigations and determining the financial responsibility of both suppliers and customers.
Establishing credit terms for sales to commercial customers.
Establishing control over payments to assignees.
Investigating new suppliers.

The Statement of Scope

The scope statement is sometimes combined with the purpose. The scope can be of particular importance in identifying any limitations of the examination. It should specifically point to areas which were not covered — areas which, because of the very title of the report, readers would consider covered in the audit unless they are told differently.

The scope is particularly important when normal auditing techniques are dispensed with and other techniques are relied upon.

Examples of two scope statements are as follows:

We confined our review of receiving activities to those carried out in the central receiving department. We did not review controls over direct deliveries, which bypass central receiving. We plan on making a separate examination of direct deliveries.

Our preliminary survey disclosed an excellent system of control over the shipping department's activities. All job instructions were up to date. The department's supervisors were required to make periodic examinations of selected transactions and report their findings to the manager who sees that deficient conditions are corrected. We discussed the shipping activities with representatives of peripheral organizations and found that they uniformly held the shipping operations in high regard. As a result, we reduced considerably the tests of transactions we normally make as a basis for our opinions.

Auditors should avoid giving a detailed account of the audit steps they take. For some activities of a sensitive nature, such disclosure may provide some people with a blueprint to follow in manipulating transactions for personal gain.

The Statement of Opinion

The opinion is the auditor's professional judgment of the activities reviewed. It provides a capsule comment of the assessment of the conditions found. Not all auditing organizations provide overall opinions on the results of their examinations, but many progressive auditing organizations believe that the failure to do so deprives management of a significant service.

It would be most natural for a president of a company who meets an auditor after the completion of an audit assignment to ask, "Well, what do you think of the activity you just reviewed?" A responsive answer would represent an overall opinion: "The activity is operating quite well" or, "I believe they're doing a poor job, because . . . " or, "Except for some minor matter which they quickly corrected, they're doing a reasonably good job."

Judgments along these lines are what executives expect from their auditing organizations. They are entitled to receive them. Certainly, auditors should not express opinions they are not capable of supporting. And, certainly, they must weigh carefully the factors supporting their opinions. The opinion should say exactly what the auditors mean, include only what they can justify, and be adequately supported by the facts. Finally, it should encompass and be responsive to the purposes of the examination set out in the purpose statement. Three examples of opinions on audits of operations follow:

> Based on the results of our review, we believe that an adequate system of control has been established over the activities of the purchasing department and that the department's assigned responsibilities were being carried out effectively and efficiently.

> In our opinion, the activities concerned with the layoff and recall of employees were well controlled and, except for inadequate explanations for monetary settlements of grievances, were performed effectively and efficiently.

> In our opinion, the system designed to ensure the timely calibration of test equipment was inadequate because no provision had been made to identify all of the equipment subject to calibration.

In expressing their opinions, auditors should not hesitate to be complimentary if the compliment is deserved. If they find a well-controlled, well-organized, well-managed, and smoothly functioning operation, they should say so. It should give evidence of their thesis that they do not seek deficiencies only. They should, of course, have adequate support for a complimentary opinion. They would not wish to see an opinion invalidated by activities they did not cover or events they should have foreseen, but if they are certain of their grounds, they should have the courage of their convictions. Here is an example of a richly deserved compliment.

> Based on the results of our review, we formed the opinion that adequate controls had been provided over the activities of the procurement services department, and that the controls were working effectively and efficiently. In fact, we consider this department to be highly effective in accomplishing its assigned mission. We believe this can be attributed to well-motivated and knowledgeable supervision and key personnel; good communication and feedback between management and subordinates; thorough on-the-job training of the individual employees, reinforced by a rotational assignment policy; up-to-date, comprehensive job instructions; constant vigilance on the part of supervision and alternates to monitor workload schedules and performance and to minimize errors; good rapport and loyalty between the manager and the group supervisors; and the participation of the manager and her supervisors in arriving at management decisions.

Findings

Findings are the source from which all opinions and recommendations flow. Findings are the results of inquiries and investigations. They are the facts produced by the auditor's efforts. They are the product of the field work. Findings may be favorable or unfavorable. They may explain a satisfactory condition that warrants explanation in the report, or they may set forth unsatisfactory conditions that need correcting.

Favorable findings, understandably, will require less explanation in the report. But they do represent an audit determination, and they are backed by the integrity and reputation of the auditor and the audit organization.

Some audit organizations do not report their favorable findings. Whether this is desirable or not is a moot point. Those auditors feel that executive management does not want to be bothered with matters that do not require their action or decision. Others feel that reporting favorable findings shows objectivity and creates a better rapport between them and operating personnel. Also, some executives wish to be told of satisfactory conditions to set their minds at rest about a particular operation or to gain more information about competent operating managers. Each view has its merits. Our view is that both favorable and unfavorable accomplishments should be recognized. Here is an example of both types of findings along with some comments on the elements to consider in drafting the finding.

The elements needed to provide the reader with background and the auditor's rationale include authority, objectives, conditions, and effect.[3]

Authority. Someone or something must have authorized the function under review. Knowing the authority permits the auditor to determine whether the function is being conducted within the bounds set. The authority may be statutory, may come from the board of directors, or may be the result of a management decision, express or implied.

Where the authority is in writing, its intent and scope are more readily ascertainable. If it is oral, the auditor would probably want to discuss it with both the one who granted the authority and the one who received it.

The auditor will ascertain, if at all possible, both the broad authority granted to the entire function and the specific authority granted to that portion of the function which is under review. For example, assume that the board of directors authorized the establishment of a new plant to make tools. The auditors, however, are concerned solely with the supply department of the plant. They would then seek to ascertain the specific authority granted to the supply department. The authority portion of the reported findings might be as follows:[4]

> The plant at Bethany was established by the board of directors to manufacture small tools. The supply department of the Bethany plant is authorized to maintain enough materials and parts to keep the production lines adequately stocked and to purchase such quantities of materials and parts as are needed for that purpose except that, by instruction of the vice president for manufacturing operations, all steel sheets and ingots are to be ordered through the main office so that quantity discounts can be obtained through consolidation of the orders of all plants.

Objectives. Having established authority, the auditors must then address themselves to the activity's objectives. Objectives are pivotal to appraisal. To know if something is done well, one must first determine what is sought to be done or what needs to be done. In audits of operations, an appraisal of an activity is often meaningless if it does not take into account the activity's mission — its reason for being.

Normally, audits have several objectives. They may be grouped under the terms *effectiveness* and *economy*. Effectiveness implies the production of a satisfactory product (one that meets specifications and standards) using *product* in its broadest sense to include services as well as tangible items. Economy generally includes efficiency. It implies spending only enough money to achieve other objectives.

Pursuing the audit of the supply department, the discussion of the objectives might be as follows:[5]

> The primary objective of the supply department is to maintain sufficient stock on hand to ensure uninterrupted production. A secondary, but almost equally important objective is economy which, for supply purposes, means keeping enough stock on hand to meet production needs but at the same time keeping the investment in inventory as low as practicable.

Certainly, the auditor must not feel precluded from appraising the objectives themselves. If they are in conflict with company aims, this conflict must be brought to light and resolved.

Condition — Favorable. In the context of audit reports, condition means the results of the auditor's appraisal of the ongoing process through observing, questioning, analyzing, and other audit techniques. The statement of condition should be relevant to the objectives considered in the auditor's examination. In a favorable finding, a simple statement of conclusion should be sufficient for management:

1. We found that stock on hand was equal to plant needs.
2. We also found that systems in effect provided assurance that inventories would be kept to a practical minimum.

Some audits of operations cover matters which may be considered by some managements to be outside the scope of the auditor's competence. In such cases the auditor may wish to set forth the criteria used in appraising the conditions found and the steps taken in measuring transactions and processes against those criteria.

Condition — Unfavorable. The auditor can take a slightly different approach to zero in directly on the deficient condition. The statements of such findings will usually include a capsule summary of the finding, the applicable criteria, the conditions found, the significance of the deficiency and its probable or actual effect, the cause of the conditions, the auditor's recommendations, and the corrective action taken.

To illustrate, assume that the auditor found the supply department's inventory records to be inaccurate and that, as a result, the department overstocked material.

Summary. The first statement would be a summary, a sort of headline that prepares the reader for what is to follow. Usually, a single sentence underlined to make it stand out, would suffice. For example:

Because of inaccurate inventory records, the supply department bought unneeded supplies costing $75,000.

Criteria. The text of the finding should begin with a statement of the standards against which the audit findings should be measured. Let us assume that the problem in the supply department was the violation of existing procedures. Thus, the procedures — which the auditor found to be reasonable — became the criteria.

Established procedures provide that excess materials returned by the production department shall be entered on the records of the supply department to show currently the levels of inventory on hand and available for issuance.

These criteria are simple and sensible. It would be hard for anyone to quarrel with them.

Facts. Then come the facts which the auditor gathered — the conditions observed.

Our tests disclosed that for a period of six months, supplies returned from production had not been entered on the supply department's records.

Effect. Unless the effect is shown, and unless that effect is significant, the attitude of management may be one of indifference. The probable or actual effect should be stated:

As a result of the inaccurate inventory records, the company bought unneeded supplies costing about $75,000.

Cause. The next question that would immediately come to the mind of the perceptive reader of the report would be: "How in the world could this happen?" This is a determination the auditor should make for any deficiency finding:

We found that the employees responsible for the posting of returned supplies had not been instructed in their duties. In addition, supervisors had not been monitoring the process.

Recommendation. Finally, the reader will ask: "Very well, Internal Auditor, you've made your point. Now what shall we do about it?" The report obligingly continues:

We reviewed the conditions with the manager of the supply department and he agreed to:
1. Bring the inventory records up to date.
2. Issue job instructions spelling out to the workers the need to record returned supplies.
3. Instruct supervisors to monitor the process in the future and to submit written reports on their periodic reviews.
Before we concluded our examination, the manager took all three steps. Our subsequent spot checks showed that the action was effective. We therefore consider this finding closed.

In sum, the auditor should be aware of the questions that a knowledgeable executive will have in mind when reading a report of a deficient condition. Recapitulating, these questions are as follows:

What is the general subject we're talking about? Orient me to the problem.

What were the people supposed to be doing?

What were they actually doing?

How badly did we get hurt? How badly could we get hurt?

How did all this come about?

What do you think should be done about it?

What did the operating manager say when you discussed these conditions and what will be done about them? Is there anything I should do?

With these questions as their own criteria, internal auditors should be able to satisfy themselves, their own supervisors, operating management, and executive management, that they have done an adequate audit job and viewed things fairly, objectively, and in their proper perspective.

Graphics

Even the most professionally written audit reports can gain from illustrations that clarify concepts and highlight interrelationships. They can provide believability to reported conditions that words could not possibly portray.

Some of the matters that can be appended to reports are as follows:
○ Bar charts showing relationships between two or more kindred sets of statistics (Exhibit 13-1).
○ Flowcharts explaining complex processes (Exhibit 13-2).
○ Pictures showing clearly the existence and extent of hazardous conditions or wasteful practices (Exhibit 13-3).

Exhibit 13-1.

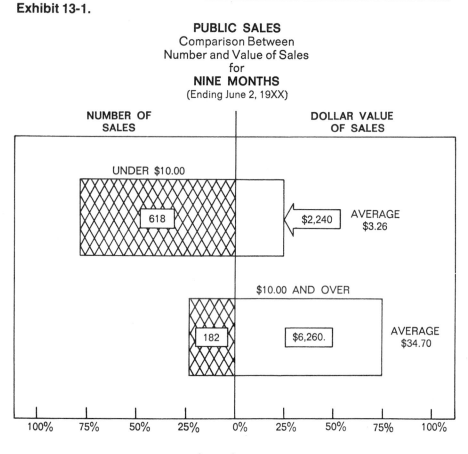

PUBLIC SALES
Comparison Between
Number and Value of Sales
for
NINE MONTHS
(Ending June 2, 19XX)

Informal Reports

Every auditing department has a need for an informal reporting system to complement its formal system. Matters may be encountered during the audit engagement that require the prompt attention of management to supplement oral reports on an ongoing project, that have no relation to an ongoing project but warrant reporting to management, and that require the postponement or abandonment of a project. These and other matters can be made the subject of interim, or progress, informal written reports.

As with other informal reports that keep communications timely, prog-

Exhibit 13-2.

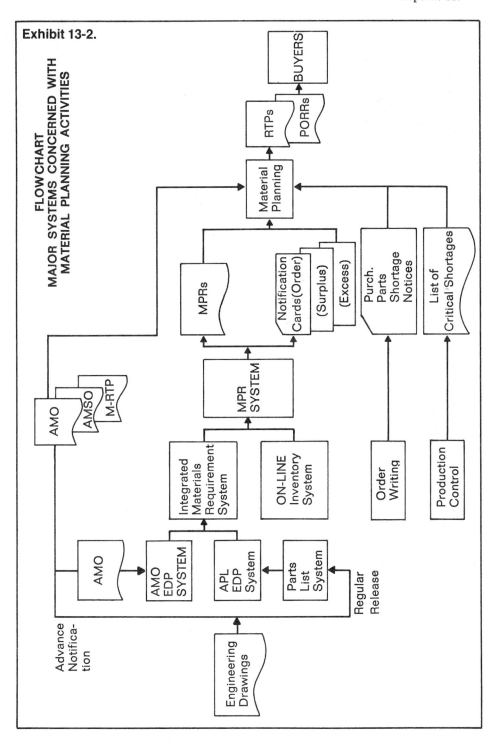

FLOWCHART
MAJOR SYSTEMS CONCERNED WITH
MATERIAL PLANNING ACTIVITIES

Exhibit 13-3.

Warehouse open to elements (note daylight through open wall). Also, product damaged in handling.

Customer's warehouse containing company's consigned products. Deterioration on the outside indicates conditions inside.

Bulk product stored in tank with evidence of corrosion at top of tank. Impurities can materially damage the product.

Open burning at plant site. Potential violation of pollution standards.

ress reports should occupy an official position in the auditing function. Readers will become accustomed to these informal reports if they follow a regular pattern, are referred to by a common designation, and are subject to some form of numerical control.

They may be designated "Informal Audit Reports" and may be given consecutive numbers for each year. The first report for the year could be designated "IAR XX-1."

The report may be of any length, depending on the subject to be covered. If it is brief it may be presented on a single typed page. If it exceeds one page, it is preferable that a brief summary act as a transmittal and outline, with the fully discussed material contained in an attachment to the informal report.

As an example, assume that the information on the supply department is being reported informally to management. The full discussion, could be incorporated in an attachment. The transmittal report could be as shown in Exhibit 13-4.

Exhibit 13-4.   **IAR 8X-10**

To: Manager
From: Auditor
Subject: Bethany Supply Department

This informal report is sent to you so that you may be currently informed on a matter which we found in our audit of the Bethany supply department, now in progress.

We found that inventory records were not being kept up to date. As a result, the supply department purchased unneeded material costing $75,000. The matter is discussed in detail in the attachment to this report.

The matter will be covered in our formal report on the Bethany supply department. We would like to acknowledge any corrective action that you take before we issue that report. Please let us know, therefore, of any action you take or intend to take. Our field work will be completed in about two or three weeks.

Oral Reports

Oral reports should not, in our opinion, replace written reports. But they do have their place, and a valuable place it is. They are being used more and more because:

They are immediate. They give management prompt assurances or current information for corrective action.

They evoke face-to-face responses. They can reveal attitudes and convictions.

They permit the auditors to counter arguments and provide additional information that the audience may require.

They can bring out inaccuracies in the auditors' thinking.

They can develop improved rapport with the auditee.

Oral reports should not be off-the-cuff. They should be prepared with care. They should show that the auditors have done their homework — that they did not arrive for a rambling discussion.

That does not mean that the auditors should make gold-plated presentations that go beyond the needs of the subject or the audience. It is possible to present them economically without the appearance of excessively expensive preparation.

Desk-top flip charts for small groups can be eminently effective. The charts can be prepared without too much effort and are extremely effective in keeping the auditors in charge of the meeting, keeping the auditees focused on what is being said, and keeping the auditors themselves on track.

The flip charts can be prepared on 8½" x 11" cards and lettered freehand with felt pens. They should not get wordy because that only serves to distract attention rather than focus it.

One means of achieving brevity is to print the material first on 3" x 5" slips of paper. There just is not sufficient room for extended comments on them.

A series of charts for the audit of the Bethany supply department, giving background, pointing out the problem, and recommending action, might be as shown in Exhibit 13-5.

The informal, desk-top presentation may not always suit the auditors' needs. They may be called upon to make formal oral presentations. Their audience may be at a level where the auditors must give considerable thought to their talk and prepare carefully for it. This should not be regarded as a catastrophe, but rather as a splendid opportunity to present another facet of the auditor's character: the articulate, practiced speaker.

These presentations deserve effort, and the results should reflect the care with which they were put together. Here are some of the considerations to take into account.

Flexibility

Keep your options open as you proceed toward your oral presentation. Be capable of cutting the presentation short. Be prepared to skip material, amplify material, and do whatever else is necessary to keep the listener interested.

Conciseness

Wordiness makes the listener's mind wander. Do not embellish or amplify beyond what is essential. Do not bring in what is not germane. When you see your listeners looking at their watches or drumming on the table with their fingers, be prepared to abbreviate the talk.

Completeness

At the same time, do not leave a subject until you have answered the obvious questions. When you say "considerable amount," the audience will

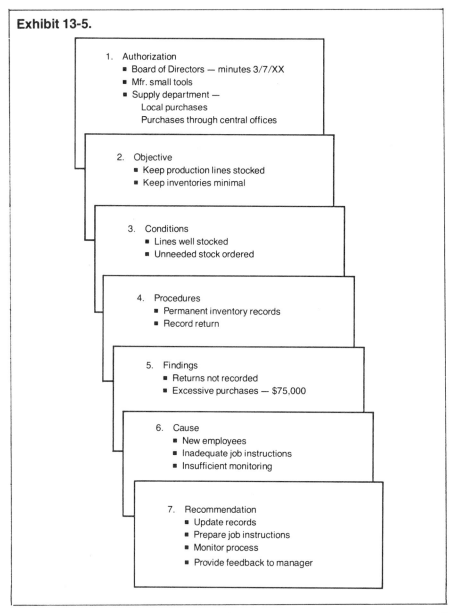

Exhibit 13-5.

1. Authorization
   - Board of Directors — minutes 3/7/XX
   - Mfr. small tools
   - Supply department —
     Local purchases
     Purchases through central offices

2. Objective
   - Keep production lines stocked
   - Keep inventories minimal

3. Conditions
   - Lines well stocked
   - Unneeded stock ordered

4. Procedures
   - Permanent inventory records
   - Record return

5. Findings
   - Returns not recorded
   - Excessive purchases — $75,000

6. Cause
   - New employees
   - Inadequate job instructions
   - Insufficient monitoring

7. Recommendation
   - Update records
   - Prepare job instructions
   - Monitor process
   - Provide feedback to manager

not be happy until you tell them just how much. When you say "long time," they will want to know how long. When you say "a number of errors," they will want to know what that number is. When you talk about a condition, they will want to know its cause and its effect.

Currency
Just before the meeting, the auditor should try to get a reading on current

conditions. There is nothing more satisfying to a questioner than to hear a response like: "I checked on that just this morning. The condition is still the way I described it."

Preparation

Careful, methodical preparation for the big day will pay off. As in any other endeavor, there are techniques that can help the tyro and remind the expert. Here are some of them:[6]

Establish objectives. Make sure you have determined precisely what your objectives are in this oral presentation. Is it to answer questions? Is it to show progress? Is it to show results? Is it to persuade and motivate toward a certain course of conduct? The objectives must be known and fixed firmly in mind. If not, the presentation may have a tendency to wander from its path and confuse the audience.

Analyze the audience. A technically perfect presentation may fail to meet its objective if it is directed toward an audience whose likes, dislikes, and backgrounds have not been considered and taken into account. As you prepare your presentation ask yourself these questions:

What does the audience know about the subject? How much background do they need? How much time can they comfortably give me?

How receptive will they be to my ideas? How much softening up do they need? How persuasive must I be?

What are their interests? Cost savings? Work reduction? Staff reduction? Improved accuracy? Improved schedules? Improved controls? Greater visibility and feedback?

What should I avoid for this audience? What are their known biases?

Prepare a preliminary plan. No matter how rough it may be, put something down in writing: a title, the objectives, the audience, the main ideas, the sub ideas, the order of presentation, and/or the form of the visual aids. It will clarify and order your thinking.

Select the material. Determine what is pertinent. Eliminate what is irrelevant. Make sure there are no gaps. Consider the transitions from one thought to another. In selecting the material, use these criteria: will it contribute to the purpose or objective of the meeting? Will it clarify the main ideas? Does it relate to this audience?

Organize the material. There are many methods of organizing material. But whatever method you use, the material **must** be organized. Good organization shines through and commands respect. Poor organization casts a gloomy pall and makes the audience restless. So you must decide early on just what form of organization you want: Chronological? Sequential? Comparison or contrast? Cause and effect? Theory versus practice?

Make sure the message is clear. Any presentation is wasted if the message does not come across clearly to the audience. Make sure the audience knows what you're trying to say and what you want of them. Keep in mind the many ways available to clarify the message and the material: analysis, definition, facts, figures, illustrations, statistics, authority, & restatement.

Plan visual aids. Visual aids have proved extremely important in getting the message across. They have many benefits: They keep the speaker on track. They save time in getting to the point. They focus attention. They support and clarify ideas. They can clearly show trends and relationships where purely oral statements cause confusion and make the listener struggle with too many concepts at once. They help the listener understand, retain data, and stay interested.

Visual aids include: chalk boards, easel displays (either the notebook-sized easel, the magnetic slap board, or the tripod which holds large cards or sheets), projection equipment (overhead, 35 mm. slides, and movie: audio-visual), and actual physical objects.

The visual aids can be used in any or a combination of the following means: words and phrases, graphs, tabulations, sketches and drawings, diagrams and flowcharts, and photographs.

Practice the presentation. Practicing the presentation before the meeting is good insurance. If possible, practice in front of several other auditors to get their reactions and suggestions. Since they are auditors, it is safe to say they will have a number of comments and recommendations.

Practice builds confidence as the material becomes more familiar. It will point up flaws and gaps. It will improve the physical handling of the visual aids. It will help timing. The matters to work on include: pauses, voice intensity, inflections, gestures, facial expressions (speaking before a mirror can be invaluable), body movement, and summaries.

Prepare for questions and answers. If you are going to entertain questions, alert the audience. They will then be prepared to note their questions as the presentation moves along. Show that you are receptive to the questions and anxious to hear them. In answering them, try to be accurate and complete, without being wordy. If you don't know the answer, say so; but add that you will try to get it. When you answer a question, watch the questioner's face to make sure that he or she appears to be satisfied. If not, ask if the question has been answered. Particularly before large groups, repeat or rephrase the question to make sure you are answering what the questioner had in mind and so that the rest of the audience has heard it.

In Sum

S. H. Thomas[7] sums up what auditors should be concerned about in oral presentations, as follows:

Think more about your listeners than yourself.

Cultivate a "lean" economical style — no needless repetition, no evasions, no weakening of force.

Carefully use transitions to carry the audience from one thought to another.

Avoid ambiguities. (The audience will be chewing on them as the presentation moves to other things.)

Speak loudly enough to be heard, clearly enough to be understood, smoothly enough to be welcome.

Good Writing

Let us emphasize once more that good writing calls for good thinking. There is no escaping it. If concepts are confused and tangled, if thoughts are muddy, and if no logical relation has been established between cause and effect, between the important and the insignificant, then the report that rises from this accumulation is bound to be an ineffectual piece of work. So before starting to write, straighten out your thinking, put things in place, and get your findings in proper perspective.

Outlines

One way of sorting things out, making sure of a logical and reasonable flow of ideas, is through the report outline. The drafting of the outline is simplified if the auditing department has developed a reasonably standardized format for its regular reports.

Standardization spells economy. It makes the writer and the reader feel comfortable. Both know the general path the report will take. Filling in the information needed to fit a particular set of circumstances becomes simplified to a considerable extent.

Outlining takes discipline. Many an auditor, instructed to outline his report, presented a completed draft with the statement "I started to outline, but when I began writing I just couldn't stop." Compassionate reviewers wind up outlining the report themselves. Hard-nosed (and probably the more effective) reviewers toss the draft back with a terse comment: "When I ask for an outline, I want an outline."

What the reviewer really wants is a crisp, simple skeleton of the report — a word or a phrase — to make sure that the thoughts flow logically and that nothing has been omitted.

A sample outline, expanding on the Bethany audit and employing the report segments previously discussed, is as follows:

Summary

A. Foreword
   1. First regular audit
   2. Covered supply department
   3. Procures, maintains supplies
      a. Locally
      b. Through headquarters
   4. Total value — $2,500,000

B. Purpose
Evaluate:
1. Procurement
2. Physical inventory
3. Records
C. Scope
1. Test purchase documents
2. Observe inventory-taking
3. Examine records
D. Opinion
1. Satisfactory on —
a. Procurements
b. Physical inventories
2. Unsatisfactory on —
a. Records
E. Findings
1. Procurements
a. Written bids
b. Approvals
c. Follow-up system
2. Physical inventories
a. Security
b. Arrangement of stock
c. Bin cards
3. Records
a. Perpetual inventory records
b. Returns from production
(1) Not recorded
(2) Overprocurement

Details

A. Summary statement re overprocurement
B. Procedures — criteria
Enter returns on records
C. Results of tests — facts
Returns not entered
D. Effect
Overprocurement — $75,000
E. Cause
Employees not instructed
Inadequate supervision
F. Recommendation
Update records
Issue instructions
Monitor performance

G. Action
   All steps taken

Prior Reports

The auditor should not overlook or fail to take counsel from any prior reports. Much thought probably went into those reports. Shades of meaning were considered. Difficult wording may have been drafted and polished. Reporting policies were probably observed. A proper format was no doubt employed.

But the prior report should be relied upon with discretion. Conditions may have changed. Procedures may have been revised. Reporting styles may have been amended. With these caveats, the prior report may be a great time saver.

The First Draft

No writer who ever held a pen or sat before a typewriter did not at one time or another get stuck. The gears slip into neutral and nothing moves. The auditor, too, may wait for inspiration, for that perfect beginning which will give character and interest to all that follows.

We may wait forever before that sterling sentence forms itself on paper. Somehow we must develop the discipline that says: "I must write. Therefore I shall."

Andre Gide, in his *Journal*, June 4, 1930, said, "Too often I wait for the sentence to finish taking shape in my mind before setting it down. It is better to seize it by the end that first offers itself, head or foot, though not knowing the rest, then pull: the rest will follow"

The writer therefore needs some spur to getting words down on paper. The outline helps. It shows where to begin and what will come after. The next step is to boldly violate the purity of the blank page with the thrust of the pencil. Some mark, some line, some word. Perhaps the title. Perhaps a heading. But something to prime the pump and get the words flowing.

The material is there. The working papers are full of facts and figures. All it takes is a dogged persistence for the draft to grow. Little matter that the first words are trite or poorly phrased. No one waits to cart them away and put them in print. They will be revised and reshaped before they reach their final form, for there is no such thing as good writing — just good rewriting. The first draft is a lump of clay to be pummeled and mauled — to be cut away here and added to there until it emerges as a monument to the auditor's persistence.

When the first draft has been written, hacked at, and interlineated, have it typed or retyped. In the interim, the ideas within the subconscious will marinate and become more palatable. Then when the new draft is received and perused, new thoughts, better thoughts, and better phrases will come. The draft will be seen with new eyes. New ways of getting ideas across will emerge, and gradually the report will take the desired form and give the hoped-for message.

Then, after dozens and dozens of painstakingly written reports, the writing improves, the chore becomes less painful, and the product becomes more professional. But at the beginning, the answer lies in good field work, a well-structured outline, and dogged persistence.

Language

No language is easy to master. It takes a long, hard apprenticeship and a flair for words. But as in any craft there are techniques that keep the writing from being inept and amateurish. Three basic rules can help any report writer: Keep your writing simple. Keep your writing clear. Keep your writing alive. Within the compass of these rules are a number of subrules which, if followed, can reward the efforts of even the poorest of writers.

Keep your writing simple. Use short sentences. It is easy for the reader to get lost in the labyrinth of a long sentence, but add some well-constructed long sentences for variety.

Use common words. Do not try to send the reader to the dictionary. If an unusual word is the only one that fits, define it.

Omit needless words.

Do not include any unnecessary ideas, phrases, or words in a sentence or a paragraph. Keep all the thoughts relevant and related.

Make the ideas flow in logical succession. Do not force the reader to mentally rearrange the ideas to clearly understand.

Avoid contradictory ideas, or thoughts that violate logic. What is said should make sense.

Avoid beginning a sentence with verb-form modifiers that require the passive tense. "The completed audit occurred in September" is improved by saying "We completed our audit in September."

Keep your writing clear. Write to communicate your findings and express your ideas, not to impress someone with your learning.

Use common words.

Don't use:	When you can use:
terminate	stop, end
optimum	best
institute	begin
initiate	start
initial	first
purchase	buy
facilitate	ease, simplify
demonstrate	show
subsequent	next
expedite	hasten, speed

prior to	before
numerous, innumerable	many
velocity	speed
accordingly, consequently	so
furthermore	then, also
nevertheless	but, however
adhere	stick, follow
likewise	and, also
conducted, effected	made
utilize	use
informed, indicated	told
implemented	carried out
reflect	show

Consider the reader's experience. Give enough information to supply background, but not so much as to belabor the obvious or be patronizing.

Express coordinate ideas in similar form. Keep related expressions in parallel. Switching between different forms for comparable thoughts troubles and confuses the reader.

Not: We made our audit by observing receipts, examining documentation, and we interviewed inspectors.

But: We observed receipts, examined documentation, and interviewed inspectors.

Make it clear which of two or more things just mentioned is being referred to or discussed.

Define clearly any technical or unfamiliar subject.

Make it clear when something happened and where it happened.

Be specific about quantities. A "substantial percentage" is not as clear as 20 out of 50.

Use the right word. Rarely do two English words mean the same. Use the one that best describes what you have in mind.

Avoid ambiguous words and phrases. Good writing should be susceptible to only one meaning. If a word or phrase can possibly be misunderstood it most likely will be.

Put words in the right place. "We only wish to improve procedures" is different from "we wish only to improve procedures."

Do not omit important details. If a finding states "The checks did not bear two signatures," it should be shown by what authority two signatures are required.

Carry out promises. If an introductory sentence says "We shall discuss three controls over the accuracy of engineering drawings," make sure all three are discussed. On the other hand, if a heading states "Accuracy of Engineering Drawings," do not discuss under that heading the timeliness with which drawings are prepared.

Lists of items should include words belonging to the same categories.

Do not use the same word in different senses in the same sentence. Avoid, for example, "There was a material amount of rubbish mixed with the scrap material."

Avoid ambiguous references. Make sure there can be no doubt about what the referent is when you use such words as "it," "they," "this," "that," "these," and "which."

Avoid dangling modifiers.
>Not: Having reported our finding, the manager took corrective action.
>But: After we reported our finding to him, the manager took corrective action.

Keep your writing alive. Use action words. They command attention. They give writing spice. The active voice is preferable, but the passive may sometimes be used for variety.

Use words that draw pictures. Avoid vague and fuzzy generalities. "Envelopes and writing paper" draws a clearer picture than "stationery."

Avoid sentences that begin with "As a result of," "Although," "Despite," "In view of," and the like. The sentences tend to get long and dreary.

Physical Characteristics

Appearance
Like any other product on the market, the report should be attractively packaged. It should have a dignified and tasteful appearance. At the same time it should not indicate excessive expense in the preparation. An expensive-looking package is inconsistent with exhortations by the auditor to practice greater economy.

Most companies follow fairly consistent formats in their report presentation, covers, and distribution sheets. Some of the reports are transmitted by memoranda. Others have the distribution sheet as the first page. Some are placed within covers with varying types of bindings.

In the main, audit reports show a good deal of "white space." Paragraphs are generally short. There is an abundant use of headings to indicate what follows and to break up the crowded lines.

Some reports are in double space; but the majority are in single space. For still others, the summaries are double spaced and the detail is single spaced.

Length
Reports come in all lengths. Long reports are generally summarized to

give executive management the gist of the audit results. Longer reports will generally have tables of contents to make their contents more accessible.

Signatures

Most reports are signed by the auditor and by the head of the auditing department. The signature may appear on the transmittal memorandum, at the end of the summary, or at the end of the entire report. Accepted practice most often calls for the signature to follow rather than to precede any opinions, thereby implying a certification of the auditor's conclusions.

Distribution

Report distributions run the gamut. They can be addressed solely to the executive to whom the manager of auditing is responsible, or they may go to every manager who is in any way involved in the matters reported. A host of variations is possible.

Some distributions merely show names of distributees. Others show the departments of the managers and indicate whether the report was reviewed in draft form with them and whether they are being asked to take corrective action.

Ratings

Some companies have adopted a plan which calls for an adjective or numerical rating for each organization audited. This idea faces opposition from many auditors. They feel that it is very difficult for the auditor to produce logically comparable ratings for the many diverse operations they review. [8]

In most instances, the rating would merely represent the auditor's subjective opinion, vulnerable to dispute and argument. To be reasonably objective, the following two factors should apply. First, the operations to be rated should be similar. Only under such conditions could standards be developed which are equally applicable to the different operations and equally applied by different auditors in the same auditing department. Second, the conditions should be quantifiable — numbers of errors or differences in inventories for example. Where audit opinions become the significant factor, ratings may be difficult to apply fairly. This is particularly true in large audit organizations with many auditors, each with different views and audit approaches.

In one company, the first item in the report is a rating (A, B, C, D) for the current audit and, for purposes of comparison, the rating for the previous audit. An explanation follows these ratings. For example:

Rating for this audit . . . . B Minus
Rating for last audit (June 28, 19XX) . . . . B Plus
This unsatisfactory rating shows a serious deterioration in controls, irregularities in the handling of estimates, and a poor credit routine performance. In addition, the work in a number of other sections is far from satisfactory.

In another firm, audit rating sheets are included in the reports of wholesale sales regions. The sheet lists the activities to be examined and shows for each activity the number of points which indicate the standard for top performance. Another column shows the number of points assigned in the current audit. The third and last column shows the percentage relationship between the current rating and the standard. An overall rating is then developed and is reported in the first paragraph of the transmittal letter.

Titles

Titles of reports deserve careful consideration. They should be sufficiently descriptive to convey clearly the subject matter of the report. They should not be so long as to be a report in themselves. Yet they should not imply coverage that is not contemplated. For example:

"Review of Warranties" — This title is so broad that it can be construed to cover both warranties to customers and warranties from suppliers.

"Review of Warranties from Suppliers" — This title restricts the field, but implies coverage of warranties on productive equipment as well as non-productive equipment such as typewriters and other office equipment.

"Review of Warranties from Suppliers of Productive Equipment" — This title may accurately convey the entire extent of the audit coverage.

Editing Reports

Reviews

In most internal audit organizations, audit reports are edited with great care. They are drafted by the auditor and then reviewed in detail by an editor, by a supervisor, by an audit manager, or any combination of the three. This review is made to put reported findings in perspective, to make sure the auditing organization's policies are followed, and to ensure accuracy, logic, and acceptable style.

The review process is a training ground for the auditor. It should point up any weaknesses in thought or in the development of facts. It should highlight the matters the auditor ought to keep in mind in the next audit. The reviewer owes it to the auditor to explain the changes and improvements made so that weaknesses can be strengthened. The reviewer should have, therefore, a thorough understanding of the factors that contribute to reporting.

Basically, the reviewer is concerned with the report's readability, correctness, and appropriateness:

Readability. The reviewer will look to see how clearly the report will get across to the reader. Does it lay a proper foundation and background? Are the sentences well constructed? Are the paragraphs lacking in topic sentences and are they overlong? Is the language clear and free from jargon? Do the thoughts flow freely and logically? Is the message clear?

Correctness. Are the grammar and punctuation correct? Are the department's reporting policies followed? Are the thoughts properly connected?

Exhibit 13-6. WRITTEN PERFORMANCE INVENTORY

I. READABILITY

READER'S LEVEL
- Too specialized in approach
- Assumes too great a knowledge of subject
- So underestimates the reader that it belabors the obvious

SENTENCE CONSTRUCTION
- Unnecessarily long in difficult material
- Subject-verb-object word order too rarely used
- Choppy, overly simple style (in simple material)

PARAGRAPH CONSTRUCTION
- Lack of topic sentences
- Too many ideas in single paragraph
- Too long

FAMILIARITY OF WORDS
- Inappropriate jargon
- Pretentious language
- Unnecessarily abstract

READER DIRECTION
- Lack of "framing" (i.e., failure to tell the reader about purpose and direction of forthcoming discussion)
- Inadequate transitions between paragraphs, thoughts, and conclusions
- Absence of subconclusions to summarize reader's progress at end of divisions in the discussion

FOCUS
- Unclear as to subject of communication
- Unclear as to purpose of message

II. CORRECTNESS

MECHANICS
- Shaky grammar
- Faulty punctuation

FORMAT
- Careless appearance of documents
- Use of unacceptable form

COHERENCE
- Sentences seem awkward owing to illogical and ungrammatical yoking of unrelated ideas
- Failure to develop a logical progression of ideas through coherent, logically juxtaposed paragraphs

SUPPORTING DETAIL
- Inadequate support for recommendations
- Too much undigested detail for busy executive

PREPARATION
- Inadequate thought given to purpose of communication prior to its final completion
- Inadequate preparation or use of data
- Failure to stick to job assigned

ANALYSIS
- Superficial examination of data leading to unconscious overlooking of important evidence
- Failure to draw obvious conclusions from data presented
- Presentation of conclusions unjustified by evidence
- Failure to qualify tenuous assertions
- Failure to identify and justify assumptions used
- Bias, conscious or unconscious, which leads to distorted interpretation of data

III. APPROPRIATENESS

TACT
- Failure to recognize differences in position between writer and receiver
- Impolitic tone — too brusque, argumentative, or insulting
- Context includes unnecessary sharpness or implications
- Overbearing attitude toward subordinates
- Insulting and/or personal references

OPINION
- Adequate research but too great an intrusion of opinions
- Too few facts (and too little research) to entitle drawing of conclusions
- Opinions not clearly identified as opinions

ATTITUDE
- Too obvious a desire to please recipients
- Too defensive in face of authority
- Too fearful of recipients to be able to do best work

PERSUASIVENESS
- Seems more convincing than facts warrant
- Seems less convincing than facts warrant
- Too obvious an attempt to sell ideas
- Lacks action-orientation and managerial viewpoint
- Too blunt an approach where subtlety and finesse called for
- Failure to identify cost/benefit relationship of recommendations

Are ideas and conclusions summarized yet properly supported? Does the report stick to its purpose? Does it make use of all the significant data accumulated in the field work? Do the working papers support the reported statements?

Appropriateness. Is the tone tactful? Are opinions separated from facts? Is the attitude objective? Are minor deficiencies given too much space — and are major deficiencies given too little? Does the report do a proper job on the ideas that need selling, while not wasting time on matters of little import?

Reviewers can use the "written performance inventory" (Exhibit 13-6) to evaluate report drafts. The inventory identifies common reporting mistakes. It clarifies for reviewers precisely what they don't like about a particular report. When the auditor asks in outrage, "What do you mean, I can't write," the reviewer can answer with authority.[9]

Proofreading

When the report is ready to be put in final form, it must be scrubbed clean of errors. It is unfortunate but true that one relatively insignificant mechanical flaw, a typographical or spelling error, can cruelly blemish and downgrade a well-written, soundly documented report. The very nature of audit reports — finding fault, exposing deficiencies, suggesting changes — magnifies in the eyes of the reader any defects within the report itself.

Typographical errors and other minor mistakes divert the reader's attention from the text and thereby lessen the force of the subject matter. Readers may begin thinking about the writer rather than about what is written. They may begin to wonder whether errors in the text may be an indication of substantive blunders in the documents behind it.

Internal auditors must therefore be exceptionally careful not only in what they say and how they say it, but also in how successfully they have purged their reports of even the slightest errors.

This is not easy to do. Sometimes we cannot trust our own eyes. In reading our own reports we would like to see them without flaws. As a result, our eyes may slip over errors because we don't really want to see them.

Also, the intelligence that makes us good internal auditors may be the very thing that blinds us to the blemishes in our own work. Intelligent people need fewer details to perceive the whole; hence, the less likely they are to plod doggedly through the individual words and letters that express a thought — a thought which they have grasped at a glance, or with which they are completely familiar.

Auditors must therefore slow themselves down and follow a careful regimen before signing their reports and sending them off to the addressees. The audit manager should establish a routine which makes sure all reasonable steps have been taken to ensure complete accuracy. The following routine can prove helpful:

Comparison. After it has been typed, the report should be compared with the draft by reading it aloud. If the typist who typed the final report is also proofreading, he or she should read the rough draft and someone else should read the final report — it is hard to detect a flaw in one's own offspring. Both people who do the proofing should initial the report, or a form prepared for the purpose, to evidence their work.

Reference check. The auditor should then "tick" on a carbon of the final report every factual statement, every number, every title, every date. The tick marks bear evidence that each item has been referenced back to basic data — to directives, organization charts, working papers, computations, and the like. Auditors will be helped if their drafts carry marginal references to their working papers. This is useful during reviews with auditees and in checking the final report.

The whole picture. Auditors should then focus their attention on the report's overall organization. This becomes quite simple if they spread out the pages of the report before them like a game of solitaire. Any inconsistencies in format, headings, and indentation will practically leap out at them. It will also simplify the verification of references within the report or between the report and supporting schedules.

Auditors should then read the report for sense and flow. Often what sounded completely logical and reasonable and what appeared in perfect sequence, when read in rough draft, assumes a most discouraging aspect in final form. Auditors who read the final report aloud may reap benefits by having to slow down and hear how the report sounds to others.

The detailed picture. After they have satisfied themselves with the organization, sense, and flow of the report, auditors should then focus on detecting the maddening typographical errors that so easily elude the eye. Here they had better have some assistance, some device to force them to focus, to keep them from reading too rapidly, to help them concentrate on letters and not on word pictures.

One such device can be made from a sheet of blank paper or cardboard. Cut a strip from the center of the sheet — a strip that is long enough and wide enough to reveal one line of type, but no more.

Lay this scanner over the line and read each line slowly, undistracted by the lines before or after it. Finally, if the report is of such significance that a single typographical or mechanical error is utterly unthinkable, read the report **backwards** through the scanner, thereby focusing on individual words, letters, and punctuation, undiverted by the sense of what was written.

Included in the techniques of the professional proofreader is a mental list of the kinds of errors that most easily escape detection. With these in mind, the auditor is less likely to overlook them.

Here are a few of the many errors to watch for:

Letters omitted (omited) or added (ommitted)

Doublets or repeaters (alllocable)

Words spelled two ways in the same report (travelled, traveled)

Improper or inconsistent capitalization

Incorrect indentation

Wrong division of words

Transposition of letters (form for from)

Inconsistent compounding ("14-foot extrusions and 7 gauge sheet stock")

Poor spacing (f. o. b. should be f.o.b.)

Headings that do not relate to the subject matter

Showing open quotes or parentheses, but no closed quotes or parentheses.

Disagreement between subject and predicate in person or number

Disagreement between pronoun and its antecedent in person or number

Pronoun with unclear referent

Using "above" or "below" when matter referred to is on another page (Use foregoing, previously, following.)

Day of week does not agree with date

Incorrect use of homonyms (principal, principle; compliment, complement; course, coarse; stationary, stationery)

Using hyphens between adverbs and adjectives (recently-revised instructions)

Using percent and % both ways in same text

Failing to place commas before and after etc., eg., i.e., when they are in the middle of a sentence

Disagreement between the total of a list of items and the specific number mentioned (we have discussed the following five deficiency findings, etc.)

Failing to put words in quotations that might otherwise be misunderstood (removing the bugs from the system)

Using both the singular and the plural when referring to the same noun

(Joseph Lasky's monumental work on proofreading gives many more.[10])

Style Manual

Every auditing department should have a style manual. It may be developed within the department or it may be a standard work. The Government Printing Office Style Manual is a respected and comprehensive text.

The cost of a good manual can easily be recovered by eliminating the time spent in arguments and differences of opinion on mechanical matters. For those departments embarking on the preparation of a style manual, here are some of the matters that should be included:

A. Report Responsibilities
   1. Preparation
   2. Client Reviews
   3. Distribution
   4. Progress Reports
   5. Checking and Proofreading
B. Report Format
   1. Distribution Sheet
   2. Report Segments
   3. Report Addenda
      a. Exhibits
      b. Appendices
      c. Schedules
   4. Elements of Style
      a. Abbreviations
      b. Apostrophes
      c. Capitalization
      d. Citations
      e. Colons
      f. Commas
      g. Connectives
      h. Dashes
      i. Hyphens
      j. Jargon
      k. Numbers
      l. Paragraphs
      m. Plurals
      n. Prepositions
      o. Quoted Material
      p. Semicolons
      q. Spelling
      r. Miscellaneous
C. Report Examples

Sample Reports

There are audit reports and there are audit reports. They come in every conceivable size and style. There is not, and there probably never will be, a standard form. Some acquire their present form from a gradual evolution. Others retain their present form because that is what people have become accustomed to and are reluctant to see changed.

We believe that the internal audit report is much too important to continue in an accustomed form year after year without considering improvements. New needs, new technology, new insights into what will attract or influence the reader should be periodically evaluated by the audit staff. Not change for change's sake, but change which will further management's needs and the auditor's objectives.

Exhibit 13-7 is a comprehensive report from an airplane manufacturer. The distribution sheet shows the broad dissemination given to the report. It specifically identifies the people who will have to take corrective action and those who are to see that the action is taken. An "audit highlights" section provides a brief summary of the report for executive consumption. The summary report gives background information, sets forth the purpose of the audit, offers an overall opinion, and summarizes the audit findings, both good and bad. The findings are keyed to the objectives of the operation; they are documented by showing how the auditors were able to arrive at their conclusions.

A supplement to the report explains in detail the four deficiency findings the internal auditors unearthed. The report concludes with a summary of findings requiring corrective action. Findings for which corrective action was not completed at the end of the audit are referred to specific individuals for action.

Exhibit 13-7.   XYZ CORPORATION
                    INTERNAL AUDIT REPORT

Audit Project R8X-18   Date: August 26, 198X

DISTRIBUTION	TAKE ACTION	SECURE ACTION	INFOR- MATION	REVIEWED PRIOR TO RELEASE
President			X	
Executive Vice President		X	X	
Vice President-Controller			X	
Director of Material		X		X
Manager, Procurement	X			X
Manager, Highway Transportation Department	X			X
Director of Industrial Relations				X
Chief, Security Division				X
Chief, Plant Protection				X

Exhibit 13-7. (Cont.)

AUDIT HIGHLIGHTS

Highway Transportation Department
(A Regularly Scheduled Review)

Prior Audit: No deficiency findings.

Audit Coverage:
1. Equipment maintenance and vehicle dispatching
2. Fuel, parts, and repair services
3. General administrative activities.

Overall Opinion: In general, the operation was functioning in a reasonably satisfactory manner.

We did find some control weaknesses. The most serious involved the lack of separation of duties in the procurement of parts and services. Steps are being taken to correct these weaknesses.

Despite the weaknesses, however, the department's activities were being performed satisfactorily.

Executive
Action Required: None.

SUMMARY REPORT

Foreword

This report covers the results of our regularly scheduled review of the activities of the Highway Transportation Department. Our last review of the Department's activities disclosed no deficiencies.

The department's primary responsibilities are (1) to transport personnel and materials, and (2) to maintain and repair automotive equipment.

At the time of our review there were about 50 employees assigned to the department. Operating costs (not including labor) for equipment rental, repair parts and services, and fuel and oil, are projected to reach about $900,000 for 19XX. Mileage for the year will total about 5 million miles.

During this review we issued one progress report to bring to management's attention certain matters requiring prompt corrective action.

Purpose

We have made an examination of the Highway Transportation Department's principal activities to determine whether they were being controlled adequately and effectively. In performing our review, we examined the system of controls concerned with the following activities:

1. Equipment maintenance and vehicle dispatching, including (a) scheduling preventive maintenance inspections, (b) performing regular maintenance and repairs, and (c) dispatching cars and trucks.

2. Ordering, receiving, and disbursing fuel and parts and obtaining automotive repair services.

3. General administrative activities concerned with (a) property accountability, (b) plant protection, (c) accident reporting, (d) insurable value reporting, (e) gasoline credit cards, and (f) petty cash.

Exhibit 13-7. (Cont.)

Opinions and Findings

We formed the opinion that adequate controls had been provided over the activities we reviewed, except for a lack of separation of duties in the procurement of parts and services. Three other matters of lesser significance likewise involved control weaknesses.

We also formed the opinion that, despite the control weaknesses we had detected, the functions we reviewed were being performed in a generally satisfactory manner.

Our conclusions and findings on each of the three groups of activities covered in our examination are summarized in the following paragraphs.

Equipment Maintenance and Vehicle Dispatching

Adequate controls have been provided which were designed to make sure that (1) automotive equipment would receive inspection and preventive maintenance in accordance with the manufacturers' recommendations, and (2) truck and car dispatching would be accomplished in accordance with established procedures.

We examined preventive maintenance reports and related control records and satisfied ourselves that maintenance was being properly scheduled, monitored, and performed. We also examined documentation supporting vehicle dispatching and observed the dispatching operations; we concluded that dispatching was being adequately controlled and performed.

Ordering, Receiving, and Disbursing Fuel and Parts, and Obtaining Vehicle Repair Services

Controls had been provided which were designed to make sure that fuel, parts, and outside repair services were (1) ordered when needed, (2) recorded upon receipt, and (3) properly approved for payment; and that the disbursement of fuel and parts was adequately documented.

We did find, however, that there was (1) a lack of appropriate separation of duties in the procurement of parts and services, and (2) what we considered to be inadequate surveillance over the withdrawal of gasoline and oil by vehicle operators. These matters are discussed more fully in the Supplement to this Summary Report.

We examined representative samples of (1) reports, records, and blanket purchase orders covering the procurement and receipt of supplies and services; and (2) the logs and records covering fuel withdrawals. Despite the control weaknesses referred to, we concluded on the basis of our tests that the functions were being performed in a reasonably satisfactory manner. We made an analysis of the fuel pump meter records and compared them with the amounts of fuel recorded by vehicle operators. The results showed little variance between the two, indicating that fuel withdrawals were in the main being properly recorded.

General Administrative Activities

Controls had been devised to provide assurance that (1) property accountability records would be complete and accurate, (2) accidents to licensed vehicles would be reported promptly, (3) gasoline credit cards would be used for the purpose issued and only when vehicles were operated away from company-owned fuel supplies, and (4) petty cash would be properly safeguarded and used only for the purpose for which the petty cash fund was established.

Exhibit 13-7. (Cont.)

It did seem to us that the area in which Highway Transportation was located was inadequately protected, and we did find that there was no provision for reporting the insurable values of repair parts and inventories. These matters are also discussed further in the Supplement.

We tested, among other things, (1) equipment information cards; (2) facilities location control cards; (3) acquisition and retirement fixed asset work orders; (4) the department's accident register; (5) the company insurance administrator's control number assignment log covering vehicle and other accidents; (6) a gasoline credit card assignment register; (7) credit card delivery tickets; (8) petty cash reimbursement request; and (9) vouchers covering petty cash disbursements, making a petty cash count as well. Based on our tests, we concluded that except for the lack of reports on insurable values, the activities we examined were carried out in a satisfactory manner.

* * *

The four deficiency findings previously mentioned are discussed in the Supplement which follows and are summarized at the end of the Supplement, along with the referrals for completion of corrective action.

Before we completed our review, provision was made to report insurable values, and steps were initiated to correct the remaining three control weaknesses.

_____Auditor-in-Charge

_____ Supervising Auditor

_____Manager of Internal Auditing

Supplement to
Summary Report

DETAILS OF DEFICIENCY FINDINGS

1. There was no separation of functional authority in the procurement of parts and services, and effective administration of labor-hour agreements was beyond the Highway Transportation Department's resources.

Blanket Purchase Orders (BPOs) have been issued for the procurement of parts and services. The cognizant purchasing department has assigned to the Highway Transportation Department all authority and responsibility for controlling (a) releases of orders under the BPOs to suppliers; (b) receipt, inspection, and acceptance upon delivery; and (c) approvals of invoices for payment.

In practice, all of these functions are performed by the department manager or by one or two people under his direct control and supervision. Thus, there is none of the protection normally afforded by the separation of such functions among personnel of independent departments; such as establishing requirements, ordering, receiving, inspection, and approving for payment.

There are about 70 currently active BPOs which require suppliers to furnish automotive parts and/or services, as requested. Expenditures for the year are budgeted at about $230,000. Many of the BPOs specify labor-hour rates for the repair of automotive equipment. In effect, these BPOs are Time and Material (T and M) agreements since no fixed number of hours is established for the orders released. Thus, the scope of work is undefined. Yet, the BPOs do not include clauses providing the company with the right of audit, something normally included in T and M agreements.

Exhibit 13-7. (Cont.)

Supplement to
Summary Report

In our opinion, these labor-hour BPOs do not appear to meet the intent of Procurement Instruction 501, in that they do not ensure the establishment of a fixed price for the order involved at the time of delivery. Furthermore, adequate and effective contract administration of these agreements is beyond the present resources of the Highway Transportation Department.

Because of the lack of separation of duties and the nature of the agreements, we made an extensive examination of the system and of transactions, but we found no basis for questioning any of the charges. Nevertheless, we recommend that Branch management review this condition with a view toward implementing some reasonable control through assignment of some of the key functions to other departments. Further, we recommend that management implement appropriate controls to preclude the use of T and M BPOs without an audit clause.

We discussed this matter with management personnel and they informed us that they intended to review the methods used at other major divisions of the company to determine whether any of their practices may warrant adoption.

2. Gasoline and oil were being withdrawn by company employees without adequate surveillance.

Since our last examination, the department reassigned elsewhere the service station attendant who had recorded gasoline and oil disbursements on the form provided for that purpose. Under present practice the vehicle operator serves himself and records his own withdrawals of gasoline and oil, without surveillance. There is no assurance, therefore, that the records are maintained accurately or that the information is always entered. Hence the dangers of misappropriation are increased. We estimate that the total yearly gasoline withdrawal will approximate 300,000 gallons at a cost of about $66,000.

We recognize that there must be a weighing of the benefits versus the costs of control. Nevertheless, we recommend that management consider some means of surveillance — even on a spot check basis — to provide minimum elements of control.

We discussed this matter with management personnel and they indicated that appropriate surveillance would be conducted over fuel pump operations.

3. The area in which the Highway Transportation Department is located was not adequately protected.

Area 10, the site of the Highway Transportation Department, is used to house vehicles, fuel pumps, oil, repair parts, and the garage. The area is completely fenced. But it has two large gates, one at the northwest corner and one at the southeast corner. At the time we began our review both gates were kept open during the regular and swing shifts. A sign at the southeast gate warned that entrance is for the company vehicles only. No such sign appeared at the other gate.

We observed that departmental employees, as well as other company employees, were allowed to park their private vehicles within the area. No guards were posted at the gates. Plant Protection personnel informed us that guards were not available for that purpose.

Exhibit 13-7. (Cont.)

Supplement to
Summary Report

After we discussed this matter with the department manager, he closed the northwest gate to strengthen security somewhat. We believe that further action should be considered, however. While there is an adequate number of employees on hand during the day shift to provide some protection for property, it is doubtful that the reduced swing shift staff can do the same. Also, permitting private cars in the area violates the posted instructions and increases the danger of losses.

We recognize that the unavailability of Plant Protection guards creates some problems. But we believe that management should consider some substitute safeguards, particularly on swing shift.

During discussions with management personnel they indicated that additional measures to strengthen plant protection would be considered.

4. The insurable value of repair parts on hand was not being reported.

We found that the value of repair parts on hand in the Highway Transportation Department had not been reported for insurance purposes since the inventory records were decontrolled in 19VV. The value of these repair parts is about $4,500.

We called the matter to the attention of the Insurance Administrator, and he requested the highway Transportation Department to report the estimated dollar value as of the end of June 19XX. He has also taken action to revise the Company Insurance Manual to show this requirement.

The Highway Transportation Department informed the Insurance Administrator of the insurable value on July 16, 19XX. Corrective action on this matter is considered complete.

SUMMARY OF FINDINGS REQUIRING CORRECTIVE ACTION

The four matters requiring corrective action are summarized as follows:

1. There was no separation of functional authority in the procurement of parts and services, and effective administration of labor-hour agreements was beyond the Highway Transportation Department's resources.

2. Gasoline and oil were being withdrawn by company employees without adequate surveillance.

3. The area in which the Highway Transportation Department is located was not adequately protected.

4. The insurable value of repair parts on hand was not being reported.

Finding 1 is referred jointly to the manager of the Procurement Department and the manager of the Highway Transportation Department for completion of corrective action. Findings 2 and 3 are referred to the manager of the Highway Transportation Department for completion of corrective action. Finding 4 has been corrected.

Exhibit 13-8 shows an interesting form of report prepared by internal auditors of a bank. Because of its length we have used excerpts from the report to show the approach and the format. The report is bound in a paperback cover. Inside the cover are standard printed instructions "How to Read This Report." The full report contains:

A distribution sheet.

A transmittal letter to the audit committees of the various boards of directors.

A table of contents.

A statement of audit scope.

The auditor's conclusion running from Excellent to Substandard. (The meanings of these adjectival ratings are explained in the instructions on the cover.)

A summary of the major findings disclosed by the audit.

A digest of recommendations summarized under three headings: loans, assets, liabilities.

The digest identifies both repeat findings and those recommendations which were previously made but which were not implemented because of limitations of staff and/or facilities.

The digest shows which recommendations had been met, which had not been carried out, and which had been agreed to and would be carried out by a given target date.

The details of the findings supporting the recommendations. Actions taken are shown in italics.

Appendices providing statistical and financial data. Among the appendices is a list of related party transactions showing the names of the directors or officers involved, the names of the borrowers, and other pertinent information.

Exhibit 13-8.

HOW TO READ THIS REPORT

This report is structured to afford you ease in identifying the seriousness of the findings of the auditor. A quick overview of the findings will be obtained by reading the CONCLUSION and SUMMARY REPORT (2 minutes). The definition of CONCLUSION statements is found below. The DIGEST (1-3 minutes) which follows the SUMMARY will give you a listing of all of the recommendations made, their status and the date by which implementation should be completed.

The SUMMARY is divided into two primary sections. The primary sections are MAJOR FINDINGS and OTHER FINDINGS. While no recommendations should be ignored, this division is intended to help the reader gain a feel for the relative importance of weaknesses found by the auditors in the course of their examina-

Exhibit 13-8. (Cont.)

tion. The MAJOR FINDINGS section is subdivided into CONTROL and COMPLI-ANCE subsections.

Findings in the CONTROL subsection indicate exposure to internal or external fraud, or exposures to error which can be costly and have material probability of occurrence.

Findings in the COMPLIANCE subsection indicate exposures created through failure to comply with laws, regulations and legal requirements which expose the bank to penalties, suits and/or judgments or which would require the bank to resort to costly legal action to maintain its rights.

Key factors to watch in the DIGEST are:

(1) The words "see comments" in the status column refers the reader to the DETAIL OF RECOMMENDATIONS section for a discussion of the two sides of an unresolved recommendation, and

(2) The symbol *** in the left margin which indicates that the recommendation was made and agreed to in the previous audit and the condition still existed at the time of this audit.

(3) When the symbol @@@ is found in the left margin of the DIGEST it denotes that this recommendation is repeated because of limitations of staff size and/or physical facilities. In such case, the most desirable control procedure will be described in the recommendation. Any alternative, cost-effective control will be described in the response by management following the recommendation.

The section titled DETAIL OF RECOMMENDATIONS is for study at your convenience and contains a detailed discussion of each recommendation and a response from management stating their intentions or actions on the implementation of the recommendations. An APPENDIX section may be placed at the end of the report which contains certain analytical and exposure information which is of interest to management and directors.

CONCLUSION STATEMENTS

The following terminology is used in the conclusion statements of XYZ Bank Holding Co. internal audit reports and is defined as follows:

EXCELLENT: Virtually all desired controls are in operation, only very minor exceptions were noted and back-up controls exist for all weaknesses noted.

GOOD: Most material controls are in operation and the exposures found are minor in extent and nature, usually backed up by other controls.

STANDARD: Attention should be given to some exposures in protective and compliance controls; however, reasonable assurance exists that current controls afford the bank adequate protection.

MARGINAL: Early attention should be given to exposures in protective and compliance controls; any deterioration in current controls can lead to serious exposures.

SUBSTANDARD*: Requires immediate attention to serious exposures in protective and compliance controls; exposures exist which could make the bank vulnerable to significant losses.

*MAY BE MODIFIED AS **SERIOUSLY** OR **DANGEROUSLY SUBSTANDARD** WHERE CONDITIONS WARRANT.

Exhibit 13-8. (Cont.)

THE AUDIT COMMITTEES OF THE BOARD OF DIRECTORS OF XYZ BANK HOLDING CO. AND THE SUBSIDIARY BANK*

Gentlemen:

Attached is the report on our recent audit of _____
_____ which began August 16, 19XX. This audit covered all departments of the bank and the major areas of three branches. All recommendations, suggestions and observations arising from the audit have been discussed in detail on December 19, 19XX, with _____
_____

_____ These discussions were held to assure a complete understanding of the contents and emphasis of the items in this report.

It should be understood that no matters in this report are intended to reflect on the honesty or integrity of any officer or employee of the bank. All recommendations have been offered as constructive suggestions for the improvement of internal control in the bank. We are sure that you will be pleased to know that we received the complete cooperation of each member of the bank's staff.

ASSIGNED AUDITORS: SENIOR AUDIT OFFICER
Supervising Auditor   DIRECTOR OF INTERNAL AUDIT
Supervising Auditor
Supervising Auditor
Senior Staff Auditor
Senior Staff Auditor
Senior Staff Auditor
Staff Auditor
Staff Auditor
Staff Auditor

REPORT DISTRIBUTION

AUDIT COMMITTEES
AUDIT COMMITTEE - XYZ BANK HOLDING CO.
AUDIT COMMITTEE - SUBSIDIARY BANK*

CORPORATE MANAGEMENT
CHAIRMAN & CHIEF EXECUTIVE OFFICER - XYZ BANK HOLDING CO.
PRESIDENT - XYZ BANK HOLDING CO.
EXECUTIVE VICE PRESIDENTS - XYZ BANK HOLDING CO.

LINE MANAGEMENT
CHAIRMAN - SUBSIDIARY BANK
PRESIDENT & CHIEF EXECUTIVE OFFICER - SUBSIDIARY BANK
CASHIER - SUBSIDIARY BANK

INFORMATIONAL COPIES
SENIOR VICE PRESIDENT, SYSTEMS & PROCEDURES - XYZ BANK HOLDING CO.
SENIOR VICE PRESIDENT, CREDIT ADMINISTRATION & LOAN REVIEW - XYZ BANK HOLDING CO.
INDEPENDENT ACCOUNTANTS
AUDIT DEPARTMENT FILES

*All names have been removed from the material reprinted here.

Exhibit 13-8. (Cont.)

TABLE OF CONTENTS

ITEM	PAGE
SCOPE OF AUDIT AND CONCLUSION OF AUDITOR	1
SUMMARY OF REPORT	2
DIGEST OF RECOMMENDATIONS	3-5
DETAIL OF RECOMMENDATIONS	
SECTION 1 - LOANS	6-8
SECTION 2 - ASSETS	8-12
SECTION 3 - LIABILITIES	12-14
SECTION 4 - PAYROLL & PERSONNEL	14-15
SECTION 5 - NON-GENERAL LEDGER ITEMS	15-18
APPENDIX I - PAST DUE COMMERCIAL LOANS	19
APPENDIX I - PAST DUE INSTALLMENT LOANS	20
APPENDIX II - OVERDRAFT ANALYSIS	21
APPENDIX III - RELATED PARTY TRANSACTIONS	22-26

SCOPE OF AUDIT

The scope of our audit was consistent with generally accepted standards of internal auditing in major banks. We reviewed operations and accounting records in all areas of the Main Office and three branch locations. Our audit tests were made to the extent we deemed necessary to establish our conclusions on the internal control structure of the bank. In several areas, we relied upon the reviews which were performed and records which were maintained by the bank's auditor, _____ whom we determined was independent of the routine banking operations and bookkeeping records.

The audit programs used in these audits were our standard audit programs which have been reviewed by the external auditors of XYZ Bank Holding Co.

CONCLUSION OF AUDITOR

In our opinion, at the time of our audit the level of internal control was GOOD at the Main Office location and STANDARD at the three branch locations. Accompanying recommendations are submitted to further enhance the bank's existing system of internal control and to establish several controls that do not now exist.

SUMMARY OF REPORT
MAJOR FINDINGS
CONTROL

TELLER FUNCTIONS AND BRANCHES: Effective dual control has not been established over a number of negotiable items at the branches: vault cash, travelers cheques, Series E Bonds, official checks, certificates of deposit, night deposit safe, preparation of night deposits, and safe deposit boxes holding branch contents. A separation of duties was not being exercised over several branch functions: deposit account opening/cash handling and approval of loans/proceeds disbursement. In general, a number of cash and teller operations controls were not functioning effectively, due primarily to high turnover and lack of proper training. In addition, night deposit records do not assure the proper disposition of each bag handled by bank personnel.

Exhibit 13-8. (Cont.)

MAIN OFFICE OPERATIONS AND LOANS: Dormant account signature cards and reserve supplies of official checks and certificates were not strictly controlled at Main Office because of an occasional lack of protection to keys. Work in transit between the bank's locations and the commercial note files are not controlled to ensure accountability for missing documents. Approval for payment of expenses is sometimes not documented, and the insider overdraft policy has not been reduced to written terms. Proper identification of new depositors is sometimes not obtained, and this sometimes results in not obtaining corporate resolutions. Nonmonetary changes to deposit account records are not being signed by the employee responsible for such changes, and no log of customer complaints is maintained. Customer safekeeping items and the supporting records do not agree with one another. Several note agreements are not accurately completed regarding purchase money security interests and collateral descriptions, and collateral documentation and information is occasionally not in file: hazard insurance, inspection reports and UCC-1 financing statements.

COMPLIANCE

Borrowers are not required to sign agreements when their loans are extended and a fee is charged. Some denials of credit are not made in writing if the application is taken orally, and two branches have not posted F.D.I.C. signs at teller windows. Standard performance review forms are not utilized, and this could result in using different criteria to judge the work performance of each bank employee.

OTHER FINDINGS

Review and documented approval controls do not exist for waiver of late charges on installment loans, and the fixed asset acquisition and employee loan policies have not been reduced to writing. Cash items were not carried in locked bags when being transported between bank locations, and some guarantors of Industrial Revenue Bond issues do not have current financial statements in file. Approval for overtime pay is not documented, and specimen signatures are not obtained from customers when accepting items to be sent for collection. A number of security procedures could be strengthened to enhance protection to employees and bank assets.

The bank's staff was most helpful and cordial during the course of our audit, and we appreciate their assistance. We also feel that bank personnel should be commended for their conscientious efforts in promptly correcting deficiencies found during the course of our audit and in correcting previous audit recommendations.

DIGEST OF RECOMMENDATIONS

RECOMMENDATION	STATUS	TARGET DATE
SECTION 1 - LOANS		
1.1 Note Completion and Credit Documentation.		
C/L*** A. Protect the bank's collateral by obtaining proper documentation.	done	
B. Complete note forms properly.	done	

Exhibit 13-8. (Cont.)

1.2	**Require customers to sign extension agreements.**	done

1.3 Internal and Recordkeeping Controls.

C/L*** A. Assign the responsibility for the commercial note files to designated employees. — done

B. Document all denials of credit in writing. — done

@@@ C. Establish a separation of duties between approval of loans and disbursement of proceeds at the branches. — see comments

D. Establish a written lending policy on employee loans. — done

E. Enhance the control over late charges waived on installment loans. — done

SECTION 2 - ASSETS

2.1 Cash

@@@ A. Provide adequate controls over large supplies of cash. — see comments

*** B. Ensure that tellers can be held accountable for assigned cash funds and transactions bearing their stamp. — see comments

C. Strengthen and strictly enforce the established administrative guidelines over tellers. — done

D. Strengthen the teller training program. — agreed — 2-15-79

C/L*** — indicates that the audit suggestion has been made in previous audit(s) to commercial loan management only.

**DETAIL OF RECOMMENDATIONS
SECTION 1
LOANS**

The recommendations in this section apply to both commercial and installment loans. If the recommendation is preceded by C/L***, it will indicate that the audit suggestion has been made in previous audit(s) to commercial loan management only. Asterisk notations without any identifying letters are explained inside the front cover of this report.

1.1 Note Completion and Credit Documentation.

C/L*** **A. Protect the bank's collateral by obtaining proper documentation.**

To perfect its interest in personal property taken as collateral, the bank must either file a UCC-1 financing statement, obtain non-filing insurance, or in the case of 1975 or newer vehicles, obtain a title. The bank

Exhibit 13-8. (Cont.)

should further ensure that its tangible collateral is protected by requiring hazard insurance from the borrower, and in certain cases, a bill of sale should be obtained for personal property which is purchased with loan proceeds and taken as collateral. Our sample review of secured loans disclosed the following conditions: many loans had no hazard insurance, nor were there bills of sale to support tangible property collateral; several loans did not have collateral inspection reports, UCC-1 financing statements or evidence of non-filing insurance coverage. To adequately secure and protect the bank's interest in personal property, we recommend that procedures be established to ensure that all collateral documentation is acquired and maintained.

B. Complete note forms properly.

The bank's note forms have been prepared by Legal Counsel of XYZ Bank Holding Co. to assure close compliance with Federal and State laws and regulations and to ensure a proper interest in collateral for secured notes. It is management's responsibility to properly complete all note forms before the customer executes the note. During a sample review of notes, we found a number of notes whose purchase money sections were not completed, and several notes had incomplete purpose of collateral sections or inadequate collateral descriptions of accounts receivable. To properly state the legal relationship between the bank and its borrowers, we recommend that all note agreements be accurately and fully completed.

Action Taken

*   and*

agreed to implement these suggestions.
also stated that the commercial loan area does not handle typical auto financing and that it was not normally bank policy to acquire bills of sale in these situations.

1.2   Require customers to sign extension agreements.

Granting loan extensions is a lending function and should be treated as such. Regulation Z also governs disclosure of extension fees to borrowers. In our review of extension procedures, we found that customer signatures are not required on extension agreements. In order to provide a better control over extensions and to be in compliance with applicable laws, we recommend that borrowers sign all extension agreements.

Action Taken

*   indicated that this has now been corrected.*

1.3   Internal and Recordkeeping Controls.

C/L*** **A.   Assign the responsibility for the commercial note file to designated employees.**

The responsibility for the commercial notes should be assigned to a designated employee(s) in order that the responsibility can be fixed for all notes. During our audit we observed that loan officers enter the note window and pull notes for review. This condition can lead to notes which are unaccounted for. We therefore recommend that a designated individual(s) be placed in charge of the commercial notes. These persons can

*All names have been removed from the material reprinted here.

Exhibit 13-8. (Cont.)

maintain a sign-out sheet for notes that must be removed from the commercial loan department and will help to eliminate the officers' direct access to the note records.

B. Document all denials of credit in writing.

The Equal Credit Opportunity Act states that all denials of credit must be made in writing. The notice must contain a statement of specific reason for the action taken or disclosure that the reasons can be obtained. During our audit we learned that some details of credit are made orally when loan applications are taken orally. In order to comply with the Equal Credit Opportunity Act, we recommend that all denials of credit be communicated with the customer in writing, using forms designed for this purpose by the holding company's legal staff.

@@@ **C. Establish a separation of duties between approval of loans and disbursement of proceeds at the branches.**

Basic internal control is provided by a separation of duties so that no one person can handle a transaction from inception to disposition. During our audit of one branch, we noted that the loan officer responsible for making a loan is also responsible for the preparation of the cashier's check for disbursement of the loan proceeds. To help provide adequate internal control, we recommend that a person who is independent of loan approval prepare the cashier's check for loan disbursement.

D. Establish a written lending policy on employee loans.

The bank should define its lending parameters and criteria through written policies and procedures. Such written policies will help to ensure that loans can be made within established guidelines set by senior management and approved by the Board of Directors. During our review of the bank's lending policy, we found that there are no written policies for employee loans. To provide guidelines for employee loans, we recommend that a written policy be prepared by management.

E. Enhance the control over late charges waived on installment loans.

An effective means for management to monitor income from waiver of late charges on installment loans is to be aware of all late charges waived by each officer. We were informed that late charge waivers are not approved by an officer. In order to provide a better control over late charges waived and loss of potential income, we recommend that a lending officer be responsible for waiving late charges and that this approval be made in writing.

Action Taken

*   *stated that approvals of late charge waivers will be properly controlled in the future.*
said that Assistant Branch Managers will prepare the cashier's checks for disbursement of loan proceeds after the Branch Managers approve loans, whenever possible; however, there will be times when this control cannot be exercised because of the small staff sizes. According to   the bank now has an employee loan policy, and management agreed to implement the remainder of the suggestions.

*All names have been removed from the material reprinted here.

Exhibit 13-8. (Cont.)

SECTION 2
ASSETS

2.1 Cash.

@@@ **A. Provide adequate controls over large supplies of cash.**

Banking authorities feel that reserve cash and large currency shipments are best protected if maintained under the joint custody of two individuals because it is the bank's most vulnerable asset. During our audit we learned that the combination to the outer vault door is known by each officer at the main office. At several branches, we noted that the vault and reserve cash is not under joint custody, and at one branch the coin vault is left open at all times during the day. To help ensure proper custodial control to vault cash supplies, we encourage management to establish effective dual control over such funds.

*** **B. Ensure that tellers can be held accountable for assigned cash funds and transactions bearing their stamps.**

Cash funds are assigned to tellers and each teller should then be able to be held accountable for all funds charged to her responsibility. Further, identification stamps and keys to tellers' machines should be equally protected to ensure that no unauthorized transaction validations are allowed to occur. During our audit we found that: tellers sometimes leave their working and reserve cash, teller identification stamps and teller machine keys unprotected when away from the teller window area; combinations and locks to the tellers' boxes and the vault have not been changed recently; and duplicate keys to teller boxes are not held under joint custody at several branches. We also noted at one branch that a large amount of cash was placed on a portable table behind the teller lines. To ensure that tellers can be held accountable for their assigned cash funds, we recommend that all cash, machine keys, and identification stamps be locked away when unattended, combinations and locks to the tellers' boxes be changed periodically, duplicate keys to teller boxes be held under joint custody, and tellers be prohibited from placing currency in an area that is visible to customers and not adequately safeguarded.

C. Strengthen and strictly enforce the established administrative guidelines over tellers.

Policies and procedures are established to assist bank personnel in performing their jobs in accordance with management's desires and with sound business practices. Further, periodic management reviews should be made to ensure that personnel are abiding by established guidelines and to review work performance and accountability for negotiable items assigned. During our audit we observed that cash limits appeared to be rather informally established and communicated to officers and tellers. Further, nearly all tellers continually exceeded these cash limits. We also noted at one of the branches that tellers do not obtain the customers' signatures or initials of approval when making out deposit slips for them. To ensure customer approval of transactions prepared by bank personnel, we suggest that they sign or initial deposit slips. We also recommend that cash limits be formally communicated to all tellers to help ensure their ability to properly comply with them.

Exhibit 13-8. (Cont.)

D. Strengthen the teller training program.

Tellers provide a vitally important service at the bank since they are frequently the only personal contact customers have with the bank. Tellers should be trained to operate effectively and efficiently and also be able to sufficiently handle depositors' needs. During our audit we observed that several tellers did not observe a number of proper cash controls; tellers' recap sheets were not legible; and tellers were frequently out of balance and in general did not seem to have an understanding of controls surrounding the cash function. To help protect the bank, tellers, and depositors from loss, we recommend that a more adequate training program be established for the teller function.

Action Taken

*   *and* *stated that the main office vault door only has a three number combination; it is therefore difficult to split the combination between two teams of people to ensure effective dual control. However, nothing is exposed when vault door is open due to the effective dual control of contents inside the vault.*   *also stated that a $10,000 cash limit has been established, and tellers sell their excess currency to the vault after closing; this is usually denoted on the bottom of the cash recap sheets. The bank is now in the process of hiring more mature and experienced tellers to improve the teller turnover situation and hopefully, some of the existing control problems will then correct themselves when stability of teller personnel occurs. Due to small branch staffs, rotating days off and Saturday banking hours, it is impossible to establish effective dual control of negotiable items at the branches; in these cases, management is ensuring effective sole control of reserve cash supplies, minimizing the amount of such cash on hand, and surprise counting of these supplies on a monthly basis. Due to the expense involved, management wishes to continue consideration of changing locks throughout the bank and will implement this suggestion at a later date. All other recommendations either have been or will be implemented.*

*All names have been removed from the material reprinted here.

Conclusion

Reports are the auditor's opportunity to get management's attention. Auditors have an admirable story to tell; they should not throw that opportunity away through inept or unprofessional reporting.

Reports will be evaluated according to their accuracy, clarity, conciseness, timeliness, and tone. Whatever their formats may be — and these formats come in many styles — they will include one or more of these elements: a summary, a foreword or introduction, a purpose, a scope, an opinion, and findings. Statements of findings should themselves contain certain elements. For satisfactory findings: authority, objectives, and conditions. For unsatisfactory findings: a summary, criteria, facts, effect, cause, and recommendation. Graphics can spice a report and provide needed illustrations.

An informal reporting system, to supplement the formal system, can be a great help to the auditor. It permits prompt and easy communication. Oral reports are of equal importance. They too present an opportunity for displaying the auditor's wares, and should be prepared with care.

Good writing takes practice and training. All writing can be improved by certain techniques: outlines to ensure logical flow, and practice to keep writing simple, clear, and alive.

Reports should present an attractive appearance. They should be easy to read. Auditors should be on the constant lookout for ways of improving their reports, making them interesting rather than dreary.

Reports need careful editing for readability, correctness, and appropriateness. The auditing organization should install a rigorous proofreading routine to make sure no errors creep into the final copy.

References

1. D. E. Browne, "Patterns for Progress in Internal Auditing," *The Internal Auditor*, Spring 1966, p. 18.
2. "Internal Audit Report Practices," Research Committee Report No. 10 (Altamonte Springs, Fla., The Institute of Internal Auditors, Inc., 1961), p. 19.
3. D. L. Scantlebury, "The Structure of a Management Audit Finding," *The Internal Auditor*, March/April 1972, p. 10.
4. *Ibid.*, p. 12.
5. *Ibid.*, p. 14.
6. P. G. Seeman, "Effective Briefing or Oral Presentation," Internal Auditing Research Study, Lockheed-California Company, 1970.
7. S. H. Thomas, "Improving the Oral Communication of Internal Auditors," *The Internal Auditor*, Spring 1966, p. 69.
8. Research Committee Report 10, p. 22.
9. J. S. Fielden, "What Do You Mean I Can't Write," *Harvard Business Review*, May-June 1964, p. 147.
10. Joseph Lasky, "Proofreading and Copy-Presentation" (New York: Mentor Press, 1941), pp. 88-176.

Supplementary Reading

Bergman, F. L. et al. *From Auditing to Editing.* Washington, D. C.: U. S. Government Printing Office, 1976.

Flesch, R. F. *The ABC of Style: A Guide to Plain English.* New York: Harper and Row, 1964.

Gallagher, W. J. *Report Writing for Management.* Reading, Mass.: Addison-Wesley Publishing Company, 1969.

O'Hayre, John. *Gobbledygook Has Gotta Go.* Washington, D. C.: U. S. Government Printing Office, 1966.

Strunk, William, Jr. and E. B. White. *The Elements of Style.* New York: The Macmillan Company, 1959.

For further study

Discussion Problems

1. A deficient condition was described as follows in the draft on an audit report:

> In our test of automotive vehicles, we found that 35 automobiles had been serviced at intervals of 9 to 12 months. We reported this matter to the manager of the transportation department.

You are reviewing the draft for the completeness of this statement of deficient condition. Although you accept the sample of 35 automobiles as being sufficient, you are concerned about whether the presentation of findings as reported is adequate.

Required: Describe five elements which are missing from the quoted statements.

2. Heretofore, senior executives have not read your internal audit reports. You believe that these executives should be interested in receiving copies of your reports, particularly because you have expanded your audit program to cover operations throughout the entire organization.

Required: Identify three qualities — in terms of form and/or content — of internal audit reports which you believe will help capture and hold the interest of senior executives.

3. Discuss two functions of the audit report.

4. Describe at least three impediments to clarity.

5. How can internal auditors make their reporting timely and still turn out thoughtful, professional, formal reports?

6. What is meant by "tone" in an internal audit report?

7. How can the statements of purpose and scope contribute to understanding the audit report?

8. Distinguish between the authorization for and the objectives of an activity.

9. Name and describe the elements in the report of an unfavorable finding.

10. Describe at least three benefits of an oral report.

Multiple Choice Problems

1. A final audit report is most useful to executive managers when it:
a. Provides an overall, appropriately supported opinion on the operations reviewed.
b. Summarizes audit results.
c. Gives appropriate space to both satisfactory and unsatisfactory conditions.
d. Recognizes remedial action taken during the course of the audit.
e. All of the above.

2. The purpose of an opinion section in an internal audit report would be to:
a. Describe the audit findings.
b. Make audit recommendations.
c. Present audit conclusions.
d. All of the above.
e. None of the above.

3. Direct support for the internal audit report is provided by the:
a. Preliminary survey.
b. Walk-through of a facility.
c. Audit working papers.
d. Preliminary interview with the auditee.
e. All of the above.

4. To assure timeliness in reporting, an internal audit should:
a. Incorporate summaries in written reports.
b. Make reports as concise as possible.
c. Provide the auditee with progress reports during field work.
d. Reduce the number of working papers prepared.
e. Always issue reports as quickly as possible after completing the field work.

5. Internal audit reports should be effective and gain management's confidence when they:
a. Contain an objective viewpoint.
b. Describe the audit scope.

c. Include recommendations.
d. Exclude insignificant findings.
e. All of the above.

6. When an auditor says "I have found," it means:
a. He or she personally, or through assistants, observed the condition.
b. The condition is a matter of record.
c. A high-placed executive informed the auditor of the condition.
d. The condition was included in the working papers of the prior audit of the same activity.
e. None of the above.

7. The function of an introduction to a report is to include:
a. The purpose and scope.
b. An opinion.
c. Stage-setting.
d. Findings of fact.
e. Overall conclusions.

8. Reporting both favorable and unfavorable findings suggests:
a. The full story, leaving out nothing.
b. Objectivity.
c. Excellent coverage.
d. The willingness to write long reports.
e. None of the above.

9. If the purpose of the sentence is to show that the auditor wants to refrain from improving anything but procedures, the word "only" should be placed as follows:
a. We only wish to improve procedures.
b. We wish only to improve procedures.
c. Only we wish to improve procedures.
d. We wish to improve procedures only.
e. None of the above.

10. Which item is out of parallel?
We made our audit by:
a. Observing receipts.
b. Examining the documentation.
c. Reviewing the receiving register.
d. Interviewing of the inspectors.
e. b. and d. above.

Case Studies

13-1 Organizing the Auditor's Notes

The following sentences appear in the auditor's notes concerning an accounts payable activity. The sentences, which are in no logical order or grouping, are to be used in the audit report.

1. Generally, we were concerned with evaluating the system of control.
2. We did not seek to determine whether discounts were being taken.
3. The review of discounts was covered in a separate audit.
4. The accounts payable department is staffed by 15 employees.
5. Specifically, we set out to verify the sufficiency of the approvals and/or documentary support for the receipt of goods.
6. We found that written procedures were current and complete.
7. We were also concerned with the adequacy of distribution of charges to accounts.
8. We believe that the system of internal control is adequate.
9. The 15 accounts payable employees process 10,000 invoices each month.
10. Our test of 200 invoices requiring management approval showed that 35 were not approved.
11. In addition, the accounts payable employees process invoices for payment amounting to $30 million annually.
12. We believe the approval and support activities were not carried out satisfactorily.
13. Of 500 paid invoices we examined, 25% showed incorrect distributions to accounts.
14. We also believe that the function of distributing charges to accounts was not carried out satisfactorily.

Required: Construct a report outline using the following section headings and putting the numbers of the sentences under the appropriate headings in a logical, consistent order: Foreword, Purpose, Scope, Opinions, Statements of condition.

13-2 Writing Somebody Else's Report

Rod Grey called Dan Sutter into his office and said, "Sit down, my friend, I've got a lovely assignment for you."

Dan looked at Rod suspiciously and said, "I'm listening."

"You'll love it," cooed Rod. "It's right up your alley, seeing as how you're one of our best report writers."

Dan's suspicions deepened. "Let's have it without the window dressing," he growled.

"Okay, if that's the way you want it. Marv Johnson just went into the hospital for a gall bladder operation."

"Hey," said Dan, immediately forgetting his suspicions. "I didn't know."

"Happened suddenly," said Rod, becoming more serious. "He'll be out for a month or more."

"He was working on that conflict-of-interest job for you, wasn't he?" asked Dan.

"Right. And that's my problem. He finished the field work and developed a report outline; but that's as far as he got. So I need somebody to carry through."

"Sure," said Dan. "Glad to help. What can I do?"

"Write the report."

"Just like that?"

"Just like that. Actually it won't be difficult. I'd do it myself if I weren't sitting in for Paul. It's keeping me jumping and I don't have the time to write Marv's report. But it'll be a breeze for you."

"Why?" asked Dan.

"Marv has all the ingredients for the report. He's got two deficiency findings; but his records of audit findings are pretty clear. The management directive on conflict of interest is quite explicit. And Marv's report outline fills in the rest."

"Marv does a real workmanlike job," conceded Dan. "I shouldn't have any problems. But what's the big deal about conflict of interest? Why do we even bother to audit it?"

"Where have you been, my boy? This is a very high risk area. As an aftermath of a big conflict-of-interest exposé in industry, just about every large company has installed its own conflict-of-interest program."

"But there's no way of getting 100% assurance that there are no such conflicts actually existing in a company," protested Dan.

"True," said Rod, "but a company must do what is reasonable and prudent to provide a system of control calculated to expose conflicts. It's the only defense a company has if a conflict really surfaced and hit the headlines or if a stockholder at a stockholder's meeting started asking embarrassing questions; and believe me, they often do. Oh yes, we take our conflict program very seriously, and we must be absolutely certain that it's working the way it should."

"I hear you," said Dan. "Now, what kind of report do you want me to write?"

"I'll tell you what I'm gonna do."

Dan was immediately suspicious again. "What have you got up your sleeve?" he asked.

"A carte blanche," said Rod.

"Just what does that mean?"

"You've always been complaining that you don't like our stereotyped format. In our supervisors' meetings recently, Paul has been urging us to experiment with something new."

Dan's face brightened. "Great. When do I start?"

"Right now. Take the report outline, the two RAF's, the management directive (Marv had excerpted the pertinent parts) and prepare a report that has professionalism and yet is easy to read, that gives executive management an overview, and that gives line management the detail. Set it up any way you want. But be proud of it and be ready to fight for it. And remember that it is going to be distributed to the:

Executive Vice President
Vice President-Controller
Director of Industrial Relations
Manager of the Salaried Personnel
Director of Finance
Our Public Accountants

"Here are the files, Dan," said Rod. "You're on your own."

Required: Prepare a written internal audit report based on the information provided and constructed along the general guidelines laid out by Rod Grey. Determine for yourself the precise format you wish to use. The information that Rod gave Dan (Management directive, outline, RAF 1 and 2) follows.

MANAGEMENT DIRECTIVE 11—CONFLICT OF INTEREST

I. It is the policy of Able Company to

• • • •

    D. Require all salaried employees to disclose to the company (by short-form conflict-of-interest questionnaire) any private interest involving present or proposed employment or business association, gifts or monetary gains, major or influential business interest, or membership on a board of directors. In the event there is no private interest, the employee is required to make a declaration of "no interests." Annually, in February, require all signatories to reaffirm their position in regard to conflict of interest.

II. Responsibility is assigned and authority granted to

    A. Industrial Relations Branch to

        1. Establish and implement a companywide system for securing a completed conflict-of-interest questionnaire from (1) all incoming salaried personnel and employees being promoted from hourly to salaried status, and (2) all salaried personnel, annually, as a means of reaffirming or reflecting any changes in regard to conflict of interest.

        2. Centrally administer the distribution, collection, processing, and filing of all conflict-of-interest questionnaires. Ensure that all potential conflicts of interest disclosed by the questionnaires are referred to the division counsel for review.

    B. Division Counsel to

        1. Review all long-form conflict-of-interest questionnaires to determine whether a potential conflict of interest does, in fact, exist. If it does, refer the matter to a conflict-of-interest committee for final action. If no conflict appears to exist, so indicate on the questionnaire.

    C. Conflict-of-Interest Committee to

        1. Review situations referred to it by the division counsel that may involve conflict of interest.

        2. Make determinations and provide counsel as required to resolve conflict-of-interest situations.

        3. Provide additional policy determinations as may be necessary to guide the administration of this directive.

MD 11

Explanatory Remarks

1. The relationship of a corporate officer or employee to his corporation is basically that of agent and principal. While not technically a trustee, an agent does stand in a fiduciary relationship to his principal and is prohibited, by law, from engaging in activities injurious to the interest of his

principal or using his agency for his own personal profit. It is a cardinal rule that an agent must not, without his principal's consent, acquire adverse interest which might influence his judgment or his action in matters where his duty is single-minded furtherance of his principal's business. The rule of law which prohibits a corporate officer or employee from acting in a dual capacity in transacting the corporate business, and from acquiring interests adverse to his corporation, is applicable irrespective of his innocence or guilt or his state of mind and without regard to whether his action caused injury to the corporation.

2. A conflict of or adverse interest arises when an officer or an employee of a corporation has such a substantial personal interest in a transaction or is a party to a transaction that it reasonably might affect the judgment he exercises upon behalf of his corporation. The personal interest may arise through the expectation of future personal gain or through the existence of a personal obligation previously created, such as, from one extreme, a monetary bribe or secret ownership of property in which his corporation is dealing or secret ownership of a company or entity dealing with his corporation to, on the other hand, mere social obligation or social ambition.

3. Any corporate transaction in which a director, officer, or other employee has a personal interest might be adjudged void or at least voidable at the election of the corporation. Additionally, any profit which a director, officer, or other employee gains by reason of his personal interest in a transaction could be recovered by the corporation. In any event, if a government contract were involved, the director, officer, or other employee might be subject to criminal prosecution for fraud.

Conflict of Interest
Outline for Report

A. Introduction
    1. Regular review.
    2. Last review two years ago.
        a. One finding then — lack of written procedures.
        b. Did not recur.
    3. Mgmt. Dir. 11 covers conflict-of-interest program.
    4. Initial disclosure.
        a. New hires.
        b. Transfers from hourly to salary.
    5. Card form for disclosures — returned to personnel.
    6. Long form submitted:
        a. If short form shows potential conflict.
        b. Sent to Legal.
        c. If Legal sees conflict, form sent to conflict-of-interest committee.

B. Purpose and Scope
   1. Did company provide good control system?
   2. Was system working as it should?
   3. Specifically,
      a. Conduct of annual survey.
      b. Disclosures from new hires and from returning and promoted employees.
      c. Legal review of long-form questionnaires.
C. Opinions and Findings
   1. Annual survey.
      a. Control is Okay.
         (1) All salaried employees furnished questionnaire cards annually.
         (2) Instructions issued on completing them.
         (3) Provision for personnel dep't to review cards and follow up.
      b. Performance was unsatisfactory.
         (1) Large number of cards not returned.
         (2) No follow up. See RAF-1.
   2. Disclosures from new hires, etc.
      a. Control inadequate in part.
         (1) Provision to request cards from all new hired, rehired employees, employees promoted from hourly to salary status.
         (2) No provision for requesting cards from employees returning from prolonged absence.
      b. Performance ineffective in part.
         (1) Cards obtained from new hires, rehired employees, employees promoted from hourly to salary status.
         (2) No cards obtained from 5 employees returned from prolonged absence. See RAF-2.
   3. Legal review.
      a. Provision made to submit to Legal long-form questionnaires involving potential conflicts.
      b. Our test disclosed prompt resolution of all items submitted to Legal.

RECORD OF AUDIT FINDING

RAF No. *1*
W/P REF. No. *C-1-3*

Organization *Salaried Personnel Dept., Industrial Relations Branch*

Nature of findings:

A large number of conflict of interest questionnaires had not been returned to Sal. Pers. Dept. after the annual conflict of interest survey and Sal. Pers. employees had not followed up to obtain the cards.

Same finding disclosed in last audit: Yes _____   No ✔_____

Directives or procedures involved:

M.D. 11, "Conflict of Interest" calls for questionnaires each year from salaried employees.

Tests made:

Population size *5,000*   Sample size *300*
Method of sample selection *Every 16th name on Sal/PR after random start.*
Discrepancies: No. *40*   % *13*

Causes:

Persons given cards had been instructed to return them directly to Sal. Pers. Dept. Ind. Rel. had given follow-up low priority.

Corrective action: *Follow-up action initiated, asking affected dept. managers to obtain the executed cards from their salaried employees. Procedures developed to prevent recurrence in the future.*

Discussion with auditee personnel:

	Name	Title	Department	Date	Auditor
(1)	*D. Richards*	*Manager*	*Sal. Pers.*	*9/10/XX*	*M.J.*
(2)					
(3)					
(4)					

Comments by auditee personnel:

(1) *Acknowledged extent and significance of problem. Said he would promptly take corrective action to obtain missing cards and prevent similar occurrences.*
(2)
(3)
(4)

_____*M.J.*_____   _____*9/12/XX*_____
Auditor   Date

RECORD OF AUDIT FINDING

RAF No. 2
W/P REF. No. D-1-2

Organization *Salaried Personnel Dept., Industrial Relations Branch*

Nature of findings: *No provision had been made to request conflict of interest questionnaires from employees returning from prolonged absence. As a result no questionnaires were obtained from all 5 such employees since the last annual survey.*

Same finding disclosed in last audit: Yes _____   No ✔ _____

Directives or procedures involved: *M.D. 11, "Conflict of Interest," calls for questionnaires each year from salaried employees.*

Tests made:

Population size *5*   Sample size *5*
Method of sample selection *All employees returning p.a. last year.*
Discrepancies: No. *5*   % *100*

Causes: *Condition had never been encountered before, and so no provision had been made for people returning from p.a.*

Corrective action: *Job instruction issued to request C. of I. questionnaires in future. Questionnaires being requested of 5 employees in our test.*

Discussion with auditee personnel:

Name	Title	Department	Date	Auditor
(1) *D. Richards*	*Manager*	*Sal. Pers.*	*9/13/XX*	*M.J.*
(2)_____	_____	_____	_____	_____
(3)_____	_____	_____	_____	_____
(4)_____	_____	_____	_____	_____

Comments by auditee personnel:

(1) *Acknowledged extent and significance of problem. Will take corrective action. Issued job instructions same day. Told his people to obtain the 5 questionnaires.*
(2)
(3)
(4)

_____*M.J.*_____   _____*9/13/XX*_____
        Auditor   Date

14

Audit Report
Reviews And Replies

Report reviews: insurance and courtesy. Responsibility for assessing the adequacy of replies. Policy statement for the internal auditing department. The objectives of report reviews. Who reviews drafts of audit reports. Documenting the reviews. The dilemma of sufficient reviews versus prompt issuance of audit reports. Setting the stage for report reviews. Preparing for the hard questions. Referencing the working papers. Rules for avoiding conflicts. Accommodating the auditee with wording changes. Audit opinions are nonnegotiable. Determining the causes of deficient conditions. Estimates of the dollar effect of deficiencies. Allowing reviews of revisions to report drafts. The right to obtain replies to audit reports. Assessing the adequacy of replies to audit reports. Policy statement on assessing replies.

Introduction

Reviewing report drafts with auditees is both a form of insurance and a form of courtesy. And due concern for replies to published audit reports is an assumption of a proper audit responsibility.

Some audit organizations — albeit a minority — still refrain from reviewing drafts of audit reports with auditees before issuing the reports in final form. This is a kind of arrogance. It assumes omniscience on the part of the auditor. One thing the auditor is certainly not, particularly in operational matters, is omniscient.

Auditors in the field spend but a minute portion of time when compared to the time spent by the auditee. Auditors can, within that short span, isolate and identify problems. They cannot possibly be aware of all the nuances, the historical reasons, the oral executive mandates, the delicate interfaces with peripheral and other organizations, and the conflicting forces throughout the company that are usually involved in company operations. The auditors may have resolved problems at the working levels during their development of the audit findings — or they may think they have — but they may not have obtained the views of line management or middle management.

People at those levels may have significant information to offer that can give perspective or a new view to reported findings. They may add an ingredient to the finding that the auditors may not themselves be able to supply: the mature experience of the managers involved and their thorough understanding of the many facets of the problem.

If they cannot be omniscient, the auditors can at least be courteous. Showing line and middle management the draft of the report which will find its way to the executive desk is a gesture of courtesy. Auditors do not owe it to the auditee to be soft and tender. They may not gloss over what is adverse and significant. But they do owe fairness, candor, and consideration of others.

Often, the very way auditees regard auditors will affect their reaction to what is said about them in the draft report. If they see in the auditors fair, honest, competent individuals doing their job without rancor or an axe to grind, then they may gulp and accept the description of the most serious of findings. Their sole response will be to take corrective action.

But if the auditees see the findings in print for the first time when they read the final report, and if they do not regard the auditor personally in a favorable light, they may be resentful, defensive, and arbitrary. They may respond to the report with denials and excuses instead of with constructive, corrective action.

So aside from any considerations of the auditee's feelings, auditors must regard draft reviews in the light of their own self interest, as a way of getting their audit job done without unfortunate repercussions.

When audit reports call for replies and for both assurances and evidence of corrective action, internal auditors have a further obligation respecting the results of their audits.

Auditors must assume — with executive blessing — the responsibility for obtaining, reviewing, and assessing the adequacy of written replies to those reports requiring replies. If written replies are not mandated by executive management, busy line management may see no reason to take the time to consider them and respond to them.

Clearly, the auditors who have reported the conditions and made the recommendations are in the best position to assess the reasonableness of the response. Certainly, they have no right to dictate line management's course of action, but they do have the responsibility for seeing that the condition is corrected irrespective of whether the audit recommendations are followed to the letter. Put simply, then, the objectives of report reviews are:

To resolve conflicts.

To reach agreement on the facts.

To prevent argumentative replies.

To permit the auditee to see in advance the written word — which sometimes will be different from the spoken word.

The auditor's objectives in reviewing and evaluating written replies to reports are to ensure the auditees' proper consideration of the auditors' findings and recommendations, and to provide assurance that matters reported remain monitored until corrected.

Report Reviews

Who Reviews Report Drafts

Who reviews report drafts depends on the nature of the report itself and on the interest or concern of the individual managers and executives.

Draft reviews of a completely satisfactory report, with no deficiency findings or recommendations, and covering some relatively small and well-defined area or function, can be limited to the line manager and is or her superior. Although some believe totally satisfactory reports either should not be written at all or do not warrant the review time, such reports demonstrate audit objectivity. They give credit where due. They raise the auditor from the level of deficiency finder to that of objective analyst. They present a permanent record of audit coverage that management can see. They bring management and auditor together under pleasant circumstances and cement the understanding between the two. Therefore, the time devoted to drafting such a report and reviewing the draft with the auditee is time well spent.

Once the satisfactory report is drafted, the draft review becomes compulsory. It is insurance — to make sure the report has not overlooked significant aspects of the operation under audit. The draft review may point up needs for shifts of emphasis of which the auditors themselves are unaware. It may raise questions on the nature of the audit coverage. It may provide needed face-to-face discussions between auditors and management to establish good rapport for the future when different circumstances may make that rapport a significant foundation on which to build. It may construct a desirable image of the auditor in the eyes of management.

The reviews of the report describing deficient conditions call for different considerations. It should be reviewed with anyone who may be able to object with validity to its contents. It should be reviewed with anyone required to take action. It should be reviewed with anyone having responsibility for the area or condition needing corrective action — whether or not they personally would take that action or would be affected by the action.

Where the conditions are restricted to specific areas, the matter presents relatively few problems. But in functional audits crossing many lines, and in organizational audits bringing extensive defects to light or calling for extensive system overhauls, the report may require reviews that go through many organizations and to the executive level.

It is well for the auditing organization to furnish its staff with written instructions on draft reviews. In large organizations it may be easy to forget who should review what and in what order the reviews should take place (see Exhibit 14-1).

In general, reviews should be made with the auditee manager and his or her superior. Yet some branch directors may wish to see all drafts of reports affecting their branches. Auditors should be glad to comply; but they should also tactfully point to the need for promptness, so that the reviews will not delay the issuance of the final report.

Reports calling for systems changes should be reviewed with the procedures people or with systems analysts such as the industrial engineers or EDP analysts.

In instances where the auditor has conducted a review at the line level, it may be well to ask whether reviews at higher levels are necessary. Auditees generally have a good idea how their superiors regard audit reports. Their views on whether or not to go higher should be given full consideration. And where line or middle management people say that no further reviews are needed, those comments should be carefully recorded in the working papers. These records can defend the auditor if he or she is accused of withholding information. After the final report is issued, the auditor may receive a call from higher management asking why the report was not reviewed in draft at that level. Having taken the proper steps, the auditor can respond by explaining normal practices, and stating exactly who said that further reviews were unnecessary, giving the time and date of the statement, and offering to ensure higher management reviews in the future — if the manager so wishes.

Experienced auditors are usually aware of those people with whom they have trouble in draft reviews. The reviews may be dreaded and the sessions may be unpleasant experiences. Sometimes these confrontations just cannot be helped, but they may be alleviated. For example, the auditor may try to include in the review conference the supervisor of the troublesome individual. This may have a salutary tendency to keep the meeting less turbulent.

In all cases the report reviews should be carefully documented. The results of the review should be recorded in the working papers immediately after the conference so that no significant matter, comment, or decision is lost. These notes can be very important in the event of later dispute.

Timing the Reviews

Obviously, the greater the number of draft reviews the longer the delay

---

Exhibit 14-1. ABC CORPORATION INTERNAL
AUDITING DEPARTMENT

REVIEWS OF DRAFT REPORTS

Policy

It is the policy of internal auditing to review drafts of audit reports with the management personnel responsible for the activities examined — in advance of the formal release of the reports.

Order

The review should begin with responsible line management and proceed, as necessary, through the branch level of management. As a minimum, the draft should be reviewed with the manager responsible for the activity and with his or her superior. Reviews may be held at levels beyond the branch director when circumstances warrant. Such reviews should be approved in advance by the audit manager.

Form of Review

The individual drafts should be reviewed to the extent necessary — in whole or in part; or through the oral or the written word, or a combination of the two. To this end the auditor should remember that the purpose of these reviews is to obtain agreement on the facts and to make sure management people understand the key statements in the report: The report is the responsibility of the auditor, not the auditee; hence, the review process is designed to ensure a proper interpretation of what the auditor has written, not what the auditee would like to see written.

Disagreement as to interpretations is another matter. The auditor should make an earnest effort to resolve such disagreements. But if all reasonable attempts at reconciling differences have proved fruitless, the report should clearly set forth the positions of both the auditor and the operating manager for the benefit of higher management.

---

in issuing the final report. This places the auditors in a dilemma. On the one hand they wish to afford all those who "need to know" the opportunity to review the draft. On the other hand, they are aware of the need for current reporting.

The problem is not insuperable, however. It does require pressure and setting deadlines, both for the auditors and the reviewers. After drafting their reports, auditors should prepare a list of distributees. Together with audit supervisors they should decide which people should review the report draft and what the order of those reviews should be.

The order is important. The list of draft reviewers should begin with those who are most closely involved in or affected by the report. They are the ones most likely to have suggestions for changes, objections to phrasing, or disputes as to facts. They are the ones with whom the report should be reviewed face to face, if possible, to iron out differences and to obtain agreement on the facts.

Thereafter, the draft can be duplicated and sent to all other concerned individuals for review. The transmittal memo should identify the report, indicate with whom it has been reviewed, offer to discuss it in person, and set a date for its return (see Exhibit 14-2).

Exhibit 14.2. TRANSMITTAL MEMORANDUM

To: Draft Reviewer
From: Auditor
Subject: Draft Report — Review of Controls Over Conflicts of Interest

Here is the subject report draft for your review. It has already been reviewed with A. B. See, E. F. Gee, and H. I. Jay. They were in agreement with the matters described in the draft which reflects changes resulting from their reviews.

If you have any questions on the draft or wish to discuss it, please call me. Otherwise, kindly have your secretary return the draft after your review.

We would appreciate your giving the draft your prompt attention, since we plan to put it in final form on Wednesday, July 10, 19XX.

_____ Internal Auditor

This memorandum can be used to submit draft reports to reviewers in other cities. Distance should not prevent draft reviews. Reviewers in other cities should be afforded the same courtesy as those in the central offices.

The Review Conference

The draft review can be either a grim confrontation or an open and courteous discussion. True, the auditor presumably has discussed all findings with the auditee. But a comprehensive written draft, showing distribution to executive management, somehow has a different impact from informal reports or oral discussions.

It is the auditor's conference. He or she can and should influence its course. No matter how serious the findings are, the auditor who is sensitive to the feelings of others can put the draft in a perspective that takes much of the harshness out of it.

No draft review should be started abruptly. There should be a setting of the stage. There should be an attempt to bring about a pleasant atmosphere. The more critical the report, the more attention is needed for proper preliminaries. Somehow, in some way, the feeling should be developed that what is reported is not said in rancor but in the spirit of correcting unfortunate conditions. Here are some of the matters to consider in orally setting the stage:

The scope of the examination.

The significance of the matters reviewed.

An acknowledgement of the difficulties which face the auditee in carrying out his responsibilities.

The cooperation obtained during the audit.

The fact that the report contains no surprises — that all findings were discussed during the field work. (If the auditor has not done so, there is no one else to blame for antagonism during the draft review.)

Comments on how many matters are already corrected, how many are in process of correction, and how many are still to be corrected.

A willingness to discuss all matters in whatever detail is necessary.

Avoiding and Resolving Conflicts

It would be wishful thinking for the auditor to expect every draft review to be conducted without conflict, no matter how well the internal auditing function may be accepted in the company. Indeed, the stronger the auditor's position, the greater the auditee's concern with what the report has to say to superiors.

Auditors must therefore be prepared — thoroughly prepared — for conflict and dispute. They must be able to retrieve information, support facts, and amplify findings without difficulty or delay. It is embarrassing to the auditor and unnerving to supervisors to see an aimless fumbling through volumes of audit working papers when it becomes necessary to offer evidence to back up reported statements. The room is hushed. The conversation has ceased. All eyes are on the hapless auditor flipping the papers, passing by the desired documents time and again in utter confusion.

Auditors can avoid these awful moments by being aware that every critical comment may evoke objection and a call for additional proof. They can rise to the challenge with forethought and preparation. Their own copy of the report draft should be copiously annotated in the margin with references to the supporting detail. This simple preparation pays big dividends.

Suppose the auditee says, "I can't believe that this particular function that you're talking about is my responsibility." Internal auditors who are prepared look for the proper marginal notation in the draft. They then turn immediately to the copy of the appropriate directive in the working papers. There, underlined in red — if they have done their homework — for all to see, is the particular statement which assigned responsibility to the auditee.

Suppose the auditee asks, "Are you sure there are no procedures on the subject?" The auditors — again, if they have done their homework — promptly turn to a work sheet which shows that on a particular date they spoke to the individual responsible for preparing such instructions and learned that indeed no procedure had been issued, and why such a condition existed.

References to records of audit findings (see Chapter 7) showing all relevant details of deficiencies can be invaluable. They can give ready information on the population sampled, the manner of sample selection, the proof that the sample was representative, the citations to directives, the causes, the effects, and the people with whom the conditions were discussed.

When auditors must go through an agony of fumbling for each piece of information needed to support their position, their credibility and the credibility of their report decline. When, on the other hand, they are able to answer each question promptly and fully, when their working papers appear to be a readily accessible storehouse of easily retrieved information, the stream of objections and questions quickly dries up.

Serious disagreements are bound to occur. The draft makes a statement. The auditee makes a contradictory statement. The auditor disagrees with it. An impasse occurs. How, then, to resolve the disagreement and go on with the business of the review?

Auditors must recognize that the auditee is on the defensive. Somehow that defensive barrier must be removed and agreement reached. Here are some rules that might help:

Have good manners. It is just plain bad manners to say bluntly "I disagree with you" or "You're wrong." It is worse manners to use such words as "idiotic," "ridiculous," or "nonsense." Besides, it is poor judgment. Under this kind of attack, the auditee either lashes back or withdraws. More important, communication is destroyed and the auditor's objectives may not be met.

Use nonpersonal phrases. In disagreeing, avoid starting a sentence with "You." That implies disagreeing with the individual rather than with the concept or idea. Use neutral phrases: "It might be worth considering . . . " "There might be a possibility that . . . " "Perhaps it might be useful to explore . . . ." These phrases, being impersonal, seldom arouse emotions — certainly not the emotions aroused by "You haven't thought of . . . " "You've forgotten . . . " "You don't realize . . . " "You don't know about . . . ." Never underestimate the emotional impact of certain words.

Get on common ground. Where an impasse appears to be reached, step back until some point can be agreed upon — even if it is just agreement that the problem is not an easy one to solve. Stand on that ground until tempers are calmed and the auditee is comfortable enough to be willing to discuss reasonably the matters at issue.

Don't back anyone into a corner. Do not press auditees for a clear statement that they have reversed themselves. If they finally go along with a point, resist the temptation. Don't say something like "I'm glad you finally see things my way." The auditors' objective is to get their conclusions and recommendations across. It doesn't really matter whether or not the auditees changed their minds.

Don't mistake airing of views with disagreement. Often all that is necessary is to let the auditees talk themselves out. Perhaps they do not really disagree but merely want a chance to justify their position or to explain the reasons for the conditions that the auditors found. After they have made their point, they might be perfectly willing to let the wording of the draft stand as written.

When there is irreconcilable disagreement, when no mutual ground can be reached, auditors have a responsibility to give the auditee's views equal prominence with their own. The auditors may then point out that they must report matters as they see them and that they will report the auditee's views as well.

In some situations, the mere offer to quote the auditee will reconcile the disagreement. If auditees secretly realize that they are in an untenable position, they would not want that position paraded before their superiors in the body of an audit report. But when there is an honest disagreement on interpretations — but never on the facts; they **must** be agreed upon — the auditee's views should be incorporated in the report.

It is common courtesy, of course, to ask the auditees to read the added material to make sure they will not feel they were misquoted.

Auditors should not be inflexible. They must recognize that people are understandably defensive. They must recognize that their reports may visit executive wrath on the head of the auditee. They must understand that words mean different things to different people. They must be sufficiently realistic to recognize that it is possible for them to be wrong. Hence, they should be willing to substitute words and phrases that do not destroy the meaning they wish to convey if, by so doing, they will make the auditee feel more comfortable.

They should also heed the auditee in matters of perspective or relevance. It may well be that what the auditor considers the heart of a function was really only a side issue. It may also be that what the auditor was told at the working level failed to take into account matters not known at that level. Auditors must be prepared to adjust accordingly. They must try to maintain a reputation for fairness, for objectivity, and for concern solely with what is factual and significant. To that end they should not be averse to changes that make for better reports.

Audit Opinions

There are some suggestions for change with which the auditor cannot agree: those affecting the audit opinion. That opinion cannot be delegated. It cannot be compromised. It can be only what the auditor can defend and support and is willing to attest to by his or her signature. Auditors cannot substitute someone else's opinion for their own.

The professional opinions of auditors cannot be negotiated. Those opinions are either what they honestly believe, based on what they have seen, or they are nothing. Thus, it must be clearly understood that while the auditors will discuss facts and the meaning of facts, the audit opinion is not subject to give and take. Of course, new facts that are brought to light may have an effect on the audit opinion, but it is still the auditor's opinion, based on all the facts.

Cause and Effect

Executive management is vitally concerned with the causes and effects of the conditions the auditor reports. The understanding of cause and effect may be a significant factor in making executive decisions. It is well, therefore, for the auditor to explore these matters during the draft review. Very often line management is in the best position to advance the reasons for the deficient conditions, and the manager's views on the subject should be sought and carefully considered.

Auditors should probe for the reasons so that they can be sure that proposed corrective action is aimed at the causes, not the symptoms. For example:

Was management aware of the problem?

Was the problem traceable to inadequate instruction or insufficient training of personnel?

Did the condition occur because supervisors were not adequately monitoring the ongoing process?

Were improper priorities assigned?

Were insufficient resources provided?

Did the need for controls go unrecognized?

Was there lack of coordination with an interfacing organization?

Were conditions caused by human error?

Were the defects attributable to the attitudes of the employees? of the supervisors? of the manager?

One source of conflict in the audit report is the auditor's statement of the effect of deficient conditions. The auditor's estimate of the amounts of money lost or potentially lost can be a source of irritation to the auditee whose superiors readily understand such numbers; and if the auditee considers them inflated, it will just be another point for dispute. Hence, it is important during the draft reviews to win agreement on the effects of deficiencies. In that vein, the auditor should come to the draft review prepared to demonstrate the validity of such estimates.

Reviewing Revisions

As the draft report goes through its course of reviews, some changes may be made. Their significance becomes a matter of judgment. So does the need to review the changed wording with those who have not seen the revisions.

Certainly, if auditees are now called upon to take action that they were unaware of in the first review, they are entitled to see the draft again as modified. They are especially entitled when, as a result of subsequent reviews, the draft places the auditee in a less favorable light or quotes the auditee or attributes an action to the auditee.

Sometimes the changes can be communicated by telephone. Auditors, in the interest of prompt report release, should try that method first. If they are unsuccessful, they will have to let the auditee see the changes. Sometimes those changes are merely word substitutions that often do not call for reviews. The chief criterion must be the maintenance of the auditor's reputation for fairness and objectivity and the assurance that no sides are taken.

Replies to Reports

The internal auditing department which does not have the authority to demand replies to its reported findings and evaluate the adequacy of the corrective action has its effectiveness diminished.

Management directives or policy statements must spell out clearly that audit reports calling for corrective action must be responded to in writing. Usually these directives and statements establish time limits for submitting replies. The distribution sheet in one company bears this statement regarding replies:

> An "x" following your name in the column "For Securing Action" means that you are responsible for seeing that satisfactory action is taken with respect to the findings which are referred for action to persons under your jurisdiction.
>
> Management Directive XX requires you to see that an adequate reply, describing the action taken, is sent to the Vice President Finance and Controller within thirty days after the audit report release date, with a copy to the Director of Internal Auditing. If action cannot be completed within this time limit, the Vice President Finance and Controller should be informed of the reason for the delay and when the final report may be expected.

It is desirable for each operating branch or division to have its own instructions regarding replies to audit reports. These instructions should state: Who should prepare the reply. Who should sign it. How the reply should be written (straightforward, addressing itself to the findings and not trying to justify the status quo). What steps should be taken if corrective action cannot be completed within the established time span.

The internal auditors should let it be known that they will be willing to discuss corrective action and review drafts of replies. At the same time, the auditors should scrupulously respect the difference between staff and line. The line people must live with the corrective action they take. The auditors are responsible for pointing out defects and recommending a course of action — not the course of action. Still, auditors must have the right to evaluate corrective action and declare it inadequate if it will not or does not cure the defect.

Exhibit 14-3. FORMAL CLOSING MEMORANDUM

To: Director of Internal Auditing

From: Auditor

Subject: Replies to report dated_____, Project No._____

          Title_____

Ref: Replies:

Date	From
_____	_____
_____	_____
_____	_____

We have received the referenced replies describing the action taken on findings discussed in the subject report. Our evaluation of this action is as follows:

	Reference to
Evaluation	Findings

Considered an Interim Reply:

    Appears satisfactory. Awaiting final reply.

    Does not appear satisfactory. We are investigating.

Considered a Final Reply:

    Appears satisfactory. Finding considered closed.

    Appears satisfactory; but the action described needs confirmation before the finding can be considered closed.

    Appears unsatisfactory; needs further investigation.

The action indicated in the referenced replies does _____ does not _____ constitute completion of satisfactory action on all the findings described in the subject report. Accordingly, we recommend that Project No. _____ be _____ not be _____ closed at this time.

                                     Auditor

Reports should remain open until the auditing organization considers the replies satisfactory. Some auditing organizations will not be satisfied solely with the statement of corrective action in a reply from the auditee. They may wish to return to the audit site to satisfy themselves that effective action has indeed been taken. They may schedule interim examinations within a period of six months or a year to make sure the reported deficiencies have not recurred.

When replies are unsatisfactory, and agreement cannot be reached orally with the auditee, the reply should be formally rejected by memorandum.

The memorandum should spell out specifically in what respects the reply is deficient. Copies of the reply should be addressed to whatever level of management is needed to see that the matter is satisfactorily resolved.

The auditing department should have a formal method of closing reports that have been satisfactorily responded to. This may be in the form of a memorandum to the director of auditing bearing the signature of the auditor. The memorandum should state that the auditor is satisfied with the response and that the report may now be closed. Exhibit 14-3 is an example of such a memorandum.

Different companies follow different reporting practices. But there seems to be a uniform feeling about the need for follow-up procedures — with management's interest and support. Exhibit 14-4 is an example of a procedure covering replies to audit reports.

Exhibit 14-4.

ABC CORPORATION
INTERNAL AUDITING DEPARTMENT
REPLIES TO AUDIT REPORTS

Policy

Internal auditors are responsible for bringing to the attention of executive management any significant risks to the Company. A reported deficiency that has not adequately been corrected is regarded as such a risk. At the same time, the responsibility for seeing that unsatisfactory conditions are properly corrected is assigned to operating management. The responsibility to evaluate the corrective action and to determine whether it is both responsive and effective is assigned to the Internal Auditing Department.

So as to have some assurance that operating managers will take corrective action promptly, they are asked in the instructions on the report distribution sheet to reply to the executive vice president in writing when there are findings requiring corrective action. The reply must outline action taken to correct the unsatisfactory conditions reported and must bear the approval of all persons responsible for securing action. If any of the corrective action described in the reply is merely proposed and not completed, or is deferred to some future date, the reply should indicate the date when corrective action will be completed. A final reply should be made when all the corrective action has been completed.

Action Required

When replies are received they will be reviewed by the auditor in charge, the supervisor concerned, and the audit manager. If the reply seems likely to dispose satisfactorily of the findings reported, the in-charge auditor should inform the director of internal auditing on the form provided for that purpose. The auditor should describe any matters subsequently discussed with operating management, such as action taken which is not clearly described in the reply, or action which does not conform to recommendations but which is felt to be worth a trial. This form should close the project.

Exhibit 14-4. (Cont.)

If the corrective action described in the reply does not seem likely to correct the conditions reported, further action on the part of the in-charge auditor or supervisor is necessary. This may take the form of discussion with the operating manager in order to clear up any questions or misunderstandings which may not have been cleared up in the review of the draft report, and to clear up any questions regarding action taken or to be taken which may not have been expressed clearly enough in the reply.

In any event, the objective is to secure some agreement or understanding as to an acceptable course of action with a minimum of further correspondence. It is therefore important to have clearly in mind what is meant by an acceptable course of action. This does not necessarily mean the adoption of all the recommendations made in a report in precisely the manner set forth. As operating management has the responsibility for correcting unsatisfactory conditions it also has been given the authority to decide how it should be done. Accordingly, in the absence of considerations of such importance as to cause the executive vice president or other members of top management to intervene, operating management will be free to accept, to accept with modifications, or to reject, any recommendations made. What is meant then is some course which at least does not seem so objectionable that it should not be given a trial.

Where no action is taken or the action taken or proposed seems clearly unsatisfactory and operating management seems unwilling to take any action which will satisfactorily dispose of the matter, a letter should be prepared for the signature of the executive vice president. It should state the auditor's position on the unsatisfactory conditions. These letters should be addressed to branch managers.

Monitoring Replies

The audit manager will delegate to the secretary or to a member of the staff the responsibility for keeping a record of replies required but not received.

When a reply has not been received within one month after the date of the report, the person responsible for keeping the record will notify the supervisor responsible. The supervisor will then make, or will have the auditor make, whatever inquiries seem to be necessary to determine when the reply might be expected. Thereafter, further inquiries will be made at intervals until different action is desirable.

At this point the supervisor may write a formal letter of inquiry for the signature of the executive vice president. That letter should be addressed to the person from whom the auditor's report requested the reply and should be forwarded through the director of internal auditing for the signature of the executive vice president. From that point on, the nature of any further action will depend on the kind of response received from operating management, or on the nature of any instructions received from the executive vice president.

The audit manager will submit a monthly report not later than the tenth of each month showing the status of replies. Copies should be provided for the executive vice president, the director of internal auditing, and the audit manager.

Conclusion

Report reviews are both insurance for the auditor and courtesy to the auditee. They are important in resolving conflicts, establishing facts, and preventing disputatious replies.

The right to obtain and review replies to reports ensures proper consideration of the auditor's findings and recommendations and sees to it that deficient conditions are monitored until corrected. The auditor must be given final responsibility for deciding on the adequacy of replies to audit reports. Management directives should spell out the auditor's authority to evaluate replies. Line management has the authority to decide what corrective action to take; internal auditors should have the authority to decide whether the action does in fact correct the deficiency.

Auditors must carefully consider the people with whom the reports should be reviewed and the order of the consecutive reviews. During the review conferences they should try to set the stage for a calm and friendly discussion. Yet they must be aware of potential conflicts and be prepared to resolve them. They must be amply equipped to present prompt and unequivocal support for their findings. They should be flexible in making word changes, but they must not relinquish their right to express their own professional opinions.

Executive management is vitally interested in the causes and effects of deficient conditions. These causes and effects should be explored and their description agreed upon in draft review.

Supplementary Reading

Hallinan, A. J. "There Is No Escape From Follow-up Except . . . ." *The Internal Auditor*, January/February 1974, pp. 31-37.

Tillman, J. R. "Preventive Controls: An Approach to Internal Auditing." *The Internal Auditor*, March/April 1973, pp. 55, 56.

For further study

Discussion Problems

1. You are conducting the first audit of the marketing activities of your organization. Your preliminary survey has disclosed indications of deficient conditions of a serious nature. You expect your field work to document the need for substantial corrective action. You feel certain that your audit report will contain descriptions of a number of serious defects.

Your preliminary meeting with the director of the marketing division and the principal subordinates gave you reason to believe that they will be defensive, that the draft of the audit report will receive a chilly reception, that your stated facts are likely to be challenged, and that any deficient conditions reported will be denied or minimized.

Required: Identify five techniques you might use to improve the chances that your draft report will be well received and that appropriate corrective action will be taken.

2. It is the policy of your company that the internal auditing department follow up its audit reports to make sure that appropriate action is taken.

Required: List five procedures for following up on audit reports.

3. You have completed an audit of a warehousing function. You found a number of deficient conditions, all of which you consider significant. You have discussed these with the warehousing manager during both the field work and the review of the report draft. The manager has told you that he will take corrective action only if his superior agrees it is warranted. The superior is a difficult person to convince and is sure to ask many pertinent questions about the findings. Accordingly you want to anticipate the questions by applying your own rigorous criteria to the findings.

Required: List at least three criteria, other than materiality, that you should apply to the statements of deficient conditions to determine whether they warrant corrective action.

4. You have made an audit of inventory storage practices. You brought to light many deficient conditions: Parts were not stacked neatly. First-in, first-out rules were not being observed. Parts were often not labeled or were labeled incorrectly. Many parts were not in their assigned bins. The bin records and the book records often disagreed.

Your report listed each individual discrepancy disclosed by your audit sample. The reply to the audit report addressed itself to each discrepancy reported and provided evidence that it had been corrected. No other action was taken.

Required: State whether you consider the reply satisfactory. Give reasons.

5. You have inaugurated an internal auditing function where none had existed before. Your first audit resulted in a number of material deficiency findings. The report review with the auditee manager went well. In fact, the operating manager congratulated you on the breadth and depth of your audit coverage and on the perception you displayed in pointing out some serious weaknesses. At the end of the report review you asked the manager when you could expect a reply to the report since none of the deficiencies had been corrected. He said casually that he'd reply or not depending on whether he could get around to it. He then rose from his desk and terminated the meeting then and there.

Required: Describe the action you will have to take to make sure that audit reports citing deficiencies will be answered and that the answers will be prompt and complete.

Multiple Choice Problems

1. One of the auditor's chief objectives in reviewing draft reports with auditees is to:
a. Eliminate typographical errors.
b. Validate the audit opinion.
c. Make sure there are no disputes with the facts.
d. Reach agreement on report distribution.
e. Both a. and b.

2. The auditor's objectives in obtaining replies to reported audit findings is to:
a. Make sure the reported unsatisfactory conditions have been corrected.

b. Complete the audit file.
c. Comply with office procedures.
d. Establish the auditor's authority.
e. Make sure the audit recommendations were adopted.

3. When a great many people should review the draft of a report, the auditor may mail the report to them with a request to:
a. Read the report carefully.
b. Return the report with comments by a given day.
c. Make a copy for their files and return the draft.
d. Certify to having read the draft.
e. Complete corrective action by a date set forth in the audit report.

4. One way the auditor can set the stage for a review conference is to:
a. State that the draft is tentative, subject to negotiation.
b. State that the review is a matter of courtesy and that no suggested changes will be accepted.
c. Explain the scope of the examination and the significance of the subject matter.
d. Set a time limit on the discussion of the audit report.
e. Arrive on time.

5. The auditor can be reasonably sure of prompt answers to the auditee's questions during the report review if he or she:
a. Memorizes all salient parts of the working papers.
b. Gives the papers to the auditee in advance of the meeting.
c. Duplicates the working papers.
d. References the report, in the margin, to the working papers.
e. Asks for the questions in advance.

6. The auditor should use phrases like this when disputes arise during the draft reviews:
a. You don't realize . . .

b. It might be worth exploring . . .
c. You haven't thought of . . .
d. You don't know about . . .
e. I really don't have all the answers . . .

7. If the auditee finally goes along with your point:
a. Don't press for acknowledgement that their position is now reversed.
b. Say "I'm glad you finally see things my way."
c. Write it down and have him or her sign it.
d. Ask for a repetition of the statement.
e. Clearly express your relief.

8. When there is irreconcilable disagreement on matters of interpretation, and when no mutual grounds can be found, the auditor should:
a. Stop the conference and issue the audit report.
b. Give the auditee's views equal prominence with the auditor's views in the report.
c. Write a special memorandum about the impasse to the auditee's superiors.
d. Report the auditor's views and state in a footnote that the auditee disagrees.
e. Not issue a report.

9. To make sure significant deficiencies have not recurred, the auditor should:
a. Set up interim reviews between the regular ones.
b. Call the auditee periodically.
c. Report the findings to the board of directors.
d. Report the findings to the chief of security.
e. All of the above.

10. The individual who should have the authority to pass on the adequacy of a reply to a reported deficiency is:
a. The controller.
b. The auditee.
c. The auditee's superior.
d. The auditor.
e. None of the above.

Case Studies

14-1 Report Reviews Without the Report

Paul Eberhardt picked up the intercom and buzzed Rod Grey. "How far have you gotten on that highway transportation job, Rod?"

"I've finished the report draft," answered Rod. "Why?"

"The Director of Materiel, Jack Hansen, knows you've been on the job and wants to review your findings with you whenever you've wrapped them up."

"I'll be happy to oblige," Rod replied.

"That's what you think," said Paul.

"Why?"

"Have you ever been in a report review with him?"

"Not yet."

"He doesn't like to read reports. He likes to be told about the findings."

"That's odd."

"Odd or not, that's the way he wants it, and we're here to oblige. On Bob's last job in the materiel area, he handed Jack Hansen the draft, and Jack handed it back and said, 'Tell me about it.' Bob was kind of taken aback, but he managed to fumble his way through."

"In that case I think I'd better make a flip chart presentation."

"Good idea," agreed Paul. "And be prepared to answer questions. Jack is pretty sharp."

"I'll have Marv Johnson, the auditor in charge of the job, work on the charts with me and then go up with me when I see Jack."

"Okay. Keep the charts simple. We don't want Jack thinking that we took a lot of time to put on a dog and pony show for him."

"Will do."

Required: Prepare flip charts of the audit findings reported in The Highway Transportation report in Chapter 13.

14-2 Be Responsive or Else

Paul stopped at Rod Grey's office and asked, "Have you seen the reply to your report on hoists and cranes?"

"Sure have," said Rod. "I got my copy this morning."

"What do you think of it?"

"It's just not responsive."

"Have you done anything about it?"

"I called Bob Seaver and told him his proposed fix falls short of doing the job."

"Good. And what did he say?"

"He told me that it was good enough and would I kindly get off his back and let him get back to his job."

"Brief me on the situation," said Paul.

"As you know, we're making a series of safety audits. This one was on hoists and cranes — different types of lifting and carrying devices."

"What are the criteria?" asked Paul.

"Before a new or repaired lifting device is put into operation, it must be proof-loaded."

"What's that?"

"Tested to see if it will lift what it's supposed to lift. They'll test it to 150% of capacity. Government safety rules call for 125%, but we're supercautious."

"How's the proof-loading done?"

"It's done with standard weights in the presence of a tool engineer and a maintenance engineer. If the lifting device doesn't check out, it is rejected. If it does check out, the tool engineer sends a copy of the tool order, signed-off to prove that the device was tested, back to maintenance. Also, he puts a tag on the device itself as evidence of the proof-loading."

"What is maintenance supposed to do?"

"They set the item up on their maintenance record, and every six months a card pops up and a preventive maintenance order (PMO) is issued to do the maintenance work."

"So if a hoist isn't proof-loaded, it might fall and cause injury. And if the approval of the hoist isn't communicated to maintenance, the hoists might not receive maintenance. Right?"

"Absolutely right," agreed Rod.

"Do the procedures spell these things out?"

"They do not," said Rod. "This is all a matter of practice."

"Did we report the lack of written procedures?"

"You bet."

"Okay," said Paul. "Now what were the facts — the conditions disclosed by your tests?"

"We have 850 lifting devices in the company. We checked 100 of them. We found that 4 out of 100 had never

been proof-tested and that 6 out of 100 had not been reported to maintenance."

"Why? What was the cause?" asked Paul.

"So far as we could tell, people goofed or had not been properly instructed. Based on our discussions with the people, I'm convinced that the lack of written procedures had something to do with it."

"What are the actual or potential results?"

"First, the six lifting devices never got their 6-month maintenance. Second, we have no assurance that the four devices won't drop things on somebody's head."

"What did Bob Seaver say?"

"He said that he has proof-loaded the four and set up maintenance records on the six. That's it, that's all," said Rod.

"And he wouldn't respond to your suggestion to go further?"

"Absolutely not," said Rod.

"We'll see about that. Prepare a memo to him for Jan Tobias's signature, setting out why we think his response is unsatisfactory."

Required: Prepare the memo to Bob Seaver, for the vice president's signature.

15
Reports To Executive Management And The Board

Summary and activity reports. Reporting requirements of the *Standards for the Professional Practice of Internal Auditing*. Administrative records and forms to help in preparing summary and activity reports. Reports of recoveries and savings. Example of a summary report. Reporting various types of audit activities. Graphic reports. Activity reports on the administrative health of the enterprise. Summarizing the various types of deficiency findings: major versus minor and control versus performance. Reporting causes of deficiencies. Reporting on the nature of deficiency findings encountered.

What Reports Do

Reports to executive management and the board of directors, usually through the audit committee, have two purposes. One is to tell what internal auditing has accomplished. The other is to tell what internal auditing has observed. In this book, we shall call the former activity reports and the latter evaluation reports.

Activity reports tell the extent to which internal auditing managed to meet the goals it set for itself. They describe the scope and the depth of the internal audit effort. They summarize corrective action taken as a result of internal audits. They demonstrate how the audits have helped protect the enterprise by monitoring the adequacy and effectiveness of the various systems of controls.

Evaluation reports supply management and the board with information about the enterprise not available elsewhere. Financial reports, audited by the independent accountants, supply objective information on the financial health of the enterprise. Operating reports describe operations from the standpoint of operating managers, and may or may not be completely objective. Evaluation reports by internal auditors, however, supply objective information on the operating health of the enterprise and serve to supplement external auditors' management letters.

Activity and evaluation reports have been used by many internal auditing departments for some time, but rarely have they been mandated. Usually, they are another service to management and the board which internal auditors of their own volition decided to provide. An air of urgency, however, was created by the *Standards for the Professional Practice of Internal Auditing.* Section 110.01 of the *Standards* spells out the obligation of directors of internal auditing to submit such reports (see Appendix A) as follows:

.5 The director of internal auditing should submit annually to management for approval and to the board for its information a summary of the department's audit work schedule, staffing plan, and financial budget. The director should also submit all significant interim changes for approval and information. Audit work schedules, staffing plans, and financial budgets should inform management and the board of the scope of internal auditing work and of any limitations placed on that scope.

.6 The director of internal auditing should submit activity reports to management and to the board annually or more frequently as necessary. Activity reports should highlight significant findings and recommendations and should inform management and the board of any significant deviations from approved audit work schedules, staffing plans, and financial budgets, and the reasons for them.

Activity Reports

Some internal auditors take the position that activity reports are unnecessary; that their current internal audit reports — those issued to show the results of specific audits — are the best evidence of audit accomplishment. These provide valuable information and point to matters needing corrective action, but they are like yesterday's newspaper. They are obscured by the rush of time and events, and rarely are they read by board members. These current audit reports need to be summarized so as to present a totality of internal audit accomplishment. When this is done artfully, it will seize and retain the interest of both executive management and the board.

Internal audit accomplishments can often boast a dollar sign, capturing more attention than most other accomplishments. When internal auditors save or recover more than their services cost, they thereby offer a potent reason to retain or even expand the audit department. Certainly, such savings and recoveries should have a prominent place in activity reports.

But dollar return is only one of the audit accomplishments — often it can be the least of them in terms of service to the organization. When a dry year passes with little or no dollar recovery; internal auditors who rely exclusively on the dollar sign may be embarrassed. Preferably the constructive and protective aspects of their work are also stressed. The Foreign Corrupt Practices Act in the United States, for example, makes systems improvement and integrity powerful objectives for internal auditing and a matter of serious concern to management and the board.

Internal auditors must periodically call to executive and board attention these summaries of accomplishments, both monetary and other, to demonstrate the value of internal audit contributions. When they put their minds to it, they can report an impressive array of steps taken and benefits provided. Here are some subjects these activity reports can address:

Comparison of work programmed with work accomplished.

Number and diversity of activities audited.

Number and kinds of reports issued.

Number of other communications to management.

Cost of operating the auditing department.

Amounts of recoveries and savings.

Number and types of special management studies.

In addition, internal auditors should be alert to those matters in which their management or board have exhibited special interest:[1] those activities subject to the highest risk, the coordination of internal and external audit activities so as to minimize total audit expense, and the comprehensiveness of coverage.

To provide information for summary or activity reports, the internal audit department will have to develop and maintain administrative records designed to permit ready accumulation of source data.

Comparisons Between Work Programmed and Accomplished

For each internal audit project, audit days programmed and expended can be compared. Programmed days can be taken from the long-range audit schedule (see Exhibits 18-1 and 18-2, page 612). Audit days expended can be summarized for each project on registers posted from individual time reports (see Exhibit 19-3, page 636).

Activities Audited

Information on the number and diversity of activities audited can be accumulated on forms prepared for each completed audit project. The form has many purposes. It provides spaces for overall audit opinions for the entire project, yet it provides for segmented opinions also. Each project is often subdivided into specific operating functions or areas. This is particularly true in functional audits. There, the audit may cross many organizational lines. Each organization, therefore, may be considered separately, even though the several organizations were involved in the same project.

Exhibit 15-1. CLASSIFICATION OF REPORT OPINIONS
AND DEFICIENCIES

Audit Project No. _____ Report Date _____
Title _____

	Opinions	OVERALL OPINIONS

		Controls		Performance	
		Sat.	Unsat.	Sat.	Unsat.
	Overall	___	___	___	___
Organization	Function	Detailed Opinions			
_____	_____	___	___	___	___
_____	_____	___	___	___	___
_____	_____	___	___	___	___
_____	_____	___	___	___	___
_____	_____	___	___	___	___
_____	_____	___	___	___	___
_____	_____	___	___	___	___
_____	_____	___	___	___	___
_____	_____	___	___	___	___
_____	_____	___	___	___	___

	Deficiencies				
		Controls		Performance	
		Major	Minor	Major	Minor
Organization	Finding No. (R)				
_____	_____	___	___	___	___
_____	_____	___	___	___	___
_____	_____	___	___	___	___
_____	_____	___	___	___	___
_____	_____	___	___	___	___
_____	_____	___	___	___	___

Totals
Open Findings _____
(R) Repeat Findings _____

_____   _____
Date   Supervisor

Some large organizational audits embrace a number of significant activities. Each activity may itself be larger than some activities which constitute a single audit project. For example, an audit of returnable containers covers one subject. An audit of purchasing may cover many different subjects: selecting suppliers, controls over competitive bidding, approvals of purchase orders, following up on the receipt of items ordered, etc. Hence, to achieve some measure of equality, the form should provide for a subdivision of the elements covered by the audit project. The form should also permit a classification of audit findings ranked major and minor.

A suggested form is shown as Exhibit 15-1. The information in the form can be used both for reports on audit activities and for reports on the company's operations. Other reports and communications to management can be summarized from information in Exhibit 15-1 and from registers of informal reports.

Costs of Operating the Auditing Department

These costs can be accumulated by recording salaries, fringe benefits, and allowances for vacations and estimated sick leave. The added overhead can be determined by discussions each year with the budget department.

Amounts of Recoveries and Savings

These amounts should be accumulated on a special record which identifies the project and analyzes the recoveries and savings. The record would show estimated recoveries at the end of the reporting period and actual recoveries after they have been finally determined.

Reports of dollar savings can be a sensitive issue. The matter is relatively simple where an overpayment is recovered; the amount is usually beyond dispute. But savings because of improved systems or elimination of unnecessary work can be given different interpretations by auditor and auditee. What is the saving when a person is taken off unproductive work but not removed from the payroll? A wise course of action is to calculate such savings conservatively and to obtain agreement with the auditee on the amounts of savings to be reported.

Example of an Activity Report

Exhibit 15-2, shown on the following pages, is an activity report. The report does contain evaluations as well, which round out the report.

This report is submitted semiannually. At the outset it declares the internal audit objectives. It then shows audit days budgeted and expended. Management and the board are provided with composite assessments of the audit functions reviewed. The assessment is based on audit opinions expressed in "segments" of audit reports. One audit report might cover several segments. For example, an audit of the receiving department might include a segment on processing documentation, one on checking receipts, one on protecting received material, and the like. Within one audit report there may be varied opinions on the different segments. This tends to level out opinions on large audits and small audits.

The report analyzes audit results and the causes of the weaknesses reported. It speaks of the special assistance provided to company managers and the amounts both saved and recovered. The report concludes with the plans for the ensuing year.

The report is notable for its brevity; it packs a good deal of material into a few pages and highlights significant matters in side comments. Hence, members of top management and the board of directors can skim or read

Exhibit 15-2. INTERNAL AUDIT HIGHLIGHTS - 19XX

The Internal Audit Department's objective is twofold: (1) to provide comprehensive, practical audit coverage of Company operations and (2) to
Audit Objectives assist Company management by conducting special reviews of Company problem areas; working with the Company's public accountants; and conducting reviews of claims, price proposals, and other data submitted by the Company's suppliers and licensees.

For the year 19XX, we expended about 3,200 audit days on our audit work. This represented 92% of the 3,500 audit days planned for initially.
Summary Information We spent some 70% of our time on audit coverage of Company operations and the remainder in assisting management. We issued a total of 121 audit reports and audit memos — an average of 10 each month; 29 of those reports and 14 of those memos dealt with the results of our management-assistance efforts.

Regular Audit Coverage

We based our 19XX audit coverage on our 19XX program, which we prepared after discussions with Branch, Program, and other management
Summary Information personnel and after review by the Audit Committee of the Board of Directors. We placed particular emphasis on sensitive control areas and on subjects covered in Corporate Policy Statement 5, "Business Ethics." We completed jobs covering significant activities for all major Company programs and involving all major functional areas and outside manufacturing locations. We also spent a significant part of our audit effort in monitoring the development of an integrated data base.

More specifically, we reviewed and reported upon 122 separate functions or audit segments:

	Coverage	Audit Segments	Percent of Satisfactory Opinions
Audit Results — Opinions	Commercial Programs	33	52%
	Government Programs	15	53
	Common Program Operations	26	65
	General Systems	48	90
	Totals	122	70%

At the mid-year, we reported over-all results showing only 65% satisfactory opinions. Although for the year over-all results rose to 70%, that level reflects deterioration from prior year results. Audit results for 19VV were, in total, 84%, and for 19WW, 81%.

We cited a total of 120 findings requiring corrective action in our 19XX audit reports. We regard one-half of those findings as having a signifi-
Audit Results - Findings cant effect on the satisfactory performance of the activity reviewed. Further analysis and study of those significant findings indicate that 60% of them dealt with the failure to follow established controls and that 40% of them dealt with shortcomings in the controls themselves. Before completing our audits, we discussed all of the findings cited with the management personnel responsible. And, in all cases, those people took corrective action which we considered satisfactory.

Exhibit 15-2. (Cont.)

We believe that the failure to follow established controls is attributable in large
measure to managers and supervisors not giving sufficient at-
Underlying   tention to training and motivating employees to do the work and
Causes   not giving sufficient attention to monitoring the work. And we believe that shortcomings in controls are attributable for the most
part to managers' lack of awareness of the need for controls. We did, however,
find and report instances in which management decisions had been made to disregard — or to de-emphasize — acceptable practice.

Special Audit Coverage

During 19XX, we assisted management in undertaking a variety of assignments.
We made reviews of supplier price and cost data, provided as-
Summary   sistance to the Company's public accountants, made examina-
Information   tions of Company-sponsored employee organizations, and
assisted Company personnel in the review of internal account-
ing controls. Other work we accomplished included a follow-on review of a subsidiary's financial reporting system, an examination of a customer's operations
under an operating cost incentive program, an investigation of material shortages, and certain other management-requested audit and investigative effort.

We issued 26 audit reports and 5 internal audit memos to report the results of our
reviews of suppliers' price and cost data. Prices negotiated by
$6,700,000   Material branch personnel using information we furnished them
Saved and   for 18 proposals we reviewed in 19XX and for 8 proposals we re-
$131,000   viewed in the prior year resulted in substantial savings. And the
Recovered   Company recovered a significant amount in connection with
prior year audit work we performed on royalty payments.

Our plans for 19YY include provision for expanded audit coverage of the ABC
Plant's operations and special provision for lending assistance
Looking   to management in the conduct of Company operations by mak-
Ahead   ing qualified audit staff available for special assignments to key
operating areas in the Company.

---

the report in a very short time. Some activity reports go into extensive narrative and quantitative detail. We question whether the executive readers
of such reports would take the time to digest the extended comments and
the detailed tables and schedules.

Some auditing organizations supply the following additional information
in their summary reports of activities:

The names and backgrounds of the internal auditors.

A listing of work objectives, including new activities or organizations, sensitive areas to be audited, and other matters outside of the normal routine.

Means of promoting coordination of the internal and external auditing efforts. An example is the establishment of a "common user" file for flowcharts, form samples, and organization charts, to be consulted by both
the external and internal auditors.

Work on questionable payments and practices.

Work on internal accounting controls to assure compliance with the provisions of the U.S. Foreign Corrupt Practices Act.

Work on audits involving equal employment opportunity and affirmative action.

Reasons for any deviations from the long-range internal audit program, such as inability to recruit personnel, heavier than budgeted training, or increases in requests for special studies.

The results of peer reviews of the internal auditing function.

Comments on audit philosophy and the broadening scope of internal auditing within the enterprise.

New professional requirements such as the *Standards for the Professional Practice of Internal Auditing.*

Examples of Graphic Reports

Another company uses graphs and charts to display the level of audit effort. Exhibit 15-3 shows audit accomplishment in terms of audit days, and compares it with what was programmed. Exhibit 15-4 shows the number of written communications, both formal (internal audit reports) and informal (internal audit memorandums) as an indicator of audit accomplishment.

Supporting these charts are status reports (not reproduced here) which describe such matter as:

Expanded use of data processing and quantitative analysis.

Extended use of visual presentations to management.

Application of management techniques to solve management problems.

Results of studies showing how to classify deficiency findings so as to isolate their causes.

Staff training sessions.

Professional activities of the staff.

Conferences with executive management and the audit committee of the board of directors.

Contacts with the external auditors.

Cost savings.

Titles of audit projects completed.

Judiciously prepared, reports of accomplishment cannot help but benefit the auditors. The reports let management know that the auditors are evaluating themselves and measuring their own achievements against approved standards. They point out that the auditors are carefully weighing what they

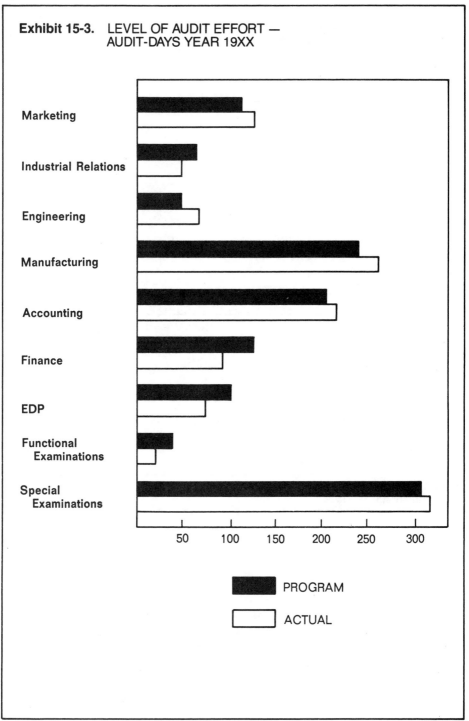

Exhibit 15-3. LEVEL OF AUDIT EFFORT —
AUDIT-DAYS YEAR 19XX

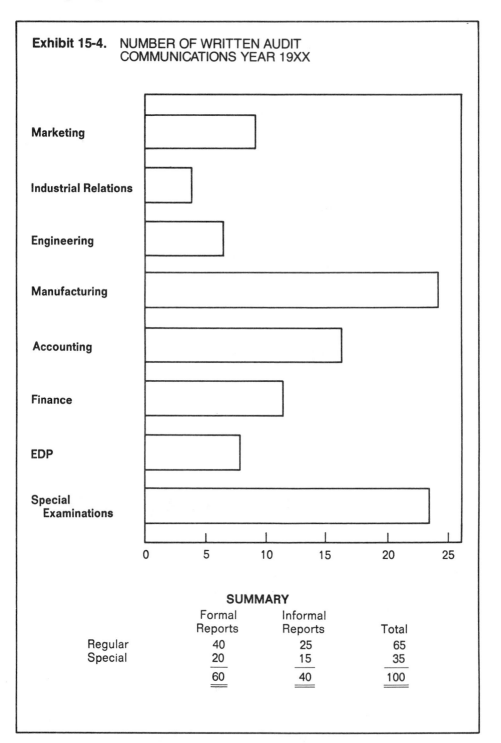

Exhibit 15-4. NUMBER OF WRITTEN AUDIT COMMUNICATIONS YEAR 19XX

SUMMARY

	Formal Reports	Informal Reports	Total
Regular	40	25	65
Special	20	15	35
	60	40	100

have done and where they are going. The reports can be written in a simple style to make reading easy. They can be illustrated by charts and diagrams to improve understanding.

These reports are not easy to devise or to prepare. They encroach upon the busy auditor's schedule of making audits. They may be started with a flourish but abandoned after a few trials because they are onerous to keep up. But the auditor must remember that, artfully prepared, they **will** be read by management, and they will keep the auditor's efforts and accomplishments before management's eyes.

Evaluation Reports

Reports on the operational health of the enterprise can be of absorbing interest to management. These can be a powerful instrument, and hence they must be used with discretion.

Management will see them as an indicator of administrative well-being or company illness. Thus they must be soundly based. Conclusions drawn from a scattering of data can be misleading. A few random numbers will give incomplete and random data. But the stability provided by large numbers can be the strong foundation on which auditors can build when they construct and present reports on the organization's operations.

It is true that executive management receives from operating management operating reports that provide information on production, schedules, quality, backlogs, staffing, and the like. These may be self-serving declarations. What executive management needs is an objective, educated, professional evaluation of what all the auditor's efforts have brought to light in terms of administering the company's affairs.

This does not imply the direct evaluation of individuals. That can be a trap. Such evaluations are difficult to support and easy to dispute. What it does imply is the accumulation of individual audit findings and conclusions and the depiction of trends and variances. There are several units of measurement for such reports. Two of these are audit opinions and audit deficiency findings.

Summarizing Audit Opinions

Not all internal auditors express overall opinions on the results of their individual audits. Some are content to report findings and recommendations only. Others, however, have taken the position that a professional opinion on the adequacy and effectiveness of the system of control within the activities audited provides useful and needed information to management. These internal auditors believe that opinions on operations are no less important than opinions on financial statements.

The latter position may be more widely adopted in the near future. The reason lies in the movement to require enterprises to express opinions in their annual reports on their systems of accounting control. The U.S. Securities and Exchange Commission (SEC) views the U.S. Foreign Corrupt Practices Act of 1977 as greatly expanding the Commission's authority to regulate public companies' internal affairs. In its 1978 *Report to Congress on the Accounting Profession and the Commission's Oversight Role*, the SEC indicated that it "is likely to require . . . a representation that an issuer's system of internal accounting control is in compliance with the provisions of the Act." The SEC goes on to say that the representation might come from management, accompanied by an opinion on its correctness from the company's independent auditors, or it might come directly from the independent auditors themselves.

Looking at it from the viewpoint of top managers in any organization, they, as well as the board, have a vital interest in knowing how well their controls can be relied on. This interest should be directed toward all the systems of controls in the enterprise — not only the internal accounting controls. After all, lack of control over production schedules or safety or quality can be far more devastating to the enterprise than weaknesses in control over petty cash or trade discounts or travel expense vouchers.

Hence, both management and the board need information — current, continuing, objective information — on how their internal auditors regard the existing systems of control. With that information the decision makers in the enterprise can take any action needed to correct weaknesses or reverse adverse trends. Based on the information and on the corrective action taken, they will be able to make representations of their systems of control.

Internal audit opinions on specific activities audited are basically satisfactory or unsatisfactory. There may be gradations, of course: highly satisfactory, satisfactory, qualified, poor, unsatisfactory. But this can be mere hair splitting. From management's point of view, the operation either measured up to standards or it did not. The job was either being done or it was not.

Therefore, audit reports should carry overall audit opinions. Also, those opinions should be summarized to provide management and the board with indications of the quality of both control and performance within an enterprise as viewed by the internal auditors.

Periodic summaries can show the total number of audit opinions expressed and the percentage which were unsatisfactory. Management is thereby given an indication as to whether corrective action is needed

Summarizing Deficiency Findings

Just where the action should be taken will be pointed out by the summaries of deficiencies which have resulted in the unsatisfactory opinions. Deficiency findings may be divided into two classifications, major and minor. Guidelines should be set to differentiate between them. Here are some usable definitions (see Chapter 7):

A **major** deficiency finding is one which affects performance or control, preventing an activity, function, or unit from meeting a substantial part of its significant goals or objectives.

A **minor** deficiency finding is one which warrants reporting and which requires corrective action but which cannot be considered as preventing the accomplishment of a significant goal or objective.

Such rules need consistent and judicious interpretation on a case-by-case basis. All deficiency findings, therefore, should be evaluated by someone in authority to ensure consistency and due deliberation at an appropriate level.

Deficiencies need one further breakdown if they are to be used effectively. Put in simple terms, management has two basic responsibilities in carrying out its operations. The first is to tell its people what needs to be done. The second is to have them do it and do it right. Implicit in the first is providing systems, standards, directives, procedures, job instructions, and other means that come under the generic heading of control. Implicit in the second is carrying out activities in accordance with these means of control; and this comes under the generic heading of performance.

Deficiency findings, therefore, may be major or minor, and they may affect control or performance. Let us give some simple examples of each.

Control-Major

The procurement organization does not require competitive bids.

Such a dereliction could seriously and adversely prevent the organization from reaching one of its primary objectives of getting required products at the best price. It affects control, rather than performance, since there is nothing to **prevent** buyers from obtaining bids. And even if, without being told to do so, experienced buyers were obtaining bids, this would not minimize the seriousness of the deficiency. New buyers might enter the procurement organization and, in the absence of rules to the contrary, give all their orders to favored suppliers. Any buyers might succumb to the blandishments of unscrupulous suppliers.

Performance-Major

Procedures required competitive bids. Yet 50% of the 200 purchase orders examined, representing a substantial portion of the amounts committed for materials, were not bid competitively, and the failure to obtain bids was not justified or otherwise documented.

This is a performance deficiency because activities were not carried out in accordance with existing instructions. There may be a related control deficiency if the procurement instruction did not require supervisory review of the orders placed, but essentially we have a performance defect which prevents the accomplishment of an important procurement objective.

Control-Minor

Instructions on preparing a statistical report to give to executive management on procurement commitments did not provide for an independent verification of the figures.

It is assumed that supervisory review of the report would prevent gross errors from being reported to management, but the missing control violates precepts of good administration and should be corrected.

Performance-Minor

Although instructions called for an independent verification of the commitment report to executive management, we found a number of errors in the report, none of which exceeded $100.

Employees should be cautioned to exercise greater care. The person who signs the report should make periodic tests of the report to ensure its accuracy. Certainly, the performance deficiency needs correcting — but it cannot be said that the errors adversely affected a significant goal or objective.

With these definitions and guidelines known by all, reports on the volume of deficiency findings can be of considerable interest to management and can indicate either deterioration or improvement in the administration of the company's activities. The information furnished can prompt management to take corrective action.

Charting Trends

Trends in opinions and deficiency findings can be charted and can provide a useful indicator of the company's administrative health. Exhibit 15-5 contains charts that graphically chronicle the records of unsatisfactory opinions. The opinions are shown separately for controls and performance.

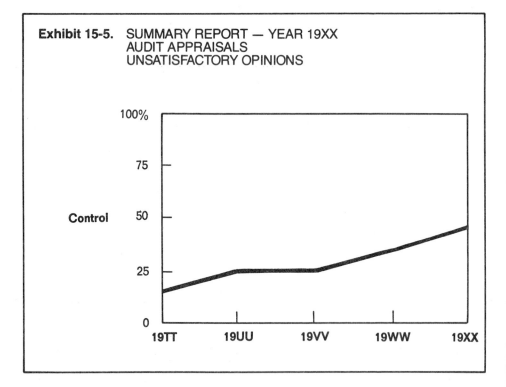

Exhibit 15-5. SUMMARY REPORT — YEAR 19XX
AUDIT APPRAISALS
UNSATISFACTORY OPINIONS

Exhibit 15-5. (Cont.)

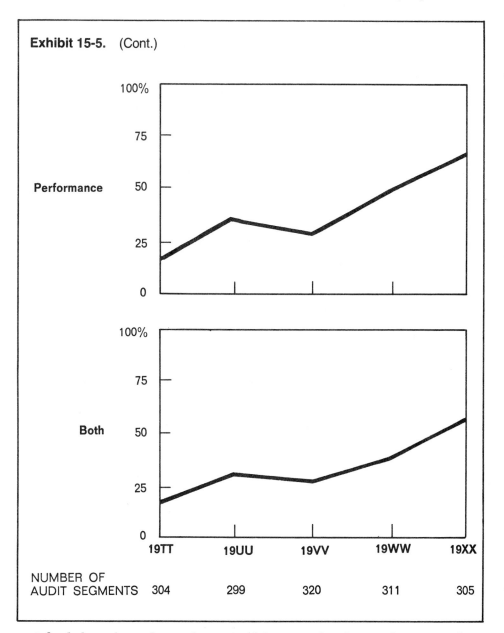

A final chart shows the combination of the two. The charts indicate a gradual deterioration of administration. They show a need to search for basic causes and to prompt management to take the action needed to reverse an unsatisfactory trend.

At the foot of the final chart is set forth the number of audit segments, those discrete parts of an audit project for which opinions can be expressed. This provides information as to the base on which the charts were constructed. Obviously, the base should be substantial enough to validate the report.

Exhibit 15-6 shows a similar chart. This one portrays the number of deficiency findings over a period of five years, and shows a condition which parallels that shown on the chart of opinions. The charts differentiate between control and performance, and major and minor deficiencies.

Summarizing Causes

Knowing that things are bad is not enough. Management should know why. Probably the most helpful information the auditor can provide management concerns causes of deficiencies. Know the cause and it is easier to prescribe the cure. Reports of deficient conditions and unsatisfactory opinions can provide management with reason for concern, but the reports can be frustrating. The executive looks at the assessment of operational weaknesses and says, "I agree with you, Internal Auditor, that conditions are bad. But why are they bad? Until I know the causes I'm not sure I can make things any better."

A good system of determining and reporting causes of deficiencies can go a long way toward helping the executive take broad corrective action. The individual audit reports set forth specific deficiencies which were then corrected. The individual deficiencies do not spell out tendencies. They do not provide management with the means of bringing a condition into focus, relating it to other deficiencies, and showing the groups of deficient conditions deserving the most attention.

Spelling out causes takes work and planning. The first step is to identify potential causes of defects. This is a matter of judgment. A dozen internal auditors presented with the problem could argue *ad infinitum* on the subject and never come to full agreement. Each auditing organization, working in entirely or slightly different environments, might find certain causes more relevant than others. The individual director of auditing must make the decisions on what best suits his or her organization.

Here is one set of causes keyed to the hierarchy of management controls:

1. Suitable objectives and plans not devised.
2. Suitable resources of manpower or materials not provided.
3. Standards not set.
4. Personnel not trained.
5. Approval system not provided.
6. Master (central) control not provided.
7. Compliance with standards not ensured.
8. The ongoing process not monitored.
9. A satisfactory system of records and reports not devised.

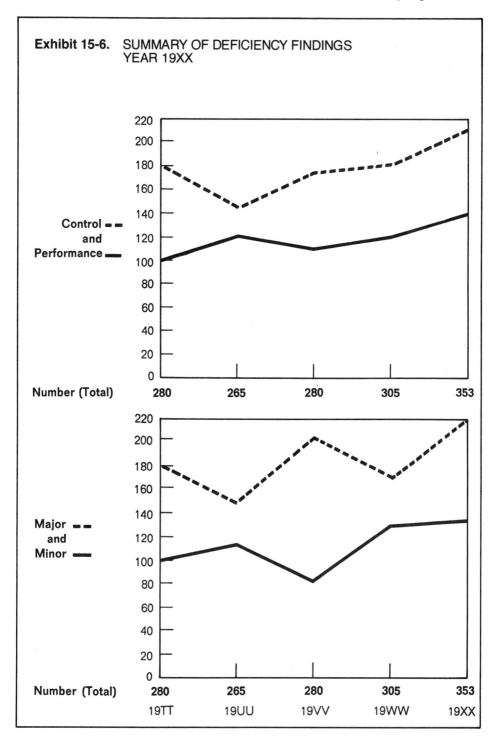

Exhibit 15-6. SUMMARY OF DEFICIENCY FINDINGS
YEAR 19XX

These causes are directed exclusively to the manager or supervisor of an activity. There is some validity to this hierarchy of causes because when all is said and done, superb managers can make almost anything happen under any circumstances. They are restricted solely by the resources at their disposal. When these restrictions seriously affect them and are beyond their control, the cause will most likely be Item 1. — the failure (by executive management) to devise suitable objectives and plans, and 2. — failure to provide suitable resources. The remaining causes cover matters generally under the operating manager's control.

Here is another set of causes which encompass the efforts of organizations, managers, and people. These causes are listed under management functions:

A. Planning and Organizing
    1. Need for controls not recognized.
    2. Management decision not to take the required action.
    3. Controls not updated.
    4. Appropriate authority not assigned.
    5. Sufficient personnel not assigned.
    6. Appropriate priority not assigned.
    7. Adequate basic training not provided.
    8. Adequate equipment not provided.
    9. Means of coordination not provided.
    10. Responsibility not assigned.
    11. Authority not assigned.
    12. Other.

B. Controlling
    1. Schedules not set or met.
    2. Adequate instructions not provided.
    3. Standards not met.
    4. Feedback about the ongoing process not obtained.
    5. Prompt corrective action not taken.
    6. Insufficient management attention.
    7. Insufficient supervisory attention.
    8. Management or supervisory attitude.
    9. Employee attitude.
    10. Human error.
    11. Other

In addition to defining the cause, it becomes necessary to determine the nature of the deficiency. True, the cause may be, for example, the failure to take prompt corrective action. But this defect could happen all the time, or part of the time. The action could be not timely or inaccurate. Finally, the

Exhibit 15-7. CAUSES OF DEFICIENCIES

CLASSIFICATION RECORD

Def. No. _____

Project No. _____ Title _____

Report Date _____ Supervisor _____ AIC _____

Functional Area _____

Deficiency: _____

_____

_____

_____

_____

_____

Corrective Action: _____

_____

_____

_____

_____

_____

Auditor's Statement of Underlying Cause: _____

_____

_____

_____

_____

_____

_____

	Major	Minor	Nature	Cause
Control	_____	_____	_____	_____
Performance	_____	_____	_____	_____

Exhibit 15-8. ANALYSIS OF DEFICIENCY FINDINGS/YEAR 19XX

	Total					
	Number	Per Cent	Contr.	Perf.	Major	Minor
Cause of Deficiency						
Planning and Organizing						
Need not recognized	78	22	110	14	60	24
Unauthorized decision by line management	37	11	22	20	30	12
Failure to update	18	5	21	—	12	4
Failure to assign appropriate priority	18	5	2	12	10	3
Failure to provide for coordination	14	4	6	4	5	5
Failure to assign responsibility	14	4	6	4	6	3
Failure to assign sufficient personnel	11	3	1	2	7	4
Failure to provide adequate training	11	3	2	3	10	5
Failure to provide adequate facilities	3	1	1	1	—	—
Subtotal	204	58	171	60	140	60
Controlling						
Insufficient supervisory attention	75	21	16	32	31	37
Insufficient management attention	25	7	13	18	22	15
Failure to provide adequate instruction	21	6	3	16	8	3
Management/Supervisory attitude	11	3	3	4	4	4
Employee attitude	7	2	2	3	6	6
Human error	3	1	2	5	5	4
Other	7	2	1	4	4	4
Subtotal	149	42	40	82	80	73
Total	353	100	211	142	220	133
Nature of Deficiency						
Control or Performance:						
Incomplete	138	39	117	57	82	61
Lacking	110	31	72	38	76	32
Not timely	55	16	11	17	30	21
Inaccurate	36	10	6	18	10	9
Inconsistent	14	4	5	12	22	10
	353	100	211	142	220	133

action could be inconsistent. So along with the cause it is of interest to know whether the control or performance was:

a. Incomplete
b. Lacking
c. Not timely
d. Inaccurate
e. Inconsistent

It becomes abundantly clear, as efforts are made to assign causes, that, like boxes within boxes within boxes, there are causes behind causes behind causes. One can easily get lost in philosophical theorizing about the cause behind the cause. Carried far enough it winds up with man's first fall from grace. But the essential cause — the cause that operating management is preoccupied with — is the cause whose removal most directly corrects the condition. Hence, it is significant, in assigning causes, to look to the action which line management took to correct the reported condition and to the nature of the deficiency.

This brings us to the use of a form that will help the auditor accumulate the data needed to prepare analyses of deficiencies for management's use. Exhibit 15-7 is one example of such a form. It provides for identifying the deficiency for purposes of control. The identification can be made at the conclusion of each audit project. It also provides spaces for showing the project number and title, the date of the report which described the deficiency, and the supervisor and auditor-in-charge responsible for it. The functional area would be the broad organizational unit concerned, usually at the branch level of finance, administration, procurement, manufacturing, and quality control, to name a few. Some organizations, however, will require further breakdowns. For example, manufacturing may be subdivided among production control, tooling, and production.

The deficiency would be stated essentially as it was summarized in the report. The corrective action would be that taken or proposed. The cause would be a narrative exposition of how the auditor — the one closest to the problem — perceived the cause of the condition.

The identification of the finding helps accumulate statistical data on whether the finding concerned control or performance and whether it is considered major or minor. If the same finding involves both control and performance, individual forms should be prepared for each category to make summarization easy. This is proper since both the cause and the corrective action may be different.

For example: If an instruction was lacking on competitive bids in the procurement organization, the corrective action is to issue one. The cause is (A-1) the failure to recognize the need, and the nature is (b) lacking. If, however, some buyers, because they were experienced and did not need to be told, were obtaining competitive bids while others were not, the entire situation changes. The corrective action, after the instruction has been issued, is closer supervisory control. The cause is (B-7) insufficient supervisory attention, and the nature is (a) incomplete.

When these forms are faithfully prepared, they can readily be summarized into a report to management. Exhibit 15-8 is an example of a report of the auditor's analysis of deficiencies. The second set of causes, just listed, is used in the sample report.

The various administrative activities and reports just discussed may seem burdensome. When auditors work feverishly to meet the deadlines for such reports they may bewail their task and berate their taskmaster. But the rewards are worth the effort. As they examine these reports, executive managers see the auditor as a continuing source of information that will help in the guidance of the enterprise. The auditor becomes more — not less — valued, moving one step closer toward the goal of being a rightful member of the councils of executive management.

Conclusion

The auditors' efforts are displayed primarily and initially in individual audit reports. But these reports do not inform management of the sum total of efforts. Auditors, therefore, owe management summary information on two fronts: one, the extent and measure of those efforts to provide adequate audit coverage and those to maintain the technical ability to cope with business problems; and two, evaluation of the administrative competence of the enterprise.

The first front involves all the auditors have done to carry out their jobs in a professional way and making sure they continue to do so. The second is more difficult. It seeks to tell management how the auditors diagnosed the administrative health of the enterprise.

With careful preparation and planning, the auditor can provide management with significant information on trends, problem areas, and the causes of the problems. Such information elevates the auditor from a finger-pointer to a source of constructive information as a member of the problem-solving team.

References

1. Paul Macciaverna, "Internal Auditing" (Research Report from the Conference Board, 1978), p. 59.

For further study

Discussion Problems

1. Describe four accomplishments that internal auditors can include in activity reports to management.

2. Describe the potential source of comparisons between work "programmed" and work "accomplished."

3. What is the potential source of information on areas covered?

4. How can the internal auditor provide management with summary reports on the effectiveness of its control systems?

5. How may the significance and the nature of deficiency findings be described?

6. How can reports on deficiencies be made more meaningful to management?

7. How can causes be related to the basic functions of management?

8. What is the essential cause which management is generally concerned with?

9. What is the difference between a major deficiency and a minor one?

10. Compare control and performance deficiencies?

Multiple Choice Problems

1. Summary reports to managment and the board of directors:
a. Describe the administrative health of the enterprise.
b. Summarize the audit findings at the end of an audit report.
c. Describe the extent to which the internal auditors met their goals.
d. Tell briefly the results of an internal audit.
e. Both b. and d.

2. A director of internal auditing submits an annual summary report of audit work:
a. To inform management of the scope of the proposed audit work for an ensuing period.
b. To set forth the audit work schedule.
c. To describe the scope of the internal audit work.
d. To report any limitation placed on the scope of the work.
e. All of the above.

3. A director of internal auditing submits annual evaluation reports:
a. To reemphasize what has been submitted in audit reports.
b. To report on significant weaknesses disclosed by internal auditors.
c. To explain proposed staffing plans.
d. To describe changes in financial budgets.
e. None of the above.

4. Activity reports should give primary emphasis on:
a. The recovery of large amounts of money.
b. Dollar savings resulting from the audits.
c. The number of deficiency findings disclosed by the auditors.
d. The protective and constructive benefits of the audit effort.
e. The educational backgrounds of the internal audit staff.

5. Since management and the board receive operating reports from their line organizations:
a. Internal auditors should be concerned primarily with reporting the financial results of their audits.

b. Internal auditors should stress their analysis of accounting matters.

c. Internal auditors should avoid summarizing findings of an operational nature.

d. Internal auditors should also report on matters of an operational nature.

e. Both a. and b. above.

Case Studies

15-1 Punitive Reporting

How would you resolve the following situation?

You are the director of internal auditing. You provide the company president with a real service by each year reporting the number of deficiency findings discussed in audit reports, the causes of the deficiencies, the kinds of deficiencies reported, how the number of deficiencies compare with those reported in prior years, and the status of corrective action.

These overall reports are in summary form and do not identify the branches or divisions responsible for the deficiencies. You would rather not show the organizations responsible because you're certain the president would use the information to punish offending organizations and thereby create problems in relationships during future audits. But this year the president asks that those organizations be identified.

Required: How would you explain your position to the president?

15-2 The Summary Report

Bob, supervising auditor, stuck his head through the doorway of Paul Eberhardt's office. "How did Jan Tobias, the vice president-controller, like your summary report on the year's activities?" he asked.

"It went over better than I had expected," said Paul, the director of internal auditing. "It was the first one

he'd ever seen out of our organization and he thought it was a great idea. He was really impressed with our accomplishments and was sympathetic to our problems."

"Did he read the whole thing?" asked Bob.

"Every single word, even though it is kind of lengthy."

"Does he want to continue receiving such reports in the future?" inquired Bob.

"He certainly does. But he wants us to go beyond that," answered Paul.

"What do you mean?" queried Bob.

"The board of directors meets in two weeks. He wants us to make a presentation to the audit committee of the board based on the summary report."

"Great, we've been trying for a long time to dream up some way of getting the board's attention. Will you give them copies of the report?"

Paul replied, "Yes, but I can't see them sitting and reading it while I just stand there."

"What do you have in mind?"

"A flip chart presentation of the salient features. Then I could answer questions as they come up."

"Sounds like a great idea," agreed Bob. "Can I help?"

"You sure can. Why don't you take the report and rough out some flip charts on those matters that you think would be of the most interest to the audit committee. Then you and I can go over them and agree on just what we'll show."

"Will do," said Bob.

Required: (1) Prepare a set of rough draft flip charts of the presentation to management, using the summary report in Exhibit 15-2. (2) Prepare a critique of Exhibit 15-2, stating what you like and don't like about it, and what you think should be included in future reports.

Part 5

Administration

16

Establishing the Auditing Organization

Foundations for internal auditing: technical excellence and service to management. The internal auditor's standing in the enterprise. The need for independence. Reporting status. The *Standards*. Moving up the management ladder. Reporting to management and the board of directors. Insulating the internal auditor. Convincing management of the need for practical independence. Assistance from the external auditor. Job descriptions: manager, supervisor, senior, associate, assistant. Audit manuals: technical, administrative, and miscellaneous functions. Promoting internal auditing to management. Steps toward increasing audit scope. Demonstrating competence in nonfinancial activities.

Foundations for Successful Internal Auditing

Successful internal auditing is constructed on a foundation of technical excellence. The structure must be firmly buttressed on the one side by demonstrated acceptance and support at the highest levels in the enterprise; on the other by continued, professional, imaginative service to management. Each of these two pillars is an integral member of the structure. Let one weaken and the structure may fall at the first hard blow from the winds of retrenchment and cost reduction.

These truisms apply equally to the auditors, seeking to provide the full benefits of internal auditing to their enterprise, and to the executives who are aware of these benefits but who are not yet obtaining them from their auditing organizations. Enterprising auditors must bring home to management the value of the service they can render in a proper climate and environment. Enlightened managers can obtain these unique services if they know what to demand of their directors of auditing and what modern internal auditing is capable of doing for them.

Both the internal auditor and the manager must understand that although technical ability may get the audit job done professionally, the auditor's findings, conclusions, and recommendations may lie impotent and ignored in the carefully prepared audit report. Proper standing in the enterprise, however, reinforced by management support, will give the job and the report full force and effect. An innovative, well-considered service to the decision makers in the company at all levels develops willing customers for the audit function, while providing the internal auditor with entree into every area of the enterprise and a seat in the councils of executive management.

Accepted standing in the organization is essential for another reason as well: It is the guarantee of independence, and for the auditing function to be effective, it must be independent of the activities it audits.

Total independence is as elusive as a perfect vacuum. Complete independence implies freedom from all dependencies, including financial dependency. As long as the auditing department is a part of the enterprise and receives its life support from the enterprise, it must relinquish some independence. The auditors' goal, therefore, is to achieve the greatest amount of practical independence in the real world situation in which they find themselves — independence which will protect them from having to compromise their audit objectives. We cannot stamp our feet when we are on our knees.

Independence, however, is more than a slogan or shibboleth. It is the climate in which the auditing organization needs to live and breathe and function. Internal auditing is a professional activity. Its task is to make professional judgments. It therefore demands the highest type of detachment, integrity, and objectivity.

These attributes atrophy in the absence of practical independence. Thus, an independent reporting status that permits the maintenance of the objectivity and removes the internal auditors from effective dependence upon the people whose activities they audit is utterly essential. This desired result is coming to pass.

Two circumstances within the last decade have accounted for increased stature of internal auditing and greater independence: One, internal auditors are reporting to higher levels of management executives; two, they are gaining access to boards of directors. A Conference Board study in 1978 showed the following changes since a similar study in 1963:[1]

Internal Auditing Reports To:	% of Respondents:	1978	1963
Controller		30%	54%
Treasurer		18	17
Senior Financial Executive		34	7
Senior Corporate Officers or Audit Committees of the Board		15	9
Dual Reporting to Audit Committees and Management Executives		4	0

In 1963 a reporting relationship between internal auditing and the board of directors was relatively rare in other than banking and insurance companies.[2] In the author's experience many companies are now adopting a dual reporting relation: a solid line to a management executive and a dotted line to the audit committee of the board. The Conference Board report of 1978 found that more than seven out of ten auditing staffs meet regularly with their audit committees to discuss auditing affairs.

Dual reporting relations are becoming more common, but the improved status may bring with it some discomfort for the director of internal auditing. Internal auditors are now reporting to auditing committees those matters which formerly were within the sole province of executive management: internal control, audit coverage, significant audit findings, corrective action or the lack of it, and restrictions placed on the internal audit function by management people.

The ability to perform objective audits and report fully and without reservation to the board will be heavily dependent on the auditor's insulation from the influence of management. That insulation will be lacking if management can hire and fire the director of internal auditing at its own pleasure.

The ideal reporting relation, therefore, should be the solid line to a top executive — to assure consideration of audit recommendations and access to all operations in the enterprise; and a dotted line to the board — to protect internal auditing from the potentially disastrous effect of unwarranted displeasure on the part of the chief executive officer.

How does the director of internal auditing go about achieving this desideratum? By a careful campaign, based on professional work and directed to the self-interest of those responsible for directing the destinies of the enterprise. Internal auditors, in their audit programs, their surveys, their field work, and their reports must display products which both management and the board will want to buy: professional, intelligent reviews that demonstrate thoroughness and objectivity. They must bring home to executive management and the board that practical independence is necessary for objectivity, and that objectivity is the prime ingredient for a believable, reliable internal audit function. This must be proclaimed in the internal auditor's charter.

To that end, the *Standards for the Professional Practice of Internal Auditing* have underscored the importance of independence and have codified what is being practiced by many advanced internal auditing organizations. Section 110.01 of the *Standards* includes these statements:

.1 The director of the internal auditing department should be responsible to an individual in the organization with sufficient authority to promote independence and to ensure broad audit coverage, adequate consideration of audit reports, and appropriate action on audit recommendations.

* * *

.3 Independence is enhanced when the board [of directors] concurs in the appointment or removal of the director of the internal auditing department.

.4 The purpose, authority, and responsibility of the internal auditing department should be defined in a formal written document (charter). The director should seek approval of the charter by management as well as acceptance by the board. The charter should (a) establish the department's position within the organization; (b) authorize access to records, personnel, and physical properties relevant to the performance of audits; and (c) define the scope of internal auditing activities.

Preparing the Functions and Responsibility Statement

Most companies maintain a set of statements which establish the authority and responsibility of the major positions in the organization. These become the charters under which each organization operates. In them is set forth, for the rest of the company to see, how executive management regards the purpose, mission, and authority of each major function within the company. Internal auditors should make certain, therefore, that the charter for their organization provides a framework within which they can function with the degree of independence that ensures objectivity.

The statement must be carefully drafted so that it affords the auditors all the authority they need, yet does not assign responsibilities which they cannot conceivably carry out. It should not restrict auditors to matters of accounting and finance. On the other hand, it should not require them to provide opinions on the effectiveness of functions of a highly technical or professional nature. For this reason, many such statements place stress on the review of management controls, rather than on the appraisal of performance. The competent internal auditor is capable of reviewing administrative and management controls over any activity within the company. This ability clearly cannot extend to the evaluation of professional performance or technical activities requiring specialized study and knowledge. At the same time, of course, they should not be barred from evaluating the performance of those administrative activities which they are competent to judge.

A sample of a functions and responsibility statement — a composite of several such statements — is shown in Exhibit 16-1.

Devising the Statement of Policy

Management support must be proclaimed clearly and categorically in the company's highest policy statement. And the policy statement should be quite specific. It should spell out clearly the scope and status of internal auditing within the enterprise, its authority to carry out audits, issue reports, make recommendations, and evaluate corrective action. Exhibit 16-2 is a composite of several published policy statements. It sets forth a

Exhibit 16-1. THE DIRECTOR OF AUDITING
STATEMENT OF AUTHORITY AND RESPONSIBILITY

Authority

The director of auditing is authorized to direct a broad, comprehensive program of internal auditing within the company. Internal auditing examines and evaluates the adequacy and effectiveness of the systems of management control provided by the company to direct its activities toward the accomplishment of its objectives in accordance with company policies and plans. In accomplishing these activities, the director of auditing and members of the audit staff are authorized to have full, free, and unrestricted access to all company functions, records, property, and personnel.

Responsibility

The director of auditing is responsible for:

Establishing policies for the auditing activity and directing its technical and administrative functions.

Developing and executing a comprehensive audit program for the evaluation of the management controls provided over all company activities.

Examining the effectiveness of all levels of management in their stewardship of company resources and their compliance with established policies and procedures.

Recommending improvement of management controls designed to safeguard company resources, promote company growth, and ensure compliance with government laws and regulations.

Reviewing procedures and records for their adequacy to accomplish intended objectives, and appraising policies and plans relating to the activity or function under audit review.

Authorizing the publication of reports on the results of audit examinations, including recommendations for improvement.

Appraising the adequacy of the action taken by operating management to correct reported deficient conditions; accepting adequate corrective action; continuing reviews with appropriate management personnel on action the director considers inadequate until there has been a satisfactory resolution of the matter.

Conducting special examinations at the request of management, including the reviews of representations made by persons outside the company.

broad-gauged charter that is consistent with the *Standards for the Professional Practice of Internal Auditing.*

The first seven missions enumerated may be regarded as core responsibilities. They are essential to the performance of comprehensive, full-scope internal audits. The remaining missions, beginning with the charge to coordinate audit efforts with those of the company's public accountants, have appeared in published policy statements of various enterprises. These define with greater particularity what executive management expects of its internal auditors. Such missions may be regarded as optional in developing a policy statement, but the concept expressed in the final paragraph dealing with corrective action is essential if the internal auditor's findings are to be accorded adequate consideration.

Not every enterprise is prepared to issue a policy statement containing all these responsibilities. Some enterprises will restrict the internal auditor's scope and reach. Certainly, all internal auditing departments must function within the environment in which they find themselves, but any subtraction from the seven core responsibilities and the requirement to respond to audit reports add to the risk of undetected, serious weaknesses. The effectiveness of the internal auditing department becomes diluted. Less reliance can be placed on its ability to function as an uninhibited monitor of enterprise controls and performance.

In seeking to secure organizational status and an effective charter, internal auditors should consider soliciting the aid of the external auditors. These independent accountants must be assured of the independence, objectivity, and unrestricted scope of the internal audit function if they are to rely fully on the internal auditor's work. They must never be apprehensive that internal auditors can be manipulated because they fear reprisals or that any weaknesses reported can go uncorrected. The external auditors have a stake in the internal audit function. Their reliance on that function will be diminished if the internal auditor's charter does not clearly set forth a comprehensive mission for the department.

Emphasizing Enterprise Policy

Policy statements describe management's apparent intentions. They do not necessarily give them urgency or demonstrate management's unequivocal support of the policy. Such a demonstration is particularly important for internal auditing. Many operating managers still regard internal auditing as a minor checking function; they do not perceive it as an extension of executive management. They must therefore be educated to that end. Management and the board must make it abundantly clear that they rely upon and support the internal audit activity.

Many large corporations underscore their policy statements with communications explaining the internal audit function. Here are some excerpts from a brochure distributed to all operating managers in a large multinational corporation. The brochure is introduced by the following statement signed by the chairman of the board and chief executive officer:*

> This brochure has been prepared to familiarize you with our Internal Auditing Department. It will help you understand the role we expect this department to perform for the company.
>
> Business, with its complexities both domestic and foreign, complicated by many external requirements, requires a staff of professionals concerned with every aspect of corporate activity.

---

*Excerpts printed, with permission, from a brochure published by The Aluminum Company of America, October 1978.

Exhibit 16-2.

POLICY STATEMENT

It is the policy of this company to establish and support an internal auditing department as an independent appraisal function to examine and evaluate company activities as a service to management and the board of directors. The internal auditing department reports administratively to executive management and functionally to the Audit Committee of the Board of Directors. In carrying out their duties and responsibilities, members of the internal auditing department will have full, free, and unrestricted access to all company activities, records, property, and personnel.

The primary objective of the internal auditing department is to assist members of management and the Board in the effective discharge of their responsibilities. To this end, internal auditing will furnish them with analyses, recommendations, counsel, and information concerning the activities reviewed.

The missions of the internal auditing department are as follows:

1. Review organizations within the company at appropriate intervals to determine whether they are efficiently and effectively carrying out their functions of planning, organizing, directing, and controlling in accordance with management instructions, policies, and procedures, and in a manner that is consonant with both company objectives and high standards of administrative practice.

2. Determine the adequacy and effectiveness of the company's systems of internal accounting and operating controls.

3. Review the reliability and integrity of financial information and the means used to identify, measure, classify, and report such information.

4. Review the established systems to ensure compliance with those policies, plans, procedures, laws, and regulations which could have a significant impact on operations and reports, and determine whether the organization is in compliance. Suggest policy where required.

5. Review the means of safeguarding assets and, as appropriate, verify the existence of such assets.

6. Appraise the economy and efficiency with which resources are employed, identify opportunities to improve operating performance, and recommend solutions to problems where appropriate.

7. Review operations and programs to ascertain whether results are consistent with established objectives and goals and whether the operations or programs are being carried out as planned.

8. Coordinate audit efforts with those of the company's public accountants.

9. Participate in the planning, design, development, implementation, and operation of major computer-based systems to determine whether (a) adequate controls are incorporated in the systems, (b) thorough system testing is performed at appropriate stages, (c) system documentation is complete

Continued

Exhibit 16-2. (Cont.)

and accurate, and (d) the needs of user organizations are met. Conduct periodic audits of computer service centers and make post-installation evaluations of major data processing systems to determine whether these systems meet their intended purposes and objectives.

10. Participate in the planning and performance of audits of potential acquisitions with the company's outside accountants and other members of the corporate staff. Follow up to assure the proper accomplishment of the audit objectives.

11. Review compliance with the company's guidelines for ethical business conduct and see that the highest standards of personal and corporate performance are met.

12. Submit annual audit plans to the President and the Audit Committee for their review and approval.

13. Report every quarter to the Audit Committee of the Board on whether:

   - Appropriate action has been taken on significant audit findings.
   - Audit activities have been directed toward the highest exposures to risk and toward increasing efficiency, economy, and effectiveness of operations.
   - Internal and external audits are coordinated so as to avoid duplications.
   - Internal audit plans are adequate.
   - There is any unwarranted restriction on the staffing and authority of the internal auditing department or on access by internal auditors to all company activities, records, property, and personnel.

14. Report to those members of management who should be informed or who should take corrective action, the results of audit examinations, the audit opinions formed, and the recommendations made.

15. Evaluate any plans or actions taken to correct reported conditions for satisfactory disposition of audit findings. If the corrective action is considered unsatisfactory, hold further discussions to achieve acceptable disposition.

16. Provide adequate follow up to make sure that adequate corrective action is taken and that it is effective.

The operating division manager is responsible for seeing that corrective action on reported weaknesses is either planned or taken within 30 days from receipt of a report disclosing those weaknesses. The division manager is also responsible for seeing that a written report of action planned or completed is sent to the executive vice president. If a plan for action is reported, a second report shall be made promptly upon completion of the plan.

Working with our independent public accountants, they evaluate the control needs of most locations and functions worldwide and develop a program of auditing that is responsive to both risk and cost effectiveness.

You should consider the Internal Audit Department an additional resource to aid in identifying problems. You can help the department help you by assuring its complete access to all records, personnel, and properties.

I encourage you to do everything possible to facilitate this work. Use this service and join me in providing full support.

(Signed)
Chairman of the Board
and Chief Executive Officer

The brochure then goes on to provide information about the internal auditing function under a number of subjects. Those subjects, and summaries of the statements about them, are as follows:

Organization. The general manager of the Internal Audit Department reports administratively to executive management and functionally to the audit committee of the Board.

Audit Committee. The manager is afforded free access to the audit committee. The committee's activities include reviewing internal audit plans and objectives and the results of audit activities.

Responsibilities. The Department provides a service to management and the audit committee which will assist them in the effective discharge of their duties and responsibilities. The principal role of internal auditing is to evaluate internal control.

Objectivity. Objectivity is assured through organizational structure, training, and careful assignment of personnel.

Scheduling/Scope. Assessment of risk, previous audit coverage, significance of exceptions, and need for regular contact are the primary considerations in audit scheduling. The scope of audit is adjusted to provide in-depth reviews in selected areas and overviews in others. Audit scope is expanding because of government laws and regulations, and management's growing responsibility to provide more specific information and to make this unique discipline available to all activities, not only the financial and regulatory area.

Planning/Execution. The common elements of the audit are listed in the brochure, from pre-audit announcement to close-out conference. The brochure emphasizes service to management, objectivity, prudence, and the striving to improve the proficiency and effectiveness of the audited department and the individual auditor.

Post-Audit Reviews. Nothing will appear in an audit report which has not been fully reviewed with the appropriate personnel of the location or function.

Audit Reports. Reporting normally is on an exception basis. But uncommonly excellent areas are also mentioned. Since recommendations are offered as ways to improve, report readers are urged not to react in alarmed fashion to other than the specifics mentioned.

Relationship With External Auditors. External and internal auditors coordinate their activities by developing common techniques, using common files, exchanging audit working papers, and participating in on-site reviews of audit work and in seminars and training.

Training/Development and Growth. Certification in interal auditing and management accounting is encouraged. Modern audit techniques are applied. Internal auditors are represented in many professional organizations. The brochure lists various in-house training methods. Internal auditors are developed for "graduation" to prominent positions in the company.

The Future. Internal auditors must demonstrate flexibility in the face of change and must constantly review their programs and objectives to produce a better product.

Statement of Responsibilities. The brochure concludes with a copy of the auditing department's statement of responsibilities, developed with the recommendation of executive management and the audit committee of the Board of Directors. The statement covers activities affected, scope, objectivity, relationship to external auditors, internal control, fraud, managerial requests, and professional standards. Under the heading of fraud, the statement points out that the internal auditors cannot assume responsibility for fraud detection or prevention; but they are expected to maintain an alertness to inadequate controls. Their evaluation of internal control should be designed to permit reasonable assurance that management will identify a material misstatement or loss of corporate assets.

This brochure seeks to remove the mystery from the internal auditing function and to inhibit any potential adversary relationships with auditees.

Such support from management is the underpinning for the internal auditing organization. Without it, auditing becomes a matter of grace, to be accepted or rejected by operating management. With it, auditing becomes binding upon operating management, ensuring action when action is called for. Acceptance must be earned, of course; but the opportunity to earn it will not exist in the absence of a clear mandate from the highest executive level of the company setting forth its support of the audit effort.

Writing Job Descriptions

Statements of function and responsibility and management directives set the stage for the directors of auditing and provide the arena in which they will function. But they cannot function at optimal levels without the right staff. The audit staff must therefore have adequate status in the company in terms of salary grades. In most companies the salary grades are established by salary review boards who make their determinations by reviewing job descriptions.

The job descriptions for the various levels of audit staff may make or break the auditing organization. Modern internal auditing demands the highest level of audit effort. Only the best auditors are able to accomplish it successfully and carry out the promise that is held forth to management by the progressive director of auditing. It has been abundantly demonstrated that it is much better to perform the internal auditing function with fewer competent staff auditors than with many mediocre ones. Indeed, the function will just plain not be accomplished without people of intelligence, imagination, and initiative — to say nothing of understanding and the ability to deal with others. Such people come high in the market place.

For this reason the job descriptions should be drafted with care. They should set forth requirements capable of being accomplished by the best auditors, not by the average auditors. Such descriptions will warrant the assignment of salary grades which will attract the best people, not only from the market place but from within the company itself.

In relatively large auditing organizations with far-flung operations and locations, the hierarchy of jobs is usually as follows:

1. Director of Auditing
2. Audit Manager
3. Audit Supervisor
4. Senior Auditor
5. Associate Auditor (sometimes called semi-senior)
6. Assistant Auditor (sometimes called junior auditor)

A typical description of the director's function was shown in Exhibit 16-1. Examples of job descriptions for the remaining positions, each a composite of several, are shown in Exhibits 16-3 through 16-7.

Exhibit 16-3.   POSITION DESCRIPTION
INTERNAL AUDITING — MANAGER

Purpose

To administer the internal auditing activity of an assigned location.

To develop a comprehensive, practical program of audit coverage for the assigned location.

To obtain accomplishment of the program in accordance with acceptable audit standards and stipulated schedules.

To maintain effective working relations with executive and operating management.

Authority and Responsibility

Within the general guidelines provided by the director of auditing:

Prepares a comprehensive, long-range program of audit coverage for the location to which assigned.

Identifies those activities subject to audit coverage, evaluates their significance, and assesses the degree of risk inherent in the activity in terms of cost, schedule, and quality.

Establishes the departmental structure.

Obtains and maintains an audit staff capable of accomplishing the internal audit function.

Assigns audit areas, staff, and budget to supervisory auditors.

Develops a system of cost and schedule control over audit projects.

Establishes standards of performance and, by review, determines that performance meets the standards.

Provides executive management within the assigned location with reports on audit coverage and the results of the audit activity, and interprets those results so as to improve the audit program and the audit coverage.

Establishes and monitors accomplishment of objectives directed toward increasing the internal auditing department's ability to serve management.

Exhibit 16-4. POSITION DESCRIPTION
INTERNAL AUDITING — SUPERVISOR

Purpose

To develop a comprehensive, practical program of audit coverage for assigned areas of audit.

To supervise the activities of auditors assigned to the review of various organizational and functional activities.

To ensure conformance with acceptable audit standards, plans, budgets, and schedules.

To maintain effective working relations with operating management.

To provide for and conduct research; develop manuals and training guides.

Authority and Responsibility

Under the general guidance of the manager of internal auditing:

Supervises the work of auditors engaged in the reviews of organizational and functional activities.

Provides a comprehensive, practical program of annual audit coverage within general areas assigned by the manager of internal auditing.

Determines areas of risk and appraises their significance in relation to operational factors of cost, schedule, and quality. Classifies audit projects as to degree of risk and significance and as to frequency of audit coverage.

Provides for flexibility in audit programs so as to be responsive to management's special needs.

Schedules projects and staff assignments so as to comply with management's needs, within the scope of the department's overall program.

Coordinates the program with the company's public accountant.

Reviews and approves the purpose, scope, and audit approach of each audit project for assigned areas of audit cognizance.

Directs audit projects to see that professional standards are maintained in the planning and execution and in the accumulation of evidentiary data.

Counsels and guides auditors to see that the approved audit objectives are met and that adequate, practical coverage is achieved.

Reviews and edits audit reports and, in company with the auditor-in-charge for the assigned project, discusses the reports with appropriate management.

Presents oral briefings to branch-level management.

Provides for and performs research on audit techniques.

Provides formal plans for the recruiting, selecting, training, evaluating, and supervising of staff personnel. Develops manuals and other training aids.

Accumulates data, maintains records, and prepares reports on the administration of audit projects and other assigned activities.

Identifies factors causing deficient conditions and recommends courses of action to improve the conditions, including special surveys and audits.

Provides for a flow of communication from operating management to the manager and to the director of auditing. Assists in evaluating overall results of the audits.

Exhibit 16-5. POSITION DESCRIPTION
INTERNAL AUDITOR — SENIOR

Purpose

To conduct reviews of assigned organizational and functional activities.

To evaluate the adequacy and effectiveness of the management controls over those activities.

To determine whether organizational units in the company are performing their planning, accounting, custodial, or control activities in compliance with management instructions, applicable statements of policy and procedures, and in a manner consistent with both company objectives and high standards of administrative practice.

To plan and execute audits in accordance with accepted standards.

To report audit findings and to make recommendations for correcting unsatisfactory conditions, improving operations, and reducing cost.

To perform special reviews at the request of management.

To direct the activities of assistants.

Authority and Responsibility

Under the general guidance of a supervising auditor:

Surveys functions and activities in assigned areas to determine the nature of operations and the adequacy of the system of control to achieve established objectives.

Determines the direction and thrust of the proposed audit effort.

Plans the theory and scope of the audit, and prepares an audit program.

Determines the auditing procedures to be used, including statistical sampling and the use of electronic data processing equipment.

Identifies the key control points of the system.

Evaluates a system's effectiveness through the application of a knowledge of business systems, including financial, manufacturing, engineering, procurement, and other operations, and his understanding of auditing techniques.

Recommends necessary staff required to complete the audit.

Performs the audit in a professional manner and in accordance with the approved audit program.

Obtains, analyzes, and appraises evidentiary data as a base for an informed, objective opinion on the adequacy and effectiveness of the system and the efficiency of performance of the activities being reviewed.

Directs, counsels, and instructs staff assistants assigned to the audit, and reviews their work for sufficiency of scope and for accuracy.

Makes oral or written presentations to management during and at the conclusion of the examination, discussing deficiencies and recommending corrective action to improve operations and reduce cost.

Prepares formal written reports, expressing opinions on the adequacy and effectiveness of the system and the efficiency with which activities are carried out.

Appraises the adequacy of the corrective action taken to improve deficient conditions.

Exhibit 16-6. POSITION DESCRIPTION
INTERNAL AUDITOR — ASSOCIATE

Purpose

To conduct or assist in conducting reviews of assigned organizational and functional activities.

To evaluate the adequacy and effectiveness of the management controls over those activities.

To determine whether organizational units in the company are performing their planning, accounting, custodial, or control activities in compliance with management instructions, applicable statements of policy and procedures, and in a manner consistent with both company objectives and high standards of administrative practice.

To plan and execute complete reviews of limited audit assignments, or conduct reviews of portions of extensive audit assignments, in accordance with accepted professional standards.

To report audit findings and to make recommendations for the correction of unsatisfactory conditions, improvements in operations, and reductions in cost.

To perform or to assist in the performance of special reviews at the request of management.

To direct, when applicable, the activities of assistants.

Authority and Responsibility

Under the guidance of a supervising or senior internal auditor:

Surveys functions and activities in assigned areas to determine the nature of operations and the adequacy of the system of control to achieve established objectives. Identifies the key control points of the system.

Determines or assists in determining the direction and thrust of the proposed audit effort. Determines or assists in determining the audit procedures to be used.

Plans or assists in planning the theory and scope of the audit, and prepares or assists in preparing an audit program.

Performs the audit in a professional manner and in accordance with the approved audit program.

Obtains, analyzes, and appraises evidentiary data as a basis for an informed, objective opinion on the adequacy and effectiveness of the system and the efficiency of performance of the activities being reviewed.

Makes, or assists in making, oral or written presentations to management during and at the conclusion of the examination, discussing deficiencies, recommending corrective action, and suggesting improvements in operations and reductions in cost.

Prepares formal written reports, as requested, expressing opinions on the adequacy and effectiveness of the system and the efficiency with which activities are carried out.

Appraises, or assists in appraising, the adequacy of the corrective action taken to improve deficient conditions.

Exhibit 16-7. POSITION DESCRIPTION
INTERNAL AUDITOR — ASSISTANT

Purpose

To verify and analyze transactions and representations while conducting reviews of assigned organizational and functional activities.

To evaluate the adequacy and effectiveness of the management controls over those activities.

To assist in determining whether organizational units in the company are performing their planning, accounting, custodial, or control activities in compliance with management instructions, applicable statements of policy and procedures, and in a manner consistent with both company objectives and high standards of administrative practice.

To prepare working papers showing the results of the audit examination.

To report audit findings on the results of the review of assigned segments of the audit and to make recommendations for the correction of unsatisfactory conditions, improvements in operations, and reductions in cost.

To assist in the performance of special reviews at the request of management.

Authority and Responsibility

Under the direct supervision of a senior internal auditor:

Assists in planning work on assigned segments of the audit.

Assists in determining records or activities to analyze, the extent of tests to apply, and the working papers to prepare.

Assists in performing the audit in accordance with the approved program and in a professional manner.

Recommends the means of obtaining, analyzing, and evaluating evidentiary data as a basis for an informed, objective opinion on the adequacy and effectiveness of the system of control and on the efficiency of performance of the activities being reviewed.

Reviews transactions, documents, records, reports, and methods for accuracy and effectiveness.

Prepares acceptable working papers which record and summarize data on the assigned audit segment.

Holds preliminary discussions of apparent deficiencies with operating personnel to verify facts and to obtain explanations of and reasons for such apparent deficiencies.

Developing the Audit Manuals

The audit manuals constitute the voice of the director of auditing. They tell staff auditors how audit duties should be carried out. They provide for stability, continuity, standards of acceptable performance, and the means of coordinating the efforts of a number of persons or of various units within the auditing organization. But in modern internal auditing the director is faced with a dilemma. On the one hand is the desirability of providing instruction and achieving some optimal level of uniformity in the organization. On the other is the possibility, through the director's pronouncements, of inhibiting imagination and innovative auditing.

Despite the dangers of stifling independent thinking, however, the staff needs guidance to prevent individuals from going off in different directions, to establish standards that lift the level of performance, and to provide assurance that the auditing department's final product meets the director's requirements.

The auditing department's statements of policies and procedures must provide instructions and guidelines in several different areas. For convenience, this body of instructions to audit staff may be divided into the following groupings:

○ Technical functions — seeing that the job of conducting internal audits meets acceptable standards of coverage.
○ Administrative functions — seeing that the internal audit department, as a group of individuals, runs smoothly.
○ Miscellaneous functions — providing answers to the complete spectrum of day-to-day problems of the auditing department, as they arise.

The audit manuals are a mirror of the life style and philosophy of the individual audit department and its director. Each manual, therefore, in each auditing organization, will be uniquely structured to carry out the ideas of the individual who charts the department's course.

Technical Functions

The technical audit manual will offer a guide to the performance of an internal audit. Without limiting the matters that may properly be included, the following subjects should probably be discussed.

Objectives of the Audit

Establish the perimeters around the audit project so that an audit program can be written which will delineate the audit area and prevent wandering off into avenues that are irrelevant to the central theme of the audit.

Theory of the Audit

Establish the idea of the audit approach. Shall it be a review of an organization or of a function? What are the auditors trying to establish or accomplish? Is the idea to make a survey with little testing, or is it to select certain suspected activities for detailed examination? Are the auditors seeking to determine the degree to which the existing structure is effective or do they want to know whether established procedures are being carried out?

Scope of the Audit

Establish the matters which should be reviewed in all examinations. For example, have responsibilities been adequately assigned? Is authority commensurate with responsibility? Have organizational or functional objectives been set? Do reports to higher management show progress in meeting established objectives? Are methods and procedures designed to facilitate meeting those objectives? Are objectives actually being met? Does management have a self-checking system to highlight deviations from acceptable performance?

Preliminary Reviews

Provide guides on the matters to be considered in the initial phase of the audit: the review of prior working papers, the research of internal auditing literature on the activity to be reviewed, and the examination of organization charts and relevant company directives.

Preliminary Discussions

Indicate the levels of management at which preliminary discussions should be held, the nature of the assistance the auditors may offer to management, and the explanations they should make of the audit objectives, approaches, and programs.

Preliminary Surveys

Indicate the nature of the preliminary survey, the kind of information to be obtained, the ways in which it can be obtained, and the uses to which the information should be put (see Chapter 4).

Audit Programs

Show the requirements for each individual audit program to be tailored to the particular assignment and to determine operating objectives and related controls; and show the detail with which the programs shall be prepared.

Budgets and Schedules

Describe the controls to be exercised over the audit project to assure compliance with budget and schedule constraints.

Working Papers

Establish standards for working papers, for methods of summarizing data, and for indexing and cross-referencing worksheets.

Draft Reviews with Auditees

Set forth policies on reviews of findings, obtaining corrective action, the evidence of corrective action needed to close a finding, and the levels at which findings should be discussed.

Report Writing

Provide guidelines on the format of reports, their length, the philosophy of reporting (problems only, or comprehensive analysis of and opinions on the activity reviewed), and the levels of management to which the reports are directed.

Replies to Reports

Provide instruction on how to deal with replies, what action to take if they are not acceptable, and how to close reports in which the replies are found to be acceptable.

Administrative Functions

Another volume of instructions is needed to provide guidance on those matters which are related to the business of performing internal audits, but which are not an actual part of performing the audit function. A separate manual, usually referred to as the administrative manual, facilitates revisions and is easier to handle. If it is combined with the audit manual it tends to become unwieldy. The administrative manual often takes the form of a compilation of staff memos, each of which can be issued or revised whenever considered desirable. Some of the matters which may be the subject of staff memos are as follows:

A. Office Administration
   1. Organization of the audit department
   2. Audit office filing system
   3. Reference library
   4. Supplies
   5. Time reports
   6. Housekeeping
   7. Security requirements
   8. Miscellaneous correspondence
   9. Periodic administrative reports
B. Personnel
   1. Personnel records
   2. Travel instructions and expense reports
   3. Staff evaluations
   4. Incentive awards
   5. Reporting injuries
   6. Jury duty
   7. Military duty
C. Audit Projects
   1. Assignment of the audit project
   2. Human relations — dealing with the auditee
   3. Permanent files for audit projects
   4. Budget estimates for audit projects

5. Requests for program revisions or budget adjustments
6. Uses of statistical sampling
7. Uses of electronic data processing on audit projects
8. Safeguarding working papers
9. Destroying working papers
10. Exit interviews with auditees
11. Closing audit projects
D. Audit Reports
1. Interim or progress reports
2. Supervisory review of audit reports
3. Proofreading, reference-checking, and processing final reports
4. Distribution of audit reports
5. Request for copies of audit reports

Miscellaneous Functions

Auditors, like most other employees, are bombarded with many instructions over and above those appearing in the technical and administrative manuals. These instructions may amplify, explain, or restrict statements in those manuals or they may cover matters not quite germane to the information in technical and administrative regulations. But whatever their relationship, these instructions appear in an unending stream.

Usually, they appear in memoranda, formal or informal, from the director's office. And since they were created by the same pen that wrote or approved the manuals, they have the same force and effect and require the same adherence.

Unfortunately, miscellaneous instructions, like comets, usually blaze across the departmental sky and then fall to rest in some correspondence file. There they lie, quiescent, to be revived only when they have been violated and are used to bludgeon the violator, or when they are vaguely remembered and take hours to locate. All such intructions, therefore, should be kept in an organized manner, capable of ready retrieval, in a miscellaneous manual.

The manual should be thoughtfully compiled and maintained, so that one, only matters of continuing significance are included; two, it is periodically and formally updated to incorporate new information and to delete superseded instructions; three, the referencing system provides for easy revisions, additions, and deletions; and four, the index is complete, easy to maintain, and facilitates prompt retrieval of information.

Clearly, each audit department's miscellaneous manual will be different, and no strict format or table of contents can be devised to be universally applicable. One for a manufacturing company would bear no recognizable relationship to one for an insurance company, for instance. But the following example of a table of contents will provide some guidance for the preparation of such a manual — a manual which can save untold hours of searching and assure closer adherence to the director's instructions (see Exhibit 16-8).

Exhibit 16-8.

MISCELLANEOUS MANUAL CONTENTS

A. Our Organization
1. Internal auditing in our company
2. Structure of our organization
3. Our responsibilities and authority
4. Our interface with other organizations

B. Our Program
1. Planning our program
2. Cooperating with our public accountants
3. Coordinating with our security department
4. Reviewing our audit program with management

C. Our Auditing Methods and Techniques
1. Areas of risk
2. Using electronic data processing in audits
3. Using statistical sampling
4. Discussing the program with the auditee
5. Discussing the deficiencies with the auditee
6. Audit time spans and budgets
7. Cost reduction suggestions
8. Recommendations for improved operations
9. Audit time spans
10. Determining causes for deficiencies
11. Reviewing draft reports with auditees

D. Audit Reports
1. Format of regular reports
2. Format of special reports
3. Distribution of audit reports
4. Replies to audit reports
5. Classifying deficiency findings according to causes and significance

E. Coordinating Among Units
1. Audits performed concurrently
2. Exchange of audit programs
3. Exchange of research information
4. Uniformity of audit programs

F. Reports of Audit Activity
1. Monthly reports
2. Quarterly reports
3. Annual reports

G. Miscellaneous
1. Professional activities
2. Budgets
3. Change of status notices
4. Travel

Each memorandum or instruction is separately numbered according to the system set out above. For example, a memorandum providing information on how to budget for research projects might be numbered G.2.1. A subsequent memorandum setting forth budgeting for employee indoctrination might be numbered G.2.2, and so forth.

Selling Modern Internal Auditing to Management

Successful selling, as every successful salesperson knows, is based on two steadfast requirements: Know your product. Know your customer. Salespeople must know every element of their product and which features make the product most salable. They must know who their customers are and what their customers want.

That is not quite as simple as it may sound in terms of internal auditing. The product will vary with the experience, tenure, and sophistication of the auditing personnel. And the customer — the real customer, executive management, those who guide the destiny of the entire enterprise — must be carefully wooed and cultivated as a part of a long-range, studied sales effort.

A major objective of the auditing organization is to be accepted as a full member in the councils of executive management, treated with respect as the provider of a product that is valuable, desirable, and unobtainable elsewhere, turned to automatically when problems within the auditor's competence arise, and looked to for current information on the state and effectiveness of the company's operating controls.

The auditors' campaign to bring their capability to the attention of management should be aggressive and dynamic. Because executive management rarely singles out the auditors, they must step forward and parade their wares. The campaign must be well founded. Let but a single hasty promise go unfulfilled, and management may become disillusioned and immune to future campaigns.

Selling modern internal auditing must start with a salable product. That product is the ability of the auditing organization to perform competently and professionally. Every audit performed in the traditional, financial area must be thorough and sound. Each auditor must function as a professional. Each audit report should carry the imprint of professional quality in terms of both form and substance. No document should be issued over the director's signature that is not of a caliber equal to what is issued over the signature of the company's chief executive officer.

Management thus learns to expect and be confident of a high level of professionalism in the traditional financial audits and in the auditors' reports. Having merited management's confidence, auditors can begin to give special character and scope to their audits, even in the financial areas. The audits can begin to adopt a management viewpoint.

For example, in a traditional financial audit it is characteristic to determine whether discounts are being taken or not taken and to make a comparison between lost discounts during current and prior accounting periods. These are serious matters, of course, but they are pedestrian, unexciting, and little deserving of high level attention. The final report on such an audit would be of interest to the chief accountant. Higher management, however, would have little reason to read it.

But what if the internal auditor applied management thinking to the examination? For example: Why are discounts being lost? How are lost discounts affected by the accounting department's workload, by any delays in the receiving department, or by the purchasing department's failure to send purchasing documents to receiving on time? Are payments to obtain discounts scheduled too far in advance of the discount dates, thereby adversely affecting cash flow? Would it be possible to save money by paying interest on borrowed funds to pay bills within discount periods? Should it be company policy to take discounts, whether they are literally earned or not, and refund the amounts only to the suppliers who complain?

When internal auditors are able to discuss matters such as these in their reports, then higher management becomes interested. Aware of this interest, auditors can and should improve the product's package. For example, they can attach to their reports charts and graphs that dramatically highlight their findings. Where a number of branches are involved, they can show the effect of the activities of an upstream organization upon a downstream organization. They can, from their advantageous position, determine where there are breakdowns in communication or where information or reports available to one organization may be of use to another.

They have the opportunity, while still hanging on to what they may regard as their lifeline — their natural base in finance — to move surefootedly into operating organizations and to disclose an understanding of operating problems as well as financial problems. At the same time, they can trace the accounting systems and records to their diverse sources, where they become palpable things and living people instead of digits and data.

As financial executives become aware of this new capability, they begin asking for studies in areas outside their authority, but within their concern — like asking for a determination as to whether the work-in-process accounts fairly reflect the cost of items actually in process in the shop. In that situation, certain financial auditors carefully dipped their toes into the operational sea and began a long and successful journey into modern internal auditing.[3]

These particular auditors found that the only way to obtain the information needed to satisfy the financial executive's question was through the production control records. The auditors were led to a searching and complete investigation of the whole spectrum of production control documents and reports and were able to learn how to grapple with factory operations. The auditors learned that there was no reason for fear. The problems were the same in operations as in finance. The questions were still "do the records fairly reflect?" and "can management rely on the information contained in the operating reports prepared from those records?" The principles of verification, analysis, and appraisal are the same for physical quantities as they are for dollars and cents.

Conclusion

Modern internal auditing, to be successful, must be grounded on management support and acceptance and on imaginative service to the organization. Also, it must have a reporting status in the company that ensures proper consideration of the findings and recommendations developed by auditors. To this end, the internal audit charter must set forth explicitly the auditors' broad authority and correlative responsibility; the charter must spell out clearly the requirement for prompt and responsive replies to internal audit reports; and the auditors' job descriptions must call for superior people, not average ones. Audit manuals should supply standards and guidelines, not detailed instructions. Auditors must mount a continuing campaign to promote their product to executive management, and the product they sell must be of the quality that will capture and keep management's interest.

References

1. Paul Macchiaverna, "Internal Auditing" (New York: The Conference Board, 1978), p. 53.
2. F. J. Walsh, Jr., *Internal Auditing* (New York: The National Industrial Conference Board, 1963), p. 17.
3. F. E. Mints, "New Developments in Operational Auditing," *The Internal Auditor*, June 1960, p. 11.

For further study

Discussion Problems

1. Under what circumstances would it be satisfactory for the internal auditor to report to the controller of an enterprise?

2. Why should internal auditors be able to display independence?

3. Can an internal auditor be completely independent of his or her organization? Why?

4. What form should the independence of the internal auditor take?

5. Why should external auditors be concerned with the internal auditor's independence?

6. Why is a formal charter within the enterprise necessary for an internal auditor?

7. What do you consider the most vital part of the charter, from the internal auditor's standpoint?

8. What are the benefits and the dangers of requiring internal auditors to use audit manuals?

9. How would you go about promoting internal auditing to executive management? To the board?

10. The internal auditing department of a large service entity is organiza-

tionally responsible to the controller, who in turn is responsible to the president. As part of the internal audit responsibility, regular audits are performed of payroll, general accounting, accounts receivable, and accounts payable.

Because these departments also report to the controller, criticism is frequently made that the internal auditor cannot be objective when auditing such activities. Listed below are two solutions that might eliminate the criticism. Describe briefly two advantages and two disadvantages of each of these solutions.

a. The internal auditing department could send directly to the president audit reports concerning activities under the supervision of the controller.

b. The director of internal auditing could discuss the organizational problem with the external auditors and ask them to make a recommendation which would eliminate the criticism.

Multiple Choice Problems

1. The internal auditor's independence is most likely to be compromised when the internal audit department is responsible directly to the:
a. Vice president - finance.
b. President.
c. Controller.
d. Executive vice president.
e. Audit committee of the board of directors.

2. The charter for an internal auditing department should indicate responsibility for:
a. Reconciling bank accounts.
b. Developing standards of control in new EDP systems.
c. Developing job descriptions in any department under review where there are no descriptions.
d. Correcting any deficient condition.
e. None of the above.

3. Internal auditing can best be described as:
a. An accounting function.
b. A compliance function.
c. An activity primarily to detect fraud.
d. An internal control function.
e. An activity that determines the integrity of financial statements.

4. An adequate statement of functions and responsibilities for the auditor is needed to:
a. Command a salary commensurate with his or her position.
b. Be on a par with other company officials.
c. Have ready access to the president of the company.
d. Have ready access to the board of directors.
e. Be permitted to review operations throughout the company.

5. The scope of work of the internal auditing department should include:
a. Reviewing the reliability and integrity of divisional financial reports.
b. Determining compliance with applicable laws and regulations.
c. Ascertaining whether operating goals and objectives are being achieved.
d. Reviewing the economy and efficiency with which resources are employed.
e. All of the above.

6. The independence of the internal auditing department is enhanced when the:
a. Board of directors concurs in the

appointment or removal of the director of internal auditing.
b. Director of internal auditing has direct communication with the board.
c. Director of internal auditing submits to management for approval, and to the board of directors for information, a summary of the department's audit work schedule, staffing plan, and financial budget.
d. All of the above.
e. a. and b. above.

7. Which of the following may compromise the independence of an internal auditor?
a. Reviewing EDP systems prior to implementation.
b. Performing an audit where the auditor recently had operating responsibilities.
c. Failing to review the audit report with the auditee prior to its distribution.
d. Following up on corrective action in response to audit findings.
e. All of the above.

8. In determining whether to rely on the work of the internal auditor, the external auditor is expected to consider which of the following:
a. Hiring practices of the internal auditing department.
b. Qualifications of the internal audit staff.
c. Recommendations made in internal audit reports.
d. Objectivity of internal auditors.
e. All of the above.

9. Which of the following should be defined in the charter of the internal auditing department?
a. Types of departmental activity reports to be prepared and to whom they should be distributed.
b. Distribution of audit reports.
c. Knowledge, skills, and disciplines required of staff auditors.

d. Scope of internal auditing activities.
e. Approval of the internal auditing department's budget.

10. Internal auditors must have independence:
a. To ensure their objectivity.
b. To be able to audit any activity in the organization.
c. To be sure they will receive replies to their reports.
d. To have access to the board of directors.
e. To be protected against threats of dismissal.

Case Studies

16-1 To Whom Should Internal Auditors Report?

Two directors of internal auditing from two different companies, Paul Eberhardt and Trevor Smith, were seated next to each other at an Institute dinner meeting.

Paul said, "I missed you last month, Trevor, what happened?"

"I was presenting a report to the board of directors of the company," said Trevor. "I just couldn't make The Institute meeting."

"Isn't a report at that level kind of unusual?" asked Paul.

"Not at all. That's where I report — to the auditing committee of the board of directors. And when they meet, I salute and say my piece. Where do you report, Paul?"

"To the vice president-controller. And I don't have to wait for a formal meeting. I can go up to him any time I get an appointment — which is just about any time I want. I like that better."

"Not me," said Trevor. "I've got a mandate from the top — there is no higher — and that's the way I like it."

"But you don't get the personal rapport and close working relationship that you have when you report to a single individual."

"True. But I've got a lot more clout," explained Trevor.

"I've got all the clout I need. It's in my statement of functions and responsibilities. And besides, I'd rather rely on hard facts and gentle persuasion than on clout," stated Paul.

"That's what you think now. But when the chips are down and you're getting into some wild management-services audit in which you're even questioning the president's policies and procedures, a little clout from the board doesn't hurt," Trevor replied.

Required: Who do you think is right? Why?

16-2 Moving Into Operations

When Paul Eberhardt was still a supervisor, his boss, Will Lohman, was about to retire. Jan Tobias, the vice president-controller, called Paul into his office.

"Hello, Paul, how are things?"

"Just fine, Mr. Tobias, although it's kind of sad to see Will leaving. He's built up a fine internal auditing organization."

"True, Paul. He's done a fine job for us. But perhaps when you pick up the ball you can carry it even further. I'm counting on that."

"I hope to, Mr. Tobias. I'd like to do a lot more work in operations."

"I'm in complete agreement, Paul. I think we're about ready for it. We've grown to $600,000,000 in sales. We've got 15,000 people working in our company. We've got finance, administration, engineering, manufacturing operations, quality assurance, procurement, and personnel organizations, not to speak of research and development and sales. I'd say we're ready for it. But I don't know about some of our entrenched directors of

those branches who have never heard of operational auditing. How do you propose to break the glad tidings to them?"

Required: How should Paul respond? Without giving a detailed outline of his plans, how can he assure Tobias that he knows what is needed?

16-3 The Audit Supervisor's Opportunity

Stu Purviss, audit supervisor for Able Company, answered his phone at 9:00 a.m. Monday.

"Mr. Purviss?"

"Yes."

"My name is Rod Walker. I work for Business Search, Incorporated. We place executives with business organizations."

"What can I do for you, Mr. Walker?"

"You're one of several people we're trying to contact for a position that might interest you."

"What kind of position?"

"General Auditor for Baker Company."

"Never heard of it. What do they do?"

"They are a large baking organization with outlets throughout the country. They're even considering penetrating foreign markets."

"What were their sales last year?"

"A little over $50,000,000. And that's up from last year by about 10%. It's a rapidly growing outfit. And they feel the time has come for them to install an internal audit staff."

"When did they get that notion?"

"This year when their outside accountants told them that they should have such a staff."

"Then they've never had an internal audit staff before?"

"No. And frankly I don't believe they are fully aware of the service a good internal audit staff could furnish them."

"Who would I report to?"

"The chief accountant."

"Not interested. I'd be going from the modern internal auditing I'm doing here to tick and checking. I passed that point years ago. I couldn't possibly consider that kind of auditing."

"Hold on. I believe that you could probably change that if you were really interested."

"Well, I'd have to talk to somebody pretty high up in the company before I could convince them of what they really need."

"Suppose I could get an appointment for you with their executive vice president Simon Cabot. I know him and he has modern, forward-looking ideas. Maybe the two of you could come to an equitable arrangement that would suit you and be of value to them."

"Fine. Make it about a week from now, so I can put together my proposition for them."

"Will do. I'll call you back as soon as I can make the arrangements."

True to his word, Rod called Stu in about a half hour. A date was set for Stu to see Mr. Cabot. Stu immediately got busy outlining what he planned to say during the interview, and what information he wanted from the executive vice president.

Required: Prepare a report to Cabot pointing out the benefits of a program of modern internal auditing.

17

Selecting and Developing the Staff

Good auditing demands good auditors. Standards for internal auditors. Professional ability; quality of character. The *Standards for the Professional Practice of Internal Auditing*. Subjects calling for proficiency, understanding, or appreciation. Adaptability, understanding, determination, integrity, objectivity, and responsibility. How internal auditors regard their own profession. Sources for internal auditors. Interviews. Rating applicants for internal auditing positions. Testing writing facility and the ability to organize thoughts. Distinguishing between fact and conjecture. Orientation for newly hired internal auditors. Program for orientation. Training for higher audit positions. Continuing education: study, staff meetings, research projects. Evaluating internal auditors. Staff rating forms.

The Need for a Superior Staff

The vision of the director of auditing and the high expectations of management are merely wistful wishes without the right staff to do the job. The dreams of improved and varied services to the organization through modern internal auditing turn into nightmares if the people who prepare the audit programs, who do the questing and the questioning, make the appraisals, and offer the recommendations are not up to the demands that modern internal auditing makes of its practitioners.

What is more, internal auditing is not static. It is expanding constantly. The subjects under review grow more difficult with each audit. As management and the board of directors rely more upon the auditor, they insist on greater depth and breadth in the audit approach.

The business of selecting the right people, orienting them, training them, promoting their development, and evaluating them accurately, must occupy much of the director's thoughts and energies.

The Qualities of Professional Internal Auditors

To build a superior staff, first one must know the standards for excellence. Modern internal auditing, with its demands for intelligence, technical competence, and the ability to deal with people at all levels of the company, sets high standards for its practitioners.

These standards should never be compromised. The organizations being audited judge all of internal auditing by the individual auditors they deal with. The audit team should, therefore, include those who will perpetuate the image that the director of internal auditing wishes to project throughout the enterprise. (See Chapter 2 for professional requirements.) It is far better to be understaffed than to hire a single internal auditor who can tear down in one assignment what took years for the rest of the team to build.

For these reasons, the director of internal auditing must consider certain attributes of professional ability and qualities of character when making personnel selections.

Education, the first step, develops professional abilities; actual experience then hones those abilities. Education for internal auditors should develop the knowledge, skills, and disciplines essential to the performance of professional internal audit work. The broad scope of internal auditing makes complete knowledge of all its subjects almost impossible for an individual to obtain. The auditing team as a whole, however, should have the needed proficiency to carry.out whatever audit engagements are assigned or approved by management — or at least have access to that proficiency. The individual auditor should be proficient in certain core skills needed for broad-based internal auditing, have an understanding of others, and an appreciation of the rest. The *Standards for the Professional Practice of Internal Auditing* explain these terms and describe their applicability. Section 250.01 of the *Standards* says:

.01 Each internal auditor should possess certain knowledge and skills as follows:

> *.1* Proficiency in applying internal auditing standards, procedures, and techniques is required in performing internal audits. Proficiency means the ability to apply knowledge to situations likely to be encountered and to deal with them without extensive recourse to technical research and assistance.
>
> *.2* Proficiency in accounting principles and techniques is required of auditors who work extensively with financial records and reports.
>
> *.3* An understanding of management principles is required to recognize and evaluate the materiality and significance of deviations from good business practice. An understanding means the

ability to apply broad knowledge to situations likely to be encountered, to recognize significant deviations, and to be able to carry out the research necessary to arrive at reasonable solutions.

.4 An appreciation is required of the fundamentals of such subjects as accounting, economics, commercial law, taxation, finance, quantitative methods, and computerized information systems. An appreciation means the ability to recognize the existence of problems or potential problems and to determine the further research to be undertaken or the assistance to be obtained.

Certain qualities of character are needed to meet the demands made by modern internal auditing. Such qualities include adaptability, understanding, and determination, among others.

To cope with the diversity of internal auditing, adaptability is needed — the ability to accommodate to the ever-changing environment internal auditors meet in their varied assignments; the facility to readily absorb the jargon that the activity being audited has spawned together with the ability to translate what they have learned into plain English; the agility to react quickly to new problems, new product lines, new management viewpoints, and new company objectives.

Because auditors are constantly dealing with people, understanding is needed — the ability to grasp what makes them react favorably or with hostility; the empathy that enables the auditor to comprehend their problems and to walk in their shoes for a while; the sensitivity to what frustrates them; the perception of how they feel about their jobs, their managers, and their company; the tact that enables the auditor to ask productive questions without raising the hackles of the person being questioned.

To deal with difficult problems and to trudge unblazed paths, determination is needed — the resistance to pressures that would sway auditors from their goals; the insistence that they and they alone must satisfy their own internal monitors before they stop their pursuit of the answers to their questions; the willingness to work as hard and as long as is necessary to establish the facts and to document them so that they will be impregnable to attack.

The knowledge that their professional opinions are a solemn affirmation demands integrity, objectivity, and responsibility — the reputation for dealing only in facts; for placing the facts in perspective; for being able to evaluate objectively the materiality of their findings; for having no personal axe to grind; for being absolutely trustworthy; for being completely responsible, because they have the power to do irreparable injury through citations of deficiencies.

Round these qualities out with the ability to communicate, both orally and in writing; a strong, positive attitude toward their profession that sells both the auditor and the audit; and the imagination and initiative that find new ways of attacking old problems — and the modern internal auditor emerges.

Professional internal auditors have a high regard for their field of work. A study carried out by a survey research company for The Institute of Internal Auditors, Inc., in 1977 had this to say:[1]

> In general, auditors' attitudes toward their jobs tend to be positive. For example, they feel their jobs give them an overview of all functions within their organization and the opportunity to make significant contributions to efficient operations.
>
> [and]
>
> The internal auditors' attitudes toward the profession are also positive. For example, more than 88% [answering a questionnaire] say they would recommend the field to a friend. Looking to the future, internal auditors have a positive attitude toward the potential of their profession. They agree that internal auditing functions will become increasingly important to organizational managers and that employment opportunities for internal auditors will significantly increase within the next five years.

The statistics in Exhibit 17-1 support these conclusions about a positive feeling toward the profession (in percentages, except for sample size):[2]

Sources

Where does one look for internal auditors? There are many sources.

Universities and Colleges

From universities and colleges one obtains the raw material and forms it into the desired likeness. Obtaining the likely graduate calls for long-range programs. The director of auditing, or an aide who is personable, enthusiastic, and speaks well before an audience, should be on a continuing program of speeches to students. There is enough excitement, adventure, and chance for advancement in the profession to form the core of an absorbing sales talk. The speaking program should be long range if it is to produce results, and it should be pursued even during those periods when staff positions are completely filled.

Certified Public Accountants

Young accountants looking for new and exciting opportunities, who have put in an apprenticeship with a public accounting firm, can be fine prospects. Advertisements in the leading accounting journals can attract the attention of the young CPAs. They may be sold on the solid prospects of modern internal auditing rather than on a position of controller or chief accountant in a small company. An excellent sales approach is to cite those managers and executives in the company who reached their present positions from the springboard of internal auditing.

Exhibit 17-1.

Statement	Stongly Agree	Agree	Neither Agree Nor Disagree	Disagree	Strongly Disagree	Number of Responses
IA (internal auditing) provides me with an overview of all functions within the organization	44.7	49.6	2.5	2.2	0.3	766
I feel that my job in IA makes a significant contribution to the efficient operation of my organization	27.9	61.3	7.9	2.7	0.3	713
My position offers opportunity for sufficient supervisory experiences	27.9	53.5	5.3	10.4	2.8	749
Sufficient funds are allocated by my organization to properly operate the IA function	21.2	48.3	10.3	15.1	4.6	740
My job provides me with excellent opportunities for promotion to management positions outside the field of IA	23.5	38.0	19.7	13.5	5.3	736
The internal auditor is often thought of as a person for special assignments	7.1	60.5	16.0	14.7	1.7	707

Within the Company

Directors of internal auditing have an excellent start by looking within their own company. They are in a position to get a first-hand look at the prospect in actual operation. The prospect already has a working knowledge of the company's policies, methods, products, and management. The audit staff should be asked to be constantly alert to people who have the basic equipment and who should be approached — through established channels, of course — for an interview.

The Institute of Internal Auditors, Inc.

The Internal Auditor, The Institute's professional journal, takes advertisements for auditors and has the advantage of being delivered to internal auditors throughout the world. In 1980 over 20,000 internal auditors received the journal.

How to Select Internal Auditors

Having attracted the prospect, what then? There are two steps that should be taken: first, interviewing; second, testing.

Interviews

An interview with applicants should be a well-planned, well-organized affair. The prospect's resume and application should have been carefully read and his or her references called. Calling the references is better than writing to them. A former employer will be more free and candid on the telephone than on paper.

The interview should be set for a time when the pressure of other work will not interfere. Directors of auditing should screen the prospects first. If they seem to be likely candidates, some of the staff supervisors should interview them also.

Interviewing is an art and takes practice to develop. It should be a two-way street. The interviewer tells about the job, the company, the opportunities, and the nature of the work. The interviewees tell about themselves.

Some people, when interviewed, need to be drawn out; some need to be guided. Questions to ask experienced candidates include:

What were some of the assignments you conducted?

How did you approach them?

What kind of reports did you write?

How have you kept up your education?

Why do you want to make a change?

What do you like about internal auditing?

What don't you like about it?

What kind of assignment do you like best?

What are your hobbies?

What are your personal goals?

Questions to ask candidates with no experience include:

What is your concept of internal auditing?

How did you hear about it?

Why do you think you'd like it?

What kinds of assignments would you like best?

What are your outside interests?

What are your personal goals?

Keep records of all interviews in an organized manner so that they can be used readily to compare the qualities and qualifications of different candidates for the same position. Exhibit 17-2 is an example of an applicant interview record. Exhibit 17-3 gives definitions of the qualities being explored and rated.

Exhibit 17-2. INTERVIEW RATING SHEET

Name_____Age_____
Degrees_____
Last two employers_____

Schools_____

Certifications_____
Will Travel?_____

	0	2	4	6	8	10
Attitude						
Appearance						
Maturity						
Sociability						
Self-Expression						
Motivation						
Intelligence						
Persuasiveness						
Self-Confidence						
Interest						
Potential						
Overall Evaluation						

Should we make this applicant an offer?_____
If so, for what position?_____
Comments_____

_____
_____

Interviewer_____
Date_____

Exhibit 17-3. INTERVIEW RATING SHEET —
DEFINITIONS

Rating Factors

Attitude — Outlook in general

Appearance — Physical appearance, neatness, dress, posture

Maturity — Behavior and apparent emotional stability

Sociability — Apparent ability to get along with others; warmth, response

Self-expression — Ability to express thoughts clearly, concisely, effectively

Motivation — Drive, initiative, enthusiasm, energy, desire to succeed

Intelligence — Mental ability, judgment, alertness, organization of thoughts

Persuasiveness — Ability to influence others

Self-confidence — Poise, interest in challenge

Interest — Indication of sincere interest in internal auditing and our company

Potential — Your impression of the applicant's potential for a management position

Overall Evaluation — Your general impression of the applicant

Rating Scores

10 — Outstanding.	Exceptional, clearly superior (applicable only in rare instances)
8 — Excellent.	Considerably above average, definitely stands out, makes immediate and lasting impression.
6 — Satisfactory Plus.	Well above average, a potential asset to the company
4 — Satisfactory.	Normal for a person of this age, experience, and education
2 — Satisfactory Minus.	A marginal rating; doesn't quite meet minimum standards
0 — Unsatisfactory.	Unsuitable for our work

Testing

With so much hanging in the balance, directors of auditing need every edge they can get to decide whether or not to hire a prospect. Only time will disclose whether the decision to hire was correct. There are no standard tests, at this writing, for internal auditors — certainly none like those given to doctors, lawyers, pharmacists, and accountants. But several tests have been developed independently by some auditing organizations to give an insight into the prospect's writing ability and thought processes.

It should be pointed out that many directors of auditing are opposed to such tests. Others, however, have used them with a fair degree of success and have validated them by comparing the grades on the tests with the evaluations subsequently given to the same employees on job rating sheets. These comparisons have shown reasonable correlations between test scores and the later evaluations.

Government laws and regulations forbid some tests for employment, but tests which bear a direct relation to the job being filled are often acceptable. Directors of internal auditing should submit their proposed tests to their industrial relations officials for review and approval before using them.

For the tests to be effective, the prospect should not be able to see them in advance. It would be unwise, therefore, to use the exact tests printed in a book in general circulation, such as this one. Each test should be separately developed by the auditing organization itself. For this reason we have developed some ideas and truncated examples in the preparation of such tests, rather than provide complete copies of those in actual use.

Test of Writing Ability

Provide applicants with a statement of an audit situation and ask them to write a report in a prescribed format, setting forth, for example, (a) background information, (b) the purpose of the audit, (c) the scope of the audit, (d) the auditor's opinion, and (e) the recommendations for corrective action. Examples of two such audit situations might be as follows:

> Envelopes are opened in the mail room by any one of several mail room employees. All remittances are placed in a box until the end of the day. At that time they are placed in an interdepartmental envelope and sent to the cashier:

> [and]

> Buyers in the purchasing department are permitted to develop their own lists of prospective bidders, prepare the requests for bids, mail them directly to the bidders being solicited, and receive the completed bids directly from the mail room.

The instructions to the applicants should tell them to write their reports in nontechnical terms which would be plain to a manager who has no accounting or purchasing background. They should also be told that their reports will be evaluated according to standards of clarity, coherence (how it hangs together), structure, and the use of appropriate language.

Evaluation and grading such tests present a problem because there are no simple mathematical criteria to rely upon. Some measure of objectivity can be obtained, however, by assigning maximum numerical grades for each of the four standards and permitting two or more people to rate the test results independently of each other. The grading criteria might be as follows:

Standard	Maximum value	Grade
Clarity	40	_____
Coherence	35	_____
Structure	15	_____
Words	10	_____
Totals	100	_____

Test of Ability to Organize Thoughts

Provide the applicant with a series of approximately 25 statements about an audit problem. The statements are numbered sequentially, but their logical order has been scrambled. Ask the applicant to rearrange the state-

---

Exhibit 17-4. TEST OF ABILITY TO ORGANIZE THOUGHTS

INSTRUCTIONS: Insert, in the spaces provided, the proper numbers in their proper order.

Purpose	Scope	Control Findings	Performance Findings	Opinion	Recommendations
( )	( )	( )	( )	( )	( )
( )	( )	( )	( )	( )	( )
( )	( )	( )	( )	( )	( )
( )	( )	( )	( )	( )	( )
( )	( )	( )	( )	( )	( )

(1) We also recommended that supervisors periodically check manuals to make sure they are kept up to date.

(2) It is also our opinion that the system was working as intended except for the fact that some manuals were not up to date.

(3) Our test of the checked drawings showed that they had all been signed off by engineering supervisors before release.

(4) We reviewed systems and procedures by reading instructions and interviewing engineering personnel.

(5) Our test of the error reports showed them to be accurate and timely.

(6) We found an adequate supply of drafting manuals for all engineers, but 20% of the manuals were not up to date.

(7) We also set out to determine whether the system was working as intended.

(8) We set out to evaluate the adequacy of the system of control over the accuracy of engineering drawings.

(9) Our test of 100 drawings showed that they had all been verified by drawing checkers.

(10) We also found that all drawings must be verified by drawing checkers for accuracy.

(11) We found that after checking, the drawings must be reviewed by engineering supervisors before release.

(12) It is our opinion that the control system was adequate.

(13) We found that a drafting manual had been developed to provide detailed instructions to engineering draftsmen.

(14) We examined 100 engineering drawings in detail.

(15) Management had developed a system of reporting the number of drawing errors based on complaints from the production organization.

(16) We recommended that all manuals be brought up to date promptly.

ments in a reasonable order under headings which have been provided. The headings may include Purpose, Scope, Control Findings, Performance Findings, Opinion, and Recommendations. An abbreviated example of the hashed statements is shown in Exhibit 17-4. The solution is shown in Exhibit 17-5.

Exhibit 17-5. SOLUTION TO TEST OF ABILITY
TO ORGANIZE THOUGHTS

Purpose

(8) We set out to evaluate the adequacy of the system of control over the accuracy of engineering drawings.

(7) We also set out to determine whether the system was working as intended.

Scope

(4) We reviewed systems and procedures by reading instructions and interviewing engineering personnel.

(14) We examined 100 engineering drawings in detail.

Control Findings

(13) We found that a drafting manual had been developed to provide detailed instructions to engineering draftsmen.

(10) We also found that all drawings must be verified by drawing checkers for accuracy.

(11) We found that after checking, the drawings must be reviewed by engineering supervisors before release.

(15) Management had developed a system of reporting the number of drawing errors based on complaints from the production organization.

Performance Findings

(6) We found an adequate supply of drafting manuals for all engineers, but 20% of the manuals were not up to date.

(9) Our test of 100 drawings showed that they had all been verified by drawing checkers.

(3) Our test of checked drawings showed that they had all been signed off by engineering supervisors before release.

(5) Our test of the error reports showed them to be accurate and timely.

Opinion

(12) It is our opinion that the control system was adequate.

(2) It is also our opinion that the system was working as intended except for the fact that some manuals were not up to date.

Recommendations

(16) We recommended that all manuals be brought up to date promptly.

(1) We also recommended that supervisors periodically check manuals to make sure they are kept up to date.

The tests can be graded by deducting, from the perfect score of 100, two points each for every statement shown in wrong sequence under the correct heading, and four points each for every statement shown under the wrong heading.

Test of Ability to Differentiate Between Fact and Conjecture

A fact is something that has actual existence, something that can be inferred with certainty, a proposition that is verified or verifiable. A conjecture is something suggesting insufficient evidence for it to be regarded as a fact. Auditors who cannot distinguish between the two need help because gathering facts, appraising them, and drawing conclusions from facts — not just making conjectures — lie at the heart of their work.

The greatest barriers to appraising the truth or falsity of a proposition are taking things for granted, jumping to conclusions, and accepting plausible appearance for hard fact. The inexperienced auditor — and quite often the old hand — may accept appearance for substance and come to improper conclusions. There is a subtle little test, full of pitfalls for the unwary, that can be devised both to trip up the conclusion jumper and to provide some good education for any auditor. It brings home sharply that what appears factual on the surface is but a signal to an experienced auditor to ask more questions.

This test can be developed along the lines set forth in Exhibit 17-6. A score of 85% or better would be Excellent; 75%, Good; 60%, Fair; 50%, Poor; and less than that, Unsatisfactory. The example shown has only five comments or questions. In practice it is well to have enough situations presented to warrant 25 or 30 questions.

How to Provide Orientation

Orientation, as distinguished from training, means pointing the new auditor in the right direction. The first days in a new organization can be traumatic. New employees want to like and respect their new environment. They want to feel that they can learn from the people around them; that these people are knowledgeable. They want to feel comfortable in their new jobs and in their new department. Their senses will be heightened to any ineptness or uncertainty. When they have been around a while, waiting for something to do is no great strain; they know how to occupy themselves. But during their first day or days, any delay, confusion, or lack of organization will be accentuated in their minds and will create an undesirable reaction.

Orientation of the new employees should therefore be carefully planned and structured. One of the people in the auditing organization with a strong teacher instinct should be assigned the task of introducing the new auditors to their surroundings and guiding them through the maze of new requirements. This mentor should be thoroughly prepared with a specific program and with well-designed materials to do the job with ease and confidence.

Generally, the period of orientation should take at least three or four days and should be organized into four phases: introduction to the staff; discussion of office policies and audit methods; reading policies, procedures, audit reports, and working papers; and feedback of what the new employee has learned.

There should be a liberal portion of each, spaced so that the new auditor is neither overwhelmed nor bored.

Immediately after the new auditors have been cleared through the personnel routines, they should have an unhurried chat about the company and

---

Exhibit 17-6. DISTINGUISHING BETWEEN FACT AND CONJECTURE

How to Take the Test

Shown below is a statement which you are to assume is completely true, although some parts are deliberately vague; so read the statement carefully. You may look back at the statement any time during the test.

Read the comments about the statement. Next to each comment indicate whether it is True (T), False (F), or Questionable (Q). Circle the letter you consider applicable. Circle T or F if you're quite sure of them. Circle Q if you are doubtful about the comment.

Answer each comment in turn. Do not change your answers once they are made.

(In this example, the answers are shown in parentheses after each comment.)

Statement

XYZ Corporation's Purchase Order 30305, dated May 15, 1981, was issued to the ABC Company for 10 castings at $10 each. The owner of the ABC Company is a brother of Joe Blow, XYZ Corporation's casting buyer.

Comments

1. An order for 10 castings was placed with ABC Company on 5/15/81. (This is questionable, since we know only the date of the purchase order, not when the order was placed. It could have been placed by telephone at an earlier date.)   T   F   Q

2. Joe Blow and the owner of ABC Company are brothers. (This is true, being categorically stated.)   T   F   Q

3. Joe Blow gave an order to his brother. (This is questionable; while Joe Blow was the castings buyer, the order could possibly have been placed by someone else — Joe might have been on vacation.)   T   F   Q

4. Purchase Order 30503 is dated May 15, 1981. (This is questionable. The purchase order in the statement, which is numbered 30305, is dated May 15, 1981. We don't know the date of Purchase Order 30503, which may or may not be May 15, 1981.)   T   F   Q

5. The value of Purchase Order 30305 is $100, without considering discount terms. (This is true.)   T   F   Q

the job with the director of auditing who should seek to set the new employees at ease. Thereafter, they should be shown to their desks by their mentor so that they have a feeling of permanence and a home base. They then should have a tour of introductions to other staff people, with the mentor briefly telling the old hands about the new auditor's background.

The mentor should provide copies of audit manuals, staff instructions, and other necessary tools, and give a brief preview of what the next few days will bring. At that point, it is well to determine what personal business the employee will have to take care of as a result of the change to a new job and, perhaps, a new locality. Provision should be made for any needed time off. Those matters should be discussed at the outset so that they will not weigh on the employee's mind and distract him or her from the orientation.

The breadth and intensity of the orientation will, of course, depend on the new auditor's prior experience. The mentor should be familiar with that experience. Clearly, an employee transferred from within the company, a newly graduated student, and an experienced auditor from another company all require different handling in their orientation.

An orientation guide, providing general information about the company and the internal auditing organization, can be an important means of furnishing general information that can be referred to as needed. Such a guide should be made available immediately to the new auditor so as to provide answers to any questions. Each company must develop its own, of course; but to assist in its development, an outline of such a guide is shown in Exhibit 17-7.

The mentor needs a formal program to help remember all the matters to be covered during the orientation. Exhibit 17-8 is an example of such a program.

Training Senior Auditors and Supervisors

Each auditing organization needs a formal program of training for the next higher position. There are at least two reasons: First, the staff personnel should be able to see physical evidence that they are being given the opportunity to show their capacity for more responsible work and to move up through the ranks. Second, no organization, including the auditing department, should leave itself open to catastrophe through the sudden loss of the "indispensable" person. Someone, and preferably more than one, should be able to step into a vacancy with the least trauma and the least dislocation of routines.

Over and above the general training program for the staff as a whole, the continuing program should provide for senior auditors to be assigned for predetermined periods to supervisory positions, and for supervisors to be assigned to manager positions. Through these training assignments the staff auditors learn the nuts and bolts of the next higher job. Management evaluates their ability to take over. They themselves develop confidence that

---

Exhibit 17-7. ORIENTATION GUIDE

Purpose

To orient you, as a new member of the internal auditing staff, to your new
environment.

To guide you through a review of pertinent administrative and technical matters
before we assign you to an audit examination.

Organization

Company

Provides an overview of the company organization and the names of key
management people.

Internal Auditing

Shows where internal auditing stands in the organization. Supplies the
names of the people most closely related to the audit function.

Administration

Hours of work	Nature of company directives
Daily notification of location	Administrative manual
Delivery of paychecks	Audit manual
Time reports	Supplies
Security matters	Desk assignments

Benefits

Vacations	Military leave
Sick leave	Retirement plan
Holidays	Insurance
Jury duty	

Exhibit 17-8. PROGRAM FOR THE ORIENTATION AND TRAINING
OF NEW EMPLOYEES

The program provided here will supplement the orientation guide and help the
training supervisor give the new auditors additional information on general administrative matters and on the more technical aspects of the department's auditing approach. The program should be supplemented by any additional
information considered desirable.

The orientation will take anywhere from three to five days, depending on the
individual's background. The oral instructions and any tours provided should be
interspersed between periods of reading so as to give some variety to the orientation period.

The Internal Auditing Organization

Introduce the new auditors to other members of the audit staff.

Discuss the auditing organization's objectives and how they are implemented.
Specifically cover opportunities for promotion and inform them of the company's policies about management selection.

Exhibit 17-8. (Cont.)

Supply the employees with copies of applicable manuals. Have them scan the manuals to familiarize themselves with their contents.
Discuss:

- The job duties and responsibilities of all members of internal auditing, from the director of auditing to the assistant auditor. Provide the new auditors with copies of their own job descriptions and answer any questions they may have about them.
- Discuss audit standards as they relate to audit coverage, audit examination, administrative records and reports, and communications.

Explain how the audit work is controlled:

- The long-range program.
- The basis for programmed jobs: areas which, by experience, require close review; chart of accounts; needs of management; and other.
- Discuss the various periodic reports to management.
- Discuss job assignments.

Review the contents of the department's library.

The Company

Have new employees attend any special orientation classes provided by the company.

- Answer any questions raised by the new auditors as a result of the class instruction.
- Provide a tour of the plant, supplementing if necessary the tour given during the company-provided classes.

Have the new auditors scan:

- Organization charts
- General information on the company
- The latest corporate annual report

Acquaint new auditors with the general ledger, subsidiary ledgers, and journal vouchers. Show them the chart and text of accounts.

Acquaint them with the work order system and with overhead accumulation and distribution.

Introduce them to management personnel with whom they may have contact on the job.

Internal Auditing

Bring to the new auditors' attention:

- The *Standards for the Professional Practice of Internal Auditing.*
- The Statement of Responsibilities.
- The Code of Ethics.
- The department's reference file of *The Internal Auditor,* the *Bibliography of Internal Auditing,* and the supplements, and the Research Reports issued by The Institute of Internal Auditors, Inc.

Exhibit 17-8. (Cont.)

Have the new auditors read pertinent articles in *The Internal Auditor* and other periodicals which relate to modern internal auditing in general.

Review the steps taken in planning an audit project.

- Explain the standard forms used in the organization.
- Explain the preliminary research undertaken, such as reviews of the relevant permanent files, the master program, organization charts, procedure manuals, and prior working papers.
- Explain how and when the audit program should be prepared, emphasizing the identification of the activity's major objectives, plans, and controls.
- Discuss the survey approach to audits, flowcharting, sampling, and computer-assisted audits.

Lead the new auditors through a selected set of working papers, showing them how the material is organized and how it is used to support the audit report.

Discuss the preparation of a segment of working papers, which will normally include:

- General information: Include applicable directives, procedures, practices, work flow (supported by flowcharts), statistics, and key controls.
- Purpose: The purpose should tie into the program and, if necessary, expand upon it. Try to cover cost, quality, and timeliness.
- Scope: Show what was done, and how much, and give the source of information and data.
- Findings: The facts evidenced by the schedules documenting the audit tests. The findings should be responsive to the questions raised in the purpose. Many findings may relate to one purpose.
- Opinions: These are the conclusions that are based on the findings. There should be an "Opinion" for each "Purpose." The opinions should be specific; either favorable or unfavorable. "No exceptions" will not suffice.
- Test work sheets: The work sheets should support the findings. They should indicate scope and sufficiency of test or the reasons why tests were limited. They should be summarized, so that the reviewer has no difficulty tracing the findings to the detail in the test schedules. Use copies of client's records, reports, tabulations, etc., whenever possible to avoid unnecessary copying.

Discuss deficiency findings. They should be thoroughly documented. The documentary evidence should show:

- Just what is wrong.
- Whether the deficiency violates some directive or is just poor administrative practice.
- The significance of the deficiency and what effect it will have if it goes uncorrected.
- What evidence has been adduced to prove the existence and extent of the deficiency.
- Who or what is responsible.

Exhibit 17-8. (Cont.)

- Whether the deficiency relates to control, performance, or both.
- The basic cause behind the deficient condition.
- What corrective action the auditor suggests.
- The client's opinion about the deficiency and what he proposes to do to correct it.

Provide new auditors with copies of typical reports and explain the various report sections and their purpose and the different formats that are used.

Discuss procedures in reviewing report drafts.

Discuss responsibilities for the evaluation of corrective action and the closure of audit projects.

Evaluation and Follow-Up

The training supervisor/mentor should keep in touch with the new auditors as they start on audit projects to see if they need answers to any of the questions that come up during actual work on the job.

In about a month, the supervisor should have a session with each new auditor, going over again the matters covered in this program and reinforcing those matters that may have been forgotten. One technique would be to use this program as a questionnaire to raise issues for the auditor to discuss or answer.

---

they can do the job or, on the other hand, decide that the higher job is not for them.

Through such training systems, the director of auditing can develop backup charts and submit them to executive management to show that the auditing organization is not encrusted with the mold of inaction, but rather is a viable entity, ready to withstand the onslaughts which may be brought about by personnel losses.

During the training periods, when the supervisory ranks are swelled temporarily, a senior supervisor may be relieved of some regular assignments to act as mentor to the supervisory trainee; to perform research on audit methods, techniques, and practices; to make reviews of working papers, reports, and executed forms to see whether standards are being met; or to develop new manuals or training aids.

Similarly, during the period when one of the supervisors is in management training, a manager may undertake long-range projects on the direction and function of the entire auditing organization or, say during a six-month "sabbatical," take a good hard look at the department to determine whether it is doing the job it is supposed to be doing or whether new approaches and areas should be explored.

How To Promote Continuing Education

Too many people — auditors included — entertain the naive notion that education is something that happens to students in a classroom. The constant winds of change should dispel that foggy notion, but apathy and lack of direction can be a frustrating and formidable barrier.

The torrents of technological changes in the business community should make it abundantly clear that the auditor must learn to breast the tide of new knowledge or remain high and dry on the shore. For those staff people not keeping up, audit management owes itself and them the duty of getting them immersed in the waters of continued learning.

Internal auditing especially — as a relatively young and growing product of business needs — must keep current to cope with the same changes that management itself must cope with. There is no excuse for a progressive auditing organization not having formal, continuing programs of education for its staff people. There are many forms this education can take.

Individual Study

Professional people must continue their formal education if they want to keep alive in their profession. When they stop learning, their professional lives start to atrophy. Modern internal auditors — like the modern business managers they serve — are fast becoming generalists in a world of specialists. New ideas and theories in all aspects of the management sciences are the sustenance on which they feed so as to remain strong enough to keep pace as the "eyes and ears of management."

New ideas and theories found in professional journals give them a taste and a hint, but it is only in formal university courses that they will get a full meal that they can convert into the useful muscle that will help them stay at the top of their profession. Every auditor should, now and again, take a formal course in a university, if one is available, or in a correspondence course if the university is not reasonably close by. There is a discipline about formal university courses — with their homework, supervision, and grades — which induces an extra effort that reading alone does not always do.

It is like anything else in the world of business and government. When the auditors see that management regards such instruction as important, they will consider the possibilities seriously. But how can the staff be motivated to take courses? The self-starter has his or her own internal motivation and desire for self-renewal. Others need help and direction.

Management can take these steps:

Point to the benefits of becoming a certified internal auditor.

Make available, in the office, catalogues of extension courses from all local universities.

Let it be known that an MBA indicates education in many of the subjects useful to internal auditors.

Ask staff auditors, at the beginning of each year, to complete a written statement of what they propose to do to improve their knowledge.

Discuss with staff auditors their own long-range and short-range plans for self-renewal.

Post lists of staff taking courses and indicate those who have completed them.

Put the names of members of the auditing organization on lists of those to be considered for management training courses sponsored by the company.

Let it be understood throughout the auditing department that the company thinks highly of, and provides opportunities for, those people who continue their education.

Not only will such courses benefit the individual concerned, but also this knowledge can be passed on to others through staff meetings.

Staff Meetings

There are different types of staff meetings, each with different purposes. They can be used to communicate or reinforce routine administrative matters, to teach new techniques, and even to let off steam.

As administrative controls within the auditing organization proliferate, it is helpful to have meetings to reinforce an understanding of existing instructions and to explain the purpose of new ones. The meetings are good forums for upgrading the staff's knowledge of bread-and-butter topics, such as report writing, audit programming, and the like.

As the use of more complex matters becomes significant, the meetings can become classrooms to teach such techniques as the use of the computer in statistical sampling, model building, probability theory, and other operations research methods.

Staff meetings can also be used as safety valves. Under careful supervision, the staff people can be given an opportunity to be heard on such matters as administrative procedures that are not working, promotion possibilities, salaries, administrative detail, lack of communication, and the many other potential sore points that should not be allowed to fester. Ground rules should be set early for such meetings. People should be asked well in advance of the meeting to develop specific questions; and, as an important step in preparation, several searching, and even impertinent questions should be "planted" so as to remove inhibitions in those who may be fearful of posing their own questions.

Staff meetings should be programmed formally. A certain amount of budget should be allotted to developing and attending the meetings. Dates for the meetings plus the personnel to conduct them should be established at the time the year's audit program is established.

A double return can be obtained from educational staff meetings by assigning each one to one or more staff auditors to research the subject, develop the lesson plan or presentation, and lead the meeting. In this way their capacities are broadened both in terms of the subject itself and learning to deal with audiences — particularly audiences who are prone to ask difficult questions.

Each assignment should be given a specific budget of audit days so that the project does not get out of hand. Also, a supervisor should be assigned so that the staff people have someone to consult with, to remove roadblocks, and to unobtrusively make sure that the objectives will be met.

Some of the topics that might be considered for such staff meetings are as follows:

Audit programming

Working paper presentation

Outlining reports

Developing deficiency findings

Describing interesting deficiency findings

Selecting samples

Determining confidence levels and precision ranges

Deciding on the sampling techniques to use under different circumstances

Surveys vs. detailed examinations

What is acceptable evidence of corrective action

New company products

New company systems

Presentations by other company personnel

Operations research techniques

The Institute of Internal Auditors

The Institute, like any other professional organization, provides opportunities for continued education. *The Internal Auditor,* The Institute's professional journal, is a primary source of information on management auditing. Its research bulletins are well-stocked warehouses of information and instruction on particular phases of the auditor's work. The Institute is the chief source of education on matters relating expressly to modern internal auditing, providing seminars and study courses in a broad spectrum of subjects which include EDP, statistical sampling, and staff improvement.

Attendance at local chapter meetings of The Institute offers opportunities to hear speakers on auditing and related topics. The interchange at the meeting's social hour can often provide an opportunity to unearth a nugget of information that can be of value to an ongoing audit project or that can give a new slant on an old problem.

The local chapter also can offer balm for that managerial itch — a balm that cannot always be found at the office. Working as a committee head or an officer adds stature to the individual, providing an opportunity to make management decisions, try out new ideas, and widen the circle of professional colleagues.

Institute relations need not be suspended because of travel. Auditors about to go on travel status should consult The Institute's *Directory of Membership*. It will show those chapters closest to the temporary duty station and the dates and places of chapter meetings.

Here again, audit management must take the initiative to plant the idea, to urge participation, to set examples, to show management approval of participation in The Institute, and to provide the necessary time and support.

Research

Research is a form of education with many side benefits. It differs from structured classroom education where often the students merely regurgitate what the instructor has fed them. Students obtain fulfillment from research accomplishments. Often, the result transcends the numerical grade given in the classroom and provides a tangible product — sometimes one that is unique. Where a class grade is soon forgotten and is, at most, of benefit or value only to the student, the research report completed outside the classroom for satisfaction, not for credit, may be of lasting value and of benefit to others. Moreover, the researcher may become both student and teacher.

The auditing department, like any other aggressive enterprise, should foster research in its own field both to widen its own vistas and to increase the capacities of its people. As in any other effort of the department, the director of auditing should give research projects the dignity and support of regularly planned programs.

Provision for specific research projects should be made in the annual program. Research projects should be given project numbers and project budgets. Researchers should be selected from among the staff with a view toward their natural proclivities and in consideration of how the research will benefit them.

Research projects can be assigned to individuals or teams. Teams should be led by staff people with the demonstrated or the potential ability to motivate themselves and others. The keynote is professionalism in approach and execution, with close management involvement to ensure a professional product.

Having selected their topics, the researchers should then present for management approval their research objectives, milestones by which to measure progress, and an estimate of the end result of the research — be it a report, a program, or a suggested course of action. Hours expended should be charged against the project, and requests for any extensions of time and budget should be made as formal as those for normal audit projects.

Research can be original — the development of brand new ideas — or it can constitute the accumulation and arraying of information to determine whether the old ways are still valid. Research topics can cover any aspect of audit activity; for example:

EDP applications to audit processes

Advanced program techniques for operational audits

Simulation and game theory as audit tools

Advanced working paper techniques

Methods of evaluating human resources

Analysis of audit report techniques

How best to audit the procurement activity

Development of a style manual for auditors

Adapting operations research techniques to audit needs

A description of an actual research project, with some excerpts from the research report, is shown in Exhibit 17-9.

Exhibit 17-9. RESEARCH REPORT ON AUDITS OF PROCUREMENT

Foreword

Procurement accounts for the majority of all company expenditures. These expenditures are committed by a large number of people working in many diverse procurement activities. Complete examinations of such activities and of the work of all the people currently is clearly infeasible. Accordingly, the audit effort must be directed toward those areas where there is the greatest risk of potential exposure to the loss or dissipation of company resources as a result of improper procurement activities.

To that end, we established a research project to determine how we could accomplish optimum coverage of the procurement activity, by identifying actual or potential risks and indicating the related controls.

Purpose and Scope

The objectives of the research project were (1) to identify the areas of major risk inherent in the procurement process, and (2) to suggest possible means of control designed to protect against such risks.

To accomplish our purpose, we used the "brainstorming" technique. The members of the research committee assembled for brainstorming sessions to list various risks, both actual and potential, that may be encountered in the procurement process. For each risk we attempted to suggest some form of control to provide protection against inadequate or improper procurement action.

We then sorted the various risk areas by major groups, and for each group we set forth the objectives of the activities and sufficient general information to give some background on how they function.

Exhibit 17-9. (Cont.)

Results of Research

Our research resulted in eight groupings and four subgroupings of risk areas and associated control. The groupings are identified as follows:

I   Bidding Procedures
II   Noncompetitive Procurements
III Decentralized Ordering and Receiving Areas
    A. Procurement Activities at Outlying Locations
    B. Direct Deliveries of Purchased Materials and Supplies
    C. Nonstocked Inventory Plan
    D. Shipments of Company-Owned Materials from Suppliers to Third Parties.
IV Outside Production
V   Blanket Purchase Orders
VI Purchase Order Changes
VII Procurements Paid for from Imprest Funds
VIII Time and Material and Labor Hour Procurements

Lists of the risk areas and the suggested controls are included. Risk areas include not only actual risks ("Selection of an unqualified supplier") but also areas of potential risk ("Sole source procurement"). For simplicity we have designated them all as "risk areas." It will be observed that the same risk areas may appear more than once, in different groupings, since the identical risk can be equally applicable to two or more different groups. The same is true of the related controls.

We have concluded that the review and evaluation of these risk areas represent the least amount of audit effort that should be expended in examining procurement activities. We wish to emphasize that the lists should not be used as check sheets which will completely satisfy audit objectives because (1) there is no substitute for imaginative, innovative auditing; (2) the lists and the associated general information which were prepared as of the date of this research report are almost certain to change with the passage of time because of the advent of new circumstances, procedures, and systems; and (3) it is a virtual impossibility to succeed in listing every conceivable risk area inherent in so broad and complex an activity as procurement.

Properly used, however, the lists should represent reasonably satisfactory audit guidelines and should provide assurance of at least minimum audit coverage within the procurement organizations assigned for audit.

Bidding Procedures

Purpose of Activity

To obtain, through competitive means, required materials, supplies, and services at the most favorable terms, giving due regard to quality, price, and schedule.

General Information

To provide assurance that materials and services will be obtained at acceptable prices on schedule from qualified suppliers, the following controls are provided by established written procedures:

■ It is the policy of the Procurement Division to solicit competitive bids for all items to be purchased except under specified conditions when the solicitation of bids is considered to be impractical.

Exhibit 17-9. (Cont.)

- In general, written quotations are to be obtained from all prospective suppliers. Written quotations are to be obtained without exception in connection with all procurements over $10,000.

- For procurements estimated to be in excess of $1,000, prior written supervisory approval is to be obtained of the prospective bidders.

- Buyers are to show on the applicable procurement request the number of bids solicited, whether the bids obtained were oral or written, and, when competitive bids are not obtained, the reasons for not obtaining them.

- Written quotations are to be obtained from the suppliers on Requests for Quotation (RFQ) forms whenever practicable, and are to be controlled by the responsible purchasing agents.

- Buyers are to select the lowest bidder capable of performing the desired work on schedule, and they are to provide adequate reasons for not selecting the low bidder.

Because of numerous pressures of varying kinds, there often is an inducement to circumvent established procedures. The circumventions may often be found in the following risk areas.

Risk Areas	Suggested Controls
Incomplete or poor initial selection of proposed sources of supply.	The review and approval of bidders' lists by procurement supervisors and by Quality Control and Finance personnel before completing and mailing the RFQ's.
Authority for the same group both to select proposed suppliers and to type and mail the RFQs.	The typing and mailing of RFQs by an organization other than the buying group.
Authority for the buying group which originated the RFQs to receive the bids directly from the mail room or from the supplier.	The receipt and retention of bids until the closing date, by an organization other than the buying group.
The receipt from suppliers of bids on other than company RFQ forms.	The analysis of terms and conditions to detect any conditions of sale which may conflict with "Terms and Conditions of Purchase."
The acceptance of oral, non-RFQ types of bids.	The review and approval of the use of this type of bid by appropriate supervision.
	The review and approval of the proposed sources of supply.
	The requirement that suppliers submit written confirmation of bids.
	The review of RTP and bid aware by appropriate management level.

Continued

Exhibit 17-9. (Cont.)

Risk Areas	*Suggested Controls*
Awards based on fewer than three bids.	The provision for written explanations and justifications of awards based on fewer than three bids, and review of those reasons by appropriate supervision.
Awards to other than low bidders.	The provision for written justifications and for supervisory approvals.
The disclosure of bid information received from some suppliers to other favored suppliers.	Bids remain sealed until opening in the presence of witnesses.
The pitting of favored suppliers against only those suppliers known to submit high bids.	Supervisory review and evaluation of list of bidders.
The submission to nonfavored suppliers of specifications, or other matters, which affect cost, that are more stringent than those submitted to favored suppliers.	Data assembled, compared, and mailed by an organization other than the buying group.
The communication of extension of bid periods or changes in RFQs only to favored suppliers.	Extensions or changes typed and mailed by same organization (other than the buying group) that handled the original RFQs.
Collusive bidding among suppliers available or selected to bid.	Estimates from using organizations of what are reasonable prices.
	Review of trade periodicals for what are going prices.
	Communication by procurement supervision with their counterparts in kindred companies to see what others are paying.

Staff Evaluations

The internal auditing profession inherits special problems when it comes to evaluating its own staff. No two projects that the auditor carries out or assists in are the same. Some projects do not even stretch a person's abilities. Others may turn out to be beyond an individual's potential or experience. Still other projects, which had previously been performed in a pedestrian and unimaginative fashion, may be raised to unsuspected heights because of an individual auditor's novel approach or innovative methods. All these factors should be considered in structuring the evaluation system so as to be fair to the employee and to the department.

To measure anything reasonably well, of course, requires objective standards and consistent methods of gauging performance. Also, as an aid to positive personnel relations, all who will be measured should be fully aware of the standards and the methods. Thus, the policy or program should be clearly set forth in a staff memorandum or directive. The instructions should make clear what is considered excellent, adequate, or unsatisfactory performance. The instructions should also establish when and how often the evaluations will be made and how they will be used.

The size of the auditing organization also has a significant bearing on how the evaluation program will be structured. A director of auditing with a half dozen staff people should have no difficulty making personal and even unstructured evaluations. A large organization, with several supervisors and a large number of in-charge auditors and assistants, presents obstacles to close contact between the staff auditor and the director. Here it is the supervisors who have the personal contact with the auditors-in-charge, while the latter have the contact with their assistants. And the greater the number of supervisors, the more remote the possibility that all evaluations in the department will be carried out in the same way.

Thus, when directors of auditing do all the evaluations, they can be completely open with their people about precisely how they rated them. When staff auditors are subject to the review of different supervisors or auditors-in-charge during the year, the directors should be careful about letting the evaluators have the last word. Hence, it would be preferable for the evaluations of an individual by more than one supervisor or auditor-in-charge to be combined and weighted by the director and then discussed with the individuals at appropriate periods. Different supervisors and different auditors-in-charge will most likely have varying standards, likes, dislikes, and prejudices. These qualities should be neutralized by having a single spokesperson for the department handle this always delicate yet essential aspect of personnel relations.

One program that has worked reasonably well — no one method is perfect where souls are bared — provides the following pattern:

At the conclusion of each audit assignment, the auditor-in-charge prepares a rating sheet for each assistant, and the supervisor prepares one for the auditor-in-charge. A rating for each assignment is necessary because of the variations among assignments. The actual numerical or adjectival ratings are not discussed, but a dialogue is conducted on the strengths and weaknesses observed on that particular project.

This dialogue can work well or poorly, depending on how it is approached. The appraisal should be constructive. The climate of the interview should be warm and supportive. An often successful ploy is for the evaluator to open the conversation by asking the staff auditors how they thought they performed, what they felt they did well, what they felt they did poorly, what they learned from the job, and what areas of improvement they see for themselves. These dialogues are valuable because it is cruel to auditors to permit them to go to another audit assignment unaware of certain defects that adversely affect their performance, and which will continue to plague their work unless they can identify their weaknesses and make a conscious effort toward improvement.

The supervisor or auditor-in-charge owes it to subordinates to help them identify their weaknesses. They also owe it to the employee to use tact and sympathy. Thus, to lead the auditor's self-evaluation toward the known defects can probably accomplish the most good. Most people like to talk about themselves, and getting staff people to do the exploring themselves can accomplish the objectives of the dialogue with the least amount of abrasion.

At the end of a 6-month or 12-month period, the director of auditing combines the various ratings for each auditor and discusses the results with them. In some organizations the periodic discussions are held when the salary adjustments are made. The purpose is to bring home the significance of the rating. In other organizations the periodic discussions are held separately from the salary adjustment interviews, thus placing the emphasis on improving the auditors, not on rewarding or punishing them.

These ratings and interviews are of extreme importance to the individual. In very large organizations, they may be the only time during the year when the staff auditor has a chance for an eye-to-eye colloquy with the director. The meeting should be carried out in an unhurried atmosphere and be pervaded by a deep and sincere interest in the auditor's problems, goals, and aspirations, and in his or her program to work them out.

When filling out rating sheets, the evaluator should seek to maintain a distinction between accomplishments and traits. While both are significant, each has a different function. The rating of accomplishments should apply to the particular project completed, since each project has different problems. The evaluation of traits deals with the qualities that auditors carry with them through their working life. Traits are harder to evaluate since the evaluator is applying subjective standards. But it is well for the director of auditing to be aware of significant traits since they may affect decisions about an auditor.

For example, a project which will require contacts at high levels in the company should not be assigned to an auditor who may be an expert but is not personable or articulate. Similarly a project which requires a large number of assistants should not be assigned to an auditor who does not possess qualities of leadership.

Many styles of rating sheets are in use. Several of them, which provide for evaluations of both accomplishments and traits, have been reproduced in Exhibits 17-10 thru 17-13.

Exhibits 17-10 and 17-11 provide numerical ratings on a large variety of subjects and qualities, with adjectival ratings to give meaning to the numbers. Exhibit 17-10 is a rating sheet for an assistant auditor. Exhibit 17-11 is a rating sheet for an in-charge auditor. Numerical ratings provide for quantitative comparisons among different auditors. The qualities being appraised on these sheets are self-explanatory. These forms also provide for an evaluation of the difficulty of the job: Class A is for a relatively simple job. Class B is for a job of normal difficulty. Class C is for a job of exceptional difficulty. These factors can be used to adjust total scores. Five per cent is deducted for easy jobs and added for difficult ones.

Exhibit 17-12 is a rating form which provides adjectival ratings only. The same form is used both for assistants and for auditors-in-charge. But certain of the factors may be marked NA (not applicable) when appropriate to distinguish between the two persons. Exhibit 17-13 provides explanations for the performance factors.

Exhibit 17-10. STAFF RATING FORM — ASSISTANT AUDITORS

Total Score_____

Name: _____ Period: From_____To_____

Job No.: _____Job Title:_____

Class (A B C)_____Signature: _____Date:_____

Planning and Organizing	Excellent	Very Good	Good	Fair	Unsatis-factory
Understanding of the procedures and problems relating to the audit segments assigned.	80	72	64	48	32
Conformance to the instructions provided by the auditor-in-charge and by the departmental manuals — yet questioning what seems illogical or unreasonable in the instructions.	60	54	48	36	24
Organizing and programming the work assigned so as to provide for coverage of the key control points in proper depth.	60	54	48	36	24
Totals	200	180	160	120	80
Field Work					
Accuracy of working papers — computations, references, statistical analyses.	90	81	72	54	36
Thoroughness of examination — yet knowing when to suggest discontinuance of the investigations.	90	81	72	54	36
Appropriateness of tests to the transactions reviewed.	60	54	48	36	24
Adequacy of documentation for work performed — showing nature, scope, and results of examination.	60	54	48	36	24
Completion of required field work — leaving no loose ends.	40	36	32	24	16
Summarization of findings — to facilitate review.	40	36	32	24	16

Exhibit 17-10. (Cont.)

	Excellent	Very Good	Good	Fair	Unsatis-factory
Evaluation of findings in forming opinion — use of judgment in assessing significance.	60	54	48	36	24
Care in preparing and organizing working papers — properly indexed, cross-referenced, initialed, dated.	60	54	48	36	24
Totals	500	450	400	300	200

Oral Expression

	Excellent	Very Good	Good	Fair	Unsatis-factory
Clarity and conciseness of oral expression.	60	54	48	36	24
Effectiveness	40	36	32	24	16
Totals	100	90	80	60	40

Writing Ability

	Excellent	Very Good	Good	Fair	Unsatis-factory
Use of clear, concise and appropriate language in working paper comments and in summaries and write-ups.	90	81	72	54	36
Organization of written material.	60	54	48	36	24
Totals	150	135	120	90	60

Administration

	Excellent	Very Good	Good	Fair	Unsatis-factory
Meeting the budget and the schedule for the work assigned.	50	45	40	30	20
Grand Totals	1,000	900	800	600	400

General Characteristics

Place check mark under appropriate adjectival rating.

Alertness, energy, and initiative.	—	—	—	—	—
Pleasantness, open-mindedness, tact, and cooperativeness.	—	—	—	—	—
Work habits — diligent application of effort to the job, and observation of company working hours.	—	—	—	—	—

Readiness for In-Charge Work

Ability to carry out work successfully with only general supervision.	—	—	—	—	—

Additional Comments

Discuss specific attributes which require strengthening so as to improve this auditor's ability to handle in-charge assignments:

Exhibit 17-11. STAFF RATING FORM — IN-CHARGE AUDITORS

Total Score_____

Name: _____ Period: From_____To_____

Job No.:_____Job Title:_____

Class (A B C)_____Signature:_____Date:_____

Planning	Excellent	Very Good	Good	Fair	Unsatis-factory
Understanding of procedures and problems relating to the activity under examination — awareness of objectives of activity under review, and relationship of those objectives to company objectives.	40	36	32	24	16
Coverage in the audit program of all key control points — giving proper weight and emphasis to most significant control points.	50	45	40	30	20
Nature of planned tests — use of imagination and economy.	30	27	24	18	12
Extent of planned tests — use of appropriate sampling techniques.	30	27	24	18	12
Totals	150	135	120	90	60

Field Work

	Excellent	Very Good	Good	Fair	Unsatis-factory
Completion of required field work — coverage of all programmed steps; adequate reasons to eliminate steps.	20	18	16	12	8
Accuracy of working papers — computations, references, statistical analyses.	70	63	56	42	28
Thoroughness of examination — yet knowing when to discontinue investigation.	70	63	56	42	28
Appropriateness of tests to the transactions reviewed.	40	36	32	24	16
Adequacy of documentation for work performed — showing nature, scope, and results of examination.	45	41	36	27	18
Summarization of findings — to facilitate review.	25	22	20	15	10

Exhibit 17-11. (Cont.)

	Excellent	Very Good	Good	Fair	Unsatis-factory
Evaluation of findings in forming opinion — judgment in assessing significance of findings.	65	59	52	39	26
Working paper preparation and organization — properly indexed, cross-referenced, initialed, dated.	40	36	32	24	16
Totals	375	338	300	225	150

Report Draft

	Excellent	Very Good	Good	Fair	Unsatis-factory
Adequacy of support for report statements — ability of findings to withstand successful attack.	60	54	48	36	24
Proper treatment of findings according to relative significance — giving greater weight and space to more serious findings.	60	54	48	36	24
Organization — presenting material in a logical and orderly sequence.	50	45	40	30	20
Compliance with departmental instructions on reporting — following rules laid down in departmental manuals.	40	36	32	24	16
Clarity and appropriateness of report language — making findings clear to nontechnical reader.	50	45	40	30	20
Accuracy in preparation and review to eliminate errors.	40	36	32	24	16
Totals	300	270	240	180	120

Oral Communication

	Excellent	Very Good	Good	Fair	Unsatis-factory
Clarity and conciseness	60	54	48	36	24
Persuasiveness	40	36	32	24	16
Totals	100	90	80	60	40

Administration

	Excellent	Very Good	Good	Fair	Unsatis-factory
Meeting Budget	40	36	32	24	16
Meeting schedule	35	31	28	21	14
Totals	75	67	60	45	30
Grand Totals	1,000	900	800	600	400

General Characteristics

(Place check mark under appropriate adjectival rating)

Alertness, energy, and initiative. ___ ___ ___ ___ ___

Pleasantness, open-mindedness, tact, and cooperativeness. ___ ___ ___ ___ ___

Work habits — diligent application of effort to the job, and observation of company working hours. ___ ___ ___ ___ ___

Additional Comments

Exhibit 17-12. STAFF PERFORMANCE APPRAISAL

Name_____ Assistant ☐ Auditor in Charge ☐

Assignment_____ Period Covered_____

Overall rating for this assignment Desirability on Another Assignment:

Desirable ___

Acceptable ___

Prefer Another Staff Member ___

Performance Factors*	NA S− S S+ E O	**Personal Characteristics***	NI FA
Quantity of Work	_____	Creativity	_____
Quality of Work	_____	Initiative	_____
Knowledge of Auditing	_____	Persistence	_____
Auditing Aptitude	_____	Ability to work	
Problem Analysis	_____	with others	_____
Decision-Making	_____	Judgment	_____
Planning	_____	Adaptability	_____
Follows Instructions	_____	Persuasiveness	_____
Communications: Oral	_____	Leadership	_____
Written	_____	Self Confidence	_____
		Attitude	_____

*See general instructions, Exhibit 17-13, for definitions and rating terms

Attributes: Circle up to five adjectives which best describe the staff member's outstanding personal characteristics. They may be desirable and/or undesirable qualities. Extra blanks are provided for adjectives which you consider more descriptive.

aggressive	enthusiastic	lazy	self-assured
articulate	erratic	loud	shallow
careless	excitable	mature	sloppy
casual	flexible	naive	steady

Exhibit 17-12. (Cont.)

cautious	flippant	neat	taciturn
clumsy	gullible	observant	tenacious
conceited	imaginative	officious	vacillating
deliberate	immature	open-minded	verbose
discreet	impulsive	overbearing	vigorous
discriminating	inarticulate	plodding	vulgar
dogmatic	indifferent	presumptuous	witty
dull	indiscreet	prim	_____
eager	inflexible	pushy	_____
energetic	inquisitive	resourceful	_____

Counseling: The completed appraisal report is confidential and should not be shown or read to the staff member even though it is required that performance on each assignment be discussed. Discuss the staff member's performance on each assignment during the course of the examination and in summary form at the end of the assignment. Please answer Yes, No, or Not Applicable (N/A) to these questions:

Have you discussed with the staff member at a meeting for that purpose: (1) Good work done?_____(2) Poor performance?_____(3) Correctable deficiencies?_____(4) Means of correcting deficiencies?_____ Give the date of the meeting_____

Matters discussed with staff member and the reaction:

_____

_____

_____

_____

_____

Comments: Comment on exceptionally outstanding performance or unsatisfactory ratings, as well as qualities not covered elsewhere. Do not include comments that are only a restatement of the various ratings: Specific illustrations are always more helpful than remarks of a general nature. Be concise.

_____

_____

_____

_____

_____

_____

_____   _____

Signature   Date

Exhibit 17-13.

General Instructions: The purpose of the staff performance appraisal form is to obtain information on the level of work the audit staff member is qualified to perform as well as on prospects for advancement. The appraisal report is necessary for knowledgeable decisions on adjustments of compensation and on promotions, as well as a means of summarizing information to assist in effectively counseling and training the staff member. The completed appraisal report is confidential and should not be shown or read to the staff member, even though it is required that performance on the assignment be discussed. There is a difference between discussion of performance and reporting, since the latter includes grading and evaluating, while the former does not.

DEFINITIONS
Rating Factors
  Performance Factors

  Quantity of work — Accomplishments measured against the requirement of the position; results measured against goals. Timely completion of work for which the auditor is responsible.

  Quality of work — The degree of excellence of the end results; thoroughness, accuracy, and overall caliber of completed assignments, including adequacy and clarity of working papers.

  Knowledge of auditing — Understanding basic auditing principles and company operational policies and procedures.

  Auditing aptitude — Understanding audit program objectives, and having the ability to analyze the systems of control to be audited.

  Problem analysis — Recognizing problems and breaking problem situations into essential parts logically and systematically. Gathering facts and getting beneath the surface to discover their full meaning.

  Decision making — Screening facts, getting to the heart of the problem, and making sound and timely decisions.

  Planning — Planning the work systematically and practically, and establishing logical priorities to do a more efficient audit job.

  Following instructions — Having the ability to follow instructions exactly and conscientiously; being proficient in comprehending instructions; knowing when to question the instructions if they seem inappropriate in a given situation.

  Communication skills — Expressing points of view clearly, logically, and convincingly in written and oral communications; and keeping superiors informed currently as the job progresses.

  Personal Characteristics

  Creativity — Ability to apply imagination and originality to the job so as to develop new and improved procedures or applications.

Exhibit 17-13. (Cont.)

Initiative — Being a self-starter.

Persistence — Being persevering. Pursuing goals resolutely. Not being easily deterred from attaining audit objectives.

Ability to work with others — Ability to get along with people. Being tactful and diplomatic and aware of effect upon others.

Judgment — Ability to comprehend all facets of a problem and to assign values to each consideration in arriving at a decision.

Adaptability — Ability to adjust to change and to meet new situations.

Persuasiveness — Ability to influence others.

Leadership — Ability to motivate subordinates and associates to take desired action.

Self-Confidence — Ability to remain at ease, self-assured, and poised.

Attitude — Enthusiasm for the job, loyalty to the company, and the ability to accept constructive criticism.

Rating Terms

Performance Factors

O - Outstanding	Exceptional, superior (would apply only in rare instances)
E - Excellent	Considerably above average; stands out; demonstrates rare ability
S+ - Satisfactory Plus	Above average
S - Satisfactory	Exhibits an acceptable degree of performance under strong direction
S− - Satisfactory Minus	A marginal rating; does not meet minimum accepted standards
NA - Not Acceptable	

Personal Characteristics

NI - Needs Improvement	Definite improvement required to reach normally accepted standards
FA - Fully Acceptable	Meets normally accepted standards in all respects.

Conclusion

The skilled internal auditor combines technical competence and education with qualities of adaptability, understanding, determination, integrity, independence, objectivity, and responsibility. He or she may be recruited from universities and colleges, from the ranks of CPAs, from within the company, and from practicing internal auditors. The recruitment program should include polished interviewing techniques and practical testing methods. The new auditor should be provided with a comprehensive orientation program that will ease the transition into the department. Adequate service to management requires a continuing training program to keep the staff abreast of new management methods and new auditing techniques. These techniques can be developed within the auditing organization through an imaginative research program. The director of auditing should provide a well-structured program of employee evaluation to keep the auditor informed of progress, strong points, and those shortcomings that need attention.

References

1. Gordon McAleer and George de Jager, *Salaries and Attitudes — a Profile of the Internal Auditing Profession* (Altamonte Springs, Fla.: The Institute of Internal Auditors, Inc., 1978) pp. 2, 3.
2. *Ibid.* p. 32.

Supplementary Reading

Barden, R. S. "Behaviorally Based Performance Appraisals." *The Internal Auditor*, February 1980, pp. 36-43.

DeMarco, V. F. "Recruiting and Developing Internal Auditors." *The Internal Auditor*, February 1980, pp. 53-57.

Macchiaverna, Paul. "Internal Auditing." New York: The Conference Board, 1978, pp. 67-94.

For further study

Discussion Problems

1. List four important points that should be included in a job description for an internal audit supervisor and briefly explain the reason for each.

2. Discuss the importance and the overall objectives of periodically evaluating the performance of the audit staff.

3. Describe the factors you would include in the above evaluation.

4. Discuss the frequency of the evaluations and the method of communicating them.

5. Discuss some of the academic requirements for a modern internal auditor and explain why they are desirable.

6. Why is adaptability an essential trait for modern internal auditors?

7. What would be the most desirable source of internal auditors for a director of internal auditing who is developing an entirely new internal auditing organization?

8. What do you think are the most important things that a prospective employer should learn about one who applies for an internal auditing position?

9. What are the desired elements of orientation for a new employee?

10. What are some of the ways of getting staff auditors interested in continuing education?

Multiple Choice Problems

1. A modern internal audit staff should preferably include individuals:
a. With an earned degree in accounting.
b. Who have had previous experience with the organization.
c. With a business administration degree and an understanding of the tools of modern management.
d. With a specialty background, such as EDP personnel.
e. Who collectively provide a reasonable balance of all the above backgrounds.

2. Orientation for a staff auditor includes:
a. Explaining the working paper format established by the auditor's organization.
b. Providing the auditor with an overview of the company organization.
c. Assigning the auditor to complete a research project.
d. Both a. and b. above.
e. None of the above.

3. Which of the following items would be the best criterion for evaluating a staff auditor's work performance?
a. Number of deficiency findings reported.
b. Ability to get along with auditees.
c. Neatness of working papers.
d. Fulfillment of requirements set forth in the approved audit programs.
e. Completion of audit assignments on schedule.

4. Which of the following best illustrates an internal auditor's professional proficiency?
a. An independent mental attitude.
b. The ability to plan audits and to meet schedules.
c. The ability to coordinate the work of the internal auditor with that of the external auditor.

d. The knowledge, skills, and disciplines needed to carry out audit responsibilities.
e. The ability to collect information to support audit results.

5. Orientation differs from training in that orientation:
a. Takes place as soon as the employee is hired.
b. Does not require an experienced teacher.
c. Helps teach new auditors how to audit.
d. Instructs trained auditors on methods applicable to their new environment.
e. Supplements training.

6. In filling out an evaluation form, the evaluator should seek to maintain a distinction between:
a. Accomplishments and traits.
b. Before and after.
c. Potential and predilection.
d. Likes and dislikes.
e. Empathy and sympathy.

7. A well-structured program of employee evaluation is designed to:
a. Help auditors keep informed of their strong points, shortcomings, and progress.
b. Ensure meetings between the manager and the auditor.
c. Keep the auditors on their toes.
d. Provide information for the auditor's personnel folder.
e. Establish a basis for promotion and salary increases.

8. To build a superior staff, one must first know:
a. The kinds of auditors available in the marketplace.
b. The kinds of courses being taught in business administration schools.
c. The standards for excellence.
d. How management regards the internal audit function.
e. How many auditors are needed

9. The essential qualities of the internal auditor do *not* include:
a. Adaptability.
b. Determination.
c. Understanding.
d. Education.
e. Objectivity.

10. With respect to their knowledge of operations research, internal auditors should have a reasonable degree of:
a. Proficiency.
b. Understanding.
c. Appreciation.
d. Sophistication.
e. Facility.

Case Studies

17-1 Rating Marv Johnson

Paul Eberhardt looked thoughtfully at the two supervisors, Bob and Rod, and then said, "Top management has given us a problem. No, strike that. They've given us an opportunity."

Bob grunted. "Something's coming and I don't like the sound of it."

"Relax," said Paul, "I'm on the hot seat, not you."

"What's the prob — I mean the opportunity?" asked Rod.

"We are now required to have an annual interview with each auditor on the staff. We are to talk about good points, weak points, potential and chances for advancement."

"Actually, I think that's been long overdue," Rod replied.

"I agree," said Paul. "Each auditor will be interviewed on the anniversary date of hire."

"Who's on first?" asked Bob.

"Marv Johnson," answered Paul. "That's why I called you in. Marv has worked for both of you. I'd like you to brief me about him. How about you, Bob?"

"He's a budget-eater. Every job he's ever done has gone way over budget."

"Why?"

"He's just slower than a tax refund."

"But he's had some high-powered jobs and some significant findings and recommendations," protested Paul.

"Yes," broke in Rod, "but he takes forever to find them and develop them."

"Doesn't he apply himself?" asked Paul.

"That's not the problem," said Bob. "He works hard, turns out great working papers, develops solid findings. But our operating managers are beginning to complain about how long he takes and how much time he demands of people."

"Haven't you guys tried to push him?" asked Paul.

"Yes," the supervisors said in unison.

"What happened?"

"He just can't operate under pressure," said Rod. "He turns out garbage when he's pushed, and his findings don't stand up."

"How's his writing?" asked Paul.

"Not bad," said Bob. "But that too takes forever; and he writes too much. With the added programs we've got, he's ruining our realization of actual versus budgeted audit-days."

Paul said nothing. But he felt that somehow the potentially important resource called Marv Johnson could be improved. Bob and Rod left. Paul told his secretary Ruth to set up a meeting with Johnson for two days hence. He then leaned back and tried to figure out what he'd say to Marv.

Required: Prepare papers discussing the matters that Paul should bring up and offering suggestions for improving Marv's methods.

17-2 There's More to Modern Auditing Than Numbers

Paul Eberhardt, director of internal auditing, fixed the audit supervisor, Rod Grey, with a baleful glare. "Terrible. Absolutely terrible."

Rod, the picture of misery, nodded agreement.

"I hadn't the slightest inkling," continued Paul, "that Bill Storm was so lacking in tact and the ability to deal with people. He blew the whole campaign sky-high — a campaign that's taken us so long to sell."

"I knew Bill was prickly," said Rod, "and gets people on edge sometimes —"

"Then why didn't you tell me about it?" demanded Paul.

"Because he's really the best auditor we've got," replied Rod. "And I was always hoping he'd mellow. But this one really tore it."

Rod was referring to a meeting with Bob Lloyd, director of production, and some of his deputies. Paul, Rod, and Bill had called the meeting to sell them on the idea of eliminating tool cabinets. Hand tools, such as drill motors and crimping tools, are assigned from centralized tool cribs to production supervisors who keep them in cabinets for their workers. Audit after audit disclosed inadequate control over the cabinet tools — large losses, failure to keep precision tools calibrated, and the like.

Bill was convinced that the cabinet system was to blame. A number of production supervisors agreed with him. But the director of production had never been convinced. He was certain there would be line-ups and delays if workers had to go to the cribs each morning for their hand tools. The auditors had seen dawdling about the cabinets in the mornings and afternoons, and so they didn't think much of the director's arguments.

This time, Bill had taken photographs of a number of badly maintained cabinets and of groups of employees hanging around the cabinets. He had truly built up a good case.

Paul and Rod, working smoothly with Bill's material, just about had Lloyd convinced at the meeting. Then Lloyd directed a question to Bill for more information. Bill incorrectly took the question to be an aspersion on his veracity and lashed back. Lloyd, antagonistic toward Bill anyway, roared his displeasure. And then the meeting became a shambles. Lloyd would not hear a further word.

Somewhat calmed by now, Paul said, "There have been other instances, not only involving Bill, where perfectly reasonably suggestions for improvement were rejected solely because of the auditor's attitude — not because of the cogency of his audit findings. We must do something about it."

"Like what?" asked Rod.

"First, we've got to educate people like Bill. Second, we've got to develop some means of screening out the prickly ones in our applicant interviews. I don't care how technically proficient an applicant looks on paper. If he can't deal with people, he'll frustrate all our efforts. He'll tear down everything we've tried to build up over the years. Our dreams of cooperative auditing will go right down the drain."

"After Bill's performance today, I've got to agree," replied Rod. "But how?"

"Sit down with Bob, our other supervisor, and brainstorm two sets of suggestions: one for training our present staff, one for an interview questionnaire. Then bring them to me."

"Will do," said Rod.

Required: Prepare the lists of suggestions Paul asked for.

18

Preparing
Long-Range Schedules

Long-range audit schedules — essential elements of internal audit planning. A guide: no significant areas overlooked. Budget justification: objective evidence. A standard: a means of measurement. Participation: management and the board. Control: goal-oriented administration. The external auditor: a basis for coordination. Building the long-range schedule. Forms of long-range schedules. Developing schedule budgets. Matrixes. The risk areas. Determining audit priorities. Raising audit capability by nonauditing objectives. Reviewing plans with management. Planning for small enterprises. Coordinating audits with security, quality control, safety, and industrial engineering organizations.

The Need for Planning and for Management Involvement

A good long-range audit schedule is an instrument having many uses. It is the auditor's guide, it is the support for budget requests, it is a way of involving management in the audit plans and obtaining its commitment to the scope of the audit, it is the standard by which auditors can measure their accomplishments, it is a visible sign to management that the audit activity is under competent control, and it is a notice to the external auditors of proposed audit coverage.

Long-range planning is not something a director of auditing can dismiss cavalierly as a needless luxury. The *Standards for the Professional Practice of Internal Auditing* provide in Section 520:

520 *Planning*

> *The director of internal auditing should establish plans to carry out the responsibilities of the internal auditing department.*

.04   Audit work schedules should include (a) what activities are to be audited; (b) when they will be audited; and (c) the estimated time required, taking into account the scope of the audit work planned and the nature and extent of audit work performed by others. Matters to be considered in establishing audit work schedule priorities should include (a) the date and results of the last audit; (b) financial exposure; (c) potential loss and risk; (d) requests by management, (f) opportunities to achieve operating benefits; and (g) changes to and capabilities of the audit staff. The work schedules should be sufficiently flexible to cover unanticipated demands on the internal auditing department.

External auditors and audit committees of the board of directors are showing considerable interest in what internal auditing intends to audit. The long-range audit schedule is the only tangible evidence of that intention.

The Schedule as a Guide

By spelling out in detail the audit projects to be carried out, the long-range schedule gives evidence of coverage of key functions at planned intervals. It provides assurance that no significant area worthy of audit will be overlooked.

The schedule also simplifies the job of assigning work to the staff. Without a detailed schedule, the audit effort can be a haphazard groping, a repeated exercise in responding to random requests or making last-minute decisions on "what do we do next?"

In large audit organizations, the schedule can be allocated equitably to different supervisors or audit managers. They in turn can assign projects to their staff people in logical order. Also, the well-constructed work schedule, stretching out for two, three or five years, can provide an air of permanence to the audit organization. It is evidence of long-term planning and the continued existence of the audit effort. Above all, it is a tangible demonstration of the place of the auditing function as the keystone in the company's structure of internal control.

In smaller organizations it relieves the directors of internal auditing from constantly having to make decisions on audit coverage. It permits them to make those decisions and settle their scheduling problems — with provision for flexibility, of course — in advance of the year's work.

The Schedule as a Justification for Budget

The long-range schedule should be specific. It should parse out in detail each audit project to be performed, while still providing for the unknown and the unanticipated. Each project listed should indicate through its title the nature of the audit to be performed and should provide an estimate of the time required.

The sum total of the allotted time for the current year is a simple demonstration of the number of auditors needed. The sum total of audit days for each of subsequent years is a projection of changes to, or continuity of, staff levels. The schedule, therefore, when accepted by executive management, becomes a commitment to the number of auditors authorized. Simple arithmetic rather than rhetoric sustains the director's request for maintaining or increasing staff levels. And the accepted audit days, together with provision for administrative expense, travel expense, and related costs, represent management's approved budget for the audit organization.

The approved work schedule provides an additional and subtle function. It defends against one of the internal auditor's constant fears — being requested to perform extraneous functions — to be at the beck and call of middle management for "fire-fighting" duties. When the audit schedule is accepted, it is tacit acknowledgment by management at the executive levels that the auditor's primary function is to carry out audit and not line activities. When such line activities become essential under emergency conditions, then the auditor can properly request top management's approval before carrying them out.

The Schedule as a Means of Obtaining Management Participation

All long-range work schedules should be reviewed up through the policy-making level of the company. The schedule reviews at the higher operating levels in the company provide management people with a preview of the audit coverage in the areas of their responsibility. During these reviews managers are given an opportunity to discuss each project and to comment on whether the scheduling is appropriate in the light of the company's present or projected activities; whether other projects — different from those listed — should be covered; whether some of the projects listed require less or no coverage; what difficulties the auditor should anticipate; what specific problems management would like to see considered; and what the thrust of a particular audit should be.

When senior managers accept the schedule, they are in effect committed to it and have provided the auditor entree into the organizations under their control and authority to subject them to the audits planned. Auditors then enter those areas and carry on their audit work with the full support of higher management; indeed, almost as a matter of contract with management.

Audit committees of boards of directors are taking a greater interest in internal auditing schedules. This concern was previously directed primarily to the audit programs of the independent public accountants alone. But as audit committees were faced with increased responsibilities and began to recognize the protection that internal auditing could afford, they became willing and eager to review and influence the scope and the depth of the audits internal auditors proposed to make. An audit committee's approval of an internal audit schedule is a powerful endorsement indeed.

The Schedule as a Means of Establishing Standards

The long-range audit schedule gives directors of internal auditing a yardstick by which to measure their own accomplishments and the accomplishments of each of their supervisors or audit managers. Current reports of work completed — in terms of audit days — provide a means of showing management and the audit committee whether the internal auditors have done what they intended to do. The comparison of audit days budgeted with audit days expended shows the degree of realization of goals. For example, overruns of budgeted audit days on audit projects can point to shortcomings either in budgeting or in accomplishment and can indicate the need for improvement in one or the other. They may be indicators that the budgets were unrealistic or that the audit projects were inadequately planned or programmed. The analysis of the variances can provide information to help in future programming or to point to needed changes in audit approach.

Further, in large auditing organizations, the work schedule can be used to measure the competence of audit managers or supervisors. At the beginning of the year the schedule may be divided among supervisors, and staff auditors may be assigned to them for specified periods. The performance of supervisors in carrying out their allotted share of the work with the staff assigned is one indicator of their ability.

The Schedule as a Means of Control

Executives are strongly trending toward scientific management. They are becoming more and more imbued with the concepts of objective- and goal-oriented administration, with adequate planning, and with sound administrative policies. Management expects that all entities within its purview will also operate in an organized, well-administered manner.

Hence, the well-structured, well-considered, long-range work schedule, with periodic reports to show that the schedule is not just window dressing but a real management tool, is one of the benchmarks of a well-controlled audit organization. It shows a setting of clear and quantifiable objectives. It implies a firm agreement with management on those objectives. Thus, when the cost-reduction itch starts, when ill-conceived and ineffective functions are subjected to the analytical glare of executive management, then the well-developed schedule of audits concentrating on key risk areas may be one of the reasons for keeping the auditing department from being reduced or eliminated.

The Schedule as Notice to the External Auditor

External auditors usually structure their own verification effort to take into account the system of internal control.

The long-range audit schedule provides them with insight as to how internal control is being monitored, how the keystone of internal control — the internal audit — is operating, and permits them to pattern their own programs so as to complement or coincide with the internal audit schedule.

Through prearrangement, specific internal audit projects may be so scheduled that they will provide the external auditors with adequate assurances and permit them to limit their own tests of internal control. This form of cooperation may provide for welcome reductions in the cost of the external audit.

The Structure of the Long-Range Schedule

The infinite variety of company structures and purposes makes a common work schedule for all an impossibility. No two companies are truly alike; in fact, most are quite different. Thus no two schedules can be alike. While production control may be of great significance to one company, it may be nonexistent in another. Inventory control will patently be more important to a retail store than it would be to an insurance company.

Hence, while no one long-range schedule will have universal applicability, an organized approach can meet the needs of many. Exhibit 18-1 gives the outline of a long-range schedule which provides a structure that can be adapted to most companies. In addition to the bare outline, a number — certainly nowhere near all — of potential areas of coverage are shown.

The schedule is divided into major areas of review. This example covers a five-year span. That span could be two, three, or four years, depending on the number of years between particular audits. If no area of coverage remains unreviewed for more than three years, then a longer span for a long-range schedule may not be applicable. Whatever the span, however, the schedule should be reevaluated every year to account for changes in company structure, product lines, and audit emphasis.

The first two columns in the program show, by project number and report date, the last time that the particular audit was performed. The third column lists the identification numbers of the applicable permanent or master program files. The fourth column describes the area of coverage. The fifth column shows the evaluation of the project in terms of urgency, from 1 (extreme urgency) to 5 (least urgency). The sixth column shows the frequency with which the audits should be made: every 1, 2, 3, 4, or 5 years. The next five columns show the years in which the audits should be made and the number of audit-days allotted to each project.

In most cases, the budgets are for specific projects. In others, as in reviews of EDP activities or follow-up reviews, lump sum budgets are set out to be expended as circumstances warrant during the year.

Exhibit 18-1 has been compressed to make it easier to understand and to make it applicable to a greater variety of companies. For example, in some companies, procurement, which is shown only as one line in the exhibit, could very easily be expanded to include such matters as material requirements, shortage controls, scrap disposition, selection of suppliers, documentation of purchases, administration of subcontracts, and so forth.

An alternative schedule format is shown in Exhibit 18-2. This suggested

Exhibit 18-1. LONG-RANGE AUDIT SCHEDULE: FIVE-YEAR SPAN

Audit Proj. No.	Rep't Date	Perm. File No.	Audit Project	Class	Freq.	Calendar Year Audit Days				
						1983	1984	1985	1986	1987
			MARKETING							
79-20	1-80	M-1	Advertising Dep't.	3	3	40	50		40	50
80-18	2-81	M-2	Sales Dep't. – Product A	3	3			50		
81-25	3-82	M-3	Sales Dep't. – Product B	3	3	30	30	30	30	30
80-2	4-80	M-4	Branch X	3	3					
81-4	5-81	M-5	Branch Y	3	3					
81-7	6-82	M-6	Branch Z	3	3					
78-1	7-78	M-7	Customer Service Dep't.	4	5	40	40			40
81-8	8-81	M-8	Contract Administration	2	3					
			Total			110	120	80	70	120
			INDUSTRIAL RELATIONS							
80-13	9-80	IR-1	Safety Dep't.	3	3	30			30	
79-19	10-79	IR-2	Personnel Records	4	4	40				40
82-20	12-82	IR-3	Employment	3	3			30		
			Total			70	—	30	30	40
			ENGINEERING							
79-15	1-80	E-1	Research and Development	2	3	50			50	
81-13	2-82	E-2	Drawings – Quality	2	2		60		60	
80-20	3-81	E-3	Drawings – Schedule	2	3		50			50
81-2	4-81	E-4	Technical Information and Data	3	4			50		
79-5	5-80	E-5	Engineering Files	4	5			50		
			Total			50	110	100	110	50
			MANUFACTURING OPERATINGS							
80-4	6-80	MO-1	Manufacturing Engineering	3	5			50		
82-1	7-82	MO-2	Procurement	1	1	100	100	100	100	100
80-9	8-80	MO-3	Quality Control	2	3	60			60	
81-5	9-81	MO-4	Production Control	2	2			50		50
81-12	10-81	MO-5	Material Control	2	3		50			50
82-13	11-82	MO-6	Stores	2	4	50				50
79-22	12-79	MO-7	Scheduling	2	4			40		
80-17	1-81	MO-8	Receiving	3	4	30				30
81-20	2-82	MO-9	Tooling	2	4			40		
81-2	3-82	MO-10	Time Studies	4	5		50			
80-3	4-80	MO-11	Traffic	3	4				50	

				3	5	240	200	280	240	280
81- 6	5-81	MO-12	**Shipping** — Total			240	200	280	240	280
			ACCOUNTING							
82- 5	6-82	A-1	Budgets and Forecasts	1	1					
82- 4	7-82	A-2	Cost Distribution	2	2					
82- 6	8-82	A-3	Inventories	2	3					
80-11	9-80	A-4	Timekeeping	3	3					
81- 3	10-81	A-5	Payroll	2	2					
82-12	11-82	A-6	Billing	1	1					
81- 9	12-81	A-7	Accounts Payable	2	2					
81-19	1-82	A-8	Accounts Receivable	2	2					
81-21	2-82	A-9	General Accounting	3	3					
			Total			200	250	170	240	210
			FINANCE							
81- 1	3-81	F-1	Mail Room	2	2					
82- 3	4-82	F-2	Cash Receipts	1	1					
82- 2	5-82	F-3	Cash Disbursements	1	1					
80- 7	6-80	F-4	Credit	2	3					
82- 7	7-82	F-5	Cash Planning	2	2					
79-12	8-79	F-6	Insurance	2	2					
			Total			120	100	90	110	90
			ELECTRONIC DATA PROCESSING							
82- 8	8-82	EDP-1	Installation	1	1					
82- 9	9-82	EDP-2	Maintenance	1	1					
			Total			100	100	100	100	100
			FUNCTIONAL EXAMINATIONS							
81-14	10-81	FE-1	Conflict of Interest	2	3					
82-11	11-82	FE-2	Rotation of Employees in Key Positions	2	3					
80-16	12-80	FE-3	Incorporation of Engineering Changes	4	3					
			Total			40	50	70	40	50
			SPECIAL EXAMINATIONS							
Various		SE-1	Special Management Requests	1	1					
Various		SE-2	Follow-up Audits	1	1					
Various		SE-3	Audits of Suppliers	1	1					
Various		SE-4	Sensitive Control Areas	1	1					
			Total			300	300	300	300	300
			Grand Total			1230	1230	1220	1240	1240

Exhibit 18-2. LONG-RANGE AUDIT SCHEDULE: THREE-YEAR SPAN

Perm. File No.	Subject	Audit Freq. (Yrs.)	Last Audit Date	Audit-days Sch.	Audit-days Act.	1983 (Quarters) 1	2	3	4	1984	1985	Defer
	Area A											
A-1	Subject 1	3	5/81	20	22					20		
A-2	Subject 2	2	4/81	20	15		15					
A-3	Subject 3	3	4/82	10	11							10
	Area B											
B-1	Subject 1	2	11/81	25	31				30			
B-2	Subject 2	3	6/82	25	26						25	
B-3	Subject 3	1	2/82	35	32			30				
	Area C											
C-1	Subject 1	1	4/82	20	24		20					
C-2	Subject 2	3	1/82	25	20							20
C-3	Subject 3	2	2/81	35	25	40						
	Area D											
D-1	Subject 1	3	10/80	10	11				10			
D-2	Subject 2	3	6/82	25	35						30	
D-3	Subject 3	2	10/82	40	39					40		
	Misc.			50	60		15	15	15	15	60	
	Special Mgm't Requests			40	80		20	20	20	20	80	

program, even more truncated for purposes of illustration, suggests using a three-year span, but allocates the coming year's budget to each of the four quarters. This program format provides for spelling out deferred projects and the time allocated to those projects. Thus, management obtains visibility on those areas of audit coverage which cannot be included in the three-year cycle in the light of current audit department budgets.

The allocated audit-days, the scheduled frequencies, and the classification of priorities in the two schedules illustrated should not be regarded as suggestions for actual use. They are all purely fictitious. Each audit organization must decide for itself what priorities to assign to its audit projects and how many days to allocate to those projects.

Schedule Budgets

One approach to budgeting is to start with the authorized level of audit personnel. Multiply that number by the available audit-hours in the year. This base must then be reduced by vacation time, sick leave, employee training, staff meetings, and the like. The remainder is available for audit work.

This remainder is broken down into scheduled and nonscheduled work. The amount of nonscheduled work is set aside — based on past experience, discussions with management, or the best available forecasts — for special requests from management, follow-up of prior deficiencies, reviews of especially sensitive activities, research, and the like.

What time remains is allotted to specific audit assignments. The budget assigned to each audit project is in essence what the director of auditing can afford to spend (or cannot afford **not** to spend) on the particular audit. Some budgets are developed intuitively. Intuition is a personal matter incapable of precise analysis, but past experience can be recorded and preserved on a simple form.

The form should be completed at the conclusion of each regularly scheduled audit assignment. It should be prepared by the person in the best position to provide the information; namely, the auditor in charge of that assignment. For at that point he or she knows more about that audit activity than anyone else.

The auditors should record on the form their conclusions as to the significance of the job (should it be repeated and, if so, how soon?); whether the job is important enough to stand on its own feet, or whether it can be combined with one or more other jobs; whether the audit thrust should be altered on future jobs; what is a reasonable budget for the job, either as a survey or as a full-scale audit assignment; what parts of the job absolutely must be done to protect the company and what parts can be slighted without excessive risk; and what parts of the job should be followed up before the next regularly scheduled assignment. Exhibit 18-3 is one example of such a form.

The executed form should be kept in the permanent file as assistance to the auditor who next does the job, and to the director of auditing or the audit managers in developing their long-range schedules.

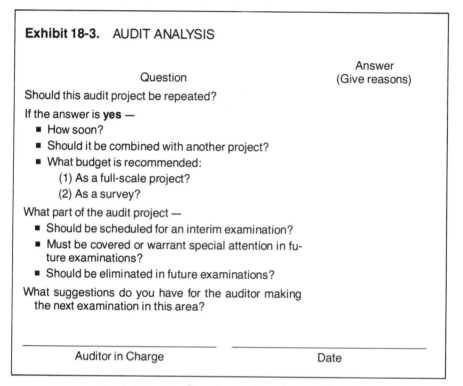

Exhibit 18-3. AUDIT ANALYSIS

Question	Answer (Give reasons)
Should this audit project be repeated?	

If the answer is **yes** —
- How soon?
- Should it be combined with another project?
- What budget is recommended:
  - (1) As a full-scale project?
  - (2) As a survey?

What part of the audit project —
- Should be scheduled for an interim examination?
- Must be covered or warrant special attention in future examinations?
- Should be eliminated in future examinations?

What suggestions do you have for the auditor making the next examination in this area?

Auditor in Charge	Date

Activities Needing Special Audit Emphasis

Certain activities within a company are particularly susceptible to improprieties, manipulation, or significant loss. These activities are usually of serious concern to executive management. They should be of equal concern to the auditor. Like weak links in a chain, they are most susceptible to failure. When breakdown occurs, the manager's lifted eyebrow is invariably turned toward the internal auditors, and the auditors who have failed to identify the activities needing special audit emphasis have nobody but themselves to blame.

Each company has its peculiar problem areas. Only that company's internal auditors can isolate and pinpoint them. These areas deserve special consideration and special assurance to management that they are being given proper audit scrutiny. These areas should be researched and listed, and the list should be regularly reviewed and revised as circumstances change.

Once identified, the sensitive areas should be interwoven into the fabric of the regular audit program and audited when the related activity is covered. An audit of deliveries bypassing the receiving department, for example — often particularly susceptible to error or manipulation — can be performed as a part of the receiving department audit. The inherent dangers in such an activity demand special assurances that direct deliveries will not be overlooked in the regular receiving audit. Other areas also may be covered in special audits.

Exhibit 18-4 is an example of a listing of activities requiring special audit emphasis. It includes sensitive control areas common to many companies. It can be expanded or revised to include areas peculiar to particular companies. The exhibit lists the activities — whose titles make them self-explanatory — along with the permanent file most applicable to that activity, the latest audit report (audit project number and report date), and the period scheduled for the next review. This period may coincide with the regular audit, or it may represent special scheduling for an interim or follow-up review.

The listing should be reviewed with management at the same time the long-range schedule is reviewed. This will offer management an opportunity to add to the list, to be made aware of the special audit coverage, and to be alerted to the penalties of reducing the audit scope.

Risk areas (see Chapter 4) are set forth here in a formal report which can be meshed with the long-range audit schedule.

One organization developed a system to determine audit priorities based on previous audit coverage, expenditures by the activity (or amounts controlled), and estimates of degree of risk (see Exhibit 18-5)[1].

Organization Development Objectives

An audit organization is no different from any other enterprise activity. It grows or it atrophies. It cannot tie its lifeline to past experience alone. The rest of the enterprise, to be successful, is learning, adapting, expanding, and testing new ideas. Directors of auditing cannot do less if they are adequately to serve their profession, their company, and their people.

Admittedly, it is hard to fit organization-development objectives into a busy and sometimes backbreaking audit schedule, but there is no choice. It is a case of improve or wither away. Somehow, some way, there are always means by which that schedule can accommodate more; especially when the need is understood, when the potential benefits are brought home to the audit group.

Such objectives must be more than wishful dreams. They must be implemented through quantifiable goals. They must call for enumerated tasks. They must result in set schedules. They must be controlled. And of equal importance, they must be keyed to certain continuing objectives that will lift auditors out of their daily routines and out of themselves, showing them that they can make themselves better than they think they are.

Exhibit 18-4. ACTIVITIES REQUIRING SPECIAL AUDIT EMPHASIS

Activity	Applicable Permanent File	Latest Report Number	Date	Scheduled for Next Review
Marketing				
No-charge sales	M-2	80-18,	2-81	1984
	M-3	81-25,	3-82	1985
Industrial Relations				
Authority to drive into plant	IR-1	80-13,	9-80	1983
Vehicle inspection — entering and leaving plant	IR-1	80-13,	9-80	1983
Control of master keys	IR-1	80-13,	9-80	1983
Conflict of interest	IR-2	79-19,	10-79	1983
Wage and salary adjustments	IR-2	79-19,	10-79	1983
Engineering				
Company proprietary data	E-1	79-15,	1-80	1983
Designation of sole procurement source	E-4	81-2,	4-81	1985
Preparation of restrictive specifications	E-4	81-2,	4-81	1985
Manufacturing Operations				
Deliveries bypassing Receiving Department	MO-8	80-17,	1-81	1985
Scrap and salvage	MO-5	81-12,	10-81	1983
Control over selection of suppliers	MO-2	81-1,	7-82	1983
Control over purchase order changes	MO-2	82-1,	7-82	1983
Transportation and routing of materials	MO-11	80-3,	4-80	1984
Supplies susceptible to pilferage	MO-6	82-13,	11-82	1985

Exhibit 18-4. (Cont.)

Activity	Applicable Permanent File	Latest Report Number	Latest Report Date	Scheduled for Next Review
Accounting				
Approval and payment of overtime	A-5	81-3,	10-81	1983
Payrolls	A-5	81-3,	10-81	1983
Bank reconciliations	A-9	81-21,	2-82	1984
Employee bonuses	A-5	81-3,	10-81	1983
Credit memo forms	A-6	82-12,	11-82	1983
Executive-approved invoices	A-7	82-9,	12-81	1983
Payments to suppliers	A-7	81-9,	12-81	1983
Accounts payable check mailing	A-7	81-9,	12-81	1983
Fixed assets	A-9	81-21,	2-82	1984
Finance				
Blank, void, and mutilated checks	F-3	82-2,	5-82	1983
Undelivered checks	F-3	82-2,	5-82	1983
Facsimile signature plate	F-3	82-2,	5-82	1983
Cashier's funds	F-3	82-2,	5-82	1983
Petty cash funds	F-3	82-2,	5-82	1983
Cash receipts	F-2	82-3,	4-82	1983
Credit approvals	F-4	80-7,	6-80	1983
Travelers checks	F-3	82-2,	5-82	1983
Metered postage	F-1	81-1,	3-81	1983
Other				
Rotation and vacations of employees in key control positions	SE-4	81-25,	3-82	1984

Exhibit 18-5.

Audit Priorities

Weight

	1. Previous Audit Coverage	
35%	Previous year	1
	First prior year	2
	Second prior year	3
	Third prior year	4
	Other	5
35	2. Yearly Expenditures Made or Dollars Controlled — Operation, Maintenance, or Capital Expenditures	
	50,000,001 +	5
	25,000,001 - 50,000,000	4
	5,000,001 - 25,000,000	3
	1,000,001 - 5,000,000	2
	1,000,000 or less	1
30	3. Exposure (Risk) — A Subjective Measure of Potential Difficulties Relating to the Expected Internal Control in the Area	
	Most Exposure	5
		4
		3
		2
100%	Least Exposure	1

The planner ranks each auditable item in each category and multiplies that number by the weighting percentage on the left. All products are summed for the total point ranking of the activity.

First, then, comes the setting of these continuing objectives — objectives that persist as long as the auditing organization shall exist. These objectives must be set by the directors of auditing and should reflect a philosophy of what they consider most significant to the growth of the internal auditing organization. The objectives should be high-minded and should make mind-stretching demands.

It would not be amiss to key these objectives to the trinity of aims mentioned in the first paragraph of this subsection — profession, company, people — stating the continuing objectives as follows:

To make the auditing organization the leader in the profession.

To expand the service to management.

To help the individual auditor achieve greater dimension and stature.

All organization-development projects could then be keyed to these fundamental objectives. In this way the development program has form and structure, and it will be balanced among plans that concern each of the three objectives.

Obviously, directors of auditing will have a selling job to do. They are asking people to take on additional work. They are hoping the work will be done to some extent on the staff's own time. They would like to see a personal commitment that can evoke the kind of effort and dedication that will accomplish the impossible and produce a superb product. They foresee people marching to the beat of the same drums that sound in the director's brain and developing a sense of pride and achievement that money itself cannot buy.

But whether these projects are undertaken through persuasion, cajolery, or outright directive, they must be undertaken; they must be a part of the long-range schedule. Resting on laurels is a debilitating posture.

There is no end to the development projects that can be pursued. Each year directors of auditing should ask their own people which projects they wish to undertake. Proposals for new projects should be carefully screened to avoid duplication, frivolous excursions into unreality, exercises not worth the effort, or projects having no reasonable relation to the continuing objectives.

Once approved, each project should be carefully controlled. The proposal should be accompanied by a schedule of specific milestones and a set of standards by which to measure accomplishments. Such standards or units of measurement might be a research report, or a new manual, or a new pro forma program. Or they might be the number of audit projects in which a particular new technique is to be employed.

Development projects should be keyed to the needs of each individual audit organization. The examples in Exhibit 18-6 are merely some ideas of the projects that can be scheduled, relating them to the three prime objectives and showing the standards or units of measurement that can be applied.

Each quarter, or at least semiannually, the director of auditing should receive status reports on these projects. When the projects are completed, appropriate recognition should be accorded those who accomplished their objectives. Also, the annual or semiannual reports to management on audit accomplishments should give prominent place to these accomplishments as well.

Reviews With Management

The audit program has significance to management to the extent that management becomes involved in its development. Reviewing the proposed program with management obtains both its involvement and its blessing. The review meetings provide for an interchange of ideas and an understanding of management's problems and needs.

Exhibit 18-6. PROJECT POSSIBILITIES RELATED TO OBJECTIVES

Project	Due date	Standard of measurement
To make the auditing organization the best in the profession.		
Expand the use of EDP in making sample selections	Dec. 19XX	5 audits
Experiment with oral presentations and visual aids	Dec. 19XX	10 audits
Develop a style manual for report writing	Dec. 19XX	Completed manual
Experiment with the use of question-naires to obtain data for audit ex-aminations	Nov. 19XX	Two proposed questionnaires
Establish dollar budget controls over various phases of audit examina-tions and reporting	June 19XX	Research report
Expand the service to manage-ment		
Develop or improve a system of clas-sifying deficiency findings to afford management a basis for broad, corrective action, throughout the company, through analysis of causes	July 19XX	List of deficiency causes
Develop or improve an annual sum-mary report to management on the adequacy and effectiveness of its controls, based on audits made during the year	Nov. 19XX	Pro forma report
Perform research into the needs of various levels of management for audit assistance	June 19XX	Research report
Develop or improve summary reports to management on audit results accumulated by families of jobs	June 19XX	Two proposed summaries
Develop or improve a system of reporting significant findings in common areas as an aid to management in perceiving poten-tial deficiencies, their causes, and the results if uncorrected	Dec. 19XX	Ten significant findings
Help auditors achieve greater di-mension and stature		
Encourage auditors to take outside courses	Dec. 19XX	Completion of 10 courses
Encourage participation in the pro-fessional organization of internal auditors	June 19XX	Two new members

Exhibit 18-6. (Cont.)		
Project	**Due date**	**Standard of measurement**
		One chapter officer
		One international officer
Develop or improve a program of counseling with staff auditors on their future education and training	Dec. 19XX	Annual counseling with all staff auditors
Establish and hold training programs for auditors on such subjects as:	Dec. 19XX	Three training programs
■ Use of EDP in audits		
■ Statistical sampling		
■ Report writing		
■ Flowcharting		
■ Audit programming		
■ Oral presentations		
■ Visual aids		
■ Referencing reports		
■ Office regulations		

These reviews should be undertaken first at the branch or division level; that is, in terms of Exhibit 18-1, they would be undertaken with the directors or vice presidents of marketing, industrial relations, engineering, operations, accounting, and finance.

The audit representatives should prepare well for the reviews. They should provide copies of the program for each functional organization. They should come prepared to answer the questions that are bound to be asked and to take notes of the suggestions which the branch or division director makes. A record of these suggestions should be deposited in the appropriate permanent or master file.

In preparation for the meeting, the audit representatives should accumulate copies of all relevant audit reports. In addition, they should prepare brief notes of the audit objectives of each of the audit projects. In this way, they will have at their fingertips the answer to such questions as "What problems did you encounter the last time in the audit of personnel records?" or "How do you propose to examine the accuracy of engineering drawings?"

In addition, the audit representatives should inquire as to what impact new programs will have on branch activities; what aspect of current programs cause the director or vice president the most problems, and which programs appear to be phasing out and do not warrant audit attention. Finally, the audit representatives should solicit advice from the branch directors as to the scheduling of the audits within their branches — which projects should be postponed, and which projects should be advanced.

After the reviews at the branch level, the proposed program should be adjusted to accommodate the needs of management or to reflect new information obtained. At that point, it should be discussed with the top company executives, at the company president level, or with the audit committee of the board of directors. A summary of the program should be prepared to support the request for audit budget for the forthcoming year.

The presentation at the summit can be sparked by visual aids summarizing the last year's results, the proposed audit effort for the coming year, and the number of auditors required to accomplish the work.

Small Internal Audit Organizations

The small audit organization is most likely to avoid the task of developing the long-range audit schedule. Yet those auditors are most likely to need the protection such schedules provide. The one- or two-auditor organizations are fair game for line assignments: help out in accounts payable when volume builds, do the legwork of external auditors, etc., etc.

If management is convinced that time away from audit projects increases business risks, the likelihood of line assignments diminishes. But the campaign for a long-range schedule must be well thought through. The internal auditors will have to do more than list audit projects. They will have to convince executive management and the board that those audit projects are significant, that if the activities are not audited, the enterprise leaves itself open to risks, that there is no assurance of reliable systems of internal control, that external audit costs might rise as a result of diminished audit activity.

Thus, internal auditors should be specific about both the audit projects and the risks. For example, management might be told:

"If we don't audit receiving, you might not know if you are paying for goods or services never received, received too early, or received damaged."

"If we don't audit shipping, you might not know that we may be packaging goods improperly, using the wrong freight routings, sending goods to the wrong destinations, or incurring needless demurrage charges."

"If we don't audit purchasing, you might not know that we may be paying too much for products, dealing with the wrong suppliers, facing the danger of improper buyer-vendor relations, buying too much or too little, or not receiving products on time."

"If we don't audit marketing, you might not know if we are expending money on market research needlessly, placing ads in the wrong media, failing to compare actual with expected benefits, dealing with the wrong advertising agencies, losing track of expensive products loaned to the agencies, or paying exorbitant prices for sales promotion items."

"If we don't audit production control, you might not know if we are meeting production schedules, or that production schedules may not be geared to sales projections, or that workers, tools, and materials are not getting together at the best time, or that production costs may be excessive."

The list can go on and on. Management often needs convincing. The convincer is a simple demonstration of an understandable risk or an audit finding that saved the company money or protected it from danger. If management has been clearly warned and insists on accepting the risk, the auditor has done all that is necessary. If one of the enumerated risks mushrooms into a loss, the auditor cannot properly be held at fault.

But the burden is on the auditor to make those risks clear and understandable. One auditor was taken to task for not having warned management of a risk which turned into a heavy loss. The auditor reminded the manager that he had indeed provided a warning of what could happen. Angrily, the manager retorted, "But you should have convinced me!"

One means of achieving internal audit objectives involves compromise — to provide formally for a certain amount of assistance to management. The internal auditors could set aside in their long-range audit program an agreed percentage of audit hours for whatever special services management needs. But internal auditors must make it clear that any violation of the remaining audit hours could destroy the internal audit function as a viable entity, make it no longer credible as a management control, provide no basis for the external auditor to rely upon it, dissipate any basis for reliance upon internal auditing as a monitor of the company's systems, and undermine its objectivity. The need to keep an excessive number of audit hours from being spent on nonauditing activities applies to all internal auditing departments. The smaller departments are the most vulnerable and need to jealously guard their auditing capability.

Coordination With Other Control Agencies in the Company

Internal auditing does not stand alone as a monitor of control. In all large companies there are other agencies which may be equally concerned with matters of control. Their interest may have a more technical aspect, but it may complement the internal auditor's interests in the administrative aspects of control.

The security department is concerned with control over irregularities. The quality control department is concerned with control over product reliability and conformance to specifications. The safety department is concerned with control over accident prevention. The industrial engineering organization is concerned with control over operating practices and procedures. Depending on the nature of the company, other agencies may have comparable control functions.

The internal auditing department should keep open a line of communications to these agencies in planning its audits. Valuable information can be obtained, either to reduce any possibility of duplicate surveillance or to point to areas where special audit emphasis may be warranted.

There are many ways in which this coordination can be accomplished. The following approaches are representative.

Security

Hold periodic meetings with security personnel. Keep them informed of the ongoing audit projects. Solicit their suggestions on where manipulations or other improprieties have occurred or can occur. Offer to assist in reviewing records relating to ongoing security investigations; the auditor usually can locate the records more readily and accumulate the data more easily. Ask to be kept informed of ongoing investigations which indicate the possibility of control breakdowns.

Quality Control

Exchange audit schedules and reports with the quality control agency. Seek to be kept informed of repetitive defects in suppliers' goods or in-house manufactured products; there may be administrative control weaknesses contributing to the difficulties.

Safety

Establish arrangements with the agency responsible for safety so that suspected dangers encountered in the audit can be immediately reported for investigation. Provide for feedback showing the nature of the corrective action.

Industrial Engineering

Provide for a pattern of preliminary discussions with the industrial engineers before engaging in audits in production areas. Clear any findings and recommendations with the industrial engineers when areas within their cognizance are involved. With their technical expertise they may be able to point to matters which the auditors may have overlooked in their findings and recommendations.

Conclusion

The long-range audit schedule is a useful instrument that helps the director of auditing justify budgets, obtain management participation, establish standards for realization of audit goals, control the audit effort, show management what will and what will not be covered, and assist the external auditors in developing their own programs.

There are many ways of structuring the schedule, but it is important to carry allotments of budget down to the individual audit projects. Each audit project should be considered in terms of its relationship to the entire audit effort. Projects should be evaluated in terms of their relative significance. This can be accomplished intuitively or on the basis of past experience.

Included in the schedule and made an integral part of it should be coverage of sensitive areas which experience teaches are subject to breakdown in control or to manipulation.

Along with the audit objectives, the director of auditing should establish long-term goals for improving the audit organization and its people and for constant upgrading of its service to management.

Reviewing the audit schedule with management affords an opportunity to determine management's needs, to obtain its involvement in the audit plans, and to highlight the auditor's service to management.

Coordinating audit plans with other control agencies in the company can add breadth and depth to the audit scope. These agencies include security, quality control, safety, and industrial engineering.

References

1. R. D. Morehead and Don W. Myers, "Audit Management and Control," *The Internal Auditor*, February 1980, p. 61.

Supplementary Reading

Darou, G. B. and J. G. Miller. "An Audit Management System." *The Internal Auditor*, January/February 1975, pp. 68-72.

Morehead, R. D. and Don W. Myers. "Audit Management and Control." *The Internal Auditor*, February 1980, pp. 58-68.

Wilson, D. E. and R. D. Ranson. "Internal Audit Scheduling — a Mathematical Model." *The Internal Auditor*, July/August 1971, pp. 42-50.

For further study

Discussion Problems

1. Describe six factors you would consider in determining the frequency and extent of the audit coverage of current assets.

2. You have been appointed to establish an internal audit function in a large national organization with 15,000 employees in various locations. The company is engaged in manufacturing and marketing commercial products. Its customers are mainly in the wholesale, manufacturing, and warehousing business. Describe five important initial steps you would take preparatory to setting up an overall audit schedule. Give a reason for each.

3. You are the director of internal auditing for a corporation with total assets of $50 million. It manufactures its products in ten strategically located regional factories and sells, distributes, and services these products

through a network of warehouses and branch offices located in most major cities.

You are preparing an audit work schedule for the coming year that will use your audit staff in a manner that will maximize its effectiveness and minimize audit costs. In the next year's work schedule, you are considering auditing the company's numerous imprest cash funds. These funds, amounting to $1,000,000, are located in the home office, ten factories, and 110 warehouses and branch offices. The average balance of the cash funds in each of the warehouses and branch offices is $5,000.

List five factors you should consider in determining how to allocate next year's internal audit staff time to an audit of the company's cash funds. Briefly discuss the rationale supporting each of these five factors.

4. Your company is a major manufacturer and distributor of television sets. It recently entered into an agreement with an advertising agency. Advertising accounts for a significant portion of your company's total expenses. Discuss four factors which will determine the audit frequency and the amount of time to budget for an audit of the advertising agency.

5. How can the internal auditor be sure that activities which are especially subject to manipulation will be reviewed during the year?

Multiple Choice Problems

1. As a monitor of the organization's control system, the internal auditor should:
a. Accept responsibility for the prevention and detection of fraud.
b. Identify all reasonably foreseeable risk areas in the organization and schedule reviews of those areas.
c. Be held responsible as a professional for extraordinary care rather than ordinary care.
d. Get to the bottom of any suspected fraud by interrogating suspects and witnesses.
e. All of the above.

2. Long-range audit schedules insure adequate audit coverage for the enterprise because they:
a. Require an inquiry into all company activities.
b. Take care to compile.
c. Are prepared every year for the ensuing 1-5 years.
d. Are reviewed at top management levels.
e. Are coordinated with the external auditor.

3. Long-range audit schedules provide justification for the internal auditing department budget because they:

a. Demonstrate an organized approach by the director of internal auditing.
b. Bring proposed programs to the attention of top-level management.
c. Show in detail the days needed to provide adequate audit coverage.
d. Are geared to the chart of accounts.
e. Are reviewed by the audit committee of the board.

4. The long-range audit schedule encourages management participation because:
a. The schedule is reviewed at the higher levels of management.
b. Management fears the auditor.
c. It covers activities throughout the company.
d. The titles of the proposed audit projects are explicit.
e. All of the above.

5. The long-range audit schedule can be used to measure audit accomplishment because it:
a. Shows the audit days that will be expended.
b. The audit days add up to the number of auditors on the staff.
c. Both audit and nonaudit projects are shown.
d. It provides a standard of comparison.
e. It is a form of planning.

6. The internal auditing department can make sure it won't overlook activities presenting special hazards by:
a. Talking to operating managers.
b. Programming audits of sensitive control areas.
c. Talking to the security people.
d. Consulting the controller.
e. Coordinating the program with the external auditors.

7. The long-range audit schedule can be considered a form of protection because:

a. If management reduces the audit budget it knows what will be eliminated.
b. Each project is assigned a specific number of audit hours of budget.
c. It has been reviewed by the external auditor.
d. It has been coordinated with the director of security.
e. The director of internal auditing has a mandate to perform operational audits.

8. Organization-development long-range objectives are concerned with:
a. Good citizenship and attention to the ecology.
b. Safety and health plans.
c. Assisting management in the discharge of its duties.
d. Developing the long-range audit program.
e. Improving auditing capabilities.

9. The agency listed below is **not** regarded as a control agency:
a. Maintenance.
b. Safety.
c. Security.
d. Quality control.
e. Industrial engineering.

10. The *Standards for the Professional Practice of Internal Auditing* states that the director of internal auditing should develop schedules which:
a. Show what activities are to be audited.
b. Are reviewed by top management.
c. Are approved by the audit committee of the board.
d. Are coordinated with the external auditors.
e. Both b. and c. above.

Case Studies

18-1 To Have or Not to Have a Long-Range Schedule

Paul Eberhardt is the head of internal auditing at Corpus Corporation, a manufacturing concern employing 5,000 people. Sales last year were $50 million. He is assisted by Irma Austen, a senior internal auditor. His secretary is Sally Clift.

Paul came into the office Monday morning to a desk full of mail that had accumulated during his absence. He rang for Sally.

"Good morning, Mr. Eberhardt. How was the conference?"

"The Institute of Internal Auditors really put on a good one this year."

"In what way?"

"I picked up a lot of good ideas."

"Sounds like more work around here."

"You bet. That's what keeps us going — the infusion of new ideas."

"What kind?"

"A number of them. But the one that really intrigues me is the idea of a long-range schedule of audits."

"What's that?"

"Setting out for a period of five years all the audits we propose to do during that time."

"It sounds like a pretty big typing job."

"That's not the half of it. We'll have to decide just what jobs we'll do, when we'll do them, and how much budget to assign to each one."

"Who'll do that?"

"I will, with the help of Irma."

"She will really love that."

"I've a notion she might, once I've sold her on the idea. Please ask her to come in."

Required: Prepare a paper setting forth both the benefits and the disadvantages of the long-range schedule.

18-2 To Audit or Not to Audit

Paul Eberhardt was ushered into the office of the director of quality assurance, carrying his long-range audit schedule for Q.A. activities. Paul was a bit apprehensive since there had been numerous problems during the past year with audit reports covering Q.A. Most deficiency findings had been bitterly fought over and the written replies had been grudging responses. Burt Meissner, the director, greeted Paul coolly and started scanning the program.

When he was through, he said, "Paul, I think this schedule is a waste of time. The problems are not in Q.A. They are in manufacturing. That's where you should direct your effort."

Paul said, "Well, Burt, we've got a schedule for manufacturing also. But that's beside the point. We have to make continuing reviews throughout the company. Your organization has not been completely without problems. I'd have no justification in eliminating Q.A. from my plans."

"Maybe so," said Burt, "but my organization has been cut to the bone. We're subject to government audits which we can't refuse. My people just don't have the time to deal with your auditors."

Required: State what Paul should say and do.

19

Controlling
Audit Projects

Discipline for auditors. Assigning projects. Identifying projects. The need for budgets and schedules. Controlling project budgets. Project time records. When budgets can be revised. Individual time records. Status reports. Bird's eye view of audits in progress. Contents of permanent files. Requirements of the *Standards for the Professional Practice of Internal Auditing* for supervision of audit projects. Supervisors: the people in the middle. Supervising planning, preliminary surveys, audit programs, field work, exit interviews, reporting, report reviews, and project closure. Project control through the computer. Computer printouts on completed assignments, audit days assigned, audit projects listed according to category and auditors, and weekly status reports. Small organizations: reports to management and the means of obtaining a form of supervision.

Audit Assignments

A well-controlled, well-structured internal audit project has a far better chance of meeting its goals than one that is haphazard and formless. True, an internal audit demands creative thinking and calls for the auditor to beat new paths and stretch old boundaries. But without control of budget and schedule and without clearly defined guides to get it going, the project tends to languish. It suffers from lack of discipline.

Discipline, from without and within, is the hallmark of professional auditors. Their profession's stated criteria impose certain disciplines; their own well-developed standards provide the rest. These disciplines include a clear understanding of the value of the audit project in relation to the needs of the enterprise. They also include an understanding of the value of timeliness and of the staleness of yesterday's news.

The long-range program has allotted a budget and schedule for the audit project assigned to the auditor. These budgets and schedules are part of the audit organization's master plan. They were established with contemplation of the value of the project to the enterprise and the timing most suitable to all concerned. Auditors must therefore fit their own audit budget and schedule into the plans mapped out by the master program.

The very initial steps in assigning and planning the audit project are controlling the audit project, meeting budgets and schedules, dealing with budget revisions, providing for progress reports on the job, maintaining an overview of the projects in process, reviewing permanent files, and devising ways of reminding auditors what they should do to launch a project on its way.

Controlling Audit Projects

The first step in controlling any audit project is "getting it on the books." This is no different from establishing a work order to authorize approved work and to permit the expenditure of money and effort on such work. A simple form, controlled by a register, should be devised for the purpose.

The form might show the number and title of the project; the assigned budget; the name of the auditor-in-charge, assistants, and supervisor; and such other information as may be considered necessary. The register will

---

Exhibit 19-1. PROJECT ASSIGNMENT ORDER

Title _____   In Charge _____

Project No. _____   Supervisor _____

Permanent File No. _____   Start Date _____

Programmed
Frequency _____

Programmed
Budget _____

Approved Budget _____
(After audit program approved)

Accounts to be Analyzed: _____

Reports to be Reviewed: _____

Special Instructions: _____

Authorized by _____

Date _____

control the assignment of project numbers and will provide a historical record of projects for ready reference. The register will remain under the control of the office secretary; copies of assignment records will be distributed to the auditor-in-charge, the supervisor, and the office file.

There is a tendency, in devising forms like these, to provide for every conceivable contingency. The forms then get complicated and forbidding. Some of the called-for information gets omitted, and the system collapses of its own weight. Worst of all, uncorrected neglect of any prescribed procedure tends to heap contempt on other procedures, resulting in incomplete records and tending to impair office administration. Exhibit 19-1 is a simple assignment record which provides essentially all the information needed to authorize a project.

Each audit organization will determine its own system of project numbering. A logical system will provide a simple means of showing the kind of project, the year, and the number of each project within each year's series. For example:

R8X-1   The first "regular" project specifically included in the long-range audit program for the year 198X.

M8X-2   The second project which was specifically requested by management during 198X.

S8X-3   The third special examination — not included in the long-range program — undertaken by the auditing organization because of special needs due to unexpected circumstances.

I8X-4   The fourth interim project, conducted between regularly programmed reviews. Interim reviews are designed to determine whether key controls or sensitive areas reviewed at intervals of two or more years are continuing to function as intended.

FU8X-5   The fifth follow-up project established to determine whether corrected deficiencies have recurred and whether the corrective action that had been instituted is still effective.

Res8X-1   The first research project of the year 198X undertaken to carry out plans for developing and expanding the effectiveness of the auditing organization.

Separate series of projects provide for more precise control over the audit organization's budget. For example, audit-days expended on regular projects can be compared with the annual budget for those projects. The same is true for the budgets established for management requests, special work, research, and the rest.

Project Budgets and Schedules

Creative souls abhor control. Modern internal auditing is largely a creative activity. The auditors engaged in that activity sometimes argue that budget and schedule constraints stifle creativity. Nonsense. Any business activity functions only so long as there are funds to pay for it, and every ac-

Exhibit 19-2. TIME RECORD

Project No. _____

TIME CHARGES IN HOURS FOR WEEK ENDED:

W/P Ref.	Budget		Total Act'l	First Week	Week	Cum.	Week	Cum.	Week	Cum.	Week	Cum.	Week	Cum.	Week	Cum.	Week	Cum.
	Orig.	Rev.																
Planning																		
Field Work																		
Audit Segment A																		
Audit Segment B																		
etc.																		
Total Field Work																		
Report Writing																		
Client Review																		
Project Closure																		
Total																		

tivity has its price tag. Even pure research in a company engaged in scientific projects must be granted a budget, and must have progress evaluated. True, the budgets may require adjustment when new conditions surface. Also true is that the project may be eliminated or halted when the budget limitations are reached and no return can be foreseen.

In all audit activities, individual project budgets and schedules are essential. Without them there is a tendency to dawdle; a tendency to give equal weight to all segments of an audit instead of determining which segments are the most significant and warrant the most attention; and a tendency to spend inordinate lengths of time to "tie up loose ends."

Accordingly, budgets and schedules on all assigned projects must become a normal way of life. Such controls, to be effective, must include a current recording and reporting system. The system should provide:

A way for the auditor-in-charge to allot budget to the various segments of the audit project and to keep a record of the time spent on those segments.

A way for each staff auditor to report time charges during the current period — usually a month.

A way for the auditing department to report currently — usually monthly — on the status of all its current audit projects.

Exhibit 19-2 is a suggested work sheet for controlling individual project budgets. It is kept in the working papers and provides for allocating the entire budget to the various segments of the project beginning with initial planning through completion of the final report.

Exhibit 19-3 is a suggested time report for every employee in the department. The report provides for an accounting of each hour in the work week. It provides for both programmed and nonprogrammed work and for vacations, holidays, and sick leave.

Exhibit 19-4 is a suggested monthly report which lists each project open at the end of the month, the budget allotted to it, the actual charges, the estimated date for completion of the field work, and the estimated date for the release of the final report. The auditor-in-charge should make an initial estimate of field work completion at least by the midpoint of the audit.

Budget Revisions

While control through budgets is essential, that control should not be so rigid as to be self-defeating. The thrust of the internal audit is such that it cannot be reduced to a mechanical exercise. New projects, not previously undertaken, are constantly added to the program. And each old project either is attacked somewhat differently from the last or faces changes in organization or activity. Thus the budget system requires some flexibility without relinquishing formal control.

The rules for budget revision should be reasonable and simple. At the

Exhibit 19-3. TIME REPORT

Name _____

5 Week Period Ended _____

	W /E						W /E					W
Programmed Work:	M	T	W	T	F	S	M	T	W	T	F	S	M
Proj. No.													
Nonprogrammed Work:													
Abandoned projects													
Follow-up on completed proj.													
Special Investigations (Desc.)													
Other (Describe)													
Other Working Time:													
New employee training													
Staff meetings and training													
Research (Describe)													
Proofreading													
Supervisory and Adminis.													
IIA													
Secretarial and clerical													
Nonworking Time:													
Vacations													
Sick Leave													
Approved time off													
Leave without pay													
Holidays													
Totals													

same time, they should not represent a cloak for incompetence or poor planning. Thus, budget adjustments should be entertained as soon as it is determined that the audit project undertaken is not the same as the project planned in the long-range program. By and large, then, budgets should generally be appraised for potential revision — either up or down — immediately after the preliminary survey and the preparation of the audit program.

The preliminary survey (see Chapter 4) establishes the subject of the review, the theory of the audit approach, and the structure of the project. If the survey discloses new activities — different from those contemplated when the audit project was first programmed — appropriate budget adjustments should be requested and authorized. If the activities remain the same, any budget overruns that do occur should be explained, but not glossed over by extending the allotted budget.

For example, the present auditor-in-charge may have uncovered substantial deficiencies which required extended investigation. He or she may have been saddled with assistants whose work had to be done over or who required considerable attention. Or the audit tests may have required expansion to establish the reliability of the audit findings. These matters, while legitimately taking more time, have no effect on the basic element in the long-range audit program. The activities subject to review remain the same.

In effect, therefore, decisions to revise budgets should be made in terms of the long-term program. The difficulties normally inherent in an internal audit project are simply a matter for consideration in evaluating the auditor's accomplishments on that job. Accordingly, requests for budget revisions should clearly spell out the structural changes in the subject under review and should provide estimates of the additional time occasioned by those changes.

Exhibit 19-4. STATUS OF CURRENT PROJECTS AND PERSONNEL ASSIGNMENTS MONTH ENDED JANUARY 31, 198X

Supervisor A

Personnel Assigned	Project	Budget	To Date	To Complete	Field Work Completion	Report Issue
			Audit-Days		Due Date	
Auditor 1	Project title	50	40	10	2-5-8X	
Ass't. A	Project Number (date started)					
Auditor 2	Project title Project Number (date started)	35	31	8	1-29-8X	2-15-8X
Auditor 3	Project title Project Number (date started)	45	10	35	(*)	

Supervisor B
etc.

(*) Not yet determined

Similarly, where the survey and the resulting audit program indicate that coverage can profitably be restricted or reduced, prompt downward adjustments should be made at that point. It would be naive to assume that auditors-in-charge will proceed with alacrity to offer to relinquish some of their treasured budget. Clearly, their jobs will be made easier if they can carry on a reduced audit with an unreduced allotment of audit-days. But in order to evaluate audit efforts, the budget should represent the time allotted for a reasonably proficient auditor to accomplish a particular examination. Accordingly, the supervisor or the audit manager should review the results of the survey and the proposed audit program to determine whether budget reductions as well as increases are in order.

Exhibit 19-5. WEEKLY STATUS REPORT

Week ended_____

Audit Project_____

	Audit-Days
Budget	_____
Prior week's cumulative total	_____
This week's total	_____
This week's cumulative total	_____
Budget still available	_____
Required to complete	_____

Audit Segments Over Budget

	Audit-Days	
Segment	Budgeted	Over
1.	_____	_____
2.	_____	_____
3.	_____	_____

Action Required to Recover

1.
2.
3.

Potential Problems

_____
Auditor-in-Charge

Note: Submit this report to the supervisor by 10 a.m. each Monday.

Progress Reports

While more formal reports of progress will be prepared monthly or quarterly, the supervisor or audit manager cannot wait that long to know how his projects are proceeding. The supervisors or managers who are suddenly caught by surprise when a budget has been used up or a schedule has slipped — and the project is nowhere near completion — must turn their criticism inward.

Audit supervisors must function under the same rules that they expect operating managers to follow. Reduced to their essentials — and perhaps oversimplified — the guideposts of the good manager read: "Feedback," "Follow-up," and "No Surprises." Hence, supervisors should expect from the auditors under their supervision a simple weekly report which provides this information. Exhibit 19-5 is an example. It is designed to show the allotted budget, the audit-days used through the prior week, the audit-days used in the week just ended, and the anticipated audit-days required to finish the job.

The form also provides for comments on anticipated problems and information concerning when assistants will be released. The latter information is quite important. It helps reduce assistants' stand-by time. The proper timing of assignments for assistants is a perennial problem; the sooner the people in charge of assignments are aware of the release of an assistant, the better they can schedule their assignments.

Schedule Boards

Scheduling staff assignments is not a simple chore at best. Slipped project schedules, unanticipated interruptions, and special requests from management complicate an already difficult task. Also, trying to get a clear picture of the current and downstream assignments of 20 or 30 auditors can boggle the mind. The project scheduler is well advised, therefore, to obtain some mechanical aid that is flexible and easy to keep up to date.

One device is a large cork board which makes use of assignment slips and numbered tack heads to show at a glance precisely what the scheduled assignments are for periods up to a year. Exhibit 19-6 pictures such a board showing only the month of January. All the auditors in charge and all the assistants are grouped separately in alphabetical order. The supervisors are shown at the bottom of the board on differently colored slips of paper to differentiate the jobs which are under their supervision.

The entire board covers a period of a year, and each of the spaces between vertical lines represents one week. The scheduled assignments for each auditor-in-charge are written on cardboard strips of the same color as that assigned to the supervisor of the job. Each assistant is assigned a number and is represented by a broad-headed tack bearing that number. A string suspended vertically across the board — moved each week — indicates the current week.

To simplify explanations, Exhibit 19-6 shows the status of jobs for only

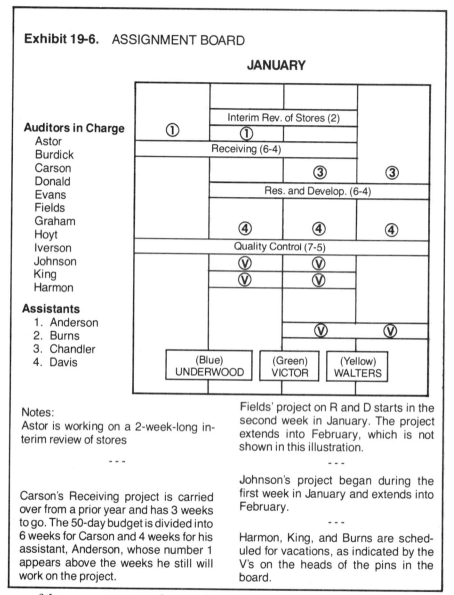

Exhibit 19-6. ASSIGNMENT BOARD

JANUARY

Auditors in Charge
Astor
Burdick
Carson
Donald
Evans
Fields
Graham
Hoyt
Iverson
Johnson
King
Harmon

Assistants
1. Anderson
2. Burns
3. Chandler
4. Davis

Interim Rev. of Stores (2)

Receiving (6-4)

Res. and Develop. (6-4)

Quality Control (7-5)

(Blue) UNDERWOOD   (Green) VICTOR   (Yellow) WALTERS

Notes:

Astor is working on a 2-week-long interim review of stores

- - -

Carson's Receiving project is carried over from a prior year and has 3 weeks to go. The 50-day budget is divided into 6 weeks for Carson and 4 weeks for his assistant, Anderson, whose number 1 appears above the weeks he still will work on the project.

Fields' project on R and D starts in the second week in January. The project extends into February, which is not shown in this illustration.

- - -

Johnson's project began during the first week in January and extends into February.

- - -

Harmon, King, and Burns are scheduled for vacations, as indicated by the V's on the heads of the pins in the board.

one of the supervisors, Underwood. Her jobs are written on blue cardboard slips. The note on Exhibit 19-6 explains the assignments.

Permanent Files

Permanent files for internal audits will vary to some extent from those used in financial audits. In financial audits there is generally a consistent pattern in the conduct of the audit and the evaluation of the accounting data. The pattern in operating departments may not be that consistent.

Operating departments are often subject to constant flux and change in their activities. Product lines change. As one activity becomes reduced it may warrant consolidation with another. Organizations become restructured to accommodate changing conditions. The emphasis that had been given to a particular function yesterday may be entirely different from what is called for today.

Accordingly, the permanent files should be useful, but economical. They should not be cluttered with matters that will not be of help either in the current audit or in planning the long-range program. Following are some of the matters that can be useful.

Prior Audit Reports and Replies

Copies of all prior audit reports and replies provide a historical record of deficiencies, recommendations, and corrective action taken or proposed. They are a good index of the audit approaches taken in prior years, the audit emphasis, and the audit findings. Where the record indicates a continuing trend of satisfactory opinions, *in toto* or in part, the current audit programs may be structured to reduce audit emphasis accordingly. Continuing difficulties, on the other hand, would be a signal for increased emphasis.

Audit Reports from other Company Divisions or Branch Offices

In multi-divisional audit organizations, where each issues its own audit reports under its own long-range program, copies of such reports give added insight into methods of attacking particular audit problems. Each internal auditor has his or her own techniques, preferences, and strengths; and each can learn from the work of another. Unique deficiencies unearthed in one division may hint of audit techniques that may not have been considered at other divisions.

Records of Reviews with Higher Management

The long-range program reviews that are held with higher management often throw a sharp light on the needs and problems of management. They can sometimes illuminate the dark corners of an audit subject and provide the auditor with a means of offering an improved service to management. Copies of the records of these reviews constitute an important part of the permanent file.

Post-Audit Reviews

Post-audit reviews (see Exhibit 18-3, the Audit Analysis form) provide conclusions and recommendations on audit approaches by the individual most qualified to make them — the auditor-in-charge who just completed the audit of the subject under consideration. These recommendations — if information indicates they are still relevant — provide helpful guides for the current program.

Auditors' Comments

All auditors, as a part of their current reviews, learn of matters which are of interest to the audit organization but which may not be germane to their own current audit purposes. Where such matters speak of emergent circumstances, they may warrant the immediate opening of a special project or the expansion of a current one. But if the demand is not immediate, the matter should be informally recorded and the record made a part of the permanent file of the appropriate audit project.

Records of Accounts and Reports

In many audit organizations, a copy of the chart of accounts is referenced to appropriate audit projects. In this way, there is assurance that the operating matters relating to these accounts will be covered in the long-range program or the accounts will be analyzed, if appropriate. Each permanent file, therefore, should contain a reference to the related accounts.

Also, management looks to the auditor to assure it of the validity and reliability of the management reports on which it leans in making its day-to-day decisions. Errors or improprieties in such reports can have serious repercussions if they contribute to incorrect decisions. Such reports should be reviewed by the auditors to the extent they consider it necessary when they engage in the audit of the particular activity. Records of these reports should likewise be referenced in the appropriate permanent files.

Miscellaneous Matters

There is considerable diversity of opinion among directors of auditing on what belongs in a permanent file. The miscellaneous matters which follow were taken from responses to our inquiries concerning program or permanent file material. They are indicative, in some ways, of how closely the auditing organization follows operating matters.

A copy of each program and the related questionnaires applicable to a particular audit project, just so long as those programs and questionnaires remain applicable.

Organization charts, which are to be replaced or corrected as changes occur.

Contracts with labor unions, and copies of long-term contracts — such as those with concessionaires.

Flowcharts and descriptions of operations and of significant equipment and facilities.

Records of wage earners' incentive plans.

List of departments or cost centers, to help in the long-range planning and to assure coverage periodically.

Historical financial information.

Basic directives or instructions applicable to specific locations or activities.

Important correspondence specifically related to the audit project.

Summaries of audit time, segregated by subject matter and program sections, as an aid in planning future audits.

Summaries of periods (weeks, months, or quarters) test checked, to avoid repeating the same periods in subsequent audits.

Summaries of operating routines, highlighting internal control points.

Schedules of accounts receivable write-offs for use in future verifications.

Descriptions of major credit problems for use in future audit examination.

Photographs of locations, copies of price lists and sales brochures, and plats of plant layouts.

The latest 12-month financial and operations reports for each location.

For separately incorporated components: copies or digests of articles of incorporation; by-laws; minutes of board meetings; minutes of stockholders' meetings; capital stock authorizations; abstracts of changes in surplus accounts; abstracts of title to property; records of the last examination of public records for transfers of title; registration of mortgages, judgments, liens, and other relevant records of judicial proceedings; lists of lands and buildings; reconciliations of changes in surplus with earnings reported for tax purposes; descriptions of pending tax assessments; and claims for tax refunds.

Supervision

No mechanical control can compare with knowledgeable, accessible, concerned supervision. Professional, experienced auditors are likely to turn out professional audits; inexperienced auditors are not. Yet an auditing department's products must be consistently and equally high. The equalizer is good supervision. A competent supervisor can warn of pitfalls, help in the audit planning, provide unbiased perspectives on audit findings, ensure the preparation of professional working papers, help maintain good auditor-auditee relations, monitor budget and schedule and help reverse adverse trends, review audit reports, and see that essential elements are not missing from the audit project.

The *Standards for the Professional Practice of Internal Auditing* speaks as follows on the subject of supervision:

230   **Supervision**
The internal auditing department should provide assurance that internal audits are properly supervised.

.01   The director of internal auditing is responsible for providing appropriate audit supervision. Supervision is a continuing process, beginning with planning and ending with the conclusion of the audit assignment.

.02   Supervision includes:

.1   Providing suitable instructions to subordinates at the outset of the audit and approving the audit program.

.2   Seeing that the approved audit program is carried out unless deviations are both justified and authorized.

.3   Determining that audit working papers adequately support the audit findings, conclusions, and reports.

.4   Making sure that audit reports are accurate, objective, clear, concise, constructive, and timely.

.5   Determining that audit objectives are being met.

.03   Appropriate evidence of supervision should be documented and retained.

.04   The extent of supervision required will depend on the proficiency of the internal auditors and the difficulty of the audit assignment.

.05   All internal auditing assignments, whether performed by or for the internal auditing department, remain the responsibility of the director.

Experienced audit supervisors are a combination of teacher and monitor. They must therefore know the people they supervise. Experienced, competent staff people require less supervision than neophytes. At the same time, oversupervision retards growth. Unreasonably tight supervision develops excessive dependence. Staff auditors then adopt the unfortunate habit of asking for solutions instead of thinking through their problems and presenting alternative solutions to their supervisors.

Supervisors are not in an enviable position. They are the ones in the middle. On the one side are the higher managers. On the other are the nonmanagement people. Management pressures them to see that audit projects are carried out efficiently, effectively, and economically. Subordinates, on the other hand, expect their supervisors to be the buffer between the auditor and the audit manager. They expect supervisors to meet the auditor's demands for security, recognition, independence, and acceptance.

The supervisors-in-the-middle know all too well the power of management, the authority of those over them in the hierarchy. They also know the power of subordinates to withhold cooperation. In a professional organization, supervisors cannot treat their subordinates as vassals, so human relations become an important aspect of the supervisory function to instill professionalism in the new auditor and to support the experienced auditors while removing roadblocks from their paths.

The supervisory job continues throughout the entire audit project. Supervisors must be involved in every phase of the audit work; for example:

Planning

Supervisors should offer their experience and their knowledge of man-

Controlling Audit Projects/**645**

agement needs and desires as the audit project is planned. Their understanding of the way line managers like to deal with internal auditors can help the staff auditor over the difficult threshhold of the initial meeting. Supervisors should attend those initial meetings, make the introductions, and lead or observe the introduction to the audit, depending on the experience of the auditor in charge.

Preliminary Survey

Supervisors should approve the plans for the preliminary survey and visit the site to see that the proper information has been obtained. Where significant findings are observed, they should counsel the auditors on how to develop them through discussions with line or management people, interim reports, and the amount of evidence needed.

Audit Programs

Auditors-in-charge should prepare the audit programs. Supervisors should approve both the initial program and any revisions to it. Supervisors should make sure, also, that all program steps are carried out or that adequate reasons are recorded for eliminating any audit steps.

Field Work

Supervisors should periodically visit the audit site and review the audit work that has been completed to date. This calls for a review of working papers. When staff auditors are aware that their papers will be reviewed, they are likely to take more care with them. Developing a high degree of respect in their subordinates for the importance of well-prepared working papers is one of the most important teaching functions supervisors can carry out. Auditors who have learned to develop professional working papers are usually those who worked under supervisors who set high standards of working papers preparation and insisted that those standards be met.

Supervisors should keep a wary eye on audit budgets and schedules both through on-site observations and periodic time reports. In their reviews during the field work, supervisors should note all questions they may have about the audit, the working papers, the findings, the unanswered program steps, and the like. The auditors should respond to every point raised, recording their responses. These documents should become part of the working paper file.

Exit Interviews

These interviews are extremely important, both in terms of corrective action and auditor-auditee relations. Supervisors should attend these meetings if at all possible. If they have kept a watchful eye on the progress of the job, they should be able to contribute usefully to the meeting.

Reporting

Before auditors prepare their audit reports, they should develop an outline for the draft. The supervisor should review it carefully and approve it before the auditor starts the report writing. The supervisor should ask the report writer to show in the draft margin the references to the applicable working papers. When they review the drafts, the supervisors should refer to the papers to make certain all statements are supported and can be authenticated.

Report Reviews

Supervisors should try to attend all report reviews. The objectivity they bring to bear can be useful if disputes develop. At the same time, supervisors can provide support for the auditor-in-charge if the auditee becomes difficult to deal with. The supervisor can also intervene if difficulties arise about the evidence of corrective action needed. Supervisors must be meticulous reviewers, and they must see to it that no errors or gaffes mar the final report.

Closing the Project

Supervisors should review the working papers to see that they are complete before the papers are filed. They should see that all forms and administrative documents have been prepared. They should be satisfied that all corrective action needed has been taken before the project is closed.

Computerized Controls

In departments with large audit staffs, manual controls over audit projects are time-consuming. Many internal auditing organizations have therefore turned to the computer to maintain time-keeping records and monitor audit projects.

Computerized records are of particular use to internal auditing organizations that bill their costs to audited facilities — both direct charges and overhead. The computerized system produces reports on audit hours budgeted and used on each project, the dollar value of those hours, and an allocation of burden.

One internal auditing organization has described its use of computerized records both for self-control and for management's information. The computer turns out reports on internal audit status and progress.1 The computer issues one weekly and four monthly reports on audit assignments. The reports are as follows:

Completed Assignments, Exhibit 19-7

Each audit assignment is given an individual number. The computer lists all projects completed the previous month. For each project, the printout shows a comparison of audit days allotted and audit days worked. Also listed is the cost of each completed project, combining both direct charges and overhead.

Report of Work Load Statistics, Exhibit 19-8

This monthly report summarizes the status of all audit assignments for a 24-month period. The report shows the estimated available audit days for the 2-year period, the assigned days for pending assignments, plus the assigned days for projects in progress, and the number of audit days committed to identified audit projects. Subtracting the committed days from available days yields the audit days available for additional commitment. The report also gives an overview of the budget status. It shows whether staff has been over- or under-assigned; that is, whether more audit hours have been allotted to projects than are available. This information serves as a guide when the director is asked to accept new assignments and when additional staff time is being assigned.

Status of Audit Assignment, Exhibit 19-9

This computer printout shows all open audit projects. The individual projects in progress are listed. For each is shown: project number, project description, month the project was last audited, name of the auditor, estimated audit days, audit days worked, audit days remaining, and estimated date report will be released.

Status of Assignments — by Auditor, Exhibit 19-10

This monthly printout lists the staff auditors in the audit department and the projects to which they were assigned. The name of each auditor is followed by the number and description of the projects on which they were working. For each project the printout shows estimated and actual audit days, the days remaining, and the estimated release date of the audit report. This printout is used to help schedule requests from management. The list shows who is available for assignment and which projects may have to be extended to fit top priority jobs into the overall schedule.

Review Status, Exhibit 19-11

This report provides the auditors each Monday with information on the review status of audit reports that were under review the previous Friday. The status report shows the time allotted for the report reviewers to complete their work, and it highlights the reports which are not meeting their target dates.

Overdue Reports, Exhibit 19-12

This printout identifies reports that are overdue, the auditor assigned to the project, and the reason why the report is delayed.

Each auditing organization will have different reporting needs and different priorities. Each would have to devise computer programs to fit its individual needs. But in large auditing organizations where keeping track of budgeted, estimated, and actual audit days and due dates is desirable, the chore of maintaining records and issuing status reports can be eased by the computer.

Exhibit 19-7.

FLORIDA DEPARTMENT OF TRANSPORTATION
INTERNAL AUDIT
COMPLETED ASSIGNMENTS
MONTH OF APRIL 1980

ASSIGN-MENT NO.	DATE COM-PLETED	DESCRIPTION	AUDITOR	AUDIT-DAYS ESTIMATE	DAYS WORKED	TOTAL COST
010055	04/08/80	FOLLOW-UP ON RECOMMENDATIONS	SHOOK	10	15	$ 2,499.30
021410	04/30/80	CONTROL OF PURCHASES	SHOOK	55	23	3,832.26
022425	04/21/80	REV. TELE. CREDIT CARD BILLINGS	SHOOK	15	21	3,599.02
022611	04/21/80	PAYROLL PROCESSING — INTERNAL CONT	HUNTER	15	10	1,666.20
060029	04/21/80	RIGHT OF WAY SUMMARY	ELLIS	8	8	1,332.96
060034	04/08/80	ALGD. ATTEMPT TO DEFRAUD	ELLIS	30	16	2,665.92
TOTAL COUNT		6		133	93	$15,495.66

Exhibit 19-8.

INTERNAL AUDIT
REPORT OF WORK LOAD STATISTICS
AS OF APRIL 30, 1980

REPORT STATUS

GOAL THROUGH CURRENT MONTH	90	REPORTS	100%
ACTUAL THROUGH CURRENT MONTH	93	REPORTS	103%
ANTICIPATED AVERAGE AUDIT-DAYS PER REPORT		20.00	
ACTUAL AVERAGE AUDIT-DAYS FOR EACH REPORT		16.48	

WORKLOAD

ESTIMATED DAYS AVAILABLE FOR 24 MONTHS		4,095	100%
LESS ASSIGNED DAYS:			
73 ASSIGNMENTS IN PROGRESS	1,548		37
72 ASSIGNMENTS PENDING	1,339		32
AUDIT DAYS COMMITTED		2,887	69
DAYS AVAILABLE FOR ADDITIONAL ASSIGNMENTS		1,208	31

Exhibit 19-9.

INTERNAL AUDIT
STATUS OF AUDIT ASSIGNMENTS
AS OF APRIL 30, 1980

ASSIGN-MENT NO.	DESCRIPTION	LAST AUDITED	AUDITOR	AUDIT-DAYS ESTIMATE	DAYS WORKED	DAYS REMAIN-ING	ESTIMATED RELEASE DATE
020204	FDOT CONTRACT CONTENT REVIEW	1279	GOODWIN	40		40	06/30/81
020205	VOUCHER PROCEDURES REVIEW	0280	URBANEK	15		15	04/30/81
021104	CONSTRUCTION - FEDERAL CITATIONS	0478	GOODWIN	30	12	18	06/30/80
021105	CURRENT BILLING REVIEW - FEDERAL	0679	WHIGHAM	45		45	02/28/81
021307	PRODUCTIVITY SURVEY		LANGFORD	10	3	7	06/30/80
021403	INVENTORY PROC-OFFICE ENG & SHOP	0377	MOORE	24		24	02/28/80
021409	TRAVEL EXPENSE VOUCHER REVIEW	0378	SHOOK	60	15	45	06/30/80
021415	FISCAL GENERAL AUDIT SECTION		SHOOK	18		18	11/30/80
021416	FISCAL ACCOUNTING SECTION		SHOOK	30		30	08/31/80
022201	PROCUREMENT OFFICE PROCEDURES	0577	LANGFORD	30		30	07/31/81
022304	REVIEW EDP FUNCTION	1178	HUNTER	45	23	22	11/30/80
022403	ADMIN SERVICES REPRODUCTION		ROLLINS	15		15	11/30/80
022410	CAFETERIA VENDING AUDIT	0478	SHOOK	5	5		07/31/80
022419	EMPLOYEE FUND — CENTRAL OFFICE	0479	GEOHAGAN	7		7	06/30/81
022420	EMPLOYEE FUND — DISTRICT I	0779	PRICE	7		7	06/30/81
022430	TELEPHONE CREDIT CARD BILLINGS		SHOOK	15		15	04/01/82
022502	CONTROL OF WAREHOUSE ISSUES		ALLIGOOD	50		50	01/31/81
022505	WAREHOUSE & DISTRIBUTION OFFICE		MYERS	40		40	11/31/81

ASSIGNMENT NO.	DESCRIPTION	LAST AUDITED	AUDITOR	AUDITOR DAYS	AUDITOR DAYS WORKED	AUDITOR DAYS REMAINING	DATE DUE FROM AUDITOR
022608	PERSONNEL OFFICE-GENERAL REVIEW	0478	FREANEY	45	2	43	09/30/81
022612	EMPLOYMENT OF RELATIVES	0778	FAIRCLOTH	25		25	09/30/81
022613	PAYROLL PROCESSING-INT. CONTROL		HUNTER	15		15	04/30/82
022702	LEGAL OFFICE REVIEW	0278	FAIRCLOTH	24		24	12/31/80
024001	REVIEW OF DOT VEHICLES CONTROL	0976	ADAMS	8		8	02/29/81
024003	INVENTORY PROCEDURES-BUILDINGS		RUNYAN	30		30	02/28/81
024019	SECURITY — CENTRAL OFFICE		LAWRENCE	3		3	10/31/80
024026	FINANCIAL MANAGEMENT SUMMARY	0380	WHIGHAM	12		12	02/10/82
TOTAL				648	60	588	

Exhibit 19-10.

INTERNAL AUDIT
STATUS OF ASSIGNMENTS — BY AUDITOR
AS OF APRIL 30, 1980

ASSIGNMENT NO.	DESCRIPTION	LAST AUDITED	AUDITOR DAYS	AUDITOR DAYS WORKED	AUDITOR DAYS REMAINING	DATE DUE FROM AUDITOR
ELLIS						
060027	RIGHT OF WAY — DISTRICT II	0978	36	35	1	05/31/80
047020	EEO — COMPLIANCE		20		20	07/31/80
060043	RIGHT OF WAY SPECIAL ASSIGNMENT		8		8	10/31/80
060038	RIGHT OF WAY — DISTRICT IV		25		25	01/31/81
060041	RIGHT OF WAY — DISTRICT VI		25		25	01/31/81
060036	RIGHT OF WAY — DISTRICT I		25		25	04/30/81
TOTAL COUNT	6		139	35	104	

Exhibit 19-11.

INTERNAL AUDIT
REVIEW STATUS — INTERNAL AUDIT REPORTS
AS OF APRIL 30, 1980

ASSIGN-MENT NO.	DESCRIPTION	UNDER REVIEW BY	DATE TO REVIEWER	DATE DUE FROM REVIEWER	DAYS LATE	STATUS	COMMENTS
010059	OFFICE PROCEDURES REVIEW - D-VI	O'DELL	04-30	05-30	000	F	
021104	CONSTRUCTION-FEDERAL CITATIONS	BROWN	05-02	06-01	000	F	
034004	RATE STRUCTURES-MATERIALS & RCH.	RUNYAN	05-15	05-29	000	P	
041002	RATE STRUCTURES - TOPOGRAPHICS	RUNYAN	05-21	06-04	000	P	
052017	CONSTRUCTION REVIEW - DISTRICT V	DAVIS	04-17	05-17	000	T	
052023	LABOR COMPLIANCE SUMMARY	BROWN	03-15	04-15	000	F	
052031	KEYS BRIDGES - CONSTRUCTION	BROWN	05-01	05-31	000	F	
060014	OUTDOOR AD. TAG PROCEDURES	DAVIS	05-16	05-30	000	T	
092029	SIGN SHOP PROCEDURAL REVIEW	BROWN	05-02	06-01	000	F	
092030	WEIGHT STATIONS REVIEW FOLLOW-UP	RUNYAN	05-21	06-04	000	P	
400011	MARCO ISLAND BRIDGE	O'DELL	04-11	05-12	000	F	
400020	DADE CO. EXPRESSWAY	LEVINGSTON	05-21	06-04	000	A	
440001	FT. DRUM CITRUS SHOP	RUNYAN	05-21	06-04	000	P	

STATUS CODE:
F = FIELD REVIEW   P = PROOFREAD   T = TYPING   A = ADMINISTRATIVE REVIEW

Exhibit 19-12.

INTERNAL AUDIT
OVER-DUE REPORTS
AS OF APRIL 30, 1980

ASSIGN-MENT NO.	DESCRIPTION	AUDIT-DAYS ESTIMATE	AUDITOR DAYS WORKED	AUDITOR	DATE DUE FROM AUDITOR	COMMENTS
060012	ALGD. TITLE COMPANY FRAUD	12	7	FAIRCLOTH	05-31-77	AWAITING COURT ACTION
092019	ALGD. ATT. TO FALSIFY SCALE WT.	138	119	FAIRCLOTH	12-31-78	LITIGATION PENDING-LEGAL
092040	MITCHELL MAINTENANCE CONTRACTS	120	30	FREANEY	04-30-79	PENDING ARBITRATION-LEGAL
092044	ALGD. MISUSE OF EQUIPMENT	18	119	KARSEBOOM	06-30-79	PENDING ADMIN. ACTION
092043	CONSTRUCTION OPERATIONAL-DIST. IV	25	8	GOODWIN	11-30-79	OTHER INVEST. ACTION REQD
052034	ALGD. ROCK HAUL FRAUD	25	10	FAIRCLOTH	12-31-79	INFO. NEEDED FROM LEGAL
092049	PUBLIC TRANSPORTATION-DIST. III	15	2	HUNTER	12-31-79	NOW UNDER REVIEW
044002	DESIGN ENGINEER-CONSUL PROJECTS	20	3	WHIGHAM	02-28-80	INSUFFICIENT STAFF TIME
092052	PRELIMINARY ENGINEERING-DIST. IX	40	10	LAWRENCE	02-28-80	OTHER PRIORITIES
021409	TRAVEL EXPENSE VOUCHER REVIEW	60	15	SHOOK	04-28-80	OTHER PRIORITIES

Small Internal Audit Organizations

Small audit organizations — those with no more than four auditors — tend to be more informal than larger ones. Their administrative records are usually less comprehensive and their own internal control mechanisms are often faulty. They justify loose procedures by citing their size and the fewer projects they deal with. This is error.

Top management and the board of directors in smaller enterprises are, or should be, as much concerned with adequate administration as are those in larger enterprises. External auditors no doubt share that concern. Reasonable administration of an internal auditing department is as necessary as the administration of an accounting department.

So audit projects of small auditing departments should be formally recorded and budgets and schedules should be used. Time records should also be maintained. Permanent files should be installed and kept up. Reminder lists for projects should be developed and used, and audits should be supervised.

External auditors dealing with small internal auditing departments will apply the same standards to them as to the larger departments: the *Standards for the Professional Practice of Internal Auditing*. The internal audit work can be relied on or it cannot. Size makes no difference.

Certainly, supervision in a one-person auditing department is not easy. A one-armed person has difficulty clapping hands, but this difficulty makes it all the more important to develop and use self-verification through check lists, reminder lists, and well-organized routines. Indeed, good administration which displays professionalism to both management and the external auditors becomes particularly important in small or one-person internal auditing departments.

Conclusion

Audit projects require management control and guidance to keep them on track and to alert audit supervisors and managers of any impending difficulties. Each auditing organization should devise the forms needed to promote project control. Not only good business practice, but The Institute's *Standards* demand supervision of all audit projects throughout their life cycles. When manual controls have proven burdensome and time-consuming, the computer has been used to provide prompt information on the status of audit projects. Supervision in small audit organizations is difficult; but with ingenuity and the cooperation of the external auditors, a form of supervision can be obtained.

References

1. A. C. Levingston, "How Well Are You Controlling Your Audit Assignments?" *The Internal Auditor*, December 1977, p. 36.

For further study

Discussion Problems

1. Discuss three factors that internal audit supervisors should consider when overseeing staff auditors on internal audit assignments.

2. Briefly describe three elements of a system for controlling staff time.

3. Why should budgets and schedules be set for each audit project?

4. Once a budget is set in the long-range audit schedule, should the director always see that it is met? Why?

5. Should budget increases be permitted when the auditor encounters unusual and time-consuming deficiencies?

6. How often should supervisors evaluate progress on a job under their supervision?

7. How can audit jobs be started in an organized fashion?

8. What two means are available for giving audit managers an overview of audit projects in process?

9. What means are available to provide auditors embarking on an audit with the history of a particular audit project?

10. What responsibility does an audit supervisor have in terms of audit reports?

Multiple Choice Problems

1. The first step in starting an audit project is to:
a. Prepare an audit program.
b. Get the project on the books.
c. Perform a preliminary survey.
d. Instruct assistants.
e. Call the auditee.

2. Differentiate among various types of projects by:
a. Distinctive color schemes.

b. Project titles.
c. Project numbering systems.
d. Names of the auditors in charge.
e. Project subject.

3. A project budget for each audit is essential because:
a. Without it a program cannot be prepared.
b. The home office needs it.
c. It is easier for the auditor in charge.
d. Without it the audit tends to drag on.
e. None of the above.

4. A budget cannot be fixed and unalterable because:
a. It is too difficult for the auditor in charge.
b. The premises for the project during planning may differ from actual experience.
c. It would adversely affect the bookkeeping on the project.
d. Budgets should be set at a level that cannot be met.
e. The long-range program is developed that way.

5. The audit supervisor should evaluate the progress of the projects for which he or she is responsible at least:
a. Every week.
b. Every month.
c. Every day.
d. At the end of the field work.
e. During the time away from reviewing audit reports.

6. The audit can be launched in an organized fashion by using:
a. The permanent file.
b. The prior audit record.
c. The applicable functions and responsibilities statements.
d. The experience of the supervisor.
e. A reminder list.

7. A schedule board showing all auditors and assignments is useful because:
a. It shows the names of the auditors.
b. It is difficult to keep all the auditors and their current and future assignments in mind.
c. It lists all current assignments.
d. It can be used as a calendar.
e. It is graphic.

8. Permanent files for audits of operations differ from those used in financial examination because:
a. Operations are more complicated.
b. Operations tend to vary more from year to year.
c. Prior histories of operations are of little importance.
d. There is little uniformity in operations.
e. It is more difficult to remember operations.

9. Audit reports from other divisions of the enterprise should be kept in the permanent file because:
a. Unique deficiencies unearthed in one division may hint of new audit techniques.
b. It is a matter of common courtesy.
c. They will be needed if questions arise about them.
d. The writing and the format of the audit reports may be worth emulating.
e. They can make good reading and be educational for new auditors.

10. Audit organizations employing a single auditor have difficulty in obtaining any form of audit supervision, and so:
a. They should not worry about it.
b. The sole auditor must supervise himself or herself.
c. They should call upon an auditor from another firm.
d. They should obtain post reviews from objective outsiders.
e. None of the above.

Case Studies

19-1. Should We Grant the Budget Increase?

Bob, the audit supervisor, dialed the number at which he could find Earl, one of the senior auditors, who was engaged in an audit of the receiving department. Bob asked Earl how the job was going.

"I was getting along pretty much on schedule, Bob. Receiving procedures are pretty good and the receiving clerks seem to know what they're doing."

"What do you mean you **were** getting along pretty well?"

"I was doing fine until I started reviewing receipts that bypass the receiving department."

"Oh, you mean direct deliveries?"

"Right. That has become a big problem."

"I thought it was going along fine the last time we audited it."

"It was. But direct deliveries were pretty light then. Now we've got a heavy development program going on, and the engineers are ordering a lot of the special parts and materials. Every order has to be delivered direct to the lab on the other side of town."

"What's the problem?"

"I'm not sure yet. Accounts payable is screaming that evidence of direct delivery receipts isn't getting to them in time and they're losing discounts."

"What do you want to do, Earl?"

"I'm going to have to spend some time at the lab and run the problem down. I figure it will take five more days than we'd budgeted the job for; so I'd like a budget increase."

"I'm not sure I can get it, Earl."

"Why not?"

"Direct deliveries were a part of the audit. The fact that there are problems shouldn't alter things."

"Seems unfair to me, Bob. I hate to

run over budget, and this thing is not under my control."

"We really haven't set a firm policy on budget increases. Let me talk to Paul and I'll get back to you."

Bob broached the problem to Paul who agreed that it was about time to set a fair, workable policy on budget increases. He set up a supervisor's meeting for the next day.

Required: Prepare a paper in the form of a staff memo setting forth policies and procedures for budget revisions.

19-2. Budgeting Creativity

Michael Stanton of ABC Company was sitting with Mark Leduc of XYZ Company at a dinner meeting of the local chapter of The Institute of Internal Auditors. Michael was grousing. He said, "That supervisor of mine is on my back about budget on my audit assignment."

Mark looked surprised. "Do you mean you work on a budget on each job?"

"You bet," said Michael. "On every single one."

"Doesn't make sense to me," replied Mark. "You can't straitjacket an operational audit. If you insist on budgets and schedules, you'll never get an in-depth audit."

"Well, I don't know," stated Michael, quick to take the other side because he loved to argue. "If you let a job hang loose, it never gets done. You have to have some discipline to bring the job in without letting the audit-hours pour down the drain."

"But operational auditing is a creative effort," explained Mark. "Budgets and schedules will stifle it. I couldn't work under such constraints."

"Oh, yes you could, if you had to. Actually, the discipline is good for you; it keeps you on your toes and gives you a goal to work toward," said Michael.

Required: State who is right. Why?

20

Quality Control

Establishing and maintaining a quality assurance program. SEC and internal accounting controls. External auditors' reliance on internal auditing. The Cohen Commission. The *Standards* — yardstick for measuring internal audit functions. Existing forms of peer reviews. The three means of assuring professional audits. Sources of peer reviews. Supervision as a form of quality control. Elements of proper supervision. Internal reviews to assess quality. Verifications of audit reports and source material. Internal audits of audit projects. Steps in project reviews. Audit programs for project reviews. The *Framework* for peer reviews. The internal audit environment. Reviewing compliance with the auditor's charter and the *Standards*. Profile of the environment. Evaluating policies and procedures in terms of independence, professional proficiency, scope of work, performance of work, and management of the audit department. Interviewing people. Analyzing completed audit projects. Reporting the results of peer reviews.

Introduction

"But who will guard the guards themselves?" mused Juvenal in the first century.[1] And he did not stop to leave a clue. Eighteen centuries later, the *Standards for the Professional Practice of Internal Auditing* supplied the answer to who is to audit the auditor. Section 560 of the *Standards* is as follows:

560 Quality Assurance

The director of internal auditing should establish and maintain a quality assurance program to evaluate the operations of the internal auditing department.

.01 The purpose of this program is to provide reasonable assurance that audit work conforms with these *Standards*, the internal auditing department's charter, and other applicable standards. A quality assurance program should include the following elements:

.1 Supervision

.2 Internal reviews

.3 External reviews

.02 *Supervision* of the work of the internal auditors should be carried out continually to assure conformance with internal auditing standards, departmental policies, and audit programs.

.03 *Internal reviews* should be performed periodically by members of the internal auditing staff to appraise the quality of the audit work performed. These reviews should be performed in the same manner as any other internal audit.

.04 *External reviews* of the internal auditing department should be performed to appraise the quality of the department's operations. These reviews should be performed by qualified persons who are independent of the organization and who do not have either a real or an apparent conflict of interest. Such reviews should be conducted at least once every three years. On completion of the review, a formal, written report should be issued. The report should express an opinion as to the department's compliance with the *Standards for the Professional Practice of Internal Auditing* and, as appropriate, should include recommendations for improvement.

But beyond the requirements of the *Standards* are the real concerns of executive management and the audit committees of boards of directors. They need assurance that they can indeed rely on this safeguard which goes by the name of internal auditing. They sit in the shadow of the U.S. Foreign Corrupt Practices Act of 1977 — an act concerned with more than bribery. The Securities and Exchange Commission has already brought an action under the internal accounting control provisions of the Act.[2] This case had no taint of bribes or payoffs; only the internal accounting controls were involved.

External auditors are basing the extent of their audits on the adequacy or inadequacy of control systems. The internal auditor is a significant part — indeed the linchpin — of an organization's control system. Without internal auditors, control systems can come apart. Late in 1975, the Auditing Standards Executive Committee of the American Institute of Certified Public Accountants issued a *Statement of Auditing Standards* (SAS) No. 9.[3] The Statement indicates that external auditors should evaluate internal audit functions and that the results of those evaluations would have a bearing on the nature, timing, and extent of their audit procedures and their reliance on internal auditing.

The Commission on Auditors' Responsibilities — the Cohen Commission — recommended that corporate management prepare a report to shareholders that would comment on a company's system of internal control.[4] Public reporting on internal control may not be too far off. The internal auditors become the final line of defense against inadequate controls and shortcomings in systems. Any such defense must be strong and capable of withstanding rigorous tests if it is to be relied upon. Management and the board need the assurances that they are not leaning on a broken reed.

With so much depending on an effective internal audit function, both top management and the director of internal auditing are vitally concerned that their internal auditors and the internal auditing department can meet reasonable tests. So the *Standards for the Professional Practice of Internal Auditing* are merely declaratory of a crucial need — the need to know whether internal auditing within the enterprise is performing professionally.

The *Standards* provide criteria against which to measure an internal auditing function. Evaluations of internal auditing departments were made before the *Standards* were adopted, but there was no accepted yardstick to measure performance.

Peer reviews are essential in any profession. In fields related to internal auditing, provisions have been made for such reviews. For example, in the United States, the Office of the Comptroller of the Currency issued a *Comptroller's Handbook for National Bank Examiners* containing instructions for the review of a bank's internal audit function.[5] The U.S. General Accounting Office issued its *Audit Standards Supplement Series No. 9, Self-Evaluation Guide for Governmental Audit Organizations.*[6] The American Institute of Certified Public Accountants prepared a *Peer Review Manual.*[7] All of these provide means of evaluating professional practitioners and their organizations.

Standards

Each of the three elements of a quality assurance program, as stated in the *Standards*, has a different purpose and a different method.

Supervision is a continuing process. It focuses on individual audits. It provides assurance to the director of internal auditing that staff auditors are doing what they are supposed to be doing in their ongoing projects. Supervision is performed by audit supervisors or managers who are responsible for assigned audit projects, but who do not themselves carry out the audit projects.

Internal reviews are a test function. They provide assurance to the director of internal auditing that the entire audit staff, including the supervisors, are doing their jobs properly. These reviews are also made to provide special assurances on specific assignments that audit representations made are accurate and reliable. These reviews are carried out by staff auditors or supervisors.

External reviews are evaluations of the entire auditing department. They are designed to tell top management and the board whether they are being served by a professional group of internal auditors whose work meets the criteria set by the *Standards for the Professional Practice of Internal Auditing*. These reviews must be performed by people outside the auditing department. According to the *Standards*, the evaluators must be "independent of the organization" and without "a real or apparent conflict of interest." Utter independence without even an apparent conflict of interest may be difficult or expensive to obtain. A number of sources for such evaluations is available. But each source has its benefits and drawbacks. Here are some of the possibilities:

Peer groups within the enterprise. These peer groups may be headquarters auditors appraising internal auditing departments in subsidiaries or regional organizations. These evaluations may be considered independent of their "auditees." They have the benefit of a short learning experience because of the headquarters auditors' overall knowledge of the enterprise. It is doubtful that they could be considered independent of the environment in which internal auditors of the entire enterprise function.

The enterprise's external auditors. These auditors provide a greater degree of objectivity than internal auditors from within the enterprise. Their learning curve is not too steep because of their familiarity with the enterprise's accounting system. There may be a question of whether they are truly independent of the internal control system which they have accepted over the years, and there is a serious question as to whether they are knowledgeable of internal auditing outside the financial and accounting sphere. These evaluations may be expensive, and for audits of operations, they may miss the mark.

External auditors from another accounting firm. These external auditors represent a high degree of independence, but the learning curve is steep because of their unfamiliarity with the enterprise systems. They, too, may have difficulty in evaluating audits of nonfinancial operations.

Reciprocal evaluations between audit groups of different enterprises. These should represent no actual or apparent conflict of interest, but the evaluators should be competent in all kinds of internal audit operations. The learning curve should not be as steep as that for external auditors, and the expense should be less. Yet, management and the board may be understandably reluctant to permit a competitor's internal auditors to gain entry to trade secrets.

Qualified consultants. These should be people with actual internal auditing experience who functioned at a management level and who can deal competently with executives and board members. They would, obviously, have a steeper learning curve than headquarters auditors, but there would be no real or apparent conflict of interest. They should be comfortable in appraising audits of all operations within the enterprise.

Complete independence and full-scope evaluations may be expensive. Management must weigh the value of the assurances it needs about the quality of its internal auditing function. Perhaps a compromise in terms of both independence and cost might be the use of headquarters auditors under the direction of a qualified consultant with a background in audits of varied operations. The background assures competence. The requirement that the consultant sign the final evaluation report assures independence. The use of personnel from within the enterprise assures a low learning curve and a less expensive evaluation.

The five standards in the *Standards for the Professional Practice of Internal Auditing* are the yardsticks against which to measure and evaluate internal audit organizations. The scope of the external review will depend on management's perceived needs. A full-scope evaluation would compare the internal audit charter of the department with the Independence and Scope-of-Work standards. It would compare actual audit performance with that prescribed in all five standards. The *Standards* call for such evaluations at least once every three years. As a practical matter, the actual reviews should not span a full three-year period. How the internal auditing organization is currently performing is more to the point. Evaluations, therefore, should not encompass more than the last six or twelve months.

Many factors will influence the cost of the evaluation and its duration. Among the variables are the size of the internal auditing department, the depth of its evaluations, travel expenses, the complexity and size of the enterprise, the amount and variety of work the department produces, the size of the sample of audits to be reviewed, the number of problems encountered, the size of the evaluation team, and the composition of its members. Also significant would be the nature and formality of the internal reviews made. If these are done often and consistently, and if they are thoroughly documented, the evaluation team could place reliance on them and reduce the extent of its own work. This is no different from the reliance placed by external auditors on the audit work done by a well-run, professional internal auditing department.

Management will have to consider carefully the scope of the evaluation. A full-scale evaluation with a broad sampling of audits will be expensive. But scope and expense can be reduced by:

Evaluating the department against only a part of the five standards.

Limiting the sample of audits to be examined during the evaluation.

Evaluating on a step basis: Test a small sample of audits and report on those before going further.

Using the reviews of individual internal audits which the external auditors made in their reviews of internal audit work. These can supplement or replace the evaluators' reviews.

Supervision

Supervision will be dealt with here only as it relates to quality assurance. All work must be supervised. Internal audits — which appraise significant controls, the safeguarding of assets, reports of information to management, and crucial operating performance — are in special need of supervision to assure professional audit work.

Supervisors must make sure that audit work is well planned, audit scope is appropriate, audit resources are economically deployed, serious defects are not being overlooked, minor matters are not being overstressed, audit representations are solidly supported, significant deficiencies are thoroughly documented, audit opinions are buttressed by unassailable evidence, the audit effort is not dissipated by forays into irrelevant or insignificant matters, and staff auditors are properly trained and evaluated.

Internal audit supervisors should monitor audit assignments from start to finish, and audit managers or the director of internal auditing should monitor the work of the supervisors. Audit managers or the director of internal auditing should be satisfied that supervision is providing needed assurances of quality control. Where appropriate, these assurances should be documented. Here are some of the elements of proper supervision:

Audit supervisors should discuss the thrust and scope of the audit before the preliminary survey. They should advise staff auditors on sources for research, on comparable audits performed elsewhere, and on management needs as they relate to the assigned audit project.

They should approve in writing the audit program and any changes to it. They should suggest revisions to the program to eliminate what is not cost effective and to include areas of significant risks.

They should be available during the audit to discuss with the staff the audit objectives, procedures, reporting, and any problems encountered.

Supervisory reviews should be conducted regularly. The extent of the reviews should be in proportion to the qualifications and experience of the audit staff.

Supervisors should review audit working papers and provide evidence of such review.

The supervisory reviews should provide assurance that the staff auditors conformed to departmental standards, that audit objectives were met, that the working papers supported findings and conclusions, and that they provided adequate information for a meaningful audit report. More specifically, supervisors should see that the audit staff:

Obtained an understanding of the objectives of the audited entity before deciding on audit tests and procedures.

Followed up findings from the prior audit to determine whether appropriate measures had been taken and were effective.

Based the extent of tests on the results of internal control evaluations.

Directed audit tests toward achieving stated audit objectives.

Considered only those matters related to the audit objectives.

Used appropriate sampling plans and selection techniques.

Interpreted statistical sample results logically.

Used the computer in the audit where appropriate and economical.

Completed all steps in the audit program or gave valid reasons for not doing so.

Supervisors should see that significant findings are brought to the attention of operating management and that progress reports are issued as needed.

They should monitor budgets and schedules to help auditors-in-charge to reverse adverse trends.

Supervisors should attend important meetings with line and executive management; current reviews should keep supervisors aware of audit findings and able to discuss them knowledgeably.

They should discuss proposed audit reports with their auditors-in-charge and approve report outlines.

They should review drafts of reports in detail and see that they meet departmental policies.

They should attend draft reviews held with auditees and with higher management whenever possible.

They should approve the adequacy of corrective action on audit findings.

They should see that all administrative documents called for by department procedures have been completed: checklists, post-audit reviews, comparisons of budget and actual audit hours, project-closure recommendations, and the like.

They should approve the filing or destruction of working papers.

Audit managers or directors of auditing should meet at least once a week with their supervisors to discuss project status and any difficulties or problems encountered in the supervised projects.

Properly supervised audit projects are the first and, perhaps, the most important step in a program of quality assurance. When supervisors do their jobs properly in the first place, the internal and external reviews should disclose no serious defects in those matters which are under the direct control of the internal auditing department.

Internal Reviews

Internal reviews can provide both quality assurance to the director of internal auditing and training for staff auditors. The reviews can take the form of verifications and internal audits. They can be done regularly or intermittently. Their frequency will depend on how concerned the director of internal auditing is about the adequacy of the supervision of audit projects and on the amount of adverse feedback from auditees.

Verification

Directors of internal auditing or audit managers who sign audit reports have an understandable concern about the accuracy and propriety of what they are signing. Their professional reputations are at stake. Audit reports are often the result of extensive and complex accumulations of data. Errors by internal auditors are not unheard of, and these can be extremely embarrassing. Those who assess blame should themselves be blameless. Yet auditors are human, and a tendency to err is a fate that no human can escape.

To protect against this tendency and to ensure blameless reports, managers and directors of internal auditing can install a verification system designed to detect mechanical errors which they are in no position to detect themselves. All drafts of internal audit reports can be subjected to an independent check. A staff auditor who was not assigned to the audit project could trace to the working papers every number, date, name, and representation to make sure these are thoroughly supported and documented.

All calculations should be recalculated. All footings and cross-footings should be footed and cross-footed again. All dates should be verified to source documents. All names and titles should be checked for spelling, accuracy, and current status. All deficiency findings should be verified to the working papers for cause, effect, significance, discussions, and evidence of corrective action.

The staff reviewer should then sign an approval slip as evidence of this independent review.

Internal Review Program

Internal reviews of audit projects are just that. They are appraisals of how well auditors and supervisors have complied with departmental policies and procedures and professional practice. Such internal reviews require more mature judgment than verifications. They encompass the work of both staff auditors and their supervisors. They are an assessment of a sample of audit reports and supporting working papers. They therefore require the attention of a senior staff auditor or a supervisor.

The results of such internal reviews can be salutary. First, of course, is the information supplied to the director of internal auditing, information on how well procedures are followed and how well the audit work and the audit reports are documented. Second is the value to the external auditors. The tests of audit projects in an external review can be reduced if those evaluators see credible evidence of internal reviews of such projects.

Hence, the internal reviews of internal audits should be carried out with the formality and discipline of any audit examination. For example:

A review project should be established with a budget and a schedule.

A review program should be prepared which sets forth the steps the evaluator will take.

An acceptable sample of audit projects should be selected which is representative of the department's production.

The evaluator should discuss any deficiencies found with the auditors and supervisors of the audit projects reviewed. Here, tact will be extremely important.

The evaluator should prepare working papers documenting the internal review.

The evaluator should also prepare a formal report on the results of the review.

The review program should be approved by the director of internal auditing. It should comply with those *Standards for the Professional Practice of Internal Auditing* which deal with the performance of audit work. For example, the evaluator should be concerned with the following matters, which are referenced to the specific *Standards:*

How well the auditors planned the audit work. (410)*

Were audit objectives and scopes of work established?

Was background information obtained and was adequate research for the audit project performed?

Was an audit budget developed and were actual audit days charged?

Were appropriate management personnel notified that the audit would take place?

Was a preliminary survey performed and were risk areas identified?

Was an audit program prepared and was the program approved by the audit supervisor?

Were audit results communicated currently either orally or in writing?

---

*Refers to paragraphs in the *Standards for the Professional Practice of Internal Auditing.*

How well the auditor collected, analyzed, interpreted, and documented information to support audit results. (420)*

Was the information collected relevant to the audit objectives?

Was the information collected sufficient, competent, and useful?

Were all the steps in the audit program followed or were adequate reasons for not following them provided?

Were appropriate sampling techniques employed, and were the sample results logically interpreted?

Were working papers prepared which adequately demonstrated the collection, analysis, and interpretation of information?

Did the working papers bear evidence of supervisory review?

How well the results of the audit work were reported. (430)*

Was the report promptly prepared and issued?

Were interim or progress reports issued on significant findings?

Were conclusions and recommendations discussed at appropriate levels of management before the final report was issued?

Were the report drafts carefully reviewed?

Were the reports written in the format required by departmental procedures?

Did the reports receive all required reviews and approvals?

Were all matters reported documented in the working papers?

How well the auditor followed up to see that appropriate action was taken on reported findings. (440)*

Was the corrective action adequately documented?

Was the corrective action complete and did it include provision for preventing a repetition of the reported weaknesses?

Was high level approval obtained in all cases when corrective action was not taken?

External Reviews

External reviews are best carried out by the peers of the practitioners evaluated. People outside the profession do not always have the education, training, and perspective to evaluate professional practice. Peer reviews, the so-called external reviews, are designed to evaluate an internal auditing organization's quality control over its internal auditing practice. These reviews seek to determine whether the quality control procedures are appro-

---

*Refers to paragraphs in the *Standards for the Professional Practice of Internal Auditing.*

priately comprehensive and suitably designed for the internal auditing department evaluated. The reviews also seek to determine whether the quality control policies and procedures are adequately documented, communicated to the staff auditors, and effectively complied with so as to provide reasonable assurance that the internal auditing department is meeting the standards of its profession within the environment it finds itself.

The Foundation for Auditability, Research, and Education, Inc. (FARE), established by The Institute of Internal Auditors, Inc., conducted a research project entitled *A Framework for Evaluating an Internal Audit Function.* [8] The purpose of the study was to supply a means of determining whether internal auditing departments were meeting the criteria established by the *Standards for the Professional Practice of Internal Auditing.*

The *Framework* provides instructions and questionnaires which can be used to evaluate any internal auditing department. These questionnaires are structured for a two-step approach to the evaluation. The first step is directed to the role of internal auditing within the enterprise — the role established by the department's charter. The *Standards* point out that internal auditing around the world is performed in diverse environments which dictate the scope of the internal audit work. Some internal auditing organizations have a broad charter. Their entree to any activity within the enterprise is without restriction. They are not hampered by any policy statement from complying fully with the *Standards* (see Exhibit 16-2, page 545).

Other organizations may function under a variety of restrictions. Some may not have access to the board of directors, may report to a low-level executive, may be barred from reviewing nonaccounting operations, may not have the authority to require replies to their audit reports, may not be responsible for following up on corrective action, or may not be authorized to review compliance with ethical business practices. The list can go on and on. Those internal auditors will be governed by their environment. They will not, therefore, be in compliance with the concepts enunciated in the *Standards* and may not be regarded as carrying out the professional practice of internal auditing within the meaning of the *Standards.* So their audit performance could not be measured by the full yardstick of the *Standards.*

But within the confines of their charter, these internal auditing organizations could be evaluated against the relevant provisions of the *Standards.* The first step in the evaluation process, therefore, will dictate the extent of the second step of the evaluation. That first step calls for comparing the work of an internal auditing department with those elements of the *Standards* that its charter permits it to comply with.

The set of questionnaires in the *Framework* is about 75 pages long and is made up of the following four sections:

Profile of the Internal Auditing Environment

The evaluators will seek to determine the environment in which the internal audit department functions by asking questions about the enterprise, the internal audit department's position in the organizational hierarchy, and the charter granted to the internal auditors by top management. Obviously, work that internal auditors are not permitted to do cannot be evaluated. But, the desirability of doing such work should be considered.

Policies and Procedures

The review team will evaluate internal audit policies and procedures to determine the independence, professional proficiency, scope of work, performance of audit work, and administration of the internal audit department.

Interviews

The evaluation team will conduct interviews with a number of people to test the adequacy of the policies and procedures. The people interviewed would include members of the board of directors, general management, the manager to whom the director of internal auditing is responsible, the director of internal auditing, internal audit supervisors, internal audit staff, auditees, and external auditors.

Review of Individual Audits

The evaluation team can obtain definitive, objective information about compliance with policies and procedures by examining the records of completed audit projects. Detailed check lists can be used to determine whether acceptable standards of professional auditing were met.

After the evaluations are completed, the evaluators should prepare a report summarizing the results of their review and expressing an opinion as to the internal auditing department's compliance with the *Standards for the Professional Practice of Internal Auditing.*

External reviews are in their infancy at this writing. The Institute's manual for evaluating an internal audit function will have to be field-tested to determine whether the questions posed are relevant and practical. The evaluators will have to exercise mature judgment. No questionnaire is completely applicable to all circumstances. The programs for external reviews will have to be developed with care and understanding. A rigorous application of the *Framework's* questionnaires might make it difficult for any internal auditing organization to receive a passing grade. The absence of a particular procedure is not necessarily an indication of an inadequate internal audit department. The evaluators will have to be able to balance what is desirable with what is practical.

External reviews, intelligently and professionally conducted, can have salutary effects. Every function in every enterprise can benefit from a knowledgeable, objective evaluation. The internal audit function is no different. Internal auditors who are placed in the position of auditees may learn some humility. They will obtain first-hand knowledge on how it feels to be reviewed, evaluated, and told about shortcomings. The experience may help to increase empathy with auditees and improve auditor-auditee relations.

Conclusion

As internal auditing receives greater latitude and authority, it must assume increased responsibilities. It must attain a high level of professionalism because it holds itself out as a professional activity. The yardstick used to measure this professionalism is the *Standards for the Professional Practice of Internal Auditing*. Internal audit functions that do not meet the criteria spelled out in the *Standards* cannot be regarded as carrying out a professional practice. Internal auditors, like other professionals, must therefore monitor themselves and subject themselves to external evaluations in the form of peer reviews. The Foundation for Auditability Research and Education has developed a *Framework* for such evaluations. It will be incumbent on directors of internal auditing to so develop and maintain professionalism within their departments that they will be able to withstand the rigorous scrutiny provided for in the FARE report, *A Framework for Evaluating an Internal Audit Function*. Through close and knowledgeable supervision and through periodic, unsparing self-assessments, an internal audit function will be prepared to pass a formal peer review.

References

1. Decimus Junius Juvenal, *Satires VI*, line 347: "Sed quis custodiet ipso custodes?"
2. *Securities Exchange Commission* v. *Aminex Resources Corporation et al.*, 78 Cir. 0410 (D. C. 1978).
3. American Institute of Certified Public Accountants, *Statement on Auditing Standards No. 9: The Effect of an Internal Audit Function on the Scope of the Independent Auditor's Examination* (New York: American Institute of Certified Public Accountants, 1975).
4. Commission on Auditors' Responsibilities, *Report, Conclusions, and Recommendations* (New York: Commission on Auditors' Responsibilities, 1978), pp. 76, 77.
5. *Comptroller's Handbook for National Bank Examiners* (Washington: Office of the Comptroller of the Currency, 1977).
6. *Audit Standards Supplement Series No. 9, Self-Evaluation Guide for Governmental Audit Organizations* (Washington: Comptroller General of the United States, 1976).
7. Division for CPA Firms Private Companies Practice Section, *Peer Review Manual* (New York: AICPA, 1978).
8. A. S. Glazer and H. R. Jaenicke, *A Framework for Evaluating an Internal Audit Function* (Altamonte Springs, Fla.: Foundation for Auditability, Research, and Education, 1980).

Supplementary Reading

Glazer, A. S. and H. R. Jaenicke. *A Framework for Evaluating an Internal Auditing Function*. Altamonte Springs, Fla.: Foundation for Auditability, Research, and Education, Inc., 1980.

Morris, Norman. "How Does Your Audit Department Rate?" *The Internal Auditor*, October 1978, p. 69.

U. S. General Accounting Office. *Audit Standards Supplement Series No. 9, Self-Evaluation Guide for Government Audit Organizations*. Washington: Comptroller General of the United States, 1976.

For further study

Discussion Problems

1. An internal audit organization has functioned successfully for a number of years. It has good rapport with its auditees and solid backing from management. At a meeting with the audit committee of the board, one of the board members, a CPA, suggests that the director consider a peer review. The director points to the success of his department and says he sees no need to undertake the cost of such a review. Looking at it from the standpoint of the board member, give five reasons why the director should consider such a review.

2. If an internal auditing organization undertakes an external review every three years, is the expense of internal reviews warranted?

3. Describe the potential legal implications of the failure of an internal auditing department in a multinational corporation to undergo external reviews.

4. Describe two ways in which the publication of the *Standards for the Professional Practice of Internal Auditing* affected peer reviews of internal auditing departments.

5. Why can audit supervision be regarded as a form of quality control?

Multiple Choice Problems

1. For audit supervision to be considered part of the system of quality control, supervisors should:
a. Approve changes to audit programs.
b. Revise report outlines.
c. Conduct all the interviews at the executive level.
d. Review all working papers after the final report is issued.
e. Follow up on corrective action.

2. An external review is beneficial in that it:
a. Indicates compliance with the *Standards for the Professional Practice of Internal Auditing*.
b. Teaches internal auditors humility.
c. Provides a scorecard for the internal auditing department.
d. Provides assurance to the board that the internal auditing function is meeting its responsibilities.
e. None of the above.

3. An external review should be relevant to the particular internal auditing department being evaluated. To that end, the first step in such a review is to compare the department's charter with the requirements set forth by the *Standards* on:
a. Independence.
b. Professional proficiency.

c. Scope of work.

d. Performance of audit work.

e. Management of the internal auditing department.

4. Enterprise management and the board are concerned with how well the internal auditing department performs the role actually assigned to it. Thus, the second step of the external review is to compare performance with:

a. The *Standards* section on independence and professional proficiency.

b. The *Standards* section on scope of work.

c. The *Standards* section on performance of work and management of the department.

d. Industry standards.

e. Both a. and c. above.

5. An independent internal review could improve the ability of management and the board to:

a. Report publicly on the system of internal accounting control.

b. Expand the internal audit function.

c. Dispense with independent audits.

d. Evaluate the status of the director of internal auditing.

e. Reduce the extent of operational audits.

Case Studies

20-1. Program for Internal Reviews

Dan Audano is director of internal auditing of an internal auditing department in a manufacturing corporation with sales of 1½ billion dollars. Last year his people carried out 100 internal audits of all sizes, both financial and operational, issuing 100 formal audit reports and 150 internal audit memos. He has a broad charter to audit all operations in the company and appraise corrective action on audit findings. He is sitting at his desk when Selma Austen, one of his audit supervisors, enters the room.

"Did you want to see me, Dan?"

"Yes, Selma. I'd like to talk to you about an internal review."

"Which one?"

"The one you're about to make."

"Oh? Which department?"

"This one, Selma."

"I'm afraid I don't understand."

"You've read the *Standards for the Professional Practice of Internal Auditing*, haven't you?"

"Yes indeed."

"Do you remember the very last section of the very last general standard?"

"Oh, yes. You mean about quality assurance."

"Exactly."

"How does that affect us?"

"There are three elements to a quality assurance program. Do you remember them?"

"Yes, I think I do. They are supervision, external reviews, and — I forget."

"The third is internal reviews. And I think it's about time we had one."

"If you don't mind my saying so, Dan, I think that would be duplication. We're scheduled to have our independent accountants make an external review about six months from now."

"Precisely. And if we have any problems, I want to know about them now rather than hearing them from those people and having them paraded before the CEO and the audit committee."

"What do you want me to do, Dan?"

"That's not the question."

"I don't understand."

"The question, I'm afraid, is what **you** want to do. In other words, how do you propose to carry out such a program."

"Oh."

"Right. So in three days I'd like you

back here with a specific program for an internal review."

Required: Prepare an audit program for an internal review of Dan's internal auditing department.

20-2. External Reviews

You are the leader of a team that has completed an external review of an internal auditing department in a large corporation. The department is headed by a director who reports to the controller. Three audit managers report to the director. Each audit manager has two supervisors. The remainder of the staff is made up of 50 internal auditors. The corporation has an audit committee of the board, and this committee retained you to carry out the review. As a result of your evaulation, you have encountered several conditions for which you will have to recommend improvements. The conditions are as follows:

1. The controller is on the same organizational level as the directors of administration, engineering, marketing, personnel, and production.

2. Semi-annual summary reports are distributed to the controller and the executive vice president.

3. During the last year, replies were not received to 14 significant findings reported to operating management. During interviews with those managers, they said they consider audit recommendations to be advisory.

4. Internal auditors are assigned to reconciling bank statements to the books of account.

5. The corporation annually develops specific goals for all branches. The internal auditors have been instructed to review these goals for mathematical accuracy.

6. During the test of specific audit projects, the evaluation team found that a number of significant audit findings had first been brought to operating management's attention in the formal audit reports.

7. The director develops a long-range audit schedule based on an analysis of the corporation's chart of accounts and organization chart.

8. The 50-person staff of internal auditors includes two CPAs, 14 bachelors of business administration, and one CMA. The director is a member of a professional organization and is a CPA and CIA.

9. Audit staff members are given oral performance appraisals which take place every one or two years.

10. The director obtains approval of the long-range audit plan from the controller.

Required: For each condition listed, indicate what action you would recommend and to whom the recommendation should be directed.

Part 6

Other Matters
Relating to Internal Auditing

21

Principles of Management

Management defined. Principles for the solution of management problems. Importance to the internal auditor. The schools of management. The models of managers. The four functions of management. The nature of planning: objectives, goals, strategies, principles, policies, procedures, rules, standards, programs, and premises. Budgets as a planning tool. Decision making. Internal audits of the planning function. The nature of organizing. Responsibility, authority, and accountability. Delegating authority and assigning responsibility. Staff and line conflicts. Functional authority. Departmentation and decentralization. Committees. Informal groups and the grapevine. Staffing. Internal audits of the organizing function. The nature of directing. Leadership, motivation, and communication. Management by objective. Internal audits of directing. The nature of controlling. Standards and measurements. Comparisons and evaluations. Correction and follow-up. Imposed control and self-control. Internal audits of the management control process.

The Nature of Management

Management deals with establishing objectives and then seeing that they are met through others. The early days of the owner-manager have evolved into the day of the professional manager. The complexities of modern enterprises have expanded the responsibilities of professional managers.

The tasks are difficult and diverse. Managers must be able to establish objectives, devise plans, develop organizations, allocate resources, direct the efforts of people, and control events so that goals will be met effectively, efficiently, and economically. Least of the skills needed is the ability to perform technical and functional activities. What managers may have been able to do comfortably and well by themselves, modern managers must now do through others. For this task they may not have the bent or the training. At the very least they should be aware of guiding principles that may make their jobs easier.

Principles

Over the years, bodies of management principles have evolved. These principles help improve the outcome of a manager's decisions. They are universal truths that can be used to solve management problems. They are statements that have stood time's test because they are based on valid causal relationships developed from logical beliefs, successful experience, and repeated experiments. They are universal in that they apply to all forms of enterprises — business, government, religious groups, educational institutions, and nonprofit organizations.

Yet, although they can be taught to everyone, not everyone so taught can manage. Successful management requires a managerial temperament — the ability and inclination to move others toward desired goals. Still, the principles are important to help managers avoid mistakes or to point to the right path.

Violating established principles of management often leads to difficulties. For that reason it is necessary for internal auditors to understand those principles. Virtually every weakness or deficiency unearthed by internal auditors can be traced to the violation of some accepted management principle. If internal auditors are well versed in those principles and can detect their violation, they can more readily identify areas of risk that need their attention. More importantly, they will be better able to carry out their own responsibilities of being counselors to and problem-solving partners with management.[1]

Theories

Many schools of thought about management have been developed by management theorists. Each has its advocates. Yet each may not be the sole answer to what makes for successful management. The student of management should be aware of these theories, not because they are the ultimate truths but because each does have something to offer. Internal auditors should be sufficiently conversant with them so that they can adjust their thinking to that of the manager who is espousing a particular school. Here are brief descriptions of some of these theories of management.

Classical

The classical (scientific) school started as a system of management in the eighteenth century. Order was imposed on haphazard organizational structure. It was developed by a number of brilliant minds and was the beginning of scientific management.

Frederick W. Taylor emphasized planning. He advocated replacing intuition and guesswork with analyzing tasks, training workers scientifically, promoting the cooperation of workers and managers, and establishing more equal divisions of responsibility among them.

The classical theory of management under Henri Fayol developed the functional sequence of planning, organizing, directing, and controlling. Based on his own experience, Fayol developed 14 principles which still have great applicability:

Division of work. Each to his or her ability.

Authority and responsibility. Wherever authority is delegated, responsibility is imposed.

Discipline. Conformity to rules.

Unity of command. One worker, one boss — single accountability.

Unity of direction. The same objectives should have the same plans.

Subordination of individual interests. The job comes first.

Remuneration of personnel. Fair pay for a fair day's work.

Centralization. Concentrating authority to be cost effective.

Scalar chain. The line of authority, like a ladder, reaches from the highest to the lowest rank.

Order. A place for everyone and everything.

Equity. Fair dealing between supervisor and worker.

Stability. A minimum of employee turnover.

Initiative. Stimulating creativity in employees.

Esprit de corps. Teamwork and morale as a result of good communication.

Ralph Currier Davis developed a unified theory of management and the concept of accountability. In addition to authority and responsibility, each subordinate must account for the proper discharge of duties.

The Gilbreths developed time and motion studies.

Henry Gantt developed charts to show the end product and then steps needed to achieve that product.

Behavioral

Observers of the management scene saw blind spots in the classical theory of management. Led by Elton Mayo and F. J. Roethlisberger, they focused on the human side of management and workers. Much research was done in the field, buttressing the view that if the needs and desires of people are satisfied, productivity will increase. Some researchers took the view that the behavioral approach canceled the concepts of the classical school of management. But many of the concepts of the classicists have defied the passage of time. Behavioral management theories should be regarded as supplements to the classical management theories, not as substitutes or the last word in management theory.

Systems

The systems theory of management regards every organization as a complex of integrated subsystems. Every system has elements of input, processing, and output. Each is affected by feedback and governed by controls. A "closed system" acts independently of its environment. An "open system" interacts with its environment. The former tends to deteriorate. The latter is designed to adjust to change. The job of the manager is to deal with this change. The orientation of the systems school is more mechanical than that of the behavioral school.

Quantitative

The quantitative school can be traced to Frederick Taylor's scientific management. Later, operations research was used to help solve management problems. With the use of calculus and the computer, answers could be obtained to extremely complex problems. Mathematical models could be developed to represent systems and assist in decision making. The techniques used include probability theory, regression analysis, linear programming, Monte Carlo simulation, inventory theory, queuing theory, sensitivity analysis, game theory, dynamic programming, and exponential smoothing.

Communication Center

Under this theory, the manager is the central point for receiving, storing, and disseminating information. It is an important aspect of management, but it is not the complete story of management.

Social System

This system is related to the behavioral theory of management. It regards the organization as a series of cultural interrelationships. It emphasizes cooperation to make decisions and solve problems. It is concerned with ethics — with what is morally right.

Many attempts have been made to integrate these various theories since each has something to offer. The fusion process points to the need for a coalescence of individual and organizational goals; both must change to meet each other's needs. The modified theory of management points to participation between the organization and the individual to dissipate the worker's alienation and thereby increase production. The organizational overlay school superimposes the informal organization on the formal organization chart. This school seeks to make use of the power residing in groups and the flow of informal communication. The contingency approach holds that management cannot be governed by a single set of principles that are universally applicable. Management is a complex and delicate process that can be affected by many factors: technology, people, and the environment. Management must take all of these into account.

Models of Managers

Four distinct models of managers have evolved during the last 100 years or so. Their evolution roughly followed the evolving theories of management.

Autocratic

The autocratic model was the result of military authority and the classical school. It was almost universal up to about 75 years ago. It is based on pure power. It has given way to more behavioral forms of management style, but for some organizations it is still effective.

Custodial

The custodial model took form in the 1930s. It was founded on the proposition that happy people are productive people. Custodial programs depended on material rewards for the worker. The workers were oriented toward pablum and the security blanket. Although people were happy, they were not fulfilled; nor were they necessarily productive. Rather, they found a relaxed way to earn a living.

Supportive

The supportive model sought to avoid the shortcomings of both the autocratic and the custodial models. Instead of obedience and happiness, the workers are pointed toward performance. They can feel participation and involvement as drives are awakened which they were not aware of. This model depends on leaders who have positive feelings toward their people — that people do want to work, grow, and achieve.

Collegial

The collegial model is still in its formative stages. It is founded on feelings of mutual contribution among members of the group. The manager is oriented toward teamwork instead of toward a superior/subordinate relationship. Each contributes to common goals. The results can be self-discipline, responsibility, self-fulfillment, and enthusiasm.

The Functions of Management

Management is exercised through four functions:

- Planning
- Organizing
- Directing
- Controlling

Some writers add staffing, but staffing can be regarded as an element of organizing. Others use "actuating" instead of the more familiar "directing." In each of the four functions, internal auditors can help managers. Their audit scope need not be limited to control systems. Many weaknesses internal auditors encounter are rooted in planning, organizing, and directing. And so a knowledge of management principles can be useful in serving management and in getting to the bottom of functional weaknesses. In the material which follows, each of the four functions is described as it relates to management. Then it is discussed to indicate how internal auditors can evaluate the function; how they can provide information useful to managers carrying out management tasks.

Planning is necessarily the first of the four functions of management. From plans flow organization, direction, and control. Every organization must fit the plans of the entity. All direction is pointed toward moving people toward planned objectives and goals. All controls should be designed to see that plans will be carried out effectively, efficiently, and economically.

Planning is the selection of the best choice from a number of choices. A significant part of modern management thinking is the increased interest in planning. An indication of good management is the determination to bridge the gap between where we are and where we ought to be — not haphazardly, but thoughtfully and rationally.

All planning is strategic or tactical. Strategic plans are long-range: tax planning, capital budgeting, personnel planning, and product planning. Tactical plans are short-range: for example, production scheduling. Yet all plans have similar characteristics. Plans are courses of action, not mere wishes. They deal with action in the future; hence a degree of uncertainty affects all plans.

Planning calls for imagination, foresight, and thought. It involves all managers from the top to the bottom of the enterprise. And because they are of necessity tentative, plans must be constantly watched and reappraised in the light of what actually comes to pass. Plans are decisions to take certain steps, yet they should be flexible, adjusting to circumstances. If they are to be successful, they should be coordinated among functions and be cost beneficial.

Plans and planning are umbrella terms that cover a number of management actions, such as:

Objectives and Goals

Objectives and goals guide the enterprise. They show how management regards what the enterprise is and where it should be. They help determine the organizational structure and the scope and direction of the enterprise. They should be understandable, easily communicated, acceptable, attainable, and capable of being implemented by subplans such as procedures and rules. They should not conflict with laws, ethical standards, public policy, or other enterprise objectives. Goals will vary among enterprises, but certain basic objectives are universal. These are to create something of value to a customer, to survive and grow, and to create values needed by members of the enterprise.

Strategies

Strategies implement objectives. They are broad, overall concepts of an operation. They often denote a general program of action and the deployment of resources.

Principles

Principles are fundamental truths. They should be acceptable to the community and should mold all policies and procedures.

Policies

Policies are general guides for action. They should influence decisions, not make them.

Procedures

Procedures are specific guides. They prescribe action but do not channel thinking. They may include a chronological sequence of events leading to the accomplishment of a task.

Rules

Rules are the simplest plans. They allow for no discretion. They must be followed as stated.

Standards

Standards are norms against which outcomes are measured. They help determine whether actions comply with plans.

Programs

Programs are a combination of goals, policies, procedures, and rules together with the resources to carry out some desired course of action.

Premises

Premises are the assumptions on which plans are based. They should be set by top management. Compatible premises should be used by everyone in the enterprise to assure coordination of plans. Since premises are predictions, they cannot be certainties. They are founded on historical information about the economy, society, government, and competition, as well as the enterprise's resources, strengths, and weaknesses.

Budgets

Budgets give quantitative expression to an entity's plans. They force an organization to identify its goals, the availability of resources, and methods of implementation. They are utterly essential to the functioning of an enterprise, yet they are almost inevitably a source of conflict. Responses to budgets are usually emotional and antagonistic. Antagonism can be reduced if budgets are based on realistic premises, if the people who are governed by them helped develop them, and if they are used to help managers help themselves.

Decision Making

Decision making is problem solving. It is a planning function and is therefore future-oriented. It is the rational selection of the best choice from among various options. The steps in decision making are as follows: Recognize and define the problem. Gather pertinent information. Develop alternative courses of action. Select the best from among feasible alternatives. Take action.

Planning and the Internal Auditor

Standards

Internal auditors should not spend all their time looking backwards at completed transactions. They can look forward with management and help in the planning process. In fact, they can evaluate the overall planning process by determining whether plans, policies, and procedures meet certain standards. For example:

All plans, policies, and procedures should be compatible with enterprise objectives.

Plans should anticipate problems and coordinate the various objectives of the enterprise.

The premises for plans should be based on accurate data and reasonable forecasting.

The benefits of plans should exceed the cost of drawing them up.

Plans should result in uniform action among interdependent organizations.

Plans should be clearly communicated to those responsible for carrying them out and should allow for initiative.

Each plan should carry a means of measuring its success.

Follow-up systems should be devised to determine whether plans were carried out as intended.

Impediments to Plans

Not all plans are devised rationally. Not all plans are prepared in an environment which gives them a chance of meeting goals. Often the planning mechanism itself is defective. Internal auditors should look for the impediments to a good planning function. Here are some:

Management is not committed to or involved in the plan.

The grass roots people were not consulted.

The plans are just not workable — conceived by people out of touch with reality.

The plans are not carried out. After being developed they are forgotten or are not monitored. The planners did not provide for feedback and control.

Plans are based on inaccurate data and information.

Plans do not take contingencies into account. The planners did not ask themselves the "what if" questions.

The plans are too rigid, allowing for no initiative.

Bridging the Gap

Internal auditors are in a position to see the work of both the planner and the doer. They can therefore bridge the gap between them. For example, internal auditors reviewing the accuracy of engineering drawings — which are essentially plans for production — can discuss them with production people to determine what problems are encountered in production because of the drawings.

In all audits of operating departments, the review can be elevated to a management-oriented audit if the auditors concern themselves with the planning activity. For example:

The auditor and the manager should agree on the primary missions, the purposes, and the objectives of the department.

The auditor should review the procedures designed to carry out departmental objectives and seek to identify those that are redundant, missing, or inconsistent.

Auditors should talk to operating people and find out if they understand the objectives, the procedures, and the instructions.

Auditors should make sure that the managers have a feedback of information which tells them how well plans are being met.

The Key Questions

Review of the development of plans, procedures, and programs can be helpful in determining whether managers considered certain key questions. For example:

Does the plan have to be carried out? Does it fill a real need?

What has to be done to best carry out the plan? Is the most logical action being taken?

Is the place where the plan is being carried out the best place?

Have schedules and due dates been set? Do long-range programs have specified milestones?

Have specific individuals been given responsibility for carrying out the plans?

Have procedures for carrying out the plans been clearly spelled out?

Change

Plans create change. People usually fear change as a threat to their security, but change can be made acceptable under certain circumstances. Internal auditors can point out the ways of easing the trauma of change. Here are some of the ways:

The need for the change should be understood by operating people.

People should be assured that the change does not threaten their security.

Those affected should participate in planning the change.

The change should result from a situation, not solely from a management fiat.

The change should follow a series of successful changes rather than a series of failures.

The change should not be a part of many other changes all going at once.

The organization should be conditioned to accept change.

Procedures

Verifying adherence to procedures is a basic internal audit function. Managers often rely on internal audit analysis to tell them how well their people are following written procedures. This is an important internal audit function. But of equal importance is determining whether the procedures are valid and useful and whether they have been carefully prepared. Standards can be applied to the development of procedures. Here are some:

Procedures should make clear who is responsible for what. A provision for accountability should be included in each procedure.

Procedures should not be empty hopes. They should be supported by adequate resources. Lack of people and equipment can prevent accomplishment of even the best procedures.

Every job needs monitoring. Every procedure should provide for surveillance and progress reporting.

When forms are developed to initiate the procedure, they should be designed so all elements in the organization can use the same forms. Paperwork should be kept to a minimum.

Budgets

Auditors are often involved in audits relating to budgets. They are concerned with the establishment of and the charges to budgets, with the recording of actual costs, with the reporting of performance, and with management's use of performance reports. In auditing the budgeting and reporting process, internal auditors can apply the following standards:

The budgeting department should be authorized to obtain information from operating departments.

Instructions and premises issued to those preparing the budgets should be understandable and consistent.

Steps in the budget development process should be scheduled to show specifically each of the steps required.

The budget department should provide all contributing departments with the same format for required information to facilitate consolidation.

Provision should be made for reviews of the budgets at higher levels in the organization.

Information sent to the budget department should be adequately supported.

All people affected by budgets should be aware of them.

Operating departments should adjust their operations to accord with budget changes.

Significant variances between budgeted and actual amounts should be explained. Steps should be taken to correct excessive variances.

Operating managers should receive adequate information to let them know how well they are meeting their budgets.

A survey by The Institute of Internal Auditors, Inc., disclosed that only 15% of over 100 large companies questioned used their internal auditors to perform audits of budgeting activities.[2] Yet substantial benefits can accrue from the audit of the budget activity — an activity no more difficult to review than many others listed in the internal audit long-range audit schedule.

Decision Making

Internal auditors can make substantial contributions to the decision-making process. They can help managers in all but the final step: the selection from among available choices. That is a management right and responsibility.

Internal auditors can help recognize the problems. Their routine audits are directed to that end. Auditors can initiate the decision-making process by pointing to matters needing management attention. Also, internal auditors are often called upon to carry out management studies of significant problems. The wise internal auditors will begin cautiously. They will make sure that they have their finger on the right problem, not necessarily on the one management — sometimes hurriedly — thought was the problem.

Internal auditors are expert information gatherers. Often they can accumulate data, obtain varying views, and define expectations better than the managers themselves.

Internal auditors can offer alternative solutions to the decision-making process. This is a normal audit function: offering possible courses of action without prescribing which course to take. Thus, internal auditors can add to the choices management has developed, making sure that all, or the most feasible, alternatives are considered.

Internal auditors can evaluate possible choices by using mathematical techniques, modeling, or simulation. Management can thus be presented with the alternative having the greatest possibility of success.

Making the final choice, as we have pointed out, is a line function. This step must be left to line management. If the internal auditor intrudes here, management may abdicate its responsibility.

Management's action — its selection of the course to take — will usually require monitoring. Here internal auditors can offer safeguards by providing feedback on the results of the action taken as they carry out their regular audits.

Organizing

Organizing brings together people and processes in logical groupings to carry out plans and meet objectives.

Good organization is no guarantee of success, but poor organization will almost inevitably bring failure because it breeds conflict and frustration.

Organizing can be done in the classical or in the behavioral style. Classical, autocratic organization creates squares and puts people into them. The behavioral style takes the individual into account; it seeks to structure organizations so as to combine the needs of both the people and the organization.

The prescription for successful organizing combines these ingredients:

The organization should be designed to carry out its objectives and plans.

The right people with the right capabilities should be placed in positions that are right for them.

Tasks and expectations should be clearly stated so that people know what is required of them and with whom they should coordinate their efforts.

The framework of operating components must be able to mesh with the environment: existing technology, society, ethics, and politics.

The final structure with its responsibility, authority, and accountability should be communicated clearly and unmistakably to those assigned to meet objectives and goals and to carry out plans.

Responsibility

Responsibility is the obligation to perform. It is an unbroken chain from superior to subordinate to subordinate. It can never be relinquished. The chief executive remains responsible for every task in the organization no matter how lowly placed that task may be. Responsibilities are grounded on tasks, and tasks are grounded on objectives. The clearer the understanding of one's objectives, the more likely will responsibilities be properly carried out.

Authority

Authority is the right to perform, to command, to enforce compliance. It derives from responsibility. There is no point to having authority to carry out a task when there is no responsibility for it. Most theories of organizational control therefore emphasize the parity between responsibility and authority.

Two forms of authority are exercised. The first is formal authority, often called "traditional authority." It stems from the right to give orders. It flourishes when jobs are scarce. Workers will then follow orders even though they may disagree with them because they need the security the job provides. The second is authority by acceptance. It depends on leadership. It works when the leader has convinced the workers that following directives will be in their own best interests. It is most desirable when workers are scarce and jobs are relatively secure. Workers may feel independent enough to ignore the orders of the authoritative (positional) leader but will follow one who has earned their respect.

Accountability

Accountability is the obligation of workers and managers to give a reckoning for what they have accomplished. Accountability derives from responsibility. People cannot properly be held accountable for what they are not responsible. And people should not be held accountable when their authority is not equal to the responsibility assigned. When responsibility is clear and authority is adequate, people should be asked to account for carrying out those responsibilities, for exercising the authority delegated to them, and for fulfilling their stewardship of the resources entrusted to them.

Delegation

Delegation includes assigning responsibility, granting authority, and exacting accountability. Obviously, only that authority legitimately possessed can be delegated, but delegation does not mean abdication. The superior is still responsible, and so delegation must be accompanied by accountability — some sort of control and feedback.

Many superiors are reluctant to delegate. This may stem from fear of being exposed, fear of having their jobs taken over, or fear of entrusting tasks to others. An understanding of the principles of delegation can help such reluctant managers. Here are some of the principles:

People must know what is expected of them.

Each delegate must know his or her delegator. The chain of command must be clear.

Once tasks are delegated, the delegate must carry through — no evasion of responsibility should be permitted.

Authority to act must equal the responsibility to accomplish.

No manager should retain supervision over more subordinates than can be comfortably dealt with. The span of control should be reasonable under the circumstances.

Only those matters should be brought to the attention of superiors which are outside the authority delegated to the subordinates.

Staff and Line

Line people make "line decisions." Staff people advise them. Line exists whenever an individual or group is responsible for an objective and makes decisions to that end. Staff exists whenever the individual or group is separated from the primary chain of command — the decision makers — to give specialized service and support.

Thus, a computer programmer in a software company, an auditor in an accounting firm, and a salesperson in a manufacturing company would be line. But a computer programmer in a brokerage firm, a secretary in an accounting department, and an internal auditor in a public utility would be staff.

Staff and line must work together to produce results. The seeds of conflict are always there. Staff is not authorized to make line decisions, but many staff people do and this breeds resentment. This lets line people shirk their responsibilities.

Both line and staff must make a concerted effort to develop and maintain reasonable working relations, otherwise conflicts are bound to erupt. This is especially true where staff people assume authority over line activities; where communication between the two breaks down; where line stubbornly resists reasonable, staff-recommended changes; where line fears punishment as a result of staff's critical reports; and where staff exhibits abrasive and critical attitudes.

Functional Authority

Between line and staff is a twilight zone called functional authority. It exists because it must. Without it the chief executive becomes overburdened. It is the assignment of some of the chief executive's authority to a staff organization or an individual. It is the right and the responsibility to prescribe processes, methods, or policies to other line or other service groups. For example, a controller has the functional authority to issue instructions to all line and staff departments on the kinds of accounting records to keep. The controller has the special education, training, and expertise needed for such tasks.

Departmentation

Departmentation divides the organization into distinct groupings to perform assigned tasks. "Flat" organizations have many groupings; they are set horizontally and report to a single superior. "Tall" organizations have a longer chain of command and a narrower span of control. They permit closer supervision, but they inhibit the development of self-reliant managers.

Departmentation can be based on number, function, territory, product, customer, processes and equipment, or project.

Decentralization

Decentralization divides large, complex organizations into smaller businesses that are relatively compact and simple. Each unit has its own management, runs its own business, and is responsible for performance and accountable for results.

Committees

A committee is a group of people who work together on some aspect of a management function. They reach decisions by consensus. They are formed at all levels. At the top level is the board of directors. At lower levels are informal committees established in a department to carry out a specific task and then disband.

Committees bring together people with different experiences and training. The total can be greater than the sum of the parts because of the interchange of information and the resulting stimulation of ideas. Committees can be a slow and expensive way of reaching a decision. The committee members may settle for the lowest common denominator to reach a consensus — achieving compromise instead of arriving at the best course.

Informal Groups

Every formal group has its informal one. Informal organizations are composed of relationships among their members that disregard the organizational chart. They are not authorized, but they exist and cannot be ignored.

Informal groups are not necessarily bad. They fill social needs and generate a feeling of belonging. But they can be disruptive. They can work against the best interests of the enterprise when group objectives are at variance with organizational objectives.

Management can do little to encourage or discourage informal groups, so managers might as well use their group's grapevine to transmit and receive information.

Staffing

Staffing is essential to organizing. It includes recruiting, selecting, and developing people to operate the organization competently. Good management requires staff planning.

Executive management should determine what management posts are available and which ones need to be filled. But it must go beyond that. Management should look to the future and see what kind of turnover in management jobs can be expected, based on past experience. Incumbents and potential managers should then be classified as follows: Those soon to retire. Those who will have to be replaced. Those who are adequate but incapable of going higher. Those ready for promotion.

Executive management must consider the entity's long-range plans and allow for changes in the organization. With this background, management can decide on the training program needed to fill the jobs anticipated. Finally, the sources of recruitment should be considered, taking into account climate, distance, and family.

Promotion from within makes for good employee relations, but it can breed sterility. An infusion of new blood can be revitalizing. A balance between the two is probably the best, and the executive who is responsible for an operation should have the authority to decide which candidates to select.

Organizing and the Internal Auditor

Internal auditors should have no responsibility for designing organizations, but their knowledge of systems and controls can be of value to those who do have that responsibility. Often those who design organizations and systems may not ask themselves questions that are central to good organization. Such questions should be natural to an experienced, management-oriented internal auditor.

What are the objectives of the proposed operation?

How do they mesh with enterprise objectives?

What controls exist or should exist to see that objectives will be met?

How is development of the organization chart keyed to the objectives of the enterprise?

Responsibility, Authority, and Accountability

Internal auditors are expected to determine what managers are responsible for, what they are authorized to do, and how they should account for their accomplishments and results.

When purchasing agents permit operating departments to deal directly with suppliers, they are shirking their own responsibility. When other departments, without the right to do so, order supplies or services without consulting purchasing, they are violating purchasing's authority to commit company funds. When executive management turns a blind eye to all this, it is relieving purchasing of its accountability.

So internal auditors have an interest in the responsibilities assigned and authority delegated to the organizations they review. Where these are not carried out, the derelictions represent a weakness that needs correcting. Also, they may find that responsibility is assigned but accountability is not required. In such cases, executive management has lost touch. Internal auditors should see that the trinity of responsibility, authority, and accountability are maintained.

Delegation

Delegation demands control. Delegation needs feedback to show how delegated tasks are carried out. Internal auditors can be the source of objective information on task accomplishment. In this analysis, internal auditors would seek answers to the following questions:

Are the delegates qualified to undertake their assignments?

Do the delegates understand their responsibilities?

Does performance meet the standards set by the delegator?

When the delegation was made, what form of control was developed to provide feedback to the delegator? Are the controls working as intended?

Staff and Line

Internal auditors have their own staff/line problems. They are responsible for identifying weaknesses. They have a commitment to assist line managers in correcting the weaknesses, but they may not dictate the specific course of action. Internal auditors may offer a course or courses of action as being one or some of many possibilities. The offer must be made with the distinct understanding that line makes the final decision, because line must live with the action taken.

Internal auditors often audit staff work. Some may be rendered by company personnel, some by suppliers. Internal auditors can assist executive management in deciding whether particular staff services should be purchased or performed by company personnel. Questions to answer would relate to comparative costs, the need for undivided attention by the staff, what to ask for in terms of services required, and the ability of in-house managers to provide the needed services. Some of these costs and benefits are measurable; some are not. The internal auditor can assist executive management in a reasonable appraisal.

Functional Authority

Internal auditors, better than any others in the organization, are in a position to determine whether functional authority is effective. The personnel department may prescribe personnel evaluation forms for all departments in the company, but may be reluctant to make sure they are being used. The purchasing department may distribute procurement stamps to ordering departments, but it may not know how those departments are protecting the stamps against misuse. The receiving department might set up rules for the receipt of deliveries directly to a using department, bypassing the receiving dock; but it does not know how well its rules are followed.

One of the functions of internal auditing is to be sure the functional authority is effective. Internal auditors can bridge the gaps and be catalysts for corrective action.

Departmentation

Internal auditors should not necessarily accept the organizational structure as they find it. Departmentation should also be questioned:

What activities are needed to carry out the department's objectives?

How are the groupings balanced to meet departmental goals?

Does departmentation provide for adequate cross-checks of important activities?

How does the grouping of activities facilitate the meeting of objectives?

What are the key activities of an organization, and have they all been assigned to specific individuals?

How well are departments or units integrated? Which ones seem to operate without surveillance or checks and balances?

Decentralization

Decentralization grants a great deal of autonomy to the decentralized units. These act like separate businesses. Yet they must be under the guidance of headquarters and be accountable to headquarters. They must conform with overall policies and procedures, such as accounting, laid down by the head office.

Senior vice presidents responsible for the decentralized units may visit them rarely. When they do, the visits may be little more than social calls. Certainly, the executive cannot review them in depth even if he or she wanted to. The link to decentralized operation must be the knowledgeable internal auditor, giving executive management reasonable assurance that common objectives will be attained, efforts will be coordinated, and decisions on matters of high policy will be controlled.

Committees

Committees should not be above audit review. Indeed, internal auditors are sometimes made members of committees to ensure conformance of committee actions with enterprise policies. Internal auditors can be helpful in determining whether committees meet certain basic standards:

The committee's charter should be in writing, should set forth its authority and responsibilities, and should show to whom the committee is accountable.

Members of the committee should have definite roles, not merely be observers. Their duties should be made clear.

Committees should be large enough to provide varied viewpoints, but not so big as to be unwieldy.

Committee members should have equal authority. None should feel dominated and fearful of expressing themselves.

An agenda should be prepared for each meeting and should be transmitted to committee members in advance of the meeting.

Minutes should be prepared for each meeting. Copies should be sent to the executives to whom the committees are responsible.

Action items should be assigned to individuals, and due dates should be scheduled.

The committee chairman should follow up on assigned tasks.

The committee should report periodically to executive management.

A committee's activities should not overlap that of other committees.

A committee should be disbanded as soon as its mission is completed.

The simplest approach to a committee audit is to ask the committee chairman how these standards are being met.

Informal Groups

Internal auditors should be sensitive to the informal organization which overlays the formal one.

Informal groups have their own cultures, their own leaders, their own forms of communication. Internal auditors, by showing empathy and understanding, can plug into the grapevine which is the mode of communication for informal groups. Then the internal auditors may be made privy to why things work the way they do, the causes for deviations from procedures, and matters needing correction which may not be evident when reviewing the system.

In foreign countries, internal auditors must become attuned to the mores of the individual cultures. Setting up meetings during siesta time in Latin America would be a waste of time. Getting upset for being kept waiting in some countries where delays are a part of life would create antagonisms that could abort a well-planned audit.

The informal organization is a fact of life. Managers have to deal with it. Internal auditors should also learn how.

Staffing

Internal auditors can be helpful in audits of staffing activities. First, they should be concerned with hiring practices. Chances are good that the villains on board were probably villains in their former jobs. Internal auditors should determine whether background checks are made. They should see that a system exists for rehires. Some standards to consider are these:

The basis for the complement of a unit should be soundly supported.

People should be in the proper position. An engineer should not be doing clerical work.

Jobs should challenge people. If the turnover rate is high, the answer may be boredom.

Internal auditors will be concerned with overstaffing, but this requires care. It is best for the statistics to speak for themselves: "This year the staff of 30 turned out 15,000 units. Last year, the same staff turned out 25,000 units."

Directing

Directing is the function of moving resources toward a goal. It includes leadership, motivation, and communication. It also includes formulating a philosophy about employees, establishing congruence of individual and organizational needs, providing a healthy leadership climate, and developing an understanding of individual and group dynamics.

It is an intricate combination of actions and concepts made all the more complicated by the complexity of human beings. They are not only complex, they are variable also. They vary from day to day and from situation to situation. Human beings respond in different ways to different management approaches, and no one approach will always bring about desired responses.

Directing is a significant element of management. When two companies have equal access to comparable technology and markets, that factor which may move one ahead can well be direction — the ability to create an environment in which people are willing to extend themselves to meet organizational goals. Getting people to do more than they think they can is the essence of successful directing.

Leadership

Leadership, properly carried out, is the art of influencing and stimulating performance. Management is responsible for giving direction to what it manages. Resources available to a manager must be led toward positive results. People must be guided toward greatest productivity and achievement. The function of leadership is therefore to stimulate people to work with zeal and confidence. Zeal is instilled by the inspiring leader. Confidence results from technical ability and is brought forth by the teacher who leads by setting good examples.

Motivation

Every manager must motivate — move people toward some common goal. The old authoritarian method, the whip, may work for a while, but it does not work when the boss's eye is turned away or when the job market for good people is tight. The modern manager must understand people — what stimulates them and what offends them.

Many theorists have performed research and drawn conclusions about what motivates workers: Douglas McGregor and the Theory Y and Theory X types of managers — Theory Y managers believe people really want to accomplish something, while Theory X managers believe all workers are lazy and must be driven. Rensis Likert and the supportive manager. Frederick Herzberg and the satisfiers which motivate people and the dissatisfiers which must be present but which really do not motivate the worker. Chris Argyris and the need for people to participate. Mary Parker Follet and the "law of the situation."

Most of these theorists believe that the job itself is the one prime motivator. By improving the job, managers can improve the desire of workers to perform. In job enrichment, a worker's assignments are made more fulfilling. In job enlargement the variety and number of tasks are expanded and made more challenging. By having workers participate in structuring and planning them, the jobs are enlarged and enriched. Workers then tend to perform to their potentials.

Communication

Communication conveys meaning and understanding. To achieve it requires a sharing and a mutual understanding of ideas, facts, and courses of action. For it to take place, people must interact.

Every communication involves a sender, a message, a receiver, and symbols. The sender wishes to convey what is in his or her mind to the mind of the receiver by couching the message in appropriate symbols. The best indicator of the effectiveness of a communication upon a receiver is a change in the receiver's behavior.

Management by Objective

Management by objective (MBO) is a term Peter Drucker coined.[3] MBO seeks to integrate company and individual objectives. The company's objectives are to achieve profits and growth. The individual's goals are to achieve self-development while contributing to company goals. But an MBO program requires considerable effort to be successful. Many hurdles stand in the way of success.

Perhaps one of the greatest hurdles is the lack of understanding of what an MBO program should be. People inaugurating such a program would probably approach it in a more enlightened way if they recalled that Drucker's full title is "Management by Objective and Self-Control." True management by objective, says Drucker, substitutes management by self-control for management by domination.

A successful MBO program should result in more cooperation among managers, improved communication between departments, more employee self-direction, and an improved sense of organizational purpose.

But many MBO programs are not successful because the basic principles of MBO are violated. Top management is not committed to it. Managers are not permitted to participate in setting objectives and goals. Managers are not provided with the information they themselves need to control. Objectives and goals are not integrated throughout the organization.

Directing and the Internal Auditor

Directing is people-oriented, not transaction-oriented. Internal audits of directing do not lend themselves to objective conclusions by documented numbers and facts. Still, internal auditors can provide counsel and assistance to the function of directing. One approach to audits of directing can be the audit of the personnel department. Here, management-oriented audits can be performed by focusing on the objectives of the department: to identify personnel needs, to train and develop manpower, and to administer personnel programs and benefits. Some standards internal auditors can use are as follows:

Jobs to be filled should be described precisely.

Uniform criteria should be used in classifying jobs.

Job compensation should be keyed to particular classifications and should be competitive with jobs in other companies and comparable to those in other departments.

Grades and compensation should be reevaluated periodically.

Department heads should be consulted on current and future personnel needs.

All significant jobs should have backup people ready to fill them.

Operating managers should have guidelines for employee orientation and training; such as, information about employee rights and obligations, what the company expects of the employee, encouragement to get additional training, tested training materials, and special training and certification for hazardous jobs.

Employee evaluations should be made periodically to match compensation and performance within the employee's grade.

Employee turnover rates should be analyzed for trends, and investigations should be made of reasons for adverse trends.

Welfare and other services should be administered in businesslike fashion. Often there is a tendency to be lax in such programs.

Leadership and Motivation

Evaluating leadership and motivation is risky. Yet such audits, wisely carried out, can provide useful information to management. Some standards for such evaluations can be borrowed from Rensis Likert. Here is what he said about evidence of good leadership:[4]

Good leaders exhibit confidence in their people, seeking and using their ideas.

Subordinates are free to talk to their superiors about their jobs.

The leader asks for employee participation.

Punishment, when needed, is immediate and fits the crime.

Employees are committed to achieving organizational goals.

Subordinates have an open line to report their problems and accomplishments upward.

People are clearly informed about the goals they are to accomplish.

Leaders learn about and understand their subordinates' problems, difficulties, and frustrations.

Employees are involved in the decision-making process.

The bases and premises for decisions come from both the top and from subordinates.

The decision-making process should motivate employees, not disaffect them.

Goals should be established by group action, not by command.

Goal establishment should not result in employee resistance.

The informal organization should have the same goals as the formal one.

Systems should provide for self-control rather than imposed control.

When internal auditors have developed the proper rapport, operating managers will be amenable to information about their performance in meeting these standards. Where operating managers will not heed, and where the violations of such standards of conduct seriously affect performance, internal auditors may have to report their conclusions to senior management.

Communication

Internal auditors recognize that managers in large organizations make decisions largely on what they are told, not on what they know of on their own. Often reports from subordinates are self-serving statements and not scrupulously accurate accounts of conditions. The internal auditor, without an axe to grind, can defend executive management from inaccurate and biased information. All reports on which management decisions are made should be reviewed for timeliness, accuracy, and usefulness.

Policies and procedures are forms of communication as well as being planning instruments. Internal auditors should determine in their audits whether policies and procedures do in fact communicate, are understandable, are not capable of being misunderstood, and meet current, not historical, conditions.

Personnel policies especially can create communication problems. Very often it is not the policy that presents the problem, but how it is perceived by employees. Personnel policy audits can be helpful to inform senior management how their personnel policies are perceived and regarded. Employees may be interviewed to obtain their views about the policies with such questions as: Have they been read? What are they perceived to mean? Do they seem reasonable? How would the employee restate the policy?

Management by Objective

Internal auditors can find out if an MBO program is working by talking to people and by comparing accomplishments with goals. Determining why an MBO program is not working may be more difficult. MBO programs fail when management violates the principles on which MBO programs should be based. Internal auditors can compare ongoing MBO programs with the following standards:

Senior management must clearly demonstrate its commitment to the program.

The objectives of all units must be in tune with the aims of the enterprise.

Goals must be expressed quantitatively.

Goals should be attainable, but people should be made to stretch.

People should have the information needed to control their own performance.

Subordinates should participate in setting goals.

Goals should be flexible. They should be changed if circumstances and premises change substantially.

Reviews of performance should be a learning experience, not punitive.

Internal auditors can use these indicators as a clue to why the program went wrong:

Executive management decrees the program and then forgets about it.

The program is not explained to participants.

Guidelines and premises were not given to operating managers and so goals are not reasonable.

The company objectives themselves are at fault because they are inconsistent, unrealistic, or unclear.

Management sets forth procedures, not goals.

Goals are not quantified and so are not measured.

Goals are either continually being changed or are completely inflexible.

Operating managers are not equipped with accurate, current information to help themselves.

Controlling

Evaluating the adequacy and effectiveness of control systems occupies much of the internal auditor's time. For that reason, Chapter 3 "Control" was devoted to the subject. That chapter examined control from the viewpoint of the internal auditor. In examining control from the manager's viewpoint, there are bound to be overlaps, but these are necessary for a rounded discussion of each point of view.

Controlling is the process of making certain that directed action is carried out as planned in order to achieve some desired objective. Controlling and planning are linked; and some devices, such as budgets, are used both as planning and controlling devices. Systems control is frequently referred to as cybernetics.

Control has been described as a closed system consisting of a series of six elements:

1. Setting performance standards to provide a means of measuring and comparing, and to establish permissible variations.

2. Measuring performance or progress to accumulate information on actual conditions.
3. Analyzing performance and comparing it with standards to determine variances.
4. Evaluating deviations and bringing them to appropriate attention in order to determine causes and take effective corrective action.
5. Correcting deviations from standards to see that goals will be met.
6. Following up on corrective action to appraise the effectiveness of action taken.

Controlling itself is a part of a closed system which includes the other functions of management: planning, organizing, and directing.

Management is responsible for establishing a control system; internal auditors are responsible for evaluating its adequacy and effectiveness. In establishing systems, managers should be concerned with the key control points. Not every part of a system needs to be under strict control. Excessive control can be burdensome and unnecessarily expensive. The control system should be adapted to the formal organizational structure, be understandable to all administrators, and be oriented more toward anticipating future mistakes than correcting past ones. When they select control points, managers should ask themselves:

What will best measure performance?

What will point out significant deviations?

What will minimize the cost of correcting errors?

What will be most efficient?

What is the lowest practicable level in the organization at which the control point should be set?

In making these determinations, managers must consider the implications of the six elements of control.

Standards

Standards translate goals into specific measurable outcomes. They inform people of what is acceptable performance. No objective measurement of performance is possible without standards. All standards derive from plans — not from policies, rules, objectives, or principles. Hence they should be linked to plans and be relevant to enterprise goals. Standards are applicable to various elements of performance. For example:

Quantity of output. Output standards specify quantitative performance. They may be based on such matters as machine-hours or worker-hours per unit of output, units per day or week, or tonnage produced.

Accuracy of quality. Accuracy of quality standards specify quality of performance, such as agreement with specifications, fastness of color, approvals required, or number of rejections.

Cost. Cost standards specify such things as material costs per unit, overhead per direct labor hour, or direct and indirect costs per unit of production.

Timeliness. Timeliness standards relate to production schedules, project completion, or meeting customers' need dates.

Capital. Capital standards apply monetary units to physical items. They deal with capital invested, not operating costs. So they relate more to the balance sheet than to the profit-and-loss statement. The standards include return on investment and such ratios as current liabilities, cash and receivables to payables, and turnover of inventory.

Revenue. Revenue standards involve monetary values assigned to sales. They include such matters as revenue per airplane passenger mile, dollars per ton of sheet steel sold, and average sale per customer.

Standards should be placed at strategic control points. The earlier the point in a process, the greater assurance that deviations will be anticipated or that they will be detected before too much time or money is lost.

Above all, performance measurement standards should be related to the primary objectives of the activity. Otherwise the key measurements are not made. For example, in a safety operation measurements can be made of the number of inspections conducted, differences reported, tests made of equipment, number of operations observed, and accidents investigated. These will point up efficiency or inefficiency of personnel, but they will not show whether the activity is moving toward its prime objective: safe operations. To that end, more relevant standards would be reductions in accident rates, reductions in the number of worker-hours lost through accidents, reduction of machine downtime resulting from accidents, and lowered worker's compensation stemming from decreases in the number of accidents.

Time and motion studies are often used in setting standards of measurement, but these are most relevant to repetitive work.

Measurements

Every end product or service can be measured. For some systems the process of setting measurable standards can be frustrating. Each task has its purpose or it should be eliminated. If that purpose can be defined and parsed out clearly, there should be some way of determining when the task has been achieved, efficiently and effectively. Where complete measurement is not desirable, as where destructive tests are used, sampling is appropriate.

Measurement should be accurately recorded and promptly communicated. It should not only inform superiors, it should also assist the subordinates being measured. Reports of measured performance should be relevant to the tasks measured. For example, factory foremen would be interested in cost analysis reports, labor distribution reports, and reports comparing budgeted and actual expenses. They would ordinarily have little interest in profitability forecast reports. Where an operating manager does not have the time to analyze reams of information, exception reporting is useful — only those matters requiring attention are brought to the manager's desk.

Although management may view certain controls and measurements as desirable, employees may regard them less kindly. They may feel that their self-esteem is damaged by controls which identify their personal weaknesses. They may believe the standards and measurements are unfair. They may resent autocratic authority, or they may perceive the controls as conflicting with group norms.

Standards should therefore consider the human factor. They should not be so loose that they present no challenge or so tight as to be unattainable and therefore frustrating. They should be acceptable to subordinates, and acceptability is improved if subordinates participate in setting the standards. For example, an MBO system will not be effective if the superiors alone establish and enforce standards and procedures, because the primary responsibility for exercising control rests with the employees charged with executing the plans. The need for control should be explained to the employees involved, and they should have a say in the standards by which they will be measured. To demonstrate fairness, standards should be reviewed periodically to ensure their continued applicability.

In considering the human factor, thought must be given to whether measurement should be performed by the people involved in the performance or by others. Each has its benefits and drawbacks. Self-measurement may create confidence and trust. It may permit fast feedback and correction, but it may also lead to distortions, concealment, and delays in reporting. Measurement by those not involved in the performance may create hostility and rebellion in those reported on. But, certainly, objective measurement may minimize bias and suspicion of the reported measurements.

Comparisons

Once standards are set and tasks are measured, performance and standards must be compared. Care must be taken to compare items that are alike in terms of time, quantity and quality. Decisions must be made on how often data should be collected and how to spot significant deviations. Continuous comparisons are expensive and objectionable to subordinates. In determining significance, judgment is needed. A simple comparison between two sets of numbers is not enough. The data must be interpreted and evaluated rationally in terms of existing circumstances — the law of the situation.

Evaluations

Evaluation calls for an analysis of the comparisons. It also calls for a look at the standards as well. Were the goals really attainable? Did unanticipated factors completely frustrate the meeting of standards thought reasonable when set? On the other hand, did luck play a part so that under the circumstances the poorest of workers could have met the standards?

In mechanized control situations, the evaluation is relatively simple and reporting is clear. In personnel and other situations calling for mature judgment, the reporting and the resulting action may be slower.

Evaluations should concentrate on the significant exceptions, those that do not conform adequately with the standards. Closely related to the exception principle is concentration on key control points. The points will vary with the enterprise, but these are the areas or functions about which activities tend to cluster or which can create bottlenecks. For example, in certain large manufacturing companies, the president concentrates attention and appraisals on shipments, customers' orders, inventories, production efficiency, and forecasts. Simple ratios can be worked out among key control points to highlight aberrations, focus attention, and conduct appraisals. Reports of comparisons and evaluations should be understandable and useful. They should include what is essential and avoid what is merely interesting.

Correction

Correction means removing the roadblocks that prevent task accomplishment, changing attitudes, and reversing adverse trends. Significant variances require vigorous and immediate action. Effective control cannot tolerate needless delays, endless compromises, or excuses. Continuing and excessive exceptions should not be countenanced.

The people in charge of performance should take the corrective action. For maximum effect, the correction should be accompanied by fixed and individual responsibility. Holding an individual rather than a group responsible improves chances of correction. The best corrective action is remedial action. The root causes should be identified and removed so as to prevent recurrence.

Follow-up

Whenever superiors or systems prescribe corrective action, a means of follow-up should take over. The pressures of an on-going system tend to push corrective action to the side. Effective follow-up sees to it that the need to take corrective action is not overlooked.

Follow-up includes surveillance of the control system itself. No control system can anticipate all possible future events. Employees may omit unintentionally or distort intentionally the feedback provided under the system. Employees may resent the system and seek to subvert it. The "unknown unknowns" may render a system inoperative. Supervisory surveillance is therefore necessary to watch for the undreamed-of aberrations. Internal auditing is useful to determine that data reported is reliable, that the feedback provided is being used, and that corrective action is prompt, adequate, and effective. Further, internal auditors are responsible for examining the standards themselves to see that they are periodically reviewed and are applicable under current conditions.

Approaches to Control

Control can be approached in two ways: imposed control and self-control.

Imposed control is traditional control: The control will measure performance against imposed standards; take corrective action through the people responsible; follow up to see that the people took action and that the action works. But that approach has one serious shortcoming: It comes **after** the performance, not before. Often the corrections are accompanied by disciplinary action. The approach therefore has negative connotations.

An emerging approach that avoids the negative and emphasizes the positive is self-control. It looks to the process of management and the function performed, and it attempts to improve the managerial process rather than to correct individual deviations. Management by objective programs, properly carried out, are good examples of this approach.

Controlling and the Internal Auditor

The internal audit of control systems to determine whether established objectives are being met is discussed in Chapter 3. Under another approach to controlling, useful both to management and the internal auditor, internal auditors determine how well managers exercise the principles of management control in handling their own operations. Here are some of the standards internal auditors can use:

Setting Standards

Provision should be made to establish and disseminate new standards of performance when the old ones are found to be inadequate or ineffective.

The systems of control should provide for feedback of significant information to managers in a timely enough manner to warn them of impending difficulties, as well as to enable them to appraise final results.

Maintaining Standards

Provision should be made to determine periodically that the lines of feedback communication are still open and functioning as intended.

A manager should have an up-to-date documented program that identifies those methods, problems, and conditions that need to be implemented, improved, corrected, or eliminated; a program that shows the status of planned solutions and the corrective action required to meet the organization's objectives and standards.

Continuing efforts should be made to eliminate or reduce the causes of exceptions and deviations rather than accepting such variances as "normal" and covering them with specially designed procedures.

Management should provide for periodic reviews of factors affecting costs of administration and operations and should see that timely and appropriate action will be taken to keep costs consistent with plans and objectives.

Training Personnel

The organization's objectives, standards, policies, procedures, and means of measuring performance should be made known to all affected personnel, and there should be provision periodically to reinforce their understanding and to provide them with the results of the feedback from downstream organizations.

Where existing practices represent interference with plans, provision should be made for prompt reinstruction of personnel.

Prescribing Approvals

Methods should be established for returning to the originator work that does not meet acceptable standards.

When interference with the execution of plans is represented by existing policies and procedures, removing the interference must be subject to the approval of the same authority which prescribed those policies or procedures in the first place.

Establishing Master Controls

Management, in establishing its feedback system, should have brought to its attention only problems of importance, not all the routine actions of subordinates.

Provision should be made for balancing and reconciling control records with subsidiary or detailed records where applicable, bringing variances and their reasons to the attention of appropriate levels of management.

Management should not only provide for reports on all of its operations but also for prompt and effective action on deviations.

Ensuring Compliance

Provision should be made for actual results to be currently evaluated with respect to the planned expectations or objectives, particularly for long-range objectives.

Provision should be made for a clear-cut assignment of responsibility for the prompt expediting and feedback of information to management on variances between established budgets and schedules and actual accomplishments.

Provision should be made for periodic spot checks (in addition to normal monitoring) of work in process and completed work, to ensure conformity with established requirements.

Provision should be made to inform personnel of their failure to comply with prescribed policies and procedures.

Monitoring Processes

Provision should be made for management's attention to be given to exceptions at the most strategic control points in the system, instead of waiting until it is found that the ultimate objective has not been achieved.

Provision should be made for all complaints and recommendations from customers and serviced organizations to be recorded upon receipt, evaluated, acted upon, and answered.

Provision should be made for all incomplete work to be systematically followed up in a timely manner to ensure removal of any interference with its completion.

Periodic status reports of work progress should be prepared for management review to determine whether work is progressing according to plan and whether established milestones are being reached.

The system of control should provide assurance that all off-schedule and missed-schedule jobs are reported promptly to affected management for corrective action and/or establishment of preventive measures against future occurrences.

Conclusion

An emerging form of internal auditing may be termed "management-oriented auditing." It goes beyond verification. Its purpose is to assist managers in carrying out their functions economically, efficiently, and effectively — in essence, to be counsellors of managers. This requires an understanding of the functions and the principles of management. One cannot counsel about a function with which one is unfamiliar. Internal auditors must be as conversant with the functions and the principles of management as any competent manager.

There is more. Almost invariably, every deficiency finding an internal auditor encounters has a root cause in some violation of a sound principle of management. Internal auditors versed in the practice of management need not laboriously test myriad transactions before they recognize the existence of some deep-seated deviations. Becoming alert to management principles and looking for their violation or neglect in systems and procedures can identify deficiencies and guide internal auditors toward the improper transactions. When the deviations are identified, the recommendations to correct the cause are elevated from being transaction-based to being management-based. Those recommendations will focus on the disease rather than on the symptoms.

References

1. L. B. Sawyer, *The Manager and the Modern Internal Auditor — A Problem-Solving Partnership* (New York: AMACOM — A Division of American Management Associations, 1979). p. 3.
2. R. S. Savich, *Internal Audit of the Budget Process* (Orlando, Fla.: The Institute of Internal Auditors, Inc., 1976), p. 1.

3. P. F. Drucker, *Management: Tasks, Responsibilities, Practices* (New York: Harper & Row, 1974). pp. 430, 440.
4. Rensis Likert, *The Human Organization: Its Management and Value* (New York: McGraw-Hill, 1967), pp. 13-24.

Supplementary Reading

Flippo, E. B. and G. M. Munsinger. *Management*. 3rd ed. Boston: Allyn and Bacon, Inc., 1975.

Koontz, Harold and Cyril O'Donnell. *Management: A Systems and Contingency Analysis of Managerial Functions*. 6th ed. New York: McGraw-Hill Book Co., 1976.

Mints, F. E. *Behavioral Patterns in Internal Audit Relationships*. Altamonte Springs, Fla.: The Institute of Internal Auditors, Inc., 1978.

Sawyer, L. B. *The Manager and the Modern Internal Auditor — A Problem-Solving Partnership*. New York: AMACOM — A Division of American Management Associations, 1979.

Terry, G. R. *Principles of Management*. 7th ed. Homewood, Illinois: Richard D. Irwin, Inc., 1977.

For further study

Discussion Problems

1. Explain why the owner-manager has had to give way to the professional manager.

2. Which statement in the introduction to the *Standards for the Professional Practice of Internal Auditing* implies that internal auditors should be conversant with management principles?

3. What are some questions an internal auditor can ask about a department's planning?

4. State a performance goal for a college instructor, a research scientist, and an engineering draftsman.

5. Which of Fayol's principles is violated by the project form of organization? Explain.

6. Describe how people in a personnel department can have both staff and line relationships in the same job position.

7. Describe an instance where an autocratic management approach might be perfectly appropriate in a research and development department composed of top-level scientists.

8. Keith Davis sees the supervisor as, among other things, "the man in the middle." Explain.

9. Self-control has been described as the most desirable form of control. Under what circumstances would imposed control be the preferable approach?

10. Control requires an evaluation of any significant variances between standards and measured performance. When managers evaluate these differences they should also evaluate the standards themselves. Does an internal auditor also have a responsibility to evaluate standards? Justify your answer.

Multiple Choice Problems

1. Which of the following is false? Management principles

a. Are statements based on valid causal relationships.
b. Help improve the outcome of a manager's decisions.
c. Come from beliefs, experiences, experimentation, and various other sources.
d. Are universal in the sense that they are found in all types of organizations.
e. Can be taught to practically all to enable them to manage effectively.

2. In an orientation session for new managers, the following comments were made. Which view is inconsistent with the contingency approach to management?
a. Management can be a very complex process.
b. Management practices can be affected by the technology used to create the final product.
c. Situational variables can explain apparent contradictions in successful managerial responses.
d. Management can be governed by a single set of prescriptive principles which are universally applicable.
e. Environmental differences can force modifications of management practices.

3. A manager is enthusiastic about a system approach to management which an organization recently adopted. Which of the following terms is least descriptive of the systems approach to management?
a. Creative.
b. Analytical.
c. Scientific.
d. Pragmatic.
e. Mechanical.

4. Planning is receiving increased attention by many organizations. Which of the following is true?
a. Long-range planning is usually performed by lower-level personnel.
b. The time devoted to planning is inversely related to the organizational level.
c. Planning requires historical and projected data.
d. The extent of detail in planning information varies directly with the organizational level.
e. Planning documents usually contain greater detail than action reports.

5. Which of the following planning aids is designed to compare actual and expected performance?
a. Taylor charts.
b. PERT charts.
c. Gantt charts.
d. PERT/cost charts.
e. CPM charts.

6. Which of the following is most likely to provide operational guidance for an EDP systems department?
a. Objectives.
b. Goals.
c. Policies.
d. Procedures.
e. None of the above.

7. Which of the following is a requirement for an effective committee?
a. Members should be selected only from those who are currently working on the problem.
b. Scheduling should take precedence over discussion.
c. The committee should have a membership of at least five persons.
d. Members should display a high level of individualism.
e. Decisions should be reached by consensus.

8. The form of organization in which some managers are responsible for planning, scheduling, and cost control

of projects while other managers are responsible for line control is called:

a. Matrix project management.
b. Line project management.
c. Venture team management.
d. Product management.
e. Territory management.

9. In what role is a controller acting when issuing specifications to departments regarding records to keep and reports to submit?

a. Line.
b. Staff service.
c. Staff advisory.
d. Functional.
e. None of the above.

10. Leadership, properly carried out, can best be described as:

a. Carefully following the managerial functions.
b. Achieving objectives.
c. Demonstrating concern for the needs of subordinates.
d. Maintaining a forthright, confident attitude.
e. The art of influencing and stimulating performance.

11. The acceptance by employees of the traditional approach to management is increased by:

a. Clear policy statements.
b. A shortage of jobs in the job market.
c. Participation on committees.
d. A surplus of jobs on the job market.
e. None of the above.

12. Which of the following is associated with the management function of directing?

a. Establishing a philosophy about employees.
b. Establishing congruence of individual needs and organizational needs.
c. Establishing a healthy leadership climate.

d. Group dynamics.
e. All of the above.

13. Which of the following activities is **not** associated with the controlling function?

a. Determining how performance will be evaluated.
b. Establishing a data collection system.
c. Developing management reports.
d. Taking corrective action.
e. Prescribing relationships among operating units.

14. Which of the following would be most likely to strengthen a control system?

a. Control exerted at the lowest practicable level.
b. A centralized flow of information to top management.
c. The use of specialized staff control groups.
d. The establishment of challenging performance standards.
e. Substandard performance publicized as a motivating factor.

15. Systems control is frequently referred to as:

a. Matrix management.
b. Integrated logistics.
c. Cybernetics.
d. Industrial dynamics.
e. Quantitative analysis.

Case Studies

21-1 Organizational Relationships

Dyag Instruments manufactures and assembles diagnostic instruments for the medical profession. The operations manager is responsible for Dyag's two production departments: manufacturing and subassembly, and final assembly. About 50% of the component parts of every diagnostic instrument is purchased from suppliers and assembled by Dyag. All other component parts are manufactured and assembled by Dyag.

The purchased subassemblies are expensive and a critical part of the instruments manufactured. The purchasing department, therefore, reports to the operations manager and to the financial services manager, who are both at the same organizational level.

The diagnostic instruments require very close tolerances in manufacture and assembly. The operations manager created a staff department, engineering services, to see that these tolerances are maintained.

Customers recently returned several defective instruments. Engineering services determined that "inconsistent assembly procedures" during final assembly caused these instruments to malfunction. As a result, the engineering services department wrote a new *Assembly Procedure Manual* and distributed it to the workers in final assembly. Engineering services then directed the implementation of the new procedures. The final assembly department manager also received a copy of the manual for his information.

Required: (1) Prepare an organization chart which reflects the portion of the Dyag organization described above. (2) Comment on the inadequacies of Dyag Instruments' organizational relationships in terms of accountability, authority, and responsibility.

21-2 Budgeting Practices

During the first review of the City of Plainview's public welfare programs by an audit team, Mary Green, a new addition to the city's internal audit staff, was assigned to review the budget formulation activity of the Vocational

Education Department. Green was just out of college and looked forward to the assignment as a means of learning about the city's budget process.

Martin Miller, director of administration of the Vocational Education Department, had the budget formulation responsibility and explained the process to Green as follows:

"The finance officer and I meet about two weeks before the budget is due. We review last year's activity and come up with some preliminary figures. We present these figures in draft form to the director of vocational education who adjusts them and returns them to us. These adjusted figures are sent to the director of finance. His budget officer then makes an across-the-board percentage increase or decrease in the line items to fit the amounts into the city's budget. It is presented to the City Council in that form.

"When the City Council enacts the budget ordinance, we then adjust the amounts by percentages to conform them to the totals for the approved line items as shown in the master line item budget.

"For example, here is the 1980 statement we used for the 1981 budget. Salaries, travel, and contractual items are types of items used." (See Fig. 1.)

Miller then added:

"The department's objective has been to train 100 welders and 50 electricians a year. This training is always useful and pays well at the journeyman level. The secretarial training program is an added objective in response to recent social pressures. We have been trying to get some figures so we can publicize how well we are doing. We will train bricklayers in 1981, because our electrician-training contractor went out of business."

With no further information, Green returned to her desk and started to document her conversation with the director of administration. In addition to identifying the factual material she had received, she planned to write certain comments about the budget system.

Required: Place yourself in Green's situation and write a specific comment about any four of the following which relate to deviations from sound budgeting practices.

1. The sources of budget information.
2. The department's stated objectives.
3. The internal structure of the budget.
4. The validity of the methods used to make adjustments.
5. Consideration of community needs.
6. The use of the budget as a tool to determine the efficiency and effectiveness of operations.

(Example: Assume that one of the listed items on which you plan to comment was "The premises on which the budgets are based." Your comment might then be written as follows: "There was no analysis of the various factors making an impact on the operation, such as social, demographic, and labor phenomena.")

Fig. 1

		1980 Budget	Actual*
Revenues			
Federal Department of Education		$100,000	$125,000
Federal Department of Labor		400,000	450,000
Plainview Dedicated Funds		200,000	200,000
	Total	$700,000	$775,000
Expenditures			
Salaries		$400,000	$400,000
Travel		10,000	15,000
Overhead		50,000	80,000
Contracting Service (Training)			
Welders		100,000	150,000
Electricians		50,000	100,000
Secretarial		75,000	75,000
	Total	$685,000	$820,000

*Projected, based on nine months actual.

Employee and
Management Fraud

Fraud, theft, and embezzlement. The costs of fraud. Impact on both the public and private sectors. Legal fraud and deceit. The elements of "white-collar crime." The environment for fraud. Conditions favoring fraud: pressures, opportunities, traits. The various forms of dishonesty and deceit. Organized crime. Forms of computer crimes. Perpetrators of computer crimes. The internal auditor's responsibility for the prevention and detection of fraud. Standards of due professional care. The need for requisite authority. Detecting dishonest acts. Practices which violate acceptable procedures. Frauds detected by internal auditors. Trend and proportional analyses. Interrogations — the hazards and the methods. Prevention — the preferred course. Deterring frauds. Hiring honest people. Human respect. Minimum means of control. Polygraphs in prevention. Created errors — pros and cons. Publishing company policy on wrongdoing. Management fraud — where it occurs, what it is, why it occurs, what to do about it, what its symptoms are, and how to control it.

Nature

Wrongdoing by deceit, in the public and private sectors, goes by many names. It has been called fraud, white-collar crime, and embezzlement, among other things. None of these embraces the full spectrum of deceptive and illegal practices encountered in business and practice.

Fraud, briefly stated, is a false representation or concealment of a material fact to induce someone to part with something of value. This definition does not include employee peculations, extortion, or the conversion to one's own use of assets already in the custody of the wrongdoer.

White-collar crime has been defined as a wrongful act or series of wrongful acts committed by nonphysical means, and by concealment or guile, to obtain money or property, to avoid the payment or loss of money or property, or to obtain business or personal advantage.[1] But many forms of wrongdoing engaged in by employees and managers are not crimes and many are perpetuated by people who do not fit the category of white-collar workers.

Embezzlement is the unlawful conversion to personal use of property which is lawfully in the custody of the wrongdoer. This is a crime with a narrow meaning. It does not include such crimes as bribery, theft, fraud against the government, obtaining property by threats of violence or disclosure, or the like.

These three terms have special meanings for the ordinary layman reader which are more useful and have greater impact than the broader terms *deceit, wrongdoing,* and *impropriety.* In this chapter, the gamut of wrong-by-deceit in the public and private sectors shall be referred to as employee and management fraud. It is distinguishable from outright theft by its active concealment of the wrongdoing.

Impact

The impact of employee and management fraud is staggering both in terms of dollar costs and effect on the victims. In 1974 the U.S. Chamber of Commerce calculated the financial cost at $41 billion annually. That amount did not take into account the cost to the public of price-fixing illegalities and industrial espionage.[2] Amounts of such magnitude dwarf into insignificance the costs of common crimes. The trauma transcends pecuniary losses. Consumer frauds undercut the ability of people to provide for food and shelter. Phony trade and occupational schools and talent agencies dash hopes for improvement. Investment frauds rob the needy of their nest eggs. Embezzlements, the most common of the white-collar crimes, may collapse the businesses in which the embezzlers are employed. Pension funds are looted. Assets can be dissipated by bribes, insider dealings, and conflicts of interest. Fake insurance claims, credit card frauds, and gigantic frauds — like the Equity Funding scandal — raise the cost of goods and services to the consumer. Computer frauds have rocked businesses to their foundations. The increasing sophistication of organized criminal syndicates makes businesses vulnerable to extortion assaults. Internal business corruption has led to increases in the frequency of large-scale stockholder suits against officers and directors of corporations and has escalated the cost of insurance to protect officers and directors.

Local, state, and federal governments are also victims. They are cheated in the collection of taxes. They lose huge sums through procurements tainted by bribery and collusion. They are victimized by corruptly negotiated contracts, by favoritism with respect to zoning ordinances, and by bribes to obtain franchises to do business. They are mulched by defrauders attacking welfare, subsistence, medical, food stamp, housing, educational, and other programs directed toward helping the needy.

Because of the enormous sums involved and the potentially disastrous effects of fraud and associated wrongdoing, internal auditors should put these unsavory activities under the spotlight of their audit surveillance.

Elements of Fraud

Fraud can take many forms. It may result from an intentional misrepresentation — the suggestion that something is true, when it is not, by someone who knows it is not. It may be a negligent misrepresentation — the assertion as a fact of that which is not true by one who has no reasonable ground for believing it to be true. It includes concealment — the suppression of a fact by one who is bound to disclose it. It also includes false promises — a promise made with no intention of fulfilling it.

The elements of legal fraud, or deceit as it was called in common law, are as follows:[3]

A false representation of a material fact, or in some cases an opinion;

Made with the knowledge of its falsity or without sufficient knowledge on the subject to warrant a representation (often referred to as "scienter");

That person acting upon the representation;

To his or her damage.

The elements of so-called white-collar crime are somewhat different. These have been described as follows:[4]

Intent to commit a wrongful act or to achieve a purpose inconsistent with law or public policy.

Disguise of purpose through falsities and misrepresentations employed to accomplish the scheme.

Reliance by the offender on the ignorance or carelessness of the victim.

Voluntary action by the victim to assist the offender as a result of the deceit practiced.

Concealment of the crime.

The Federal Bureau of Investigation defines white-collar crime as "those illegal acts characterized by deceit, concealment, violation of trust, and not dependent upon the application or threat of physical force or violence. Such crimes are committed to obtain money, property, or services; or to secure personal or business advantage."[5]

Environment

Employee and management fraud is a noxious weed which flourishes best in a permissive climate where the seeds of fraud are helped, even invited, to blossom and mature.

The environment within an enterprise is generally developed and maintained by senior management and the board of directors. To deter fraud the environment should be a rigorous one. Management should set forth clearly in written policies its commitment to fair dealing, its position on conflicts of interest, its requirement that only honest employees be hired, its insistence on strong internal controls that are well policed, and its resolve to prosecute the guilty.

Too often, members of senior management cannot bring themselves to believe that any of their people could conceivably commit dishonest acts. When evidence of dishonesty is brought before them, they may refuse to believe it — they refuse to think ill of some favored employee. Management's negligence or refusal to be realistic can generate a climate for fraud to germinate. Climate is one of the key conditions under which fraud grows. It is generally believed that three conditions combine to move people to commit fraudulent acts:

Situational pressures experienced by employees of enterprises. Employees may be in debt or may be pressured (externally or internally) to improve their positions. The employees of companies faced with lost sales, competition, rigorous schedules or specifications, harsh regulations, or falling profits, may do what is illegal or unethical to reverse their positions.

Uncontrolled access to assets, coupled with management's indifference. One of the strongest deterrents to employee and management fraud is the certainty of detection and punishment. Strong controls and monitoring increase that certainty.

Personality traits undermining personal integrity. Some people have a tendency to take the crooked path. When others see no obstacles placed in that path, they are inclined to take it too.

Neither managers nor internal auditors can do much about an individual's situational pressures. These are not usually communicated readily. But managers can reduce the perceived opportunities by installing appropriate controls; and internal auditors can evaluate the adequacy and effectiveness of these controls.

One of the most effective ways of deterring dishonest conduct is by not hiring dishonest employees. The least management can do is to try to verify backgrounds. Too often personnel departments fail to check references or get in touch with former employers, even when employees are hired for sensitive positions. Senior management should insist on proper hiring practices; internal auditors should see that those practices are carried out as intended.

Organized Crime

Employees may be induced to steal under the direction of organized crime. One method used to rob a company is to have extra cartons, rolls, or other merchandise loaded on a truck of a given purchaser. Organized crime takes the difference. The criminals refer to employees who help steal disposable merchandise as "10 percenters." The employees receive 10% of the value of the stolen goods.

Organized crime obtains lucrative gains from stolen credit cards. In one company, strict control was maintained over credit cards from the time the blanks were purchased until the cards were sent to the post office for mailing to customers. A postal employee diverted the credit cards to an organized crime mailing address for the purpose of fraud. Companies in the credit card business also suffer losses by reason of counterfeit credit cards. A comparison of identification numbers with a central record to detect duplication is an important form of protection.[6]

Computer Crimes

Computer crimes are in their ascendancy. The methods and means are legion (see Chapter 11). Some of the methods involve:

Unauthorized intervention in consoles and remote terminals.

Fraudulent changes in program routines.[7]

Manipulating input data.[8]

Improper actions by systems programmers, computer operators, maintenance personnel, and users.[9]

Responsibility

Historical Perspectives

In early years, the attention of auditors was directed primarily to the detection of erroneous and fraudulent transactions. By and large theirs was a policing action. Their function was protective and detective rather than constructive. No formal standards had been established for internal auditors which imposed a responsibility to prevent and detect fraud. But the subject had been addressed by the courts with respect to an external auditor's responsibility. As far back as nineteenth century England, the courts applied the rule of reason: What can be expected of a reasonably proficient auditor under the circumstances. The same rule is equally applicable to internal auditors.

In the case of *In re London and General Bank* (No. 2), (1895, 2 Ch. 673), an auditor was required to pay to the Official Receiver of the London & General Bank, whose affairs were being concluded, the amount of certain dividends paid out on the basis of the auditor's certified balance sheet which did not properly state the provision for bad debts. Had provision properly been made, the dividends would never have been declared. In reversing the trial court and holding the auditor blameless with respect to one of the dividends, the appellate court said:

An auditor . . . is not bound to do more than exercise reasonable care and skill in making enquiries and investigations. He is not an insurer . . . Such I take to be the duty of the auditor: he must be honest — that is he must not certify what he does not believe to be true, and he must take reasonable care and skill before he believes that what he certifies is true.

In the same vein, the court spoke as follows in the case of *In re Kingston Cotton Mill Co., Limited (No. 2), (1896 2 Ch. 279)*:

It is the duty of an auditor to bring to bear on the work he has to perform that skill, care and caution which a reasonably competent, careful, cautious auditor would use . . . An auditor is not bound to be a detective, or, as was said, to approach his work with suspicion or with a forgone conclusion that there is something wrong. He is a watchdog, but not a bloodhound . . . If there is anything calculated to excite suspicion he should probe it to the bottom, but in the absence of anything of that kind, he is only bound to be reasonably cautious and careful . . .

Standards

Nevertheless, for years internal auditors spent most of their time looking for suspicious transactions in financial records. Then came the swing to operational auditing. The desire to show the constructive side of internal auditing resulted in a downplaying of attention to fraud. Then the business volcano erupted. In the lava flow that scorched a host of companies were such major frauds as Equity Funding and National Student Marketing. The liability of corporate executives, board members, and external auditors grew heavier. Heads began to turn to the internal auditor — the so-called "eyes and ears of management." The internal auditor's responsibility for the prevention and detection of wrongdoing had to be reconsidered. It had to be set forth with particularity. This coincided with the drafting of the *Standards for the Professional Practice of Internal Auditing.* In Section 280, Due Professional Care, the drafters set forth these responsibilities:

Internal auditors should exercise due professional care in performing internal audits.

.01 Due professional care calls for the application of the care and skill expected of a reasonably prudent and competent internal auditor in the same or similar circumstances. Professional care should, therefore, be appropriate to the complexities of the audit being performed. In exercising due professional care, internal auditors should be alert to the possibility of intentional wrongdoing, errors and omissions, inefficiency, waste, ineffectiveness, and conflicts of interest. They should also be alert to those conditions and activities where irregularities are most likely to occur. In addition, they should identify inadequate controls and recommend improvements to promote compliance with acceptable procedures and practices.

.02 Due care implies reasonable care and competence, not infallibility or extraordinary performance. Due care requires the auditor to conduct examinations and verifications to a reasonable extent, but does not require detailed audits of all transactions. Accordingly, the internal auditor cannot give absolute assurance that noncompliance or irregularities do not exist. Nevertheless, the possibility of material irregularities or noncompliance should be considered whenever the internal auditor undertakes an internal auditing assignment.

.03 When an internal auditor suspects wrongdoing, the appropriate authorities within the organization should be informed. The internal auditor may recommend whatever investigation is considered necessary in the circumstances. Thereafter, the auditor should follow up to see that the internal auditing department's responsibilities have been met.

These standards set responsibilities not much different from the rules laid down in the English court cases in the nineteenth century. Internal auditors are monitors of their enterprise's control systems; they are not insurers against fraud, embezzlement, theft, and noncompliance with procedures. They must exercise ordinary prudence when devising audit programs and carrying them out. They are not responsible for anticipating or unearthing every devious, hidden defect that escaped an examination carried out in a professional manner.

Some frauds would be impossible to detect by even the best auditors. These are forgery, collusion, and unrecorded transactions. Auditors cannot be charged with being handwriting experts. When skillfully prepared false documents are presented to auditors who have no reason to doubt their validity, it is reasonable for auditors to rely on them. When a system of control depends on separation of duties, the auditor has no way of knowing that the people charged with those duties have conspired to subvert the system. Neither can they be expected to detect collusion between people inside and outside the enterprise. Acceptable auditing techniques cannot provide assurance that there are no unrecorded transactions. How could auditors discover an unrecorded payable unless they requested confirmations from all potential creditors? Absolute certainty is no more an attainable goal of auditing than it is of any other professional endeavor.[10]

Yet the responsibility remains to do more than accept representations from others. Certainly, an auditor who carefully reviews a reasonable sample of transactions cannot be held responsible for subsequently discovered fraudulent documents in the transactions not examined. And, unless the auditors have reason for suspicion, they may accept the truth of the representations made to them and the genuineness of the documents they inspect. But internal auditors are responsible for discoverable fraud — discoverable by a reasonably skilled and prudent auditor — and for any looseness of the system of control. Where suspicion is aroused or there are reasonable grounds for suspicion, internal auditors are responsible for going behind the documents, behind the numbers, to track down improprieties. The comments of the court in *State Street Trust Company* vs. *Ernst* about the responsibility of accountants has equal applicability to internal auditors.[11]

> A representation certified as true knowledge of the accountants when knowledge there is none, a reckless misstatement, or an opinion based on grounds so flimsy as to lead to the conclusion that there was no genuine belief in its truth are all sufficient upon which to base liability. A refusal to see the obvious, a failure to investigate the doubtful, if sufficiently gross, may furnish evidence leading to an inference of fraud . . . In other words, heedlessness and reckless disregard of consequences may take the place of deliberate intention.

The dangers of fraud are too great, the risks too high to accept a passive role. As the *Standards* say, the internal auditor must be **alert.** Hence, when an audit finding reveals the breakdown of controls, it is only the beginning of the deficiency's development. If approval requirements are not followed, if improperly developed shipping documents destroyed the control over merchandise, if the billing of invoices was in arrears, if competitive bids were not obtained, if checks received in the mailroom were not listed, if one who maintains records also has control over the recorded assets, then the internal auditor should be alerted to the possibility of intentional wrongdoing and start digging further.

Internal auditors may not merely report these derelictions to operating management and move on. First of all, management may not be particularly control-oriented. Second, unit managers can very well be involved in wrongdoing themselves. Third, managers often find it very difficult to believe that the very people they trusted could possibly be guilty of intentional wrongdoing. Hence the need to follow the dictates of the *Standards,* when fraud is evident or suspected, that "the appropriate authorities within the organization should be informed," and that, "thereafter, the auditor should follow up to see that the internal auditing department's responsibilities have been met."

Authority

Responsibility for fraud detection can extend only as far as the authority to probe potential areas of fraud. Internal auditors cannot be expected to roam far afield if they are shackled by restrictions. Just as important, internal auditors cannot properly be held responsible for an obligation rightfully imposed on management or to seek the authority to meet such an obligation.[12]

Management sets the moral climate in which the enterprise functions.

Management provides the organization to accomplish its plans and follow its policies.

Management establishes and maintains internal controls.

Management determines the cost vs. control ratios, keeping in mind the equation: Exposure minus safeguards = risks.

Management establishes the personnel policies of the organization, the qualifications of people, and the working conditions.

Management determines the accounting systems and the records to be kept.

Management has the responsibility for establishing and maintaining the lines of communications and systems of reporting within the organization and for knowing what is going on.

The internal auditor will be responsible for determining whether all these actions have been taken and whether they were carried out efficiently and effectively. But internal auditors can make those determinations only if management authorizes them to do so. Responsibility may not properly be imposed if coequal authority is not assigned.

Different companies take different approaches to this responsibility.[13] At a large bank holding company the internal auditors refer all suspected frauds to lawyers who are members of the internal audit unit. A separate security section of the internal auditing department in an insurance company conducts fraud investigations. A special auditing section in a public utility deals both with fraud investigations and with special auditing assignments not a part of the regular audit program.

Delegating authority for fraud investigations and organizing for them become more and more important as wrongdoing increases and as technology becomes more complex. Electronic fund transfer systems and remote terminals will increase exposure to fraud and escalate the hazards.

In some companies, responsibility and authority have been made clear by high-level policy pronouncements.[14]

In one company the general auditor is to be notified immediately of any irregularities found by his own auditors or by any other person. He then is authorized to decide whether to investigate or not to investigate, depending on the potential losses and recoveries. If investigation is warranted, he will notify senior management of the fact and use either local personnel or recommend the use of outside investigators or law enforcement agencies.

In another company the audit manager is assigned responsibility for the fraud investigation, is authorized to direct the procedures, and is exclusively responsible for substantiating facts and informing the proper authorities.

If internal auditors learn that top management in their enterprise are committing fraudulent acts, they should have the authority, clearly spelled out, to consult with immediate supervision, outside directors, or public accountants. Without this specific authority, they would be — with impunity — unable to comply with Article II of the internal auditor's Code of Ethics. Members, in holding the trust of their employer, shall exhibit loyalty in all matters pertaining to the affairs of the employer or to whomever they may be rendering a service. **However, members shall not knowingly be a party to any illegal or improper activity.** (Emphasis supplied.)

Hence, if internal auditors are to be held responsible for the investigation of potential wrongdoing at all levels in the enterprise, they should be authorized by the board of directors to carry out the following duties:[15]

Review and comment on annual reports from managers at all levels in the enterprise responsible for authorizing the payment of funds.

Audit all consulting arrangements and evaluate both their documentation and justification.

Analyze the enterprise's procedures and practices for opening and maintaining bank accounts. Recommend any needed controls.

Test the documentation supporting financial reports.

Monitor compliance with the company's record-retention policies.

Ask managers whether there have been any illegal political contributions or questionable practices.

Monitor the enterprise's conflict-of-interest policy, questioning an employee's possible relations with suppliers, contractors, and customers, including family alliances and outside business dealings.

Detection

The Difficulties

A head teller in a bank managed to take more than $1 million over a three-year period by manipulating the bank's computer. The bank's normal internal controls did not detect the defalcations. He was apprehended simply because Federal agents, investigating the activities of a known gambling place, found he was gambling as much as $30,000 a day. By following him they found out where he was getting the money. The detection was by happenstance, not design. Some losses based on dishonesty escaped as many as 15 examinations by independent public accountants. Others remained undiscovered for as long as 25 years despite regular state and federal examiners' efforts.[16]

An auditing firm analyzed 100 selected losses resulting from embezzlement and it found that only 29% of the losses were found by auditors:[17]

Means of Discovery	Percent
Internal checks	11
Management inquiries	16
Public accountants and internal auditors	29
Plain luck	36
Unknown	8
	100

If internal auditors are to be more successful in detecting fraud, they will have to develop a greater awareness of how it occurs and why. The first step is to devote more time determining what the systems of control are and how they are established by prescribed procedures. Then the auditors must determine whether procedures are violated in actual practice. Some examples of fraud are as follows:[18]

Cash Receipts

An analysis of 485 cases involving losses of all sizes showed that 333, over 68%, consisted of embezzlement of cash receipts. Mechanical bookkeeping devices are intended to prevent thefts of cash receipts but they do not always work. In one supermarket the cash register stubs usually checked out perfectly, but not all else was perfect. The supermarket chain had equipped the store with six cash registers. Seven, however, were in use. The seventh was the property of the store manager and his assistant. They had set up their own checkout counter. Their share-the-wealth scheme defied detection for 27 months. Meanwhile the extra cash register funnelled $70,000 into the pockets of the conspirators.

Mail

Checks received by mail should be under the supervision of a responsible official other than a cashier or bookkeeper. A machine company in Michigan sustained a loss totaling $117,000 because no control was maintained over incoming mail. The defaulter took one or two checks daily over a period of five years. Accounts receivable had never been properly verified.

Deliveries

Losses involving deliveries are difficult to control because of collusion between people inside and outside the enterprise. Drivers should never fill their own orders. A weighmaster conspired with junk dealers to share in the proceeds of scrap he gave them for which they did not have to pay. He inflated the listed weight of each truck by 200 pounds, loading them with that amount of "extra" scrap. This scrap was hauled away in the dealers' trucks.

Detected Frauds

These three defalcations had not necessarily been detected by internal auditors. Such things usually come to light when the towering fraud collapses of its own weight, when somebody blows the whistle, or when pure chance occasions discovery. Yet some cases have been brought to light by alert auditors who could spot the signals and run down the evidence. Here are some samples.

Purchasing

By using computer analyses, internal auditors were able to highlight suspicious aberrations pointing to fraud by a purchasing agent. The analyses showed that many identical small orders were placed with one supplier. The sequence of invoice numbers indicated that the supplier had few if any other customers. The supplier received an unusually large portion of the number and value of the orders for the commodities supplied. Following through on these indicators the internal auditors were able to obtain evidence of a purchasing fraud. [19]

Conflict of Interest

Open and friendly communications with operating employees can produce useful information. One employee in a department store confided to the internal auditor that there were significant problems in a custom-decorating department.

Investigation confirmed that the manager of the department owned a local drapery company that the department store used to fabricate drapery. The manager was paid for a 50-hour week but spent 30 of these hours working for his own company. The manager used drapery and lining belonging to the department store for his other accounts. Custom-decorating supplies that should have been furnished by the fabricator were improperly billed to the department store.

The manager admitted to his defalcations. The estimated loss amounted to about $45,000. [20]

Inventory Sheets

A sharp-eyed internal auditor observed that some pencil impressions on inventory sheets were darker than others. For example, the first 1 in the number 114 was darker than the other two numbers; the number 12 appeared to have been altered to 42; the last 0 in the number 300 appeared darker. A test of inventories disclosed 14 items instead of 114, 12 items instead of 42, and 30 items instead of 300. The inventory clerk admitted to padding the inventory in the amount of $7,600 to cover mistakes. [21]

False Invoices

A relatively small company used a janitorial service for some years. One day the owner of the janitorial service told the company's head janitor he was discontinuing the service. The head janitor decided to take on the work himself without canceling the contract. He had a printer run off copies of the invoices used by the janitorial service. Each month he mailed an invoice for $1,000 to accounts payable, using the former janitorial service's name but his own address. Accounts payable sent the invoice to him for his approval. He was happy to do so. He opened a bank account in the name of the janitorial service to which he deposited the checks. He thus received $1,000 a month for 13 years — $156,000 — until he was caught. A purchasing procedure requiring annual renegotiation of all such contracts and blanket purchase orders would have limited the fraud considerably. [22]

Segregation of Duties

A bookkeeper in a foreign subsidiary was considered a jewel of an employee. A grateful management had given her several salary increases for her ambition and willingness to take on additional jobs. At the time of the audit she was handling accounts receivable, issuing monthly statements, preparing the accounts receivable trial balance, handling the checking account, making all bank deposits, and acting as full-time cashier. A confirmation of customers' accounts disclosed the feet of clay. She had been taking all currency brought into the office by small accounts and covering them with payments made by large and very active accounts. Shortages in these large accounts were covered by payments made by other large accounts so that no account balance ever became delinquent. At the end of each month she sent statements to the customers which showed the payments they had actually made. But her trial balance was inflated by the amount she had taken. Hence it agreed with the general ledger in the home office. At the time the defalcation was discovered the bookkeeper had taken over $85,000.[23]

These are drops in an ocean of wrongdoing. For every defalcation revealed an untold number remain concealed. No audit activity, no matter how feverish, can be calculated to bring all wrongdoing to light. The possibility of detecting fraud increases with auditor awareness of where fraud may occur, with the use of modern techniques, and with an inquisitive audit approach that runs down every suspicious condition.

Awareness

Auditors should be aware of the kinds of fraud being practiced. Exhibit 22-1 lists forty common forms of fraud. These run the gamut of pilfering stamps for small amounts to dealing with favored suppliers who may increase contract prices by huge amounts and give kickbacks to a fraudulent purchasing agent. Exhibit 22-2 lists the telltale signs that should raise suspicions in the minds of internal auditors — from the open and constant borrowing of money from other employees to the surreptitious rewriting of records under the guise of making them look neat.

Exhibit 22-1.   FORTY COMMON FORMS OF FRAUD

1. Pilfering stamps.
2. Stealing merchandise, tools, supplies, and other items of equipment.
3. Removing small amounts from cash funds and registers.
4. Failing to record sales of merchandise, and pocketing the cash.
5. Creating overages in cash funds and registers by under-recording.
6. Overloading expense accounts or diverting advances to personal use.
7. Lapping collections on customers' accounts.
8. Pocketing payments on customers' accounts, issuing receipts on scraps of paper or in self-designed receipt books.

Exhibit 22-1. (Cont.)

9. Collecting an account, pocketing the money, and charging it off; collecting charged-off accounts and not reporting.
10. Charging customers' accounts with cash stolen.
11. Issuing credit for false customer claims and returns.
12. Failing to make bank deposits daily, or depositing only part of the money.
13. Altering dates on deposit slips to cover stealing.
14. Making round sum deposits — attempting to catch up by end of month.
15. Carrying fictitious extra help on payrolls, or increasing rates or hours.
16. Carrying employees on payroll beyond actual severance dates.
17. Falsifying additions on payrolls; withholding unclaimed wages.
18. Destroying, altering, or voiding cash sales tickets and pocketing the cash.
19. Withholding cash sales receipts by using false charge accounts.
20. Recording unwarranted cash discounts.
21. Increasing amounts of petty-cash vouchers and/or totals in accounting for disbursements.
22. Using personal expenditure receipts to support false paid-out items.
23. Using copies of previously used original vouchers, or using a properly approved voucher of the prior year by changing the date.
24. Paying false invoices, either self-prepared or obtained through collusion with suppliers.
25. Increasing amounts of suppliers' invoices through collusion.
26. Charging personal purchases to company through misuse of purchase orders.
27. Billing stolen merchandise to fictitious accounts.
28. Shipping stolen merchandise to an employee or relative's home.
29. Falsifying inventories to cover thefts or delinquencies.
30. Seizing checks payable to the company or to suppliers.
31. Raising cancelled bank checks to agree with fictitious entries.
32. Inserting fictitious ledger sheets.
33. Causing erroneous footings of cash receipts and disbursement books.
34. Deliberately confusing postings to control and detail accounts.
35. Selling waste and scrap materials and pocketing proceeds.
36. "Selling" door keys or the combinations to safes or vaults.
37. Creating credit balances on ledgers and converting to cash.
38. Falsifying bills of lading and splitting with carrier.
39. Obtaining blank checks (unprotected) and forging the signature.
40. Permitting special prices or privileges to customers, or granting business to favored suppliers, for "kickbacks."

Exhibit 22-2. TWENTY DANGER SIGNS OF EMBEZZLEMENT

1. Borrowing small amounts from fellow employees.
2. Placing personal checks in change funds — undated, postdated — or requesting others to "hold" checks.
3. Personal checks cashed and returned for irregular reasons.
4. Collectors or creditors appearing at the place of business, and excessive use of telephone to "stall off" creditors.
5. Placing unauthorized I.O.U's in change funds, or prevailing on others in authority to accept I.O.U's for small, short-term loans.
6. Inclination toward covering up inefficiencies or "plugging" figures.
7. Pronounced criticism of others, endeavoring to divert suspicion.
8. Replying to questions with unreasonable explanations.
9. Gambling in any form beyond ability to stand the loss.
10. Excessive drinking and nightclubbing or associating with questionable characters.
11. Buying or otherwise acquiring through "business" channels expensive automobiles and extravagant household furnishings.
12. Explaining a higher standard of living as money left from an estate.
13. Getting annoyed at reasonable questioning.
14. Refusing to leave custody of records during the day; working overtime regularly.
15. Refusing to take vacations and shunning promotions for fear of detection.
16. Constant association with, and entertainment by, a member of a supplier's staff.
17. Carrying an unusually large bank balance, or heavy buying of securities.
18. Extended illness of self or family, usually without a plan of debt liquidation.
19. Bragging about exploits, and/or carrying unusual amounts of money.
20. Rewriting records under the guise of neatness in presentation.

Indicators

Other indicators can be developed by experienced auditors. These come in the form of trend and proportional analyses.[24]

Trend Analysis

Trend analysis is a diagnostic tool. The auditor charts operating data for prior years to evaluate the reasonableness of current income or expense. Here are some examples:

An auditor charted sales and freight costs for a period of seven years. Sales had increased by 130%. But outbound freight — which had a direct relationship to sales — was up by 300%. The auditor checked freight bills for several months and found they did not add up to the inflated amount. Investigation disclosed that amounts purportedly for freight had been stolen.

An auditor charted sales to customers and sales to employees. The first was increasing dramatically, mirroring the company's excellent growth. The sales to employees were decreasing. Investigation disclosed no control over sales to employees. The office manager had been pocketing a good deal of the cash received from employees.

Proportional Analysis

Proportional analysis, like trend analysis, is also a diagnostic tool. It is a method which appraises certain income and expenses by relating them to other income and expenses. For example, the cost of shipping cartons should bear a proportional relationship to the number of units sold and shipped.

One auditor, within a few hours after his arrival at a brewery, discovered that the quantity of hops charged to costs was twice the amount necessary to produce the annual output of beer. Investigation disclosed that the thief was the treasurer. He was paying for hops delivered to another brewery in which he had an interest.

Some proportional comparisons are based on ratios from other organizations or on industry averages. Trade associations often compile average costs for the information of their members. Several universities compile and issue valuable studies about certain industries. Often personal experience provides indicators of what is reasonable or unreasonable.

A new manager took charge of a business and one of his first acts was to compare expense ratios with statistics compiled during his previous employment in the same industry. The comparisons revealed excessive payroll costs. Investigation showed that a cashier had been stealing $200 to $900 each week and concealing the thefts by overstating the totals of weekly payrolls.

Internal auditors must be cautious in using these analyses. Variables may enter into the calculations — such as a great deal of overtime pay in one period and none in others. Moreover, most of these ratios are limited to relating only two variables to each other. But used cautiously, such analyses may provide useful indicators with this additional caveat. Trend and proportional analyses do not produce substantive evidence. Like a divining rod in the hands of a dowser seeking water, these analyses merely show where to dig.

Interrogations

The Hazards

Once a serious wrongdoing is suspected, and after the evidence is gathered, the suspect will have to be confronted and interrogated. This can be hazardous to the interrogator and to his or her company. Employees suspected of theft or fraud have certain common law and statutory rights. If these are infringed upon — whether or not the employees are guilty — the suspects have a perfect right to sue the interrogator and the company. Here are some of the legal dangers:

Libel and Slander

An accused employee can sue in a civil action if the employer/defendant has made defamatory utterances. Libel is a written defamation. Slander is an oral defamation. A suit for defamation can be brought if:

The utterances by the employer/defendant contained defamatory words calculated to injure the employee/plaintiff's business reputation or cause him or her to be regarded with scorn or contempt.

The defamatory words were communicated to someone other than the plaintiff/employee.

The employee/plaintiff was actually damaged, losing money as a result of the defamation. The law states that some utterances are so defamatory that damage is conclusively presumed — they are libelous or slanderous per se.

Sometimes the truth of the defamatory words is no defense; the employer/defendant would have to show that the utterance was not communicated out of malice. Hence, open accusations should be avoided. To a certain extent internal auditors' communications are privileged when they are justified or necessary under the circumstances for the performance of legitimate duties of the person (auditor) communicating the defamatory words. But an action of slander or libel can be brought if the communication of suspicion of a crime goes beyond that justified for investigation or for notification to management.

Thus, suspicions should not be broadcast. Written reports should be kept to a minimum and labeled "Personal and Confidential." It should be remembered that dictating a report to a secretary may be a "communication" within the meaning of libel statutes. Unnecessary "publications" of defamatory statements can be construed as being malicious or vindictive.

False Imprisonment

An employer can be sued for false arrest or false imprisonment when he or she unreasonably restrains an employee's freedom of mobility. The restraint need not be a physical touching or a locking of a person in a room. Intimidating plaintiff-employees or telling them they cannot leave the room or **even leave the city** has been held to constitute false imprisonment. Indeed, just causing great inconvenience can be the basis for a civil action. In one case, draining water from the employee's car radiator was considered false imprisonment. The employee could have emerged from the car, but he could not have taken it with him. No extensive restraint is necessary. According to one authority: "The imprisonment need not be for more than an appreciable length of time and it is not necessary that any damage result from it, since the tort is complete with even a brief restraint of the plaintiff's freedom."[25]

Malicious Prosecution

This action — also called malicious use of process or abuse of process — arises from the groundless institution of criminal or civil proceedings against the employee so as to cause damage. A suit against the employer can be brought when these elements of the civil wrong exist: The employer causes a criminal prosecution or a civil suit to be brought against an employee. The employer is motivated by malice. (The absence of probable cause for the suit is proof of malice.) The employee is acquitted of the criminal charge or prevails in the civil suit. And the employee suffers damage to his or her person, property, or reputation.

It has been held that probable cause can be established by proof of good-faith reliance on the advice of counsel. A good rule for internal auditors to follow is to seek advice of counsel before proceeding with charges.

Compounding a Felony

The law in the United States provides that the right to punish or to forgive a criminal is reserved to the state. Defrauded employers cannot take those rights upon themselves. Agreeing for a consideration not to prosecute a criminal is itself a crime. It is called compounding a felony and can result in legal punishment for employer, auditor, or both. In one state, for example, it is punishable by fines and maximum prison terms of three to five years.[26] The elements of the crime are as follows: A crime actually committed by one person; and the receipt of something of value by another; under an agreement not to prosecute for the crime, or to limit or handicap such a prosecution.

An employer may lawfully accept restoration of the amounts lost as a result of fraud or theft, but the employer may not lawfully bargain for the restoration by telling the employee no prosecution will take place. Consider this not unlikely scenario:

An employee defrauds an employer. The employee gives the employer a note promising to make good the loss. The employee is terminated. The note, or an installment, comes due; but the employee does not pay. The wrathful employer sues on the note. The ex-employee, to whom the employer was quite benevolent, defends the suit by now claiming that the employer compounded a felony — that the employer and the internal auditor who participated in the agreement should go to jail for their offense. The fact that the employer did not inform the police or prosecute the employee lends credence to the employee's claim of compounding a felony. Any determination not to prosecute an employee for fraud, theft, or other illegal actions should be under advice of counsel.

Confessions

Confessions are not the most trustworthy forms of evidence. They can be repudiated in court by showing mistake, bewilderment, or the fear of the interrogators; hallucination that the defendant thought he or she had committed a crime when actually they had not; or coercion through brutality, threats, prolonged questioning, or any form of intimidation.

In order that a statement may constitute a confession, it must be made voluntarily after the offense, and it must be of such a nature that no inference other than the guilt of the confessor may be drawn from the confession.

A confession should be distinguished from an admission. A confession is a complete acknowledgement of guilt of a crime. An admission is any other statement by the defendant of a fact which is relevant to the charge and which is offered against the defendant as evidence of the fact.

Questioning Suspects

With all these hazards in mind — libel, slander, false imprisonment, and the rest — if internal auditors still wish to question suspects and witnesses, they should follow certain procedures.

Interviews with suspected employees should be conducted in private. The tone should never be heated. It should never be accusatory. It should proceed as an even-tempered, sympathetic search for information. It should provide the suspect with an opportunity to explain and make a clean breast of things. Often this is really what guilt-ridden wrongdoers want.

Thus, internal auditors should be patient, persistent, and pleasantly conversational. They should listen as long as the employee wishes to talk. The interviewing internal auditor should be sympathetic and understanding. After all, the employee may not be a professional thief, but someone who started down the wrong path through a mistake which gradually turned into a pattern. Besides, the employer may have contributed by poor controls which put temptation in the way of the employee.

Internal auditors should make sure the documentary proof is absolutely airtight. Never ask a question to which you do not know the true answer. Never let the employee know exactly how much evidence has been gathered about the fraud or theft. The questioner should always give the impression that additional evidence is in reserve.

The interviewer should be in possession of the facts and the nuances of the case, should possess an inquisitive, logical mind, and be capable of objective, immediate evaluation of what is being said. Unless the internal auditors qualify, they are advised to give the task of questioning to a professional.

Prevention

The Better Part of Valor

How much better it is not to lose something than to have to go to the trouble of finding it after it is lost. How much better to prevent a person from stealing than to detect the theft, recover the loss, and jail the miscreant. How much better to remove temptation than to punish someone for having been tempted. How much better for the internal auditor to be regarded as a constructive consultant than as a policeman or a prosecutor.

For these reasons and more, this author feels that it is far more profitable for internal auditors to concentrate on constructive and preventive services for their enterprises than to neglect these and be forced into the role of a detective or bloodhound. It is far better to require the installation of adequate and effective controls than to track down miscreants whose thefts went undetected by inadequate controls.

Every embezzler starts playing the game fully aware that he or she may be caught in due course. Those odds must be increased to the point where, no matter how much of a gambler the potential thief, defalcator, or embezzler may be, the odds loom up as being prohibitive. What increases the odds against the thief or embezzler is control and surveillance.

The Deterrent

Controls are important; but they are not complete insurance. They make the perpetration of fraud difficult, but not impossible. Neither management nor internal auditors should be lulled into a sense of false security because certain controls are in force. Any barricade can be breached by a determined and crafty thief, but good controls make the job of the thief, embezzler, or defrauder more difficult.

One of the strongest motivators for honesty is the fear of being caught. Make apprehension a certainty and inducement to steal becomes dissipated. But even that certainty can be a chimera. All one can hope for is deterrence.

Actually, the routine tests and checks in any audit program rarely turn up thefts. Many manipulatory thefts start as a mistake that does not get caught by the system. For example, a bookkeeper may make an error which results in a cash overage, assuming that sooner or later someone will detect the error and direct the disposition of the overage, but nobody does. The bookkeeper may then go back to find out what caused the overage and suddenly realize that if the mistake were made intentionally nobody would know the difference. And so it starts. Had the control system thrown the spotlight on the error, the thought of manipulation might never have entered the bookkeeper's mind.

Honest People

Defense against fraud begins with hiring honest people — determining their honesty as far as possible by checking backgrounds and references. It continues through systems of control and through a rigorous environment which makes honesty an essential attribute of the enterprise. Remove temptation. Install strict rules. Refuse to tolerate that perfectly natural inclination to reduce surveillance out of human respect:

The office manager who is reluctant to have petty cash audited on a surprise basis — a reflection on the cashier.

The plant superintendent who will not have trash containers spot checked — a reflection on the maintenance people.

The accounting people who do not supervise physical inventories — they see the inventories as the purchasing department's responsibility.

The foreman who does not install a tool check system whereby an employee surrenders a tool check whenever a tool is borrowed — the workers are such a "swell bunch of guys."

Misplaced confidence and the failure to install or maintain reasonable controls become allies of dishonest employees, or tempt honest ones to become dishonest. The results of good systems are to make thieves aware of greater odds against concealment. Fraud is thereby more likely to be exposed at the early stages. Data for business decisions is made more reliable. On the other hand, as an insurance executive pointed out, the lack of a system of internal controls may make a company uninsurable or may impose conditions difficult to live with, such as large deductibles or surcharged premiums.[27]

Minimum Controls

Certain minimum, well-established forms of control should always be in force. Embezzlement seldom builds to large sums unless the embezzler is able to cover peculations by manipulating accounting records. And so:

Those responsible for the physical receipt of goods should not be responsible for paying for those goods.

Those responsible for the collection of receivables should not be responsible for entries in the books of accounts.

Those responsible for issuing checks should not also be responsible for reconciling the bank statements to the books of account.

Nevertheless, internal auditors should be fully aware that the controls erected through such separation of duties can be circumvented by collusion between the two or more people who represent the control. They are also circumvented when fellow employees are reluctant to tell on the perpetrator or do not want to get involved in a messy situation.

In reporting on a client's sytem of internal control, one public accounting firm made this statement in its report:[28]

There are inherent limitations that should be recognized in considering the potential effectiveness of any system of internal accounting control. In the performance of most control procedures, errors can result from misunderstanding of instructions, mistakes of judgment, carelessness, or other personal factors. Control procedures whose effectiveness depends upon segregation of duties can be circumvented by collusion. Similarly, control procedures can be circumvented intentionally by management with respect either to the execution and recording of transactions or with respect to the estimates and judgments required in the preparation of financial statements. Further, projection of any evaluation of internal accounting control to future accounting periods is subject to the risk that the procedures may become inadequate because of changes in conditions and that the degree of compliance with the procedures may deteriorate.

This statement respecting internal accounting control is equally applicable to internal administrative controls. In the absence of constant vigilance, they too can be rendered ineffective.

Polygraphs

Polygraphs are instruments which simultaneously record certain body responses — pulse rate, blood pressure, the rate and depth of breathing, and skin resistance.[29] They are often referred to as "lie detectors." Actually they do not detect lies, but rather the responses of the body to questions. These responses are not completely accurate, because there is a possibility that a response may be erroneously interpreted. Polygraph evidence is generally inadmissible in court cases.

Nevertheless, private use of the polygraph has become widespread. In 1965 there were about 500 commercial polygraph firms, and one estimate indicated that 80% of their income was from private business.

Probably the most extensive use of the polygraph is in preemployment testing. The questions range from whether the applicant ever stole anything from a previous employer or lied on the application to whether he or she uses narcotics or intends to stay long with the organization if hired.

The polygraph is also used when known thefts have occurred. These usually take the form of nine or ten questions which can be answered by a yes or no response. Questions include: "Do you know who stole the money?" and "Did you participate in the theft?" In one case cited, $10,000 in checks were stolen from a treasurer's desk. Sixteen people had access to the checks. By polygraphic examination the thief was identified; the 15 others were proved innocent.

Polygraph tests must be administered by experts. The possibility of error even in the hands of experts is everpresent. Undue reliance cannot be placed on polygraphs. The polygraph can detect only wrongs of which the employee tested is aware. It cannot detect errors resulting from inefficiency or carelessness. Also, only certain selected employees are tested. The theft may be the work of an untested employee who may be high in the company's echelons. Then, too, there is the possibility of polygraphic error. Some people have been known to "beat the machine." The author of the article cited believes that internal auditors can use the device profitably in their investigations. This author urges great caution. First, an employee's constitutional rights should not be jeopardized. Second, the test should be administered by a qualified expert. Third, any polygraphic findings should be corroborated by objective evidence.

Created Errors

Another test of internal control can be made through created errors, sometimes called custom-made frauds. Improper documents are introduced into a system: Invoices marked paid or cancelled. Purchase orders not approved. Requests to purchase not bearing proper authorization. A blank check prepared on a typewriter to a fictitious payee with a note attached saying, "Please rush — support will follow."

Proponents of the plan point out that the escalation of fraud and theft demand desperate remedies. They reason that if computerized systems are so tested, why shouldn't manual systems be tested in the same way?[30]

Opponents of the system cite the adverse effect the procedure will have on the internal auditor's reputation, the undue emphasis on employee fraud, the reputation of sneakiness on the part of management, the difficulty of controlling the management group that introduces the errors, the impossibility of keeping such plans secret, the alienation of honest employees, the objections by unions, and the accusation that the company is practicing entrapment.[31]

All of these arguments against the use of created errors are valid, except the last. The defense of entrapment can be used only when an officer of the law actively induced and enticed a victim to commit some crime which the victim had no intention to commit and would not have committed except for the enticement. The defense is inapplicable when company officials seek merely·to test the efficacy of a system of control.

It is possible, of course, for the management team or the individuals who introduce the errors to do so to their own advantage and, when caught, protest that they were only testing the system. This can be prevented. Three members of top management should be brought into the plan, including a personnel and legal executive. They should initial the planned test and any changes to it. No deviations from the plan should be permitted. They should be kept informed currently of the results of the tests.

The enormity of thefts and embezzlements in some companies may impel the use of created errors to test systems and the alertness of employees. If they are carried out, all those participating in the plan should be made abundantly aware of the risks.

Publicity

Fear of punishment is a deterrent, but that is a matter of company policy. That policy, if it is to be rigorous, should be publicized in advance to all employees. As a minimum, management should publicize these matters:

If periodic credit checks are to be made on certain employees such as cashiers, claims adjusters, and buyers, those people should be told in advance that these checks go with the job.

Employees should be made abundantly aware that fraud will be vigorously investigated and prosecuted.

Employees should be told that security people must be notified immediately of any suspicion of employee fraud.

All employees are expected to cooperate with fraud investigations.

Management, by its actions, should publicize to its employees that dishonesty will not be tolerated and will be punished. Too often management policy is simply to fire the dishonest employee and hope to recover the amounts stolen from the bonding company or from the employee.

Management Fraud

Management fraud requires special consideration. It is a form of fraud that goes beyond the narrow legal definitions of embezzlement, fraud, and theft. It comprises all the forms of deception practiced by managers to benefit themselves to the detriment of the enterprise. Deception by managers, people in positions of power and trust, is not often talked about. It is more often concealed then revealed. It is usually covered up by its victims to avoid the adverse effects of publicity.[32]

Where It Takes Place

Management fraud can be found wherever managers have the opportunity and the need to better their purse, their status, or their ego through deception. The opportunity lies largely in the fiduciary position that managers have in the organization. In a position of trust, they command belief and respect; their motives are rarely questioned; and their explanations are rarely disputed. Their respected roles as profit center managers — heads of autonomous units — place them above suspicion. They are often immune to the ordinary checks and balances imposed on their subordinates.

In decentralized organizations, division presidents, vice presidents, and general managers are vested with relatively complete authority. They are judged by the central corporate executive group and by boards of directors in terms of performance. Such performance is generally portrayed in reports and financial statements. The artful imagination of the deceiver has little difficulty making red appear black.

The deception can continue for years. It goes on where there is no thoroughgoing surveillance. It goes on where group vice presidents who visit the decentralized organizations use those visits to make social calls, not to ask the hard questions. It goes on where there are no top-flight internal auditors who analyze and dissect both operations and reports. When it finally surfaces, or where suspicions trigger investigations, the harm is done and the miscreant usually moves on to browse in other pastures. The damage left behind can be incalculable.

The Reasons Behind Management Fraud

Different pressures push managers into deception. These pressures can be internal or external. The manager may have the inner drive to outperform all others, to exceed the performance displayed during the last fiscal year, to beat a rival to a coveted promotion, or to receive a larger incentive bonus. Grasp may exceed reach. The goals set may be beyond the manager's capacity to achieve.

Similar pressures may come from superiors. Goals may be set by centralized management that are unrealistic. These goals filter down to subordinate managers who are forced to meet what they had never committed to. Since they cannot achieve these goals fairly, they manage to appear to meet them through deception. A summary of some the reasons behind management fraud is as follows:

Executives sometimes take rash steps from which they cannot retreat. In one instance, the president of a large conglomerate unthinkingly asserted before a group of financial analysts that profits for the current year would be X dollars a share. The assertion became a company goal, and the independent public accountants were talked into writing off an inventory adjustment over a five-year period. The transaction increased the current year's profits, but it caused a distortion in the corporate financial statement. Corporate management was unaware of the deception until it was unearthed by consultants.

Profit centers may distort facts to hold off divestment. One profit center was running into hard times. Corporate management was looking only at the bottom line, judging the worth of the division by what it brought into the corporate coffers. When the line started turning from black to red, corporate executives started thinking about amputation.

But the division comprised more than numbers and things; it was also made up of people. They were fully aware that poor performance could bring drastic action; that their jobs, their status, their seniority, and their futures were in jeopardy. The first law of nature is self-preservation. Those with much to lose and the opportunity to protect themselves resorted to "cooking the books" to turn actual red into ostensible black.

Incompetent managers may deceive in order to survive. Nothing stands still. Ours is a galloping technology. Good managers keep abreast of change. Poor ones slip back. In a number of instances, consultants found that what some managers could not produce on merit they spelled out in reports that puffed up their performance in defiance of the existing facts.

Performance may be distorted to warrant larger bonuses. Managers in many organizations participate in management incentive plans. The better the performance, the larger the bonus. In large organizations performance is demonstrated by numbers in a report. The temptation dangles before all of us to put the best face on our accomplishments. When the size of the reward hangs on the size of the reported numbers, and where managers feel that they can manipulate the numbers without detection, some of them may succumb to temptation.

The need to succeed can turn managers to deception. Ambition is a worthy trait. It can move ordinary people to do extraordinary things. But when ambition drives with an unmerciful whip and when self-advancement is more important than solid accomplishment, some managers will betray the stewardship of the resources entrusted to them. To the detriment of reasonable long-range performance, some managers have shown superior short-range performance and then moved on before the long-range effects could catch up with them. Their methods included inadequate funding of research and development, so that the company ultimately lost its share of the market; deterioration of machinery and equipment, so that production faltered; and the loss of good, well-paid people, replaced by low-salaried hacks.

Unscrupulous managers may serve interests which conflict. A manager should be loyal to one master only. That loyalty must never be fractionated. The chief engineer who requires all potential suppliers of goods to use a testing company he or she personally owns, the purchasing agent who specifies products only a favored and compliant supplier will produce, the inspector who certifies a low quality supplier for a price — all these contribute to the hiding or falsification of records which will hush the cry of conflict of interest.

Profits may be inflated to obtain advantages in the market place. The financial officers or executives who wish their company's stock to make a splash in the market or seek to obtain unwarranted credit lines, may inflate profits unfairly. They take this path if they bow to temptation, have the opportunity, and are unafraid of being detected. Consultants have found that those who do deceive have a supreme contempt for the abilities of those who have the job of detecting improprieties. Their belief in their own abilities transcends any fear of detection.

The one who controls both the assets and their records is in a perfect position to falsify the latter. When managers are in a strategic position both to control physical assets and adjust the records of those assets, they may make away with large amounts without being detected.

Each of these reasons for deception exists in abundance in the business world. But deceptions sprout only under the rains of opportunity. The umbrella against the downpour is constructed of good business practice, adherence to accepted principles of management, knowledge of what goes on in the enterprise, and reports that are independently reviewed. Let any corporate executives forget their responsibility to **manage** — a responsibility they dare not delegate — and they reap a bitter harvest.

When Management Fraud Occurs

An immediate result of management fraud, after it is detected, is the cruel drain on the time and nervous systems of the senior executives or the members of the boards of directors who must excise the cancer and bind up the wound. All the cost and the time spent on curing most likely exceed by far that which was needed for preventive medicine. All auditors and investigators who have worked on fraud cases will recall the pain that top executives experience and exhibit when they find that valued subordinates betrayed their trust. It is a trauma no executive seeks.

When management fraud occurs, executive management, in its outrage, may take swift and drastic action. This can be a fatal error. The tendency is to focus on the legal aspects, turn loose the authorities, dismiss the ostensible miscreant, and thus abort a methodical, thorough, productive investigation.

Corporate heads, including the board of directors, should regard the occurence as a business problem, not a legal problem. The latter comes afterwards. Key personnel should not be dismissed before the problem is solved. There may be innocents among the guilty. Only a fair investigation can sort them out. Both the professional investigator and the internal auditor have a duty to protect the innocent as well as to identify the guilty.

Corporate heads should seek to minimize losses so that they can honestly tell the bonding company that all efforts were exerted to prevent any extension of losses and to mitigate damages.

They must look at a broader picture than that which focuses solely on the cancer within the body corporate. They must be concerned with the possible loss of credibility in the market place — the assessment that financial analysts will place upon the circumstances. They should be concerned with the premiums on new fidelity insurance and the impact on new coverage. And so they should be able to point out to the insurance carrier that the steps taken in the wake of the investigation will see to it that no more harsh surprises are in the offing.

They should concern themselves with the disruption of business. Herds of auditors and investigators descending on a profit center can have a devastating effect. Hence, an executive should be assigned to coordinate the efforts of all groups involved in the investigation. These efforts, among others, are as follows:

External Auditors

Have them verify financial reports. Request the external auditors to perform a "heavy review" as compared to an audit. Since the matter may result in litigation, the corporate legal staff should arrange to have access to the external auditors' working papers.

Internal Auditors

Have them supplement the work of the external auditors, analyze operating records and reports — as distinguished from financial records and reports — and support any consultants used in gathering information and helping to analyze data.

Legal Counsel

Have corporate attorneys determine the need for disclosure and for compliance with SEC and other regulatory requirements. Premature disclosure, before it is determined with certainty that fraud exists and that there is adequate evidence to support the finding, may prejudice the company's case and reputation. The attorneys can determine, as a matter of law, when the facts demand disclosure and when disclosure can properly be delayed. The attorneys should also evaluate the legal aspect of recoveries under any fidelity policies and what action may be taken against third parties whose negligence or participation contributed to the difficulties.

Outside Consultants

Have consultants skilled in the identification of fraudulent acts carry out the delicate task of interrogating witnesses. Consultants can provide an aura of objectivity and neutrality needed to obtain the cooperation of witnesses. They can advise the internal auditors which avenues to explore, what information to obtain, and what records to analyze. They can guide the analysis of third-party records — documents submitted by people outside the organization. They can help determine whether those documents are valid, and they can go behind supporting documents to dredge up the whole truth. Also, since they are external to the organization and may never again be seen, they can obtain information an insider might be denied.

The Symptoms of Management Fraud

Investigative consultants have identified a set of symptoms which are usually reliable indicators of an improper condition. The symptom is but a surface lesion. The cancerous condition lies below it, but the lesions have to be recognized for what they imply. Here are a few of these indicators, some explanations, and some examples.

Consistently late reports. Honest reports can usually be issued on time since their purpose is to inform, not deceive. But in order for a deceiver to know where figures need to be plugged, he or she must analyze the reported data in order to know just where that data is to be manipulated. These analyses take time. Continuing late reports cry for in-depth investigations and a search for the reasons for delays.

Managers who regularly assume subordinates' duties. In one company, a vice president of administration never relinquished the comptrollership function. The nominal comptroller was a flunky. The V.P. also overrode the credit manager and acted as warehouse manager. Even worse, he preempted the cash manager's responsibilities and took deposits to the bank. Some of the purported deposits, most of it in cash, were never made to the company's account. An alert internal auditing department might have detected the symptom and done some digging. But the company, large enough to generate $400,000,000 in sales, apparently did not feel that it needed any internal auditors.

Noncompliance with corporate directives and procedures. A chief financial officer of a subsidiary was directed by corporate executives to install a standard cost system. He gave excuse after excuse for the delay. Three years went by while he was able to hide the cost problems which a standard cost system would have exposed.

Managers dealing in matters outside their profit center's scope. A division manager acted as a broker on products outside his cost center's product line. He needed the cash to hide other manipulations. Such an action should have been an indicator to corporate managers or internal auditors. But the corporate group's executive responsible for the profit center visited it for social calls only, and there was no internal audit function. The corporate headquarters relied on the external auditors to ferret out such matters. The normal financial audit by external auditors is not designed for that purpose.

Payments to trade creditors supported by copies instead of originals. One subsidiary had a practice of doctoring the support for payments to its creditors. Some of the payments it supported with an original invoice but a copy of a receiving memo. Others it supported with the original receiving memo but a duplicate invoice. The duplicates and the originals were artfully mixed so as to avoid a pattern which might have alerted the external auditors. The company employed no internal auditors. Because of the clever mixture of originals and copies, and in the absence of the deterrent effect of competent internal auditors, duplicate payments and kickbacks flourished.

Negative debit memos. At one profit center, credit memos were generated by the computer. When the financial officer wished to write off a credit memo, he would generate a negative debit memo. The external auditors were dutifully provided with all credit memos. They were not made aware of the debit memos.

Commissions not in line with increased sales. In one corporation, sales skyrocketed. But most of the increase was the result of cranking fictitious contracts into the computer. At the same time commissions to salesmen were valid and accurate. The sales and commissions were supposed to be interrelated. So the picture was there for anyone to see: Contracts escalating but commissions hardly rising.

In all the cases just described, the symptoms were there. The indicators could be plotted and the data behind them could be verified. An alert internal auditing group should be able to determine the types of indicators needed for top management surveillance.

Controlling Management Fraud

The cornerstone in the structure designed to control management fraud is an environment created by the organization's policy makers. It is an environment that fosters morality and high business ethics. Let sharp practices flourish at the top — income smoothing, lavish entertainment, bribes to officials — and the seeds for management fraud are sown.

Senior management must also understand that the manager of a profit center has autonomy and opportunity. The greater the freedom, the easier it is to fall into temptation. Without constricting managers so that imagination and innovation are squeezed out of them, the systems should provide checks and balances and reports that cause flares to streak across the corporate sky if improprieties are practiced. Some of the control measures which executive managers should install are as follows:

Establish standards, budgetary and statistical, and investigate all material deviations.

Use quantitative and analytical techniques (time series analyses, regression and correlation analyses, and random sampling) to highlight aberrant behavior. Develop indicators, such as space used, time required, weight limitations imposed, usage and output compared. Where possible, develop management information systems that supply the data needed for such analyses.

Compare performance with industry norms as well as with the performance of comparable profit centers within the organization.

Identify critical process indicators: Melt loss in smelting, death loss in feed lots, rework in manufacturing and assembly, and gross profit tests in buy-sell or retail operations.

Analyze carefully performance that looks too good as well as performance that does not meet standards.

Establish a professional internal auditing department. Provide it with a charter, signed by the chief executive officer and approved by the audit committee of the board of directors, which gives it independence of the activities it audits, guarantees objectivity, authorizes the periodic review of **all** operations, and demands the appropriate consideration of all deficiency findings and audit recommendations.

Conclusion

Fraud and theft have grown too big to be ignored. The internal auditor has a definite responsibility for its prevention and detection. It is a rational, not a complete responsibility. It is the responsibility to act prudently and inquisitively, to be aware of the activities and locations where fraud is likely to occur. It is not the responsibility of an insurer or guarantor against fraud. Certain kinds of frauds are impossible for either internal or external auditors to detect. The most useful course an internal auditor can advocate is that fraud should be deterred. Internal auditors can promote deterrence by reviewing personnel policies, recommending adequate control systems and evaluating their effectiveness, and seeing that temptation and opportunity are not offered to employees.

Management fraud is a form of fraud not often discussed, but the huge amounts which are lost thereby make it an important consideration for internal auditors. They should have a charter which gives them the authority to go to the highest levels of the enterprise if they have well-founded suspicions of fraud. They should have the right to ask pertinent questions of people in every echelon of the enterprise.

References

1. U.S. Department of Justice, *The Investigation of White-Collar Crime* (Washington, D.C., Government Printing Office, April 1977) p.4.
2. *White-Collar Crime: Everyone's Problem, Everyone's Loss*, publication of the Chamber of Commerce of the United States (1974), pp. 4-6.
3. Wm. L. Prosser, *Handbook of the Law of Torts*, 4th Ed. (St. Paul, Minn.: West Publishing Co., 1971) pp. 685, 686.
4. *The Investigation of White-Collar Crime*, p. 124.
5. C. M. Kelley, "Accountants and Auditors vs. White Collar Crime", *The Internal Auditor*, June 1976, p. 35.
6. D. B. Niestrath, "Catch That Thief," *The Internal Auditor*, January/February 1974, p. 67.
7. D. R. Carmichael, "Fraud in EDP Systems," *The Internal Auditor*, May/June 1969, p. 32.
8. D. R. Carmichael, p. 33.
9. *The Investigation of White-Collar Crime*, pp. 209, 210.
10. American Institute of Certified Public Accountants. "Report of the Special Committee on Equity Funding." American Institute of Certified Public Accountants, 1974.
11. *State Street Trust Company* vs. *Ernst*, 15 N.E. 2nd 416, 1938.
12. O. A. Hill, Jr., "The Role of the Auditor With Respect to Internal Control and Fraud," *The Internal Auditor*, May/June 1968, p. 38.
13. Paul Macciaverna, *Internal Auditing*, (New York: The Conference Board, 1978), p. 17.
14. *Ibid.*, pp. 20, 21.
15. *Ibid.*
16. W. E. Henderson, Jr. "Employee Thefts and Fidelity Bonding." *The Internal Auditor*, November/December 1974, p. 24.
17. *Ibid.*, p. 25.
18. *Ibid.*, p. 29.
19. "The Round Table," *The Internal Auditor*, December 1979, p. 66.
20. "The Round Table," December 1979, p. 67.
21. "The Round Table," August 1978, p. 74.
22. "The Round Table," April 1977, p. 67.
23. "The Round Table," May/June 1972, p. 72.
24. Harvey Cardwell, *The Principles of Audit Surveillance* (Princeton, N.J.: D. Van Nostrand Company, Inc., 1960), Chapter 20.
25. Wm. L. Prosser, p. 43.
26. Deering's California Penal Code, Sec. 153.
27. W. E. Henderson, Jr. "Employee Thefts and Fidelity Bonding," *The Internal Auditor*, November/December 1974, p. 31.
28. H. F. Russell, *Foozles & Frauds* (Altamonte Springs, Fla.: The Institute of Internal Auditors, Inc., 1977), p. 146.
29. C. B. Cheatham, "Is the Polygraph a Valid Internal Control Device?" *The Internal Auditor*, January/February 1974, pp. 39-48.
30. "Readers Problem Clinic," *The Internal Auditor*, Fall 1961, pp. 66-69.

31. "Readers Problem Clinic," *The Internal Auditor*, Spring 1961, pp. 71-76.
32. L. B. Sawyer, A. A. Murphy, Michael Crossley, "Management Fraud: The Insidious Specter," *The Internal Auditor*, April 1979, pp. 11-25.

Supplementary Reading

Albrecht, W. S. "Analytical Reviews for Internal Auditors." *The Internal Auditor*, August, 1980, pp. 20-25.

Cardwell, Harvey. *The Principles of Audit Surveillance*. Princeton, N.J.: D. Van Nostrand Company, Inc., 1960.

Parker, Donn B. *Crime by Computer*. New York: Charles Scribner's Sons, 1976.

Russell, H. F. *Foozles & Frauds*. Altamonte Springs, Fla.: The Institute of Internal Auditors, 1977.

The Investigation of White-Collar Crime, A Manual for Law Enforcement Agencies, 1977. (For sale by Superintendent of Documents, U.S. Government Printing Office, Washington, D.C., 20402. Stock No. 027-000-00507-1, Catalog No. J 1.8/2; W58.)

For further study

Discussion Problems

1. Distinguish between embezzlement and robbery.

2. Distinguish between legal fraud and management fraud.

3. What two forms of pressure can cause managers to defraud their companies?

4. An internal auditor tells management: "The courts have held that an auditor cannot be regarded as an insurer against fraud. Ergo, I can take no responsibility for its prevention or detection in this company." Comment.

5. May internal auditors consider their responsibilities for the prevention and detection of fraud discharged if they find written procedures which provide satisfactory controls designed to eliminate the risk? Give reasons.

6. A supervisor dictates to her secretary in the privacy of a secure office: "John Smith is a crook." Is the supervisor guilty of a crime? Why?

7. One company has posted a $5,000 reward to anyone who can breach its EDP security system. Give a reason for and against this idea.

8. In what way can having a high regard for people increase the possibility of fraud?

9. Give an example of trend analysis in a purchasing department.

10. Give an example of proportionate analysis in a labor pool.

Multiple Choice Problems

1. An internal auditor has reason to believe a fraud is being committed in the bill-paying unit of the Controller's Department. Which of the following actions best describes the way the internal auditor should proceed?

a. Immediately start an audit and interrogate suspected employees.

b. Inform the controller of suspicions and schedule an audit within 30 days.

c. Consider the present work load of the controller's department before scheduling an audit.

d. Inform the supervisor of the bill-paying unit that an audit is being scheduled immediately.

e. None of the above.

2. In conducting a fraud investigation, the internal auditor should first:

a. Identify the perpetrator.

b. Get the facts.

c. Obtain a confession.

d. Notify a law-enforcement agency.

e. Obtain restitution.

3. An embezzler draws a check on Bank A as of the fiscal period closing date and deposits it in Bank B the same day. This form of embezzlement is termed:

a. Double-checking.

b. Lapping.

c. Kiting.

d. Floating.

e. Larceny

4. After the whistle has blown, a manager calls an employee into his office, locks the door, and accuses the employee of being a thief. The manager has committed the crime of:

a. False imprisonment.

b. Slander.

c. Malicious prosecution.

d. Libel.

e. Compounding a felony.

5. Certain frauds are almost impossible to detect through normal audit routines. These are:

a. Collusion.

b. Lapping.

c. Forgery.

d. a. and c.

e. None of the above.

6. As soon as he or she becomes suspicious of potential management fraud, the Chief Executive Officer should:

a. Suspend the suspect.

b. Notify the police.

c. Treat the matter as a legal problem.

d. Treat the matter as a management problem.

e. Both a. and b. above.

7. A good way of identifying management fraud in an autonomous profit center is to:

a. Use questionnaires.

b. Hire ex-FBI agents.

c. Identify critical process indicators.

d. Analyze both very good and very bad performance.

e. Both c. and d.

8. In a corporation an internal auditor finds that the cashier is also reconciling bank statements. To which of the following people should the matter be communicated before the auditor is justified in closing the matter without corrective action?

a. The controller.

b. The treasurer.

c. The executive vice president.

d. The president.

e. The board of directors.

9. The difference between an error and a fraud is:

a. The size of the amounts lost.

b. The suspect's position in the organization.

c. Intent.

d. Predilection.

e. Need.

10. The best defense against fraud is:

a. Hiring honest people.

b. Restricting opportunities for fraud.

c. Surveillance.

d. Certainty of detection.

e. All of the above.

Case Studies

22-1 Inventory Shortages

During the audit of purchasing and inventory operations, the internal auditor discovers that significant quantities of purchased materials are not actually in stock, nor are they accounted for. Stock records, controlled by the warehouse supervisor, do not reflect shortages; and the inventory reports seem to have been altered. The internal auditor suspects that the warehouse supervisor, who has the greatest opportunity to remove materials for personal gain, altered the reports.

The auditor immediately notifies the department manager, and together they confront the suspected supervisor. The supervisor offers no explanation for the shortages and denies any wrongdoing. The department manager immediately suspends the supervisor, pending further investigation, and informs the warehouse employees of the situation. Since no adequate explanation for the shortages was obtained, the auditor contacts the security unit for assistance.

Required: The actions of the auditor and the department manager could hinder the conduct of a successful investigation and could subject the company to legal proceedings. List four of their improper actions and briefly discuss the possible adverse effect of each.

22-2 Indicators

It has been said that internal auditors are not responsible for detecting defalcation, embezzlement, or fraud. Yet when fraud is uncovered, the question is usually asked, "Where were the auditors?"

While it is obvious that an internal auditor cannot be expected to guarantee that there is no fraud, there are a number of indicators which an alert internal auditor might spot and investigate as a deterrent to fraud or as an early disclosure of possible fraud.

Discuss the following six indicators or danger signs, including the potential fraud which could be involved, and the initial approach to take in each case:

1. Employees living beyond their apparent means.

2. Reluctance by a key employee to take a vacation.

3. Unreasonable association with supplier's personnel by member of the Purchasing Department.

4. Erasures, changes, or manually inserted entries on time cards.

5. Date of deposits per cash book is significantly different from date of deposits on bank statements.

6. Lack of cooperation in relinquishing records for audit.

23

Dealing With People

Relations between internal auditors and others in the enterprise. The conflicting objectives. Churchill and Cooper's study. Mints' study. Fears stemming from the line/staff relation. Negative connotations of control. Causes of antagonism. Why bad relations can lead to bad audits. Traditional versus participative auditing. The auditee's perception of the auditor. Dealing with fraud. Dispelling fear and mistrust. Dealing with the intransigent auditee. The importance of learning to listen. Aggressive listening. Barriers to listening. Means of concentrating. Obtaining participation from the auditee. A case history. Conflicting duties: Executive management vs. the board. Problem-solving partner vs. investigator. Dealing with operating managers but issuing reports on their work.

Introduction

Financial auditors deal mainly with figures. Modern internal auditors deal mainly with people. Internal auditors must develop and maintain good relations with auditees to gain information and to ensure corrective action on audit findings. Yet internal auditors can find themselves buffeted by conflicting objectives that appear to be in complete opposition. The problem is a knotty one: on the one hand, to secure cooperation from auditees; on the other hand, to be alert to the possibility of fraud and to root it out when it becomes evident; on the one hand, to gain the confidence of an operating manager, on the other hand, to record deficiency findings in a report going to the manager's superior; on the one hand, to be on the chief executive officer's payroll, on the other hand, to report to the board of directors derelictions in an enterprise for which the CEO has complete responsibility.

Meeting these conflicting aims can be difficult. Yet they must be met if internal auditors are to carry out the responsibilities assigned to them. This chapter discusses the problems and explores solutions. Specifically:

○ How auditees regard auditors.
○ The causes of low esteem.
○ The importance of developing and maintaining good auditor/auditee relations.
○ The effects of both good and bad relations.
○ Some suggestions for improving relations.
○ Listening.
○ Participative auditing.
○ Special dilemmas for internal auditors.

How Auditees Regard Auditors

For many years auditors have known in a general way that their advent brings no joy and their leaving brings no tears. It was not until 1965 that a research study was published which gave specificity to this common understanding.[1] Churchill and Cooper reported a pilot study of seven firms in the Pittsburgh area. Among the questions they asked of people in those firms were these: What is your attitude toward internal auditors? What role do you perceive them as playing?

Exhibit 23-1 is a summary of their findings.

Exhibit 23-1.

ATTITUDES TOWARD AUDITORS

Description	Number	% of Total
Negative	11	26
Neutral	20	48
Positive	10	24
Mixed	1	2
	42	100

ROLE

	Number	% of Total
Teacher	3	11
Policeman	15	58
Attorney	6	23
Mixed	2	8
	26	100

These responses indicate that only 24% of the respondents had positive attitudes toward auditors. With respect to roles, the question about attorney is not clear-cut. It is dubious, based on the responses to the attitude question, that the respondents had a **defense** attorney in mind. In this view, at least 81% of the respondents saw internal auditors in an unfavorable light.

In 1972, Mints published the results of a far more comprehensive study of auditee attitudes.[2] As part of his research project, he asked audit managers how they felt their auditees regarded internal auditors. Usable responses were received from 76 respondents. The results are summarized in Exhibit 23-2.

Exhibit 23-2. STUDY OF AUDITEE ATTITUDES

Auditee Occupation	Percentage of Respondents		
	Favorable	**Neutral**	**Unfavorable**
Managers:			
Accounting	26%	46%	16%
Non-accounting	29	39	19
Subordinates:			
Accounting	13	34	40
Non-accounting	16	35	37

(The three percentages on each line do not add to 100% because of the nature of many of the responses.)

These 1972 results show little if any improvement over Churchill and Cooper's findings some seven years earlier. The picture held by auditees about auditors — particularly the views of subordinates — is pretty bleak. The view by auditees of audit effectiveness is equally bleak.

In 1980, Clancy, Collins, and Rael conducted a survey of perceptions about internal auditing.[3] Here are three of the questions asked of auditees and the "mean responses."

1. In evaluating the effectiveness of past reviews performed by independent work organizations (such as internal audits), how effective would you say the reviews have been?   3.3*

2. Do you agree that fundamental organizational problems are generally identified as a result of reviews performed by independent work organizations (such as internal audit)?   2.4*

3. In terms of benefit to the firm, how would you classify the overall contribution of internal auditing to accomplishment of company goals and objectives?   3.4*

Obviously, internal auditors need to improve their image and the perception others have of them. Internal auditors need to know the reasons why many people hold them in low esteem. Improvement comes hard without a thorough understanding of root causes. These causes are found in the organizational status of internal auditors, the way they perceive their own function, and how they practice their profession.

---

*The mean of auditees responses. A score of 1 indicates "not at all," and 5 indicates "a great deal."

Reasons and Causes

Staff/Line Conflicts

The staff/line relationship is inherently prone to conflict. The very aspect of most staff people is not endearing to line personnel. Staff people are usually younger. They generally have a better formal education. They are more individualistic. They have a more formal dress mode. They report to higher echelons than do line personnel. Being specialists in their field, they may think their answers are the only answers. They tend to discount the difficulty line people may face if called on to act on their ideas. And they may feel that they must point out defects to prove themselves to upper management.[4]

Line personnel, under such circumstances, will most likely regard staff with animosity. The aspect of the staff person is but one reason; they also have reason to fear staff. They fear being shown up for not having thought of the improvements themselves. They fear that proposed changes may disrupt comfortable routines and existing cliques. They fear that revised methods may expose inefficiencies and/or forbidden practices.

Mostly they fear change. Change is a window to the unknown. Better the devil we know than the devil we don't. Better the old, accustomed ways than the disruptions and dislocations line people perceive as attending change.

Internal auditors are staff. And line people — in this sense, all auditees — are likely to regard internal auditors the same as they regard other staff people. Chris Argyris could have been talking about internal auditors in his study of conflicts between budget staff people and operating line people.[5] Budget people, like internal auditors, can perceive their role as being "watchdogs" for the company. Their gain is somebody else's loss. Their identification of faults and weaknesses shows management they are doing their job well. It also implies, however, that the line people are doing theirs badly. Budget people — and internal auditors — hold up their findings for all the world to see. At the same time, the line people are left naked and shivering before the cold glare of senior management. As Argyris summed it up: " . . . to add insult to injury, the entire incident is made permanent and exhibited to top officials by being placed in a formal report circulated through many top channels."

Control

Line people may bow to control, but they do not have to like it. Control has negative connotations. Line people regard internal auditors as part of the control system. Indeed, internal auditors have made no attempt to downplay that role. Their Statement of Responsibilities declares at the outset that internal auditing "is a managerial control which functions by measuring and evaluating the effectiveness of other controls." People almost universally dislike both control and those who exert control over them. Control therefore breeds antagonism as a result of auditee perception of, or personal experiences with, audits. Mints points out the causes of antagonism, based on his research findings.[6]

Fear of criticism stemming from adverse audit findings.

Fear of changes in day-to-day working habits because of changes resulting from audit recommendations.

Punitive action by superiors prompted by reported deficiencies.

Insensitive audit practices: reports which are overly critical, reports which focus on deficiencies only, the air of mystery cloaking some audits, and the perception that auditors gain personally from reporting deficiencies.

Hostile audit style: a cold and distant aspect, a lack of understanding of the auditee's problems, an absence of empathy, an air of smugness or superiority, an excessive concentration on insignificant errors, a prosecutorial style when asking questions, and a greater concern with parading defects than helping constructively to improve conditions.

Many internal auditors contribute to these perceptions through their failure to understand why people act as they do in the presence of an auditor. Nearly all conscious behavior is motivated or caused. Internal auditors who have no understanding of motivational theory will cause behavior which places roadblocks in front of their audit objectives. People receive motivation from their underlying needs and act in a way to satisfy those needs. They react negatively and hostilely when those needs are threatened.

D. R. Carmichael has shown that internal control systems usually make the assumption that "employees have inherent mental, moral, and physical weaknesses."[7] He also showed that these assumptions can be self-fulfilling. They cause the employee to behave in the same undesirable manner which the system sought to prevent. Employees may feel threatened because internal audit findings will result in punishment, loss of personal goals, and deprivation of need satisfaction. Hence, they may resort to dishonesty to meet standards, or they may bury their errors and inefficiencies in the hope that the internal auditor will not find them.

The Need For Good Relations

Assuming that the behaviorists are right, assuming that line people dislike staff people in general and internal auditors in particular, and assuming that controls — especially in the form of an internal auditor — will cause people to be fearful, defensive, and dishonest, does it matter? Isn't it the job of internal auditors to carry out their audits despite difficulties? Isn't it their job to exhume what was covered up? Isn't it their job to report what they found?

The answer to all of these questions is yes. But why make the job more difficult than necessary? Why do in a spirit of animosity what can be carried out in a spirit of cooperation?

The conflict is compounded with the auditor's move into operations. Perhaps auditee's fears and distrust may not keep a financial auditor in an accounting area from achieving audit objectives, but audits of operations present different problems.

When internal auditors perform comprehensive audits of operations throughout their enterprises, they cannot possibly be as well informed about such operations as a financial auditor in a financial department. Operating processes may be unfamiliar, complex, and bewildering. The operating people may be speaking a language and using terms that are foreign to the auditor's experience. Then too, the corrective action required is likely to demand the whole-hearted commitment of operating personnel if it is to be effective. Yet operating people are less accustomed to internal auditors and are less likely to accept them and their recommendations.

Stephen Keating, president of Honeywell, Inc., saw clearly the importance of cooperation between auditor and auditee when he said: " . . . real progress cannot be made in an environment of conflict and friction . . . Resentment, mistrust, even fear . . . are typical responses . . . Finding the trouble is only half the battle — the other half is putting recommendations to work. This requires understanding and confidence."[8]

W. G. Phillips, also a corporate president, said that the auditor: " . . . must approach his job in a constructive manner, realizing that mistakes are guides for improvement, not crimes . . . He must consider himself a partner with those involved in the audit, not an adversary."[9]

The ability to deal effectively with others goes beyond pleasant relations. It goes beyond people being nice to each other. It means the ability to get a job done with the least adverse effect on others.

Harmeyer cites a study by psychologists of 4,000 employees who had been discharged.[10] The study showed, surprisingly, that only 38% had been discharged for technical incompetence. Almost two thirds, 62%, had been discharged for social unsuitability. Yet most organizations — including the Institute of Internal Auditors, Inc. — spend about 95% of the time concentrating on technical skills.

What profits the auditor to develop a sound audit finding only to see it bitterly fought by operating management because the auditor, wittingly or unwittingly, had created a feeling of conflict and distrust?

The Effects of Auditor/Auditee Relations

Mints' research study evoked abundant evidence of the importance of conducting audits without animosity. His study included test audits in which some teams of auditors used a cool, superior, impersonal style and other teams used a participative, teamwork approach. After each audit, auditees were asked to evaluate the auditors in terms of their audit style. For example, did they regard the auditor as a policeman or a teacher? After the audits had been made, after the auditors had been evaluated, and after sufficient time had elapsed for the effect of the audits to be known, one of the general auditors involved in the study wrote to the researcher:

> Within six months of the completion of an audit, the auditees send a memo to the corporate controller and division manager in which they report action taken or otherwise. We noted a direct correlation between the auditee ratings of the auditors and these replies. When the auditors were highly rated, action was normally taken on practically all items, and vice versa. Since motivating personnel is one of our major objectives, I'd say this is a most important finding, which substantiates our need to improve auditor acceptance by auditee.[11]

The research study demonstrated, as clinically as such studies can, that poor relations defeat the audit purpose and that good relations promote it. Two examples from the study offer evidence of this conclusion:

> One auditor who used the cold, aloof style, performed an audit which was professional and technically outstanding. It was characterized by imaginative and potentially profitable work. Yet eight months after the audit, the operating organization had not implemented the audit recommendations. The operating people were apparently seething over the methods which the auditor had used.
>
> On the other hand, in an audit which followed — in which the cooperative approach was used — the controller of the division audited called the director of auditing to compliment him and to say that the operating people were enthusiastic about implementing the suggestions. The audit director was convinced that the differences in styles were responsible for the diverse results.[12]

Another of the general auditors also evaluated the results of the audits conducted for the research study. He was able to say without reservation that the results obtained from the warm, empathetic style were significantly better than those obtained from the cold, reserved style. He also said that one of the sad things coming out of his correlation was that from a technical point of view the work performed by the reserved auditors was judged superior in some respects to that performed by the empathetic auditors. Yet the results from the empathetic audit groups showed that management accepted and implemented their ideas readily. He concluded:

> Putting it another way, the results of our audits depend a good deal on how we are perceived by others, rather than how we perceive ourselves. Further, we can positively influence the "how we are perceived by others" by getting ourselves involved with the auditees, by having empathy with them, and by considering what's best for them rather than us.[13]

There seems little doubt that intelligent, imaginative internal audit work in and of itself is not enough to ensure improvements in operations. The auditee must want to implement the audit recommendations. So the auditor's style may be as important as his or her technical competence.

Solutions

Relations between auditor and auditee may improve if the auditor, the expert on control, appreciates the difference between imposed control and self-control. The principle of self-control requires that a staff group never be the instrument for policing — for being the conduit through which the procedures developed by upper echelons flow down on the heads of operating managers and people.

Rather, they should act and be perceived as a means of transmitting the reasons for needed procedures. They should seek to help managers control themselves. This help includes informing operating people that they are out of line, but it also includes helping them get themselves back in line, motivating them to want to do so. Internal auditors are in the middle. They find themselves between top management controls on the one hand and those who are being controlled on the other. The way they conduct themselves — as helpful buffers or abrasive forces — may make the difference between effective and ineffective audits.

Consultative Attitudes

A favored behavioral solution to line and staff, and therefore to auditee/ auditor relations, is the adoption of a consulting rather than a policing attitude. If staff specialists, including internal auditors, are to succeed in achieving their objectives, they must demonstrate that their knowledge and their efforts can work to the benefit of the operating people. Participation can succeed where imposition will not. Exhibit 23-3 compares the traditional (hard-line) and the participative audit approaches.

Internal auditors will have to emphasize to operating managers their constructive, participative role. This calls for continued, innovative methods to bring the message to operating people. The importance of the proper perception by the auditee is highlighted in a statement by Comptroller General Elmer B. Staats on July 25, 1978, to a congressional committee in connection with the Inspector General (IG) Act of 1978. Mr. Staats said:

> I cannot stress too strongly to you the need to revise the inspector general's title in this bill. This may seem a minor point, but I can assure you that what this subcommittee does in the matter is going to have far-reaching consequences in the years to come. We believe that the name of the organizations established by the bill will set the tone for how they operate. If you call them "office of inspector general," you are going to find that future hiring of personnel for those offices will be concentrated on persons with investigative backgrounds, and future operations will increasingly be centered on investigations for the purpose of detecting fraud. . . . what the federal agencies need are strong internal controls to minimize the opportunities to defraud the government . . . [14]

Conflicting Demands

Fraud prevention and detection are important. The losses resulting from fraud are enormous. Their effect on enterprises can be staggering, and internal auditors have a responsibility to be alert for its existence and take appropriate action when it is suspected (see Chapter 22). In short, internal auditors must act as a capable manager acts.

Exhibit 23-3. AUDIT APPROACH COMPARISONS

Traditional	Participative
Reduced costs and improved efficiency are the traditional audit objectives.	Providing better means by which managers can reduce costs and improve efficiency are the participative audit objectives.
Procedures and controls are imposed from above and policed by the internal auditors.	Procedures and controls belong to operating managers. The internal auditor is a professional consultant dedicated to helping managers improve **their** controls and procedures.
The internal auditor sets the standards by which operations will be managed. The manager provides only the knowledge of operations.	Both the manager and the internal auditor agree on the standards of measurement and how the standards will be applied.
The internal auditor issues reports describing deficiencies only, reporting audit recommendations to top management.	The internal auditor issues balanced reports and describes what line management is doing to correct any weaknesses found.
Improved conditions will result from focusing on deficiencies disclosed by the internal auditor.	Improved conditions will result from corrective action in which both auditor and auditee participate.
The internal auditor sees that all procedures and policies are strictly adhered to.	The internal auditor examines procedures and policies for relevance, viability, and good sense; proposes appropriate changes; and points out to operating managers and their employees the desirability of following acceptable policies and procedures.
The internal auditor acts as an outside expert.	The internal auditor acts as an internal consultant.

The fact that an admirable manager will not countenance reprehensible conduct does not make him or her less admirable to desirable employees. We believe that the internal auditors' rooting out wrongdoing when wrongdoing occurs should not affect the way they are regarded if, in their regular audits, they function in a participative manner.

Indeed, in some internal auditing organizations separate internal auditing groups are employed for the protective and the constructive audit phases. Thus, those performing the regular internal audit functions, not related to fraud, are not identified with investigative tactics. They are free to carry out participative audits with no tinge of an adversary relationship.

Considering the Audit Impact

Internal auditors who seek cooperation will have to plan their approach carefully. They will have to recognize that definite behavioral effects surface in three different steps in the audit: the anticipation of the audit, the conduct of the audit, and the report on the audit.

The anticipation of the audit and the mystery attached can be defused by positive steps on the part of the internal auditors. They can keep surprise audits to a minimum, restricting them to such activities as cash and negotiable securities or where fraud is suspected. They can provide information in advance to auditees, explaining the audit process and how to prepare for it. They can explain to the auditees the positive results of the audit and the benefits the auditees can expect. Jarvis describes an approach which was used in a bank:[15] An article was distributed in advance to all bank employees. The article was designed to give branch employees a capsule view of what internal auditors do and don't do and thus put them at ease when they see that "here come the auditors."

During an audit, people are given a feeling of importance if they are asked people-type rather than control-type questions. For example:

What tasks do you perform?

What tasks does your immediate supervisor perform?

What tasks do the people directly under your supervision perform?

Which of the people in your own work group do you see most often outside of work?

When you want a job done in a hurry whom do you turn to?

This type of inquiry has additional benefits. It provides a window to the informal organization. It shows the network of relationships which overlays the formal, structured organization chart, and it helps the internal auditor understand not only how things are supposed to work, but also how they actually do work.

The Management View

During the audit, internal auditors should take a managerial approach to deficiencies. They should downplay the insignificant findings, search for the causes of significant ones, and work with operating managers to correct weaknesses. Internal auditors should keep in mind that operating people usually have a pretty good idea of what is going on. No matter what ideas the auditors may have about improvements, the chances are that the operating people have already considered them. Relations are improved immeasurably when the internal auditors openly adopt these ideas, filter them through their own experience, and then present them as the result of a team effort between auditor and auditee.

During the reporting phase, no deficiency finding should be formally reported which was not thoroughly discussed with operating management. No weakness should be overstated. No nitpicking findings should appear in the formal report. Credit for outstanding achievements by the auditee should find a place in the report.

The Investigative Audit

Not all audits can be carried out in the participative mode. Some are frankly critical or problem-finding audits. Even here, the behavioral aspects should be considered.[16]

Be sure the nature and scope of the investigation are understood in advance by those being audited, if at all possible.

Be sure the examination or investigation is supported by higher management and that the support has been communicated to those concerned.

Before the work starts, meet with the responsible manager in charge of the functions being audited to discuss the range and scope of the audit, the time required, and the work to be done.

Conduct the audit with the least possible disruption of day-to-day operations.

If the audit is prolonged, keep management currently informed of progress.

At the end of the audit, report as fully as may be permissible to the manager involved.

Meeting Hostile Opposition

Despite all the good will in the world, internal auditors are still bound to find antagonism. The auditors may seek reasonably and logically to present their point of view, but the auditee will remain adamant, unhearing, unconvinced, and completely negative. These confrontations happen. They are bound to happen, now and again, so long as people remain people. It is the closed-mind syndrome, and there is no master key. The following suggestions may be useful.

Select the right time. Do not try to open the closed mind to reason when the owner is angry or tired or distracted.

Never take a locked-in-concrete position. All that does is seal the closed mind from any possible penetration.

Don't rely on logic. Logic never opened a closed mind. If it were agreeable to logic it could not be characterized as a closed mind.

Never paint yourself into a corner. Never take a position from which you cannot gracefully retreat.

Abjure force and embrace persuasion.

At the outset, find a point of agreement. Opposition is useless; agreement is the opening wedge. There must be some things on which auditor and auditee agree, even if it is that you are in disagreement.

Invite the auditees to spell out their position. Listen and try to understand, really listen. Don't be a closed mind yourself.

Make an active effort to put yourself in their place. Sincerely try to understand.

When you understand where they stand, when you have put yourself in their shoes, then try to make them feel the position you want them to take is the position they themselves want to take. Help them to be right. That is what the closed mind wants above all.

When all else fails, when the deficiency or weakness is serious, when the risks are great and correction cannot be compromised, then the internal auditors must remember their responsibilities and carry the matter to higher authority. The time bombs of potential risk to the enterprise **must** be defused. It is best to try persuasion first, because internal auditors must remember that one day they may have to return to deal with the closed mind again.

Listening

Audit derives from the Latin *auditus* — to hear. Initially it meant a judicial hearing of complaints, a judicial examination. Later it meant an official examination of accounts with verification by reference to witnesses and vouchers. Accounts were originally oral. Later practices of auditing increased the reliance on written records and decreased the weight given oral witness.

The wheel has turned. In audits of operations the emphasis is on people as much as it is on documents. Auditors have become adept at analyzing, comparing, and evaluating the written words and numbers; they are not, however, equally adept at evaluating the spoken word. That is not necessarily their fault. Little has been written and less has been taught about listening. Nichols reported that 12 months of research on the subject disclosed that 3,000 scientific and experimental researches had been published on reading. Only one had been published on listening.[17]

Yet studies have confirmed the greater importance of listening. Paul Rankin of Ohio University conducted the pioneer study on listening in 1927 when he decided to find out what proportion of our waking day is spent in communication. He asked 65 white-collar workers to keep a log of all their waking daytime activities at 15-minute intervals for two months. He found that 70% of our conscious waking day is spent in communication. Of this 70%, 9% is spent in writing, 16% in reading, 30% in talking, and 45% in listening.[18]

Most of schooling is spent in teaching students reading, writing, and arithmetic. Little if any is spent on teaching listening, and yet this is how we spend almost half our waking day. The obvious question here is, "So what?" Is lack of formal listening training such a problem?

The answer is yes. An experiment by Professor Harry Jones of Columbia

University proved that we recall but 50% of what we have just heard. In two weeks we recall only 25%.[19] This presents a problem to all people, but it is especially serious for internal auditors. They must gain their understanding of operations chiefly by listening to people, really listening.

A sales maxim has it that "the foolish salesman would sell me with his reasons; the wise salesman with my own." How does the wise salesman — or the wise internal auditor — learn "my own" reasons? By listening, not by talking.

Listening, then, is as important to an internal auditor as is the ability to verify, compare, and evaluate. Indeed, those very abilities can be used in aggressive, attentive listening. First, however, internal auditors should know the barriers to good listening — the bad habits that bar a comprehension of what was heard.

Dr. Nichols carried out a research project at the University of Minnesota which identified ten bad listening habits. Other studies at Michigan State University and in Colorado confirmed his findings. Here are some of the barriers to good listening which are of particular interest to internal auditors.[20]

Criticizing the speaker's delivery. Internal auditors must often listen, for their very livelihood, to people who are dull, who fail to come to the point, who wander, and who murder the king's English. Yet among all the chaff may be kernels which will be significant to an effective audit.

Getting overstimulated. Evaluation should be withheld until comprehension is complete. The internal auditors' naturally critical faculty impel them to criticize and rebut, but if the mind is on rebuttal, there is no listening and no comprehension.

Listening only for the facts. The inept listener tries to absorb the many facts a speaker uses to support the central ideas being conveyed. In the mad scramble to remember the facts, the poor listeners lose the central concept — the hook on which the facts hang. The good listener is the idea listener. The facts tend to be appended to the threads connected to the ideas.

Trying to write down everything. Most inept listeners will try to write down everything the speaker says. Good listeners seek out the central premises and record those, spending the rest of the time listening for how well the speaker will support these premises.

Letting emotion-laden words get between us and the speaker. An emotion-laden word can have such an impact on the listener that the speaker is completely tuned out. Aggressive listening can overcome this tendency to concentrate on the hated words rather than what the speaker is trying to say.

Wasting the differential between speech and thought speed. People speak at about 125 words a minute. But thought cruises along easily at 400 words a minute. For college-educated people, the cruising speed is well over

800 words a minute. Most internal auditors have a college education or its equivalent. This differential can be a liability if it lets the listener randomly tune out and in to the speaker. Important information may be lost. This liability can be converted to an asset by three mental forms of concentration:

1. Anticipate the speaker's next point. Run ahead of the speaker mentally. Try to guess the point that will be made. Then compare your guess with that point. Learning is thereby reinforced. One of the oldest laws of learning is to contrast or compare one fact or idea with another.

2. Identify evidence. The speaker's points should not be accepted at face value. Merely because they have been asserted does not make them true. They should be supported by facts. The time differential can be used to identify the facts.

3. Recapitulate periodically as you listen. The good listener will tune the speaker in, listen hard for four or five minutes, and then take a quick mental time out. In that interval the listener, with that enormous thought speed, can summarize in ten seconds what was said in five minutes. Several of these summaries increase the ability of the listener to understand and recall what was heard.

Participative Auditing

People are willing to assist others when they feel they will share in the benefits, when they are all working toward the same goal. Operating people have less animosity towards budgets when they participate in establishing them. People work more enthusiastically toward goals when they help set them. Line looks more kindly toward staff when it sees staff as an aid and not a control.

The same is true of internal auditing. The fear, the distrust, the mystery are all dissipated when auditor and auditee work together in a spirit of cooperation and self-evaluation.

Mints urges some method of establishing teamwork relationships so that auditees may feel a real share and interest in the audit projects. Specifically he suggests:

> For example, the truly participative auditor might do such things as: (1) take the auditees into his confidence at the beginning of the examination by discussing his program along with his objectives and the reasoning behind his approach; (2) solicit suggestions and assistance from them; (3) discuss all findings currently with those directly concerned and actively seek their help in developing proposed solutions; (4) provide the auditees with interim reports of findings so that steps toward implementation of corrective action might be taken before issuance of the final report; and (5) review his reports with all those concerned at each level and carefully consider their suggestions for modification before going to the next higher level. When he does not agree with their suggestions for changes he would explain his views and attempt to persuade them of the reasonableness of his position.[21]

The conduct Mints suggests in performing audits would appear basic to establishing a useful relationship between auditor and auditee. We believe, however, that a truly participative audit implies that operating personnel will personally take part in the audit itself. The internal auditors must guide and direct the audit since the audit opinion, in the final analysis, is theirs. Their direction is essential to ensure independence and objectivity. But within that framework, participation can still take place. It calls for an aggressive program of involving the auditee personnel in the gathering of information, the identification of weaknesses, and the correction of defects. This can be done and has been done with some success.[22]

A company president requested the audit of research and development (R & D) activities. The people assigned to the audit reviewed R & D methods and interviewed scientists and engineers in other divisions and companies. As a result the auditors were able to construct a body of standards which, if met, would provide evidence that the R & D activities were being carried out in a professional and businesslike manner. Here, for example, are two of such standards from about thirty:

1. The technological requirements for R & D should be identified, and the personnel responsible for the work should have the requisite knowledge and skills in their technologies.

2. Managers should be provided with adequate systems of financial control to assist them in accomplishing their goals and missions within allocated budgets.

Once the standards were developed, the auditors met with auditee personnel and convinced them of the desirability of a teamwork approach: The auditees would contribute their technical knowledge; the auditors would contribute their administrative and management knowledge.

The auditees then gathered pertinent and useful information about each of the 30 standards. The information was provided by accumulating such things as procedures, instructions, manuals, statistics, job descriptions, employee histories, and the like. In accordance with the agreement, the auditors validated the information gathered, making such independent checks as they deemed necessary.

During their gathering of information, the auditees found deviations from acceptable standards. Without any prompting, they initiated corrective action. Before the audit was completed, most of the weaknesses had been strengthened and most of the deviations had been corrected. Auditee and auditor worked together in harmony to achieve mutual goals. The exercise in participative auditing paid off.

With the increasing complexity of enterprise systems, and with the broadening scope of internal audit work to include all manner of operations within the enterprise, such participative audits may become the norm rather than the exception. A wedding of technical expertise contributed by the auditee and the management expertise contributed by internal auditors may be the only effective way to make thorough audits of complex, technical activities.

Special Problems in Audit Relationships

Internal auditors find themselves torn by conflicting forces and faced by duties and responsibilities that may seem completely irreconcilable.[23]

They owe a duty to executive management whose work they appraise and whose pay they accept. They also owe a duty to keep the audit committee of the board of directors informed of serious weaknesses that are detected during their appraisals.

They are admonished to be problem-solving partners of operating managers and help them improve their operation. Yet they have a duty to be the watchdogs of the enterprise, alert for management inefficiency, ineptitude, and even fraud.

They are urged to work together in participative teamwork with operating managers. Yet they are required to report deficiencies to the managers' superiors.

These opposing claims on the auditor's loyalties and responsibilities can create audit schizophrenia. The solutions may not be simple, but solutions will have to be found so auditors can do their jobs with the least possible friction.

Management and the Board

In 1978, the *Standards for the Professional Practice of Internal Auditing* pronounced internal auditing to be "an independent appraisal function within an organization to examine and evaluate its activities as a service to the organization." This was a departure from the earlier Statement of Responsibilities which held internal auditing to be "a service to management." This change signaled the internal auditor's new responsibility to both management and the board of directors.

In earlier years the distinction may not have been significant, but recent pressures upon boards of directors have forced them to face responsibilities they may have shrugged off previously. The U.S. Securities and Exchange Commission (SEC) recommended in 1972 that all publicly held companies have audit committees composed of outside directors. Accordingly, no members of management would be involved in the review of certain matters which were once solely the prerogative of management. For example, many audit committees review the scope of both internal and external audit work and the content of internal audit reports. Also of interest to them is the review of internal accounting and operating controls. The committee will be highly interested in any breakdowns in internal controls. The U.S. Foreign Corrupt Practices Act of 1977 makes concern for good internal controls an imperative for audit committees.

Indeed, these suggested actions may become mandated. In April 1977, in the case of SEC vs. Killearn Properties, Inc., a United States District Court judge handed down a final judgment and order which decreed that:

The majority of the board of directors are not to be employees of Killearn.

The board maintain an audit committee of outside directors.

The audit committee become involved in internal control and improvements suggested both by the independent auditor and the internal staff.

The committee meet at least twice a year with the company's financial staff and discuss with them the scope of internal accounting and auditing procedures in effect and the extent to which recommendations made by the independent accountants and the internal staff have been implemented.

The last two matters used to be the sole concern of management. When brought before the board they were usually dutifully approved. They are still a matter of concern to managers at all levels, but management is now being forced to share the review function with nonmanagement board members. This has become an unpleasant fact of life to many members of senior management.

Internal auditors often have a dotted-line reporting relation to the audit committee. These internal auditing watchdogs, who probably know more about what is going on in the company than anybody else, have unrestricted access to the audit committee and can report to the committee in private without asking permission of senior management.

This puts internal auditors in the middle. They owe an allegiance both to management and the board; yet their salaries are paid by management. How can they meet their responsibilities to both bodies and still keep their jobs and their sanity? The answer is not easy, but there is an answer. It involves status, professionalism, and candor.

Status

For operating personnel to understand the internal auditor's authority and responsibilities, these must be set forth in writing and with particularity. This writing, this charter, should be signed by the chief executive officer **and** approved by the board of directors.

The drafters of the *Standards for the Professional Practice of Internal Auditing* were fully aware of the dilemma that can perplex internal auditors. They recognized that without adequate protection the director of internal auditing would be in peril any time a report to the audit committee was not pleasing to the CEO. Section 110 of the *Standards* states that internal auditors must be independent of the activities they audit. They should be responsible to an officer in the organization with sufficient authority to promote independence. They should have direct communication with the board. And the board should concur in the appointment or removal of the director of the internal auditing department (see Chapter 16).

Professionalism

Internal auditors should reflect the same posture of professionalism — of adherence to a professional code of ethics — as the ethical attorney or doctor. Neither will break the law for his or her client or patient.

Internal auditors cannot break faith with their own code of ethics. That code dictates that members of the internal auditing profession have an obligation to exercise honesty, objectivity, and diligence in the performance of their duties and responsibilities. They shall not knowingly be a part of any illegal or improper activity. In their reporting, they shall reveal such material facts known to them which, if not revealed, could either distort the results of operations under review or conceal unlawful practice. They shall in the practice of their profession be mindful of their obligation to maintain standards of competence, morality, and dignity.

This is a heavy burden every professional is expected to carry. When both management and the board are aware of the dictates of the profession, the job of the professional internal auditor may be easier to handle.

Candor

The internal auditor must be completely open with the chief executive officer. The CEO should never be surprised by what is reported to the board — unless the CEO is involved in wrongdoing. But, fraud excepted, keeping the CEO informed is a matter of courtesy if not pure survival. The CEO may not be enthralled by the parading of soiled linen before the board, but if the CEO is informed of it in advance, and his or her views and proposed actions are dutifully reported to the board, the sting will thereby be made less galling.

The answer to the dilemma is three-fold: one, a strong position in the organization by reason of status and charter; two, the understanding in management circles that the internal auditors are professionals bound by a professional code of ethics; and three, an open, candid aspect maintained by the auditors toward all with whom they deal.

The Partner and the Watchdog

In recent years, the stress in the internal auditing profession has been on having a concern for, and dealing openly and fairly with, people. Present auditor/auditee relations still reflect some basic conflicts and hostility. These attitudes limit the auditor's ability to contribute to overall organizational goals.

Many senior executives see the internal auditor's role as more than a detector of wrongdoing. They want their internal auditors to be a part of the problem-solving team, working shoulder-to-shoulder with operating managers to correct weaknesses and deficiencies. But senior managers also want to be assured of the internal auditor's protective role. Internal auditors must make sure that systems are properly controlled and protected. The *Standards* require internal auditors to be alert to the possibility of intentional wrongdoing, errors, omissions, inefficiency, waste, ineffectiveness, and conflicts of interest. Further, when internal auditors suspect wrongdoing, they should inform appropriate authorities within the organization. The internal auditor does have a watchdog function and must be aware of the ever-present danger of management fraud.

No internal auditor can be so naive as to think every manager is a model of probity and rectitude. Too often operating reports are self-serving declarations by the operating manager instead of precise statements of fact. Some managers, including those holding high positions, have been known to be less than ethical in the transactions they become involved in.

The quandary is painful but clear: The behaviorists admonish us to improve staff/line relations; yet there is the responsibility to identify risks and to be alert for wrongdoing. Again, the internal auditors must go back to their charter in the company, to the statement of their *Standards*, and to their professionalism.

The charter must provide internal auditors with free access to all persons, records, systems, and facilities. This provision is for access, not suspicion. The first approach, the first contacts, the preliminary surveys — without prior indicators of misbehavior — should be carried out openly and cordially. The purpose here is to gather information; and particularly where the activities are esoteric, the internal auditors will need the assistance of operating managers and their subordinates to familiarize themselves with the objectives, controls, and standards that have been set or established. If there is naught to persuade otherwise, the auditors may continue their role of problem-solving partners and complete the audit in that manner.

But what if all is not well? What if the indicators of impropriety begin to raise their heads? Then the internal auditors must heed the requirements of their *Standards*. Although they are not responsible as insurers against fraud, they must be alert to what may be shown by the indicators as possible wrongdoing. The steps to be taken will vary with the circumstances. The law of the situation will dictate the program to follow. Here are some suggestions:

Seek out or establish standards, both budgetary and statistical, and investigate all material deviations.

Use quantitative and analytical techniques (time series analyses, regression and correlation analyses, and random sampling) to highlight aberrant behavior. What stands out like a candle in the darkness? Develop benchmarks, such as space used, time required, weight limitations imposed, wage and output compared.

Compare performance with industry norms as well as with performance in comparable profit centers within the organization.

Identify critical process indicators: melt loss in smelting, death loss in feed lots, rework in assembly, scrap in manufacturing, and gross profit tests in buy-sell operations.

Analyze carefully not only performance that does not meet standards, but also performance that looks too good.

Then, if the indicators proclaim aberrant behavior, the internal auditor has no choice but to follow the *Standards*.

280 *Due Professional Care*

.03   When an internal auditor suspects wrongdoing, the appropriate authorities within the organization should be informed. The internal auditor may recommend whatever investigation is considered necessary in the circumstances. Thereafter, the auditor should follow up to see that the internal auditing department's responsibilities have been met.

When senior management, made aware of the problem, is coping with it, the internal auditor should wait a seemly time to make sure it is corrected. This may not be the appropriate time to notify the board or suggest that senior management do so. Every company has its problems. The internal auditors should not cry wolf each time they see a problem.

But if management is not taking care of the difficulty in a timely manner, further audit action may be necessary. The internal auditor should heed Ward Burns who said that internal auditors must have guts. They must have the fortitude to stand up and be heard even if it means going to the top.[24] That top may be the chief executive officer or the audit committee of the board, depending on the circumstances. Knowing to whom to go and when to go calls for professionalism. Here too, resolving the dilemma calls for status, an unequivocal charter, professional conduct, and fairness to all.

Operating Managers and their Superiors

The commandment to employ humanistic behavior toward auditees is not only to show that the internal auditor is a human being. It is also to provide an atmosphere of trust and fair dealing.

But fair dealing must not equate with whitewashing. No matter how pleasant the relations with the manager and no matter how charming the manager is personally, a significant deficiency in his or her shop is still a deficiency. It must, therefore, be brought up to the cold light of day, and it cannot be forgotten until it is corrected.

What happens when the internal auditor sees on the one side a hard-working accounts payable manager who has been helpful and pleasant during the audit and then sees on the other side an unacceptable series of duplicate payments of significant amounts? It depends on how the internal auditor handles the situation. The overpayments can cause chaos or they can create an opportunity for auditor and auditee to roll up their sleeves and then be able to say to the auditee's superiors, "We fixed it!"

Such a relationship has to be developed early and nurtured carefully. It starts at the preliminary meeting. It points out the way the internal auditor operates: fairly and objectively. For example, the auditor could say:

"I'm going to keep my audit open and above board. Absent fraud, which vitiates everything, you'll be kept currently aware of all my findings, both good and bad. If I or my assistants come up with some minor deviation or haphazard human error, we'll point it out to the individual who caused the error and we'll not bother reporting it. But let's face it, significant deviations occur in the best-run organizations. If we find one that will continue to hurt our company if not corrected, then we must report it. My charter, my professional code, require that I report it and discuss it with whomever I feel should know. This I will do for you: You'll be the first to know. We'll discuss it in whatever depth you wish. We'll present you with all the evidence we gathered. If you like, we'll show you our working papers. We'll search together for the causes.

"We'll explore together the effect, both actual and potential. I'll offer my counsel, based on my experience, on how to correct the difficulty and solve the problem. The corrective action will, of course, be yours, not mine. If I receive evidence of action taken or action begun with a due date for completion, I will stress that to your superiors and I certainly will not exaggerate the matter in my report. Can I be fairer than that, and still do my job?"

Most operating managers will welcome this attitude, this openness, and sincerity. The fact that defects will be communicated to superiors need not be fatal to the problem-solving partnership. But it is a sad fact of internal auditing life that some managers will not respond to this offer of good working relations. Where these managers are encountered, the internal auditor must maintain professionalism.

Internal auditors must ask themselves, "What is our basic objective as an auditor?" The answer is obvious: "To make an audit." From that the auditor may not be deterred. Internal auditors can but hold out the olive branch. If it is dashed from their hands, their choice is clear: They must still do their field work, they must still develop deficiency findings, they must still discuss them with whomever is a party of interest, and they must still include their significant findings in their reports.

The internal auditor is an extension of management. How would top management expect their internal auditors to act? Most likely they would want their internal auditors to act like themselves: Treat sterling operating managers and employees with praise. Guide erring people into the paths of righteousness. But castigate the unregenerate villains. There can be no problem-solving partnership with villains.

If all managers are educated to know what to expect, then the results do not come as a surprise. Unnecessary surprises are what are unfair. Operating managers have a right to be treated fairly, but they have no right to have the deficiencies in their shops hidden from the light of day. Internal auditors are bound to uncover the hidden defects by their charter, by their Statement of Responsibilities, and by their *Standards for the Professional Practice of Internal Auditing*.

Internal auditors must be prepared to look both ways. They must deal openly and fairly with operating managers, yet they must disclose and help drive out chicanery and wrongdoing. They must seek out defects in operations, while also helping managers correct them so that superiors do not visit unfair punishment on their subordinates as a result of audits.

Conclusion

Research studies have proven what internal auditors have known for a long time: They are not high on the list of close friends of line personnel. This stems from inherent staff/line conflicts and from the approach internal auditors often take toward their audits.

The research studies have also shown that the difference between an effective and an ineffective audit may often lie in the way the auditee regards the auditor. Potentially good audits with significant audit findings have resulted in no corrective action because of the hostility the auditors themselves engendered. Internal auditors who adopt a participative posture have a better chance of reaching their audit objectives than those who do not.

Internal auditors often find themselves in the middle. They are affected by conflicts between executive management and the board of directors, by the need to be empathetic with managers and still report serious defects, and by the requirement that the serious errors of the operating manager be brought to the attention of the manager's superiors. The answer to the dilemma is not simple. It can be alleviated by adequate status for the internal auditors in the enterprise, by their recognition as professional practitioners, and by an open, candid approach to their audits.

References

1. N. C. Churchill and W. W. Cooper, "A Field Study of Internal Auditing," *The Accounting Review*, Vol. XL, No. 4 (October 1965) pp. 267-281.
2. F. E. Mints, *Behavioral Patterns in Internal Audit Relationships*, Research Committee Report 17 (Altamonte Springs, Fla: The Institute of Internal Auditors, Inc. 1972), p. 37.
3. D. K. Clancy, Frank Collins, and Selimo C. Rael, "Some Behavioral Perceptions of Internal Auditing," *The Internal Auditor*, June 1980, p. 50.
4. Melville Dalton, "Conflicts between Staff and Line Managerial Officers," *American Sociological Review*, Vol. 15 (1950), pp. 342-351.
5. Chris Argyris, *The Impact of Budgets on People* (New York: Controllership Foundation, 1952).
6. F. E. Mints, "Cooperative Auditing: The Key to the Future," *The Internal Auditor*, November/December 1973, p. 35.
7. D. R. Carmichael, "Behavioral Hypothesis of Internal Control," *The Accounting Review*, April 1970, pp. 235-245.
8. S. F. Keating, "How Honeywell Management Views Operational Auditing," *The Internal Auditor*, September/October 1969, pp. 43-51.
9. W. G. Phillips, "The Internal Auditor and the Changing Needs of Management," *The Internal Auditor*, May/June 1970, pp. 55-56.
10. W. J. Harmeyer, "Some of My Best Friends are Auditors, But . . . ," *The Internal Auditor*, January/February 1973, p. 8.
11. F. E. Mints, "Behavioral Patterns," p. 60.
12. *Ibid.*, p. 67.
13. *Ibid.*

14. W. R. DeZerne, "Will the I.G. Act Improve Internal Auditing in Federal Agencies?" *The Internal Auditor*, June 1980, p. 100.
15. J. E. Jarvis, "Here Come the Auditors," *The Internal Auditor*, August 1980, p. 43.
16. J. J. Butler, "Human Relations in Auditing," *The Internal Auditor*, Spring 1963, p. 66.
17. R. G. Nichols, "Listening Is Good Business," *The Internal Auditor*, March/April 1970, p. 32.
18. R. G. Nichols, pp. 31-32; and Robert Haakenson, "The Art of Listening," *The Internal Auditor*, August 1976, p. 33.
19. *Ibid.*, pp. 33-34.
20. *Ibid.*, pp. 38-42.
21. F. E. Mints, "Behavioral Patterns," p. 86.
22. L. B. Sawyer, "Tomorrow's Internal Auditor," *The Internal Auditor*, June 1978, pp. 20-23.
23. L. B. Sawyer, "Janus, or the Internal Auditor's Dilemma," *The Internal Auditor*, December 1980, pp. 19-27.
24. Ward Burns, "What Management Expects of Internal Audit Now!" *The Internal Auditor*, May/June 1975, p. 23.

Supplementary Reading

Clancy, D. K., Frank Collins, and Selimo C. Real. "Some Behavioral Perceptions of Internal Auditing." *The Internal Auditor*, June 1980, pp. 44-52.

Harmeyer, W. J. "Some of My Best Friends are Auditors, But. . . ." *The Internal Auditor*, January/February 1973, pp. 8-17.

Mints, F. E. "Behavioral Patterns in Internal Audit Relationships." Research Committee Report 17. Altamonte Springs, Fla.: The Institute of Internal Auditors, Inc., 1972.

Nichols, R. G. "Listening is Good Business." *The Internal Auditor*, March/April 1970, pp. 31-42.

Sawyer, L. B. "Tomorrow's Internal Auditor." *The Internal Auditor*, June 1978, pp. 11-23.

Sawyer, L. B. "Janus, or the Internal Auditor's Dilemma." *The Internal Auditor*, December 1980, pp. 19-27.

For further study

Discussion Problems

1. The internal audit manager sent a team of auditors to perform a first-time audit of a computer center at one of the regional offices. The audit supervisor, after his preliminary discussion with local supervision, proceeded to carry out the audit without enlisting the cooperation of the technically qualified employees. At the conclusion of the audit when the findings were discussed, there were serious differences of opinion between auditees and auditors which cast doubt on the effectiveness of the audit findings and recommendations.

Required: Describe three ways in which the auditors might have modified their approach to gain more harmonious and effective relations between auditors and auditees.

2. An internal auditor should be conscious of the obligation to be objective and of the need for constructive and practical audit opinions and recommendations. The auditor also should be conscious of the need for good auditor/auditee relationships. Assume that the auditor is concluding an audit of the engineering division. The major audit findings indicate a tendency to

bypass other departments that should be involved in decision making; some shortcomings in control practices; and a lack of liaison among the engineering, purchasing, and accounting departments.

Required: Describe five actions the internal auditor should take to conclude the assignment in such a way as to preserve reasonably good auditor/auditee relationships.

3. List five opportunities provided by the opening internal audit conference for establishing good auditor/auditee relationships.

4. Many internal auditors find it a good practice to review the draft of the internal audit report with the auditees. In order to have a productive review, these auditors orally set the stage by commenting upon a number of matters concerning the audit, such as the scope of the examination and so forth.

Required: List four additional matters appropriate for internal auditors to comment on when orally setting the stage for a draft review.

5. One audit manager says to another, "I hear a lot about developing harmonious relations with auditees. I disagree. An audit, like taxes, should hurt. That's the way I play it in my company. When I'm through with them they know they've been audited. Besides, maintaining satisfactory relations with auditees is not professional. We are under no obligation to empathize with the people we audit." Comment.

Multiple Choice Problems

1. The internal auditor may contribute to poor auditor/auditee relationships by:
a. Not discussing audit findings with auditees.
b. Not giving due credit to auditees for improvements made.

c. Failing to give the auditee sufficient time to respond to audit findings.
d. All of the above.
e. None of the above.

2. Which of the following is likely to cause the least resistance to internal audit activity?
a. Surprise audits.
b. Oral audit reports.
c. A judgmental attitude by the auditee.
d. Contrived questions to the auditee.
e. An attitude of superiority by the auditor

3. The Mints study, carried out about seven years after the Churchill and Cooper study, showed that the auditee's perception of internal auditors was:
a. Much improved.
b. Somewhat improved.
c. About the same.
d. Somewhat worse.
e. Much worse.

4. A study conducted by Clancy, et al., showed that in the views of auditees, internal auditors:
a. Have demonstrated no great ability to identify organizational problems.
b. Do not concern themselves with organizational problems.
c. Are especially adept at dealing with organizational problems.
d. Can teach managers a great deal about the function of organizing.
e. None of the above.

5. Line people fear staff people because:
a. They believe their superiors will believe they should have thought of the improvements themselves.
b. They dread the unknown quantities inherent in change.
c. They are apprehensive that any revisions to current procedures will unveil ineptitude.

d. All of the above.

e. None of the above.

6. One of the chief reasons auditees fear internal auditors is because they perceive them as:

a. Emissaries of management.

b. Out to do them harm.

c. Smarter than they.

d. Part of the control system.

e. Better dressed.

7. When internal auditors find themselves torn between duties to the CEO and the board, they should:

a. Resign.

b. Follow the *Standards*.

c. Lean toward the board.

d. Lean toward the CEO.

e. Keep quiet.

8. Auditors can achieve more lasting good relations with auditees if:

a. They downplay all adverse audit findings.

b. They report all audit defects.

c. They refrain from reporting some of their findings.

d. They issue oral reports only.

e. They report all serious defects fairly and candidly.

9. The ability to maintain satisfactory relations basically means:

a. Being nice to people.

b. Getting the job done with the least adverse effect.

c. Turning all unpleasant jobs over to a special investigative unit.

d. Not reporting deficiencies to executive management.

e. Meeting auditees socially.

10. True participative audits call for:

a. The auditee to participate in gathering data.

b. The auditee to participate in forming the audit opinion.

c. The auditee to participate in writing the audit report.

d. The auditor to carry out corrective action.

e. All of the above.

Case Studies

23-1 A Directed Audit

In the ABC Company Director of Internal Auditing Ina Austin is organizationally responsible to Director of Financial Operations Frank Oppenheim. Frank asked Ina to his office where the following discussion took place:

"Ina, what's the last time you audited the purchasing department?"

"Two years ago, Frank."

"When are you going to audit it again?"

"Next year."

"Well, I'd like you to move it up immediately or else do a special review."

"Why?"

"My chief accountant has been having problems with purchasing."

"Chet Ackroyd?"

"Right. He tells me that purchase order change notices coming to accounts payable are often late and that some of them look suspicious."

"Suspicious in what way?"

"It seems to our accounts payable people that some of the price increases are not justified."

"How late are these change notices?"

"Late enough to cause underpayments and create bad relations with suppliers."

"Has Chet talked to Perry Agee, the purchasing agent?"

"He says he has and that Perry promised improvements, but there have been none."

"Have you talked to Derek Matheson, director of material, Perry's boss?"

"Damn it, Ina, do I have to make your audit for you?"

"Not at all. I'd like to get as much background as possible before I send someone out on this assignment."

"Well, that's your assignment. Hop

to it. And get this mess cleaned up. Another thing."

"Yes?"

"Don't tell Derek or Perry that I asked for this audit. What those two jokers don't know won't hurt them."

"Yes sir."

Ina left the meeting feeling disturbed. She had always had good relations with Perry and Derek. They had been open with her, and she and her auditors had always dealt openly and candidly with them. She felt that Perry usually tried to do a good job. But he had 45 buyers working for him and they were not all equally competent and dedicated.

Yet, when well-documented findings and reasonable recommendations were brought to Perry's attention, he always saw to it that appropriate corrective action was taken. Ina decided to give the assignment to Art Chaney, one her best auditors in charge.

Required: What instructions should Ina give Art?

23-2 Conflict of Interest

Art Chaney, Jr., is an internal auditor for Astro Corporation, a company listed on the New York Stock Ex-change. While auditing the engineering branch, Art found out what seemed to be pretty general knowledge in engineering. Charles De La Fontaine, the chief engineer for the Astro Corporation, had a half interest in a testing laboratory. The laboratory apparently had a good reputation in the community and its rates were competitive. Last year the lab did over $25,000 worth of business for the Astro Corporation.

Charles had openly declared this interest in his annual conflict-of-interest declaration. Each year every salaried employee is required to complete such a declaration. It is a questionnaire about potential conflicts. One of the questions is: Do you have any financial interest in a supplier with which our company does business? Charles had answered "yes" to the question and his statement had gone up to the review committee made up of the general counsel, the vice-president of administration, and the president of the corporation, Richard De La Fontaine. The review committee had decided there was no conflict.

Required: What action should internal auditing take?

24

Relationships with
External Auditors

Objectives of external and internal auditors. The scope of their work. The different missions. Concerns with internal controls. Changing times and the greater importance of coordination. The U.S. Foreign Corrupt Practices Act. The needs of senior management and the audit committee of the board. Statement of Auditing Standards (SAS)9. Practice under SAS-9. Criteria to be met by internal auditors: Qualifications, independence, and competence. Specific standards. How to achieve coordination. Company policies on internal/external audit relations. Internal auditors as an information network. Mutual respect and integrity. Building blocks for cooperation. Common user files. Statistical sampling. Computer audits. Mandated and personal obstacles. Opportunities for improved cooperation.

Introduction

External auditors and internal auditors have different objectives, but they reach them by similar means. External auditors express an independent expert's opinion as to the fairness of their clients' financial statements. They serve a number of entities because their opinion is relied on by management, directors, shareholders, suppliers, creditors, and the government. Internal auditors serve the organization by measuring and evaluating its operations. External auditors normally restrict their audit scope to the financial records and the accounting areas. Internal auditors have a wider scope; they may review any records, any activities, and any areas in the organization.*

*See Chapter 1 for a summary of distinctions between the two.

In the early years, the work of internal auditors closely paralleled that of the external auditors. Now the focus on operations expands the scope of internal auditing: to measure the effectiveness of existing systems throughout the enterprise, to appraise efficiency and economy in all operations, and to evaluate operating performance. This new focus became necessary to carry out the mission of the modern internal auditor: to serve both senior management and the board of directors. The mission has a dual thrust: to protect enterprise assets and to offer constructive recommendations for improved operations. Internal auditors are therefore concerned with any weaknesses, both large and small, which keep enterprise operations from meeting their objectives.

The external auditors' mission is primarily to offer an independent audit opinion. To that end they are concerned with only those matters which have a material effect on that opinion.

The missions of both disciplines are supportive of each other. The internal and external auditors are both concerned with internal controls — the external auditors with internal accounting controls, the internal auditors with the entire internal control system, including internal accounting controls. Still, the depth of concern varies. To the internal auditor the adequacy and effectiveness of control systems are of primary concern. To the external auditor, they are secondary. Internal controls interest external auditors vitally; they affect the extent of their substantive tests of transactions, but these controls are secondary to the primary mission of expressing an opinion on financial statements. If controls are poor the external auditor may have to make more substantive tests. The internal auditor, on the other hand, will make recommendations to improve the controls and follow up to see that the weaknesses are corrected. This is not to say external auditors do not make similar recommendations. It is just that the recommendations are a secondary consideration.

Importance of Coordination

Neither form of audit can take the place of the other. The two areas of concern impinge on each other; hence coordination becomes essential to reduce duplications and overlaps.

The need for coordination is becoming more pressing each day. Modern business is becoming more complex. Financial reporting standards have stretched the time needed for financial audits. Inflationary trends have increased the personnel costs of public accounting firms. Fees have risen accordingly and this does not sit well with management.

Rising costs are not the only reason for coordination. The U.S. Foreign Corrupt Practices Act of 1977 placed rigorous requirements on organizations to ensure adequate systems of internal accounting control. The penalties attached to violations of the act give impetus to a united effort from both disciplines to comply with the law. The advanced techniques developed by independent accounting firms, melded to the internal auditor's expertise and intimate knowledge of the organization, can provide greater comfort to management and the board.

The expanded responsibilities of boards of directors add pressures that demand assurances of no surprises. A well-coordinated effort by professional external and internal auditors can provide nervous board members with welcome and needed assurances that weaknesses in control systems will be detected and that failures to comply with adequate systems will be promptly brought to light.

A research study for The Institute of Internal Auditors, Inc., by Brink and Barrett, appraised relations between external and internal auditors. As a part of their study they questioned chief financial officers (CFOs), chief executive officers (CEOs), and chairmen of audit committees (CACs). Questions asked of these officials included their perception of the internal audit services currently provided and desired in these two areas: one, assuring sound internal financial control, and two, assisting external auditors.

Respondents to these questions were asked for their ratings of the desirability of these outcomes on a scale of 1 to 5, with 1 equalling the lowest and 5 equalling the highest rating. A rating of 3.1 to 3.9 was considered moderately high. One of 4.0 to 5.0 was considered very high. The ratings by CFOs, CEOs, and CACs were as follows:[1]

	Current Evaluation by			Optimum Evaluation by		
Internal Audit Services	CFOs	CEOs	CACs	CFOs	CEOs	CACs
1. Assure sound internal financial control	4.3	4.4	4.4	4.8	4.7	4.7
2. Assist external auditors	3.5	3.8	3.9	3.8	4.0	4.0

Clearly, there is a high degree of interest in assuring sound internal control. At the CEO and CAC levels, particularly, there is a strong desire to see internal auditors cooperate with external auditors.

Prerequisites for Coordination

There is need for cooperation between the internal and the external auditor. The external auditor needs to use the work of the internal auditor, but that use is limited by certain prohibitions and is conditioned on certain prerequisites. These are spelled out in the Statement of Auditing Standards 9 (SAS-9) issued December 1975 by the American Institute of Certified Public Accountants (AICPA). SAS-9 superseded the AICPA's Statement on Auditing Standards No. 1, section 320.74.[2]

The Statement begins negatively: "The work of internal auditors cannot be substituted for the work of the independent auditor." This flat denial is puzzling to those internal auditors who came from public accounting and who are as well equipped as external auditors by training, experience, and continuing education to perform acceptable financial audits. SAS-9 continues, however, by saying that independent auditors in determining the nature, timing, and extent of their own auditing procedures, should consider the procedures, if any, which internal auditors perform.

If independent auditors decide that the work of internal auditors may have a bearing on their own procedures, then SAS-9 cautions that these independent auditors should consider the competence and objectivity of internal auditors and evaluate their work.

When considering the competence of internal auditors, independent auditors should inquire about the qualifications of the internal audit staff. They should consider the client's practices for hiring, training, and supervising that staff.

When addressing objectivity, independent auditors should take into account two matters: first, the organizational level to which internal auditors report the results of their work; second, the organizational level to which they report administratively. SAS-9 observes that this is frequently an indication of the extent of their ability to act independently of those responsible for the functions being audited. The higher the reporting level, the greater the reliance independent auditors will place on the objectivity of the internal auditor. For example, Brink and Barrett asked external auditors about the level of their satisfaction concerning internal auditors reporting to the chief financial officer, the chief executive officer, and the chairman of the audit committee. The responses were tabulated as follows (1 being lowest and 5 highest):[3]

Responses by:	Level of Satisfaction if Internal Auditors Report to:		
	CFO	CEO	CAC
Independent auditors	2.9	3.9	4.7

Obviously, the typical independent auditor would like to see internal auditors reporting to the CAC. Neither the CAC nor the internal auditor shares that enthusiasm. Chairmen of audit committees gave that choice a ranking of 3.7. Internal auditors gave it a ranking of 3.6. Brink and Barrett attribute the rankings by CACs to a reluctance to take over the direct supervision of internal auditing activities. They attribute the internal auditors' moderate enthusiasm to the possibility that such a reporting relationship might isolate them from management and thereby make their day-to-day activities more difficult to carry out.[4]

In evaluating the work of internal auditors, the independent auditor is required by SAS-9 to test the documentation of the audit work. These tests should include such factors as scope of work, adequacy of audit programs and of working papers, appropriateness of conclusions reached, and the agreement between reports issued and results of work performed.

SAS-9 states that independent auditors intending to rely on the work of internal auditors should at the outset of an engagement inform the internal auditors of the reports and working papers they will need and determine the internal auditor's plans. Where external auditors make use of internal auditors to provide direct assistance, SAS-9 states that the independent auditors should consider the internal auditors' competence and objectivity and supervise and test their work as appropriate.

SAS-9 concludes with a cautionary note about the judgments independent auditors make when considering the work of internal auditors. These must be the independent auditors' judgments so long as they affect the independent auditors' reports on the financial statements.

We have spoken with independent accountants and with internal auditors about SAS-9. It seems to us that where independent auditors and internal auditors respect each other's competence and objectivity, the rigorous requirements of SAS-9 are softened in actual practice. Certainly, with the emerging role of the internal auditor as an independent professional, a sharing of some of the external auditor's work with the internal auditor would be more appropriate than the restrictive language of SAS-9 indicates.

Assessing Internal Audit Competence and Objectivity

It is only reasonable for independent auditors to evaluate the work and status of internal auditors before they rely on their work. The wise internal auditors would want independent auditors to have sufficient reason to regard them as professionals. Only then can the coordination desired by CEOs and CACs take place.

Hence, internal auditors should demonstrate to external auditors that they are able to meet certain criteria of professional qualifications, of independence through status and objectivity, and of professional competence. These criteria are as follows:

Qualifications

The internal auditing department should possess or should obtain the knowledge, skills, and disciplines needed to carry out its audit responsibilities. Internal auditors who work extensively with financial records and reports should be proficient in accounting principles and techniques. They should be able to apply financial and accounting knowledge to situations likely to be encountered and to deal with them without extensive recourse to technical research and assistance. To be able to coordinate its work with that of the independent accountants, the internal auditing organization should be able to meet these qualifications:

Job descriptions should define the duties and responsibilities of the internal audit staff.

Internal auditors should meet prescribed standards of educational background and audit experience.

Internal auditors should be active in professional organizations.

Periodic training courses should be given to keep internal auditors informed about current business, company, accounting, and auditing developments.

Newly hired internal auditors should participate in formal, supervised, on-the-job training.

A significant percentage of the internal audit staff should be Certified Internal Auditors, Certified Public Accountants, or Chartered Accountants.

At least one internal auditor should have public accounting experience.

Internal auditors should have a knowledge of and be able to apply generally accepted auditing principles.

Internal auditors' performance should be periodically reviewed to assess their strengths and weaknesses in terms of specified standards.

Independence

Internal auditors should have practical independence which permits them to carry out their work freely and objectively. Independence permits internal auditors to render the impartial and unbiased judgments essential to the proper conduct of audits. It is achieved through organizational status and objectivity. The organizational status of the internal auditing department should be sufficient to permit the accomplishment of its audit responsibilities. Objectivity implies a mental attitude that views events on a purely factual basis without influence by one's personal feelings, prejudices, opinions, or interests. Objectivity requires internal auditors to have an honest belief in their work product and to feel certain that no significant quality compromises are made. Internal auditors are not to subordinate their judgment on audit matters to that of others. In terms of independence, internal auditors should be able to meet the following specific standards:

The director of the internal auditing department should be responsible to an individual in the organization with sufficient authority to promote independence and to ensure broad audit coverage, adequate consideration of audit reports, and appropriate action on audit recommendations.

The director of internal auditing should have ready access to the board of directors.

The purpose, authority, and responsibility of the internal auditing department should be defined in a formal written document (charter). The charter should establish the department's position within the organization; authorize access to records, personnel, and physical properties relevant to the performance of audits; and define the scope of internal auditing activities.

Audit findings and recommendations should be reviewed with management on a higher level than that of the function or organization audited.

Audit reports should be routed to senior executives.

Competence

Internal auditors should be competent in planning and conducting audit assignments, subject to supervisory review and approval. Internal auditors should be able to prepare formal audit plans which establish the objectives and scope of audit work. They should be able to collect, analyze, interpret, and document information to support audit results. They should be able to communicate effectively the results of their audit work, and they should follow up to ascertain that appropriate action is taken on reported audit findings. They should be able to meet these specific standards:

Audit staff should be properly instructed before they begin an audit project.

Internal auditors should be supervised from the planning of the audit work until the conclusion of the audit.

Audit work, including the evaluation of operating and control procedures, should be adequately documented in the audit working papers.

Working papers should contain appropriate evidence of follow-up and disposition of deficiency findings.

Audit reports should be supported by competent, sufficient, and relevant evidence in the working papers.

Working papers should be retained for a reasonable period or in accordance with contractual or statutory requirements.

By and large these criteria of qualifications, independence, and competence are already spelled out in the *Standards for the Practice of Internal Auditing*. Adherence to these standards — issued after SAS-9 — together with some standards specifically applicable to financial audits, should meet the requirements of SAS-9 for coordination of the work of internal auditors with external auditors.

Degrees of coordination between internal and external auditors vary widely. The Conference Board's 1978 research report on internal auditing found no unanimity on how the two groups achieved coordination:[5]

Type of Coordination	Number	Percent*
External auditors regularly receive reports of internal audit findings	234	82%
External auditors meet regularly with internal auditors:	247	87
To discuss the scope of internal audits	214	75
To review internal audit findings	174	61
To discuss the internal audit organization	108	38

*Percentage of 284 companies

In some companies the relationship between internal auditors and external auditors are prescribed by company policy and specific steps are spelled out. Here are some of these prescribed steps.[6]

Discuss audit plans and schedules to avoid conflicts and duplication of effort.

Arrange for the review of the latest working papers of the independent accountants and for discussion of the intended scope of audit coverage.

Distribute audit reports to independent public accountants and make internal audit working papers available on request.

Meet periodically with the public accountants to discuss developments affecting the internal audit function and to exchange other pertinent information.

In one company, the internal audit organization is given a considerable measure of authority over the external audit engagement. For example:[7]

Internal audit is responsible for the audit plans at all locations.

Internal audit is to approve all audit budgets; but it is not permitted to enter into any contractual arrangements on behalf of the company without the express approval of the corporate controller.

Internal audit is to approve all audit fees before they are paid.

Internal audit is responsible for coordination among the various audit firms.

All correspondence between the company and any outside audit firms must clear through internal audit.

Internal auditors can be a source of useful information which external auditors might have difficulty obtaining for themselves. The external auditors could accumulate facts, but they might not obtain the depth of understanding which internal auditors have absorbed about systems and the organization. The cost of obtaining such information can be reduced by appropriate coordination between the audit staffs.

This coordination must be based on mutual respect and integrity. Each group must be able to regard the other as professionals of equal competence. Each must be able to respect the other's independence. Moreover, the internal auditor should not be dragged off at the peremptory call of management to leave the external auditor high, dry, and alone.

Trust must be a keystone of the cooperative bridge. Neither should try any tricks with the other. Neither should be ashamed or reluctant to admit to not having been especially clever in the way they handled a particular task. With a feeling of mutual respect and trust, they can soundly construct the cooperative bridge. Here are some of the building blocks that will help make it strong:

Awareness of each other's plans requires close coordination at the very outset, but the internal auditor must accept the fact of some surprises. External auditors must have the right to keep some audit features to themselves until they are ready to carry them out. If both are aware of each other's understanding of this prerogative, such surprises should not be fatal to a wholesome relationship.

Communication should continue throughout the engagement between both staffs. Each should tell the other of accounting and auditing developments. Certainly the external auditors should be informed of important accounting decisions of the enterprise.

External auditors should be kept informed of any conditions which may affect the qualifications, independence, and competence of the internal audit staff.

The client's system of internal accounting control is the foundation on which all independent audits are built. The external auditors must be absolutely certain they have reliable, unbiased information about the system. Hence, it has been suggested that the internal auditors fill out the independent auditor's internal control questionnaires. The internal auditors must accept it as professional practice for the external auditors to test the information the internal auditors give them so that they are in a position to make independent judgments and express independent opinions. This form of cooperation leads to "common user" files which contain internal control questionnaires, flowcharts, audit programs, records of weaknesses and of corrective action, and similar matters.

Both groups could make use of the same or similar statistical sampling techniques and of computer software designed to extract statistical samples and compute statistical results.

Internal and external auditors should pool their knowledge of computer installations and applications. Each should be aware of the organization's systems for making sure that the proper information goes into the computer, the information is correctly processed in the computer, the information that comes out of the computer is controlled and dealt with properly, and the computer hardware and software are secure.

External auditors can be particularly helpful to internal auditors by supplying an outsider's viewpoint, unobstructed by the close contacts internal auditors have with the affairs of their enterprise; by providing advice on current developments in accounting and financial auditing; by supporting internal audit recommendations; and by supporting the internal auditor's need for a sufficiently high status in the organization to ensure independence.

Internal auditors can be particularly helpful to external auditors by exchanging ideas and providing an informed viewpoint on conditions and developments in the organization; by conducting plant tours and explaining processes and procedures; by providing briefings on audit activities and findings; and by participating in the year-end audits.

Conditions to Cooperation

Conditions to complete cooperation come in two forms: mandated and personal.

Mandated conditions are those included in the independent auditor's general standard requiring independence of mental attitude and the standard of field work relating to the extent of supervision. Hence, external auditors are **not** permitted to delegate certain work to the internal auditors. Such work may include:[8]

Confirmation of trade accounts receivable.

Observation of physical inventories at major locations.

Examination of corporate minutes.

Evaluation of internal controls (as distinguished from testing).

Verification of material account balances.

Verification of long-term debt, including confirmation and compliance reviews.

Rendering professional judgments, such as determining the adequacy of bad debt reserves, provisions for inventory obsolescence, and consideration of disclosures for contingent liabilities.

Personal conditions to cooperation include mutual respect, an understanding of each other's roles, and adherence to professional practice.

Some external auditors have been known to regard internal auditors as poor relations and treat them accordingly. They have not yet been made aware of the fact that modern internal auditing is a distinctive discipline and not a junior sibling to public accounting. Such attitudes breed resentment and destroy cooperation.

Poor or infrequent contact is also an obstacle to coordination. For example, certain external auditors issued "management letters" to senior executives of the client firm without discussing the draft with the internal auditors. These letters pointed out perceived system weaknesses. If the drafts were discussed with them in advance of issuance, internal auditors would be in a position to point out flaws. Certainly, the external auditor would want to purge such letters of inaccuracies before releasing them. Yet external auditors will on occasion bypass the internal auditors. Then the internal auditors become adversaries rather than allies; they will be as eager as the controller to dispute the allegations in the letter. Had the draft been reviewed with the internal auditors they might want to support the external auditors in those matters with which they agree.

Internal auditors can also place obstacles in the path of coordination by not performing professionally. For example, Winter comments:

> . . . I have observed many internal audit groups that do not establish a set plan of operations for the year and they lack complete, detailed audit programs which prescribe the audit objectives and procedures they intend to follow. Without this basic documentation, it is nearly impossible for the independent public accountant to give the proper recognition to internal audit activities in the scope of their work. Furthermore, I find that the working papers of internal auditors are often deficient and do not provide the degree of support we need to satisfy ourselves as to the actual audit procedures employed.[9]

Conclusion

Coordination and cooperation between external and internal auditors are essential. The potential for it exists, but it needs a firm foundation. It calls for the mutual understanding of each other's roles and objectives. It calls for respect for each other's professionalism. And it calls for professional conduct and professional competence.

Next must come communication: discussion of plans and programs, exchanging reports and working papers, meeting to resolve mutual problems, attending joint technical sessions, and keeping each other informed on what is new both in the accounting profession and in the client organization.

A healthy cooperative attitude can have a synergistic effect, yielding in concert more than the sum of the efforts of both staffs.

References

1. M. J. Barrett and V. Z. Brink, *Evaluating Internal/External Audit Services and Relationships*, Research Report 24 (Altamonte Springs, Fla.: The Institute of Internal Auditors, Inc., 1980), p. 26.
2. "Statement on Auditing Standards 9" (New York: American Institute of Certified Public Accountants, Inc., 1976).
3. Barrett and Brink, p. 39.
4. *Ibid.*
5. Paul Macchiaverna, *Internal Auditing* (New York: The Conference Board 1978), p. 64.
6. Paul Macchiaverna, p. 63.
7. *Ibid.*, p. 64.
8. W. B. Haase, "Cooperation Makes the Difference," *The Internal Auditor*, July/August 1973, p. 47.
9. J. W. Winter, "Coordination Between Internal and External Auditors," *The Internal Auditor*, December 1976, p. 21.

Supplementary Reading

Barrett, M. J., and V. Z. Brink. *Evaluating Internal/External Audit Services and Relationships*, Research Report 24. Altamonte Springs, Fla.: The Institute of Internal Auditors, Inc., 1980.

Haase, W. B. "Cooperation Makes the Difference." *The Internal Auditor*, July/August 1973, pp. 41-48.

"Statement on Auditing Standards 9." New York: American Institute of Certified Public Accountants, Inc., 1976.

For further study

Discussion Problems

1. The agenda of a forthcoming meeting of the audit committee of the board of directors indicates that you are to discuss coordination between external and internal auditors.

Required: (a) List five advantages of a program of coordination between external and internal auditors. (b) List five essential ingredients in establishing coordination between external and internal auditors.

2. Contrast competence and qualifications.

3. If external auditors are given copies of all audit reports, and if they have satisfied themselves of the internal auditors' competence, why would they want to review working papers as well?

4. Name three types of documents that should be kept in a "common user" file.

5. Under what circumstances would external auditors refuse to accept the internal auditors' conclusions, even if they regarded the internal auditors as being highly qualified, competent, and objective? Why?

Multiple Choice Problems

1. The independence of the internal auditing department will most likely be assured if it reports to the:
a. President.
b. Controller.
c. Treasurer.
d. Audit committee of the board of directors.
e. Vice president of finance.

2. The scope of work of the internal auditing department, as contrasted to that of the independent public accountant, should include:

a. Reviewing the reliability and integrity of financial and operating reports.
b. Determining compliance with applicable laws and regulations.
c. Ascertaining whether operating goals and objectives are being achieved.
d. Reviewing the economy and efficiency with which resources are employed.
e. All of the above.

3. The external auditors' mission is primarily to:
a. Prepare financial statements and reports.
b. Offer an opinion on financial statements.
c. Issue "management letters" on control weaknesses.
d. Validate operating reports.
e. Offer an opinion on the books of account.

4. According to an Institute of Internal Auditors' study, those with the least desire to have internal auditors assist external auditors are:
a. Chairmen of Audit Committees.
b. Chief Executive Officers.
c. Chief Financial Officers.
d. External auditors.
e. Both a. and b.

5. SAS-9 provides that if independent auditors permit the work of the internal auditors to have a bearing on their own procedures, they should:
a. Consider their competence.
b. Consider their objectivity.
c. Evaluate their work.
d. Consider their qualifications.
e. All of the above.

6. Full compliance by internal auditors with the *Standards of Professional*

Practice of Internal Auditing should satisfy independent auditors of the internal auditors':

a. Objectivity.
b. Independence.
c. Qualifications.
d. Competence.
e. All of the above.

7. Internal auditors work for the organization on whose statements the independent auditor is to express an opinion. Yet the internal auditors may be considered independent if they report to an individual in the company with sufficient authority to:

a. Assure broad audit coverage.
b. Pay adequate salaries.
c. Assure consideration of audit reports.
d. Assure an appropriate title for the chief internal auditor.
e. Both a. and c.

Case Study

24-1 Cementing Relations

Irwin Austin, director of internal auditing for Ace Manufacturing, called in his two audit supervisors, Steve and Sandy.

"Why so gloomy, Irwin?" asked Sandy.

"You'd be too if you just got raked over the coals by Frank O'Farrell," growled Irwin.

"The director of financial operations?" asked Steve.

"Who else could make my life so miserable?"

"What was it this time?" asked Sandy.

"He just got back from a meeting with the audit committee of the board. They asked him why external audit fees were skyrocketing and what were his internal auditors doing about it."

"That's what you get for reporting to the DFO and not having direct com-

munication with the audit committee yourself," said Steve smugly.

"Pretty smart. You know how often I've tried that without success."

"What did Frank tell the chairman?" asked Sandy.

"He said the audit fees were going up because of inflation and that we have had little contact with the external auditors."

"That's because our chief executive officer has been very happy with our concentration on operations instead of on financial audits," protested Steve.

"I know," said Irwin, "and I told Frank that, but he paid no attention. He wants us to make a definite move toward coordination. And he wants us to brief him by Friday on what we plan to do about it. It's now Tuesday."

"It's not that easy," said Sandy. "We have some special problems with the external auditors."

"Nobody said it would be easy," said Irwin. "If life were easy for you then you wouldn't be getting your fat salary. But what problems are you referring to?"

"Well, they never forgave us for the way we teamed up with the controller a few years ago and really laid them low," said Steve.

"Yes," agreed Sandy. "When they issued their Management Letter without giving us the courtesy of reviewing it with us in draft, we thought we'd teach them a lesson."

"I remember that," said Irwin. "We were mainly responsible for writing the response which proved that half of what they said was wrong and the rest was inconsequential. What else?"

"My brother works with them," said Sandy. "And he told me that the partner in charge of this audit doesn't think we're independent, qualified, or competent."

"How the devil would he know?"

roared Steve. "Did he ever talk to us? Did he ever see our five-year audit plan? Did he ever see our working papers? Did he ever see our audit reports? Did he ever see the millions in savings and recoveries we've made through our audits? Does he know that a third of our staff of 30 are CPAs? Does he know that every one of us are keeping up on our continuing education? Does he know that another third of our staff are CIAs?"

"You know," said Irwin, "it could be our fault in part. Independence depends on reporting relationships. And in this day and age, we're a little behind the times there. Competence is a matter of how we are perceived. And they've never seen the results of our work. Qualification is a matter of education and training; they've never inquired about it and we've never offered to tell them. But that's neither here nor there. We've got a job to do and we're going to do it."

"We?" asked Sandy.

"You and Steve," said Irwin, fixing them both with a hard stare. "I want you to have a written program of coordination on my desk by Thursday morning. And I want suggestions on how we hurdle the barriers we've built up between the external auditors and us."

"Yes, sir," said Sandy and Steve in unison as they closed the door behind them.

Required: (1) Prepare a detailed plan by which the internal and external auditors could develop a mutual blueprint of coordination. (2) Develop a program to sell the external auditors on the benefits of the plan and the ability of the internal auditors to participate in a program of coordination.

25

Relationships with Boards of Directors

Corporations and boards of directors. Why the figureheads? The results of board indifference. The winds of change. BarChris and the new responsibilities. Outside directors taking over. SEC's influence. The tasks of the board. Asking the hard questions. Shaping the environment. The audit committee of the board — recent growth. Reasons for formation. The Mautz and Neumann study. Policies and practices of audit committees. Different view of committee tasks. Establishing internal audit functions. What concerns the board of directors. Providing comfort to the board. The quality of internal audit service. Addressing the board's concerns. Answering the committee's questions. Looking to the future. Educating the audit committee. The difference between internal and external audit services. Taking the initiative. The internal audit bill of rights. The internal audit charter.

Authority

The Passive Board

A corporation is created by law. The law endows it with the capacity to act as a single person, separate from those who formed it. The corporation is governed by a board of directors who are accountable to the owners and who act as the stewards of the assets of the owners. Some boards make decisions which affect the very life of the corporation. Others are merely approval bodies for top management.

Different countries have different names for this body of stewards: board of directors, supervisory board, and *conseil d'aministration*. In Germany, members of management cannot sit on the board; they can under American, British, and Japanese law. Most boards have one thing in common, according to Peter Drucker who said in 1974: "They do not function."[1] However, the figurehead boards — the result of the large, publicly held corporation — are now showing some signs of life.

Boards are supposed to represent the owners. They did when corporations were small, when but a few people owned the corporate stock, and when each owner had a substantial stake in the business. Owners devoted their time to their boards and, because they sat on very few, they had a personal concern.

As corporations multiplied, grew larger, and went public, the typical board became staffed with members of management, with people doing business with the company, or with people invited to sit because of the luster which glossed their names. But such people are reluctant to probe deeply or ask embarrassing questions. Besides, they often sit on so many boards that they cannot do their homework and do not know the questions to ask. As far back as 1776 the problem was identified by Adam Smith who said in *Wealth of Nations*:[2]

> The trade of a joint stock company is always managed by a court of directors. This court, indeed, is frequently subject, in many respects, to the control of a general court of proprietors. But the greater part of those proprietors seldom pretend to understand anything of the business of the company . . . Being the managers of other people's money than their own, it cannot be well expected that they should watch over it with the same anxious vigilance with which the partners of a co-partnery watch over their own . . . Negligence and profusion, therefore, must always prevail, more or less, in the management of the affairs of such a company.

In 1951 the picture was no better. A study by a management institute resulted in this statement:[3]

> The Institute, after studies of thousands of corporations, is convinced the greatest single weakness in American business organization lies in the composition of the average board of directors . . . In fact, more than one-half of the correspondence of the American Institute of Management, in answer to inquiries from the outside, is now concerned with matters regarding directors.

The results of the indifference of board members is evident in business catastrophes: The board was the last to know. Drucker cites the Austrian Credit Anstalt, Rolls Royce in England, the Penn Central Railroad in the United States, and Montacatini in Italy.[4] To this list can be added Franklin National Bank, San Diego National Bank, W. T. Grant, and Hamilton Bank of Chattanooga.[5]

The Active Board

The board's role used to be what the president wanted it to be. That is still true in many companies, but a change is making itself apparent. General Electric gave the signal in 1972 by forming five new committees of the board, each chaired by an outside director: audit, management development and compensation, public issues, science and technology, and operations.[6] In 1972, Monsanto's top management was changed. According to rumor, the change was instigated by a disgruntled group of directors.[7]

The winds of change may well have been spawned by the blast in the 1968 BarChris decision where the court uncompromisingly proclaimed the responsibilities of directors of publicly held corporations.[8]

Responsibility

The Awakening

In BarChris, the court said of a new director who pleaded unfamiliarity with the corporation:

> The liability of a director who signs a registration statement does not depend upon whether or not he read it or, if he did, whether he understood what he was reading. Section 11 (of the Securities Act of 1933) imposes liability in the first instance on directors whether new or not. He can escape liability only by using reasonable care to investigate the facts which a prudent man would employ in the management of his own property.

Thereafter, a large number of articles in business publications emphasized the expanding scope of directors' responsibility. A 1974 editorial in *Business Week* pointed out:[9]

> The Securities and Exchange Commission's [SEC] suit against the old management of the bankrupt Penn Central Railroad abruptly extends responsibility for corporate misdeeds to a broad new area. In effect, the SEC is saying that anyone connected with the company who was in a position to know what was going on and to do something about it will be held liable along with those who actually committed the offense.
>
> Applying this philosophy to the Penn Central case, the SEC did not stop with bringing suit against Stewart T. Saunders, the former president, and David C. Bevin, the former top financial officer. It also included as defendants three outside directors of the company. . . .

Directors have seen the handwriting. The placid, passive board is being replaced. Courtney C. Brown, dean emeritus of Columbia University's Graduate School of Business, observed that, "boards are becoming increasingly more assertive." Jeremy Bacon of the Conference Board said that "They [outside directors] are no longer satisfied with what management tells them." Outside directors are becoming a potent force on many boards. In 1979, a study showed that 70% of the nation's 1,000 largest companies have boards composed of a majority of outside directors.[10]

This fact has created confrontations between boards and chief executive officers in which the CEOs came off second-best. In 1979, the outside directors of General Automation, Inc., ousted the CEO who was also the founder. The same year, the board of Itel Corporation removed all operating authority from the president and the vice chairman, both founders of the company.[11]

The SEC is helping to increase the population of outside directors. On August 16, 1979, the Rapid-American Corporation signed a consent decree with SEC under which the company agreed to add four outside directors, giving them a majority on the board.[12]

Tasks of the Board

No specific responsibilities for directors have been established which have the force and effect of law, but the problem has been addressed. Peter Drucker sees these three tasks as being central to an effective board:[13]

1. To be a review organ. Without such an organ, top management has no way to control itself.

2. To remove top management when it fails to perform. A board capable of removing nonperforming top management has real power.

3. To be a public relations and community relations organ. The board needs easy and direct access to the various publics and constituents.

The prestigious Business Roundtable, made up of the top business executives in the United States, adds a fourth task:[14]

4. To develop policy and the implementing procedures necessary to limit conflicts of interest and to ensure compliance with both the law and ethical principles at all levels of the enterprise.

Asking the Hard Questions

Beyond these specific tasks, a special capability is essential for an effective board and is one of the most important contributions by directors to the management process. It is the ability and the inclination to ask discerning questions. A discerning question opens up a situation. It results in executive action or a review of policy. It forces corporate executives to consider matters they may have neglected. It compels them to give further thought to the possible alternative solutions to a problem. A board that does not have a keen questioner in its membership is not likely to be a strong board.[15]

Shaping the Environment

Probably the greatest effect a board of directors can have is to influence and shape the environment within the company. In one firm, a special review committee appointed by the board conducted an investigation of corporate activities. In its report, the committee recommended a series of corrective actions, saying that "the board of directors has a heavy and continuing obligation to see that necessary initiatives are taken and to monitor and assess the actions taken by management in working toward the achievement of this broad objective [of open and constructive communication]. The board has already taken an important first step in this direction by adopting . . . a statement of 'Principles of Business Conduct . . . '"[16]

The statement adopted by the board is directed toward creating an environment designed to foster ethical conduct and to deter conflicts of interest. The words are clear and unmistakable. For example:

We believe [the Company's] management has an obligation to articulate the general principles which should guide and motivate [the company's] people. We are clearly stating them now as a mark of our determination to conduct the company's business on an ethical basis and as an imperative signal to every man and woman in the corporation that they must share these principles.

[The corporate] business will be fully recorded in the corporate records, and open to appropriate inspection. Our people not only must scrupulously avoid any conflict of interest, but must avoid even the appearance of conflict.

Boards of directors are finding themselves in the harsh light of public and judicial criticism. Many of them are responding affirmatively to the challenge and making of it an opportunity to improve the management of their companies.

The Growth of Audit Committees

Historical Perspectives

One sign that boards are taking their review function seriously is the rising number of audit committees of the board. Boards of directors are recognizing the value of an audit committee as an instrument of control and as a means of improving the quality of a company's financial reporting practices. The growth is recent, brought about by pressures from the New York Stock Exchange (NYSE), the American Institute of Certified Public Accountants (AICPA), and the Securities and Exchange Commission:

In the NYSE, a report of the Subcommittee on Independent Audits and Audit Procedures of the Committee on Stock List, accepted by the Board of Governors on August 23, 1939, said: "Where applicable, the selection of the [independent] auditors by a special committee composed of directors who are not officers of the company seems desirable."

The AICPA Executive Committee's statement of July 20, 1967, published in the *Journal of Accountancy,* September 1967, was in part as follows: "The executive committee of the American Institute of Certified Public Accountants recommends that publicly owned corporations appoint committees composed of outside directors . . . to nominate the independent auditors . . . and to discuss the auditors' work with them.

"Audit committees can assist their full board of directors in matters involving financial statements and control over financial operations. They can also strengthen the positions of managements by providing assurance that all possible steps have been taken to provide independent review of the managements' financial policies and operation. This is good for the company and good for the public."

In Canada, Section 182(1) of the 1970 Business Corporations Act prescribed that the directors of a corporation offering securities to the public should establish audit committees composed of not fewer than three directors. A majority must be outside directors.

In the United States, SEC Accounting Series Release No. 123, March 23, 1972, "Standing Audit Committees Composed of Outside Directors," states in part: " . . . The Commission . . . endorses the establishment by all publicly held companies of audit committees composed of outside directors. . . . "

In a White Paper published in 1973, the NYSE said: "The Exchange first suggested the concept of an audit committee back in 1940. The Securities and Exchange Commission and the AICPA subsequently added their support. The Exchange believes that the idea no longer represents a corporate luxury but has become a necessity, and we strongly recommend that each listed company form an Audit Committee."

In January 1977, the NYSE adopted an "Audit Committee Policy Statement," which was in part as follows: "Each domestic company with common stock listed on the Exchange, as a condition of listing and continued listing of its securities on the Exchange, shall establish no later than June 30, 1978 and maintain thereafter an Audit Committee comprised solely of directors independent of management and free from any relation that, in the opinion of the Board of Directors, would interfere with the exercise of independent judgment as a committee member."

The Growth

The rapid growth of audit committees is impressive, as attested to by a number of recent surveys.

A Coopers and Lybrand study showed that 45% of respondents in a diverse sample had audit committees in 1972, and 67% had them in 1974.[17]

A NYSE survey showed that 80% of responding companies had audit committees in 1975 and 96% in 1979. Almost 90% of these committees were made up entirely of nonmanagement board members.[18]

In some cases the SEC was instrumental in the formation of audit committees. In *SEC v. Mattel, Inc.*, the SEC alleged false financial reporting. As a part of the settlement, SEC directed the appointment of unaffiliated directors and the establishment of an audit committee.[19] In the consent decree arising out of *SEC v. Lum's Inc., et al.*, the court ordered that an audit committee be established. It was to consist of two or more members of the board of directors who were not officers or employees of the company.[20] (See *SEC v. Killearn*, Chapter 23.)

The excellent survey by Mautz and Neumann on audit committees delved into the reasons for their formation. A majority of respondents to questionnaires said that management itself brought the committees into being. The report on the survey, however, urges caution in accepting the raw responses. A careful reading of the replies indicates that the NYSE, the SEC, and the AICPA probably influenced the management decisions to form audit committees.[21]

Most of the responses to the Mautz and Neumann survey showed acceptance of and even enthusiasm for audit committees. Many of the people queried saw the committees as useful devices with potential for real service.

Still, the committees are recognized as playing a limited role, a role that needs better definition which will come as all concerned gain more experience.[22]

The growth of audit committees can be viewed as comparable to the growth of internal auditing. Audit committees started as a bridge between the independent auditor and the board of directors. They restricted their activities to financial and accounting matters. Similarly, internal auditing started as a function dedicated to verifying financial and accounting transactions. It expanded its reach to encompass the appraisal of all operations — supplying information to help management in the planning, organizing, directing, and controlling functions.

The Broadening Scope of Interest

With growing sophistication, audit committees may expand their field of interest in the same way. For example, Perry sees audit committees as going through a continuum of ascending involvement as they grow into their comprehensive oversight role (see Exhibit 25-1):[23]

Exhibit 25-1. EXPANDING ROLE OF AUDIT COMMITTEES

Steps	Functions	Tasks
1	Nominate external auditors (EAs).	Review performance of EAs.
2	Review EA's audit scope.	Meet with EA, review locations to be visited, and review scope of work.
3	Review results of EA's examination.	Review interim and year-end reports.
4	Review internal auditor's (IA's) audit objectives and means of achieving objectives.	Meet with IAs, review annual audit plans and audit results.
5	Review IA reports.	Receive copies of IA reports, raise questions, make comments.
6	Review interaction with government agencies.	Receive copies of applicable reports before issuance, raise questions, make comments.
7	Accept responsibility for IA function.	Approve audit plans, scheduling, staffing; supervise general auditor; invite general auditor to attend most audit committee meetings.
8	Review selected number of the organization's internal controls.	Review copies of policies and procedures and meet with company officials as needed.

Functions of Audit Committees

The Different Views

Studies disclose little consensus on the specific practices and policies of a viable audit committee. Diverse practices are due, no doubt, to the many changes taking place in the corporate scene. Practices are dictated by the outlook of the individuals involved — the attitudes of executive management and of the board members themselves.

Many voices are raised in support of this or that function for audit committees. As time goes by, as the courts define more specifically how audit committees function, some consensus may emerge. In the meantime, it is instructive to listen to what the voices are saying and to seek to identify some direction for audit committees.

H. L. Aikin says that the audit committee is to act as " . . . management's conscience as to what is right or wrong in the company, providing assurances that [Board] policies and objectives are being complied with."[24]

One board director feels that the audit committee should be auditing the internal auditors — that the committee should be a vehicle for assuring the stockholders and directors that audit programs are appropriate; the auditors have indeed audited the affairs of the company; the auditors' reports have been reviewed and acted on; the auditors' communications with the directors (through the audit committee) are direct, uninhibited, and in no way subject to management veto or censorship; the auditors' access to the directors and top management is indeed adequate; and the auditors are receiving the full cooperation of top management.[25]

Another director said, "Don't expect it right away, but performance audits will probably become a major focus for corporate audit committees."[26] He refers to Peter Drucker's concept of performance audits as dealing with performance in the following four areas:[27]

1. Performance in appropriating capital. Determining what has happened on specific projects after capital spending has been approved. Measuring results against expected outcomes.

2. Performance on people decisions. Measuring the performance of people against what was expected of them when they were hired.

3. Innovation performance. Measuring the outcome of research efforts after one to five years, based on what was expected at the inception.

4. Planning performance. Determining how well management predicted and prepared for the future.

A survey by a public accounting firm showed the following incidence of audit committee functions among respondents to its questions about audit committee functions:[28]

Incidence of Committee Functions

Review outside auditor's management letter.	65%
Meet with independent auditor:	
To discuss scope of engagement before it begins.	43
To review financial statements:	
Before publication.	40
After publication.	25
Meet with the company's financial officer:	
To discuss implementing independent auditor's recommendations	48
To discuss internal controls, procedures, et cetera.	40
To review alternative accounting policies.	30
Meet with the company's internal auditor:	
To discuss adequacy of internal audit program.	34
To review findings of internal audit investigations.	40
To discuss adequacy of staff.	38
Discuss recent AICPA, SEC, and other regulatory pronouncements and their impact on the company's financial statements.	43
Discuss performance and staffing of accounting and financial departments.	43
Appoint or nominate the independent auditor.	60
Participate in the establishment of fees.	28

Establishing Internal Audit Functions

A public accounting firm report points out that the internal audit function is an important element of the internal control system. Accordingly, the firm suggests that the committee or the whole board may want to establish an internal auditing department where none exists. The report goes further and suggests a statement of functions to guide a newly established internal audit department:[29]

Set policies for the audit activity.

Develop and execute a comprehensive long-range audit program.

Examine management's stewardship at all levels for effectiveness and for compliance with company policies and procedures.

Recommend improvements in management controls to safeguard assets, promote corporate growth, and increase profits.

Review functional operations to evaluate internal and management controls and the accomplishment of objectives.

Issue audit reports on the results of reviews, including appropriate recommendations for improvement.

Appraise the effectiveness of actions taken to correct deficiencies until satisfactorily resolved.

Conduct special examinations into areas such as conflict-of-interest situations at the request of management or the independent auditors.

Investigate all discovered defalcations to determine cause and extent of loss and to recommend appropriate action.

Assist the chief financial officer in facilitating and expediting the work of the independent auditors. Also, provide assistance, as needed, to the company's audit committee.

The Committee's Role

Responses to the Mautz and Neumann 1976 survey showed that the most important attributes of a successful corporate audit committee were considered to be as follows:

Ready access by independent auditors.

Regular briefings by independent auditors.

Availability to the committee of relevant information and the prompt receipt of data requested.

Prompt notice of problems by independent auditors.

Ready access by internal auditors.

When asked what would be considered the most desirable expansion of the audit committee's role, the respondents replied most often: " . . . to obtain greater interaction with the internal auditors, including a firm follow-up on their recommendations when warranted."

Mautz and Neumann conclude that for the most part the audit committee is viewed as a link between the board of directors and the auditors. They found that respondents and the people interviewed emphasized direct communication between auditors and nonofficer directors as the most important feature. The audit committee's greater attention to the audit function has served to strengthen audit independence and motivate high-level performance. As a result, management has become more responsive to auditors' suggestions and audit committee requests for information.[30]

Mautz and Neuman report that the most widely held view by respondents and those interviewed has been one of warm acceptance for audit committees. What Mautz and Neumann saw in 1976 is an indication of what is to come as nonofficer directors assume a more important role in corporate affairs.

Internal Audit Services

Internal auditors must have a clear understanding of the philosophy and the functions of the audit committees in their corporations. Also, they should be aware of the direction audit committees are taking and the pressures upon them to increase the scope of their review functions. Without this knowledge, internal auditors may be blind to the needs of the committees they are seeking to serve and fail to provide the services that may be urgently needed and expected.

What Worries Audit Committees

In the five years since Penn Central, the number of claims against corporate directors jumped 300%, according to W. K. Brown, vice president of Marsh & McLennan, Inc., an insurance brokerage firm.[31] These claims and the actions of the courts have raised the anxiety temperature of directors to the fever point.

Mace details the specific matters today's directors are worried about. Those relevant here are as follows:[32]

Legal action. The possibility of some sort of legal action when directors fail to exercise due diligence.

Information systems. The adequacy of the corporation's management information systems.

Standards. Compliance with ethical and legal standards.

Capital items. Requests for capital expenditures.

Performance. Unsatisfactory performance by the chief executive officer.

Company background. Unfamiliarity with the company background.

Corey points out that audit committees are interested in reviewing areas where the firm is in serious trouble, especially where either the integrity of the assets or the future course of the business is involved. He cites as an example General Electric's unsuccessful attempt to break into computers. Audit committees are vitally concerned with such matters. They have a duty to see that significant, controversial problems are not ignored. They have a right to look to the internal auditors for the identification of such problems.[33] One director supports the belief that internal audit operations could have prevented scandals like those at Penn Central and Equity Funding.[34] This assumes, of course, that the internal auditor had access both to the information and to the ear of an independent audit committee.

Internal auditors are being required to have detailed understanding of management objectives, of the various conditions essential to their achievement, and of the barriers that might prevent achievement. Audit committees want to be informed of the barriers. Within one corporation, a member of the audit committee conducts an exit interview with any member of the internal audit team who leaves the company for any reason whatsoever.[35]

A director who studied section 118(4) of the Canada Business Corporation Act, which provides a new statutory duty for directors and officers to exercise due care, is looking for a great deal more than the external auditor is prepared to give. He understood the limited role of the external auditor, saying he "can get some comfort from the external auditors and considerable comfort from the internal audit staff."[36]

Audit committee members, according to one source, should see The Institute of Internal Auditors' *Standards for the Professional Practice of Internal Auditing* as an answer to a prayer. It makes clear that internal auditing is a service to the organization, not only to management. Mautz said that if he were a member of a corporate audit committee he would ask the chief internal auditor two questions:[37] Do you accept these [IIA] standards? Can you meet them?

Prescription: The Internal Auditor

An internal auditing department, organized and staffed to meet the *Standards*, should be able to alleviate many of the worries afflicting audit committee members whose number one concern is how to keep themselves informed and to be sure the information they receive is reliable. To this end they are turning to internal auditors. Here are two examples:

At CBS, Inc., fraud was discovered in one of the operating divisions. The external auditors said they were unable to give guarantees where fraud or noncompliance was concerned. Accordingly, the board of directors and the management of CBS established a new executive position of vice president - general auditor who reports to a three-member audit committee. The internal audit staff was increased from 11 to 40. More people of various skills were recruited, including generalists with operational backgrounds. At the beginning, outsiders with security experience were retained; but the internal auditing department soon developed that expertise itself. CBS believes it is doing what other corporate managements one day will get around to doing.[38]

Lockheed's special review committee made the following specific recommendation: "The internal audit function should be significantly upgraded. Its budget should be independent of the budgets of the operating divisions and subsidiaries which it audits. The audit function should report to the Company's chief executive officer, at least for the present. The director of the internal audit function should have direct access to the audit committee of the board of directors (and, when necessary, to the board itself), and should make reports to the audit committee on a regular basis."[39]

Services Internal Auditors Can Perform

Perhaps the most significant ingredient of the services internal auditors provide audit committees is quality: quality services rendered with objectivity and integrity.

Certified internal auditors (CIAs) must subscribe to a Code of Ethics embraced by The Institute of Internal Auditors, Inc. This code obligates members to exercise honesty, objectivity, and diligence and to exhibit loyalty in all matters concerning the affairs of the employer or to whomever they may be rendering services. They shall not be imprudent in the use of information acquired in the course of their duties. They shall use all reasonable care to obtain sufficient factual evidence. In their reporting, they shall reveal such material facts known to them which, if not revealed, could either distort the report of the results of operations under review or conceal unlawful practices.[40]

The Code of Ethics emphasizes the quality of the services professional internal auditors can render to provide some measure of comfort to audit committees. Here is how internal auditors can help alleviate concerns which beset board members:

Legal Action

Internal auditors can supply the committee with copies of audit reports or summaries of those reports. These can convey to the committee the problems being encountered and the actions taken to correct identified defects and weaknesses. These reports, together with informal meetings between the auditors and the committee, can demonstrate to the outside world that the committee is acting prudently in the discharge of its duties by acquainting itself with identified problems and the steps taken to solve them. If it has made sure of the internal auditor's independence and free access to all activities, the committee's regular receipt of such information can be a defense against claims that it did not exercise due care in the discharge of its duties.

Also, deep and basic policy controversies can exist in a corporation which may adversely affect the interests of stockholders and lead to law suits. Competent, professional internal auditors should be able to bring such controversies to the attention of the committee without taking sides and without unnecessarily reflecting on the ability of management.

Information System

In compliance with their standards, internal auditors are responsible for reviewing the reliability and integrity of financial and operating information and the means used to identify, measure, classify, and report such information. The committee is thus able to obtain assurances about the corporation's management information system or be alerted to weaknesses which need attention. To obtain that information currently, however, the committee would have to establish regular communication with the internal auditors.

Standards of Conduct

Internal auditors are responsible for complying with standards of due professional care. In so doing, they are required to be alert to the possibility of intentional wrongdoing, errors and omissions, inefficiency, waste, ineffectiveness, and conflicts of interest. When internal auditors suspect wrongdoing, they should see that the appropriate authorities within the organization are informed. Such authorities can include the audit committee of the board wherever access to the committee is guaranteed.

Capital Items

Internal auditors review budgeted and actual expenditures as a matter of course. Capital budgets are no different. If the audit committee is concerned about specific capital expenditures or proposals, internal auditors can perform special studies to provide information in individual cases.

Performance

No internal auditors who wish to retain their jobs will hold themselves out as appraisers of their chief executive's performance. But the internal auditor's *Standards* call for a review of the accomplishment of established objectives. Internal auditors, performing a full-scope audit, regularly review operations and programs to ascertain whether results are consistent with established objectives and goals and whether the operations are being carried out as planned. This audit function, together with the review of financial and operating reports, will ensure the flow of accurate information to the committee so that it may make a knowledgeable evaluation of CEO performance.

Company Background

Properly prepared, internal audit reports can provide audit committees with insight into company background. Directors, particularly outside directors, often have difficulty in comprehending the operations of a large organization. One of the biggest barriers to understanding operations is the unique jargon each organization uses, jargon that is usually unintelligible to the uninitiated. Internal auditors can be the translators the directors need. Fully conversant with the local argot, the auditors can translate gobbledygook into plain English. More important, their reports can provide clear statements of what the entity does and how well or poorly it does it.

Internal auditors will have to learn about the liabilities facing board members and about what the courts are expecting of them. This will be a constantly evolving process as the courts address themselves to corporate liability. Internal auditors will be called upon to exercise judgment as to the extent and quantity of information a corporation should provide each director. That information should be sufficient to enable the director to exercise the reasonable care of a prudent man or woman in the discharge of his or her duties. In fact, some people advocate that internal auditors should evaluate the adequacy of management's disclosure of information to directors. The auditors should then express their opinions as to whether the information presented and its form of presentation will lead to proper conclusions.[41]

Anticipating the Questions

Internal auditors should be sensitive to the questions an audit committee is likely to ask, and bring certain information to the committee's attention even before the questions such as these are posed:

What frauds, thefts, and defalcations have been attempted against the company since the last meeting of the audit committee?

How were they disposed of?

What were the losses?

What litigation took place before the last meeting?

Which of the company's operating areas are most vulnerable to loss, misappropriation of assets, misstatements of financial condition, and the like?

Past history may not be enough. Internal auditors should be able to bring to the committee's attention matters about the future course of the business. The committee should be alerted to any developments which may have an adverse effect on the company. One director said that the unhappy outcome in three specific instances might have been different if the auditors had been diligent in bringing the following matters to the attention of the directors:[42]

Montgomery Wards' failure to enter the suburban shopping centers in the early 1950s.

A & P's failure to move promptly into the supermarket area during the same period.

The failure of certain railroads to use their tax losses to enable them to move into profitable areas outside railroading during the postwar years.

Certainly, the identification of such information may be beyond the capacity of many internal auditors. But the growing needs of the audit committees demand equally expanding abilities on the part of internal auditors: to think like managers, to understand economics as well as auditing, and to assist members of the board in carrying out their responsibilties both to shareholders and the public.

Educating the Audit Committee

The Need for Education

To many audit committees, relations with internal auditors have a very low priority. Responses of nonofficer directors to the Mautz and Neumann survey saw "attention to the audit function performed by the internal auditors" as number five on their list of five priorities.[43] Yet the evidence is abundant that mature audit committees are able to perceive the benefits of the internal audit function. Indeed, the most frequently proposed reason for expanding audit committees was "to obtain greater interaction with the internal auditors, including a firm follow-up on their recommendations when warranted."[44]

One chairman of an audit committee admitted that he had considered internal auditing as a supplement to external auditing. Then he observed that some outside auditors had "been backing away as fast as possible from taking responsibility for evaluating accounting systems and controls in place as a part of their annual audit; and this has occurred almost simultaneously with the SEC's heightened interest in the subject and its efforts to require public management certification of such controls." The chairman added that his forays into internal auditing publications and activities have "changed considerably the way I will, in the future, look at the internal audit function and the way I am required to rely on it."[45]

The Need for Comfort

Management and the board are responsible for evaluating controls. Their needs go beyond the degree of satisfaction an external auditor requires in the normal audit. Management and the board must understand there is a point beyond which they cannot rely on the external audit. The external auditors are concerned with that aspect of internal control which may have an effect on their opinions. Their responsibilities and liabilities point to the cogency of that position. The concerns of management, the board, and the internal auditors are much broader, having a much lower threshhold to pain. A significant control weakness may be signalled by a relatively low dollar loss. Yet some small-dollar risks — too immaterial to concern the external auditor — might have a material affect on the image of the corporation.

Internal auditors must sell to the audit committees the comfort only they can provide. Audit committees must become educated to the activities of the internal audit function and to the internal auditors' role as guardians of and counsellors to the board.

Taking the Initiative

Internal auditors must take the initiative in the education program. The first step in developing the right relationship with the audit committee is getting the matter on the table. That first step is the draft of a proposed charter, if there isn't one, or a revised charter which makes it quite clear that interal auditing has unrestricted access both to the acitivites it needs to audit and to the ear of the audit committee. That charter should contain the internal auditor's bill of rights: the right to inquire, the right to be heard, and the right to adequate resources to do both.

In many cases, the improvement of the internal audit function can be attributed to the board of directors itself. The mature board will ask: Does the internal audit department need strengthening? Does the director of internal auditing have ready access to the board through the audit committee?

Many internal audit units have embarked on courses of education for audit committee members, bringing to the committee's attention what the internal audit department is now doing and what it is capable of doing. The results have been increased status and improved effectiveness for the audit group with correspondingly greater comfort to the audit committee.[46]

A senior vice president, secretary, and general counsel of a large bank said that "the specific duties and responsibilities of both the general auditor and the audit committee should be reduced to writing and approved by the board of directors and spread upon the minutes. And not forgotten that they're on the minutes — but updated regularly."[47]

One course of action is for the director of internal auditing to work with the company's finance committee, attorneys, and external auditors to promote a discussion with the audit committee and the adoption of the formal charter. As appropriate, the director of internal auditing should educate the audit committee concerning SEC, FCPA, and similar requirements. The professional stature of internal auditing should be presented along with information about The Institute of Internal Auditors, Inc., and the *Standards for the Professional Practice of Internal Auditing,* the internal auditors' Code of Ethics, the Common Body of Knowledge, the Certified Internal Auditor program, and the external auditor's review of the internal function. This action will emphasize the fact that internal auditing is a quality function vital to the management process.

Using the *Standards*

The *Standards for the Professional Practice of Internal Auditing* have been used to good effect in such an educational program. At General Motors, before 1978, the general auditor's responsibilities were not specifically set forth in any formal policy statements. The responsibilities had simply evolved over the years. But in 1978 the *Standards* were issued. These prescribed the adoption of an internal audit charter spelling out the nature and objectives of the internal auditing function, the unrestricted scope of its work, its responsibility and authority, the reporting relationship of the general auditor, and the independence from activities that are audited.

Upon issuance of the *Standards,* GM's director of internal auditing drafted a charter patterned after them but tailored to GM's needs. Included in the charter was provision for complete and independent access to the audit committee of the board. It provided for periodic reports on audit coverage to the audit committee. It declared that the director has both the right and the duty to report at any time directly to the audit committee on any matters he feels should be brought to their attention.

The audit committee reviewed the proposed responsibility statement and it was then approved by the whole board. The chairman of the board signed a letter transmitting the policy statement to general managers of divisions, general operating officers, group executives, staff executives, and heads of staff sections. [48]

The maturation of both audit committees and internal auditing departments will bring about a heightened awareness of the need for a close relationship between them. The union of their interests should bring about more enlightened corporate governance.

Conclusion

Boards of directors have been shocked into an awareness of responsibilities they may have shrugged off in prior years. Speaking of corporate misdeeds, the courts have said that the directors either knew or should have known of their companies' derelictions. Ignorance was no excuse. This has given rise to the audit committee of the board composed of outside directors. But committee members stand naked in the wind without the protective cloak of adequate, accurate, timely information about corporate operations. The information external auditors provide is often not enough. The committees will have to turn to the internal auditors for information and for comfort, and internal auditors will have to meet their own increased responsibilities. Part of these responsibilities is educating the audit committees about the risks they face and about the counsel internal auditors can supply in defusing those risks. The new relationship will have a profound effect on corporate governance.

References

1. P. F. Drucker, *Management: Tasks, Responsibilities, Practices* (New York: Harper & Row, Publishers, Inc., 1974), pp. 627, 628.
2. Adam Smith, *Wealth of Nations* (New York: Modern Library, Inc., 1937), pp. 699-700.
3. American Institute of Management, *The Corporate Director*, Special Issue 15, December 1951, p. 4.
4. Drucker, p. 628.
5. J. A. Alexander, In *The Audit Committee Interface With the Internal Auditor* Transcript of the National Association of Corporate Directors and The Institute of Internal Auditors' Conference in Boca Raton on November 19-21, 1979 (Altamonte Springs, Florida: National Association of Corporate Directors, a division of American Management Associations, and The Institute of Internal Auditors, 1980), p. 149.
6. "GE's New Strategy for Faster Growth," *Business Week*, No. 2236, July 8, 1972, p. 53.
7. "Monsanto Searches for a Fresh Face," *Business Week*, No. 2218, March 4, 1972, pp. 28, 29.
8. *Escott* vs. *BarChris Construction Corp.*, 283 F. Supp. 643, 1968.
9. "A New Sterner Standard," *Business Week*, No. 2230, May 11, 1974, p. 158.
10. "End of the Directors' Rubber Stamp," *Business Week*, No. 2602, September 10, 1979, pp. 72-83.
11. *Business Week*, September 10, 1979, pp. 72-83.
12. *Ibid.*, p. 73.
13. Drucker, p. 631.
14. "Core Functions of a Board," *Harvard Business Review*, September/October 1978, p. 26.
15. M. T. Copeland and A. R. Towl, *The Board of Directors and Business Management* (Cambridge: Harvard University Press, 1947), p. 95.
16. "Report of the Special Review Committee of the Board of Directors — Lockheed Aircraft Corporation" (Burbank, Calif.: Lockheed Aircraft Corporation, May 16, 1977).
17. D. Klock and C. Bellas, "Director Liability and the Audit Committee," *California Management Review*, Winter 1976, pp. 34-43.
18. J. W. Fuller, In *The Audit Committee Interface With the Internal Auditor*, p. 42.
19. CCH Federal Securities Law Reporter, Sec. 94,807, October 1, 1974.
20. CCH Federal Securities Law Reporter, Sec. 94,504, April 11, 1974.
21. R. K. Mautz and F. L. Neumann, *Corporate Audit Committees: Policies and Practices* (New York: Ernst & Ernst, 1977).
22. Mautz and Neumann, p. 117.
23. W. E. Perry, "Effective Audit Committees," *The Internal Auditor*, August 1977, pp. 12, 13.
24. H. L. Aikin, "Focus: The Board of Directors and the Internal Auditors," *CPA Journal*, June 1974, p. 7.

25. G. R. Corey, "The Directors' Audit Committee and the Audit Function," *The Internal Auditor*, January/February 1975, pp. 30, 31.
26. E. H. Fram, "An Insider's View of Audit Committees," *The Internal Auditor*, April 1978, pp. 43, 44.
27. P. F. Drucker, "A New Score Card for Management," *Wall Street Journal*, September 24, 1976, p. 15.
28. "The Coopers and Lybrand Audit Committee Guide" 2nd Edition, (New York: Coopers and Lybrand, 1976), p. 13.
29. *Ibid.*, pp. 17, 18.
30. Mautz and Neumann, p. 117.
31. *Business Week*, September 10, 1979, p. 73.
32. M. L. Mace, "What Today's Directors Worry About," *Harvard Business Review*, July/August 1978, pp. 30-51.
33. Corey, p. 32.
34. Fram, p. 45. (See, also, in this connection, R. L. Colegrove, "The Functions and Responsibilities of the Corporate Audit Committee," *The Internal Auditor*, June 1976, p. 19.)
35. Francine Neff, In *The Audit Committee Interface With the Internal Auditor*, p. 112.
36. W. A. Bradshaw, "Who Has the Ball?" *The Business Quarterly*, Winter 1978, p. 39.
37. R. K. Mautz, "First Conference on Audit Committees" (Altamonte Springs, Fla.: The Institute of Internal Auditors, Inc., 1977), p. 182.
38. "Strengthening the Functions of Internal Auditors," *Harvard Business Review*, July/August 1977, pp. 46, 47.
39. Lockheed Aircraft Corporation, p. 25.
40. "Certified Internal Auditor Code of Ethics" (Altamonte Springs, Fla.: The Institute of Internal Auditors, Inc., 1976).
41. W. A. Bradshaw, p. 41.
42. Corey, p. 35.
43. Mautz and Neumann, p. 53.
44. *Ibid.*, p. 71.
45. J. S. Wright, In *The Audit Committee Interface With the Internal Auditor*, p. 93.
46. Mautz and Neumann, p. 96.
47. J. B. Wynne, In *The Audit Committee Interface With the Internal Auditor*, p. 115.
48. G. R. Troost, In *The Audit Committee Interface With the Internal Auditor*, pp. 134, 135.

Supplementary Reading

Corey, G. R. "The Directors' Audit Comittee and the Audit Function." *The Internal Auditor*, January/February 1975, pp. 29-37.

Fram, E. H. "An Insider's View of Audit Committees." *The Internal Auditor*, April 1978, pp. 40-46.

Mautz, R. K., and F. L. Neumann. *Corporate Audit Committees: Policies and Practices.* New York: Ernst & Ernst, 1977.

Perry, W. E. "Effective Audit Committees." *The Internal Auditor*, August 1977, pp. 9-20.

The Audit Committee Interface With the Internal Auditor Transcript of the National Association of Corporate Directors' and The Institute of Internal Auditors' Conference in Boca Raton on November 19-21, 1979. Altamonte Springs, Florida: National Association of Corporate Directors, a division of American Management Associations, and The Institute of Internal Auditors, 1980.

For further study

Discussion Problems

1. Compare the attitudes of boards of directors before and after the BarChris decision.

2. Cite two specific examples that would seem to dispute Peter Drucker's statement that boards of directors do not function.

3. Former Supreme Court Justice Goldberg left the board of TWA because he believed he needed more information about the company's operations and a staff to provide such information. How could Mr. Goldberg have obtained that information without employing a private staff?

4. Name at least five different kinds of committees that are being used by boards of directors.

5. Compare the maturing of boards of directors with the maturing of internal auditors.

Multiple Choice Problems

1. By law, boards of directors are primarily accountable to:
a. Management.
b. Society.
c. Stockholders.
d. Courts.
e. None of the above.

2. Internal auditors should be aware of the tasks of their company's audit committees so that they can:
a. Anticipate the committee's questions.
b. Evaluate the committee's performance.
c. Act as a buffer between the committee and management.
d. Bypass the CEO in connection with those tasks.
e. Improve their own standing.

3. As a result of the Penn Central Railroad affair, the SEC took the position that:
a. Only those board directors personally involved in wrongdoing would be held liable.
b. Board directors should take over active administration of financial operations.
c. Audit committees should meet at least annually with the external auditors.
d. Internal auditors should have uninhibited access to the audit committee.
e. Any director who is in a position to know what wrongdoing was going on and to do something about it would be held liable.

4. The tasks of an effective board have been said to:
a. Be a review organ.
b. Remove top management for failure to perform.
c. Be a public relations and community relations organ.
d. Develop policies to ensure ethical practices.
e. All of the above.

5. The growth of audit committees can be attributed to the influence of the:
a. SEC.
b. AICPA.
c. NYSE.
d. All of the above.
e. None of the above.

6. Various surveys have indicated that between 1972 and 1979, the number of audit committees increased by about:
a. 5%.
b. 10%.
c. 30%.
d. 40%.
e. 50%.

7. Audit committee members can receive the greatest comfort about internal accounting control from:

a. Management.
b. Internal auditors.
c. External auditors.
d. Personal review.
e. Reading the text of accounts.

Case Study

25-1 Meeting With the Audit Committee

Don Anderson is director of internal auditing for a large, multinational manufacturing corporation. He reports both administratively and functionally to the chief financial officer of the corporation. Don has a staff of 50 auditors and a broad charter which permits him access to all domestic installations of the corporation. Audits overseas are conducted by an external auditing firm; a decision made by the chief executive officer who is also chairman of the board of directors.

The board recently appointed an audit committee composed of three outside directors. The CEO did not disguise his displeasure at seeing this step taken. The audit committee has indicated no interest in the internal audit staff. And the external auditors, with whom Don has a good working relation, have told Don privately that they consider the audit committee quite immature: The members are not fully aware of the implications of the Bar-Chris decision, and they think of the internal auditors as merely a shadow of the external auditors. From one of his friends in the independent auditing firm, Don learned that the committee is considering engaging the external accountants to perform a special review of internal accounting controls.

Don believes the time has come to educate the audit committee on what his staff has to offer. At the same time, he is unsure of the support he could get from the CEO and the independent auditors.

Required: Develop a program that Don should follow to achieve his objectives.

Appendices

Appendix A

Standards for the Professional Practice of Internal Auditing

Introduction

Internal auditing is an independent appraisal function established within an organization to examine and evaluate its activities as a service to the organization. The objective of internal auditing is to assist members of the organization in the effective discharge of their responsibilities. To this end, internal auditing furnishes them with analyses, appraisals, recommendations, counsel, and information concerning the activities reviewed.

The members of the organization assisted by internal auditing include those in management and the board of directors. Internal auditors owe a responsibility to both, providing them with information about the adequacy and effectiveness of the organization's system of internal control and the quality of performance. The information furnished to each may differ in format and detail, depending upon the requirements and requests of management and the board.

The internal auditing department is an integral part of the organization and functions under the policies established by management and the board. The statement of purpose, authority, and responsibility (charter) for the internal auditing department, approved by management and accepted by the board, should be consistent with these *Standards for the Professional Practice of Internal Auditing*.

The charter should make clear the purposes of the internal auditing department, specify the unrestricted scope of its work, and declare that auditors are to have no authority or responsibility for the activities they audit.

Throughout the world internal auditing is performed in diverse environments and within organizations which vary in purpose, size, and structure.

In addition, the laws and customs within various countries differ from one another. These differences may affect the practice of internal auditing in each environment. The implementation of these *Standards*, therefore, will be governed by the environment in which the internal auditing department carries out its assigned responsibilities. But compliance with the concepts enunciated by these *Standards* is essential before the responsibilities of internal auditors can be met.

"Independence," as used in these *Standards*, requires clarification. Internal auditors must be independent of the activities they audit. Such independence permits internal auditors to perform their work freely and objectively. Without independence, the desired results of internal auditing cannot be realized.

In setting these *Standards*, the following developments were considered:

1. Boards of directors are being held increasingly accountable for the adequacy and effectiveness of their organizations' systems of internal control and quality of performance.

2. Members of management are demonstrating increased acceptance of internal auditing as a means of supplying objective analyses, appraisals, recommendations, counsel, and information on the organization's controls and performance.

3. External auditors are using the results of internal audits to complement their own work where the internal auditors have provided suitable evidence of independence and adequate, professional audit work.

In the light of such developments, the purposes of these *Standards* are to:

1. Impart an understanding of the role and responsibilities of internal auditing to all levels of management, boards of directors, public bodies, external auditors, and related professional organizations

2. Establish the basis for the guidance and measurement of internal auditing performance

3. Improve the practice of internal auditing

The *Standards* differentiate among the varied responsibilities of the organization, the internal auditing department, the director of internal auditing, and internal auditors.

The five general *Standards* are expressed in italicized statements in upper case. Following each of these general *Standards* are specific standards expressed in italicized statements in lower case. Accompanying each specific standard are guidelines describing suitable means of meeting that standard. The *Standards* encompass:

1. The independence of the internal auditing department from the activities audited and the objectivity of internal auditors

2. The proficiency of internal auditors and the professional care they should exercise

3. The scope of internal auditing work

4. The performance of internal auditing assignments

5. The management of the internal auditing department

The *Standards* and the accompanying guidelines employ three terms which have been given specific meanings. These are as follows:

The term *board* includes boards of directors, audit committees of such boards, heads of agencies or legislative bodies to whom internal auditors report, boards of governors or trustees of nonprofit organizations, and any other designated governing bodies of organizations.

The terms *director of internal auditing* and *director* identify the top position in an internal auditing department.

The term *internal auditing department* includes any unit or activity within an organization which performs internal auditing functions.

100 INDEPENDENCE

INTERNAL AUDITORS SHOULD BE INDEPENDENT OF THE ACTIVITIES THEY AUDIT.

.01 Internal auditors are independent when they can carry out their work freely and objectively. Independence permits internal auditors to render the impartial and unbiased judgments essential to the proper conduct of audits. It is achieved through organizational status and objectivity.

110 Organizational Status

The organizational status of the internal auditing department should be sufficient to permit the accomplishment of its audit responsibilities.

.01 Internal auditors should have the support of management and of the board of directors so that they can gain the cooperation of auditees and perform their work free from interference.

.1 The director of the internal auditing department should be responsible to an individual in the organization with sufficient authority to promote independence and to ensure broad audit coverage, adequate consideration of audit reports, and appropriate action on audit recommendations.

.2 The director should have direct communication with the board. Regular communication with the board helps assure independence and provides a means for the board and the director to keep each other informed on matters of mutual interest.

.3 Independence is enhanced when the board concurs in the appointment or removal of the director of the internal auditing department.

.4 The purpose, authority, and responsibility of the internal auditing department should be defined in a formal written document (charter). The director should seek approval of the charter by management as well as acceptance by the board. The charter should (a) establish the department's position within the organization; (b) authorize access to records, personnel, and physical properties relevant to the performance of audits; and (c) define the scope of internal auditing activities.

.5 The director of internal auditing should submit annually to management for approval and to the board for its information a summary of the department's audit work schedule, staffing plan, and financial budget. The director should also submit all significant interim changes for approval and information. Audit work schedules, staffing plans, and financial budgets should inform management and the board of the scope of internal auditing work and of any limitations placed on that scope.

.6 The director of internal auditing should submit activity reports to management and to the board annually or more frequently as necessary. Activity reports should highlight significant audit findings and recommendations and should inform management and the board of any significant deviations from approved audit work schedules, staffing plans, and financial budgets, and the reasons for them.

120 **Objectivity**

Internal auditors should be objective in performing audits.

.01 Objectivity is an independent mental attitude which internal auditors should maintain in performing audits. Internal auditors are not to subordinate their judgment on audit matters to that of others.

.02 Objectivity requires internal auditors to perform audits in such a manner that they have an honest belief in their work product and that no significant quality compromises are made. Internal auditors are not to be placed in situations in which they feel unable to make objective professional judgments.

.1   Staff assignments should be made so that potential and actual conflicts of interest and bias are avoided. The director should periodically obtain from the audit staff information concerning potential conflicts of interest and bias.

.2   Internal auditors should report to the director any situations in which a conflict of interest or bias is present or may reasonably be inferred. The director should then reassign such auditors.

.3   Staff assignments of internal auditors should be rotated periodically whenever it is practicable to do so.

.4   Internal auditors should not assume operating responsibilities. But if on occasion management directs internal auditors to perform nonaudit work, it should be understood that they are not functioning as internal auditors. Moreover, objectivity is presumed to be impaired when internal auditors audit any activity for which they had authority or responsibility. This impairment should be considered when reporting audit results.

.5   Persons transferred to or temporarily engaged by the internal auditing department should not be assigned to audit those activities they previously performed until a reasonable period of time has elapsed. Such assignments are presumed to impair objectivity and should be considered when supervising the audit work and reporting audit results.

.6   The results of internal auditing work should be reviewed before the related audit report is released to provide reasonable assurance that the work was performed objectively.

.03   The internal auditor's objectivity is not adversely affected when the auditor recommends standards of control for systems or reviews procedures before they are implemented. Designing, installing, and operating systems are not audit functions. Also, the drafting of procedures for systems is not an audit function. Performing such activities is presumed to impair audit objectivity.

200   PROFESSIONAL PROFICIENCY

INTERNAL AUDITS SHOULD BE PERFORMED WITH PROFICIENCY AND DUE PROFESSIONAL CARE

.01   Professional proficiency is the responsibility of the internal auditing department and each internal auditor. The department should assign to each audit those persons who collectively possess the necessary knowledge, skills, and disciplines to conduct the audit properly.

The Internal Auditing Department
210 Staffing

The internal auditing department should provide assurance that the technical proficiency and educational background of internal auditors are appropriate for the audits to be performed.

.01 The director of internal auditing should establish suitable criteria of education and experience for filling internal auditing positions, giving due consideration to scope of work and level of responsibility.

.02 Reasonable assurance should be obtained as to each prospective auditor's qualifications and proficiency.

220 Knowledge, Skills, and Disciplines

The internal auditing department should possess or should obtain the knowledge, skills, and disciplines needed to carry out its audit responsibilities.

.01 The internal auditing staff should collectively possess the knowledge and skills essential to the practice of the profession within the organization. These attributes include proficiency in applying internal auditing standards, procedures, and techniques.

.02 The internal auditing department should have employees or use consultants who are qualified in such disciplines as accounting, economics, finance, statistics, electronic data processing, engineering, taxation, and law as needed to meet audit responsibilities. Each member of the department, however, need not be qualified in all of these disciplines.

230 Supervision

The internal auditing department should provide assurance that internal audits are properly supervised.

.01 The director of internal auditing is responsible for providing appropriate audit supervision. Supervision is a continuing process, beginning with planning and ending with the conclusion of the audit assignment.

.02 Supervision includes:

> *.1* Providing suitable instructions to subordinates at the outset of the audit and approving the audit program
>
> *.2* Seeing that the approved audit program is carried out unless deviations are both justified and authorized
>
> *.3* Determining that audit working papers adequately support the audit findings, conclusions, and reports

.4 Making sure that audit reports are accurate, objective, clear, concise, constructive, and timely

.5 Determining that audit objectives are being met

.03 Appropriate evidence of supervision should be documented and retained.

.04 The extent of supervision required will depend on the proficiency of the internal auditors and the difficulty of the audit assignment.

.05 All internal auditing assignments, whether performed by or for the internal auditing department, remain the responsibility of its director.

The Internal Auditor

240 Compliance with Standards of Conduct

Internal auditors should comply with professional standards of conduct.

01. The *Code of Ethics* of The Institute of Internal Auditors sets forth standards of conduct and provides a basis for enforcement among its members. The *Code* calls for high standards of honesty, objectivity, diligence, and loyalty to which internal auditors should conform.

250 Knowledge, Skills, and Disciplines

Internal auditors should possess the knowledge, skills, and disciplines essential to the performance of internal audits.

.01 Each internal auditor should possess certain knowledge and skills as follows:

.1 Proficiency in applying internal auditing standards, procedures, and techniques is required in performing internal audits. Proficiency means the ability to apply knowledge to situations likely to be encountered and to deal with them without extensive recourse to technical research and assistance.

.2 Proficiency in accounting principles and techniques is required of auditors who work extensively with financial records and reports.

.3 An understanding of management principles is required to recognize and evaluate the materiality and significance of deviations from good business practice. An understanding means the ability to apply broad knowledge to situations likely to be encountered, to recognize significant deviations, and to be able to carry out the research necessary to arrive at reasonable solutions.

.4 An appreciation is required of the fundamentals of such

subjects as accounting, economics, commercial law, taxation, finance, quantitative methods, and computerized information systems. An appreciation means the ability to recognize the existence of problems or potential problems and to determine the further research to be undertaken or the assistance to be obtained.

260 Human Relations and Communications

Internal auditors should be skilled in dealing with people and in communicating effectively.

.01 Internal auditors should understand human relations and maintain satisfactory relationships with auditees.

.02 Internal auditors should be skilled in oral and written communications so that they can clearly and effectively convey such matters as audit objectives, evaluations, conclusions, and recommendations.

270 Continuing Education

Internal auditors should maintain their technical competence through continuing education.

.01 Internal auditors are responsible for continuing their education in order to maintain their proficiency. They should keep informed about improvements and current developments in internal auditing standards, procedures, and techniques. Continuing education may be obtained through membership and participation in professional societies; attendance at conferences, seminars, college courses, and in-house training programs; and participation in research projects.

280 Due Professional Care

Internal auditors should exercise due professional care in performing internal audits.

.01 Due professional care calls for the application of the care and skill expected of a reasonably prudent and competent internal auditor in the same or similar circumstances. Professional care should, therefore, be appropriate to the complexities of the audit being performed. In exercising due professional care, internal auditors should be alert to the possibility of intentional wrongdoing, errors and omissions, inefficiency, waste, ineffectiveness, and conflicts of interest. They should also be alert to those conditions and activities where irregularities are most likely to occur. In addition, they should identify inadequate controls and recommend improvements to promote compliance with acceptable procedures and practices.

.02 Due care implies reasonable care and competence, not infallibility or extraordinary performance. Due care requires the auditor to conduct examinations and verifications to a reasonable extent, but does not require detailed audits of all transactions. Accordingly, the internal auditor cannot give absolute assurance that noncompliance or irregularities do not exist. Nevertheless, the possibility of material irregularities or noncompliance should be considered whenever the internal auditor undertakes an internal auditing assignment.

.03 When an internal auditor suspects wrongdoing, the appropriate authorities within the organization should be informed. The internal auditor may recommend whatever investigation is considered necessary in the circumstances. Thereafter, the auditor should follow up to see that the internal auditing department's responsibilities have been met.

.04 Exercising due professional care means using reasonable audit skill and judgment in performing the audit. To this end, the internal auditor should consider:

.1 The extent of audit work needed to achieve audit objectives

.2 The relative materiality or significance of matters to which audit procedures are applied

.3 The adequacy and effectiveness of internal controls

.4 The cost of auditing in relation to potential benefits

.05 Due professional care includes evaluating established operating standards and determining whether those standards are acceptable and are being met. When such standards are vague, authoritative interpretations should be sought. If internal auditors are required to interpret or select operating standards, they should seek agreement with auditees as to the standards needed to measure operating performance.

300 SCOPE OF WORK

THE SCOPE OF THE INTERNAL AUDIT SHOULD ENCOMPASS THE EXAMINATION AND EVALUATION OF THE ADEQUACY AND EFFECTIVENESS OF THE ORGANIZATION'S SYSTEM OF INTERNAL CONTROL AND THE QUALITY OF PERFORMANCE IN CARRYING OUT ASSIGNED RESPONSIBILITIES

.01 The scope of internal auditing work, as specified in this standard, encompasses what audit work should be performed. It is recognized, however, that management and the board of directors provide general direction as to the scope of work and the activities to be audited.

.02 The purpose of the review for adequacy of the system of internal control is to ascertain whether the system established provides reasonable assurance that the organization's objectives and goals will be met efficiently and economically.

.03 The purpose of the review for effectiveness of the system of internal control is to ascertain whether the system is functioning as intended.

.04 The purpose of the review for quality of performance is to ascertain whether the organization's objectives and goals have been achieved.

.05 The primary objectives of internal control are to ensure:

.1 The reliability and integrity of information

.2 Compliance with policies, plans, procedures, laws, and regulations

.3 The safeguarding of assets

.4 The economical and efficient use of resources

.5 The accomplishment of established objectives and goals for operations or programs

310 Reliability and Integrity of Information

Internal auditors should review the reliability and integrity of financial and operating information and the means used to identify, measure, classify, and report such information.

.01 Information systems provide data for decision making, control, and compliance with external requirements. Therefore, internal auditors should examine information systems and, as appropriate, ascertain whether:

.1 Financial and operating records and reports contain accurate, reliable, timely, complete, and useful information.

.2 Controls over record keeping and reporting are adequate and effective.

320 Compliance with Policies, Plans, Procedures, Laws and Regulations

Internal auditors should review the systems established to ensure compliance with those policies, plans, procedures, laws, and regulations which could have a significant impact on operations and reports, and should determine whether the organization is in compliance.

.01 Management is responsible for establishing the systems designed to ensure compliance with such requirements as policies, plans, procedures, and applicable laws and regulations. Internal auditors are responsible for determining whether the systems are adequate and effective and whether the activities audited are complying with the appropriate requirements.

330 Safeguarding of Assets

Internal auditors should review the means of safeguarding assets

and, as appropriate, verify the existence of such assets.

.01 Internal auditors should review the means used to safeguard assets from various types of losses such as those resulting from theft, fire, improper or illegal activities, and exposure to the elements.

.02 Internal auditors, when verifying the existence of assets, should use appropriate audit procedures.

340 **Economical and Efficient Use of Resources**

Internal auditors should appraise the economy and efficiency with which resources are employed.

.01 Management is responsible for setting operating standards to measure an activity's economical and efficient use of resources. Internal auditors are responsible for determining whether:

> *.1* Operating standards have been established for measuring economy and efficiency.
>
> *.2* Established operating standards are understood and are being met.
>
> *.3* Deviations from operating standards are identified, analyzed, and communicated to those responsible for corrective action.
>
> *.4* Corrective action has been taken.

.02 Audits related to the economical and efficient use of resources should identify such conditions as:

> *.1* Underutilized facilities
>
> *.2* Nonproductive work
>
> *.3* Procedures which are not cost justified
>
> *.4* Overstaffing or understaffing

350 **Accomplishment of Established Objectives and Goals for Operations or Programs**

Internal auditors should review operations or programs to ascertain whether results are consistent with established objectives and goals and whether the operations or programs are being carried out as planned.

.01 Management is responsible for establishing operating or program objectives and goals, developing and implementing control procedures, and accomplishng desired operating or program results. Internal auditors should ascertain whether such objectives and goals conform with those of the organization and whether they are being met.

.02 Internal auditors can provide assistance to managers who are developing objectives, goals, and systems by determining whether the

underlying assumptions are appropriate; whether accurate, current, and relevant information is being used; and whether suitable controls have been incorporated into the operations or programs.

400   PERFORMANCE OF AUDIT WORK

AUDIT WORK SHOULD INCLUDE PLANNING THE AUDIT, EXAMINING AND EVALUATING INFORMATION, COMMUNICATING RESULTS, AND FOLLOWING UP.

.01   The internal auditor is responsible for planning and conducting the audit assignment, subject to supervisory review and approval.

410 Planning the Audit

Internal auditors should plan each audit.
.01   Planning should be documented and should include:

.1   Establishing audit objectives and scope of work

.2   Obtaining background information about the activities to be audited

.3   Determining the resources necessary to perform the audit

.4   Communicating with all who need to know about the audit

.5   Performing, as appropriate, an on-site survey to become familiar with the activities and controls to be audited, to identify areas for audit emphasis, and to invite auditee comments and suggestions

.6   Writing the audit program

.7   Determining how, when, and to whom audit results will be communicated

.8   Obtaining approval of the audit work plan

420 Examining and Evaluating Information

Internal auditors should collect, analyze, interpret, and document information to support audit results.
.01   The process of examining and evaluating information is as follows:

.1   Information should be collected on all matters related to the audit objectives and scope of work.

.2   Information should be sufficient, competent, relevant, and useful to provide a sound basis for audit findings and recommendations.

Sufficient information is factual, adequate, and convincing so that a prudent, informed person would reach the same conclusions as the auditor.

Competent information is reliable and the best attainable through the use of appropriate audit techniques.

Relevant information supports audit findings and recommendations and is consistent with the objectives for the audit.

Useful information helps the organization meet its goals.

.3 Audit procedures, including the testing and sampling techniques employed, should be selected in advance, where practicable, and expanded or altered if circumstances warrant.

.4 The process of collecting, analyzing, interpreting, and documenting information should be supervised to provide reasonable assurance that the auditor's objectivity is maintained and that audit goals are met.

.5 Working papers that document the audit should be prepared by the auditor and reviewed by management of the internal auditing department. These papers should record the information obtained and the analyses made and should support the bases for the findings and recommendations to be reported.

430 Communicating Results

Internal auditors should report the results of their audit work.

.1 A signed, written report should be issued after the audit examination is completed. Interim reports may be written or oral and may be transmitted formally or informally.

.2 The internal auditor should discuss conclusions and recommendations at appropriate levels of management before issuing final written reports.

.3 Reports should be objective, clear, concise, constructive, and timely.

.4 Reports should present the purpose, scope, and results of the audit; and, where appropriate, reports should contain an expression of the auditor's opinion.

.5 Reports may include recommendations for potential improvements and acknowledge satisfactory performance and corrective action.

.6 The auditee's views about audit conclusions or recommendations may be included in the audit report.

.7 The director of internal auditing or designee should review and approve the final audit report before issuance and should decide to whom the report will be distributed.

440 Following Up

Internal auditors should follow up to ascertain that appropriate action is taken on reported audit findings.

.01 Internal auditing should determine that corrective action was taken and is achieving the desired results, or that management or the board has assumed the risk of not taking corrective action on reported findings.

500 MANAGEMENT OF THE INTERNAL AUDITING DEPARTMENT

THE DIRECTOR OF INTERNAL AUDITING SHOULD PROPERLY MANAGE THE INTERNAL AUDITING DEPARTMENT.

.01 The director of internal auditing is responsible for properly managing the department so that:

    .1 Audit work fulfills the general purposes and responsibilities approved by management and accepted by the board.

    .2 Resources of the internal auditing department are efficiently and effectively employed.

    .3 Audit work conforms to the *Standards for the Professional Practice of Internal Auditing.*

510 Purpose, Authority, and Responsibility

The director of internal auditing should have a statement of purpose, authority, and responsibility for the internal auditing department.

.01 The director of internal auditing is responsible for seeking the approval of management and the acceptance by the board of a formal written document (charter) for the internal auditing department.

520 Planning

The director of internal auditing should establish plans to carry out the responsibilities of the internal auditing department.

.01 These plans should be consistent with the internal auditing department's charter and with the goals of the organization.

.02 The planning process involves establishing:

    .1 Goals

    .2 Audit work schedules

    .3 Staffing plans and financial budgets

    .4 Activity reports

.03 The *goals* of the internal auditing department should be capable of being accomplished within specified operating plans and budgets and, to the extent possible, should be measurable. They should be accompanied by measurement criteria and targeted dates of accomplishment.

.04 *Audit work schedules* should include (a) what activities are to be audited; (b) when they will be audited; and (c) the estimated time required, taking into account the scope of the audit work planned and the nature and extent of audit work performed by others. Matters to be considered in establishing audit work schedule priorities should include (a) the date and results of the last audit; (b) financial exposure; (c) potential loss and risk; (d) request by management; (e) major changes in operations, programs, systems, and controls; (f) opportunities to achieve operating benefits; and (g) changes to and capabilities of the audit staff. The work schedules should be sufficiently flexible to cover unanticipated demands on the internal auditing department.

.05 *Staffing plans and financial budgets,* including the number of auditors and the knowledge, skills, and disciplines required to perform their work, should be determined from audit work schedules, administrative activities, education and training requirements, and audit research and development efforts.

.06 *Activity reports* should be submitted periodically to management and to the board. These reports should compare (a) performance with the department's goals and audit work schedules and (b) expenditures with financial budgets. They should explain the reasons for major variances and indicate any action taken or needed.

530 Policies and Procedures

The director of internal auditing should provide written policies and procedures to guide the audit staff.

.01 The form and content of written policies and procedures should be appropriate to the size and structure of the internal auditing department and the complexity of its work. Formal administrative and technical audit manuals may not be needed by all internal auditing departments. A small internal auditing department may be managed informally. Its audit staff may be directed and controlled through daily, close supervision and written memoranda. In a large internal auditing department, more formal and comprehensive policies and procedures are essential to guide the audit staff in the consistent compliance with the department's standards of performance.

540 Personnel Management and Development

The director of internal auditing should establish a program for selecting and developing the human resources of the internal auditing department.

.01 The program should provide for:

.1 Developing written job descriptions for each level of the audit staff

.2 Selecting qualified and competent individuals

.3 Training and providing continuing educational opportunities for each internal auditor

.4 Appraising each internal auditor's performance at least annually

.5 Providing counsel to internal auditors on their performance and professional development

550 External Auditors

The director of internal auditing should coordinate internal and external audit efforts.

.01 The internal and external audit work should be coordinated to ensure adequate audit coverage and to minimize duplicate efforts.

.02 Coordination of audit efforts involves:

.1 Periodic meetings to discuss matters of mutual interest

.2 Access to each other's audit programs and working papers

.3 Exchange of audit reports and management letters

.4 Common understanding of audit techniques, methods, and terminology

560 Quality Assurance

The director of internal auditing should establish and maintain a quality assurance program to evaluate the operations of the internal auditing department.

.01 The purpose of this program is to provide reasonable assurance that audit work conforms with these *Standards*, the internal auditing department's charter, and other applicable standards. A quality assurance program should include the following elements:

.1 Supervision

.2 Internal reviews

.3 External reviews

.02 *Supervision* of the work of the internal auditors should be carried out continually to assure conformance with internal auditing standards, departmental policies, and audit programs.

.03 *Internal reviews* should be performed periodically by members of the internal auditing staff to appraise the quality of the audit work performed. These reviews should be performed in the same manner as any other internal audit.

.04   *External reviews* of the internal auditing department should be performed to appraise the quality of the department's operations. These reviews should be performed by qualified persons who are independent of the organization and who do not have either a real or an apparent conflict of interest. Such reviews should be conducted at least once every three years. On completion of the review, a formal, written report should be issued. The report should express an opinion as to the department's compliance with the *Standards for the Professional Practice of Internal Auditing* and, as appropriate, should include recommendations for improvement.

Appendix B-1
Table of 105,000 Random Decimal Digits, Statement 4914, Interstate Commerce Commission, May 1949. Reproduced with the permission of Bureau of Transport Economics and Statistics, Interstate Commerce Commission, Washington.

Line	Col.	(1)	(2)	(3)	(4)	(5)	(6)	(7)	(8)	(9)	(10)	(11)	(12)	(13)	(14)
1															
2															
3															
4															
5															
6															
7															
8															
9															
10															
11															
12															
13															
14															
15															
16															
17															
18															
19															
20															
21															
22															
23															
24															
25															
26															
27															
28															
29															
30															
31															
32															
33															
34															
35															
36															
37															
38															
39															
40															
41															
42															
43															
44															
45															
46															
47															
48															
49															
50															

Appendix B-2

Line	(1)	(2)	(3)	(4)	(5)	(6)	(7)	(8)	(9)	(10)	(11)	(12)	(13)	(14)
51	16408	81899	04153	53381	79401	21438	83035	92350	36693	31238	59649	91754	72772	02338
52	18629	81953	05520	91962	04739	13092	97662	24822	94730	06496	35090	04822	86774	98289
53	73115	35101	47498	87637	99016	71060	88824	71013	18735	20286	23153	72924	35165	43040
54	57491	16703	23167	49323	45021	33132	12544	41035	80780	45393	44812	12515	98931	91202
55	30405	83946	23792	14422	15059	45799	22716	19792	09983	74353	68668	30429	70735	25499
56	16631	35006	85900	98275	32388	52390	16815	69298	82732	38480	73817	32523	41961	44437
57	96773	20206	42559	78985	05300	22164	24369	54224	35083	19687	11052	91491	60383	19746
58	38935	64202	14349	82674	66523	44133	00697	35552	35970	19124	63318	29686	03387	59846
59	31624	76384	17403	53363	44167	64486	64758	75366	76554	31601	12614	33072	60332	92325
60	78919	19474	23632	27889	47914	02584	37680	20801	72152	39339	34806	08930	85001	87820
61	03931	33309	57047	74211	63445	17361	62825	39908	05607	91284	68833	25570	38818	46920
62	74426	33278	43972	10119	89917	15665	52872	73823	73144	88662	88970	74492	51805	99378
63	09066	00903	20795	95452	92648	45454	09552	88815	16553	51125	74461	63990	78095	83197
64	42238	12426	87025	14267	20979	04508	64535	31355	86064	29472	47689	05974	52468	16834
65	16153	08002	26504	41744	81959	65642	74240	56302	00033	67107	77510	70625	28725	34191
66	21457	40742	29820	96783	29400	21840	15035	34537	33310	06116	95240	15957	16572	06004
67	21581	57802	02050	89728	17937	37621	47075	42080	97403	48626	68995	43805	33386	21597
68	55612	78095	83197	33732	05810	24813	89093	54099	47520	68331	09251	27427	51821	62706
69	44657	66967	19847	37883	43575	20562	15910	15347	29640	00900	05211	00880	12683	17471
70	91340	84979	46949	81973	37949	61023	43997	15263	80644	43079	92217	64731	19885	45501
71	91227	21199	31935	27022	84067	05462	35216	14486	29891	68607	41867	14951	91696	85065
72	50001	38140	66321	19924	72163	09538	12151	06878	91903	18749	34405	56087	82790	70925
73	65390	05224	72958	28609	81406	39147	25549	48542	42627	45233	57202	94617	23772	07896
74	27504	96131	83944	41575	10573	08619	64482	73923	36152	05184	94142	25299	84387	34925
75	37169	94851	39117	89632	00959	16487	65536	49071	39782	17095	02330	74301	00275	48280
76	11508	70225	51111	38351	19444	66499	71945	05422	13442	78675	84081	66938	93654	59894
77	37449	30362	06694	54690	04052	53115	62757	95348	78662	11163	81651	50245	34971	52924
78	46515	70331	85922	38329	57015	15765	97161	17869	45349	61796	66345	81073	49106	79860
79	30986	81223	42416	58353	21532	30502	32305	86482	05174	07901	88824	71013	18735	20286
80	63798	64995	46583	09785	44160	78128	83991	42865	92520	83531	80377	35909	81250	54238
81	82486	84846	99254	67632	43218	50076	21361	64816	51202	88124	41870	52689	51275	83556
82	21885	32906	92431	09060	64297	51674	64126	62570	26123	05155	59194	52799	28225	85762
83	60336	98782	07408	53458	13564	59089	26445	29789	85205	41001	12535	12133	14645	23541
84	43937	46891	24010	25560	86355	33941	25786	54990	71899	15475	95434	98227	21824	19585
85	97656	63175	89303	16275	07100	92063	21942	18611	47348	20203	18534	03717	44540	13056
86	03299	01221	05418	38982	55758	92237	26759	86367	21216	98442	08303	56613	91511	75928
87	79626	06486	03574	17668	07785	76020	79924	25651	83325	88815	16553	51125	79375	97596
88	85636	68335	47539	03129	65651	11977	02510	26113	99447	68645	34327	15152	55230	93448
89	18039	14367	61337	06177	12143	46609	32989	74014	64708	00533	35398	58408	13261	47908
90	08362	15656	60627	36478	65648	16764	53412	09013	07832	41574	17639	82163	60859	75567
91	79556	29068	04142	16268	15387	12856	66227	38358	22478	73373	88732	09443	82558	05250
92	92608	82674	27072	32534	17075	27698	98204	63863	11951	34648	88022	56148	34925	57031
93	23982	25835	40055	67006	12293	02753	14827	23235	35071	99704	37543	11601	35503	85171
94	09915	96306	05908	97901	28395	14186	00821	80703	70426	75647	76310	88717	37890	40129
95	59037	33300	26695	62247	69927	76123	50842	43834	86654	70959	79725	93872	22302	60721
96	46766	78077	62935	77712	31267	63792	62568	13516	07983	64905	99718	14049	83350	82651
97	46764	86273	63003	93017	31204	36692	40202	35273	07586	55543	79936	63387	83935	80334
98	03237	45430	55201	56627	66672	05440	88298	90183	36600	78406	06216	95787	42579	90730
99	86591	81482	52667	61582	14972	90053	89534	76036	49199	43716	97548	04379	46370	28672
100	38534	01715	94964	87288	65680	43772	39560	12918	86537	62738	19636	51132	25739	56947

Appendix B-3

Line/Col.	(1)	(2)	(3)	(4)	(5)	(6)	(7)	(8)	(9)	(10)	(11)	(12)	(13)	(14)
101	13284	16834	74151	92027	24670	36665	00770	22878	02179	51602	07270	76517	97275	45960
102	21026	91683	84463	60563	79640	65667	32422	21571	22295	61035	84353	24077	52345	24122
103	00513	58636	68541	49523	50241	44130	63329	19445	70542	31068	18541	63533	67285	81983
104	60570	68335	47487	11767	03162	95233	10282	35043	12406	28085	82240	70401	11059	
105	91366	85040	46009	38094	37788	94005	17702	67523	51211	95411	50248			
106	91240	18312	17441	01929	03945	36265	31216	54245	02290	17318	67524	90412	72126	62077
107	97458	42029	12204	17044	99678	36060	31234	55367	37150	05626	36269	91154	14094	62413
108	35249	38605	83859	37743	33004	67275	12489	55927	32929	78614	83758	51438	03451	52637
109	38980	46600	13174	23337	65435	49396	87209	19529	47250	09927	85896	68038	49812	37005
110	10750	52745	43785	18835	31035	19631	10297	34062	11312	02194	62210	74047	29812	83126
111	36247	27850	73958	20673	37800	63835	71051	84724	52420	21342	18802	07033	96104	18327
112	70963	60647	79709	26633	30615	42409	11062	25051	02560	25110	89017	31257	59605	59605
113	92018	45573	91468	71849	30675	30068	41058	15200	01062	06935	08175	98145	68525	68525
114	21036	71475	60213	50807	20710	49359	42930	12054	02913	24260	09189	90477	44280	44286
115	24033	65445	12408	03210	37804	90894	95397	03515	20134	95312	39082	24164	34675	32286
116	76500	51300	80357	05236	91102	37178	60513	14064	07892	76567	51700	59472	36104	57676
117	36755	69088	07945	80648	19141	31057	31024	54235	12310	08892	57026	71036	44702	21366
118	35681	71685	26035	63451	10940	60599	63806	20614	54307	80498	46771	94801	75305	67640
119	10146	67500	87512	81643	44831	63308	83867	35112	58759	39520	49475	00555	34698	71800
120	06578	89048	55038	03231	47039	79599	36036		60855					
121	90301	58632	14961	22603	30864	63020	82852	37966	06766	00809	72288	11972	98975	30761
122	35157	64072	49561	23183	38481	48025	16432	30751	32925	13177	67287	73456	96554	53623
123	47669	85524	97045	48279	76014	45438	74690	64017	31017	47805	45577	27451	35321	54660
124	11651	79705	46957	28568	48713	43820	85091	20615	58557	58664	45671	72364	86954	55580
125	19675	80095	32863	71199	09911	79566	62561	32819	77142	21554	49475			
126	91664	86340	69009	74036	69604	63601	72508	90313	24655	10278	15234	46704	58975	30107
127	35067	52907	49613	20531	64805	38702	62408	99594	08090	91540	05105	89522	81204	03584
128	62814	66409	35617	23089	68087	65438	26540	34617	05805	59864	01003	96601	43008	53464
129	25557	60829	09710	16257	07671	43009	54571	49295	89899	70694	30098	00155	81892	55580
130		22955	15227	83290	41170	13609	22273	71845	86817	21554	24290			
131	68700	38318	02740	80147	91776	51817	14980	09188	73410	14283	15234	03791	57048	54148
132	17940	81064	68915	09812	57117	30578	55813	01776	26167	73007	52036	57123	03098	07623
133	54649	45706	63513	06808	96476	84051	31448	37784	37940	03791	30574	89322	09956	95442
134	25946	66911	91258	66041	82710	14360	24273	25554	95241	07694	85476	92926	03726	60251
135						83658	14273		86036					
136	09547	90928	02740	92510	91720	26908	14398	76518	32410	18608	48981	31962	97764	75091
137	52651	93363	27430	26664	95476	97568	55420	01377	09315	03957	34681	54480	97322	80642
138	78705	33363	68105	08594	03155	93672	31436	38806	81804	09211	34687	11258	14857	96473
139	05282	46626	82796	85111	07820	13658	53461	04164	11611	48712	57674	16308	54786	29015
140		81666	82973	60041			02415	33222	66036		46795			
141	78108	90948	02763	23259	03175	46552	14399	30884	32010	02169	72811	53359	28513	86932
142	02560	33363	62876	26656	80624	16955	82261	24772	09212	93182	77020	91692	15557	82655
143	85197	93363	82936	85114	13567	93658	58471	33322	98712	48221	10202	16308	15693	29167
144	41317	81666		60041	71020	83658	02415		66036		46795			

Appendix B-4

Line / Col.	(1)	(2)	(3)	(4)	(5)	(6)	(7)	(8)	(9)	(10)	(11)	(12)	(13)	(14)
151	38128	51178	75096	13609	16110	73530	42564	59874	29353	67834	05175	74797	51107	11611
152	60592	10455	72542	13606	76179	13870	12210	24060	21358	31802	02187	99177	90705	89264
153	00529	01732	29830	29780	57793	25350	30224	48905	80572	39299	91378	35597	97582	05370
154	49284	18278	98332	39408	97058	43558	02302	96052	62097	43668	91375	54798	90975	05314
155	18409	82709	67160	19468	97056	45787	47939	09122	98768	04369	00438	05105	22840	82897
156	65337	72984	30171	37741	70203	09441	87261	30568	54117	70131	89636	30552	91572	09075
157	51065	12232	04213	15782	95330	55797	76451	01770	52457	11512	12181	38051	09744	09033
158	51645	22032	56358	44587	31337	53178	76439	67336	80544	31652	73620	21924	51745	07642
159	69748	93907	26258	74580	43332	50748	51842	47310	47538	16692	02620	91126	40015	74716
160	58012	23007	67448	18407	47992	09469	58424	11710	47538	13452	22620	24246	40155	82897
161	18334	19855	42887	14549	63205	47077	42637	45603	11811	66200	72560	82534	92735	56383
162	59058	19793	58017	05498	58384	49750	70752	56602	72756	01512	45600	67460	92768	59116
163	13906	20892	06374	25406	34463	57658	07980	62031	72931	16902	54808	91924	54641	97777
164	06009	02802	69145	76589	54634	50619	55417	81375	47538	19908	22620	35593	09801	00497
165	73965	37864	57960	74350	54634	50619	55417	81375	47538	19908	26687	35593	09805	00497
166	16948	11128	76163	59037	87513	87007	19067	67590	11087	68570	22534	65277	91018	91499
167	21507	10853	65178	36176	85893	53790	91721	73126	47808	47607	95760	67466	91685	96142
168	20635	61843	80203	60987	80689	73893	70549	66601	30725	32257	60216	14760	92041	97920
169	00987	57410	23806	66572	20628	49995	30150	89561	76887	41215	11664	35933	48779	00497
170	68130	67841	39571	40489	43775	55217	15417	89561	76887	19908	66687	67466	98779	00497
171	89933	11128	61114	72755	80084	90303	02945	90027	93186	22590	36568	65247	96957	91499
172	15036	01853	80357	46192	74815	35889	17701	99194	81435	60609	22566	30748	21468	96142
173	49206	05213	03573	21937	06465	44776	05010	91643	31296	76330	76736	67460	96934	97920
174	20069	80213	66513	56972	20902	73895	73116	96113	15126	60408	30886	24173	96884	00497
175	21068	12169	37237	45697	20628	35217	30150	89561	47726	33226	41415	35938	87687	00497
176	99194	11128	37560	72755	47547	96303	08148	45817	67867	18047	87453	17228	72004	90251
177	45568	08213	48581	55066	73206	58098	18558	96015	65202	26269	59602	25010	39861	53892
178	13222	06806	45903	66572	08635	89826	50836	25185	95193	62469	68246	51681	90484	36061
179	36095	57418	65936	56974	00925	84476	13079	31357	15296	04263	24016	28317	91914	21120
180	16761	23169	90903	46807	20606	36430	31085	98958	01726	32262	27021	35938	00497	21120
181	09066	26830	37560	80809	30016	37776	90869	34810	08710	45305	95594	06816	95094	82118
182	74713	22573	48581	80937	01630	85851	42566	92219	36096	90460	81886	92966	90484	05627
183	42041	57519	85048	93051	85710	71412	50866	98522	03589	55110	25209	79526	63097	27954
184	31448	48942	03806	01738	15553	85872	08718	10897	00519	55735	21089	53170	14858	13444
185	11870	23169	90903	15137	13313	51888	35965	06241	26491	15800	37248	96117	41258	21130
186	78935	26830	37560	69546	38060	77556	20896	35655	55209	90607	59941	36538	05976	15378
187	27153	25782	48548	16651	81658	85817	42558	61487	73096	59846	25260	57998	86906	27956
188	17313	62803	96038	65726	85510	93071	80815	92801	26389	72541	51210	79865	63937	61141
189	29587	16844	20063	72535	22615	80712	09807	69635	00335	31026	08080	95205	62562	13311
190	11181	09424	84490	51291	23565	64278	13685	32965	57616	85096	82619	73527	41252	21126
191	04910	56302	55974	16502	10078	31725	03056	30750	47305	96601	70857	36533	17057	18099
192	81946	25716	98925	12304	55755	80712	58856	57504	48307	59246	77708	94942	96750	92708
193	12147	30308	58205	11322	21553	43701	41864	77628	87325	27066	90706	58732	99760	92708
194	46544	16683	44439	15257	55553	50712	05416	69637	06046	08012	36895	20545	63556	27048
195	12391	06858	44472	22377	03755	84278	04196	69046	70457	16350	35005	51879	64357	30628
196	03035	47183	55974	91023	10070	31752	03056	30372	81035	01561	76093	57717	42510	03003
197	08194	07466	85205	21522	01682	09105	07420	69538	67235	06810	07608	46812	98763	58164
198	32181	20690	80205	12235	11289	03031	70417	52307	10604	38812	65935	15818	54354	10683
199	10659	06680	14449	72234	16809	58541	72976	60633	30457	62136	68051	68721	36704	21983
200	02339	81908	41442	83497	25266	94208	91961	50097	60409	69161	65053	51807	64357	21983

Appendix B-5

Line Col.	(1)	(2)	(3)	(4)	(5)	(6)	(7)	(8)	(9)	(10)	(11)	(12)	(13)	(14)
2001														
2002														
2003														
2004														
2005														
2006														
2007														
2008														
2009														
2010														
2011														
2012														
2013														
2014														
2015														
2016														
2017														
2018														
2019														
2020														
2021														
2022														
2023														
2024														
2025														
2026														
2027														
2028														
2029														
2030														
2031														
2032														
2033														
2034														
2035														
2036														
2037														
2038														
2039														
2040														
2041														
2042														
2043														
2044														
2045														
2046														
2047														
2048														
2049														
2050														

Appendix B-6

Line Col.	(1)	(2)	(3)	(4)	(5)	(6)	(7)	(8)	(9)	(10)	(11)	(12)	(13)	(14)
251	89485	26726	15567	72667	78735	29397	60521	31037	23728	37647	16476	11707	68737	56874
252	43578	25413	25587	49770	87480	44706	05138	31826	04262	76051	44957	41827	40783	60115
253	58578	81245	51846	81267	77637	14065	28038	52287	06212	30654	23667	63903	87241	33060
254	61888	71102	24097	16190	26827	98065	63882	97257	62166	66541	19363	78780	88265	33062
255	73891	47025	40937	71907	26827	98065	63882	97257	62166	66541	19363	78780	88265	33062
256	40953	73894	08549	19807	93814	33390	31734	56849	43707	75293	89549	39355	54339	57203
257	98074	73138	14639	81277	54563	03020	23310	31442	48382	92265	86405	30730	54413	99742
258	59776	20749	63043	16009	92549	00650	32444	99257	90602	93205	04551	30746	97985	10725
259	09774	45205	63077	59230	95409	13640	83044	97062	90806	01443	34551	15030	03307	72003
260	38991	64502	24770	02155	76911	46610	44941	95921	25406	71429	66911	15123	79798	22203
261	25622	22100	56128	62140	02388	19771	97604	13628	01314	71717	32858	98708	97165	02810
262	31661	27100	66064	35299	60744	32730	87685	19809	58847	28073	85185	92600	90307	92365
263	81187	75630	28061	55655	29808	02080	69540	80317	69001	43330	91617	91360	90307	95060
264	69878	52810	80534	10215	29650	54150	17410	13371	73947	13129	41007	27720	23707	95047
265	27848	51107	05761	02155	95311	16610	49927	93920	05796	13129	11309	05123	09307	95047
266	29418	93967	82648	31456	67524	04236	97660	13628	21286	13736	32858	99708	77857	93041
267	69408	61408	21813	78044	60247	31306	87665	19809	24735	35920	89549	04002	50223	64449
268	38220	44225	64133	74946	62282	14486	89189	80047	78035	00944	09941	30756	80234	44656
269	94725	45256	43410	48541	13010	16596	19133	11218	93201	08021	93354	53766	90694	79561
270	45275	16852	56299	48541	13010	16596	64136	11218	24901	08021	33354	94015	90694	79561
271	97260	09552	82841	44042	58235	44055	13337	53850	92345	56024	75307	99708	77857	00080
272	01930	65309	21284	78044	55160	51727	62826	81625	84773	92265	95198	24060	66941	80190
273	24650	65467	42353	07445	55160	59067	62803	96164	07005	63869	17948	53740	96941	46240
274	98071	33147	41030	54854	54573	26596	62800	81846	03036	00821	93015	05123	66941	80190
275	34101	79442	56299	48541	13010	16596	72800	81846	03036	00821	93015	79601	66941	80190
276	42116	86593	25918	03670	90574	45055	06097	53850	93195	56024	15785	99708	58679	93048
277	23118	61400	48030	51937	80554	31772	02185	08802	34375	55047	51147	24060	50523	71668
278	11985	72610	44102	16603	76555	53832	11863	55852	34735	69286	79668	31640	96941	18899
279	62575	72610	81638	54651	61501	20110	97420	36164	70035	92265	05020	37640	96941	11899
280	65925	26450	55299	00170	43010	16596	97200	53850	70035	82265	03015	37640	96941	02940
281	42163	33271	21804	10788	90906	23726	11216	15457	32055	56451	15785	51069	58679	95967
282	35946	28571	10688	16700	05674	27258	10987	55800	38790	91300	11498	62388	52388	52388
283	25910	36127	16303	30605	81640	58587	07885	08802	37000	62098	56148	51069	58679	57855
284	31196	30815	10816	17000	13010	08017	73764	36164	30034	34275	09146	40438	19807	03753
285	91106	95455	23880	01700	13010	16596	73150	36164	30034	32275	03015	10547	66941	50935
286	31138	74676	08940	91803	90600	70330	48510	30418	21805	49224	46568	44534	24334	74866
287	71130	34811	67930	47930	65723	59780	85630	80047	16304	25088	44031	98930	52620	43626
288	62573	32212	39838	70323	76000	53882	56338	30047	30298	05840	05018	50430	93113	43344
289	65925	08943	23810	24695	74156	33457	87968	80447	57300	15823	39186	99317	90077	74450
290	91106	95455	35577	99067	03835	48662	31500	54829	51473	11177	35387	57342	68915	15864
291	97978	74676	44257	56975	15773	96301	85110	16557	15801	95645	49568	10699	15660	15973
292	01930	70034	38622	82486	78559	14782	87636	55820	16304	25008	44031	97855	56947	81485
293	68570	83016	34715	83412	54040	59780	56338	08080	56938	50834	93113	19314	61602	14526
294	54701	34640	64702	44695	73415	39347	81968	37710	30209	15823	39186	57342	13702	45064
295	79954	87186	83577	99067	03835	48662	31500	54829	51473	11177	35387	57342	68915	15864
296	55479	01059	44257	56975	67810	80203	26060	16801	77652	95642	04951	10699	06238	15973
297	38180	70630	16757	82495	46245	97845	82614	48006	58051	76815	31162	62395	71171	81485
298	05454	83640	62157	81680	37365	78200	97630	31565	90524	82577	18288	95112	73180	14526
299	31772	64640	34772	44695	73415	39347	31500	54829	95473	51177	39186	73737	54118	46884
300	77522	87186	83577	99067	03835	48662	31500	54829	51473	11177	15387	57342	68915	15864

Appendix C FACTORS REQUIRED TO ACHIEVE GIVEN CONFIDENCE LEVELS

(Confidence levels in percentages converted to standard deviation units, based on the normal distribution curve.)

Confidence level	Factor
99.9	3.2905
99.7	3.0000
99.5	2.8070
99.0	2.5758
98.0	2.3263
95.5	2.0000
95.0	1.9600
90.0	1.6449
85.0	1.4395
80.0	1.2816
75.0	1.1503
70.0	1.0364
68.3	1.0000
60.0	0.8416
50.0	0.6745
40.0	0.5244
30.0	0.3853
20.0	0.2534
10.0	0.1257

Appendix D-1 SQUARE ROOT OF SAMPLE SIZE AND PRECISION
FOR MEAN VALUES IN STANDARD DEVIATION
UNITS FOR AN INFINITE UNIVERSE

Reprinted with permission of Department of
Defense, Defense Contract Audit Agency.

Sample Size (n)	Square Root of Sample Size	Precision for Confidence Level of:[*]			
		80%	90%	95%	99%
30	5.4772	+ .2394	+ .3102	+ .3734	+ .5032
31	5.5678	.2351	.3046	.3662	.4930
32	5.6569	.2312	.2996	.3599	.4836
33	5.7446	.2275	.2949	.3539	.4770
34	5.8309	.2240	.2900	.3484	.4685
35	5.9161	.2208	.2857	.3431	.4604
36	6.0000	.2175	.2815	.3380	.4548
37	6.0828	.2144	.2775	.3331	.4463
38	6.1644	.2115	.2737	.3283	.4396
39	6.2450	.2087	.2698	.3238	.4336
40	6.3246	.2060	.2663	.3196	.4276
41	6.4031	.2036	.2628	.3154	.4218
42	6.4807	.2009	.2595	.3114	.4163
43	6.5574	.1986	.2564	.3075	.4110
44	6.6332	.1962	.2533	.3038	.4060
45	6.7082	.1939	.2503	.3002	.4010
46	6.7823	.1917	.2476	.2968	.3910
47	6.8556	.1896	.2448	.2935	.3915
48	6.9282	.1876	.2421	.2903	.3871
49	7.0000	.1856	.2393	.2871	.3829
50	7.0710	.1837	.2370	.2841	.3787
51	7.1414	.1818	.2346	.2812	.3747
52	7.2111	.1800	.2323	.2783	.3708
53	7.2801	.1783	.2300	.2755	.3670
54	7.3485	.1766	.2277	.2728	.3632
55	7.4162	.1749	.2256	.2702	.3598
56	7.4833	.1733	.2235	.2677	.3564
57	7.5498	.1717	.2215	.2652	.3529
58	7.6158	.1702	.2195	.2628	.3497
59	7.6811	.1687	.2177	.2605	.3466
60	7.7460	.1673	.2157	.2582	.3434
61	7.8102	.1658	.2139	.2560	.3403
62	7.8740	.1645	.2121	.2539	.3374
63	7.9373	.1631	.2103	.2517	.3346
64	8.0000	.1619	.2086	.2497	.3319
65	8.0623	.1606	.2068	.2477	.3292
66	8.1240	.1593	.2054	.2457	.3266
67	8.1853	.1582	.2038	.2437	.3240
68	8.2462	.1569	.2022	.2418	.3215
69	8.3066	.1558	.2007	.2399	.3190
70	8.3666	.1547	.1992	.2383	.3165

[*]Multiply applicable factor by standard deviation computed from sample. The
result is the precision at the indicated confidence level.

Appendix D-2

Sample Size (n)	Square Root of Sample Size	Precision for Confidence Level of: 80%	90%	95%	99%
71	8.4261	± .1535	± .1978	± .2366	± .3143
72	8.4853	.1525	.1963	.2349	.3120
73	8.5440	.1514	.1949	.2332	.3097
74	8.6023	.1504	.1936	.2316	.3075
75	8.6602	.1494	.1923	.2300	.3053
76	8.7178	.1484	.1910	.2284	.3032
77	8.7750	.1474	.1897	.2269	.3011
78	8.8318	.1464	.1885	.2254	.2990
79	8.8882	.1454	.1872	.2240	.2970
80	8.9443	.1445	.1860	.2225	.2951
81	9.0000	.1435	.1847	.2211	.2932
82	9.0554	.1427	.1836	.2198	.2913
83	9.1104	.1418	.1825	.2183	.2894
84	9.1651	.1409	.1814	.2170	.2876
85	9.2195	.1401	.1806	.2157	.2858
86	9.2736	.1392	.1795	.2145	.2840
87	9.3274	.1385	.1785	.2131	.2822
88	9.3808	.1376	.1774	.2119	.2807
89	9.4340	.1369	.1761	.2107	.2790
90	9.4868	.1361	.1752	.2094	.2774
91	9.5394	.1353	.1741	.2083	.2758
92	9.5917	.1346	.1732	.2070	.2742
93	9.6436	.1338	.1722	.2059	.2726
94	9.6954	.1331	.1713	.2048	.2712
95	9.7468	.1324	.1704	.2038	.2696
96	9.7980	.1317	.1694	.2026	.2681
97	9.8489	.1310	.1685	.2016	.2666
98	9.8995	.1303	.1677	.2005	.2652
99	9.9499	.1296	.1668	.1995	.2640
100	10.0000	.1290	.1660	.1984	.2626
101	10.0499	.1284	.1651	.1974	.2613
102	10.0995	.1277	.1643	.1964	.2600
103	10.1489	.1271	.1635	.1955	.2587
104	10.1980	.1265	.1627	.1945	.2574
105	10.2469	.1259	.1619	.1936	.2562
106	10.2956	.1253	.1611	.1927	.2550
107	10.3441	.1247	.1604	.1918	.2537
108	10.3923	.1241	.1596	.1908	.2525
109	10.4403	.1236	.1589	.1899	.2514
110	10.4881	.1230	.1581	.1891	.2502

Appendix D-3

Sample Size (n)	Square Root of Sample Size	Precision for Confidence Level of: 80%	90%	95%	99%
111	10.5356	± .1224	± .1574	± .1882	± .2490
112	10.5830	.1219	.1567	.1874	.2479
113	10.6301	.1214	.1560	.1865	.2468
114	10.6771	.1208	.1553	.1857	.2457
115	10.7238	.1203	.1546	.1848	.2445
116	10.7703	.1198	.1539	.1840	.2434
117	10.8166	.1193	.1533	.1832	.2424
118	10.8628	.1188	.1526	.1825	.2414
119	10.9087	.1183	.1520	.1817	.2403
120	10.9544	.1178	.1514	.1809	.2393
121	11.0000	.1173	.1507	.1801	.2383
122	11.0454	.1168	.1501	.1794	.2373
123	11.0905	.1163	.1495	.1786	.2362
124	11.1355	.1158	.1489	.1779	.2353
125	11.1803	.1153	.1483	.1772	.2343
126	11.2250	.1148	.1476	.1765	.2334
127	11.2694	.1144	.1470	.1756	.2324
128	11.3137	.1139	.1465	.1751	.2315
129	11.3578	.1134	.1459	.1744	.2306
130	11.4018	.1130	.1453	.1737	.2297
131	11.445	.1126	.1448	.1730	.2287
132	11.4891	.1122	.1442	.1723	.2279
133	11.5326	.1118	.1437	.1717	.2270
134	11.5758	.1114	.1431	.1710	.2262
135	11.6189	.1109	.1426	.1704	.2252
136	11.6619	.1105	.1421	.1698	.2244
137	11.7047	.1101	.1416	.1692	.2236
138	11.7473	.1097	.1410	.1685	.2228
139	11.7898	.1093	.1405	.1679	.2220
140	11.8322	.1089	.1400	.1672	.2211
141	11.8743	.1086	.1395	.1667	.2203
142	11.9164	.1081	.1390	.1661	.2195
143	11.9583	.1078	.1385	.1655	.2188
144	12.0000	.1074	.1380	.1649	.2179
145	12.0416	.1070	.1375	.1643	.2172
146	12.0830	.1067	.1371	.1638	.2164
147	12.1244	.1063	.1366	.1631	.2157
148	12.1655	.1060	.1361	.1626	.2149
149	12.2066	.1056	.1357	.1620	.2141
150	12.2474	.1052	.1352	.1615	.2134

Appendix D-4

Sample Size (n)	Square Root of Sample Size	Precision for Confidence Level of:			
		80%	90%	95%	99%
151	12.2882	± .1048	± .1348	± .1610	± .2127
152	12.3288	.1045	.1343	.1604	.2119
153	12.3693	.1041	.1339	.1599	.2112
154	12.4097	.1038	.1334	.1594	.2106
155	12.4499	.1035	.1330	.1588	.2098
156	12.4900	.1031	.1326	.1583	.2091
157	12.5300	.1028	.1322	.1578	.2085
158	12.5698	.1025	.1317	.1573	.2077
159	12.6095	.1021	.1313	.1568	.2071
160	12.6491	.1018	.1309	.1563	.2064
161	12.6886	.1015	.1305	.1558	.2058
162	12.7279	.1012	.1301	.1552	.2051
163	12.7671	.1009	.1296	.1549	.2045
164	12.8062	.1006	.1292	.1544	.2038
165	12.8452	.1003	.1288	.1538	.2032
166	12.8841	.1000	.1285	.1534	.2026
167	12.9228	.0997	.1281	.1529	.2020
168	12.9615	.0994	.1277	.1524	.2013
169	13.0000	.0991	.1273	.1520	.2007
170	13.0384	.0988	.1269	.1515	.2001
171	13.0767	.0985	.1266	.1510	.1992
172	13.1149	.0982	.1262	.1506	.1989
173	13.1529	.0979	.1258	.1502	.1983
174	13.1909	.0976	.1255	.1497	.1977
175	13.2288	.0974	.1250	.1493	.1971
176	13.2664	.0970	.1247	.1489	.1965
177	13.3041	.0967	.1243	.1484	.1960
178	13.3417	.0965	.1240	.1480	.1943
179	13.3791	.0962	.1236	.1476	.1949
180	13.4164	.0959	.1233	.1472	.1942
181	13.4536	.0957	.1229	.1467	.1937
182	13.4907	.0954	.1226	.1463	.1932
183	13.5277	.0951	.1223	.1459	.1926
184	13.5647	.0949	.1219	.1455	.1920
185	13.6015	.0946	.1216	.1451	.1915
186	13.6382	.0944	.1213	.1447	.1910
187	13.6748	.0941	.1210	.1444	.1905
188	13.7113	.0939	.1206	.1440	.1899
189	13.7477	.0936	.1202	.1436	.1894
190	13.7840	.0934	.1199	.1431	.1889

Appendix D-5

Sample Size (n)	Square Root of Sample Size	\- Precision for Confidence Level of:			
		80%	90%	95%	99%
191	13.8203	± .0931	± .1196	± .1428	± .1884
192	13.8564	.0929	.1193	.1424	.1879
193	13.8924	.0926	.1190	.1420	.1874
194	13.9284	.0924	.1187	.1417	.1869
195	13.9642	.0922	.1184	.1413	.1864
196	14.0000	.0919	.1181	.1409	.1859
197	14.0357	.0917	.1178	.1406	.1854
198	14.0712	.0915	.1175	.1402	.1849
199	14.1067	.0912	.1172	.1399	.1845
200	14.1421	.0909	.1168	.1394	.1839
201	14.1774	.0907	.1165	.1391	.1835
202	14.2127	.0904	.1162	.1387	.1830
203	14.2478	.0903	.1159	.1384	.1826
204	14.2829	.0900	.1157	.1381	.1820
205	14.3178	.0898	.1154	.1377	.1816
206	14.3527	.0896	.1151	.1374	.1811
207	14.3875	.0894	.1148	.1371	.1807
208	14.4222	.0892	.1145	.1367	.1803
209	14.4568	.0890	.1143	.1364	.1798
210	14.4914	.0887	.1140	.1361	.1794
211	14.5258	.0885	.1137	.1358	.1790
212	14.5602	.0883	.1135	.1354	.1786
213	14.5914	.0881	.1132	.1351	.1782
214	14.6287	.0879	.1129	.1348	.1777
215	14.6629	.0877	.1127	.1345	.1772
216	14.6969	.0875	.1124	.1342	.1768
217	14.7309	.0873	.1121	.1339	.1764
218	14.7648	.0871	.1119	.1336	.1760
219	14.7986	.0869	.1116	.1333	.1756
220	14.8324	.0867	.1114	.1330	.1752
221	14.8661	.0865	.1111	.1326	.1748
222	14.8997	.0863	.1109	.1324	.1744
223	14.9332	.0861	.1106	.1321	.1740
224	14.9666	.0859	.1104	.1318	.1737
225	15.0000	.0857	.1101	.1315	.1733
226	15.0333	.0855	.1099	.1312	.1729
227	15.0665	.0853	.1096	.1309	.1725
228	15.0997	.0852	.1094	.1306	.1721
229	15.1327	.0850	.1092	.1303	.1717
230	15.1657	.0848	.1089	.1300	.1713

Appendix D-6

Sample Size (n)	Square Root of Sample Size	Precision for Confidence Level of:			
		80%	90%	95%	99%
231	15.1987	± .0846	± .1087	± .1297	± .1709
232	15.2315	.0844	.1085	.1295	.1706
233	15.2643	.0842	.1082	.1292	.1702
234	15.2971	.0841	.1080	.1289	.1698
235	15.3297	.0839	.1078	.1286	.1695
236	15.3623	.0837	.1075	.1284	.1691
237	15.3948	.0835	.1073	.1280	.1688
238	15.4278	.0834	.1071	.1278	.1684
239	15.4596	.0832	.1069	.1275	.1680
240	15.4919	.0830	.1066	.1272	.1676
241	15.5242	.0828	.1064	.1270	.1673
242	15.5563	.0827	.1062	.1267	.1669
243	15.5885	.0825	.1060	.1264	.1666
244	15.6205	.0823	.1058	.1262	.1663
245	15.6525	.0822	.1055	.1259	.1659
246	15.6844	.0820	.1053	.1257	.1656
247	15.7162	.0818	.1051	.1254	.1652
248	15.7480	.0817	.1049	.1252	.1649
249	15.7797	.0815	.1047	.1249	.1646
250	15.8114	.0813	.1045	.1247	.1642
251	15.8430	.0812	.1043	.1244	.1639
252	15.8745	.0810	.1041	.1242	.1635
253	15.9060	.0808	.1039	.1239	.1632
254	15.9374	.0807	.1036	.1237	.1629
255	15.9687	.0805	.1035	.1234	.1626
256	16.0000	.0804	.1033	.1232	.1622
257	16.0312	.0802	.1030	.1229	.1619
258	16.0624	.0801	.1028	.1227	.1616
259	16.0935	.0799	.1026	.1225	.1613
260	16.1245	.0797	.1025	.1222	.1609
261	16.1555	.0796	.1023	.1220	.1606
262	16.1864	.0794	.1021	.1218	.1603
263	16.2173	.0793	.1019	.1215	.1600
264	16.2481	.0791	.1017	.1213	.1597
265	16.2788	.0790	.1015	.1211	.1594
266	16.3095	.0788	.1013	.1208	.1591
267	16.3401	.0787	.1011	.1206	.1588
268	16.3707	.0785	.1009	.1204	.1585
269	16.4012	.0784	.1007	.1202	.1582
270	16.4317	.0783	.1005	.1199	.1579

Appendix D-7

Sample Size (n)	Square Root of Sample Size	80%	Precision for Confidence Level of: 90%	95%	99%
271	16.4621	± .0781	± .1004	± .1197	± .1576
272	16.4924	.0780	.1002	.1195	.1573
273	16.5227	.0778	.1000	.1193	.1570
274	16.5529	.0777	.0998	.1191	.1567
275	16.5831	.0775	.0996	.1189	.1564
276	16.6132	.0774	.0994	.1186	.1561
277	16.6433	.0773	.0993	.1184	.1559
278	16.6733	.0771	.0991	.1182	.1556
279	16.7033	.0770	.0989	.1180	.1553
280	16.7332	.0769	.0987	.1178	.1550
281	16.7631	.0767	.0985	.1176	.1547
282	16.7929	.0766	.0984	.1174	.1544
283	16.8226	.0764	.0982	.1172	.1541
284	16.8523	.0763	.0980	.1170	.1539
285	16.8819	.0762	.0979	.1167	.1536
286	16.9115	.0760	.0977	.1165	.1533
287	16.9411	.0759	.0975	.1163	.1531
288	16.9706	.0758	.0973	.1161	.1528
289	17.0000	.0756	.0972	.1159	.1525
290	17.0294	.0755	.0970	.1157	.1522
291	17.0587	.0754	.0968	.1155	.1519
292	17.0880	.0753	.0967	.1153	.1517
293	17.1172	.0751	.0965	.1151	.1514
294	17.1464	.0750	.0963	.1149	.1512
295	17.1756	.0749	.0962	.1147	.1509
296	17.2046	.0747	.0960	.1145	.1507
297	17.2337	.0746	.0959	.1143	.1504
298	17.2627	.0745	.0957	.1141	.1501
299	17.2916	.0744	.0955	.1139	.1498
300	17.3205	.0742	.0954	.1137	.1496
325	18.0278	.0713	.0916	.1092	.1437
350	18.7083	.0686	.0882	.1052	.1384
375	19.3649	.0664	.0852	.1016	.1337
400	20.0000	.0642	.0825	.0983	.1294
425	20.6155	.0623	.0800	.0954	.1255
450	21.2132	.0605	.0777	.0927	.1220
475	21.7945	.0589	.0757	.0902	.1187
500	22.3607	.0574	.0737	.0879	.1156
525	22.9129	.0560	.0719	.0858	.1129
550	23.4521	.0547	.0703	.0838	.1103

Appendix D-8

Sample Size (n)	Square Root of Sample Size	Precision for Confidence Level of: 80%	90%	95%	99%
575	23.9792	± .0535	± .0687	± .0819	± .1078
600	24.4949	.0524	.0673	.0802	.1055
625	25.0000	.0513	.0659	.0786	.1034
650	25.4951	.0503	.0646	.0770	.1014
675	25.9808	.0494	.0634	.0756	.0995
700	26.4575	.0485	.0623	.0742	.0977
725	26.9258	.0476	.0611	.0729	.0960
750	27.3861	.0468	.0601	.0717	.0944
775	27.8388	.0461	.0592	.0705	.0928
800	28.2843	.0454	.0582	.0694	.0913
825	28.7228	.0447	.0573	.0684	.0899
850	29.1548	.0440	.0565	.0674	.0886
875	29.5804	.0434	.0557	.0664	.0873
900	30.0000	.0428	.0549	.0654	.0861
925	30.4138	.0422	.0542	.0645	.0849
950	30.8221	.0416	.0534	.0637	.0838
975	31.2250	.0411	.0527	.0628	.0827
1000	31.6228	.0405	.0520	.0620	.0816
1100	33.1662	.0387	.0496	.0592	.0778
1200	34.6410	.0370	.0475	.0566	.0745
1300	36.0555	.0356	.0450	.0544	.0716
1400	37.4166	.0343	.0440	.0524	.0690
1500	38.7298	.0331	.0425	.0507	.0666
1600	40.0000	.0321	.0411	.0490	.0645
1700	41.2311	.0311	.0399	.0476	.0625
1800	42.4264	.0302	.0388	.0462	.0608
1900	43.5890	.0294	.0378	.0450	.0592
2000	44.7214	.0287	.0368	.0438	.0576
2500	50.0000	.0256	.0329	.0392	.0516
3000	54.7723	.0234	.0300	.0358	.0471
3500	59.1608	.0217	.0278	.0332	.0436
4000	63.2455	.0203	.0260	.0310	.0408
4500	67.0820	.0191	.0245	.0292	.0384
5000	70.7107	.0183	.0233	.0277	.0365
5500	74.1620	.0173	.0222	.0264	.0348
6000	77.4597	.0165	.0212	.0253	.0333
6500	80.6226	.0159	.0204	.0243	.0320
7000	83.6660	.0153	.0197	.0234	.0308
7500	86.6025	.0148	.0190	.0226	.0298
8000	89.4427	.0143	.0184	.0219	.0288
8500	92.1954	.0139	.0178	.0213	.0280
9000	94.8683	.0135	.0173	.0207	.0272
9500	97.4679	.0132	.0169	.0201	.0264
10000	100.0000	.0128	.0164	.0196	.0255

Appendix E-1 FINITE UNIVERSE CORRECTION FACTOR

Reprinted with permission of Department of
Defense, Defense Contract Audit Agency.

Sampling Fractions n/N	Finite Universe Correction Factor	Sampling Fractions n/N	Finite Universe Correction Factor	Sampling Fractions n/N	Finite Universe Correction Factor
		(Read Table Across)			
.0001	1.00000	.0005	.99980	.0010	.99955
.0015	.99930	.0020	.99905	.0025	.99980
.0030	.99855	.0035	.99830	.0040	.99805
.0045	.99780	.0050	.99755	.0055	.99730
.0060	.99705	.0065	.99780	.0070	.99654
.0075	.99629	.0080	.99604	.0085	.99579
.0090	.99554	.0095	.99529	.0100	.99504
.0105	.99479	.0110	.99454	.0115	.99428
.0120	.99403	.0125	.99378	.0130	.99353
.0135	.99328	.0140	.99303	.0145	.99277
.0150	.99252	.0155	.99227	.0160	.99202
.0165	.99177	.0170	.99151	.0175	.99126
.0180	.99101	.0185	.99076	.0190	.99050
.0195	.99025	.0200	.99000	.0205	.98975
.0210	.98949	.0215	.98924	.0220	.98899
.0225	.98874	.0230	.98848	.0235	.98823
.0240	.98798	.0245	.98772	.0250	.98747
.0255	.98722	.0260	.98696	.0265	.98671
.0270	.98646	.0275	.98620	.0280	.98595
.0285	.98570	.0290	.98544	.0295	.98519
.0300	.98494	.0305	.98468	.0310	.98443
.0315	.98417	.0320	.98392	.0325	.98367
.0330	.98341	.0335	.98316	.0340	.98290
.0345	.98265	.0350	.98239	.0355	.98214
.0360	.98188	.0365	.98163	.0370	.98138
.0375	.98112	.0380	.98087	.0385	.98061
.0390	.98036	.0395	.98010	.0400	.97985
.0405	.97959	.0410	.97933	.0415	.97908
.0420	.97882	.0425	.97857	.0430	.97831
.0435	.97806	.0440	.97780	.0445	.97755
.0450	.97729	.0455	.97703	.0460	.97678
.0465	.97652	.0470	.97627	.0475	.97601
.0480	.97575	.0485	.97550	.0490	.97524
.0495	.97499	.0500	.97473	.0505	.97447
.0510	.97422	.0515	.97396	.0520	.97370
.0525	.97345	.0530	.97319	.0535	.97293
.0540	.97267	.0545	.97242	.0550	.97216
.0555	.97190	.0560	.97165	.0565	.97139
.0570	.97113	.0575	.97087	.0580	.97062
.0585	.97036	.0590	.97010	.0595	.97934
.0600	.96953	.0605	.96933	.0610	.96907
.0615	.96881	.0620	.96855	.0625	.96829
.0630	.96804	.0635	.96778	.0640	.96752
.0645	.96726	.0650	.96700	.0655	.96674
.0660	.96649	.0665	.96623	.0670	.96597
.0675	.96571	.0680	.96545	.0685	.96519
.0690	.96493	.0695	.96467	.0700	.96441

Appendix E-2

Sampling Fractions n/N	Finite Universe Correction Factor	Sampling Fractions n/N	Finite Universe Correction Factor	Sampling Fractions n/N	Finite Universe Correction Factor
		(Read Table Across)			
.0705	.96415	.0710	.96390	.0715	.96364
.0720	.96338	.0725	.96312	.0730	.96286
.0735	.96260	.0740	.96234	.0745	.96208
.0750	.96182	.0755	.96156	.0760	.96130
.0765	.96104	.0770	.96078	.0775	.96052
.0780	.96026	.0785	.96000	.0790	.95974
.0795	.95948	.0800	.95921	.0805	.95895
.0810	.95869	.0815	.95843	.0820	.95817
.0825	.95791	.0830	.95765	.0835	.95739
.0840	.95713	.0845	.95687	.0850	.95660
.0855	.95634	.0860	.95608	.0865	.95582
.0870	.95556	.0875	.95530	.0880	.95504
.0885	.95477	.0890	.95451	.0895	.95425
.0900	.95399	.0905	.95373	.0910	.95346
.0915	.95320	.0920	.95294	.0925	.95268
.0930	.95241	.0935	.95215	.0940	.95189
.0945	.95163	.0950	.95136	.0955	.95110
.0960	.95084	.0965	.95057	.0970	.95031
.0975	.95005	.0980	.94978	.0985	.94952
.0990	.94926	.0995	.94899	.1000	.94873
.1005	.94847	.1010	.94820	.1015	.94794
.1020	.94768	.1025	.94741	.1C30	.94715
.1035	.94688	.1040	.94662	.1045	.94636
.1050	.94609	.1055	.94583	.1060	.94556
.1065	.94530	.1070	.94503	.1075	.94477
.1080	.94451	.1085	.94424	.1090	.94398
.1095	.94371	.1100	.94345	.1105	.94318
.1110	.94292	.1115	.94265	.1120	.94239
.1125	.94212	.1130	.94185	.1135	.94159
.1140	.94132	.1145	.94106	.1150	.94079
.1155	.94053	.1160	.94026	.1165	.93999
.1170	.93973	.1175	.93946	.1180	.99920
.1185	.99893	.1190	.99866	.1195	.93840
.1200	.93813	.1205	.93786	.1210	.93760
.1215	.93733	.1220	.93706	.1225	.93680
.1230	.93653	.1235	.93626	.1240	.93600
.1245	.93573	.1250	.93546	.1255	.93519
.1260	.93493	.1265	.93466	.1270	.93439
.1275	.93412	.1280	.93386	.1285	.93359
.1290	.93332	.1295	.93305	.1300	.93279
.1305	.93252	.1310	.93225	.1315	.93198
.1320	.93171	.1325	.93144	.1330	.93118
.1335	.93091	.1340	.93064	.1345	.93037
.1350	.93010	.1355	.92983	.1360	.92956
.1365	.92929	.1370	.92902	.1375	.92876
.1380	.92849	.1385	.92822	.1390	.92795

Appendix E-3

Sampling Fractions n/N	Finite Universe Correction Factor	Sampling Fractions n/N	Finite Universe Correction Factor	Sampling Fractions n/N	Finite Universe Correction Factor
		(Read Table Across)			
.1395	.92768	.1400	.92741	.1405	.92714
.1410	.92687	.1415	.92660	.1420	.92633
.1425	.92606	.1430	.92579	.1435	.92552
.1440	.92525	.1445	.92498	.1450	.92471
.1455	.92444	.1460	.92417	.1465	.92390
.1470	.92363	.1475	.92336	.1480	.92309
.1485	.92281	.1490	.92259	.1495	.92227
.1500	.92200	.1505	.92173	.1510	.92146
.1515	.92119	.1520	.92092	.1525	.92064
.1530	.92037	.1535	.92010	.1540	.91983
.1545	.91956	.1550	.91929	.1555	.91901
.1560	.91874	.1565	.91847	.1570	.91820
.1575	.91792	.1580	.91765	.1585	.91738
.1590	.91711	.1595	.91683	.1600	.91656
.1605	.91629	.1610	.91602	.1615	.91574
.1620	.91547	.1625	.91520	.1630	.91492
.1635	.91465	.1640	.91438	.1645	.91410
.1650	.91383	.1655	.91356	.1660	.91328
.1665	.91301	.1670	.91273	.1675	.91246
.1680	.91219	.1685	.91191	.1690	.91164
.1695	.91136	.1700	.91109	.1705	.91081
.1710	.91054	.1715	.91027	.1720	.90999
.1725	.90972	.1730	.90944	.1735	.90917
.1740	.90889	.1745	.90862	.1750	.90834
.1755	.90807	.1760	.90779	.1765	.90751
.1770	.90724	.1775	.90696	.1780	.90669
.1785	.90641	.1790	.90614	.1795	.90586
.1800	.90558	.1805	.90531	.1810	.90503
.1815	.90476	.1820	.90448	.1825	.90420
.1830	.90393	.1835	.90365	.1840	.90337
.1845	.90310	.1850	.90282	.1855	.90254
.1860	.90227	.1865	.90199	.1870	.90171
.1875	.90143	.1880	.90116	.1885	.90088
.1890	.90060	.1895	.90032	.1900	.90005
.1905	.89977	.1910	.89949	.1915	.89921
.1920	.89893	.1925	.89866	.1930	.89838
.1935	.89810	.1940	.89782	.1945	.89754
.1950	.89726	.1955	.89698	.1960	.89671
.1965	.89643	.1970	.89615	.1975	.89587
.1980	.89559	.1985	.89531	.1990	.89503
.1995	.89475	.2000	.89447	.2005	.89419
.2010	.89391	.2015	.89363	.2020	.89335
.2025	.89307	.2030	.89279	.2035	.89251
.2040	.89223	.2045	.89195	.2050	.89167
.2055	.89139	.2060	.89111	.2065	.89083
.2070	.89055	.2075	.89027	.2080	.88999
.2085	.88971	.2090	.88943	.2095	.88915
.2100	.88886	.2105	.88858	.2110	.88830

Appendix F-1 TABLES OF PROBABILITIES FOR USE IN STOP-OR-GO SAMPLING

PROBABILITY THAT ERROR RATE IN UNIVERSE SIZE OF OVER 2000 IS LESS THAN:

SIZE OF SAMPLE EXAMINED	NO. OF ERRORS FOUND	1%	2%	3%	4%	5%	6%	7%	8%	9%	10%	12%	14%	16%	18%	20%
50	0	39.50	63.58	78.19	87.01	92.31	95.47	97.34	98.45	99.10	99.49	99.83	99.95	99.96	100.00	100.00
	1	8.94	26.42	44.47	59.95	72.06	81.00	87.35	91.73	94.68	96.62	98.69	99.52	99.83	99.94	99.98
	2	1.38	7.84	18.92	32.33	45.95	58.38	68.92	77.40	83.95	88.83	94.87	97.79	99.10	99.65	99.87
	3	0.16	1.78	6.28	13.91	23.96	35.27	46.73	57.47	66.97	74.97	86.55	93.30	96.88	98.64	99.43
	4	0.02	0.32	1.68	4.90	10.36	17.94	27.10	37.11	47.23	56.88	73.21	84.72	91.92	96.01	98.15
	5		0.05	0.37	1.44	3.78	7.76	13.51	20.81	29.28	38.39	56.47	71.86	83.23	90.71	95.20
	6		0.01	0.07	0.36	1.18	2.89	5.83	10.19	15.96	22.98	39.35	56.16	70.81	81.99	89.66
70	0	50.52	75.69	88.14	94.26	97.24	98.69	99.38	99.71	99.86	99.94	99.99	100.00	100.00	100.00	100.00
	1	15.53	40.96	62.47	77.51	87.03	92.81	96.10	97.93	98.92	99.45	99.86	99.97	99.99	100.00	100.00
	2	3.34	16.50	35.08	53.44	68.63	79.87	87.59	92.60	95.72	97.58	99.28	99.80	99.95	99.99	100.00
	3	0.54	5.19	15.87	30.71	46.61	61.15	73.07	82.10	88.53	92.88	97.48	99.19	99.76	99.93	99.98
	4	0.07	1.32	5.93	14.85	27.21	41.13	54.77	66.80	76.61	84.12	93.36	97.51	99.16	99.74	99.92
	5		0.28	1.86	6.12	13.72	24.27	36.58	49.24	61.06	71.28	85.94	93.92	97.64	99.17	99.73
	6		0.05	0.50	2.18	6.04	12.61	21.75	32.70	44.40	55.82	74.98	87.57	94.50	97.81	99.20
	7			0.12	0.68	2.34	5.80	11.54	19.54	29.33	40.12	61.33	78.13	89.04	95.08	98.00
	8			0.02	0.19	0.80	2.38	5.49	10.54	17.59	26.37	46.66	66.03	80.85	90.36	95.63
	9				0.05	0.25	0.88	2.36	5.14	9.60	15.86	32.88	52.46	70.10	83.23	91.55
100	0	63.40	86.74	95.25	98.31	99.41	99.80	99.93	99.98	99.99	100.00	100.00	100.00	100.00	100.00	100.00
	1	26.42	59.67	80.54	91.28	96.29	98.48	99.40	99.77	99.91	99.97	100.00	100.00	100.00	100.00	100.00
	2	7.94	32.33	58.02	76.79	88.17	94.34	97.42	98.87	99.52	99.81	99.97	100.00	100.00	100.00	100.00
	3	1.84	14.10	35.28	57.05	74.22	85.70	92.56	96.33	98.27	99.22	99.86	99.98	100.00	100.00	100.00
	4	0.34	5.08	18.22	37.11	56.40	72.32	83.68	90.97	95.26	97.63	99.47	99.90	99.98	100.00	100.00
	5	0.05	1.55	8.08	21.16	38.40	55.93	70.86	82.01	89.55	94.24	98.48	99.66	99.93	99.99	100.00
	6	0.01	0.41	3.12	10.64	23.40	39.37	55.57	69.68	80.60	88.48	96.33	99.03	99.78	99.96	99.99
	7		0.09	1.06	4.75	12.80	25.17	40.12	55.29	68.72	79.40	92.39	97.67	99.39	99.86	99.97
	8		0.02	0.32	1.90	6.31	14.63	26.60	40.74	55.06	67.91	86.14	95.08	98.53	99.62	99.91
	9			0.09	0.68	2.82	7.75	16.20	27.80	41.25	54.87	77.44	90.78	96.84	99.08	99.77
	10			0.02	0.22	1.15	3.76	9.08	17.57	28.82	41.68	66.63	84.40	93.93	98.00	99.43
	11				0.07	0.43	1.68	4.69	10.29	18.76	29.70	54.58	75.91	89.39	96.05	98.74
	12				0.02	0.15	0.69	2.24	5.59	11.38	19.82	42.39	65.66	82.97	92.89	97.47
	13					0.05	0.26	0.99	2.82	6.45	12.39	31.14	54.36	74.69	88.19	95.31
	14					0.01	0.09	0.41	1.33	3.41	7.26	21.60	42.94	64.90	81.77	91.96
	15						0.03	0.16	0.59	1.69	3.99	14.15	32.27	54.20	73.70	87.15

Appendix F-2

PROBABILITY THAT ERROR RATE IN UNIVERSE SIZE OF OVER 2000 IS LESS THAN:

SIZE OF SAMPLE EXAMINED: 120

NO. OF ERRORS FOUND	1%	2%	3%	4%	5%	6%	7%	8%	9%	10%	12%	14%	16%	18%	20%
0	70.06	91.15	97.41	99.25	99.79	99.94	99.98	100.00	100.00	100.00	100.00	100.00	100.00	100.00	100.00
1	33.77	69.46	87.82	95.53	98.45	99.48	99.83	99.95	99.98	100.00	100.00	100.00	100.00	100.00	100.00
2	11.96	43.13	70.16	86.28	94.25	97.75	99.17	99.71	99.90	99.97	100.00	100.00	100.00	100.00	100.00
3	3.30	22.00	48.67	71.13	85.56	93.40	97.19	98.87	99.60	99.84	99.98	100.00	100.00	100.00	100.00
4	0.74	9.38	29.24	52.67	72.18	85.27	92.83	96.75	98.61	99.44	99.92	99.99	100.00	100.00	100.00
5	0.14	3.41	15.29	34.83	55.85	73.23	85.23	92.47	96.42	98.40	99.72	99.96	99.99	100.00	100.00
6	0.02	1.07	7.03	20.57	39.37	58.50	74.26	85.35	92.26	96.18	99.21	99.87	99.98	100.00	100.00
7		0.30	2.86	10.90	25.24	43.20	60.81	75.25	85.57	92.16	98.08	99.62	99.94	100.00	100.00
8		0.07	1.04	5.21	14.74	29.39	46.51	62.85	76.21	85.86	95.89	99.05	99.82	99.97	100.00
9		0.02	0.34	2.26	7.86	18.43	33.12	49.44	64.70	77.14	92.18	97.89	99.53	99.91	99.99
10			0.10	0.89	3.85	10.66	21.93	36.49	52.06	66.39	86.56	95.79	98.94	99.78	99.96
11			0.03	0.32	1.73	5.70	13.50	25.23	39.56	54.45	78.90	92.39	97.80	99.48	99.90
12			0.01	0.11	0.72	2.83	7.75	16.33	28.23	42.39	69.41	87.35	95.83	98.88	99.75
13				0.03	0.28	1.31	4.15	9.64	19.11	31.27	58.66	80.53	92.71	97.78	99.44
14				0.01	0.10	0.56	2.07	5.64	12.13	21.82	47.45	72.05	88.17	95.95	98.86
15					0.03	0.23	0.97	3.01	7.26	14.40	36.66	62.30	82.06	93.10	97.82
16					0.01	0.09	0.43	1.51	4.10	8.99	26.99	51.88	74.42	89.00	96.12
17						0.03	0.18	0.72	2.18	5.31	18.93	41.50	65.52	83.49	93.53
18						0.01	0.07	0.32	1.10	2.97	12.64	31.84	55.82	76.57	89.81

SIZE OF SAMPLE EXAMINED: 150

NO. OF ERRORS FOUND	1%	2%	3%	4%	5%	6%	7%	8%	9%	10%	12%	14%	16%	18%	20%
0	77.86	95.17	98.96	99.78	99.95	99.99	100.00	100.00	100.00	100.00	100.00	100.00	100.00	100.00	100.00
1	44.30	80.39	94.15	98.41	99.60	99.90	99.98	100.00	100.00	100.00	100.00	100.00	100.00	100.00	100.00
2	19.05	57.91	83.07	94.16	98.19	99.48	99.86	99.96	99.99	100.00	100.00	100.00	100.00	100.00	100.00
3	6.47	35.28	66.16	85.42	94.52	98.14	99.42	99.83	99.95	99.99	100.00	100.00	100.00	100.00	100.00
4	1.80	18.30	46.93	72.04	87.44	95.01	98.20	99.40	99.81	99.95	100.00	100.00	100.00	100.00	100.00
5	0.42	8.19	29.57	55.76	76.56	89.17	95.52	98.31	99.41	99.81	99.98	99.99	100.00	100.00	100.00
6	0.08	3.20	16.60	39.37	62.71	80.16	90.66	96.03	98.45	99.44	99.94	99.99	100.00	100.00	100.00
7	0.02	1.11	8.34	25.32	47.72	68.34	83.12	91.94	96.50	98.60	99.82	99.98	100.00	100.00	100.00
8		0.34	3.78	14.85	33.62	54.84	72.98	85.58	93.04	96.93	99.52	99.94	99.99	100.00	100.00
9		0.10	1.55	7.97	21.91	41.26	60.93	76.85	87.65	94.00	98.89	99.84	99.98	100.00	100.00
10		0.02	0.58	3.93	13.22	29.03	48.15	66.16	80.13	89.40	97.66	99.61	99.95	100.00	100.00
11		0.01	0.20	1.79	7.40	19.09	35.90	54.32	70.66	82.91	95.54	99.14	99.87	100.00	100.00
12			0.06	0.75	3.85	11.74	25.23	42.40	59.82	74.55	92.19	98.25	99.70	99.97	100.00
13			0.02	0.29	1.87	6.77	16.70	31.39	48.43	64.70	87.34	96.70	99.35	99.92	99.99
14				0.11	0.85	3.66	10.42	22.03	37.41	53.98	80.86	94.25	98.70	99.77	99.97
15				0.04	0.36	1.86	6.13	14.64	27.53	43.18	72.85	90.62	97.58	99.52	99.92
16				0.01	0.14	0.89	3.40	9.22	19.28	33.06	63.64	85.63	95.78	99.05	99.83
17					0.05	0.40	1.79	5.51	12.86	24.19	53.74	79.24	93.07	98.24	99.65
18					0.02	0.17	0.89	3.13	8.16	16.92	43.76	71.54	89.26	96.92	99.31
19					0.01	0.07	0.42	1.68	4.93	11.30	34.31	62.84	84.21	94.90	98.72
20						0.03	0.19	0.86	2.84	7.21	25.87	53.56	77.92	92.01	97.76
21						0.01	0.08	0.42	1.56	4.40	18.74	44.22	70.50	88.08	96.28
22							0.03	0.20	0.82	2.56	13.04	35.29	62.22	83.02	94.10
23							0.01	0.09	0.41	1.43	8.72	27.20	53.43	76.84	91.07
24								0.04	0.20	0.76	5.60	20.24	44.58	69.66	87.06

Appendix F-3

PROBABILITY THAT ERROR RATE IN UNIVERSE SIZE OF OVER 2000 IS LESS THAN:

SIZE OF SAMPLE EXAMINED	NO. OF ERRORS FOUND	1%	2%	3%	4%	5%	6%	7%	8%	9%	10%	12%	14%	16%	18%	20%
180	0	83.62	97.37	99.58	99.94	99.99	100.00	100.00	100.00	100.00	100.00	100.00	100.00	100.00	100.00	100.00
	1	53.84	87.69	97.27	99.45	99.90	99.98	100.00	100.00	100.00	100.00	100.00	100.00	100.00	100.00	100.00
	2	26.91	70.01	90.86	97.65	99.46	99.89	99.98	100.00	100.00	100.00	100.00	100.00	100.00	100.00	100.00
	3	10.77	48.61	79.10	93.20	98.10	99.52	99.89	99.98	100.00	100.00	100.00	100.00	100.00	100.00	100.00
	4	3.56	29.28	63.01	84.99	94.93	98.50	99.60	99.90	99.98	100.00	100.00	100.00	100.00	100.00	100.00
	5	1.00	15.39	45.49	72.95	89.05	96.21	98.84	99.68	99.92	99.98	100.00	100.00	100.00	100.00	100.00
	6	0.24	7.13	29.69	58.32	80.02	91.93	97.16	99.11	99.75	99.93	100.00	100.00	100.00	100.00	100.00
	7	0.05	2.93	17.54	43.17	68.21	85.15	94.03	97.88	99.32	99.80	99.99	100.00	100.00	100.00	100.00
	8	0.01	1.08	9.41	29.51	54.77	75.79	88.92	95.57	98.42	99.49	99.96	100.00	100.00	100.00	100.00
	9		0.36	4.61	18.64	41.26	64.37	81.58	91.72	96.70	98.82	99.88	99.99	100.00	100.00	100.00
	10		0.11	2.07	10.89	29.09	51.90	72.13	86.00	93.81	97.55	99.71	99.98	100.00	100.00	100.00
	11		0.03	0.86	5.90	19.20	39.61	61.13	78.32	89.38	95.37	99.35	99.94	100.00	100.00	100.00
	12		0.01	0.33	2.98	11.86	28.56	49.48	68.91	83.21	91.96	98.65	99.84	99.99	100.00	100.00
	13			0.12	1.40	6.87	19.44	38.14	58.33	75.33	87.06	97.42	99.65	99.96	100.00	100.00
	14			0.04	0.62	3.74	12.50	27.96	47.36	66.03	80.57	95.42	99.27	99.92	99.99	100.00
	15			0.01	0.25	1.92	7.59	19.48	36.81	55.86	72.59	92.41	98.58	99.81	99.99	100.00
	16				0.10	0.92	4.36	12.90	27.34	45.48	63.44	88.17	97.43	99.60	99.98	100.00
	17				0.04	0.42	2.38	8.12	19.40	35.57	53.63	82.59	95.62	99.23	99.96	100.00
	18				0.01	0.18	1.23	4.87	13.15	26.70	43.77	75.69	92.95	98.57	99.79	99.98
	19					0.08	0.60	2.78	8.51	19.22	34.42	67.68	89.25	97.52	99.52	99.95
	20					0.03	0.28	1.51	5.26	13.27	26.06	58.89	84.40	95.89	99.22	99.89
	21					0.01	0.13	0.78	3.11	8.78	18.98	49.75	78.39	93.54	98.62	99.78
	22						0.05	0.39	1.76	5.57	13.30	40.74	71.31	90.29	97.66	99.59
	23						0.02	0.18	0.96	3.40	8.96	32.31	63.40	86.05	96.21	99.25
	24						0.01	0.08	0.50	1.99	5.81	24.78	54.97	80.76	94.13	98.69
	25							0.04	0.25	1.12	3.62	18.38	46.41	74.47	91.27	97.83
	26							0.02	0.12	0.60	2.18	13.17	38.10	67.34	87.54	96.54
	27							0.01	0.06	0.31	1.26	9.12	30.39	59.58	82.87	94.70
	28								0.02	0.16	0.70	6.11	23.52	51.51	77.27	92.19
	29								0.01	0.08	0.38	3.95	17.67	43.45	70.82	88.90

Appendix F-4

PROBABILITY THAT ERROR RATE IN UNIVERSE SIZE OF OVER 2000 IS LESS THAN:

SIZE OF SAMPLE EXAMINED	NO. OF ERRORS FOUND	1%	2%	3%	4%	5%	6%	7%	8%	9%	10%	12%	14%	16%	18%	20%
220	0	89.04	98.83	99.88	99.99	100.00	100.00	100.00	100.00	100.00	100.00	100.00	100.00	100.00	100.00	100.00
	1	64.69	93.55	99.04	99.87	99.98	100.00	100.00	100.00	100.00	100.00	100.00	100.00	100.00	100.00	100.00
	2	37.76	81.77	96.21	99.35	99.90	99.99	100.00	100.00	100.00	100.00	100.00	100.00	100.00	100.00	100.00
	3	17.99	64.30	89.84	97.75	99.58	99.93	99.99	100.00	100.00	100.00	100.00	100.00	100.00	100.00	100.00
	4	7.15	44.96	79.15	94.15	98.66	99.74	99.95	99.99	100.00	100.00	100.00	100.00	100.00	100.00	100.00
	5	2.42	27.91	64.88	87.67	96.58	99.21	99.84	99.97	99.99	100.00	100.00	100.00	100.00	100.00	100.00
	6	0.71	15.43	49.06	77.99	92.66	97.99	99.53	99.90	99.98	99.99	100.00	100.00	100.00	100.00	100.00
	7	0.19	7.65	34.10	65.67	86.34	95.61	98.81	99.72	99.94	99.97	100.00	100.00	100.00	100.00	100.00
	8	0.04	3.43	21.78	51.99	77.48	91.57	97.38	99.30	99.83	99.90	99.99	100.00	100.00	100.00	100.00
	9	0.01	1.39	12.81	38.57	66.51	85.50	94.83	98.43	99.59	99.76	99.98	100.00	100.00	100.00	100.00
	10		0.52	6.95	26.77	54.32	77.32	90.79	96.85	99.07	99.45	99.92	99.97	100.00	100.00	100.00
	11		0.18	3.50	17.38	42.07	67.35	84.98	94.21	98.09	98.85	99.81	99.94	100.00	100.00	100.00
	12		0.06	1.63	10.57	30.84	56.27	77.36	90.22	96.40	97.78	99.59	99.86	99.99	100.00	100.00
	13		0.02	0.71	6.03	21.39	44.96	68.19	84.67	93.72	96.02	99.18	99.71	99.98	100.00	100.00
	14			0.29	3.23	14.03	34.28	57.98	77.53	89.82	93.35	98.46	99.43	99.95	100.00	100.00
	15			0.11	1.63	8.71	24.92	47.43	69.00	84.51	89.54	97.28	98.94	99.90	100.00	100.00
	16			0.04	0.78	5.13	17.26	37.25	59.50	77.78	84.46	95.47	98.15	99.80	99.99	100.00
	17			0.01	0.35	2.86	11.40	28.06	49.59	69.80	78.09	92.85	96.93	99.61	99.97	100.00
	18				0.15	1.52	7.18	20.26	39.87	60.89	70.57	89.25	95.12	99.29	99.93	100.00
	19				0.06	0.77	4.31	14.02	30.89	51.53	62.17	84.58	92.59	98.76	99.86	100.00
	20				0.02	0.37	2.48	9.29	23.04	42.22	53.29	78.82	89.21	97.93	99.74	100.00
	21				0.01	0.17	1.36	5.91	16.53	33.46	44.36	72.06	84.90	96.69	99.52	100.00
	22					0.07	0.71	3.60	11.42	25.61	35.81	64.49	79.63	94.93	99.17	100.00
	23					0.03	0.36	2.11	7.59	18.94	28.02	56.40	73.47	92.51	98.62	100.00
	24					0.01	0.17	1.19	4.85	13.52	21.23	48.12	66.56	89.34	97.69	99.98
	25						0.08	0.64	2.99	9.31	15.58	40.01	59.11	85.34	96.56	99.95
	26						0.04	0.33	1.78	6.20	11.06	32.39	51.39	80.49	94.85	99.91
	27						0.02	0.17	1.02	3.98	7.60	25.51	43.69	74.83	92.56	99.83
	28						0.01	0.08	0.56	2.47	5.06	19.54	36.28	68.46	89.58	99.69
	29							0.04	0.30	1.48	3.26	14.54	29.41	61.54	85.86	99.45
	30							0.02	0.15	0.86	2.03	10.52	23.26	54.30	81.37	99.09
	31							0.01	0.08	0.48	1.23	7.40	17.94	46.97	76.13	98.52
	32								0.04	0.26	0.72	5.05	13.49	39.80	70.21	97.69
	33								0.02	0.14	0.41	3.36				96.50
	34								0.01	0.07	0.23	2.17				94.86
	35									0.04	0.12					92.69
	36									0.02						89.90

Appendix F-5

PROBABILITY THAT ERROR RATE IN UNIVERSE SIZE OF OVER 2000 IS LESS THAN:

SIZE OF SAMPLE EXAMINED: 240

NO. OF ERRORS FOUND	1%	2%	3%	4%	5%	6%	7%	8%	9%	10%	12%	14%	16%	18%	20%
0	91.04	99.22	99.93	99.99	100.00	100.00	100.00	100.00	100.00	100.00	100.00	100.00	100.00	100.00	100.00
1	69.31	95.38	99.44	99.94	99.99	100.00	100.00	100.00	100.00	100.00	100.00	100.00	100.00	100.00	100.00
2	43.08	86.01	97.60	99.66	99.96	99.99	100.00	100.00	100.00	100.00	100.00	100.00	100.00	100.00	100.00
3	22.06	70.85	93.10	98.75	99.81	99.97	100.00	100.00	100.00	100.00	100.00	100.00	100.00	100.00	100.00
4	9.49	52.52	84.85	96.49	99.34	99.90	99.99	100.00	100.00	100.00	100.00	100.00	100.00	100.00	100.00
5	3.49	34.86	72.81	90.04	98.19	99.66	99.94	99.99	100.00	100.00	100.00	100.00	100.00	100.00	100.00
6	1.12	20.75	58.23	84.79	95.80	99.06	99.82	99.97	99.99	100.00	100.00	100.00	100.00	100.00	100.00
7	0.32	11.12	43.15	74.69	91.60	97.78	99.51	99.91	99.98	100.00	100.00	100.00	100.00	100.00	100.00
8	0.08	5.40	29.57	62.44	85.16	95.40	98.83	99.74	99.95	99.99	100.00	100.00	100.00	100.00	100.00
9	0.02	2.39	18.74	49.27	76.43	91.49	97.50	99.38	99.87	99.98	100.00	100.00	100.00	100.00	100.00
10		0.97	11.00	36.60	65.82	85.73	95.20	98.65	99.68	99.93	100.00	100.00	100.00	100.00	100.00
11		0.36	6.00	25.56	54.14	78.04	91.58	97.33	99.28	99.83	99.99	100.00	100.00	100.00	100.00
12		0.12	3.05	16.78	42.40	68.67	86.38	95.14	98.53	99.62	99.98	100.00	100.00	100.00	100.00
13		0.04	1.45	10.37	31.57	58.17	79.51	91.79	97.24	99.20	99.96	100.00	100.00	100.00	100.00
14		0.01	0.64	6.04	22.33	47.32	71.13	87.07	95.16	98.46	99.90	100.00	100.00	100.00	100.00
15			0.27	3.32	15.00	36.88	61.63	80.88	92.07	97.21	99.77	99.99	100.00	100.00	100.00
16			0.11	1.72	9.57	27.50	51.57	73.32	87.76	95.25	99.54	99.97	100.00	100.00	100.00
17			0.04	0.85	5.81	19.62	41.60	64.65	82.15	92.39	99.11	99.94	100.00	100.00	100.00
18			0.01	0.40	3.36	13.39	32.30	55.32	75.28	88.45	98.40	99.87	99.99	100.00	100.00
19				0.18	1.85	8.74	24.11	45.83	67.34	83.33	97.26	99.74	99.98	100.00	100.00
20				0.07	0.97	5.46	17.31	36.72	58.66	77.06	95.55	99.50	99.96	100.00	100.00
21				0.03	0.49	3.27	11.94	28.42	49.66	69.75	93.10	99.09	99.93	100.00	100.00
22				0.01	0.23	1.87	7.92	21.23	40.81	61.66	89.77	98.43	99.85	99.99	100.00
23					0.11	1.03	5.06	15.31	32.51	53.15	85.47	97.42	99.72	99.98	100.00
24					0.05	0.55	3.10	10.65	25.09	44.59	80.17	95.92	99.49	99.96	100.00
25					0.02	0.28	1.84	7.15	18.74	36.38	73.92	93.82	99.12	99.92	100.00
26					0.01	0.14	1.05	4.64	13.56	28.84	66.88	90.99	98.52	99.85	99.99
27						0.06	0.57	2.90	9.49	22.19	59.27	87.24	97.63	99.72	99.98
28						0.03	0.30	1.76	6.43	16.58	51.37	82.82	96.33	99.51	99.96
29						0.01	0.16	1.03	4.22	12.01	43.50	77.44	94.53	99.17	99.92
30							0.08	0.58	2.68	8.45	35.95	71.28	92.11	98.64	99.85
31							0.04	0.32	1.65	5.77	28.98	64.48	88.99	97.86	99.73
32							0.02	0.17	0.98	3.82	22.76	57.26	85.11	96.74	99.54
33							0.01	0.09	0.57	2.45	17.43	49.85	80.45	95.19	99.24
34								0.04	0.32	1.53	12.99	42.50	75.05	93.12	98.78
35								0.02	0.17	0.93	9.44	35.46	68.99	90.45	98.10
36								0.01	0.09	0.55	6.67	28.94	62.42	87.11	97.14
37									0.05	0.31	4.60	23.08	55.52	83.06	95.81
38									0.02	0.17	3.08	17.99	48.50	78.32	94.04
39									0.01	0.09	2.02	13.70	41.57	72.92	91.74
40										0.05	1.28	10.18	34.94	66.97	88.86

Appendix F-6

PROBABILITY THAT ERROR RATE IN UNIVERSE SIZE OF OVER 2000 IS LESS THAN:

SIZE OF SAMPLE EXAMINED	NO. OF ERRORS FOUND	1%	2%	3%	4%	5%	6%	7%	8%	9%	10%	12%	14%	16%	18%	20%
260	0	92.67	99.48	99.96	100.00	100.00	100.00	100.00	100.00	100.00	100.00	100.00	100.00	100.00	100.00	100.00
	1	73.42	96.70	99.67	99.97	100.00	100.00	100.00	100.00	100.00	100.00	100.00	100.00	100.00	100.00	100.00
	2	48.23	89.36	98.50	99.83	99.98	100.00	100.00	100.00	100.00	100.00	100.00	100.00	100.00	100.00	100.00
	3	26.36	76.48	95.39	99.31	99.91	99.99	100.00	100.00	100.00	100.00	100.00	100.00	100.00	100.00	100.00
	4	12.16	59.59	89.20	97.93	99.68	99.96	99.99	100.00	100.00	100.00	100.00	100.00	100.00	100.00	100.00
	5	4.82	41.94	79.39	94.99	99.06	99.86	99.98	100.00	100.00	100.00	100.00	100.00	100.00	100.00	100.00
	6	1.66	26.64	66.51	89.79	97.67	99.57	99.93	99.99	100.00	100.00	100.00	100.00	100.00	100.00	100.00
	7	0.51	15.30	52.05	81.92	95.02	98.92	99.81	99.99	100.00	100.00	100.00	100.00	100.00	100.00	100.00
	8	0.14	7.99	37.91	71.54	90.60	97.60	99.50	99.91	99.99	99.99	100.00	100.00	100.00	100.00	100.00
	9	0.03	3.81	25.67	59.44	84.09	95.24	98.86	99.77	99.96	99.99	100.00	100.00	100.00	100.00	100.00
	10	0.01	1.67	16.16	46.79	75.49	91.46	97.64	99.46	99.89	99.98	100.00	100.00	100.00	100.00	100.00
	11		0.67	9.48	34.80	65.21	85.98	95.55	98.85	99.75	99.94	100.00	100.00	100.00	100.00	100.00
	12		0.25	5.19	24.44	53.97	78.72	92.30	97.74	99.44	99.88	99.99	100.00	100.00	100.00	100.00
	13		0.09	2.66	16.21	42.69	69.88	87.63	95.90	98.87	99.74	99.99	100.00	100.00	100.00	100.00
	14		0.03	1.28	10.15	32.22	59.92	81.42	93.09	97.88	99.45	99.98	100.00	100.00	100.00	100.00
	15		0.01	0.58	6.01	23.18	49.50	73.76	89.07	96.26	98.93	99.94	100.00	100.00	100.00	100.00
	16			0.25	3.38	15.89	39.31	64.94	83.73	93.82	98.04	99.88	99.99	100.00	100.00	100.00
	17			0.10	1.80	10.39	29.98	55.40	77.05	90.35	96.62	99.74	99.99	100.00	100.00	100.00
	18			0.04	0.91	6.48	21.94	45.71	69.22	85.71	94.49	99.49	99.97	100.00	100.00	100.00
	19			0.01	0.44	3.86	15.40	36.42	60.54	79.87	91.47	99.07	99.94	100.00	100.00	100.00
	20				0.20	2.19	10.37	28.00	51.45	72.91	87.44	98.36	99.88	99.99	100.00	100.00
	21				0.09	1.19	6.71	20.75	42.42	65.05	82.31	97.27	99.77	99.99	100.00	100.00
	22				0.04	0.62	4.16	14.82	33.88	56.60	76.12	95.64	99.56	99.97	100.00	100.00
	23				0.01	0.31	2.48	10.21	26.21	47.95	69.01	93.35	99.22	99.95	100.00	100.00
	24					0.15	1.42	6.78	19.61	39.50	61.21	90.27	98.67	99.89	100.00	100.00
	25					0.07	0.78	4.34	14.20	31.62	53.02	86.29	97.83	99.80	99.99	100.00
	26					0.03	0.42	2.68	9.94	24.57	44.80	81.40	96.59	99.64	99.98	100.00
	27					0.01	0.21	1.60	6.74	18.53	36.89	75.61	94.83	99.37	99.95	100.00
	28						0.11	0.92	4.42	13.55	29.57	69.05	92.46	98.94	99.91	99.99
	29						0.05	0.51	2.80	9.62	23.06	61.88	89.37	98.30	99.83	99.99
	30						0.02	0.28	1.72	6.62	17.50	54.37	85.49	97.35	99.71	99.98
	31						0.01	0.14	1.03	4.44	12.91	46.76	80.81	96.00	99.50	99.96
	32							0.07	0.59	2.87	9.26	39.33	75.36	94.17	99.17	99.93
	33							0.04	0.33	1.81	6.46	32.34	69.23	91.77	98.68	99.87
	34							0.02	0.18	1.10	4.38	25.97	62.56	88.70	97.96	99.77
	35							0.01	0.09	0.66	2.89	20.36	55.56	84.94	96.93	99.61
	36								0.05	0.38	1.85	15.58	48.43	80.46	95.52	99.36
	37								0.02	0.21	1.16	11.64	41.40	75.28	93.65	98.99
	38								0.01	0.12	0.70	8.48	34.69	69.51	91.24	98.44
	39									0.06	0.42	6.03	28.47	63.24	88.22	97.66
	40									0.03	0.24	4.18	22.88	56.65	84.57	96.57
	41									0.02	0.13	2.83	17.99	49.91	80.26	95.12
	42									0.01	0.07	1.87	13.85	43.21	75.34	93.23
	43										0.04	1.20	10.42	36.75	69.85	90.84

Appendix F-7

PROBABILITY THAT ERROR RATE IN UNIVERSE SIZE OF OVER 2000 IS LESS THAN:

SIZE OF SAMPLE EXAMINED: 300

NO. OF ERRORS FOUND	1%	2%	3%	4%	5%	6%	7%	8%	9%	10%	12%	14%	16%	18%	20%
0	95.10	99.77	99.99	100.00	100.00	100.00	100.00	100.00	100.00	100.00	100.00	100.00	100.00	100.00	100.00
1	80.24	98.34	99.89	99.99	100.00	100.00	100.00	100.00	100.00	100.00	100.00	100.00	100.00	100.00	100.00
2	57.79	93.98	99.43	99.96	100.00	100.00	100.00	100.00	100.00	100.00	100.00	100.00	100.00	100.00	100.00
3	35.28	85.15	98.01	99.80	99.98	100.00	100.00	100.00	100.00	100.00	100.00	100.00	100.00	100.00	100.00
4	18.39	71.77	94.76	99.32	99.93	99.99	100.00	100.00	100.00	100.00	100.00	100.00	100.00	100.00	100.00
5	8.29	55.59	88.80	98.14	99.77	99.99	100.00	100.00	100.00	100.00	100.00	100.00	100.00	100.00	100.00
6	3.28	39.37	79.74	95.72	99.34	99.92	99.99	100.00	100.00	100.00	100.00	100.00	100.00	100.00	100.00
7	1.15	25.46	67.97	91.49	98.40	99.77	99.97	100.00	100.00	100.00	100.00	100.00	100.00	100.00	100.00
8	0.36	15.07	54.64	85.03	96.59	99.41	99.92	100.00	100.00	100.00	100.00	100.00	100.00	100.00	100.00
9	0.10	8.18	41.26	76.30	93.50	98.68	99.79	100.00	100.00	100.00	100.00	100.00	100.00	100.00	100.00
10	0.03	4.10	29.22	65.71	88.77	97.32	99.50	99.99	100.00	100.00	100.00	100.00	100.00	100.00	100.00
11	0.01	1.90	19.40	54.07	82.20	95.03	98.93	99.97	100.00	100.00	100.00	100.00	100.00	100.00	100.00
12		0.82	12.09	42.40	73.88	91.50	97.91	99.82	100.00	100.00	100.00	100.00	100.00	100.00	100.00
13		0.33	7.08	31.63	64.17	86.52	96.19	99.15	99.85	100.00	100.00	100.00	100.00	100.00	100.00
14		0.12	3.90	22.42	53.70	80.00	93.54	98.37	99.67	100.00	100.00	100.00	100.00	100.00	100.00
15		0.04	2.03	15.11	43.19	72.07	89.74	97.08	99.33	100.00	100.00	100.00	100.00	100.00	100.00
16		0.01	1.00	9.69	33.34	63.05	84.64	95.08	98.74	99.74	99.99	100.00	100.00	100.00	100.00
17			0.46	5.91	24.67	53.43	78.23	92.17	97.76	99.48	99.98	100.00	100.00	100.00	100.00
18			0.21	3.43	17.50	43.77	70.65	88.19	96.24	99.03	99.96	100.00	100.00	100.00	100.00
19			0.09	1.90	11.91	34.63	62.18	83.05	94.01	98.29	99.92	100.00	100.00	100.00	100.00
20			0.03	1.01	7.76	26.43	53.22	76.78	90.91	97.13	99.84	99.99	100.00	100.00	100.00
21			0.01	0.51	4.86	19.45	44.23	69.51	86.82	95.42	99.69	99.99	100.00	100.00	100.00
22				0.25	2.92	13.79	35.65	61.49	81.69	93.01	99.43	99.98	100.00	100.00	100.00
23				0.12	1.68	9.44	27.84	53.06	75.56	89.77	99.01	99.95	100.00	100.00	100.00
24				0.05	0.94	6.22	21.05	44.60	68.56	85.61	98.34	99.90	100.00	100.00	100.00
25				0.02	0.50	3.96	15.42	36.47	60.92	80.51	97.33	99.81	100.00	100.00	100.00
26				0.01	0.26	2.43	10.93	29.00	52.92	74.52	95.88	99.67	99.99	100.00	100.00
27					0.13	1.44	7.50	22.41	44.90	67.76	93.87	99.43	99.98	100.00	100.00
28					0.06	0.83	4.99	16.82	37.16	60.44	91.20	99.04	99.95	100.00	100.00
29					0.03	0.46	3.21	12.26	29.99	52.81	87.78	98.46	99.90	100.00	100.00
30					0.01	0.25	2.00	8.68	23.58	45.16	83.57	97.59	99.81	100.00	100.00
31						0.13	1.21	5.97	18.05	37.75	78.57	96.36	99.68	99.98	100.00
32						0.06	0.71	3.99	13.46	30.83	72.84	94.69	99.46	99.97	100.00
33						0.03	0.40	2.59	9.77	24.58	66.49	92.47	99.12	99.94	100.00
34						0.02	0.22	1.63	6.91	19.14	59.69	89.63	98.61	99.90	100.00
35						0.01	0.12	1.00	4.75	14.53	52.65	86.12	97.87	99.82	99.99
36							0.06	0.60	3.19	10.77	45.57	81.92	96.84	99.70	99.98
37							0.03	0.35	2.08	7.79	38.69	77.03	95.44	99.50	99.97
38							0.02	0.20	1.32	5.49	32.20	71.53	93.59	99.21	99.94
39							0.01	0.11	0.82	3.78	26.25	65.51	91.22	98.77	99.90
40								0.06	0.50	2.54	20.96	59.12	88.28	98.15	99.83
41								0.03	0.29	1.66	16.38	52.52	84.73	97.25	99.72
42								0.02	0.17	1.06	12.53	45.90	80.56	96.11	99.56
43								0.01	0.09	0.67	9.39	39.43	75.79	94.57	99.31
44									0.05	0.41	6.88	33.27	70.49	92.60	98.94
45									0.03	0.24	4.93	27.58	64.74	90.13	98.42
46									0.01	0.14	3.46	22.44	58.68	87.12	97.70
47										0.08	2.38	17.91	52.43	83.56	96.72
48										0.04	1.60	14.01	46.16	79.43	95.43

Appendix F-8

PROBABILITY THAT ERROR RATE IN UNIVERSE SIZE OF OVER 2000 IS LESS THAN:

SIZE OF SAMPLE EXAMINED	NO. OF ERRORS FOUND	1%	2%	3%	4%	5%	6%	7%	8%	9%	10%	12%	14%	16%	18%	20%
400	0	98.20	99.97	100.00	100.00	100.00	100.00	100.00	100.00	100.00	100.00	100.00	100.00	100.00	100.00	100.00
	1	90.95	99.72	99.99	100.00	100.00	100.00	100.00	100.00	100.00	100.00	100.00	100.00	100.00	100.00	100.00
	2	76.34	98.69	99.95	100.00	100.00	100.00	100.00	100.00	100.00	100.00	100.00	100.00	100.00	100.00	100.00
	3	56.75	95.91	99.79	99.99	100.00	100.00	100.00	100.00	100.00	100.00	100.00	100.00	100.00	100.00	100.00
	4	37.12	90.27	99.30	99.97	100.00	100.00	100.00	100.00	100.00	100.00	100.00	100.00	100.00	100.00	100.00
	5	21.41	81.15	98.10	99.88	99.99	100.00	100.00	100.00	100.00	100.00	100.00	100.00	100.00	100.00	100.00
	6	10.96	68.91	95.65	99.65	99.98	100.00	100.00	100.00	100.00	100.00	100.00	100.00	100.00	100.00	100.00
	7	5.02	54.85	91.38	99.10	99.94	100.00	100.00	100.00	100.00	100.00	100.00	100.00	100.00	100.00	100.00
	8	2.08	40.74	84.90	97.99	99.83	99.99	100.00	100.00	100.00	100.00	100.00	100.00	100.00	100.00	100.00
	9	0.78	28.21	76.16	95.97	99.58	99.97	100.00	100.00	100.00	100.00	100.00	100.00	100.00	100.00	100.00
	10	0.27	18.21	65.60	92.67	99.06	99.92	99.99	100.00	100.00	100.00	100.00	100.00	100.00	100.00	100.00
	11	0.08	10.97	54.01	87.80	98.10	99.80	99.98	100.00	100.00	100.00	100.00	100.00	100.00	100.00	100.00
	12	0.02	6.19	42.40	81.23	96.45	99.56	99.96	100.00	100.00	100.00	100.00	100.00	100.00	100.00	100.00
	13	0.01	3.27	31.68	73.05	93.86	99.10	99.91	99.99	100.00	100.00	100.00	100.00	100.00	100.00	100.00
	14		1.62	22.52	63.63	90.10	98.28	99.79	99.98	100.00	100.00	100.00	100.00	100.00	100.00	100.00
	15		0.76	15.23	53.53	85.01	96.95	99.57	99.96	100.00	100.00	100.00	100.00	100.00	100.00	100.00
	16		0.34	9.80	43.40	78.56	94.90	99.18	99.90	99.99	100.00	100.00	100.00	100.00	100.00	100.00
	17		0.14	6.01	33.87	70.88	91.94	98.50	99.80	99.98	100.00	100.00	100.00	100.00	100.00	100.00
	18		0.06	3.51	25.42	62.29	87.93	97.42	99.61	99.96	100.00	100.00	100.00	100.00	100.00	100.00
	19		0.02	1.96	18.34	53.20	82.78	95.78	99.27	99.91	100.00	100.00	100.00	100.00	100.00	100.00
	20		0.01	1.04	12.72	44.09	76.51	93.43	98.71	99.81	99.98	100.00	100.00	100.00	100.00	100.00
	21			0.53	8.49	35.41	69.27	90.23	97.83	99.65	99.96	100.00	100.00	100.00	100.00	100.00
	22			0.26	5.45	27.54	61.32	86.08	96.52	99.37	99.91	100.00	100.00	100.00	100.00	100.00
	23			0.12	3.37	20.73	52.97	80.95	94.64	98.91	99.83	100.00	100.00	100.00	100.00	100.00
	24			0.06	2.00	15.10	44.60	74.88	92.07	98.20	99.69	100.00	100.00	100.00	100.00	100.00
	25			0.02	1.15	10.65	36.56	68.02	88.72	97.14	99.46	99.99	100.00	100.00	100.00	100.00
	26			0.01	0.64	7.27	29.16	60.56	84.50	95.63	99.08	99.98	100.00	100.00	100.00	100.00
	27				0.34	4.80	22.62	52.79	79.43	93.56	98.51	99.96	100.00	100.00	100.00	100.00
	28				0.18	3.07	17.06	44.99	73.56	90.83	97.65	99.93	100.00	100.00	100.00	100.00
	29				0.09	1.90	12.51	37.47	67.01	87.37	96.43	99.87	100.00	100.00	100.00	100.00
	30				0.04	1.14	8.92	30.46	59.96	83.14	94.76	99.78	100.00	100.00	100.00	100.00
	31				0.02	0.67	6.18	24.17	52.65	78.15	92.54	99.62	100.00	100.00	100.00	100.00
	32				0.01	0.38	4.16	18.71	45.31	72.45	89.70	99.37	99.98	100.00	100.00	100.00
	33					0.21	2.73	14.12	38.20	66.17	86.18	98.99	99.97	100.00	100.00	100.00
	34					0.11	1.74	10.40	31.53	59.47	81.95	98.43	99.95	100.00	100.00	100.00
	35					0.06	1.08	7.47	25.46	52.53	77.04	97.64	99.91	100.00	100.00	100.00
	36					0.03	0.65	5.23	20.11	45.58	71.51	96.54	99.84	100.00	100.00	100.00
	37					0.01	0.38	3.57	15.53	38.81	65.47	95.07	99.74	99.99	100.00	100.00
	38						0.22	2.38	11.73	32.42	59.05	93.15	99.58	99.99	100.00	100.00
	39						0.12	1.55	8.66	26.55	52.44	90.72	99.33	99.98	100.00	100.00

Appendix F-9

PROBABILITY THAT ERROR RATE IN UNIVERSE SIZE OF OVER 2000 IS LESS THAN:

SIZE OF SAMPLE EXAMINED	NO. OF ERRORS FOUND	1%	2%	3%	4%	5%	6%	7%	8%	9%	10%	12%	14%	16%	18%	20%
400 (Cont.)	40						0.07	0.98	6.25	21.31	45.80	87.73	98.97	99.96	100.00	100.00
	41						0.04	0.61	4.41	16.77	39.33	84.15	98.45	99.94	100.00	100.00
	42						0.02	0.37	3.04	12.92	33.18	79.98	97.73	99.89	100.00	100.00
	43						0.01	0.22	2.05	9.76	27.49	75.24	96.75	99.83	100.00	100.00
	44							0.13	1.36	7.21	22.37	70.00	95.46	99.72	99.99	100.00
	45							0.07	0.88	5.23	17.86	64.35	93.80	99.56	99.99	100.00
	46							0.04	0.55	3.71	14.00	58.40	91.71	99.33	99.98	100.00
	47							0.02	0.34	2.58	10.76	52.29	89.15	98.99	99.96	100.00
	48							0.01	0.21	1.76	8.12	46.16	86.09	98.52	99.93	100.00
	49								0.12	1.17	6.01	40.16	82.51	97.88	99.89	100.00
	50								0.07	0.77	4.36	34.42	78.41	97.01	99.82	99.99
	51								0.04	0.49	3.11	29.04	73.84	95.89	99.72	99.99
	52								0.02	0.31	2.17	24.12	68.84	94.45	99.57	99.98
	53								0.01	0.19	1.49	19.71	63.50	92.65	99.35	99.97
	54									0.12	1.00	15.85	57.91	90.45	99.05	99.96
	55									0.07	0.66	12.54	52.18	87.81	98.62	99.93
	56									0.04	0.43	9.75	46.44	84.71	98.06	99.89
	57									0.02	0.27	7.46	40.80	81.15	97.30	99.82
	58									0.01	0.17	5.62	35.38	77.14	96.32	99.73
	59										0.11	4.16	30.25	72.71	95.08	99.59
	60										0.06	3.03	25.51	67.91	93.52	99.39
	61										0.04	2.17	21.21	62.82	91.62	99.12
	62										0.02	1.52	17.38	57.52	89.34	98.75
	63										0.01	1.06	14.04	52.10	86.65	98.25
	64											0.72	11.18	46.67	83.54	97.59
	65											0.48	8.76	41.32	80.01	96.74
	66											0.32	6.77	36.15	76.08	95.67
	67											0.21	5.15	31.24	71.78	94.32
	68											0.13	3.86	26.65	67.16	92.68
	69											0.08	2.86	22.45	62.28	90.70
	70											0.05	2.08	18.67	57.21	88.36

PROBABILITY THAT ERROR RATE IN UNIVERSE SIZE OF OVER 2000 IS LESS THAN:

Appendix F-10

SIZE OF SAMPLE EXAMINED: 500

NO. OF ERRORS FOUND	1%	2%	3%	4%	5%	6%	7%	8%	9%	10%	12%	14%	16%	18%	20%
0	99.34	100.00	100.00	100.00	100.00	100.00	100.00	100.00	100.00	100.00	100.00	100.00	100.00	100.00	100.00
1	96.02	99.95	100.00	100.00	100.00	100.00	100.00	100.00	100.00	100.00	100.00	100.00	100.00	100.00	100.00
2	87.66	99.74	100.00	100.00	100.00	100.00	100.00	100.00	100.00	100.00	100.00	100.00	100.00	100.00	100.00
3	73.64	99.02	99.98	100.00	100.00	100.00	100.00	100.00	100.00	100.00	100.00	100.00	100.00	100.00	100.00
4	56.04	97.19	99.92	100.00	100.00	100.00	100.00	100.00	100.00	100.00	100.00	100.00	100.00	100.00	100.00
5	38.40	93.48	99.75	99.99	100.00	100.00	100.00	100.00	100.00	100.00	100.00	100.00	100.00	100.00	100.00
6	23.71	87.24	99.30	99.98	100.00	100.00	100.00	100.00	100.00	100.00	100.00	100.00	100.00	100.00	100.00
7	13.23	78.25	98.32	99.94	100.00	100.00	100.00	100.00	100.00	100.00	100.00	100.00	100.00	100.00	100.00
8	6.71	66.95	96.46	99.82	99.99	100.00	100.00	100.00	100.00	100.00	100.00	100.00	100.00	100.00	100.00
9	3.11	54.33	93.31	99.56	99.98	100.00	100.00	100.00	100.00	100.00	100.00	100.00	100.00	100.00	100.00
10	1.32	41.70	88.52	99.03	99.95	100.00	100.00	100.00	100.00	100.00	100.00	100.00	100.00	100.00	100.00
11	0.52	30.21	81.93	98.05	99.89	100.00	100.00	100.00	100.00	100.00	100.00	100.00	100.00	100.00	100.00
12	0.19	20.65	73.62	96.38	99.74	99.99	100.00	100.00	100.00	100.00	100.00	100.00	100.00	100.00	100.00
13	0.06	13.33	63.97	93.77	99.45	99.97	100.00	100.00	100.00	100.00	100.00	100.00	100.00	100.00	100.00
14	0.02	8.14	53.59	89.98	98.92	99.93	100.00	100.00	100.00	100.00	100.00	100.00	100.00	100.00	100.00
15	0.01	4.70	43.19	84.87	98.01	99.85	99.99	100.00	100.00	100.00	100.00	100.00	100.00	100.00	100.00
16		2.57	33.44	78.42	96.57	99.69	99.98	100.00	100.00	100.00	100.00	100.00	100.00	100.00	100.00
17		1.34	24.85	70.76	94.41	99.40	99.96	100.00	100.00	100.00	100.00	100.00	100.00	100.00	100.00
18		0.66	17.73	62.20	91.35	98.90	99.91	99.99	100.00	100.00	100.00	100.00	100.00	100.00	100.00
19		0.31	12.14	53.16	87.28	98.10	99.83	99.99	100.00	100.00	100.00	100.00	100.00	100.00	100.00
20		0.14	7.98	44.09	82.12	96.87	99.67	99.98	100.00	100.00	100.00	100.00	100.00	100.00	100.00
21		0.06	5.04	35.46	75.91	95.07	99.40	99.95	100.00	100.00	100.00	100.00	100.00	100.00	100.00
22		0.02	3.06	27.62	68.79	92.58	98.95	99.90	99.99	100.00	100.00	100.00	100.00	100.00	100.00
23		0.01	1.79	20.84	61.01	89.26	98.25	99.82	99.99	100.00	100.00	100.00	100.00	100.00	100.00
24			1.01	15.22	52.86	85.06	97.20	99.67	99.97	100.00	100.00	100.00	100.00	100.00	100.00
25			0.55	10.76	44.71	79.96	95.71	99.42	99.95	99.99	100.00	100.00	100.00	100.00	100.00
26			0.28	7.37	36.86	74.00	93.65	99.02	99.91	99.99	100.00	100.00	100.00	100.00	100.00
27			0.14	4.89	29.61	67.33	90.92	98.42	99.82	99.98	100.00	100.00	100.00	100.00	100.00
28			0.07	3.14	23.17	60.13	87.46	97.54	99.68	99.97	100.00	100.00	100.00	100.00	100.00
29			0.03	1.96	17.65	52.65	83.22	96.28	99.46	99.95	100.00	100.00	100.00	100.00	100.00
30			0.02	1.18	13.09	45.16	78.21	94.57	99.11	99.90	100.00	100.00	100.00	100.00	100.00
31			0.01	0.69	9.44	37.91	72.50	92.32	98.60	99.82	100.00	100.00	100.00	100.00	100.00
32				0.40	6.64	31.13	66.19	89.45	97.85	99.70	100.00	100.00	100.00	100.00	100.00
33				0.22	4.54	24.99	59.46	85.90	96.80	99.50	100.00	100.00	100.00	100.00	100.00
34				0.12	3.03	19.61	52.49	81.67	95.38	99.21	100.00	100.00	100.00	100.00	100.00
35				0.06	1.96	15.03	45.52	76.78	93.50	98.77	99.99	100.00	100.00	100.00	100.00
36				0.03	1.24	11.26	38.74	71.27	91.10	98.14	99.98	100.00	100.00	100.00	100.00
37				0.02	0.77	8.24	32.33	65.27	88.13	97.26	99.97	100.00	100.00	100.00	100.00
38				0.01	0.46	5.90	26.46	58.92	84.55	96.07	99.95	100.00	100.00	100.00	100.00
39					0.27	4.12	21.23	52.37	80.35	94.50	99.85	100.00	100.00	100.00	100.00
40					0.16	2.81	16.69	45.81	75.56	92.49	99.75	100.00	100.00	100.00	100.00
41					0.09	1.88	12.85	39.40	70.26	89.99	99.61	100.00	100.00	100.00	100.00
42					0.05	1.23	9.70	33.32	64.52	86.95	99.39	99.99	100.00	100.00	100.00

Appendix F-11

PROBABILITY THAT ERROR RATE IN UNIVERSE SIZE OF OVER 2000 IS LESS THAN:

SIZE OF SAMPLE EXAMINED	NO. OF ERRORS FOUND	1%	2%	3%	4%	5%	6%	7%	8%	9%	10%	12%	14%	16%	18%	20%
500 (Cont.)	43					0.02	0.78	7.17	27.68	58.47	83.35	99.07	99.98	100.00	100.00	100.00
	44					0.01	0.49	5.19	22.59	52.26	79.20	98.62	99.97	100.00	100.00	100.00
	45						0.30	3.68	18.11	46.04	74.53	98.01	99.96	100.00	100.00	100.00
	46						0.18	2.56	14.25	39.96	69.40	97.17	99.93	100.00	100.00	100.00
	47						0.10	1.75	11.01	34.14	63.88	96.07	99.88	100.00	100.00	100.00
	48						0.06	1.17	8.35	28.71	58.10	94.65	99.81	100.00	100.00	100.00
	49						0.03	0.76	6.22	23.76	52.18	92.87	99.70	100.00	100.00	100.00
	50						0.02	0.49	4.55	19.34	46.24	90.68	99.55	100.00	100.00	100.00
	51						0.01	0.31	3.26	15.49	40.42	88.04	99.32	99.99	100.00	100.00
	52							0.19	2.30	12.19	34.84	84.94	99.00	99.98	100.00	100.00
	53							0.12	1.59	9.44	29.59	81.36	98.57	99.96	100.00	100.00
	54							0.07	1.08	7.19	24.77	77.32	97.98	99.94	100.00	100.00
	55							0.04	0.72	5.38	20.42	72.86	97.21	99.91	100.00	100.00
	56							0.02	0.47	3.96	16.58	68.02	96.21	99.86	100.00	100.00
	57							0.01	0.30	2.87	13.26	62.87	94.94	99.78	100.00	100.00
	58								0.19	2.04	10.44	57.52	93.96	99.67	100.00	100.00
	59								0.12	1.43	8.10	52.05	91.43	99.51	99.99	100.00
	60								0.07	0.98	6.18	46.57	89.12	99.29	99.98	100.00
	61								0.04	0.67	4.65	41.17	86.42	98.99	99.97	100.00
	62								0.03	0.44	3.44	35.97	83.30	98.58	99.96	100.00
	63								0.02	0.29	2.50	31.03	79.76	98.03	99.93	100.00
	64								0.01	0.19	1.80	26.44	75.84	97.32	99.90	100.00
	65									0.12	1.27	22.23	71.55	96.42	99.84	100.00
	66									0.07	0.88	18.45	66.95	95.28	99.77	100.00
	67									0.05	0.60	15.11	62.10	93.88	99.66	99.99
	68									0.03	0.41	12.22	57.08	92.18	99.50	99.99
	69									0.02	0.27	9.74	51.95	90.16	99.29	99.98
	70									0.01	0.18	7.67	46.82	87.78	99.00	99.97
	71										0.11	5.95	41.76	85.04	98.62	99.95
	72										0.07	4.56	36.84	81.93	98.13	99.93
	73										0.04	3.44	32.16	78.46	97.49	99.89
	74										0.03	2.56	27.75	74.64	96.68	99.84
	75										0.02	1.88	23.68	70.51	95.67	99.76
	76										0.01	1.37	19.98	66.11	94.42	99.66
	77											0.98	16.65	61.50	92.92	99.51
	78											0.69	13.72	56.73	91.14	99.31
	79											0.48	11.17	51.88	89.05	99.05
	80											0.33	8.99	47.02	86.63	98.70
	81											0.22	7.14	42.22	83.88	98.25
	82											0.15	5.61	37.54	80.79	97.68

Appendix G-1 TABLES OF PROBABILITIES FOR USE IN EXPLORATORY SAMPLING

Reprinted with permission of
the United States Air Force Auditor General.

PROBABILITY, IN PER CENT, OF FINDING AT LEAST ONE ERROR IF TOTAL NO. OF ERRORS IN UNIVERSE IS AS INDICATED

TOTAL ERRORS IN UNIVERSE SIZE OF 1000.

SAMPLE SIZE	2	3	4	5	10	15	20	25	30	40	50	75	100	200	300	500	1000	2000
5	1.0	1.5	2.0	2.5	4.9	7.3	9.6	11.9	14.2	18.5	22.7	32.3	41.0	67.3	83.3	96.9	100.0	—
10	2.0	3.0	3.9	4.9	9.6	14.1	18.4	22.5	26.4	33.6	40.3	54.3	65.3	89.4	97.2	99.9	100.0	—
15	3.0	4.4	5.9	7.3	14.1	20.4	26.3	31.8	36.9	46.0	53.9	69.2	79.7	96.6	99.5	100.0	100.0	—
20	4.0	5.9	7.8	9.6	18.4	26.3	33.5	40.0	45.9	56.2	64.5	79.3	88.1	98.9	99.9	100.0	100.0	—
25	4.9	7.3	9.6	11.9	22.5	31.8	40.0	47.3	53.7	64.4	72.7	86.1	93.1	99.6	100.0	100.0	100.0	—
30	5.9	8.7	11.5	14.2	26.4	36.9	45.9	53.7	60.4	71.2	79.0	90.7	96.0	99.9	100.0	100.0	100.0	—
35	6.9	10.1	13.3	16.3	30.1	41.6	51.3	59.4	66.2	76.6	83.9	93.8	97.7	100.0	100.0	100.0	100.0	—
40	7.8	11.5	15.1	18.5	33.6	46.0	56.2	64.4	71.2	81.1	87.7	95.9	98.6	100.0	100.0	100.0	100.0	—
45	8.8	12.9	16.8	20.6	36.9	50.1	60.5	68.8	75.4	84.7	90.6	97.2	99.2	100.0	100.0	100.0	100.0	—
50	9.8	14.3	18.6	22.7	40.3	53.9	64.5	72.7	79.0	87.7	92.8	98.2	99.6	100.0	100.0	100.0	100.0	—
55	10.7	15.6	20.3	24.7	43.4	57.5	68.1	76.1	82.1	90.1	94.5	98.8	99.7	100.0	100.0	100.0	100.0	—
60	11.6	17.0	22.0	26.7	46.3	60.7	71.3	79.1	84.8	92.0	95.8	99.2	99.8	100.0	100.0	100.0	100.0	—
65	12.6	18.3	23.6	28.6	49.1	63.8	74.3	81.8	87.1	93.6	96.8	99.5	99.9	100.0	100.0	100.0	100.0	—
70	13.5	19.6	25.2	30.5	51.8	66.6	76.9	84.1	89.0	94.8	97.6	99.7	99.9	100.0	100.0	100.0	100.0	—
75	14.4	20.9	26.8	32.3	54.3	69.2	79.3	86.1	90.7	95.9	98.2	99.8	100.0	100.0	100.0	100.0	100.0	—
80	15.4	22.2	28.4	34.1	56.7	71.6	81.4	87.9	92.0	96.7	98.6	99.8	100.0	100.0	100.0	100.0	100.0	—
85	16.3	23.4	29.9	35.9	59.0	73.9	83.4	89.5	93.2	97.3	98.9	99.9	100.0	100.0	100.0	100.0	100.0	—
90	17.2	24.7	31.5	37.7	61.2	75.9	85.1	90.8	94.3	97.9	99.2	99.9	100.0	100.0	100.0	100.0	100.0	—
95	18.1	25.9	33.0	39.4	63.3	77.9	86.7	92.0	95.2	98.3	99.4	100.0	100.0	100.0	100.0	100.0	100.0	—
100	19.0	27.1	34.4	41.0	65.3	79.7	88.1	93.1	96.0	98.6	99.6	100.0	100.0	100.0	100.0	100.0	100.0	—
125	23.4	33.0	41.4	48.8	73.9	86.7	93.3	96.6	98.3	99.6	99.9	100.0	100.0	100.0	100.0	100.0	100.0	—
150	27.8	38.6	47.8	55.7	80.5	91.4	96.3	98.3	99.3	99.9	100.0	100.0	100.0	100.0	100.0	100.0	100.0	—
175	32.0	43.9	53.7	61.9	85.5	94.5	98.0	99.2	99.7	100.0	100.0	100.0	100.0	100.0	100.0	100.0	100.0	—
200	36.0	48.8	59.1	67.3	89.4	96.6	98.9	99.6	99.9	100.0	100.0	100.0	100.0	100.0	100.0	100.0	100.0	—
225	40.0	53.5	64.0	72.1	92.3	97.9	99.4	99.8	100.0	100.0	100.0	100.0	100.0	100.0	100.0	100.0	100.0	—
250	43.8	57.9	68.4	76.3	94.5	98.7	99.7	99.9	100.0	100.0	100.0	100.0	100.0	100.0	100.0	100.0	100.0	—
275	47.5	61.9	72.4	80.0	96.1	99.2	99.8	100.0	100.0	100.0	100.0	100.0	100.0	100.0	100.0	100.0	100.0	—
300	51.0	65.7	76.1	83.3	97.2	99.5	99.9	100.0	100.0	100.0	100.0	100.0	100.0	100.0	100.0	100.0	100.0	—
325	54.5	69.3	79.3	86.1	98.1	99.7	100.0	100.0	100.0	100.0	100.0	100.0	100.0	100.0	100.0	100.0	100.0	—
350	57.8	72.6	82.2	88.5	98.7	99.9	100.0	100.0	100.0	100.0	100.0	100.0	100.0	100.0	100.0	100.0	100.0	—
375	61.0	75.6	84.8	90.5	99.1	99.9	100.0	100.0	100.0	100.0	100.0	100.0	100.0	100.0	100.0	100.0	100.0	—
400	64.0	78.4	87.1	92.3	99.4	100.0	100.0	100.0	100.0	100.0	100.0	100.0	100.0	100.0	100.0	100.0	100.0	—
425	67.0	81.0	89.1	93.8	99.6	100.0	100.0	100.0	100.0	100.0	100.0	100.0	100.0	100.0	100.0	100.0	100.0	—
450	69.8	83.4	90.9	95.0	99.8	100.0	100.0	100.0	100.0	100.0	100.0	100.0	100.0	100.0	100.0	100.0	100.0	—
475	72.5	85.6	92.3	96.0	99.8	100.0	100.0	100.0	100.0	100.0	100.0	100.0	100.0	100.0	100.0	100.0	100.0	—
500	75.0	87.5	93.8	96.9	99.9	100.0	100.0	100.0	100.0	100.0	100.0	100.0	100.0	100.0	100.0	100.0	100.0	—
550	79.8	90.9	95.8	98.2	100.0	100.0	100.0	100.0	100.0	100.0	100.0	100.0	100.0	100.0	100.0	100.0	100.0	—
600	84.0	93.6	97.5	99.0	100.0	100.0	100.0	100.0	100.0	100.0	100.0	100.0	100.0	100.0	100.0	100.0	100.0	—
650	87.8	95.7	98.5	99.5	100.0	100.0	100.0	100.0	100.0	100.0	100.0	100.0	100.0	100.0	100.0	100.0	100.0	—
700	91.0	97.3	99.2	99.8	100.0	100.0	100.0	100.0	100.0	100.0	100.0	100.0	100.0	100.0	100.0	100.0	100.0	—
750	93.8	98.5	99.6	99.9	100.0	100.0	100.0	100.0	100.0	100.0	100.0	100.0	100.0	100.0	100.0	100.0	100.0	—
800	96.0	99.2	99.8	100.0	100.0	100.0	100.0	100.0	100.0	100.0	100.0	100.0	100.0	100.0	100.0	100.0	100.0	—
850	97.8	99.7	100.0	100.0	100.0	100.0	100.0	100.0	100.0	100.0	100.0	100.0	100.0	100.0	100.0	100.0	100.0	—
900	99.0	99.9	100.0	100.0	100.0	100.0	100.0	100.0	100.0	100.0	100.0	100.0	100.0	100.0	100.0	100.0	100.0	—
950	99.8	100.0	100.0	100.0	100.0	100.0	100.0	100.0	100.0	100.0	100.0	100.0	100.0	100.0	100.0	100.0	100.0	—
1000	100.0	100.0	100.0	100.0	100.0	100.0	100.0	100.0	100.0	100.0	100.0	100.0	100.0	100.0	100.0	100.0	100.0	—
1100	—	—	—	—	—	—	—	—	—	—	—	—	—	—	—	—	—	—
1200	—	—	—	—	—	—	—	—	—	—	—	—	—	—	—	—	—	—
1300	—	—	—	—	—	—	—	—	—	—	—	—	—	—	—	—	—	—
1400	—	—	—	—	—	—	—	—	—	—	—	—	—	—	—	—	—	—
1500	—	—	—	—	—	—	—	—	—	—	—	—	—	—	—	—	—	—
1600	—	—	—	—	—	—	—	—	—	—	—	—	—	—	—	—	—	—
1700	—	—	—	—	—	—	—	—	—	—	—	—	—	—	—	—	—	—
1800	—	—	—	—	—	—	—	—	—	—	—	—	—	—	—	—	—	—
1900	—	—	—	—	—	—	—	—	—	—	—	—	—	—	—	—	—	—
2000	—	—	—	—	—	—	—	—	—	—	—	—	—	—	—	—	—	—

Appendix G-2

PROBABILITY, IN PER CENT, OF FINDING AT LEAST ONE ERROR IF TOTAL NO. OF ERRORS IN UNIVERSE IS AS INDICATED

TOTAL ERRORS IN UNIVERSE SIZE OF 3000

SAMPLE SIZE	1	2	3	4	5	10	15	20	25	30	40	50	75	100	200	300	500	1000	2000
5.	0.2	0.3	0.5	0.7	0.8	1.7	2.5	3.3	4.1	4.9	6.5	8.1	11.9	15.6	29.2	41.0	59.8	86.9	99.6
10.	0.3	0.7	1.0	1.3	1.7	3.3	4.9	6.5	8.0	9.6	12.6	15.5	22.4	28.8	49.9	65.2	83.9	98.3	100.0
15.	0.5	1.0	1.5	2.0	2.5	4.9	7.3	9.6	11.8	14.0	18.3	22.3	31.7	39.9	64.6	79.5	93.6	99.8	100.0
20.	0.7	1.3	2.0	2.6	3.3	6.5	9.6	12.6	15.5	18.3	23.6	28.6	39.8	49.3	75.0	87.9	97.4	100.0	100.0
25.	0.8	1.7	2.5	3.3	4.1	8.0	11.8	15.5	18.9	22.3	28.4	34.4	47.0	57.3	82.3	92.9	99.0	100.0	100.0
30.	1.0	2.0	3.0	3.9	4.9	9.6	14.2	18.3	22.6	26.1	33.4	39.8	53.4	64.0	87.5	95.8	99.6	100.0	100.0
35.	1.2	2.3	3.5	4.6	5.7	11.1	16.2	21.0	25.5	29.8	37.7	44.7	59.0	69.7	91.2	97.9	99.8	100.0	100.0
40.	1.3	2.6	3.9	5.2	6.5	12.6	18.3	23.6	28.6	33.3	41.8	49.2	63.9	74.5	93.8	98.6	99.9	100.0	100.0
45.	1.5	3.0	4.4	5.8	7.3	14.0	20.3	26.1	31.5	36.6	45.6	53.3	68.3	78.5	95.6	99.3	100.0	100.0	100.0
50.	1.7	3.3	4.9	6.5	8.1	15.5	22.3	28.6	34.4	39.8	49.2	57.1	72.1	81.9	96.9	99.6	100.0	100.0	100.0
55.	1.8	3.6	5.4	7.1	8.8	16.9	24.3	31.0	37.2	42.8	52.5	60.7	75.5	84.8	97.8	99.7	100.0	100.0	100.0
60.	2.0	4.0	5.9	7.8	9.6	18.3	26.2	33.3	39.8	45.5	55.7	63.9	78.4	87.2	98.5	99.8	100.0	100.0	100.0
65.	2.2	4.3	6.4	8.4	10.4	19.7	28.1	35.6	42.3	48.3	58.6	66.9	81.1	89.2	99.0	99.9	100.0	100.0	100.0
70.	2.3	4.6	6.9	9.1	11.3	21.1	29.9	37.7	44.7	50.9	61.4	69.6	83.4	90.9	99.2	99.9	100.0	100.0	100.0
75.	2.5	4.9	7.3	9.6	11.9	22.4	31.7	39.8	47.0	53.4	63.9	72.1	85.4	92.4	99.5	100.0	100.0	100.0	100.0
80.	2.7	5.3	7.8	10.3	12.6	23.7	33.4	41.9	49.3	55.7	66.3	74.4	87.2	93.6	99.7	100.0	100.0	100.0	100.0
85.	2.8	5.6	8.3	10.9	13.4	25.0	35.1	43.8	51.4	58.0	68.4	76.5	88.7	94.6	99.8	100.0	100.0	100.0	100.0
90.	3.0	5.9	8.7	11.5	14.1	26.0	36.7	45.7	53.4	60.1	70.7	78.5	90.1	95.2	99.8	100.0	100.0	100.0	100.0
95.	3.2	6.2	9.2	12.1	14.9	27.6	38.4	47.6	55.4	62.1	72.6	80.3	91.3	95.9	99.9	100.0	100.0	100.0	100.0
100.	3.3	6.6	9.7	12.7	15.6	28.8	39.9	49.3	57.3	64.0	74.5	81.9	92.4	96.8	99.9	100.0	100.0	100.0	100.0
125.	4.2	8.2	12.0	15.7	19.2	34.7	47.3	57.4	65.5	72.2	82.0	88.3	96.1	98.7	100.0	100.0	100.0	100.0	100.0
150.	5.0	9.8	14.3	18.6	22.6	40.2	53.8	64.3	72.4	78.7	87.3	92.5	97.8	99.5	100.0	100.0	100.0	100.0	100.0
175.	5.8	11.3	16.5	21.4	26.0	45.2	59.5	70.1	77.9	83.7	91.1	95.2	98.8	99.8	100.0	100.0	100.0	100.0	100.0
200.	6.7	12.9	18.7	24.1	29.2	49.9	64.6	75.0	82.3	87.5	93.8	96.9	99.3	99.9	100.0	100.0	100.0	100.0	100.0
225.	7.5	14.4	20.9	26.8	32.3	54.2	69.0	79.1	85.9	90.5	95.4	98.0	99.7	100.0	100.0	100.0	100.0	100.0	100.0
250.	8.3	16.0	23.0	29.4	35.3	58.2	73.0	82.6	88.7	92.6	96.5	98.7	99.8	100.0	100.0	100.0	100.0	100.0	100.0
275.	9.2	17.5	25.1	31.9	38.2	61.8	76.4	85.5	90.9	94.3	97.2	99.1	99.9	100.0	100.0	100.0	100.0	100.0	100.0
300.	10.0	19.0	27.1	34.4	41.0	65.2	79.5	87.9	92.9	95.8	97.9	99.4	99.9	100.0	100.0	100.0	100.0	100.0	100.0
325.	10.8	20.5	29.1	36.8	43.7	68.3	82.2	90.0	94.4	96.6	98.5	99.6	100.0	100.0	100.0	100.0	100.0	100.0	100.0
350.	11.7	22.0	31.1	39.1	46.2	71.1	84.5	91.7	95.6	97.6	98.9	99.7	100.0	100.0	100.0	100.0	100.0	100.0	100.0
375.	12.5	23.4	33.0	41.4	48.7	73.7	86.6	93.1	96.5	98.2	99.2	99.8	100.0	100.0	100.0	100.0	100.0	100.0	100.0
400.	13.3	24.9	34.9	43.6	51.1	76.1	88.4	94.3	97.2	98.7	99.4	99.9	100.0	100.0	100.0	100.0	100.0	100.0	100.0
425.	14.2	26.3	36.8	45.7	53.4	78.3	89.9	95.2	97.8	99.0	99.6	99.9	100.0	100.0	100.0	100.0	100.0	100.0	100.0
450.	15.0	27.8	38.6	47.8	55.7	80.2	91.3	96.2	98.3	99.3	99.7	100.0	100.0	100.0	100.0	100.0	100.0	100.0	100.0
475.	15.8	29.2	40.4	49.8	57.8	82.2	92.5	96.9	98.7	99.4	99.8	100.0	100.0	100.0	100.0	100.0	100.0	100.0	100.0
500.	16.7	30.6	42.1	51.8	59.8	83.3	93.4	97.4	99.0	99.6	99.8	100.0	100.0	100.0	100.0	100.0	100.0	100.0	100.0
550.	18.3	33.3	45.5	55.5	63.7	86.4	95.2	98.4	99.4	99.8	99.9	100.0	100.0	100.0	100.0	100.0	100.0	100.0	100.0
600.	20.0	36.0	48.8	59.1	67.3	89.1	96.5	98.9	99.6	99.9	100.0	100.0	100.0	100.0	100.0	100.0	100.0	100.0	100.0
650.	21.7	38.6	51.9	62.4	70.5	91.3	97.5	99.3	99.8	99.9	100.0	100.0	100.0	100.0	100.0	100.0	100.0	100.0	100.0
700.	23.3	41.2	55.0	65.5	73.3	93.0	98.2	99.5	99.9	100.0	100.0	100.0	100.0	100.0	100.0	100.0	100.0	100.0	100.0
750.	25.0	43.8	57.8	68.4	76.3	94.4	98.7	99.7	99.9	100.0	100.0	100.0	100.0	100.0	100.0	100.0	100.0	100.0	100.0
800.	26.7	46.2	60.6	71.1	78.8	95.5	99.1	99.8	100.0	100.0	100.0	100.0	100.0	100.0	100.0	100.0	100.0	100.0	100.0
850.	28.3	48.6	63.2	73.6	81.1	96.4	99.3	99.9	100.0	100.0	100.0	100.0	100.0	100.0	100.0	100.0	100.0	100.0	100.0
900.	30.0	51.0	65.7	76.0	83.2	97.2	99.5	99.9	100.0	100.0	100.0	100.0	100.0	100.0	100.0	100.0	100.0	100.0	100.0
950.	31.7	53.3	68.1	78.2	85.1	97.8	99.6	100.0	100.0	100.0	100.0	100.0	100.0	100.0	100.0	100.0	100.0	100.0	100.0
1000.	33.3	55.6	70.4	80.3	86.9	98.3	99.8	100.0	100.0	100.0	100.0	100.0	100.0	100.0	100.0	100.0	100.0	100.0	100.0
1100.	36.7	59.9	74.6	83.9	89.9	99.0	99.9	100.0	100.0	100.0	100.0	100.0	100.0	100.0	100.0	100.0	100.0	100.0	100.0
1200.	40.0	64.0	78.4	87.1	92.2	99.4	100.0	100.0	100.0	100.0	100.0	100.0	100.0	100.0	100.0	100.0	100.0	100.0	100.0
1300.	43.3	67.9	81.8	89.7	94.2	99.7	100.0	100.0	100.0	100.0	100.0	100.0	100.0	100.0	100.0	100.0	100.0	100.0	100.0
1400.	46.7	71.6	84.8	91.9	95.7	99.8	100.0	100.0	100.0	100.0	100.0	100.0	100.0	100.0	100.0	100.0	100.0	100.0	100.0
1500.	50.0	75.0	87.5	93.8	96.9	99.9	100.0	100.0	100.0	100.0	100.0	100.0	100.0	100.0	100.0	100.0	100.0	100.0	100.0
1600.	53.3	78.2	89.8	95.3	97.8	99.9	100.0	100.0	100.0	100.0	100.0	100.0	100.0	100.0	100.0	100.0	100.0	100.0	100.0
1700.	56.7	81.2	91.9	96.5	98.5	100.0	100.0	100.0	100.0	100.0	100.0	100.0	100.0	100.0	100.0	100.0	100.0	100.0	100.0
1800.	60.0	84.0	93.6	97.4	99.0	100.0	100.0	100.0	100.0	100.0	100.0	100.0	100.0	100.0	100.0	100.0	100.0	100.0	100.0
1900.	63.3	86.6	95.1	98.2	99.3	100.0	100.0	100.0	100.0	100.0	100.0	100.0	100.0	100.0	100.0	100.0	100.0	100.0	100.0
2000.	66.7	88.8	96.3	98.8	99.6	100.0	100.0	100.0	100.0	100.0	100.0	100.0	100.0	100.0	100.0	100.0	100.0	100.0	100.0

Appendix G-3

PROBABILITY, IN PER CENT, OF FINDING AT LEAST ONE ERROR IF TOTAL NO. OF ERRORS IN UNIVERSE IS AS INDICATED

TOTAL ERRORS IN UNIVERSE SIZE OF 5000.

SAMPLE SIZE	1	2	3	4	5	10	15	20	25	30	40	50	75	100	200	300	500	1000	2000
5.	0.1	0.2	0.3	0.4	0.5	1.0	1.5	2.0	2.5	3.0	3.9	4.9	7.3	9.6	18.5	26.6	41.0	67.2	92.2
10.	0.2	0.4	0.6	0.8	1.0	2.0	3.0	3.9	4.9	5.8	7.7	9.6	14.0	18.3	33.5	46.2	65.2	89.3	99.4
15.	0.3	0.6	0.9	1.2	1.5	3.0	4.4	5.8	7.3	8.6	11.4	14.0	20.3	26.2	45.8	60.5	79.5	96.5	100.0
20.	0.4	0.8	1.2	1.6	2.0	3.9	5.8	7.7	9.6	11.4	14.9	18.2	26.1	33.3	55.8	71.1	87.9	98.9	100.0
25.	0.5	1.0	1.5	2.0	2.5	4.9	7.3	9.6	11.8	14.0	18.2	22.3	31.5	39.7	64.1	78.8	92.9	99.6	100.0
30.	0.6	1.2	1.8	2.4	3.0	5.8	8.6	11.4	14.0	16.6	21.5	26.1	36.5	45.5	70.7	84.6	95.8	99.8	100.0
35.	0.7	1.4	2.1	2.8	3.5	6.8	10.0	13.1	16.1	19.1	24.6	29.7	41.2	50.8	76.2	88.6	97.5	100.0	100.0
40.	0.8	1.6	2.4	3.2	3.9	7.7	11.4	14.9	18.2	21.5	27.6	33.2	45.5	55.6	80.6	91.7	98.5	100.0	100.0
45.	0.9	1.8	2.7	3.6	4.4	8.7	12.7	16.6	20.3	23.8	30.4	36.5	49.5	59.9	84.2	93.9	99.1	100.0	100.0
50.	1.0	2.0	3.0	3.9	4.9	9.6	14.0	18.2	22.3	26.1	33.2	39.6	53.2	63.8	87.1	95.5	99.5	100.0	100.0
55.	1.1	2.2	3.3	4.3	5.4	10.5	15.3	19.9	24.2	28.3	35.9	42.6	56.6	67.3	89.5	96.7	99.7	100.0	100.0
60.	1.2	2.4	3.6	4.7	5.9	11.4	16.6	21.5	26.1	30.5	38.4	45.5	59.8	70.5	91.5	97.6	99.8	100.0	100.0
65.	1.3	2.6	3.9	5.1	6.3	12.3	17.8	23.1	28.0	32.5	40.9	48.2	62.8	73.3	93.1	98.3	99.9	100.0	100.0
70.	1.4	2.8	4.1	5.5	6.8	13.2	19.1	24.6	29.8	34.6	43.2	50.8	65.5	75.9	94.4	98.7	99.9	100.0	100.0
75.	1.5	3.0	4.4	5.9	7.3	14.0	20.3	26.1	31.5	36.5	45.5	53.2	68.1	78.3	95.4	99.1	100.0	100.0	100.0
80.	1.6	3.2	4.7	6.2	7.8	14.9	21.5	27.6	33.2	38.4	47.7	55.5	70.4	80.4	96.3	99.3	100.0	100.0	100.0
85.	1.7	3.4	5.0	6.6	8.2	15.8	22.7	29.1	34.9	40.3	49.8	57.8	72.6	82.3	97.0	99.5	100.0	100.0	100.0
90.	1.8	3.6	5.3	7.0	8.7	16.6	23.9	30.5	36.6	42.1	51.8	59.9	74.7	84.0	97.5	99.6	100.0	100.0	100.0
95.	1.9	3.8	5.6	7.4	9.1	17.5	25.0	31.9	38.2	43.9	53.7	61.9	76.5	85.6	98.0	99.7	100.0	100.0	100.0
100.	2.0	4.0	5.9	7.8	9.6	18.3	26.2	33.3	39.7	45.5	55.6	63.8	78.3	87.0	98.4	99.8	100.0	100.0	100.0
125.	2.5	4.9	7.3	9.6	11.9	22.4	31.6	39.8	47.0	53.3	63.8	72.0	85.2	92.3	99.4	100.0	100.0	100.0	100.0
150.	3.0	5.9	8.7	11.5	14.1	26.3	36.7	45.8	53.4	60.0	70.6	78.4	90.0	95.4	99.8	100.0	100.0	100.0	100.0
175.	3.5	6.9	10.1	13.3	16.3	30.0	41.4	51.0	59.1	65.8	76.1	83.3	93.2	97.3	99.9	100.0	100.0	100.0	100.0
200.	4.0	7.8	11.5	15.1	18.6	33.5	45.8	55.7	64.1	70.7	80.6	87.1	95.4	98.4	100.0	100.0	100.0	100.0	100.0
225.	4.5	8.8	12.9	16.8	20.6	36.9	49.9	60.3	68.5	75.0	84.3	90.1	96.9	99.0	100.0	100.0	100.0	100.0	100.0
250.	5.0	9.8	14.3	18.6	22.6	40.2	53.7	64.2	72.3	78.6	87.3	92.4	97.9	99.4	100.0	100.0	100.0	100.0	100.0
275.	5.5	10.7	15.6	20.3	24.6	43.2	57.2	67.8	75.8	81.8	89.7	94.2	98.6	99.7	100.0	100.0	100.0	100.0	100.0
300.	6.0	11.6	16.9	21.9	26.6	46.2	60.5	71.1	78.8	84.5	91.7	95.5	99.1	99.8	100.0	100.0	100.0	100.0	100.0
325.	6.5	12.6	18.3	23.6	28.6	49.0	63.6	74.0	81.4	86.8	93.3	96.6	99.4	99.9	100.0	100.0	100.0	100.0	100.0
350.	7.0	13.5	19.6	25.2	30.4	51.6	66.4	76.6	83.8	88.7	94.6	97.4	99.6	99.9	100.0	100.0	100.0	100.0	100.0
375.	7.5	14.4	20.9	26.8	32.3	54.2	69.0	79.0	85.8	90.4	95.6	98.0	99.7	100.0	100.0	100.0	100.0	100.0	100.0
400.	8.0	15.3	22.1	28.4	34.1	56.6	71.4	81.2	87.6	91.9	96.5	98.5	99.8	100.0	100.0	100.0	100.0	100.0	100.0
425.	8.5	16.3	23.4	29.9	35.9	58.9	73.7	83.1	89.2	93.1	97.2	98.9	99.9	100.0	100.0	100.0	100.0	100.0	100.0
450.	9.0	17.2	24.6	31.4	37.6	61.1	75.7	84.9	90.6	94.1	97.7	99.1	99.9	100.0	100.0	100.0	100.0	100.0	100.0
475.	9.5	18.1	25.9	32.9	39.3	63.2	77.7	86.5	91.8	95.0	98.2	99.3	100.0	100.0	100.0	100.0	100.0	100.0	100.0
500.	10.0	19.0	27.1	34.4	41.0	65.2	79.5	87.9	92.9	95.8	98.5	99.5	100.0	100.0	100.0	100.0	100.0	100.0	100.0
550.	11.0	20.8	29.5	37.3	44.2	68.9	82.6	90.3	94.6	96.9	99.1	99.7	100.0	100.0	100.0	100.0	100.0	100.0	100.0
600.	12.0	22.6	31.9	40.2	47.2	72.2	85.3	92.3	96.0	97.9	99.4	99.8	100.0	100.0	100.0	100.0	100.0	100.0	100.0
650.	13.0	24.3	34.2	42.8	50.2	75.2	87.7	93.9	97.0	98.5	99.6	99.9	100.0	100.0	100.0	100.0	100.0	100.0	100.0
700.	14.0	26.0	36.4	45.3	52.0	77.9	89.6	95.1	97.7	98.9	99.8	99.9	100.0	100.0	100.0	100.0	100.0	100.0	100.0
750.	15.0	27.8	38.6	47.8	55.6	80.3	91.3	96.2	98.3	99.2	99.9	100.0	100.0	100.0	100.0	100.0	100.0	100.0	100.0
800.	16.0	29.4	40.7	50.2	58.2	82.5	92.7	97.0	98.7	99.5	99.9	100.0	100.0	100.0	100.0	100.0	100.0	100.0	100.0
850.	17.0	31.1	42.8	52.6	60.6	84.5	93.9	97.6	99.1	99.6	100.0	100.0	100.0	100.0	100.0	100.0	100.0	100.0	100.0
900.	18.0	32.8	44.9	54.8	62.9	86.3	94.9	98.1	99.3	99.7	100.0	100.0	100.0	100.0	100.0	100.0	100.0	100.0	100.0
950.	19.0	34.4	46.9	57.0	65.1	87.9	95.8	98.5	99.5	99.8	100.0	100.0	100.0	100.0	100.0	100.0	100.0	100.0	100.0
1000.	20.0	36.0	48.8	59.1	67.2	89.3	96.5	98.9	99.6	99.8	100.0	100.0	100.0	100.0	100.0	100.0	100.0	100.0	100.0
1100.	22.0	39.2	52.6	63.0	71.1	91.7	97.6	99.3	99.8	99.9	100.0	100.0	100.0	100.0	100.0	100.0	100.0	100.0	100.0
1200.	24.0	42.2	56.1	66.7	74.7	93.6	98.4	99.6	99.9	100.0	100.0	100.0	100.0	100.0	100.0	100.0	100.0	100.0	100.0
1300.	26.0	45.2	59.2	70.0	77.8	94.9	98.9	99.7	100.0	100.0	100.0	100.0	100.0	100.0	100.0	100.0	100.0	100.0	100.0
1400.	28.0	48.2	62.7	73.1	80.7	96.3	99.3	99.8	100.0	100.0	100.0	100.0	100.0	100.0	100.0	100.0	100.0	100.0	100.0
1500.	30.0	51.0	65.7	76.0	83.2	97.2	99.5	99.8	100.0	100.0	100.0	100.0	100.0	100.0	100.0	100.0	100.0	100.0	100.0
1600.	32.0	53.8	68.6	78.6	85.5	97.9	99.7	99.9	100.0	100.0	100.0	100.0	100.0	100.0	100.0	100.0	100.0	100.0	100.0
1700.	34.0	56.4	71.3	81.0	87.5	98.4	99.8	99.9	100.0	100.0	100.0	100.0	100.0	100.0	100.0	100.0	100.0	100.0	100.0
1800.	36.0	59.0	73.8	83.2	89.3	98.9	99.8	100.0	100.0	100.0	100.0	100.0	100.0	100.0	100.0	100.0	100.0	100.0	100.0
1900.	38.0	61.6	76.2	85.2	90.8	99.2	99.9	100.0	100.0	100.0	100.0	100.0	100.0	100.0	100.0	100.0	100.0	100.0	100.0
2000.	40.0	64.0	78.4	87.1	92.2	99.4	99.9	100.0	100.0	100.0	100.0	100.0	100.0	100.0	100.0	100.0	100.0	100.0	100.0

Appendix G-4

PROBABILITY, IN PER CENT, OF FINDING AT LEAST ONE ERROR IF TOTAL NO. OF ERRORS IN UNIVERSE IS AS INDICATED

TOTAL ERRORS IN UNIVERSE SIZE OF 10000.

SAMPLE SIZE	1	2	3	4	5	10	15	20	25	30	40	50	75	100	200	300	500	1000	2000
5.	0.1	0.1	0.1	0.2	0.2	0.5	0.7	1.0	1.2	1.5	2.0	2.5	3.7	4.9	9.6	14.1	22.6	41.0	67.2
10.	0.1	0.2	0.3	0.4	0.5	1.0	1.5	2.0	2.5	3.0	3.9	4.9	7.3	9.6	18.3	26.7	40.7	65.1	89.3
15.	0.2	0.3	0.4	0.6	0.7	1.5	2.2	3.0	3.7	4.4	5.8	7.2	10.7	14.0	26.2	36.7	53.7	79.4	96.5
20.	0.2	0.4	0.6	0.8	1.0	2.0	3.0	3.9	4.9	5.8	7.7	9.5	14.0	18.2	33.2	45.1	64.2	87.9	98.9
25.	0.3	0.5	0.7	1.0	1.2	2.5	3.7	4.9	6.1	7.2	9.5	11.8	17.2	22.2	39.7	53.3	72.3	92.8	99.6
30.	0.3	0.6	0.9	1.2	1.5	3.0	4.4	5.8	7.2	8.6	11.3	14.0	20.2	26.1	45.5	60.0	78.6	95.5	99.9
35.	0.4	0.7	1.0	1.4	1.7	3.4	5.1	6.8	8.4	10.0	13.1	16.1	23.2	29.7	50.8	65.6	83.4	97.5	100.0
40.	0.4	0.8	1.2	1.6	2.0	3.9	5.8	7.7	9.5	11.3	14.8	18.2	26.0	33.2	55.5	70.5	87.2	98.5	100.0
45.	0.5	0.9	1.3	1.8	2.2	4.4	6.5	8.6	10.7	12.7	16.5	20.2	28.8	36.4	59.8	74.7	90.1	99.1	100.0
50.	0.5	1.0	1.5	2.0	2.5	4.9	7.2	9.5	11.8	14.0	18.2	22.2	31.4	39.6	63.7	78.3	92.4	99.5	100.0
55.	0.6	1.1	1.6	2.2	2.7	5.4	7.9	10.5	12.9	15.3	19.8	24.0	34.0	42.6	67.2	81.4	94.1	99.7	100.0
60.	0.6	1.2	1.8	2.4	3.0	5.8	8.6	11.4	14.0	16.5	21.4	26.0	36.4	45.4	70.4	84.0	95.4	99.8	100.0
65.	0.7	1.3	1.9	2.6	3.2	6.3	9.3	12.2	15.0	17.8	23.8	27.9	38.8	48.1	72.0	86.3	96.5	99.9	100.0
70.	0.7	1.4	2.1	2.8	3.5	6.8	10.0	13.1	16.1	19.0	24.5	29.7	41.1	50.6	75.8	88.2	97.3	99.9	100.0
75.	0.8	1.5	2.2	3.0	3.7	7.3	10.7	14.0	17.2	20.2	26.0	31.4	43.3	53.1	78.1	89.9	97.9	100.0	100.0
80.	0.8	1.6	2.4	3.2	3.9	7.7	11.4	14.7	18.2	21.4	27.5	34.0	45.4	55.4	80.3	91.4	98.3	100.0	100.0
85.	0.9	1.7	2.5	3.4	4.2	8.2	11.9	15.6	19.2	22.8	29.0	34.8	47.4	57.6	82.2	92.6	98.7	100.0	100.0
90.	0.9	1.8	2.7	3.6	4.4	8.6	12.7	16.6	20.3	23.8	30.4	36.4	49.1	59.7	83.9	93.6	99.0	100.0	100.0
95.	1.0	1.9	2.8	3.7	4.7	9.1	13.3	17.4	21.3	25.0	31.8	38.0	51.3	61.7	85.5	94.5	99.3	100.0	100.0
100.	1.0	2.0	3.0	3.9	4.9	9.6	14.0	18.4	22.2	26.0	33.2	39.6	53.1	63.0	86.9	95.3	99.4	100.0	100.0
125.	1.3	2.5	3.7	4.9	6.1	11.8	17.2	22.3	27.0	31.5	39.0	46.8	61.2	71.8	92.1	97.8	99.8	100.0	100.0
150.	1.5	3.0	4.4	5.9	7.3	14.0	20.3	26.1	31.5	36.5	45.4	53.1	67.9	78.1	95.3	99.0	100.0	100.0	100.0
175.	1.8	3.5	5.2	6.8	8.5	16.2	23.3	29.8	35.7	41.2	50.7	58.7	73.5	82.5	97.2	99.5	100.0	100.0	100.0
200.	2.0	4.0	5.9	7.8	9.6	18.3	26.2	33.3	39.7	45.5	55.5	63.0	78.1	86.9	98.3	99.8	100.0	100.0	100.0
225.	2.3	4.4	6.6	8.7	10.8	20.4	28.9	36.4	43.3	49.5	59.0	68.0	82.0	89.5	99.0	99.9	100.0	100.0	100.0
250.	2.5	4.9	7.3	9.6	11.8	22.2	31.6	39.6	47.0	53.3	63.1	71.6	85.0	92.0	99.4	100.0	100.0	100.0	100.0
275.	2.8	5.4	7.9	10.5	13.0	24.3	34.2	42.6	50.2	56.7	66.6	75.1	87.5	93.4	99.6	100.0	100.0	100.0	100.0
300.	3.0	5.9	8.7	11.5	14.1	26.3	36.7	45.4	53.3	60.0	70.5	78.3	89.7	95.3	99.8	100.0	100.0	100.0	100.0
325.	3.3	6.4	9.4	12.4	15.2	28.1	39.1	48.4	56.3	62.9	73.4	80.9	91.7	96.4	99.9	100.0	100.0	100.0	100.0
350.	3.5	6.9	10.1	13.3	16.3	30.0	41.4	51.0	59.0	65.7	76.0	83.2	93.2	97.2	99.9	100.0	100.0	100.0	100.0
375.	3.8	7.4	10.8	14.2	17.4	31.8	43.7	53.5	61.6	68.3	78.4	85.3	94.4	97.9	100.0	100.0	100.0	100.0	100.0
400.	4.0	7.8	11.5	15.1	18.5	33.5	45.8	55.8	64.0	70.7	80.5	87.1	95.4	98.3	100.0	100.0	100.0	100.0	100.0
425.	4.3	8.3	12.2	16.0	19.5	35.2	47.9	58.1	66.3	72.9	82.5	88.7	96.2	98.7	100.0	100.0	100.0	100.0	100.0
450.	4.5	8.8	12.9	16.8	20.6	36.9	49.9	60.2	68.4	74.9	84.2	90.1	96.9	98.9	100.0	100.0	100.0	100.0	100.0
475.	4.8	9.3	13.6	17.7	21.6	38.5	51.8	62.3	70.4	76.8	85.8	91.3	97.4	99.2	100.0	100.0	100.0	100.0	100.0
500.	5.0	9.8	14.3	18.6	22.6	40.1	53.7	64.2	72.3	78.6	87.2	92.4	97.9	99.4	100.0	100.0	100.0	100.0	100.0
550.	5.5	10.7	15.6	20.3	24.6	43.2	57.2	67.8	75.7	81.7	89.5	94.1	98.5	99.6	100.0	100.0	100.0	100.0	100.0
600.	6.0	11.6	16.9	21.9	26.6	46.2	60.5	71.0	78.7	84.4	91.3	95.5	98.9	99.8	100.0	100.0	100.0	100.0	100.0
650.	6.5	12.6	18.3	23.6	28.6	49.1	63.5	73.9	81.4	86.7	92.8	96.4	99.2	99.8	100.0	100.0	100.0	100.0	100.0
700.	7.0	13.5	19.6	25.2	30.5	51.6	66.1	76.6	83.7	88.7	94.1	97.3	99.4	100.0	100.0	100.0	100.0	100.0	100.0
750.	7.5	14.4	20.9	26.8	32.3	54.2	68.5	79.0	85.8	90.4	95.0	98.0	99.5	100.0	100.0	100.0	100.0	100.0	100.0
800.	8.0	15.4	22.1	28.4	34.1	56.6	71.4	81.2	87.6	91.8	95.8	98.5	99.7	100.0	100.0	100.0	100.0	100.0	100.0
850.	8.5	16.3	23.4	29.9	35.9	58.9	73.6	83.2	89.2	93.1	96.6	98.8	99.8	100.0	100.0	100.0	100.0	100.0	100.0
900.	9.0	17.2	24.6	31.4	37.6	60.9	75.5	84.9	90.6	94.1	97.2	99.1	99.8	100.0	100.0	100.0	100.0	100.0	100.0
950.	9.5	18.1	25.9	32.9	39.3	63.2	77.3	86.5	91.8	95.0	97.7	99.3	99.9	100.0	100.0	100.0	100.0	100.0	100.0
1000.	10.0	19.0	27.1	34.4	41.0	65.1	79.0	87.9	92.8	95.8	98.1	99.4	99.9	100.0	100.0	100.0	100.0	100.0	100.0
1100.	11.0	20.8	29.5	37.3	44.2	68.6	82.0	90.3	94.6	97.0	98.7	99.7	100.0	100.0	100.0	100.0	100.0	100.0	100.0
1200.	12.0	22.6	31.9	40.0	47.2	72.2	85.3	92.6	96.3	98.0	99.1	99.8	100.0	100.0	100.0	100.0	100.0	100.0	100.0
1300.	13.0	24.3	34.2	42.7	50.2	75.2	87.3	93.8	96.9	98.5	99.4	99.9	100.0	100.0	100.0	100.0	100.0	100.0	100.0
1400.	14.0	25.9	36.4	45.3	52.9	77.8	89.0	94.8	97.7	98.8	99.6	99.9	100.0	100.0	100.0	100.0	100.0	100.0	100.0
1500.	15.0	27.8	38.6	47.8	55.6	80.2	90.5	95.8	98.2	99.2	99.7	100.0	100.0	100.0	100.0	100.0	100.0	100.0	100.0
1600.	16.0	29.4	40.8	50.2	58.2	82.6	92.3	96.6	98.7	99.4	99.8	100.0	100.0	100.0	100.0	100.0	100.0	100.0	100.0
1700.	17.0	31.1	42.8	52.5	60.6	84.5	93.2	97.2	98.9	99.6	99.9	100.0	100.0	100.0	100.0	100.0	100.0	100.0	100.0
1800.	18.0	32.8	44.9	54.8	62.9	86.3	94.4	97.8	99.2	99.7	99.9	100.0	100.0	100.0	100.0	100.0	100.0	100.0	100.0
1900.	19.0	34.4	46.9	57.0	65.1	87.7	95.2	98.3	99.4	99.8	100.0	100.0	100.0	100.0	100.0	100.0	100.0	100.0	100.0
2000.	20.0	36.0	48.8	59.0	67.2	89.3	96.5	98.9	99.6	99.9	100.0	100.0	100.0	100.0	100.0	100.0	100.0	100.0	100.0

Appendix G-5

PROBABILITY, IN PER CENT, OF FINDING AT LEAST ONE ERROR IF TOTAL NO. OF ERRORS IN UNIVERSE IS AS INDICATED

TOTAL ERRORS IN UNIVERSE SIZE OF 15000.

SAMPLE SIZE	1	2	3	4	5	10	15	20	25	30	40	50	75	100	200	300	500	1000	2000
5.	0.0	0.1	0.1	0.1	0.2	0.3	0.5	0.7	0.8	1.0	1.3	1.7	2.5	3.3	6.5	9.6	15.6	29.2	51.1
10.	0.1	0.1	0.2	0.3	0.3	0.7	1.0	1.3	1.7	2.0	2.6	3.3	4.9	6.5	12.6	18.3	28.8	49.9	76.1
15.	0.1	0.2	0.3	0.4	0.5	1.0	1.5	2.0	2.3	2.9	3.9	4.9	7.2	9.6	18.2	26.2	39.9	64.5	88.3
20.	0.1	0.3	0.4	0.5	0.7	1.3	2.0	2.6	3.3	3.9	5.2	6.5	9.5	12.5	23.6	33.3	49.3	74.9	94.3
25.	0.2	0.3	0.5	0.7	0.8	1.7	2.5	3.3	4.1	4.9	6.5	8.0	11.8	15.4	28.5	39.7	57.2	82.0	97.2
30.	0.2	0.4	0.6	0.8	1.0	2.0	2.9	3.9	4.9	5.8	7.7	9.5	14.0	18.2	33.2	45.1	63.9	87.4	98.6
35.	0.3	0.5	0.7	0.9	1.1	2.3	3.4	4.6	5.7	6.7	8.9	11.0	16.1	20.9	37.5	50.7	69.5	91.1	99.3
40.	0.3	0.5	0.8	1.1	1.3	2.6	3.9	5.1	6.3	7.5	10.1	12.5	18.2	23.5	41.6	55.5	74.3	93.7	99.7
45.	0.3	0.6	0.9	1.2	1.5	3.0	4.4	5.8	7.2	8.6	11.3	14.0	20.2	26.0	45.4	59.8	78.3	95.5	99.8
50.	0.3	0.7	1.0	1.3	1.7	3.3	4.9	6.5	8.0	9.5	12.5	15.4	22.2	28.5	48.9	63.6	81.7	96.8	99.9
55.	0.4	0.7	1.1	1.5	1.8	3.6	5.4	7.1	8.8	10.4	13.7	16.8	24.1	30.8	52.3	67.1	84.6	97.8	100.0
60.	0.4	0.8	1.2	1.6	2.0	3.9	5.8	7.7	9.5	11.3	14.8	18.2	26.0	33.1	55.4	70.3	87.0	98.4	100.0
65.	0.4	0.9	1.3	1.7	2.1	4.3	6.3	8.3	10.3	12.2	16.0	19.5	27.9	35.3	58.3	73.2	89.0	98.9	100.0
70.	0.5	0.9	1.4	1.9	2.3	4.6	6.8	8.9	11.0	13.1	17.1	20.9	29.7	37.5	61.0	75.8	90.7	99.2	100.0
75.	0.5	1.0	1.5	2.0	2.5	4.9	7.2	9.5	11.8	14.0	18.2	22.2	31.4	39.5	63.6	78.1	92.2	99.4	100.0
80.	0.5	1.1	1.6	2.1	2.6	5.2	7.7	10.1	12.5	14.8	19.3	23.5	33.1	41.5	65.8	80.1	93.4	99.6	100.0
85.	0.6	1.1	1.7	2.2	2.8	5.5	8.2	10.7	13.3	15.7	20.4	24.8	34.8	43.4	68.2	82.0	94.4	99.7	100.0
90.	0.6	1.2	1.8	2.4	3.0	5.8	8.7	11.4	14.0	16.5	21.5	26.0	36.4	45.3	70.2	83.9	95.3	99.8	100.0
95.	0.6	1.3	1.9	2.5	3.1	6.2	9.1	12.0	14.7	17.4	22.5	27.3	38.0	47.1	72.2	85.4	96.0	99.9	100.0
100.	0.7	1.3	2.0	2.6	3.3	6.5	9.6	12.5	15.4	18.2	23.5	28.5	39.5	48.9	74.0	86.7	96.7	99.9	100.0
125.	0.8	1.7	2.5	3.3	4.1	8.0	11.8	15.4	18.9	22.2	28.5	34.3	46.7	56.8	81.5	92.1	98.6	100.0	100.0
150.	1.0	2.0	3.0	3.9	4.9	9.6	14.0	18.2	22.2	26.1	33.1	39.5	53.0	63.5	86.8	95.2	99.4	100.0	100.0
175.	1.2	2.3	3.4	4.6	5.7	11.1	16.1	20.9	25.4	29.7	37.5	44.4	58.6	69.2	90.6	97.1	99.7	100.0	100.0
200.	1.3	2.6	3.9	5.2	6.5	12.6	18.2	23.6	28.5	33.2	41.6	48.9	63.6	74.0	93.3	98.1	99.9	100.0	100.0
225.	1.4	3.0	4.4	5.9	7.3	14.0	20.3	26.1	31.5	36.5	45.4	53.1	67.3	78.1	95.2	98.8	99.9	100.0	100.0
250.	1.7	3.3	4.9	6.5	8.1	15.5	22.3	28.6	34.3	39.6	49.0	56.9	71.1	81.5	96.6	99.4	100.0	100.0	100.0
275.	1.8	3.6	5.4	7.1	8.8	16.8	24.2	30.7	37.1	42.5	52.3	60.4	75.1	84.4	97.6	99.6	100.0	100.0	100.0
300.	2.0	3.9	5.9	7.8	9.6	18.3	26.0	33.3	39.7	45.5	55.5	63.6	78.1	86.9	98.3	99.8	100.0	100.0	100.0
325.	2.1	4.3	6.3	8.4	10.4	19.7	28.0	35.5	42.2	48.2	58.0	66.6	80.7	88.8	98.8	99.8	100.0	100.0	100.0
350.	2.3	4.6	6.8	9.0	11.1	21.0	29.8	37.7	44.6	50.8	61.2	69.3	83.1	90.6	99.1	99.9	100.0	100.0	100.0
375.	2.5	4.9	7.3	9.6	11.9	22.4	31.6	39.8	46.9	53.2	63.7	71.9	85.1	92.1	99.4	99.9	100.0	100.0	100.0
400.	2.7	5.2	7.8	10.2	12.6	24.0	33.3	41.8	49.1	55.6	66.1	74.2	86.9	93.4	99.6	99.9	100.0	100.0	100.0
425.	2.8	5.6	8.3	10.9	13.4	25.0	35.5	43.7	51.3	57.8	68.4	76.3	88.3	94.4	99.7	100.0	100.0	100.0	100.0
450.	3.0	5.9	8.7	11.5	14.1	26.3	36.7	45.5	53.5	59.9	70.5	78.2	89.5	95.3	99.8	100.0	100.0	100.0	100.0
475.	3.2	6.2	9.2	12.1	14.9	27.5	38.2	47.5	55.3	62.0	72.4	80.0	90.8	96.0	99.8	100.0	100.0	100.0	100.0
500.	3.2	6.6	9.7	12.5	15.6	28.8	39.9	49.3	57.2	63.9	74.3	81.7	92.2	96.7	99.8	100.0	100.0	100.0	100.0
550.	3.7	7.2	10.6	13.9	17.0	31.2	42.9	52.6	60.7	67.4	77.6	84.6	94.2	97.6	99.9	100.0	100.0	100.0	100.0
600.	4.0	7.8	11.5	15.1	18.5	33.8	45.8	55.8	64.0	70.6	80.5	87.1	95.8	98.3	100.0	100.0	100.0	100.0	100.0
650.	4.3	8.1	12.4	16.2	19.9	35.8	48.6	58.8	67.0	73.6	83.0	89.1	96.9	98.8	100.0	100.0	100.0	100.0	100.0
700.	4.7	8.8	13.6	17.5	21.3	38.0	51.6	61.6	69.5	76.2	85.2	90.6	97.6	99.2	100.0	100.0	100.0	100.0	100.0
750.	5.0	9.8	14.3	18.6	22.6	40.1	53.7	64.2	72.3	78.6	87.2	92.3	98.3	99.4	100.0	100.0	100.0	100.0	100.0
800.	5.3	10.4	15.2	19.7	24.0	42.2	56.1	66.6	74.6	80.7	88.9	93.6	98.7	99.6	100.0	100.0	100.0	100.0	100.0
850.	5.7	11.0	16.6	20.8	25.5	44.2	58.3	68.9	76.8	82.7	90.3	94.6	99.0	99.7	100.0	100.0	100.0	100.0	100.0
900.	6.0	11.6	16.9	21.9	26.6	46.1	60.5	71.0	78.7	84.4	91.6	95.5	99.3	99.8	100.0	100.0	100.0	100.0	100.0
950.	6.3	12.3	17.8	23.0	27.9	48.0	62.5	73.0	80.5	86.0	92.7	96.2	99.5	99.8	100.0	100.0	100.0	100.0	100.0
1000.	6.7	12.9	18.7	24.1	29.2	49.8	64.2	74.9	82.0	87.4	93.7	96.8	99.6	99.9	100.0	100.0	100.0	100.0	100.0
1100.	7.2	13.9	20.2	25.8	31.2	53.3	68.1	78.2	85.1	89.8	95.3	97.8	99.7	99.9	100.0	100.0	100.0	100.0	100.0
1200.	7.8	15.4	22.1	28.4	34.1	56.6	71.4	81.2	87.6	91.8	96.5	98.5	99.8	100.0	100.0	100.0	100.0	100.0	100.0
1300.	8.7	16.6	23.8	30.4	36.4	59.6	74.3	83.7	89.7	93.4	97.4	98.9	99.9	100.0	100.0	100.0	100.0	100.0	100.0
1400.	9.3	17.8	25.5	32.4	38.7	62.1	77.0	85.9	91.4	94.7	98.0	99.3	99.9	100.0	100.0	100.0	100.0	100.0	100.0
1500.	10.0	19.0	27.1	34.1	41.0	65.0	79.4	87.9	92.8	95.8	98.5	99.5	100.0	100.0	100.0	100.0	100.0	100.0	100.0
1600.	10.7	20.2	28.7	36.3	43.1	67.6	81.6	89.5	94.1	96.6	98.9	99.6	100.0	100.0	100.0	100.0	100.0	100.0	100.0
1700.	11.3	21.6	30.3	38.2	45.2	70.0	83.5	90.9	95.1	97.3	99.2	99.7	100.0	100.0	100.0	100.0	100.0	100.0	100.0
1800.	12.0	22.6	31.9	40.0	47.2	72.0	85.3	92.3	96.0	97.8	99.4	99.8	100.0	100.0	100.0	100.0	100.0	100.0	100.0
1900.	12.7	23.7	33.4	41.8	49.2	74.2	86.9	93.4	96.6	98.3	99.6	99.9	100.0	100.0	100.0	100.0	100.0	100.0	100.0
2000.	13.3	24.9	34.9	43.6	51.1	76.1	88.3	94.3	97.2	98.6	99.7	99.9	100.0	100.0	100.0	100.0	100.0	100.0	100.0

Appendix G-6

PROBABILITY, IN PER CENT, OF FINDING AT LEAST ONE ERROR IF TOTAL NO. OF ERRORS IN UNIVERSE IS AS INDICATED

UNIVERSE SIZE OF 25000.

SAMPLE SIZE	TOTAL ERRORS IN UNIVERSE																	
	2	3	4	5	10	15	20	25	30	40	50	75	100	200	300	500	1000	2000
5	0.0	0.1	0.1	0.1	0.2	0.3	0.4	0.5	0.6	0.8	1.0	1.5	2.0	3.9	5.9	9.6	18.5	34.1
10	0.1	0.1	0.2	0.2	0.4	0.6	0.8	1.0	1.2	1.6	2.0	3.0	3.9	7.7	11.4	18.3	33.5	56.6
15	0.1	0.2	0.2	0.3	0.6	0.9	1.2	1.5	1.8	2.4	3.0	4.4	5.8	11.3	16.6	26.1	45.8	71.4
20	0.2	0.2	0.3	0.4	0.8	1.2	1.6	2.0	2.4	3.2	3.9	5.8	7.7	14.8	21.5	33.2	55.8	81.1
25	0.2	0.3	0.4	0.5	1.0	1.5	2.0	2.5	3.0	3.9	4.9	7.2	9.5	18.2	26.1	39.7	64.0	87.6
30	0.2	0.4	0.5	0.6	1.2	1.8	2.4	3.0	3.5	4.7	5.8	8.6	11.3	21.4	30.4	45.5	70.6	91.8
35	0.3	0.4	0.6	0.7	1.4	2.1	2.8	3.4	4.1	5.5	6.8	10.0	13.1	24.5	34.5	50.7	76.0	94.6
40	0.3	0.5	0.6	0.8	1.6	2.4	3.2	3.9	4.7	6.2	7.7	11.3	14.8	27.5	38.3	55.4	80.5	96.4
45	0.4	0.5	0.7	0.9	1.8	2.7	3.5	4.4	5.3	7.0	8.6	12.6	16.5	30.4	41.9	59.7	84.1	97.7
50	0.4	0.6	0.8	1.0	2.0	3.0	3.9	4.9	5.8	7.7	9.5	13.9	18.2	33.1	45.4	63.6	87.0	98.5
55	0.4	0.7	0.9	1.1	2.2	3.2	4.3	5.4	6.4	8.4	10.4	15.2	19.8	35.7	48.5	67.1	89.4	99.0
60	0.5	0.7	1.0	1.2	2.4	3.5	4.7	5.8	7.0	9.2	11.3	16.5	21.4	38.3	51.6	70.2	91.4	99.3
65	0.5	0.8	1.0	1.3	2.6	3.8	5.1	6.3	7.5	9.9	12.2	17.8	23.0	40.7	54.4	73.1	93.0	99.6
70	0.6	0.8	1.1	1.4	2.8	4.1	5.4	6.8	8.1	10.6	13.1	19.0	24.5	43.1	57.1	75.7	94.3	99.7
75	0.6	0.9	1.2	1.5	3.0	4.4	5.8	7.2	8.6	11.3	13.9	20.2	26.0	45.3	59.6	78.0	95.3	99.8
80	0.6	1.0	1.3	1.6	3.2	4.7	6.2	7.7	9.2	12.0	14.8	21.4	27.4	47.4	62.0	80.2	96.2	99.9
85	0.7	1.0	1.4	1.7	3.3	5.0	6.6	8.2	9.7	12.7	15.7	22.6	28.9	49.5	64.2	82.1	96.9	99.9
90	0.7	1.1	1.4	1.8	3.5	5.3	7.0	8.6	10.2	13.4	16.5	23.7	30.3	51.5	66.3	83.8	97.5	99.9
95	0.8	1.1	1.5	1.9	3.7	5.5	7.3	9.1	10.8	14.1	17.3	24.8	31.7	53.4	68.3	85.4	97.9	100.0
100	0.8	1.2	1.6	2.0	3.9	5.8	7.7	9.5	11.3	14.8	18.2	26.0	33.0	55.2	70.1	86.7	98.3	100.0
125	1.0	1.5	2.0	2.5	4.9	7.2	9.5	11.8	13.9	18.1	22.1	31.3	39.4	63.4	77.9	92.0	99.4	100.0
150	1.2	1.8	2.4	3.0	5.8	8.6	11.3	13.9	16.5	21.4	25.9	36.3	45.2	70.0	83.7	95.2	99.8	100.0
175	1.4	2.1	2.8	3.4	6.8	10.0	13.1	16.1	19.0	24.4	29.6	40.9	50.4	75.5	87.9	97.1	99.9	100.0
200	1.6	2.4	3.1	3.9	7.7	11.3	14.8	18.1	21.3	27.4	33.0	45.2	55.1	79.9	91.1	98.2	100.0	100.0
225	1.8	2.7	3.5	4.4	8.6	12.6	16.5	20.2	23.7	30.3	36.3	49.1	59.4	83.6	93.4	98.9	100.0	100.0
250	2.0	3.0	3.9	4.9	9.5	13.9	18.1	22.1	25.9	33.0	39.4	52.8	63.3	86.6	95.1	99.4	100.0	100.0
275	2.2	3.2	4.3	5.4	10.4	15.2	19.8	24.0	28.1	35.6	42.3	56.2	66.8	89.0	96.4	99.6	100.0	100.0
300	2.4	3.5	4.7	5.8	11.3	16.5	21.3	25.9	30.3	38.2	45.2	59.4	70.0	91.0	97.3	99.8	100.0	100.0
325	2.6	3.8	5.1	6.3	12.2	17.7	22.9	27.8	32.3	40.6	47.8	62.3	72.8	92.6	98.0	99.9	100.0	100.0
350	2.8	4.1	5.4	6.8	13.1	19.0	24.4	29.6	34.3	42.9	50.4	65.1	75.4	94.0	98.5	99.9	100.0	100.0
375	3.0	4.4	5.8	7.2	13.9	20.2	25.9	31.3	36.3	45.1	52.8	67.6	77.8	95.1	98.9	99.9	100.0	100.0
400	3.1	4.7	6.2	7.7	14.8	21.3	27.4	33.0	38.1	47.3	55.1	69.9	79.9	96.0	99.2	100.0	100.0	100.0
425	3.3	5.0	6.6	8.2	15.6	22.5	28.8	34.6	40.0	49.4	57.3	72.1	81.8	96.7	99.4	100.0	100.0	100.0
450	3.5	5.3	6.9	8.6	16.5	23.7	30.3	36.3	41.7	51.4	59.4	74.1	83.5	97.3	99.6	100.0	100.0	100.0
475	3.7	5.5	7.3	9.1	17.3	24.8	31.6	37.8	43.5	53.3	61.4	76.0	85.1	97.8	99.7	100.0	100.0	100.0
500	3.9	5.8	7.7	9.5	18.1	25.9	33.0	39.4	45.1	55.1	63.2	77.7	86.5	98.2	99.8	100.0	100.0	100.0
550	4.3	6.4	8.4	10.4	19.8	28.1	35.6	42.3	48.3	58.6	66.8	80.8	89.0	98.8	99.9	100.0	100.0	100.0
600	4.7	6.9	9.2	11.3	21.3	30.3	38.1	45.1	51.3	61.7	69.9	83.5	91.0	99.2	99.9	100.0	100.0	100.0
650	5.1	7.5	9.9	12.2	22.9	32.3	40.6	47.8	54.2	64.7	72.8	85.8	92.6	99.5	100.0	100.0	100.0	100.0
700	5.4	8.1	10.6	13.1	24.4	34.3	42.9	50.4	56.8	67.4	75.4	87.8	93.9	99.6	100.0	100.0	100.0	100.0
750	5.8	8.6	11.3	13.9	25.9	36.3	45.1	52.8	59.4	69.9	77.7	89.5	95.1	99.8	100.0	100.0	100.0	100.0
800	6.2	9.2	12.0	14.8	27.4	38.1	47.3	55.1	61.7	72.2	79.8	91.0	96.0	99.8	100.0	100.0	100.0	100.0
850	6.6	9.7	12.7	15.6	28.8	40.0	49.4	57.3	64.0	74.4	81.8	92.2	96.7	99.9	100.0	100.0	100.0	100.0
900	6.9	10.2	13.4	16.5	30.3	41.7	51.3	59.4	66.1	76.3	83.5	93.3	97.3	99.9	100.0	100.0	100.0	100.0
950	7.3	10.8	14.1	17.3	31.6	43.5	53.3	61.3	68.0	78.2	85.1	94.2	97.8	100.0	100.0	100.0	100.0	100.0
1000	7.7	11.3	14.8	18.1	33.0	45.1	55.1	63.2	69.9	79.8	86.5	95.1	98.2	100.0	100.0	100.0	100.0	100.0
1100	8.4	12.4	16.1	19.8	35.6	48.3	58.5	66.7	73.3	82.8	88.9	96.3	98.8	100.0	100.0	100.0	100.0	100.0
1200	9.2	13.4	17.5	21.3	38.1	51.3	61.7	69.9	76.3	85.4	91.0	97.3	99.2	100.0	100.0	100.0	100.0	100.0
1300	9.9	14.4	18.8	22.9	40.6	54.2	64.7	72.8	79.0	87.5	92.6	98.0	99.5	100.0	100.0	100.0	100.0	100.0
1400	10.6	15.5	20.1	24.4	42.9	56.8	67.4	75.4	81.4	89.4	93.9	98.5	99.6	100.0	100.0	100.0	100.0	100.0
1500	11.3	16.5	21.3	25.9	45.1	59.4	69.9	77.7	83.5	90.9	95.0	98.9	99.8	100.0	100.0	100.0	100.0	100.0
1600	12.0	17.5	22.6	27.4	47.3	61.7	72.2	79.8	85.4	92.3	95.9	99.2	99.8	100.0	100.0	100.0	100.0	100.0
1700	12.7	18.5	23.8	28.8	49.4	64.0	74.4	81.7	87.0	93.4	96.7	99.4	99.9	100.0	100.0	100.0	100.0	100.0
1800	13.4	19.4	25.0	30.3	51.3	66.1	76.3	83.5	88.5	94.4	97.3	99.6	99.9	100.0	100.0	100.0	100.0	100.0
1900	14.1	20.4	26.2	31.6	53.3	68.0	78.2	85.1	89.8	95.2	97.8	99.7	100.0	100.0	100.0	100.0	100.0	100.0
2000	14.8	21.3	27.4	33.0	55.1	69.9	79.8	86.5	90.9	95.9	98.2	99.8	100.0	100.0	100.0	100.0	100.0	100.0

Appendix G-7

PROBABILITY, IN PER CENT, OF FINDING AT LEAST ONE ERROR IF TOTAL NO. OF ERRORS IN UNIVERSE IS AS INDICATED

TOTAL ERRORS IN UNIVERSE SIZE OF 50000.

SAMPLE SIZE	1	2	3	4	5	10	15	20	25	30	40	50	75	100	200	300	500	1000	2000
5.	0.0	0.0	0.0	0.0	0.0	0.1	0.1	0.2	0.2	0.3	0.4	0.5	0.7	1.0	2.0	3.0	4.9	9.6	18.5
10.	0.0	0.0	0.0	0.1	0.1	0.2	0.3	0.4	0.5	0.6	0.8	1.0	1.5	2.0	3.9	5.8	9.6	18.3	33.5
15.	0.0	0.1	0.1	0.1	0.1	0.3	0.4	0.6	0.7	0.9	1.2	1.5	2.2	3.0	5.8	8.6	14.0	26.1	45.8
20.	0.0	0.1	0.1	0.2	0.2	0.4	0.6	0.8	1.0	1.2	1.6	2.0	3.0	3.9	7.7	11.3	18.2	33.2	55.8
25.	0.1	0.1	0.1	0.2	0.2	0.5	0.7	1.0	1.2	1.5	2.0	2.5	3.7	4.9	9.5	14.0	22.2	39.7	64.0
30.	0.1	0.1	0.2	0.2	0.3	0.6	0.9	1.2	1.5	1.8	2.4	3.0	4.4	5.8	11.3	16.5	26.0	45.5	70.6
35.	0.1	0.1	0.2	0.3	0.3	0.7	1.0	1.4	1.7	2.1	2.8	3.4	5.1	6.7	13.1	19.0	29.7	50.7	76.1
40.	0.1	0.2	0.2	0.3	0.4	0.8	1.2	1.6	2.0	2.4	3.2	3.9	5.8	7.6	14.8	21.4	33.1	55.4	80.5
45.	0.1	0.2	0.3	0.4	0.4	0.9	1.3	1.8	2.2	2.7	3.5	4.4	6.5	8.6	16.5	23.7	36.4	59.7	84.1
50.	0.1	0.2	0.3	0.4	0.5	1.0	1.5	2.0	2.5	3.0	3.9	4.9	7.2	9.5	18.2	26.0	39.5	63.6	87.0
55.	0.1	0.2	0.3	0.4	0.6	1.1	1.6	2.2	2.7	3.2	4.3	5.4	7.9	10.4	19.8	28.2	42.5	67.1	89.4
60.	0.1	0.2	0.4	0.5	0.6	1.2	1.8	2.4	3.0	3.5	4.7	5.8	8.6	11.3	21.4	30.3	45.3	70.3	91.4
65.	0.1	0.3	0.4	0.5	0.6	1.3	1.9	2.6	3.2	3.8	5.1	6.3	9.3	12.2	22.9	32.4	48.0	73.1	93.0
70.	0.1	0.3	0.4	0.6	0.7	1.4	2.1	2.8	3.4	4.1	5.5	6.8	10.0	13.1	24.5	34.4	50.5	75.7	94.3
75.	0.2	0.3	0.4	0.6	0.7	1.5	2.2	3.0	3.7	4.4	5.8	7.2	10.7	14.0	26.0	36.3	53.0	78.0	95.3
80.	0.2	0.3	0.5	0.6	0.8	1.6	2.4	3.2	3.9	4.7	6.2	7.7	11.3	14.8	27.5	38.2	55.3	80.2	96.2
85.	0.2	0.3	0.5	0.7	0.8	1.7	2.5	3.3	4.2	5.0	6.6	8.2	12.0	15.7	28.9	40.1	57.5	82.1	96.9
90.	0.2	0.4	0.5	0.7	0.9	1.8	2.8	3.7	4.4	5.3	7.0	8.6	12.6	16.5	30.3	41.8	59.6	83.8	97.5
95.	0.2	0.4	0.6	0.8	0.9	2.0	2.8	3.7	4.6	5.5	7.3	9.1	13.3	17.3	31.7	43.6	61.5	85.4	97.9
100.	0.2	0.4	0.6	0.8	1.0	2.0	3.0	3.9	4.9	5.8	7.7	9.5	14.0	18.2	33.0	45.3	63.4	86.8	98.3
125.	0.3	0.5	0.7	1.0	1.2	2.5	3.7	4.9	6.1	7.2	9.5	11.8	17.1	22.2	39.4	52.9	71.6	92.0	99.4
150.	0.3	0.6	0.9	1.2	1.5	3.0	4.4	5.8	7.2	8.6	11.3	14.0	20.2	26.0	45.2	59.5	77.5	95.2	99.8
175.	0.4	0.7	1.0	1.4	1.7	3.4	5.1	6.8	8.4	10.0	13.1	16.1	23.1	29.6	50.5	65.2	82.8	97.1	99.9
200.	0.4	0.8	1.2	1.6	2.0	3.9	5.8	7.7	9.5	11.3	14.8	18.2	26.0	33.0	55.2	70.1	86.7	98.3	100.0
225.	0.5	0.9	1.3	1.8	2.2	4.4	6.5	8.6	10.7	12.7	16.2	20.2	28.7	36.3	59.5	74.3	89.6	98.9	100.0
250.	0.5	1.0	1.5	2.0	2.5	4.9	7.2	9.5	11.8	14.0	18.2	22.2	31.4	39.5	63.4	77.9	91.9	99.4	100.0
275.	0.6	1.1	1.6	2.2	2.7	5.4	7.9	10.4	12.9	15.3	19.8	24.1	33.9	42.4	66.9	81.0	93.7	99.6	100.0
300.	0.6	1.2	1.8	2.4	3.0	5.8	8.6	11.3	14.0	16.5	21.4	26.0	36.3	45.3	70.1	83.6	95.1	99.8	100.0
325.	0.7	1.3	1.9	2.6	3.2	6.3	9.3	12.2	15.0	17.8	23.0	27.9	38.7	47.9	72.9	85.7	96.2	99.8	100.0
350.	0.7	1.4	2.1	2.8	3.5	6.8	10.0	13.1	16.1	19.0	24.6	29.6	41.0	50.5	75.5	87.5	97.1	99.9	100.0
375.	0.8	1.5	2.2	3.0	3.7	7.2	10.7	14.0	17.2	20.2	26.0	31.4	43.2	52.9	77.9	89.0	97.7	100.0	100.0
400.	0.8	1.6	2.4	3.2	3.9	7.7	11.3	14.8	18.2	21.4	27.5	33.1	45.3	55.2	80.0	91.1	98.2	100.0	100.0
425.	0.9	1.7	2.5	3.4	4.2	8.2	12.0	15.7	19.2	22.6	28.9	34.8	47.3	57.4	81.9	92.3	98.6	100.0	100.0
450.	0.9	1.8	2.7	3.6	4.4	8.6	12.7	16.5	20.2	23.8	30.4	36.4	49.3	59.5	83.7	93.4	98.9	100.0	100.0
475.	1.0	1.9	2.8	3.7	4.7	9.1	13.3	17.4	21.2	24.9	31.7	38.0	51.2	61.5	85.2	94.3	99.2	100.0	100.0
500.	1.0	2.0	3.0	3.9	4.9	9.6	14.0	18.2	22.2	26.0	33.1	39.5	53.0	63.4	86.8	95.1	99.4	100.0	100.0
550.	1.1	2.2	3.3	4.3	5.4	10.5	15.3	19.8	24.0	28.2	35.8	42.6	56.4	67.0	89.1	96.4	99.6	100.0	100.0
600.	1.2	2.4	3.6	4.7	5.9	11.4	16.6	21.3	26.1	30.4	38.3	45.3	59.6	70.1	91.0	97.1	99.8	100.0	100.0
650.	1.3	2.6	3.8	5.1	6.3	12.3	17.8	23.0	27.9	32.5	40.8	48.0	62.5	73.0	92.7	98.1	99.9	100.0	100.0
700.	1.4	2.8	4.1	5.5	6.8	13.2	19.1	24.6	29.7	34.5	43.1	50.6	65.2	75.6	94.1	98.6	99.9	100.0	100.0
750.	1.5	3.0	4.4	5.9	7.3	14.0	20.3	26.1	31.3	36.5	45.4	53.0	67.8	78.0	95.1	99.2	100.0	100.0	100.0
800.	1.6	3.2	4.7	6.2	7.7	14.9	21.5	27.6	33.2	38.6	47.6	55.4	70.2	80.0	96.0	99.2	100.0	100.0	100.0
850.	1.7	3.4	5.0	6.6	8.2	15.8	22.7	29.0	34.9	40.2	49.6	57.4	72.4	82.0	96.8	99.4	100.0	100.0	100.0
900.	1.8	3.6	5.3	7.0	8.7	16.6	24.0	30.5	36.5	42.0	51.7	59.7	74.4	83.8	97.4	99.6	100.0	100.0	100.0
950.	1.9	3.8	5.6	7.4	9.1	17.5	25.0	31.8	38.1	43.8	53.6	61.7	76.3	85.2	97.9	99.7	100.0	100.0	100.0
1000.	2.0	4.0	5.9	7.8	9.6	18.3	26.1	33.2	39.7	45.5	55.4	63.6	78.0	86.8	98.3	99.8	100.0	100.0	100.0
1100.	2.2	4.4	6.5	8.5	10.5	18.9	28.4	35.5	42.7	48.7	58.2	67.1	80.9	89.2	98.8	99.9	100.0	100.0	100.0
1200.	2.4	4.7	7.0	9.3	11.5	21.9	30.7	38.5	45.9	50.8	62.2	70.3	83.4	91.2	99.3	99.9	100.0	100.0	100.0
1300.	2.8	5.1	7.6	10.0	12.3	23.2	32.7	41.0	48.3	54.6	65.2	73.2	86.2	92.8	99.5	100.0	100.0	100.0	100.0
1400.	2.8	5.5	8.2	10.7	13.2	24.7	34.7	43.3	50.8	57.4	67.5	75.8	86.6	94.2	99.7	100.0	100.0	100.0	100.0
1500.	3.0	5.9	8.7	11.5	14.1	26.3	36.7	45.5	53.3	59.2	70.4	78.2	89.3	95.1	99.8	100.0	100.0	100.0	100.0
1600.	3.2	6.3	9.3	12.2	15.0	27.6	38.6	47.8	55.3	62.3	72.8	80.2	91.3	96.1	99.9	100.0	100.0	100.0	100.0
1700.	3.4	6.7	9.9	12.9	15.9	28.7	40.5	49.0	57.9	64.6	74.9	82.3	92.6	96.9	99.9	100.0	100.0	100.0	100.0
1800.	3.6	7.1	10.4	13.6	16.8	29.7	42.0	52.0	59.4	66.7	76.9	84.0	93.6	97.5	99.9	100.0	100.0	100.0	100.0
1900.	3.8	7.5	11.0	14.4	17.6	32.1	44.3	53.8	62.0	68.7	78.8	85.6	94.5	97.9	100.0	100.0	100.0	100.0	100.0
2000.	4.0	7.8	11.5	15.1	18.5	33.5	45.8	55.8	64.0	70.6	80.5	87.0	95.3	98.3	100.0	100.0	100.0	100.0	100.0

Appendix G-8

PROBABILITY, IN PER CENT, OF FINDING AT LEAST ONE ERROR IF TOTAL NO. OF ERRORS IN UNIVERSE IS AS INDICATED

TOTAL ERRORS IN UNIVERSE SIZE OF 100000.

SAMPLE SIZE	1	2	3	4	5	10	15	20	25	30	40	50	75	100	200	300	500	1000	2000
5	0.0	0.0	0.0	0.0	0.0	0.0	0.1	0.1	0.1	0.1	0.2	0.2	0.4	0.5	1.0	1.5	2.5	4.9	9.6
10	0.0	0.0	0.0	0.0	0.0	0.1	0.1	0.2	0.2	0.3	0.4	0.5	0.7	1.0	2.0	3.0	4.9	9.6	18.3
15	0.0	0.0	0.0	0.1	0.1	0.1	0.2	0.3	0.4	0.4	0.6	0.7	1.1	1.5	3.0	4.4	7.2	14.0	26.1
20	0.0	0.0	0.1	0.1	0.1	0.2	0.3	0.4	0.5	0.6	0.8	1.0	1.5	2.0	3.9	5.8	9.5	18.2	33.2
25	0.0	0.0	0.1	0.1	0.1	0.2	0.4	0.5	0.6	0.7	1.0	1.2	1.9	2.5	4.9	7.2	11.8	22.2	39.7
30	0.0	0.1	0.1	0.1	0.1	0.3	0.4	0.6	0.7	0.9	1.2	1.5	2.2	3.0	5.8	8.6	14.0	26.0	45.5
35	0.0	0.1	0.1	0.1	0.2	0.3	0.5	0.7	0.9	1.0	1.4	1.7	2.6	3.4	6.8	10.0	16.1	29.7	50.7
40	0.0	0.1	0.1	0.2	0.2	0.4	0.6	0.8	1.0	1.2	1.6	2.0	3.0	3.9	7.7	11.3	18.2	33.1	55.4
45	0.0	0.1	0.1	0.2	0.2	0.4	0.7	0.9	1.1	1.3	1.8	2.2	3.3	4.4	8.6	12.6	20.2	36.4	59.7
50	0.0	0.1	0.1	0.2	0.2	0.5	0.7	1.0	1.2	1.5	2.0	2.5	3.7	4.9	9.5	13.9	22.2	39.5	63.6
55	0.1	0.1	0.2	0.2	0.3	0.5	0.8	1.1	1.4	1.6	2.2	2.7	4.0	5.4	10.4	15.2	24.1	42.4	67.1
60	0.1	0.1	0.2	0.2	0.3	0.6	0.9	1.2	1.5	1.8	2.4	3.0	4.4	5.8	11.3	16.5	26.0	45.2	70.3
65	0.1	0.1	0.2	0.3	0.3	0.6	1.0	1.3	1.6	1.9	2.6	3.2	4.8	6.3	12.2	17.7	27.8	47.9	73.1
70	0.1	0.1	0.2	0.3	0.3	0.7	1.0	1.4	1.7	2.1	2.8	3.4	5.1	6.8	13.1	19.0	29.6	50.4	75.7
75	0.1	0.1	0.2	0.3	0.4	0.7	1.1	1.5	1.9	2.2	3.0	3.7	5.5	7.2	13.9	20.2	31.4	52.8	78.0
80	0.1	0.2	0.2	0.3	0.4	0.8	1.2	1.6	2.0	2.4	3.1	3.9	5.8	7.7	14.8	21.4	33.1	55.1	80.1
85	0.1	0.2	0.3	0.3	0.4	0.8	1.3	1.7	2.1	2.5	3.3	4.2	6.2	8.1	15.7	22.6	34.8	57.2	82.0
90	0.1	0.2	0.3	0.4	0.4	0.9	1.3	1.8	2.2	2.7	3.5	4.4	6.5	8.6	16.5	23.7	36.4	59.3	83.6
95	0.1	0.2	0.3	0.4	0.5	0.9	1.4	1.9	2.3	2.8	3.7	4.6	6.9	9.1	17.3	24.9	38.0	61.2	85.3
100	0.1	0.2	0.3	0.4	0.5	1.0	1.5	2.0	2.5	3.0	3.9	4.9	7.2	9.5	18.1	26.0	39.5	63.4	86.7
125	0.1	0.2	0.4	0.5	0.6	1.2	1.9	2.5	3.1	3.7	4.9	6.1	9.0	11.8	22.1	31.3	46.6	71.5	92.0
150	0.1	0.3	0.4	0.6	0.7	1.5	2.2	3.0	3.7	4.4	5.8	7.2	10.6	13.9	25.9	36.3	52.8	77.9	95.2
175	0.2	0.3	0.5	0.7	0.9	1.7	2.6	3.4	4.3	5.1	6.8	8.4	12.3	16.1	29.6	40.9	58.4	82.8	97.1
200	0.2	0.4	0.6	0.8	1.0	2.0	3.0	3.9	4.9	5.8	7.7	9.5	13.9	18.1	33.0	45.2	63.3	86.6	98.2
225	0.2	0.4	0.7	0.9	1.1	2.2	3.3	4.4	5.5	6.5	8.6	10.6	15.5	20.1	36.3	49.1	67.6	89.6	98.9
250	0.2	0.5	0.7	1.0	1.2	2.5	3.7	4.9	6.1	7.2	9.5	11.8	17.1	22.1	39.4	52.8	71.4	91.9	99.4
275	0.3	0.5	0.8	1.1	1.4	2.7	4.0	5.4	6.6	7.9	10.4	12.8	18.6	24.0	42.3	56.2	74.8	93.7	99.6
300	0.3	0.6	0.9	1.2	1.5	3.0	4.4	5.8	7.2	8.6	11.3	13.9	20.1	25.9	45.2	59.4	77.8	95.1	99.8
325	0.3	0.6	1.0	1.3	1.6	3.2	4.8	6.3	7.8	9.3	12.2	15.0	21.6	27.7	47.8	62.3	80.4	96.2	99.9
350	0.3	0.7	1.0	1.4	1.7	3.4	5.1	6.8	8.4	10.0	13.1	16.1	23.1	29.5	50.4	65.1	82.7	97.0	99.9
375	0.4	0.7	1.1	1.5	1.9	3.7	5.5	7.2	9.0	10.6	13.9	17.1	24.5	31.3	52.8	67.6	84.7	97.7	99.9
400	0.4	0.8	1.2	1.6	2.0	3.9	5.8	7.7	9.5	11.3	14.8	18.1	25.9	33.0	55.1	69.9	86.5	98.2	100.0
425	0.4	0.8	1.3	1.7	2.1	4.2	6.2	8.1	10.1	12.0	15.6	19.1	27.3	34.6	57.3	72.1	88.1	98.6	100.0
450	0.4	0.9	1.3	1.8	2.2	4.4	6.5	8.6	10.6	12.6	16.5	20.1	28.7	36.2	59.4	74.1	89.5	98.9	100.0
475	0.5	0.9	1.4	1.9	2.3	4.6	6.9	9.1	11.2	13.3	17.3	21.1	30.0	37.8	61.4	76.0	90.8	99.2	100.0
500	0.5	1.0	1.5	2.0	2.5	4.9	7.2	9.5	11.8	13.9	18.1	22.1	31.3	39.3	63.3	77.8	91.8	99.3	100.0
550	0.5	1.1	1.6	2.2	2.7	5.4	7.9	10.4	12.8	15.2	19.7	24.0	34.0	42.3	66.7	80.8	93.7	99.6	100.0
600	0.6	1.2	1.8	2.4	3.0	5.8	8.6	11.3	13.9	16.5	21.3	25.9	36.2	45.1	69.9	83.5	95.1	99.8	100.0
650	0.6	1.3	1.9	2.6	3.2	6.3	9.3	12.2	15.0	17.7	22.9	27.7	38.6	47.8	72.8	85.8	96.2	99.9	100.0
700	0.7	1.4	2.1	2.8	3.4	6.8	10.0	13.1	16.1	18.9	24.4	29.5	40.8	50.3	75.4	87.8	97.0	99.9	100.0
750	0.7	1.5	2.2	3.0	3.7	7.2	10.6	13.9	17.1	20.1	25.9	31.3	43.0	52.8	77.7	89.5	97.7	99.9	100.0
800	0.8	1.6	2.4	3.1	3.9	7.7	11.3	14.8	18.1	21.3	27.4	33.0	45.1	55.1	79.8	91.0	98.2	100.0	100.0
850	0.8	1.7	2.5	3.3	4.2	8.1	12.0	15.6	19.1	22.5	28.8	34.6	47.1	57.3	81.7	92.2	98.6	100.0	100.0
900	0.9	1.8	2.7	3.5	4.4	8.6	12.6	16.5	20.1	23.7	30.2	36.2	49.1	59.3	83.5	93.3	98.9	100.0	100.0
950	0.9	1.9	2.8	3.7	4.6	9.1	13.3	17.3	21.1	24.8	31.6	37.8	51.0	61.3	85.1	94.2	99.1	100.0	100.0
1000	1.0	2.0	3.0	3.9	4.9	9.5	13.9	18.1	22.1	25.9	33.0	39.3	52.8	63.2	86.5	95.0	99.3	100.0	100.0
1100	1.1	2.2	3.2	4.3	5.4	10.4	15.2	19.7	24.0	28.1	35.6	42.3	56.2	66.7	88.9	95.9	99.6	100.0	100.0
1200	1.2	2.4	3.5	4.7	5.8	11.3	16.5	21.3	25.9	30.2	38.1	45.1	59.3	69.9	91.0	97.3	99.8	100.0	100.0
1300	1.3	2.6	3.8	5.1	6.3	12.2	17.7	22.9	27.7	32.3	40.5	47.8	62.3	72.7	92.6	98.0	99.9	100.0	100.0
1400	1.4	2.8	4.1	5.4	6.8	13.1	18.9	24.4	29.5	34.3	42.9	50.3	65.0	75.3	93.9	98.5	99.9	100.0	100.0
1500	1.5	3.0	4.4	5.8	7.2	13.9	20.1	25.9	31.3	36.2	45.1	52.8	67.5	77.7	95.0	98.9	99.9	100.0	100.0
1600	1.6	3.1	4.7	6.2	7.7	14.8	21.3	27.4	33.0	38.1	47.3	55.1	69.9	79.8	95.9	99.2	100.0	100.0	100.0
1700	1.7	3.3	5.0	6.6	8.1	15.6	22.5	28.8	34.6	39.9	49.3	57.3	72.1	81.7	96.7	99.4	100.0	100.0	100.0
1800	1.8	3.5	5.3	6.9	8.6	16.5	23.7	30.2	36.2	41.7	51.3	59.3	74.1	83.5	97.3	99.6	100.0	100.0	100.0
1900	1.9	3.7	5.5	7.3	9.1	17.3	24.8	31.6	37.8	43.4	53.2	61.3	75.9	85.0	97.8	99.7	100.0	100.0	100.0
2000	2.0	3.9	5.8	7.7	9.5	18.1	25.9	33.0	39.3	45.1	55.1	63.2	77.7	86.5	98.2	99.8	100.0	100.0	100.0

TOTAL ERRORS IN UNIVERSE SIZE OF 100000.

Appendix G-9

PROBABILITY, IN PER CENT, OF FINDING-AT LEAST ONE ERROR IF TOTAL NO. OF ERRORS IN UNIVERSE IS AS INDICATED

TOTAL ERRORS IN UNIVERSE SIZE OF 150000.

SAMPLE SIZE	1	2	3	4	5	10	15	20	25	30	40	50	75	100	200	300	500	1000	2000
5.	0.0	0.0	0.0	0.0	0.0	0.0	0.0	0.1	0.1	0.1	0.1	0.2	0.2	0.3	0.7	1.0	1.7	3.3	6.5
10.	0.0	0.0	0.0	0.0	0.0	0.1	0.1	0.1	0.2	0.2	0.3	0.3	0.5	0.7	1.3	2.0	3.3	6.5	12.6
15.	0.0	0.0	0.0	0.1	0.1	0.1	0.2	0.2	0.2	0.2	0.4	0.5	0.7	1.0	2.0	3.0	4.9	9.5	18.2
20.	0.0	0.1	0.1	0.1	0.1	0.2	0.2	0.3	0.3	0.4	0.5	0.7	1.0	1.3	2.6	3.9	6.5	12.5	23.5
25.	0.0	0.1	0.1	0.1	0.1	0.2	0.3	0.3	0.4	0.5	0.7	0.8	1.2	1.7	3.3	4.9	8.0	15.4	28.5
30.	0.0	0.1	0.1	0.1	0.2	0.2	0.3	0.4	0.5	0.6	0.8	1.0	1.5	2.0	3.9	5.8	9.5	18.2	33.2
35.	0.0	0.1	0.1	0.1	0.2	0.3	0.3	0.4	0.6	0.7	0.9	1.1	1.8	2.3	4.6	6.7	11.0	20.9	37.5
40.	0.0	0.1	0.1	0.1	0.2	0.3	0.4	0.5	0.7	0.8	1.1	1.3	2.0	2.6	5.2	7.7	12.5	23.5	41.6
45.	0.0	0.1	0.1	0.1	0.2	0.3	0.4	0.6	0.7	0.8	1.2	1.5	2.3	3.0	5.8	8.6	14.0	26.0	45.3
50.	0.0	0.1	0.1	0.2	0.2	0.3	0.5	0.7	0.8	1.0	1.3	1.7	2.5	3.3	6.5	9.5	15.4	28.4	48.9
55.	0.0	0.1	0.1	0.2	0.2	0.4	0.5	0.7	0.9	1.1	1.5	1.8	2.7	3.6	7.1	10.4	16.8	30.8	52.2
60.	0.0	0.1	0.1	0.2	0.2	0.4	0.6	0.8	1.0	1.2	1.6	2.0	3.0	3.9	7.7	11.3	18.2	33.1	55.3
65.	0.0	0.1	0.1	0.2	0.2	0.4	0.7	0.9	1.1	1.3	1.7	2.1	3.2	4.2	8.3	12.2	19.5	35.3	58.2
70.	0.0	0.1	0.1	0.2	0.2	0.5	0.7	0.9	1.2	1.4	1.9	2.3	3.4	4.6	8.9	13.1	20.8	37.4	60.9
75.	0.1	0.1	0.2	0.3	0.3	0.5	0.8	1.0	1.3	1.5	2.0	2.5	3.7	4.9	9.5	13.9	22.2	39.5	63.5
80.	0.1	0.1	0.2	0.3	0.3	0.5	0.8	1.1	1.3	1.6	2.1	2.6	3.9	5.2	10.1	14.8	23.4	41.4	65.8
85.	0.1	0.1	0.2	0.3	0.3	0.6	0.9	1.2	1.4	1.7	2.2	2.8	4.2	5.5	10.7	15.7	24.7	43.4	68.1
90.	0.1	0.1	0.2	0.3	0.3	0.6	1.0	1.3	1.5	1.9	2.4	3.0	4.4	5.8	11.3	16.5	26.0	45.2	70.1
95.	0.1	0.1	0.2	0.3	0.3	0.6	1.0	1.3	1.6	1.9	2.5	3.1	4.6	6.1	11.9	17.3	27.2	47.0	72.1
100.	0.1	0.2	0.2	0.3	0.4	0.7	1.0	1.3	1.7	2.0	2.6	3.3	4.9	6.5	12.5	18.1	28.4	48.8	73.9
125.	0.1	0.2	0.3	0.3	0.4	0.8	1.1	1.7	2.1	2.5	3.3	4.1	6.1	8.0	15.4	22.1	34.1	56.7	81.3
150.	0.1	0.2	0.3	0.4	0.5	1.0	1.4	2.0	2.5	3.0	3.9	4.9	7.2	9.5	18.1	26.0	39.4	63.4	86.7
175.	0.1	0.2	0.3	0.4	0.5	1.2	1.7	2.3	2.9	3.4	4.6	5.8	8.4	11.0	20.8	29.6	44.3	69.0	90.5
200.	0.2	0.3	0.4	0.5	0.6	1.3	2.0	2.6	3.3	3.9	5.2	6.5	9.5	12.5	23.4	33.0	48.7	73.8	93.2
225.	0.2	0.3	0.4	0.6	0.7	1.5	2.2	3.0	3.7	4.4	5.8	7.2	10.7	13.9	25.9	36.3	52.8	77.8	95.1
250.	0.2	0.3	0.5	0.7	0.8	1.7	2.5	3.3	4.1	4.9	6.5	8.0	11.8	15.4	28.4	39.4	56.6	81.2	96.5
275.	0.2	0.4	0.5	0.7	0.9	1.8	2.7	3.6	4.5	5.4	7.1	8.8	12.9	16.8	30.7	42.4	60.1	84.1	97.5
300.	0.2	0.4	0.6	0.8	1.0	2.0	3.0	3.9	4.9	5.8	7.7	9.5	13.9	18.1	33.0	45.2	63.3	86.6	98.2
325.	0.2	0.4	0.6	0.8	1.1	2.1	3.2	4.2	5.3	6.3	8.3	10.3	15.0	19.5	35.2	47.9	66.3	88.7	98.7
350.	0.2	0.5	0.7	0.9	1.2	2.3	3.4	4.6	5.7	6.8	8.9	11.0	16.1	20.8	37.3	50.4	69.0	90.4	99.1
375.	0.3	0.5	0.7	1.0	1.2	2.5	3.7	4.9	6.1	7.2	9.5	11.8	17.1	22.2	39.4	52.8	71.5	91.9	99.4
400.	0.3	0.5	0.8	1.1	1.3	2.6	3.9	5.2	6.5	7.7	10.1	12.5	18.2	23.4	41.4	55.2	73.7	93.1	99.5
425.	0.3	0.6	0.8	1.1	1.4	2.8	4.1	5.5	6.8	8.2	10.7	13.2	19.2	24.7	43.3	57.3	75.9	94.2	99.7
450.	0.3	0.6	0.9	1.2	1.5	3.0	4.4	5.8	7.2	8.6	11.3	14.0	20.2	26.0	45.2	59.4	77.8	95.1	99.8
475.	0.3	0.6	0.9	1.3	1.6	3.1	4.6	6.1	7.6	9.1	11.9	14.7	21.2	27.2	47.0	61.4	79.6	95.9	99.8
500.	0.3	0.7	1.0	1.3	1.7	3.3	4.9	6.5	8.0	9.5	12.5	15.4	22.2	28.4	48.7	63.3	81.2	96.5	99.9
550.	0.4	0.7	1.1	1.5	1.8	3.6	5.4	7.1	8.8	10.4	13.7	16.8	24.1	30.8	52.2	66.8	84.1	97.5	99.9
600.	0.4	0.8	1.1	1.6	2.0	3.9	5.8	7.7	9.5	11.3	14.8	18.2	26.1	33.0	55.2	70.0	86.6	98.2	100.0
650.	0.4	0.9	1.3	1.7	2.1	4.2	6.3	8.3	10.3	12.2	15.9	19.5	27.8	35.2	58.1	72.9	88.6	98.7	100.0
700.	0.5	0.9	1.4	1.9	2.3	4.6	6.8	8.9	11.0	13.1	17.1	20.8	29.6	37.4	60.8	75.5	90.4	99.1	100.0
750.	0.5	1.0	1.5	2.0	2.5	4.9	7.2	9.5	11.8	14.0	18.2	22.2	31.3	39.4	63.3	77.8	91.9	99.3	100.0
800.	0.6	1.1	1.6	2.1	2.6	5.2	7.7	10.1	12.5	14.8	19.3	23.5	33.0	41.4	65.7	79.9	93.1	99.5	100.0
850.	0.6	1.1	1.7	2.2	2.8	5.5	8.2	10.7	13.2	15.7	20.3	24.7	34.7	43.4	67.9	81.9	94.2	99.5	100.0
900.	0.6	1.2	1.8	2.4	3.0	5.8	8.6	11.3	14.0	16.6	21.4	26.0	36.3	45.2	70.0	83.6	95.1	99.7	100.0
950.	0.6	1.3	1.9	2.5	3.1	6.2	9.1	11.9	14.7	17.4	22.2	27.2	37.9	47.0	72.0	85.2	95.8	99.7	100.0
1000.	0.7	1.3	2.0	2.6	3.3	6.5	9.5	12.5	15.4	18.2	23.5	28.4	39.5	48.8	73.8	86.6	96.5	99.8	100.0
1100.	0.7	1.5	2.2	2.9	3.6	7.1	10.5	13.7	16.8	19.8	25.5	30.8	42.1	52.1	77.0	89.0	97.5	99.9	100.0
1200.	0.8	1.6	2.4	3.2	3.9	7.7	11.4	14.8	18.2	21.4	27.5	33.1	45.3	55.2	80.0	91.0	98.2	99.9	100.0
1300.	0.9	1.7	2.6	3.4	4.3	8.3	12.2	16.0	19.6	23.0	29.4	35.3	48.0	58.1	82.5	92.7	98.7	100.0	100.0
1400.	0.9	1.9	2.8	3.7	4.6	9.0	13.1	17.1	20.9	24.5	31.3	37.4	50.5	60.9	84.6	94.0	99.1	100.0	100.0
1500.	1.0	2.0	3.0	3.9	4.9	9.6	14.0	18.2	22.2	26.0	33.1	39.5	53.0	63.4	86.7	95.1	99.3	100.0	100.0
1600.	1.1	2.1	3.2	4.2	5.2	10.2	14.9	19.3	23.5	27.5	34.9	41.5	55.3	65.8	88.3	96.0	99.5	100.0	100.0
1700.	1.1	2.3	3.4	4.5	5.5	10.8	15.7	20.4	24.9	29.0	36.6	43.5	57.5	68.0	89.6	96.7	99.6	100.0	100.0
1800.	1.2	2.4	3.6	4.7	5.9	11.4	16.6	21.5	26.1	30.4	38.3	45.3	59.6	70.1	91.1	97.3	99.7	100.0	100.0
1900.	1.3	2.5	3.8	5.0	6.2	12.0	17.4	22.5	27.3	31.8	39.9	47.1	61.6	72.1	92.2	97.8	99.8	100.0	100.0
2000.	1.3	2.6	3.9	5.2	6.5	12.6	18.2	23.5	28.5	33.2	41.5	48.9	63.5	73.9	93.2	98.2	99.9	100.0	100.0

Appendix G-10

PROBABILITY, IN PER CENT, OF FINDING AT LEAST ONE ERROR IF TOTAL NO. OF ERRORS IN UNIVERSE IS AS INDICATED

TOTAL ERRORS IN UNIVERSE SIZE OF 200000.

SAMPLE SIZE	1	2	3	4	5	10	15	20	25	30	40	50	75	100	200	300	500	1000	2000
5.	0.0	0.0	0.0	0.0	0.0	0.0	0.0	0.1	0.1	0.1	0.1	0.1	0.2	0.2	0.5	0.7	1.2	2.5	4.9
10.	0.0	0.0	0.0	0.0	0.0	0.0	0.0	0.1	0.1	0.1	0.1	0.2	0.4	0.5	1.0	1.5	2.5	4.9	9.6
20.	0.0	0.0	0.0	0.0	0.1	0.1	0.1	0.1	0.2	0.3	0.3	0.4	0.6	0.7	1.5	2.2	3.7	7.2	14.0
25.	0.0	0.0	0.0	0.0	0.1	0.1	0.1	0.2	0.3	0.3	0.4	0.5	0.7	1.0	1.9	3.0	4.9	9.5	18.2
30.	0.0	0.0	0.0	0.0	0.1	0.1	0.2	0.3	0.4	0.4	0.5	0.6	0.9	1.2	2.5	3.7	6.1	11.8	22.2
35.	0.0	0.0	0.0	0.1	0.1	0.2	0.3	0.3	0.4	0.5	0.7	0.9	1.3	1.7	3.4	5.1	7.2	14.0	26.0
40.	0.0	0.0	0.0	0.1	0.1	0.2	0.3	0.4	0.5	0.6	0.8	1.0	1.5	2.0	3.9	5.8	8.5	16.1	29.7
45.	0.0	0.0	0.1	0.1	0.1	0.2	0.3	0.4	0.6	0.7	1.0	1.1	1.7	2.2	4.4	6.5	10.7	20.2	33.1
50.	0.0	0.0	0.1	0.1	0.2	0.3	0.4	0.5	0.6	0.7	1.0	1.2	1.9	2.5	4.9	7.2	11.8	22.2	36.4
55.	0.0	0.1	0.1	0.1	0.2	0.3	0.4	0.5	0.7	0.8	1.1	1.4	2.0	2.7	5.4	7.9	12.9	24.1	39.5
60.	0.0	0.1	0.1	0.1	0.2	0.3	0.4	0.6	0.7	0.9	1.2	1.5	2.2	3.0	5.8	8.6	12.9	24.1	42.5
65.	0.0	0.1	0.1	0.1	0.2	0.3	0.5	0.6	0.8	1.0	1.3	1.6	2.4	3.2	6.3	9.3	15.0	26.0	45.3
70.	0.0	0.1	0.1	0.2	0.2	0.3	0.5	0.7	0.9	1.0	1.4	1.7	2.6	3.4	6.8	10.0	15.0	27.8	48.0
80.	0.0	0.1	0.1	0.2	0.2	0.4	0.6	0.8	1.0	1.1	1.6	2.0	3.0	3.9	7.7	11.3	17.1	29.6	50.5
85.	0.0	0.1	0.1	0.2	0.2	0.4	0.6	0.8	1.0	1.2	1.6	2.1	3.1	4.1	8.2	12.0	18.2	33.0	52.9
90.	0.0	0.1	0.1	0.2	0.3	0.4	0.7	0.9	1.1	1.3	1.8	2.2	3.3	4.4	8.6	12.6	20.2	34.7	55.3
95.	0.0	0.1	0.2	0.2	0.3	0.5	0.7	0.9	1.2	1.4	1.8	2.3	3.3	4.6	8.6	13.9	20.2	36.3	57.4
100.	0.1	0.1	0.2	0.2	0.3	0.5	0.7	1.0	1.2	1.5	2.0	2.5	3.7	4.9	9.5	13.9	22.1	37.9	59.5
125.	0.1	0.1	0.2	0.3	0.3	0.6	0.9	1.2	1.6	1.9	2.5	3.1	4.6	6.1	11.8	17.1	26.9	39.4	61.5
150.	0.1	0.1	0.2	0.3	0.4	0.7	1.1	1.5	1.9	2.2	3.0	3.7	5.5	7.2	14.0	19.2	31.3	46.6	63.4
175.	0.1	0.2	0.3	0.3	0.4	0.9	1.3	1.7	2.2	2.6	3.4	4.3	6.4	8.4	16.1	23.1	35.5	52.9	71.5
200.	0.1	0.2	0.3	0.4	0.5	1.0	1.5	2.0	2.5	3.0	3.9	4.9	7.2	9.5	18.1	25.9	39.4	58.4	77.9
225.	0.1	0.2	0.3	0.4	0.6	1.1	1.7	2.2	2.8	3.3	4.4	5.5	8.1	10.6	20.2	28.7	43.1	63.3	82.8
250.	0.1	0.2	0.4	0.5	0.6	1.2	1.9	2.5	3.1	3.7	4.9	6.1	9.0	11.8	22.1	31.3	46.5	67.6	86.6
275.	0.1	0.3	0.4	0.5	0.7	1.4	2.0	2.7	3.4	4.0	5.4	6.6	9.8	12.9	24.1	33.8	49.8	71.5	89.6
300.	0.1	0.3	0.4	0.6	0.7	1.5	2.2	3.0	3.7	4.4	5.8	7.2	10.6	13.9	25.9	36.3	52.8	74.8	91.9
325.	0.2	0.3	0.5	0.6	0.8	1.6	2.4	3.2	4.0	4.8	6.3	7.8	11.5	15.0	27.8	38.6	55.7	77.8	93.7
350.	0.2	0.3	0.5	0.7	0.9	1.7	2.6	3.4	4.3	5.1	6.8	8.4	12.2	16.1	29.6	40.9	58.4	80.4	95.1
375.	0.2	0.4	0.6	0.7	0.9	1.9	2.8	3.7	4.6	5.5	7.2	9.0	13.1	17.1	31.3	43.1	60.9	82.7	96.2
400.	0.2	0.4	0.6	0.8	1.0	2.0	3.0	3.9	4.9	5.8	7.7	9.5	13.9	18.1	33.0	45.2	63.3	84.8	97.0
425.	0.2	0.4	0.6	0.8	1.1	2.1	3.1	4.2	5.2	6.2	8.2	10.1	14.7	19.2	34.7	47.2	65.5	86.6	97.7
450.	0.2	0.5	0.7	0.9	1.1	2.2	3.3	4.4	5.5	6.5	8.6	10.7	15.5	20.2	36.3	49.1	67.6	88.1	98.2
475.	0.2	0.5	0.7	0.9	1.2	2.3	3.5	4.6	5.8	6.9	9.1	11.2	16.3	21.2	37.9	51.0	69.6	89.5	98.6
500.	0.3	0.5	0.7	1.0	1.2	2.5	3.7	4.9	6.1	7.2	9.5	11.8	17.1	22.1	39.4	52.8	71.4	90.8	98.9
550.	0.3	0.5	0.8	1.1	1.4	2.7	4.0	5.4	6.7	7.9	10.4	12.9	18.7	24.1	42.4	56.3	74.8	91.9	99.3
600.	0.3	0.6	0.9	1.2	1.5	3.0	4.4	5.8	7.2	8.6	11.3	14.0	20.2	26.0	45.2	59.4	77.8	93.7	99.6
650.	0.3	0.6	1.0	1.3	1.6	3.2	4.8	6.3	7.8	9.2	12.2	15.0	21.7	27.8	47.9	62.2	80.4	95.1	99.8
700.	0.4	0.7	1.1	1.4	1.7	3.5	5.1	6.8	8.4	10.0	13.1	16.1	23.2	29.6	50.4	65.1	82.7	96.2	99.9
750.	0.4	0.7	1.1	1.5	1.9	3.7	5.5	7.2	9.0	10.7	14.0	17.1	24.6	31.3	52.4	67.6	84.8	97.0	99.9
800.	0.4	0.8	1.2	1.6	2.0	3.9	5.8	7.7	9.5	11.3	14.8	18.2	26.0	33.0	55.2	70.0	86.6	97.7	99.9
850.	0.4	0.9	1.3	1.7	2.1	4.2	6.2	8.2	10.2	12.1	15.7	19.2	27.4	34.7	57.4	72.2	88.1	98.2	100.0
900.	0.5	0.9	1.3	1.8	2.2	4.4	6.5	8.6	10.7	12.7	16.5	20.2	28.7	36.3	59.4	74.2	89.5	98.6	100.0
950.	0.5	0.9	1.4	1.9	2.3	4.6	6.9	9.1	11.2	13.3	17.3	21.2	30.0	37.9	61.4	76.1	90.8	98.9	100.0
1000.	0.5	1.0	1.5	2.0	2.4	4.9	7.2	9.5	11.8	14.0	18.2	22.2	31.3	39.4	63.3	77.8	91.9	99.3	100.0
1100.	0.6	1.1	1.6	2.2	2.7	5.4	7.9	10.4	12.9	15.3	19.8	24.1	33.9	42.4	66.8	80.9	93.7	99.6	100.0
1200.	0.6	1.2	1.8	2.4	3.0	5.9	8.6	11.3	14.0	16.5	21.4	26.0	36.3	45.2	70.0	83.6	95.1	99.8	100.0
1300.	0.7	1.3	1.9	2.6	3.2	6.3	9.3	12.2	15.0	17.8	23.0	27.8	38.7	47.9	72.9	85.9	96.2	99.9	100.0
1400.	0.7	1.4	2.1	2.8	3.5	6.8	10.0	13.1	16.1	19.0	24.5	29.6	41.0	50.5	75.5	87.9	97.0	99.9	100.0
1500.	0.8	1.5	2.2	3.0	3.7	7.3	10.7	14.0	17.2	20.2	26.0	31.3	43.1	52.9	77.8	89.6	97.7	99.9	100.0
1600.	0.8	1.6	2.4	3.2	3.9	7.7	11.4	14.8	18.2	21.4	27.5	33.1	45.3	55.2	80.0	91.9	98.2	100.0	100.0
1700.	0.9	1.7	2.5	3.4	4.2	8.2	12.0	15.7	19.2	22.6	28.9	34.7	47.3	57.4	81.9	92.3	98.6	100.0	100.0
1800.	0.9	1.8	2.7	3.6	4.4	8.6	12.7	16.5	20.2	23.8	30.3	36.4	49.2	59.5	83.6	95.1	98.9	100.0	100.0
1900.	1.0	1.9	2.8	3.7	4.7	9.1	13.3	17.4	21.2	24.9	31.7	38.0	51.1	59.5	85.2	94.3	99.2	100.0	100.0
2000.	1.0	2.0	3.0	3.9	4.9	9.6	14.0	18.2	22.2	26.0	33.1	39.5	52.9	63.4	86.6	95.1	99.3	100.0	100.0

Index

Index

A

A & P, 801
abstract of deficiency finding, 228-229 exhib.
acceptance, authority by, 689
accountability
  and the internal auditor, 692
  in management theory, 679, 689
accounting controls, *see also* Controls, 57-58, 65
accounting Dept., 560
accounts payable dept., 98, 218, 304
  computer-assisted audit, 423
accounts receivable
  and controls, 60 exhib.
accuracy of reports, 434-435
activities audited, 515-517 exhib.
activity reports, 514-523, 517-519 exhib.
adaptability and staff
  development, 569
Additional GAO Standards, 345
adjustment factors, 300 app.
administration
  control questionnaire, 116 exhib.
administrative control, 57
administrative functions, 556-557
advertising audit, 154-155 exhib.
AICPA, *see* American Institute of Certified Public Accountants
Aikin, H. L., 794
Air Force, U.S., 305, 307, 366

ambiguities in the audit programs 160-161
American Gas Assoc., 18
American Institute of Certified Public Accountants, 57, 68, 70, 660-661
American Institute of Management, 788
analytical evidence, 205
analyzing technique
  in transactions examination, 179-180
ancient times, and internal auditing, 3-4
application controls, EDP, 387-406
application programs, EDP, 398-399
appraisals of staff, 592-602 exhib.
approvals, prescribing of, 706
Argyris, Chris, 696, 750
Arkin, Herbert, 304
arrangement of working papers, 249-251
arrest, 729
assets; access to, 716
assets, fixed, 198
assignment record, 632-633 exhib.
assignments completed, 646, 648 exhib.
attitude of auditees toward auditors, 748-749 exhib.
attitudes of auditors toward their jobs, 570-571 exhib.
attributes sampling, 296-298
audit
  assignments, 631-632

1

audit assignments status, 647, 650-651 exhib.
audit committees, *see* Boards of Directors, 55, 513-536
  education of, 801-803
  functions of, 794-796
  growth of, 791-793
  and audit planning, 608
  role of, 796
audit days expend, 515 exhib.
audit evidence, 204-205
audit manuals, 554-559
audit objectives, 554
audit programs, 143 168, 555
  ambiguities, 160-161
  criteria, 1580160
  relation to final audit report, 161
  guidelines for preparation, 163-164
  preparation of, 144-145
  program mechanics, 161-162
  small audit staffs, 162-163
audit reports
  reviews and replies, 493-511
audit scope, 555
audit theory, 554-555
audit trails, 352-354
audit unit sampling, 304
auditees
  dealing with, 747-772
  defensive barrier removal, 500-501
  regard of auditor, 748-749
auditing organization
  establishment, 539-565
auditos ('a hearing'), 4
Austrian Credit Anstalt, 788
authority
  of audit findings, 442-443
  and corrective action, 233-234
  and the internal auditor, 692
  in management, 688-689
authorization of audit project, 632-633 exhib.
Automatic Data Processing Risk Assessment, 400
autocratic model of managers, 681

B

backup EDP plan, 381
Bacon, Jeremy, 789
balance-sheet audit, inception of, 4
bank accounts auditing, 214
BarChris, 789
batch EDP controls, 357
batch-processing computer systems, 347
behavioral theories, 751
behavioral theory of management 679
bell-shaped curve, 291, 294

benefits, definition of, 193
Bennett, George E., 57
best evidence, 200-201
Bevin, David C., 789
binomial probability distribution, 310
Boards of Directors
  audit committees, 540-541
  relations with, 787-807
bonuses and fraud, 737
Brink and Barrett, 775-776
British Companies Act, 4
Brown, Dudley E., 432
Brown, Wm. K., 797
budgeting
  and long-range audit schedules, 608-609, 615-616 exhib.
budgets
  and control, 65-66
  and management planning, 683
  and planning by auditor, 686-687
  of projects, 633-635
  revisions of, 635-638
  and schedules, 555
Burns, Ward, 766
Business Corp. Act of Canada, 791
Business Roundtable, 790

C

Canada, 791
Canadian Business Corp. Act, 69
Canadian Institute of Chartered Accountants, 58
candor in auditing, 764
canned program, *see* Pro-Forma Audit
capital items
  and boards of directors, 799
capital records EDP plan, 381
capital standards, 702
Carmichael, D. R., 751
Carolus, Roger N., 39
cash
  audits, 9-10, 11
  and controls, 60 exhib.
  risks, 95
cash receipts and fraud, 723
Catholic Univ. of America, 37-38
cause
  in audit reports, 445
  of deficiency finding, 222
  and effect in audit reports, 502
CBS, Inc., 798
CEO, 789
  and candor, 764
Certificate in Management Accounting, 38
certification program, 30-35
Certified Internal Auditor, 26-28 exhib., 30-35

examination, 31-35
Certified Publec Accountants
  to select staff, 570
chairmen of audit committees
  (CAC), 775
Chamber of Commerce, U.S., 714
change
  and planning by auditor, 685-686
changes in EDP systems, 398-399,
  400-406
character qualities and staff
  development, 569
chart of accounts, 642
charter of internal auditing dept., 802
charter of internal auditors, 233, 541,
  669
charts, 520-523 exhib.
charts in reports, 446 exhib., 447
  exhib., 450-451 exhib.
chief executive officer; see CEO, 789
chief executive officers (CEO), 775
chief financial officers (CFO), 775
CIA, see Certified Internal Auditor
circumstantial evidence, 201
clarity of reports, 435-436
classical theory of management,
  678-680
closing audit reports, 504-505 exhib.
cluster sampling, 287
CMA, See Certificate in Management
  Accounting
code of ethics, 23, 24-28 exhib.
Cohen Commission, 661
collegial model of managers, 681
collusion, 719
combined attributes variables
  asmpling, 303
comments of auditors, 641-642
Commission on Auditors'
  Responsibilities, 661
commissions and fraud, 740
committees
  and the internal auditor, 694
  in management, 691
common body of knowledge, 28-30, 32
common ground
  in review conference, 500
common user file, 519
common user files, 781
communication in auditing, 758-760
communications
  of deficiency findings, 234-235
  in EDP auditing, 367
  evaluation of, 699
  in management, 697
  in reports, 433
communications center theory of
  management, 680

company accountants
  to select staff, 571
company background
  of directors, 800
comparisons
  and standards, 703
  technique, 396
competence of internal auditing
  dept., 779-782
competency test, 205
competition studies, 336
completeness of
  corrective action, 232
compliance
  ensuring, 706
comprehensive audits, 153-158
Comptoller General of the U.S., 31
Comptroller of the Currency, U.S, 661
computerized controls, 646-653
computers
  assisted auditing, 415-428
  for auditors, 425
  auditing, 343-413
  and control, 59-60 exhib.
  crime by, 717
  risk assessment, 103
  for sampling, 287
  security, 375-376
  simulation, 417-419
  techniques, 326
concealment, 715
conciseness of reports, 436-437
conclusions of deficiency finding, 223
conclusive evidence, 201
condition statement in audit
  reports, 443-445
conditions
  of deficiency finding, 220-221
conference
  for review of reports, 498-499
Conference Board, 540-541, 779
confessions and fraud, 731
confidence level in sampling, 288-296
confirmation technique, 396
conflict of interest and fraud, 724
conflict of interest programs
  audit of, 173-174
conflict of interests and fraud, 738
conflicts
  in report reviews, 499-501
Congress, U.S., acts, see names of laws
construction contracts audit, 181,
  195-198, 214
consultants, 188, 194-195
  and fraud, 740
  and quality control, 662-663
consultative attitudes, 754
contingency plans in EDP activity 381

continuing corrective action, 232
continuing education and staff
    development, 584-585
contract audits, 195-198
control
  achieving, 63-67
  approaches to, 705
  of audit projects, 631-657
  and auditees, 750-751
  computer documentation, 370
  deficiencies, 525
  definition of, 56-59
  elements of, 59-63
  internal operating controls, 71-80
  and long-range audit schedules, 610
  significance of, 53-56
  in Statement of Responsibilities,
    23-24
  tests for EDP weaknesses, 395-406
  over working papers, 258
controlling
  as a function of management,
    700-707
  improprieties, 92
  information for preliminary surveys,
    123-124
  and the internal auditor, 705-707
controls, see also Risks
  accounting, 7
  over administration, 356-357
  benefits of, 55-56
  for computer system design and
    development, 354-362
  computerized, 646-653
  over EDP procedures, 357-358,
    382-384, 384-387
  financial, 55
  in flow chart, 131
  identification of, 149-153
  inadequate, 91-92
  master controls establishment, 706
  in the preliminary survey, 101-103
  to prevent fraud, 731-736
  questionnaire for preliminary audit,
    116-117 exhib.
conversion of data, 392-393
cooperation with external auditors, 782
cooperative approach, 752-753
coopers and Lybrand, 792
coordination with external auditor,
    774-777
correction
  and standards, 704
corrective action, 502
  to deficiency findings, 232
correlation analysis, 329-330
correspondence courses and sraff
    development, 585

corroborative evidence, 202
corruption, see Foreign Corrupt
    Practices Act
cost accounting systems, 363
cost-benefit analysis, 362, 393, 399
cost effectiveness study, definition
    of, 192
cost reductions
  in reminder list, 108, 111 exhib.
cost standards, 702
cost-type contracts, 195-196
courses, see also Review Courses, 35-39
court cases and fraud, 717-719
Courtney, Robert H., Jr., 103
created errors and fraud, 735
creditors and fraud, 741
crime
  by computer, 717
  organized, 716-717
criteria, see also standards
  for audit programs, 158-160
  for reports, 433-438
critical path method, 334-335
cross-referencing working papers,
    253-255
cryptography, 368
cultural interrelationships, 680
cumulative monetary amounts
    sampling, 303
curricula, see University Curricula
custodial model of managers, 681
cycle approach to controlling, 58,
    70-71, 76

D

data conversion, 393, 395
data processing, See EDP
Davis, Ralph Currier, 679
deceit; see also fraud, 713-746
decentralization
  and the internal auditor, 694
  in management, 690-691
deception and fraud, 738
decision making
  and management planning, 683
  and planning by auditor, 687-688
defamation of character, 729
defects
  causes of, 528
  and deficiency findings, 213-214
Defense Dept., U.S., 399
deficiencies
  causes of, 528-534 exhib.
  summaries of, 253, 306-307
deficiency findings, 213-242, 495, 502
  approach to, 216-217
  degrees of significance, 217-219
  discussing findings, 224-225

elements of, 219-224
follow-up, 230-234
major, 524
minor, 525
nature of, 213-216
reporting deficiencies, 230
selling audit findings, 234-235
summaries of findings, 225-228
summarizing of, 524-525
supervisory reviews, 228-230
definition of internal auditing, 6-7
delegation
and the internal auditor, 692-693
in management, 689
deliveries and fraud, 723
demands of auditng, 754-755
departmentation
and the internal auditor, 693-694
in management, 690
descriptive OR models, 326
design standards, EDP, 388-389, 393
details in audit reports, 455-456
detection controls, 59-60 exhib.
detection safeguards, EDP, 380-381
determination and staff
development, 569
Detroit Edison, 18
development of internal auditing, 3-16
development projects
and long-range audit schedules,
617-621
deviations and deficiency findings
213-214
diagnostic tools, 727-278
dialogues with audit staff, 593-594
Dicksee, L. R., 57
direct evidence, 201
directed sample, 281
directing
as a function of management,
695-700
improprieties, 92
and the internal auditor, 697-700
disagreement
in review conference, 501
disaster plans in EDP activity, 381
discounts audit, 559-560
discussion of deficiency findings,
224-225
disputes in report reviews, 499-501
distribution problems, 334
divestment and fraud, 737
document security dept. audit, 174
documentary evidence, 204-205
documentation
of EDP systems, 369-371, 421
standards as EDP controls, 356
dollar estimation sampling, 298

dollar return, 514-515
dollar unit sampling, 303-305
Domtar Ltd. (Canada), 29
draft reviews, 555
drafts of reports, 495-496
drawings in engineering dept.,
258-269 exhib.
Drucker, Peter, 697, 787, 790, 794
due professional care, 41, 766
due professional care, 718-719
duties segregation and fraud, 724-725
dynamic programming, 336

E

economical working papers, 24801606
248 249
economy, definition of, 147
economy of EDP systems, 362-366
Edison Electric Institute, 18
editing audit reports, 461-466, 462
exhib.
EDP, see Computers
education, see also Courses
of internal auditor, 379-380
and staff development, 584-585
education and staff development, 568
effect in audit reports, 444-445
effect of deficiency finding, 222-223
effectiveness, definition of, 147
efficiency
definition of, 147
of EDP systems, 362-366
electronic data processing, see
Computers
embezzlement; see also fraud, 714
emergency EDP plan, 381
employee
fraud, 713-746
payments to, see Payroll
turnover, 199
employment costs, 199
encryption, 368
engineer, industrial, see Industrial
Engineer
engineering dept. audit, 258-269
exhib.
enterprise policy, 544-553
environments of EDP audit, 347-348
Equity Funding, 718, 797
errors created, and fraud, 735
ethics, see also Code of Ethics
in management, 680
evaluating
in transactions examination, 182-184
evaluation
definition of, 192
and field work, 172-173
reports, 523-526

evaluations
of staff, 592-602 exhib., 703-704
evalusting
sample results, 308-309
event concept of auditing on-line
systems, 353
evidence
audit, 204-206
legal, 200-204
standards of, 205-206
examination of transactions, 176
exit interviews
and supervision, 645
expected error rate principle, 296
expenditure cycle audit, 71, 72 exhib.,
146-147
experts
in OR auditing, 339
exploratory sampling, 306-307
explosives handling auditing, 232-233
exponential smoothing, 336
external auditor
and the internal auditor, 8-11
external auditors
and fraud, 739
and audit planning, 608
relationahip with, 773-786
external reviews
and quality assurance, 668-671

F

facts in audit reports, 444
false promises, 715
Fayol, Henri, 55-56, 679
feasibility studies
EDP, 361
internal audit, 351-352
managemant policies during, 349
felony, compounding, 730
field work, 169-211
audit evidence, 204-206
audit modes, 184-198
forms of, 173-174
indicators, 198-200
legal evidence, 200-204
nature of, 169-173
in reminder list, 110 exhib.
and supervision, 645
testing, 174-184
file documentation standards, 356
file dumps, 421
final audit report
relation to audit programs, 161
financial audit, 559-560
financial controls, see Controls
findings, deficiency, see deficiency
findings
findings of audit reports, 442

finite population correction factor, 298
finite universe correction factor, 300
app.
flowcharting, 519
formal, 128, 132-133 exhib.
informal, 130 exhib.
in the preliminary survey, 124,
128-131 exhib.
symbols, 128, 128-129 exhib.
vertical, 134 exhib.
Follet, Mary Parker, 696
follow-up
to deficiency findings, 230-234
procedures, 505 exhib.
and standards, 704
Foreign Corrupt Practices Act,
U.S., 8, 55, 67-70, 67-71, 77, 105, 153,
206, 245, 270, 345, 367, 368, 402-403,
515, 520, 524, 660, 774
foreword in reports, 439-440
forgery, 719
formal
authority, 689
reports, 439-446
formats of reports, 438-439
Foundation for Auditability
Research and Education, Inc., 669
*Framework for Evaluating an
Internal Audit Function,* 669
Franklin National Bank, 788
fraud
detection of, 722-728
employee, 713-746
management, 713-746
prevention of, 731-736
fraud prevention and detection,
754-755
Freedom of Information Act, 367
fuel sampling, 281-282
functional audits, 114, 185-187, 496
functional authority
and the internal auditor, 693
in management, 690
functional reports, 515
functions and responsibility
statement, 542-543 exhib.

G

game theory, 336
Gantt, Henry L., 12, 679
GAO, see General Accounting Office
General Accounting Office, U.S., 327,
345, 661
general EDP controls, 372-387
General Electric, 788
General Motors, 803
generalized computer audit
programs, 419-420

Gilbreth, Frank & Lillian, 12
glossary of terms of working
  papers, 249
goals
  of management planning, 682
  of the preliminary survey, 98-101
Gobeil, Robert E., 29
Goodfellow, J. L., 305
Government Printing Office, U.S.,
  417-418
Grandfather clause of certification
  program, 30
W. T. Grant, 788
graphics in audit reports, 445-446
  exhib., 520-523 exhib.
groups, informal
  and the internal auditor, 695
  in management, 691
Guidelines for Automatic Data
  Processing Physical Risk Asse, 400
Guidelines for Model Evaluation,
  338-339

H

Hamilton Bank, 788
hardware, EDP, controls, 384-387
Harmeyer, W. James, 20, 121-122
Haskins & Sells, 304
health plan auditing, 214
hearsay evidence, 203-204
H. J. Heinz Co., 334
Herzberg, Frederick, 696
history of internal auditing, 3-6
honesty and fraud, 732-733
hospital costs, 330-331
hotel operations audit, 180
humanistic behavior, 766

I

illustrations in audit reports, 445-446
  exhib.
image of internal auditing, 748-749
imaginative theory of the audit,
  148-149
impacts, definition of, 193
imposed control, 705
impressions record, 108, 111-112
  exhib.
imprisonment, false, 729-730
improvement suggestions, 214-215
independence of internal auditing
  dept., 778-779
independence of internal auditors
  40-41, 541-542
indexing working papers, 253-255
indicators in field work, 198-200
industrial engineer and the
  internal auditor, 12-13

industrial engineering
  and long-range schedule, 626
industrial revolution and internal
  auditing, 4
informal audit reports, 446-449
informal groups
  and the internal auditor, 695
  in management, 691
informal organization, 756
information
  obtained at preliminary surveys,
    122-125
  sources of, 125
  in working papers, 250-251
information systems
  and boards of directors, 799
  input EDP controls, 357-358
inspections, physical, 126-128
Inspector General Act of 1978, 754
Institute of Internal Auditors, Inc.
  formation, 4, 18-19
  growth, 19
  publications, 19-20, 587-588
  to select staff, 572
integrated tests, 392
integrity EDP controls, 362
intergity
  and fraud, 716
interim audit reports, 446-449
internal auditing
  auditing operations, 7
  certification program, 30-3k
  code of ethics, 24-48
  common body of knowledge, 28-30
  concerns of, 13
  courses, 35-39
  definition of, 6-7
  and the external auditor, 8-11
  history of, 3-6
  and the industrial engineer, 12-13
  management of departments, 43
  professional organization, 18-20
  professionalism, 17-18
  related desciplines, 7
  standards, 39-47
  statement of responsibilities, 20-24
  success of, 539-542
  The Internal Auditor, 19, 587
  responsibilities of, 90-91
internal control
  and audit trails, 352-353
  of computer controls, 354-362
  computer systems, 348-351
internal controls, see also Controls, 774
internal operating controls, 71-80
Internal Revenue Service, 353
internal review
  and control, 66-67

and quality assurance, 666-668
International Business Machines
  Co., 103
interrogations for fraud, 728-731
Interstate Commerce
  Commission, U.S., 283
interval sampling, 284-285
interviewing
  at preliminary meeting, 121-122
  and staff selection, 572-574 exhib.
introduction in reports, 439 440
inventory
  auditing, 417-418
  and controls, 60 exhib.
  theory, 335
  turnover, 199
inventory sheets and fraud, 724
investigating technique in
  transactions examination, 181-182
investigative audits, 757
Investment Co. Act of 1940, 4
invoices, false, and fraud, 724
Itel Corp., 789
Ivers, John B., 18

J

job descriptions, 548-553 exhib.
job enlargement, 696
job enrichment, 696
Johnson, Samuel, 56-57
judgment sampling, 307-308

K

Keating, Stephen, 752
keypunching standards, 356
*In Re Kingston Cotton Mill Co.,
  Ltd,* 718
knowledge, *see* Common Body of
  Knowledge

L

law of the situation, 696
leadership
  evaluation of, 698-699
  in management, 696
least squares methods, 328-329
legal action
  and boards of directors, 799
legal counsel
  and fraud, 740
legal evidence, 200-204
legal requirements in EDP
  auditing, 366-368
legislation, *see* names of laws
libel, 729
librarians of EDP files, 355
library EDP documentation, 370

lie detectors and fraud, 734
Likert, Rensis, 696
limit tests technique, 396
line and staff
  and the internal auditor, 693
  in management, 690
line/staff conflicts, 750
linear programming, 332-334
listening habits in auditing, 758-760
Lockheed, 798
Loebbecke, J. K., 305
In Re London and General Bank,
  717-718
long-range audit schedule, 515 exhib.
long-range audit schedules, 607-630
  format of, 611-613 exhib.
  structure of, 611-615
lump-sum contracts, 195-196

M

mail and fraud, 723
maintenance of EDP, 385-386
management
  accounting, *see also* Certificate in
    Management Accounting
  auditing, 8, 11, 122-123, 216
  by objective, 697
  controls on, 91-92
  fraud, 713-746
  functions and control, 74-76
  functions of, 681-684
  good, constraints on, 94
  ineffectiveness of, 92-93
  and long-range audit schedules, 609
  long-range planning review, 621-624
  models, 680-681
  nature of, 677-681
  overrides, 77-80
  poor, indicators of, 93-94
  principles of, 677-712
  records of reviews, 641
  studies, 188-192 exhib.
  theories of, 678
mandated conditions, 782
manners
  in review conference, 500
manuals, audit, 554-559
marketing dept.
  and the audit program, 153-155
    exhib.
  questionnaire, 119-120 exhib.
Marsh & McLennan, Inc., 797
Master's Degree in Internal
  Auditing, 37-38
material records, 199
mathematical models, 325-342
matrixes, 334
Mautz and Neumann survey, 792

maximization theory, 336
Maynard, H. B., 12
Mayo, Elton, 679
MBO, *see* Management by Objective
McGregor, Douglas, 696
measurement
  in field work, 170-171
  and standards, 702-703
mechanized sampling, 287
meetings, *see also* Preliminary Meeting
  interviews at preliminary meeting,
    121-122
  of staff for staff development,
    586-587
  summaries, 252
memos to close audit reports, 504-505
  exhib.
Middle Ages and internal auditing 4
minicomputers and security, 378-379,
  382
minor deficiency, 218
Mints, F. E., 760
miscellaneous manual, 557-559 exhib.
misuse, intentional EDP, 399-400
Mocern Internal Auditing, 163
modeling techniques, 325-342
models of managers, 680-681
modes of auditing, 184-198
monitoring
  corrective action, 232
  processes, 706-707
Monsanto, 788
Montacatini, 788
monte carlo simulation, 335
Montgomery Ward, 11, 801
monthly reports, 635, 637 exhib.
motivation
  evaluation of, 698-699
  in management, 696
motivation of personnel, 753
motor vehicles sampling, 281-282
multiple regression analysis, 329
multiprogramming computer
  systems, 348

N

National Bureau of Standards, U.S, 368
National Safety Council, 171
National Student Marketing, 718
neatness of working papers, 246
negligent misreprensentation, 715
Neter, J., 305
network analysis, 334-335
New School for Social Research, 38-39
New York City financial crisis, 55
New York Stock Exchange, 791
nonpersonal phrases
  in review conference, 500

normal distribution, 294
North American Co., 18
Northwest Bancorp., 39
numbering of projects, 633

O

objective, management by, *see*
  management by objective
objectives
  of audit reports, 443
  of control, 61
  identification of, 149-153
  of management planning, 682
  of the preliminary survey, 98-101
  statement in EDP control, 148-149,
    362
objectives of organization
  and long-range audit schedules,
    617-621
objectivity in auditing, 775-776
observation technique
  in transactions examination, 176-177
observations, *see* IMPRESSIONS
operating controls, internal, 71-80
operating costs of auditing dept., 517
operating documentation
  standards, 356
operating systems controls, 382-384
operations, auditing, 7
operations, EDP
  controls, 372
operations research
  auditing methods of, 325-327,
    337-339, 680
operators of EDP systems, 358
opinion evidence, 202
opinion statement in reports, 441-442
opinions in auditing, 501-502
oral questions in auditing, 178
oral reports, 449-454
oral setting of review conference,
  498-499
organization
  and control, 63-64
organizational audits, 114, 187-188,
  496
organizational control
  of computer controls, 355
  of EDP, 372-374
organizational overlay school of
  management, 680
organizing
  as a function of management, 688
  improprieties, 91-92
  information for preliminary surveys,
    123
  and the internal auditor, 692-695
  and staff selection, 576-578 exhib.

orientation program for mew staff 578-584 exhib.
outlining reports, 454-456
output controls, EDP, 359, 388
output standards, 701
outputs, definition of, 192-193
outside directors, 762
overcontrolling, 77

P

papers, *see* working papers
parallel simulation, 392, 416-417
parametric linear programming, 336
participative auditing approach, 754-755 exhib.
payments
  to or for employees, 94-95
  to suppliers, 95
payroll dept.
  audit of, 148-149
  computer audit, 360
  risks, 97, 102-103 exhib.
pedestrian theory of the audit, 148
peer reviews, 245, 661
Penn Central Railroad, 788
people, *see* Personnel
people; *see also* auditees, 747-772
perceptions about internal auditing, 748-749
performance
  deficiencies, 525-526
  of employees in audit, 113
  factors of staff, 599-602 exhib.
  measurement standards, 702
  standards as EDP controls, 355
performance audits, 794
performance of CEO
  and boards of directors, 800
permanemt files, 640-643
personality traits
  and fraud, 716
personnel
  and control, 65
  and the preliminary survey, 125-126
  training of, 706
personnel dept., 697
  statistics as indicators, 198-199
personnel relations of staff, 592-602
PERT/CPM, 334-335
Phillips, W. G., 752
photographs as evidence, 240
physical characteristics of audit reports, 459-461
physical evidence, 204
physical inspections, 126-128
physical security
  of EDP activity, 375

planning
  audit assignments, 145-146
  EDP, documention, 371
  as a function of management, 681-688
  impec 'ments to, 684
  impro_.ieties, 91
  information for preliminary surveys, 123
  and the internal auditor, 684-688
  in management, 678, 680
  OR models, 327
  for the preliminary survey, 105-107
  and quality control, 667
planning audit work, 607-608
  and supervision, 644-645
policies
  and control, 64
  of management planning, 683
policy statements, 542-546 exhib.
  on internal control, 78-80 exhib.
polygraphs and fraud, 734
population
  definition, 282
  proportions, 309-313
  in sampling, 310-312
  to be tested, 175-176
populations
  unknown, 312-313
Porter, Dauid, 12
post-audit reviews, 641
practices
  and deficiency finding, 221-222
precision in sampling, 288-296
predicting hospital costs, 330-331
predictive OR models, 327
preliminary discussion, 555
preliminary meeting, 117-122
preliminary reviews, 555
preliminary survey, 87-141, 555
  conclusions, 135-136
  controls, 101-103
  flowcharting, 128-131 exhib.
  obtaining information, 122-125
  objectives, goals and standards, 98-101
  people, 125-126
  physical inspections, 126-128
  preliminary meeting, 117-122
  preparing for the survey, 105-117
  purpose of the survey, 87-89
  risks in- the survey, 90-98
  and supervision, 645
premises of management planning, 683
preprinted working papers, 255-256
prevention controls, 59
prevention safeguards EDP, 381

preventive maintenance, EDP, 385-386
prices audit, 151-153 exhib.
principles of management, 677-712
principles of management planning, 683
prior audit reports, 641
Privacy Act of 1974, 366
pro-forma audit programs, 144, 145
pro-forma working papers, 255-256
probability theory, 281, 334
procedures
  and control, 64-65
  and deficiency finding, 221-222
  of management planning, 683
  and planning by auditor, 686
process auditing, 185-187
processing, EDP
  controls, 358
  efficiencies, 389-390
  testing, 396-397
procurement of materials
  flow chart, 130 exhib.
production, EDP, controls, 372
production services
  control questionnaire, 116 exhib., 117 exhib.
profession of internal auditing, 17-47
professional organization, 18-20
professional proficiency, 41-42
professionalism, 17-18, 568-570
proffesionalism, 763-764
profits and fraud, 738
program audits, 192-194
program EDP documentation, 370
program evaluation and review techniques, 334-335
program evaluation, definition of, 192
program mechanics, 161-162
program summaries, 252-253
program test procedures, 357
programmed audit days, 515 exhib.
programming documentation standards, 356
programming, linear, 332-334
programs, audit
  and supervision, 645
programs of management planning, 683
progress audit reports, 437-438, 446-449
progress reports, 638-639 exhib.
project budgets, 633-635
project closing
  and supervision, 646
project development EDP controls, 372
project numbering, 633

proofreading audit reports, 463
proportional analysis and fraud, 728
prosecution, malicious, 730
prudent management, 147
public accountants, 36, 57-58
  and internal control, 57-58
Public Holding Co. Act of 1935, 4
public utility industry, 18
publicity and fraud, 735-736
purchasing and fraud, 723-724
purchasing dept.
  and the audit programs, 150-152 exhib.
  computer-assisted audit, 423
  controls measurement, 173
  questionnaire, 118-119 exhib.
  risks, 96, 97, 102-103 exhib.
purpose statement in reports, 440
purposive sampling, 281
purposive tests, 309

Q

quaestors ('one who inquires'), 4
qualifications of internal auditing dept., 777-778
quality assurance program, 43
quality control, 245, 659-674
  control questionnaire, 117 exhib.
  and long-range schedule, 626
quality standards, 701
quantification, 325-342
quantitative school of management, 680
questioning suspects, 731
questioning technique
  in transactions examination, 177-179
questionnaires
  for preliminary survey, 113-117
queuing theory, 335-336

R

RAF, see record of audit finding
railroad company audit, 360
Rand Corp., 399
random number
  sampling, 2811645
  tables, 283-284
Rankin, Paul, 758
Rapid-American Corp., 789
rating of staff, 595-599 exhib.
real-time systems, 357-358
receiving memos, 306
reciprical evaluations, 662
recommendations in audit reports 445
recommendations of deficiency finding, 223-224
recording system, 635

records
  EDP, security, 376-378
  of impressions, 108, 111-112 exhib.
Records of Audit Finding, 131-135,
  225-227 exhib., 252-254 exhib., 438,
  500
recoveries
  amounts, 517
  in contract audits, 197-198
recovery plan for EDP, 377, 381
regression analysis, 328-332
regulatory requirements in EDP
  auditing, 368
relationships in auditing, 761-768
relevance test, 205-206
relevancy of working papers, 247
reminder list for auditing, 105 exhib.,
  107-108, 109-110 exhib.
remote-access computer systems,
  347-348
replies to audit reports, 503-506
report reviews
  and supervision, 646
reporting
  and control, 66
  of deficiencies, 230
  relationships, 541
  and supervision, 645-646
reports, 431-492
  to board of directors, 513-536
  criteria for, 433-438
  to executive management, 513-536
  overdue, 647, 653 exhib.
  replies, 556
  reviews and replies, 493-511
  writing, 556
  writing and staff selection, 575
reports of time spent, 634-637 exhib.
reproting system, 635
research and development
  control procedures, 74, 75-76 exhib.
research and development dept., 761
research projects and staff
  development, 588-592 exhib.
resource allocation problems, 332
resource-sharing computer
  systems, 348
responses to audit reports, 503-506
responsibilities, *see$also* Statement of
  Responsibilities
responsibility
  for audit programs, 145-146
  and functions statement, 542-543
  exhib.
  and the internal auditor, 692
  in management, 688
responsiveness of corrective
  action, 232

results testing for EDP controls, 396
retention procedure for working
  papers, 270
returnable containers audit, 177
revenue cycle, 71, 72 exhib.
revenue standards, 702
review courses for CIA
  examination, 34
review status, 647, 652 exhib.
reviewing revisions of audit
  reports, 502-503
reviews by supervisors, 228-230
reviews of audit reports, 495-503,
  496-497 exhib.
  review conference, 498-499
  timing of, 496-498
reviews of staff, 592-602 exhib.
reviews of working papers, 256-258
revisions in audit reports, 502-503
risks, *see also* Controls
  assessment of, 103-105
  in contract agreements, 196-197
  identification of, 149-153
  in the payroll dept., 103 exhib.
  in the preliminary survey, 90-98,
  102-103 exhib.
  in the Purchasing Dept., 102-103
  exhib.
Roethlisberger, F. J., 679
rolling stock, 199
Rolls Royce, 788
Royal Melbourne Institute of
  Technology, 36-67
rule of reason, 71
rules of management planning, 683

S

safeguards in EDP activity, 380-381
safety
  and long-range schedule, 626
safety control audit, 171-172, 180
safety deposit boxes audit program, 159
  exhib.
salvage and scrap generation and
  disposition, 96
sample audit reports, 466-482 exhib.
sample working papers, 258-269 exhib.
samples
  selection of for testing, 176
sampling, 279-324, 280
  of EDP operations, 365
  evaluating results, 308-309
  population proportions, 309-313
  selection, 281-287
  sizes, 287-308
Sampling Manual for Auditors, 286,
  296, 300
San Diego National Bank, 788

SAS-9, AICPA, 775-776
satisfiers, 696
Saunders, Stewart T., 789
savings reported, 517
scatter diagram, 328
schedule, *see* Long-Range Audit
  Schedules
schedule boards, 639-640 exhib.
schedules
  of projects, 633-635
scheduling of EDP operations, 364
schizophrenia in auditing, 762
schools, *see* Courses, and University
  Curricula
scientific school of management,
  678-680
scope of audits, 146-147
scope statement in reports, 440-441
scrap and salvage generation and
  disposition, 96
scrap sales
  audit of, 174
  and control, 62-63
Sears Roebuck & Co., 11
SEC v. Killearn Properties, Inc,
  762-763, 792
secondary evidence, 201
Securities Act of 1933, 4
Securities and Exchange Act of
  1934, 4, 68, 69
Securities & Exchange
  Commission, U.S., 40, 69, 367,
  523-524, 660, 740, 762
security
  of EDP activity, 374-382
  of EDP systems, 367
  and long-range schedule, 626
  of plant, 95
  problems, 127
  and working papers, 25,
*Security; Risk Assessment in EDP
  System,* 103
selection
  of samples, 281-287
  of staff, 572-578
self-control, 705
self-evaluation of audit staff, 245,
  593-594
selling internal auditing to
  management, 559-561
seminars, *see* Courses
senior auditors and staff
  development, 580-584
sensitive control areas
  and long-range audit schedules,
  617-619 exhib.
sensitive payments, 55
sensitivity analysis, 336

service units system distribution,
  335-336
shipments audit, 156-157 exhib.
simple regression analysis, 329
simplification of working papers, 249
simulation computer tests, 392
simulation in computer auditing,
  416-419
simulation, monte carlo, 335
situational pressures
  and fraud, 716
sizes of samples, 287-308
slander, 729
small audit staffs, 162-163
small internal audit organizations
  and long-range schedule, 624-625
  and supervision, 654
Smith, Adam, 788
Smith, William S., 31
snapshot computer tests, 392
social system theory of
  management, 680
software for auditing, 419-420
sources
  of information, 125
  for staff, 570-572
special audit programs, 420-421
special services
  and long-range schedule, 625
split-page form, 113
Staats, Elmer B., 754
staff and line
  and the internal auditor, 693
  in management, 690
staff/line conflicts, 750
staff selection and development,
  567-606
staffing
  and the internal auditor, 695
  in management, 691-692
standard deviation, 293, 299
standards
  in audit measurement, 171-172
  conformance, EDP, 387-395
  in control, 61-62
  in deficiency finding, 220
  development of, 171-172
  as EDP controls, 355-356
  EDP design, 393
  of evidence, 205-206
  and fraud, 718-720
  and long-range audit schedules, 610
  maintaining, 705
  of management planning, 683,
  699-700
  for OR auditing, 337
  and planning by auditor, 684
  of the preliminary survey, 98-101

in quality control, 661-664
setting of, 705
for staff excellence, 568-570
in testing, 175
in working paper reviews, 257-258
*Standards for Audit of
Governmental Organizations..*, 345
*Standards for the Professional
Practice of Internal Audi*, 24, 39-47,
74, 90, 100, 145-146, 230-231,
344-345, 514, 520, 541-542, 543,
568-569, 607-608, 643-644, 659-660,
662, 663, 667, 718-719, 762, 763,
765-766, 767, 779, 798
standards of conduct
and boards of directors, 799
Stanford Research Institute, *399-400*
State Street Trust Co. vs. Ernst, 720
state employment insurance
charges audit, 184
*Statement of Responsibilities of
Internal Auditors*, 20-24 exhib., 231,
360-361
Statement on Auditing Standards,
57-58, 68, 775
statements in reports, *see* specific
name
stationery, 199
statistical models, 325-342
statistical sampling, *see* Sampling
statistical summaries, 252
statistical theory, 288-296
status of auditor, 763
status reports, 520
statutory requirements in EDP
auditing, 368
steering committees
for management overview, 349
stock room audit, 174
stop-or-go sampling, 305-306
strategies of management
planning, 682
stratified sampling, 285-286
studying and staff development,
585-592
style manual, 465-466
styles of auditing, 752-753
sufficiency test, 205
suggestions for improvement, 214-215
summaries
in audit reports, 454-455, 523-524
of causes, 528-534 exhib.
of deficiency findings, 225-228,
524-525
in reports, 439
in working papers, 251-253
summary reports
in preliminary survey, 131-135

summary statement in audit
reports, 444
supervision
and control of audit projects, 643-646
and EDP testing controls, 394
and quality assurance, 664-666
and staff development, 580-584
supervisory reviews
of deficiency findings, 228-230
of working papers, 256-258
suppliers, *see* Purchasing Dept.
supply inventory auditing, 214
supply stores, 199
supportive model of managers, 681,
696
survey, preliminary, *see* Preliminary
Survey
system computer tests, 392
system design and development;
computer auditing, 347-371
system EDP documentation, 355, 369
system studies, EDP, 361
systematic sampling, 284-285
systems theory of management,
679-680
systems, unsatisfactory, 214

T

t factors, 297
table of contents for working
papers, 105-107 exhib.
table of digits, 282-283 app.
*Table of 150,000 Random Decimal
Digits*, 283-284
tailor-made program, 153
Taylor, Frederick W., 678, 680
teamwork relationships in
auditing, 760
technical audit manual, 554
technical services EDP controls, 373
telephones, 199-200
10 percenters, 717
test pilots, and audit measurement,
170-171
testimonial evidence, 204
testing and staff selection, 574-578
exhib.
tests
of computer controls, 391-392
of EDP disaster plan, 381, 395-406
of evidence, 205-206
and field woek, 174-184
theories of management, 678
theory of the audit, 148-149
Theory X&Y types of managers, 696
Thomas, S.H., 453-454
thriftiness, 147
thrust of the audit, 148

Thurston, John B., 4, 18-19
time and material contracts audit, 182
time reports, 634-636 exhib.
time-sharing computer systems, 348
timeliness
  of reports, 437-438
  standards, 702
tone of reports, 438
traceability of transactions, 352-353
traditional authority, 689
traffic department audit program,
  156-157 exhib.
trails of transactions, 352-353
training systems for staff
  development, 580-584
transactions to be examined, 176
transmittal memo
  for draft reports, 498 exhib.
  for questionnaires, 115 exhib.
transmittal report, 449 exhib.
transportation problems, 333-334
trapdoors in EDP auditing, 362
trend analysis and fraud, 727-728
trend charting of findings, 526-528
  exhib.
Trojan horses in EDP auditing, 362

U

U.S. Government agencies, *see* names
  of agencies
U.S. laws, *see* names of laws
understandable working papers, 247
understanding and staff
  development, 569
uniformity of working papers, 246-247
unit-price contracts, 192, 195-196
universities and colleges used to
  select staff, 570
university curricula, 31, 34
University of South Carolina, 38
unrecorded transactions, 719
users of EDP documentation, 370
utility computer programs, 420

V

validity for OR auditing, 337-338
variability in sampling, 290-296
variables
  methods, 329
  sampling, 298-303
vehicles audit, 421-422
verification
  in transactions examination, 180-181
  for OR auditing, 338-339
  and quality control, 666

W

walk through inspection, 102, 127-128
water meters audit, 220
Wealth of Nations, 788
weekly reports, 635-636 exhib.
white-collar crime; *see also* fraud, 714
Williams, Harold M., 40
women in internal auditing, 24
work load statistics report, 647
work sampling study, 365
working papers, 105-107 exhib.,
  243-276, 555
  control over, 258
  documentation in, 246-251
  indexing and cross-referencing,
    253-255
  pro forma, 255-256
  retention of, 270
  in review conference, 500
  reviews of, 256 258
  samples of, 258-259
  summarization, 251-253
  writing, 259-270
writing
  as the audit progresses, 259, 270
  reports, 454-459
  and staff selection, 575
  in working papers, 249

Y

Yellow Book, 345

Z

z factors, 297